CIVIL PROCEDURE

CASES, PROBLEMS AND EXERCISES

By

John T. Cross

Professor of Law
University of Louisville, Louis D. Brandeis School of Law

Leslie W. Abramson

Professor of Law
University of Louisville, Louis D. Brandeis School of Law

Ellen E. Deason

Professor of Law
The Ohio State University, Michael E. Moritz College of Law

AMERICAN CASEBOOK SERIES®

THOMSON

™

WEST

Mat #40286187

American Casebook Series and West Group are trademarks registered in the U.S. Patent and Trademark Office.

© 2006 Thomson/West
 610 Opperman Drive
 P.O. Box 64526
 St. Paul, MN 55164–0526
 1–800–328–9352

Printed in the United States of America

ISBN–13: 978–0–314–15547–4
ISBN–10: 0–314–15547–3

 TEXT IS PRINTED ON 10% POST CONSUMER RECYCLED PAPER

To my parents, who never let me think for a moment
that there was anything I could not do,
provided I tried hard enough.

JTC

For Lisa, Sam, Shel & Will.

LWA

To my mother, Elizabeth McGregor Deason,
and my grandmother, Gertrude Ellen McGregor,
from whom I received my names
and so much more.

EED

*

Preface

Civil Procedure can be one of the most difficult courses in law school, both for the student and for the professor. And yet, it also can prove to be among the most rewarding. This book is designed to help both the student and the professor overcome the challenges and reap the rewards. We have tapped into our many years of combined experience teaching Civil Procedure to produce a book that we hope is highly "teachable," while also providing a solid foundation in the subject matter.

What makes Civil Procedure difficult? The difficulty is really not the subject matter. Although Procedure is not easy, the rules and doctrines are by and large no more difficult than in most of the other courses in law school. Instead, the real problem in learning—and teaching—Procedure is one of perspective. Most students dealing with the subject for the first time have one of two vastly different preconceptions of the course. Some students think that Procedure will be their one practical or "hands on" course. Those in this camp are surprised to learn that Procedure, no less than their other courses, is laden with difficult policy concerns. While they readily adapt to making policy-based arguments in their other courses, such arguments may seem somehow out of place in a rules-dominated course like Procedure.

The second group of students has quite a different preconception. To those in this camp, Civil Procedure's apparent complexity is intimidating. Overwhelmed by the arcane nature of the subject, students in this group tend to want to approach the subject as a Herculean task of remembering hundreds of individual rules.

Both of these views represent a problem of perspective. It is an inescapable fact that Procedure may seem like a foreign language to most students. Everyone has a rough idea of what a tort, contract, or property interest is. More importantly, most students have their own basic notions as to how the law ought to treat those matters. Although those ideas may not be correct, it is much easier to learn a legal rule when you have a preconceived notion of what that rule ought to be. Students rarely have such preconceived notions for rules of Civil Procedure. Indeed, students often think that the rules of Procedure are mainly arbitrary choices about time limits, wording, and motions. Of course, nothing could be further from the truth. Although it may be difficult for the newcomer to spot, Civil Procedure is a system in which choices as to individual rules are generally made with the overall litigation structure in mind.

This book provides students a more accurate perspective on Civil Procedure. For those intimidated by the subject, it makes an effort to start with the basics, and only then to proceed to the more difficult issues. On the other hand, the book pays considerable attention to the underlying policy concerns, both to deal with the group of students who thinks of Procedure as merely practical, and to foster a greater appreciation of the subject in all students. Moreover, the book presents Procedure as a unified whole, something that is much greater than the sum of its seemingly unrelated parts. This approach provides a better long-term understanding of the subject. After all, although the actual *rules* of Procedure may change with some regularity, the basic system has remained remarkably stable. Studying Procedure as a system will help the student throughout a career that may span forty or more years.

This book differs from other Civil Procedure casebooks in five main ways. The first, and most significant, is the extensive use of problems and exercises. Most sections include not only an Introductory Problem, which encourages students to think about the issues, but also review problems at the end of the section. These problems serve two primary purposes. First, they help the students become comfortable in *applying* the rules they have learned. Such application aids immensely in overcoming any fear of Procedure and gaining a deeper understanding of the underlying rule. Second, of all the first-year courses, Civil Procedure is the most "statutory" in nature. Given that many doctrines are governed by statutes and especially the Federal Rules, problems give the students the incentive to look closely at the language of the positive law itself, rather than simply relying on how that (sometimes outdated) language is paraphrased in a judicial opinion. The exercises go one step further, typically asking the students to use their recently acquired skills to research local law, which may differ from the Federal Rule being discussed.

The second main feature of this book is the extensive notes. Although some of the notes help explain the preceding case, most provide additional information that provide a fuller understanding of the doctrine in question. Although this book cannot completely replace a good secondary source, the extensive notes should greatly reduce the frequency with which students will need to refer to outside sources to understand what is being discussed.

Third, the book whenever possible uses newer cases. Most of the cases in the book were decided during the last decade. In some cases, we replaced an old Supreme Court case that established a rule with a newer lower court decision that applies that rule to a new situation. In our view, using these newer cases affords two advantages. First, the newer decisions often do an excellent job explaining the earlier cases, providing the students a good exposition of the rules and policies. Second, and more subtly, using newer cases reinforces in the reader's mind that Civil Procedure remains a vibrant, changing field of the law. The old Supreme Court "chestnuts" that populate many of the other Procedure casebooks rarely resolve the policy clash for all time. Instead, courts must continue to deal with the policy concerns even today.

Fourth, we present dispute resolution methods like mediation, not as a recent curiosity at the book's end, but as part of the overall procedural context. Despite media depictions that all cases go to trial, settlement and dispute resolution are essential elements for keeping the American litigation system moving.

Finally, you will find that although this book by and large follows the traditional chronological order of a Civil Procedure book, we have diverged from that order in certain places. Three of these are especially worth noting. First, rather than overwhelming the students with a discussion of jurisdiction, we start (in Chapter 2) with an introduction to the basic rules of joinder (multiple plaintiffs and defendants, counter and cross-claims, and impleader). In our experience, joinder is one of the few topics in Procedure that requires no knowledge of any other topic. Moreover, knowing what parties and claims can be in a case helps the students immensely when they deal later with questions of jurisdiction and venue. Second, we divided the discussion of two issues unique to the federal courts—federal question jurisdiction and *Erie*—into a relatively straightforward basic discussion (Chapters 3 and 5.D, respectively), and a more in-depth discussion (Chapter 13). This treatment affords the professor considerable flexibility in how to teach that material. Third, we lump all of the various ways to resolve a case without a jury—from dismissals and defaults to the judgment as a matter of law—in a single chapter. Although these methods of resolution occur at different times, studying them as a group helps students immensely in learning the nuances of, and proper roles for, each. This in turn reinforces an idea that we are trying to stress: namely, that Civil Procedure is a unified system.

These differences make for what we feel is a highly teachable book, as well as an excellent desk reference for the students. Although this is only the first edition, the materials have been "field tested" in the classroom for two years. Several changes were made in response to student reaction. Of course, we would also welcome any input that you might offer as to how the book could be improved. Although everyone teaches Civil Procedure in his or her own unique way, we hope that this book proves useful to many of you.

Finally, we would be ungrateful if we failed to acknowledge that several student research assistants helped us in the production of this book. We are especially grateful to Katherine Vesely for her keen eyes, hard work, and encouragement. We likewise appreciate the unflagging support of Reva Campbell, Amanda Hartley, Barbara Kehoe, Karen Paulin, and Elizabeth Worthing.

JOHN T. CROSS
LESLIE W. ABRAMSON
ELLEN E. DEASON

February 2006

*

Acknowledgements

We gratefully acknowledge permission to reprint the following:

Lon L. Fuller, "Mediation—Its Forms and Functions," 44 *Southern California Law Review* 305–326 (1971), reprinted with the permission of the *Southern California Law Review*.

Marc Galanter, "The Vanishing Trial: An Examination of Trials and Related Matters in Federal and State Courts," 1 *Empirical Legal Studies* 459 (2004), reprinted with permission from Marc Galanter and Blackwell Publishing.

"'The Vanishing Trial' Report: An Alternative View of the Data" by John Lande, published in *Dispute Resolution*, Volume 10, No. 4, Summer 2004. © 2004 by the American Bar Association. Reprinted with permission.

Joseph B. Stulberg, "The Theory and Practice of Mediation: A Reply to Professor Susskind," 6 *Vermont Law Review* 85 (1981), reprinted with the permission of Joseph B. Stulberg and the *Vermont Law Review*.

"The Senate Table: An Introductory Adjudication/Mediation Exercise," is used by permission of Gary A. Weissman, attorney, mediator, and adjunct professor of ADR at William Mitchell College of Law (Minnesota). The teaching materials are adapted with permission from those authored by Barbara McAdoo, Hamline University School of Law.

*

Summary of Contents

_____

	Page
PREFACE	v
ACKNOWLEDGEMENTS	ix
TABLE OF CASES	xxvii

Chapter 1. An Overview of Civil Procedure — **1**
A. The Role of Procedure — 1
B. Dealing With Civil Procedure — 6
C. State and Federal Rules of Procedure — 8

Chapter 2. Basic Joinder of Claims and Parties — **9**
A. Multiple Plaintiffs and Defendants — 10
B. Counterclaims — 18
C. Cross–Claims — 26
D. Adding Third Parties: Impleader — 29
E. Multiple Claims — 37
F. Making Optional Claims Compulsory: An Overview of Merger and Bar — 43

Chapter 3. Federal Subject Matter Jurisdiction — **51**
A. The Concept of Subject Matter Jurisdiction — 51
B. Federal Question Jurisdiction — 54
C. Diversity Jurisdiction — 64
D. Supplemental Jurisdiction — 87
E. Removal — 109
F. Challenging Subject Matter Jurisdiction — 117

Chapter 4. Personal Jurisdiction and Venue — **120**
A. Exercising Jurisdiction Over Defendants — 120
B. Service of Process on Defendants — 216
C. Venue — 238
D. Rule 12(b) Procedural Challenges — 259

Chapter 5. Pleading — **262**
A. Philosophy and History of Pleading — 263
B. Pleading a Claim Under the Federal Rules — 273
C. Objecting to the Statement of a Claim — 305
D. Determining the Applicable Law — 310
E. Responding to the Complaint — 333
F. Veracity Standards for Filed Documents — 351
G. Amended and Supplemental Pleadings — 368

Page

Chapter 6. Advanced Joinder 387
A. Intervention 387
B. Necessary Parties 400
C. Interpleader 412
D. Class Actions 430

Chapter 7. Discovery 456
A. The Scope of Discovery 457
B. Discovery Devices 487
C. Discovery Sanctions 517

Chapter 8. Alternative Dispute Resolution and Settlement 525
A. Introduction 525
B. Alternative Dispute Resolution Processes 526
C. Case Settlement 542
D. Legal Rules That Support Settlement 563

Chapter 9. Jury Trial 576
A. The Constitutional Right to a Jury Trial in Civil Cases 577
B. Demanding a Jury Trial 610
C. Selecting a Group of Prospective Jurors 612
D. Challenging Individual Prospective Jurors 617
E. Jury Instructions and Jury Verdicts 635

Chapter 10. Dispositive and Post–Trial Motions 647
A. Dismissals 647
B. Default Judgments 663
C. Resolving the Case Based on the Pleadings Alone 672
D. Summary Judgment 674
E. Judgment as a Matter of Law 694
F. New Trial 705
G. Relief From Judgment 716

Chapter 11. The Effect of a Judgment 729
A. Enforcing a Judgment 729
B. Preclusive Effect of a Judgment: An Overview 730
C. Claim Preclusion 732
D. Issue Preclusion 744
E. Parties Affected by Claim and Issue Preclusion 762
F. Applying Preclusion Across State Lines 776
G. Doctrines Similar to Preclusion 790

Chapter 12. Appeals 797
A. Who May Appeal 797
B. The Timing of an Appeal—The ''Final Decision'' Rule 802
C. Scope of Appellate Review 819
D. United States Supreme Court Review 826

Page

Chapter 13.   Special Issues in Federal Court ---------------------- **833**
A.   Advanced Issues in Federal Question Jurisdiction ------------------ 833
B.   An In–Depth Look at the *Erie* Doctrine ------------------------------- 849

INDEX -- 897

*

Table of Contents

Page

PREFACE --- v
ACKNOWLEDGEMENTS -- ix
TABLE OF CASES -- xxvii

Chapter 1. An Overview of Civil Procedure ----------------- **1**
A. The Role of Procedure --- 1
    Nolph v. Scott -- 1
    Notes and Questions --- 5
B. Dealing With Civil Procedure ------------------------------------ 6
C. State and Federal Rules of Procedure --------------------------- 8

Chapter 2. Basic Joinder of Claims and Parties ------------ **9**
A. Multiple Plaintiffs and Defendants ------------------------------ 10
    Introductory Problem -- 10
    Apache County v. Superior Court --------------------------------- 11
    Alexander v. Fulton County -------------------------------------- 13
    Notes and Questions --- 16
B. Counterclaims -- 18
    Introductory Problem -- 18
    Simmons v. Simmons --- 19
    Notes and Questions --- 22
C. Cross–Claims --- 26
    Introductory Problem -- 26
    Rainbow Management Group, Ltd. v. Atlantis Submarines Hawaii, L.P. -- 27
    Notes and Questions --- 28
D. Adding Third Parties: Impleader --------------------------------- 29
    Introductory Problem 1 -- 29
    Introductory Problem 2 -- 30
    Lopez de Robinson v. United States ------------------------------ 31
    Notes and Questions --- 35
E. Multiple Claims -- 37
    Introductory Problem -- 37
    McCoy v. Like --- 38
    Notes and Questions --- 40
    Problems -- 41
    Exercise -- 42
F. Making Optional Claims Compulsory: An Overview of Merger
    and Bar --- 43
    Introductory Problem -- 43
    Huffey v. Lea --- 44
    Notes and Questions --- 49

Chapter 3. Federal Subject Matter Jurisdiction ------------ **51**
A. The Concept of Subject Matter Jurisdiction --------------------- 51
B. Federal Question Jurisdiction ---------------------------------- 54

                                                                    Page
B. Federal Question Jurisdiction—Continued
    Introductory Problem --- 54
    1. How Does a Party Invoke Federal Question Jurisdiction? ----- 56
        Louisville & Nashville Railroad v. Mottley --------------- 56
        Notes and Questions -------------------------------------- 58
    2. What Types of Claims Present a "Federal Question?" --------- 61
        a. United States Constitution ----------------------------- 61
        b. Treaties --- 61
        c. International Law --------------------------------------- 62
        d. Federal Common Law ------------------------------------- 62
        e. Problematic Federal Statutes --------------------------- 62
        f. State Law -- 63
            Problems --- 63
C. Diversity Jurisdiction --- 64
    Introductory Problem --- 64
    1. The Policy Underlying Diversity Jurisdiction -------------- 64
    2. Determining Diversity ------------------------------------- 66
        Lundquist v. Precision Valley Aviation, Inc. ------------- 66
        Notes and Questions -------------------------------------- 70
        Montrose Chemical Corp. v. American Motorists Insurance Co. ------- 71
        Notes and Questions -------------------------------------- 74
    3. The Amount in Controversy --------------------------------- 76
    4. Additional Issues in Diversity Jurisdiction --------------- 79
        a. Alienage Jurisdiction ---------------------------------- 79
        b. Time for Determining Diversity ------------------------- 80
        c. Manipulating § 1332 ------------------------------------ 81
        d. States --- 83
        e. Exceptions to Diversity Jurisdiction ------------------- 84
            Problems --- 85
            Exercise --- 86
D. Supplemental Jurisdiction -- 87
    Introductory Problem --- 87
    1. Theoretical Bases for Supplemental Jurisdiction ----------- 88
        United Mine Workers v. Gibbs ----------------------------- 88
        Notes and Questions -------------------------------------- 92
    2. The Supplemental Jurisdiction Statute --------------------- 93
        Exxon Mobil Corp. v. Allapattah Services, Inc. ---------- 95
        Notes and Questions -------------------------------------- 102
        Problems --- 104
    3. Supplemental Jurisdiction and Other Forms of Joinder ------- 106
        Problems --- 108
E. Removal -- 109
    Introductory Problem --- 109
    1. General Rules Governing Removal --------------------------- 109
        Caterpillar Inc. v. Williams ---------------------------- 109
        Notes and Questions -------------------------------------- 111
    2. Removal in Diversity Cases -------------------------------- 114
    3. Procedure for Removal ------------------------------------- 115
        Problems --- 116
F. Challenging Subject Matter Jurisdiction -------------------------- 117
    Introductory Problem --- 117
    Notes and Questions --- 118

Page

Chapter 4. Personal Jurisdiction and Venue ------------- **120**
A. Exercising Jurisdiction Over Defendants------------------- 120
  Introductory Problem #1 ------------------------------- 120
  Introductory Problem #2 ------------------------------- 121
    1. Jurisdiction Over Defendants: The Early Decisions------------ 122
      Notes and Questions -------------------------------- 124
      Problems --- 125
      International Shoe Co. v. Washington ----------------- 127
      Notes and Questions -------------------------------- 131
    2. Jurisdiction Over Nonresident Defendants -------------- 133
      a. Specific Jurisdiction--------------------------- 134
      b. General Jurisdiction ------------------------- 136
        Exercise --------------------------------- 137
        Problems -------------------------------- 138
    3. Emerging Personal Jurisdiction Principles------------ 140
      Shaffer v. Heitner ---------------------------- 142
      Notes and Questions --------------------------- 149
      World–Wide Volkswagen Corp. v. Woodson ------------ 150
      Notes and Questions --------------------------- 156
      Problems ------------------------------------ 157
      Calder v. Jones------------------------------- 159
      Notes and Questions --------------------------- 162
      Problems ------------------------------------ 163
      Helicopteros Nacionales de Colombia, S.A. v. Hall ----- 164
      Notes and Questions --------------------------- 170
      Problems ------------------------------------ 171
      Burger King v. Rudzewicz----------------------- 172
      Notes and Questions --------------------------- 180
      Problem ------------------------------------- 182
      Asahi Metal Industry Co. v. Superior Court ---------- 183
      Notes and Questions --------------------------- 188
      Problems ------------------------------------ 190
      Burnham v. Superior Court---------------------- 191
      Notes and Questions --------------------------- 197
    4. To the Internet—and Beyond!------------------------ 198
      Young v. New Haven Advocate-------------------- 200
      Notes and Questions --------------------------- 205
      Problems ------------------------------------ 205
      Gator.com Corp. v. L.L. Bean, Inc.-------------- 206
      Toys "R" Us, Inc. v. Step Two, S.A. -------------- 210
      Notes and Questions --------------------------- 215
      Exercise ------------------------------------- 216
B. Service of Process on Defendants ----------------------- 216
  Introductory Problem ----------------------------------- 217
    1. Constitutional Standards ------------------------- 217
      Mullane v. Central Hanover Bank & Trust Co. ---------- 217
      Notes and Questions --------------------------- 221
    2. Procedural Standards for Service of Process-------------- 222
      Larsen v. Mayo Medical Center ------------------- 223
      Notes and Questions --------------------------- 226
      Cox v. Quigley-------------------------------- 227
      Notes and Questions --------------------------- 231
      Problems ------------------------------------ 235
      Exercise ------------------------------------- 237

	Page
C. Venue	238
Introductory Problem	238
1. Federal Venue Standards	239
Uffner v. La Reunion Francaise, S.A.	240
Notes and Questions	241
Problems	243
2. Transferring the Lawsuit	244
a. By Statute	244
Meteoro Amusement Corp. v. Six Flags	244
Notes and Questions	248
b. By Forum Non Conveniens	251
Piper Aircraft Co. v. Reyno	251
Notes and Questions	256
Problems	258
D. Rule 12(b) Procedural Challenges	259
Problems	260
Chapter 5. Pleading	**262**
A. Philosophy and History of Pleading	263
1. Historical English Pleading	264
Charles E. Clark, Handbook of the Law of Code Pleading	265
Robert Wyness Millar, Civil Procedure of the Trial Court in Historical Perspective	267
Notes	268
2. Code Pleading	270
Charles E. Clark, Handbook of the Law of Code Pleading	271
Notes and Questions	272
B. Pleading a Claim Under the Federal Rules	273
Introductory Problem	273
1. General Rule	275
Swierkiewicz v. Sorema, N.A.	278
Notes and Questions	281
Daniels v. USS Agri–Chemicals	282
Roe v. Aware Woman Center for Choice, Inc.	285
Notes and Questions	290
2. Heightened Pleading Standards	291
Alternative System Concepts, Inc. v. Synopsys, Inc.	291
Notes and Questions	294
Browning v. Clinton	296
Notes and Questions	298
3. The Prayer for Relief	299
4. The Form of the Complaint	300
Notes and Questions	303
Problems	304
C. Objecting to the Statement of a Claim	305
Introductory Problem	305
1. When a Pleading "Fails to State a Claim"	307
2. Procedural Aspects of the 12(b)(6) Motion	308
3. Motion for a More Definite Statement and Motion to Strike	309
Problems	309
Exercise	310
D. Determining the Applicable Law	310
Introductory Problem	310
1. Choice of Law	313
Paul v. National Life	313

D. Determining the Applicable Law—Continued
    Notes and Questions --- 318
  2. An Introduction to *Erie* -- 319
    Houben v. Telular Corporation -- 320
    Notes and Questions --- 324
    Chamberlain v. Giampapa -- 326
    Notes and Questions --- 331
    Problems -- 332
E. Responding to the Complaint --- 333
    Introductory Problem -- 333
  1. Menu of Responses -- 334
    King Vision Pay Per View, Ltd. v. J.C. Dimitri's Restaurant, Inc. ---- 337
    Problems -- 338
    Exercise --- 339
  2. Affirmative Defenses --- 340
    Red Deer v. Cherokee County, Iowa --------------------------------- 341
    Notes and Questions --- 345
  3. Responding to the Answer --- 346
    Reyes v. Sazan --- 346
    Notes and Questions --- 348
    Exercise --- 350
F. Veracity Standards for Filed Documents ------------------------------- 351
    Ruszala v. Walt Disney World Co. --------------------------------------- 353
    Notes and Questions --- 356
    Exercise --- 358
    Christian v. Mattel, Inc. --- 358
    Notes and Questions --- 364
    Problems -- 367
G. Amended and Supplemental Pleadings ----------------------------------- 368
    Introductory Problem -- 369
  1. Amending Pleadings With (or Without) the Court's Permission -- 369
    Beeck v. Aquaslide 'N' Dive Corp. ------------------------------------- 369
    Notes and Questions --- 372
  2. Amendments to Add Issues at Trial --------------------------------- 374
    Otness v. United States -- 374
    Notes and Questions --- 376
    Problems -- 376
  3. Amendments Filed After the Limitations Period Has Expired --- 377
    Singletary v. Pennsylvania Dept. of Corrections --------------------- 377
    Notes and Questions --- 382
  4. Supplemental Pleadings --- 383
    Stewart v. Shelby Tissue, Inc. -- 383
    Notes and Questions --- 385
    Exercise --- 386

Chapter 6. Advanced Joinder -- **387**
A. Intervention --- 387
    Introductory Problem -- 387
    Chiles v. Thornburgh -- 388
    Notes and Questions --- 394
    Problems -- 400

                                                                        Page
B. Necessary Parties -- 400
    Introductory Problem --- 400
    *Dawavendewa v. Salt River Project Agricultural Improvement and
        Power District* -- 402
    Notes and Questions -- 407
    Problems --- 411
C. Interpleader --- 412
    Introductory Problem --- 412
    Star Insurance Co. v. Cedar Valley Express, LLC ---------------- 413
    1. When a Party May Use Interpleader ------------------------- 419
        Notes and Questions --------------------------------------- 421
    2. Jurisdiction and Venue ----------------------------------- 423
        Notes and Questions --------------------------------------- 426
    3. Enjoining Other Litigation ------------------------------- 427
    4. The Subsequent Proceeding -------------------------------- 428
        Problems -- 429
D. Class Actions -- 430
    Introductory Problem --- 430
    1. Problems with Representational Litigation --------------- 432
        Hansberry v. Lee -- 432
        Notes and Questions --------------------------------------- 435
        Problem --- 437
    2. The Protection Afforded by Rule 23 --------------------- 437
        Szabo v. Bridgeport Machines, Inc. ------------------------ 438
        Notes and Questions --------------------------------------- 446
    3. Other Issues in Class Actions ------------------------- 451
        a. Personal Jurisdiction ------------------------------ 451
        b. Federal Subject Matter Jurisdiction ---------------- 451
            Exxon Mobil Corp. v. Allapattah Services, Inc. ------- 453
            Notes and Questions ------------------------------- 453
        c. Resolving the Class Action ------------------------- 453
            Problems -- 454

Chapter 7. Discovery --- **456**
A. The Scope of Discovery -- 457
    1. Mandatory Disclosure ----------------------------------- 457
        Introductory Problem -------------------------------------- 457
    2. Discovery of Relevant and Non–Privileged Information ---- 459
        Introductory Problem #1 ----------------------------------- 459
        Introductory Problem #2 ----------------------------------- 459
        Thompson v. Department of Housing and Urban Devel. -------- 460
        Notes and Questions --------------------------------------- 464
        Problems -- 468
    3. Discovery of Attorney Work Product --------------------- 469
        Introductory Problem -------------------------------------- 469
        Hickman v. Taylor --- 469
        Notes and Questions --------------------------------------- 473
        Gutshall v. New Prime, Inc. ------------------------------- 476
        Problems -- 478
    4. Discovery About Experts -------------------------------- 480
        Introductory Problem -------------------------------------- 480
        Lehan v. Ambassador Programs, Inc. ------------------------ 481
        Notes and Questions --------------------------------------- 485
        Problems -- 486

Page

A. The Scope of Discovery—Continued
Exercise --- 487
B. Discovery Devices -- 487
   1. Depositions -- 487
     Alexander v. F.B.I. -- 488
     Notes and Questions -- 492
   2. Interrogatories -- 495
     O'Connor v. Boeing North American, Inc. ------------------ 495
     Notes and Questions -- 500
     Exercise -- 502
   3. Request for Production of Documents ----------------- 502
     Playboy Enterprises, Inc. v. Welles ---------------------- 502
     Notes and Questions -- 506
     Exercise -- 508
   4. Request for Admissions -------------------------------- 508
     Asea, Inc. v. Southern Pac. Transp. Co. ---------------- 508
     Notes and Questions -- 512
     Exercise -- 513
   5. Physical and Mental Examinations ------------------- 513
     Ali v. Wang Laboratories, Inc. ---------------------------- 513
     Notes and Questions -- 516
C. Discovery Sanctions --- 517
   Lee v. Walters -- 517
   Notes and Questions -- 522

Chapter 8. Alternative Dispute Resolution and Settlement 525
A. Introduction --- 525
B. Alternative Dispute Resolution Processes --------------- 526
   1. Arbitration -- 526
     Bowen v. Amoco Pipeline Company ----------------------- 527
     Notes and Questions -- 535
     Exercise -- 536
   2. Mediation --- 536
     Lon L. Fuller, Mediation—Its Forms and Functions ----- 537
     Joseph B. Stulberg, The Theory and Practice of Mediation: A Reply
       to Professor Susskind ------------------------------------- 539
     Notes and Questions -- 541
     Exercise -- 542
C. Case Settlement -- 542
   Introductory Problem --- 542
   1. Trends in Judicial Activity ------------------------------ 544
     Marc Galanter, The Vanishing Trial: An Examination of Trials and
       Related Matters in Federal and State Courts ----------- 544
     John Lande, 'The Vanishing Trial' Report: An Alternative View of
       the Data --- 548
     Notes and Questions -- 550
   2. Court-annexed ADR ------------------------------------- 551
     In re Atlantic Pipe Corporation ------------------------- 552
     Notes and Questions -- 560
     Exercise -- 563
D. Legal Rules That Support Settlement --------------------- 563
   Problems --- 564
   Marek v. Chesny --- 565
   Notes and Questions -- 575

Page

Chapter 9.   Jury Trial... **576**
A. The Constitutional Right to a Jury Trial in Civil Cases 577
   1. Applying the Seventh Amendment: A Historical Analysis 578
   2. Problems in Applying the Historical Approach to a Modern
      Procedural System 581
     a. Statutory Claims 581
       Introductory Problem 581
       City of Monterey v. Del Monte Dunes at Monterey, Ltd. 582
       Notes and Questions 588
     b. Problems Arising from the Merger of Law and Equity 590
       Introductory Problem 590
       Marseilles Hydro Power, LLC v. Marseilles Land and Water
         Company 592
       Notes and Questions 594
     c. The Effect of the Federal Rules on Historically Equitable
       Claims 596
       Ross v. Bernhard 596
       Notes and Questions 599
     d. Public Rights 600
       Introductory Problem 600
       Granfinanciera, S.A. v. Nordberg 603
       Notes and Questions 606
   3. The Reexamination Clause 608
     Problems 609
B. Demanding a Jury Trial 610
  Marseilles Hydro Power, LLC v. Marseilles Land and Water Company .. 610
  Notes and Questions 611
  Problems 612
C. Selecting a Group of Prospective Jurors 612
  Floyd v. Garrison 614
  Notes and Questions 616
  Exercise 617
D. Challenging Individual Prospective Jurors 617
  Introductory Problem 617
  Thompson v. Altheimer & Gray 619
  Notes and Questions 622
  Exercise 624
  Alverio v. Sam's Warehouse Club, Inc. 629
  Notes and Questions 632
  Problems 633
  Exercise 634
E. Jury Instructions and Jury Verdicts 635
   1. Requesting and Objecting to Jury Instructions 635
     Jarvis v. Ford Motor Co. 636
     Notes and Questions 640
   2. Jury Verdicts 640
     Lavoie v. Pacific Press & Shear Co. 640
     Notes and Questions 643
     Problems 645
     Exercise 646

Page

Chapter 10. Dispositive and Post–Trial Motions _____ **647**
A. Dismissals _____ 647
  Introductory Problem _____ 647
    1. Voluntary Dismissals _____ 648
      Marques v. Federal Reserve Bank of Chicago _____ 648
      Notes and Questions _____ 650
      Hinfin Realty Corp. v. Pittston Co. _____ 651
      Notes and Questions _____ 655
    2. Involuntary Dismissals _____ 655
      Aura Lamp & Lighting Inc. v. International Trading Corp. ____ 656
      Notes and Questions _____ 661
      Problems _____ 662
      Exercise _____ 662
B. Default Judgments _____ 663
  Introductory Problem _____ 663
  KPS & Associates, Inc. v. Designs by FMC, Inc. _____ 663
  Notes and Questions _____ 669
  Problems _____ 671
  Exercise _____ 672
C. Resolving the Case Based on the Pleadings Alone _____ 672
  Introductory Problem _____ 672
D. Summary Judgment _____ 674
  Introductory Problem _____ 674
  Celotex Corp. v. Catrett _____ 675
  Notes and Questions _____ 681
  Jorgensen v. Epic/Sony Records _____ 686
  Notes and Questions _____ 692
  Problems _____ 693
E. Judgment as a Matter of Law _____ 694
  Introductory Problem One _____ 694
  Introductory Problem Two _____ 695
  Kinserlow v. CMI Corp., Bid–Well Div. _____ 696
  Notes and Questions _____ 701
  Problems _____ 704
F. New Trial _____ 705
  Introductory Problem _____ 705
  Piesco v. Koch _____ 706
  Notes and Questions _____ 711
  Problems _____ 715
  Exercise _____ 715
G. Relief From Judgment _____ 716
  Tate v. Riverboat Services, Inc. _____ 716
  Jones v. Lincoln Elec. Co. _____ 722
  Notes and Questions _____ 726
  Exercise _____ 728

Chapter 11. The Effect of a Judgment _____ **729**
A. Enforcing a Judgment _____ 729
B. Preclusive Effect of a Judgment: An Overview _____ 730
C. Claim Preclusion _____ 732
  Introductory Problem _____ 732
    1. The Basics of Claim Preclusion _____ 733
      Rodgers v. St. Mary's Hospital _____ 733
      Notes and Questions _____ 735
    2. Precluding Counterclaims, Cross-claims, and Defenses _____ 738
    3. Final Judgment on the Merits _____ 741

Page

C. Claim Preclusion—Continued
    4. Exceptions to Claim Preclusion ----------------------------- 742
       Problems --- 742
D. Issue Preclusion --- 744
    Introductory Problem ------------------------------------- 744
    1. Same Issue -- 745
       Williams v. City of Jacksonville Police Dept. ------------ 745
       Notes and Questions -------------------------------- 751
    2. Actually Litigated ------------------------------------- 752
    3. Actually Decided --------------------------------------- 753
    4. Necessary to the Judgment ----------------------------- 754
       Stemler v. Florence --------------------------------- 754
       Notes and Questions -------------------------------- 758
    5. Exceptions -- 760
       Problems --- 761
E. Parties Affected by Claim and Issue Preclusion ------------- 762
    Introductory Problem ------------------------------------- 763
    1. Who is Bound by an Adverse Judgment? --------------- 763
       Richards v. Jefferson County ----------------------- 763
       Notes and Questions -------------------------------- 770
    2. Who Can Take Advantage of a Judgment? -------------- 771
       Parklane Hosiery Co., Inc. v. Shore ---------------- 771
       Notes and Questions -------------------------------- 775
       Problems --- 776
F. Applying Preclusion Across State Lines --------------------- 776
    Introductory Problem ------------------------------------- 776
    Sentinel Acceptance Ltd., L.P. v. Hodson Auto Sales & Leasing, Inc. ---- 778
    Notes and Questions ------------------------------------- 781
    Durfee v. Duke --- 785
    Notes and Questions ------------------------------------- 788
    Problems --- 789
G. Doctrines Similar to Preclusion --------------------------- 790
    Introductory Problem ------------------------------------- 790
    1. Law of the Case --------------------------------------- 790
    2. Judicial Estoppel -------------------------------------- 791
       New Hampshire v. Maine ---------------------------- 791
       Notes and Questions -------------------------------- 796

Chapter 12. Appeals --------------------------------------- **797**
A. Who May Appeal --- 797
    Introductory Problem ------------------------------------- 797
    In re DES Litigation ------------------------------------- 798
    Notes and Questions ------------------------------------- 801
B. The Timing of an Appeal—The "Final Decision" Rule ------- 802
    Introductory Problem ------------------------------------- 802
    1. The Basic Rule -- 802
    2. Limitations on and Exceptions to the Rule ------------- 804
       N.A.A.C.P. v. American Family Mutual Insurance Co. ----- 804
       Notes and Questions -------------------------------- 806
       United States v. Bear Marine Services -------------- 809
       Notes and Questions -------------------------------- 811
       In re Diet Drugs (Phentermine/Fenfluramine/Dexfenfluramine)
          Products Liability Litigation --------------------- 813
       Notes and Questions -------------------------------- 817
       Problems --- 818

Page

C. Scope of Appellate Review — 819
 1. Need to Raise the Issue Below — 819
 2. The Standard of Review — 821
  Notes and Questions — 824
D. United States Supreme Court Review — 826
 1. Supreme Court Review of the Federal Courts of Appeal — 826
 2. Supreme Court Review of the States' High Courts — 827
  Michigan v. Long — 828
  Notes and Questions — 831
  Problems — 832

Chapter 13. Special Issues in Federal Court — **833**
A. Advanced Issues in Federal Question Jurisdiction — 833
 Introductory Problem — 833
 Nicodemus v. Union Pacific Corporation — 835
 Notes and Questions — 840
 Beneficial National Bank v. Anderson — 842
 Notes and Questions — 846
 Problems — 848
B. An In–Depth Look at the Erie Doctrine — 849
 1. Genesis of the Doctrine — 849
  Notes and Questions — 851
  Erie R. Co. v. Tompkins — 852
  Notes and Questions — 857
  Guaranty Trust Co. of New York v. York — 860
  Notes and Questions — 865
  Notes and Questions — 868
  Hanna v. Plumer — 869
  Notes and Questions — 874
 2. Applying the Modern Doctrine — 877
  Stewart Organization v. Ricoh Corporation — 877
  Notes and Questions — 880
  Notes and Questions — 883
  Semtek International Inc. v. Lockheed Martin Corp. — 883
  Notes and Questions — 887
 3. Federal Common Law — 888
  Texas Industries, Inc. v. Radcliff Materials, Inc. — 889
  Notes and Questions — 892
  Problems — 894

INDEX — 897

*

Table of Cases

The principal cases are in bold type. Cases cited or discussed in the text are roman type. References are to pages. Cases cited in principal cases and within other quoted materials are not included.

Ackermann v. Levine, 788 F.2d 830 (2nd Cir.1986), 235

Acridge v. Evangelical Lutheran Good Samaritan Soc., 334 F.3d 444 (5th Cir. 2003), 71

Adlman, United States v., 134 F.3d 1194 (2nd Cir.1998), 473

Aetna Casualty and Sur. Co. v. Leahey Const. Co., 219 F.3d 519 (6th Cir.2000), 823

Aetna Ins. Co. v. Meeker, 953 F.2d 1328 (11th Cir.1992), 357

Air Crash Disaster Near Roselawn, Indiana, In re, 96 F.3d 932 (7th Cir.1996), 601

Alexander v. F.B.I., 186 F.R.D. 148 (D.D.C.1999), **488**

Alexander v. Fulton County, Georgia, 207 F.3d 1303 (11th Cir.2000), **13**

Alfa Financial Corp. v. Key, 927 F.Supp. 423 (M.D.Ala.1996), 421

Ali v. Wang Laboratories, Inc., 162 F.R.D. 165 (M.D.Fla.1995), **513**

Alisal Water Corp., United States v., 370 F.3d 915 (9th Cir.2004), 397

Allen v. R & H Oil & Gas Co., 63 F.3d 1326 (5th Cir.1995), 78

Alternative System Concepts, Inc. v. Synopsys, Inc., 374 F.3d 23 (1st Cir. 2004), **291**

Alverio v. Sam's Warehouse Club, Inc., 253 F.3d 933 (7th Cir.2001), **629**

Amchem Products, Inc. v. Windsor, 521 U.S. 591, 117 S.Ct. 2231, 138 L.Ed.2d 689 (1997), 454

American Cyanamid Co. v. McGhee, 317 F.2d 295 (5th Cir.1963), 650

American Family Mutual Ins. Co. v. Roche, 830 F.Supp. 1241 (E.D.Wis.1993), 424

American Financial Life Ins. and Annuity Co. v. Youn, 2001 WL 369826 (10th Cir. 2001), 427

American Fire & Casualty Co. v. Finn, 341 U.S. 6, 71 S.Ct. 534, 95 L.Ed. 702 (1951), 113

American Motorcycle Assn. v. Superior Court, 146 Cal.Rptr. 182, 578 P.2d 899 (Cal.1978), 36

American National Red Cross v. S.G., 505 U.S. 247, 112 S.Ct. 2465, 120 L.Ed.2d 201 (1992), 847

American Ry. Express Co., United States v., 265 U.S. 425, 44 S.Ct. 560, 68 L.Ed. 1087 (1924), 820

American Soccer Co., Inc. v. Score First Enterprises, 187 F.3d 1108 (9th Cir. 1999), 650

American States Insurance Co. v. Dastar Corp., 318 F.3d 881 (9th Cir.2003), 373

Amoco Egypt Oil Co. v. Leonis Nav. Co., Inc., 1 F.3d 848 (9th Cir.1993), 137

Anderson v. Liberty Lobby, Inc., 477 U.S. 242, 106 S.Ct. 2505, 91 L.Ed.2d 202 (1986), 683

Anderson v. Smithfield Foods, Inc., 353 F.3d 912 (11th Cir.2003), 365

Andrews v. Daw, 201 F.3d 521 (4th Cir. 2000), 770

Ankenbrandt v. Richards, 504 U.S. 689, 112 S.Ct. 2206, 119 L.Ed.2d 468 (1992), 84

Apache County v. Superior Court, 163 Ariz. 54, 785 P.2d 1242 (Ariz.App. Div. 1 1989), **11**

Appelbaum v. Milwaukee Metropolitan Sewerage Dist., 340 F.3d 573 (7th Cir. 2003), 702

Arakaki v. Cayetano, 324 F.3d 1078 (9th Cir.2003), 396

ARCO Environmental Remediation, L.L.C. v. Department of Health and Environmental Quality of Montana, 213 F.3d 1108 (9th Cir.2000), 842

Aristech Chemical Intern. Ltd. v. Acrylic Fabricators Ltd., 138 F.3d 624 (6th Cir. 1998), 138

Art Press, Ltd. v. Western Printing Machinery Co., 791 F.2d 616 (7th Cir.1986), 626

Asahi Metal Industry Co., Ltd. v. Superior Court of California, Solano

County, 480 U.S. 102, 107 S.Ct. 1026, 94 L.Ed.2d 92 (1987), **183**

Asea, Inc. v. Southern Pacific Transp. Co., 669 F.2d 1242 (9th Cir.1981), **508**

Atlantic Pipe Corp., In re, 304 F.3d 135 (1st Cir.2002), **552**

Atlantis Development Corp. v. United States, 379 F.2d 818 (5th Cir.1967), 398, 408

Atlas Roofing Co., Inc. v. Occupational Safety and Health Review Com'n, 430 U.S. 442, 97 S.Ct. 1261, 51 L.Ed.2d 464 (1977), 602

Aura Lamp & Lighting Inc. v. International Trading Corp., 325 F.3d 903 (7th Cir.2003), **656**

A.V. Imports, Inc. v. Col De Fratta, S.p.A., 171 F.Supp.2d 369 (D.N.J.2001), 191

Ayres v. Jacobs & Crumplar, P.A., 99 F.3d 565 (3rd Cir.1996), 223

Baker v. General Motors Corp., 209 F.3d 1051 (8th Cir.2000), 476

Baker v. Gold Seal Liquors, Inc., 417 U.S. 467, 94 S.Ct. 2504, 41 L.Ed.2d 243 (1974), 23

Bank of Credit and Commerce International (OVERSEAS) Ltd. v. State Bank of Pakistan, 273 F.3d 241 (2nd Cir.2001), 257

Bankston v. Toyota Motor Corp., 889 F.2d 172 (8th Cir.1989), 235

Barrett v. Catacombs Press, 44 F.Supp.2d 717 (E.D.Pa.1999), 206

Basco v. Wal–Mart Stores, Inc., 216 F.Supp.2d 592 (E.D.La.2002), 447

Beacon Theatres, Inc. v. Westover, 359 U.S. 500, 79 S.Ct. 948, 3 L.Ed.2d 988 (1959), 595

Bear Marine Services, United States v., 696 F.2d 1117 (5th Cir.1983), **809**

Bearry v. Beech Aircraft Corp., 818 F.2d 370 (5th Cir.1987), 171

Beckstrom v. Coastwise Line, 14 Alaska 190, 13 F.R.D. 480 (D.Alaska Terr.1953), 350

Beeck v. Aquaslide 'N' Dive Corp., 562 F.2d 537 (8th Cir.1977), **369**

Belleville Catering Co. v. Champaign Market Place, L.L.C., 350 F.3d 691 (7th Cir. 2003), 364

Beneficial National Bank v. Anderson, 539 U.S. 1, 123 S.Ct. 2058, 156 L.Ed.2d 1 (2003), **842**

Bills v. Aseltine, 52 F.3d 596 (6th Cir.1995), 644

Bivens v. Six Unknown Named Agents of Federal Bureau of Narcotics, 403 U.S. 388, 91 S.Ct. 1999, 29 L.Ed.2d 619 (1971), 61

Bleecker v. Standard Fire Ins. Co., 130 F.Supp.2d 726 (E.D.N.C.2000), 507

Boggs v. West, 188 F.3d 1335 (Fed.Cir. 1999), 820

Borden v. CSX Transportation, Inc., 843 F.Supp. 1410 (M.D.Ala.1993), 693

Bouchard Transportation Co. v. Florida Dept. of Environmental Protection, 91 F.3d 1445 (11th Cir.1996), 562

Bowen v. Amoco Pipeline Co., 254 F.3d 925 (10th Cir.2001), **527,** 535

Bowen v. Parking Authority of City of Camden, 214 F.R.D. 188 (D.N.J.2003), 516

Boyce, United States v., 148 F.Supp.2d 1069 (S.D.Cal.2001), 468

Bradley v. Kochenash, 44 F.3d 166 (2nd Cir.1995), 422

Brandon, Jones, Sandall, Zeide, Kohn, Chalal & Musso, P.A. v. MedPartners, Inc., 312 F.3d 1349 (11th Cir.2002), 803

Bridgeport Music, Inc. v. Still N The Water Publishing, 327 F.3d 472 (6th Cir.2003), 136, 215

Bridgestone/Firestone, Inc., In re, 288 F.3d 1012 (7th Cir.2002), 449

Bristol–Myers Squibb Securities Litigation, In re, 205 F.R.D. 437 (D.N.J.2002), 507

Brown v. Webster, 156 U.S. 328, 15 S.Ct. 377, 39 L.Ed. 440 (1895), 76

Browning v. Clinton, 292 F.3d 235, 352 U.S.App.D.C. 4 (D.C.Cir.2002), **296**

Buffalo Courier–Express, Inc. v. Buffalo Evening News, Inc., 601 F.2d 48 (2nd Cir.1979), 825

Burford v. Sun Oil Co., 319 U.S. 315, 63 S.Ct. 1098, 87 L.Ed. 1424 (1943), 84

Burger King Corp. v. Rudzewicz, 471 U.S. 462, 105 S.Ct. 2174, 85 L.Ed.2d 528 (1985), **172**

Burlington Northern Railroad Co. v. Woods, 480 U.S. 1, 107 S.Ct. 967, 94 L.Ed.2d 1 (1987), 332, 876

Burlington Northern & Santa Fe Ry. Co. v. United States Dist. Court for Dist. of Montana, 408 F.3d 1142 (9th Cir.2005), 466

Burnham v. Superior Court of California, County of Marin, 495 U.S. 604, 110 S.Ct. 2105, 109 L.Ed.2d 631 (1990), **191**

Business Guides, Inc. v. Chromatic Communications Enterprises, Inc., 498 U.S. 533, 111 S.Ct. 922, 112 L.Ed.2d 1140 (1991), 357

Byrd v. Blue Ridge Rural Electric Co-op., Inc., 356 U.S. 525, 78 S.Ct. 893, 2 L.Ed.2d 953 (1958), 867

Caldarera v. Eastern Airlines, Inc., 705 F.2d 778 (5th Cir.1983), 712

Calder v. Jones, 465 U.S. 783, 104 S.Ct. 1482, 79 L.Ed.2d 804 (1984), **159**

Campania Management Co., Inc. v. Rooks, Pitts & Poust, 290 F.3d 843 (7th Cir. 2002), 373

Capron v. Van Noorden, 6 U.S. 126, 2 L.Ed. 229 (1804), 118

Cardtoons, L.C. v. Major League Baseball Players Ass'n, 95 F.3d 959 (10th Cir. 1996), 60

Carnival Cruise Lines, Inc. v. Shute, 499 U.S. 585, 111 S.Ct. 1522, 113 L.Ed.2d 622 (1991), 132

Caterpillar Inc. v. Lewis, 519 U.S. 61, 117 S.Ct. 467, 136 L.Ed.2d 437 (1996), 75, 80

Caterpillar Inc. v. Williams, 482 U.S. 386, 107 S.Ct. 2425, 96 L.Ed.2d 318 (1987), **109**

Catlin v. United States, 324 U.S. 229, 65 S.Ct. 631, 89 L.Ed. 911 (1945), 803

Cauley v. Ingram Micro, Inc., 216 F.R.D. 241 (W.D.N.Y.2003), 516

Celotex Corp. v. Catrett, 477 U.S. 317, 106 S.Ct. 2548, 91 L.Ed.2d 265 (1986), **675**

Chamberlain v. Giampapa, 210 F.3d 154 (3rd Cir.2000), **326**

Chambers v. NASCO, Inc., 501 U.S. 32, 111 S.Ct. 2123, 115 L.Ed.2d 27 (1991), 351, 561

Chauffeurs, Teamsters and Helpers, Local No. 391 v. Terry, 494 U.S. 558, 110 S.Ct. 1339, 108 L.Ed.2d 519 (1990), 589

Chicot County Drainage Dist. v. Baxter State Bank, 308 U.S. 371, 60 S.Ct. 317, 84 L.Ed. 329 (1940), 119

Chiles v. Thornburgh, 865 F.2d 1197 (11th Cir.1989), **388**

Christian v. Mattel, Inc., 286 F.3d 1118 (9th Cir.2002), **358**

Christy v. Pennsylvania Turnpike Com'n, 912 F.Supp. 148 (E.D.Pa.1996), 811

Chrysler Motors Corp. v. Thomas Auto Co., Inc., 939 F.2d 538 (8th Cir.1991), 804

Cincinnati Ins. Co. v. Reybitz, 205 Ga.App. 174, 421 S.E.2d 767 (Ga.App.1992), 18

Citizens for Open Access to Sand and Tide, Inc. v. Seadrift Ass'n, 71 Cal.Rptr.2d 77 (Cal.App. 1 Dist.1998), 736

City of (see name of city)

Clune v. Alimak AB, 233 F.3d 538 (8th Cir.2000), 137

Coleman v. Parkman, 349 F.3d 534 (8th Cir.2003), 818

Colgrove v. Battin, 413 U.S. 149, 93 S.Ct. 2448, 37 L.Ed.2d 522 (1973), 617

Columbia Gas Transmission Corp. v. Drain, 191 F.3d 552 (4th Cir.1999), 841

Commercial Space Management Co., Inc. v. Boeing Co., Inc., 193 F.3d 1074 (9th Cir.1999), 650

Commercial Union Insurance Co. v. United States, 999 F.2d 581, 303 U.S.App.D.C. 33 (D.C.Cir.1993), 427, 428

Commonwealth Edison Co. v. Train, 71 F.R.D. 391 (N.D.Ill.1976), 398

Computer Access Technology Corp. v. Catalyst Enterprises, Inc., 273 F.Supp.2d 1063 (N.D.Cal.2003), 702

Cooter & Gell v. Hartmarx Corp., 496 U.S. 384, 110 S.Ct. 2447, 110 L.Ed.2d 359 (1990), 364

Cox v. Quigley, 141 F.R.D. 222 (D.Me. 1992), **227**

CSX Transportation, Inc. v. Union Tank Car Co., 247 F.Supp.2d 833 (E.D.Mich. 2002), 172

Curry v. Regents of University of Minnesota, 167 F.3d 420 (8th Cir.1999), 396

Curtis v. Loether, 415 U.S. 189, 94 S.Ct. 1005, 39 L.Ed.2d 260 (1974), 579

Curtiss–Wright Corp. v. General Elec. Co., 446 U.S. 1, 100 S.Ct. 1460, 64 L.Ed.2d 1 (1980), 807

Dairy Queen, Inc. v. Wood, 369 U.S. 469, 82 S.Ct. 894, 8 L.Ed.2d 44 (1962), 598

Dandridge v. Williams, 397 U.S. 471, 90 S.Ct. 1153, 25 L.Ed.2d 491 (1970), 820

Daniels v. USS Agri–Chemicals, 965 F.2d 376 (7th Cir.1992), **282**

Davey v. Lockheed Martin Corp., 301 F.3d 1204 (10th Cir.2002), 633

Davis v. Hutchins, 321 F.3d 641 (7th Cir. 2003), 446

Dawavendewa v. Salt River Project Agricultural Improvement and Power District, 276 F.3d 1150 (9th Cir.2002), **402**

Day & Zimmermann, Inc. v. Challoner, 423 U.S. 3, 96 S.Ct. 167, 46 L.Ed.2d 3 (1975), 877

Dennis v. Dillard Dept. Stores, Inc., 207 F.3d 523 (8th Cir.2000), 373

DES Litigation, In re, 7 F.3d 20 (2nd Cir.1993), **798**

Dice v. Akron, Canton, and Youngstown R. Co., 342 U.S. 359, 72 S.Ct. 312, 96 L.Ed. 398 (1952), 868

Diet Drugs (Phentermine/Fenfluramine/Dexfenflurammine) Products Liability Litigation, In re, 401 F.3d 143 (3rd Cir.2005), **813**

Dimick v. Schiedt, 293 U.S. 474, 55 S.Ct. 296, 79 L.Ed. 603 (1935), 713

Donaldson v. United States, 400 U.S. 517, 91 S.Ct. 534, 27 L.Ed.2d 580 (1971), 396

Donnelly v. Glickman, 159 F.3d 405 (9th Cir.1998), 394

Dunlap v. G&L Holding Group, Inc., 381 F.3d 1285 (11th Cir.2004), 842

Duren v. Missouri, 439 U.S. 357, 99 S.Ct. 664, 58 L.Ed.2d 579 (1979), 616

Durfee v. Duke, 375 U.S. 106, 84 S.Ct. 242, 11 L.Ed.2d 186 (1963), 119, **785**

Eastman Kodak Co. v. Kavlin, 978 F.Supp. 1078 (S.D.Fla.1997), 257

EDIAS Software Intern., L.L.C. v. BASIS Intern. Ltd., 947 F.Supp. 413 (D.Ariz. 1996), 205

E.E.O.C. v. Kohler Co., 335 F.3d 766 (8th Cir.2003), 702

E.E.O.C. v. Lutheran Social Services, 186 F.3d 959, 337 U.S.App.D.C. 373 (D.C.Cir.1999), 474

Eiland v. Westinghouse Elec. Corp., 58 F.3d 176 (5th Cir.1995), 712

Eisen v. Carlisle and Jacquelin, 417 U.S. 156, 94 S.Ct. 2140, 40 L.Ed.2d 732 (1974), 450

Eldredge v. Martin Marietta Corp., 207 F.3d 737 (5th Cir.2000), 806

Ellington, Estate of v. EMI Music Publishing, 282 F.Supp.2d 192 (S.D.N.Y.2003), 429

Emcasco Ins. Co. v. Davis, 753 F.Supp. 1458 (W.D.Ark.1990), 421

EOI Corp. v. Medical Marketing Ltd., 172 F.R.D. 133 (D.N.J.1997), 235

Erie R. Co. v. Tompkins, 304 U.S. 64, 58 S.Ct. 817, 82 L.Ed. 1188 (1938), **852**

ESAB Group, Inc. v. Centricut, Inc., 126 F.3d 617 (4th Cir.1997), 164

ESI, Inc. v. Coastal Power Production Co., 13 F.Supp.2d 495 (S.D.N.Y.1998), 693

Estate of (see name of party)

Estes v. Midwest Products, Inc., 24 F.Supp.2d 621 (S.D.W.Va.1998), 159

Ex parte (see name of party)

Exxon Mobil Corp. v. Allapattah Services, Inc., ___ U.S. ___, 125 S.Ct. 2611, 162 L.Ed.2d 502 (2005), **95, 453**

Faber v. Menard, Inc., 267 F.Supp.2d 961 (N.D.Iowa 2003), 811

Fanselow v. Rice, 213 F.Supp.2d 1077 (D.Neb.2002), 250

Far West Capital, Inc. v. Towne, 46 F.3d 1071 (10th Cir.1995), 164

Faulkner v. Caledonia County Fair Ass'n, 869 A.2d 103 (Vt.2004), 732

Fauntleroy v. Lum, 210 U.S. 230, 28 S.Ct. 641, 52 L.Ed. 1039 (1908), 782

Federated Department Stores, Inc. v. Moitie, 452 U.S. 394, 101 S.Ct. 2424, 69 L.Ed.2d 103 (1981), 673, 741

Ferens v. John Deere Co., 494 U.S. 516, 110 S.Ct. 1274, 108 L.Ed.2d 443 (1990), 249

Fierro v. Grant, 53 F.3d 338 (9th Cir.1995), 397

Finley v. United States, 490 U.S. 545, 109 S.Ct. 2003, 104 L.Ed.2d 593 (1989), 103

First American First, Inc. v. National Ass'n of Bank Women, 802 F.2d 1511 (4th Cir.1986), 163

First Interstate Bank of Oregon, N.A. v. United States By and Through I.R.S., 891 F.Supp. 543 (D.Or.1995), 420

First Nat. Bank of Pulaski v. Curry, 301 F.3d 456 (6th Cir.2002), 115

FleetBoston Financial Corp. v. FleetBostonFinancial.com, 138 F.Supp.2d 121 (D.Mass.2001), 150

Floyd v. Garrison, 996 F.2d 947 (8th Cir. 1993), **614**

Ford Motor Co., In re, 344 F.3d 648 (7th Cir.2003), 818

Ford Motor Co., In re, 110 F.3d 954 (3rd Cir.1997), 475

Franchise Tax Board of State of California v. Construction Laborers Vacation Trust, 463 U.S. 1, 103 S.Ct. 2841, 77 L.Ed.2d 420 (1983), 841

Franklin America, Inc. v. Franklin Cast Products, Inc., 94 F.R.D. 645 (E.D.Mich. 1982), 232

Frew ex rel. Frew v. Hawkins, 540 U.S. 431, 124 S.Ct. 899, 157 L.Ed.2d 855 (2004), 727

Gambelli v. United States, 904 F.Supp. 494 (E.D.Va.1995), 71

Garrett v. Fleming, 362 F.3d 692 (10th Cir. 2004), 383

Garvie v. City of Ft. Walton Beach, Florida, 366 F.3d 1186 (11th Cir.2004), 578

Gasperini v. Center for Humanities, Inc., 518 U.S. 415, 116 S.Ct. 2211, 135 L.Ed.2d 659 (1996), 609, 881

Gator.Com Corp. v. L.L. Bean, Inc., 341 F.3d 1072 (9th Cir.2003), **206**

Genentech, Inc. v. Novo Nordisk A/S, 907 F.Supp. 97 (S.D.N.Y.1995), 811

Getter v. Wal–Mart Stores, Inc., 66 F.3d 1119 (10th Cir.1995), 625

Glancy v. Taubman Centers, Inc., 373 F.3d 656 (6th Cir.2004), 409

Gomez v. Toledo, 446 U.S. 635, 100 S.Ct. 1920, 64 L.Ed.2d 572 (1980), 345

Gorman v. Ameritrade Holding Corp., 293 F.3d 506, 352 U.S.App.D.C. 229 (D.C.Cir.2002), 215

Grable & Sons Metal Products, Inc. v. Darue Engineering & Mfg., ___ U.S. ___, 125 S.Ct. 2363, 162 L.Ed.2d 257 (2005), 847

Grace v. MacArthur, 170 F.Supp. 442 (E.D.Ark.1959), 125

Granfinanciera, S.A. v. Nordberg, 492 U.S. 33, 109 S.Ct. 2782, 106 L.Ed.2d 26 (1989), **603**

Gray v. St. Martin's Press, Inc., 929 F.Supp. 40 (D.N.H.1996), 189

Great American Ins. Co. v. Spraycraft, Inc., 844 F.Supp. 1188 (S.D.Ohio 1994), 429

Greene v. Lindsey, 456 U.S. 444, 102 S.Ct. 1874, 72 L.Ed.2d 249 (1982), 222

Greene v. United States, 996 F.2d 973 (9th Cir.1993), 396

Griffin v. McCoach, 313 U.S. 498, 61 S.Ct. 1023, 85 L.Ed. 1481 (1941), 877

Grupo Dataflux v. Atlas Global Group, L.P., 541 U.S. 567, 124 S.Ct. 1920, 158 L.Ed.2d 866 (2004), 80

Guaranty Trust Co. of New York v. York, 326 U.S. 99, 65 S.Ct. 1464, 89 L.Ed. 2079 (1945), **860**

Gully v. First Nat. Bank, 299 U.S. 109, 57 S.Ct. 96, 81 L.Ed. 70 (1936), 56

Gutshall v. New Prime, Inc., 196 F.R.D. 43 (W.D.Va.2000), **476**

Hadges v. Yonkers Racing Corp., 48 F.3d 1320 (2nd Cir.1995), 365

Hamling v. United States, 418 U.S. 87, 94 S.Ct. 2887, 41 L.Ed.2d 590 (1974), 617

Hanna v. Plumer, 380 U.S. 460, 85 S.Ct. 1136, 14 L.Ed.2d 8 (1965), **869**

Hansberry v. Lee, 311 U.S. 32, 61 S.Ct. 115, 85 L.Ed. 22 (1940), **432**

Hanson v. Denckla, 357 U.S. 235, 78 S.Ct. 1228, 2 L.Ed.2d 1283 (1958), 141

Harris v. Interstate Brands Corp., 348 F.3d 761 (8th Cir.2003), 578

Hayduk v. Lanna, 775 F.2d 441 (1st Cir. 1985), 331

Hazel–Atlas Glass Co. v. Hartford–Empire Co., 322 U.S. 238, 64 S.Ct. 997, 88 L.Ed. 1250 (1944), 726

Headwaters Forest Defense v. County of Humboldt, 240 F.3d 1185 (9th Cir.2000), 704

Helicopteros Nacionales de Colombia, S.A. v. Hall, 466 U.S. 408, 104 S.Ct. 1868, 80 L.Ed.2d 404 (1984), **164**

Heller Financial, Inc. v. Prudential Ins. Co. of America, 371 F.3d 944 (7th Cir.2004), 428

Henry v. Mississippi, 379 U.S. 443, 85 S.Ct. 564, 13 L.Ed.2d 408 (1965), 831

Herb v. Pitcairn, 324 U.S. 117, 65 S.Ct. 459, 89 L.Ed. 789 (1945), 827

Hernandez v. New York, 500 U.S. 352, 111 S.Ct. 1859, 114 L.Ed.2d 395 (1991), 632

Hess v. Pawloski, 274 U.S. 352, 47 S.Ct. 632, 71 L.Ed. 1091 (1927), 126, 133

Hickman v. Taylor, 329 U.S. 495, 67 S.Ct. 385, 91 L.Ed. 451 (1947), **469**

Hicks v. Long Island R.R., 165 F.R.D. 377 (E.D.N.Y.1996), 37

Higgins v. E.I. DuPont de Nemours & Co., 863 F.2d 1162 (4th Cir.1988), 114

Hilton v. Guyot, 159 U.S. 113, 16 S.Ct. 139, 40 L.Ed. 95 (1895), 784

Hinderlider v. La Plata River & Cherry Creek Ditch Co., 304 U.S. 92, 58 S.Ct. 803, 82 L.Ed. 1202 (1938), 892

Hinfin Realty Corp. v. Pittston Co., 206 F.R.D. 350 (E.D.N.Y.2002), **651**

Hipp v. Liberty Nat. Life Ins. Co., 252 F.3d 1208 (11th Cir.2001), 451

Hoffman v. Blaski, 363 U.S. 335, 80 S.Ct. 1084, 4 L.Ed.2d 1254 (1960), 249

Holland v. Illinois, 493 U.S. 474, 110 S.Ct. 803, 107 L.Ed.2d 905 (1990), 614

Hollis v. Florida State University, 259 F.3d 1295 (11th Cir.2001), 243

Honda Motor Co., Ltd. v. Oberg, 512 U.S. 415, 114 S.Ct. 2331, 129 L.Ed.2d 336 (1994), 824

Hossler v. Barry, 403 A.2d 762 (Me.1979), 775

Houben v. Telular Corp., 309 F.3d 1028 (7th Cir.2002), **320**

Howard Johnson International, Inc. v. Wang, 7 F.Supp.2d 336 (S.D.N.Y.1998), 233

Howard Motor Co., Inc. v. Swint, 214 Ga. App. 682, 448 S.E.2d 713 (Ga.App.1994), 17

Hudson, United States v., 11 U.S. 32, 3 L.Ed. 259 (1812), 562

Huffey v. Lea, 491 N.W.2d 518 (Iowa 1992), **44**

Humble Oil & Refining Co. v. Copeland, 398 F.2d 364 (4th Cir.1968), 423

Hurd v. American Hoist and Derrick Co., 734 F.2d 495 (10th Cir.1984), 702

Hutchinson, In re, 5 F.3d 750 (4th Cir. 1993), 589

Illinois v. City of Milwaukee, Wisconsin, 406 U.S. 91, 92 S.Ct. 1385, 31 L.Ed.2d 712 (1972), 62, 893

Indianapolis, City of v. Chase Nat. Bank of City of New York, 314 U.S. 63, 62 S.Ct. 15, 86 L.Ed. 47 (1941), 82

Indianapolis Colts v. Mayor and City Council of Baltimore, 741 F.2d 954 (7th Cir. 1984), 420

In re (see name of party)

Integra Realty Resources, Inc., In re, 262 F.3d 1089 (10th Cir.2001), 437

International Action Center v. United States, 365 F.3d 20, 361 U.S.App.D.C. 108 (D.C.Cir.2004), 818

International Brotherhood of Teamsters, Chauffeurs, Stablemen and Helpers of America, Local Union No. 523, of Tulsa, Oklahoma v. Keystone Freight Lines, 123 F.2d 326 (10th Cir.1941), 409

International Controls Corp. v. Vesco, 593 F.2d 166 (2nd Cir.1979), 227

International Shoe Co. v. Washington, 326 U.S. 310, 66 S.Ct. 154, 90 L.Ed. 95 (1945), **127**

Irvin v. Dowd, 366 U.S. 717, 81 S.Ct. 1639, 6 L.Ed.2d 751 (1961), 624

Jacobs v. Felix Bloch Erben Verlag fur Buhne Film und Funk KG, 160 F.Supp.2d 722 (S.D.N.Y.2001), 258

Jaffe and Asher v. Van Brunt, 158 F.R.D. 278 (S.D.N.Y.1994), 231

Jarvis v. Ford Motor Co., 283 F.3d 33 (2nd Cir.2002), **636**

J.E.B. v. Alabama ex rel. T.B., 511 U.S. 127, 114 S.Ct. 1419, 128 L.Ed.2d 89 (1994), 632

Jinks v. Richland County, South Carolina, 538 U.S. 456, 123 S.Ct. 1667, 155 L.Ed.2d 631 (2003), 104

Jones v. Lincoln Elec. Co., 188 F.3d 709 (7th Cir.1999), **722**

Jorgensen v. Epic/Sony Records, 351 F.3d 46 (2nd Cir.2003), **686**

Kadic v. Karadzic, 70 F.3d 232 (2nd Cir. 1995), 62

Kalb v. Feuerstein, 308 U.S. 433, 60 S.Ct. 343, 84 L.Ed. 370 (1940), 119

Karahalios v. National Federation of Federal Employees, 489 U.S. 527, 109 S.Ct. 1282, 103 L.Ed.2d 539 (1989), 840

Kasap v. Folger Nolan Fleming & Douglas, Inc., 166 F.3d 1243, 334 U.S.App.D.C. 280 (D.C.Cir.1999), 62

Keeton v. Hustler Magazine, Inc., 465 U.S. 770, 104 S.Ct. 1473, 79 L.Ed.2d 790 (1984), 163

King Vision Pay Per View, Ltd. v. J.C. Dimitri's Restaurant, Inc., 180 F.R.D. 332 (N.D.Ill.1998), **337**

Kinserlow v. CMI Corp, 217 F.3d 1021 (8th Cir.2000), **696**

Klaxon Co. v. Stentor Electric Mfg. Co., 313 U.S. 487, 61 S.Ct. 1020, 85 L.Ed. 1477 (1941), 325, 859

Kolb v. Scherer Bros. Financial Services Co., 6 F.3d 542 (8th Cir.1993), 28

Kopke v. A. Hartrodt S.R.L., 245 Wis.2d 396, 629 N.W.2d 662 (Wis.2001), 190

KPS & Associates, Inc. v. Designs By FMC, Inc., 318 F.3d 1 (1st Cir.2003), **663**

Kramer v. Caribbean Mills, Inc., 394 U.S. 823, 89 S.Ct. 1487, 23 L.Ed.2d 9 (1969), 83

Kuhn v. Fairmont Coal Co., 215 U.S. 349, 30 S.Ct. 140, 54 L.Ed. 228 (1910), 856

Kwoczak, United States v., 210 F.Supp.2d 638 (E.D.Pa.2002), 702

Kyocera Corp. v. Prudential–Bache Trade Services, Inc., 341 F.3d 987 (9th Cir. 2003), 536

Lakin v. Prudential Securities, Inc., 348 F.3d 704 (8th Cir.2003), 170

LAK, Inc. v. Deer Creek Enterprises, 885 F.2d 1293 (6th Cir.1989), 181

Larsen v. Mayo Medical Center, 218 F.3d 863 (8th Cir.2000), **223**

Larson v. Domestic & Foreign Commerce Corp., 337 U.S. 682, 69 S.Ct. 1457, 93 L.Ed. 1628 (1949), 61

Lavoie v. Pacific Press & Shear Co., a Div. of Canron Corp., 975 F.2d 48 (2nd Cir.1992), **640, 821**

League of United Latin American Citizens v. Wilson, 131 F.3d 1297 (9th Cir.1997), 395

Leasetec Corp. v. Cumberland, 896 F.Supp. 35 (D.Me.1995), 34

Leatherman v. Tarrant County Narcotics Intelligence and Coordination Unit, 507 U.S. 163, 113 S.Ct. 1160, 122 L.Ed.2d 517 (1993), 295

Lee v. Walters, 172 F.R.D. 421 (D.Or. 1997), **517**

Lehan v. Ambassador Programs, Inc., 190 F.R.D. 670 (E.D.Wash.2000), **481**

Lehman v. Nakshian, 453 U.S. 156, 101 S.Ct. 2698, 69 L.Ed.2d 548 (1981), 601

LeSane v. Hall's Security Analyst, Inc., 239 F.3d 206 (2nd Cir.2001), 656

Lesnick v. Hollingsworth & Vose Co., 35 F.3d 939 (4th Cir.1994), 190

Levin v. Ruby Trading Corp., 248 F.Supp. 537 (S.D.N.Y.1965), 235

Liljeberg v. Health Services Acquisition Corp., 486 U.S. 847, 108 S.Ct. 2194, 100 L.Ed.2d 855 (1988), 728

Limon–Hernandez v. Lumbreras, 171 F.R.D. 271 (D.Or.1997), 233

Lincoln Property Co. v. Roche, ___ U.S. ___, 126 S.Ct. 606 (2005), 114

Link v. Wabash R. Co., 370 U.S. 626, 82 S.Ct. 1386, 8 L.Ed.2d 734 (1962), 661

Local Union No. 11 v. G.P. Thompson Elec., Inc., 363 F.2d 181 (9th Cir.1966), 25

Lopez de Robinson v. United States, 162 F.R.D. 256 (D.Puerto Rico 1995), **31**

Louisiana Power & Light Co. v. City of Thibodaux, 360 U.S. 25, 79 S.Ct. 1070, 3 L.Ed.2d 1058 (1959), 84

Louisville & Nashville Railroad Co. v. Mottley, 219 U.S. 467, 31 S.Ct. 265, 55 L.Ed. 297 (1911), 59

Louisville & Nashville Railroad Co. v. Mottley, 211 U.S. 149, 29 S.Ct. 42, 53 L.Ed. 126 (1908), **56**

Lundquist v. Precision Valley Aviation, Inc., 946 F.2d 8 (1st Cir.1991), **66**

Mann v. Lewis, 108 F.3d 145 (8th Cir.1997), 662

Marek v. Chesny, 473 U.S. 1, 105 S.Ct. 3012, 87 L.Ed.2d 1 (1985), **565**

Markman v. Westview Instruments, Inc., 517 U.S. 370, 116 S.Ct. 1384, 134 L.Ed.2d 577 (1996), 590

Marlar, In re, 267 F.3d 749 (8th Cir.2001), 768

Marques v. Federal Reserve Bank of Chicago, 286 F.3d 1014 (7th Cir.2002), **648**

Marrese v. American Academy of Orthopaedic Surgeons, 470 U.S. 373, 105 S.Ct. 1327, 84 L.Ed.2d 274 (1985), 784

Marseilles Hydro Power, LLC v. Marseilles Land and Water Co., 299 F.3d 643 (7th Cir.2002), **592, 610**

Martin v. Wilks, 490 U.S. 755, 109 S.Ct. 2180, 104 L.Ed.2d 835 (1989), 411

Massachusetts School of Law at Andover, Inc. v. American Bar Ass'n, 142 F.3d 26 (1st Cir.1998), 737

McCoo v. Denny's Inc., 192 F.R.D. 675 (D.Kan.2000), 466

McCoy v. Like, 511 N.E.2d 501 (Ind.App. 1 Dist.1987), 17, **38**

McDonough Power Equipment, Inc. v. Greenwood, 464 U.S. 548, 104 S.Ct. 845, 78 L.Ed.2d 663 (1984), 623

McGee v. International Life Ins. Co., 355 U.S. 220, 78 S.Ct. 199, 2 L.Ed.2d 223 (1957), 140

Mejdrech v. Met–Coil Systems Corp., 319 F.3d 910 (7th Cir.2003), 449

Melkaz International Inc. v. Flavor Innovation Inc., 167 F.R.D. 634 (E.D.N.Y. 1996), 234

Memphis, In re City of, 293 F.3d 345 (6th Cir.2002), 811

Mendoza, United States v., 464 U.S. 154, 104 S.Ct. 568, 78 L.Ed.2d 379 (1984), 776

Merrill Lynch, Pierce, Fenner & Smith, Inc. v. Curran, 456 U.S. 353, 102 S.Ct. 1825, 72 L.Ed.2d 182 (1982), 840

Mesa v. California, 489 U.S. 121, 109 S.Ct. 959, 103 L.Ed.2d 99 (1989), 60, 113

Metcalf v. Lawson, 148 N.H. 35, 802 A.2d 1221 (N.H.2002), 206

Meteoro Amusement Corp. v. Six Flags, 267 F.Supp.2d 263 (N.D.N.Y. 2003), **244**

Metropolitan Life Ins. Co. v. Ditmore, 729 F.2d 1 (1st Cir.1984), 408

Metropolitan Life Ins. Co. v. Robertson–Ceco Corp., 84 F.3d 560 (2nd Cir.1996), 137

Metropolitan Property and Casualty Ins. Co. v. Shan Trac, Inc., 324 F.3d 20 (1st Cir.2003), 423

Mexico Money Transfer Litigation, In re, 267 F.3d 743 (7th Cir.2001), 449

Michigan v. Long, 463 U.S. 1032, 103 S.Ct. 3469, 77 L.Ed.2d 1201 (1983), **828**

Michigan Nat. Bank v. Quality Dinette, Inc., 888 F.2d 462 (6th Cir.1989), 171

Migra v. Warren City School Dist. Board of Education, 465 U.S. 75, 104 S.Ct. 892, 79 L.Ed.2d 56 (1984), 784

Miller–El v. Dretke, ___ U.S. ___, 125 S.Ct. 2317, 162 L.Ed.2d 196 (2005), 633

Milliken v. Meyer, 311 U.S. 457, 61 S.Ct. 339, 85 L.Ed. 278 (1940), 133

M.K. v. Tenet, 216 F.R.D. 133 (D.D.C.2002), 17

Mobile, In re City of, 75 F.3d 605 (11th Cir.1996), 113

Mohr v. Chicago School Reform Board of Trustees of Board of Education of City of Chicago, 155 F.Supp.2d 923 (N.D.Ill. 2001), 702

Mollan v. Torrance, 22 U.S. 537, 6 L.Ed. 154 (1824), 80

Montana v. United States, 440 U.S. 147, 99 S.Ct. 970, 59 L.Ed.2d 210 (1979), 437, 771

Monterey, City of v. Del Monte Dunes at Monterey, Ltd., 526 U.S. 687, 119 S.Ct. 1624, 143 L.Ed.2d 882 (1999), **582**

Montgomery v. City of Ardmore, 365 F.3d 926 (10th Cir.2004), 820

Montrose Chemical Corp. of California v. American Motorists Insurance Co., 117 F.3d 1128 (9th Cir.1997), **71**

Morguard Investments Ltd. v. De Savoye (S.C.C.1990), 783

Morton v. Mancari, 417 U.S. 535, 94 S.Ct. 2474, 41 L.Ed.2d 290 (1974), 407

Moses H. Cone Memorial Hosp. v. Mercury Const. Corp., 460 U.S. 1, 103 S.Ct. 927, 74 L.Ed.2d 765 (1983), 62

Mt. Hawley Ins. Co. v. Federal Sav. & Loan Ins. Corp., 695 F.Supp. 469 (C.D.Cal. 1987), 421

Mullane v. Central Hanover Bank & Trust Co., 339 U.S. 306, 70 S.Ct. 652, 94 L.Ed. 865 (1950), **217**

Municipal Mortgage & Equity v. Southfork Apartments Ltd. Partnership, 93 F.Supp.4th 622 (D.Md.2000), 183

Murphy v. Florida, 421 U.S. 794, 95 S.Ct. 2031, 44 L.Ed.2d 589 (1975), 624

Mutual Federal Savings and Loan Ass'n v. Richards & Associates, Inc., 872 F.2d 88 (4th Cir.1989), 524

N.A.A.C.P. v. American Family Mutual Ins. Co., 978 F.2d 287 (7th Cir.1992), **804**

Nanda v. Board of Trustees of University of Illinois, 303 F.3d 817 (7th Cir.2002), 818

National Hockey League v. Metropolitan Hockey Club, Inc., 427 U.S. 639, 96 S.Ct. 2778, 49 L.Ed.2d 747 (1976), 524

National Mutual Ins. Co. of Dist. of Col. v. Tidewater Transfer Co., 337 U.S. 582, 69 S.Ct. 1173, 93 L.Ed. 1556 (1949), 83

Natural Resources Defense Council, Inc. v. United States Nuclear Regulatory Commission, 578 F.2d 1341 (10th Cir.1978), 398

New Hampshire v. Maine, 532 U.S. 742, 121 S.Ct. 1808, 149 L.Ed.2d 968 (2001), **791**

New Jersey Sports Productions, Inc. v. Don King Productions, Inc., 15 F.Supp.2d 534 (D.N.J.1998), 426

Nichols v. G.D. Searle & Co., 991 F.2d 1195 (4th Cir.1993), 171

Nick v. Morgan's Foods, Inc., 270 F.3d 590 (8th Cir.2001), 562

Nicodemus v. Union Pacific Corp., 318 F.3d 1231 (10th Cir.2003), **835**

Nippon Credit Bank, Ltd. v. Matthews, 291 F.3d 738 (11th Cir.2002), 23

Nolph v. Scott, 725 S.W.2d 860 (Ky.1987), **1**

North Cent. F.S., Inc. v. Brown, 951 F.Supp. 1383 (N.D.Iowa 1996), 117

Norwood v. Kirkpatrick, 349 U.S. 29, 75 S.Ct. 544, 99 L.Ed. 789 (1955), 257

Nuovo Pignone, SpA v. Storman Asia M/V, 310 F.3d 374 (5th Cir.2002), 234

O'Connor v. Boeing North American, Inc., 185 F.R.D. 272 (C.D.Cal.1999), **495**

Oliver v. Haas, 777 F.Supp. 1040 (D.Puerto Rico 1991), 79

Oneida Indian Nation of New York State v. Oneida County, New York, 414 U.S. 661, 94 S.Ct. 772, 39 L.Ed.2d 73 (1974), 847

Oppenheimer Fund, Inc. v. Sanders, 437 U.S. 340, 98 S.Ct. 2380, 57 L.Ed.2d 253 (1978), 450

Orange Beach, Alabama, City of v. Scottsdale Ins. Co., 166 F.R.D. 506 (S.D.Ala. 1996), 35

Oregon Trail Elec. Consumers Co-op, Inc. v. Co–Gen Co., 168 Or.App. 466, 7 P.3d 594 (Or.App.2000), 823

Otness v. United States, 23 F.R.D. 279 (D.Alaska Terr.1959), **374**

Paige v. Henry J. Kaiser Co., 826 F.2d 857 (9th Cir.1987), 841

Panavision Intern., L.P. v. Toeppen, 141 F.3d 1316 (9th Cir.1998), 206

Parklane Hosiery Co., Inc. v. Shore, 439 U.S. 322, 99 S.Ct. 645, 58 L.Ed.2d 552 (1979), **771**

Parsons v. Bedford, Breedlove & Robeson, 28 U.S. 433, 7 L.Ed. 732 (1830), 579

Paul v. National Life, 177 W.Va. 427, 352 S.E.2d 550 (W.Va.1986), **313**

Paul, Hastings, Janofsky & Walker, LLP v. City of Tulsa, Oklahoma, 245 F.Supp.2d 1248 (N.D.Ga.2002), 171

Pavelic & LeFlore v. Marvel Entertainment Group, 493 U.S. 120, 110 S.Ct. 456, 107 L.Ed.2d 438 (1989), 357

Pennoyer v. Neff, 95 U.S. 714, 24 L.Ed. 565 (1877), 122

Peralta v. Heights Medical Center, Inc., 485 U.S. 80, 108 S.Ct. 896, 99 L.Ed.2d 75 (1988), 669, 728

Peterson Novelties, Inc. v. City of Berkley, 305 F.3d 386 (6th Cir.2002), 785

Philip Morris Inc., United States v., 314 F.3d 612, 354 U.S.App.D.C. 171 (D.C.Cir.2003), 817

Phillips Petroleum Co. v. Shutts, 472 U.S. 797, 105 S.Ct. 2965, 86 L.Ed.2d 628 (1985), 312, 450, 451

Piazza v. Major League Baseball, 836 F.Supp. 269 (E.D.Pa.1993), 811

Piedra v. Mentor Graphics Corp., 979 F.Supp. 1297 (D.Or.1997), 655

Piesco v. Koch, 12 F.3d 332 (2nd Cir. 1993), **706**

Pioneer Inv. Services Co. v. Brunswick Associates Ltd. Partnership, 507 U.S. 380, 113 S.Ct. 1489, 123 L.Ed.2d 74 (1993), 727

Piper Aircraft Co. v. Reyno, 454 U.S. 235, 102 S.Ct. 252, 70 L.Ed.2d 419 (1981), **251**

Pizza Time Theatre Securities Litigation, In re, 113 F.R.D. 94 (N.D.Cal.1986), 486

Plant v. Blazer Financial Services, Inc. of Georgia, 598 F.2d 1357 (5th Cir.1979), 25

Playboy Enterprises, Inc. v. Welles, 60 F.Supp.2d 1050 (S.D.Cal.1999), **502**

Portage II v. Bryant Petroleum Corp., 899 F.2d 1514 (6th Cir.1990), 644

Porter v. Warner Holding Co., 328 U.S. 395, 66 S.Ct. 1086, 90 L.Ed. 1332 (1946), 589

Poynter by Poynter v. Ratcliff, 874 F.2d 219 (4th Cir.1989), 623

Procter & Gamble Co., United States v., 356 U.S. 677, 78 S.Ct. 983, 2 L.Ed.2d 1077 (1958), 456

Pryer v. C.O. 3 Slavic, 251 F.3d 448 (3rd Cir.2001), 713

Ptaszynki v. Ferrell, 277 F.Supp. 969 (E.D.Tenn.1967), 250

Public Service Co. of New Hampshire v. Patch, 136 F.3d 197 (1st Cir.1998), 397

Railcar, Ltd. v. Southern Illinois Railcar Co., 42 F.Supp.2d 1369 (N.D.Ga.1999), 172

Rainbow Management Group, Ltd. v. Atlantis Submarines Hawai'i, L.P., 158 F.R.D. 656 (D.Hawai'i 1994), **27**

Red Deer v. Cherokee County, Iowa, 183 F.R.D. 642 (N.D.Iowa 1999), **341**

Reed v. United Transp. Union, 488 U.S. 319, 109 S.Ct. 621, 102 L.Ed.2d 665 (1989), 866

Religious Technology Center v. Gerbode, 1994 WL 228607 (C.D.Cal.1994), 367

Reppert v. Marvin Lumber and Cedar Co., Inc., 359 F.3d 53 (1st Cir.2004), 437

Republican National Committee v. Taylor, 299 F.3d 887, 353 U.S.App.D.C. 236 (D.C.Cir.2002), 412

Reyes v. Sazan, 168 F.3d 158 (5th Cir. 1999), **346**

Reynolds v. International Amateur Athletic Federation, 23 F.3d 1110 (6th Cir.1994), 164

Rhode Island v. United States Environmental Protection Agency, 378 F.3d 19 (1st Cir.2004), 400

Richards v. Jefferson County, Alabama, 517 U.S. 793, 116 S.Ct. 1761, 135 L.Ed.2d 76 (1996), 450, **763**

Rink v. Cheminova, Inc., 203 F.R.D. 648 (M.D.Fla.2001), 449

Rio Properties, Inc. v. Rio Intern. Interlink, 284 F.3d 1007 (9th Cir.2002), 235

Roadway Package System, Inc. v. Kayser, 257 F.3d 287 (3rd Cir.2001), 536

Rockefeller Center Properties, Inc. Securities Ligitation, In re, 311 F.3d 198 (3rd Cir.2002), 295

Rodgers v. St. Mary's Hospital of Decatur, 149 Ill.2d 302, 173 Ill.Dec. 642, 597 N.E.2d 616 (Ill.1992), **733**

Rodriguez–Diaz v. Sierra–Martinez, 853 F.2d 1027 (1st Cir.1988), 70

Roe v. Aware Woman Center for Choice, Inc., 253 F.3d 678 (11th Cir. 2001), **285**

Rosario Ortega v. Star–Kist Foods, Inc., 370 F.3d 124 (1st Cir.2004), 77

Rose v. Giamatti, 721 F.Supp. 906 (S.D.Ohio 1989), 82

Ross v. Bernhard, 396 U.S. 531, 90 S.Ct. 733, 24 L.Ed.2d 729 (1970), **596**

Roth v. District of Columbia Courts, 160 F.Supp.2d 104 (D.D.C.2001), 62

Roy v. Inhabitants of City of Lewiston, 42 F.3d 691 (1st Cir.1994), 693

Ruszala v. Walt Disney World Co., 132 F.Supp.2d 1347 (M.D.Fla.2000), **353**

Ruvalcaba v. City of Los Angeles, 64 F.3d 1323 (9th Cir.1995), 711

Saadeh v. Farouki, 107 F.3d 52, 323 U.S.App.D.C. 239 (D.C.Cir.1997), 80

Safeco Ins. Co. of America v. City of White House, Tenn., 36 F.3d 540 (6th Cir. 1994), 82

Sailor v. Hubbell, Inc., 4 F.3d 323 (4th Cir.1993), 589

Schlagenhauf v. Holder, 379 U.S. 104, 85 S.Ct. 234, 13 L.Ed.2d 152 (1964), 516

Schnabel v. Abramson, 232 F.3d 83 (2nd Cir.2000), 702

Schultea v. Wood, 47 F.3d 1427 (5th Cir. 1995), 349

Sealed Case, In re, 146 F.3d 881, 330 U.S.App.D.C. 368 (D.C.Cir.1998), 474

Security Ins. Co. of Hartford v. Schipporeit, Inc., 69 F.3d 1377 (7th Cir.1995), 394

Semtek International Inc. v. Lockheed Martin Corp., 531 U.S. 497, 121 S.Ct. 1021, 149 L.Ed.2d 32 (2001), 784, **883**

Sentinel Acceptance, Ltd., L.P. v. Hodson Auto Sales & Leasing, Inc., 45 S.W.3d 464 (Mo.App. W.D.2001), **778**

Shaffer v. Heitner, 433 U.S. 186, 97 S.Ct. 2569, 53 L.Ed.2d 683 (1977), **142**

Sharpe v. United States, 936 F.2d 1178 (11th Cir.1991), 693

Shaver v. Operating Engineers Local 428 Pension Trust Fund, 332 F.3d 1198 (9th Cir.2003), 372

Shelley v. Kraemer, 334 U.S. 1, 68 S.Ct. 836, 92 L.Ed. 1161 (1948), 436

Sierra Club v. United States E.P.A., 995 F.2d 1478 (9th Cir.1993), 397

Simeon v. T. Smith & Son, Inc., 852 F.2d 1421 (5th Cir.1988), 712

Simmons v. Simmons, 773 P.2d 602 (Colo.App.1988), **19**

Singletary v. Continental Illinois Nat. Bank and Trust Co. of Chicago, 9 F.3d 1236 (7th Cir.1993), 71

Singletary v. Pennsylvania Dept. of Corrections, 266 F.3d 186 (3rd Cir. 2001), **377**

Skipper v. French, 130 F.3d 603 (4th Cir. 1997), 820

Smith v. Marsh, 194 F.3d 1045 (9th Cir. 1999), 395

Smith Kline & French Laboratories Ltd v. Bloch (Interlocutory Injunction), 1982 WL 222260 (CA (Civ Div) 1982), 256

Societe Internationale Pour Participations Industrielles Et Commerciales, S.A. v.

Rogers, 357 U.S. 197, 78 S.Ct. 1087, 2 L.Ed.2d 1255 (1958), 522

Sokaogon Gaming Enterprise Corp. v. Tushie–Montgomery Associates, Inc., 86 F.3d 656 (7th Cir.1996), 811

Southern Construction Co. v. Pickard, 371 U.S. 57, 83 S.Ct. 108, 9 L.Ed.2d 31 (1962), 25

Spectacor Management Group v. Brown, 131 F.3d 120 (3rd Cir.1997), 78

Star Insurance Co. v. Cedar Valley Express, LLC, 273 F.Supp.2d 38 (D.D.C. 2002), **413**

State Farm Mutual Auto. Ins. Co. v. Narvaez, 149 F.3d 1269 (10th Cir.1998), 76

Steel v. United States, 813 F.2d 1545 (9th Cir.1987), 137

Stemler v. Florence, 350 F.3d 578 (6th Cir.2003), **754**

Steward v. Up North Plastics, Inc., 177 F.Supp.2d 953 (D.Minn.2001), 250

Stewart v. Ramsay, 242 U.S. 128, 37 S.Ct. 44, 61 L.Ed. 192 (1916), 198

Stewart v. Shelby Tissue, Inc., 189 F.R.D. 357 (W.D.Tenn.1999), **383**

Stewart Organization, Inc. v. Ricoh Corp., 487 U.S. 22, 108 S.Ct. 2239, 101 L.Ed.2d 22 (1988), **877**

St. Paul Mercury Indem. Co. v. Red Cab Co., 303 U.S. 283, 58 S.Ct. 586, 82 L.Ed. 845 (1938), 77

Strawbridge v. Curtiss, 7 U.S. 267, 2 L.Ed. 435 (1806), 75

Sullivan v. School Board of Pinellas County, 773 F.2d 1182 (11th Cir.1985), 589

Supreme Tribe of Ben Hur v. Cauble, 255 U.S. 356, 41 S.Ct. 338, 65 L.Ed. 673 (1921), 452

Swierkiewicz v. Sorema N.A., 534 U.S. 506, 122 S.Ct. 992, 152 L.Ed.2d 1 (2002), **278**

Swift v. Tyson, 41 U.S. 1, 10 L.Ed. 865 (1842), 849

Swope v. Columbian Chemicals Co., 281 F.3d 185 (5th Cir.2002), 804

Szabo v. Bridgeport Machines, Inc., 199 F.R.D. 280 (N.D.Ind.2001), **438**

Taco Bell Corp. v. Continental Casualty Co., 2003 WL 124454 (N.D.Ill.2003), 408

Tahfs v. Proctor, 316 F.3d 584 (6th Cir. 2003), 366

Tahoe Sierra Preservation Council, Inc. v. Tahoe Regional Planning Agency, 322 F.3d 1064 (9th Cir.2003), 769

Tate v. Riverboat Services, Inc., 305 F.Supp.2d 916 (N.D.Ind.2004), **716**

Taylor v. Anderson–Tully Co., 151 F.R.D. 295 (W.D.Tenn.1993), 486

Ten Taxpayer Citizens Group v. Cape Wind Associates, LLC, 373 F.3d 183 (1st Cir. 2004), 63

Texaco, Inc. v. Ponsoldt, 118 F.3d 1367 (9th Cir.1997), 429

Texas Industries, Inc. v. Radcliff Materials, Inc., 451 U.S. 630, 101 S.Ct. 2061, 68 L.Ed.2d 500 (1981), **889**

Textile Workers Union of America v. Lincoln Mills of Alabama, 353 U.S. 448, 77 S.Ct. 912, 1 L.Ed.2d 972 (1957), 893

Thompson v. Altheimer & Gray, 248 F.3d 621 (7th Cir.2001), **619,** 623

Thompson v. Department of Housing and Urban Development, 199 F.R.D. 168 (D.Md.2001), **460**

Toys "R" Us, Inc. v. Step Two, S.A., 318 F.3d 446 (3rd Cir.2003), **210**

Treinies v. Sunshine Mining Co., 308 U.S. 66, 60 S.Ct. 44, 84 L.Ed. 85 (1939), 783

Tulip Computers Intern., B.V. v. Dell Computer Corp., 210 F.R.D. 100 (D.Del. 2002), 512

Uffner v. La Reunion Francaise, S.A., 244 F.3d 38 (1st Cir.2001), **240**

Ugarriza v. Schmieder, 414 N.Y.S.2d 304, 386 N.E.2d 1324 (N.Y.1979), 692

Union Carbide Corp. Gas Plant Disaster at Bhopal, India, In re, 634 F.Supp. 842 (S.D.N.Y.1986), 257

UNI Storebrand Ins. Co., UK Ltd. v. Star Terminal Corp., 1997 WL 391125 (S.D.N.Y.1997), 409

United Mine Workers of America v. Gibbs, 383 U.S. 715, 86 S.Ct. 1130, 16 L.Ed.2d 218 (1966), **88**

United Paperworkers Intern. Union, AFL–CIO v. Misco, Inc., 484 U.S. 29, 108 S.Ct. 364, 98 L.Ed.2d 286 (1987), 535

United States v. _____ (see opposing party)

Unum Life Ins. Co. of America v. Kelling, 170 F.Supp.2d 792 (M.D.Tenn.2001), 429

Upjohn Co. v. United States, 449 U.S. 383, 101 S.Ct. 677, 66 L.Ed.2d 584 (1981), 465

Van Dusen v. Barrack, 376 U.S. 612, 84 S.Ct. 805, 11 L.Ed.2d 945 (1964), 249

Vermont Teddy Bear Co., Inc. v. 1–800 Beargram Co., 373 F.3d 241 (2nd Cir. 2004), 681

Vess v. Ciba–Geigy Corp. USA, 317 F.3d 1097 (9th Cir.2003), 330

Vitamins Antitrust Litigation, In re, 216 F.R.D. 168 (D.D.C.2003), 494

Walker v. Armco Steel Corp., 446 U.S. 740, 100 S.Ct. 1978, 64 L.Ed.2d 659 (1980), 876

Wanderer v. Johnston, 910 F.2d 652 (9th Cir.1990), 524

Weisgram v. Marley Co., 528 U.S. 440, 120 S.Ct. 1011, 145 L.Ed.2d 958 (2000), 714

Wheaton v. Peters, 33 U.S. 591, 8 L.Ed. 1055 (1834), 851

Whitacre Partnership v. Biosignia, Inc., 358 N.C. 1, 591 S.E.2d 870 (N.C.2004), 796

Whitaker v. Ameritech Corp., 129 F.3d 952 (7th Cir.1997), 736

White v. Nix, 43 F.3d 374 (8th Cir.1994), 811

Williams v. City of Jacksonville Police Dept., 165 N.C.App. 587, 599 S.E.2d 422 (N.C.App.2004), **745**

Wilmington Trust v. United States District Court for Dist. of Hawaii, 934 F.2d 1026 (9th Cir.1991), 601

World–Wide Volkswagen Corp. v. Woodson, 444 U.S. 286, 100 S.Ct. 559, 62 L.Ed.2d 490 (1980), **150**

Wyman v. Newhouse, 93 F.2d 313 (2nd Cir.1937), 198

Young, Ex parte, 209 U.S. 123, 28 S.Ct. 441, 52 L.Ed. 714 (1908), 61

Young v. New Haven Advocate, 315 F.3d 256 (4th Cir.2002), **200**

Zahn v. International Paper Co., 414 U.S. 291, 94 S.Ct. 505, 38 L.Ed.2d 511 (1973), 75, 452

Zervos v. Verizon New York, Inc., 252 F.3d 163 (2nd Cir.2001), 825

Zinser v. Accufix Research Institute, Inc., 253 F.3d 1180 (9th Cir.2001), 448

Zippo Mfg. Co. v. Zippo Dot Com, Inc., 952 F.Supp. 1119 (W.D.Pa.1997), 199

Zubulake v. UBS Warburg LLC, 216 F.R.D. 280 (S.D.N.Y.2003), 467

Zuk v. Eastern Pennsylvania Psychiatric Institute of the Medical College of Pennsylvania, 103 F.3d 294 (3rd Cir.1996), 365

CIVIL PROCEDURE

CASES, PROBLEMS AND EXERCISES

*

Chapter 1

AN OVERVIEW OF CIVIL PROCEDURE

A. THE ROLE OF PROCEDURE

NOLPH v. SCOTT

725 S.W.2d 860 (Ky. 1987)

STEPHENS, Justice.

The issue on this appeal is whether CR 15.03 permits an amended complaint, substituting movant Michael Nolph for an "unknown defendant," to relate back to the time of the original complaint where "unknown defendants" were constructively served by appointment of a warning order attorney.

The trial court ruled relation back was not permitted and granted Movant's motion for summary judgment. The Court of Appeals reversed. We hold CR 15.03 does not permit relation back under the circumstances of this case and reverse the decision of the Court of Appeals.

Respondent Scott instituted this medical malpractice action against the University of Louisville, University Hospital, Drs. Selvoy Fillerup and Richard Albert, and other unknown defendants. The unknown defendants were identified as "being certain persons who were careless and negligent in treating Helen Scott at the University Hospital. . . ." The complaint alleged medical malpractice for injuries sustained as a result of surgery performed on March 9, 1982, at University Hospital. Michael Nolph was not identified by name in the original complaint.

On March 2, 1983, Respondent sought constructive service on the unknown defendants through the appointment of a warning order attorney. A letter of the warning order attorney directed to the unknown defendants was sent to University Hospital on or about March 7, 1983. The trial court found that Nolph did not receive notice of the lawsuit prior to March 11, 1983, when the limitations period expired.

On July 14, 1983, appellee took the deposition of Dr. Fillerup who identified Michael Nolph as being present during Scott's surgery. On September 9, 1983, Respondent deposed Nolph and verified that he was

1

the supervising physician in the operating room during her surgery. On November 7, 1983, Respondent filed an amended complaint naming Michael Nolph as a party defendant. Nolph was finally served with summons on December 23, 1983, approximately nine months past the limitations period. By his own admission Nolph first learned of the lawsuit, informally, in May or June, 1983.

In order for an amended pleading to relate back to the time of filing of the original complaint, the requirements of CR 15.03 must be met. The relevant sections of the rule are as follows:

> (1) Whenever the claim or defense asserted in the amended pleading arose out of the conduct, transaction, or occurrence set forth or attempted to be set forth in the original pleading, the amendment relates back to the date of the original pleading.

> (2) An amendment changing the party against whom a claim is asserted relates back if the condition of paragraph (1) is satisfied and, within the period provided by law for commencing the action against him, the party to be brought in by amendment (a) has received such notice of the institution of the action that he will not be prejudiced in maintaining his defense on the merits, and (b) knew or should have known that but for mistake concerning the identity of the proper party, the action would have been brought against him. . . .

There is no dispute among the parties that the requirement of section (1) is met. The present controversy involves the requirements of section (2).

Scott contends the amended complaint relates back to the earlier filing date because Nolph received constructive notice of the lawsuit. We disagree. Constructive service on unknown defendants through appointment of a warning order attorney is not sufficient notice for the purposes of CR 15.03.

The warning order rules provide for constructive service on a person unknown to the plaintiff. While strict compliance with these rules is required, actual notice to the defendant is not necessary. Appointment of a warning order attorney is a procedural device permitting an action to proceed, in certain circumstances, unknown to the defendant.

However, the relation back rule mandates that the party to be named in an amended pleading knew or should have known about the action brought against him. CR 15.03(2)(b). Actual, formal notice may not be necessary. Nevertheless, knowledge of the proceedings against him gained during the statutory period must be attributed to the defendant. As noted by the United States Supreme Court in its review of the federal relation back rule,[2] "The linchpin is notice, and notice within

---

2. Civil Rule 15.03 is substantially the same as Federal Rule of Civil Procedure 15(c).

the limitations period." Schiavone v. Fortune aka Time, Inc., 477 U.S. 21 (1986).

Movant Nolph lacked notice of the lawsuit within the limitations period. Thus, a key ingredient of CR 15.03 is missing. The trial court did not err in refusing to permit the amended pleading to relate back to the time of the original complaint. The decision of the Court of Appeals is reversed.

LEIBSON, J., DISSENTING

Respectfully, I dissent.

This decision is a triumph of form over substance, a victory for those who favor the "sporting theory" of law over the "search for the truth."

The new rules of civil procedure in general, and the rule of relation back (CR 15.03) in particular, were designed for the opposite result to avoid victory through technicality and achieve trial on the merits.

The plaintiff seeks to add Dr. Nolph by name to a law suit in which he has been an integral part from the beginning. He functioned in a teaching hospital in a supervisory capacity, charged by the defendant/hospital with the duty of teaching and supervising the defendants/residents whose names appear on the typewritten operating report. Reason and common sense dictate that this group of defendants share a community of interests and should be charged with common knowledge such that there is no prejudice when Dr. Nolph is replaced by name for the "unknown defendants" referred to in the complaint. Surely the good doctor should have been the first person apprised of the law suit in the ordinary course of events. If this did not occur, through design or inadvertence, nevertheless the people defending the remaining defendants were in effect representing his interests as well. Our Court should not reward with victory those who play games to conceal the identity of a key player until it is too late to name him in the law suit. Leaving Dr. Nolph's name off of the surgical report—the only legible identification of the participants in the surgery which is the gravamen of this action—is such a game.

I agree with the Majority Opinion that adding "unknown defendants" and attempting service upon them through a letter sent by a Warning Order Attorney to the Hospital did not achieve constructive service on Dr. Nolph. * * * But this step did serve as a signal, clear as a bell, that the plaintiff's law suit meant to include all those responsible for her surgical treatment, persons whom the hospital could be reasonably expected to notify, and Dr. Nolph surely fits in that classification.

In this opinion our Court has elected to cause a harsh and unjust result where the law itself does not require such a result. There is ample authority to sustain the decision of the Court of Appeals that service on Dr. Nolph was not time barred by the one year statute of limitations because of the saving provisions found in CR 15.03, "relation back of amendments." This authority includes:

* * *

3) A significant number of federal decisions with fact situations more in point than the Schiavone case which is cited in the majority opinion as controlling authority. These include inter alia, *Ingram v. Kumar*, 585 F.2d 566 (CA 2d 1978), cert. denied 440 U.S. 940; *Kirk v. Cronvich*, 629 F.2d 404 (C.A.5th 1980); and *Travelers Indemnity Co. v. United States*, 382 F.2d 103 (C.A.10th 1967).

All of the above authorities would apply the rule of relation back of amendments provided in CR 15.03 to the present situation because there is such a community of interests between Dr. Nolph and the originally named defendants that it is patently unreasonable to insulate him from their notice of the lawsuit.

As stated in *Travelers Indemnity Co. v. United States*, the "purpose of the federal rules [is not] furthered by denying the addition of a party who has a close identity of interest with the old party when the added party will not be prejudiced. The ends of justice are not served when forfeiture of just claims because of technical rules is allowed."

The facts here cry out for a different result. The plaintiff filed a medical negligence action against University of Louisville Hospital and two physicians, the only two, whose names appeared on the official typewritten operative report. Although Dr. Nolph's name appears elsewhere in the hospital records, it is illegibly written and ambiguously connected to the medical procedure which is the gravamen of the plaintiff's complaint. A suit against him in the circumstances would have invited a physicians' countersuit for malicious prosecution under the invitation to countersue which we extended in *Raine v. Drasin*, Ky., 621 S.W.2d 895 (1981).

* * * The physician's countersuit is available as punishment if a physician is named as a defendant without foundation in fact. Now this present decision imposes an equally severe penalty if claimant's counsel, faced with the one year statute of limitations, fails to name every physician whose name appears anywhere in the hospital record. We have indeed presented the injured claimant with a Hobson's Choice. "The logic of words should yield to the logic of realities." Justice Louis D. Brandeis in *Di Santo v. Pennsylvania*, 273 U.S. 34, 43 (1927).

The "logic of realities" applied in the present situation is found in the Court of Appeals' opinion; there is no reasonable possibility that Dr. Nolph would not be among those immediately informed when the hospital received the letter from the warning order attorney asking it to respond for "unknown defendants." He was their agent and supervisory employee and the first person logically to be consulted about this matter. In present circumstances, the fact that service by Warning Order Attorney is only constructive service is irrelevant. The Court of Appeals' opinion is based on informal notice, not the technicalities of constructive service. * * *

Under CR 15.03 service of process is not required. Indeed, the purpose for CR 15.03 is to take care of this problem by relation back where personal service was not obtained in the first instance but it is fair to hold in a party served at a later time, after the statute of limitations has run, because there is an identity or community of interest with the named defendants such that the later named party undoubtedly would know of the action, despite protestations to the contrary, unless the named parties sharing the same interest intentionally concealed the law suit from the unnamed party. * * *

In the present case the later named party was the supervising agent for the teaching hospital, which was a named defendant, and the teacher in the operating room supervising the surgery being performed by the two residents, also named defendants. Unless the law condones pretense, Dr. Nolph should be prepared to defend this case on the merits.

* * * Note that the same law firm represents Dr. Fillerup as represents University Hospital. No doubt it would also represent Dr. Albert if he gets served and Dr. Nolph if his counsel were not seeking to interpose the present technicality. It is reasonable to conclude that there is an identity of interest at the end of the road either through self-insurance under the University of Louisville Medical Malpractice Act or through some insurance carrier, or both. It is quite likely that one entity shares financial responsibility and controls the case for all involved.

This is yet another unfortunate decision in a line of recent cases from our Court using an unnecessarily harsh and overly technical approach to the detriment of the person who has been wronged. * * * This case, like these others named, harkens back to 19th Century "mechanical jurisprudence," condemned by Roscoe Pound. See Pound, Mechanical Jurisprudence, 8 Colum. L. Rev. 605 (1908).

The nadir of mechanical jurisprudence is reached when conceptions are used, not as premises from which to reason, but as ultimate solutions. So used, they cease to be conceptions and become empty words.

Lambert, J., joins in this dissent.

Notes and Questions

1. The plaintiff was trying to amend the complaint in her *original* action to add Nolph as an additional defendant. Do you understand why plaintiff chose this difficult route instead of simply filing a new, separate lawsuit against Nolph?

2. What would plaintiff have had to do, and by when, in order to bring a claim against Nolph in the original lawsuit?

3. The core issue upon which this case turns is whether Nolph had "received such notice of the institution of the action that he will not be prejudiced in maintaining his defense on the merits." Kentucky Civil Rule 15.03(2)(b). Why does the majority find that this requirement is not satisfied? Didn't Nolph receive notice?

Could you argue that the rule could be interpreted not to require *any* notice to Nolph prior to the date upon which plaintiff wanted to add him? Note that the rule is designed to reduce prejudice to the added party. How, if at all, was Nolph "prejudiced" by not receiving timely notice?

4.   Federal Rule of Civil Procedure 15(c), upon which the Kentucky rule is based, was amended after the decision in *Nolph* to extend the time period for relation back when a party is changed.

B. DEALING WITH CIVIL PROCEDURE

Nolph v. Scott deals with what at first glance may appear to be a fairly narrow and technical issue of court procedure. However, the vigorous dissent reminds us that the real impact of the case goes far beyond merely construing the language of Rule 15. The case is, after all, an actual dispute between living people, under a legal system that proudly calls itself a system of justice. Yet, that system strictly applies its own rules to take away completely and permanently Ms Scott's claim against Nolph, before she even had a chance to present it to the court.

Never lose sight of these broader concerns. Students often protest that Civil Procedure is one of the most difficult of the courses required in law school. However, although the subject is by no means easy, the rules of Procedure are no more numerous or complex than those in other required courses. The problem in learning Procedure is that the subject-matter is almost entirely foreign to most law students. Courses such as Contracts, Torts, Criminal Law, and Constitutional Law present real-life issues to which students can relate. In addition, because they understand the underlying issue, students more often than not have a "gut" feeling as to what the rule of law ought to be. Although these hunches are not always correct, it is easier to learn a rule with which you strongly agree or disagree.

The rules of Civil Procedure may seem cold and mechanical in comparison. The outcome of a dispute concerning whether an amended complaint "relates back" has no immediately obvious effect on the greater social good. Procedure students therefore often find that they do not have a hunch as to how most issues should be resolved. This can lead to the perception that Civil Procedure comprises a mass of arbitrary rules that must be memorized. Like many non-lawyers, students may view the subject-matter as a "bag of tricks" that a crafty litigator can use to win an otherwise weak case.

That view misses the essence of Procedure. Civil Procedure is much more than a collection of rules setting standards for mundane minutia such as filing deadlines and paper size. It is instead a coordinated system that sets out a particular way in which disputes are to be resolved. As with other types of systems, an individual component cannot be fully understood or appreciated until you see how it fits into the overall system.

As just one example, consider pleading, the topic of Chapter 5 of the casebook. Pleadings are the papers that a litigant serves on the other side to inform them of the claims and defenses that are being asserted. One basic issue in pleading is how detailed a pleading should have to be. The system could require simply a bare-bones notice of what the suit is about—"I'm suing you because you hit me last Wednesday"—or could instead require a detailed exposition of the facts and the legal theories on which the claimant relies. The choice between the two extremes may at first glance seem arbitrary. Realize, however, that pleading is merely one stage in a lawsuit. Once the other stages, especially the processes of discovery and summary judgment, are considered, it becomes clear that the choice of a standard for pleading has implications throughout the remainder of the lawsuit.

Throughout this course, then, you may find it useful to ask yourself how a given rule fits into the overall system of dispute resolution. In so doing, you will soon come to realize that the *system* of Civil Procedure does have basic underlying principles that guide the content of the rules.

Another factor to consider is that the system of Procedure exists not for its own sake, but in order to resolve disputes that for whatever reason were not resolved by society's informal methods of dispute resolution. Any system of dispute resolution must balance two basic concerns. The first is *efficiency*. The court system should operate as smoothly and quickly as possible, so that people can afford to have their disputes resolved by the official mechanism.

The second concern is *fairness*. Society will continue to accept the legal system only as long as it produces outcomes that in most cases comport with people's expectations of how disputes should be resolved. Part of this, of course, involves the "substantive" law, the legal rules that you learn in other law school courses. Courts must select the proper rule to apply in a given case, and apply it correctly. However, disputes that find their way to the courts rarely involve only a disagreement as to the rule of law. In most cases, the parties also disagree on exactly what happened. The role of the court is to ferret out the "truth" of what happened, an often arduous and time-consuming process. Reaching a fair result in a given case, then, involves both determining what happened, and selecting the proper rule of law to govern the rights and liabilities of the parties.

The rules of Civil Procedure attempt to strike a balance between efficiency and fairness. It would be tremendously costly in all cases—and probably impossible in most—to reach the "perfect" result. The rules of litigation place limits on litigation in order to ensure that the system works efficiently, while still reaching a result that comports with society's expectations in most cases. This is obviously a difficult balance to maintain.

When reviewing a particular procedural rule, ask yourself whether it strikes what you consider to be the best balance between efficiency and fairness. Does the rule sacrifice the ultimate truth in an effort to speed up the process? Or does the result drag out the process of litigation, perhaps helping courts reach a "better" result in some cases, but at a cost of making the process more burdensome for *all* litigants? There are no right or wrong answers to these questions. Nevertheless, by reminding yourself from the outset that there are underlying normative goals in

Civil Procedure, you will have a much better grasp of both the overall process and the constituent rules.

Nolph v. Scott is an interesting case to lead off the course because it touches upon these broader issues. The majority considers the rule to be clear. The dissenting justice, on the other hand, argues that the court should consider the *purpose* underlying the written rule. The dissenter feels that purpose would be satisfied by allowing relation back of the amendment under the facts of the case. From a broader perspective, one could frame the debate as one concerning what makes a system "just". Does justice mean doing whatever is possible to reach the right result in each case? Or is a system just when it takes fair rules and applies them in a consistent manner? That basic theme will recur throughout this course.

C. STATE AND FEDERAL RULES OF PROCEDURE

The *Nolph* case turns on an interpretation of Kentucky Civil Rule 15.03. Note, however, that both the majority and dissent cite *federal* cases dealing with Federal Rule of Civil Procedure 15(c). Although that federal rule does not apply in state court litigation, the majority indicates in footnote 2 that the federal precedent is important because the two rules are "substantially the same."

State courts regularly cite to federal practice. It is no mere coincidence that state and federal procedural rules use identical language. The Federal Rules of Civil Procedure, enacted in 1938, have had a tremendous impact on civil litigation in the United States, both in the federal and state court systems. The 1938 rules fundamentally altered a number of traditional concepts in civil litigation. Because the system offered many advantages, a number of states adopted the language of the federal rules virtually wholesale (although many, like Kentucky, alter the numbering scheme to some extent). Other states, while not copying the language of the federal rules, have borrowed many of the underlying concepts. As a result, there is a significant similarity among many United States courts in the basic issues of civil procedure.

Do not assume, however, that all states follow the federal approach. Some of the largest states, including California, Illinois, and New York, have their own systems of procedure, systems that differ in many important ways from the federal. Other states, although structuring their systems on the federal model, have tinkered with one or more of the rules in significant ways. In fact, the differences between the federal rules and the states have tended to increase over the past few years. Recent amendments to some of the Federal Rules of Civil Procedure have proven controversial. Many states have adopted a "wait and see" approach to these changes, refusing to amend their rules until the wisdom of those changes is borne out by experience. Nevertheless, a basic similarity remains.

Chapter 2

BASIC JOINDER OF CLAIMS AND PARTIES

Much of the analysis in your law school classes assumes that the case in question involves one plaintiff, one defendant, and a single claim. The discussion focuses on how these parties have interacted prior to the case and whether the defendant ought to be liable to the plaintiff. Distilling the case to a two-party dispute is undoubtedly the easiest way to learn the legal rules in courses such as Torts, Contracts, Property, and Civil Procedure. But this pedagogical tool can be somewhat unrealistic when measured from a "real world" perspective. Lawsuits involving only one claim, one plaintiff and one defendant are becoming less and less common. Instead, many lawsuits today involve several plaintiffs, a bevy of defendants, and perhaps even other parties bearing names such as "third-party defendant" and "intervenor". Once all of these parties are in the case, the trend is for them to file claims against each other. As a result, courts are increasingly called upon to resolve complex cases involving myriad joined claims and parties.

Several different factors may underlie this trend toward increasingly complex lawsuits. A major cause is the increased prevalence of large corporations in the national and international economy. A large corporation can injure many different people in similar ways, whether they be employees or consumers. In addition, the substantive law itself is partly to blame for the growing trend toward complex lawsuits. For reasons that you will discuss in your other courses, during the twentieth century the law has increasingly held multiple parties responsible for a single injury. Similarly, the procedural rules governing joinder of parties and claims have become far more flexible over the past thirty years.

Not everyone agrees on whether this trend toward larger and more complex cases is desirable. Allowing joinder of everyone who is in any way connected with a dispute certainly has some benefits. The primary benefit is efficiency. A great deal of judicial time can be saved if one court can wrap up all of the disputes that may arise from, for example, a complex commercial transaction. But these benefits are not without cost. A bigger lawsuit is not always more efficient. At some point, allowing

9

uncontrolled joinder of claims and parties will result in a case so unwieldy that justice cannot be properly administered. The court rules governing joinder, then, are an attempt to balance the benefits of consolidated litigation with the effects on fair litigation.

A. MULTIPLE PLAINTIFFS AND DEFENDANTS

INTRODUCTORY PROBLEM

The Divine School of Law is a private law school operated by a religious group. Because this religion has very strong beliefs, all faculty and staff must be practicing members of the religious group. However, the school admits students regardless of their religious beliefs. In fact, the application form for the school does not ask about religion.

Notwithstanding the school's stated policy, three students at Divine School of Law feel that they have been the victims of religious discrimination by Divine faculty members. None of the three is a member of the particular religion that operates Divine. Andrew, an atheist, received a very low grade in Professor Jackson's Law and Religion class. Andrew is sure that Professor Jackson reduced his grade because Andrew often expressed his views during class discussions.

Cathy, a Roman Catholic, also feels that Professor Jackson discriminated against her. Cathy was taking Evidence from Professor Jackson. However, her complaint has nothing to do with her grade. In fact, Cathy never received a grade in Evidence. During the course of the semester, Cathy missed the Evidence class four times in order to travel out of town for job interviews. Because Divine School of Law rules allow a student to miss class only three times, Professor Jackson dropped her from the course. However, Cathy knows of several other students in the Evidence class who also missed four or more times and were not dropped from the course. All of these other students are members of the religion that operates Divine.

The third aggrieved party, Jacob, is Jewish. Jacob received a very low grade in Professor Wang's Civil Procedure class. Jacob is convinced that Professor Wang lowered his grade once she discovered Jacob's religious beliefs.

Because federal law forbids religious discrimination, Andrew, Cathy, and Jacob are all considering bringing discrimination claims in federal court. They would prefer to bring all of their claims in a single action. Tactically, what advantages might the three plaintiffs realize by suing together? Do the joinder rules allow Andrew, Cathy, and Jacob to join in order to sue Professors Jackson and Wang?

Governing Law: Federal Rule of Civil Procedure 20

Federal Rule 20 sets forth three separate criteria that must be satisfied in order to bring a case involving multiple plaintiffs and/or defendants. Although these criteria may overlap to some extent, each deals with a distinct concern.

The first criterion, that the right to recover (in the case of multiple plaintiffs) or the liability (in the case of multiple defendants) be *joint, several, or in the alternative*, may at first glance seem the most complex. Other courses, especially the basic Torts course, discuss the precise meanings of these terms. For our purposes at this point, however, it is safe to conclude that taken together, joint, several, and in the alternative comprise all the possible ways in which liability can be imposed or relief granted. Because Rule 20 requires that only one of these be present, this part of the test rarely presents a problem.

Turning to the third part of the test, all claims by or against the joined parties must share a *common question of law or fact*. This criterion illustrates the underlying purpose of Rule 20, which is to encourage judicial efficiency by reducing the extent to which the same issue is litigated in separate lawsuits. Later we will explore the difference between a question of "law" and "fact." The issue of whether a question is one of law or fact—or a "mixed" question involving both— has a number of important consequences; for example, as discussed in Chapter 9 it determines whether the judge or jury will decide the question. But the difference is not that important for purposes of Rule 20. As long as claims by or against joined parties share a common question of law *or* fact, joinder is proper.

It is the second element of the test, the requirement that the claims arise out of the *same transaction, occurrence, or series of transactions or occurrences*, that ordinarily proves the most difficult to satisfy. What exactly is a "transaction" or "occurrence"? And how closely must several separate transactions or occurrences be connected before they will be considered a "series"? Note that this concept of a "single transaction or occurrence" appears not only in Rule 20, but also in Rules 13(a) (compulsory counterclaims), 13(g) (cross-claims), 14 (claims involving third-party defendants), and 24(b) (when outsiders may intervene in the suit). Moreover, roughly the same principle guides courts when they apply the doctrine of claim preclusion, which is discussed in Part G of this chapter. Because this core concept will arise throughout this chapter, consider carefully how the courts in the following two cases interpret the phrase "same transaction, occurrence, or series of transactions or occurrences."

APACHE COUNTY v. SUPERIOR COURT

785 P.2d 1242 (Ariz. App. 1989)

SHELLEY, Judge

Samaritan Health Services, Inc. (Samaritan) filed a 294–count complaint against 11 different counties in the Maricopa County Superior

Court seeking payment for emergency medical services rendered to 291 allegedly indigent persons. Only 17 of the counts involve patients for which Apache County is alleged to be responsible. Apache County [claimed that] . . . . joinder of the counts against it was improper under Rule 20(a), Arizona Rules of Civil Procedure . . . .

We hold that the trial court erred in denying [Apache County's] motion . . . because joinder under Rule 20(a) was improper.

The State of Arizona requires Samaritan and other private health care providers to provide necessary emergency medical services to all patients regardless of their ability to pay. Pursuant to A.R.S. § 11–291, et seq., the counties are obligated to provide or pay for necessary emergency services rendered to the indigent sick of their respective counties. Many of Arizona's rural counties lack necessary medical facilities to treat critically ill or injured patients. These patients are therefore routinely transferred to Samaritan and other health care providers in Phoenix or Tucson for treatment.

Apache County asserts that there is no factual or legal basis for joining the counts against Apache County with the remaining 277 against the ten other counties. [The court quoted A.R.C.P. 20(a), which is identical to Federal Rule 20(a).]

Samaritan asserts:

Samaritan's claims against the county defendants arise from and involve the application of the identical statutory basis of liability. The claims involve a varying, but repetitious, set of legal and factual questions, such as whether a patient resided in a given county, whether Samaritan gave the required notice to the county, whether the patient was qualified to receive medical assistance at county expense, and so on. The counties' liability is also premised on the identical statute, A.R.S. § 11–297.01. * * * Samaritan submits that its daily and routine treatment of Arizona's indigent population constitutes a series of transactions or occurrences within the meaning of Rule 20. * * * Samaritan's treatment of indigent patients constitutes a series of transactions or occurrences under State mandate, and joinder of these claims is thus permissible.

We disagree.

* * * This case does not involve the same litigable event with respect to any of the claims against the defendants. Under the allegations in this case, there will be no duplicate presentation of evidence relating to facts common to more than one demand for relief. * * * Each county's sole interest is in the claims for which it is alleged to be responsible. * * * [T]he transactions are perhaps similar but they are not the same. The operative facts of each transaction are distinct from any other.

There is no concert of action alleged between any of defendants in evaluating or processing the indigent medical claims presented to them. Each claim presents facts occurring at different times with circumstances peculiar to each claim. There is no "common thread" running between or through each of the claims which is necessary to permit permissive joinder. The questions to be resolved with respect to each patient named in the 294 counts are the same, to-wit: (1) Was he/she a resident of the county in question at the time of the hospitalization? (2) Was the patient an indigent as defined by statute? (3) Did the hospital give the county notice as required by the statute? (4) On what dates did the hospitalization commence and end for each named patient? Also, there may be other factual issues involved. The testimony with respect to factual issues relative to each patient will apply only to that patient. Therefore, none of the counts arises out of the same transaction or series of transactions. Samaritan's daily and routine treatment of Arizona's indigent population does not constitute the same transactions or series of transactions as required by Rule 20(a).

Even though the allegations in all 294 counts are based upon the same statutory duty, this is not sufficient by itself to bring the case within the requirement that joinder must arise out of the same transaction, occurrence, or series of transactions or occurrences. It is only when this requirement is met, coupled with a common question of law or fact, that joinder is proper. This requirement was not met. Therefore, joinder was improper. * * *

The case of *United States v. Mississippi*, 380 U.S. 128 (1965), is relied on by Samaritan for its assertion that its 294–count lawsuit involves the same transaction or series of transactions. We disagree. In that case, the Supreme Court upheld the joinder of different voting registrars based upon the allegation of a common practice or scheme in Mississippi to deny blacks the right to vote. In this case, there is no allegation of a common practice or scheme on the part of any of the defendants to avoid paying hospital claims for indigent emergency medical services. * * *

The order of the trial court denying Apache County's motion . . . is reversed. * * *

ALEXANDER v. FULTON COUNTY

207 F.3d 1303 (11th Cir. 2000)

MARCUS, Circuit Judge:

This case involves various claims of race discrimination brought by eighteen current and former Fulton County Sheriff's Department employees individually and on behalf of all similarly situated white employees of the Sheriff's Department against Fulton County, Georgia and Sheriff Jacquelyn H. Barrett, in her official and individual capacities (collectively, "Defendants"). Plaintiffs sued Fulton County and Sheriff Barrett alleging that Fulton County maintained a "policy or custom" of racial discrimination in employment decisions, that Fulton County and the Sheriff's Department engaged in a "pattern or practice" of employment discrimination, and specifically that Fulton County and Sheriff

Barrett intentionally discriminated on the basis of race with respect to discipline, promotions, transfers, reclassifications, promotional examinations, restorations of rank, and appointments to unclassified positions. Defendants now appeal from a jury verdict entered for most of the Plaintiffs finding that Fulton County maintained a policy or custom of discrimination against white employees and that Sheriff Barrett intentionally discriminated against white employees. After a thorough review of the record, we affirm in part, reverse in part, and remand for further proceedings consistent with this opinion. * * *

[Defendants]   broadly allege that the district court erred in so far as it tried each of the Plaintiffs' claims together. After discovery, Defendants moved to sever Plaintiffs' individual claims of discrimination contending that the joint trial of these claims would confuse the jury and unfairly prejudice their defense. The district court rejected this motion. We review a district court's joinder of Plaintiffs' claims and denial of severance for abuse of discretion. Although we recognize that unfair prejudice may result from trying together the claims of multiple Plaintiffs alleging different types of discrimination, we discern no abuse of discretion in the district court's decision to join the Plaintiffs' claims in this case.

Among other things, the Federal Rules of Civil Procedure provide that "all persons may join in one action as plaintiffs if they assert any right to relief jointly, severally, or in the alternative in respect of or arising out of the same transaction, occurrence, or series of transactions or occurrences and if any question of law or fact common to all these persons will arise in the action." Federal Rule 20(a). A party seeking joinder of claimants under Rule 20 must establish two prerequisites: 1) a right to relief arising out of the same transaction or occurrence, or series of transactions or occurrences, and 2) some question of law or fact common to all persons seeking to be joined. Plainly, the central purpose of Rule 20 is to promote trial convenience and expedite the resolution of disputes, thereby eliminating unnecessary lawsuits. See *Mosley v. General Motors Corp.*, 497 F.2d 1330, 1332 (8th Cir. 1974). The Federal Rules, however, also recognize countervailing considerations to judicial economy. Rule 42(b), for example, provides for separate trials where the efficiency of a consolidated trial is outweighed by its potential prejudice to the litigants. The Supreme Court has instructed the lower courts to employ a liberal approach to permissive joinder of claims and parties in the interest of judicial economy: "Under the Rules, the impulse is towards entertaining the broadest possible scope of action consistent with fairness to the parties; joinder of claims, parties and remedies is strongly encouraged." *United Mine Workers v. Gibbs*, 383 U.S. 715, 724 (1966). * * *

" '[T]ransaction' is a word of flexible meaning. It may comprehend a series of many occurrences, depending not so much upon the immediateness of their connection as upon their logical relationship." *Moore v. New York Cotton Exchange*, 270 U.S. 593, 610 (1926). Accordingly, "all 'logically related' events entitling a person to institute a legal action against another generally are regarded as comprising a transaction or occurrence." *Mosley*, 497 F.2d at 1333. Several courts have concluded that allegations of a "pattern or practice" of discrimination may describe such logically related events and satisfy the same transaction requirement. In *Mosley*, perhaps the leading case on the joinder of Title VII plaintiffs under Rule 20, ten black plaintiffs alleged that General Motors had a general policy of discrimination against black employees. The trial court had ordered the severance of the claims, concluding that the allegations presented a variety of issues and had little relationship to one another. The Eighth Circuit reversed the trial court's order to sever plaintiffs' claims, concluding that, based on its reading of Rule 20, the General Motors policy "purportedly designed to discriminate against blacks in employment ... [arose] out of the same series of transactions and occurrences." Id. at 1334. The court held that "a company-wide policy purportedly designed to discriminate against blacks in employment ... arises out of the same series of transactions or occurrences." Id. at 1333–34.

The second prong of Rule 20 does not require that all questions of law and fact raised by the dispute be common, but only that some question of law or fact be common to all parties. Several courts have found that the question of the discriminatory character of Defendants' conduct can satisfy the commonality requirement of Rule 20.

On the other hand, the prejudicial effects of other witnesses' alleged discriminatory experiences may outweigh their probative value where, for example, the alleged discrimination occurs during different time periods, different supervisors make the challenged decisions, or the alleged discrimination happens at geographically removed places. None of these concerns is presented here.

In this case, the district court did not abuse its discretion in finding that the Plaintiffs satisfied both requirements for joinder. As for the first requirement, all of the Plaintiffs' claims stem from the same core allegation that they were subject to a *systemic* pattern or practice of race-based discrimination against white law enforcement officers by Sheriff Barrett in her first year in office. Plaintiffs all seek relief based on the same series of discriminatory transactions by the same decision-maker in the same department during the same short time frame. As for the second requirement, the discriminatory character of Defendants' conduct is plainly common to each plaintiff's recovery. The fact that the Plaintiffs suffered different effects–in this case, discrimination in promotions, transfers, assignments, or discipline–from the alleged policy of discrimination did not preclude the trial court from finding a common question of law and fact.

Alternatively, the Defendants argue that even if the district court did not abuse its discretion in finding proper joinder under Rule 20(a), it did err in failing to sever the Plaintiffs' cases for trial under Fed.R.Civ.P. 42(b). As Rule 42(b) requires the district court to balance considerations of convenience, economy, expedition, and prejudice, the decision to order separate trials naturally depends on the peculiar facts and circumstances of each case. Again, we disturb a district court's decision not to order separate trials only upon a showing of abuse of discretion. We can discern no abuse of discretion here.

Defendants suggest that there was no way to try together the individual claims of the eighteen Plaintiffs, each involving different work histories, employment decisions and prayers for relief, without unfairly prejudicing their defense and confusing the jury. While we acknowledge the real potential for confusion among jurors and for unfair prejudice to a defendant where there are large numbers of Plaintiffs, claims, and defenses, and urge care in joining together in one case multiple claims and multiple claimants, we conclude that in this case the potential for prejudice was minimized because of the core similarities in Plaintiffs' claims. As we have stated, the claims all center on the core allegation of a systemic pattern of race-based discrimination against white law enforcement officers instigated by Sheriff Barrett during her first year in office. Moreover, the Plaintiffs' specific claims also overlap substantially. Each plaintiff, with the exception of Major A.M. Alexander, challenged on the grounds of race discrimination Sheriff Barrett's alleged failure to consider him or her for appointment to unclassified positions. Thirteen Plaintiffs claimed the Sheriff discriminated against each of them in assignments or transfers. In addition to these two main claims, three of the Plaintiffs alleged that they were discriminated against with respect to reclassifications, two claimed that they were discriminated against when Sheriff Barrett failed to restore their rank after voluntary demotions, and two claimed they were disciplined in a discriminatory manner. Furthermore, several of the claims–discriminatory denial of reclassification, discriminatory denial of restoration of rank, and denial of promotion claims–logically relate or overlap. Finally, each of the Plaintiffs' claims and the evidence of discrimination undoubtedly are relevant to every other plaintiff's core allegation of systemic discrimination.

Given the common core of allegations, the substantial overlap of the particular claims, and the logical interconnection of several of the different forms the alleged discrimination took, we are satisfied that the district court did not abuse its discretion in finding that the efficiency of a consolidated trial outweighed the potential for unfair prejudice or jury confusion. * * *

[The court of appeals then reversed in part on other grounds and ordered a remand.]

Notes and Questions

1. The Arizona and federal rules governing joinder of multiple defendants are virtually identical. Yet the *Apache County* and *Alexander* courts reach different results. Can the cases be reconciled on their facts? Although the courts are applying the same provision, do they interpret the words in the same way?

2. One difference between the cases is the way the courts construe the phrase "same transaction, occurrence, or series of transactions or occur-

rences." Do you understand the difference in the way the courts interpret this language? What test does each court use to determine whether the requirement is satisfied?

Like *Apache County* and *Alexander*, most courts have avoided coming up with a precise definition of the phrase. They instead look to the general purpose of the rule—to promote judicial economy—and attempt to ascertain whether that purpose would be served by allowing joinder under the facts of a particular case. The tests used in the two main cases reflect different ways of answering the question of what it actually means to promote judicial economy. *Apache County* recognizes that the greatest demand placed upon a court in litigation is to hear and consider the evidence. The court's "same evidence" approach attempts to measure the extent to which the claims involved share the same evidence.

Alexander's "logical relationship" test does not limit itself to considering the evidence, but instead considers all factors that may exist in a particular case. Because of this flexibility, one influential treatise on federal civil procedure commends the logical relationship test as the best approach. 7 Wright, Miller, and Kane, Federal Practice and Procedure: Civil 2d § 1653 (1990). Many state courts also use this test. *See, e.g., McCoy v. Like*, 511 N.E.2d 501 (Ind. App. 1987).

Of course, flexibility has its price. One problem with any case-by-case approach is a lack of predictability to attorneys and parties who must use the rule in later cases. What exactly does *Alexander* mean by a "logical" relationship? The court is not using the term logic in its formal sense, is it? If not strictly "logical," then in what sense are the claims related?

On the other hand, does ambiguity really present a serious concern in the context of Rule 20? What happens if two plaintiffs erroneously think they can—or cannot—join under Rule 20?

3. Would the *Alexander* court, with its broader test for determining what constitutes the "same transaction," have allowed joinder in *Apache County*? Or is there another difference in the cases? What about the way in which the plaintiffs framed their complaints? Does that affect your analysis of the Introductory Problem?

4. For two other cases relying on the distinction suggested in the prior note, compare *Howard Motor Co. v. Swint*, 448 S.E.2d 713 (Ga. App. 1994) (employees of a company alleging sexual harassment by a single individual could not join) with *M.K. v. Tenet*, 216 F.R.D. 133 (D.D.C. 2002) (former employees of CIA could join to sue director and others for constitutional violations).

5. Although Rule 20(a) may allow multiple parties to be joined, it does not guarantee that all of the claims thus joined will be tried together. Rules 20(b) and 42(b) give a judge considerable discretion to dissect a case into convenient trial units, and to conduct a separate trial for each unit. Some of the reasons the rule gives for separate trials—"in furtherance of convenience" and "to avoid delay"—are obvious. After all, litigation, like most activities, does not enjoy unlimited economies of scale. A case that involves multiple parties can be both cumbersome and confusing, especially when the case is to be tried to a jury.

On the other hand, both rules also allow severance of claims or parties to avoid "prejudice." How might a party be prejudiced by having claims by or against it heard at the same time as other claims?

6.   Rule 42(a) is the converse of Rules 20(b) and 42(b). It allows a judge to consolidate separate cases for a single trial. The standard for consolidation is much easier to satisfy than Rule 20. Does this offer a back-door way around Rule 20? Can a party achieve joinder of a case that does not satisfy Rule 20 by the simple expedient of filing separate cases and consolidating them? Practically speaking, what is the crucial difference between this option and Rule 20(a)?

7.   Even when multiple claims meet the standards of Rule 20, other factors may cause a court to deny joinder. For example, in *Cincinnati Ins. Co. v. Reybitz*, 421 S.E.2d 767 (Ga. App. 1992), the court refused to allow a plaintiff, who was claiming that he had been struck by a large sports utility vehicle while riding his bicycle, to sue both the driver of the vehicle and the driver's insurance company in the same lawsuit. In most states, a party is precluded from introducing evidence that the defendant has insurance coverage (do you see why?). The court in *Cincinnati Insurance* held that allowing the plaintiff to name the insurance company as a second defendant would effectively evade this strict rule excluding evidence of insurance coverage.

8.   The plaintiff in *Apache County* had not only filed claims against multiple defendants, but also had filed several claims against each individual defendant. Note that this does not mean that the suit will be divided into 294 independent actions. Under the Federal Rules and similar state regimes, the rule governing joinder of *claims* against a single defendant is considerably more lenient than Rule 20. Thus, the seventeen claims against Apache County can be litigated in one suit even though they do not arise from the same transaction. Joinder of claims is discussed in Section E of this chapter.

B.   COUNTERCLAIMS

INTRODUCTORY PROBLEM

Midway Motors, Inc. ["Midway"], operates a large car dealership. To be competitive, all car dealers must keep a large inventory on the lot at all times. Maintaining that inventory is extremely expensive. To help it meet these costs, in August of last year Midway borrowed money from Financial Bank ["Financial"], pursuant to a rolling line of credit agreement.

Midway decided to expand its showroom a few months later. Because the line of credit agreement did not allow funds to be used for this sort of expense, Midway entered into a second loan agreement, called a building loan, with Financial in March of this year. Midway owes large sums of money to Financial under both loan agreements.

When rising fuel prices dampen demand for cars, Midway cannot make the required payments under either loan. Financial therefore sues Midway ["Case #1"]. However, because it is still negotiating with

Midway on a way to pay the building loan, Financial sues only for the outstanding balance on the line of credit. Midway files an answer which both denies liability and asserts a counterclaim. In this counterclaim, Midway claims that Financial failed to make certain disbursements to the plumber and electrician who worked on the showroom expansion, as called for by the explicit terms of the building loan agreement. Midway paid these parties itself, and now seeks reimbursement. Before filing a reply, Financial moves to dismiss the counterclaim, arguing that the rules of procedure do not allow Midway to file a counterclaim that involves a different transaction than that which gave rise to the complaint.

Midway then files a new case against Financial ["Case #2"]. In this action, Midway seeks damages from Financial for failure to make the disclosures required by federal law in connection with the line of credit. Even though it has not yet responded to Midway's counterclaim in Case #1, Financial files an answer in Midway's new case. Financial's answer asks the court to dismiss Case #2, arguing that Midway was required to bring the disclosure claim as a counterclaim in the action involving the line of credit.

Financial's next step is to file another suit against Midway ["Case #3"], in which it seeks to recover the outstanding balance on the building loan. Midway moves to dismiss this action, arguing that Financial was required to bring this claim in response to Midway's counterclaim in Case #1.

How should the court resolve the challenges that Financial and Midway have raised in these three separate actions?

Governing Rule: Federal Rules of Civil Procedure 13(a) and (b).

SIMMONS v. SIMMONS

773 P.2d 602 (Colo. App. 1988)

JONES, Judge

Defendant, James J. Simmons, former husband of plaintiff, Linda K. Simmons, appeals the judgment entered on a jury verdict awarding plaintiff $15,000 in compensatory damages and $100,000 in punitive damages against the defendant for assault and battery, intentional infliction of emotional distress, and outrageous conduct. Because of prejudicial error to defendant in the conduct of the trial, we reverse.

The parties were married in 1976, and in June 1982, a petition for dissolution of marriage was filed by defendant, with the hearing on final dissolution orders set for February 1983.

Before the hearing date, plaintiff filed the civil complaint in this matter. In it, she alleged that, one year earlier, defendant had assaulted her by throwing coffee on her; that on May 10, 1982, defendant without provocation, intentionally kicked, slapped, and hit her, and tore her ear; and finally, that during the last years of the marriage defendant intentionally caused plaintiff to suffer emotional distress by his outrageous conduct.

During 1983, the two separate cases between these parties remained pending before two separate trial courts. In this case, defendant filed a motion to dismiss on grounds that plaintiff's claims should be pursued in the pending dissolution proceedings. That motion was denied. On April 11, 1983, the trial court presiding over the dissolution proceeding granted the motion of James (defendant here) for partial summary judgment, upholding the parties' antenuptial agreement. Later, a decree of dissolution was entered, allocating the parties' property in accordance with the agreement. On March 21, 1985, the trial court in this case entered judgment against defendant. From that judgment, defendant appeals.

I.

Defendant first contends that since the parties to this action were married, the trial court erred when it allowed an independent civil action alleging the tort of intentional infliction of emotional distress. We disagree.

In Colorado a wife may sue her husband for damages for personal injuries caused by the conduct of the husband. Thus, plaintiff's marriage to defendant does not preclude her from maintaining the action for damages against him.

II.

Defendant next contends that plaintiff should have been required to assert her present claims in the prior dissolution proceedings because (1) they are compulsory counterclaims under C.R.C.P. 13; and (2) the Uniform Marriage and Dissolution Act requires the resolution of all disputes arising out of a marriage to be resolved in a single proceeding. We disagree.

No Colorado appellate decision has squarely addressed this precise issue. Although the few cases decided in other jurisdictions reveal no clear majority position, they do reveal that consideration of judicial economy and efficiency has been central to their results.

In *Tevis v. Tevis*, 79 N.J. 422, 400 A.2d 1189 (1979), the New Jersey Supreme Court held that a suit in tort by the plaintiff ex-spouse was barred, stating that:

> Since the circumstances of the marital tort and its potential for money damages were relevant in the matrimonial proceedings, the claim should not have been held in abeyance; it should, under the 'single controversy' doctrine, have been presented in conjunction with that action as part of the overall dispute between the parties in order to lay at rest all their legal differences in one proceeding and avoid the prolongation and fractionalization of litigation.

Conversely, the Supreme Court of Utah has held that actionable torts between married persons should not be litigated in divorce proceedings. *Walther v. Walther*, 709 P.2d 387 (Utah 1985); Lord v. Shaw, 665 P.2d 1288 (Utah 1983). In both these cases, the court reasoned that:

> Divorce actions will become unduly complicated in their trial and disposition if torts can be or must be litigated in the same action. * * * The administration of justice will be better served by keeping the two proceedings separate.

The Supreme Court of Arizona reached the same conclusion, basing its holding on "the peculiar and special nature of a divorce action." *Windauer v. O'Connor*, 485 P.2d 1157 (Ariz. 1971).

We note that in Utah, as in New Jersey, divorce is grounded in fault. Nevertheless, the Utah Supreme Court focused on the distinctions between dissolutions and matters at law, rather than the relevancy of potential tort money damages in dissolution proceedings. The court's high regard for the equitable nature of dissolutions—in a statutory fault context—is highly persuasive.

In a state governed by the Uniform Dissolution of Marriage Act, such as Colorado, moreover, the reasoning in *Tevis* is inapposite. Considerations of fault or misconduct would be appropriate only in the context of child custody proceedings and, even then, only when directly bearing on the issue of the best interests of the child the custody of whom is at issue.

Accordingly, we adopt the reasoning of the Utah and Arizona courts, and hold that the efficient administration of dissolution cases requires their insulation from the peculiarities of matters at law. The joinder of marriage dissolution actions with claims sounding in tort or, for instance, contract would require our trial courts to address many extraneous issues, including trial by jury, and the difference between the "amicable settlement of disputes that have arisen between parties to a marriage," and the adversarial nature of other types of civil cases. Moreover, such would create tension between the acceptance of contingent fees in tort claims and our strong and longstanding public policy against contingent fees in domestic cases. We conclude that sound policy considerations preclude either permissive or compulsory joinder of interspousal tort claims, or non-related contract claims, with dissolution of marriage proceedings.

[The court then held that plaintiff's counsel had engaged in a number of improper actions that had prejudiced the trial.] Hence, although there was no error in plaintiff's pursuing her claims against defendant in this independent action, the judgment is reversed, and the cause is remanded for a new trial consistent with the views expressed in this opinion.

JUDGE VAN CISE concurring in part and dissenting in part.

I disagree with Part II of the majority opinion. Therefore, although I concur in the reversal of the judgment, I would remand with directions to dismiss the complaint.

I agree with defendant husband's contention that plaintiff wife should have asserted her tort claims as counterclaims when she filed her answer in the dissolution action. Since she did not so plead, the instant case based on these claims should have been dismissed under the doctrine of res judicata.

The district court in the dissolution action is a trial court of general jurisdiction. * * * [T]he Uniform Dissolution of Marriage Act (the Act) states that: "The Colorado Rules of Civil Procedure apply to all proceedings under this article, except as otherwise specifically provided in this article." There is no language in the Act prohibiting joinder of other claims with proceedings under the Act. Therefore, C.R.C.P. 13(a) pertaining to compulsory counterclaims is applicable as in any other type of civil action.

The complained of acts arose out of the failed marital relationship and, therefore, came under the category of compulsory counterclaims as defined in C.R.C.P. 13(a). Not having been raised in the dissolution proceeding, they are barred. This is so even though the evidence needed to establish these tort claims is quite different from that pertaining to the dissolution action, as here, there is a logical relationship between the claim for dissolution and the claims for torts committed during the marriage.

Also, § 106(1)(b) of the Act directs the court to "consider, approve, or make provision for. . . . the disposition of property" in conjunction with the entry of a decree of dissolution. These tort claims are choses in action and, therefore, are property to be disposed of in the dissolution proceeding. And, since one of the underlying purposes of the Act, as stated in § 102(2)(a), is "to promote the amicable settlement of disputes that have arisen between parties to a marriage," the dissolution court is the proper court to decide all claims and disputes that may exist between the parties.

Notes and Questions

1. Do you find the reasoning of the majority or the dissent more convincing? Note that the majority goes further than holding that the counterclaim is not "compulsory." The court instead suggests in *dictum* that such a tort claim is not even permissive, *i.e.*, it could not be asserted in the divorce case even if the defendant chose to assert it. Does that make sense? Isn't the *Tevis* court correct when it says that a court must consider the behavior of the parties when determining a divorce action? If the court needs to consider that behavior, why not let it decide any liability that may flow from that behavior? Or is that reasoning too simplistic?

Reread Federal Rule 13(b). Given the clear language of the rule, does a court have any authority to refuse to hear a tort counterclaim like the one in *Simmons*, assuming that it is properly presented to the court in a divorce proceeding?

2. *Compulsory and Permissive Counterclaims.* Because Rule 13(b) places no restrictions on the claims that a defendant can file as a counter-

claim, there is relatively little case law dealing with permissive counter-claims. The vast majority of case law under Rule 13 deals instead with compulsory counterclaims.

Rule 13(a) is somewhat unusual. Aside from Rule 19, a complex provision that does not apply in that many cases, joinder of claims and parties is usually optional, not mandatory. Why should counterclaims be any different? Are "compulsory" counterclaims logically necessary to the main case in the sense that the court must determine the merits of the counterclaim before it can rule on plaintiff's claim?

3.   There are relatively few reported cases dealing with the question of what happens when a party fails to file a "compulsory" counterclaim. The reason is practical: once litigation is commenced, attorneys tend to file all available claims.

In cases like *Simmons* where this does not happen, the court must determine the consequences of failing to comply with Rule 13. The rule itself does not clearly state that a party who fails to file such a counterclaim loses it. Courts seem to assume, however, that this is the only sanction that makes sense. *See Nippon Credit Bank, Ltd. v. Matthews*, 291 F.3d 738, 755 (11th Cir. 2002). The United States Supreme Court appears to agree, although only in *dictum. Baker v. Gold Seal Liquors*, 417 U.S. 467, 469 n. 1, 94 S.Ct. 2504, 41 L.Ed.2d 243 (1974). Can you conceive of any possible sanctions for failing to file a compulsory counterclaim other than barring the omitted claim?

4.   Rules 20 and 13(a) both use the "same transaction or occurrence" test. Partly because of the drastic consequences of failing to file a compulsory counterclaim, that phrase has added importance in the Rule 13 context. Most courts use something akin to the "logical relationship" test that we saw in *Alexander*. A leading treatise, although favoring the logical relationship test, also acknowledges that there are at least three other tests in use:

a.   Will substantially the same evidence support or refute the claim and the counterclaim? This approach is similar to that employed in *Apache County*.

b.   Are the issues of fact and law raised by the claim and counterclaim largely the same?

c.   If there were no compulsory counterclaim rule, would the common-law doctrine of claim preclusion bar a subsequent suit on defendant's claim? The doctrine of claim preclusion is introduced in section G of this Chapter.

6 Wright, Miller, and Kane, *Federal Practice and Procedure: Civil 2d* § 1410 (1990). Are any of these preferable to the majority "logical relationship" test? If you were an attorney who concentrated on representing defendants, which test would you prefer? Or, given your unfettered ability to file any counterclaim under Rule 13(b), would the difference between the tests have any effect on how you would structure your case?

Should courts interpret the phrase "same transaction or occurrence" the same way under Rules 13 and 20? After all, the consequences of failing to meet the two rules are quite different. Should a court therefore be more hesitant to conclude that two claims arise from the same transaction under

Rule 13, in order to avoid dismissal of possibly meritorious claims on technical procedural grounds? But does it make sense that the same words could have different meanings in the same set of rules?

5.   One possible difference between Rules 13 and 20 is that the latter refers not only to the same transaction or occurrence, but also to a *series* of transactions or occurrences. Although this language seems to be broader, in practice courts do not interpret Rule 20 any more broadly than other permissive joinder rules that use the "same transaction" test. 2 Moore, Vestal, & Kurland, Moore's Manual: Federal Practice and Procedure § 14.21 at 14–40 (2000).

6.   Are defendants the only parties required to counterclaim? What if defendant counterclaims against plaintiff, and plaintiff has another claim against defendant that arises from the same transaction as that counterclaim?

In addition to plaintiffs and defendants, other parties may be required to counterclaim. For example, Rule 14, which is explored later in this Chapter, requires "third party defendants" to file compulsory counterclaims.

7.   Not all counterclaims that arise from the same transaction as the original claim are compulsory. Rule 13 contains four explicit exceptions. First, because the rule covers only those claims that the defendant has on the date it files its answer, *unmatured* claims are not compulsory. Suppose, for example, that Tenant sues Landlord for failing to maintain the roof of Tenant's apartment building. If Tenant has failed to pay rent during the term of the lease, many courts would treat Landlord's claim for the rent as a compulsory counterclaim in Tenant's suit. However, Landlord cannot sue for any rent payments that are not yet due. What if Tenant fails to pay rent while its suit is pending? Rule 13(e) admittedly allows Landlord to amend its answer to add the counterclaim. However, because the claim is not matured on the day the answer was filed, Landlord is not *required* to add the counterclaim by amendment.

The second exception involves situations in which the counterclaim cannot be adjudicated without joining unavailable third parties. In certain cases, especially those involving multiple claimants to a will, a piece of property, or a fund, the rules require that certain parties be joined. The doctrine of necessary parties is discussed in Chapter 6.

Third, a claim is not a compulsory counterclaim if it is already pending before a court at the time the original complaint is filed. For example, suppose that X and Y both claim the other breached a contract. X sues first, in a jurisdiction that does not have a compulsory counterclaim rule. If Y then sues X for breach of contract in a jurisdiction that follows Rule 13(a), X does not have to counterclaim for breach because his claim is already being heard by another court.

Fourth, counterclaims are not compulsory in cases where the court acquires jurisdiction by seizing property. As you will see in Chapter 4, a court cannot litigate a case unless it has acquired jurisdiction over the objects of the suit. In most cases, the court acquires jurisdiction over the parties to the case. In some situations, however, the court acquires jurisdiction not over the parties, but over property owned or claimed by those parties. In such a case, it is the property, not the person, that is technically the "party" to the case. Although courts have eviscerated many of the historical differences between suits against individuals and suits against property, see *Shaffer v. Heitner* on p. 142, some differences still remain. One of these is reflected in Rule 13(a): if the court's jurisdiction arises from attachment of property, any claims belonging to the *owner* of that property need not be filed as counterclaims.

8. *Simmons* deals not with an explicit exception to Rule 13(a), but instead with a judge-made exception. Courts have recognized a few such exceptions. In addition to divorce cases, see *Local Union No. 11, IBEW v. G.P. Thompson Electric, Inc.*, 363 F.2d 181 (9th Cir. 1966) (a party that chooses to submit a claim arising under a collective bargaining agreement to arbitration instead of a court does not lose the claim, because of the federal policy encouraging arbitration) and *Southern Construction v. Pickard*, 371 U.S. 57, 83 S.Ct. 108, 9 L.Ed.2d 31 (1962) (where a party is sued in two related cases, and has a claim that arises out of the same transaction as *both* complaints, it can elect to bring its counterclaim in either the first or second suit). See also *Plant v. Blazer Financial Services*, 598 F.2d 1357 (5th Cir. 1979) (although concluding that a defendant lender's counterclaim for failure to pay a loan does not arise from the same transaction as the borrower's claim that lender violated federal Truth-in-Lending laws in making that loan, also suggests in *dictum* that it would contravene the policies underlying the federal law if lender were even allowed to bring the counterclaim). To what extent should a court have the authority to modify the clear requirements of Rule 13 based on its own perceptions of public policy? Cf. Rule 13(f), which gives the court some flexibility.

9. P and D are involved in an automobile accident. P works for X, and was running an errand for X when the accident happened. P sues D for her injuries. If D also suffered injuries, his claim against P is a compulsory counterclaim. But is there any way D may also file a claim against X in the same case? Federal Rule 13(h) provides that a party who files a counterclaim or cross-claim may join additional parties to that claim if the party could have joined both the existing parties and the new parties as co-defendants under Rule 20. In our example, D could have sued both P and X for his injuries, as joinder of P and X would satisfy Rule 20. However, P filed her lawsuit first. Under these circumstances, it makes sense to allow D to add X as an additional party to the case. The resulting case is the same as the suit that would have occurred had D filed first, suing P and X as codefendants.

Of course, X must formally be made a party to the case. When a plaintiff sues a defendant, he must serve her with the complaint and other court papers. A party joined under Rule 13(h) will likewise be served with a copy of the claim against it. In addition, he receives copies of the other pleadings filed in the case. X may file counterclaims and cross-claims of his own against D and P; possibly resulting in the addition of still other parties under Rule 13(h) or other joinder rules.

10. The issue of whether a counterclaim arises from the same transaction as the original claim can have an additional twist in federal court, as you will see in Chapter 3.

C. CROSS–CLAIMS

INTRODUCTORY PROBLEM

Attorney has represented Client in numerous legal matters during the last ten years. One day, the two decide to meet at 7:00 a.m. at Attorney's office to discuss a new issue. While walking down the hallway in Attorney's office building, both slip and fall, suffering serious injuries. An investigation reveals that Janitor, an independent maintenance contractor, had experimented with a new and terribly slippery silicone-based floor wax that very morning. Attorney and Client therefore join to sue Janitor and Sili Co., the company that manufactured the wax. They allege negligence against both defendants.

Janitor files a cross-claim against Sili Co. Several weeks before the accident, Sili Co. approached Janitor to try to persuade him to try out the new silicone wax. Although initially reluctant, Janitor eventually agreed to use the product. However, Janitor insisted that the parties sign a contract in which Sili Co. agreed to indemnify and hold harmless Janitor for any losses that Janitor might suffer due to using the wax. Janitor's cross-claim seeks indemnity under this contract.

Sili Co. then files a permissive counterclaim against Client. Eleven months prior to the accident, Client had written a scathing newspaper article detailing Sili Co.'s use of animal testing for one of its other products, a silicone-based hair spray. Because of this article, the market for the product disappeared, causing Sili Co. to suffer significant losses. Sili Co.'s counterclaim seeks recovery for these losses under a theory of defamation.

After being served with the counterclaim, Client files a legal malpractice cross-claim against Attorney. Client had vetted the newspaper article with Attorney before submitting it for publication. Attorney had assured Client that the article was not defamatory. In the cross-claim, Client seeks reimbursement for any damages she must pay Sili Co.

Attorney and Sili Co. move to dismiss the cross-claims filed against them, arguing that they are not proper under the procedural rules governing cross-claims. How should the court rule on these motions?

Governing Law: Federal Rule of Civil Procedure 13(g).

––––––––––

In addition to mastering the rules, the newcomer to joinder must also deal with a technical and sometimes arcane terminology. We have already discussed "counterclaims," which are governed by Rule 13. Yet, Rule 13(g) also allows parties to file "cross-claims." What is the difference between a counterclaim and a cross-claim? A careful review of Rule 13 indicates that cross-claims are filed against a "co-party," whereas counterclaims are filed against an "opposing party." However, these terms are nowhere defined in the rules.

Courts themselves often confuse the terminology. There are a number of cases in which courts mislabel a counterclaim as a "cross-claim" or "countersuit." Usually the mistake does not affect the outcome of the case. However, given that counterclaims, unlike cross-claims, can be compulsory, it is important to exercise care in applying the proper label.

Counterclaims and cross-claims are not the only confusing terms in joinder. Later in the course you will learn about impleader, interpleader, and intervention; three very different joinder devices that share confusingly similar labels.

RAINBOW MANAGEMENT GROUP, LTD. v. ATLANTIS SUBMARINES HAWAII, L.P.

158 F.R.D. 656 (D. Haw. 1994)

Harold M. Fong, District Judge

[Atlantis conducted submarine tours off Waikiki Beach. A separate company, Rainbow Management Group ["RMG"] ferried passengers from the shore to the submarine. On January 27, 1992, RMG's vessel, the Elua, collided with the Boston Whaler, a ship owned by Haydu. The Boston Whaler was destroyed, and several of its passengers injured. The Elua was also damaged in the collision. A Boston Whaler passenger, George Berry, sued RMG and Atlantis [the "Berry case"]. Atlantis filed a cross-claim against RMG, both for indemnity and for breach of contract. The Berry case was eventually resolved.

RMG then filed the instant action against Atlantis and Haydu, seeking compensation for the damage to the Elua.]

Atlantis argues that RMG's claims are compulsory counterclaims, barred by Fed. R. Civ. P. 13(a) because RMG failed to assert them in the Berry case. * * * Atlantis argues that, after it filed its initial cross-claim against RMG, RMG became an "opposing party" within the meaning of Rule 13(a), and thereafter was required to plead any claims against Atlantis that arose out of the same transaction or occurrence as the initial cross-claims.

In response, RMG argues that its Elua claim is not a compulsory counterclaim, but is instead a permissive cross-claim pursuant to Fed. R. Civ. P. 13(g). Rule 13(g) provides in pertinent part:

> Cross–Claim Against a Co–Party. A pleading may state as a cross-claim any claim by one party against a coparty arising out of the transaction or occurrence that is the subject matter either of the original action or of a counterclaim therein. . . .

RMG argues that Atlantis was a co-party in the Berry case, not an opposing party. Thus, RMG could have asserted its Elua claim in the Berry case, but it was not required to do so.

This issue appears to be an open question in the Ninth Circuit, and the case law from other circuits is limited and contradictory. See, e.g., *U.S. v. Confederate Acres Sanitary Sewage & Drainage Sys.*, 935 F.2d 796, 799 (6th Cir. 1991) ("cross-claims against co-defendants are permissive") ; *Earle M. Jorgenson Co. v. T.I. United States, Ltd.*, 133 F.R.D. 472, 474 (E.D.Penn. 1991) ("Once a cross-claim has been pleaded, the cross-claimant becomes an opposing party, and 'the party against whom the cross-claim is asserted must plead as a counterclaim any right to relief that party has against the cross-claimant that arise from the same transaction or occurrence.' " (internal citations omitted))

Professor James W. Moore addresses this problem in his treatise, and concludes that co-parties become opposing parties within the meaning of Rule 13(a) after one party pleads a crossclaim against the other. 3 James W. Moore and Jo Desha Lucas, Moore's Federal Practice, ¶ 13.34, at 13–209–210 (2d. ed. 1985).

The Supreme Courts of Kansas and Alaska have also adopted this approach. See *Miller v. LHKM*, 751 P.2d 1356 (Alaska 1988); *Mohr v. State Bank of Stanley*, 241 Kan. 42, 734 P.2d 1071 (Kansas 1987). Furthermore, this approach is consistent with the goal of judicial economy and reducing unnecessary litigation, because it encourages parties to plead all claims arising out of a single incident and to resolve such claims in a single lawsuit.

The court finds Professor Moore's approach to this issue to be persuasive, and, accordingly, adopts the following rule: Co-parties become opposing parties within the meaning of Fed. R. Civ. P. 13(a) after one such party pleads an initial cross-claim against the other. The court holds, however, that this rule should be limited to situations in which the initial cross-claim includes a substantive claim (as opposed to merely a claim for contribution and indemnity). The reason for this modification is that an unlimited rule may actually increase the amount or complexity of litigation. * * *

In the instant case, Atlantis' initial cross-claim included a claim for contribution and indemnity, as well as an additional substantive claim for breach of contract. RMG was therefore on notice that it would have to defend against claims other than its own original claim. Accordingly, under the rule adopted today, the court GRANTS Atlantis' motion for summary judgment. * * *

Notes and Questions

1. Rule 13(g) states that a party "may" bring a cross-claim. Compare Rule 13(a), which requires a party to bring certain counterclaims. Given the clear language, how can the court in *Rainbow* conclude that a party was required to bring a cross-claim in the earlier action? Is the court, like others discussed in the introductory notes to this section, confusing counterclaims and cross-claims, or is something more involved?

2. Parties can be treated as opposing parties even when neither has filed a claim against the other. In *Kolb v. Scherer Bros. Financial Services*

Co., 6 F.3d 542 (8th Cir. 1993), a subcontractor, seeking payment for work it had performed, began foreclosure proceedings on its mechanics lien. (Under the law of most states, anyone who performs work to improve real property has a lien on that property in the amount that the owner agreed to pay for the work. That lien may be foreclosed like a mortgage.) The subcontractor named as defendants all other lienholders, including Kolb and Scherer. Kolb and Scherer filed answers in that case. Once that case was complete, Kolb then commenced a new action challenging Scherer's liens on the property. Although Kolb and Scherer were both defendants in the action, the court held that Kolb's new action was barred because he failed to bring his claims as cross-claims in the first action:

> Although all parties in a mechanic's lien action, other than the one who originally files the complaint, are designated as codefendants [under Minnesota law], it would be pure fiction to conclude that no adversity in fact exists between the parties merely because they are all designated as defendants. * * * Minnesota law is unambiguous. Any party who files an answer in a mechanic's lien action, though nominally a defendant, may actually function as a plaintiff with regard to other named defendants.

Because Kolb and Scherer were adverse, the court held that Rule 13(a) required him to bring the claim in the first case.

3.   Perhaps the best way to keep track of claims in complicated cases is always to remain focused on exactly who is claiming what against whom. Labels are important only insofar as they help you determine what rule to apply when considering if the claim is properly before the court. Once the claim is part of the suit, the label is no longer relevant. A tort claim, for example, will be resolved the same way regardless of whether it is filed as an original claim, counterclaim, or cross-claim.

D. ADDING THIRD PARTIES: IMPLEADER

INTRODUCTORY PROBLEM 1

Consummate Cosmetics Corporation has recently developed a new face moisturizing cream. Consummate assigns Jean Gull, an employee in the company's marketing department, the daunting task of coming up with a name for the cream. Gull names the product "Fountain of Youth." Without consulting with the company president or board, Gull arranges for the cream to be distributed under that name to the public.

Soon after Fountain of Youth hits the shelves, Consummate Cosmetics is sued for false advertising by one its competitors. This competitor charges that use of the name "Fountain of Youth" suggests that the product will actually make skin look younger, which simply is not the case. The competitor also cites a provision of governing law that makes a company liable for false advertising caused by one of its employees in the course of that employee's duties.

Consummate does not dispute that the ad is a "false advertisement" as that term is used in governing law. However, it wants to bring three separate parties into this lawsuit. First, it seeks to bring in Jean Gull, claiming that she was really responsible for the advertisement. Second, Consummate wants to bring in its insurance carrier. Although Consummate has a liability insurance policy, the insurance carrier has denied coverage, arguing that the policy does not extend to false advertising.

Finally, Consummate wants to join Barry Sterr, an attorney who represents Consummate in most of its business dealings. Consummate has learned that Gull asked Sterr about the proposed product name. Without doing any research, Sterr assured Gull that the name would be perfectly acceptable. The bill for this work was sent to Consummate. Consummate argues that Sterr's malpractice in giving advice to an employee of the company led to this lawsuit and Consummate's likely liability to the competitor.

Can Consummate join any or all of these parties to the case? Assuming that at least one can be joined, what motion should Consummate use to add it to the suit?

Governing Rule: Federal Rule 14.

INTRODUCTORY PROBLEM 2

Refer to the facts of Introductory Problem 1. Assume (without affecting the prior question) that Consummate successfully joins Gull and the insurance company.

The competitor now wants to file two claims against the new parties. First, it wants to file a false advertising claim against Gull based on her role in marketing the product. Second, it wants to add a claim against the insurance company. Under governing law, however, the competitor could not sue the insurance company directly at the present time. It could only sue the insurance company if it recovered a judgment against Consummate.

Gull also has a claim that she wants to bring against the competitor. Gull was injured when a tube of toothpaste manufactured by the competitor exploded, ruining her best suit.

Can the competitor and Gull bring any or all of their claims?

———————

Part A of this Chapter demonstrated that a plaintiff whose injuries were caused by two or more people could join all of the actors as defendants in the same case. However, a plaintiff may be able to obtain full recovery without joining all responsible parties to the case. As you have learned or will learn in Torts, some states hold tortfeasors "jointly and severally liable." This phrase means that each defendant is responsible for all of plaintiff's damages even though the actions of others may have contributed to those injuries. Plaintiffs in these states may obtain full recovery against any one of the defendants, which can save the plaintiff considerable time and trouble. Although Rule 20 allows the plaintiff to join the others, nothing in the Federal Rules requires it to join them (the mandatory joinder provisions of Rule 19, which are discussed in Chapter 6, are extremely narrow and would not apply to joint tortfeasors).

Often, however, tort law allows a defendant who must pay the entire amount of the injury to recover against the other responsible people. Depending on the situation, the defendant's right is labeled one of *contribution* (partial reimbursement) or *indemnification* (full reimbursement). Defendant can, of course, wait until the original suit by plaintiff is complete, and bring a separate suit for contribution or indemnity. However, recognizing that it is often more efficient to take care of both the original claim and the claim for contribution or indemnity at the same time, Rule 14 allows the defendant to bring in the other responsible party or parties.

Do not assume that Rule 14 applies only to cases of joint tortfeasors. It allows the defendant to bring in an additional party whenever that party may be liable to defendant for all or part of defendant's liability to plaintiff. Another common situation in which impleader may be proper is when one party agrees by contract to indemnify another. A carrier who agrees to transport a dangerous substance, for example, might negotiate a term in the contract for carriage in which the party who ships the substance indemnifies the carrier for any harm. If the carrier is sued, it may bring in the party who shipped the substance as a third-party defendant.

LOPEZ DE ROBINSON v. UNITED STATES
162 F.R.D. 256 (D. P.R. 1995)

PIERAS, JR., U.S. DISTRICT JUDGE

This is a medical malpractice action brought pursuant to the Federal Tort Claims Act. During July 1989, plaintiff's husband, Mr. Vance Le Roy Robinson, was suffering from acute abdominal pain. Plaintiff took her husband to the Veterans Administration Medical Center ("VAMC") in San Juan, Puerto Rico. He was denied admission to VAMC, however, because there were no hospital beds available. Thereafter, he was admitted to Hospital San Pablo ("San Pablo") where he was treated. Seven days later, Mr. Robinson died. Plaintiff alleges that the VAMC's negligent failure to admit her husband caused his death or aggravated the conditions leading to his death. Defendant denies all liability and has brought a third-party complaint against San Pablo alleging that negligent actions of San Pablo were the actual and proximate cause of decedent's death. The question currently before the Court is whether defendant/third-party plaintiff's third-party complaint is valid pursuant to Rule 14(a) of the Federal Rules of Civil Procedure. * * *

The parties disagree about what was the cause of Mr. Robinson's death. The death certificate states that the cause of decedent's death was carcinomatosis, which is the existence of malignant tumors derived from the epithelial tissue, a membranous tissue covering internal surfaces and organs. Plaintiffs, on the other hand, assert that an autopsy performed by Dr. Yocasta Brugal in 1991, after Mr. Robinson's body was exhumed, revealed that myocarditis, an inflammation of the muscle tissue of the heart, not carcinomatosis, was the cause of death. * * *

The historical evolution of Rule 14(a) of the Federal Rules of Civil Procedure illuminates the underlying purposes and policies of contemporary third-party pleading practice. In 1937, Rule 14(a) was added to the Federal Rules of Civil Procedure as an adaptation of Admiralty Rule 56. Originally, the rule provided that defendant/third-party plaintiff may implead a party "who is or may be liable to him [the original defendant] or to the plaintiff for all or part of plaintiff's claim" against defendant/third-party plaintiff. Therefore, the rule initially permitted a defendant/third-party plaintiff to implead a party who was directly liable exclusively to plaintiff.

By 1946, however, Rule 14(a) had been amended to the current version which reads in pertinent part:

> At any time after commencement of the action a defending party, as a third-party plaintiff, may cause a summons and complaint to be served upon a person not a party to the action who is or may be liable to the third-party plaintiff for all or part of the plaintiff's claim against the third-party plaintiff.

The amendment thus eliminated defendant/third-party plaintiff's ability to join a party whose sole liability was to the plaintiff.

In the case at bar, plaintiff presents the following legal theory. First, plaintiff alleges that VAMC had a duty to admit a veteran patient when emergency hospitalization is required. Plaintiff asserts that decedent's condition required emergency hospitalization. Thus, plaintiff argues, VAMC breached its duty when it failed to admit decedent on either July 7, 10, or 11, 1989, causing decedent pain and suffering on those days, and further aggravating the conditions which caused his death.

In an attempt to shield itself from any potential liability, defendant/third-party plaintiff brought this third-party complaint against San Pablo asserting that San Pablo was negligent by failing to properly diagnose decedent's condition, failing to provide decedent with proper medical care, and failing to maintain the premises in a safe condition, thereby causing decedent to slip and fall. Thus, defendant/third-party plaintiff contends that San Pablo is entirely liable to plaintiff for decedent's injury and death since San Pablo's negligence alone caused all injury. In the alternative, defendant/third-party plaintiff argues that San Pablo's negligence fused with VAMC's alleged negligence, so that the combined negligence of both entities caused decedent's death. Consequently, defendant/third-party plaintiff argues, San Pablo is jointly and severally liable with VAMC for plaintiff's damages as a joint tortfeasor.

For this third-party complaint to be properly lodged under Fed. R.Civ.P. 14(a), defendant/third-party plaintiff must allege that if VAMC were held liable to plaintiff under the original complaint, then VAMC has a right under substantive law to transfer all or a portion of its liability to third-party defendant, San Pablo. Defendant/third-party plaintiff attempts to forge a link between itself and San Pablo based upon the substantive right of contribution between joint tortfeasors.

Pursuant to Puerto Rico law, two or more individuals whose combined negligence causes plaintiff's injuries can be held jointly and severally liable as joint tortfeasors for plaintiff's damages. See *Garcia v. Gobierno de la Capital*, 72 D.P.R. 138 (1951). If judgment is entered for plaintiff to have and recover from defendants, jointly and severally, plaintiff may recover the full amount from one of the joint tortfeasors in execution of the judgment. Then, the paying tortfeasor has a right of contribution against the other joint tortfeasor, to recover a portion of the judgment. *Sanchez Rodriguez v. Lopez Jimenez*, 87 J.T.S. 36, 118 D.P.R. 701 (1987).

VAMC and San Pablo, however, are not joint tortfeasors. Defendant/third-party plaintiff's alleged tortious activity is neither geographically or temporally linked to the alleged tortious activity of San Pablo. Decedent visited the VAMC, in San Juan, Puerto Rico, during the early evening of Friday, July 7, 1989, and later on Monday, July 10, 1989, and Tuesday, July 11, 1989. On all three occasions, decedent was not admitted to the VAMC because there were no hospital beds available. Plaintiff is currently suing to recover compensation for the injury plaintiff's decedent sustained which is directly attributable to any potential negligence resulting from the VAMC's denial of admission on those three specific dates. By contrast, any potential negligent action or omission on the part of San Pablo would have occurred after decedent had already been denied admission at the VAMC, or during the period after decedent had been hospitalized at San Pablo, in Bayamon, Puerto Rico, on July 11, 1989. Therefore, the injury which San Pablo could have caused would have occurred after the injury for which plaintiff is seeking compensation in the case at bar.

Furthermore, neither party was in a position to control and prevent the allegedly negligent actions of the other party. There was no explicit or implicit contractual relationship between VAMC and San Pablo. Nor was San Pablo acting as VAMC's agent when it admitted decedent. As an independent entity, VAMC had no control over the type of care and attention San Pablo gave decedent nor over the conditions of the premises at San Pablo. Therefore, VAMC could not have actually prevented any negligent actions of San Pablo which may have caused plaintiff's injuries.

Finally, different evidence would be necessary to prove the cause of action against each separate party. In order to sustain the claim against VAMC, plaintiffs need to present evidence that VAMC had a duty to admit decedent for hospitalization, and that the failure to admit decedent as a patient in the hospital constituted a breach of that duty, leading to the injuries incurred. On the other hand, in order to sustain a claim of negligence against San Pablo, plaintiffs need to present evidence demonstrating that the actions taken by San Pablo failed to reach the appropriate standard of medical care. * * *

Defendant/third-party plaintiff, VAMC, has not successfully alleged any basis upon which San Pablo might be liable to VAMC. VAMC has merely asserted that San Pablo caused the injury to plaintiff, thus VAMC should not be held ultimately liable to plaintiff. Defendant/third-party plaintiff is not precluded from raising the argument that San Pablo's negligence was the sole cause of plaintiff's death. The argument, however, must be raised as an affirmative defense, not as the basis for a third-party complaint. See *Parr v. Great Lakes Express Co.*, 484 F.2d 767, 769 (7th Cir. 1973) ("if the accident was solely and proximately caused by someone else's negligence this would seem to be a complete defense to the original action and would not seem to be the basis of a third-party action, which presupposes liability on the part of the original defendant which he is attempting to pass on to the third-party defendant.").

As a final consideration, the Court notes that third-party pleading is within the discretion of the trial court. In the case at bar, allowing the third-party complaint to proceed would cause unnecessary confusion and would require fact development which is not salient to the relevant legal issues. The third-party complaint would cause inordinate cost and delay to this litigation, rather than to consolidate and simplify factual and legal issues for trial. For the foregoing reasons, the third-party complaint is hereby DISMISSED.

LEASETEC CORP. v. COUNTY OF CUMBERLAND, 896 F.Supp. 35 (D. Me. 1995). In an effort to computerize its records, a county entered into a contract with a computer vendor and a leasing company. Under this contract, the vendor sold a computer system to the leasing company, which in turn leased it to the county. When the system failed to perform to expectations, the county refused to make its lease payments. The leasing company sued the county, which in turn tried to implead the vendor. The county claimed that because it had breached the contract, the vendor was obligated either to indemnify the county or to provide contribution.

The court refused to allow the impleader. Under governing law, a right to indemnity or contribution could arise in two ways: (i) by contract, or (ii) by implication. The court found no duty to indemnify in the contract. Nor could the court find an implied duty to indemnify or contribute. Because the leasing company was suing the county for breach of contract, the county could not seek contribution on the basis that the leasing company was a "joint tortfeasor." The court also rejected the county's claim that a breach of warranty in the sale of a product creates any right to indemnification.

CITY OF ORANGE BEACH V. SCOTTSDALE INSURANCE CO., 166 F.R.D. 506 (S.D. Ala. 1996). In this case, a city had sued its insurance company for refusing to settle a previous lawsuit that had been filed against the city. That case resulted in a judgment of $4.5 million against the city, an amount far in excess of the insurance policy's liability limits. The insurance company in turn attempted to implead the law firm that it had hired to represent the city in the suit. The insurance company claimed that the law firm was also negligent, thereby making it a joint tortfeasor.

The court in this case also refused to allow the impleader. Even though the law firm may well have been a joint tortfeasor, Alabama law did not allow contribution among joint tortfeasors who were both "actively" negligent. It only allowed a claim for contribution by a "passive" joint tortfeasor against an "active" one. Because the insurance company itself was responsible for the decision, it was an active tortfeasor. Therefore, the company had no legal claim against the attorneys for contribution.

The court also rejected a malpractice claim that the defendant insurance company had attempted to assert by the process of impleader. Although the insurance company might have a viable claim for malpractice, it could not be brought in the process of impleader. Like in the *Leasetec* case above, the court held that the malpractice claim involved an independent liability owed by the law firm to the insurance company, which was not logically connected with the underlying claim by the city against the insurer.

Notes and Questions

1. *Rule 14 and the Substantive Law.* The *Lopez de Robinson* court devotes considerable discussion to the underlying law of torts. Analysis of the substantive law is necessary because Rule 14 does not itself *create* a right of indemnity or contribution. Instead, the party seeking impleader must show that such a right already exists in the substantive law. Rule 14 simply provides a procedure by which defendant's otherwise existing right of indemnity or contribution can be litigated along with the suit establishing defendant's liability.

Generally, a substantive right to indemnity or contribution can arise in two ways. First, it can be created by contract. Insurance contracts are but one form of a contractual right; other examples include contracts of surety, payment or performance bonds, and indemnity agreements. Second, the law may imply a duty of indemnity or contribution. The law will impose a right of indemnity when one party is held "vicariously" or "secondarily" liable for the actions of another, such as an employer's liability for acts of an employee. Contribution generally arises in tort cases.

2. Do you agree with the court in *Orange Beach* that the malpractice claim did not comply with Rule 14? In the operative part of its opinion, the court stated as reasoned:

> While such malpractice claim is related to the Orange Beach claims against Scottsdale, the malpractice claim is separate and independent from the Orange Beach claim against Scottsdale. As stated above Scottsdale has an independent duty to its insured to exercise honest judgment with regard to the settlement of claims. If Scottsdale breached its duty it did so by its own actions or inactions. Therefore, Scottsdale could be found to have acted negligently or in bad faith regardless of whether Stone Granade was guilty of professional malpractice. In fact, Scottsdale could be victorious in the main claim even if Stone Granade committed the alleged professional malpractice. The above is true because advice of counsel is only one of the many factors that an insurance company must consider when denying to settle a claim. The claim for professional malpractice is not dependent upon Orange Beach's claims against Scottsdale for negligent and bad faith failure to settle a claim. Therefore, Count I is a separate and independent claim that cannot serve as a proper impleader claim under Rule 14(a).

Is the malpractice claim really separate and independent? If Scottsdale won the underlying suit, was there really "malpractice"? What damages would Scottsdale suffer if it won the suit against the city?

3. One of the more difficult issues to arise in the area of impleader is that of so-called "comparative negligence." In recent years, many legislatures and courts have abandoned the traditional doctrine of joint and several liability, under which each defendant could conceivably be held liable for the entire amount of the injury. They have substituted a system in which the court attempts to assign a precise percentage of fault to each defendant, and if appropriate, to the plaintiff. Each party is liable *only* for the percentage of injury that it caused. You will explore the intricacies of, and problems with, this doctrine of comparative negligence in your Torts class. For purposes of impleader, however, one of the crucial facets of comparative negligence is its effect on contribution and indemnity. For an in-depth analysis of California's comparative negligence rule and its effect in impleader, see *American Motorcycle Ass'n v. Superior Court*, 20 Cal.3d 578, 578 P.2d 899 (1978).

4. When a substantive right to indemnity or contribution does exist, Rule 14 promotes efficiency by allowing two suits that would otherwise be litigated back-to-back to be merged into a single proceeding. In addition to efficiency, however, this joinder may also help prevent the injustice that can result from separate lawsuits. There is no guarantee that two courts will decide the same basic facts in the same way. In some situations, splitting the dispute into two or more cases can result in unfairness.

Suppose, for example, that plaintiff is injured by a defectively-designed product. Rather than sue the manufacturer, plaintiff elects to sue the retail store where she purchased the product. As you will learn in Torts, many states would apply the doctrine of vicarious liability, and hold the retailer responsible for plaintiff's injury even though it was not careless in any way. If the plaintiff demonstrates that the product was indeed defective, the retailer can be required to pay plaintiff's full damages.

The law also allows the retailer to seek full indemnity from the manufacturer. Absent impleader, the retailer would have to pursue its indemnity claim in a separate action. The problem, however, is that there is no way to guarantee that the second case will come out the same way as the first. Suppose, for example, that the manufacturer convinces the jury in the second case that the product was not defective. In this case, the retailer would end up holding the bag for an injury for which it was not responsible.

Impleader helps to avoid this sort of unfairness by assigning one court the duty to determine the core issue of whether the product is defective. That determination applies not only to plaintiff's claim against defendant, but also to defendant's third-party claim.

5. Impleader does not always result in more efficiency. As the final paragraph of the opinion in *Lopez de Robinson* notes, a court has the discretion to refuse to hear a third-party claim even though the claim complies with the requirements of Rule 14. A court will typically use this discretion when the new claim would make the case unduly complicated. For an example of a court dismissing a claim that satisfied Federal Rule 14, see *Hicks v. Long Island Railroad*, 165 F.R.D. 377 (E.D.N.Y. 1996).

6. Defendant's claim against a third-party defendant is treated as if it were a complaint. The third-party defendant is required to answer the third-party complaint, Rule 7(a), and to bring any compulsory counterclaims that it may have against the defendant, Rule 13(a). In addition, once a third-party defendant is joined, plaintiff and the third-party defendant may be able to bring related claims that they have against each other, Rule 14(a).

E. MULTIPLE CLAIMS

INTRODUCTORY PROBLEM

The Springfield Dome is the newest landmark in the City of Springfield. The Dome is a modern marvel, an inflatable dome stadium equipped with the latest in technology and creature comforts. The City hired Contractor to build the dome. However, because inflatable domes are tricky to build, Contractor subcontracted the roof work to Subcontractor.

Disaster struck when Springfield residents packed the Dome on opening day. The City had arranged for a fireworks display to inaugurate the new stadium. One of the fireworks pierced the roof, causing it to collapse on the crowd below.

The City sues Contractor for $1,000,000 in damages, based on the harm caused by the fallen roof. Contractor in turn impleads Subcontractor, arguing that the subcontract requires Subcontractor to reimburse Contractor for any damages that Contractor has to pay because of a faulty roof.

City wants to file two additional claims in the case. First, two years ago City hired Contractor to perform minor improvements to City Hall. Because the work was performed in shoddy fashion, City had to have another company repair the problem. City therefore wants to add a claim for $50,000 to cover the costs of repair.

Second, City wants to file a claim against Subcontractor for $10,000 in unpaid city property taxes, which are due and owing on Subcontractor's office building.

May City file these two additional claims in the case?

Governing Rule: Federal Rule 18(a).

The theme of this chapter thus far has been determining what claims a party to a lawsuit may bring against the other parties. We have assumed all along that each claimant has only one claim against a given party. In many cases, however, there are multiple claims. For example, a plaintiff may have been injured on more than one occasion by a given defendant, resulting in several separate claims. Even where there has been but a single injury, the law may allow recovery under more than one theory. As just one example, a business that discovers that one of its competitors has been engaging in false advertising may be entitled to recover under a federal statute,[1] state statutes,[2] and the common-law of unfair competition. Finally, you will see in Chapter 6 that the Rules allow a pleader to plead inconsistent theories of recovery, something like, "Defendant breached a contract; however if this court should find that there was no contract, defendant committed an intentional tort."

In all of these situations, a plaintiff might prefer to bring its claims in a single action. After all, litigation is not free. Parties in the United States are ordinarily required to pay their own attorneys. One suit will generally be cheaper than several. On the other hand, allowing multiple claims to be litigated together can confuse the jury, especially when the claims involve similar but unrelated transactions or inconsistent legal theories. How do the rules resolve this tension between efficiency and accuracy?

McCOY v. LIKE

511 N.E.2d 501 (Ind. App. 1987)

RATLIFF, Chief Judge

The facts as set forth in the plaintiffs' amended complaint reveal that Martha McCoy died in a nursing home at the age of seventy-nine (79) in Knox County on July 11, 1985. The following day, her will, dated February 16, 1984, was probated in the Knox Circuit Court. Dr. Jerry Like was appointed personal representative of the estate pursuant to the terms of the will. Dr. Like exercised Martha McCoy's power of attorney from November 17, 1983 until her death. Also on November 17, 1983,

1. Lanham Act § 43(a), 15 USC § 1125(a).

2. See, e.g., the Uniform Deceptive Trade Practices Act.

Martha, as seller, entered into a contract for the conditional sale of over 120 acres of real estate with Dr. Like and his wife, Georgialee. Martha McCoy was Georgialee's aunt. Less than one month later, the same parties amended the agreement by lowering substantially the purchase price. Dr. Like and his wife never made any payments to Martha on the contract. * * *

William McCoy, George McCoy, Mildred Robison, and Betty Hayes (hereinafter referred to as the plaintiffs), were Martha McCoy's nephews and nieces who were legatees under the 1984 will. They filed a complaint to contest the will on several grounds, including fraud and undue influence. All other heirs and beneficiaries were named as defendants as well as Dr. Like in his capacity as Martha's personal representative. * * *

After taking Dr. Like's deposition, the plaintiffs filed an amended complaint which was served upon all of the defendants, and added as a defendant Dr. Like as an individual. The amended complaint added several claims to the will contest. In Count I, the original will contest allegations were restated and a claim was made against Dr. Like for his exertion of undue influence and fraud in the will's execution. Count II sought to set aside the land contract because of Dr. Like's undue influence and fraud and to impose a constructive trust. Finally, Count III alleged Dr. Like's failure to act during Martha McCoy's lifetime in her best interests and other alleged acts of misconduct and breaches of his fiduciary duty. The amended complaint requested compensatory and punitive damages against Dr. Like individually. * * *

The defendants argue that a will contest is not subject to the rules of joinder of claims. They rely upon very old cases. [*Summers v. Copeland* 125 Ind. 466 (1890)] is cited for the proposition that joinder of claims is improper for will contests. . . . However, *Summers* is predicated upon the civil code predating our current Trial Rules which were enacted into law on January 1, 1970. Trial Rule 18(A) speaks in very broad terms; it does not delineate any exceptions. "An era of past Indiana procedural law will be wiped out by this rule which permits unlimited joinder of claims. . . ." 2 W. Harvey, Indiana Practice 185 (2d ed. 1987), quoting from the Civil Code Study Commission Comments. See also 6 C. Wright and A. Miller Federal Practice and Procedure § 1582 (1971) (no restriction on claims that may be joined under federal counterpart to T.R. 18(A)). Furthermore, "[i]f the action involves multiple parties, joinder is also freely permitted, subject to the restrictions contained in Rule 19, 20, and 22, relating to necessary and permissive joinder and interpleader." Harvey, at 190. Thus, once a person is properly made a party, joinder of claims is unfettered.

In the present case, Dr. Like as an individual was properly joined as a defendant under T.R. 20(A), thus enabling the plaintiffs to assert against him any and all claims they have under T.R. 18(A) as a matter of right. The holding of *Summers* clearly is no longer applicable under our present, liberal joinder provisions. Therefore, since joinder of Dr. Like in his individual capacity was proper, the trial court erred when it dismissed Dr. Like as an individual defendant and the portions of the amended complaint dealing with claims other than the will contest. If all of the plaintiffs' allegations as set forth in their amended complaint are taken as true, the plaintiffs certainly are entitled to the relief they seek.

It must be noted that T.R. 18(A) joinder is an initial matter. For trial convenience or to avoid confusion or prejudice, the trial court has broad discretion in deciding whether certain claims which have been joined with other claims should be tried together or severed into separate trials. Ind. Rules of Procedure, Trial Rule 42(B)[3]. * * * Thus, in the present case, the trial court can exercise its discretion in deciding whether to sever the will contest action from any of the other issues under T.R. 42(B).

Judgment reversed and remanded for further proceedings not inconsistent with this opinion.

Notes and Questions

1. Compare Rule 18 (joinder of claims) with Rule 20 (joinder of plaintiffs and defendants). Why should there be a difference? Is there any possible justification for a joinder rule as liberal as Rule 18? Will there be any real gains in efficiency from allowing the claim against Dr. Like to be joined, or by allowing joinder in the Introductory Problem? Isn't jury confusion likely?

2. As the Introductory Problem demonstrates, Rule 18 deals not only with plaintiffs, but also with many other claimants in a suit. Note, however, that Rule 18 does not stand alone. Instead, whenever you have a party who wants to file several claims against another party, you must first determine whether she can bring *any* of the claims under the applicable rule. If any one of the claims is proper, the party can join *all* of the other claims with it under Rule 18, regardless of any transactional relationship.

To illustrate, suppose that two parties, D1 and D2, have been sued by a single plaintiff. D1 has several claims that he wants to file against D2. Because D1 and D2 are co-parties, D1 must first look to the cross-claim rule, Rule 13(g), and determine whether any of the claims arise from the same transaction as the original case. As long as any of the claims satisfies 13(g), Rule 18 also allows him to bring all of the remaining claims, regardless of whether those additional claims are related. However, if none of the claims are related, D1 cannot bring any of them in the action.

3. In practice, one must consider factors other than Rule 18 to determine if claims can be joined. One is the issue of *subject-matter jurisdiction*. Until now we have been assuming that a court can hear every possible claim.

---

3. Trial Rule 42(B) provides:

"(B) Separate Trials. The court, in furtherance of convenience or to avoid prejudice, or when separate trials will be conducive to expedition and economy, may order a separate trial of any claim, cross-claim, counterclaim, or third-party claim, or of any separate issue or of any number of claims, cross-claims, counterclaims, third-party claims, or issues, always preserving inviolate the right of trial by jury."

However, that is often not the case. Every state assigns certain types of claims to specialized courts. For example, cases involving wills or domestic matters may be confined to Probate or Family courts. Similarly, in some states minor cases may be assigned to a Small Claims court. Joinder of two claims is proper only if the court has jurisdiction over all of the claims.

Subject matter jurisdiction is a special problem when the case is filed in federal court. Federal courts have a very carefully-defined jurisdiction, which is discussed in Chapter 3.

Problems

1.　P, who leases a house and yard from D1, is upset when D2 practices "offroading" with her large SUV in P's yard. P learns that after D1 leased the property to P, he gave D2 a license to drive on the property. P sues D1 and D2. P's claim against D2 is for trespass. His claim against D1 arises under the lease, in which D1 promised that he would do nothing to disturb P's exclusive possession of the house and yard. D1 and D2 object to joinder, arguing that the trespass and contract claims are too dissimilar in nature and origin to be joined. How should the court rule?

2.　P, D1, and D2 are involved in a three-way car accident at an intersection. P sues both D1 and D2. D1 was also injured in the accident. Because it is not clear who is responsible, D1 wants to file claims against P and D2. May D1 file either or both claims in this action? Must D1 file either or both claims?

3.　Same facts as Problem 2. Assume that the court allows D1 to file his claims against P and D2. Once the case is complete, D2 sues D1 for the injuries that D2 suffered in the accident. D1 argues that the claim should have been brought in the first action. How should the court rule?

4.　Same facts as Problem 2. D2 wants to file a counterclaim against P for the injuries that D2 suffered in the accident, arguing that P failed to have the brakes on his car maintained. D2 would also like to join P's mechanic to this counterclaim. May D2 do so?

5.　P1 and P2 were both injured when they were struck by city buses. However, their injuries were caused by different drivers, operating different buses, at different locations, on different days. P1 and P2 would like to join as plaintiffs in order to sue the drivers and the city for their injuries. May they join as plaintiffs to sue all three of these defendants?

6.　D is a caterer who obtains produce from X and Y. After several of its employees contract food poisoning at a luncheon catered by D, P sues D and X for negligence. Under governing law, D is entitled to be reimbursed by its supplier for any damages that D must pay because of food poisoning. However, D is unsure whether the produce in question came from X or Y. Is there any way D may bring claims against both X and Y in D's case?

7.　P, a landlord in a shopping mall, sues D, one of the tenants, for breach of lease. D immediately impleads X. D has incontrovertible proof that he assigned the lease to X weeks before the alleged breach occurred. Therefore, D claims, X is responsible for the breach. X objects to the impleader, arguing that the joinder rules do not allow impleader under these circumstances. Is X correct?

8.   P sues D for patent infringement after D uses P's patented part as a component in D's product. D properly impleads 3PD1 and 3PD2, two parties who supplied the patented part to D. 3PD1 cross-claims against 3PD2 for unfair competition, alleging that 3PD2 falsely represented to D that its components were of higher quality than those supplied by 3PD1. 3PD2 objects to the claim, arguing that the joinder rules do not allow one third-party defendant to allege this sort of claim against another third-party defendant. Is 3PD2 correct?

9.   Same facts as Problem 8. After the 3PDs are joined, P files a claim against 3PD1 (but not 3PD2) for patent infringement, based on her manu-facture and sale of the part. P also includes a second claim against 3PD1. P's place of business is located immediately adjacent to that of 3PD1. P claims that because 3PD1 failed to maintain its property, a large tree on 3PD1's lot fell onto P's factory, causing extensive damage. 3PD1 objects to both of P's claims against her, arguing that they are improper under the rules of joinder. Is 3PD1 correct?

10.   Same facts as Problem 8. 3PD1 files a claim against P in the case, arguing that P's attempt to enforce its patent was in bad faith, and therefore in violation of federal antitrust laws. P argues that the joinder rules do not allow 3PD1 to bring that claim in this case. Is P correct?

11.   Same facts as Problem 8. Both third-party defendants answer, and the case goes to trial. The trial court enters judgment for D against P, finding that the part used by D was not similar enough to P's patented part to infringe. Because D won on the main claim, D recovers nothing on the third-party claims. After the case is complete, 3PD1 discovers that D never paid it for the last two shipments of the part in question. 3PD1 wants to sue D for these payments. May it?

12.   P sues D for personal injury, after P was injured by an exploding beer bottle in D's tavern. Because the bottle shattered into such small pieces, D is unsure whether it was produced by 3PD1 or 3PD2, two of D's suppliers. D impleads both 3PD1 and 3PD2, arguing that one of the two is responsible for indemnifying D for any damages D must pay P. Both third-party defendants object, arguing that the rules do not allow impleader in this situation. How should the court rule?

Exercise

Because the federal rules permit litigants much flexibility in bringing claims, it is useful to inquire about whether state rules are equally permis-sive. For the state a) where you intend to practice after graduation, b) where your law school is located, and/or c) your professor assigns, go to that state's annotated statutes and research the procedural rules by which joinder of parties and claims occurs. Based on your research, print the rules and bring them to class for discussion. In addition, answer the following questions.

1.   Identify the minimum requirements for:

A.   Joinder of parties.

B. Joinder of claims.

2. Identify whether the following are compulsory or merely permissive, as well as whether they must arise from the same transaction as the claim brought by the plaintiff:

A. Counterclaims

B. Cross-claims

C. Third party claims

3. Identify whether additional parties may be added for counterclaims and cross-claims.

F. MAKING OPTIONAL CLAIMS COMPULSORY: AN OVERVIEW OF MERGER AND BAR

INTRODUCTORY PROBLEM

After reading a particularly scurrilous article about himself in *Mogul Magazine*, Celebrity sues Publisher, the company that edits and prints the magazine, for defamation. The case eventually goes to trial. The trial court enters judgment for Celebrity, and Publisher does not appeal.

Several months later, Celebrity is contemplating bringing several other cases. First, he would like to sue Publisher again for defamation, based on the same article. Since the judgment in the first case, Celebrity has learned that the damages he had suffered at the time he filed the first suit were far greater than he originally thought. Therefore, the judgment in the first case did not begin to compensate Celebrity for the full harm.

Second, Celebrity would like to sue Publisher for the tort of intentional infliction of emotional distress, based on the same magazine article. Unlike the tort of defamation, Celebrity can prevail on the tort of intentional infliction only if he can show that Publisher published the article with the intent to upset Celebrity. However, the tort of intentional infliction would also allow Celebrity to recover punitive damages, a remedy not available for defamation.

Third, Celebrity has not received his copy of *Mogul Magazine* for several months. He would like to sue Publisher for breach of the subscription agreement.

Fourth, Celebrity also wants to bring a defamation claim against Author, the person who wrote the magazine article in question.

Does the first action bar Celebrity from bringing any or all of these claims?

The rules governing joinder of claims and parties are typically framed in permissive, rather than compulsory, terms. Rule 18, for example, only tells a party whether it *may* bring a claim; it nowhere requires the party to do so. Likewise, Rules 20 (joinder of multiple plaintiffs and defendants), 13(g) (cross-claims), and 13(h) allow, but do not require, joinder. The only exceptions to the rule that joinder is optional are Rule 13(a) (compulsory counterclaims) and Rule 19 (mandatory joinder of parties, discussed in Chapter 6).

The rules are in this respect somewhat deceiving. Even though the majority of the joinder rules are merely permissive, there are other doctrines in the law of Civil Procedure that *require* a party with related claims to join them into a single lawsuit. These rules, commonly referred to in the collective by the term *res judicata* (also known as claim preclusion), are dealt with in detail in Chapter 11. It is nevertheless worthwhile to take a brief look at some of the basic rules at this juncture, to illustrate how they interact with the joinder rules.

In most jurisdictions, *res judicata* is a court-created doctrine. The rules and principles typically derive from case law rather than statutes and written rules. Indeed, the Federal Rules of Civil Procedure and their state counterparts are largely devoid of rules dealing with preclusion. Nevertheless, the framers of the Federal Rules were acutely aware of the common-law principles, and crafted the rules against the backdrop of the common-law rules.

Unlike most of the joinder rules that we have studied so far, the rules of *res judicata* operate retrospectively rather than prospectively. That is, the court that applies the doctrine is the *second* court to become involved in adjudicating a certain basic dispute. This court will determine if a party is precluded from litigating a claim because of what that party did during the first suit.

Technically, we are concerned here with only one branch of the overall doctrine of *res judicata*, under which a party may sometimes lose a claim by failing to bring it in the first action. Confusingly, this subset of the overall doctrine of *res judicata* was itself also called *res judicata*, as distinguished from the other main subset of the doctrine, "collateral estoppel." To avoid this confusion, many courts and scholars refer to the first branch of the doctrine of *res judicata* under the more descriptive name "claim preclusion."

Under what circumstances will a party lose a claim by failing to assert it in a case? The following case contains a good discussion of both the basic rules of, and policy underlying, claim preclusion.

HUFFEY v. LEA

491 N.W.2d 518 (Iowa 1992)

SCHULTZ, Justice

The principal issue on appeal is whether the doctrine of claim preclusion prevents an action for tortious interference with a bequest when the action is not brought with the underlying will contest. The district court and the court of appeals held that the failure to join the tort action with the will contest bars a later action. We disagree.

This is a dismissal of the action based on the pleadings; therefore, we accept those allegations as true. We also take judicial notice of the appellate decision involving the will contest, *Matter of Estate of Olson,* 451 N.W.2d 33 (Iowa App.1989).

This appeal has its genesis in the wills of Hjalmar Olson and his wife Margaret, whose maiden name was Lea. Following their marriage in 1946, Margaret and Hjalmar lived on a farm until their deaths in 1986. The Olsons did not have children; however, they had a close relationship with Hjalmar's nephew, George Huffey. Huffey lived with the Olsons for several years and after that was a tenant on the Olson farm.

On June 18, 1986, two days after Hjalmar's death, Margaret executed a will. Under this will, she, like her husband before her, provided that the Olson farm should become the property of George Huffey. In July 1986, Margaret executed a new will revoking her June 18 will. Under the new will, George Huffey would not receive the Olson farm and her brother, Ambrose Lea, and his children would receive the bulk of her estate.

Margaret died in August 1986 and the July will was admitted to probate. George and Jean Huffey (Huffeys) commenced an action contesting the will. The case was tried to a jury which found that Margaret lacked testamentary capacity and that the July will was procured by undue influence. The defendants to the will contest successfully moved for a judgment notwithstanding the verdict and a new trial. On appeal, the court of appeals reinstated the jury verdict.

On December 5, 1990, plaintiffs commenced this action against defendants Ambrose Lea, Eunice Lea, his wife, and their children (Leas). We are concerned with the tort actions which are counts one and two of the petition, maintaining that the defendants unduly influenced Margaret and tortiously interfered with her intent to devise her farm to George. They seek money damages for legal fees, loss of farming time, mental anguish and embarrassment. * * * .

As previously indicated, the fighting issue involves application of the doctrine of claim preclusion to Huffeys' tort action. Leas defend the district court's ruling by asserting that the tort action involves the same "claim" that was advanced in Huffeys' prior will contest. As an initial matter, we discuss the doctrine of claim preclusion.

As a general rule, the doctrine of claim preclusion bars further litigation on the same "claim" or cause of action. See *Leuchtenmacher v. Farm Bureau Mut. Ins. Co.,* 460 N.W.2d 858, 859–60 (Iowa 1990). Under this doctrine, an adjudication in a former suit between the same parties on the same claim "is final as to all matters which could have been presented to the court for determination, and a party must litigate all matters growing out of its claim at one time rather than in separate actions." *Id.* at 860. The court explained:

Claim preclusion under the doctrine of res judicata is based on the principle that a party may not split or try his claim piecemeal, but must put in issue and try his entire claim or put forth his entire defense in the case on trial.

* * *

[To make that determination, it] is necessary to determine whether plaintiff's first and second actions were the same claim or cause of action within the meaning of this principle.

Id. (quoting *B & B Asphalt Co. v. T.S. McShane Co.*, 242 N.W.2d 279, 286 (Iowa 1976)). A second claim is likely to be considered the same as a first claim, and therefore precluded, "if the acts complained of, and the recovery demanded, are the same, or when the same evidence will support both actions." *Leuchtenmacher*, 460 N.W.2d at 860. We now examine whether the will contest and the tort action are the same claim or cause of action within the meaning of claim preclusion. We do not believe that they are.

When a will is contested on grounds of undue influence and lack of testamentary capacity, as it was here, the required proof focuses on the testator's mental strength and intent and whether infirmities or undue influence have affected the disposition of property under the will. The necessary proof in an action for intentional interference with a bequest or devise focuses on the fraud, duress, or other tortious means intentionally used by the alleged wrongdoer in depriving another from receiving from a third person an inheritance or gift. Stated simply, in a will contest, the testator's intent or mental state is the key issue; in an intentional interference case, the wrongdoer's unlawful intent to prevent another from receiving an inheritance is the key issue. Because of the differences in proof, the actions are not the same nor will the same evidence necessarily support both actions.

In addition, the recovery demanded in the will contest and in this action for intentional interference is not the same. In the will contest, the recovery demanded was the setting aside of the will procured by undue influence. In this action for intentional interference, the recovery demanded is for attorney fees, value of Huffey's time lost in his farm operation, and mental anguish incurred in contesting the will. Obviously, the setting aside of the will did not provide Huffey with recovery of his consequential damages. Huffey also requested an award of punitive damages based on intentional and malicious conduct of defendants. An adequate remedy has not been provided by the mere setting aside of the will. [The court then reviewed cases from other courts dealing with the issue, finding no clear majority rule.] * * *

Although there is some overlap, we do not believe the same evidence supports the will contest and the action for intentional interference with a bequest. Further, we agree with plaintiffs that a complete remedy could not be provided in the will contest because of additional costs involved in the appeals process. Therefore, we hold the district court erred in dismissing Huffeys' action against these defendants under the doctrine of claim preclusion. * * *

McGIVERIN, Chief Justice (dissenting in part)

I respectfully dissent in part from the result of the majority opinion and would affirm the district court's dismissal of plaintiffs' petition in its entirety.

I. The main issue in division II of the majority opinion involves whether plaintiff George Huffey should be able to maintain the present action for tortious interference with a bequest. For the reasons that follow, I believe he should be precluded from doing so.

* * * [R]es judicata, specifically claim preclusion, precludes Huffey from pursuing a claim for tortious interference with a bequest because those tort elements are virtually identical to those for undue influence, the claim upon which he contested the July will.

As a general rule, the doctrine of claim preclusion bars further litigation on the same "claim" or cause of action. * * *

A second claim is likely to be considered the same as a first claim, and therefore precluded, "if the acts complained of, and the recovery demanded, are the same, or when the same evidence will support both actions." *Leuchtenmacher*, 460 N.W.2d at 860. More specifically, when a valid and final judgment rendered in an action extinguishes the plaintiff's claim, "the claim extinguished includes all rights of the plaintiff to remedies against the defendant with respect to all or any part of the transaction, or series of connected transactions, out of which the action arose." *Id.* (quoting Restatement (Second) of Judgments, s 24, at 196).

I believe Huffey's action for tortious interference with a bequest constitutes basically the same "claim" as the undue influence claim upon which his prior will contest was based. An examination of the elements of each claim reveals that they are in substance the same. We have said that the elements necessary to sustain a finding of undue influence in the execution of a will in a will contest in probate include: (1) the testator's susceptibility to undue influence; (2) opportunity to exercise such influence and effect the wrongful purpose; (3) disposition to influence unduly for the purpose of procuring an improper favor; and (4) a result clearly the effect of undue influence. Similarly, an action for intentional interference with a bequest or devise may be maintained where "[o]ne who by fraud, duress or other tortious means intentionally prevents another from receiving from a third person an inheritance or gift that he would otherwise have received. . . ." *See* Restatement (Second) of Torts s 774B, at 58.

Although the legal elements of each claim do not parallel one another with mathematical precision, it is apparent from the general nature of each, and from review of the pleaded facts in this case, that a law action for tortious interference with a bequest necessarily must be supported by the same facts and evidence supporting a will contest in probate based on undue influence. The Restatement specifically provides that a law action for tortious interference applies "when a testator has been induced by tortious means to make his first will or not to make it; and it applies also when he has been induced to change or revoke his will or not to change or revoke it." Restatement (Second) of Torts s 774B comment b, at 58.

The majority states that an action for undue influence focuses on the testator's intent. However, I point out that the second and third elements of undue influence (opportunity to exercise undue influence and effect a wrongful purpose, and disposition to unduly influence) specifically address the wrongdoer's intent, rather than the testator's intent. The wrongdoer's disposition (intent) to unduly influence the testator in undue influence is necessarily the same intent exhibited in a claim involving tortious interference with a bequest or a devise. Thus, both actions involve the same "claim" for purposes of applying the doctrine of claim preclusion.

This conclusion is not altered by the mere fact that Huffey is presently seeking a remedy (damages) different from the remedy sought in the will contest (the setting aside of the will). This is because the rule barring subsequent actions on the same claim applies even though the plaintiff in a subsequent action is prepared to "present evidence or grounds or theories of the case not presented in the first action" or to "seek remedies or forms of relief not demanded in the first action."

See Restatement (Second) of Judgments s 25, at 209.

> Where the plaintiff may in one action claim two or more remedies cumulatively rather than alternatively, all arising from the same transaction, but seeks fewer than all of these remedies, and a judgment is entered that extinguishes the claim under the rules of merger or bar, he is precluded from maintaining another action for the other remedies.

See Restatement (Second) of Judgments s 25 comments c and j, at 211, 221. Attorney fees are simply one additional remedy Huffey could have sought at the same time he sought to have the July will set aside. * * *

Finally, there is nothing in our probate code that would have precluded Huffey from pursuing his law action in conjunction with his will contest. Therefore, the district court would have had jurisdiction of both claims had they both been brought at the same time.

Thus, I would hold that will contestants such as George Huffey must join with his probate action any claim against alleged wrongdoers for tortious interference with a bequest if he seeks a remedy beyond the mere setting aside of the will. * * *

Because the same facts and evidence may be used to prove both undue influence and tortious interference with a bequest by an alleged wrongdoer, judicial economy policies and claim preclusion rules require that both claims be brought and heard together. * * *

NEUMAN, J., joins this dissent.

Notes and Questions

1. What is the basic test that the *Huffey* court uses to determine if a claim is barred by failure to include it in an earlier lawsuit? Do the majority and dissent disagree on the test, or the application of that test?

2. We have already seen rules that look somewhat similar to the test used in *Huffey.* Several of the Rules governing joinder employ the "same transaction or occurrence" test. *See, e.g.,* Rules 13(a), 13(g), 14(a), and 20(a). Under the more restrictive minority test used to interpret this key phrase, courts look to see if the claims involve the same evidence. *See Apache County* at page 11. Therefore, there is admittedly some overlap in the analysis used in joinder and claim preclusion cases.

However, the degree of overlap may be less than you might assume. As a rule, the test for claim preclusion is significantly more restrictive than that used in joinder. That is, courts are considerably less likely to conclude that two given claims are sufficiently intertwined so that both must be heard in the same case than they are to conclude that the same claims may be joined under the same transaction or occurrence test. To the extent that there is overlap between joinder and claim preclusion, it is only at the fringes of each doctrine.

Can you guess why the test for preclusion is more restrictive than the test for joinder? Consider the consequences of each decision.

3. Another reason why preclusion is construed more restrictively than joinder is that the policies underlying the two doctrines differ. The joinder rules are, generally speaking, concerned with efficiency. Efficiency concerns are also certainly relevant to preclusion. However, in the realm of preclusion, efficiency is only a secondary or collateral aim. Historically, the policy underlying preclusion has been a desire for consistency. To the extent that two claims are litigated in separate cases, there is the possibility of inconsistent results. Apply that logic to *Huffey v. Lea.* Would allowing the Huffeys to pursue their intentional interference claim in a separate proceeding pose a threat of inconsistent results?

4. There are other requirements that must be satisfied before a court will apply claim preclusion. These additional requirements are discussed in Chapter 11.

5. You will also see in Chapter 11 that claim preclusion has a sister doctrine called "issue preclusion." As the name implies, issue preclusion bars not entire claims, but instead only issues. Issue preclusion applies when two different claims share certain factual sub-issues. Although the rules governing issue preclusion may seem technical, they are strongly based on the notions of consistency discussed in note 3.

6. If the common-law doctrine of claim preclusion bars a party from bringing a claim that is related to a claim already litigated in a prior suit, you may be wondering why the Federal Rules have a compulsory counter-claim rule. The answer is primarily historical: the common-law doctrine applied only to claims brought by someone who was a plaintiff in the first action. With one significant exception to be discussed in Chapter 11, the

doctrine did not require a party who was a defendant to bring any counter-claims. Because plaintiff picked the court, courts deemed it unfair to require defendant to litigate its claims in a court that was not of its choosing.

Rule 13(a) clearly rejects the common-law rule. Now, a defendant is required to bring all of its related counterclaims in its answer, unless one of the rule's exceptions apply.

The rule only applies to counterclaims. Other types of joinder are never mandatory. A party is therefore free to withhold cross-claims from the dispute as it sees fit. Of course, concerns of efficiency may well prompt the party to go ahead and file whatever claims it has available. Why did the framers of the rules choose to diverge from the common-law rules for counterclaims, but not for other claims?

7.   The second major limitation on common-law claim preclusion is that it did not require joinder of new *parties*. With one narrow exception to be discussed in Chapter 11, a party is never prevented from suing a party that it did not sue in the first action.

Chapter 3

FEDERAL SUBJECT MATTER JURISDICTION

A. THE CONCEPT OF SUBJECT MATTER JURISDICTION

In the next two chapters, you will learn about three factors that dictate which court may hear a particular case. Personal jurisdiction and venue, covered in Chapter 4, focus mainly on the parties. They attempt to locate the litigation in a physical location that is fair to the defendant and relatively convenient for all parties and witnesses. Subject matter jurisdiction, by contrast, deals more with institutional, rather than individual, concerns. The rules governing subject matter jurisdiction determine which of two or more courts, located in the same geographic area, has the authority to hear the particular type of dispute in question.

This Chapter explores the allocation of authority between the state courts and the federal courts. That this question even arises is due to a somewhat unique feature of United States federalism; namely, parallel systems of state and federal courts with substantially overlapping authority. Some federal systems have no federal courts. In others, such as Canada and Australia, federal courts do exist, but their role is confined to hearing certain narrow categories of cases. Only in the United States do federal courts have the authority to hear a broad array of tort, contract, and property cases between private parties.

Of course, allowing cases to be litigated in federal court diminishes the influence of the state courts. Therefore, it will be no great surprise to learn that the United States Constitution itself sets limits on the subject matter jurisdiction of the federal courts. The main constitutional provision is Article III.[1] This provision establishes the basic paradigm: federal courts are courts of *limited jurisdiction*, with the authority to hear only those categories of cases specifically allocated to them. State courts, by

---

1. The eleventh amendment, enacted in 1793, also places an important limit on federal court jurisdiction. However, that amendment is beyond the scope of this course. It is usually covered in a course called Federal Courts or Federal Jurisdiction.

contrast, may hear all cases, unless the U.S. Constitution, Congress, or their state legislature has taken a particular category of case from them.

Article III confines federal subject matter jurisdiction to nine categories of cases. For our purposes, the most important three are:

- "all Cases, in Law and Equity, arising under this Constitution, the Laws of the United States, and Treaties made, or which shall be made, under their Authority;"
- "Controversies ... between Citizens of different States;" and
- "Controversies ... between a State, or the Citizens thereof, and foreign States, Citizens, or Subjects."

Taken together, the nine constitutional categories of Article III cover a wide range of cases. However, there are two types of cases that are notably missing. Unless the case involves claims under federal law, the Constitution, or a treaty, a federal court cannot hear a case involving a single plaintiff and single defendant from the *same state*, or a single plaintiff and single defendant who are *not citizens of the United States*. These cases must be heard in the state courts.

Although it is not apparent from the constitutional text, Article III does not itself give the lower federal courts jurisdiction over any cases. Instead, Congress allocates that jurisdiction by statute. In fact, Congress has never given the federal courts the full authority authorized by Article III. Because of the need for a statutory enablement, any analysis of subject matter jurisdiction will involve two steps. First, there must be a statute giving the court the authority to hear the dispute in question. Second, even if a statute allows for jurisdiction, the case must fall within one of the nine categories of Article III. As Congress has generally crafted the jurisdiction statutes to fit the limits of Article III, the second question rarely affects whether the court has jurisdiction. Nevertheless, you will encounter one provision—28 U.S.C. § 1441(c), discussed in Part E of this chapter—that arguably exceeds constitutional limits.

This Chapter deals exclusively with the subject matter jurisdiction of the United States District Courts, the trial courts in the federal system. There are many statutes allocating subject matter jurisdiction to these courts. *See, e.g.*, 28 U.S.C. §§ 1330 (actions against foreign nations), 1343 (civil rights cases), and 1344 (election disputes). However, this chapter will concentrate on the four most important provisions. Early in the Chapter (in Parts B and C), you will deal with §§ 1331 and 1332 of the Judicial Code (the "Judicial Code" is title 28 of the United States Code). § 1331 is the general statute implementing the first of the three categories of Article III jurisdiction quoted above, namely, jurisdiction over cases arising under federal law, the Constitution, or a treaty. This type of jurisdiction is commonly called "federal question" jurisdiction. § 1332 implements the second and third of the categories quoted above. Because these categories both turn on the citizenship of the parties, § 1332 is commonly referred to as "diversity of citizenship" or simply "diversity" jurisdiction. However, sometimes a court will refer to this jurisdiction as "alienage" jurisdiction in a case between a United States citizen and a citizen of another nation.

Part D of the chapter discusses § 1367, which creates a form of jurisdiction called "supplemental." As the name suggests, supplemental jurisdiction adds to other forms of jurisdiction. A party will usually invoke supplemental jurisdiction when she has some claims that qualify for federal question or diversity jurisdiction, and other claims that do not. If the claims all arise from the same set of facts, § 1367 may allow the federal court to hear all of them as part of a single case.

One important point to remember about jurisdiction under all of these provisions is that it is *concurrent*, not exclusive. The federal courts share jurisdiction under these sections with the state courts. Because the federal and state courts have concurrent jurisdiction over diversity and alienage cases, those cases may be litigated in either state or federal court. Similarly, state courts usually even have the authority to hear cases arising under federal law. However, there are some claims, which either arise under federal law or involve some strong federal interest, for which the federal courts have exclusive jurisdiction. *See, e.g.,* 28 U.S.C. § 1334 (cases arising under federal bankruptcy laws); § 1338 (patent and copyright infringement claims); and § 1351 (claims (including state-law claims) against foreign diplomats). On the other hand, if the only basis for federal jurisdiction over the claim is § 1331 or § 1332, the federal and state courts will always have concurrent jurisdiction.

Note that the fact that jurisdiction is shared does not necessarily give plaintiff an unfettered ability to choose state or federal court. True, a plaintiff alone makes the initial choice of state or federal court. However, another federal statute, 28 U.S.C. § 1441 (discussed in Part E of this Chapter), may give the defendant the option to *remove* a case filed in state court to federal court. Conversely, as we will see later, in certain rare situations a federal court may abstain from hearing a case, even though it has clear subject matter jurisdiction under the statutes. If a federal court abstains, the state courts will decide all or part of the dispute.

The Judicial Code also contains provisions governing the jurisdiction of the federal Courts of Appeal and the United States Supreme Court. The statutes governing the Courts of Appeal and the Supreme Court are not discussed until Chapter 12, as they usually apply only when the case is being appealed. Nevertheless, it may be useful—both for Procedure and for your other courses—to touch upon two important points concerning the United States Supreme Court. Many people labor under certain misconceptions concerning what we commonly call the "nation's high court." First, the Supreme Court is not really a supreme court. It is instead a supreme *federal* court. Like the lower federal courts, the Supreme Court is bound by the strictures of Article III. Although there are differences between the Supreme Court and the lower federal courts—for example, the Supreme Court's original jurisdiction vests automatically, without the need for a grant from Congress—never forget that the Supreme Court's authority is limited to the nine categories of cases set out in Article III. Second, although the Supreme Court, unlike the lower courts, has the power to hear appeals of cases heard in the state courts, Congress has not given the Supreme Court the authority to hear state-court cases that do not involve some question of federal law, the United States Constitution, or a treaty. As a result, the state courts are the highest authority for interpreting state law.

Finally, the fact that this chapter deals only with the allocation of subject matter jurisdiction between the state and federal courts should not lead you into thinking that the state systems are a monolithic whole. Questions of subject matter jurisdiction also arise frequently in actions heard in the state courts. For example, many states have specialized family courts or probate courts that hear matters such as divorces, child custody, and wills. Many also have small claims courts that provide an abbreviated, simplified procedure for claims involving less than a certain amount. However, because the jurisdiction of state courts is not bound by Article III or any other provision of the Constitution, there will always be one court in a state—often called a district or circuit court—that may hear any claim not assigned to some other court. This court is often referred to as a "court of general jurisdiction."

B. FEDERAL QUESTION JURISDICTION

INTRODUCTORY PROBLEM

Penny owns a large tract of forest land in upstate Vermont. She makes a very good living selling maple syrup, which she extracts from trees located on her property. Recently, however, two events have occurred that have threatened Penny's comfortable and profitable living. Unable to remedy the problem by negotiation, Penny has filed two cases in federal district court.

The first case is Penny v. Daniel. Penny sells her maple syrup using the trademark MAPLE LEAF. When Penny discovered that Daniel had begun selling his own maple syrup under the exact same trademark, she sued him for trademark infringement under the federal trademark laws. Daniel admits that he used the MAPLE LEAF mark on maple syrup. He also concedes that federal trademark laws clearly impose liability on a party who uses an identical mark on a similar product. Nevertheless, Daniel claims that Penny granted him an oral license to use the MAPLE LEAF mark. Penny argues that the license is invalid under state contract law because it is not in writing. The sole issue in the case is whether the oral license is valid.

Penny's second case is against the giant company Dynamic Dynamos, Inc. ("DDI"). DDI manufactures guidance systems for missiles and other weapons used by the military. Penny sued DDI for trespass when she discovered that DDI was constructing a new factory on a remote section of her property. DDI admits that it is building the plant on the land described by Penny. However, DDI raises two separate arguments in denying liability. First, although conceding that the land used to belong to Penny, DDI asserts that it now owns Penny's land. DDI claims that the federal government seized Penny's land for nonpayment of federal income taxes, and later sold the land at a tax sale to DDI. In response to this first argument, Penny responds that the tax sale was invalid under the United States Constitution and federal law because the IRS never gave her notice that she had not paid her taxes.

But DDI is prepared for this response. Second, and in the alternative, DDI claims that even if the tax sale was invalid and Penny owns the land, it is protected by the federal contractor's defense. Under this defense, which is set out in federal statutes and case law, a court cannot impose liability on a military contractor that acted in good faith. DDI argues that it thought the tax sale was valid.

Penny relied on 28 U.S.C. § 1331 as the sole basis for federal jurisdiction in both cases. Daniel and DDI each file a timely objection to the federal court's jurisdiction in their respective case. How will the federal courts rule?

Governing Laws: U.S. Const. Article III, § 2, cl. 1; 28 U.S.C. § 1331.

———————

In some ways, it is redundant for a federal nation to operate separate federal and state court systems. State courts are perfectly competent to deal with cases arising under both state and federal law. Other federal nations such as Canada and Australia operate only a very limited federal court system, and rely on the state courts to handle the vast majority of cases that arise.

The United States, however, has since its inception maintained a comprehensive system of lower federal courts. Every state has at least one federal district court, which often sits in a courthouse just down the street from the state courts. The decision to have federal courts is largely due to a sense that federal courts offer certain advantages that might not be available in the state systems. Those advantages are most readily apparent in situations requiring the interpretation of federal law. First, if most cases arising under federal law go to federal court, federal judges may acquire a deeper understanding of the nuances of federal law. Second, in some cases one might suspect that state judges, who are beholden to their constituencies, might prove hostile to enforcing federal laws. A state judge facing a re-election or retention vote might well be reluctant to enforce a federal civil rights claim or a claim in which an Indian tribe seeks superior rights to scarce water resources. Giving these cases to the federal courts, while not removing politics entirely from the decision, at least provides the appearance of a more neutral forum.

This section focuses almost exclusively on § 1331, the "general" federal question statute. This section gives the federal courts jurisdiction over all matters arising under federal law, regardless of the federal law in question. However, a quick glance at the statutes following § 1331 will reveal a number of other statutes that allocate jurisdiction over matters arising under specific federal laws. See 28 U.S.C. §§ 1333 (admiralty), 1334 (bankruptcy), 1337 (commerce and antitrust), 1338 (patents, copyrights, and trademarks), 1339 (postal matters), 1343 (civil rights), and 1355 (fines and penalties under federal laws). If § 1331 affords jurisdiction over all federal matters, why are these specific provisions necessary? First, as noted above, a few of these statutes make federal jurisdiction exclusive. Jurisdiction under § 1331, however, is shared with the state courts.

Second, until fairly recently § 1331 required a minimum amount in controversy (in fact, the caption for § 1331 in the United States Code still refers to "amount in controversy"). Many of the specific statutes had a lower threshold, or often no minimum amount at all. Thus, Congress created a special jurisdiction provision for federal civil rights claims to allow parties with small claims to avail themselves of federal court. Now that there is no minimum amount in controversy under § 1331, these statutes are redundant.

Third, as the following discussion indicates, jurisdiction under § 1331 is subject to significant limitations. Jurisdiction under these other provisions is not necessarily subject to the same limits. Therefore, a party may sometimes be better off invoking one of the other federal question subject matter statutes.

The following sections explore how courts have interpreted § 1331. Although these same principles will often apply to the other federal question statutes, you should not immediately assume that the other statutes are interpreted the same way.

1. How Does a Party Invoke Federal Question Jurisdiction?

Suppose you have a case like the Introductory Problem, in which the ultimate outcome depends on how the court interprets the Constitution and federal law. Can such a case automatically go to federal court under § 1331? As the Supreme Court has stated, "How and when a case arises 'under the Constitution or laws of the United States' has been much considered in the books." *Gully v. First National Bank in Meridian*, 299 U.S. 109, 112, 57 S.Ct. 96, 81 L.Ed. 70 (1936). As we will see, the answer depends on exactly who is bringing the underlying claim, as well as the way in which federal law applies to that claim.

LOUISVILLE & NASHVILLE RAILROAD
v. MOTTLEY
211 U.S. 149, 29 S.Ct. 42, 53 L.Ed. 126 (1908)

Statement by Mr. Justice MOODY:

The appellees (husband and wife), being residents and citizens of Kentucky, brought this suit in equity in the circuit court of the United States for the western district of Kentucky against the appellant, a railroad company and a citizen of the same state. * * *

The bill alleged that in September, 1871, plaintiffs, while passengers upon the defendant railroad, were injured by the defendant's negligence, and released their respective claims for damages in consideration of the agreement for transportation during their lives, expressed in * * * [a] contract. It is alleged that the contract was performed by the defendant up to January 1, 1907, when the defendant declined to renew the passes. The bill then alleges that the refusal to comply with the contract was based solely upon that part of the act of Congress of June 29, 1906, which forbids the giving of free passes or free transportation. The bill further alleges: First, that the act of Congress referred to does not prohibit the giving of passes under the circumstances of this case; and, second, that, if the law is to be construed as prohibiting such passes, it is in conflict with the 5th Amendment of the Constitution, because it deprives the plaintiffs of their property without due process of law. The defendant demurred to the bill. The judge of the circuit court overruled the demurrer, entered a decree for the relief prayed for, and the defendant appealed directly to this court.

Mr. Justice MOODY, after making the foregoing statement, delivered the opinion of the court.

Two questions of law were raised by the demurrer to the bill, were brought here by appeal, and have been argued before us. They are, first, whether that part of the act of Congress of June 29, 1906, which forbids the giving of free passes or the collection of any different compensation for transportation of passengers than that specified in the tariff filed, makes it unlawful to perform a contract for transportation of persons who, in good faith, before the passage of the act, had accepted such contract in satisfaction of a valid cause of action against the railroad; and, second, whether the statute, if it should be construed to render such a contract unlawful, is in violation of the 5th Amendment of the Constitution of the United States. We do not deem it necessary, however, to consider either of these questions, because, in our opinion, the court below was without jurisdiction of the cause. Neither party has questioned that jurisdiction, but it is the duty of this court to see to it that the jurisdiction of the circuit court, which is defined and limited by statute, is not exceeded. This duty we have frequently performed of our own motion.

There was no diversity of citizenship, and it is not and cannot be suggested that there was any ground of jurisdiction, except that the case was a "suit ... arising under the Constitution or laws of the United States." It is the settled interpretation of these words, as used in this statute, conferring jurisdiction, that a suit arises under the Constitution and laws of the United States only when the plaintiff's statement of his own cause of action shows that it is based upon those laws or that Constitution. It is not enough that the plaintiff alleges some anticipated defense to his cause of action, and asserts that the defense is invalidated by some provision of the Constitution of the United States. Although such allegations show that very likely, in the course of the litigation, a question under the Constitution would arise, they do not show that the suit, that is, the plaintiff's original cause of action, arises under the Constitution. In *Tennessee v. Union & Planters' Bank*, 152 U.S. 454, the plaintiff, the state of Tennessee, brought suit in the circuit court of the United States to recover from the defendant certain taxes alleged to be due under the laws of the state. The plaintiff alleged that the defendant claimed an immunity from the taxation by virtue of its charter, and that therefore the tax was void, because in violation of the provision of the Constitution of the United States, which forbids any state from passing a law impairing the obligation of contracts. The cause was held to be beyond the jurisdiction of the circuit court, the court saying, by Mr. Justice Gray: "A suggestion of one party, that the other will or may set up a claim under the Constitution or laws of the United States, does not make the suit one arising under that Constitution or those laws." Again, in *Boston & M. Consol. Copper & S. Min. Co. v. Montana Ore Purchasing Co.*, 188 U.S. 632 [1903] the plaintiff brought suit in the circuit court of the United States for the conversion of copper ore and for an injunction against its continuance. The plaintiff then alleged, for the purpose of showing jurisdiction, in substance, that the defendant would set up in defense certain laws of the United States. The cause was held to be beyond the jurisdiction of the circuit court, the court saying, by Mr. Justice Peckham [188 U.S. at 638, 639]:

> It would be wholly unnecessary and improper, in order to prove complainant's cause of action, to go into any matters of defense which the defendants might possibly set up, and then attempt to reply to such defense, and thus, if possible, to show that a Federal question might or probably would arise in the course of the trial of the case. * * *

> Conforming itself to that rule, the complainant would not, in the assertion or proof of its cause of action, bring up a single Federal question. The presentation of its cause of action would not show that it was one arising under the Constitution or laws of the United States.

> The only way in which it might be claimed that a Federal question was presented would be in the complainant's statement of what the defense of defendants would be, and complainant's answer to such defense. * * *

The application of this rule to the case at bar is decisive against the jurisdiction of the circuit court.

It is ordered that the judgment be reversed and the case remitted to the circuit court with instructions to dismiss the suit for want of jurisdiction.

Notes and Questions

1. As *Mottley* demonstrates, courts use the "well-pleaded complaint" rule to determine whether a case qualifies for federal question jurisdiction under § 1331. First, the case must turn on an issue of federal law, the

United States Constitution, or a treaty. Second, that issue of federal law must appear in plaintiff's well-pleaded complaint. Which part of this test did the Mottleys fail?

2. The "well-pleaded complaint" rule does not evaluate whether the complaint complies with the procedural rules that govern pleadings. Under the rule that governs the complaint, the complaint filed by the Mottleys would be perfectly proper, even though it anticipated defendant's statutory and Constitutional defenses. See Federal Rule 8(a), which is discussed in Chapter 5, part B. A complaint is proper under this rule even if it includes superfluous or irrelevant material. However, under the well-pleaded complaint rule, any material that is superfluous or irrelevant to plaintiff's claim(s) will not be considered when determining whether the court has federal jurisdiction. A well-pleaded complaint, then, is one in which plaintiff says everything it needs to say to plead the claims it is bringing, and nothing more.

3. Note that it is also irrelevant to the question of jurisdiction whether plaintiff ultimately prevails on its claim. Federal question jurisdiction is the power to decide a claim arising under federal law. The court does not lose jurisdiction merely because it finds that no violation of federal law has occurred.

On the other hand, plaintiff must file a good-faith claim to invoke federal question jurisdiction. If plaintiff's claim is frivolous, the court may refuse to exercise jurisdiction or impose sanctions. See Chapter 5.

4. The Supreme Court in *Mottley* ordered that the case be dismissed for lack of subject matter jurisdiction. As you will learn in Chapter 11, such dismissals do not prevent the plaintiff from filing the case again in a proper court. Therefore, the Mottleys could—and in fact *did*—file the same action against the railroad in a state court. What issues would the state court decide? The railroad had filed a "demurrer." What is that? Does the railroad deny giving the Mottleys a lifetime pass? Does it deny that it refused to honor that pass? Aren't the only substantive issues in dispute questions of federal and Constitutional law? Does it make sense to say that this case does not involve a federal question?

5. The Mottleys' battle with the railroad continued in the state courts. The Kentucky trial court found for the Mottleys, and the state's high court affirmed. The railroad then appealed the case to the United States Supreme Court, which reversed and found for the railroad. *Louisville & Nashville R. Co. v. Mottley*, 219 U.S. 467, 31 S.Ct. 265, 55 L.Ed. 297 (1911). But how could the United States Supreme Court have jurisdiction to decide the merits of the case? Like the lower federal courts, the Supreme Court is a federal court, with jurisdiction limited by Article III of the Constitution. If the case set out above did not involve a federal question, and the second case was framed the same way, how could a federal question have been involved in that second case?

The answer requires one to distinguish between Article III and the statutes assigning that constitutional jurisdiction to the federal courts. Although *Mottley* is not clear on this point, the case is generally interpreted as an interpretation of § 1331, not Article III. The Supreme Court's jurisdiction to review state court decisions comes from § 1257, not § 1331. Moreover, although Article III uses the same language as § 1331—cases "arising under" the Constitution or federal law—the Constitutional language is interpreted far more broadly. A case satisfies Article III as long as its resolution turns on a question of federal law, regardless of whether that federal issue is a necessary part of the complaint. *Mesa v. California*, 489 U.S. 121, 109 S.Ct. 959, 103 L.Ed.2d 99 (1989). Therefore, because the dispute between the Mottleys and the railroad did turn on questions of federal law, the case qualified as a federal question under Article III, and was within the Supreme Court's power to decide.

Does it make sense that Congress would parrot the language of Article III when drafting § 1331, but intend for that language to mean something considerably narrower in the statute?

6. *Declaratory judgment cases.* Consider a variation on the facts of *Mottley*. Suppose that after the enactment of the federal law mentioned in the opinion, the Louisville & Nashville Railroad considered adopting a policy telling its conductors to quit accepting lifetime passes. However, the railroad fears that if it adopts this policy, it will be sued by the Mottleys. Historically, there was nothing the railroad could do to determine whether its proposed policy would withstand a challenge. Its only option was adopt the policy and hope for the best once it was sued.

Today, however, the railroad might be able to sue for a *declaratory judgment*. Under 28 U.S.C. § 2201 and analogous state statutes, a person may ask a court to declare the respective rights of the parties to an upcoming dispute. Conceptually, a declaratory judgment is like an ordinary case, except that the court does not grant a money judgment, injunction, or other traditional remedy. Instead, the only remedy is the declaration of rights. However, should the parties later get into a dispute involving the same basic legal rights, the result in the earlier declaratory judgment case is binding.

There are a number of limits and special rules dealing with use of the declaratory judgment device. For now, we need only consider the effect of a declaratory judgment on the well-pleaded complaint rule. Suppose that the railroad brings a declaratory judgment suit against the Mottleys, arguing that the federal statute bars it from honoring lifetime passes, and that the statute is constitutional. Railroad's complaint in this declaratory judgment case must invoke federal law. Do you see why? Does the fact that a federal issue now appears in the complaint mean that the dispute now presents a federal question? The analysis is not quite that straightforward:

> District courts have original federal question jurisdiction over complaints that contain a claim that arises under federal law. In actions for declaratory judgment, however, the position of the parties is often reversed: the plaintiff asserts a defense to an anticipated action by the declaratory judgment defendant. It is the character of the impending action, not the plaintiff's defense, that determines whether there is federal question jurisdiction. Thus, federal question jurisdiction exists in a declaratory judgment action if the potential suit by the declaratory judgment defendant would arise under federal law.

Cardtoons, L.C. v. Major League Baseball Players Ass'n, 95 F.3d 959 (10th Cir. 1996). Therefore, a court looks beyond the declaratory judgment to the coercive action that would otherwise occur to determine if the case involves a federal question. Under this analysis, would Railroad's declaratory judgment case qualify for federal question jurisdiction?

2. What Types of Claims Present a "Federal Question?"

The prior case demonstrated that jurisdiction under § 1331 exists only if there is a federal question on the face of the plaintiff's complaint. But what do we mean by a federal question? Although usually fairly straightforward, that issue can at times prove to be extraordinarily difficult. The simplest, and most common, example of a federal question case is when a plaintiff sues a defendant for relief afforded by a statute enacted by Congress, e.g., alleging employment discrimination. However, that classic case does not begin to exhaust the scope of what § 1331 means by a federal question. Some cases arising under federal statutes do not qualify as federal questions under § 1331, while other cases involving claims arising under other bodies of law sometimes will qualify. The following discussion briefly summarizes various sources of § 1331 federal questions.

a. United States Constitution

By its very terms, § 1331 also allows federal courts to hear claims asserting rights provided by the United States Constitution. Unlike the Canadian Constitution and those of some other nations, the United States Constitution does not explicitly give people a right to sue in court to enforce its provisions. Nevertheless, courts have for many years assumed that a person may sue for an injunction to prevent a government official from violating the Constitution. See, e.g., *Larson v. Domestic & Foreign Commerce Corp.*, 337 U.S. 682, 69 S.Ct. 1457, 93 L.Ed. 1628 (1949) (federal officials); *Ex parte Young*, 209 U.S. 123, 28 S.Ct. 441, 52 L.Ed. 714 (1908) (state officials). More recently, the Court has held that a party may in certain circumstances also sue for money damages for a violation of Constitutional rights. *Bivens v. Six Unknown Named Agents of Federal Bureau of Narcotics*, 403 U.S. 388, 91 S.Ct. 1999, 29 L.Ed.2d 619 (1971) (victim of search that violated the Fourth Amendment may sue the searching officers under the Constitution).

Note that it is technically inaccurate to refer to constitutional claims as "federal" questions. The United States Constitution is not federal law. Instead, it is a body of national law, created by the states and the people, and amended only with the consent of a supermajority of the states. As a matter of convenience, however, courts and commentators call all claims falling within § 1331 "federal" questions.

b. Treaties

§ 1331 also allows for federal jurisdiction over claims arising under treaties. The main issue to consider when treaties are involved is whether the treaty itself creates a legally enforceable claim. Most treaties ratified by the United States are not "self-implementing," which means that the treaty itself does not have the force of law in the courts.

Instead, the treaty must be implemented by a statute. Therefore, the vast majority of claims involving treaties will actually arise under the implementing statute rather than the treaty itself.

c. International Law

International law is the set of rules that govern relations between sovereign nations, as well as human rights rules that limit how sovereigns may treat individuals and groups. It comprises a collection of treaties, conventions, and customary international law. Even though international law does not owe its origin to Congress, international law is treated as federal law for purposes of federal question jurisdiction. Thus, a claim arising under international law qualifies as a federal question under § 1331. An interesting example of this principle is *Kadic v. Karadzic*, 70 F.3d 232 (2d Cir. 1995), which involves claims by Bosnian victims against a Serb leader during the Serbian conflict in the 1990s. The court ruled that the case qualified for federal question jurisdiction under a statute analogous to § 1331.

d. Federal Common Law

As you will discover in Chapter 13, the *Erie* doctrine greatly limits a federal court's ability to fashion independent rules of substantive law. Nevertheless, even after *Erie* there are certain areas in which federal judge-made rules will decide a case. When a party's claim arises under this federal common law, the case presents a federal question. *Illinois v. City of Milwaukee*, 406 U.S. 91, 92 S.Ct. 1385, 31 L.Ed.2d 712 (1972).

e. Problematic Federal Statutes

The above examples demonstrate that a claim need not arise under a federal statute in order to present a federal question under § 1331. Conversely, there are some situations where a case does not present a federal question even though it clearly arises under a federal statute. The first situation is a case brought to enforce the requirements of the Federal Arbitration Act, 9 U.S.C. §§ 1–16. The Federal Arbitration Act provides that a provision in a contract that requires disputes to be submitted to arbitration is enforceable in certain circumstances, notwithstanding what state law may provide. The Act also gives a party the right to sue to compel arbitration (§ 4) and to vacate an improper arbitration award (§ 10). Although federal law clearly creates the rights to compel and vacate, the courts have uniformly held that suits to enforce these rights do not create a federal question for purposes of § 1331. *Moses H. Cone Mem. Hosp. v. Mercury Constr. Corp.*, 460 U.S. 1, 25 n. 32, 103 S.Ct. 927, 74 L.Ed.2d 765 (1983); *Kasap v. Folger Nolan Fleming & Douglas, Inc.*, 166 F.3d 1243 (D.C. Cir. 1999).

Second, although Congress acts as legislature for the District of Columbia, claims arising under federal statutes for the District are not considered federal questions. 28 U.S.C. § 1366; see *Roth v. District of Columbia Courts*, 160 F.Supp.2d 104 (D. D.C. 2001).

f. State Law

As odd as it may seem at first glance, there are even situations where a case that ostensibly turns exclusively on state law may involve a federal question. For example, Congress will often "borrow" state law as governing law for lands and other areas under exclusive federal control, such as military bases. The borrowed rules become the federal law for that area, and can support federal question jurisdiction. See, e.g., *Ten Taxpayer Citizens Group v. Cape Wind Associates, LLC*, 373 F.3d 183 (1st Cir. 2004) (because Congress borrowed state law for the Outer Continental Shelf, suit alleging that construction project was improper because it did not comply with Massachusetts statute was a federal question). In other situations, a state-law claim will be treated as a federal question because it involves a federal element. Suppose, for example, that plaintiff sues defendant (a manufacturer) for negligence, claiming that defendant's products were not labeled as required by federal law. In some cases, this federal element may transform the state-law negligence claim into a federal question. Finally, in certain rare situations, a state claim may be a federal questions because it has been completely preempted by federal law. These last two situations (federal element and complete preemption) present additional complexities, and discussion of them has therefore been deferred to Chapter 13.

Problems

1. When P learns that his employee D has been revealing certain sensitive company information, P sues D under state trade secret laws. P brings his action in federal court, seeking $50,000 in damages. D immediately files a $100,000 counterclaim. D's counterclaim arises under the federal "whistleblower" statute, which provides a cause of action for employees who reveal information that shows that their employers are committing a crime. Does the court have subject-matter jurisdiction?

2. P, a pharmaceutical company, produces a drug called Absinthozene. P recently entered into a contract to sell 10,000 lots of Absinthozene to D, a pharmacy distribution company. However, after the contract was entered, the federal government banned the production and sale of Absinthozene based on evidence that it could cause brain damage. P obviously does not want to go to the expense of producing the drug if there is no real market. Nevertheless, because D can sell the drug in other nations where it is still legal, P worries that D will sue it for breach of contract if it does not honor the terms of the contract. P therefore wants to bring a declaratory judgment action in which it will ask the court for a declaration that the contract is void because of illegality. May P bring this action in federal court, based on federal question jurisdiction?

3. P, a private person, sues the D Tribe of American Indians in federal court for breach of contract. Under federal law, Indian tribes enjoy immunity to most civil actions. In his complaint, however, P argues the immunity should not apply to "commercial activities" such as those that gave rise to the contract between P and D. D moves to dismiss for lack of subject-matter jurisdiction. Will the court grant D's motion?

C. DIVERSITY JURISDICTION

INTRODUCTORY PROBLEM

While preparing her garden for planting, Gardner was seriously injured when her power rototiller malfunctioned. Gardner decides to sue both Cultivate, Inc. (the manufacturer of the rototiller) and Vendor (the individual who sold the rototiller to her) to recover for her injuries. For several reasons she would prefer to bring this action in a federal court.

The injury occurred at Gardner's home in Iowa. However, like many others in the Midwest, Gardner prefers to spend her winters in Florida. In fact, Gardner spends seven months of every year at a vacation condominium in Florida. Although Gardner owns the condominium, she considers her house in Iowa as her "true home."

Gardner bought the rototiller from Vendor's lawn supply store in Iowa. At the time of the sale and the injury, Vendor was domiciled in Iowa. Since the accident, however, Vendor has retired to Mexico. Vendor sold both his business and his home in Iowa and bought a new house on a Mexico beach. In addition, he gave up his United States citizenship and acquired Mexican citizenship.

Cultivate, Inc. is a corporation that was incorporated under the laws of the State of Iowa. The company also maintains a small office in that state, where the company president and some officers do business. Most major decisions emanate from the Iowa office. However, the vast majority of the day-to-day operations of the company are in New Mexico. Cultivate, Inc. operates a plant in New Mexico, and all of its employees live and work in that state.

Gardner suffered injuries of $74,000 in the rototilling accident. She would like to sue both defendants for this injury. In addition, however, Gardner wants to add a second claim to the action. When Gardner bought the rototiller, she was entitled to a $1000 rebate. Under governing law, both Vendor and Cultivate, Inc. are responsible for paying the rebate. Because applicable joinder rules would allow her to join these two claims into a single action, Gardner plans to bring both claims against the two defendants.

May Gardner bring her action in federal court?

Governing Law: 28 U.S.C. § 1332.

1. The Policy Underlying Diversity Jurisdiction

Diversity jurisdiction is the second main branch of federal subject matter jurisdiction. Diversity and federal question are alternatives: a party may sue in federal court if the requirements of *either* the federal question statute (§ 1331) *or* the diversity statute (§ 1332) are satisfied. In some cases, both § 1331 and § 1332 may provide jurisdiction. Like federal question jurisdiction, diversity jurisdiction is explicitly authorized by Article III of the Constitution. The "general" diversity statute—the only one with which we will be concerned at this juncture—is § 1332. Unlike federal question jurisdiction, diversity jurisdiction is not concerned with the legal source of the plaintiff's claim. Instead, it looks to the citizenship of the parties. If the parties are citizens of different states, the dispute can possibly be heard in federal court.

As you might expect, the justifications for diversity jurisdiction are quite different than the justifications for federal question jurisdiction. Because federal courts sitting in diversity can hear virtually any claim (with some exceptions to be discussed later), there is no reason to think that the federal courts will have any greater expertise with the case. Nor is there any particular federal interest in private disputes between citizens of different states. Instead, diversity jurisdiction exists because of a historical fear of state-court bias. State judges are government officials. In many states they are elected by the people of that state, while in the others they are appointed by the governor or other state official. Therefore, there is some reason to suspect that state judges might favor in-state litigants when those litigants are involved in a dispute with someone from out of state. Federal judges, by contrast, are protected by certain systemic safeguards designed to ensure their neutrality. Federal judges are national appointments; nominated by the President and confirmed by the Senate. Of equal or perhaps even greater importance, federal judges are appointed for life, subject only to impeachment.

Whether federal diversity jurisdiction actually helps prevent state-court bias is subject to some debate. Is a state court in rural southern Illinois more likely to be biased against someone who lives a few miles away in rural Indiana or a fellow Illinoisan who lives in Chicago? State judges today certainly have political leanings, but it is not clear that many have a strong home-state bias. And even if there is home-state loyalty, federal district court judges, like their state-court counterparts, are almost always selected from the bar of the state where they will serve. Moreover, as § 1332 is crafted, diversity jurisdiction exists regardless of whether any of the litigants are citizens of the state where the case is heard. Therefore, a federal court in Alaska may hear a dispute between a citizen of Florida and a citizen of Georgia. For all of these reasons, there is reason to doubt whether diversity jurisdiction serves its intended purpose.

Nevertheless, diversity jurisdiction is firmly established in the federal courts. In fact, diversity jurisdiction is actually considerably older than general federal question jurisdiction. Congress established diversity jurisdiction in section 11 of the Judiciary Act of 1789, Congress's very first comprehensive federal statute dealing with the federal courts. General federal question jurisdiction, by contrast, dates back only to 1875. Although the federal courts had jurisdiction over narrow categories of federal questions prior to 1875, for the first 85 years of the nation a significant number of federal question claims could be heard only in state courts.

Another difference between diversity and federal question jurisdiction is that the diversity statute has an amount in controversy requirement. Therefore, even if the parties are diverse, the federal courts may hear the case only if the amount at stake exceeds $75,000. Calculating the amount in controversy can be tricky, especially in cases involving multiple claims or those seeking injunctive relief.

Over the past half-century, there have been repeated efforts to abolish diversity jurisdiction. The push for abolition comes from several different sources. First, as noted above, there is some doubt as to whether state-court bias is a real problem. Second, diversity cases occupy a significant percentage of the federal court's workload; time that could perhaps be better devoted to cases requiring interpretation of federal law. Compounding this problem is the fact that diversity cases present a number of unique and idiosyncratic issues. As you progress through Civil Procedure, take a moment to make note of the number of special rules that apply to diversity cases. We will see two examples in this chapter—the special rules that apply in supplemental jurisdiction (§ 1367(b)) and removal (§ 1441(b)). Another example is the special venue rule for diversity cases. And the *Erie* doctrine, discussed in Chapter 5, is a problem that arises mainly in diversity cases. Therefore, removing diversity jurisdiction would not only lighten the load on the federal courts, but also significantly simplify certain aspects of federal litigation.

2. Determining Diversity

Because of the wording of § 1332, ascertaining whether diversity jurisdiction exists involves two basic issues. First, you must ensure that the litigants are of "diverse citizenship." Second, you must determine that the amount in controversy exceeds $75,000. The following two cases explore the question of diversity.

LUNDQUIST v. PRECISION VALLEY AVIATION, INC.

946 F.2d 8 (1st Cir. 1991)

PER CURIAM

Plaintiff-appellant Courtney Lundquist filed an action on March 20, 1987 in the District of Massachusetts against defendants-appellees Precision Valley Aviation, Inc., Winnipesaukee Airlines, Inc., Walter Fawcett, and Susan Fawcett, to recover on promissory notes relating to a sale of stock in Winnipesaukee Airlines, Inc., by Lundquist to defendants. Lundquist's complaint alleged federal jurisdiction on the basis of diversity of citizenship under 28 U.S.C. § 1332. The complaint did not allege citizenship but did state that Lundquist resided in Arlington, Massachusetts.

On November 5, 1990, defendants filed a motion to dismiss for lack of subject matter jurisdiction on the ground that complete diversity of citizenship did not exist. The motion, which included affidavits and other evidentiary documents, alleged that Lundquist, like the defendants, was a citizen of New Hampshire. Lundquist filed an objection to the motion to dismiss, including affidavits, in which he alleged that he was a citizen of Florida. Lundquist asked that the district court permit him to amend his complaint to assert Florida citizenship. * * *

Under 28 U.S.C. § 1332(a)(1), there is diversity of citizenship if the plaintiff is a "citizen" of a different state than all of the defendants. *Sweeney v. Westvaco Co.*, 926 F.2d 29, 32–33, 41 (1st Cir. 1991). "Citizenship" in a state is the equivalent of "domicile." *Valedon Martinez v. Hospital Presbiteriano de la Comunidad, Inc.*, 806 F.2d 1128, 1132 (1st Cir. 1986). Where a party changes domicile, "domicile at the time suit is filed [here, March 20, 1987] is the test and jurisdiction once established is not lost by a subsequent change in citizenship." *Id.* Moreover, "the burden of proof is on the plaintiff to support allegations of jurisdiction with competent proof when the allegations are challenged by the defendant." *O'Toole v. Arlington Trust Co.*, 681 F.2d 94, 98 (1st Cir. 1982).

Defendants' primary evidence that Lundquist was a New Hampshire citizen was as follows: (1) that Lundquist owned real property in Melvin Village, New Hampshire and paid taxes on that property; (2) that Lundquist maintained a functioning telephone in Melvin Village; (3) that Lundquist had had a New Hampshire driver's license since 1986; (4) that Lundquist was registered to vote in New Hampshire from 1976 until at least 1990, and has actually voted in New Hampshire during that time; and (5) that Lundquist or Lundquist's wife stated his address to be in Melvin Village, New Hampshire on 1986, 1987, and 1988 annual reports filed with the New Hampshire Secretary of State by Amphibair, Inc., a corporation of which Lundquist was sole director, President, and Treasurer, and Lundquist's wife was Secretary.

Lundquist presented affidavits of himself and his wife setting forth primarily the following evidence that Lundquist was a citizen not of New Hampshire, but of Florida: (1) that Lundquist purchased real property in Florida and moved there in 1984, keeping his New Hampshire property as a summer home; (2) that since 1984 Lundquist has maintained several Florida bank accounts; (3) that Lundquist has a Florida driver's license; (4) that Lundquist's wife has run a horse farm continuously in Florida since 1984; (5) that Lundquist and/or his wife belong to several social organizations in Florida; (6) that Lundquist has summered in New Hampshire, in some years spending as little as two to three weeks there; (7) that all of Lundquist's personal belongings are in Florida except for certain bank accounts and for sparse furnishings in the Melvin Village, New Hampshire residence; and (8) that Lundquist listed a Florida residence on his federal tax returns for 1987, 1988, and 1989.

The district court, in its brief order finding New Hampshire citizenship, noted that Lundquist had lived in Florida at material times. The court placed weight, however, on Lundquist's voting registration in New Hampshire and on Lundquist's representations of New Hampshire residence on corporate filings. * * *

As an initial matter, Lundquist attacks this district court ruling by asserting that the district court applied the wrong legal standard. Lundquist correctly notes that the relevant standard is "citizenship," i.e., "domicile," not mere residence; a party may reside in more than one state but can be domiciled, for diversity purposes, in only one. Because the district court did not expressly use the term "citizenship" or "domicile" in its order, but instead twice stated that Lundquist represented himself to be "a resident of New Hampshire," Lundquist argues that the district court improperly based its ruling on a finding of mere residence in New Hampshire.

The district court's order, however, is silent as to the legal analysis employed by the district court. It discusses only the facts of the case. The district court's references to residence were employed in the course of setting forth findings as to the facts. Since residence is highly relevant to the issue of domicile, the district court's discussion was fully consistent with application of the correct legal standard. Nothing else in the district court's order, beyond this mere accident of language, would suggest that the district court employed the wrong legal standard. We cannot find that the district court committed legal error in the absence of any significant indication that it did so. * * *

The remaining question is whether the district court applied that standard correctly. The district court's determination that Lundquist was a citizen of New Hampshire at the time he commenced the action "is a mixed question of law and fact and as such may not be set aside unless clearly erroneous."

There are, of course, many factors that courts have deemed relevant to the determination of a party's domicile.

> While it is impossible to catalogue all factors bearing on the issue, they include the place where civil and political rights are exercised, taxes paid, real and personal property (such as furniture and automobiles) located, driver's and other licenses obtained, bank accounts maintained, location of club and church membership and places of business or employment.

1 *Moore's Federal Practice* 3.–3, at 788 (2nd ed. 1991). Just as no single factor is controlling, id. at 787–88, domicile need not be determined by mere numerical comparison of the number of factors that may appear to favor each side of the issue.

In the instant case there is no question that a number of important factors do suggest domicile in Florida. For example, defendants introduced nothing to contradict Lundquist's assertion that most of Lundquist's personal property is in Florida, Lundquist has several bank accounts in Florida, Lundquist belongs to social organizations in Florida, and Lundquist listed a Florida residence on his federal tax returns for relevant years. Although Lundquist stated he had a Florida driver's license, defendants introduced uncontradicted evidence that he also had a New Hampshire license. On the other hand, the factors relied on by the district court—Lundquist's registration to vote and actual voting in

New Hampshire, and his representation of New Hampshire residence on corporate reports to the New Hampshire Secretary of State—are also weighty ones.

For example, "some opinions have given special weight to the state in which a party is registered to vote, occasionally stating that such registration raises a presumption of domicile." We need establish no such presumption to agree that Lundquist's voting registration carries weight. The applicable New Hampshire statute provides,

> Every inhabitant of the state, having a fixed and permanent established domicile, . . . shall have a right at any meeting or election, to vote in the town, ward, or unincorporated place in which he is domiciled. The determinant of one's domicile is a question of factual physical presence incorporating an intention to reside for an indefinite period. This domicile is the voter's residence to which, upon temporary absence, he has the intention of returning. This domicile is that place in which he dwells on a continuing basis for a significant portion of each year.

N.H. Rev. Stat. Ann. 654:1. Given this statute, Lundquist's voting behavior is tantamount to a representation of New Hampshire domicile to voting officials.

In addition, we have held in *O'Toole*, 681 F.2d at 98, that a party's own representation of domicile on corporate reports is "strong evidence." In *O'Toole*, appellants had filed corporate reports with the state of Massachusetts listing their "domicile" as in Massachusetts. We upheld as not clearly erroneous the district court's determination of Massachusetts domicile, stating,

> Although the term "domicile" on the corporate filing form may not have the exact legal meaning that it has in the § 1332 context, appellants' designation of domicile in Massachusetts on the forms is strong evidence that appellants have the burden of overcoming. The paucity of appellants' presentation of evidence justifies the district court's conclusion that they had not met that burden.

Id.

In the instant case, to be sure, the contrary evidence as to domicile is stronger than it was in *O'Toole*. Also, neither the corporate report forms nor the governing New Hampshire statutes use the word "domicile." New Hampshire law requires that at least one director be an "actual resident" of New Hampshire, N.H. Rev. Stat. Ann. § 296:3, and that the corporation "continuously maintain in this state a secretary, . . . who shall be an individual resident in this state. . . ." N.H. Rev. Stat. Ann. § 293–A:12 (emphasis added). Again, Lundquist was the corporation's sole director, and Lundquist's wife held the office of Secretary. Thus, although Lundquist's and his wife's representations on these corporate reports cannot be said to have been representations of "domicile," they were representations not only of mere residence but of continuous, "actual" residence. Accordingly, while *O'Toole* certainly is not on all fours with this case, *O'Toole* does support the proposition that Lundquist's representations to state officials on corporate reports, as well as for voting purposes, are entitled to significant weight.

Given the substantial evidence on both sides of the issue, we cannot say that the district court committed clear error in making the determination that it did. Although Lundquist in his affidavit put forth strong evidence of an intent to remain in Florida, Lundquist's voting registration and representations on corporate reports constitute significant countervailing evidence of intent to remain in New Hampshire and maintain New Hampshire domicile. * * *

The judgment of the district court is affirmed.

Notes and Questions

1. *Lundquist* explores what § 1332 means by a "citizen of a state." In the case of United States citizens, a person's citizenship is measured by her domicile. As the court indicates, domicile is not the same as residence. In one sentence, describe the difference between domicile and residence.

2. Bonnie was born in Oregon to Oregon citizens, and has lived in that state her entire 35–year life. However, for as long as she can remember, she has hated Oregon's gray and dreary climate. In fact, for the past thirty years Bonnie has intended to leave Oregon and relocate to Arizona. Unfortunately, she still has not saved enough money to make the change. What is Bonnie's domicile? Does she even have a domicile?

Rethink your answers to these questions in light of the following general principles of the law of domicile:

a. A person always has one—and only one—domicile.

b. An infant acquires a domicile at birth, which is almost always the domicile of his parents.

c. In order to change his domicile, a person must both establish residence in a new state and have the intent to remain in that state. The residence and the intent to remain must exist at the same time, even if only for a moment.

3. *Intent.* Domicile's focus on a person's subjective intent creates special problems in certain situations. In some cases, a person will not have the legal capacity to form the required intent. Therefore, a minor will usually keep the domicile of his parents until the age of majority. Of course, the age of majority differs from state to state, which can lead to convoluted analysis, especially in cases where a person moves from a state where he is a minor to one in which he would be old enough to form the required intent. See, e.g., *Rodriguez–Diaz v. Sierra–Martinez*, 853 F.2d 1027 (1st Cir. 1988).

People with diminished mental capacity also cannot themselves form the intent to change domicile. Because people with diminished capacity are limited in their ability to effect a legal transfer of property and enter into contracts, a legal guardian is often appointed to manage their affairs. In some cases, the guardian may move the ward to a new state. Courts are split as to whether the guardian can change the ward's domicile. For an excellent discussion of the competing views, see *Acridge v. The Evangelical Lutheran Good Samaritan Society*, 334 F.3d 444 (5th Cir. 2003).

What about military personnel and prisoners who are serving jail terms in states other than their previous home? For these people, of course, the problem is not capacity. Instead, the problem is that their change of residence is not voluntary. Nevertheless, both military personnel and prisoners may form the intent to remain in their new state of residence. See *Gambelli v. United States*, 904 F.Supp. 494 (E.D. Va. 1995) (military); *Singletary v. Continental Illinois National Bank*, 9 F.3d 1236 (7th Cir. 1993) (prisoner).

The prior case dealt with a natural person. However, the legal concept of a "person" is not limited to individuals. Corporations and government bodies may also have legal rights, and can sue and be sued in court. If a case involves a legal person such as a corporation, how does the court determine the entity's citizenship? After all, a corporation is a legal fiction that does not truly "live" anywhere.

MONTROSE CHEMICAL CORP. v. AMERICAN MOTORISTS INSURANCE CO.

117 F.3d 1128 (9th Cir. 1997)

MAGILL, Judge:

* * * Montrose is a Delaware corporation that used to manufacture, among other chemicals, the pesticide DDT. Montrose's manufacturing operations were conducted primarily in California and Nevada. Although Montrose still owns a chemical facility in Nevada that it leases to another corporation, Montrose's main activity for the past decade has been defending itself against environmental damages claims. Because of the liabilities flowing from this litigation, Montrose has become an almost entirely inactive corporation.

The rental income that Montrose receives from its Nevada facility is its only source of operating income. Montrose's only other stream of income comes from financial investments. Both of these activities are managed by Montrose's only officer and only full-time employee, Frank C. Bachman, who works out of Montrose's sole office in Trumbull, Connecticut. The office in Trumbull is also Montrose's sole mailing address.

Travelers, AMICO, and INA are three of Montrose's comprehensive general liability insurance carriers, and the dispute in the present action revolves around the obligation of these insurance companies to provide coverage to Montrose. * * *

[During August of 1994, Montrose filed seven different actions against Travelers, AMICO, and INA in the Central District of California, alleging that the defendants had failed to defend Montrose in several different cases brought against Montrose for environmental harm.] In each of the seven complaints filed by Montrose, Montrose alleged federal subject matter jurisdiction based solely upon diversity of citizenship. Montrose pled each defendant's state of incorporation and each defendant's principal place of business. Specifically, Montrose pled that: (1) Travelers is incorporated in Connecticut and that Travelers's principal place of business is Connecticut; (2) AMICO is incorporated in Illinois and that AMICO's principal place of business is Illinois; and (3) INA is incorporated in Pennsylvania and that INA's principal place of business is Pennsylvania. Montrose, however, did not identify its own principal place of business in any of the complaints that it filed with the court. Montrose merely pled that it is incorporated in Delaware. * * *

On October 21, 1994, Travelers, AMICO, and INA ... filed a motion to dismiss each of Montrose's seven actions for lack of subject matter jurisdiction, arguing that there was not complete diversity of citizenship between the opposing parties. Travelers, AMICO, and INA argued that, because both Travelers and Montrose are citizens of Connecticut, the district court lacked diversity jurisdiction. In response to the motion to dismiss, Montrose filed, on November 7, 1994, an opposition brief in which Montrose claimed that it is a citizen of both Delaware and Nevada, but not Connecticut. Montrose claimed that, because it is incorporated in Delaware, Montrose is a citizen of Delaware and that, because its principal place of business is Nevada, Montrose is also a citizen of Nevada.

On June 20, 1995, the district court dismissed Montrose's actions for lack of subject matter jurisdiction. The district court determined that "Montrose's business activities are threefold: (1) managing investment accounts, (2) supervising lawyers handling their pollution liability and insurance lawsuits, and (3) leasing the Nevada facility." The district court further determined that "all of these activities are conducted by Mr. Frank C. Bachman and his small staff, from Montrose's headquarters and sole office in Connecticut." The district court concluded that "it is clear that Montrose's principal place of business is Connecticut." Thus, because Travelers's principal place of business is also Connecticut, the district court held that "the requisite diversity jurisdiction is lacking" and dismissed Montrose's actions. * * *

For the district court to have diversity jurisdiction over the seven actions brought by Montrose, the citizenship of Montrose must be different than the citizenship of each of the three defendants. To identify a corporation's citizenship for purposes of diversity jurisdiction, "a corporation shall be deemed to be a citizen of any State by which it has been incorporated and of the State where it has its principal place of business...." 28 U.S.C. § 1332(c)(1). For this reason, "a corporation is typically a citizen of two states for determining the existence of diversity jurisdiction: the state of incorporation and the state in which it has its principal place of business." *Breitman v. May Co. California*, 37 F.3d 562, 564 (9th Cir. 1994).

It is undisputed that Montrose is diverse with respect to both AMICO and INA. In addition, it is undisputed that Montrose and Travelers are diverse with respect to their states of incorporation. Finally, it is undisputed that Travelers's principal place of business is Connecticut. Accordingly, the only potential bar to complete diversity is the district court's conclusion that Montrose's principal place of business is also Connecticut.

This Court generally applies "one of two tests to determine in which state a corporation has its principal place of business: the place of operations test and the nerve center test." *Breitman*, 37 F.3d at 564. "Under the place of operations test, a corporation's principal place of business is the state in which it performs a 'substantial predominance' of corporate operations." *Breitman*, 37 F.3d at 564. Under the nerve center test, "a corporation's principal place of business is the state in which the executive and administrative functions are performed." *Id.* However, "the 'nerve center' test should be used only when no state contains a substantial predominance of the corporation's business activities." *Industrial Tectonics*, 912 F.2d at 1094.

In *Industrial Tectonics*, this Court explained further that:

One must keep in mind that the purpose of diversity jurisdiction is to avoid the effects of prejudice against outsiders. *Thus, the principal place of business should be the place where the corporation conducts the most activity that is visible and impacts the public*, so that it is least likely to suffer from prejudice against outsiders. Many factors are relevant to determining the location of the majority of corporate activity and greatest contact with the public. Certainly the location of employees, tangible property, and production activities are relevant factors. Additional relevant factors include the locations where income is earned, purchases are made, and sales take place.

Id. (emphasis added)

Because Nevada arguably "contains a substantial predominance of [Montrose's] business activities," *id.*, we apply the place of operations test to determine whether [the] * * * assertion of diversity jurisdiction was baseless. Under this test and under the principles set forth in Industrial Tectonics, we hold that [the] * * * assertion of subject matter jurisdiction did not "completely lack[ ] a factual foundation...." *Orange Production*, 792 F.2d at 801.

First, with respect to Montrose's tangible property, ownership of a chemical facility in Nevada that produces rental income is likely more visible than the performance of various administrative functions out of an office in Connecticut. Furthermore, with respect to Montrose's production activities, Nevada is the ultimate source of Montrose's only operating income—the rental income from the Nevada chemical facility. As the ultimate source of its only operating income, Nevada is arguably the site of Montrose's most important "production activity" within the meaning of the Industrial Tectonics principles. Finally, with respect to the locations where income is earned, although Montrose collects the rental income in Connecticut and oversees its financial investments from there, its operating income is generated entirely by means of its ownership of the chemical facility in Nevada. Consequently, [the] * * * argument that Nevada is Montrose's principal place of business is not completely without factual foundation. Cf. *Danjaq, S.A. v. Pathe Communications Corp.*, 979 F.2d 772, 776 (9th Cir. 1992) (holding that, under the standard enunciated in *Industrial Tectonics*, California was the principal place of business of a developer and producer of James Bond films because the company's "central figure" made all the arrangements and decisions regarding production of the films in Los Angeles, notwithstanding that Switzerland was where administrative and ministerial duties were performed). * * *

Notes and Questions

1. Plaintiff Montrose clearly has a citizenship diverse from defendants AMICO and INA. Therefore, wasn't the action one "between citizens of different states" for purposes of § 1332 regardless of whether Montrose was diverse from Travelers? Why did diversity between Montrose and Travelers matter?

2. The "complete diversity" rule applied in *Montrose Chemical* requires that no plaintiff may share citizenship with any defendant. Like the "well-pleaded complaint" rule that applies in federal question cases, the complete diversity rule is a rule of statutory, not constitutional, interpretation. The courts have interpreted the diversity language in Article III of the Constitution to require only "minimal," rather than complete diversity. Minimal diversity exists when one plaintiff is diverse from any one defendant; the citizenship of the other parties to the case does not matter. Because the Constitution requires only minimal diversity, Congress could change the requirements for diversity jurisdiction under § 1332. In fact, under other specialized diversity statutes Congress sometimes does not require complete diversity. See, for example, § 1335, which requires less than complete diversity in interpleader cases.

Similarly, in 2002 Congress enacted the Multiparty, Multiforum Jurisdiction Act of 2002, which gives the district courts subject-matter jurisdiction over certain cases arising out of an accident in which 75 or more people died. 28 U.S.C. § 1369. The statute explicitly requires only "minimal diversity," which is defined as any situation where at least one plaintiff is diverse from any defendant. 28 U.S.C. § 1369(c)(1). However, if a substantial majority of the plaintiffs are citizens of the same state as the primary defendant or defendants, the federal court must decline to hear the case. In addition, the statute also applies only if the accident did not occur in defendant's home state, or, if there are two or more defendants, at least two reside in different states.

Finally, Congress recently amended § 1332 to give the district courts jurisdiction over large class actions (involving an amount in controversy greater than $5,000,000) in which at least one member of the plaintiff class is diverse from the defendant. This amendment, codified at § 1332(d), is discussed in Chapter 6 in the material dealing with class actions.

3. The complete diversity rule has a long heritage, tracing its roots to the Supreme Court's decision in *Strawbridge v. Curtiss*, 7 U.S. (3 Cranch) 267, 2 L.Ed. 435 (1806). *Strawbridge* has often been criticized. Nevertheless, the rule has never been overturned. One reason cited for retaining the rule is that Congress has amended § 1332 on a number of occasions since 1806, but did nothing in these amendments to overturn the rule. That silence, the courts reason, constitutes acquiescence. Moreover, as we will see in Part D of this chapter, the adoption of § 1367 in 1990 provides more positive proof that Congress is content with the complete diversity rule in ordinary diversity cases.

4. Imagine a case where two plaintiffs sue two defendants. P1 is diverse from both defendants. While P2 is diverse from D1, P2 and D2 are citizens of the same state. However, P2 has not filed a claim against D2. May the case be brought in federal court under diversity jurisdiction? For a number of years, many lower courts allowed diversity jurisdiction under these circumstances. However, in *Caterpillar Inc. v. Lewis*, 519 U.S. 61, 117 S.Ct. 467, 136 L.Ed.2d 437 (1996), the Supreme Court made it clear that the complete diversity rule applied regardless of whether the non-diverse parties had filed claims against each other. Therefore, in the above example, the case cannot proceed in federal court as long as P2 and D2 are still in the case. Either P2 or D2 must be dropped if the case is to stay in federal court.

5. The complete diversity rule deals with citizenship. What about the other main requirement of § 1332—the amount in controversy? For many years, the courts held that every plaintiff's claim against every defendant had to satisfy the amount in controversy requirement. *Zahn v. International Paper Co.*, 414 U.S. 291, 94 S.Ct. 505, 38 L.Ed.2d 511 (1973). However, the adoption of the supplemental jurisdiction statute, 28 U.S.C. § 1367, has relaxed this requirement in part. See *Exxon Mobil Corp. v. Allapattah Services, Inc.* in Part D of this Chapter.

6. The other main issue addressed in *Montrose* is how to determine the citizenship of a corporation. § 1332(c) provides the governing rule. After reviewing that section, do you see why the *Montrose* court says that a corporation is often a citizen of two states? Can you conceive of a situation where a corporation could have only one citizenship? Note, however, that a corporation will almost never have more than two citizenships. There can, by definition, be only one "principal" place of business. And a corporation is almost always incorporated under the laws of only one state. If the parties who operate the corporation file incorporation papers in more than one state, they will create two separate corporations.

Sometimes you will see reference to a corporation being "chartered" in a state. This is an older term that means the same as "incorporated."

7. If a corporation may have two citizenships, then why wasn't Montrose diverse from Travelers regardless of its principal place of business? Wasn't Montrose a citizen of Delaware by virtue of its incorporation in that state? Wasn't Travelers a citizen of Connecticut?

8. *Partnerships and unincorporated associations.* Partnerships and other unincorporated associations present special issues. First, unlike a corporation, these entities are usually not a "person" in the eyes of the law, which means they can neither sue nor be sued in their own name. Second, even if

the partnership or unincorporated association is considered a legal person, in determining diversity courts look to the citizenship of all the partners or members of the association.

9. *Foreign corporations.* What if a corporation is chartered under the laws of another nation, but has its principal place of business in the United States? If the normal rules applied, such a party would be both an alien (a citizen of the laws of the nation of incorporation) and a citizen of a state. Most courts, however, do not apply the principal place of business test to foreign corporations. Such corporations are citizens only of the nation in which they were incorporated.

3. The Amount in Controversy

The other primary requirement of § 1332 is that the amount in controversy exceed $75,000. Throughout its history, diversity jurisdiction has been subject to an amount in controversy requirement. The Judiciary Act of 1789 established a minimum of $500. Congress has periodically increased the floor over the years to its present amount. This increase represents more than inflation. At times, Congress has agreed to increase the amount in controversy as a way to appease those who would abolish diversity jurisdiction altogether. Confining diversity to the larger, and ostensibly more important, cases helps to reduce the drain on federal judicial resources.

What amounts are considered. Generally speaking, a court applying the amount in controversy requirement attempts to ascertain the total value of the dispute. Claims for both compensatory and punitive damages are counted in determining whether the requirement is satisfied. However, other payments that one side may be required to make to the other following the case may not count. § 1332 makes it clear that the amount in controversy is "exclusive of interest and costs." The term costs means the various expenses charged by the judicial system. Courts often require the losing party to pay the winner's costs.

Contrary to what a literal reading of the statute might suggest, not all interest is excluded from the calculation. As one court restated the rule:

> The purpose of excluding interest is to prevent the delaying of a suit merely to accumulate the necessary amount for federal jurisdiction. Thus, interest is not counted if it "was an incident arising solely by virtue of a delay in payment" of the underlying amount in controversy.

State Farm Mutual Auto Ins. Co. v. Narvaez, 149 F.3d 1269 (10th Cir. 1998). Conversely, to the extent that the claim arises from a loan or other obligation that earns interest, any interest that is an essential ingredient of the claim does count. *Brown v. Webster*, 156 U.S. 328, 15 S.Ct. 377, 39 L.Ed. 440 (1895). Therefore, a suit to collect $80,000 in unpaid interest coupons on a note would satisfy the amount in controversy, even though the entire amount is made up of interest. In short, interest counts if it is imposed by agreement, but not if it is imposed by law.

Claims for relief other than money. What if the case seeks an injunction or other non-monetary relief? Courts in these situations determine the amount in controversy by attempting to approximate the monetary value of the relief being sought. In the case of an injunction, the courts are split as to how to determine the value. Depending on the jurisdiction, the court will use one of the following tests: (a) the value of injunctive relief to the plaintiff (the majority view), (b) the cost of the injunction to the defendant, (c) the greater of the value to plaintiff or expense to defendant, or (d) the worth of the "object in controversy"; i.e. the subject of the dispute. 1 Moore's Manual, Federal Practice and Procedure § 5.72(3) (2000).

What evidence the court considers. In determining whether the amount in controversy requirement is satisfied, a court usually looks solely to the face of plaintiff's complaint. If the plaintiff simply alleges an amount in excess of $75,000, exclusive of interest and costs, the requirement is usually deemed satisfied. Even if plaintiff's demand for relief seems high, the court will accept it unless it appears to a legal certainty that the plaintiff cannot recover the amount sought. *St. Paul Mercury Indem. Co. v. Red Cab Co.*, 303 U.S. 283, 288–89, 58 S.Ct. 586, 82 L.Ed. 845 (1938). It is very difficult for defendant to overcome the presumption that plaintiff's request is in good faith. For an excellent recent decision applying this principle to several claims, finding some sufficient and others insufficient, see *Rosario Ortega v. Star–Kist Foods, Inc.*, 370 F.3d 124 (1st Cir. 2004), *overturned on other grounds* ___ U.S. ___, 125 S.Ct. 2611, 162 L.Ed.2d 502 (2005).

Conversely, a plaintiff can keep a case out of court by specifically alleging that she demands an amount not to exceed $75,000. This is especially helpful when the plaintiff wants to prevent defendant from removing the case, as discussed in Part E of this chapter.

In some situations, the court may consider pleadings other than the complaint in determining whether the amount in controversy is satisfied. This usually arises in situations of aggregation, which is discussed just below.

When amount determined. Because the court considers the complaint, a party need only show that the amount in controversy is satisfied on the date the case is filed. The court does not lose jurisdiction if it eventually determines that plaintiff will actually recover $75,000 or less. However, if plaintiff recovers $75,000 or less, § 1332(b) gives the court the option of requiring the plaintiff to pay both its costs and those of the defendant.

Aggregation. The discussion to this point has been considering only single plaintiff-single defendant-single claim cases. Today, few cases fit that mold. How does the court apply the amount in controversy rules to cases involving multiple claims and parties? The rules governing aggregation are complex, and can require a fairly sophisticated knowledge of both property rights and the substantive law underlying the claim. The following is but a brief summary of the basic principles.

1. *Single plaintiff-single defendant.* Generally, a plaintiff may aggregate all claims she has against a single defendant to meet the $75,000 floor. Aggregation is possible regardless of whether the claims are in any way related, and regardless of whether any individual claim by itself exceeds $75,000. However, if a plaintiff seeks recovery for the same injury using two or more claims that present alternate legal theories, the damages sought under each of those claims is not aggregated. Suppose, for example, that plaintiff, who was injured by a defective product, sues defendant for breach of warranty and negligence. Plaintiff suffered $50,000 in damages. Because these claims are merely alternate ways to recover for the same injury, the $50,000 in damages is counted only once. These two claims would not be aggregated.

2. *Multiple plaintiffs.* Two or more plaintiffs ordinarily cannot aggregate their claims. However, there are two exceptions to this rule. First, as discussed in Part D of this Chapter, to the extent that the claims are factually related, a plaintiff with a claim of $75,000 or less may be able to join with a plaintiff whose claim exceeds $75,000 by virtue of the supplemental jurisdiction statute. Second, if two or more plaintiffs hold a joint and undivided interest in property that has a value in excess of $75,000, the court will consider the amount in controversy to be the value of the property rather than the value of each plaintiff's separate share. For an excellent discussion of the principles that apply to multiple plaintiffs, see *Allen v. R & H Oil and Gas Co.*, 63 F.3d 1326 (5th Cir. 1995).

Class actions involving multiple plaintiffs are governed by special rules. See Chapter 6. However, these special rules only apply if at least one of the class members have a claim in excess of $75,000. If no member of the class has a claim that meets the requirement, the class action may be brought in federal court based on diversity only if the claims of the class members can be aggregated under the rules set out in the prior paragraph. Claims of class members will rarely satisfy the requirements of aggregation.

3. *Multiple defendants.* A plaintiff may aggregate claims against multiple defendants only if the total injury suffered by plaintiff exceeds $75,000, and under governing law defendants can be held jointly liability for the entire injury. If a state still follows the traditional rule of joint and several liability for multiple tortfeasors, aggregation is possible.

4. *Counterclaims.* As discussed above, a court usually considers only the complaint in determining whether the amount in controversy requirement is satisfied. However, several courts have indicated that the requirement may also be met if defendant asserts a compulsory counterclaim that, when added to the prayer in the complaint, totals more than $75,000. Other courts disagree, holding that only the complaint counts for determining the amount in controversy. Compare *Spectator Mgmt. Group v. Brown*, 131 F.3d 120 (3d Cir. 1997) (considers counterclaim)

with *Oliver v. Haas*, 777 F.S. 1040 (D. P.R. 1991) (counterclaim does not factor into calculation). Even courts like *Spectator Mgmt.* apply the logic only to compulsory counterclaims, not to permissive counterclaims, cross-claims, or other forms of joinder.

4. Additional Issues in Diversity Jurisdiction

a. *Alienage Jurisdiction*

§ 1332 does not apply only to United States citizens. It also allows the federal courts to exercise jurisdiction over certain cases involving citizens or subjects (technically, a "subject" is a person who lives under a monarchy) of foreign nations. The rationale for this so-called alienage jurisdiction is in many respects the same as that for ordinary diversity jurisdiction; namely, that state courts might favor their own citizens in suits between them and foreign citizens.

1. Review § 1332 and determine whether a federal court may hear the following disputes:

a. P1 (a citizen of Mississippi) and P2 (a citizen of France) sue D, a citizen of Louisiana.

b. P (a citizen of North Dakota) sues D1 (a citizen of Sweden) and D2 (a citizen of Brazil).

c. P (a citizen of Indonesia) sues D (a citizen of India).

d. P1 (a citizen of Indonesia) and P2 (a citizen of Indiana) sue D (a citizen of India).

e. P1 (a citizen of Finland) and P2 (a citizen of Florida) sue D1 (a citizen of Minnesota) and D2 (a citizen of Finland).

2. Note that § 1332 contains language that treats an alien who has been admitted "for permanent residence" as a citizen of the state in which she is domiciled. This provision applies only when the alien has been granted permanent resident alien status by the federal government. Merely establishing a domicile, without government approval, is not enough. Therefore, in Problem 1.b above, if the Swedish defendant had been granted permanent resident alien status, he would be treated as a citizen of the state in which he established domicile. If the state of domicile was North Dakota, this would destroy complete diversity.

Now consider Problem 1.c. Suppose the Indian defendant in that problem was a permanent resident alien who lived in West Virginia. Could the federal court then exercise jurisdiction? Many courts would answer no. These courts interpret the permanent resident alien language in a way that serves only to defeat jurisdiction rather than establish it. In other words, if a West Virginia plaintiff sued our permanent resident alien who lived in West Virginia, the federal courts would not have alienage jurisdiction. The rationale for this result is that any fear of state-court bias would be mitigated since both parties lived in the same state. However, in Problem 1.c, the person would still be treated as an alien, and no diversity would exist. See *Saadeh v. Farouki*, 107 F.3d 52 (D.C. Cir. 1997).

3. Do not forget that state courts may also hear cases involving aliens. In fact, a state court could hear any of the cases set out in Note 1.

4. As we have seen, § 1332 applies to both United States citizens and people who live in other countries. What about a United States citizen who is domiciled abroad? May that person avail herself of diversity jurisdiction? The somewhat surprising answer is no. Because that person does not have a domicile in any state, she is not a "citizen of a state." And because that person is a citizen of the United States, she cannot be a citizen or subject of a foreign state. Thus, the United States citizen domiciled abroad may not avail herself of diversity jurisdiction. Of course, like anyone else she may invoke federal question jurisdiction.

b. *Time for Determining Diversity*

"[T]he jurisdiction of the Court depends upon the state of things at the time of the action brought." *Mollan v. Torrance*, 22 U.S. (9 Wheat) 537, 6 L.Ed. 154 (1824). We already saw that the amount in controversy is measured as of the date the complaint is filed. Similarly, for purposes of determining diversity a court will look only to the citizenship of the parties on the date the case begins. Post-filing changes of residence do not affect the court's jurisdiction.

What happens if the requirements for diversity are not satisfied on the date the case is commenced, but the problem is cured by the time the case is tried? Under application of the traditional rule, those post-filing events would not matter, and the case would have to be dismissed. However, in *Caterpillar Inc. v. Lewis*, 519 U.S. 61, 117 S.Ct. 467, 136 L.Ed.2d 437 (1996), the Supreme Court held that a federal court could exercise jurisdiction over a case where the complete diversity requirement was not met when the case began in federal court, but the non-diverse defendant had been dismissed before the time of trial.

Caterpillar created a potentially significant loophole in the traditional time-of-filing rule, and the Court explained the scope of its earlier decision in 2004. In *Grupo Dataflux v. Atlas Global Group, L.P.*, 541 U.S. 567, 124 S.Ct. 1920, 158 L.Ed.2d 866 (2004), a partnership sued a corporation. The corporation was a citizen of Mexico. As discussed above, a partnership's citizenship is determined by the citizenship of its members. At the time the case was commenced, two of the partners were from Mexico, while the others were citizens of states in the United States. The case accordingly failed the complete diversity requirement because there were aliens on both sides.

For some reason, however, defendant did not challenge jurisdiction in the early stages of the case. A month before trial, the two Mexican partners left the partnership, leaving only United States citizens as partners. The case went to trial, and a judgment was rendered against defendant.

After judgment, defendant challenged subject-matter jurisdiction, invoking the time-of-filing rule. Plaintiff argued that under *Caterpillar*, the jurisdictional defect had been "cured" when the two alien partners left the partnership. The Court agreed with defendant and dismissed the case, finding *Caterpillar* distinguishable. In *Caterpillar*, there had been a change in the people who were parties to the suit. In *Grupo*, by contrast, the parties remained the same, but meanwhile their citizenship had changed:

> To our knowledge, the Court has never approved a deviation from the rule articulated by Chief Justice Marshall in 1829 that "where there is *no* change of party, a jurisdiction depending on the condition of the party is governed by that condition, as it was at the commencement of the suit." *Conolly*, 27 U.S. 556, 2 Pet., at 556, (emphasis added). Unless the Court is to manufacture a brand-new exception to the time-of-filing rule, dismissal for lack of subject-matter jurisdiction is the only option available in this case. The purported cure arose not from a change in the parties to the action, but from a change in the citizenship of a continuing party. Withdrawal of the Mexican partners from Atlas did not change the fact that Atlas * * * remained a party to the action. True, the composition of the partnership, and consequently its citizenship, changed. But allowing a citizenship change to cure the jurisdictional defect that existed at the time of filing would contravene the principle articulated by Chief Justice Marshall in *Conolly*. We decline to do today what the Court has refused to do for the past 175 years.

c. *Manipulating § 1332*

In many cases, parties attempt to tinker with the structure of the underlying dispute in an attempt to create or destroy diversity. As you might imagine, there have been efforts to control the most egregious examples of this manipulation. A federal court can avail itself of several different tools to deal with attempts to evade the requirements of § 1332.

Nominal parties. The easiest way for a party to prevent a federal court from exercising diversity jurisdiction is to make sure that at least one of the plaintiffs is from the same state as one of the defendants. In that case, the complete diversity rule bars jurisdiction. Therefore, a plaintiff who wants to make sure that her case is heard in state court will join with another plaintiff who is not diverse from the defendant, or join a second defendant who is from the same state as the plaintiff. Note that this option is available only to plaintiffs. Although we saw in Chapter 2 that defendants may also join parties, any parties joined by defendants will not destroy diversity over the original case.

In most cases, a plaintiff can keep a case out of federal court by joining nondiverse parties. However, if the additional party is merely a nominal party with no real claim or liability in the matter, the court may ignore that party in determining whether diversity exists. Perhaps the best-known case involving this issue is *Rose v. Giamatti*, 721 F.Supp. 906 (S.D. Ohio 1989). In this case, the famous baseball player Pete Rose brought an action challenging his exclusion from baseball. Rose sued the Commissioner of Baseball, the Cincinnati Reds, and Major League Baseball. The latter two defendants were, like Rose, citizens of Ohio. The court nevertheless held that diversity jurisdiction existed. The court reasoned that because Rose had no real claim against the Reds or Major League Baseball, the citizenship of those nominal defendants would be ignored.

Realignment of parties. The complete diversity rule requires that no plaintiff be from the same state as any defendant. Whether a plaintiff is from the same state as another plaintiff—or whether a defendant is from the same state as another defendant—is irrelevant. In some situations, the parties may erect a case in which two parties who are at odds with each other nevertheless end up as co-plaintiffs or defendants. Note that this is not always done in bad faith, as in certain types of disputes it may be difficult to ascertain whether a party is properly a plaintiff or a defendant. In situations where a party is wrongly joined, a court has considerable power to realign the parties, putting them into their proper role. As one court stated:

> A plaintiff's alignment of the parties, however, is not determinative. In considering whether there is complete diversity, a federal court must look beyond the nominal designation of the parties in the pleadings and should realign the parties according to their real interests in the dispute.

Safeco Ins. Co. v. City of White House, 36 F.3d 540, 545 (6th Cir. 1994). See also *Indianapolis v. Chase Nat'l Bank*, 314 U.S. 63, 62 S.Ct. 15, 86 L.Ed. 47 (1941). Realignment is especially likely to occur in cases involving declaratory relief. In *Chase National Bank*, for example, a lender who had been granted a mortgage on certain leased property sued both the landlord and a tenant for a declaration that the lease between the two defendants was valid and enforceable. The Court held that because both the lender and the landlord were interested in having a lease be held enforceable, the landlord should be realigned as a plaintiff rather than a defendant. However, the landlord and the tenant were from the same state. Because the case no longer satisfied the complete diversity rule after the realignment of the landlord, the federal courts had no diversity jurisdiction.

Collusive joinder. Another powerful tool in the federal court's arsenal is § 1359, which provides that a federal court cannot exercise diversity jurisdiction over a case "in which any party, by assignment or otherwise, has been improperly or collusively ... joined to invoke the jurisdiction of such court." Most cases in which the court invokes § 1359 involve assignments of claims. If a party from state A makes a genuine assignment of her claim to a party from state B, the court will consider the citizenship of the assignee. However, if the assignment is a mere sham, the assignment will be ignored, and the court will use the assignor's citizenship. An example of a sham assignment is one where the price paid for the assignment is 95% of whatever assignee recovers when it sues on the obligation. *Kramer v. Caribbean Mills, Inc.*, 394 U.S. 823, 89 S.Ct. 1487, 23 L.Ed.2d 9 (1969).

Legal representatives. In some situations, a party is appointed to represent the rights of another. If the representation involves litigation, the action is brought in the name of the representative. Therefore, a party could create or destroy diversity by the simple expediency of appointing a legal representative who lives in a different state than the represented party. § 1332(c)(2) greatly curtails this "back door" way into federal court. Under that section, the legal representative of an infant, incompetent, and the estate of a decedent is treated as having the same citizenship as the represented party.

Insurance. § 1332(c)(1) contains a special rule that applies to insurance companies. If a plaintiff brings a direct action against an insurance company, the insurance company will be a citizen not only of its state of incorporation and principal place of business, but also a citizen of the insured's state(s) of domicile. Like the rule governing personal representatives discussed in the prior note, this provision makes it more difficult for the parties to get a dispute into federal court by a judicious choice of insurance company. Note that this provision only applies to liability insurance. Moreover, only a few states allow direct actions against insurance companies. In most states, plaintiffs sue the insured even though the case will actually be defended by—and any judgment paid by—the insurance company.

d. States

Both § 1332 and Article III of the Constitution speak in terms of citizens of a "State." However, the United States includes a number of regions that are not technically states, namely the District of Columbia, Puerto Rico, various federal territories, and federal protectorates. May citizens who are domiciled in these areas qualify for diversity jurisdiction? § 1332(e) explicitly addresses this question. It provides that the term "State" in § 1332 "includes the Territories, the District of Columbia, and the Commonwealth of Puerto Rico." Therefore, Congress clearly wants citizens of these areas to enjoy the benefits of diversity jurisdiction at the same level as citizens of the states.

Whether Congress has the authority to extend diversity to these parties, however, is another matter. After all, Article III also limits diversity jurisdiction to disputes between citizens of States. And the notion of a State is a term of art in the Constitution. If the territories, Puerto Rico, and the District are not "States" within the meaning of Article III, Congress has no authority to give the federal courts diversity jurisdiction in state-law suits involving these parties.

The Supreme Court considered the constitutionality of § 1332(e) in its 1949 decision in *National Mutual Insurance Co. v. Tidewater Transfer Co.*, 337 U.S. 582, 69 S.Ct. 1173, 93 L.Ed. 1556 (1949). Although the

Court upheld the statute, the decision was badly fractured, producing no majority vote. Two Justices concluded that the District of Columbia was a "State" for purposes of Article III. The remaining seven disagreed. Three other Justices concluded that Congress could give the federal courts jurisdiction over the dispute even if the District was not a state. The remaining six rejected this view. Nevertheless, because a total of five Justices voted that § 1332(e) was constitutional, the decision upheld the statute, even though a majority of the Justices rejected each of the two theories offered to sustain the statute.

e. Exceptions to Diversity Jurisdiction

Generally speaking, federal courts sitting in diversity may hear any claim regardless of the nature of the dispute. However, there are exceptions to this rule. The Supreme Court has held that cases involving certain issues fall outside of the diversity jurisdiction of the federal court. These exceptions fall within two broad categories, neither of which can be gleaned from the language of § 1332.

The first exception includes domestic relations and probate cases. Federal courts will not exercise diversity jurisdiction over the probate of a will. In addition, in *Ankenbrandt v. Richards*, 504 U.S. 689, 112 S.Ct. 2206, 119 L.Ed.2d 468 (1992), the Court reaffirmed older cases which held that federal courts may not exercise diversity jurisdiction over cases involving core issues of family law. However, this family law exception applies only to divorce, alimony, and child custody. Thus, although a federal court may not adjudicate a divorce, it may hear a breach of contract or a tort suit between spouses connected to a divorce proceeding, provided the other requirements of § 1332 are satisfied. The Court's rationale in *Ankenbrandt* turned in part on the fact that divorce, alimony, and child custody were historically matters that fell outside the authority of the English Chancery court. Therefore, when Congress granted the federal courts a similar chancery jurisdiction in the Judiciary Act of 1789, it did not intend for the federal courts to hear these cases. Although divorce, alimony, and child custody are now routinely heard in secular courts in the states, the Court noted that Congress had never acted to change § 1332 in a way that would extend federal jurisdiction to these matters.

The second exception to diversity jurisdiction involves situations where the federal courts must abstain from exercising jurisdiction. In rare cases, a federal court sitting in diversity may be required to abstain from a case in situations where the underlying state law is unclear and where there are important state interests at stake. See *Louisiana Power and Light Co. v. City of Thibodaux*, 360 U.S. 25, 79 S.Ct. 1070, 3 L.Ed.2d 1058 (1959); *Burford v. Sun Oil Co.*, 319 U.S. 315, 63 S.Ct. 1098, 87 L.Ed. 1424 (1943). Abstention is a complex topic that is far beyond the scope of an introductory Civil Procedure course. Note, however, that unlike the domestic relations/probate exception, abstention is a court-created doctrine, rather than an interpretation of § 1332.

Problems

1. P, a citizen of Michigan, sues D, a citizen of Wisconsin, for $100,000. P brings her case in state court. Does the state court have jurisdiction to hear the case?

2. P plans to sue D for $100,000 for medical malpractice. At the time of the medical procedure, P and D were citizens of Maryland. After the accident, however, P decided to move to Delaware. P has purchased a new home in Delaware, and a moving van is scheduled to come to P's home tomorrow to pack and move her belongings. If P files her action today, may she sue in federal court?

3. P sues D for $250,000 for breach of contract. When the action was commenced, P was a citizen of the District of Columbia, while D was a citizen of Idaho. The day after the action was commenced, however, P moved to Idaho and established a domicile in that state. D makes a timely request to dismiss the action for lack of subject-matter jurisdiction. How should the court rule?

4. P is a retired salesman. After retiring, P left his home in snowy North Dakota and established domicile in Costa Rica. However, P has kept his United States citizenship. When P fails to receive his commission check for sales he made during his last year on the job, he sues D, his boss, for $85,000. D is a citizen of North Dakota. May the action be heard in federal court?

5. Same as Problem 4, except that P gave up his United States citizenship and became a citizen of Costa Rica.

6. P, a citizen of Pennsylvania, files a products liability action against D Corp. in federal court. P seeks $150,000 in damages. D Corp. was chartered in the state of Delaware. D Corp. has large factories in Massachusetts, Tennessee, and Nevada. The corporate offices, from which all significant decisions are made, are located in Pennsylvania. However, other than the corporate offices, D Corp. has no facilities in Pennsylvania. Nor does D Corp. sell its product in Pennsylvania (P bought the product while on a business trip to New York). D Corp. files a timely request to have P's case dismissed for lack of subject-matter jurisdiction. How should the court rule?

7. Same as Problem 6, except that P does not sue D Corp., but instead brings a direct action against Umbrella Insurance Company, a corporation that has issued a liability insurance policy covering D Corp. Umbrella is a Utah corporation with its principal place of business in Texas. Umbrella files a timely request to have P's case dismissed for lack of subject-matter jurisdiction. How should the court rule?

8. Same as Problems 6 and 7, except that (i) P is a citizen of Texas, and (ii) P sues both D Corp. and Umbrella Insurance Company in a single action.

9. Lender sues Borrower for failure to make the final payment on a home loan. Lender is a citizen of Washington, and Borrower is a citizen of Alaska. Lender's complaint asks for the past-due payment ($70,000), $6,000 in interest accruing under the terms of the loan agreement prior to judg-

ment, and $5,500 in post-judgment interest, measured at the judgment rate. After being served with the complaint, Borrower files a counterclaim for $90,000. Borrower claims that because Lender violated federal lending laws by making incorrect disclosures in the loan application process, Lender must return to Borrower all interest payments that Borrower made under the loan. Lender then moves to dismiss the case for lack of subject matter jurisdiction. How should the court rule?

10. P, a citizen of Connecticut, sues D, a citizen of Florida, in federal court. P asserts two claims. In the main claim, P alleges that D owes him $70,000 for breach of contract. In the second count, P seeks $8,000 in damages for trespass, based upon the fact that D regularly walks his dog across a corner of the lot of P's Florida vacation home. The contract and trespass claims have nothing to do with each other. Moreover, no court in this state has ever awarded more than $150 in damages for a trespass claim involving someone walking across property. D files a timely request to dismiss the case for lack of subject-matter jurisdiction. How should the court rule?

11. P, a citizen of California, wants to sue D, a citizen of Georgia, for divorce. Because P and D are rich and famous celebrities, the court will be called upon to dispense with over ten million dollars worth of property. May P file the action in a federal court?

Exercise

Just as the federal statutes you have been studying define the types of cases a federal court can hear, there are state standards defining the various types of cases which can be heard by state courts. Typically, a state court of "general jurisdiction" can hear only cases involving a threshold amount of damages, or more. For example, a threshold amount for damages may be $5,000. The enabling statutes for state courts also describe categories of cases which are not heard by the courts of "general jurisdiction." For example, probate cases are commonly excepted from "general jurisdiction" cases.

For the state a) where you intend to practice after graduation, b) where your law school is located, and/or c) your professor assigns, go to that state's annotated statutes and research the standards defining how it is determined which courts hear which types of cases. Based on your research, print the rule and bring it to class for discussion. In addition, answer the following questions.

1. Identify the threshold amount of damages for a court of "general jurisdiction."

2. Identify whether there are certain types of cases recognized as exceptions to cases of "general jurisdiction."

D. SUPPLEMENTAL JURISDICTION

INTRODUCTORY PROBLEM

After he loses his life savings in a bad investment, Ian Investor decides to sue Brenda Broker, the person who recommended the investment. Ian would strongly prefer to sue in federal court. However, because Ian and Brenda are citizens of the same state, and because only state law affords Ian a remedy, Ian's case, standing by itself, would not qualify for either diversity or federal question jurisdiction. Ian comes to you, his attorney, to discuss his options.

During the conversation, Ian tells you about two friends of his who are also about to sue Brenda. Both of these soon-to-be plaintiffs made an investment similar to Ian's, relying on the exact same misleading representations by Brenda. Unlike Ian, however, these other plaintiffs can file in federal court. The first plaintiff, Irene, is of diverse citizenship from Brenda, and has a claim in excess of $75,000. The second, Isaak, can rely on federal question jurisdiction. Because Brenda made the representation to Isaak by mail, rather than face-to-face as in the case of Ian and Irene, Isaak has a cause of action under the federal mail fraud provisions.

Ian asks whether he might be able to get his dispute into federal court by "piggybacking" on either Irene's or Izaak's case. The cases are, after all, very closely related. Irene and Isaak have each told Ian that they are willing to have him as a co-plaintiff in their cases. Your quick review of Rule 20 assures you that Ian could join with either plaintiff. If Ian joins with either Irene or Izaak, may he bring his case in federal court?

Ian also has one other concern. Brenda told Izaak that if anyone were to sue her, she would immediately file a counterclaim for any unpaid brokerage fees. Ian owes Brenda $9,000 in brokerage fees. Ian asks you whether the federal court would be able to hear a state-law counterclaim against him.

What will you tell Ian?

Governing law: 28 U.S.C. §§ 1331, 1332, and 1367.

One of the cardinal rules of federal subject-matter jurisdiction is that a federal court must have jurisdiction over every claim presented to it as part of a single case. Therefore, what may have seemed the easy answer to the preceding problem will not work. The court would not have jurisdiction over Ian's claim—or Brenda's counterclaims—merely because they were part of Irene's or Izaak's proper diversity or federal question action. Instead, the court would have to dismiss Ian's and

Brenda's claims unless they could demonstrate a source of federal jurisdiction.

To this point, we have considered only two bases for federal jurisdiction, federal question and diversity. When determining whether federal question jurisdiction exists, courts analyze each claim separately to see if the claimant is asserting rights under federal law. In diversity cases, the complete diversity rule requires that no plaintiff can be from the same state as any defendant. Therefore, aside from the aggregation rules in diversity, neither § 1331 nor § 1332 allows a party to piggyback claims that do not qualify for federal jurisdiction with those that do qualify.

This section introduces a third source of federal subject-matter jurisdiction, called "supplemental" jurisdiction. The name is actually quite informative. Supplemental jurisdiction supplements federal question and diversity jurisdiction. In order for supplemental jurisdiction to work, there must be at least one claim by one plaintiff that independently qualifies for federal question or diversity jurisdiction. If such a claim exists, the court may be able to use supplemental jurisdiction to hear other claims in the case that do not by themselves qualify for federal subject-matter jurisdiction. Supplemental jurisdiction will never be the sole basis for jurisdiction in the case; instead, it always works in conjunction with one of the other forms.

If left unchecked, supplemental jurisdiction could undermine the limitations on federal question and diversity jurisdiction that you learned in the prior sections. For example, in the Introductory Problem, allowing Ian to use supplemental jurisdiction to join with Irene would contradict the complete diversity rule. As you will see, Congress has placed important limits on the use of supplemental jurisdiction in order to preserve some of the limits on federal question and diversity jurisdiction.

1. Theoretical Bases for Supplemental Jurisdiction

UNITED MINE WORKERS v. GIBBS

383 U.S. 715, 86 S.Ct. 1130, 16 L.Ed.2d 218 (1966)

Justice BRENNAN delivered the opinion of the Court.

Respondent Paul Gibbs was awarded compensatory and punitive damages in this action against petitioner United Mine Workers of America (UMW) for alleged violations of § 303 of the Labor Management Relations Act, 1947, as amended, and of the common law of Tennessee. The case grew out of the rivalry between the United Mine Workers and the Southern Labor Union over representation of workers in the southern Appalachian coal fields. Tennessee Consolidated Coal Company, not a party here, laid off 100 miners of the UMW's Local 5881 when it closed one of its mines in southern Tennessee during the spring of 1960. Late that summer, Grundy Company, a wholly owned subsidiary of Consolidated, hired respondent as mine superintendent to attempt to open a new mine on Consolidated's property at nearby Gray's Creek through use of members of the Southern Labor Union. As part of the arrangement, Grundy also gave respondent a contract to haul the mine's coal to the nearest railroad loading point.

On August 15 and 16, 1960, armed members of Local 5881 forcibly prevented the opening of the mine, threatening respondent and beating an organizer for the rival union. The members of the local believed Consolidated had promised them the jobs at the new mine; they insisted that if anyone would do the work, they would. * * * There was no further violence at the mine site; a picket line was maintained there for nine months; and no further attempts were made to open the mine during that period.

Respondent lost his job as superintendent, and never entered into performance of his haulage contract. He testified that he soon began to lose other trucking contracts and mine leases he held in nearby areas. Claiming these effects to be the result of a concerted union plan against him, he sought recovery not against Local 5881 or its members, but only against petitioner, the international union. The suit was brought in the United States District Court for the Eastern District of Tennessee, and jurisdiction was premised on allegations of secondary boycotts* under § 303. The state law claim, for which jurisdiction was based upon the doctrine of pendent jurisdiction, asserted 'an unlawful conspiracy and an unlawful boycott aimed at him and (Grundy) to maliciously, wantonly and willfully interfere with his contract of employment and with his contract of haulage.' * * *

The jury's verdict was that the UMW had violated both § 303 and state law. * * * On motion, the trial court set aside the award of damages with respect to the haulage contract on the ground that damage was unproved. It also held that union pressure on Grundy to discharge respondent as supervisor would constitute only a primary dispute with Grundy, as respondent's employer, and hence was not cognizable as a claim under § 303. Interference with the employment relationship was cognizable as a state claim, however, and a remitted award was sustained on the state law claim. The Court of Appeals for the Sixth Circuit affirmed. We granted certiorari. We reverse.

A threshold question is whether the District Court properly entertained jurisdiction of the claim based on Tennessee law. * * *

The Court held in *Hurn v. Oursler*, 289 U.S. 238, that state law claims are appropriate for federal court determination if they form a separate but parallel ground for relief also sought in a substantial claim based on federal law. The Court distinguished permissible from nonpermissible exercises of federal judicial power over state law claims by contrasting 'a case where two distinct grounds in support of a single

---

* A "secondary boycott" occurs when a union with a labor dispute with Employer X pickets, refuses to work for, or otherwise deal with Employer Y, in an attempt to convince Y to quit dealing with X. Secondary boycotts are illegal under federal labor law. [Eds.]

cause of action are alleged, one only of which presents a federal question, and a case where two separate and distinct causes of action are alleged, one only of which is federal in character. In the former, where the federal question averred is not plainly wanting in substance, the federal court, even though the federal ground be not established, may nevertheless retain and dispose of the case upon the nonfederal ground; in the latter it may not do so upon the nonfederal cause of action.' The question is into which category the present action fell.

Hurn was decided in 1933, before the unification of law and equity by the Federal Rules of Civil Procedure. At the time, the meaning of 'cause of action' was a subject of serious dispute; the phrase might 'mean one thing for one purpose and something different for another.' *United States v. Memphis Cotton Oil Co.*, 288 U.S. 62, 67–68. The Court in *Hurn* identified what it meant by the term by citation of *Baltimore S.S. Co. v. Phillips*, 274 U.S. 316, a case in which 'cause of action' had been used to identify the operative scope of the doctrine of res judicata. In that case the Court had noted that "the whole tendency of our decisions is to require a plaintiff to try his whole cause of action and his whole case at one time," 274 U.S., at 320. It stated its holding in the following language, quoted in part in the *Hurn* opinion:

> A cause of action does not consist of facts, but of the unlawful violation of a right which the facts show. The number and variety of the facts alleged do not establish more than one cause of action so long as their result, whether they be considered severally or in combination, is the violation of but one right by a single legal wrong. The mere multiplication of grounds of negligence alleged as causing the same injury does not result in multiplying the causes of action. "The facts are merely the means, and not the end. They do not constitute the cause of action, but they show its existence by making the wrong appear."

Id., at 321.

With the adoption of the Federal Rules of Civil Procedure and the unified form of action, Fed.Rule Civ.Proc. 2, much of the controversy over "cause of action" abated. * * * Under the Rules, the impulse is toward entertaining the broadest possible scope of action consistent with fairness to the parties; joinder of claims, parties and remedies is strongly encouraged. Yet because the *Hurn* question involves issues of jurisdiction as well as convenience, there has been some tendency to limit its application to cases in which the state and federal claims are, as in *Hurn*, "little more than the equivalent of different epithets to characterize the same group of circumstances." 289 U.S., at 246.

This limited approach is unnecessarily grudging. Pendent jurisdiction, in the sense of judicial power, exists whenever there is a claim 'arising under (the) Constitution, the Laws of the United States, and Treaties made, or which shall be made, under their Authority * * *,' U.S.Const., Art. III, § 2, and the relationship between that claim and the state claim permits the conclusion that the entire action before the court comprises but one constitutional 'case.' The federal claim must have substance sufficient to confer subject matter jurisdiction on the court. The state and federal claims must derive from a common nucleus of operative fact. But if, considered without regard to their federal or state character, a plaintiff's claims are such that he would ordinarily be expected to try them all in one judicial proceeding, then, assuming substantiality of the federal issues, there is power in federal courts to hear the whole.

That power need not be exercised in every case in which it is found to exist. It has consistently been recognized that pendent jurisdiction is a doctrine of discretion, not of plaintiff's right. Its justification lies in considerations of judicial economy, convenience and fairness to litigants; if these are not present a federal court should hesitate to exercise jurisdiction over state claims. * * * Needless decisions of state law should be avoided both as a matter of comity and to promote justice between the parties, by procuring for them a surer-footed reading of applicable law. Certainly, if the federal claims are dismissed before trial, even though not insubstantial in a jurisdictional sense, the state claims should be dismissed as well. Similarly, if it appears that the state issues substantially predominate, whether in terms of proof, of the scope of the issues raised, or of the comprehensiveness of the remedy sought, the state claims may be dismissed without prejudice and left for resolution to state tribunals. There may, on the other hand, be situations in which the state claim is so closely tied to questions of federal policy that the argument for exercise of pendent jurisdiction is particularly strong. In the present case, for example, the allowable scope of the state claim implicates the federal doctrine of pre-emption; while this interrelationship does not create statutory federal question jurisdiction, its existence is relevant to the exercise of discretion. Finally, there may be reasons independent of jurisdictional considerations, such as the likelihood of jury confusion in treating divergent legal theories of relief, that would justify separating state and federal claims for trial. If so, jurisdiction should ordinarily be refused.

The question of power will ordinarily be resolved on the pleadings. But the issue whether pendent jurisdiction has been properly assumed is one which remains open throughout the litigation. Pretrial procedures or even the trial itself may reveal a substantial hegemony of state law claims, or likelihood of jury confusion, which could not have been anticipated at the pleading stage. * * * Once it appears that a state claim constitutes the real body of a case, to which the federal claim is only an appendage, the state claim may fairly be dismissed.

We are not prepared to say that in the present case the District Court exceeded its discretion in proceeding to judgment on the state claim. We may assume for purposes of decision that the District Court was correct in its holding that the claim of pressure on Grundy to terminate the employment contract was outside the purview of § 303. Even so, the § 303 claims based on secondary pressures on Grundy relative to the haulage contract and on other coal operators generally were substantial. * * *

It is true that the § 303 claims ultimately failed and that the only recovery allowed respondent was on the state claim. We cannot confidently say, however, that the federal issues were so remote or played such a minor role at the trial that in effect the state claim only was tried. * * * The jury returned verdicts against petitioner on those § 303 claims, and it was only on petitioner's motion for a directed verdict and a judgment n.o.v. that the verdicts on those claims were set aside. * * * Moreover, the question whether the permissible scope of the state claim was limited by the doctrine of pre-emption afforded a special reason for the exercise of pendent jurisdiction; the federal courts are particularly appropriate bodies for the application of pre-emption principles. We thus conclude that although it may be that the District Court might, in its sound discretion, have dismissed the state claim, the circumstances show no error in refusing to do so.

[The Court then reversed the lower court's decision on the merits.]

Notes and Questions

1. *Terminology*. The title of this section is "supplemental jurisdiction." But the Court in *Gibbs* never uses that term, speaking instead in terms of "pendent" jurisdiction. Other cases dealt with what was called "ancillary" jurisdiction. Although there were important differences between pendent and ancillary jurisdiction, those differences are of little more than historical interest. As you will see in the next subsection, Congress eventually passed a statute that merged both pendent and ancillary jurisdiction into a concept called supplemental jurisdiction.

2. At one level, the Court's decision in *Gibbs* is fairly straightforward. Earlier Supreme Court decisions allowed a federal court to hear state-law claims between non-diverse parties as long as there was a sufficient connection between those claims and claims arising under federal law. *Gibbs* simply changes the test for how close the connection must be between the claims. Under *Hurn*, the test was whether the claimant was for all practical purposes required to try them together. If the non-federal claims would be barred by claim preclusion if not raised, then it certainly makes sense that the federal court should be able to hear all the claims in a single proceeding. *Gibbs*'s "common nucleus of operative fact" test, by contrast, asks whether a party would ordinarily be expected to join the claims, even if the claims would not be lost if omitted. This test turns more on considerations of efficiency than it does on claim preclusion.

3. Beneath that veneer of simplicity lie some complex and difficult issues. Federal subject-matter jurisdiction involves much more than efficiency. As noted in the Introduction to this chapter, federal jurisdiction is kept in check in order to preserve the role of the state judiciaries. The limits on federal subject-matter jurisdiction arise from both the United States Constitution and federal statute law. Is *Gibbs* ignoring these limitations when it concludes that a federal court should be able to exercise jurisdiction over a

claim that does not by itself qualify for federal question or diversity jurisdiction? How can "considerations of judicial economy, convenience, and fairness to litigants," which the Court says are the justifications for pendent jurisdiction, override the clear provisions in the Constitution and federal law?

4. *Gibbs* does deal with the Constitution. How does the Court conclude that pendent jurisdiction is consistent with Article III? Compare the Court's brief discussion of Article III with the actual terminology of Article III, § 2. The issue in *Gibbs* is whether the court can exercise jurisdiction over a claim. Notice that Article III does not speak in terms of "claims," but instead gives the federal courts jurisdiction over "cases" and "controversies." According to Gibbs, what is the difference between a claim and a case or controversy?

Incidentally, there is a difference between the terms "case" and "controversy" in Article III. A case includes both civil and criminal matters. A controversy is a civil dispute. Article III allows the federal courts to exercise jurisdiction over "all cases" arising under federal law, but only controversies involving diverse citizens, or states and the citizens of another state. One practical implication of this difference is that while federal courts may hear criminal prosecutions involving violations of federal law, they may not hear criminal cases brought by a state against a citizen of another state or a foreigner.

2. The Supplemental Jurisdiction Statute

Pendent and ancillary jurisdiction evolved in the federal courts, in cases like *Gibbs* and *Hurn v. Ousler*. As a result, there was a sort of tension between pendent and ancillary jurisdiction and the federal statutes allocating jurisdiction to the federal courts, which made no mention of this expanded jurisdiction. However, the long history of pendent and ancillary jurisdiction helped to validate it. After all, if Congress did not approve of the doctrines, it could always enact legislation to abolish it.

Congress eventually *did* act—not to overturn the doctrine established in *Gibbs* and the other cases, but expressly to authorize it. In 1990, Congress enacted 28 U.S.C. § 1367, which creates a form of jurisdiction called "supplemental" jurisdiction.*

One of Congress's main goals in enacting § 1367 was to unify and simplify the courts' jurisdiction over pendent and ancillary claims. However, Congress also hoped to clean up the law by rejecting some of the limits and distinctions adopted over the years by the courts. Unfortunately, the statute as written is not a model of clarity. Although § 1367 does get rid of some of the problems that arose in the case law, it creates other new problems that the courts are still struggling to resolve.

---

* Note that § 1367 is not the only source of "supplemental" jurisdiction. § 1338(b), which gives the federal courts jurisdiction over state-law unfair competition claims brought in connection with claims under federal intellectual property law, is another example. Moreover, although §§ 1367 and 1338(b) apply only to the federal district courts, the statutes governing appellate court and Supreme Court jurisdiction give those courts the power to hear the entire case being appealed, including not only the federal claims but also the state claims.

The most obvious change that § 1367 makes is in terminology. § 1367 substitutes the single term "supplemental" for both of the older terms "ancillary" and "pendent." More importantly, the statute also abolishes the analytical distinctions that used to exist between pendent and ancillary jurisdiction. Now, a case is dealt with the same way under § 1367 regardless of whether it historically would have been considered a case of pendent or ancillary—or "pendent party," yet another variation—jurisdiction.

Section 1367 establishes a two-part test for supplemental jurisdiction. First, the court applies § 1367(a). This section asks whether the claim in question (that is, the claim that could not be heard by a federal court on its own), and another claim in the case that the federal court can hear, "form part of the same case or controversy under Article III of the United States Constitution." In determining whether the two claims form part of the same Article III case, most courts use *Gibbs*'s "common nucleus of operative fact" test. The Court in *Gibbs* used that test in explaining how supplemental jurisdiction fit within the jurisdiction that Article III allows federal courts to exercise.

The second part of the analysis asks whether the case falls into one of the exceptions listed in § 1367(b) and (c). Although these two subsections are both exceptions, they are very different in nature. § 1367(b) is an issue of power. If a claim is barred by that subsection, a federal court cannot hear it, no matter how efficient it would be to hear the claims in one case. § 1367(c), by contrast, reflects the discussion of discretion in *Gibbs*. If the court determines that the state-law claim is the heart and soul of the case, for example, the federal court may refuse to hear the state-law claim. Note that although some of the factors listed in § 1367(c) match those discussed in *Gibbs*, the statute also brings in new factors to consider. Take a moment to review the statute, identifying which of the § 1367(c) factors are mentioned in *Gibbs* and which were added by Congress.

Section 1367(b) often proves exceptionally difficult to students dealing with it for the first time. Admittedly, the provision is worded in a very technical fashion. However, if you are careful and work through it mechanically, the provision is relatively straightforward. As a bit of advice, you should fight the temptation to fashion broad rules to paraphrase that section—the number of tricky permutations make that approach dangerous. Basically, § 1367(b) uses a three-step analysis to determine if a claim is barred. First, § 1367(b) precludes supplemental jurisdiction only if the *sole* basis for federal jurisdiction over the original claim is § 1332 diversity jurisdiction. If the related federal claim is a federal question, § 1367(b) simply does not apply. Second, the claim in question must be a claim by a plaintiff. Ordinarily, this will be relatively obvious. But you will see that even this issue can be tricky. Third, the claim must be brought against a party joined under the listed rules. Part of the confusion that has arisen in applying § 1367 is that the rules listed do not exhaust all of the joinder provisions in the Federal Rules. The following case illustrates the ambiguity.

EXXON MOBIL CORP. v. ALLAPATTAH SERVICES, INC.

—— U.S. ——, 125 S.Ct. 2611, 162 L.Ed.2d 502 (2005)

JUSTICE KENNEDY delivered the opinion of the Court.

These consolidated cases present the question whether a federal court in a diversity action may exercise supplemental jurisdiction over additional plaintiffs whose claims do not satisfy the minimum amount-in-controversy requirement, provided the claims are part of the same case or controversy as the claims of plaintiffs who do allege a sufficient amount in controversy. Our decision turns on the correct interpretation of 28 U.S.C. § 1367. The question has divided the Courts of Appeals, and we granted certiorari to resolve the conflict.

We hold that, where the other elements of jurisdiction are present and at least one named plaintiff in the action satisfies the amount-in-controversy requirement, § 1367 does authorize supplemental jurisdiction over the claims of other plaintiffs in the same Article III case or controversy, even if those claims are for less than the jurisdictional amount specified in the statute setting forth the requirements for diversity jurisdiction. We affirm the judgment of the Court of Appeals for the Eleventh Circuit in No. 04–70, and we reverse the judgment of the Court of Appeals for the First Circuit in No. 04–79.

I

In 1991, about 10,000 Exxon dealers filed a class-action suit against the Exxon Corporation in the United States District Court for the Northern District of Florida. The dealers alleged an intentional and systematic scheme by Exxon under which they were overcharged for fuel purchased from Exxon. The plaintiffs invoked the District Court's § 1332(a) diversity jurisdiction. After a unanimous jury verdict in favor of the plaintiffs, the District Court certified the case for interlocutory review, asking whether it had properly exercised § 1367 supplemental jurisdiction over the claims of class members who did not meet the jurisdictional minimum amount in controversy.

The Court of Appeals for the Eleventh Circuit upheld the District Court's extension of supplemental jurisdiction to these class members. * * * This decision accords with the views of the Courts of Appeals for the Fourth, Sixth, and Seventh Circuits. See *Rosmer* v. *Pfizer, Inc.*, 263 F.3d 110 (CA4 2001); *Olden* v. *LaFarge Corp.*, 383 F.3d 495 (CA6 2004); *Stromberg Metal Works, Inc.* v. *Press Mechanical, Inc.*, 77 F.3d 928 (CA7 1996); *In re Brand Name Prescription Drugs Antitrust Litigation*, 123 F.3d 599 (CA7 1997). The Courts of Appeals for the Fifth and Ninth Circuits, adopting a similar analysis of the statute, have held that in a diversity class action the unnamed class members need not meet the amount-in-controversy requirement, provided the named class members do. These decisions, however, are unclear on whether all the named plaintiffs must satisfy this requirement. *In re Abbott Labs.*, 51 F.3d 524 (CA5 1995); *Gibson* v. *Chrysler Corp.*, 261 F.3d 927 (CA9 2001).

In the other case now before us the Court of Appeals for the First Circuit took a different position on the meaning of § 1367(a). In that case, a 9–year-old girl sued Star–Kist in a diversity action in the United States District Court for the District of Puerto Rico, seeking damages for unusually severe injuries she received when she sliced her finger on a tuna can. Her family joined in the suit, seeking damages for emotional distress and certain medical expenses. The District Court granted summary judgment to Star–Kist, finding that none of the plaintiffs met the minimum amount-in-controversy requirement. The Court of Appeals for the First Circuit, however, ruled that the injured girl, but not her family members, had made allegations of damages in the requisite amount.

The Court of Appeals then addressed whether, in light of the fact that one plaintiff met the requirements for original jurisdiction, supplemental jurisdiction over the remaining plaintiffs' claims was proper under § 1367. The court held that § 1367 authorizes supplemental jurisdiction only when the district court has original jurisdiction over the action, and that in a diversity case original jurisdiction is lacking if one plaintiff fails to satisfy the amount-in-controversy requirement. * * * The Court of Appeals for the First Circuit's view of § 1367 is, however, shared by the Courts of Appeal for the Third, Eighth, and Tenth Circuits, and the latter two Courts of Appeals have expressly applied this rule to class actions. See *Meritcare Inc.* v. *St. Paul Mercury Ins. Co.*, 166 F.3d 214 (CA3 1999); *Trimble* v. *Asarco, Inc.*, 232 F.3d 946 (CA8 2000); *Leonhardt* v. *Western Sugar Co.*, 160 F.3d 631 (CA10 1998).

II

* * * The complete diversity requirement is not mandated by the Constitution, or by the plain text of § 1332(a). The Court, nonetheless, has adhered to the complete diversity rule in light of the purpose of the diversity requirement, which is to provide a federal forum for important disputes where state courts might favor, or be perceived as favoring, home-state litigants. The presence of parties from the same State on both sides of a case dispels this concern, eliminating a principal reason for conferring § 1332 jurisdiction over any of the claims in the action. The specific purpose of the complete diversity rule explains both why we have not adopted [*United Mine Workers* v.] *Gibbs*' expansive interpretive approach to this aspect of the jurisdictional statute and why *Gibbs* does not undermine the complete diversity rule. In order for a federal court to invoke supplemental jurisdiction under *Gibbs*, it must first have original jurisdiction over at least one claim in the action. Incomplete diversity destroys original jurisdiction with respect to all claims, so there is nothing to which supplemental jurisdiction can adhere.

In contrast to the diversity requirement, most of the other statutory prerequisites for federal jurisdiction, including the federal-question and amount-in-controversy requirements, can be analyzed claim by claim.

True, it does not follow by necessity from this that a district court has authority to exercise supplemental jurisdiction over all claims provided there is original jurisdiction over just one. Before the enactment of § 1367, the Court declined in contexts other than the pendent-claim instance to follow *Gibbs'* expansive approach to interpretation of the jurisdictional statutes. * * *

Thus, with respect to plaintiff-specific jurisdictional requirements, the Court held in *Clark* v. *Paul Gray, Inc.*, 306 U.S. 583 (1939), that every plaintiff must separately satisfy the amount-in-controversy requirement. Though *Clark* was a federal-question case, at that time federal-question jurisdiction had an amount-in-controversy requirement analogous to the amount-in-controversy requirement for diversity cases. "Proper practice," *Clark* held, "requires that where each of several plaintiffs is bound to establish the jurisdictional amount with respect to his own claim, the suit should be dismissed as to those who fail to show that the requisite amount is involved." *Id.*, at 590. The Court reaffirmed this rule, in the context of a class action brought invoking § 1332(a) diversity jurisdiction, in *Zahn* v. *International Paper Co.*, 414 U.S. 291 (1973). * * *

As the jurisdictional statutes existed in 1989, then, here is how matters stood: First, the diversity requirement in § 1332(a) required complete diversity; absent complete diversity, the district court lacked original jurisdiction over all of the claims in the action. Second, if the district court had original jurisdiction over at least one claim, the jurisdictional statutes implicitly authorized supplemental jurisdiction over all other claims between the same parties arising out of the same Article III case or controversy. Third, even when the district court had original jurisdiction over one or more claims between particular parties, the jurisdictional statutes did not authorize supplemental jurisdiction over additional claims involving other parties. * * *

§ 1367(a) is a broad grant of supplemental jurisdiction over other claims within the same case or controversy, as long as the action is one in which the district courts would have original jurisdiction. The last sentence of § 1367(a) makes it clear that the grant of supplemental jurisdiction extends to claims involving joinder or intervention of additional parties. The single question before us, therefore, is whether a diversity case in which the claims of some plaintiffs satisfy the amount-in-controversy requirement, but the claims of others plaintiffs do not, presents a "civil action of which the district courts have original jurisdiction." If the answer is yes, § 1367(a) confers supplemental jurisdiction over all claims, including those that do not independently satisfy the amount-in-controversy requirement, if the claims are part of the same Article III case or controversy. If the answer is no, § 1367(a) is inapplicable and, in light of our holdings in *Clark* and *Zahn*, the district court has no statutory basis for exercising supplemental jurisdiction over the additional claims.

We now conclude the answer must be yes. When the well-pleaded complaint contains at least one claim that satisfies the amount-in-controversy requirement, and there are no other relevant jurisdictional defects, the district court, beyond all question, has original jurisdiction over that claim. The presence of other claims in the complaint, over which the district court may lack original jurisdiction, is of no moment. If the court has original jurisdiction over a single claim in the complaint, it has original jurisdiction over a "civil action" within the meaning of § 1367(a), even if the civil action over which it has jurisdiction comprises fewer claims than were included in the complaint. Once the court determines it has original jurisdiction over the civil action, it can turn to the question whether it has a constitutional and statutory basis for exercising supplemental jurisdiction over the other claims in the action. * * *

If § 1367(a) were the sum total of the relevant statutory language, our holding would rest on that language alone. The statute, of course, instructs us to examine § 1367(b) to determine if any of its exceptions apply, so we proceed to that section. While § 1367(b) qualifies the broad rule of § 1367(a), it does not withdraw supplemental jurisdiction over the claims of the additional parties at issue here. The specific exceptions to § 1367(a) contained in § 1367(b), moreover, provide additional support for our conclusion that § 1367(a) confers supplemental jurisdiction over these claims. § 1367(b), which applies only to diversity cases, withholds supplemental jurisdiction over the claims of plaintiffs proposed to be joined as indispensable parties under Federal Rule of Civil Procedure 19, or who seek to intervene pursuant to Rule 24. Nothing in the text of § 1367(b), however, withholds supplemental jurisdiction over the claims of plaintiffs permissively joined under Rule 20 (like the additional plaintiffs in No. 04–79) or certified as class-action members pursuant to Rule 23 (like the additional plaintiffs in No. 04–70). The natural, indeed the necessary, inference is that § 1367 confers supplemental jurisdiction over claims by Rule 20 and Rule 23 plaintiffs. This inference, at least with respect to Rule 20 plaintiffs, is strengthened by the fact that § 1367(b) explicitly excludes supplemental jurisdiction over claims against defendants joined under Rule 20.

We cannot accept the view, urged by some of the parties, commentators, and Courts of Appeals, that a district court lacks original jurisdiction over a civil action unless the court has original jurisdiction over every claim in the complaint. As we understand this position, it requires assuming either that all claims in the complaint must stand or fall as a single, indivisible "civil action" as a matter of definitional necessity— what we will refer to as the "indivisibility theory"—or else that the inclusion of a claim or party falling outside the district court's original jurisdiction somehow contaminates every other claim in the complaint, depriving the court of original jurisdiction over any of these claims–what we will refer to as the "contamination theory."

The indivisibility theory is easily dismissed, as it is inconsistent with the whole notion of supplemental jurisdiction. If a district court must have original jurisdiction over every claim in the complaint in order to have "original jurisdiction" over a "civil action," then in *Gibbs* there was no civil action of which the district court could assume original jurisdiction under § 1331, and so no basis for exercising supplemental jurisdiction over any of the claims. * * *

The contamination theory, as we have noted, can make some sense in the special context of the complete diversity requirement because the presence of nondiverse parties on both sides of a lawsuit eliminates the justification for providing a federal forum. The theory, however, makes little sense with respect to the amount-in-controversy requirement, which is meant to ensure that a dispute is sufficiently important to warrant federal-court attention. The presence of a single nondiverse party may eliminate the fear of bias with respect to all claims, but the presence of a claim that falls short of the minimum amount in controversy does nothing to reduce the importance of the claims that do meet this requirement.

It is fallacious to suppose, simply from the proposition that § 1332 imposes both the diversity requirement and the amount-in-controversy requirement, that the contamination theory germane to the former is also relevant to the latter. There is no inherent logical connection between the amount-in-controversy requirement and § 1332 diversity jurisdiction. After all, federal-question jurisdiction once had an amount-in-controversy requirement as well. If such a requirement were revived under § 1331, it is clear beyond peradventure that § 1367(a) provides supplemental jurisdiction over federal-question cases where some, but not all, of the federal-law claims involve a sufficient amount in controversy. In other words, § 1367(a) unambiguously overrules the holding and the result in *Clark*. If that is so, however, it would be quite extraordinary to say that § 1367 did not also overrule *Zahn*, a case that was premised in substantial part on the holding in *Clark*. * * *

It follows from this conclusion that the threshold requirement of § 1367(a) is satisfied in cases, like those now before us, where some, but not all, of the plaintiffs in a diversity action allege a sufficient amount in controversy. We hold that § 1367 by its plain text overruled *Clark* and *Zahn* and authorized supplemental jurisdiction over all claims by diverse parties arising out of the same Article III case or controversy, subject only to enumerated exceptions not applicable in the cases now before us.

The proponents of the alternative view of § 1367 insist that the statute is at least ambiguous and that we should look to other interpretive tools, including the legislative history of § 1367, which supposedly demonstrate Congress did not intend § 1367 to overrule *Zahn*. We can reject this argument at the very outset simply because § 1367 is not ambiguous. For the reasons elaborated above, interpreting § 1367 to foreclose supplemental jurisdiction over plaintiffs in diversity cases who do not meet the minimum amount in controversy is inconsistent with the text, read in light of other statutory provisions and our established jurisprudence. Even if we were to stipulate, however, that the reading these proponents urge upon us is textually plausible, the legislative history cited to support it would not alter our view as to the best interpretation of § 1367. [Discussion of legislative history omitted.] * * *

The judgment of the Court of Appeals for the Eleventh Circuit is affirmed. The judgment of the Court of Appeals for the First Circuit is reversed, and the case is remanded for proceedings consistent with this opinion.

JUSTICE STEVENS, with whom JUSTICE BREYER joins, dissenting.

JUSTICE GINSBURG's carefully reasoned opinion demonstrates the error in the Court's rather ambitious reading of this opaque jurisdictional statute. She also has demonstrated that "ambiguity" is a term that may have different meanings for different judges, for the Court has made the remarkable declaration that its reading of the statute is so obviously correct—and Justice Ginsburg's so obviously wrong—that the text does not even qualify as "ambiguous." Because ambiguity is apparently in the eye of the beholder, I remain convinced that it is unwise to treat the ambiguity *vel non* of a statute as determinative of whether legislative history is consulted. Indeed, I believe that we as judges are more, rather than less, constrained when we make ourselves accountable to *all* reliable evidence of legislative intent. * * *

JUSTICE GINSBURG, with whom JUSTICE STEVENS, JUSTICE O'CONNOR, and JUSTICE BREYER join, dissenting.

* * * The Court adopts a plausibly broad reading of § 1367, a measure that is hardly a model of the careful drafter's art. There is another plausible reading, however, one less disruptive of our jurisprudence regarding supplemental jurisdiction. If one reads § 1367(a) to instruct, as the statute's text suggests, that the district court must first have "original jurisdiction" over a "civil action" before supplemental jurisdiction can attach, then *Clark* and *Zahn* are preserved, and supplemental jurisdiction does not open the way for joinder of plaintiffs, or inclusion of class members, who do not independently meet the amount-in-controversy requirement. For the reasons that follow, I conclude that this narrower construction is the better reading of § 1367. * * *

II

§ 1367, by its terms, operates only in civil actions "of which the district courts have original jurisdiction." The "original jurisdiction" relevant here is diversity-of-citizenship jurisdiction, conferred by § 1332. The character of that jurisdiction is the essential backdrop for comprehension of § 1367.

The Constitution broadly provides for federal-court jurisdiction in controversies "between Citizens of different States." Art. III, § 2, cl. 1. This Court has read that provision to demand no more than "minimal diversity," *i.e.*, so long as one party on the plaintiffs' side and one party on the defendants' side are of diverse citizenship, Congress may authorize federal courts to exercise diversity jurisdiction. Further, the Constitution includes no amount-in-controversy limitation on the exercise of federal jurisdiction. But from the start, Congress, as its measures have been construed by this Court, has limited federal court exercise of diversity jurisdiction in two principal ways. First, unless Congress specifies otherwise, diversity must be "complete," *i.e.*, all parties on plaintiffs' side must be diverse from all parties on defendants' side. Second, each plaintiff's stake must independently meet the amount-in-controversy specification * * *.

The statute today governing federal court exercise of diversity jurisdiction in the generality of cases, § 1332, like all its predecessors, incorporates both a diverse-citizenship requirement and an amount-in-controversy requirement.[5] This Court has long held that, in determining whether the amount-in-controversy requirement has been satisfied, a single plaintiff may aggregate two or more claims against a single defendant, even if the claims are unrelated. But in multiparty cases, including class actions, we have unyieldingly adhered to the nonaggregation rule stated in *Troy Bank* [*v. G.A. Whitehead & Co.*, 222 U.S. 39 (1911)]. See *Clark*, 306 U.S., at 589 (reaffirming the "familiar rule that when several plaintiffs assert separate and distinct demands in a single suit, the amount involved in each separate controversy must be of the requisite amount to be within the jurisdiction of the district court, and that those amounts cannot be added together to satisfy jurisdictional requirements") * * *.

These cases present the question whether Congress abrogated the nonaggregation rule long tied to § 1332 when it enacted § 1367. In answering that question, "context [should provide] a crucial guide." *Rosario Ortega* v. *Star-Kist Foods, Inc.*, 370 F.3d 124, 135 (2004). The Court should assume, as it ordinarily does, that Congress legislated against a background of law already in place and the historical development of that law. Here, that background is the statutory grant of diversity jurisdiction, the amount-in-controversy condition that Congress, from the start, has tied to the grant, and the nonaggregation rule this Court has long applied to the determination of the "matter in controversy." * * *

As explained by the First Circuit in *Ortega*, and applied to class actions by the Tenth Circuit in *Leonhardt*, § 1367(a) addresses "civil

---

5. Endeavoring to preserve the "complete diversity" rule first stated in *Strawbridge* v. *Curtiss*, 7 U.S. 267 (1806), the Court's opinion drives a wedge between the two components of 28 U.S.C. § 1332, treating the diversity-of-citizenship requirement as essential, the amount-in-controversy requirement as more readily disposable. § 1332 itself, however, does not rank order the two requirements. What "ordinary principle of statutory construction" or "sound canon of interpretation," allows the Court to slice up § 1332 this way? In partial explanation, the Court asserts that amount in controversy can be analyzed claim-by-claim, but the diversity requirement cannot. It is not altogether clear why that should be so. The cure for improper joinder of a nondiverse party is the same as the cure for improper joinder of a plaintiff who does not satisfy the jurisdictional amount. In both cases, original jurisdiction can be preserved by dismissing the nonqualifying party.

actions of which the district courts have original jurisdiction," a formulation that, in diversity cases, is sensibly read to incorporate the rules on joinder and aggregation tightly tied to § 1332 at the time of § 1367's enactment. On this reading, a complaint must first meet that "original jurisdiction" measurement. If it does not, no supplemental jurisdiction is authorized. If it does, § 1367(a) authorizes "supplemental jurisdiction" over related claims. In other words, § 1367(a) would preserve undiminished, as part and parcel of § 1332 "original jurisdiction" determinations, both the "complete diversity" rule and the decisions restricting aggregation to arrive at the amount in controversy. § 1367(b)'s office, then, would be "to prevent the erosion of the complete diversity [and amount-in-controversy] requirements that might otherwise result from an expansive application of what was once termed the doctrine of ancillary jurisdiction." See Pfander, *Supplemental Jurisdiction and § 1367: The Case for a Sympathetic Textualism*, 148 U. Pa. L. Rev. 109, 114 (1999). In contrast to the Court's construction of § 1367, which draws a sharp line between the diversity and amount-in-controversy components of § 1332, the interpretation presented here does not sever the two jurisdictional requirements. * * *

The less disruptive view I take of § 1367 also accounts for the omission of Rule 20 plaintiffs and Rule 23 class actions in § 1367(b)'s text. If one reads § 1367(a) as a plenary grant of supplemental jurisdiction to federal courts sitting in diversity, one would indeed look for exceptions in § 1367(b). Finding none for permissive joinder of parties or class actions, one would conclude that Congress effectively, even if unintentionally, overruled *Clark* and *Zahn*. But if one recognizes that the nonaggregation rule delineated in *Clark* and *Zahn* forms part of the determination whether "original jurisdiction" exists in a diversity case, then plaintiffs who do not meet the amount-in-controversy requirement would fail at the § 1367(a) threshold. Congress would have no reason to resort to a § 1367(b) exception to turn such plaintiffs away from federal court, given that their claims, from the start, would fall outside the court's § 1332 jurisdiction. * * *

What is the utility of § 1367(b) under my reading of § 1367(a)? § 1367(a) allows parties other than the plaintiff to assert *reactive* claims once entertained under the heading ancillary jurisdiction. As earlier observed, § 1367(b) stops plaintiffs from circumventing § 1332's jurisdictional requirements by using another's claim as a hook to add a claim that the plaintiff could not have brought in the first instance. * * *

For the reasons stated, I would hold that § 1367 does not overrule *Clark* and *Zahn*. I would therefore affirm the judgment of the Court of Appeals for the First Circuit and reverse the judgment of the Court of Appeals for the Eleventh Circuit.

Notes and Questions

1. As the Court indicates, when Congress enacted § 1367, it meant to change some of the rules that had applied in pendent and ancillary jurisdic-

tion. One of the reasons Congress enacted § 1367 was to overturn the Supreme Court's decision in *Finley v. United States*, 490 U.S. 545, 109 S.Ct. 2003, 104 L.Ed.2d 593 (1989). In *Finley*, plaintiff had a federal question claim against the United States, and a state-law claim against another, non-diverse defendant. The federal courts had exclusive jurisdiction over the claim against the United States. Therefore, if the federal courts could not hear the state-law claim, plaintiff would be forced to divide her action into two separate suits. The Supreme Court nevertheless refused to allow the courts to exercise pendent jurisdiction, arguing that allowing jurisdiction would be inconsistent with the complete diversity requirements of § 1332. Section 1367 clearly overrules *Finley*. Do you see how? What part of § 1367 overrules *Finley*?

2.   Unlike *Finley*, the claims in *Exxon Mobil* were brought in federal court on the basis of diversity jurisdiction. In diversity cases, § 1367(b) adds an additional complication to the analysis. At least in part because of that additional factor, it is not clear whether Congress meant to overturn the pre-§ 1367 case law that denied jurisdiction over claims like those in *Zahn* that did not independently meet the requirements of the diversity statute.

3.   Both the majority and the dissents base their arguments mainly on the language of § 1367(a), not § 1367(b). Restate each of these arguments in your own words. Do you find either argument more faithful to the language of § 1367?

4.   Note that even under the majority's argument, it is essential that all claims involved in the supplemental jurisdiction analysis arise out of a common nucleus of operative fact. However, in the typical case involving joinder of plaintiffs under Federal Rule 20, this requirement will always be satisfied. Why? (If you are unsure, review Federal Rule 20.)

5.   Would the majority allow supplemental jurisdiction in the following cases (assuming in every case that all claims arise from a common nucleus of operative fact)?

a.   P1 and P2 sue D in federal court. P1 and P2 are both citizens of State Alpha, while D is a citizen of State Beta. P1's claim is $60,000, but P2's claim is only $30,000.

b.   P1, from State Alpha, sues D1 and D2, both of whom are from State Beta, in federal court. P's claim against D1 is for $100,000, while her claim against D2 is only for $50,000.

c.   P1 and P2 sue D in federal court. P1 is from State Alpha, while P2 and D are both from State Beta. Each plaintiff claims over $100,000 in damages.

d.   P, from State Alpha, sues D, from State Beta, in federal court. P seeks $100,000 in damages. D impleads 3PD, a citizen of State Alpha. P files a claim against 3PD, as authorized by Federal Rule 14.

e.   P, from State Alpha, sues D, from State Beta, in federal court. P seeks $100,000 in damages. D impleads 3PD, a citizen of State Gamma. 3PD has signed a guaranty under which it is liable for up to $50,000 of D's liability. P accordingly sues 3PD for $50,000.

f. P1 and P2, both from State Alpha, sue D, from State Beta, in federal court. P1 then files a $100,000 cross-claim against P2.

6. Do you understand the majority's distinction (explored in Problem 5b above) between the "amount in controversy" and "complete diversity" requirements of § 1332? According to the majority, why is complete diversity between plaintiffs and defendants still required even given the language of § 1332 which could be read to dispense with the requirement?

7. If a court determines that supplemental jurisdiction is unavailable, it dismisses the state-law claim or claims. Note, however, that the court does not dismiss the entire case. Any claims that independently qualify for federal question or diversity jurisdiction remain before the federal court, and the court dismisses *only* the state-law claims that needed supplemental jurisdiction. At that point, what option(s) does the plaintiff have?

8. What happens if the federal court dismisses the state claims after the statute of limitations has expired on those claims? § 1367(d) provides the plaintiff some protection. Under this provision, plaintiff will have at least 30 days to refile the dismissed claims in a state court. The statute of limitations is tolled during this period. Although several commentators have questioned Congress's authority to legislate regarding state statutes of limitations, the Supreme Court upheld the constitutionality of § 1367(d) in *Jinks v. Richland County*, 538 U.S. 456, 123 S.Ct. 1667, 155 L.Ed.2d 631 (2003). In addition, many states have "savings statutes" that toll the statute of limitations whenever a plaintiff mistakenly files her case in a jurisdiction that lacks either subject matter jurisdiction or personal jurisdiction. These savings statutes also give the plaintiff a certain period of time to file the case in a proper forum after the first case is dismissed. If such a savings statute is in force, a plaintiff may not need the protection provided by § 1367(d).

Problems

Scenario One. During the 1960s, the United States experienced a rash of incidents where library patrons kept books long beyond the due date. In response to this major issue, Congress enacted the Federal Overdue Book Act ["FOBA"]. FOBA gives librarians a federal cause of action against patrons who keep books beyond the due date. The statute provides statutory damages for overdue books.

Marion is the librarian at State University School of Law. For years, Marion has had trouble with Professor Tardy. Professor Tardy checks out books, but never returns them on time. Fed up, Marion sues Tardy for $1,000 under FOBA, based on materials that Tardy checked out on August 15th. Marion is a citizen of Illinois, and Tardy is a citizen of Missouri.

1. In addition to the FOBA claim, Marion's complaint includes a second claim for $10, which arises out of a bet between her and Tardy concerning the outcome of the World Series. Will the federal court have subject-matter jurisdiction over both claims?

2. The materials that Tardy checked out included not only books, but also legal materials stored on CD–ROM. All the materials were due on September 15th. Of course, Tardy failed to return any of the materials on time. However, because it was written in the 1960s, FOBA does not cover

CD–ROMs. Undaunted, Marion brings two claims: a FOBA claim for the books, and a claim under state conversion law for the CD–ROM. She alleges total damages of $6,500: $6,000 under FOBA, and $500 under state law. Will the federal court have subject-matter jurisdiction over both claims?

3. Same as Problem 2, except that Tardy checked out the CD–ROMs two weeks after he checked out the books. Because the circulation period for CD–ROMs is shorter, however, all the materials were due on September 15th. Will the federal court have subject-matter jurisdiction over both claims?

4. Same as Problem 2, except that Marion does not immediately run off to court. Instead, she first tries to speak to Tardy in private. Her efforts prove fruitless. To make matters worse, Tardy begins to spread rumors about Marion, claiming that she is purposefully lying about Tardy keeping the materials beyond the due date. Marion sues Tardy under FOBA, but only for the overdue books. In addition, she adds a second claim: a state-law defamation claim based on the rumors that Tardy has been spreading about her. She seeks $6,000 under FOBA and $20,000 for defamation. Will the federal court have subject-matter jurisdiction over both claims?

5. Same as Problem 4, except that FOBA only provides damages of $1 a book, so that Marion's FOBA claim seeks only $12 in damages.

Scenario 2. Marion's problems are not limited to overdue books. Recently, Bonnie and Clyde, two students at State University, have been using the library's computers to download music and movies from the Internet. Bonnie, a citizen of Louisiana, downloads the music. Once she is done, she turns the computer over to Clyde, a citizen of Illinois, who uses the computer's CD-burner to make copies of the downloaded materials for their friends. A recently-enacted federal statute, the Federal Internet Piracy Act ["FIPA"] provides the owner of a computer a cause of action against anyone who, without permission, uses the owner's computer to download materials from the Internet. As written, however, FIPA provides a cause of action against a person who uses a computer to download material, but not against someone who uses the computer to make a copy of the downloaded material. Therefore, Marion may sue only Bonnie under FIPA.

6. Marion, a citizen of Illinois, sues both Bonnie and Clyde in federal court. Her claim against Bonnie relies on FIPA, and seeks $25,000. Her claim against Clyde is based on the state law of misappropriation, and seeks $100,000 in damages. May the federal court hear both claims?

7. Because the damages afforded by FIPA are capped at $25,000, Marion foregoes her federal claim and brings state-law misappropriation claims against both Bonnie and Clyde. She seeks $100,000 in damages from each defendant. May the federal court hear both claims?

8. Now assume Clyde is a citizen of Kentucky. Doris, a citizen of Indiana, is the dean of State University Law School. Because she would be considered a co-owner of the library's computers for purposes of FIPA, Doris joins with Marion as a co-plaintiff in her suit against Bonnie and Clyde. Their claim against Bonnie relies on FIPA, and seeks damages of $25,000. Their claim against Clyde relies on state misappropriation law, and seeks damages of $100,000. May the federal court hear all claims in the case?

3. Supplemental Jurisdiction and Other Forms of Joinder

The prior section demonstrated how supplemental jurisdiction can facilitate bringing a case involving multiple plaintiffs and/or defendants in federal court. Of course, the joinder provisions of the Federal Rules deal with much more than claims by plaintiffs against defendants. Those rules also allow for counterclaims and cross-claims among the plaintiffs and defendants. Moreover, the defendant may add additional parties to the suit through the process of impleader. This section deals with how supplemental jurisdiction applies to these other forms of joinder.

At first glance, there may seem to be a discrepancy between what the Federal Rules allow and the limits set out in the supplemental jurisdiction statute. Rule 20, for example, appears to allow a plaintiff to sue multiple defendants, as long as the claims arise from the same transaction or occurrence and meet the other requirements of Rule 20. As the prior section demonstrates, however, § 1367(b) does not allow plaintiff to bring claims against a non-diverse defendant.

The key to resolving this seeming contradiction lies in Federal Rule 82. That Rule makes it clear that the Federal Rules do not affect subject-matter jurisdiction. (Although the Rule speaks of jurisdiction in general terms, which would seem to include personal jurisdiction (the topic of the next chapter), you will see in that chapter that the Federal Rules do affect personal jurisdiction directly.) Therefore, all the Federal Rules deal with is the procedural issue of joinder. Whether the federal court can exercise jurisdiction over the various joined claims can only be answered by looking to the jurisdiction statutes, such as §§ 1331, 1332, and 1367.

Although the Federal Rules do not deal with jurisdiction, there nevertheless is a significant parallel between the liberal joinder provisions of the Federal Rules and the concept of supplemental jurisdiction. Many of the joinder rules allow joinder of claims that arise from the "same transaction or occurrence." § 1367(a), the first step in any analysis of supplemental jurisdiction, allows a party to join a claim that the federal court could not hear on its own with another that the federal court could hear, provided the two claims arise from a "common nucleus of operative fact." These two concepts, although worded differently, are construed the same way. Therefore, the analyses of joinder and supplemental jurisdiction will dovetail, at least in part.

As a rule of thumb, if a joinder rule conditions joinder on satisfying the "same transaction or occurrence" test, the claims in question will ordinarily satisfy § 1367(a). The only exception, set out in *Exxon Mobil*, is a case involving multiple plaintiffs and/or defendants, where jurisdiction is based solely on diversity but complete diversity is lacking. Aside from that exception, § 1367(a) will be satisfied for all of the following claims:

- joinder of plaintiffs or defendants under Rule 20, when jurisdiction is based on a federal question or there is complete diversity;

- compulsory counterclaims (Rule 13(a));

- any cross-claims that arise from the same transaction or occurrence as plaintiff's claim (recall that a cross-claim is also proper if it arises from the same transaction as a counterclaim; because § 1367(a) requires factual overlap with the plaintiff's claim, these cross-claims may not satisfy § 1367(a));

- parties joined to counterclaims or cross-claims under Rule 13(h); and

- claims by a third-party defendant against plaintiff, and by plaintiff against third-party defendant, under Rule 14(a).

But here it is crucial that you keep two *caveats* in mind. First, do not assume that supplemental jurisdiction is the only way for a court to obtain jurisdiction over a joined claim. Supplemental jurisdiction is a last resort; to be used only if diversity and federal question jurisdiction do not work for all claims. You should first analyze each claim separately, to see whether diversity or federal question applies. You should turn to supplemental jurisdiction only if you find claims that do not qualify for federal question or diversity jurisdiction. Also, do not forget that § 1367(a) requires that there is at least one claim by plaintiff that does qualify for federal question or diversity.

Using supplemental jurisdiction only as a last resort does more than possibly save you the trouble of undertaking a difficult § 1367 analysis. Remember that § 1367(c) makes jurisdiction over the supplemental claims discretionary. If those claims qualify for federal question or diversity jurisdiction, by contrast, the federal court does not have discretion to dismiss them.

The second *caveat* is equally important. Too many students try to simplify the analysis by assuming that there will always be supplemental jurisdiction over claims falling within the joinder rules listed above. Concluding that one of the above joinder rules is satisfied only means that you have also met the requirements of § 1367(a). It is still essential to analyze whether the case satisfies §§ 1367(b) and (c). § 1367(b) in particular will prevent the court from exercising jurisdiction over a number of claims, even though joinder may be proper under the Federal Rules. Under that provision, some claims by a plaintiff in a diversity case—whether brought against a third-party defendant, a second, nondiverse defendant, or another plaintiff as a cross-claim—will not qualify for supplemental jurisdiction.

Conversely, there are certain situations in which a court may exercise supplemental jurisdiction over claims that do not fall into the above joinder rules. Suppose P sues D in federal court. D has a claim against P that arises out of the same transaction or occurrence. Ordinarily, that claim would be a compulsory counterclaim. However, if D had already filed that claim in a state proceeding, Rule 13(a) provides that the claim is not compulsory. Nevertheless, because the claim is still a permissive counterclaim, most defendants will choose to file it anyway, for purposes of efficiency, even if they are not required to. In this situation, the court may exercise supplemental jurisdiction over the claim (subject always to its discretion to dismiss the state claim under § 1367(c)), even though it is a permissive rather than a compulsory counterclaim.

Problems

1. P1 and P2 both sue D in federal court. P1's claim qualifies for federal jurisdiction. Although P2's claim arises from the same event as P1's, it would not qualify for either federal question or diversity jurisdiction on its own. May P2 bring her claim in federal court along with P1's claim? What additional information do you need to answer this question?

2. After they were involved in an automobile accident, P sues D in federal court, relying on diversity jurisdiction. P seeks $100,000 in damages. D files a counterclaim in the action, seeking $15,000 for the injuries that D suffered in the same collision. P moves to dismiss D's counterclaim for lack of subject-matter jurisdiction. How should the court rule?

3. P, a farmer, hired D1 to treat his crops with an herbicide. D1 obtained the herbicide from D2. Because of a labelling mistake, the herbicide turns out to be Agent Orange, a product that kills every plant, including P's crops. P therefore brings a diversity action against both D1 and D2 in federal court, seeking $250,000 in damages. D1 files a cross-claim against D2 in this action, arguing that D2 must reimburse D1 for any injuries that D1 is required to pay. This cross-claim clearly meets the requirements of Rule 13(g). However, because D1 and D2 are citizens of the same state, D2 moves to dismiss the cross-claim for lack of subject-matter jurisdiction. How should the court rule?

4. Same basic facts as Problem 3. D2 impleads Ins. Co., its liability insurance carrier, into the action. D2 and Ins. Co. are citizens of the same state. Ins. Co. accordingly moves to dismiss for lack of subject-matter jurisdiction. How should the court rule?

5. P1 and P2 sue D in federal court, relying on diversity jurisdiction. P1 then files a proper cross-claim against P2. Because P1 and P2 are citizens of the same state, P2 moves to dismiss the cross-claim for lack of subject-matter jurisdiction. How should the court rule?

6. P sues D in federal court, relying on diversity jurisdiction, for injuries incurred by P in an automobile accident. D files a counterclaim against P for the injuries that D suffered in the same accident. D also uses Rule 13(h) to join O, the owner of the automobile driven by P, as an additional party to the counterclaim. Because P and O are from the same state, D's counterclaim qualifies for diversity jurisdiction. P then files a claim against O, arguing that O must reimburse P for any sums that P must pay D. O moves to dismiss P's claim for lack of subject-matter jurisdiction. How should the court rule?

E. REMOVAL

INTRODUCTORY PROBLEM

Porthos sues Athos and Aramis in an Arizona state court for injuries that Porthos suffered in a swordfight. Porthos is a citizen of Pennsylvania, Athos is a citizen of Nebraska, and Aramis is a citizen of Arizona. Athos and Aramis would rather have the case litigated in federal court. Is there any way they can force the action into federal court?

Governing Law: 28 U.S.C. § 1441.

As we saw in sections B–D of this chapter, in many cases a plaintiff will have the option of suing in either state or federal court. For a variety of reasons—greater familiarity with the state procedural system and plaintiff-favoring juries being perhaps the most common—many plaintiffs will elect to bring their case in state rather than federal court. However, plaintiff does not have absolute control over the choice of forum. The removal statutes may level the playing field by giving defendant the right to move the case to a federal court.

The effect of removal is to allow defendants to avail themselves of the federal courts to roughly the same extent as plaintiffs. Note that there is no counterpart to removal if plaintiff originally files in federal court. If a plaintiff selects federal court, there is nothing defendant can do to transfer the case to state court.

1. General Rules Governing Removal

CATERPILLAR INC. v. WILLIAMS

482 U.S. 386, 107 S.Ct. 2425, 96 L.Ed.2d 318 (1987)

Justice BRENNAN delivered the opinion of the Court. * * *

I

At various times between 1956 and 1968, Caterpillar Tractor Company (Caterpillar) hired respondents to work at its San Leandro, California, facility. Initially, each respondent filled a position covered by the collective-bargaining agreement between Caterpillar and Local Lodge No. 284, International Association of Machinists (Union). Each eventually became either a managerial or a weekly salaried employee, positions outside the coverage of the collective-bargaining agreement. Respondents held the latter positions for periods ranging from 3 to 15 years; all but two respondents served 8 years or more.

Respondents allege that, "[d]uring the course of [their] employment, as management or weekly salaried employees," Caterpillar made oral and written representations that "they could look forward to indefinite and lasting employment with the corporation and that they could count on the corporation to take care of them." More specifically, respondents claim that, "while serving Caterpillar as managers or weekly salaried employees, [they] were assured that if the San Leandro facility of Caterpillar ever closed, Caterpillar would provide employment opportunities for [them] at other facilities of Caterpillar, its subsidiaries, divisions, or related companies." Respondents maintain that these "promises were continually and repeatedly made," and that they created "a total employment agreement wholly independent of the collective-bargaining agreement pertaining to hourly employees." In reliance on these promises, respondents assert, they "continued to remain in Caterpillar's employ rather than seeking other employment."

* * * On December 15, 1983, Caterpillar notified respondents that its San Leandro plant would close and that they would be laid off.

On December 17, 1984, respondents filed an action based solely on state law in California state court, contending that Caterpillar "breached [its] employment agreement by notifying [respondents] that the San Leandro plant would be closed and subsequently advising [respondents] that they would be terminated" without regard to the individual employment contracts. Caterpillar then removed the action to federal court, arguing that removal was proper because any individual employment contracts made with respondents "were, as a matter of federal substantive labor law, merged into and superseded by the ... collective bargaining agreements."* Respondents denied that they alleged any federal claim and immediately sought remand of the action to the state court. In an oral opinion, the District Court held that removal to federal court was proper, and dismissed the case when respondents refused to amend their complaint to attempt to state a claim under § 301 of the LMRA.

The Court of Appeals for the Ninth Circuit reversed, holding that the case was improperly removed. The court determined that respondents' state-law claims were not grounded, either directly or indirectly, upon rights or liabilities created by the collective-bargaining agreement. Caterpillar's claim that its collective-bargaining agreement with the Union superseded and extinguished all previous individual employment contracts alleged by respondents was deemed irrelevant. The court labeled this argument a "defensive allegation," "raised to defeat the [respondents'] claims grounded in those independent contracts." Since respondents' cause of action did not require interpretation or application of the collective-bargaining agreement, the court concluded that the complaint did not arise under § 301 and was not removable to federal court. * * *

II

A

* * * Only state-court actions that originally could have been filed in federal court may be removed to federal court by the defendant.

---

* A claim for breach of a collective bargaining contract arises under § 301 of the Labor Management Relations Act (LMRA), and is accordingly a federal question. *Eds.*

Absent diversity of citizenship, federal-question jurisdiction is required. The presence or absence of federal-question jurisdiction is governed by the "well-pleaded complaint rule," which provides that federal jurisdiction exists only when a federal question is presented on the face of the plaintiff's properly pleaded complaint. The rule makes the plaintiff the master of the claim; he or she may avoid federal jurisdiction by exclusive reliance on state law.

Ordinarily federal pre-emption is raised as a defense to the allegations in a plaintiff's complaint. Before 1887, a federal defense such as pre-emption could provide a basis for removal, but, in that year, Congress amended the removal statute. We interpret that amendment to authorize removal only where original federal jurisdiction exists. Thus, it is now settled law that a case may not be removed to federal court on the basis of a federal defense, including the defense of pre-emption, even if the defense is anticipated in the plaintiff's complaint, and even if both parties concede that the federal defense is the only question truly at issue. * * * [The Court then considered a narrow exception to this rule—the "complete preemption" doctrine discussed in Chapter 13—but concluded that it did not apply.]

It is true that when a defense to a state claim is based on the terms of a collective-bargaining agreement, the state court will have to interpret that agreement to decide whether the state claim survives. But the presence of a federal question, even a § 301 question, in a defensive argument does not overcome the paramount policies embodied in the well-pleaded complaint rule—that the plaintiff is the master of the complaint, that a federal question must appear on the face of the complaint, and that the plaintiff may, by eschewing claims based on federal law, choose to have the cause heard in state court. When a plaintiff invokes a right created by a collective-bargaining agreement, the plaintiff has *chosen* to plead what we have held must be regarded as a federal claim, and removal is at the defendant's option. But a *defendant* cannot, merely by injecting a federal question into an action that asserts what is plainly a state-law claim, transform the action into one arising under federal law, thereby selecting the forum in which the claim shall be litigated. If a defendant could do so, the plaintiff would be master of nothing. Congress has long since decided that federal defenses do not provide a basis for removal.

III

Respondents' claims do not arise under federal law and therefore may not be removed to federal court. The judgment of the Court of Appeals is Affirmed.

Notes and Questions

1. Before evaluating the particular issue of federal question jurisdiction presented by the main case, consider the basic process of removal. What is the threshold test that § 1441(a) establishes for all attempts to remove?

2.   Because § 1441(a) makes removal turn on whether the case could have been filed originally in federal court, every removal situation may require application of the rules dealing with federal question, diversity, and supplemental jurisdiction. However, removal and original jurisdiction are not perfectly parallel. There are a number of cases that cannot be removed even though they could have been filed originally in federal court. Conversely, there are some cases that can be removed even though they could not have been filed originally in federal court.

3.   *Non-removable cases.* § 1441(a) provides the possibility that Congress may enact exceptions to its general rule. § 1445 lists a few narrow categories of cases that cannot be removed even if they could have originally been filed in federal court. §§ 1445(a) and (b), dealing with certain actions filed against railroads and other carriers, represent historical political compromises. But what about §§ 1445(c) and (d)? Why would Congress forbid the removal of workers compensation actions? Is there something special about workers compensation that suggests the action should remain in state court? And what might explain § 1445(d), which forbids removal of certain civil actions under the Violence Against Women Act of 1994? Is Congress sending a message that these cases are somehow "beneath" the federal courts? Is it merely a coincidence that domestic relations cases also lie outside the federal courts' jurisdiction, as discussed in Part C of this chapter?

4.   *Preemption.* Now, consider why the plaintiffs' claim in *Caterpillar* was not treated as a federal question. The Court's analysis focuses on the doctrine of preemption, which you will study in greater depth in Constitutional Law. Preemption stems from the "supremacy clause" of Article VI of the United States Constitution, which provides that the United States Constitution and federal statute law are the "Supreme Law of the Land." Therefore, a state law that is inconsistent with the Constitution or federal law is preempted, and has no effect. Do you see why the issue of whether plaintiffs' claims were preempted by federal labor law did not affect the jurisdictional analysis?

5.   You may recall that although federal question jurisdiction is ordinarily shared with the state courts, federal courts have exclusive jurisdiction over certain actions arising under federal law, such as antitrust and patent and copyright infringement cases. If a plaintiff mistakingly brings one of those claims in a state court, may defendant remove to federal court? For many years, the surprising answer was often no: many courts refused to allow removal under the argument that if the action was not properly before the state court, it could not be removed. The defendant had to dismiss the case, and plaintiff would then refile in federal court. Congress remedied this anomaly when it enacted § 1441(f), which allows removal regardless of whether the state court has jurisdiction.

6.   Suppose that P sues D in state court, alleging both federal and state law claims. P and D are citizens of the same state. If the state and federal claims are sufficiently related, may the case be removed? Could the entire case have been brought in federal court originally?

7.   D tries to remove based on supplemental jurisdiction. The federal court determines that although the claims satisfy §§ 1367(a) and (b), the

state claim presents a novel and complex issue of state law within the meaning of § 1367(c). Does the federal court remand the entire case or only the state claim? See *In re City of Mobile*, 75 F.3d 605 (11th Cir. 1996).

8. Consider again the situation posed in note 7, but suppose that the claims are not sufficiently related to qualify for supplemental jurisdiction. Can this case be removed? Recall that a defendant must remove the entire case, not selected claims. This case, however, could not be filed originally in federal court. Logic would therefore dictate that it could not be removed.

However, § 1441(c) indicates to the contrary. Under that section, a defendant may remove "separate and independent" claims, as long as one of the claims arises under federal law. If you are troubled by this provision, you are by no means alone. Indeed, several have argued that the provision could well be unconstitutional. Can you recreate the argument as to why § 1441(c) is unconstitutional?

The Supreme Court has held that "separate and independent" is a strict standard, and that the section requires "complete dissociation" between the claims. *American Fire & Casualty Co. v. Finn*, 341 U.S. 6, 71 S.Ct. 534, 95 L.Ed. 702 (1951). This strict interpretation limits the number of cases where § 1441(c) is available. In addition, even if separate and independent claims are present, § 1441(c) gives the court the discretion to remand the state-law claims. Given that the claims will share little factual overlap, a court may be more inclined to remand the state-law claims and thereby avoid jury confusion.

9. *Other types of removal.* Although § 1441 is far and away the most-commonly used removal statute, it is by no means the only one. In some situations, Congress passes new legislation, and explicitly provides for removal of state-court actions in that legislation. One example of such a statute is the Price–Anderson Act, 42 U.S.C. § 2014(hh), which allows defendants to remove state court actions involving tort claims stemming from nuclear accidents. Unlike § 1441, the Price–Anderson Act allows removal regardless of whether the case satisfies the requirements for either diversity or federal question jurisdiction.

In addition to the Price–Anderson Act, 28 U.S.C. §§ 1442, 1442a, 1443, and 1452 are more specialized removal statutes that apply in enumerated situations. These removal provisions are also not always subject to the same rules that apply to removal under § 1441. It is especially interesting to compare the federal officer removal statute, § 1442, to § 1441. Unlike the general statute, § 1442 allows removal of not only civil actions, but also criminal prosecutions. In addition, on its face § 1442 allows removal regardless of whether the parties are diverse or if a federal question is involved. However, to avoid a possible constitutional problem with that broad definition, the Supreme Court in *Mesa v. California*, 489 U.S. 121, 109 S.Ct. 959, 103 L.Ed.2d 99 (1989), construed § 1442 to allow removal of claims based solely on state law only when the defendant officer actually raised a federal defense. Therefore, even though the case might not qualify as a federal question under § 1331 because of the face of the complaint rule, it did qualify under the broader definition of federal question used under Article III of the Constitution.

2. Removal in Diversity Cases

Application of § 1441 is fairly routine when jurisdiction is based on a federal question. In diversity cases, however, there are a few special rules that often prove to be traps for the unwary. The most obvious special rule is § 1441(b), which prevents removal of a case based on diversity if any of the defendants is a citizen of the state where the state-court action is pending. Can you think of a good policy reason that may have led Congress to include this provision?

Second, the rules governing the time at which diversity is determined differ in removal. When plaintiff files a diversity case originally in federal court, all that matters is that the parties are diverse on the date the case was filed. *Higgins v. E.I. DuPont de Nemours & Co.*, 863 F.2d 1162, 1166 (4th Cir. 1988). Post-filing acts do not affect jurisdiction. In removal cases, by contrast, diversity must be present both on the date the case was filed and the date on which removal occurs. The only exception is a voluntary act by the plaintiff that creates diversity.

To illustrate, suppose P sues D. Both parties are from the same state. If D moves to another state after the case is commenced, the case is not removable. However, if P moves to another state, defendant has 30 days to remove, subject to § 1441(b). Other acts by a plaintiff, such as dismissing all non-diverse defendants, may also make the case removable.

What if all the existing parties are diverse, but there are also other potential defendants who would destroy diversity? In *Lincoln Property Co. v. Roche*, ___ U.S. ___, 126 S.Ct. 606 (2005), the Supreme Court held that the possible existence of unnamed non-diverse parties did not prevent removal.

Another special rule that applies to diversity removal is the one-year bar of § 1446(b), which is discussed in the section on procedure.

Finally, the amount in controversy requirement can also present problems in diversity removal cases. Many states do not allow a plaintiff to state a specific amount of damages in the complaint. Instead, the court will determine the actual damages based on the evidence adduced at trial. The purpose of this rule is to prevent plaintiffs from trying to win the sympathies of the jury by grossly exaggerating their injuries. However, the absence of any dollar figure makes it difficult for a federal court to determine whether removal was proper. Many courts in this situation presume that the amount in controversy requirement is satisfied unless plaintiff (the party opposing removal) demonstrates that he cannot recover more than $75,000.

A plaintiff who wants to keep his case in state court may be able to preempt any removal attempts by limiting his prayer for relief in the complaint. For example, if plaintiff's complaint specifically alleges that he is entitled to recover "an amount not to exceed $50,000," a court may not allow the defendant to remove based on diversity.

3. Procedure for Removal

How exactly does a defendant remove a case to federal court? § 1441 itself provides part of the answer. In addition, you should carefully review §§ 1446 and 1447, which set out time constraints, additional requirements, and certain limits, on removal.

Timing. Perhaps the most important limits relate to time. § 1446(b) provides that a defendant has only 30 days following service to remove a case. However, this 30 days only begins to run when the defendant receives a pleading that indicates that the case may be removed. In most cases, the plaintiff's original complaint will show that the case qualifies for federal question, diversity, and/or supplemental jurisdiction. However, suppose that the original complaint is based on state law, and one of the plaintiffs is from the same state as the defendant. In this situation, the case could not have originally been filed in federal court because of the complete diversity rule. However, if the non-diverse plaintiff later drops out of the case, and an amended complaint is served that does not name the dropped plaintiff, defendant's 30–day time period begins to run with service of the amended complaint.

The rule stated just above is subject to an important—and often forgotten—exception. The last clause of § 1446(b) provides that no action may be removed based on diversity after one year following *filing* of the *original* complaint. Therefore, a plaintiff in a diversity case may defeat removal by joining both a diverse and a non-diverse defendant, waiting for a year, and then dropping the non-diverse defendant. As long as that non-diverse defendant is not a nominal party, the case cannot be removed.

Multiple defendants. § 1441 provides that an action may be removed by "the defendant or defendants." How does this language operate in the case of multiple defendants? The courts have uniformly held that in a case involving multiple defendants, *all* defendants must join in the removal. If even one defendant refuses to cooperate, the case cannot be removed. However, you do not always need the consent of everyone named as a defendant in the complaint. If a defendant is named in the complaint but has not yet been served, that defendant need not join in the removal.

What exactly is a "defendant"? Courts have consistently held that a plaintiff cannot remove even when the defendant files a counterclaim against her. More recently, a federal appellate court held that a third-party defendant was not a defendant within the meaning of § 1441, and therefore could not remove. *First National Bank of Pulaski v. Curry*, 301 F.3d 456 (6th Cir. 2002).

Assuming all necessary defendants agree, the case is removed by filing a notice of removal with the proper federal court, serving it on all adverse parties, and filing a copy of the notice with the state court. A "notice" is just what it implies—it is not a request to remove, but instead a statement that defendant is exercising her right to remove the case. Until fairly recently, a party had to file a motion asking for removal. Therefore, many of the older, but still influential, removal cases will speak in terms of a motion.

Once the case is properly removed, the state court loses jurisdiction over the case. § 1446(d). In fact, any rulings that the state court issues from that point forward have no effect whatsoever.

Although removal gives the defendant the option of moving the case to federal court, it does not give the defendant any choice as to which federal court will hear the case. § 1441 is crystal clear in this regard: the case is removed to "the district and division embracing the place where [the state] action is pending." Thus, a defendant who removes a case from the state courts in Louisville, Kentucky must remove the case to the Western District of Kentucky, Louisville division. In Chapter 5, you will study the concept of venue, which in the federal courts comprises various statutes that dictate where an action must be filed. Because the removal statutes specify a particular district, they are treated as overriding the venue statutes. Therefore, if our defendant properly removes the case to the Western District of Kentucky, that court will have venue even if it would have not been a proper venue under the venue statutes had the same action been filed originally in federal court.

What happens if defendant's removal is improper? In that situation, the federal court may remand the case to state court. Here again, the issue of timing is important. If removal was improper because the underlying case is not one that could have been filed originally in federal court, the objection is actually a challenge to the federal court's subject matter jurisdiction. Thus, like other challenges to subject matter jurisdiction, the motion for remand may be made at any time (even on appeal), and by either side (including the removing defendant itself) or by the court. Similarly, if something happens in the case that causes the federal court to lose subject matter jurisdiction—for example, if the sole federal question in the case is dismissed voluntarily—the federal court may remand. All other objections, however, such as objections to the content of the notice or timeliness, must be raised within 30 days following filing of the notice of removal. 28 U.S.C. § 1447(c).

Problems

1.   P, a citizen of Nebraska, sues D, a citizen of Kansas, in state court. P seeks $500,000 in damages from D for breach of contract and unjust enrichment. D files a timely notice of removal. P moves for a remand. What additional facts do you need before you can determine whether the court will remand the case to the state court?

2.   Same facts as Problem 1. Would your analysis differ if P had brought both a federal question claim and a diversity claim against D?

3.   P, a citizen of Indiana, sues D1, a citizen of South Dakota, and D2, a citizen of Indiana, in an Indiana state court. P seeks $200,000 in damages from the defendants for conspiring to commit an intentional tort against P. Two weeks after the case is commenced, P and D2 settle. P immediately

amends her complaint to drop D2 from the case. May D1 now remove the case? If so, what must D1 do, and when?

4. Same as Problem 3, except that P waits for over a year after the settlement before filing the papers dismissing D2 from the case. Would it matter if P's tardiness was purposeful or merely an oversight?

F. CHALLENGING SUBJECT MATTER JURISDICTION

INTRODUCTORY PROBLEM

P, a citizen of Hawaii, sues D Corp. in federal court. After a long and bitter trial, the jury returns a verdict for D. P then immediately moves to dismiss the case for lack of subject matter jurisdiction. P has recently discovered that while D Corp. has its sole place of business in Oregon, it was incorporated in Hawaii. The incorporation records are a public record, which P could easily have found prior to filing his suit. However, P without checking simply guessed that the corporation was also incorporated in Oregon. Will the court grant P's request to dismiss for lack of subject matter jurisdiction?

Governing Law: Federal Rule 12(h).

NORTH CENTRAL F.S., INC. v. BROWN, 951 F.Supp. 1383 (N.D. Iowa 1996). North Central operated grain elevators in various locations in Iowa. North Central had entered into "hedge-to-arrive" ("HTA") agreements with grain producers, under which the producers would sell grain to North Central. The producers declared that the HTA agreements violated federal law, and were therefore unenforceable. North Central then sued the producers in a federal district court in Iowa. Neither of the parties challenged the court's jurisdiction. The court nevertheless raised the question of its own jurisdiction *sua sponte*, stating:

> The federal district courts have always been courts of limited jurisdiction. See U.S. CONST., Art. III, § 1. "Federal courts are not courts of general jurisdiction and have only the power that is authorized by Article III of the Constitution and the statutes enacted by Congress pursuant thereto." *Marine Equip. Management Co. v. United States*, 4 F.3d 643, 646 (8th Cir.1993). A federal court therefore has a duty to assure itself that the threshold requirement of subject matter jurisdiction has been met in every case.

> The parties ... may not confer subject matter jurisdiction upon the federal courts by stipulation, and lack of subject matter jurisdiction cannot be waived by the parties or ignored by the court. *Pacific Nat'l Ins. Co. v. Transport Ins. Co.*, 341 F.2d 514, 516 (8th Cir.), *cert. denied*, 381 U.S. 912 (1965); see also *Pennsylvania v. Union*

Gas Co., 491 U.S. 1, 25 (1989) (Stevens, J., concurring) ("[T]he cases are legion holding that a party may not waive a defect in subject-matter jurisdiction or invoke federal jurisdiction simply by consent," citing *Owen Equip. & Erection Co. v. Kroger*, 437 U.S. 365, 377 n. 21 (1978). Even where " 'the parties did not raise any jurisdictional issues[, t]his court is obligated to raise such jurisdictional issues if it perceives any.' " *White v. Nix*, 43 F.3d 374, 376 (8th Cir.1994). The federal courts have a duty to examine the substantiality of the federal claim throughout the litigation, and must dismiss all claims if the federal claim proves patently meritless even after the trial begins.* * *

The court eventually held that it lacked jurisdiction over North Central's claims.

Notes and Questions

1. *North Central* illustrates one of the most important features of subject matter jurisdiction: unlike every other defense in a case, subject matter jurisdiction cannot be waived by the parties. Any party may raise the issue at any time during the course of a proceeding, even on appeal. Not only may either party raise the issue of subject matter jurisdiction at any time, but a court may raise it of its own accord, or "sua sponte." As a result, a court may dismiss a case for lack of subject matter jurisdiction even though both parties are willing to have it heard in that court. Nor can the parties create subject matter jurisdiction where it would not otherwise exist by consenting in a contract to have claims under that contract heard by a particular court. Compare this lenient rule to that governing challenges to personal jurisdiction and venue, discussed in Part D of Chapter 4. A defendant must raise those defenses no later than the answer, which occurs very early in the case. Similarly, courts rarely raise these issues of their own accord.

2. *Challenges by plaintiff.* Even more unusual is the fact that a plaintiff may challenge subject matter jurisdiction. This result makes sense, of course, in a removal case, where the defendant has taken the case to federal court. But a plaintiff may also challenge subject matter jurisdiction in cases where the plaintiff himself has chosen federal court. Moreover, the plaintiff may challenge jurisdiction at any time. Note that this rule means that a party can bring a case in federal court, lose on a crucial issue concerning the merits of the case, and then move to dismiss the action for lack of jurisdiction. If the court dismisses, the earlier ruling on the crucial issue is not binding. *Capron v. Van Noorden*, 6 U.S. (2 Cranch) 126, 2 L.Ed. 229 (1804).

3. Whether the parties may by agreement *deprive* a court of the power to hear a dispute is a more complicated matter. Courts typically treat the issue as a question of venue rather than subject matter jurisdiction.

4. The principles discussed in the prior notes are reflected in Federal Rule 12(h)(3). That Rule allows the issue of lack of subject matter jurisdiction to be raised at any time ("whenever it appears") and by either the parties or the court itself ("by suggestion of the parties or otherwise"). All

other Rule 12 defenses are subject to time limits, as set out in Rules 12(h)(1) and (2). Moreover, unlike the other defenses, a party need not raise the issue in a pleading or formal motion. A mere suggestion will suffice.

5. The *North Central* opinion discusses why the rule governing challenges to subject matter jurisdiction is so accommodating. Do these same arguments apply to *diversity* cases? Although diversity jurisdiction is an allocation of authority, the justifications for diversity jurisdiction are noticeably different than for other types of cases. Diversity jurisdiction exists not to ensure the supremacy of federal law, but because the framers feared that the state courts might tend to side with in-state litigants when those parties were embroiled in litigation with out-of-staters. Given this different justification, should parties from the same state be able to litigate their state law claims in federal court if both are willing to do so? Construct an argument that even this situation presents a threat to state authority.

6. The above principles only apply to *direct attacks*, i.e., challenges made while the case in question is still pending at the trial court or on appeal. Once that case is entirely complete (either because no appeal was taken or because the appellate courts have finished with the case), a party's ability to challenge the subject matter jurisdiction of the court that decided the case is more limited. A situation in which a person challenges a prior case in a separate and distinct case is referred to as a *"collateral attack."* If a party actually litigated the court's subject matter jurisdiction in the first proceeding, that party is bound by the court's determination, even if that determination later proves to be clearly incorrect. *Durfee v. Duke*, 375 U.S. 106, 84 S.Ct. 242, 11 L.Ed.2d 186 (1963) (*Durfee* is in Chapter 11).

The law is less clear when the issue of subject matter jurisdiction was not litigated in the first case. If a party shows up and litigates the case, but never raises the question of subject-matter jurisdiction, she will usually be precluded from challenging the court's jurisdiction in a collateral proceeding. *Chicot County Drainage Dist. v. Baxter State Bank*, 308 U.S. 371, 60 S.Ct. 317, 84 L.Ed. 329 (1940). The only exception is a case like *Kalb v. Feuerstein*, 308 U.S. 433, 60 S.Ct. 343, 84 L.Ed. 370 (1940), where Congress had explicitly provided by statute that the court had no jurisdiction, and that any action by the court was not valid.

The Supreme Court has never directly ruled on the issue of where the party simply never shows up at all in the action. Although several commentators have suggested that collateral attack would be available in this case, the law is not clear. As you will see in the next chapter, a party is always free to challenge personal jurisdiction by taking a default in the first action. For that reason alone, the commentators may be correct that collateral attack is available.

Why are the rules that apply to collateral attacks different? These cases present a clash between two constitutional principles: the notions of cooperative sovereignty that underlie subject matter jurisdiction, and the competing notion that courts in a federal system should respect the decisions of other courts. This latter principle is set out in the Constitution's full faith and credit provision (Article IV), as well as in federal statutes (most notably 28 U.S.C. § 1738). If a court could ignore the judgment of another court simply by ruling that the earlier court had no jurisdiction, it would undermine the entire structure of the full faith and credit system.

Chapter 4

PERSONAL JURISDICTION AND VENUE

A. EXERCISING JURISDICTION OVER DEFENDANTS

INTRODUCTORY PROBLEM #1

Jaye Bizer was a cruise ship passenger who has brought suit in the U.S. District Court for the Western District of Washington against the DizzyWhiz Cruise Lines for damages sustained in a slip and fall case. The defendant cruise line has filed a motion to dismiss based upon improper personal jurisdiction.

DizzyWhiz Cruise Lines is a Colombian corporation with its principal place of business in Miami, Florida. DizzyWhiz is not registered to do business in the state of Washington. It owns no property in Washington, maintains no office or bank account in Washington, and pays no business taxes in Washington. It has never operated ships which have called at Washington ports. It has no exclusive agent in Washington. Dizzy-Whiz does, however, advertise its cruises in local Washington newspapers. It also provides brochures to travel agents in Washington, which in turn are distributed to potential customers. DizzyWhiz also holds seminars for travel agents in the State of Washington to inform them about, and encourage them to sell DizzyWhiz cruises. DizzyWhiz pays travel agencies a 10% commission on proceeds from tickets sold for DizzyWhiz cruises.

Jaye Bizer is a Washington resident who purchased her ticket through the Jesse Boyer Travel Agency in Tacoma, Washington, for a seven-day cruise on a DizzyWhiz Cruise Lines ship called the SENECA. She was to embark in Los Angeles, California, sailing from there to Puerto Vallarta, Mexico. The tickets were purchased through the travel agent, who forwarded payment to DizzyWhiz in Miami. The tickets were issued in Florida, then forwarded to Jaye Bizer in Washington.

Ms. Bizer suffered injuries when she slipped on a deck mat while on a guided tour of the ship's galley. The incident occurred in international waters off the coast of Mexico. Ms. Bizer alleges that the fall was due to the negligence of DizzyWhiz and its employees, and she requests damages arising out of her personal injuries. Washington's jurisdictional statute has been construed by the Washington Supreme Court to permit the assertion of jurisdiction to the extent permitted by due process.

You are the judge in this case. Write your opinion granting or denying the defendant's motion to dismiss.

INTRODUCTORY PROBLEM #2

Defendant Wendy Baker is a Tennessee attorney who, in 2001, performed legal services for plaintiff, Mrs. Susan James, in connection with her deceased husband's estate. Mrs. James was at that time a resident of Tennessee. As part of her services, Baker set up and supervised a "discretionary investment account" for Mrs. James in a Tennessee bank.

In 2002, Mrs. James moved to California and Baker handled (in Tennessee) the closing on the sale of Mrs. James's Tennessee home. In 2003, Baker recommended that Mrs. James close the investment account in the Tennessee bank and place the funds instead with a newly established investment firm (also in Tennessee). Baker subsequently recommended the investment of these funds in various real estate investment trusts, and Mrs. James followed these recommendations.

At the end of 2003, Mrs. James became concerned about the steady decline in the value of her investment as indicated by the quarterly reports, and asked Baker to take corrective action. Baker did not do this and, allegedly as a result of Baker's negligent inaction, Mrs. James's funds were substantially dissipated. Baker communicated with Mrs. James by telephone and e-mail on most occasions, but in some instances they exchanged letters between Mrs. James's home in California and Baker's office when it became necessary for her to execute investment contracts.

In 2004, Mrs. James commenced a lawsuit against Baker in a federal court in California, which has a "due process" long-arm statute. Can a California federal court exercise personal jurisdiction over Baker in a lawsuit filed by Mrs. James?

––––––––––

One of the important decisions that you will make in deciding to file a lawsuit on behalf of a client is to determine which court(s) would have the authority to bind the defendant to a judgment after your client prevails at trial. By filing a lawsuit, *your* client has consented to the power of the court to issue binding orders and judgments. But usually the defendant has not consented to being sued in a particular state. (As discussed later in this chapter, the defendant may consent to be sued in a particular court.)

Because the defendant has neither invoked the authority of the court nor consented to be sued in a particular court, your goal is to file the lawsuit in a court that can exercise power over the defendant. If a defendant cannot be served within the state where the lawsuit is filed, the court will be unable to adjudicate the plaintiff's claim unless it obtains *in rem* jurisdiction over the defendant's property.

When a court has personal jurisdiction over a defendant, its judgment in the case is valid and is enforceable locally, or in another state by virtue of the Full Faith and Credit Clause of the United States Constitution. Conversely, a judgment from a court lacking personal jurisdiction is invalid and cannot be enforced in the place where the issuing court sits, another part of the same state, or another state. However, if the court has jurisdiction and your client prevails at trial and is awarded damages, you can enforce the judgment for damages locally, elsewhere in the state, and/or in another state by identifying property belonging to the defendant that can be used to satisfy the judgment.

1. Jurisdiction Over Defendants: The Early Decisions

PENNOYER v. NEFF, 95 U.S. (5 Otto) 714, 24 L.Ed. 565 (1877) is the landmark case in personal jurisdiction. Mitchell, an Oregon attorney, sued Neff in an Oregon state court for failing to pay him for his services. Mitchell served Neff by publishing an advertisement containing information about the lawsuit in an Oregon newspaper for six weeks, and Mitchell did not attach Neff's Oregon property. A nonresident, Neff probably never saw the ad and therefore never knew that he had been sued. As a result, when Neff did not answer Mitchell's complaint or otherwise appear to defend, Mitchell obtained a default judgment against Neff, and was able to have Neff's land in Oregon sold at a sheriff's auction to satisfy the judgment. Pennoyer obtained title to Neff's land at the sale. Neff responded to Pennoyer's claim to the land by suing him in an Oregon federal court to reclaim the land. The trial court in *Neff v. Pennoyer* decided in Neff's favor; Pennoyer appealed to the United States Supreme Court, claiming that the prior sheriff's sale from *Mitchell v. Neff* was valid. Neff claimed that the service by publication was ineffective to give the Oregon state court jurisdiction over him. Justice Field first identified

> two well-established principles of public law respecting the jurisdiction of an independent State over persons and property. * * * [E]xcept as restrained and limited by that instrument, they possess and exercise the authority of independent States, and the principles of public law to which we have referred are applicable to them. One of these principles is, that every State possesses exclusive jurisdiction and sovereignty over persons and property within its territory. * * * The other principle of public law referred to follows from the one mentioned; that is, that no State can exercise direct jurisdiction and authority over persons or property without its territory. * * * And so it is laid down by jurists, as an elementary principle, that the laws of one State have no operation outside of its territory, except so

far as is allowed by comity; and that no tribunal established by it can extend its process beyond that territory so as to subject either persons or property to its decisions.

So the State, through its tribunals, may subject property situated within its limits owned by non-residents to the payment of the demand of its own citizens against them; and the exercise of this jurisdiction in no respect infringes upon the sovereignty of the State where the owners are domiciled. Every State owes protection to its own citizens; and, when non-residents deal with them, it is a legitimate and just exercise of authority to hold and appropriate any property owned by such non-residents to satisfy the claims of its citizens. It is in virtue of the State's jurisdiction over the property of the non-resident situated within its limits that its tribunals can inquire into that non-resident's obligations to its own citizens, and the inquiry can then be carried only to the extent necessary to control the disposition of the property. If the non-residents have no property in the State, there is nothing upon which the tribunals can adjudicate.

Substituted service by publication, or in any other authorized form, may be sufficient to inform parties of the object of proceedings taken where property is once brought under the control of the court by seizure or some equivalent act. The law assumes that property is always in the possession of its owner, in person or by agent; and it proceeds upon the theory that its seizure will inform him, not only that it is taken into the custody of the court, but that he must look to any proceedings authorized by law upon such seizure for its condemnation and sale. * * * In other words, such service may answer in all actions which are substantially proceedings in rem. But where the entire object of the action is to determine the personal rights and obligations of the defendants, that is, where the suit is merely in personam, constructive service in this form upon a non-resident is ineffectual for any purpose. * * * Process sent to him out of the State, and process published within it, are equally unavailing in proceedings to establish his personal liability. * * *

The force and effect of judgments rendered against non-residents without personal service of process upon them, or their voluntary appearance, have been the subject of frequent consideration in the courts of the United States and of the several States, as attempts have been made to enforce such judgments in States other than those in which they were rendered, under the provision of the Constitution requiring that "full faith and credit shall be given in each State to the public acts, records, and judicial proceedings of every other State" * * *

It follows from the views expressed that the personal judgment recovered in the State court of Oregon against the plaintiff herein, then a non-resident of the State, was without any validity, and did not authorize a sale of the property in controversy.

To prevent any misapplication of the views expressed in this opinion, it is proper to observe that we do not mean to assert, by any thing we have said, that a State may not authorize proceedings to determine the status of one of its citizens towards a non-resident, which would be binding within the State, though made without service of process or personal notice to the non-resident. The jurisdiction which every State possesses to determine the civil status and capacities of all its inhabitants involves authority to prescribe the conditions on which proceedings affecting them may be commenced and carried on within its territory. The State, for example, has absolute right to prescribe the conditions upon which the marriage relation between its own citizens shall be created, and the causes for which it may be dissolved. * * *

Neither do we mean to assert that a State may not require a nonresident entering into a partnership or association within its limits, or making contracts enforceable there, to appoint an agent or representative in the State to receive service of process and notice in legal proceedings instituted with respect to such partnership, association, or contracts, or to designate a place where such service may be made and notice given, and provide, upon their failure, to make such appointment or to designate such place that service may be made upon a public officer designated for that purpose, or in some other prescribed way, and that judgments rendered upon such service may not be binding upon the nonresidents both within and without the State. * * *

Notes and Questions

1. With *in personam* jurisdiction, a court has the authority to enter a judgment against a defendant that is personally binding and which can be taken to other parts of the same state or to another state to be enforced. With *in rem* jurisdiction, a court has the power to determine the rights of the parties in specific property within the state's boundary. Using *quasi in rem* jurisdiction enables a court to exercise power over a defendant's property by attachment, and use it to satisfy a plaintiff's personal claim against the defendant. However, quasi in rem jurisdiction limits the plaintiff to recovering an amount not exceeding the value of the property.

What did *Pennoyer* hold? Which type of jurisdiction (*in rem*, *in personam*, or *quasi in rem*) was being asserted? Why did the assertion of that jurisdiction not succeed?

After *Pennoyer*, states could exercise personal jurisdiction over any defendant served while present in the state where a claim was filed. Courts could not serve nonresident defendants who were outside the forum state, because service would assume the sovereign power of the other states. Any judicial decision without the proper use of "power" was void and unenforceable. *Pennoyer* protected a nonresident defendant from being sued in a state where he could not be served and owned no property.

2. Based on the *Pennoyer* dicta, describe the two exceptions to the general rule that are available to invoke the jurisdiction of the court over the nonresident defendant.

3. After *Pennoyer*, what type of service of process is necessary for a personal judgment against a defendant? When, if ever, is constructive service

of process permitted? In *Mitchell v. Neff*, what could Mitchell have done to protect the validity of any judgment he obtained?

What is the purpose of notice to the defendant? For example under the Court's "principles of public law" as to an *in personam* judgment, even if Neff had learned about the lawsuit when he was outside Oregon, the Oregon court still would have lacked the power to enter a binding judgment against Neff. By contrast, if Mitchell had seized Neff's property (with notice by publication to Neff) before the judgment was entered, the seizure itself would have been sufficient, because the property's seizure has the effect of informing the owner about the seizure. Does either of these notice concepts make sense?

4. What practical limitations does the *Pennoyer* principle impose on plaintiffs who want to sue nonresident defendants? What options does a plaintiff have to sue a nonresident defendant?

5. In dicta, the Court referred to the Fourteenth Amendment, but that provision was not in effect until 1868, after the sheriff sold Neff's property. However, the Court left no doubt that the Due Process Clause of the Fourteenth Amendment would be important in future decisions about the exercise of jurisdiction over nonresident defendants.

6. When is a nonresident defendant considered to be within a state? Suppose that a nonresident is on a jet going from California to New York. He has recently been sued in a Kansas state court. Can the Kansas sheriff sitting next to the defendant on the flight validly invoke the jurisdiction of the Kansas court by serving him with the court papers when the jet is flying over Kansas? See *Grace v. MacArthur*, 170 F.Supp. 442 (E.D. Ark. 1959), where the court upheld jurisdiction because it had occurred when the defendant was within the "territorial limits" of the forum state. The court noted that "a time may come ... when commercial aircraft will fly at altitudes so high that it would be unrealistic to consider them as being within the territorial limits" of a particular state. Does the jet's altitude matter under *Pennoyer* if the defendant's presence "within" the state can be determined?

7. For an entertaining discussion about the parties in *Pennoyer*, read Wendy Collins Perdue, "Sin, Scandal, and Substantive Due Process: Personal Jurisdiction and *Pennoyer* Reconsidered," 62 Wash. L. Rev. 479 (1987).

Problems

Based on your reading of *Pennoyer*, check on your understanding of the scope of its holding by thinking about the following problems.

1. If a Florida resident sues a North Carolina resident in a Florida state court, where does the defendant have to be served?

2. Can the North Carolina defendant be served while traveling through Florida?

3. The North Carolina defendant owns property in Florida. What can the Florida plaintiff do to obtain jurisdiction?

4. What if the defendant voluntarily appears in Florida to contest the merits of the plaintiff's claim?

5. If the Florida plaintiff notifies the defendant by publication and obtains a default judgment, can the Florida judgment be enforced against the defendant in North Carolina?

6. The claim in the Florida lawsuit seeks a divorce, and the defendant is served with court papers in North Carolina. Is the defendant's objection to the location of the notice proper?

7. The claim in the Florida lawsuit seeks a divorce, plus maintenance, custody, and child support. The defendant is served with court papers in North Carolina. Is the defendant's objection to the location of the notice proper?

As interstate travel expanded and as corporations from other states increased, legislators decided that it was important to exercise state authority over the nonresident person or entity causing harm to their citizens. "Eventually the pressures of a rapidly growing country attenuated the need to reduce the restrictions placed on amenability by the sovereignty theory in *Pennoyer*, and the law of amenability began its complex evolution." Diane Kaplan, "Paddling Up the Wrong Stream: Why the Stream of Commerce Theory Is Not Part of the Minimum Contacts Doctrine," 55 Baylor L.Rev. 503 (2003). There were numerous assertions of jurisdiction over persons who could not be served while physically in the forum state. The enacted statutes authorized courts to assert personal jurisdiction over nonresident defendants in specified circumstances that were limited in scope.

Fifty years after *Pennoyer v. Neff*, the Court extended the explicit, knowing appointment of an agent within a state for business dealings to the implicit appointment of an agent within the state resulting from a nonresident driving in another state. *Hess v. Pawloski*, 274 U.S. 352, 47 S.Ct. 632, 71 L.Ed. 1091 (1927) upheld a Massachusetts nonresident motorist statute that specifically deemed driving within the state as implied consent to being sued there for any claim arising from that driving. Even though the nonresident driver was unlikely to have been present at the time the lawsuit was filed, at least the driver had been present in the state at the time of the relevant conduct.

The Court stressed that because "[m]otor vehicles are dangerous machines, even when skillfully and carefully operated, . . . the use of the highway by the nonresident is the equivalent of the appointment of [an agent] on whom process may be served." Despite the policy reasons for implied consent, the consent is a fiction because the defendant probably does not understand that consent has occurred. The Court also noted the statute provides a plaintiff from the forum state "a convenient method" to enforce his rights, i.e., by suing in a state that he may never have left. Many states retain nonresident motorist statutes, even though additional, broader "long-arm" statutes have supplanted the need for the older legislation. A discussion about long-arm statutes occurs in the next section.

The next case, *International Shoe v. Washington,* also addressed the application of a long-arm statute in a specific factual context. The Court announced a test that still governs whether a state's exercise of jurisdiction over a nonresident is consistent with Fourteenth Amendment due process.

INTERNATIONAL SHOE CO. v. WASHINGTON

326 U.S. 310, 66 S.Ct. 154, 90 L.Ed. 95 (1945)

Mr. Chief Justice STONE delivered the opinion of the Court.

The questions for decision are (1) whether, within the limitations of the due process clause of the Fourteenth Amendment, appellant, a Delaware corporation, has by its activities in the State of Washington rendered itself amenable to proceedings in the courts of that state to recover unpaid contributions to the state unemployment compensation fund exacted by state statutes, and (2) whether the state [has the power to tax the defendant].

The statutes in question set up a comprehensive scheme of unemployment compensation, the costs of which are defrayed by contributions required to be made by employers to a state unemployment compensation fund. Section 14(c) of the Act, Wash.Rev.Stat. 1941 Supp., s 9998—114c, authorizes respondent Commissioner to issue an order and notice of assessment of delinquent contributions upon prescribed personal service of the notice upon the employer if found within the state, or, if not so found, by mailing the notice to the employer by registered mail at his last known address. * * *

In this case notice of assessment for the years in question was personally served upon a sales solicitor employed by appellant in the State of Washington, and a copy of the notice was mailed by registered mail to appellant at its address in St. Louis, Missouri. Appellant appeared specially before the office of unemployment and moved to set aside the order and notice of assessment. . . . * * *

The motion was heard on evidence and a stipulation of facts by the appeal tribunal which denied the motion and ruled that respondent Commissioner was entitled to recover the unpaid contributions. That action was affirmed by the Commissioner; both the Superior Court and the [Washington] Supreme Court affirmed. Appellant in each of these courts assailed the statute as applied, as a violation of the due process clause of the Fourteenth Amendment, and as imposing a constitutionally prohibited burden on interstate commerce. * * *

Appellant is a Delaware corporation, having its principal place of business in St. Louis, Missouri, and is engaged in the manufacture and sale of shoes and other footwear. It maintains places of business in several states, other than Washington, at which its manufacturing is carried on and from which its merchandise is distributed interstate through several sales units or branches located outside the State of Washington.

Appellant has no office in Washington and makes no contracts either for sale or purchase of merchandise there. It maintains no stock of merchandise in that state and makes there no deliveries of goods in intrastate commerce. During the years from 1937 to 1940, now in question, appellant employed eleven to thirteen salesmen under direct supervision and control of sales managers located in St. Louis. These salesmen resided in Washington; their principal activities were confined to that state; and they were compensated by commissions based upon the amount of their sales. The commissions for each year totaled more than $31,000. Appellant supplies its salesmen with a line of samples, each consisting of one shoe of a pair, which they display to prospective purchasers. On occasion they rent permanent sample rooms, for exhibiting samples, in business buildings, or rent rooms in hotels or business buildings temporarily for that purpose. The cost of such rentals is reimbursed by appellant.

The authority of the salesmen is limited to exhibiting their samples and soliciting orders from prospective buyers, at prices and on terms fixed by appellant. The salesmen transmit the orders to appellant's office in St. Louis for acceptance or rejection, and when accepted the merchandise for filling the orders is shipped f.o.b. from points outside Washington to the purchasers within the state. All the merchandise shipped into Washington is invoiced at the place of shipment from which collections are made. No salesman has authority to enter into contracts or to make collections.

* * *

Appellant ... insists that its activities within the state were not sufficient to manifest its 'presence' there and that in its absence the state courts were without jurisdiction, that consequently it was a denial of due process for the state to subject appellant to suit. It refers to those cases in which it was said that the mere solicitation of orders for the purchase of goods within a state, to be accepted without the state and filled by shipment of the purchased goods interstate, does not render the corporation seller amenable to suit within the state. * * * And appellant further argues that since it was not present within the state, it is a denial of due process to subject it to taxation or other money exaction. It thus denies the power of the state to lay the tax or to subject appellant to a suit for its collection.

Historically the jurisdiction of courts to render judgment in personam is grounded on their de facto power over the defendant's person. Hence his presence within the territorial jurisdiction of court was prerequisite to its rendition of a judgment personally binding him. *Pennoyer v. Neff*, 95 U.S. 714, 733. But now that the *capias ad respondendum* has given way to personal service of summons or other form of notice, due process requires only that in order to subject a defendant to a judgment in personam, if he be not present within the territory of the forum, he have certain minimum contacts with it such that the maintenance of the suit does not offend 'traditional notions of fair play and substantial justice.' *Milliken v. Meyer*, 311 U.S. 457, 463. See Holmes, J., in *McDonald v. Mabee*, 243 U.S. 90, 91.

* * * To say that the corporation is so far 'present' there as to satisfy due process requirements, for purposes of taxation or the maintenance of suits against it in the courts of the state, is to beg the question to be decided. For the terms 'present' or 'presence' are used merely to symbolize those activities of the corporation's agent within the state which courts will deem to be sufficient to satisfy the demands of due process. L. Hand, J., in *Hutchinson v. Chase & Gilbert*, 2 Cir., 45 F.2d 139, 141. Those demands may be met by such contacts of the corporation with the state of the forum as make it reasonable, in the context of our federal system of government, to require the corporation to defend the particular suit which is brought there. An 'estimate of the inconveniences' which would result to the corporation from a trial away from its 'home' or principal place of business is relevant in this connection.

"Presence" in the state in this sense has never been doubted when the activities of the corporation there have not only been continuous and systematic, but also give rise to the liabilities sued on, even though no consent to be sued or authorization to an agent to accept service of process has been given. Conversely it has been generally recognized that the casual presence of the corporate agent or even his conduct of single or isolated items of activities in a state in the corporation's behalf are not enough to subject it to suit on causes of action unconnected with the activities there. To require the corporation in such circumstances to defend the suit away from its home or other jurisdiction where it carries on more substantial activities has been thought to lay too great and unreasonable a burden on the corporation to comport with due process. * * *

Finally, although the commission of some single or occasional acts of the corporate agent in a state sufficient to impose an obligation or liability on the corporation has not been thought to confer upon the state authority to enforce it, other such acts, because of their nature and quality and the circumstances of their commission, may be deemed sufficient to render the corporation liable to suit.

It is evident that the criteria by which we mark the boundary line between those activities which justify the subjection of a corporation to suit, and those which do not, cannot be simply mechanical or quantitative. The test is not merely, as has sometimes been suggested, whether the activity, which the corporation has seen fit to procure through its agents in another state, is a little more or a little less. Whether due process is satisfied must depend rather upon the quality and nature of the activity in relation to the fair and orderly administration of the laws which it was the purpose of the due process clause to insure. That clause does not contemplate that a state may make binding a judgment in personam against an individual or corporate defendant with which the state has no contacts, ties, or relations.

But to the extent that a corporation exercises the privilege of conducting activities within a state, it enjoys the benefits and protection of the laws of that state. The exercise of that privilege may give rise to obligations; and, so far as those obligations arise out of or are connected with the activities within the state, a procedure which requires the corporation to respond to a suit brought to enforce them can, in most instances, hardly be said to be undue.

Applying these standards, the activities carried on in behalf of appellant in the State of Washington were neither irregular nor casual. They were systematic and continuous throughout the years in question. They resulted in a large volume of interstate business, in the course of which appellant received the benefits and protection of the laws of the state, including the right to resort to the courts for the enforcement of its rights. The obligation which is here sued upon arose out of those very activities. It is evident that these operations establish sufficient contacts or ties with the state of the forum to make it reasonable and just according to our traditional conception of fair play and substantial justice to permit the state to enforce the obligations which appellant has incurred there. * * *

Affirmed.

Mr. Justice BLACK delivered the following opinion.

* * *

I believe that the Federal Constitution leaves to each State, without any "ifs" or "buts", a power to tax and to open the doors of its courts for its citizens to sue corporations whose agents do business in those States. Believing that the Constitution gave the States that power, I think it a judicial deprivation to condition its exercise upon this Court's notion of "fair play", however appealing that term may be. Nor can I stretch the meaning of due process so far as to authorize this Court to deprive a State of the right to afford judicial protection to its citizens on the ground that it would be more "convenient" for the corporation to be sued somewhere else.

There is a strong emotional appeal in the words "fair play", "justice", and "reasonableness." But they were not chosen by those who wrote the original Constitution or the Fourteenth Amendment as a measuring rod for this Court to use in invalidating State or Federal laws passed by elected legislative representatives. No one, not even those who most feared a democratic government, ever formally proposed that courts should be given power to invalidate legislation under any such elastic standards. Express prohibitions against certain types of legislation are found in the Constitution, and under the long settled practice, courts invalidate laws found to conflict with them. This requires interpretation, and interpretation, it is true, may result in extension of the

Constitution's purpose. But that is no reason for reading the due process clause so as to restrict a State's power to tax and sue those whose activities affect persons and businesses within the State, provided proper service can be had. * * *

Notes and Questions

1.   Near the end of the majority opinion Chief Justice Stone stated:

Whether due process is satisfied must depend rather upon the quality and nature of the activity in relation to the fair and orderly administration of the laws which it was the purpose of the due process clause to insure. That clause does not contemplate that a state may make binding a judgment in personam against an individual or corporate defendant with which the state has no contacts, ties, or relations.

After *International Shoe*, is *Pennoyer*'s holding about power or presence still sound? Is the minimum contacts standard relevant when a nonresident defendant is served in the forum state? *International Shoe* appears to assume that jurisdiction over a defendant could be based on his physical presence alone:

[D]ue process requires only that in order to subject a defendant to a judgment in personam, *if he be not present within the territory of the forum*, he have certain minimum contacts with it such that the maintenance of the suit does not offend "traditional notions of fair play and substantial justice." [emphasis added]

Did the Court intend the minimum contacts standard to control jurisdiction over nonresident defendants, regardless of whether they are served inside the forum state?

2.   What did the Court hold? Was there an implied consent statute in Washington, providing for service of process on a nonresident, similar to the Massachusetts provision in *Hess*? Pursuant to the statute, how was the defendant served with the papers about the lawsuit?

3.   How did International Shoe raise its objection to Washington's assertion of jurisdiction over it? What is meant when the Court states that the defendant appeared "specially"?

4.   The Court says that a nonresident defendant must have minimum contacts with a state in order to be required to defend itself in that distant place. What is a "contact"? Does a contact have to be a literal contact between two vehicles? Does "contact" include doing business within a state? Making solicitation phone calls? Publishing a periodical? Does *any* relationship of a defendant with a state or with persons inside the state satisfy the definition of a contact, or is something more required to constitute a contact relevant to personal jurisdiction?

5.   In its opinion, the Court describes several basic principles depicting the connection or relationship between the nature of the nonresident defendant's activities in the forum state, on the one hand, and the relation of the plaintiff's claim to the defendant's activities within the state. Those principles do not so much provide a set rule as they furnish a guide by which each case may be decided on its particular facts.

Draw a square with four cells, identifying the nature of the nonresident's activities in the forum state across the top, dividing them as either continuous and systematic activities or as isolated activity. Then, down the left side, divide the square into claims arising from the defendant's activity in the forum state and claims that do not arise from the activity there.

Cell #1 represents the situation when the defendant has continuous and systematic activities within the forum state and the plaintiff's claim arises from those activities by the defendant. Within Cell #2, the defendant again has continuous and systematic activities, but this time the plaintiff's claim does not arise from those activities. Cell #3 would involve only an isolated contact by the defendant in the forum state and the plaintiff's claim does not arise from that activity. Cell #4 indicates isolated activity by the defendant, but this time the plaintiff's claim arises from that activity.

Into which cells/parts of the fourfold table does *International Shoe* case belong? The Court's opinion suggests that the more closely related the defendant's contacts are to the plaintiff's claim, the fewer contacts that a plaintiff has to show in order to satisfy the notion of fair play and substantial justice. Where does *Hess* belong?

For the next few cases, identify which cell in which each case belongs. Does plotting the placement of the cases follow any pattern relating to the Court's conclusion about the propriety of asserting jurisdiction over the nonresident? Does that pattern provide some predictability about how a court may decide a distinct yet comparable fact pattern?

6.   Under the facts, was there anything inconvenient for International Shoe about defending itself in Washington state against Washington's attempt to collect its unemployment compensation fund premiums?

7.   What was Justice Black's concern in his dissent? Was his concern legitimate? From a practical perspective, what potential problems accompany a vague legal standard? As general counsel for a corporation doing business in a variety of states, how do you advise your client about anticipating its legal obligations in different locales when the legal standard in each state is vague?

8.   One method to limit the places a business can be sued by a consumer is to include a "forum selection" clause in the contract. The clause constitutes consent by a consumer that any claim against the business based on the contract must be brought only in a federal or state court of a particular state. In CARNIVAL CRUISE LINES, INC. v. SHUTE, 499 U.S. 585, 111 S.Ct. 1522, 113 L.Ed.2d 622 (1991), the Court presumed that in a maritime case any forum selection clause is valid, even a clause in an adhesion contract (a contract where one party has no bargaining power), if it is reasonably communicated to the claimant. In *Shute*, the forum selection clause was printed on a cruise passenger ticket and required the Washington plaintiff to bring suit in Florida. However, the claimant did not have the opportunity to review the clause until after she had paid for the ticket.

The Court cited several reasons justifying a forum selection clause in travel contexts: because passengers are from many places, in case of a mass disaster the business could be sued in many places; the clause clarifies where any claim should be brought, thereby reducing the time and expense of litigation; and any savings to the business by limiting the courts where it could be sued would result in lower passenger fares.

The *Shute* forum selection clause prescribing Florida as the forum for litigation was not overreaching or unreasonably inconvenient to the Washington resident, because in the absence of fraud the plaintiff "presumably retained the option of rejecting the contract with impunity." Do you agree? Does it matter that many of the cruise line's trips departed from Florida? Does the option of rejecting the contract exist when the ticket is non-refundable? In terms of inconvenience, suppose the clause designates a foreign court system as the "agreed" forum? Do the plaintiff's limited resources to pursue a distant claim under a forum selection clause constitute an unreasonable inconvenience to the claimant?

---

2. Jurisdiction Over Nonresident Defendants

The concept of domicile already was discussed regarding diversity of citizenship subject matter jurisdiction. Domicile is also relevant to personal jurisdiction. When a defendant's domicile is in the forum state, the state has power to decide all claims of whatever nature against the defendant. An individual who lives in the state or a corporation that is incorporated there is domiciled in that state, giving the state the power to adjudicate claims brought against either the individual or corporation. The rationale for exercising this power is that, because the state provides privileges to its citizens and protects them, the citizens have a reciprocal duty to defend lawsuits brought in the courts where they reside. See *Milliken v. Meyer*, 311 U.S. 457, 61 S.Ct. 339, 85 L.Ed. 278 (1940).

A second method of exercising jurisdiction over an individual or a business defendant occurs when either type of defendant consents to be sued in the courts of the state. As noted earlier, the consent may occur prior to the filing of the lawsuit. In *Hess v. Pawloski*, 274 U.S. 352, 47 S.Ct. 632, 71 L.Ed. 1091 (1927), the Court approved the fiction of implied consent to jurisdiction by a nonresident who consents to being sued in a state where he drives.

Explicit consent also provides authority for a trial court to adjudicate disputes. For example, a contract between business entities or even an airline ticket may include a provision that the parties to the contract consent to a particular state's authority, i.e., a forum selection clause. Another method of consent was mentioned in *Pennoyer*: a person or entity seeking to do business in a state must appoint a local agent to accept service of process.

It is also possible for a defendant to consent to the jurisdiction of a court following the filing of a lawsuit. As discussed later in this Chapter, the effect of a defendant's waiver of service of process operates as consent to the jurisdiction of the court where the lawsuit was filed. Frequently, in divorce cases for example a defendant will enter his appearance in a case and waive service of process in order to reduce the costs of the litigation.

a. *Specific Jurisdiction*

Courts use specific jurisdiction to exercise authority over a plaintiff's claim that arises out of or relates to a nonresident defendant's activities within a state. The type of conduct by a defendant that can subject him to the jurisdiction of the court is diverse. For example, the plaintiff's claim may be that the defendant has engaged in a tortious act, some illegal business activity, or improper property ownership. In *International Shoe*, the obligation to pay unemployment compensation taxes arose from the activities of International Shoe Co.'s salesmen in the forum state

The nature of the analysis for specific jurisdiction cases is twofold. The plaintiff must show that 1) her claim arises from the defendant's conduct, which fits the language of the state's "long-arm" statute, and 2) the exercise of jurisdiction by the court over the nonresident does not offend the Due Process Clause of the Fourteenth Amendment.

The Due Process Clause defines the outer boundaries of permissible jurisdictional power. It is left to the legislatures within each state to grant power to its courts to exercise specific personal jurisdiction through long-arm statutes. What is meant by a "long-arm" statute? As to the nature and scope of long-arm statutes, you already have read about two of them. The implied consent nonresident motorist statute in *Hess* was an early example of a long-arm statute that has a precise scope. The unemployment compensation statute in *International Shoe* also permitted a state judiciary to reach beyond its borders to exert its authority over a nonresident defendant based on that defendant's activities in the state. As you will read later in this chapter, a plaintiff also typically uses a long-arm statute to achieve service of process over a nonresident defendant who may not be physically present in the forum state.

There are two types of modern long-arm statutes. A "laundry list" long-arm simply lists the types of particular activity by the defendant which the legislature has decided justifies subjecting the nonresident defendant to jurisdiction there. With a laundry-list long-arm, the plaintiff's task is to match the legislative language with the defendant's conduct within the state (e.g., the plaintiff's claim arises from a defendant "transacting business" in the forum). If the facts fit at least one of the provisions of the laundry list long-arm statute, the legal analysis can progress to the next step. A plaintiff's inability to convince the court of that fit will end the inquiry as to specific jurisdiction.

In the early 1960s, the National Conference of Commissioners on Uniform State Laws adopted a uniform long-arm statute, which provided:

(1) A court may exercise personal jurisdiction over a person, who acts directly or by an agent, as to a claim for relief arising from the person's

(a) transacting any business in this state;

(b) contracting to supply services or things in this state;

(c) causing tortious injury by an act or omission in this state;

(d) causing tortious injury in this state by an act or omission outside this state if he regularly does or solicits business, or engages in any other persistent course of conduct, or derives substantial revenue from goods used or consumed or services rendered, in this state;

(e) having an interest in, using or possessing real property in this state; or

(f) contracting to insure any person, property or risk located within this state at the time of contracting.

While few states adopted the precise language of the uniform act, it served as a model for many early attempts by states to draft a broad, yet constitutional, long-arm laundry list long-arm statute.

Consider the scope of the uniform statute. Its language may preclude filing a claim against a nonresident based on a breach of warranty, a common alternative claim for relief to negligence. For example, does the uniform act include a claim against a nonresident arising from injuries to any person in the state by an express or implied breach of warranty made in sale of goods *outside* the state, when the seller knew that the person would use the goods *in* the state? A section of the uniform act deals with tortious injuries, but not injuries from a breach of warranty. It appears that neither the "transacting any business" or "contracting to supply ... goods" sections would apply to a breach of warranty made outside the state.

The second type of long-arm statute is known as a "due process" long-arm. Instead of listing situations when jurisdiction over a nonresident is proper, the statute merely states that the particular state can exercise personal jurisdiction over a nonresident to the extent permitted by due process (the second step of the specific jurisdiction analysis). Two examples of due process long-arm statutes follow. California Code of Civil Procedure § 410.10 states:

A court of this state may exercise jurisdiction on any basis not inconsistent with the Constitution of this state or of the United States.

Rhode Island General Laws Annotated § 9–5–33(a) declares:

Every foreign corporation, every individual not a resident of this state or his executor or administrator, and every partnership or association, composed of any person or persons, not such residents, that shall have the necessary minimum contacts with the state of Rhode Island, shall be subject to the jurisdiction of the state of

Rhode Island, and the courts of this state shall hold such foreign corporations and such nonresident individuals or their executors or administrators, and such partnerships or associations amenable to suit in Rhode Island in every case not contrary to the provisions of the constitution or laws of the United States.

The effect of a due process long-arm statute on the judicial analysis is to reduce an otherwise two step procedure into one step. Analysis under the due process long-arm and constitutional due process is identical. See, e.g., *Bridgeport Music, Inc. v. Still N The Water Publishing*, 327 F.3d 472 (6th Cir. 2003). Instead of insuring compliance with both a laundry list long-arm statute and constitutional due process, a court in a state using a due process long-arm only needs to apply the constitutional due process analysis to the case.

Even if the defendant's activities satisfy the long-arm statute, it is still possible that exercising jurisdiction over the nonresident defendant nevertheless will fail because of a due process violation. As you read in *International Shoe*, due process requires that, in order to subject a nonresident defendant to the jurisdiction of the court, the defendant must have minimum contacts with the forum state and entering a judgment against that defendant will not violate "fair play and substantial justice."

b. General Jurisdiction

Besides specific jurisdiction, the other focus of jurisdictional case law is general jurisdiction, under which a plaintiff's claim does not have to arise from the activities of the defendant in the forum state. In other words, a court in Ohio can exercise jurisdiction over a defendant even if the plaintiff's claim arose from the defendant's activities outside Ohio, because the defendant has so many contacts with the forum state that it is fair to subject that defendant to suit in Ohio on every possible claim. The nature of the legal analysis for general jurisdiction centers on constitutional due process alone. General jurisdiction may function as a back-up to specific jurisdiction in the event that a nonresident defendant's conduct in the forum state does not satisfy the language of the long-arm statute. Due to the defendant's continuous and systematic contacts with the jurisdiction, states use the normal service of process rules to notify the defendant within the state

The evolution of case law for general jurisdiction has produced a test by which the nonresident's contacts with the forum state must be "continuous and systematic," rather than the minimum contacts test used for specific jurisdiction. (Domicile is an example of the applicability of general jurisdiction, because of the extent of the domiciliary's contacts with the place where she lives.) Even though the state can exercise general jurisdiction over a nonresident defendant when the plaintiff's claim does not arise from the defendant's activities there, the due process trade-off is that the plaintiff must prove more than minimum contacts; the plaintiff must prove that the defendant's contacts with the forum state are continuous and systematic. The *Helicopteros* case in the next section will expand on this point.

Using either specific jurisdiction or general jurisdiction, even if the requisite contacts with the forum have been shown by the plaintiff, the defendant still can try to prove that exercising jurisdiction over him is nonetheless constitutionally unreasonable, i.e., it violates fair play and substantial justice to exert authority over the nonresident defendant. See, e.g., *Amoco Egypt Oil Co. v. Leonis Nav. Co.*, 1 F.3d 848 (9th Cir. 1993). Courts have identified at least five factors that are relevant to a fair play analysis: the burden on the defendant, the plaintiff's interest, the forum state's interest, the interstate judicial system's interest in obtaining the most efficient resolution of controversies, and the common interests of the states in promoting substantive social policies.

Recall that in the case of subject matter jurisdiction, its propriety consistently is determined at the time that a suit is filed. Personal jurisdiction cases are not as uniform. The case law is clear that post-filing contacts are irrelevant to the determination of personal jurisdiction. Some cases assert alternative rules, see, e.g., *Clune v. Alimak AB*, 233 F.3d 538, 544 n.8 (8th Cir. 2000) ("minimum contacts must occur at the time the cause of action arose, the time the suit is filed, or a reasonable period of time immediately prior to the filing of the lawsuit"). Other cases distinguish between specific jurisdiction and general jurisdiction cases. See, e.g., *Metropolitan Life Ins. v. Robertson–Ceco Corp.*, 84 F.3d 560, 569–70 (2d Cir.1996) (in general jurisdiction case, the court "should examine a defendant's contacts with the forum state over a period that is reasonable under the circumstances—up to and including the date the suit was filed—to assess whether they satisfy the 'continuous and systematic' standard"); *Steel v. United States*, 813 F.2d 1545, 1549 (9th Cir.1987) (to determine whether specific jurisdiction is proper, the court must examine the defendant's contacts with the forum at the time of the events underlying the dispute).

Exercise

For the state a) where you intend to practice after graduation, b) where your law school is located, and/or c) your professor assigns, go to that state's annotated statutes and research the long-arm statute typically used for exercising specific jurisdiction over nonresident defendants. Based on your research, print the statutory portion of the statute and bring it to class for discussion. In addition, answer the following questions.

1. Identify whether the type of long-arm statute in your state is a laundry list or due process long-arm.

2. If it is a due process long-arm statute:

A) Does the legislative history of the statute show that at one time there was a laundry list long-arm used in the state instead of a due process long-arm statute?

B) If the answer to part A) is yes, was the adoption of a due process long-arm made in response to a judicial decision that the former laundry list long-arm should be construed as if it were a due process long-arm statute?

3.   If it is a laundry list long-arm statute:

A) Note the types of statutory conduct available for a plaintiff's counsel to try to fit with the nonresident defendant's factual conduct.

B) Note the specificity or generality of some or all of the provisions, e.g., "transacting business," "contracting for services."

C) Note whether the list includes the possibility that jurisdiction can be exercised over a nonresident defendant whose conduct outside the state has caused some harm within the state.

D) Note when it was enacted as well as how many times the legislature has amended the long-arm statute since it was enacted.

E) Note how the federal and/or state courts have interpreted the laundry list long-arm statute, i.e., despite its laundry list specificity, have the courts nevertheless interpreted the long-arm statute as if it were a due process long-arm statute? See, e.g., *Aristech Chemical Intern. Ltd. v. Acrylic Fabricators Ltd.*, 138 F.3d 624 (6th Cir. 1998) (state laundry list long-arm statute extends as far as the federal due process clause).

Problems

1.   An Illinois resident's automobile collides in Georgia with a truck driven by a Georgia resident who has never been outside Georgia. If the Georgia resident sues the Illinois resident in an Illinois state court, can an Illinois court adjudicate the claim under jurisdiction based on:

A.   Domicile?

B.   Specific jurisdiction?

C.   General jurisdiction?

2.   In #1, if the Georgia resident sues the Illinois resident in a Georgia state court, can a Georgia court adjudicate the claim under jurisdiction based on:

A.   Domicile?

B.   Specific jurisdiction?

C.   General jurisdiction?

3.   In #1, if the Illinois resident sues the Georgia resident in a Georgia state court, can a Georgia court adjudicate the claim under jurisdiction based on:

A.   Domicile?

B.   Specific jurisdiction?

C.   General jurisdiction?

4.   In #1, if the Illinois resident sues the Georgia resident in an Illinois state court, can an Illinois court adjudicate the claim under jurisdiction based on:

A.   Domicile?

B.   Specific jurisdiction?

C.   General jurisdiction?

5.   Randy was driving on I–65 from his home in Indianapolis, Indiana to his Spring Break condominium in Mobile, Alabama. At Exit 2 in Franklin, Kentucky, he went to Ben's Franklin full service gas station to have his brakes checked. In a very short time, Ben replaced the brake shoes on Randy's SUV. After Ben wrote down Randy's license plate number when Randy paid him with a credit card, Randy resumed his trip to the Gulf of Mexico. Still traveling on I–65, Randy tried to apply his brakes, swerved and hit the center median. The SUV and Randy were both damaged in the Alabama wreck, which a later investigation revealed was caused by improperly installed brake shoes.

You are Randy's attorney, trying to determine your client's options for where to file a claim for personal injuries and property damage against Ben Brakeman, doing business as Ben's Franklin Gas Station. Assume that Indiana, Kentucky, and Alabama all have long-arm statutes identical to the Uniform Long-arm Act. Without reaching the due process issue, can a court in any of the states assert jurisdiction over Ben under the long-arm statute? Because laundry list long-arm statutes are phrased in the disjunctive, remember that it is necessary to identify only one statutory basis for invoking a long-arm statute.

6.   In #5, assume that instead of having his brakes immediately repaired, Randy had to leave his SUV with Ben and take a bus to Alabama for his vacation. Before leaving his SUV with Ben, Randy signed a contract with Ben agreeing to pay for the brake shoes and the labor for installing the brake shoes. When he returned to the gas station a week later, he refused to pay the bill because he thought it was well in excess of Ben's original estimate. This time, you are counsel for Ben. Again, assume that the Uniform Long-arm Act applies in all three states. Can a court in any of the states assert jurisdiction over Randy under a long-arm statute? Using domicile?

7.   An Ohio resident read a product advertisement in her local newspaper, and ordered the product from a Pennsylvania manufacturer that advertises every Sunday in all major Ohio Sunday newspapers. The customer offered to pick up the product in Pittsburgh. On the outskirts of Pittsburgh, the Ohio resident collided with the Pennsylvania manufacture's minivan. To make things worse, after returning to Ohio, the product malfunctioned but the manufacturer refused to return the purchase price. In an Ohio state court, the Ohio plaintiff sues the Pennsylvania manufacturer for negligence in connection with the wreck and for breach of contract in connection with the defective product. Can the Ohio court exert jurisdiction over the manufacturer, using domicile, specific jurisdiction, or general jurisdiction?

8.   Same facts as #7, except that the plaintiff's claim was for the vehicular collision only. In addition to the Pennsylvania manufacturer, the plaintiff also names the manufacturer's employee who was driving the minivan as a co-defendant. The employee lives in eastern Ohio. Can the Ohio

court exert jurisdiction over the defendants, using domicile, specific jurisdiction, or general jurisdiction?

9.   Fly-by-Night Insurance Co. operates a large bank of telephones in Michigan to solicit persons throughout the northeastern United States to purchase term life insurance policies. Each evening between 5:00 p.m. and 8:00 p.m., Fly-by-Night's agents interrupt countless families and individuals to sell them life insurance policies. You work for the Attorney General of Massachusetts considering a lawsuit to enjoin such telephone solicitations. Under the Uniform Long-arm Act, can your office file its claim in Massachusetts or in Michigan? If you were a state legislator who wanted to amend the long-arm statute to be more explicit about jurisdiction over telephone solicitors, what language would you propose to amend the statute?

---

3.   Emerging Personal Jurisdiction Principles

Following *International Shoe*, the Court decided several cases which led to confusion about the scope of the due process standard for exercising specific jurisdiction over a nonresident defendant under newly adopted long-arm statutes. In *McGee v. International Life Insurance Co.*, 355 U.S. 220, 78 S.Ct. 199, 2 L.Ed.2d 223 (1957), a Texas insurance company had bought out another company after it sold a life insurance policy by mail to an insured living in California. After the death of the insured, his mother attempted to collect the proceeds of the policy by suing the insurer in a California state court and serving the insurance company under the California long-arm statute. When the Texas company did not appear to defend the lawsuit, the California court awarded a default judgment to the insured's mother. However, because the Texas company had no assets in California, the insured's mother had to go to Texas to try to enforce the California judgment against the insurer. The precise issue before the Court was whether a Texas court had to enforce the California default judgment. If the California court had personal jurisdiction, the Texas court was required by the Full Faith and Credit Clause to enforce the California judgment.

The Supreme Court held that the insurer's isolated contact through the sale of the policy was sufficient contact with California to subject the insurer to the authority of the California courts. Even though the insurer had no office or agent in California, the Court upheld the jurisdiction of the California court, because the insurance contract had a substantial connection with California: the contract was delivered there, the premiums were mailed there, and the insured was a California resident when he died. From a convenience viewpoint, the insured's mother could not bear the cost of going to Texas to litigate the validity of the insurance contract as easily as the Texas company could afford to hire counsel in California to defend the lawsuit. The connection of the nonresident insurance company was the most tenuous of any case in which the Court has upheld jurisdiction.

A year later, *Hanson v. Denckla*, 357 U.S. 235, 78 S.Ct. 1228, 2 L.Ed.2d 1283 (1958) checked the expansion of jurisdiction under *McGee's* economic rationale, and showed that there are limits beyond which due process cannot be stretched. After a Pennsylvania woman executed a trust in Delaware with a Delaware bank as trustee, she moved to Florida where she exercised her power to appoint the beneficiaries of the trust. Following her death, her children fought over whether her assets should pass to them under her will, or whether her grandchildren should receive her estate through the trust. The children challenged her appointment of trust beneficiaries by suing the Delaware trustee and the grandchildren in Florida, and having them served under the Florida long-arm statute. Several defendants challenged Florida's jurisdiction over the trustee. Before a Florida judgment for the plaintiffs was rendered, a parallel lawsuit was brought by the grandchildren in Delaware. The Florida judgment winners took their judgment to Delaware for enforcement, arguing that the Florida judgment operated as *res judicata* on the Delaware case. However, the Delaware court refused to give it full faith and credit because the Florida court lacked personal jurisdiction over the Delaware trustee.

Were the bank's activities in Florida regarding the trust sufficient for the Florida court to have jurisdiction over the nonresident trustee? The Supreme Court held that the Delaware trustee lacked the necessary minimal contacts with Florida. Therefore, the Delaware court was under no obligation to give full faith and credit to the Florida judgment because it was invalid under the due process clause of the Fourteenth Amendment. The trustee had no office in Florida, no trust assets were administered or held there, and the claim did not arise from any act done or transaction consummated in Florida by the Delaware trustee. It was immaterial to jurisdiction over the trustee that the deceased and most of the beneficiaries lived in Florida, or that she exercised the power of appointment unilaterally in Florida. The *Hanson* opinion noted that

> the unilateral activity of those who claim some relationship with a nonresident defendant cannot satisfy the requirement of contact with the forum State.... [I]t is essential in each case that there be some act by which the defendant *purposely avails* itself of the privilege of conducting activities within the forum State, thus invoking the privileges and protections of its laws. [emphasis supplied]

To compare the two cases, *McGee* and *Hanson* each involved an out-of-state corporate defendant that had only one customer in the forum state. However, the relationships in each case began differently. In *McGee*, the insurance company solicited the insured by sending an offer to insure him in California. In *Hanson*, the Delaware trustee did not seek business in Florida; the trustee's contact with Florida began when the customer moved there.

SHAFFER v. HEITNER

433 U.S. 186, 97 S.Ct. 2569, 53 L.Ed.2d 683 (1977)

Mr. Justice MARSHALL delivered the opinion of the Court.

[Plaintiff Heitner brought a shareholders' derivative suit in Delaware against 28 present or former nonresident officers and directors of Greyhound Corporation, a Delaware corporation with its national headquarters in Arizona, for damages they had caused the corporation through mismanagement in Oregon. (The Court noted in fn. 37 of its opinion that the case did not raise and it was not considering the issue of "whether the presence of a defendant's property in a State is a sufficient basis for jurisdiction when no other forum is available to the plaintiff.") Delaware law permitted Heitner to ask the trial court for an order sequestering (an equity term for attachment) a defendant's property in the state. Because Heitner was unable to acquire personal jurisdiction over the nonresident defendants, the sequestration allowed him to proceed against any of their property located within Delaware by using quasi in rem jurisdiction.

The trial court ordered that the defendants' Greyhound stock be subject to "stop transfer orders" on Greyhound's records. The orders had an effect similar to a seizure of 82,000 shares of Greyhound stock by the court. Under Delaware law, the location of all Greyhound stock was deemed to be in the state, due to Greyhound being a Delaware corporation, even though the stock certificates were located elsewhere. The controversy in the case concerned the constitutionality of the Delaware sequestration statute. The defendant made a special appearance to quash service and to vacate the trial court's order of sequestration. Delaware state courts all rejected the defendants' due process arguments.]

II

The Delaware courts rejected appellants' jurisdictional challenge by noting that this suit was brought as a quasi in rem proceeding. Since quasi in rem jurisdiction is traditionally based on attachment or seizure of property present in the jurisdiction, not on contacts between the defendant and the State, the courts considered appellants' claimed lack of contacts with Delaware to be unimportant. This categorical analysis assumes the continued soundness of the conceptual structure founded on the century-old case of *Pennoyer v. Neff*, 95 U.S. 714 (1878).

* * *

From our perspective, the importance of *Pennoyer* is not its result, but the fact that its principles and corollaries derived from them became the basic elements of the constitutional doctrine governing state-court jurisdiction. As we have noted, under *Pennoyer* state authority to adjudicate was based on the jurisdiction's power over either persons or property. This fundamental concept is embodied in the very vocabulary which we use to describe judgments. If a court's jurisdiction is based on its authority over the defendant's person, the action and judgment are denominated "*in personam*" and can impose a personal obligation on the defendant in favor of the plaintiff. If jurisdiction is based on the court's power over property within its territory, the action is called "*in rem*" or "*quasi in rem*." The effect of a judgment in such a case is limited to the property that supports jurisdiction and does not impose a personal liability on the property owner, since he is not before the court. In *Pennoyer*'s terms, the owner is affected only "indirectly" by an *in rem* judgment adverse to his interest in the property subject to the court's disposition.

By concluding that "(t)he authority of every tribunal is necessarily restricted by the territorial limits of the State in which it is established," *Pennoyer* sharply limited the availability of in personam jurisdiction over defendants not resident in the forum State. If a nonresident defendant could not be found in a State, he could not be sued there. On the other hand, since the State in which property was located was considered to have exclusive sovereignty over that property, *in rem* actions could proceed regardless of the owner's location. Indeed, since a State's process could not reach beyond its borders, this Court held after *Pennoyer* that due process did not require any effort to give a property owner personal notice that his property was involved in an *in rem* proceeding.

* * *

The question in *International Shoe* was whether the corporation was subject to the judicial and taxing jurisdiction of Washington. Mr. Chief Justice Stone's opinion for the Court began its analysis of that question by noting that the historical basis of in personam jurisdiction was a court's power over the defendant's person. That power, however, was no longer the central concern:

> But now that the *capias ad respondendum* has given way to personal service of summons or other form of notice, due process requires only that in order to subject a defendant to a judgment in personam, if he be not present within the territory of the forum, he have certain minimum contacts with it such that the maintenance of the suit does not offend "traditional notions of fair play and substantial justice."

Thus, the inquiry into the State's jurisdiction over a foreign corporation appropriately focused not on whether the corporation was "present" but on whether there have been "such contacts of the corporation with the state of the forum as make it reasonable, in the context of our federal system of government, to require the corporation to defend the particular suit which is brought there." Mechanical or quantitative evaluations of the defendant's activities in the forum could not resolve the question of reasonableness:

> Whether due process is satisfied must depend rather upon the quality and nature of the activity in relation to the fair and orderly administration of the laws which it was the purpose of the due process clause to insure. That clause does not contemplate that a

state may make binding a judgment in personam against an individual or corporate defendant with which the state has no contacts, ties, or relations.

Thus, the relationship among the defendant, the forum, and the litigation, rather than the mutually exclusive sovereignty of the States on which the rules of *Pennoyer* rest, became the central concern of the inquiry into personal jurisdiction. The immediate effect of this departure from *Pennoyer*'s conceptual apparatus was to increase the ability of the state courts to obtain personal jurisdiction over nonresident defendants.

No equally dramatic change has occurred in the law governing jurisdiction in rem. There have, however, been intimations that the collapse of the in personam wing of Pennoyer has not left that decision unweakened as a foundation for in rem jurisdiction. Well-reasoned lower court opinions have questioned the proposition that the presence of property in a State gives that State jurisdiction to adjudicate rights to the property regardless of the relationship of the underlying dispute and the property owner to the forum. The overwhelming majority of commentators have also rejected *Pennoyer*'s premise that a proceeding "against" property is not a proceeding against the owners of that property. * * *

It is clear, therefore, that the law of state-court jurisdiction no longer stands securely on the foundation established in *Pennoyer*. We think that the time is ripe to consider whether the standard of fairness and substantial justice set forth in *International Shoe* should be held to govern actions in rem as well as in personam.

III

The case for applying to jurisdiction in rem the same test of "fair play and substantial justice" as governs assertions of jurisdiction in personam is simple and straightforward. It is premised on recognition that "(t)he phrase, 'judicial jurisdiction over a thing', is a customary elliptical way of referring to jurisdiction over the interests of persons in a thing." Restatement (Second) of Conflict of Laws s 56, Introductory Note (1971) (hereafter Restatement). This recognition leads to the conclusion that in order to justify an exercise of jurisdiction *in rem*, the basis for jurisdiction must be sufficient to justify exercising "jurisdiction over the interests of persons in a thing." The standard for determining whether an exercise of jurisdiction over the interests of persons is consistent with the Due Process Clause is the minimum-contacts standard elucidated in *International Shoe*.

This argument, of course, does not ignore the fact that the presence of property in a State may bear on the existence of jurisdiction by providing contacts among the forum State, the defendant, and the litigation. For example, when claims to the property itself are the source of the underlying controversy between the plaintiff and the defendant, it would be unusual for the State where the property is located not to have jurisdiction. In such cases, the defendant's claim to property located in the State would normally indicate that he expected to benefit from the State's protection of his interest. The State's strong interests in assuring the marketability of property within its borders and in providing a procedure for peaceful resolution of disputes about the possession of that property would also support jurisdiction, as would the likelihood that important records and witnesses will be found in the State. The presence of property may also favor jurisdiction in cases such as suits for injury suffered on the land of an absentee owner, where the defendant's ownership of the property is conceded but the cause of action is otherwise related to rights and duties growing out of that ownership.

It appears, therefore, that jurisdiction over many types of actions which now are or might be brought *in rem* would not be affected by a holding that any assertion of state-court jurisdiction must satisfy the *International Shoe* standard. For the type of *quasi in rem* action typified by * * * the present case, however, accepting the proposed analysis would result in significant change. These are cases where the property which now serves as the basis for state-court jurisdiction is completely unrelated to the plaintiff's cause of action. Thus, although the presence of the defendant's property in a State might suggest the existence of other ties among the defendant, the State, and the litigation, the presence of the property alone would not support the State's jurisdiction. * * *

Since acceptance of the *International Shoe* test would most affect this class of cases, we examine the arguments against adopting that standard as they relate to this category of litigation. Before doing so, however, we note that this type of case also presents the clearest illustration of the argument in favor of assessing assertions of jurisdiction by a single standard. For in cases such as ... this one, the only role played by the property is to provide the basis for bringing the defendant into court. Indeed, the express purpose of the Delaware sequestration procedure is to compel the defendant to enter a personal appearance. In such cases, if a direct assertion of personal jurisdiction over the defendant would violate the Constitution, it would seem that an indirect assertion of that jurisdiction should be equally impermissible.

The primary rationale for treating the presence of property as a sufficient basis for jurisdiction to adjudicate claims over which the State would not have jurisdiction if International Shoe applied is that a wrongdoer "should not be able to avoid payment of his obligations by the expedient of removing his assets to a place where he is not subject to an in personam suit." Restatement s 66, Comment a. This justification, however, does not explain why jurisdiction should be recognized without regard to whether the property is present in the State because of an effort to avoid the owner's obligations. Nor does it support jurisdiction to adjudicate the underlying claim. At most, it suggests that a State in which property is located should have jurisdiction to attach that property, by use of proper procedures, as security for a judgment being sought in a forum where the litigation can be maintained consistently with *International Shoe*. Moreover, we know of nothing to justify the assumption that a debtor can avoid paying his obligations by removing his property to a State in which his creditor cannot obtain personal jurisdiction over him. The Full Faith and Credit Clause, after all, makes the valid in personam judgment of one State enforceable in all other States.[36]

* * *

We therefore conclude that all assertions of state-court jurisdiction must be evaluated according to the standards set forth in International Shoe and its progeny.

IV

* * *

Appellee Heitner did not allege and does not now claim that appellants have ever set foot in Delaware. Nor does he identify any act related to his cause of action as having taken place in Delaware. Nevertheless, he contends that appellants' positions as directors and officers of a corporation chartered in Delaware provide sufficient "contacts, ties, or relations" with that State to give its courts jurisdiction over appellants in this stockholder's derivative action. This argument is based primarily on what Heitner asserts to be the strong interest of Delaware in supervising the management of a Delaware corporation. * * * In order to protect this interest, appellee concludes, Delaware's courts must have jurisdiction over corporate fiduciaries such as appellants.

This argument is undercut by the failure of the Delaware Legislature to assert the state interest appellee finds so compelling. Delaware law bases jurisdiction, not on appellants' status as corporate fiduciaries, but rather on the presence of their property in the State. * * * If Delaware perceived its interest in securing jurisdiction over corporate fiduciaries to be as great as Heitner suggests, we would expect it to have enacted a statute more clearly designed to protect that interest.

Moreover, even if Heitner's assessment of the importance of Delaware's interest is accepted, his argument fails to demonstrate that Delaware is a fair forum for this litigation. The interest appellee has identified may support the application of Delaware law to resolve any controversy over appellants' actions in their capacities as officers and directors. But we have rejected the argument that if a State's law can properly be applied to a dispute, its courts necessarily have jurisdiction over the parties to that dispute.

Appellee suggests that by accepting positions as officers or directors of a Delaware corporation, appellants performed the acts required by *Hanson v. Denckla*. He notes that Delaware law provides substantial benefits to corporate officers and directors, and that these benefits were at least in part the incentive for appellants to assume their positions. It

---

36. Once it has been determined by a court of competent jurisdiction that the defendant is a debtor of the plaintiff, there would seem to be no unfairness in allowing an action to realize on that debt in a State where the defendant has property, whether or not that State would have jurisdiction to determine the existence of the debt as an original matter.

is, he says, "only fair and just" to require appellants, in return for these benefits, to respond in the State of Delaware when they are accused of misusing their power.

But like Heitner's first argument, this line of reasoning establishes only that it is appropriate for Delaware law to govern the obligations of appellants to Greyhound and its stockholders. It does not demonstrate that appellants have "purposefully avail(ed themselves) of the privilege of conducting activities within the forum State," *Hanson v. Denckla*, in a way that would justify bringing them before a Delaware tribunal. Appellants have simply had nothing to do with the State of Delaware. Moreover, appellants had no reason to expect to be haled before a Delaware court. Delaware, unlike some States, has not enacted a statute that treats acceptance of a directorship as consent to jurisdiction in the State. And "[i]t strains reason ... to suggest that anyone buying securities in a corporation formed in Delaware 'impliedly consents' to subject himself to Delaware's ... jurisdiction on any cause of action." Appellants, who were not required to acquire interests in Greyhound in order to hold their positions, did not by acquiring those interests surrender their right to be brought to judgment only in States with which they had had "minimum contacts." * * *

Delaware's assertion of jurisdiction over appellants in this case is inconsistent with that constitutional limitation on state power. The judgment of the Delaware Supreme Court must, therefore, be reversed.

Mr. Justice POWELL, concurring.

    * * *

I would explicitly reserve judgment, however, on whether the ownership of some forms of property whose situs is indisputably and permanently located within a State may, without more, provide the contacts necessary to subject a defendant to jurisdiction within the State to the extent of the value of the property. In the case of real property, in particular, preservation of the common-law concept of quasi in rem jurisdiction arguably would avoid the uncertainty of the general *International Shoe* standard without significant cost to " 'traditional notions of fair play and substantial justice.' "Subject to the foregoing reservation, I join the opinion of the Court.

Mr. Justice STEVENS, concurring in the judgment.

    * * *

One who purchases shares of stock on the open market can hardly be expected to know that he has thereby become subject to suit in a forum remote from his residence and unrelated to the transaction. As a practical matter, the Delaware sequestration statute creates an unacceptable risk of judgment without notice. * * * I therefore agree with the Court that on the record before us no adequate basis for jurisdiction exists and that the Delaware statute is unconstitutional on its face.

How the Court's opinion may be applied in other contexts is not entirely clear to me. I agree with Mr. Justice POWELL that it should not be read to invalidate quasi in rem jurisdiction where real estate is involved. I would also not read it as invalidating other long-accepted methods of acquiring jurisdiction over persons with adequate notice of both the particular controversy and the fact that their local activities might subject them to suit. My uncertainty as to the reach of the opinion, and my fear that it purports to decide a great deal more than is necessary to dispose of this case, persuade me merely to concur in the judgment.

Mr. Justice BRENNAN, concurring in part and dissenting in part.

I join Parts I–III of the Court's opinion. I fully agree that the minimum-contacts analysis developed in *International Shoe Co. v. Washington* represents a far more sensible construct for the exercise of state-court jurisdiction than the patchwork of legal and factual fictions that has been generated from the decision in *Pennoyer v. Neff*. It is precisely because the inquiry into minimum contacts is now of such overriding importance, however, that I must respectfully dissent from Part IV of the Court's opinion.

I

* * * [T]he Court in Part IV reaches the minimum-contacts question and finds such contacts lacking as applied to appellants. Succinctly stated, once having properly and persuasively decided that the quasi in rem statute that Delaware admits to having enacted is invalid, the Court then proceeds to find that a minimum-contacts law that Delaware expressly denies having enacted also could not be constitutionally applied in this case.

In my view, a purer example of an advisory opinion is not to be found. * * *

II

Nonetheless, because the Court rules on the minimum-contacts question, I feel impelled to express my view. * * * I am convinced that as a general rule a state forum has jurisdiction to adjudicate a shareholder derivative action centering on the conduct and policies of the directors and officers of a corporation chartered by that State. Unlike the Court, I therefore would not foreclose Delaware from asserting jurisdiction over appellants were it persuaded to do so on the basis of minimum contacts.

* * *

I, therefore, would approach the minimum-contacts analysis differently than does the Court. Crucial to me is the fact that appellants voluntarily associated themselves with the State of Delaware, "invoking the benefits and protections of its laws", *Hanson v. Denckla*. I thus do not believe that it is unfair to insist that appellants make themselves available to suit in a competent forum that Delaware might create for vindication of its important public policies directly pertaining to appellants' fiduciary associations with the State.

Notes and Questions

1. Where does the *Shaffer* decision leave *Pennoyer*'s principles? Justice Marshall stated, "It is clear, therefore, that the law of state-court jurisdiction no longer stands securely on the foundation established in *Pennoyer*." Prior to that statement, he had noted that "the relationship among the defendant, the forum, and the litigation, rather than the mutually exclusive sovereignty of the States on which the rules of *Pennoyer* rest, became the central concern of the inquiry into personal jurisdiction." He then cited language from *International Shoe* that the exercise of jurisdiction over nonresidents required "contacts, ties, or relations" with the forum.

After *Shaffer*, an *in rem* claim is no longer about the property; instead the jurisdictional inquiry addresses whether the court has jurisdiction over the person who *owns* the property. The fact that the defendant owns property in the state may be sufficient proof that the defendant can satisfy a minimum contacts analysis there. Why?

After *Shaffer*, can you argue that there is anything left of *Pennoyer*'s rules about power? Do the principles about power over persons and property in the forum state survive *Shaffer*?

2. The plaintiff argued that the defendants' positions as directors and officers of a Delaware corporation gave the Delaware courts a sufficient tie to a shareholders' derivative suit, thereby rendering jurisdiction constitutional. The Court responded simply that Delaware had no implied consent statute asserting such an interest in the management of a Delaware corporation. Shortly after *Shaffer* was decided, the Delaware legislature passed an implied consent law that formed the basis of Heitner's position. Doesn't Justice Marshall's recognition that acceptance of a directorship is the equivalent of consent to be sued simply perpetuate consent as a legal fiction?

3. Justice Powell's concurrence maintained that when the attached property "is undisputably and permanently located within a State, a court of that State, without more, might constitutionally invoke *quasi in rem* jurisdiction." Did Justice Powell make clear whether he felt that *Pennoyer*'s rationale survived to that extent, or whether the indisputable presence of real property within a state satisfied the *International Shoe* test?

Similarly, Justice Stevens emphasized the connection between the type of property at issue and the expectations of the owner. Someone who acquired realty or opened a bank account might assume the risk that the state would assert jurisdictional power over him. But under *Shaffer*'s facts, did Justice Stevens explain how the expectations of the parties could be identified (e.g., could a purchaser of stock be expected to know that he is subject to suit in a remote forum on an unrelated claim merely because the stock was in a corporation chartered in the forum state)? Are the *Shaffer* defendants' expectations different because they were not merely purchasers of stock on the open market? Do the expectations turn on the existence of a particularly worded statute or on the nature of the defendants' contacts? Even if the former were dispositive, how does a due process long-arm statute satisfy *Shaffer*'s expectation requirement?

4. After *Shaffer*, what if anything remains of a meaningful distinction between *in personam* and *quasi in rem* jurisdiction? Unlike *quasi in rem* jurisdiction, an *in personam* claim would be more attractive because the plaintiff's recovery is not limited to the value of any property that was attached. The plaintiff also can try to recover his damages by going elsewhere in the jurisdiction or to another jurisdiction to enforce the judgment. Nevertheless, one remaining benefit of *quasi in rem* jurisdiction and its accompanying attachment of property is the pressure placed on a defendant to settle that results from "tying up" the attached property.

Shaffer also leaves open the possibility that the presence of defendant's property in the forum would support jurisdiction even if the plaintiff's claim is unrelated to the defendant's property there. Therefore, jurisdiction in the forum is proper if no other forum is available to the plaintiff.

5. The Anticybersquatting Consumer Protection Act (ACPA) became law in 1999, as an amendment to the federal Trademark Act. Its purpose was to end the registration, traffic, or use of domain names by "cybersquatters," i.e., entities that act in bad faith to profit from the value of others' existing trademarks. To resolve Internet domain name disputes for names registered to persons who are difficult to find or beyond the purview of American courts, the ACPA provides for *in rem* jurisdiction. Under the statute, domain names possess a property interest capable of standing as a res for *in rem* jurisdiction, and the situs of the res is deemed to be the jurisdiction hosting the domain name registrar used by the alleged cybersquatter. An *in rem* action can be filed "in the judicial district in which the domain name registrar, domain name registry, or other domain name authority that registered or assigned the domain name is located...." When none of those is located in the federal district where the lawsuit is filed, the court lacks *in rem* jurisdiction to adjudicate the claims. *FleetBoston Financial Corp. v. Fleetbostonfinancial.com*, 138 F.Supp.2d 121 (D. Mass. 2001) (jurisdiction does not exist where documents are merely deposited with court).

WORLD–WIDE VOLKSWAGEN CORP. v. WOODSON

444 U.S. 286, 100 S.Ct. 559, 62 L.Ed.2d 490 (1980)

Mr. Justice WHITE delivered the opinion of the Court.

The issue before us is whether, consistently with the Due Process Clause of the Fourteenth Amendment, an Oklahoma court may exercise in personam jurisdiction over a nonresident automobile retailer and its wholesale distributor in a products-liability action, when the defendants' only connection with Oklahoma is the fact that an automobile sold in New York to New York residents became involved in an accident in Oklahoma.

I

Respondents Harry and Kay Robinson purchased a new Audi automobile from petitioner Seaway Volkswagen, Inc. (Seaway), in Massena,

N. Y., in 1976. The following year the Robinson family, who resided in New York, left that State for a new home in Arizona. As they passed through the State of Oklahoma, another car struck their Audi in the rear, causing a fire which severely burned Kay Robinson and her two children.

The Robinsons subsequently brought a products-liability action in the District Court for Creek County, Okla., claiming that their injuries resulted from defective design and placement of the Audi's gas tank and fuel system. They joined as defendants the automobile's manufacturer, Audi NSU Auto Union Aktiengesellschaft (Audi); its importer Volkswagen of America, Inc. (Volkswagen); its regional distributor, petitioner World–Wide Volkswagen Corp. (World–Wide); and its retail dealer, petitioner Seaway. Seaway and World–Wide entered special appearances, claiming that Oklahoma's exercise of jurisdiction over them would offend the limitations on the State's jurisdiction imposed by the Due Process Clause of the Fourteenth Amendment.

The facts presented to the District Court showed that World–Wide is incorporated and has its business office in New York. It distributes vehicles, parts, and accessories, under contract with Volkswagen, to retail dealers in New York, New Jersey, and Connecticut. Seaway, one of these retail dealers, is incorporated and has its place of business in New York. Insofar as the record reveals, Seaway and World–Wide are fully independent corporations whose relations with each other and with Volkswagen and Audi are contractual only. Respondents adduced no evidence that either World–Wide or Seaway does any business in Oklahoma, ships or sells any products to or in that State, has an agent to receive process there, or purchases advertisements in any media calculated to reach Oklahoma. In fact, as respondents' counsel conceded at oral argument, there was no showing that any automobile sold by World–Wide or Seaway has ever entered Oklahoma with the single exception of the vehicle involved in the present case.

Despite the apparent paucity of contacts between petitioners and Oklahoma, the District Court rejected their constitutional claim and reaffirmed that ruling in denying petitioners' motion for reconsideration. Petitioners then sought a writ of prohibition in the Supreme Court of Oklahoma to restrain the District Judge, respondent Charles S. Woodson, from exercising in personam jurisdiction over them. They renewed their contention that, because they had no "minimal contacts," with the State of Oklahoma, the actions of the District Judge were in violation of their rights under the Due Process Clause.

The Supreme Court of Oklahoma denied the writ, holding that personal jurisdiction over petitioners was authorized by Oklahoma's "long-arm" statute. Although the court noted that the proper approach was to test jurisdiction against both statutory and constitutional standards, its analysis did not distinguish these questions, probably because [the long-arm statute] has been interpreted as conferring jurisdiction to the limits permitted by the United States Constitution. The court's rationale was contained in the following paragraph:

> In the case before us, the product being sold and distributed by the petitioners is by its very design and purpose so mobile that petitioners can foresee its possible use in Oklahoma. This is especially true of the distributor, who has the exclusive right to distribute such automobile in New York, New Jersey and Connecticut. The evidence presented below demonstrated that goods sold and distributed by the petitioners were used in the State of Oklahoma, and under the facts we believe it reasonable to infer, given the retail value of the automobile, that the petitioners derive substantial income from automobiles which from time to time are used in the State of Oklahoma. This being the case, we hold that under the facts presented, the trial court was justified in concluding that the petitioners derive substantial revenue from goods used or consumed in this State.

We granted certiorari to consider an important constitutional question with respect to state-court jurisdiction and to resolve a conflict between the Supreme Court of Oklahoma and the highest courts of at least four other States. We reverse.

II

* * *

As has long been settled, and as we reaffirm today, a state court may exercise personal jurisdiction over a nonresident defendant only so long as there exist "minimum contacts" between the defendant and the forum State. *International Shoe Co. v. Washington.* The concept of minimum contacts, in turn, can be seen to perform two related, but distinguishable, functions. It protects the defendant against the burdens of litigating in a distant or inconvenient forum. And it acts to ensure that the States through their courts, do not reach out beyond the limits imposed on them by their status as coequal sovereigns in a federal system.

The protection against inconvenient litigation is typically described in terms of "reasonableness" or "fairness." We have said that the defendant's contacts with the forum State must be such that maintenance of the suit "does not offend 'traditional notions of fair play and substantial justice.'" *International Shoe Co. v. Washington.* The relationship between the defendant and the forum must be such that it is "reasonable ... to require the corporation to defend the particular suit which is brought there." Implicit in this emphasis on reasonableness is the understanding that the burden on the defendant, while always a primary concern, will in an appropriate case be considered in light of other relevant factors, including the forum State's interest in adjudicating the dispute, see *McGee v. International Life Ins. Co.*, the plaintiff's interest in obtaining convenient and effective relief, at least when that interest is not adequately protected by the plaintiff's power to choose the forum, the interstate judicial system's interest in obtaining the most efficient resolution of controversies, and the shared interest of the several States in furthering fundamental substantive social policies. * * *

Nevertheless, we have never accepted the proposition that state lines are irrelevant for jurisdictional purposes * * * Even if the defendant would suffer minimal or no inconvenience from being forced to litigate before the tribunals of another State; even if the forum State has a strong interest in applying its law to the controversy; even if the forum State is the most convenient location for litigation, the Due Process Clause, acting as an instrument of interstate federalism, may sometimes act to divest the State of its power to render a valid judgment. *Hanson v. Denckla.*

III

Applying these principles to the case at hand, we find in the record before us a total absence of those affiliating circumstances that are a necessary predicate to any exercise of state-court jurisdiction. Petitioners carry on no activity whatsoever in Oklahoma. They close no sales and perform no services there. * * * In short, respondents seek to base jurisdiction on ... the fortuitous circumstance that a single Audi automobile, sold in New York to New York residents, happened to suffer an accident while passing through Oklahoma.

It is argued, however, that because an automobile is mobile by its very design and purpose it was "foreseeable" that the Robinsons' Audi would cause injury in Oklahoma. Yet "foreseeability" alone has never been a sufficient benchmark for personal jurisdiction under the Due Process Clause. In *Hanson v. Denckla,* it was no doubt foreseeable that the settlor of a Delaware trust would subsequently move to Florida and seek to exercise a power of appointment there; yet we held that Florida courts could not constitutionally exercise jurisdiction over a Delaware trustee that had no other contacts with the forum State. * * *

This is not to say, of course, that foreseeability is wholly irrelevant. But the foreseeability that is critical to due process analysis is not the mere likelihood that a product will find its way into the forum State. Rather, it is that the defendant's conduct and connection with the forum State are such that he should reasonably anticipate being haled into court there. The Due Process Clause, by ensuring the "orderly administration of the laws," *International Shoe Co. v. Washington* gives a degree of predictability to the legal system that allows potential defendants to structure their primary conduct with some minimum assurance as to where that conduct will and will not render them liable to suit.

When a corporation "purposefully avails itself of the privilege of conducting activities within the forum State," *Hanson v. Denckla,* it has clear notice that it is subject to suit there, and can act to alleviate the risk of burdensome litigation by procuring insurance, passing the expected costs on to customers, or, if the risks are too great, severing its connection with the State. Hence if the sale of a product of a manufacturer or distributor ... is not simply an isolated occurrence, but arises from the efforts of the manufacturer or distributor to serve directly or indirectly, the market for its product in other States, it is not unreasonable to subject it to suit in one of those States if its allegedly defective merchandise has there been the source of injury to its owner or to others. The forum State does not exceed its powers under the Due Process Clause if it asserts personal jurisdiction over a corporation that delivers its products into the stream of commerce with the expectation that they will be purchased by consumers in the forum State.

* * * In our view, whatever marginal revenues petitioners may receive by virtue of the fact that their products are capable of use in Oklahoma is far too attenuated a contact to justify that State's exercise of in personam jurisdiction over them. * * *

Reversed.

[The dissenting opinions of Justice Marshall and Justice Blackmun are omitted.]

Justice BRENNAN, dissenting.

* * *

I

The Court's opinions focus tightly on the existence of contacts between the forum and the defendant. In so doing, they accord too little weight to the strength of the forum State's interest in the case and fail to explore whether there would be any actual inconvenience to the defendant.

* * * Because lesser burdens reduce the unfairness to the defendant, jurisdiction may be justified despite less significant contacts. * * * Due process limits on jurisdiction do not protect a defendant from all inconvenience of travel, *McGee*, and it would not be sensible to make the constitutional rule turn solely on the number of miles the defendant must travel to the courtroom. Instead, the constitutionally significant "burden" to be analyzed relates to the mobility of the defendant's defense. For instance, if having to travel to a foreign forum would hamper the defense because witnesses or evidence or the defendant himself were immobile, or if there were a disproportionately large number of witnesses or amount of evidence that would have to be transported at the defendant's expense, or if being away from home for the duration of the trial would work some special hardship on the defendant, then the Constitution would require special consideration for the defendant's interests.

That considerations other than contacts between the forum and the defendant are relevant necessarily means that the Constitution does not require that trial be held in the State which has the "best contacts" with the defendant. The defendant has no constitutional entitlement to the best forum or, for that matter, to any particular forum. Under even the most restrictive view of *International Shoe*, several States could have jurisdiction over a particular cause of action. We need only determine whether the forum States in these cases satisfy the constitutional minimum.

II

* * * I would find that the forum State has an interest in permitting the litigation to go forward, the litigation is connected to the forum, the defendant is linked to the forum, and the burden of defending is not unreasonable. Accordingly, I would hold that it is neither unfair nor unreasonable to require these defendants to defend in the forum State.

* * *

* * * [T]he interest of the forum State and its connection to the litigation is strong. The automobile accident underlying the litigation occurred in Oklahoma. The plaintiffs were hospitalized in Oklahoma when they brought suit. Essential witnesses and evidence were in Oklahoma. The State has a legitimate interest in enforcing its laws designed to keep its highway system safe, and the trial can proceed at least as efficiently in Oklahoma as anywhere else.

The petitioners are not unconnected with the forum. Although both sell automobiles within limited sales territories, each sold the automobile which in fact was driven to Oklahoma where it was involved in an accident. It may be true, as the Court suggests, that each sincerely intended to limit its commercial impact to the limited territory, and that each intended to accept the benefits and protection of the laws only of those States within the territory. But obviously these were unrealistic hopes that cannot be treated as an automatic constitutional shield.

An automobile simply is not a stationary item or one designed to be used in one place. An automobile is intended to be moved around. * * *

The Court accepts that a State may exercise jurisdiction over a distributor which "serves" that State "indirectly" by "deliver[ing] its products into the stream of commerce with the expectation that they will be purchased by consumers in the forum State." It is difficult to see why the Constitution should distinguish between a case involving goods which reach a distant State through a chain of distribution and a case involving goods which reach the same State because a consumer, using them as the dealer knew the customer would, took them there. In each case the seller purposefully injects the goods into the stream of commerce and those goods predictably are used in the forum State. * * *

III

* * *

The plaintiffs * * * brought suit in a forum with which they had significant contacts and which had significant contacts with the litigation. I am not convinced that the defendants would suffer any "heavy and disproportionate burden" in defending the suits. Accordingly, I would hold that the Constitution should not shield the defendants from appearing and defending in the plaintiffs' chosen fora.

Notes and Questions

1. Did the New York distributor and the retailer purposely avail themselves of conducting activities in Oklahoma? Could (or should) they be able to foresee being subject to the jurisdiction of the Oklahoma court?

2. Why does foreseeability matter? Should a defendant be subject to suit anywhere a product malfunctions, even if it had nothing to do with the product's location? What is the relationship between minimum contacts and foreseeability? Why did the manufacturer and the importer not contest jurisdiction in Oklahoma?

3. A) As plaintiffs' counsel, what factual argument supports jurisdiction over the manufacturer and the importer in Oklahoma?

B) As defendants' counsel, what factual argument opposes jurisdiction over the manufacturer and the importer in Oklahoma?

C) As plaintiffs' counsel, what factual argument supports jurisdiction over the New York retailer in Oklahoma?

4. How would you argue that *World–Wide Volkswagen* is not a stream-of-commerce case? Were the defendants present in Oklahoma? Did any of them use a sales or distribution scheme in which their vehicles would reach Oklahoma as products for sale? Was the chain of events leading to the arrival of the Robinson's vehicle in Oklahoma commercial in nature? Was the vehicle's arrival in Oklahoma entirely due to the Robinson's unilateral activity?

5. Is a stream-of-commerce analysis different in the case of a manufacturer of a finished product, as opposed to the manufacturer of a component product? What is the nature of the distinction? Can the manufacturer of a finished product structure its conduct to limit the geographic scope of its liability? Can a component part manufacturer do the same?

6. In *World–Wide Volkswagen*, the Court begins to explain the meaning of "fair play and substantial justice." The Court's relevant balancing criteria for evaluating the "fair play" factors are:

A) "[T]he burden on the defendant" of litigating the claim in a place removed from its principal place of business. Modern transportation tempers this burden, which also is mitigated when a defendant already has ongoing connections in the forum. Even though all defendants attempt to articulate the burden of going to a distant place to litigate, courts seriously consider this factor for a foreign defendant who has to travel a long distance in another nation's legal system. When an alternative forum within the federal court system would not constitute a burden, a change of venue to another trial court accommodates the interest.

B) "[T]he forum state's interest in" deciding the case. States have an interest in providing a place for their residents to seek a remedy for injuries caused by nonresident persons. The forum also has an interest if its law will apply to the case. When the interest is satisfied by settlement of the resident's claim, the forum's interest no longer is nearly as strong.

C) "[T]he plaintiff's interest in obtaining convenient and effective relief." This factor is especially important when the plaintiff's chances of recovery would be greatly reduced by forcing her to litigate elsewhere because of the latter forum's laws. It is also promoted when the plaintiff is financially unable to litigate elsewhere.

D) "[T]he interstate judicial system's interest in obtaining the most efficient resolution of controversies." Courts generally consider where the witnesses and evidence are likely to be located, although there is always some inefficiency in having one side travel to the other's forum state. To avoid piecemeal litigation, when numerous defendants are from diverse locations, a court may evaluate whether, as in *World–Wide Volkswagen*, it is better for plaintiffs to maintain the case in Oklahoma against the two defendants and sue the other two in New York, or whether it would be more efficient to dismiss the Oklahoma case and sue all four defendants in a New York court. If much of the evidence is documentary and can easily be sent to the forum, this factor is less important.

E) "[T]he shared interest of the several States in furthering fundamental substantive social policies." This is a positive factor when there is a common interest in dealing with a common problem. Courts have the most difficulty articulating this factor, but it is peculiar to the type of lawsuit, e.g., hazardous waste, bad drivers, bad air, ensuring that valid contracts are not breached. When the subject of the litigation is the conduct of foreign defendants so that foreign law might apply, this factor works against invoking the jurisdiction of the court over the foreign defendant.

See Leslie W. Abramson, "Clarifying 'Fair Play and Substantial Justice': How the Courts Apply the Supreme Court Standard for Personal Jurisdiction," 18 Hastings Const. L.Q. 441 (1991).

In *World–Wide Volkswagen*, why did the majority merely refer to the "fair play" factors, while the dissent discussed their applicability in detail?

7. With the Court's decision, what options remain for the plaintiffs? If you were plaintiffs' counsel, would you continue to pursue damages in Oklahoma against the manufacturer and the importer and file a separate claim in New York against the distributor and the retailer? Or, would it be more efficient to voluntarily dismiss the claims against the remaining Oklahoma parties and file against all four defendants in New York?

Problems

Evaluate the following problems from the perspective of due process contacts, for specific or general jurisdiction.

1. Tater Computer Chips, Inc. is a Delaware corporation manufacturing its products in Delaware and selling computer and electronic components to Swell Computer Corporation (which is incorporated in Tennessee). Tater

Computer has assembly facilities in Maryland, Delaware, and Pennsylvania. Swell Computers uses the components to manufacture computers that it advertises and sells in every state except Alaska and Hawaii. Because of Swell's nationwide sales, Tater Computer Chips has become a very profitable company. Klausing lives in Delaware and delivers the components to Swell in all three states. On his way to make a delivery in Pennsylvania, his truck collides with Grossman who lives in Pennsylvania but has never ventured outside the Erie, Pennsylvania metropolitan area.

A) As counsel for Klausing, can Klausing sue Grossman in Delaware? In Pennsylvania?

B) As counsel for Grossman, can Grossman sue Klausing in Pennsylvania? In Maryland?

2. Loeb lives in Texas and is vacationing in Miami Beach, where he purchased a Swell Computer at a local store. At the time of the purchase, Loeb told the store manager that he was from Dallas and intended to take the computer back to his home. During the transaction, Loeb also tells the manager to call his sister-in-law Fidelow in Colorado who would be very interested in the Swell Computer products.

The computer exploded while Loeb was still in Florida, injuring Loeb seriously. A consumer products safety investigation revealed that the cause of the injuries was a malfunctioning component part made by Tater Computer Chips.

A) As counsel for Loeb, can Loeb sue Tater Computer Chips, Inc. in Florida? In Texas? In Delaware?

B) As counsel for Loeb, can Loeb sue Swell Computer Corporation in Florida? In Texas? In Delaware?

3. Fidelow, who lives in Colorado, receives a call from the Miami store promoting Swell's new line of laptop computers. Fidelow orders two of the laptops for her children, but neither of them ever works as speedily as the store manager had told her. When Fidelow calls the Miami store to complain, the only message is that the phone number has been disconnected. When Fidelow calls the Swell U.S. national service center, the Swell representative denies that Swell ever had a Swell store in Miami Beach.

A) As counsel for Fidelow, can she sue the Miami Beach store for fraud in a Colorado court?

B) As counsel for Fidelow, can she sue Swell Computer Corporation for fraud in a court in Colorado? In Florida?

4. Swell Computer Corporation wants to begin selling computers in Alaska. It buys advertising in Anchorage, Alaska's daily newspaper starting on September 1. Watson lives in Anchorage. In early August of the same year, Watson's cousin e-mails Watson to persuade Watson to buy a Swell desktop computer system. The next day, Watson calls Swell's 800 number, 1–800–COMPUTR (1–800–266–7887), from his home and orders a Swell desktop. After delivery, Watson discovers that Swell has sent him a laptop instead. When Watson calls the Swell U.S. national service center, the Swell representative cannot locate Watson's order and refuses to help him.

A) As counsel for Watson, can he sue Swell Computer Corporation for breach of contract in a court in Alaska?

B) If Watson had written a letter to the national Swell headquarters in August to order a computer instead of calling the 800 number, would it be easier for an Alaska court to exercise personal jurisdiction over Swell?

5. A West Virginia resident purchased an air tank manufactured by Shelton Products, Inc. in Missouri. Shortly thereafter, as a service station attendant attempted to fill the tank in West Virginia, the tank exploded, seriously injuring Estes. Estes filed a products liability action based on negligence in the design, manufacture, and sale of the air tank, and the breach of numerous warranties.

Shelton is a Missouri corporation with its sole place of business in Branson, Missouri. Shelton has no salesmen visiting West Virginia, no contracts for the sale of its products directly to West Virginia businesses, and no direct advertising in West Virginia. Shelton does direct its products to "the national market" by selling its products to national retail chains such as Wal–Mart, Target, and Auto Zone. The retail chains sell to residents of the states they serve through individual stores within those states. Contracts between Shelton and the retail chains are made at the corporate level either at Shelton's Missouri office or at the retail chains' corporate offices. By common carrier, Shelton delivers products to the purchasers' distribution centers where the products are warehoused for shipment directly to the purchasers' individual retail stores.

Shelton filed a motion to dismiss for lack of personal jurisdiction. Assume that West Virginia has a due process long-arm statute. Applying *World–Wide Volkswagen*, how should the trial court rule on the motion? See *Estes v. Midwest Products, Inc.*, 24 F.Supp.2d 621 (S.D.W.Va. 1998).

CALDER v. JONES

465 U.S. 783, 104 S.Ct. 1482, 79 L.Ed.2d 804 (1984)

Justice REHNQUIST delivered the opinion of the Court.

Respondent Shirley Jones brought suit in California Superior Court claiming that she had been libeled in an article written and edited by petitioners in Florida. The article was published in a national magazine with a large circulation in California. Petitioners were served with process by mail in Florida and caused special appearances to be entered on their behalf, moving to quash the service of process for lack of personal jurisdiction. The superior court granted the motion on the ground that First Amendment concerns weighed against an assertion of jurisdiction otherwise proper under the Due Process Clause. The California Court of Appeal reversed, rejecting the suggestion that First Amendment considerations enter into the jurisdictional analysis. We now affirm.

Respondent lives and works in California. She and her husband brought this suit against the National Enquirer, Inc., its local distributing company, and petitioners for libel, invasion of privacy, and intentional infliction of emotional harm. The Enquirer is a Florida corporation with its principal place of business in Florida. It publishes a national weekly newspaper with a total circulation of over 5 million. About 600,000 of those copies, almost twice the level of the next highest State, are sold in California. Respondent's and her husband's claims were based on an article that appeared in the Enquirer's October 9, 1979 issue. Both the Enquirer and the distributing company answered the complaint and made no objection to the jurisdiction of the California court.

Petitioner South is a reporter employed by the Enquirer. He is a resident of Florida, though he frequently travels to California on business. South wrote the first draft of the challenged article, and his byline appeared on it. He did most of his research in Florida, relying on phone calls to sources in California for the information contained in the article. Shortly before publication, South called respondent's Home and read to her husband a draft of the article so as to elicit his comments upon it. Aside from his frequent trips and phone calls, South has no other relevant contacts with California.

Petitioner Calder is also a Florida resident. He has been to California only twice—once, on a pleasure trip, prior to the publication of the article and once after to testify in an unrelated trial. Calder is president and editor of the Enquirer. He "oversee[s] just about every function of the Enquirer." He reviewed and approved the initial evaluation of the subject of the article and edited it in its final form. He also declined to print a retraction requested by respondent. Calder has no other relevant contacts with California.

In considering petitioners' motion to quash service of process, the superior court surmised that the actions of petitioners in Florida, causing injury to respondent in California, would ordinarily be sufficient to support an assertion of jurisdiction over them in California. But the court felt that special solicitude was necessary because of the potential "chilling effect" on reporters and editors which would result from requiring them to appear in remote jurisdictions to answer for the content of articles upon which they worked. The court also noted that respondent's rights could be "fully satisfied" in her suit against the publisher without requiring petitioners to appear as parties. The superior court, therefore, granted the motion.

The California Court of Appeal reversed. The court agreed that neither petitioner's contacts with California would be sufficient for an assertion of jurisdiction on a cause of action unrelated to those contacts. But the court concluded that a valid basis for jurisdiction existed on the theory that petitioners intended to, and did, cause tortious injury to respondent in California. The fact that the actions causing the effects in California were performed outside the State did not prevent the State from asserting jurisdiction over a cause of action arising out of those effects. The court rejected the superior court's conclusion that First

Amendment considerations must be weighed in the scale against jurisdiction.

* * * The plaintiff's lack of "contacts" will not defeat otherwise proper jurisdiction, but they may be so manifold as to permit jurisdiction when it would not exist in their absence. Here, the plaintiff is the focus of the activities of the defendants out of which the suit arises.

The allegedly libelous story concerned the California activities of a California resident. It impugned the professionalism of an entertainer whose television career was centered in California. The article was drawn from California sources, and the brunt of the harm, in terms both of respondent's emotional distress and the injury to her professional reputation, was suffered in California. In sum, California is the focal point both of the story and of the harm suffered. Jurisdiction over petitioners is therefore proper in California based on the "effects" of their Florida conduct in California.

Petitioners argue that they are not responsible for the circulation of the article in California. A reporter and an editor, they claim, have no direct economic stake in their employer's sales in a distant State. Nor are ordinary employees able to control their employer's marketing activity. The mere fact that they can "foresee" that the article will be circulated and have an effect in California is not sufficient for an assertion of jurisdiction. They do not "in effect appoint the [article their] agent for service of process." Petitioners liken themselves to a welder employed in Florida who works on a boiler which subsequently explodes in California. Cases which hold that jurisdiction will be proper over the manufacturer, should not be applied to the welder who has no control over and derives no direct benefit from his employer's sales in that distant State.

Petitioners' analogy does not wash. Whatever the status of their hypothetical welder, petitioners are not charged with mere untargeted negligence. Rather, their intentional, and allegedly tortious, actions were expressly aimed at California. Petitioner South wrote and petitioner Calder edited an article that they knew would have a potentially devastating impact upon respondent. And they knew that the brunt of that injury would be felt by respondent in the State in which she lives and works and in which the National Enquirer has its largest circulation. Under the circumstances, petitioners must "reasonably anticipate being haled into court there" to answer for the truth of the statements made in their article. An individual injured in California need not go to Florida to seek redress from persons who, though remaining in Florida, knowingly cause the injury in California.

Petitioners are correct that their contacts with California are not to be judged according to their employer's activities there. On the other hand, their status as employees does not somehow insulate them from jurisdiction. Each defendant's contacts with the forum State must be assessed individually. In this case, petitioners are primary participants in an alleged wrongdoing intentionally directed at a California resident, and jurisdiction over them is proper on that basis.

We also reject the suggestion that First Amendment concerns enter into the jurisdictional analysis. The infusion of such considerations would needlessly complicate an already imprecise inquiry. Moreover, the potential chill on protected First Amendment activity stemming from libel and defamation actions is already taken into account in the constitutional limitations on the substantive law governing such suits. To reintroduce those concerns at the jurisdictional stage would be a form of double counting. We have already declined in other contexts to grant special procedural protections to defendants in libel and defamation actions in addition to the constitutional protections embodied in the substantive laws.

We hold that jurisdiction over petitioners in California is proper because of their intentional conduct in Florida calculated to cause injury to respondent in California. The judgment of the California Court of Appeal is affirmed.

Notes and Questions

1.   The Court rejected the analogy to the "welder employed in Florida who works on a boiler which subsequently explodes in California," because the welder at most would have been liable for "mere untargeted negligence." By contrast, the Court characterized the defendants' conduct as intentional and expressly aimed at California. Would the welder be subject to a lawsuit for negligence in Florida? In California? Would the welder have "reasonably anticipated being haled into court" in either state for his work?

The Court ruled that nonresident executive and staff employees could be subject to jurisdiction in their individual roles. For the president and editor of the *National Enquirer*, perhaps that may not be a surprising conclusion. While jurisdiction over the reporter is not likely to affect the liability of the main defendant or the ability to collect a judgment, is there likely to be an effect on the reporter who wrote the story? When he wrote the story, did the reporter "reasonably anticipate being haled into court" in California, even if he knew that the newspaper would be distributed there?

2.   An important element of the *Calder* analysis is that the defendant must have committed an intentional tort. From your reading of *Calder*, what is the relevance of the nature of a plaintiff's claim? In other words, is it sufficient to show jurisdiction over the defendant merely by alleging an intentional tort by the defendant? Lower courts have recognized that *Calder*'s "effects" test is just another way of evaluating the defendant's contacts with the forum. The effects of the claim against the defendant are part of the analysis.

3.   A second factor in *Calder* requires that the plaintiff show that it felt the brunt (or effects) of the harm from the defendant's tortious behavior in the forum state. How was this element satisfied in *Calder*? Does it matter where the plaintiff lives in relation to the allegedly defamatory article? What does *Calder* suggest about the importance of whether the article referred to

the forum state was related to the forum state activities of the plaintiff, and/or was directed at forum state readers as opposed to readers from other states?

4.   The third *Calder* factor demands a showing that the defendant "expressly aimed" its tortious conduct at the forum. In the context of traditional due process analysis concepts like "purposeful availment" and "foreseeability," what is the significance of the defendant's knowledge about the place where his conduct is directed, e.g., whether the defendant knows the plaintiff resides in the forum state? Does the Court's language go further than merely assessing the defendants' ability to foresee that the article would be circulated and have an effect in the forum state in order to establish personal jurisdiction?

5.   Assess the significance of the Court's reliance on the forum state being the *National Enquirer*'s largest distribution market. Does that portion of the *Calder* opinion indicate a narrow range of application? For example, suppose the plaintiff had sued the defendants in the market where the *National Enquirer* had its second or third largest circulation. Would jurisdiction be upheld? Or, was the Court's reference to the defendant's circulation a convenient coincidence? Does *Calder* restrict jurisdiction to the forum where the effects of the alleged defamation are felt the most? Or, is it enough that the effects of the defamation are felt at all?

6.   In *Keeton v. Hustler Magazine, Inc.*, 465 U.S. 770, 104 S.Ct. 1473, 79 L.Ed.2d 790 (1984), decided the same day as *Calder*, the Court held that New Hampshire could exercise jurisdiction over a non-resident corporation, based on allegedly libelous material printed in its magazine. The Court noted that circulation within the state consisted of more than 10,000 copies every month. (Presumably, the magazine had larger circulations in many other states, thereby diluting the impact of *Calder*'s concern about the *National Enquirer*'s largest distribution being in the forum state.) The corporation's "regular monthly sales of thousands of magazines cannot by any stretch of the imagination be characterized as random, isolated, or fortuitous," and were more than sufficient to satisfy the minimum contacts requirement. The decision also confirms the possibility of bringing a defamation action in any forum with adequate minimum contacts.

7.   In the Internet cases discussed in the next section, *Calder* is often cited in judicial analysis about issues such as whether posting information on a website that is read by a plaintiff in another forum is sufficient to invoke the jurisdiction of the reader's forum.

Problems

Using the *Calder* principle, decide whether personal jurisdiction exists in the following cases.

1.   In a Virginia court, Virginia resident Dave sued an Illinois defendant named Andrew for sending defamatory letters written and mailed from Illinois to Dave's colleagues in Virginia. Does the Virginia court have personal jurisdiction over Andrew by virtue of the effects in Virginia of his conduct? See *First Am. First, Inc. v. National Ass'n of Bank Women*, 802 F.2d 1511 (4th Cir. 1986).

2. A South Carolina corporation sued a New Hampshire company in South Carolina, claiming that the defendant had conspired to steal its customer lists. The co-conspirators were Florida and New Hampshire residents who engaged in a mail order business, but they had no customers in South Carolina. The defendant's only contact that the plaintiff could identify was the defendant's knowledge that possession of the lists could have the effect of lowered sales for the plaintiff. Is that sufficient for jurisdiction over the New Hampshire defendant? See *ESAB Group, Inc. v. Centricut, Inc.*, 126 F.3d 617 (4th Cir. 1997).

3. At a track meet in Monaco, world-class runner Reynolds tested positive for drugs, resulting in his removal from International Amateur Athletic Federation (IAAF) track meets for two years. After the group issued a press release describing the test results, media outlets in Ohio and other places disseminated the report. In an Ohio federal court, Reynolds sued the group for defamation and interference with his contractual relations with product manufacturers. Is jurisdiction proper in Ohio because the IAAF could foresee an effect of its actions there? See *Reynolds v. International Amateur Athletic Fed'n*, 23 F.3d 1110 (6th Cir. 1994).

4. Nevada resident Towne, who owned real property there, had negotiated with the Utah corporation FWC to develop Towne's land. The site of the negotiations was Nevada, but Towne corresponded with FWC by fax and letter on numerous occasions. Towne hired a Utah consultant who went to FWC's offices to pick up materials for Towne. The negotiations produced a lease with a provision that Nevada law would apply to any disputes about the lease. After Towne interfered with FWC's later negotiations with a California group about financing the project on Towne's property, FWC sued Towne in Utah. Was personal jurisdiction over Towne proper there? See *Far W. Capital, Inc. v. Towne*, 46 F.3d 1071 (10th Cir. 1995).

HELICOPTEROS NACIONALES DE COLOMBIA, S.A. v. HALL

466 U.S. 408, 104 S.Ct. 1868, 80 L.Ed.2d 404 (1984)

Justice BLACKMUN delivered the opinion of the Court.

We granted certiorari in this case to decide whether the Supreme Court of Texas correctly ruled that the contacts of a foreign corporation with the State of Texas were sufficient to allow a Texas state court to assert jurisdiction over the corporation in a cause of action not arising out of or related to the corporation's activities within the State.

I

Petitioner Helicopteros Nacionales de Colombia, S.A. (Helicol), is a Colombian corporation with its principal place of business in the city of Bogota in that country. It is engaged in the business of providing helicopter transportation for oil and construction companies in South America. On January 26, 1976, a helicopter owned by Helicol crashed in

Peru. Four United States citizens were among those who lost their lives in the accident. Respondents are the survivors and representatives of the four decedents.

At the time of the crash, respondents' decedents were employed by Consorcio, a Peruvian consortium, and were working on a pipeline in Peru. Consorcio is the alter ego of a joint venture named Williams–Sedco–Horn (WSH). The venture had its headquarters in Houston, Tex. Consorcio had been formed to enable the venturers to enter into a contract with Petro Peru, the Peruvian state-owned oil company. Consorcio was to construct a pipeline for Petro Peru running from the interior of Peru westward to the Pacific Ocean. Peruvian law forbade construction of the pipeline by any non-Peruvian entity.

Consorcio/WSH needed helicopters to move personnel, materials, and equipment into and out of the construction area. In 1974, upon request of Consorcio/WSH, the chief executive officer of Helicol, Francisco Restrepo, flew to the United States and conferred in Houston with representatives of the three joint venturers. At that meeting, there was a discussion of prices, availability, working conditions, fuel, supplies, and housing. Restrepo represented that Helicol could have the first helicopter on the job in 15 days. The Consorcio/WSH representatives decided to accept the contract proposed by Restrepo. Helicol began performing before the agreement was formally signed in Peru on November 11, 1974. The contract was written in Spanish on official government stationery and provided that the residence of all the parties would be Lima, Peru. It further stated that controversies arising out of the contract would be submitted to the jurisdiction of Peruvian courts. In addition, it provided that Consorcio/WSH would make payments to Helicol's account with the Bank of America in New York City.

Aside from the negotiation session in Houston between Restrepo and the representatives of Consorcio/WSH, Helicol had other contacts with Texas. During the years 1970–1977, it purchased helicopters (approximately 80% of its fleet), spare parts, and accessories for more than $4 million from Bell Helicopter Company in Fort Worth. In that period, Helicol sent prospective pilots to Fort Worth for training and to ferry the aircraft to South America. It also sent management and maintenance personnel to visit Bell Helicopter in Fort Worth during the same period in order to receive "plant familiarization" and for technical consultation. Helicol received into its New York City and Panama City, Fla., bank accounts over $5 million in payments from Consorcio/WSH drawn upon First City National Bank of Houston.

Beyond the foregoing, there have been no other business contacts between Helicol and the State of Texas. Helicol never has been authorized to do business in Texas and never has had an agent for the service of process within the State. It never has performed helicopter operations in Texas or sold any product that reached Texas, never solicited business in Texas, never signed any contract in Texas, never had any employee based there, and never recruited an employee in Texas. In addition,

Helicol never has owned real or personal property in Texas and never has maintained an office or establishment there. Helicol has maintained no records in Texas and has no shareholders in that State. None of the respondents or their decedents were domiciled in Texas, but all of the decedents were hired in Houston by Consorcio/WSH to work on the Petro Peru pipeline project.

Respondents instituted wrongful-death actions in the District Court of Harris County, Tex., against Consorcio/WSH, Bell Helicopter Company, and Helicol. Helicol filed special appearances and moved to dismiss the actions for lack of in personam jurisdiction over it. The motion was denied. After a consolidated jury trial, judgment was entered against Helicol on a jury verdict of $1,141,200 in favor of respondents.

The Texas Court of Civil Appeals, Houston, First District, reversed the judgment of the District Court, holding that in personam jurisdiction over Helicol was lacking. The Supreme Court of Texas * * * reversed the judgment of the intermediate court. In ruling that the Texas courts had in personam jurisdiction, the Texas Supreme Court first held that the State's long-arm statute reaches as far as the Due Process Clause of the Fourteenth Amendment permits. Thus, the only question remaining for the court to decide was whether it was consistent with the Due Process Clause for Texas courts to assert in personam jurisdiction over Helicol.

II

* * * Due process requirements are satisfied when in personam jurisdiction is asserted over a nonresident corporate defendant that has "certain minimum contacts with [the forum] such that the maintenance of the suit does not offend 'traditional notions of fair play and substantial justice.'" When a controversy is related to or "arises out of" a defendant's contacts with the forum, the Court has said that a "relationship among the defendant, the forum, and the litigation" is the essential foundation of in personam jurisdiction.

Even when the cause of action does not arise out of or relate to the foreign corporation's activities in the forum State, due process is not offended by a State's subjecting the corporation to its in personam jurisdiction when there are sufficient contacts between the State and the foreign corporation. * * *

All parties to the present case concede that respondents' claims against Helicol did not "arise out of," and are not related to, Helicol's activities within Texas. We thus must explore the nature of Helicol's contacts with the State of Texas to determine whether they constitute the kind of continuous and systematic general business contacts the Court found to exist in *Perkins* [v. *Benguet Consol. Mining Co.*, 342 U.S. 437 (1952)]. We hold that they do not.

It is undisputed that Helicol does not have a place of business in Texas and never has been licensed to do business in the State. Basically, Helicol's contacts with Texas consisted of sending its chief executive officer to Houston for a contract-negotiation session; accepting into its New York bank account checks drawn on a Houston bank; purchasing helicopters, equipment, and training services from Bell Helicopter for substantial sums; and sending personnel to Bell's facilities in Fort Worth for training.

The one trip to Houston by Helicol's chief executive officer for the purpose of negotiating the transportation-services contract with Consorcio/WSH cannot be described or regarded as a contact of a "continuous and systematic" nature, as *Perkins* described it, and thus cannot support an assertion of in personam jurisdiction over Helicol by a Texas court. Similarly, Helicol's acceptance from Consorcio/WSH of checks drawn on a Texas bank is of negligible significance for purposes of determining whether Helicol had sufficient contacts in Texas. There is no indication that Helicol ever requested that the checks be drawn on a Texas bank or that there was any negotiation between Helicol and Consorcio/WSH with respect to the location or identity of the bank on which checks would be drawn. Common sense and everyday experience suggest that, absent unusual circumstances, the bank on which a check is drawn is generally of little consequence to the payee and is a matter left to the discretion of the drawer. Such unilateral activity of another party or a third person is not an appropriate consideration when determining whether a defendant has sufficient contacts with a forum State to justify an assertion of jurisdiction.

The Texas Supreme Court focused on the purchases and the related training trips in finding contacts sufficient to support an assertion of jurisdiction. We do not agree with that assessment, for the Court's opinion in *Rosenberg Bros. & Co. v. Curtis Brown Co.*, 260 U.S. 516 (1923) (Brandeis, J., for a unanimous tribunal), makes clear that purchases and related trips, standing alone, are not a sufficient basis for a State's assertion of jurisdiction.

* * * In accordance with *Rosenberg*, we hold that mere purchases, even if occurring at regular intervals, are not enough to warrant a State's assertion of in personam jurisdiction over a nonresident corporation in a cause of action not related to those purchase transactions. Nor can we conclude that the fact that Helicol sent personnel into Texas for training in connection with the purchase of helicopters and equipment in that State in any way enhanced the nature of Helicol's contacts with Texas. The training was a part of the package of goods and services purchased by Helicol from Bell Helicopter. The brief presence of Helicol employees in Texas for the purpose of attending the training sessions is no more a significant contact than were the trips to New York made by the buyer for the retail store in *Rosenberg*.

III

We hold that Helicol's contacts with the State of Texas were insufficient to satisfy the requirements of the Due Process Clause of the

Fourteenth Amendment. Accordingly, we reverse the judgment of the Supreme Court of Texas.

It is so ordered.

Justice BRENNAN, dissenting.

* * * Based on essentially undisputed facts, the Court concludes that petitioner Helicol's contacts with the State of Texas were insufficient to allow the Texas state courts constitutionally to assert "general jurisdiction" over all claims filed against this foreign corporation. Although my independent weighing of the facts leads me to a different conclusion, the Court's holding on this issue is neither implausible nor unexpected.

What is troubling about the Court's opinion, however, are the implications that might be drawn from the way in which the Court approaches the constitutional issue it addresses.

* * * I believe that the undisputed contacts in this case between petitioner Helicol and the State of Texas are sufficiently important, and sufficiently related to the underlying cause of action, to make it fair and reasonable for the State to assert personal jurisdiction over Helicol for the wrongful-death actions filed by the respondents. Given that Helicol has purposefully availed itself of the benefits and obligations of the forum, and given the direct relationship between the underlying cause of action and Helicol's contacts with the forum, maintenance of this suit in the Texas courts "does not offend [the] 'traditional notions of fair play and substantial justice,'" that are the touchstone of jurisdictional analysis under the Due Process Clause. I therefore dissent.

I

* * * As active participants in interstate and foreign commerce take advantage of the economic benefits and opportunities offered by the various States, it is only fair and reasonable to subject them to the obligations that may be imposed by those jurisdictions. And chief among the obligations that a nonresident corporation should expect to fulfill is amenability to suit in any forum that is significantly affected by the corporation's commercial activities.

As a foreign corporation that has actively and purposefully engaged in numerous and frequent commercial transactions in the State of Texas, Helicol clearly falls within the category of nonresident defendants that may be subject to that forum's general jurisdiction. Helicol not only purchased helicopters and other equipment in the State for many years, but also sent pilots and management personnel into Texas to be trained in the use of this equipment and to consult with the seller on technical matters. Moreover, negotiations for the contract under which Helicol provided transportation services to the joint venture that employed the respondents' decedents also took place in the State of Texas. Taken together, these contacts demonstrate that Helicol obtained numerous benefits from its transaction of business in Texas. In turn, it is eminently fair and reasonable to expect Helicol to face the obligations that attach to its participation in such commercial transactions. Accordingly, on the basis of continuous commercial contacts with the forum, I would conclude that the Due Process Clause allows the State of Texas to assert general jurisdiction over petitioner Helicol.

II

The Court also fails to distinguish the legal principles that controlled our prior decisions in *Perkins* and *Rosenberg*. In particular, the contacts between petitioner Helicol and the State of Texas, unlike the contacts between the defendant and the forum in each of those cases, are significantly related to the cause of action alleged in the original suit filed by the respondents. Accordingly, in my view, it is both fair and reasonable for the Texas courts to assert specific jurisdiction over Helicol in this case.

By asserting that the present case does not implicate the specific jurisdiction of the Texas courts, the Court necessarily removes its decision from the reality of the actual facts presented for our consideration. Moreover, the Court refuses to consider any distinction between contacts that are "related to" the underlying cause of action and contacts that "give rise" to the underlying cause of action. In my view, however, there is a substantial difference between these two standards for asserting specific jurisdiction. Thus, although I agree that the respondents' cause of action did not formally "arise out of" specific activities initiated by Helicol in the State of Texas, I believe that the wrongful-death claim filed by the respondents is significantly related to the undisputed contacts between Helicol and the forum. On that basis, I would conclude that the Due Process Clause allows the Texas courts to assert specific jurisdiction over this particular action.

The wrongful-death actions filed by the respondents were premised on a fatal helicopter crash that occurred in Peru. Helicol was joined as a defendant in the lawsuits because it provided transportation services, including the particular helicopter and pilot involved in the crash, to the joint venture that employed the decedents. Specifically, the respondent Hall claimed in her original complaint that "Helicol is ... legally responsible for its own negligence through its pilot employee." Viewed in light of these allegations, the contacts between Helicol and the State of Texas are directly and significantly related to the underlying claim filed by the respondents. The negotiations that took place in Texas led to the contract in which Helicol agreed to provide the precise transportation services that were being used at the time of the crash. Moreover, the helicopter involved in the crash was purchased by Helicol in Texas, and the pilot whose negligence was alleged to have caused the crash was actually trained in Texas. This is simply not a case, therefore, in which a state court has asserted jurisdiction over a nonresident defendant on the basis of wholly unrelated contacts with the forum. Rather, the contacts between Helicol and the forum are directly related to the negligence that was alleged in the respondent Hall's original complaint. * * *

Limiting the specific jurisdiction of a forum to cases in which the cause of action formally arose out of the defendant's contacts with the State would subject constitutional standards under the Due Process Clause to the vagaries of the substantive law or pleading requirements of each State. For example, the complaint filed against Helicol in this case alleged negligence based on pilot error. Even though the pilot was trained in Texas, the Court assumes that the Texas courts may not assert jurisdiction over the suit because the cause of action "did not 'arise out of,' and [is] not related to," that training. If, however, the applicable substantive law required that negligent training of the pilot was a necessary element of a cause of action for pilot error, or if the respondents had simply added an allegation of negligence in the training provided for the Helicol pilot, then presumably the Court would concede that the specific jurisdiction of the Texas courts was applicable.

Our interpretation of the Due Process Clause has never been so dependent upon the applicable substantive law or the State's formal pleading requirements. At least since *International Shoe Co. v. Washington*, 326 U.S. 310 (1945), the principal focus when determining whether a forum may constitutionally assert jurisdiction over a nonresident defendant has been on fairness and reasonableness to the defendant. To this extent, a court's specific jurisdiction should be applicable whenever the cause of action arises out of or relates to the contacts between the defendant and the forum. It is eminently fair and reasonable, in my view, to subject a defendant to suit in a forum with which it has significant contacts directly related to the underlying cause of action. Because Helicol's contacts with the State of Texas meet this standard, I would affirm the judgment of the Supreme Court of Texas.

Notes and Questions

1. Under general jurisdiction, a nonresident's contacts with the forum state must be "continuous and systematic," rather than the minimum contacts test used for specific jurisdiction. So, even though the state can exercise general jurisdiction over a nonresident defendant when the plaintiff's claim does not arise from the defendant's activities there, the due process trade-off is that the plaintiff must prove more than minimum contacts; the plaintiff must prove that the defendant's contacts with the forum state are continuous and systematic.

2. Are contacts for general jurisdiction simpler to measure than for specific jurisdiction? Does the volume of the defendant's business in the forum matter? In *Lakin v. Prudential Securities, Inc.*, 348 F.3d 704, 709 (8th Cir. 2003), defendant did more than $10 million of business in the forum, making up one percent of its total loan portfolio. The court noted.

Percentage of a company's sales in a given state are generally irrelevant.... Many companies conduct millions of dollars in sales worldwide yet only do a small percentage of their sales in any one state. However, our relevant inquiry is not whether the percentage of a company's contacts is substantial for that company; rather, our inquiry focuses on whether the company's contacts are substantial for the forum.

Other circuits do consider the percentage of a defendant's total business as one factor in a general jurisdiction analysis. See, e.g., *Nichols v. G.D. Searle & Co.*, 991 F.2d 1195 (4th Cir.1993) (company with two percent of total sales in Maryland, when coupled with other factors had insufficient contacts); *Michigan Nat'l Bank v. Quality Dinette, Inc.*, 888 F.2d 462 (6th Cir.1989) (defendant with three percent of its total sales in Michigan, when combined with other factors, had sufficient contacts).

3. Courts apply the "fair play and substantial justice" factors to general jurisdiction cases, as well as specific jurisdiction cases. See, e.g., *Bearry v. Beech Aircraft Corp.*, 818 F.2d 370, 377 (5th Cir. 1987).

Problems

Evaluate the following problems from the perspective of due process contacts, for general jurisdiction. If you and your fellow classmates disagree about jurisdiction in a particular case, you should remember that reasonable judges can reach different conclusions from the same fact situation, based on the quality of advocacy and/or their own perspectives on an issue.

1. The Atlanta, Georgia office of a large law firm sued its former client, the city of Tulsa, Oklahoma, for nonpayment of its legal fees, in a Georgia court. The city hired the law firm to assist in defending a class action lawsuit filed in an Oklahoma court. During the four years of representation, the City of Tulsa "sent at least one hundred letters and e-mail messages to employees" of the law firm in Atlanta. Officials of the city of Tulsa visited Atlanta once.

The city spent millions of dollars in Georgia for goods and services in the seven years before the lawsuit was filed. It sent a variety of employees to Atlanta for official business trips. It also collected taxes from Georgia residents and businesses. Tulsa also maintains agreements with Georgia businesses to advertise in magazines distributed primarily in European countries. The City of Tulsa filed a motion to dismiss for lack of personal jurisdiction. How should the trial court rule? See *Paul, Hastings, Janofsky & Walker, LLP v. City of Tulsa, Oklahoma*, 245 F.Supp.2d 1248 (N.D. Ga. 2002).

2. After CSX Transportation, Inc., a railroad company, settled claims against it arising from one of its rail tank cars exploding and causing considerable damage in Kansas, the company sued Procor, the Canadian inspector of that car, in a Michigan court to recover its costs from the earlier litigation. Procor moved to dismiss the complaint for lack of personal jurisdiction. CSX attempted to prove that Procor had continuous and systematic contacts with Michigan from the following: Procor's rail cars travel on Michigan track for millions of miles per year, producing significant revenue (millions of dollars) to Procor for activities occurring in Michigan. Seventy-nine of Procor's lessees directed their leased rail cars through the state of Michigan in 2000. In addition, Procor paid more than $150,000 to have 816 of its rail cars repaired in Michigan during 2000.

Procor counters that it has no facilities in the United States, is not required to have an agent in Michigan, performed repairs in Michigan only in the previous eight years, owns no real estate or bank accounts in

Michigan, has no telephone listing or warehouse space there, and does no advertising of its rail cars there. Also, it states that only one of its largest twenty leases is in the U.S., and that only one of its lessees was not a Canadian company. How should the trial court rule on Procor's motion? See *CSX Transportation, Inc. v. Union Tank Car Company*, 247 F.Supp.2d 833 (E.D. Mich. 2002).

3. A Georgia lessor of rail cars sued an Illinois lessee for breach of contract in a Georgia court. The defendant has its principal place of business in Illinois. It owns no real estate in Georgia, does not advertise in Georgia, and is not registered to do business there, and has no offices, employees or operations there. The plaintiff contends that the defendant appointed it as defendant's agent to negotiate two contracts in Georgia which were substantially performed there. It states that the defendant has transported goods on Georgia railroads, it has used a Georgia maintenance facility for its rail cars, and has purchased labor, materials and services in Georgia in the previous three years worth $500,000. Finally, the defendant pays ad valorem taxes to Georgia based on the rail cars it owns that transport goods there.

The defendant argues that its contacts in Georgia are random and sporadic, because it is inevitable that its cars and business cross many state lines and enter numerous states. Less than 5% of the car wheel miles traveled by the defendant were in Georgia, and it spent only .24% of its maintenance costs there. How should the court rule on the defendant's motion to dismiss? See *Railcar, Ltd. v. Southern Illinois Railcar Company*, 42 F.Supp.2d 1369 (N.D. Ga. 1999).

Until 1984, the Court had referred to "fair play and substantial justice," but it had not indicated 1) the role of the "fair play" factors in the due process analysis, or 2) how a trial court should allocate the burden of proof on that issue. The *Burger King* case addressed these issues.

BURGER KING v. RUDZEWICZ

471 U.S. 462, 105 S.Ct. 2174, 85 L.Ed.2d 528 (1985)

Justice BRENNAN delivered the opinion of the Court.

The State of Florida's long-arm statute extends jurisdiction to "[a]ny person, whether or not a citizen or resident of this state," who, *inter alia*, "[b]reach [es] a contract in this state by failing to perform acts required by the contract to be performed in this state," so long as the cause of action arises from the alleged contractual breach. Fla.Stat. § 48.193(1)(g) (Supp.1984). The United States District Court for the Southern District of Florida, sitting in diversity, relied on this provision in exercising personal jurisdiction over a Michigan resident who allegedly had breached a franchise agreement with a Florida corporation by failing to make required payments in Florida. The question presented is whether this exercise of long-arm jurisdiction offended "traditional conception[s] of fair play and substantial justice" embodied in the Due Process

Clause of the Fourteenth Amendment. *International Shoe Co. v. Washington . . . .*

I

A

Burger King Corporation is a Florida corporation whose principal offices are in Miami. It is one of the world's largest restaurant organizations, with over 3,000 outlets in the 50 States, the Commonwealth of Puerto Rico, and 8 foreign nations. Burger King conducts approximately 80% of its business through a franchise operation that the company styles the "Burger King System"—"a comprehensive restaurant format and operating system for the sale of uniform and quality food products." Burger King licenses its franchisees to use its trademarks and service marks for a period of 20 years and leases standardized restaurant facilities to them for the same term. In addition, franchisees acquire a variety of proprietary information concerning the "standards, specifications, procedures and methods for operating a Burger King Restaurant." They also receive market research and advertising assistance; ongoing training in restaurant management; and accounting, cost-control, and inventory-control guidance. By permitting franchisees to tap into Burger King's established national reputation and to benefit from proven procedures for dispensing standardized fare, this system enables them to go into the restaurant business with significantly lowered barriers to entry.

* * *

Rudzewicz and MacShara jointly applied for a franchise to Burger King's Birmingham, Michigan, district office in the autumn of 1978. Their application was forwarded to Burger King's Miami headquarters, which entered into a preliminary agreement with them in February 1979. During the ensuing four months it was agreed that Rudzewicz and MacShara would assume operation of an existing facility in Drayton Plains, Michigan. MacShara attended the prescribed management courses in Miami during this period, and the franchisees purchased $165,000 worth of restaurant equipment from Burger King's Davmor Industries division in Miami. Even before the final agreements were signed, however, the parties began to disagree over site-development fees, building design, computation of monthly rent, and whether the franchisees would be able to assign their liabilities to a corporation they had formed. During these disputes Rudzewicz and MacShara negotiated both with the Birmingham district office and with the Miami headquarters. With some misgivings, Rudzewicz and MacShara finally obtained limited concessions from the Miami headquarters, signed the final agreements, and commenced operations in June 1979. By signing the final agreements, Rudzewicz obligated himself personally to payments exceeding $1 million over the 20–year franchise relationship. * * *

The Drayton Plains facility apparently enjoyed steady business during the summer of 1979, but patronage declined after a recession began later that year. Rudzewicz and MacShara soon fell far behind in their monthly payments to Miami. Headquarters sent notices of default, and an extended period of negotiations began among the franchisees, the Birmingham district office, and the Miami headquarters. After several Burger King officials in Miami had engaged in prolonged but ultimately unsuccessful negotiations with the franchisees by mail and by telephone, headquarters terminated the franchise and ordered Rudzewicz and MacShara to vacate the premises. They refused and continued to occupy and operate the facility as a Burger King restaurant.

B

Burger King commenced the instant action in the United States District Court for the Southern District of Florida in May 1981, invoking that court's diversity jurisdiction pursuant to 28 U.S.C. § 1332(a) and its original jurisdiction over federal trademark disputes pursuant to § 1338(a). Burger King alleged that Rudzewicz and MacShara had breached their franchise obligations "within [the jurisdiction of] this district court" by failing to make the required payments "at plaintiff's place of business in Miami, Dade County, Florida," and also charged that they were tortiously infringing its trademarks and service marks through their continued, unauthorized operation as a Burger King restaurant. Burger King sought damages, injunctive relief, and costs and attorney's fees. Rudzewicz and MacShara entered special appearances and argued, inter alia, that because they were Michigan residents and because Burger King's claim did not "arise" within the Southern District of Florida, the District Court lacked personal jurisdiction over them. The District Court denied their motions after a hearing, holding that, pursuant to Florida's long-arm statute, "a non-resident Burger King franchisee is subject to the personal jurisdiction of this Court in actions arising out of its franchise agreements." * * *

After a 3–day bench trial, the court again concluded that it had "jurisdiction over the subject matter and the parties to this cause." Finding that Rudzewicz and MacShara had breached their franchise agreements with Burger King and had infringed Burger King's trademarks and service marks, the court entered judgment against them, jointly and severally, for $228,875 in contract damages. The court also ordered them "to immediately close Burger King Restaurant Number 775 from continued operation or to immediately give the keys and possession of said restaurant to Burger King Corporation," found that they had failed to prove any of the required elements of their counterclaim, and awarded costs and attorney's fees to Burger King.

Rudzewicz appealed to the Court of Appeals for the Eleventh Circuit. A divided panel of that Circuit reversed the judgment, concluding that the District Court could not properly exercise personal jurisdiction over Rudzewicz pursuant to Fla.Stat. § 48.193(1)(g) (Supp.1984) because "the circumstances of the Drayton Plains franchise and the negotiations which led to it left Rudzewicz bereft of reasonable notice and financially unprepared for the prospect of franchise litigation in Florida." *Burger King Corp. v. MacShara*, 724 F.2d 1505, 1513 (1984). Accordingly, the panel majority concluded that "[j]urisdiction under these circumstances would offend the fundamental fairness which is the touchstone of due process." *Ibid.*

Treating the jurisdictional statement as a petition for a writ of certiorari, we grant the petition and now reverse.

II

A

The Due Process Clause protects an individual's liberty interest in not being subject to the binding judgments of a forum with which he has established no meaningful "contacts, ties, or relations." *International Shoe Co. v. Washington.* By requiring that individuals have "fair warning that a particular activity may subject [them] to the jurisdiction of a foreign sovereign," the Due Process Clause "gives a degree of predictability to the legal system that allows potential defendants to structure their primary conduct with some minimum assurance as to where that conduct will and will not render them liable to suit," *World–Wide Volkswagen Corp. v. Woodson.*

Where a forum seeks to assert specific jurisdiction over an out-of-state defendant who has not consented to suit there, this "fair warning" requirement is satisfied if the defendant has "purposefully directed" his activities at residents of the forum, and the litigation results from alleged injuries that "arise out of or relate to" those activities, *Helicopteros Nacionales de Colombia, S.A. v. Hall.* Thus "[t]he forum State does not exceed its powers under the Due Process Clause if it asserts personal jurisdiction over a corporation that delivers its products into the stream of commerce with the expectation that they will be purchased by consumers in the forum State" and those products subsequently injure forum consumers. *World–Wide Volkswagen Corp. v. Woodson.* Similarly, a publisher who distributes magazines in a distant State may fairly be held accountable in that forum for damages resulting there from an allegedly defamatory story. *Keeton v. Hustler Magazine, Inc.,* see also *Calder v. Jones.* And with respect to interstate contractual obligations, we have emphasized that parties who "reach out beyond one state and create continuing relationships and obligations with citizens of another state" are subject to regulation and sanctions in the other State for the consequences of their activities. *Travelers Health Assn. v. Virginia,* 339 U.S. 643, 647 (1950). See also *McGee v. International Life Insurance Co.*

[T]he constitutional touchstone remains whether the defendant purposefully established "minimum contacts" in the forum State. *International Shoe Co. v. Washington.* Although it has been argued that foreseeability of causing injury in another State should be sufficient to establish such contacts there when policy considerations so require, the Court has consistently held that this kind of foreseeability is not a "sufficient benchmark" for exercising personal jurisdiction. *World–Wide Volkswagen Corp. v. Woodson.* Instead, "the foreseeability that is critical to due process analysis ... is that the defendant's conduct and connection with the forum State are such that he should reasonably anticipate being haled into court there." *Id.*, at 297. In defining when it is that a potential defendant should "reasonably anticipate" out-of-state litigation, the Court frequently has drawn from the reasoning of *Hanson v. Denckla*:

> The unilateral activity of those who claim some relationship with a nonresident defendant cannot satisfy the requirement of contact with the forum State. The application of that rule will vary with the quality and nature of the defendant's activity, but it is essential in each case that there be some act by which the defendant purposefully avails itself of the privilege of conducting activities within the forum State, thus invoking the benefits and protections of its laws.

This "purposeful availment" requirement ensures that a defendant will not be haled into a jurisdiction solely as a result of "random," "fortuitous," or "attenuated" contacts. *World-Wide Volkswagen Corp. v. Woodson*, or of the "unilateral activity of another party or a third person," *Helicopteros Nacionales de Colombia, S.A. v. Hall*. Jurisdiction is proper, however, where the contacts proximately result from actions by the defendant himself that create a "substantial connection" with the forum State. *McGee v. International Life Insurance Co.* Thus where the defendant "deliberately" has engaged in significant activities within a State, *Keeton v. Hustler Magazine, Inc.*, or has created "continuing obligations" between himself and residents of the forum, *Travelers Health Assn. v. Virginia*, he manifestly has availed himself of the privilege of conducting business there, and because his activities are shielded by "the benefits and protections" of the forum's laws it is presumptively not unreasonable to require him to submit to the burdens of litigation in that forum as well.

Jurisdiction in these circumstances may not be avoided merely because the defendant did not *physically* enter the forum State. Although territorial presence frequently will enhance a potential defendant's affiliation with a State and reinforce the reasonable foreseeability of suit there, it is an inescapable fact of modern commercial life that a substantial amount of business is transacted solely by mail and wire communications across state lines, thus obviating the need for physical presence within a State in which business is conducted. So long as a commercial actor's efforts are "purposefully directed" toward residents of another State, we have consistently rejected the notion that an absence of physical contacts can defeat personal jurisdiction there.

Once it has been decided that a defendant purposefully established minimum contacts within the forum State, these contacts may be considered in light of other factors to determine whether the assertion of personal jurisdiction would comport with "fair play and substantial justice." *International Shoe Co. v. Washington*. Thus courts in "appropriate case[s]" may evaluate "the burden on the defendant," "the forum State's interest in adjudicating the dispute," "the plaintiff's interest in obtaining convenient and effective relief," "the interstate judicial system's interest in obtaining the most efficient resolution of controversies,'' and the ''shared interest of the several States in furthering fundamental substantive social policies.'' *World–Wide Volkswagen Corp. v. Woodson.* These considerations sometimes serve to establish the reasonableness of jurisdiction upon a lesser showing of minimum contacts than would otherwise be required. See, e.g., *McGee v. International Life Insurance Co.* On the other hand, where a defendant who purposefully has directed his activities at forum residents seeks to defeat jurisdiction, he must present a compelling case that the presence of some other considerations would render jurisdiction unreasonable. Most such considerations usually may be accommodated through means short of finding jurisdiction unconstitutional. For example, the potential clash of the forum's law with the ''fundamental substantive social policies'' of another State may be accommodated through application of the forum's choice-of-law rules. Similarly, a defendant claiming substantial inconvenience may seek a change of venue. * * *

B

(1)

Applying these principles to the case at hand, we believe there is substantial record evidence supporting the District Court's conclusion that the assertion of personal jurisdiction over Rudzewicz in Florida for the alleged breach of his franchise agreement did not offend due process. At the outset, we note a continued division among lower courts respecting whether and to what extent a contract can constitute a ''contact'' for purposes of due process analysis. If the question is whether an individual's contract with an out-of-state party alone can automatically establish sufficient minimum contacts in the other party's home forum, we believe the answer clearly is that it cannot. The Court long ago rejected the notion that personal jurisdiction might turn on ''mechanical'' tests, *International Shoe Co. v. Washington.* or on ''conceptualistic . . . theories of the place of contracting or of performance.'' Instead, we have emphasized the need for a ''highly realistic'' approach that recognizes that a ''contract'' is ''ordinarily but an intermediate step serving to tie up prior business negotiations with future consequences which themselves are the real object of the business transaction.'' * * *

In this case, no physical ties to Florida can be attributed to Rudzewicz other than MacShara's brief training course in Miami. Rudzewicz did not maintain offices in Florida and, for all that appears from the record, has never even visited there. Yet this franchise dispute grew directly out of ''a contract which had a *substantial* connection with that State.'' *McGee v. International Life Insurance Co ..* (emphasis added). Eschewing the option of operating an independent local enterprise, Rudzewicz deliberately ''reach[ed] out beyond'' Michigan and negotiated with a Florida corporation for the purchase of a long-term franchise and the manifold benefits that would derive from affiliation with a nationwide organization. *Travelers Health Assn. v. Virginia.* Upon approval, he entered into a carefully structured 20–year relationship that envisioned continuing and wide-reaching contacts with Burger King in Florida. In light of Rudzewicz' voluntary acceptance of the long-term and exacting regulation of his business from Burger King's Miami headquarters, the "quality and nature" of his relationship to the company in Florida can in no sense be viewed as "random," "fortuitous," or "attenuated." *Hanson v. Denckla*; *World–Wide Volkswagen Corp. v. Woodson*. Rudzewicz' refusal to make the contractually required payments in Miami, and his continued use of Burger King's trademarks and confidential business information after his termination, caused foreseeable injuries to the corporation in Florida. For these reasons it was, at the very least, presumptively reasonable for Rudzewicz to be called to account there for such injuries.

The Court of Appeals concluded, however, that in light of the supervision emanating from Burger King's district office in Birmingham, Rudzewicz reasonably believed that "the Michigan office was for all intents and purposes the embodiment of Burger King" and that he therefore had no "reason to anticipate a Burger King suit outside of Michigan." This reasoning overlooks substantial record evidence indicating that Rudzewicz most certainly knew that he was affiliating himself with an enterprise based primarily in Florida. The contract documents themselves emphasize that Burger King's operations are conducted and supervised from the Miami headquarters, that all relevant notices and payments must be sent there, and that the agreements were made in and enforced from Miami. Moreover, the parties' actual course of dealing repeatedly confirmed that decisionmaking authority was vested in the Miami headquarters and that the district office served largely as an intermediate link between the headquarters and the franchisees. When problems arose over building design, site-development fees, rent computation, and the defaulted payments, Rudzewicz and MacShara learned that the Michigan office was powerless to resolve their disputes and could only channel their communications to Miami. Throughout these disputes, the Miami headquarters and the Michigan franchisees carried on a continuous course of direct communications by mail and by telephone, and it was the Miami headquarters that made the key negotiating decisions out of which the instant litigation arose.

Moreover, we believe the Court of Appeals gave insufficient weight to provisions in the various franchise documents providing that all disputes would be governed by Florida law. * * * Nothing in our cases ... suggests that a choice-of-law provision should be ignored in considering whether a defendant has "purposefully invoked the benefits and protections of a State's laws" for jurisdictional purposes. Although such a provision standing alone would be insufficient to confer jurisdiction, we believe that, when combined with the 20–year interdependent relationship Rudzewicz established with Burger King's Miami headquarters, it reinforced his deliberate affiliation with the forum State and the reasonable foreseeability of possible litigation there. * * *

(2)

Nor has Rudzewicz pointed to other factors that can be said persuasively to outweigh the considerations discussed above and to establish the unconstitutionality of Florida's assertion of jurisdiction. We cannot conclude that Florida had no "legitimate interest in holding [Rudzewicz] answerable on a claim related to" the contacts he had established in that State. * * *

The Court of Appeals also concluded, however, that the parties' dealings involved "a characteristic disparity of bargaining power" and "elements of surprise," and that Rudzewicz "lacked fair notice" of the potential for litigation in Florida because the contractual provisions suggesting to the contrary were merely "boilerplate declarations in a lengthy printed contract." * * * To the contrary, Rudzewicz was represented by counsel throughout these complex transactions and, as Judge Johnson observed in dissent below, was himself an experienced accountant "who for five months conducted negotiations with Burger King over the terms of the franchise and lease agreements, and who obligated himself personally to contracts requiring over time payments that exceeded $1 million." Rudzewicz was able to secure a modest reduction in rent and other concessions from Miami headquarters; moreover, to the extent that Burger King's terms were inflexible, Rudzewicz presumably decided that the advantages of affiliating with a national organization provided sufficient commercial benefits to offset the detriments.

III

Notwithstanding these considerations, the Court of Appeals apparently believed that it was necessary to reject jurisdiction in this case as a prophylactic measure, reasoning that an affirmance of the District Court's judgment would result in the exercise of jurisdiction over "out-of-state consumers to collect payments due on modest personal purchases" and would "sow the seeds of default judgments against franchisees owing smaller debts." We share the Court of Appeals' broader concerns and therefore reject any talismanic jurisdictional formulas; "the facts of each case must [always] be weighed" in determining whether personal jurisdiction would comport with "fair play and substantial justice." The "quality and nature" of an interstate transaction may sometimes be so "random," "fortuitous," or "attenuated" that it cannot fairly be said that the potential defendant "should reasonably anticipate being haled into court" in another jurisdiction. *World–Wide Volkswagen Corp. v. Woodson.* We also have emphasized that jurisdiction may not be grounded on a contract whose terms have been obtained through "fraud, undue influence, or overweening bargaining power" and whose application would render litigation "so gravely difficult and inconvenient that [a party] will for all practical purposes be deprived of his day in court." * * *

For the reasons set forth above, however, these dangers are not present in the instant case. Because Rudzewicz established a substantial and continuing relationship with Burger King's Miami headquarters, received fair notice from the contract documents and the course of dealing that he might be subject to suit in Florida, and has failed to demonstrate how jurisdiction in that forum would otherwise be fundamentally unfair, we conclude that the District Court's exercise of jurisdiction pursuant to Fla.Stat. § 48.193(1)(g) (Supp.1984) did not offend due process. The judgment of the Court of Appeals is accordingly reversed, and the case is remanded for further proceedings consistent with this opinion.

Justice STEVENS, with whom Justice WHITE joins, dissenting.

In my opinion there is a significant element of unfairness in requiring a franchisee to defend a case of this kind in the forum chosen by the franchisor. It is undisputed that appellee maintained no place of business in Florida, that he had no employees in that State, and that he was not licensed to do business there. Appellee did not prepare his French fries, shakes, and hamburgers in Michigan, and then deliver them into the stream of commerce "with the expectation that they [would] be purchased by consumers in" Florida. To the contrary, appellee did business only in Michigan, his business, property, and payroll taxes were payable in that State, and he sold all of his products there.

Throughout the business relationship, appellee's principal contacts with appellant were with its Michigan office. Notwithstanding its disclaimer, the Court seems ultimately to rely on nothing more than standard boilerplate language contained in various documents, to establish that appellee " 'purposefully availed himself of the benefits and protections of Florida's laws.' " Such superficial analysis creates a potential for unfairness not only in negotiations between franchisors and their franchisees but, more significantly, in the resolution of the disputes that inevitably arise from time to time in such relationships.

Accordingly, I respectfully dissent.

Notes and Questions

1. *Burger King* differed from prior decisions for three reasons. First, the lawsuit was filed in a federal court. The court invoked jurisdiction over the Michigan franchisees based on Federal Rule of Civil Procedure 4, which permits a federal court to use the long-arm statute of the state in which it is sitting to reach nonresident defendants. Rule 4 allows a federal court to exercise personal jurisdiction to the extent the state in which the federal court is sitting can exert jurisdiction under its long-arm statute. See Part B of this Chapter for more on service of process.

Second, the decision describes the chronology of due process analysis. Initially, the burden of raising the issue of lack of personal jurisdiction is on the defendant who meets that burden by moving to dismiss the complaint. The burden of proof then moves to the plaintiff to establish that the defendant has the requisite contact(s) with the forum state that put the defendant on notice about the foreseeability of being sued.

If the plaintiff sustains its burden of proof on the minimum contacts issue, the burden of proof on the issue of fair play and substantial justice switches to the defendant. The defendant has the opportunity to show "a compelling case" that even though he has minimum contacts with the forum state, it is nevertheless constitutionally unreasonable for him to defend where the litigation related contacts occurred. In *Burger King*, the Court quickly disposed of the "fair play" analysis by observing that the defendant failed to point "to other factors that can be said persuasively to . . . establish the unconstitutionality of" the forum state's assertion of jurisdiction. Given the Court's articulation of the governing burdens for the first time in *Burger King*, it was not surprising that counsel for the franchisees may have been unaware of their obligations to present a "compelling" case of unreasonableness.

Third, the Court measured the trial court's findings of fact against the Federal Rule 52(a) standard of clearly erroneous, which "requires that '[f]indings of fact shall not be set aside unless clearly erroneous.' . . . [N]either Rudzewicz nor the Court of Appeals has pointed to record evidence that would support a 'definite and firm conviction' that the District Court's findings are mistaken." The effect of using the "clearly erroneous" standard is that appellate courts are more deferential to the trial court's findings of fact on issues of foreseeability, purposeful availment, and fair play and substantial justice.

2. A finding that jurisdiction over a nonresident defendant is reasonable effectively means that the defendant failed to present a compelling reason to rebut the presumption of reasonableness of asserting jurisdiction. Because this fact-specific approach lacks predictability and precision, it is subject to strong criticism from lower courts that are bound to apply it. For example, the court in *LAK, Inc. v. Deer Creek Enterprises*, 885 F.2d 1293 (6th Cir. 1989) remarked that:

> If it suggests nothing else, this case may suggest that there is a downside, as well as an upside, to the judicially imposed requirement that each and every question of personal jurisdiction over a non-resident defendant be decided "on its own facts," with counsel and court sifting through each new complex of facts in search of "contacts" demonstrating that the plaintiff's choice of a forum does or does not accord with the notions of "reasonableness" and "fair play" reflected in a vast number of fact-specific judicial opinions. More sharply defined standards might well reduce miscalculations on the part of lawyers who, not surprisingly, normally seek a home court advantage if they think they see some chance of getting it—and it is not inconceivable that clearer standards might lead to more expeditious and efficient resolution of those jurisdictional questions that counsel choose to fight out in court. In this particular case, diligent lawyers have favored us with several hundred case citations; scholarship that comprehensive carries obvious costs, both in time and in money.

3. Since *Burger King*, in contract cases the key evaluative factors in determining whether a nonresident defendant has purposefully established the requisite contacts in the forum state are prior negotiations and contemplated future consequences, the terms of the contract, and the parties' actual

course of dealing. What is the meaning of prior negotiations and contemplated future consequences? Courts have considered several factors in the contract situation, such as where the parties contemplated that the work would be performed, where the negotiations were conducted, where payment was made, and whether the defendant initiated the business relationship in some way. The last factor appears to be the strongest factor.

A. Who initiated the business relationship? Does the record establish that the plaintiff pursued the nonresident defendant? For example, did a representative of the plaintiff travel to the defendant's location in another state to secure the defendant as a developer of a project after arrangements with a first developer fell apart?

B. Prior negotiations—Did all prior face-to-face negotiations between the parties occur in the defendant's state by local counsel for all parties? Were documents executed there as well?

C. Where did the parties contemplate that performance was to occur? For example, was the project designed by an engineer in the defendant's state, constructed by local contractors, and managed by a defendant's state's municipality?

D. Parties' course of dealing. Did the defendant avail itself of the benefits and protections of the law where the lawsuit was filed? Does the franchise agreement include terms regarding regulation of the franchise by the headquarters in the forum state?

E. Does the agreement contain a provision that the laws of the forum state would govern the agreement?

4. If the two franchisees had sued Burger King, what state courts would have jurisdiction over Burger King? Would general jurisdiction enable them to sue in any state where there are franchises?

5. The contract at issue in *Burger King* contained a choice of law clause, meaning that the parties agreed that regardless of where a lawsuit was filed, Florida law would apply to resolve the dispute. A choice of law clause is comparable to the forum selection clause already discussed in conjunction with the *Shute* case, (see the Notes after *International Shoe*). Indeed, many contracts contain both types of clauses, prescribing not only what state's law applies but also where any lawsuit arising from the contract must be filed.

Problem

How would you resolve the following case, applying the principles from *Burger King*?

Municipal Mortgage & Equity, LLC, a Delaware limited liability company with its principal place of business in Maryland [MuniMae] brought a diversity action in Maryland federal court against Southfork Apartments Limited Partnership, a limited partnership organized under the laws of Minnesota. MuniMae seeks a declaratory judgment pursuant to federal law establishing that Southfork owes certain amounts of money pursuant to loan agreements entered into by the parties in 1999. The contract was to secure funds necessary to develop a multi-family public housing project in a small town in Minnesota. MuniMae had initially chosen a party other than Southfork to develop the Project. When the financing arrangements with that party fell through, MuniMae approached Southfork in Minnesota to apply for MuniMae funding.

Under the contract, the defendant was required during construction to request funds from MuniMae which was located in Maryland. Following completion of the Project's construction, Southfork sent interest payments and fees to MuniMae in Maryland. (Later, Southfork sent payments to a successor Trustee in New York.) In addition, the loan documents required Southfork to send the Project's progress and operating reports to MuniMae in Maryland. The contract also included a provision that Minnesota law (rather than Maryland law) should govern the interpretation of any contract provision.

Southfork moved to dismiss the complaint due to improper personal jurisdiction. Applying the factors discussed in *Burger King*, how should the court rule? Did the communications between Southfork and MuniMae rise to the level of "exacting regulations of every conceivable aspect of . . . operations," characteristic of the "wide-reaching" relationships in the franchise context that was important to the exercise of personal jurisdiction in *Burger King*? Did Southfork purposely avail itself of the benefits and protections of Maryland law? See *Municipal Mortgage & Equity LLC v. Southfork Apartments Limited Partnership*, 93 F.Supp.2d 622 (D.Md. 2000).

Reading the next case, *Asahi Metal Industry Co. v. Superior Court*, requires you to do something you probably have yet to do in reading appellate cases—figure out which justices and how many justices are on which side of which issues. In *Asahi*, watch how the results of your calculation change as the question moves from one of minimum contacts to a discussion of the fair play and substantial justice factors.

ASAHI METAL INDUSTRY CO.
v. SUPERIOR COURT

480 U.S. 102, 107 S.Ct. 1026, 94 L.Ed.2d 92 (1987)

Justice O'CONNOR announced the judgment of the Court and delivered the unanimous opinion of the Court with respect to Part I, the opinion of the Court with respect to Part II–B, in which THE CHIEF JUSTICE, Justice BRENNAN, Justice WHITE, Justice MARSHALL, Justice BLACKMUN, Justice POWELL, and Justice STEVENS join, and an opinion with respect to Parts II–A and III, in which THE CHIEF JUSTICE, Justice POWELL, and Justice SCALIA join.

This case presents the question whether the mere awareness on the part of a foreign defendant that the components it manufactured, sold, and delivered outside the United States would reach the forum State in the stream of commerce constitutes "minimum contacts" between the defendant and the forum State such that the exercise of jurisdiction "does not offend 'traditional notions of fair play and substantial justice.'" *International Shoe Co. v. Washington*, 326 U.S. 310, 316 (1945), quoting *Milliken v. Meyer*, 311 U.S. 457, 463 (1940).

I

Zurcher lost control of his Honda motorcycle and collided with a tractor. He sued, alleg[ing] that the accident was caused by a sudden loss of air and an explosion in the rear tire of the motorcycle, and alleged that the motorcycle tire, tube, and sealant were defective. Zurcher's complaint named, Cheng Shin Rubber Industrial Co., Ltd. (Cheng Shin), the Taiwanese manufacturer of the tube. Cheng Shin in turn filed a cross-complaint seeking indemnification from its codefendants and from petitioner, Asahi Metal Industry Co., Ltd. (Asahi), the manufacturer of the tube's valve assembly. Zurcher's claims against Cheng Shin and the other defendants were eventually settled and dismissed, leaving only Cheng Shin's indemnity action against Asahi.

California's long-arm statute authorizes the exercise of jurisdiction "on any basis not inconsistent with the Constitution of this state or of the United States." Asahi moved to quash Cheng Shin's service of summons, arguing the State could not exert jurisdiction over it consistent with the Due Process Clause of the Fourteenth Amendment.

In relation to the motion, the following information was submitted by Asahi and Cheng Shin. Asahi is a Japanese corporation. It manufactures tire valve assemblies in Japan and sells the assemblies to Cheng Shin, and to several other tire manufacturers, for use as components in finished tire tubes. Asahi's sales to Cheng Shin took place in Taiwan. The shipments from Asahi to Cheng Shin were sent from Japan to Taiwan. Cheng Shin bought and incorporated into its tire tubes 150,000 Asahi valve assemblies in 1978; 500,000 in 1979; 500,000 in 1980; 100,000 in 1981; and 100,000 in 1982. Sales to Cheng Shin accounted for 1.24 percent of Asahi's income in 1981 and 0.44 percent in 1982. Cheng Shin alleged that approximately 20 percent of its sales in the United States are in California. Cheng Shin purchases valve assemblies from other suppliers as well, and sells finished tubes throughout the world.

* * *

[T]he Superior Court denied the motion to quash summons, stating: "Asahi obviously does business on an international scale. It is not unreasonable that they defend claims of defect in their product on an international scale."

The Court of Appeal of the State of California issued a peremptory writ of mandate commanding the Superior Court to quash service of summons. The court concluded that "it would be unreasonable to require Asahi to respond in California solely on the basis of ultimately realized foreseeability that the product into which its component was embodied would be sold all over the world including California."

The Supreme Court of the State of California reversed and discharged the writ issued by the Court of Appeal. The court observed: "Asahi has no offices, property or agents in California. It solicits no business in California and has made no direct sales [in California]." Moreover, "Asahi did not design or control the system of distribution that carried its valve assemblies into California." Nevertheless, the court found the exercise of jurisdiction over Asahi to be consistent with the Due Process Clause. It concluded that Asahi knew that some of the valve assemblies sold to Cheng Shin would be incorporated into tire tubes sold in California, and that Asahi benefitted indirectly from the sale in California of products incorporating its components. The court considered Asahi's intentional act of placing its components into the stream of commerce—that is, by delivering the components to Cheng Shin in Taiwan—coupled with Asahi's awareness that some of the components would eventually find their way into California, sufficient to form the basis for state court jurisdiction under the Due Process Clause.

We granted certiorari, and now reverse.

II

A

* * * Since *World–Wide Volkswagen*, lower courts have been confronted with cases in which the defendant acted by placing a product in the stream of commerce, and the stream eventually swept defendant's product into the forum State, but the defendant did nothing else to purposefully avail itself of the market in the forum State. Some courts have understood the Due Process Clause, as interpreted in *World–Wide Volkswagen*, to allow an exercise of personal jurisdiction to be based on no more than the defendant's act of placing the product in the stream of commerce. Other courts have understood the Due Process Clause and . . . *World–Wide Volkswagen* to require the action of the defendant to be more purposefully directed at the forum State than the mere act of placing a product in the stream of commerce.

* * * The "substantial connection" between the defendant and the forum State necessary for a finding of minimum contacts must come about by an action of the defendant purposefully directed toward the forum State. The placement of a product into the stream of commerce, without more, is not an act of the defendant purposefully directed toward the forum State. Additional conduct of the defendant may indicate an intent or purpose to serve the market in the forum State, for example, designing the product for the market in the forum State, advertising in the forum State, establishing channels for providing regular advice to customers in the forum State, or marketing the product through a distributor who has agreed to serve as the sales agent in the forum State. But a defendant's awareness that the stream of commerce may or will sweep the product into the forum State does not convert the mere act of placing the product into the stream into an act purposefully directed toward the forum State.

Assuming, arguendo, that respondents have established Asahi's awareness that some of the valves sold to Cheng Shin would be incorporated into tire tubes sold in California, respondents have not demonstrated any action by Asahi to purposefully avail itself of the California market. Asahi does not do business in California. It has no office, agents, employees, or property in California. It does not advertise or otherwise solicit business in California. It did not create, control, or employ the distribution system that brought its valves to California. There is no evidence that Asahi designed its product in anticipation of sales in California. On the basis of these facts, the exertion of personal jurisdiction over Asahi by the Superior Court of California exceeds the limits of due process.

B

* * *

We have previously explained that the determination of the reasonableness of the exercise of jurisdiction in each case will depend on an evaluation of several factors. A court must consider the burden on the defendant, the interests of the forum State, and the plaintiff's interest in obtaining relief. It must also weigh in its determination "the interstate judicial system's interest in obtaining the most efficient resolution of controversies; and the shared interest of the several States in furthering fundamental substantive social policies."

A consideration of these factors in the present case clearly reveals the unreasonableness of the assertion of jurisdiction over Asahi, even apart from the question of the placement of goods in the stream of commerce.

Certainly the burden on the defendant in this case is severe. Asahi has been commanded by the Supreme Court of California not only to traverse the distance between Asahi's headquarters in Japan and the Superior Court of California in and for the County of Solano, but also to submit its dispute with Cheng Shin to a foreign nation's judicial system. The unique burdens placed upon one who must defend oneself in a foreign legal system should have significant weight in assessing the reasonableness of stretching the long arm of personal jurisdiction over national borders.

When minimum contacts have been established, often the interests of the plaintiff and the forum in the exercise of jurisdiction will justify even the serious burdens placed on the alien defendant. In the present case, however, the interests of the plaintiff and the forum in California's assertion of jurisdiction over Asahi are slight. All that remains is a claim for indemnification asserted by Cheng Shin, a Taiwanese corporation, against Asahi. The transaction on which the indemnification claim is based took place in Taiwan; Asahi's components were shipped from Japan to Taiwan. Cheng Shin has not demonstrated that it is more convenient for it to litigate its indemnification claim against Asahi in California rather than in Taiwan or Japan.

Because the plaintiff is not a California resident, California's legitimate interests in the dispute have considerably diminished. The Supreme Court of California argued that the State had an interest in "protecting its consumers by ensuring that foreign manufacturers comply with the state's safety standards." The State Supreme Court's definition of California's interest, however, was overly broad. The dispute between Cheng Shin and Asahi is primarily about indemnification rather than safety standards. * * *

World–Wide Volkswagen also admonished courts to take into consideration the interests of the "several States," in addition to the forum State, in the efficient judicial resolution of the dispute and the advancement of substantive policies. In the present case, this advice calls for a court to consider the procedural and substantive policies of other nations whose interests are affected by the assertion of jurisdiction by the California court. The procedural and substantive interests of other nations in a state court's assertion of jurisdiction over an alien defendant will differ from case to case. In every case, however, those interests, as well as the Federal interest in Government's foreign relations policies, will be best served by a careful inquiry into the reasonableness of the assertion of jurisdiction in the particular case, and an unwillingness to find the serious burdens on an alien defendant outweighed by minimal interests on the part of the plaintiff or the forum State. "Great care and reserve should be exercised when extending our notions of personal jurisdiction into the international field."

Considering the international context, the heavy burden on the alien defendant, and the slight interests of the plaintiff and the forum State, the exercise of personal jurisdiction by a California court over Asahi in this instance would be unreasonable and unfair.

III

Because the facts of this case do not establish minimum contacts such that the exercise of personal jurisdiction is consistent with fair play and substantial justice, the judgment of the Supreme Court of California is reversed, and the case is remanded for further proceedings not inconsistent with this opinion.

Justice BRENNAN, with whom Justice WHITE, Justice MARSHALL, and Justice BLACKMUN join, concurring in part and concurring in the judgment.

I do not agree with the interpretation in Part II–A of the stream-of-commerce theory, nor with the conclusion that Asahi did not "purposely avail itself of the California market." I do agree, however, with the Court's conclusion in Part II–B that the exercise of personal jurisdiction over Asahi in this case would not comport with "fair play and substantial justice," This is one of those rare cases in which "minimum requirements inherent in the concept of 'fair play and substantial justice' . . . defeat the reasonableness of jurisdiction even [though] the defendant has purposefully engaged in forum activities." I therefore join

Parts I and II–B of the Court's opinion, and write separately to explain my disagreement with Part II–A.

* * * The stream of commerce refers not to unpredictable currents or eddies, but to the regular and anticipated flow of products from manufacture to distribution to retail sale. As long as a participant in this process is aware that the final product is being marketed in the forum State, the possibility of a lawsuit there cannot come as a surprise. Nor will the litigation present a burden for which there is no corresponding benefit. * * *

Justice STEVENS, with whom Justice WHITE and Justice BLACK-MUN join, concurring in part and concurring in the judgment.

The judgment of the Supreme Court of California should be reversed for the reasons stated in Part II–B of the Court's opinion. While I join Parts I and II–B, I do not join Part II–A for two reasons. First, it is not necessary to the Court's decision. An examination of minimum contacts is not always necessary to determine whether a state court's assertion of personal jurisdiction is constitutional. Part II-B establishes, after considering the factors set forth in *World–Wide Volkswagen Corp. v. Woodson* that California's exercise of jurisdiction over Asahi in this case would be "unreasonable and unfair." This finding alone requires reversal; this case fits within the rule that "minimum requirements inherent in the concept of 'fair play and substantial justice' may defeat the reasonableness of jurisdiction even if the defendant has purposefully engaged in forum activities." *Burger King*. Accordingly, I see no reason in this case for the plurality to articulate "purposeful direction" or any other test as the nexus between an act of a defendant and the forum State that is necessary to establish minimum contacts.

Second, even assuming that the test ought to be formulated here, Part II–A misapplies it to the facts of this case. The plurality seems to assume that an unwavering line can be drawn between "mere awareness" that a component will find its way into the forum State and "purposeful availment" of the forum's market. Over the course of its dealings with Cheng Shin, Asahi has arguably engaged in a higher quantum of conduct than "[t]he placement of a product into the stream of commerce, without more. . . ." Whether or not this conduct rises to the level of purposeful availment requires a constitutional determination that is affected by the volume, the value, and the hazardous character of the components. In most circumstances I would be inclined to conclude that a regular course of dealing that results in deliveries of over 100,000 units annually over a period of several years would constitute "purposeful availment" even though the item delivered to the forum State was a standard product marketed throughout the world.

Notes and Questions

1. *Asahi*'s opinions contain three conceptions of purposeful availment and the stream of commerce. The most stringent approach for establishing

jurisdiction is found in Justice O'Connor's plurality opinion, and concludes that placing a product into stream of commerce must include additional conduct indicating intent or purpose to serve the market in the forum state. "A defendant's awareness that the stream of commerce may or will sweep the product into the forum State does not convert the mere act of placing the product into the stream into an act purposefully directed toward the forum State."

If you were general counsel for a corporation that manufactures finished products or component parts for installation in finished products, which view would enable you to advise your corporation better about predicting where it could be required to defend damage claims or how it could conform its conduct to avoid specific places to defend such claims?

2.   What argument can be made that the stream of commerce concept in either *World–Wide Volkswagen* or *Asahi* does not represent the law? In other words, based on the structure and support for each opinion's discussion of the stream of commerce theory, can you argue that a lower federal or state court does not have to adopt either Justice O'Connor or Justice Brennan's perspectives from *Asahi*? Is it significant to your argument that no one supporting Justice Brennan's view still sits on the Court?

3.   Do you agree with the Court's (unusual) unanimity in disposing of the fair play issue?

4.   Combining the factual context of the *Calder* and *Keeton* cases (number of copies of a work distributed to a state) with Justice O'Connor's *Asahi* approach, is there a threshold number of copies of the allegedly offensive work necessary to satisfy jurisdiction, or is that number relevant at all to the stream of commerce approach?

In *Gray v. St. Martin's Press, Inc.*, 929 F.Supp. 40 (D. N.H. 1996), the trial court upheld jurisdiction based on the sale of sixty-one copies of a book in New Hampshire, despite the author's argument that she merely placed the book into the stream of commerce when she gave her publisher the right to publish her book and that she had done nothing further to indicate purposeful availment. In rejecting her argument, the court noted that she had retained the copyright when she signed a contract with a national publisher, and that "national distribution, including distribution within the State of New Hampshire, was the raison d'etre of the Contract." This was not, the court stated, "a simple stream of commerce scenario." Instead, the author had engaged in sufficient "additional conduct" to indicate purposeful availment.

5.   Assume that the original plaintiff Zurcher had not settled with the defendant and dropped away from the claims. Would the Court's opinion on minimum contacts or fair play have differed?

Would the case have been decided differently if the component part manufacturer was a U.S. corporation and the component part itself had been made in the United States?

Problems

Using the stream of commerce plus and the stream of commerce approaches from *Asahi*, does personal jurisdiction exist in the following cases?

1. After her husband died from lung cancer, Mrs. Lesnick filed a lawsuit in the federal district of Maryland, alleging that Kent brand cigarettes manufactured by Lorillard, Inc. and Vose Corp. were the cause of her husband's death. Her complaint included claims of negligence, strict liability, negligent misrepresentation, and breach of express warranty. Specifically, she alleged that his death was caused by asbestos inserted into Kent cigarettes' "Micronite Filter" between 1972 and 1976. Vose Corp., a Massachusetts corporation, manufactured the filter material in Massachusetts and shipped it to Lorillard plants in Kentucky and New Jersey.

Lorillard and Vose jointly shared the costs of developing the Micronite Filter and jointly own the patent. Vose has no office, employees, or customers in Maryland, and it is not registered to do business there. Less than one percent of Vose's income is the result of Lorillard's sale of cigarettes in Maryland. Vose knew that Kent cigarettes with its filter material would be sold in Maryland. Vose Corp. filed a motion to dismiss the complaint, alleging that it had insufficient contacts with Maryland to subject it to personal jurisdiction there. Maryland has a due process long-arm statute. How should the trial court decide the motion to dismiss? Does Vose's work with Lorillard constitute "additional conduct" beyond the mere sale of the filters by Vose to Lorillard, per Justice O'Connor's *Asahi* opinion? See *Lesnick v. Hollingsworth & Vose Co.*, 35 F.3d 939 (4th Cir. 1994).

2. In May, 2004, Samuel, a truck driver, was seriously injured when he opened an ocean-going cargo container and a pallet loaded with paper fell out of the container and onto Samuel. The paper had been shipped from Crusinello, Italy, by its manufacturer, Binda Corp. (Binda), an Italian company. The paper had been purchased from Binda's Crusinello mill by CTI Paper, Inc. (CTI), which had been purchasing paper product from the Crusinello mill for ten years. L'Arciere had a contract with Binda to supply workers for the purpose of loading cargo containers. In a Wisconsin state court, Samuel asserts that L'Arciere workers in Italy negligently loaded the pallet into the container that was shipped to this forum. L'Arciere files a motion to dismiss Samuel's claim for lack of personal jurisdiction. How should the trial court rule on the motion? How is this fact situation (un)like *Asahi*? If no one from L'Arciere had ever visited Wisconsin, what is its probable argument about awareness? How should Samuel counter that argument? See *Kopke v. A. Hartrodt*, 629 N.W.2d 662 (Wis. 2001).

3. A.V. Imports is a Maryland corporation, which imports and distributes wines. Defendant Cielo is an Italian corporation exporting wines from Italy to the United States. "Maestro Italiano Merlot–Cabernet" is among the wines Cielo produces for export. Cielo knew that its product is imported into and sold in New Jersey. However, Cielo does not have offices, property, or employees in New Jersey, and does not pay any taxes in or to New Jersey.

Dufour, doing business in New Jersey as Maestro Italiano, is a Massachusetts corporation and imports wines into the United States. Dufour imports into the United States and New Jersey the "Maestro Italiano Merlot Cabernet" produced by Cielo. Cielo and Dufour share the trademark on "Maestro Italiano Merlot Cabernet" and jointly market it in the United States. Cielo advertises the wine in national publications, and the ad showing the wine specifies that it is "Imported by Maestro Italiano, North Bergen, N.J."

Plaintiff filed suit against the defendants in federal court for (1) federal trade dress infringement under 15 U.S.C. § 1125, (2) deceptive practices in violation of New Jersey state law, and (3) unjust enrichment. "Maestro Italiano Merlot Cabernet" allegedly infringes the trade dress of plaintiff's wine identified as "Luna di Luna Merlot Cabernet Blend." Cielo has moved to dismiss the complaint based on a lack of personal jurisdiction. How should the trial judge rule, applying Justice O'Connor's plurality opinion in *Asahi*? See *A.V. Imports, Inc. v. Col De Fratta, S.p.A.*, 171 F.Supp.2d 369 (D.N.J. 2001).

––––––––––

The Supreme Court cases after *Pennoyer* appeared to reverse many of the 19th century territorial principles of jurisdiction over defendants. A court in one state now can assert jurisdiction over defendants who have never physically been in the state, either when the claim arose or when the suit was filed. What happens when a nonresident defendant is served while visiting the forum state? The next (and most recent) decision by the Supreme Court in the area of personal jurisdiction is a reminder that portions of *Pennoyer*'s jurisprudence survive. Although the Court is split on the reason for upholding jurisdiction over a defendant who is served while inside the forum state, there is agreement about the vitality of "transient" jurisdiction.

BURNHAM v. SUPERIOR COURT

495 U.S. 604, 110 S.Ct. 2105, 109 L.Ed.2d 631 (1990)

Justice SCALIA announced the judgment of the Court and delivered an opinion in which THE CHIEF JUSTICE and Justice KENNEDY join, and in which Justice WHITE joins with respect to Parts I, II–A, II–B, and II–C.

The question presented is whether the Due Process Clause of the Fourteenth Amendment denies California courts jurisdiction over a nonresident, who was personally served with process while temporarily in that State, in a suit unrelated to his activities in the State.

I

Petitioner Dennis Burnham married Francie Burnham in 1976 in West Virginia. In 1977 the couple moved to New Jersey, where their two children were born. In July 1987 the Burnhams decided to separate.

They agreed that Mrs. Burnham, who intended to move to California, would take custody of the children. Shortly before Mrs. Burnham departed for California that same month, she and petitioner agreed that she would file for divorce on grounds of "irreconcilable differences."

In October 1987, petitioner filed for divorce in New Jersey state court on grounds of "desertion." Petitioner did not, however, obtain an issuance of summons against his wife and did not attempt to serve her with process. Mrs. Burnham, after unsuccessfully demanding that petitioner adhere to their prior agreement to submit to an "irreconcilable differences" divorce, brought suit for divorce in California state court in early January 1988.

In late January, petitioner visited southern California on business, after which he went north to visit his children in the San Francisco Bay area, where his wife resided. He took the older child to San Francisco for the weekend. Upon returning the child to Mrs. Burnham's home on January 24, 1988, petitioner was served with a California court summons and a copy of Mrs. Burnham's divorce petition. He then returned to New Jersey.

Later that year, petitioner made a special appearance in the California Superior Court, moving to quash the service of process on the ground that the court lacked personal jurisdiction over him because his only contacts with California were a few short visits to the State for the purposes of conducting business and visiting his children. The Superior Court denied the motion, and the California Court of Appeal denied mandamus relief, rejecting petitioner's contention that the Due Process Clause prohibited California courts from asserting jurisdiction over him because he lacked "minimum contacts" with the State. The court held it to be "a valid jurisdictional predicate for in personam jurisdiction" that the "defendant [was] present in the forum state and personally served with process." We granted certiorari.

II

A

* * * To determine whether the assertion of personal jurisdiction is consistent with due process, we have long relied on the principles traditionally followed by American courts in marking out the territorial limits of each State's authority. That criterion was first announced in *Pennoyer v. Neff.* * * * Since *International Shoe*, we have only been called upon to decide whether these "traditional notions" permit States to exercise jurisdiction over absent defendants in a manner that deviates from the rules of jurisdiction applied in the 19th century. We have held such deviations permissible, but only with respect to suits arising out of the absent defendant's contacts with the State.[1] The question we must

---

1. We have said that "[e]ven when the cause of action does not arise out of or relate to the foreign corporation's activities in the forum State, due process is not of-fended by a State's subjecting the corporation to its in personam jurisdiction when there are sufficient contacts between the State and the foreign corporation." Heli-

decide today is whether due process requires a similar connection between the litigation and the defendant's contacts with the State in cases where the defendant is physically present in the State at the time process is served upon him.

B

Among the most firmly established principles of personal jurisdiction in American tradition is that the courts of a State have jurisdiction over nonresidents who are physically present in the State. The view developed early that each State had the power to hale before its courts any individual who could be found within its borders, and that once having acquired jurisdiction over such a person by properly serving him with process, the State could retain jurisdiction to enter judgment against him, no matter how fleeting his visit. * * *

Particularly striking is the fact that, as far as we have been able to determine, not one American case from the period (or, for that matter, *not one* American case until 1978) held, or even suggested, that in-state personal service on an individual was insufficient to confer personal jurisdiction. * * *

This American jurisdictional practice is, moreover, not merely old; it is continuing. It remains the practice of, not only a substantial number of the States, but as far as we are aware all the States and the Federal Government * * * We do not know of a single state or federal statute, or a single judicial decision resting upon state law, that has abandoned in-state service as a basis of jurisdiction. * * *

C

Despite this formidable body of precedent, petitioner contends, in reliance on our decisions applying the *International Shoe* standard, that in the absence of "continuous and systematic" contacts with the forum, a nonresident defendant can be subjected to judgment only as to matters that arise out of or relate to his contacts with the forum. This argument rests on a thorough misunderstanding of our cases.

* * * The short of the matter is that jurisdiction based on physical presence alone constitutes due process because it is one of the continuing traditions of our legal system that define the due process standard of "traditional notions of fair play and substantial justice." That standard was developed by analogy to "physical presence," and it would be

copteros Nacionales de Colombia v. Hall, 466 U.S., at 414. Our only holding supporting that statement, however, involved "regular service of summons upon [the corporation's] president while he was in [the forum State] acting in that capacity." See Perkins v. Benguet Consolidated Mining Co., 342 U.S. 437, 440 (1952). It may be that whatever special rule exists permitting "continuous and systematic" contacts, id., at 438, to support jurisdiction with respect to matters unrelated to activity in the forum applies only to corporations, which have never fitted comfortably in a jurisdictional regime based primarily upon "de facto power over the defendant's person." International Shoe Co. v. Washington, 326 U.S. 310, 316 (1945). We express no views on these matters—and, for simplicity's sake, omit reference to this aspect of "contacts"-based jurisdiction in our discussion.

perverse to say it could now be turned against that touchstone of jurisdiction.

D

Petitioner's strongest argument, though we ultimately reject it, relies upon our decision in *Shaffer v. Heitner*, 433 U.S. 186 (1977). * * *

It goes too far to say, as petitioner contends, that *Shaffer* compels the conclusion that a State lacks jurisdiction over an individual unless the litigation arises out of his activities in the State. *Shaffer*, like *International Shoe*, involved jurisdiction over an *absent defendant*, and it stands for nothing more than the proposition that when the "minimum contact" that is a substitute for physical presence consists of property ownership it must, like other minimum contacts, be related to the litigation. Petitioner wrenches out of its context our statement in *Shaffer* that "all assertions of state-court jurisdiction must be evaluated according to the standards set forth in International Shoe and its progeny." * * * The logic of *Shaffer*'s holding—which places all suits against absent nonresidents on the same constitutional footing, regardless of whether a separate Latin label is attached to one particular basis of contact—does not compel the conclusion that physically present defendants must be treated identically to absent ones. * * *

It is fair to say, however, that while our holding today does not contradict *Shaffer*, our basic approach to the due process question is different. We have conducted no independent inquiry into the desirability or fairness of the prevailing in-state service rule, leaving that judgment to the legislatures that are free to amend it; for our purposes, its validation is its pedigree, as the phrase "traditional notions of fair play and substantial justice" makes clear. *Shaffer* did conduct such an independent inquiry, asserting that " 'traditional notions of fair play and substantial justice can be as readily offended by the perpetuation of ancient forms that are no longer justified as by the adoption of new procedures that are inconsistent with the basic values of our constitutional heritage." * * * Where, however, as in the present case, a jurisdictional principle is both firmly approved by tradition and still favored, it is impossible to imagine what standard we could appeal to for the judgment that it is "no longer justified." While in no way receding from or casting doubt upon the holding of *Shaffer* or any other case, we reaffirm today our time-honored approach. * * * For new procedures, hitherto unknown, the Due Process Clause requires analysis to determine whether "traditional notions of fair play and substantial justice" have been offended. But a doctrine of personal jurisdiction that dates back to the adoption of the Fourteenth Amendment and is still generally observed unquestionably meets that standard.

III

A few words in response to Justice Brennan's opinion concurring in the judgment: It insists that we apply "contemporary notions of due process" to determine the constitutionality of California's assertion of jurisdiction. * * * The "contemporary notions of due process" applicable to personal jurisdiction are the enduring "*traditional* notions of fair play and substantial justice" established as the test by *International Shoe*. By its very language, that test is satisfied if a state court adheres to jurisdictional rules that are generally applied and have always been applied in the United States.

But the concurrence's proposed standard of "contemporary notions of due process" requires more: It measures state-court jurisdiction not only against traditional doctrines in this country, including current state-court practice, but also against each Justice's subjective assessment of what is fair and just. Authority for that seductive standard is not to be found in any of our personal jurisdiction cases. It is, indeed, an outright break with the test of "traditional notions of fair play and substantial justice," which would have to be reformulated "*our* notions of fair play and substantial justice."

* * * Because the Due Process Clause does not prohibit the California courts from exercising jurisdiction over petitioner based on the fact of in-state service of process, the judgment is affirmed.

Justice WHITE, concurring in part and concurring in the judgment.

I join Parts I, II–A, II–B, and II–C of Justice SCALIA's opinion and concur in the judgment of affirmance. The rule allowing jurisdiction to be obtained over a nonresident by personal service in the forum State, without more, has been and is so widely accepted throughout this country that I could not possibly strike it down, either on its face or as applied in this case, on the ground that it denies due process of law guaranteed by the Fourteenth Amendment. * * *

Justice BRENNAN, with whom Justice MARSHALL, Justice BLACKMUN, and Justice O'CONNOR join, concurring in the judgment.

I agree with Justice SCALIA that the Due Process Clause of the Fourteenth Amendment generally permits a state court to exercise jurisdiction over a defendant if he is served with process while voluntarily present in the forum State. I do not perceive the need, however, to decide that a jurisdictional rule that " 'has been immemorially the actual law of the land,' " automatically comports with due process simply by virtue of its "pedigree." * * * Unlike Justice SCALIA, I would undertake an "independent inquiry into the . . . fairness of the prevailing in-state service rule." I therefore concur only in the judgment.

I

I believe that the approach adopted by Justice Scalia's opinion today—reliance solely on historical pedigree—is foreclosed by our decisions in *International Shoe Co. v. Washington*, and *Shaffer v. Heitner*. * * * The critical insight of *Shaffer* is that all rules of jurisdiction, even ancient ones, must satisfy contemporary notions of due process. * * * I agree with this approach and continue to believe that "the minimum-contacts analysis developed in *International Shoe* represents a far more sensible construct for the exercise of state-court jurisdiction than the patchwork of legal and factual fictions that has been generated from the decision in *Pennoyer v. Neff*."

While our *holding* in *Shaffer* may have been limited to *quasi in rem* jurisdiction, our mode of analysis was not. Indeed, that we were willing in *Shaffer* to examine anew the appropriateness of the *quasi in rem* rule—until that time dutifully accepted by American courts for at least a century—demonstrates that we did not believe that the "pedigree" of a jurisdictional practice was dispositive in deciding whether it was consistent with due process. * * * Notwithstanding the nimble gymnastics of Justice Scalia's opinion today, it is not faithful to our decision in *Shaffer*.

II

Tradition, though alone not dispositive, is of course relevant to the question whether the rule of transient jurisdiction is consistent with due process. Tradition is salient not in the sense that practices of the past are automatically reasonable today.

Rather, I find the historical background relevant because, however murky the jurisprudential origins of transient jurisdiction, the fact that American courts have announced the rule for perhaps a century * * * provides a defendant voluntarily present in a particular State *today* "clear notice that [he] is subject to suit" in the forum. * * * The transient rule is consistent with reasonable expectations and is entitled to a strong presumption that it comports with due process.

By visiting the forum State, a transient defendant actually "avail[s]" himself, of significant benefits provided by the State. His health and safety are guaranteed by the State's police, fire, and emergency medical services; he is free to travel on the State's roads and waterways; he likely enjoys the fruits of the State's economy as well. Moreover, the Privileges and Immunities Clause of Article IV prevents a state government from discriminating against a transient defendant by denying him the protections of its law or the right of access to its courts. Subject only to the doctrine of forum non conveniens, an out-of-state plaintiff may use state courts in all circumstances in which those courts would be available to state citizens. Without transient jurisdiction, an asymmetry would arise: A transient would have the full benefit of the power of the forum State's courts as a plaintiff while retaining immunity from their authority as a defendant.

The potential burdens on a transient defendant are slight. * * * That the defendant has already journeyed at least once before to the forum—as evidenced by the fact that he was served with process there—is an indication that suit in the forum likely would not be prohibitively inconvenient. Finally, any burdens that do arise can be ameliorated by a variety of procedural devices. For these reasons, as a rule the exercise of personal jurisdiction over a defendant based on his voluntary presence in the forum will satisfy the requirements of due process.

In this case, it is undisputed that petitioner was served with process while voluntarily and knowingly in the State of California. I therefore concur in the judgment.

Justice STEVENS, concurring in the judgment.

As I explained in my separate writing, I did not join the Court's opinion in *Shaffer v. Heitner* because I was concerned by its unnecessarily broad reach. The same concern prevents me from joining either Justice Scalia's or Justice Brennan's opinion in this case. For me, it is sufficient to note that the historical evidence and consensus identified by Justice Scalia, the considerations of fairness identified by Justice Brennan, and the common sense displayed by Justice White, all combine to demonstrate that this is, indeed, a very easy case. Accordingly, I agree that the judgment should be affirmed.

Notes and Questions

1. *Burnham* confirms a fourth basis for the modern exercise of jurisdiction, in addition to domicile, minimum contacts, and consent. As subsequent decisions had eroded *Pennoyer*, lower courts and commentators had questioned the continued viability of transient jurisdiction. When a defendant is personally served with process while physically present (however briefly) in the forum state, personal service is sufficient to confer personal jurisdiction without violating due process.

Justice Scalia said that it is a firmly established principle that a state has jurisdiction over nonresidents who are physically present (however briefly) in the state, regardless of whether the plaintiff's claim is related to the defendant's activities there. Was that principle so firmly established after the cases decided between *Pennoyer* and *Burnham*? Or, did Justice Scalia reinstate the *Pennoyer* idea that each state can automatically exert authority over anyone served within the state borders, and the state retains that authority to enter a judgment against the person?

2. From the nonresident defendant's point of view, how fair is it to be forced to defend in a place where the defendant has no contacts aside from being served during a brief presence there? Your client is a lifelong resident of New York whose commitment to his business never allowed him time for a vacation. A possible buyer of your client's business communicates with him one day from his corporate offices in Texas and insists that he travel to Houston to close the deal. Your client departs for Houston, but to save money instead of a non-stop flight he had booked a one-stop flight there with a brief stop in Miami. When he deplanes, he is served with a summons and complaint to defend a wrongful discharge lawsuit filed by a former employee who has moved to Miami. What is fair to your client about that situation? Is it fair for him to have to choose between finding a lawyer in Florida and taking a default judgment? Did he assume the risk of being served with process and subject to Florida jurisdiction by his stop at the Miami airport? Could you argue for your client that he was not *voluntarily* present when he was served? What interest could Florida possibly have in the outcome of litigation arising in New York and filed by a disgruntled former employee who had been in Florida a short time?

What are the competing arguments? Doesn't your client receive the benefits and protections of Florida law while there, however briefly? Doesn't your client assume the risk of being served when entering the state? Isn't the transient jurisdiction rule far more predictable than the minimum contacts/foreseeability/purposeful availment doctrine for personal jurisdiction?

3. Legislatures and courts have imposed two non-constitutional limits on service of process out of a sense of fairness. One historical restriction on transient jurisdiction is that a defendant is not obligated to defend a lawsuit when she has been fraudulently induced to enter the forum state. In *Wyman v. Newhouse*, 93 F.2d 313 (2d Cir. 1937), Newhouse, a New York resident, received a telegram and a letter from his paramour, Wyman, falsely saying that her mother was ill in Ireland and that she needed to see him before she went to be with her mother permanently. He promised to go to Florida to see her, arriving at 6:00 a.m. at the Miami Airport. Before he could get to her, a deputy sheriff served him with process in a suit for $500,000. A stranger then offered to take him to his home, and stated that he knew a lawyer familiar with her attorney. He did not retain the Florida attorney, but instead returned to New York that evening and consulted his New York counsel, who advised him to ignore the Florida summons. A default judgment was entered against him. Wyman took the Florida judgment to a New York federal court to give the judgment full faith and credit and enforce it. On appeal from denial of the enforcement action, the appellate court concluded that Newhouse was persuaded to enter Florida by a fraud perpetrated upon him by Wyman falsely representing the situation.

> A judgment procured fraudulently, as here, lacks jurisdiction and is null and void. A fraud affecting the jurisdiction is equivalent to a lack of jurisdiction.... A judgment recovered in a sister state, through the fraud of the party procuring the appearance of another, is not binding on the latter when an attempt is made to enforce such judgment in another state.... The appellee was not required to make out a defense on the merits to the suit in Florida. We are not here concerned with such rule, applicable to alleged fraud in the proceedings after valid jurisdiction of the person and the subject matter has been obtained. Here the court did not duly acquire jurisdiction and no such defense to the merits need be shown.

The other limitation on transient jurisdiction applies to nonresidents who are present in a state in order to participate in a legal proceeding. Whether a party, a witness, or an attorney, the person is generally immune from effective service of process for other lawsuits and claims for a reasonable time before and after the actual time of the proceedings. Thus, a person's presence in a forum to attend another proceeding immunizes her from even transient jurisdiction of the court during the immunity period. See *Stewart v. Ramsay*, 242 U.S. 128, 37 S.Ct. 44, 61 L.Ed. 192 (1916). The primary justification for the immunity is to prevent disruption of the ongoing proceeding and to encourage persons to attend that proceeding.

4. To the Internet—and Beyond!

Should courts be reluctant to apply the traditional due process, personal jurisdiction standards to Internet activity? Are pages on the

World Wide Web comparable to postal addresses or phone numbers? Does the creator of a Web page broadcast information on the page to everyone, or does its transmission depend on a request by another? If the mere development of a Web page constitutes a broadcast, a court may be inclined to regard that creation as a type of contact by the Web creator, thereby subjecting the creator of even a passive site to personal jurisdiction in a faraway court.

On the other hand, in order to access a Web page, a person types the Web "address" on a Web browser or clicks on a link, and the computer retrieves the appropriate or desired page from the home computer of the page. Like telephone usage, a Web user obtains information on the Web only by requesting that information. Thus, except for "spam" that appears as electronic mail, viewing Web material depends on the Web user seeking it. Does characterizing Web viewing in this manner expose the Web creator to the jurisdiction of a distant court?

There are several legal approaches to the issue of personal jurisdiction over nonresident defendants for Internet activities. Under the effects test originating in *Calder v. Jones*, courts focus on the effects purposely caused within the forum state by the defendant's conduct outside the forum. The occurrence of some effect or the foreseeability that the defendant's conduct may have an effect is outside the meaning of *Calder*. Even if the effects of a defendant's conduct are felt in the forum state, the exercise of jurisdiction requires that the defendant direct that conduct at the forum state. A court also may find satisfaction of the effects test when the defendant's conduct causes harm to a person known by the defendant to be living there.

In *Zippo Mfg. Co. v. Zippy Dot Com, Inc.*, 952 F.Supp. 1119 (W.D.Pa. 1997), the court adopted a sliding scale approach to World Wide Web sites. Citing the Supreme Court's due process cases, the court stated that the exercise of jurisdiction is proper over Web sites and their operators when contracts on the Internet result. Jurisdiction is improper for passive Web sites merely providing information. Accessibility to a Web site or its actual usage in the forum state is insufficient to confer jurisdiction. Those are the "easy" cases, which are consistent with the cases precluding the exercise of jurisdiction for placement of an advertisement, without more, in a national publication.

Between those extreme cases, there are interactive Web sites where no commercial transaction occurs but there is some exchange of information between the user and the host. The *Zippy* analytical approach is to determine "the level of interactivity and commercial nature of the exchange of information that occurs on the Web site. * * * [The] likelihood that personal jurisdiction can be constitutionally exercised is directly proportionate to the nature and quality of the commercial activity that an entity conducts over the Internet."

Does that standard offer guidance to attorneys who are expected to provide legal advice to their clients about the clients' amenability to suit in some distant courtroom? Yes, but only for Web sites on the extreme ends of the spectrum of activity. Even at the extremes, though, is the type of Web site more important than the nature of the contacts by the Web site? Even for "active" Web sites, is the capability of exchanging information more important than the exchange itself of material? Can a risk-averse defendant be successful in trying to limit its exposure to suit based on a web page by requiring customers to call rather than order online?

As the case law under *Zippy* has developed, any defendant trying to avoid being sued limits the usefulness of its web page. A defendant providing product information but requiring a telephone call to finalize an order, is likely to shield itself from exposure to a lawsuit based on the operation of its website. Increasingly, courts are turning away from the sliding scale approach of *Zippy* and focusing instead on the defendant's purposeful conduct directed toward the forum.

YOUNG v. NEW HAVEN ADVOCATE

315 F.3d 256 (4th Cir. 2002)

MICHAEL, Circuit Judge.

The question in this appeal is whether two Connecticut newspapers and certain of their staff (sometimes, the "newspaper defendants") subjected themselves to personal jurisdiction in Virginia by posting on the Internet news articles that, in the context of discussing the State of Connecticut's policy of housing its prisoners in Virginia institutions, allegedly defamed the warden of a Virginia prison. * * * [W]e hold that a court in Virginia cannot constitutionally exercise jurisdiction over the Connecticut-based newspaper defendants because they did not manifest an intent to aim their websites or the posted articles at a Virginia audience. Accordingly, we reverse the district court's order denying the defendants' motion to dismiss for lack of personal jurisdiction.

I

Sometime in the late 1990s the State of Connecticut was faced with substantial overcrowding in its maximum security prisons. To alleviate the problem, Connecticut contracted with the Commonwealth of Virginia to house Connecticut prisoners in Virginia's correctional facilities. Beginning in late 1999 Connecticut transferred about 500 prisoners, mostly African–American and Hispanic, to the Wallens Ridge State Prison, a "supermax" facility in Big Stone Gap, Virginia. The plaintiff, Stanley Young, is the warden at Wallens Ridge. Connecticut's arrangement to incarcerate a sizeable number of its offenders in Virginia prisons provoked considerable public debate in Connecticut. Several Connecticut legislators openly criticized the policy, and there were demonstrations against it at the state capitol in Hartford.

Connecticut newspapers, including defendants the New Haven Advocate (the Advocate) and the Hartford Courant (the Courant), began reporting on the controversy. On March 30, 2000, the Advocate published a news article, written by one of its reporters, defendant Camille Jackson, about the transfer of Connecticut inmates to Wallens Ridge. The article discussed the allegedly harsh conditions at the Virginia prison and pointed out that the long trip to southwestern Virginia made visits by prisoners' families difficult or impossible. In the middle of her lengthy article, Jackson mentioned a class action that inmates transferred from Connecticut had filed against Warden Young and the Connecticut Commissioner of Corrections. The inmates alleged a lack of proper hygiene and medical care and the denial of religious privileges at Wallens Ridge. Finally, a paragraph at the end of the article reported that a Connecticut state senator had expressed concern about the presence of Confederate Civil War memorabilia in Warden Young's office. At about the same time the Courant published three columns, written by defendant-reporter Amy Pagnozzi, questioning the practice of relocating Connecticut inmates to Virginia prisons. The columns reported on letters written home by inmates who alleged cruelty by prison guards. In one column Pagnozzi called Wallens Ridge a "cut-rate gulag." Warden Young was not mentioned in any of the Pagnozzi columns.

On May 12, 2000, Warden Young sued the two newspapers, their editors (Gail Thompson and Brian Toolan), and the two reporters for libel in a diversity action filed in the Western District of Virginia. He claimed that the newspapers' articles imply that he "is a racist who advocates racism" and that he "encourages abuse of inmates by the guards" at Wallens Ridge. Young alleged that the newspapers circulated the allegedly defamatory articles throughout the world by posting them on their Internet websites.

The newspaper defendants filed motions to dismiss the complaint under Federal Rule of Civil Procedure 12(b)(2) on the ground that the district court lacked personal jurisdiction over them. In support of the motions the editor and reporter from each newspaper provided declarations establishing the following undisputed facts. The Advocate is a free newspaper published once a week in New Haven, Connecticut. It is distributed in New Haven and the surrounding area, and some of its content is published on the Internet. The Advocate has a small number of subscribers, and none of them are [sic] in Virginia. The Courant is published daily in Hartford, Connecticut. The newspaper is distributed in and around Hartford, and some of its content is published on the Internet. When the articles in question were published, the Courant had eight mail subscribers in Virginia. Neither newspaper solicits subscriptions from Virginia residents. No one from either newspaper, not even the reporters, traveled to Virginia to work on the articles about Connecticut's prisoner transfer policy. The two reporters, Jackson of the Advocate and Pagnozzi of the Courant, made a few telephone calls into Virginia to gather some information for the articles. Both interviewed by telephone a spokesman for the Virginia Department of Corrections. All other interviews were done with people located in Connecticut. The two reporters wrote their articles in Connecticut. The individual defendants (the reporters and editors) do not have any traditional contacts with the

Commonwealth of Virginia. They do not live in Virginia, solicit any business there, or have any assets or business relationships there. The newspapers do not have offices or employees in Virginia, and they do not regularly solicit or do business in Virginia. Finally, the newspapers do not derive any substantial revenue from goods used or services rendered in Virginia.

* * *

The district court denied the newspaper defendants' motions to dismiss, concluding that it could exercise personal jurisdiction over them under Virginia's long-arm statute, because "the defendants' Connecticut-based Internet activities constituted an act leading to an injury to the plaintiff in Virginia." The district court also held that the defendants' Internet activities were sufficient to satisfy the requirements of constitutional due process. With our permission the newspaper defendants are taking this interlocutory appeal. The facts relating to jurisdiction are undisputed, and the district court's decision that it has personal jurisdiction over these defendants presents a legal question that we review de novo. * * *

II

A

A federal court may exercise personal jurisdiction over a defendant in the manner provided by state law. Because Virginia's long-arm statute extends personal jurisdiction to the extent permitted by the Due Process Clause, "the statutory inquiry necessarily merges with the constitutional inquiry, and the two inquiries essentially become one." *Stover v. O'Connell Assocs., Inc.*, 84 F.3d 132, 135–36 (4th Cir.1996). The question, then, is whether the defendant has sufficient "minimum contacts with [the forum] such that the maintenance of the suit does not offend 'traditional notions of fair play and substantial justice.'" *Int'l Shoe Co. v. Washington*, 326 U.S. 310, 316 (1945) (quoting *Milliken v. Meyer*, 311 U.S. 457, 463 (1940)). * * * In determining whether specific jurisdiction exists, we traditionally ask (1) whether the defendant purposefully availed itself of the privileges of conducting activities in the forum state, (2) whether the plaintiff's claim arises out of the defendant's forum-related activities, and (3) "whether the exercise of personal jurisdiction over the defendant would be constitutionally reasonable." * * *

B

We turn to whether the district court can exercise specific jurisdiction over the newspaper defendants, namely, the two newspapers, the two editors, and the two reporters. To begin with, we can put aside the few Virginia contacts that are not Internet based because Warden Young does not rely on them. Thus, Young does not claim that the reporters' few telephone calls into Virginia or the Courant's eight Virginia subscribers are sufficient to establish personal jurisdiction over those defendants. Nor did the district court rely on these traditional contacts.

Warden Young argues that the district court has specific personal jurisdiction over the newspaper defendants (hereafter, the "newspapers") because of the following contacts between them and Virginia: (1) the newspapers, knowing that Young was a Virginia resident, intentionally discussed and defamed him in their articles, (2) the newspapers posted the articles on their websites, which were accessible in Virginia, and (3) the primary effects of the defamatory statements on Young's reputation were felt in Virginia. Young emphasizes that he is not arguing that jurisdiction is proper in any location where defamatory Internet content can be accessed, which would be anywhere in the world. Rather, Young argues that personal jurisdiction is proper in Virginia because the newspapers understood that their defamatory articles, which were available to Virginia residents on the Internet, would expose Young to public hatred, contempt, and ridicule in Virginia, where he lived and worked. As the district court put it, "[t]he defendants were all well aware of the fact that the plaintiff was employed as a warden within the Virginia correctional system and resided in Virginia," and they "also should have been aware that any harm suffered by Young from the circulation of these articles on the Internet would primarily occur in Virginia."

* * * *Calder* [*v. Jones*, 465 U.S. 783 (1984),] though not an Internet case, has particular relevance here because it deals with personal jurisdiction in the context of a libel suit. In *Calder* a California actress brought suit there against, among others, two Floridians, a reporter and an editor who wrote and edited in Florida a National Enquirer article claiming that the actress had a problem with alcohol. The Supreme Court held that California had jurisdiction over the Florida residents because "California [was] the focal point both of the story and of the harm suffered." *Calder*, 465 U.S. at 789. The writers' "actions were expressly aimed at California," the Court said, "[a]nd they knew that the brunt of [the potentially devastating] injury would be felt by [the actress] in the State in which she lives and works and in which the National Enquirer has its largest circulation," 600,000 copies. *Calder*, 465 U.S. at 789–90.

Warden Young argues that *Calder* requires a finding of jurisdiction in this case simply because the newspapers posted articles on their Internet websites that discussed the warden and his Virginia prison, and he would feel the effects of any libel in Virginia, where he lives and works. Calder does not sweep that broadly, as we have recognized. * * * We thus had no trouble in concluding in *ALS Scan* that application of *Calder* in the Internet context requires proof that the out-of-state defendant's Internet activity is expressly targeted at or directed to the forum state. *ALS Scan*, 293 F.3d at 714. In *ALS Scan* we went on to adapt the traditional standard (set out in part II.A., supra) for establishing specific jurisdiction so that it makes sense in the Internet context. We "conclude[d] that a State may, consistent with due process, exercise judicial power over a person outside of the State when that person (1) directs electronic activity into the State, (2) with the manifested intent of engaging in business or other interactions within the State, and (3) that activity creates, in a person within the State, a potential cause of action cognizable in the State's courts." *ALS Scan*, 293 F.3d at 714.

When the Internet activity is, as here, the posting of news articles on a website, the *ALS Scan* test works more smoothly when parts one and two of the test are considered together. We thus ask whether the newspapers manifested an intent to direct their website content—which included certain articles discussing conditions in a Virginia prison—to a Virginia audience. As we recognized in *ALS Scan*, "a person's act of placing information on the Internet" is not sufficient by itself to "subject[ ] that person to personal jurisdiction in each State in which the information is accessed." *Id.* at 712. Otherwise, a "person placing information on the Internet would be subject to personal jurisdiction in every State," and the traditional due process principles governing a State's jurisdiction over persons outside of its borders would be subverted. Thus, the fact that the newspapers' websites could be accessed anywhere, including Virginia, does not by itself demonstrate that the newspapers were intentionally directing their website content to a Virginia audience. Something more than posting and accessibility is needed to "indicate that the [newspapers] purposefully (albeit electronically) directed [their] activity in a substantial way to the forum state," Virginia. *Panavision Int'l, L.P. v. Toeppen*, 141 F.3d 1316, 1321 (9th Cir.1998). The newspapers must, through the Internet postings, manifest an intent to target and focus on Virginia readers.

We therefore turn to the pages from the newspapers' websites that Warden Young placed in the record, and we examine their general thrust and content. The overall content of both websites is decidedly local, and neither newspaper's website contains advertisements aimed at a Virginia audience. For example, the website that distributes the Courant, ctnow.com, provides access to local (Connecticut) weather and traffic information and links to websites for the University of Connecticut and Connecticut state government. The Advocate's website features stories focusing on New Haven, such as one entitled "The Best of New Haven." In sum, it appears that these newspapers maintain their websites to serve local readers in Connecticut, to expand the reach of their papers within their local markets, and to provide their local markets with a place for classified ads. The websites are not designed to attract or serve a Virginia audience.

We also examine the specific articles Young complains about to determine whether they were posted on the Internet with the intent to target a Virginia audience. The articles included discussions about the allegedly harsh conditions at the Wallens Ridge prison, where Young was warden. One article mentioned Young by name and quoted a Connecticut state senator who reported that Young had Confederate Civil War memorabilia in his office. The focus of the articles, however, was the Connecticut prisoner transfer policy and its impact on the transferred prisoners and their families back home in Connecticut. The articles reported on and encouraged a public debate in Connecticut about whether the transfer policy was sound or practical for that state and its citizens. Connecticut, not Virginia, was the focal point of the articles. * * *

The facts in this case establish that the newspapers' websites, as well as the articles in question, were aimed at a Connecticut audience. The newspapers did not post materials on the Internet with the manifest intent of targeting Virginia readers. Accordingly, the newspapers could not have "reasonably anticipate[d] being haled into court [in Virginia] to answer for the truth of the statements made in their article[s]." *Calder*, 465 U.S. at 790. In sum, the newspapers do not have sufficient Internet contacts with Virginia to permit the district court to exercise specific jurisdiction over them.

We reverse the order of the district court denying the motions to dismiss for lack of personal jurisdiction made by the New Haven Advocate, Gail Thompson (its editor), and Camille Jackson (its reporter) and by the Hartford Courant, Brian Toolan (its editor), and Amy Pagnozzi (its reporter). Reversed.

Notes and Questions

1. Is *Young* consistent with *Calder*? Why did the court of appeals refuse to endorse jurisdiction over a nonresident defendant in a defamation suit on the basis of a mere website contact with the forum state? What is the effect on liability for web publishers?

2. Does *Young* provide a shield behind which defamers could always hide? Does a specific jurisdiction inquiry remain in place to raise personal jurisdiction over a nonresident defendant who intentionally aimed its tortious conduct at the forum state through the website? Is there a lesson to be learned about what needs to be stated in the complaint to sustain personal jurisdiction? In *Young*, the plaintiff alleged only that the Newspapers' acts caused harm in Virginia. Would the court more likely have sustained personal jurisdiction in Virginia if the plaintiff had included in his complaint an allegation that the defendant intended to harm the plaintiff there?

3. Is it logical that general jurisdiction should apply to the Internet cases? What prevents a defendant from being subject to jurisdiction anywhere, based on the subscribers to the World Wide Web in any forum?

Problems

1. A New Mexico software distributor posted on its Web site and e-mailed to Arizona material that allegedly defamed the plaintiff there. The complaint alleged that the defamatory information in the e-mail was sent to Arizona with both the intent to harm the plaintiff there and the effect of actually causing harm. Is personal jurisdiction over the New Mexico defendant proper in an Arizona federal court? Is a defamatory statement on a passive Web site different from a printed periodical? See *EDIAS Software International, LLC v. BASIS International Ltd.*, 947 F.Supp. 413 (D. Ariz. 1996).

2.   An Illinois defendant registered exclusive Internet domain names containing registered trademarks belonging to others. He demanded fees from well-known California corporation Panavision as his price for relinquishing rights to domain names that matched Panavision's existing trademark registrations. Panavision sued the defendant in California. Is personal jurisdiction proper there? See *Panavision Int'l, L.P. v. Toeppen*, 141 F.3d 1316 (9th Cir. 1998).

3.   A Pennsylvania psychiatrist who had spoken out against health care fraud and supported the fluoridation of water sources sued an Oregon resident in Pennsylvania federal court for defamatory statements on the defendant's Oregon Web site. Is jurisdiction over the Oregonian proper in Pennsylvania? See *Barrett v. Catacombs Press*, 44 F.Supp.2d 717 (E.D.Pa. 1999).

4.   A New Jersey defendant advertised a solar powered ice cream maker on the eBay auction site. A New Hampshire plaintiff exchanged several e-mails with the defendant about the quality of the maker. After the plaintiff bid on the item online and won it, he went to New Jersey and took the maker to New Hampshire where it malfunctioned. The plaintiff sued the New Jersey defendant in New Hampshire. Does listing the ice cream maker on an Internet auction site subject the seller to personal jurisdiction where the buyer lives? See *Metcalf v. Lawson*, 802 A.2d 1221 (N.H. 2002).

GATOR.COM CORP. v. L.L. BEAN, INC.

341 F.3d 1072 (9th Cir. 2003)

FERGUSON, Circuit Judge.

* * *

I

A.   *Factual Background*

Defendant/Appellee L.L. Bean is a Maine corporation with its principal place of business in that state. Its corporate offices, distribution facilities, and manufacturing facilities are all located in Maine. L.L. Bean sells clothing and outdoor equipment and maintains stores in Maine, Delaware, New Hampshire, Oregon, and Virginia. In total, L.L. Bean sells over one billion dollars worth of merchandise annually to consumers in 150 different countries.

A very large percentage of L.L. Bean's sales come from mail-order and internet business. The company ships approximately 200 million catalogs each year. In 2000, its website sales accounted for over two hundred million, or about 16 percent, of its total sales. * * *

L.L. Bean is not authorized to do business in California, has no agent for service of process in California, and is not required to pay taxes in California. However, in the year 2000 alone, L.L. Bean sold millions of dollars worth of products in California (about six percent of its total sales) through "its catalog, its toll-free telephone number, and its Internet website." In the same year, L.L. Bean also mailed a substantial number of catalogs and packages to California residents, targeted substantial numbers of California residents for direct email solicitation, and maintained substantial numbers of "on-line" accounts for California consumers. Like other internet customers, California residents may view and purchase products on-line as well as interact with L.L. Bean customer service representatives "live" over the internet if they have questions or concerns with an L.L. Bean product.

In addition, L.L. Bean conducts national print and broadcast marketing efforts that include, but according to L.L. Bean do not target, California. L.L. Bean also maintains relationships with numerous California vendors from whom they purchase products. Other than for the year 2000, L.L. Bean has not provided information regarding the contacts its employees have had with California or any purchases of goods from California.

Plaintiff/Appellant Gator.com Corp. is a Delaware corporation with its principal place of business in California. Gator develops and distributes software ("the Gator program") to consumers who purchase goods or services over the Internet. The Gator program provides a "digital wallet" which stores computer user passwords to various websites, user personal information, and credit card information. In addition, when a user visits a website on the Internet, the Gator program analyzes the Uniform Resource Locator ("URL") associated with that web page. When it recognizes certain URLs that have been pre-selected by Gator, the program displays a pop-up window offering a coupon for a competitor. Gator users who visit L.L. Bean's website are offered coupons for one of L.L. Bean's competitors, Eddie Bauer, via a pop-up window that at least partially obscures L.L. Bean's website. * * *

B.   Procedural History

On March 19, 2001, Gator filed a declaratory judgment action in the District Court for the Northern District of California, requesting a judgment that the Gator program "does not infringe, or dilute, directly or contributorily, any trademark held by [L.L. Bean] and does not constitute unfair competition, a deceptive or unfair trade or sales practice, false advertising, fraud, or any other violation of either federal or state law." On July 16, 2001, L.L. Bean filed a Motion to Dismiss, along with a Declaration of Support, alleging that the District Court lacked personal jurisdiction. On November 21, 2001, after a hearing, the District Court granted L.L. Bean's motion, finding that neither general nor specific jurisdiction existed. On December 21, 2001, Gator filed this timely appeal.

II

* * * It is the plaintiff's burden to establish that a district court has jurisdiction. For purposes of a Motion to Dismiss, the plaintiff's version of the facts are assumed to be true unless directly controverted. * * *

III

* * *

A. *Substantial or Continuous and Systematic Contacts Test*

In applying the "substantial" or "continuous and systematic" contacts test, courts have focused primarily on two areas. First, they look for some kind of deliberate "presence" in the forum state, including physical facilities, bank accounts, agents, registration, or incorporation. See *Perkins*. In addition, courts have looked at whether the company has engaged in active solicitation toward and participation in the state's markets, i.e., the economic reality of the defendant's activities in the state. * * *

Given the high standard the Ninth Circuit has set, the presence of general jurisdiction in the instant case is a close question. Admittedly, L.L. Bean has few of the factors traditionally associated with physical presence, such as an official agent or incorporation.

* * * The facts as alleged by Gator indicate that L.L. Bean meets the first set of factors set out in these cases: it makes sales, solicits business in the state, and serves the state's markets. In addition, * * * Gator alleges that L.L. Bean "targets" its electronic advertising at California and maintains a highly interactive, as opposed to "passive," website from which very large numbers of California consumers regularly make purchases and interact with L.L. Bean sales representatives. L.L. Bean has not merely made a single "package" purchase from a forum vendor or cashed a check on a forum bank; instead, it ships very large numbers of products to California and maintains ongoing contacts with numerous California vendors. Nor are any of L.L. Bean's contacts occasional or infrequent. L.L. Bean's contacts are part of a consistent, ongoing, and sophisticated sales effort that has included California for a number of years.

The District Court erred in concluding that there was no general jurisdiction in this case. We now proceed to consider whether assertion of general jurisdiction over L.L. Bean is reasonable.

B. *Reasonableness Test*

Even if there are sufficient contacts to support general jurisdiction in a particular case, it is still limited by a reasonableness analysis. The reasonableness test * * * is the same as the test for reasonableness in the specific jurisdiction context, requiring an analysis of seven factors:

> [T]he extent of purposeful interjection, the burden on the defendant to defend the suit in the chosen forum, the extent of conflict with the sovereignty of the defendant's state, the forum state's interest in the dispute; the most efficient forum for judicial resolution of the dispute; the importance of the chosen forum to the plaintiff's interest in convenient and effective relief; and the existence of an alternative forum.

The burden is on the defendant to present a "compelling case" that the assertion of jurisdiction is not reasonable. Although L.L. Bean did not specifically address the issue of reasonableness in the general jurisdiction context, with the exception of the "purposeful interjection" factor, its arguments in the specific jurisdiction context are germane since the same standard applies.

L.L. Bean asserts that three of the above factors cut in its favor: the extent of purposeful interjection, the burden on L.L. Bean of litigating in California, and the availability of an alternative forum. L.L. Bean concedes that the remaining factors are either neutral or cut in Gator's favor.

* * *

L.L. Bean also argues that defending this litigation would impose a substantial burden on it because its principal place of business and its corporate records and personnel are all located in Maine. This argument lends little support to L.L. Bean's case, given that it is a multi-million dollar company that concedes that its agents regularly do business around the country, including flying to California to meet with vendors. Nor does this case present issues whose disposition will rely on access to L.L. Bean's facilities or records. Moreover, the burden on Gator if it were forced to proceed in Maine would be at least equal to, if not more severe, than the burden faced by L.L. Bean. In short, L.L. Bean presents no evidence that the " 'inconvenience is so great as to constitute a deprivation of due process[.]' "

Finally, L.L. Bean asserts that because Gator has filed an almost identical declaratory action in the District Court of Oregon, Gator has failed to show that there is no alternative forum available. While this factor does cut in L.L. Bean's favor, it does not make assertion of jurisdiction unreasonable. We therefore find that L.L. Bean has not presented a compelling case that general jurisdiction is unreasonable.

IV

It is increasingly clear that modern businesses no longer require an actual physical presence in a state in order to engage in commercial activity there. With the advent of "e-commerce," businesses may set up shop, so to speak, without ever actually setting foot in the state where they intend to sell their wares. Our conceptions of jurisdiction must be flexible enough to respond to the realities of the modern marketplace. "As technological progress . . . increase[s] the flow of commerce between States, the need for jurisdiction over nonresidents [undergoes] a similar increase. . . . In response to these changes, the requirements for personal jurisdiction over nonresidents [evolve]." *Hanson v. Denckla*, 357 U.S. 235, 250–251 (1958). Businesses who structure their activities to take full advantage of the opportunities that virtual commerce offers can reasonably anticipate that these same activities will potentially subject them to suit in the locales that they have targeted.

We find that the facts as alleged by Gator demonstrate that L.L. Bean has substantial or continuous and systematic contacts with California sufficient to support a finding of general jurisdiction. The decision of the District Court is reversed and we remand for further proceedings consistent with this opinion.

TOYS "R" US, INC. v. STEP TWO, S.A.

318 F.3d 446 (3d Cir. 2003)

OBERDORFER, District Judge.

Toys "R" Us, Inc. and Geoffrey, Inc. ("Toys") brought this action against Step Two, S.A. and Imaginarium Net, S.L. ("Step Two"), alleging that Step Two used its Internet web sites to engage in trademark infringement, unfair competition, misuse of the trademark notice symbol, and unlawful "cybersquatting," in violation of the Lanham Act, 15 U.S.C. § 1501 et seq., and New Jersey state law. The District Court denied Toys' request for jurisdictional discovery and, simultaneously, granted Step Two's motion to dismiss for lack of personal jurisdiction. We hold that the District Court should not have denied Toys' request for jurisdictional discovery. We therefore reverse and remand for limited jurisdictional discovery, relating to Step Two's business activities in the United States, and for reconsideration of personal jurisdiction with the benefit of the product of that discovery, with a view to its renewing administration of the case, in the event the District Court finds that it does have jurisdiction.

I

Toys, a Delaware corporation with its headquarters in New Jersey, owns retail stores worldwide where it sells toys, games, and numerous other products. In August 1999, Toys acquired Imaginarium Toy Centers, Inc., which owned and operated a network of "Imaginarium" stores for the sale of educational toys and games. As part of this acquisition, Toys acquired several Imaginarium trademarks, and subsequently filed applications for the registration of additional Imaginarium marks. Prior to Toys' acquisition, the owners of the Imaginarium mark had been marketing a line of educational toys and games since 1985 and had first registered the Imaginarium mark with the United States Patent and Trademark Office in 1989. Toys currently owns thirty-seven freestanding Imaginarium stores in the U.S., of which seven are located in New Jersey. In addition, there are Imaginarium shops within 175 of the Toys "R" Us stores in the U.S., including five New Jersey stores.

Step Two is a Spanish corporation that owns or has franchised toy stores operating under the name "Imaginarium" in Spain and nine other countries. It first registered the Imaginarium mark in Spain in 1991, and opened its first Imaginarium store in the Spanish city of Zaragoza in November 1992. Step Two began expanding its chain of Imaginarium stores by means of a franchise system in 1994. It has registered the Imaginarium mark in several other countries where its stores are located. There are now 165 Step Two Imaginarium stores. The stores have the same unique facade and logo as those owned by Toys, and sell the same types of merchandise as Toys sells in its Imaginarium stores. However, Step Two does not operate any stores, maintain any offices or bank accounts, or have any employees anywhere in the United States. Nor does it pay taxes to the U.S. or to any U.S. state. Step Two maintains that it has not directed any advertising or marketing efforts towards the United States. The record does, however, indicate some contacts between Step Two and the United States: for example, a portion of the merchandise sold at Step Two's Imaginarium stores is purchased from vendors in the United States. Additionally, Felix Tena, President of Step Two, attends the New York Toy Fair once each year.

In the mid–1990s, both parties turned to the Internet to boost their sales. In 1995, Imaginarium Toy Centers, Inc. (which Toys later acquired) registered the domain name <imaginarium.com> and launched a web site featuring merchandise sold at Imaginarium stores. In 1996, Step Two registered the domain name <imaginarium.es>, and began advertising merchandise that was available at its Imaginarium stores. In April 1999, Imaginarium Toy Centers registered the domain name <imaginarium.net>, and launched another web site where it offered Imaginarium merchandise for sale. In June 1999, Step Two registered two additional "Imaginarium" domain names, <imaginarium-world.com> and <imaginarium-world.com>. In May 2000, Step Two registered three more domain names: <imaginariumnet.com>, <imaginariumnet.net>, and <imaginariumnet.org>. Step Two's web sites are maintained by Imaginarium Net, S.L., a subsidiary of Step Two, S.A. formed in 2000.

At the time this lawsuit was filed, four of the aforementioned sites operated by Step Two were interactive, allowing users to purchase merchandise online. When buying merchandise via Step Two's web sites, purchasers are asked to input their name and email address, as well as a credit card number, delivery address, and phone number. At no point during the online purchase process are users asked to input their billing or mailing address. The web sites provide a contact phone number within Spain that lacks the country code that a user overseas would need to dial. Moreover, the prices are in Spanish pesetas and Euros, and goods ordered from those sites can be shipped only within Spain. Step Two's Imaginarium web sites are entirely in Spanish.

* * *

Mr. Tena submitted an affidavit stating that Step Two had not made any sales via its web sites to U.S. residents. Toys, however, adduced evidence of two sales to residents of New Jersey conducted via Step Two's Imaginarium web sites. These purchases were initiated by Toys. Lydia Leon, a legal assistant in the Legal Department of Geoffrey, Inc., made the first purchase. Ms. Leon, a resident of New Jersey, purchased a toy via <www.imaginariumworld.com> on January 23, 2001. The second purchase was made in February 2001 by Luis M. Lopez, an employee of

Darby & Darby P.C., attorneys for Toys. Mr. Lopez is also a resident of New Jersey, and accessed <www.imaginarium.es> to make his purchase.

For both of these sales, the items were shipped to Angeles Benavides Davila, a Toys employee in Madrid, Spain; Ms. Benavides Davila then forwarded the items to the offices of Geoffrey, Inc. in New Jersey. Both purchases were made with credit cards issued by U.S. banks. Additionally, both purchasers received in New Jersey an email confirming their purchases, and a subsequent email with a login and password to access Club Imaginarium. One of the two purchasers also separately registered for Club Imaginarium, exchanged emails with a Step Two employee about his purchase, and received a copy of an email newsletter from Step Two. Aside from these two sales, there is no evidence in the record of a sale to anyone in the United States. After learning of these two sales, Mr. Tena submitted a second affidavit stating that his company does not know where its purchasers reside, as that information is not apparent from a purchaser's email address, and Step Two keeps records only of shipping addresses.

On February 7, 2001, Toys filed the instant complaint against Step Two in federal district court. Step Two moved to dismiss for lack of personal jurisdiction on April 10, 2001. Toys opposed the motion, and requested discovery on the issue of jurisdiction. After hearing oral argument on July 30, 2001, the District Court denied the discovery request and granted the motion to dismiss. Toys appealed these decisions on August 28, 2001.

II

In the following discussion, we first consider the standard for personal jurisdiction based upon a defendant's operation of a commercially interactive web site, as articulated by courts within this circuit and other Courts of Appeals. In light of that standard and the arguments presented in the proceeding below, we then assess the propriety of the District Court's denial of jurisdictional discovery.

A. *Personal Jurisdiction Based on the Operation of a Web Site*

* * * The precise question raised by this case is whether the operation of a commercially interactive web site accessible in the forum state is sufficient to support specific personal jurisdiction, or whether there must be additional evidence that the defendant has "purposefully availed" itself of the privilege of engaging in activity in that state. Prior decisions indicate that such evidence is necessary, and that it should reflect intentional interaction with the forum state. If a defendant web site operator intentionally targets the site to the forum state, and/or knowingly conducts business with forum state residents via the site, then the "purposeful availment" requirement is satisfied. * * *

2. Non–Internet Contacts

In deciding whether to exercise jurisdiction over a cause of action arising from a defendant's operation of a web site, a court may consider the defendant's related non-Internet activities as part of the "purposeful availment" calculus. One case that relies on non-Internet contacts for the exercise of jurisdiction—a case Toys repeatedly cites—is *Euromarket Designs, Inc. v. Crate and Barrel Ltd.*, 96 F.Supp.2d 824 (N.D.Ill.2000). In *Euromarket*, the court exercised jurisdiction over an Irish manufacturer based on its commercially interactive web site, even though the products purchased through the web site could not be shipped to Illinois. The court identified a number of non-Internet contacts between the defendant and Illinois, including the fact that the defendant's vendors included Illinois suppliers, its attendance at trade shows in Illinois, and its advertisement in publications that circulate in the United States (albeit originating outside). The *Euromarket* court also relied on the fact that the defendant billed Illinois customers, collected revenues from Illinois customers, and recorded sales from goods ordered from Illinois, and that the web site was designed to accommodate addresses in the United States.

Thus far, Toys has not shown that Step Two maintained the type of contacts that supported jurisdiction in *Euromarket*—i.e., that the defendant intentionally and knowingly transacted business with residents of the forum state, and had significant other contacts with the forum besides those generated by its web site. This limited record does not provide an occasion for us to spell out the exact mix of Internet and non-Internet contacts required to support an exercise of personal jurisdiction. That determination should be made on a case-by-case basis by assessing the "nature and quality" of the contacts. However, non-Internet contacts such as serial business trips to the forum state, telephone and fax communications directed to the forum state, purchase contracts with forum state residents, contracts that apply the law of the forum state, and advertisements in local newspapers, may form part of the "something more" needed to establish personal jurisdiction. It is noteworthy that the Supreme Court in *Burger King Corp.*, when expounding on the "minimum contacts" requirement, referred generally to a defendant's "activities" in the forum state—a term that includes the aforementioned non-Internet contacts.

3. Personal Jurisdiction over Step Two

* * * Based on the facts established in this case thus far, Toys has failed to satisfy the purposeful availment requirement. Step Two's web sites, while commercial and interactive, do not appear to have been designed or intended to reach customers in New Jersey. Step Two's web sites are entirely in Spanish; prices for its merchandise are in pesetas or Euros, and merchandise can be shipped only to addresses within Spain. Most important, none of the portions of Step Two's web sites are designed to accommodate addresses within the United States. While it is possible to join Club Imaginarium and receive newsletters with only an

email address, Step Two asks registrants to indicate their residence using fields that are not designed for addresses in the United States.

Moreover, the record may not now support a finding that Step Two knowingly conducted business with residents of New Jersey. The only documented sales to persons in the United States are the two contacts orchestrated by Toys, and it appears that Step Two scarcely recognized that sales with U.S. residents had been consummated.

At best, Toys has presented only inconclusive circumstantial evidence to suggest that Step Two targeted its web site to New Jersey residents, or that it purposefully availed itself of any effort to conduct activity in New Jersey. Many of the grounds for jurisdiction that Toys advanced below have been deemed insufficient by the courts. First, the two documented sales appear to be the kind of "fortuitous," "random," and "attenuated" contacts that the Supreme Court has held insufficient to warrant the exercise of jurisdiction. * * * Non–Internet contacts, such as Mr. Tena's visits to New York and the relationships with U.S. vendors, have not been explored sufficiently to determine whether they are related to Toys' cause of action, or whether they reflect "purposeful availment."

Absent further evidence showing purposeful availment, Toys cannot establish specific jurisdiction over Step Two. However, any information regarding Step Two's intent vis-a-vis its Internet business and regarding other related contacts is known by Step Two, and can be learned by Toys only through discovery. The District Court's denial of jurisdictional discovery is thus a critical issue, insofar as it may have prevented Toys from obtaining the information needed to establish personal jurisdiction. We next turn to whether the District Court properly denied Toys' request for jurisdictional discovery.

B. Jurisdictional Discovery

[The court granted Toys' request for] jurisdictional discovery for the purpose of establishing either specific personal jurisdiction, or jurisdiction under the federal long-arm statute, Fed.R.Civ.P. 4(k)(2). * * *

We are persuaded that the District Court erred when it denied Toys' request for jurisdictional discovery. The court's unwavering focus on the web site precluded consideration of other Internet and non-Internet contacts—indicated in various parts of the record—which, if explored, might provide the "something more" needed to bring Step Two within our jurisdiction. * * *

Given the allegations as to Step Two's mimicry of Toys' ventures on the Internet and its copy-cat marketing efforts, it would be reasonable to allow more detailed discovery into Step Two's business plans for purchases, sales, and marketing. Limited discovery relating to these matters would shed light on the extent, if any, Step Two's business activity—including, but not limited to, its web site—were aimed towards the United States. This information, known only to Step Two, would speak to an essential element of the personal jurisdiction calculus.

* * * Although Step Two does not appear to have widespread contacts with the United States, this limited discovery will also help determine whether jurisdiction exists under the federal long-arm statute. Accordingly, on remand, the District Court should consider whether any newly discovered facts will support jurisdiction under traditional jurisdictional analysis, or under Rule 4(k)(2).

Notes and Questions

1. In *Gorman v. Ameritrade Holding Corp.*, 293 F.3d 506 (D.C. Cir. 2002), the Court of Appeals provided the standard by which a claim of general jurisdiction on the basis of website activity should be evaluated. After noting that the general jurisdiction doctrine is flexible enough to expand to incorporate developing technologies such as the internet and electronic commerce, the court concluded that the jurisdictional test remained whether the plaintiff had alleged "continuous and systematic" contacts with the federal district.

Initially, a court must determine whether the non-resident defendant's website is more "passive," that is, for example, merely informational in nature, or more "active," whereby the defendant actually transacts business of a systematic and continuous nature with customers in the District of Columbia through the website. Even if it is interactive, the website must be used by a defendant to do business with residents in the forum state in a continuous and systematic way. Mere access by forum residents to a non-resident defendant's website is not enough, by itself, to establish minimum contacts with the forum. The question is not whether District of Columbia residents "can" transact business in the district with the non-resident defendant through the defendant's website, but if they actually "do" engage in sustained business activities in a continuous and systematic way.

The court concluded that general jurisdiction likely existed over a brokerage firm where resident customers freely accessed the firm's website to open brokerage accounts, to transmit funds to those accounts electronically, to use the accounts to buy and sell securities, and to enter into binding contracts with the defendant.

2. Why do so few cases recognize the application of general jurisdiction based on an Internet presence? Are courts concerned about large corporations being subject to litigation in so many places that are unrelated to the claim? If general jurisdiction is easily available, what can a defendant do to eliminate being subject to jurisdiction in a particular forum? With Internet access, a defendant is subject to being sued in any state based on conduct occurring worldwide. Should inexpensive Internet access for everyone establish that a defendant purposefully avails itself of the market in every forum? Would general jurisdiction based on Internet transactions be more attractive for a court if the defendant had appointed an agent or had a business in the forum?

3. In *Bridgeport Music, Inc. v. Still N the Water Publishing*, 327 F.3d 472 (6th Cir. 2003), plaintiff brought a copyright infringement lawsuit, in which it claimed that the defendant music publisher knew that a defendant music distributor was likely to distribute the plaintiff-publisher's composi-

tions nationally. The court held that that fact, coupled with its lack of objection to sales in the forum state, was insufficient conduct upon which to prove purposeful availment in the forum state, under *Asahi*'s stream of commerce "plus" approach.

4. Shortly after *Gator.com* was published, the Ninth Circuit vacated its decision and granted a rehearing *en banc*. 366 F.3d 789 (9th Cir. 2004). After the briefs were filed but before oral arguments, the parties did what parties often do while a case is on appeal. They settled the case, and the court soon dismissed the appeal as moot. 398 F.3d 1125 (9th Cir. 2005) (en banc).

Exercise

You are general counsel for a corporation that has an Internet website, and you recently sent the following memorandum to the CEO of your corporation. Write a follow-up memo to the CEO.

Date: _____, 200_

To: President and Chief Executive Officer

From: General Counsel

Re: Limiting the Corporation's Exposure to Lawsuits

I am writing in response to your recent memorandum of concern about the company's growing litigation costs. After personally reading several recent court decisions, I am planning a meeting with my legal team this morning to explore ways to reduce or eliminate the company's potential exposure to litigation as a result of our Internet Website which the company began to use two years ago.

Thus far, we have been extremely fortunate that very few Website-related lawsuits have been filed against the company. I recognize that my office's suggestions may be outweighed by the need to maximize the company's business/selling efforts. However, that is a business decision that you will ultimately be making in response to my proposal.

I will send you a minimum of five recommendations about changes in the way the company does business. Enjoy your weekend.

B. SERVICE OF PROCESS ON DEFENDANTS

Service of process relates to the notice a defendant receives about the filing of a lawsuit. Historically, service was satisfied by placing a copy of the complaint and a summons in the hands of the defendant. Over time, the law recognized that there are circumstances when a defendant is deemed to have been notified through "substituted" service or "constructive" service of process. With any method of service, the goal is to ensure that the party being served acquires the relevant documents. As with personal jurisdiction issues, service of process must satisfy both constitutional and rule standards, or it may be waived by the defendant's entering an appearance before the court.

The federal rules do not address issues about whether the defendant can be served within the federal district where the lawsuit was filed, or whether a particular type of service of process satisfies the Due Process Clause of the United States Constitution. The federal rule merely describes the procedure for serving the papers, and assumes that the defendant can be served in a constitutionally acceptable manner.

INTRODUCTORY PROBLEM

Kennedy, a citizen of Massachusetts, sued four Virginia defendants (Harrison, Tyler, Taylor, and Wilson) in a Virginia federal court for breach of contract connected with purchase of a large local business. The United States Marshal notified Harrison by delivering a summons and a copy of the complaint to him personally. She notified Tyler by sending him a copy of those two documents by first class mail. She attempted to notify Taylor about the lawsuit by going to his home, but when she realized he was out of town, she left the documents with the person who answered the door. Wilson proved to be difficult to notify. When the Marshal attempted to leave the documents at the address listed by Kennedy as Wilson's residence on the complaint, she could not find such a street listing anywhere within the commonwealth of Virginia, much less within the boundaries of the federal district and division where the complaint was filed. Knowing that defendants should be notified about lawsuits brought against them, the Marshal called the cellphone providers and found a cell number under Wilson's name. She called him and told him that he had been sued and that he could pick up the papers at her office in the local federal building.

Assess whether the defendants were provided with proper notice about the filing of the complaint.

Governing Law: Federal Rule 4.

1. Constitutional Standards

MULLANE v. CENTRAL HANOVER BANK & TRUST CO.

339 U.S. 306, 70 S.Ct. 652, 94 L.Ed. 865 (1950)

Mr. Justice JACKSON delivered the opinion of the Court.

[A petition was filed in a New York court to settle the 113 accounts of the trustee of a common trust fund. A number of the beneficiaries were nonresidents of New York and their addresses were unknown. Pursuant to New York law which was the legal basis for establishing the trusts, notice about the proceeding was by publication in a local newspaper. The guardian appointed by the court on behalf of some of the trust beneficiaries appeared specially and objected to the assertion of jurisdiction on the ground that the nonresidents had not been served personally.]

Personal service of written notice within the jurisdiction is the classic form of notice always adequate in any type of proceeding. But the vital interest of the State in bringing any issues as to its fiduciaries to a final settlement can be served only if interests or claims of individuals who are outside of the State can somehow be determined. A construction of the Due Process Clause which would place impossible or impractical obstacles in the way could not be justified.

Against this interest of the State we must balance the individual interest sought to be protected by the Fourteenth Amendment. This is defined by our holding that "The fundamental requisite of due process of law is the opportunity to be heard." *Grannis v. Ordean*, 234 U.S. 385, 394 (1914). This right to be heard has little reality or worth unless one is informed that the matter is pending and can choose for himself whether to appear or default, acquiesce or contest.

The Court has not committed itself to any formula achieving a balance between these interests in a particular proceeding or determining when constructive notice may be utilized or what test it must meet. Personal service has not in all circumstances been regarded as indispensable to the process due to residents, and it has more often been held unnecessary as to nonresidents. We disturb none of the established rules on these subjects. No decision constitutes a controlling or even a very illuminating precedent for the case before us. But a few general principles stand out in the books.

An elementary and fundamental requirement of due process in any proceeding which is to be accorded finality is notice reasonably calculated, under all the circumstances, to apprise interested parties of the pendency of the action and afford them an opportunity to present their objections. The notice must be of such nature as reasonably to convey the required information, *Grannis v. Ordean*, and it must afford a reasonable time for those interested to make their appearance. But if with due regard for the practicalities and peculiarities of the case these conditions are reasonably met the constitutional requirements are satisfied. * * *

But when notice is a person's due, process which is a mere gesture is not due process. The means employed must be such as one desirous of actually informing the absentee might reasonably adopt to accomplish it. The reasonableness and hence the constitutional validity of any chosen method may be defended on the ground that it is in itself reasonably certain to inform those affected, or, where conditions do not reasonably permit such notice, that the form chosen is not substantially less likely to bring home notice than other of the feasible and customary substitutes.

It would be idle to pretend that publication alone as prescribed here, is a reliable means of acquainting interested parties of the fact that their rights are before the courts. It is not an accident that the greater number of cases reaching this Court on the question of adequacy of notice have been concerned with actions founded on process constructively served through local newspapers. Chance alone brings to the attention of even a local resident an advertisement in small type inserted in the back pages of a newspaper, and if he makes his home outside the area of the newspaper's normal circulation the odds that the information will never reach him are large indeed. The chance of actual notice is further reduced when as here the notice required does not even name those whose attention it is supposed to attract, and does not inform acquaintances who might call it to attention. In weighing its sufficiency on the basis of equivalence with actual notice we are unable to regard this as more than a feint.

Nor is publication here reinforced by steps likely to attract the parties' attention to the proceeding. It is true that publication tradition-ally has been acceptable as notification supplemental to other action which in itself may reasonably be expected to convey a warning. The ways of an owner with tangible property are such that he usually arranges means to learn of any direct attack upon his possessory or proprietary rights. Hence, libel of a ship, attachment of a chattel or entry upon real estate in the name of law may reasonably be expected to come promptly to the owner's attention. When the state within which the owner has located such property seizes it for some reason, publication or posting affords an additional measure of notification. A state may indulge the assumption that one who has left tangible property in the state either has abandoned it, in which case proceedings against it deprive him of nothing, or that he has left some caretaker under a duty to let him know that it is being jeopardized. * * *

In the case before us there is, of course, no abandonment. On the other hand these beneficiaries do have a resident fiduciary as caretaker of their interest in this property. But it is their caretaker who in the accounting becomes their adversary. Their trustee is released from giving notice of jeopardy, and no one else is expected to do so. Not even the special guardian is required or apparently expected to communicate with his ward and client, and, of course, if such a duty were merely transferred from the trustee to the guardian, economy would not be served and more likely the cost would be increased.

This Court has not hesitated to approve of resort to publication as a customary substitute in another class of cases where it is not reasonably possible or practicable to give more adequate warning. Thus it has been recognized that, in the case of persons missing or unknown, employment of an indirect and even a probably futile means of notification is all that the situation permits and creates no constitutional bar to a final decree foreclosing their rights.

Those beneficiaries represented by appellant whose interests or whereabouts could not with due diligence be ascertained come clearly within this category. As to them the statutory notice is sufficient. However great the odds that publication will never reach the eyes of such unknown parties, it is not in the typical case much more likely to fail than any of the choices open to legislators endeavoring to prescribe the best notice practicable.

Nor do we consider it unreasonable for the State to dispense with more certain notice to those beneficiaries whose interests are either conjectural or future or, although they could be discovered upon investigation, do not in due course of business come to knowledge of the common trustee. Whatever searches might be required in another situation under ordinary standards of diligence, in view of the character of the proceedings and the nature of the interests here involved we think them unnecessary. We recognize the practical difficulties and costs that would be attendant on frequent investigations into the status of great numbers of beneficiaries, many of whose interests in the common fund are so remote as to be ephemeral; and we have no doubt that such impracticable and extended searches are not required in the name of due process. The expense of keeping informed from day to day of substitutions among even current income beneficiaries and presumptive remaindermen, to say nothing of the far greater number of contingent beneficiaries, would impose a severe burden on the plan, and would likely dissipate its advantages. These are practical matters in which we should be reluctant to disturb the judgment of the state authorities.

Accordingly we overrule appellant's constitutional objections to published notice insofar as they are urged on behalf of any beneficiaries whose interests or addresses are unknown to the trustee.

As to known present beneficiaries of known place of residence, however, notice by publication stands on a different footing. Exceptions in the name of necessity do not sweep away the rule that within the limits of practicability notice must be such as is reasonably calculated to reach interested parties. Where the names and post office addresses of those affected by a proceeding are at hand, the reasons disappear for resort to means less likely than the mails to apprise them of its pendency.

The trustee has on its books the names and addresses of the income beneficiaries represented by appellant, and we find no tenable ground for dispensing with a serious effort to inform them personally of the accounting, at least by ordinary mail to the record addresses. Certainly sending them a copy of the statute months and perhaps years in advance does not answer this purpose. The trustee periodically remits their income to them, and we think that they might reasonably expect that with or apart from their remittances word might come to them personally that steps were being taken affecting their interests.

We need not weigh contentions that a requirement of personal service of citation on even the large number of known resident or nonresident beneficiaries would, by reasons of delay if not of expense, seriously interfere with the proper administration of the fund. Of course personal service even without the jurisdiction of the issuing authority serves the end of actual and personal notice, whatever power of compulsion it might lack. However, no such service is required under the circumstances. This type of trust presupposes a large number of small interests. The individual interest does not stand alone but is identical with that of a class. The rights of each in the integrity of the fund and the fidelity of the trustee are shared by many other beneficiaries. Therefore notice reasonably certain to reach most of those interested in objecting is likely to safeguard the interests of all, since any objections sustained would inure to the benefit of all. We think that under such circumstances reasonable risks that notice might not actually reach every beneficiary are justifiable. * * *

The statutory notice to known beneficiaries is inadequate, not because in fact it fails to reach everyone, but because under the circumstances it is not reasonably calculated to reach those who could easily be informed by other means at hand. However it may have been in former times, the mails today are recognized as an efficient and inexpensive means of communication. Moreover, the fact that the trust company has been able to give mailed notice to known beneficiaries at the time the common trust fund was established is persuasive that postal notification at the time of accounting would not seriously burden the plan.

In some situations the law requires greater precautions in its proceedings than the business world accepts for its own purposes. In few, if any, will it be satisfied with less. Certainly it is instructive, in determining the reasonableness of the impersonal broadcast notification here used, to ask whether it would satisfy a prudent man of business, counting his pennies but finding it in his interest to convey information to many persons whose names and addresses are in his files. We are not satisfied that it would. Publication may theoretically be available for all the world to see, but it is too much in our day to suppose that each or any individual beneficiary does or could examine all that is published to see if something may be tucked away in it that affects his property interests. We have before indicated in reference to notice by publication that, "Great caution should be used not to let fiction deny the fair play that can be secured only by a pretty close adhesion to fact." *McDonald v. Mabee*, 243 U.S. 90 (1917).

We hold the notice of judicial settlement of accounts required by the New York Banking Law is incompatible with the requirements of the Fourteenth Amendment as a basis for adjudication depriving known persons whose whereabouts are also known of substantial property rights. Accordingly the judgment is reversed and the cause remanded for further proceedings not inconsistent with this opinion.

Reversed.

Notes and Questions

1. What did the Court hold? Why is the Court willing to validate a mode of service (first-class mail) that is not the best available? Why does the Court conclude that it is unnecessary for every beneficiary to receive notice about the lawsuit? Is service by publication ever sufficient, and if so, under what circumstances? How can notice never received comply with due process?

2. The United States is a country where many languages are spoken by its citizens. Is it consistent with due process for the notice about a lawsuit to be in English? When a non-English speaking defendant receives a summons and complaint in English, does the face of the "official looking" documents convey enough information for the defendant to be on notice to have it translated? What problems would be created if court systems began to print forms in languages other than English?

3. In *Greene v. Lindsey*, 456 U.S. 444, 102 S.Ct. 1874, 72 L.Ed.2d 249 (1982), a Kentucky statute permitted service of process in a landlord-tenant eviction proceeding by posting a summons "in a conspicuous place on the premises," if the defendant or a member of the defendant's family over 16 years of age could not be located. The landlord posted the summons in a public housing project on the door of each of the tenants' apartments. The tenants claimed they never saw the summonses and did not know of the eviction proceedings until after default judgments had been entered against them and the time for filing an appeal had expired. The tenants filed a federal civil rights class action against public officials, claiming in part that the notice procedures used violated due process.

The Supreme Court held that under *Mullane* the procedures failed to afford the tenants adequate notice of the proceedings against them under the circumstances of the case. Because the notices were often removed from the doors before the tenants could see them, merely posting the notices on the doors failed to satisfy minimum standards of due process. The Court, though, did not hold that posting notices were always an inappropriate method of service under due process. The Court endorsed notice by mail to ensure that the tenants would have the opportunity to present a defense. Wouldn't the lack of mail box security in a public housing project present potentially the same due process problems for missing or stolen notices as the posting procedures? Some jurisdictions reacted to *Greene* by requiring that the notice in eviction cases be both posted *and* mailed to the tenant.

2. Procedural Standards for Service of Process

When a plaintiff files a claim against a defendant, it is necessary to notify the defendant about the lawsuit. The notice function of service of process is essential to ensuring that a defendant has a fair opportunity to respond to the complaint and to raise defenses and objections. Federal Rule 4 requires that the defendant be served, i.e., receive a copy of a summons and a copy of the complaint.

An objection to the method of service and/or to the process itself can occur in two contexts. First, a motion can be made to dismiss the complaint due to insufficient service of process or insufficient process, per Federal Rule 12(b)(4)-(5). Second, a plaintiff often obtains a default judgment against a defendant who never answered the complaint. After the plaintiff tries to enforce the judgment, e.g., by garnishing the defendant's wages, the defendant may learn about the lawsuit for the first time and file a motion with the court to vacate the default judgment. The premise for the motion is that the default judgment was improper because the court lacked jurisdiction over the defendant due to the improper service of process.

While an important goal of service of process is to notify the defendant that a lawsuit has been filed, a defendant's knowledge about the lawsuit is usually regarded as insufficient to dispense with the service of process requirements. For example, in *Ayres v. Jacobs & Crumplar,* 99 F.3d 565, 568–70 (3d Cir. 1996), the court held that a defendant's actual notice about the lawsuit, as shown by the defendant's later participation in discovery, failed to confer jurisdiction on the court, because no proper summons was issued and signed by the clerk or stamped with the seal of the court. The formal requirements of Rule 4 for proper service must be satisfied, and actual knowledge of the lawsuit does not cure a defective service of process. Not all courts agree with that judicial approach. See, e.g., note 2, after *Cox v. Quigley,* infra.

The summons has several requirements. It must 1) be issued by the clerk of court, bearing the court's seal and the clerk's signature; 2) identify the district court, name the parties, and list the name and address of the plaintiff or the plaintiff's attorney; 3) be directed to the specific defendant; 4) state the time within which the defendant must appear and defend the lawsuit; and caution about the consequences of the defendant's failure to appear. A sample of a federal summons is found in your rules supplement as Federal Rules of Civil Procedure Form 1.

At or about the same time that a complaint is filed, plaintiff has the obligation to prepare a summons and submit it to the clerk for signing and sealing. In multiple defendant cases, copies of the summons must be issued for each defendant. The summons and complaint are served together, and plaintiff is responsible for effective service. In federal court, because the plaintiff himself cannot serve the papers on the defendant, the plaintiff selects an appropriate person, typically a commercial process server who works for a fee, to serve the defendant. A United States Marshal serves process only when ordered by the court.

Federal Rule 4(d) imposes a duty on defendants to avoid unnecessary costs of formal service of process. To avoid costs, the plaintiff can notify the defendant about filing the lawsuit and ask that the defendant waive service. The plaintiff must make a formal request to the defendant to waive formal service of process. The request must be in writing, conform to the approved form, identify the court, describe the consequences of both waiver and the refusal to waive, contain a copy of the complaint, sent by first-class mail or "other reliable means," and be addressed directly to the defendant. Federal Rules of Civil Procedure Form 1A, Notice of Lawsuit and Request for Waiver of Service of Summons, shows a plaintiff how to make the request. The next case illustrates potential problems with relying on the waiver procedure.

LARSEN v. MAYO MEDICAL CENTER

218 F.3d 863 (8th Cir. 2000)

HEANEY, Circuit Judge.

Patricia Larsen contracted an illness from medication administered to her during her hospitalization at the Mayo Medical Center ("Mayo").

She sued Mayo for medical malpractice. Mayo moved for summary judgment on the basis that Larsen's claim was time-barred. The district court granted the motion, and Larsen appeals. Because Larsen failed to serve Mayo within the two-year statute of limitations, we affirm.

* * * Larsen filed her complaint against Mayo on May 29, 1998 wherein she alleged medical malpractice. On June 1, 1998, Larsen attempted to serve Mayo by mailing a copy of the summons and complaint and enclosing an Acknowledgment of Service form for Mayo to return. Mayo received the materials two days later, but did not sign and return the acknowledgment form. On June 15, 1998, Larsen's counsel contacted Mayo's in-house counsel, who informed him that Mayo would not admit service or assist Larsen in any way in suing his client.

On June 22, 1998, Larsen filed an amended complaint, which she again mailed to Mayo with an Acknowledgment of Service form. Mayo did not return the form, and on September 3, 1998, Larsen's counsel again contacted Mayo's counsel, who again told him that Mayo would not execute the form.

On September 4, 1998, Larsen mailed copies of the amended summons and complaint to the Olmstead County Sheriff's Department. The Sheriff's Department received the materials on September 8, 1998 and served Mayo the following day.

* * * [T]he district court considered whether service was timely. It concluded that service was not effective until September 8, 1998, the date the Olmstead County Sheriff's Department received the summons and complaint for service on Mayo, and thus that Larsen's claims were time-barred. Larsen appeals the district court's grant of Mayo's summary judgment motion.

* * *

Larsen contends that service was timely even if the limitations period began to run on July 24, 1996. She argues that under the Federal Rules of Civil Procedure a civil action is commenced by filing a complaint with the court, see Fed.R.Civ.P. 3, and that since she filed her complaint on May 29, 1998, her action is timely. This argument fails to recognize the case law of both the Supreme Court and our court.

Larsen correctly points out that the Federal Rules of Civil Procedure determine the date from which various timing requirements begin to run. They do not, however, affect the commencement of a lawsuit. See *Walker v. Armco Steel Corp.*, 446 U.S. 740, 750–52 (1980). Rather, state commencement rules apply because they are "part and parcel of the statute of limitations." *Walker*, 446 U.S. at 752. Accordingly, Minnesota's commencement rule, rather than the federal commencement rule, governs in this case.

Under Minnesota's Rules of Civil Procedure, a civil action is commenced:

(a) when the summons is served upon that defendant, or

(b) at the date of acknowledgment of service if service is made by mail, or

(c) when the summons is delivered to the sheriff in the county where the defendant resides for service....

Minn. R. Civ. P. 3.01.

Although Minnesota law controls the commencement of a lawsuit, service of process in federal diversity actions is procedural, and therefore, governed by the Federal Rules. Under the Federal Rules, a plaintiff may, among other things, notify the defendant of the commencement of the action and request that the defendant waive service of the summons. See Fed.R.Civ.P. 4(d)(2). If the defendant returns the waiver and the plaintiff files the waiver with the court, "the action shall proceed ... as if a summons and complaint had been served at the time of filing the waiver." *Id.* at 4(d)(4). However, if the defendant does not waive service, service has not been effected.

In this case, Larsen twice mailed copies of the summons and complaint to Mayo, first on June 1, 1998 and again on June 22, 1998. Both times she enclosed an acknowledgment form, and both times, Mayo refused to execute the form. Because Mayo did not waive service by returning the acknowledgment form, the requirements for service by mail were not met. Mayo then was not served until the Olmstead County Sheriff's Department received a copy of the summons and complaint on September 8, 1998, more than a month after the two-year limitations period expired.

Larsen makes two alternative arguments, both of which are without merit. She claims that service was effective under Fed.R.Civ.P. 4(m), which states:

Time Limit for Service. If service of the summons and complaint is not made upon a defendant within 120 days after the filing of the complaint, the court, upon motion or on its own initiative after notice to the plaintiff, shall dismiss the action without prejudice as to that defendant or direct that service to be effected within a specified time....

Larsen argues that Rule 4(m) conflicts with Minnesota's commencement rule, and thus, that the federal rule, not the state rule, governs.

First, Fed.R.Civ.P. 4(m) is irrelevant. The rule is only a time restriction that requires the summons and complaint to be served within 120 days of the filing of the complaint. It does not address how or when a lawsuit is properly commenced.

Second, even if relevant, Fed.R.Civ.P. 4(m) does not conflict with Minnesota's commencement rule. In *Walker*, the Supreme Court interpreted a state commencement rule identical to that of Minnesota and held that the state rule did not conflict with the Federal Rules. See 446 U.S. at 752 ("[Each] can exist side by side, therefore, each controlling its own intended sphere of coverage without conflict.''). Because the rules do not conflict, Minn. R.Civ.P. 3.01 governs the commencement of Larsen's lawsuit.

Finally, Larsen argues that service was effective under Fed.R.Civ.P. 4(h), which provides for service on a corporation by delivering a copy of the summons and complaint to an officer, manager or authorized agent of the corporation. This argument also is meritless because the summons and complaint were mailed and not personally served on anyone during the limitations period. Further, they were not even mailed to an officer, manager or authorized agent of Mayo Clinic, but addressed to "Medical/Legal Department, Mayo Clinic." Thus, service was ineffective under Rule 4(h).

The statute of limitations began to run in this case no later than July 24, 1996. The lawsuit was not commenced until September 8, 1998, over a month after the limitations period expired. Thus, the district court correctly concluded that Larsen's medical malpractice claim against Mayo is time-barred, and we affirm its decision to grant summary judgment.

Notes and Questions

1. As in *Larsen*, if a defendant refuses to waive service of process under Rule 4(d), plaintiff must proceed with normal service of process using Rules 4(e), (f), and (h). The case also makes the point that Rule 4(m)'s 120–day period for completing service is running while the waiver of service request is made.

A plaintiff has 120 days after filing to serve the defendant with the summons and complaint. When the 120 days have passed, the lawsuit can be dismissed. but the period may be extended for "good cause." The dismissal may be harmful to the plaintiff because filing another complaint may occur after the running of the statute of limitations. The trial court has discretion to determine whether "good cause" exists. For example, if the plaintiff can show that the limitations period has run, the court has the discretion to decide against dismissal and instead grant a motion to extend the time for service.

2. Carefully reading Rule 4(d) discloses the non-economic inducement to waive formal service of process: a longer time for responding to the complaint. While a defendant has 20 days to answer a complaint following personal service, 60 days are available for a defendant with a United States address to answer the complaint following a waiver of service.

3. If the defendant agrees to waive service of process, he is expected to return the waiver form, which is Federal Rules of Civil Procedure Form 1B, Waiver of Service of Summons. When a defendant has agreed to waive service and returns the waiver form, the date of service is deemed the date when the plaintiff files the form with the court. Regardless of which procedure is used, the waiver of service or formal service must occur within the 120–day period after filing the complaint. In *Larsen*, even if the defendant had returned the waiver of service form, if the 120–day time period had

passed before the form was filed, the case would have to be dismissed, thereby creating a risk that refiling the lawsuit could occur after expiration of the limitations period.

Federal Rule 4 governs most of the service of process standards in federal courts. Specifically, Rule 4(e) and (h) regulate service on individuals, corporations and other associations. It is important to remember, though, that the descriptive techniques under the federal rules are merely one method by which service can be made. The federal rules clearly indicate that service on defendants may be effected by the law of the state in which the federal district court is held or in which service occurs. State rules, for example, may authorize service by mail—certified, registered, first-class, express, or electronic.

The most desirable method of service for individuals is to serve them personally. Personal service avoids any question about whether a defendant has received notice about the lawsuit, and it is unlikely to produce due process objections. In-hand delivery is not always essential. What happens if a defendant attempts to evade service, or refuses to accept delivery after being informed by the process server of the nature of the papers? It is sufficient service that the process server touches the party to be served with the papers, or, if touching is impossible, leaves the papers in the defendant's physical proximity. The defendant does not have to possess the papers for effective service.

International Controls Corp. v. Vesco, 593 F.2d 166 (2d Cir. 1979), is an example of the difficulties posed by a possession requirement. The process server came across a bolted gate and two bodyguards in front of the defendant's home, and the defendant refused to come outside so he could be served. The process server attached the papers to a blue ribbon and threw them over the defendant's fence on the front lawn. The papers were also mailed to the defendant at his residence. The court found that the defendant had actual notice of the proceedings against him, and upheld the service.

The federal rules also permit substituted service of process alternatives to personal delivery. One option for the process server under Federal Rule 4(e)(2) is to leave the papers at the defendant's "dwelling house or usual place of abode with some person of suitable age and discretion then residing therein."

COX v. QUIGLEY

141 F.R.D. 222 (D.Me. 1992)

HORNBY, District Judge.

Where is the dwelling house or usual place of abode of a young person who has recently graduated from college, has left home and is serving on board ship in the Military Sealift Command for most of the year and spends his time off visiting various relatives and vacationing in different parts of the country or abroad? That is the question on this motion to vacate default judgment. Concluding that at the time service was attempted the defendant had no dwelling house or usual place of abode except perhaps for his ship, I find that the plaintiff failed to make proper service of process under [current Rule 4(e)] when the process server left the papers with the defendant's father at his parents' home. As a result, the court never obtained personal jurisdiction over the defendant and the default judgment must be vacated.

Growing up, Joseph Quigley lived with his family on Cayuga Heights Road in Ithaca, New York. He attended Maine Maritime Academy in Castine, Maine and graduated in the spring of 1987. Earlier that year, his parents moved to a new house in Ithaca on Iradell Road where there was no bedroom for their son. When he returned to Ithaca after graduation and took a summer job, Quigley slept on a cot in the basement. In the fall of 1987, he obtained a position with the Military Sealift Command and went to sea. In May, 1988, he notified his employer that he was changing his address to Florida, specifically Port Richie, his grandparents' address. At the same time he registered to vote in Florida and proceeded to cast a Florida absentee ballot. He has only voted once. He also filed his federal income tax return listing a Florida address in May, 1988. All of these events occurred before the relevant developments in this lawsuit.

In June, 1988, the plaintiff's lawyer attempted to serve process on Quigley in connection with this lawsuit. The plaintiff's lawyer had a sheriff deliver the process to Quigley's parents' home on Iradell Road in Ithaca. Quigley's father, who has the same first name and middle initial as his son, declined to accept the process after determining that the lawsuit did not involve him. He told the deputy sheriff that his son was at sea for several months. The lawyer's secretary next wrote the deputy sheriff to determine if Quigley's parents' home was his usual place of abode and, if so, to leave the process there. This time the deputy sheriff left the process with Quigley's father and apparently also sent a copy by mail. Quigley's father took the process to his own lawyer who returned it by mail to the plaintiff's lawyer informing him that Quigley did not reside with his father and that his father did not accept service on his behalf.

[Current Rule 4(e)(2)] provides that service can be made upon an individual by serving him personally "or by leaving copies [of the summons and complaint] at the individual's dwelling house or usual place of abode...." The issue, therefore, is whether Iradell Road was Quigley's dwelling house or usual place of abode in June, 1988. The parties also presented evidence to me concerning events that occurred after June, 1988. My decision is limited to Quigley's status as of June, 1988. Nevertheless, his later activities may shed light on what took place earlier and may also affect his credibility.

Quigley's later activities include the following: He continued to hold his New York driver's license until it was stolen from him in Greece in the summer of 1988. On October 14, 1988, Quigley obtained a replacement Virginia license while his ship was in port in Norfolk, Virginia. Apparently Virginia makes such licenses available to nonresidents because of the large number of Navy personnel stationed there. The Virginia license listed New York as Quigley's residence. I draw no conclusions from these driver's licenses. The original New York license did not expire until March, 1989, and it is not unusual that a graduating college student in the process of locating a job and ultimately a place to live does not immediately obtain a new driver's license. The apparent New York residence on the Virginia license is also explainable as a reference to the pre-existing New York license.

Quigley arranged for his grandmother in Florida to forward all his financial and business mail to his mother in New York and gave his mother a power-of-attorney. His mother was the joint account holder of his bank accounts and paid his bills. Through his father, a real estate broker, Quigley engaged in real estate transactions, buying a house, accepting a mortgage and renting property. All the documents reflecting these transactions listed Iradell Road as his address. I draw no conclusion from the real estate transactions carried on by Quigley's parents in his absence. His parents would logically use their own New York address for ease of payments.

When Quigley was arrested for OUI in Maine in the spring of 1989, he gave both his sister's Maine address and his ship as his address. During leave periods, Quigley spent approximately equal amounts of time with his parents, his grandparents and his sister. Most of his leave time was spent elsewhere, however, such as Virginia or Brazil. When Quigley upgraded his Coast Guard license in April, 1989, he gave his Iradell Road address. Most of Quigley's employment-related documents were addressed to the Florida address. His federal tax returns filed in 1989 and 1990 listed Florida as his address. Quigley maintains that when his mother became seriously ill he moved back to Iradell Road in late 1990. His New York driver's license issued on August 30, 1991, lists Iradell Road as his address but his interrogatory answers signed in this case on September 3, 1991, list Florida as both his residence and post office address.

In fact, I do not find Quigley to be a particularly credible witness when it comes to statements about his dwelling house and place of abode or about his contacts with New York. Several of his previous statements in affidavits or interrogatory answers were equivocal or made material omissions in failing to reveal that his financial mail was forwarded by his grandmother unopened to his mother in New York, in understating the number of times he visited Ithaca and in later referring to his residence as Florida when he had already changed it back to New York. Confronted with the default in this lawsuit, I conclude that Quigley has been at best cavalier in his statements seeking to avoid the default judgment. Nevertheless, many of the factors that control my decision whether Iradell Road is his dwelling house or usual place of abode are based on documentary evidence and, in many cases, predate his notice of the lawsuit.

I conclude from the evidence that Quigley's goal in May, 1988, was to change his tax residence to Florida in order to avoid New York income taxes. Although tax residence alone is not determinative of the location of a dwelling house or usual place of abode, I conclude for that and other reasons that Quigley was no longer dwelling or maintaining a usual place of abode at Iradell Road in Ithaca, New York by June, 1988. The obvious purpose of [current Rule 4(e)(2)'s] provision for service upon a responsible person at a defendant's dwelling house or usual place of abode is to provide some assurance that timely notice of the lawsuit will reach a defendant who has not been served personally. Leaving the process with a responsible person where the defendant is living is a good way to accomplish this objective. But in no sense was Quigley dwelling at Iradell Road or maintaining a place of abode there any longer in June, 1988. He had left home the fall after graduation and had taken up a new tax and voting residence. He maintained only a minimal connection to his parents' home. Quigley visited Iradell Road only briefly and treated his parents on his off-duty time to the same share of his time as his sister and grandmother. His grandmother at his Florida address forwarded certain categories of mail to his mother. But Quigley's parents had no effective way of reaching him at sea except through the Red Cross in case of a medical emergency. Thus, Iradell Road was not a location where process would reach Quigley in a timely manner. Quigley's father told the deputy sheriff that Quigley no longer lived there and the lawyer's letter to the plaintiff's lawyer confirmed the situation.

By the same token, I do not suggest that Florida had become Quigley's dwelling or usual place of abode. Quigley had no particular connection with his grandparents' house except the ability to sleep there when he was in the United States, a privilege he seldom used after May, 1988, and to use the address for his mail and to have his grandmother forward financial and business mail to his mother. He was obviously not dwelling there or maintaining an abode in Florida. If Quigley had a dwelling house or usual place of abode in June, 1988, it was his ship while he was not on leave. I do not mean to suggest that the ship furnished the plaintiff with an attractive option for service. As Quigley testified, he was often at sea for months at a time in the Military Sealift Command and his destinations and the dates of returning to port were often secret. I recognize that [current Rule 4(e)(2)] is designed to provide plaintiffs an alternative method to serve a defendant who is avoiding personal service. Its permission for service at a dwelling house or usual place of abode is probably based on the assumption that these are usually not quickly or easily moved. Therefore, even though a defendant may avoid the process server in person, some other responsible person in the house can receive the papers. Courts and commentators have referred to our society's mobility and affluence as grounds for enlarging this method of service by recognizing that defendants may have two or more dwelling houses or places of abode for purposes of service. But there is a limit to the scope of this service option. Unfortunately, our mobile and affluent society has a large number of transient or homeless people. For them, there may be no dwelling house or usual place of abode. Although they are not the object of a lawsuit as frequently as the affluent, the Rule's language covers all categories. The last shelter at which a homeless person slept will often not furnish reasonable assurance that process will reach the defendant. For such defendants service at the dwelling house or place of abode is unavailable; personal service may be a plaintiff's only option then, no matter how difficult.

Quigley, of course, was not homeless. He was, however, transient. As the plaintiff has conceded, it is her burden of proof to show that Iradell Road in Ithaca was his dwelling house or usual place of abode in June, 1988. I conclude that under the circumstances here that was no longer the case. Quigley had graduated from college, left home, found a job, obtained a new tax residence, voted in a different state, and maintained employment records with a new Florida address. Although he used his parents' address in some other respects, such as to obtain financial documents and have his mother manage his financial affairs (there is no suggestion that the power-of-attorney authorized her to accept service of process or answer a complaint), and although his behavior with his driver's and Coast Guard licenses was inconsistent, I conclude that these factors are not sufficient to show that he was dwelling or maintaining a place of abode at Iradell Road. This conclusion may mean that it will be difficult for plaintiffs to serve some highly mobile or transient defendants. But ease of service cannot displace the need to find a method that will reasonably assure timely notice of the lawsuit.

Finally, the plaintiff has not satisfied me that Quigley had timely notice of this lawsuit. Although it seems incomprehensible that Quigley's father did not notify him of the lawsuit even later when he ultimately did visit home, family and father-son relationships encompass many possibilities. I do find credible Quigley's parents' failure to contact him while he was at sea given the difficulties of using the mail and ship-to-shore phone with a person in the Military Sealift Command.

Default judgment is therefore vacated.

Notes and Questions

1. In *Jaffe and Asher v. Van Brunt*, 158 F.R.D. 278 (S.D.N.Y. 1994), the defendant tried to vacate a default judgment obtained in a lawsuit by a law firm suing him to collect an attorney's fee. The court denied the motion, concluding that the law firm "properly effected service at Van Brunt's usual place of abode" in Connecticut at his parents' residence, which also was the site where the defendant asked for the law firm's bill to be sent.

Defendant argued that he had resided in California for several years preceding the lawsuit, supporting his contention with copies of his California driver's license and his income tax returns. The law firm argued that his parents' home was defendant's "usual place of abode," because he maintained a private phone line and fax machine there, he used a private bedroom and clothing he kept there when he visited the New York metropolitan area, and he received mail there.

Our highly mobile and affluent society has relegated to history the days when an individual had but a single residence. Thus, as the Second Circuit acknowledged, "it is unrealistic to interpret [the federal rule] so that the person to be served has only one dwelling house or usual place of abode at which process may be left." *National Development Co. v. Triad Holding Corp.*, 930 F.2d 253, 257 (2d Cir.1991). A strictly literal interpretation of the rule may thwart the purpose of [the federal rule]— to insure that service is reasonably calculated to provide a defendant with actual notice of the action. Hence, for purposes of effecting service under Rule 4(e), an individual can have multiple " 'dwelling houses or usual places of abode,' provided each contains sufficient indicia of permanence." *Id.*, 930 F.2d at 257.

The court found "sufficient indicia of permanence" at his parents' home to make service there reasonably calculated to provide their son with actual notice of the action. "[E]ven if the parents' home were not one of defendant's 'usual places of abode,' his numerous representations that that location was his address estop him from challenging service there."

2. Under the federal rule, a person can receive substituted service if she is "residing" in the defendant's usual residence or place of abode. In *Franklin America, Inc. v. Franklin Cast Products,* 94 F.R.D. 645 (E.D. Mich. 1982), service was made on the defendant's part-time housekeeper, Mrs. Bannon. Defendant Schwartz claimed "that service was invalid because (1) Mrs. Bannon was not 'residing' in the Schwartz home in January 1982; and (2) Mrs. Bannon was not appointed by Schwartz as his agent to receive service of process." In granting the defendant's motion to dismiss, the court made several observations.

The term "residing therein" has been broadly and naturally interpreted to apply to a landlord, an apartment manager, a housemaid whose usual place of residence was the defendant's home, and a live-in maid. On the other hand, the term "residing therein" has been held not to encompass a janitor or a ranch employee.

It appears the common theme in the cases is not only whether the defendant is reasonably likely to receive the papers served, but whether the person to whom they are handed is a full-time resident of the defendant's dwelling house or usual place of abode.

"Residing therein" has long been held to require the recipient of the papers to be actually living in the same place as defendant. Thus, service on an employee of defendant who spends only a part of his time at defendant's residence is defective.

Here it is undisputed that Mrs. Bannon was a part-time housekeeper who did not live in the Schwartz home. She cannot be deemed to have been "residing therein" without placing an artificial construction on the language of the rule. Thus Mrs. Bannon was not "residing" in the Schwartz home to properly accept service intended for Schwartz.

While [the federal rule] authorizes service upon "an agent authorized by appointment ... to receive service of process", it is undisputed that Schwartz never so appointed Mrs. Bannon. Whether or not his wife appointed Mrs. Bannon as an agent for her husband by virtue of her telephone conversation with the Deputy United States Marshal is immaterial, since there is simply no evidence to indicate Schwartz ever gave his wife that power and an appointment must be made or authorized by the defendant. Thus the service cannot be upheld on the theory that Mrs. Bannon was an agent authorized to accept service of process for Schwartz. * * *

The trial judge granted the plaintiff thirty days in which to "re-serve" the defendant. Why?

By contrast, in *Limon–Hernandez v. Lumbreras*, 171 F.R.D. 271 (D. Or. 1997), the process server gave the papers to an adult male who answered the door at the home of the defendant. After quoting from Federal Rule 4(e)(2), the court upheld the propriety of service by stating simply that the papers were left "with an adult male who was inside of the Lumbreras residence." The court failed to inquire into whether the person who received the papers actually resided there. And in *Howard Johnson International, Inc. v. Wang*, 7 F.Supp.2d 336 (S.D.N.Y. 1998), the court found it to be a "minor point" that the recipient of service did not actually live at the defendant's residence or place of abode.

3. Federal Rule 4(e)(2) also authorizes substituted service on a defendant by delivery of a copy of the summons and complaint to an agent of the defendant. The rule applies only to service on individuals, and should be distinguished from Rule 4(h)(1)'s service on an organization's managing or general agent. Courts look to whether an agency relationship exists, i.e., there must be evidence that the defendant intended to confer authority to receive process on an agent. For example, an agency relationship may be implied from the terms of a power of attorney or from other circumstances.

Rule 4(e)(2) also permits service on an agent authorized by law. For example, a statute may provide that a nonresident corporation which registers to do business in a state can (or must) designate an agent for service, or if none is appointed the Secretary of State becomes the agent who accepts service on behalf of the business. Operation of a long-arm statute is another example of an agent authorized by law, because the Secretary of State is designated as the defendant's agent who mails the papers by certified mail to the defendant at the address listed on the complaint.

4. Service within the United States on a corporation, partnership, or unincorporated association subject to being sued under a common name is made by 1) the waiver of service provision for individuals; or 2) delivery of the summons and complaint to an officer, managing or general agent, or to any other agent appointed to receive service or authorized by law to receive service. Because the summons and complaint must be served on the designated person, it is insufficient merely to address the papers to the corporation generally. As the *Larsen* case indicated, mailing the legal papers to the "Medical/Legal Department, Mayo Clinic" was ineffective service under the federal rules.

For effective service of a corporate officer or managing or general agent, specific authorization by the corporation to accept service is unnecessary. Whether a person is regarded as a managing or general agent depends on the person's duties and authority rather than the name of the office. The governing principle is that service is to be made on someone who realizes her responsibilities to the corporation and knows what to do with the legal papers she receives. To uphold service of process, the person served must fit within the personnel categories listed in Rule 4(h) and therefore has the authority to accept service of process on the defendant's behalf. The record should show that the recipient of the summons and complaint had discretion in the operation of the defendant business, and that the recipient recognized the obligation to deliver the summons promptly to the defendant's appropriate personnel.

Service upon corporations and other entities is separate from considerations of service on individuals. For example, while it is permissible to serve an individual at his usual place of abode with a person of suitable age and discretion, the same type of service is not specifically authorized in the federal rules for corporations. Thus, service on a corporation is improper when a copy of the summons and complaint are left with a person (who is not a managing agent or a designated person for service of process) at the corporation's headquarters.

5.　Some courts adopt a flexible approach to personal service upon corporations, known as "redelivery." Service on a corporation is upheld if: (a) the process server acts with due diligence in trying to meet the statutory requirements by establishing that the recipient is a company employee; (b) the process server nevertheless serves a person not authorized to accept service; and (c) the recipient then redelivers the papers to one who *is* authorized to accept service. The redelivery must be close in time and space so that it can be classified as part of the same act. See, e.g., *Melkaz International Inc. v. Flavor Innovation Inc.*, 167 F.R.D. 634 (E.D.N.Y. 1996).

6.　Rule 4 sets forth a series of methods for serving process on individuals in a foreign country. As with other provisions, Rule 4(f) addresses only the *manner* of service and not whether a particular defendant is subject to suit. Rule 4(f)(1) allows service of process pursuant to the 1969 Hague Convention on the Service of Process Abroad of Judicial and Extrajudicial Documents in Civil or Commercial Matters international litigation in actions governed by the federal rules. Because it specifically refers to the Hague Convention as among the permissible means of service of process in a foreign country, service made pursuant to that treaty explicitly is within the foreign service exception to the 120–day time limit for completing process in Rule 4(m). The Hague Convention, however, does not preempt all other methods of service on defendants residing in another signatory nation.

Articles 2 through 7 of the Hague Convention set out the manner in which service should be executed in a signatory nation. Article 2 requires that all signatory nations must designate a "Central Authority" whose responsibility is to accept requests of service from any other signatory nation. The Hague Convention provides for alternate methods of service: 1) service through the Central Authority of member states; 2) service through consular channels; 3) service by mail if the receiving nation does not object; and 4) service pursuant to the internal laws of the nation.

Article 10(a) of the Hague Convention states that, if the "state of destination does not object," the Convention "shall not interfere with the freedom to send judicial documents, by postal channels, directly to persons abroad." See, e.g., *Nuovo Pignone v. Storman Asia M/V*, 310 F.3d 374 (5th

Cir. 2002) (service by FedEx in Italy); *Bankston v. Toyota Motor Corp.*, 889 F.2d 172 (8th 1989) (registered mail to Japan); *Ackermann v. Levine*, 788 F.2d 830 (2d Cir. 1986) (registered mail to Germany); *EOI Corp. v. Medical Mktg. Ltd.*, 172 F.R.D. 133 (D.N.J.1997) (service by DHL in England).

The ability to request a waiver of service under Rule 4(e) may be particularly beneficial for service that is to occur outside the United States. If a foreign defendant waives service, the costs associated with serving process abroad can be reduced or eliminated. Waiver of service also eliminates the risk that the costs of service will be taxed against him for being unsuccessful in the lawsuit. A foreign defendant has ninety days following the mailing date to submit its defenses instead of the twenty days a defendant has to answer a complaint.

Rule 4(f)(2) sets forth several methods for serving process in a foreign country that are neither signatories to the Hague Convention nor parties to any other applicable international agreement: 1) the manner prescribed by the law of the foreign country for service in an action in that nation in any of its courts of general jurisdiction; 2) as directed by the foreign authority in response to a formal letter of request from the forum court that proceeds through diplomatic channels and invokes the aid of the addressee court in the country in which service would take place (a time consuming, cumbersome and expensive method of service); and 3) personal delivery upon an individual in a foreign country by any form of mail requiring a signed receipt, to be addressed and dispatched to the party to be served by the clerk of the court.

Rule 4(f)(3) gives the court discretion to order service by any method that is not prohibited by international agreement. For all of the methods, due process requirements of reasonable notice and opportunity to be heard must be satisfied. Courts have approved alternative methods of service such as first-class mail, electronic mail, publication, and telex. See, e.g., *Rio Properties, Inc. v. Rio International Interlink*, 284 F.3d 1007 (9th Cir. 2002) (service by electronic mail was reasonably calculated to inform the defendant about the pendency of the lawsuit as well as the method most likely to reach the defendant). The flexibility of Rule 4(f)(3) is illustrated by *Levin v. Ruby Trading Corporation*, 248 F.Supp. 537 (S.D.N.Y. 1965). The defendant was Canadian, and the plaintiff had tried unsuccessfully to serve him under Rule 4(f)(2) by registered mail and by personal service. Pursuant to a court order, service was then attempted by ordinary mail to the defendant at his Canadian residence. The court upheld the service under the existing version of Rule 4(f)(3), because it provided an alternative to the signed receipt mailing in Rule 4(f)(2).

Problems

1. Adams sues Bursen in federal court. Must or may the process server give the complaint and summons to Bursen personally?

2. Adams sues Bursen in federal court, and Adams personally takes the papers to Bursen's home, leaving them with a 10-year-old girl who answers the door. Was service of process proper?

3. Adams sues Bursen in federal court for trespassing on his large estate, but the process server hands the papers to Bursen at his weekend lakefront cottage in a nearby county. Was service of process proper?

4. Adams sues Bursen in federal court, and the process server leaves the papers with Bursen's limousine driver who answered the door at Bursen's home, because she mistook the driver for Bursen. The driver does not live at Bursen's home. Was service of process proper?

5. Adams sues Bursen in federal court. A procedural rule in the state where the federal court is located permits a process server to leave the papers at the defendant's home, regardless of whether anyone is present at the time. The process server leaves the papers at Bursen's house when no one was at home. Was service of process proper?

6. A state rule allows service by publication if personal service and substituted service methods are unsuccessful. Bursen has avoided numerous attempts by a privately-retained process server to serve him. Adams then invokes the service by publication rule for the required time period, receives no response from Bursen, and then obtains a default judgment against Bursen. When Adams seeks to enforce the judgment by garnishing Bursen's wages, Bursen moves to set aside the default judgment because the notice by publication procedure violates due process. Applying *Mullane*, how should the court rule?

7. Adams sues Bursen in federal court, and Adams properly solicits Bursen to waive service of process. If Bursen fails to respond to Adams's request, is Adams obligated to do anything further?

8. After filing a federal claim against the defendant, Adams attempted to serve Bursen by sending him copies of the summons and complaint, along with the proper forms for waiver of service under Rule 4(d). Bursen fails to return the acknowledgment required by Rule 4. Now that Bursen is aware of the lawsuit, he also manages to avoid Adams's various attempts to have him served under Rule 4(e). However, Adams knows that a procedural rule in his state permits service by publication for defendants who seek to avoid service. Can Adams serve Bursen under the state rule and obtain a default judgment if Bursen fails to answer?

9. Adams sues Bursen, who does business as Bursen's Bike Shop. The process server leaves the papers with Cohn at one of the three bike shops owned by Bursen. Cohn is the manager of the store where he receives the papers intended for Bursen. Was service of process proper?

10. Adams sues Bikes 'R Me, Inc., in federal court. Bursen is President of the corporation. The process server leaves the papers with Bursen's father at the home they share. Was service of process proper?

11. Adams sues Bikes 'R Me, Inc., in federal court. Bursen is President of the corporation. The process server leaves the papers with Cohn at the corporate office. Was service of process proper?

12. Describe the difference between the defense of insufficiency of service of process under Rule 12(b)(5) and the defense of insufficiency of process under Rule 12(b)(4).

Exercise

Because the federal rules permit a plaintiff to serve a defendant under the methods described in the federal rules as well as using the techniques allowed by the state encompassing the federal district where the case is filed or where service is made, it is important to be familiar with the service of process standards in state courts as well. For the state where a) you intend to practice after graduation, b) your law school is located, and/or c) your professor assigns, go to that state's annotated statutes and research the procedural rules by which service of process is made. Based on your research, print the rule and bring it to class for discussion. In addition, answer the following questions.

1.   Identify the minimum requirements for who can serve process.

2.   Identify the methods of service described by rule for serving individuals.

A) Is personal service required?

B) Is substituted (some method other than personal) service permitted? If so, by what method?

1.   First-class mail?

2.   Electronic mail?

3.   Registered or certified mail?

4.   Facsimile transmission?

5.   Serving another person? If so, who, where, and how is the service to be accomplished?

C) Is service by publication permitted? If so, under what circumstances?

1.   Must plaintiff show that attempts to serve by other means were unsuccessful?

2.   Must the papers also be mailed to the defendant to increase likelihood of receipt of the notice?

3.   What types of notice? Posting? Newspaper? Certain types of cases?

3.   Identify the methods of service described by the rule for serving corporations. Are specific persons associated with the corporate entity designated for service, or can anyone in the corporation be served? If the former is true, which corporate positions are designated?

4.   Is waiver of service of process addressed specifically with a set of procedures similar to Federal Rule 4(d)?

5.   Find the long-arm statute you researched earlier in this chapter. Many long-arm statutes specify the method by which service of process using the long-arm must be achieved. Identify the method for service of process under your long-arm statute, and compare it to the methods in your state for serving individuals and corporations.

C. VENUE

Venue relates to the place or places where a lawsuit may be properly instituted. In state practice, venue may be geared to factors such as the county where a defendant resides or where the claim arose. In federal courts, venue is geared to the federal district or the division (where a district is divided into divisions). Unlike subject matter jurisdiction and personal jurisdiction which have their source based in constitutional law, venue is exclusively statutorily based. Venue connotes locality, and places a limitation on the otherwise free choice a plaintiff has to commence a lawsuit in any court which has both subject matter and personal jurisdiction. In general, venue statutes afford a defendant some protection from being forced to defend in a place remote from her residence or remote from the place where the events underlying the controversy occurred. The venue concept developed from the early concept of a jury trial, i.e., that the case be tried in the vicinity of the events giving rise to the claim.

Federal venue generally is governed by 28 U.S.C. § 1391. Unlike diversity of citizenship subject matter jurisdiction and personal jurisdiction, which concentrate on states, federal venue focuses on federal judicial districts. §§ 1391(a)(1) and 1391(b)(1) define proper venue "where any defendant resides," and for individual defendants the majority of courts equates residence with the domicile/citizenship analysis from diversity of citizenship subject matter jurisdiction.

As with personal jurisdiction, venue can be waived, via the Federal Rules (through a failure to raise the issue) or via a contract's forum selection provision (for a forum which otherwise would not be proper under § 1391). Some areas of federal law have their own specialized venue provisions, which explains why § 1391 begins by stating "except as otherwise provided by law..." That "law" would be a specialized venue provision such as 28 U.S.C. § 1400(b), dealing with venue in patent cases.

The defendant's remedy for the plaintiff's selection of an improper venue is to file a timely motion to dismiss based on improper venue under Federal Rule 12(b)(3) or 28 U.S.C. § 1406(a). Another remedy available is to seek a transfer due to improper venue, pursuant to 28 U.S.C. § 1406(a). Even if the venue is proper, a defendant can seek a transfer under 28 U.S.C. § 1404(a). The propriety of venue and the alternative remedies is discussed in the following sections.

INTRODUCTORY PROBLEM

Bob Bigelow had an unfortunate accident on July 1, 2003. While cleaning his home with some friends in Dallas, Texas in preparation for a party, the vacuum cleaner he was using exploded. The blast seriously injured Bigelow, sending him to the hospital for almost a month. The vacuum cleaner was a product of the Sucker Corporation of America (SCOA), which sells its wares in hundreds of its own stores in each state throughout the United States. Indeed, Bigelow purchased the vacuum which detonated at one of SCOA's six Dallas stores. SCOA was incorporated in Delaware in 1927, and its national offices and factories are located in Rhode Island.

Shortly after being discharged from the hospital, Bigelow met with his attorney to discuss a lawsuit against SCOA. After numerous unsuccessful negotiation sessions with SCOA, Bigelow decided to sue SCOA for $1,000,000 on product liability theories (negligence, breach of warranty, strict liability) in the state trial court in Dallas, Texas. Following proper service of process on the managing agent of one of its Dallas stores, SCOA's chief corporate and trial attorneys in Rhode Island decided that a trial in the Texas state court would be a nuisance for SCOA. Because the essence of the lawsuit was an attack on the design and manufacture of the vacuum cleaner, SCOA's attorneys concluded that a trial closer to the corporate offices and the available expert witnesses that SCOA always used would be preferable. In addition, a quick trial is a priority in order to minimize the damage to SCOA's nationwide goodwill. Those attorneys also have concluded that there are no substantive or procedural grounds which can result in the lawsuit being thrown out of state court. They have come to you with the following problem—figure out a way for the case to be tried in the federal court in nearby New Hampshire (which has only one federal district and a relatively clear trial docket).

Governing Law: 28 U.S.C. § 1391.

1. Federal Venue Standards

§ 1391 lists several venue options for a plaintiff to consider. § 1391(a) applies to diversity of citizenship cases, and § 1391(b) applies to federal question cases, even if there is also diversity of citizenship. The first venue option in § 1391(a) and (b) is a district where any defendant resides, with the proviso that when there are several defendants all of them must be shown to reside in the same state. If they do reside in the same state, the district of residence of any one of them is a proper venue. The proviso obviously applies to any state with two or more federal districts. If they do not live in the same state, the defendants' residence is inapplicable, and a plaintiff will have to turn to other criteria.

Under §§ 1391(a)(2) and (b)(2), venue is proper in a district in which a "substantial part" of the activities took place, and there may be several districts that qualify as a situs of "substantial activities." The fact that substantial activities took place in one district does not disqualify another district as a proper venue as long as "substantial" activities took place there, too.

UFFNER v. LA REUNION FRANCAISE, S.A.

244 F.3d 38 (1st Cir. 2001)

TORRUELLA, Chief Judge.

[Uffner filed a diversity action in federal district court in Puerto Rico against his insurer and underwriters for wrongful denial of an insurance claim. The court granted defendants' motions to dismiss due to improper personal jurisdiction and improper venue.]

* * * On June 14, 1997, Uffner departed from Fajardo, Puerto Rico on a voyage to St. Thomas, U.S. Virgin islands. When he was positioned near Isla Palominos, a small island approximately one mile off the coast of Puerto Rico, a fire broke out in the engine room, forcing Uffner to abandon the vessel. The yacht subsequently sank in the same location. Shortly thereafter, Uffner contacted his insurance broker, International Marine Insurance Services ("IMIS") to file a claim for the loss of the boat. After a series of written communications and telephone calls between IMIS and appellees, the claim was denied due to the alleged absence of a "current out-of-water survey."

[The appellate court found the trial court's conclusions about personal jurisdiction were erroneous, and then discussed the venue issue.]

* * * Specifically, the court found that the appellant's claim sounded in contract rather than tort. As such, the court observed, the claim was wholly unrelated to Puerto Rico: the "triggering event" was the denial of the claim and "[t]he issue at bar is the interpretation of the contract." The court also noted that the contract was neither negotiated nor formed in Puerto Rico. Finally, according to the court, the occurrence of the fire in Puerto Rican waters was "a tenuous connection at best."

To begin, the distinction between tort and contract is immaterial to the requirements for venue set forth in the general venue statute, 28 U.S.C. § 1391(a). * * * There is no dispute that § 1391(a)(1) is inapplicable in this case. The question, then, is whether "a substantial part of the events ... giving rise to the claim occurred" in Puerto Rico.

Prior to 1990, § 1391(a) provided venue in "the judicial district ... in which the claim arose." 28 U.S.C. § 1391(a) (1988). * * * The pre-amendment statute ... engendered a plethora of tests to determine the single venue in which the claim "arose." By contrast, many circuits have interpreted the legislative history of the 1990 amendment as evincing Congress's recognition that when the events underlying a claim have taken place in different places, venue may be proper in any number of districts. We look, therefore, not to a single "triggering event" prompting the action, but to the entire sequence of events underlying the claim.

In so doing, we consider the following acts: (1) appellant, a resident of the Virgin Islands, obtained an insurance policy for his yacht, La Mer; (2) the insured vessel caught fire and sank in Puerto Rican waters; (3)

appellant filed a claim with appellees through his insurance broker demanding payment for this loss; and (4) the claim was ultimately denied because it was allegedly not covered by the policy. Though this is merely a skeletal outline of events leading to the claim, for purposes of this appeal, we need just establish that the sinking of La Mer was one part of the historical predicate for the instant suit. It is the only event, however, that occurred in Puerto Rico. For venue to be proper in that district, therefore, the loss of La Mer must be "substantial."

Appellees argue that Uffner's complaint alleges a bad faith denial of his insurance claim, not that the loss itself was due to their fault or negligence. Consequently, they reason, the sinking of the vessel cannot be considered "substantial." It is true, as the district court pointed out, that the legal question in the suit is "whether [an out-of-water survey] was necessary under the terms of the insurance contract." Resolving this issue does not require an investigation into how, when, or why the accident occurred. In this sense, the sinking of Uffner's yacht is not related to the principal question for decision.

However, an event need not be a point of dispute between the parties in order to constitute a substantial event giving rise to the claim. In this case, Uffner's bad faith denial claim alleges that the loss of his yacht was covered by the contract and the payment due to him wrongfully denied. Thus, although the sinking of La Mer is itself not in dispute, the event is connected to the claim inasmuch as Uffner's requested damages include recovery for the loss. We conclude that, in a suit against an insurance company to recover for losses resulting from a vessel casualty, the jurisdiction where that loss occurred is "substantial" for venue purposes.

We add that our conclusion does not thwart the general purpose of statutorily specified venue, which is "to protect the defendant against the risk that a plaintiff will select an unfair or inconvenient place of trial." *Leroy v. Great W. United Corp.*, 443 U.S. 173, 183–84 (1979). First, appellees have not alleged—either below or on appeal—that continuing the suit in the district of Puerto Rico would confer a tactical advantage to appellant or prejudice their own case in any way. We also highlight the absence of a forum-selection clause in the insurance policy indicating appellees' preferred forum for litigation. Finally, appellees conceded at oral argument that they would not object to litigating in the Virgin Islands, suggesting that traveling to the Caribbean would not be unduly burdensome. We therefore hold that venue properly lies in the district of Puerto Rico. * * *

Notes and Questions

1. If tangible property is the subject of the claim, e.g., title to property or damage to property, proper venue lies in any district in which a "substantial part" of the property lies. The physical presence of the property can support venue when the property is the subject of the claim, even if the conduct that made the claim actionable took place elsewhere, e.g., a breach

of contract about a land purchase when negotiations and the signing of the contract occurred in a district different from where the property is located.

2. § 1391(a)(3) provides that in diversity cases, venue is proper in any district in which any defendant is subject to personal jurisdiction. The term "subject" suggests that venue is proper in a district where a defendant could be served, even if she is not actually served there. The good news is that the provision makes venue available merely because personal jurisdiction is available. The bad news is that the provision is available *only* when neither § 1391(a)(1) nor (a)(2) applies. When does § 1391(a)(3) ever apply? It applies when a substantial part of the events occurred outside the United States and either multiple defendants reside in different states or an individual defendant resides outside the United States.

§ 1391(b)(3) applies to federal question cases for all the parties where any defendant may be found, e.g., where a transient defendant is found. The effect of § 1391(b)(3)'s application is to make that district a proper venue for the whole case with respect to all the parties, assuming that there is a method to obtain personal jurisdiction over all defendants in that district. As with § 1391(a)(3), § 1391(b)(3) applies when no other district qualifies as a proper venue under the other two options of § 1391(b).

3. How does § 1391(c) fit in the scheme for defining venue? It is important to note that it does not provide separately for venue in cases involving corporations. Instead, it serves to define corporate residency for § 1391(a) or § 1391(b). Its language applies only to cases in which corporations are defendants, the rationale being that it was added to make it easier to sue a corporation, not to make it easier for corporations to sue. § 1391(c) applies, then, to define the residency of a corporate defendant as any district where the corporation could be served, meaning anywhere personal jurisdiction over the corporation exists. Thus, anywhere that personal jurisdiction exists over a corporation for the instant case, venue will be proper as under § 1391(a)(1) or § 1391(b)(1), regardless of whether personal jurisdiction is based on incorporation, specific jurisdiction, or general jurisdiction.

The relatively complicated part of § 1391(c) comes next. In deciding whether a corporation is subject to personal jurisdiction, the test under § 1391(c) is whether its contacts within that federal *district* (not within that state) were sufficient, if that district were a separate state. If the contacts are satisfied for more than one federal district in the state, the corporation is deemed a resident of each of those districts. However, if the contacts with a state are sufficient but there is not one district where the contacts are sufficient, the corporation is deemed to reside in the district which has the most significant contacts. For a corporation that is incorporated in the state, aren't the contacts equal throughout the state, so that venue is proper in any federal district in the state? However, for specific jurisdiction or general jurisdiction, it would be necessary to establish the requisite contacts in the respective districts.

4. The general removal statute, 28 U.S.C. § 1441, provides that the venue of a removed case is "the district and division embracing the place where such action is pending." Because § 1391 limits venue to the district in which an action was "brought," a case filed in a state court and removed to federal court was not "brought" in the federal court. Thus, once a case is

properly removed to federal court, a defendant cannot move to dismiss on § 1391 venue grounds. See, e.g., *Hollis v. Florida State Univ.*, 259 F.3d 1295 11th Cir. 2001). It is immaterial that the federal court to which the action is removed would not have been in a district of proper venue if the action had been brought there originally.

Problems

After reviewing 28 U.S.C. § 1391, in the following problems identify the districts in which proper venue lies. You may assume that all requirements of federal subject matter jurisdiction are satisfied.

1.   Warner, a resident of Virginia, sues Edwards, a resident of the Western District of North Carolina, on a claim arising out of an automobile accident. Edwards has substantial land holdings in New Mexico. The accident occurred in the Northern District of Illinois when Edwards's brakes apparently failed. Edwards's car, usually serviced in western North Carolina, had been checked by a service station in Minnesota a few days before the accident.

2.   Warner, a resident of Northern District of Virginia, sues Edwards, a resident of the Western District of North Carolina, on a claim based on a federal civil rights violation occurring in the Northern District of Georgia.

3.   Trudeau, a Canadian citizen, sues Stoops, a resident of the Eastern District of Oklahoma, based on a personal injury damage claim arising from an automobile accident in the Western District of Kansas.

4.   In #3, suppose that Stoops had sued Trudeau in a federal court. Where is (are) the proper venue(s)?

5.   Stoops, a resident of the Eastern District of Oklahoma, sues Dole, a citizen of the Western District of Kansas, alleging personal injury damages from an accident in western Kansas.

6.   Clinton, a resident of the Southern District of New York, wants to sue Hillary, Inc., a New York corporation that conducts significant business throughout Virginia and nowhere else. Clinton's claim arises out of that business and is based on federal law.

7.   Boxer, a resident of the Central District of California, and Schmidt, a resident of the Eastern District of Colorado, suffer injuries in a boating accident in Oregon. They sue Moboat Corporation, the boat's manufacturer, alleging negligent design of the boat. The boat was purchased in central California after it was manufactured in the Southern District of Florida at its only factory. Moboat Corporation has its headquarters and is incorporated in Florida. It sells boats in all fifty states, but does continuous and systematic business only in Michigan, Wisconsin, and Pennsylvania.

8.   McCain, a resident of the Southern District of Arizona, wants to sue the *New York Times Corporation* and its publisher, Angus Sulzburger. The *Times* does sufficient business in every district in New York state to be subject to personal jurisdiction there. Sulzburger lives and conducts most business from his home in the Eastern District of New York; he only occasionally visits the offices of the *Times* in the Southern District of New

York. McCain's claim is for common law defamation based on an article in the newspaper.

2. Transferring the Lawsuit

a. By Statute

Regardless of whether venue is proper, it may be possible to transfer a case elsewhere within the same court system. For example, a case filed in the Southern District of New York may be transferred to another federal district if statutory requirements are met. A forum shopping plaintiff may file a claim where venue is proper, but the district where it is filed may have little to do with the parties or the litigation, and may be distant from the locale of the key witnesses.

28 U.S.C. § 1404(a) is the most important of the various statutes providing for transfer of a case, allowing transfer of a case on a defendant's motion to either another federal district or to another federal division in the same district. The premise for using § 1404(a) is that venue is proper under § 1391 or some specialized venue statute where the case currently sits. The statute potentially applies to all civil cases, even cases that were initially filed in a state court but were removed properly to a federal court. A § 1404(a) motion for transfer may be made at any time, but delay in filing the motion is an element considered in a ruling on the motion.

One limitation on transferring a case elsewhere in the system is that it can be shifted only to another district "where it might have been brought." The statute bars transfer unless the transferee court would have 1) been a proper venue, usually measured by any provision of § 1391, not just the one that was used to obtain venue where the case was originally filed; 2) had proper subject matter jurisdiction, which is no problem because the transfer is to another district in the *same court system;* and 3) been a place where the defendant is subject to personal jurisdiction, and specific or general jurisdiction may be used to satisfy personal jurisdiction in the transferee court.

In addition to whether a case "might have been brought" in the transferee court, § 1404(a) contains three explicit standards for the court to consider and balance in exercising its discretion about whether to grant a motion to transfer: the convenience of the parties, the convenience of the witnesses, and the interest of justice.

METEORO AMUSEMENT CORP. v. SIX FLAGS

267 F.Supp.2d 263 (N.D.N.Y. 2003)

MCCURN, Senior District Judge.

Plaintiff, Meteoro Amusement Corp. ("Meteoro"), a New Mexico Corporation with its principal place of business in Lansing, New York, filed this civil action against defendant, Six Flags, Inc. ("SFI"), a Delaware corporation, on July 31, 2002. * * *

The following are the facts as set forth in the complaint. Meteoro is the assignee of the patent, entitled "Modularized Amusement Ride and Training Simulation Device", issued on May 14, 2002. The Modularized Amusement Ride and Training Simulation Device is defined in the abstract of the patent as "[a]n amusement device comprising a modular pod, in which one or more riders sit and are restrained, and which spins under power about a horizontal axis according to the passenger's active control" and "may be used in conjunction with many different types of amusement devices, including, but not limited to roller coasters". Meteoro offered to sell SFI, as well as other companies such as Premier Rides and Arrow Dynamics, Inc., the technology embodied in the patent. In 1998, copies of a video which illustrated this technology were distributed to and presumed viewed by Premier Rides, Arrow Dynamics and SFI, and in 1999 the video was made available for public viewing on Meteoro's website.

In December 2000, defendant SFI announced the anticipated debut of a roller coaster called "X" at its theme park, Magic Mountain, located in Valencia, California. The roller coaster was being manufactured by Arrow Communications. Passengers of the X roller coaster are strapped into vehicles that move 360 degrees forward or backward along a central carriage. * * *

In November 2001, the United States Patent and Trademark Office published the application. The following month, X was opened to a limited audience at Magic Mountain, and was opened to the general public in January 2002. SFI has promoted, and continues to promote X, utilizing, among other things, its website to do so. * * *

Presently before the court [are several preliminary motions to dismiss, which the court denied.] Alternatively, defendant moves this court to transfer venue pursuant to 28 U.S.C. § 1404(a). Plaintiff opposes this motion. * * * The court now ... exercises its discretion to transfer venue to the Western District of Oklahoma pursuant to 28 U.S.C. § 1404(a).

* * * Defendant moves in the alternative for a transfer of venue pursuant to 28 U.S.C. § 1404(a) to the Western District of Oklahoma, or alternatively to the Central District of California or the Southern District of New York. Defendant has made clear that the foregoing is its order of preference, such that its first choice for venue is the Western District of Oklahoma.

[The court found that the case might have been brought in any of the three districts.]

Once the threshold is met, as it is here, the court has discretion to transfer the case, but such a motion will not be granted absent a clear showing by defendant that the balance of convenience factors weighs in favor of a transfer. Moreover, the burden is on the moving party to establish that there should be a change in venue. In determining whether to grant a motion to transfer venue, the following factors may be considered by the court: the convenience to parties; the convenience of witnesses; the relative ease of access to sources of proof; the availability of process to compel attendance of unwilling witnesses; the cost of obtaining willing witnesses; practical problems that make trial of a case easy, expeditious, and inexpensive; and the interests of justice. Further, in this circuit, when a party seeks a transfer based on convenience of witnesses pursuant to [section] 1404(a) he must clearly specify the key witnesses to be called and must make a general statement of their testimony. * * * [T]he relative financial hardship on the litigants and their respective abilities to prosecute or defend an action in a particular forum are legitimate factors to consider. The consideration of comparative calender conditions is also relevant. Finally, the plaintiff's choice of forum is an additional consideration.

Meteoro argues that their choice of forum should be given great weight. * * * [T]he most substantial weight is given to the convenience of witnesses.

Here, defendant SFI argues that the convenience of witnesses militates in favor of transfer to the Western District of Oklahoma. Since the majority of witnesses will be from Oklahoma City, where SFI's corporate offices are located, and presumably plaintiff will only have two witnesses, SFI argues it will be much more convenient for them to travel to the local federal courthouse than to the Northern District of New York.

* * * Defendant's list includes two categories of witnesses: those who will testify about the purchase of X from Arrow Communications, and those who will testify about its "design, development, structure, function, manufacture and operation". Additionally, defendant expects eight witnesses from Arrow Communications to testify regarding "the design, development, structure, function and manufacture of the X–Coaster ride, the sale of the ride to SFTPI, the documents and circumstances surrounding that sale, the financial and business records of Arrow, the cost, profits, and revenues relating to the sale of the X coaster." These witnesses are all located in Utah.

Plaintiff argues that the majority of "relevant" testimony will come from its witnesses, including its CEO and inventor of the patented devices at issue in this case, John F. Mares. Mr. Mares resides in the Northern District of New York and is the only person active in the operation of the plaintiff corporation. In addition to operating Meteoro, Mr. Mares is employed as a Vice President for a corporation located in Ithaca, New York. Mr. Mares avers that for the foregoing reasons, it would be a severe hardship for him to litigate his claim in another district. At oral argument, plaintiff's counsel identified an additional witness, Bob Perls, who is associated with Meteoro but resides in New Mexico. Counsel for plaintiff also suggested that Meteoro may require expert testimony and would seek to find such an expert within this District.

Defense counsel noted at oral argument that Mr. Mares will be deposed in this district "no matter what." Moreover, defendant argues that for the majority of witnesses, including Mr. Perls and the attorney who prosecuted one of the patents at issue in this case, who also resides in New Mexico, it would be more inconvenient to travel to the Northern District of New York than it would to travel to Oklahoma or California. Plaintiff counters that for most of the potential witnesses defendant identifies, deposition testimony can be taken where they are located, so the inconvenience of travel will be on the parties, not the witnesses. In addition, whichever venue the court chooses, some witnesses will be inconvenienced by travel, and the costs associated with a longer traveling distance are not a substantial enough showing of inconvenience to outweigh the plaintiff's choice of forum.

SFI also argues that the availability of process to compel the testimony of unwilling witnesses is an important factor. Plaintiff contends that any testimony proffered by defendant regarding the design and construction of X is irrelevant, since the roller coaster was built prior to the issuance of the patents defendant allegedly infringed, although defendant counters such testimony is relevant to plaintiff's allegation of willfulness. Moreover, as plaintiff previously argued, and the court tends to agree, non-party witnesses would be deposed where they are located, and defendant failed to identify any reason why this would not be so.

There is also disagreement between the parties as to whether a firsthand viewing of the alleged infringing roller coaster would be necessary, a factor that if proved important would militate in favor of the Central District of California as the proper venue. At oral argument, Defense counsel argued that photographs or design blueprints of the alleged infringing roller coaster will not be sufficient to show a jury whether said coaster, as it currently exists, is infringing plaintiff's patents.

Additionally, defense counsel argues the location of most documents needed for litigation is SFI's headquarters in Oklahoma City. Although the documents can be shipped, this involves an added cost and inconvenience that should weigh in favor of a transfer of venue to the Western District of Oklahoma.

Finally, Meteoro argues that the disparities in the financial means of the parties weighs greatly in favor of denying SFI's motion to transfer. Plaintiff cites the affidavit of its president as evidence of the hardship a transfer would cause, but cites no authority for its allegation that defendant has over one billion dollars in annual revenue. Counsel for plaintiff argues that a transfer to any of the three districts defendant suggests would require that Meteoro retain local counsel, and thereby incur additional costs.

The court finds, after weighing the evidence before it, that venue is most proper in the Western District of Oklahoma. Defendant's headquarters, as well as a near majority of potential witnesses, are located in Oklahoma City. The only factor weighing in favor of the Central District of California, aside from it being the location of a small number of potential witnesses, is that it is the location of the alleged infringing roller coaster. However, there is disagreement as to the evidentiary significance of a viewing of the roller coaster by being in its presence instead of viewing photographs or design blueprints. Further, very little evidence was submitted regarding the appropriateness of the Southern District of New York as a venue, except that defendant has offices there. Finally, the court has already found that the Northern District is an improper venue. Plaintiff's main witness, John Mares, who resides in the Northern District, will be inconvenienced regardless of the forum the Court chooses. The only additional witness specified by plaintiff is located in New Mexico and will likewise be inconvenienced by the Court's choice of forum. * * * Based on the foregoing, defendant's . . . request for a transfer of venue to the Western District of Oklahoma is hereby granted. * * *

Notes and Questions

1. Did the court apply the correct statute? Notice that the court observed that venue in the Northern District of New York was "improper."

2. *Convenience of the parties.* If the transfer's effect would merely shift any inconvenience from the defendant to the plaintiff, the motion to transfer is likely to be denied. The defendant moving for transfer must show that the original forum is inconvenient for it and that the plaintiff would not be substantially inconvenienced by the transfer. The trial court may consider the parties' financial strength as well as their physical condition. Indeed, sometimes it will condition the transfer on the willingness of the defendant to bear specified expenses of the plaintiff to transfer the case.

3. *Convenience of the witnesses.* It is a powerful argument against transfer if the forum chosen by the plaintiff will be the most convenient for the witnesses. The evaluation is based on the convenience for the key witnesses, as opposed to the convenience for all the witnesses. Because a motion to transfer is usually filed early in the life of a lawsuit, the identities of the key witnesses still may be unclear.

What type of proof would persuade a court that a transfer for the "convenience of the witnesses" should be granted? Of what relevance is it to know 1) what helpful testimony a distant witness would provide; 2) the availability of expert witnesses in the transferee district; and 3) the convenience for counsel?

4. *Interest of justice.* Your ability to argue that the interest of justice favors your client should be limited only by your creativity, but most of the case law giving importance to this factor falls into two categories. The "interest of justice" may be served by the avoidance of multiple lawsuits from a single transaction. It may be in the "interest of justice" to transfer a case to a forum where other cases are pending from the same transaction so that the pending cases and the transferred case possibly can be consolidated. If Able sues Baker in the Eastern District of Florida, and Charlie has sued Baker in the Northern District of Tennessee and both cases are based on the same transaction, Baker may attempt to transfer one of the cases to the location of the other case. Or, transfer may be in the "interest of justice" if transfer enables the plaintiff to gain personal jurisdiction over an additional

defendant who was not subject to process in the original forum. Able sued Baker in the Eastern District of Florida and Baker moves for a change of venue to the Northern District of Tennessee so that Able would be able to join Charlie as a co-defendant along with Baker.

The second category of case where the "interest of justice" may be served by transfer is where an earlier trial date is easier to obtain because of a less crowded docket in the transferee court. Keep in mind that these three balancing factors are relevant only if the lawsuit "might have been brought" by the plaintiff in the district where your client would like to have the case transferred.

The interest of justice also may relate to a party's inability to obtain a fair trial, e.g., from media attention. See Chapter 9, dealing with the right to trial by jury.

5.   Recall that when a lawsuit is filed, venue could have been achieved by the defendant's consent to be sued in that district. However, the United States Supreme Court in *Hoffman v. Blaski*, 363 U.S. 335, 80 S.Ct. 1084, 4 L.Ed.2d 1254 (1960) held that the defendant's consent to have a case transferred is irrelevant in determining whether a district is one in which the suit "might have been brought." That phrase directs the court's attention to the situation that existed when the lawsuit was filed, i.e., where the plaintiff could have sued, independent of the defendant's wishes.

Hoffman established that a defendant's consent does not permit transfer to a forum where the lawsuit could not originally have been brought. Does that result follow from the statutory language? Not likely. On the other hand, wouldn't an opposite conclusion effectively strike the words "where it might have been brought" from the statute? Wouldn't an opposite holding also turn § 1404(a) into a method for forum shopping by defendants? A defendant sued in a forum that is not the most convenient could choose whether to consent to transfer or insist that the case remain in the inconvenient court.

6.   One potential motive for seeking a change of venue is that the defendant would count on a different substantive law applying in a federal district located in another state. The Supreme Court took care of that tactic in *Van Dusen v. Barrack*, 376 U.S. 612, 84 S.Ct. 805, 11 L.Ed.2d 945 (1964) by holding that the same law applies after a transfer as applied prior to the change of venue. The *Van Dusen* principle applies in diversity cases and regardless of which party moves for transfer. *Ferens v. John Deere Company*, 494 U.S. 516, 110 S.Ct. 1274, 108 L.Ed.2d 443 (1990).

The procedural transfer therefore is strictly procedural without any accompanying substantive advantage for the moving party. If the substantive law in the district where the case is filed is unclear, does that argue against transfer? If so, the assumption is that the original judge is better able to figure out the law than a judge would in the transferee state. If the effect of *Van Dusen* is not to change the applicable law after transfer, the "interest of justice" argument that transfer can facilitate consolidation with a case already filed in the transferee district is doubtful.

The effect of *Van Dusen* may raise another concern, though, about the expanded scope of available districts for venue created by the provisions in

§§ 1391(a)(2) and (b)(2). Assuming that the "substantial part" standard increases the number of districts where a case could be filed, what prevents a plaintiff from filing in the (proper venue) district that also supplies the preferred substantive law and then not caring much about a defendant's motion to transfer under § 1404(a)? In other words, by the time the motion for transfer is filed, the plaintiff has the benefit of the law that would produce the best result.

7. § 1406(a) transfer is an alternative change of venue statute to § 1404(a). The primary difference between the two provisions is that the premise for using § 1406(a) is that venue where the case currently sits is *improper,* e.g., it violates § 1391. Another difference in the statutes is that the remedy available under § 1406(a) is to either transfer the case or to dismiss it. Why the latter remedy? Because venue in the current district is improper. Both § 1406(a) and Federal Rule 12(b)(3) provide for dismissal of a lawsuit in which the venue is improper. Is a motion to dismiss under § 1406(a) permitted, even when the time for filing a motion under Rule 12(b)(3) to dismiss the complaint has passed? Compare *Steward v. Up No. Plastics, Inc.*, 177 F.Supp.2d 953 (D.Minn. 2001)(passage of significant time and motion practice precludes § 1406 motion) with *Ptaszyneki v. Ferrell*, 277 F.Supp. 969 (E.D.Tenn. 1967)(transfer permitted even though objection to improper venue was waived).

§ 1406(a) transfer may be used by a court as an alternative remedy to a defendant's motion to dismiss under Federal Rule 12(b)(3). The criteria for granting a motion to transfer under § 1406(a) is the "interest of justice" and whether the lawsuit "could have been brought" in the district where to which transfer is attempted. When might it be in the "interest of justice" to transfer a case to a proper forum rather than dismiss the lawsuit? The main example of the criterion's application occurs when the statute of limitations has already run on the plaintiff's claim. Dismissal would prevent a new lawsuit from being refiled by the plaintiff, but transferring the case is deemed to be a continuation of the original filing.

An assessment of whether a case "could have been brought" in the transferee district under § 1406(a) is comparable to the analysis under § 1404(a): whether the transferee court would have 1) been a proper venue; 2) had proper subject matter jurisdiction; and 3) been a place where the defendant is subject to personal jurisdiction.

8. Does the *Van Dusen* principle mentioned in note 6 apply in the § 1406(a) context? Should the law of the place where the lawsuit was originally filed apply if the case was filed in the wrong place (venue)? Wouldn't that result reward the plaintiff for filing in the wrong court? See, e.g., *Fanselow v. Rice*, 213 F.Supp.2d 1077 (D. Neb. 2002) (law of transferee court applies).

9. As with personal jurisdiction, venue is decided on a party-by-party basis. The trial court may dismiss the lawsuit as to one party as a result of improper venue, and continue the litigation for the other parties for whom venue is proper. Or, in the context of a motion to transfer, a court may transfer a case under § 1404(a) for the defendant for whom venue is proper, and approve the transfer under § 1406 for the party for whom venue is currently improper.

b. *By Forum Non Conveniens*

Sometimes, a distant and inconvenient forum may have personal jurisdiction over a defendant, but the mere existence of power to adjudicate a claim against a defendant does not necessarily mean that the court should exercise that power. "Forum non conveniens" is a common law doctrine that in its modern conception allows a court to dismiss a claim so that it can be brought in a more appropriate forum *in another court system*. Its application is discretionary with the trial court.

PIPER AIRCRAFT CO. v. REYNO

454 U.S. 235, 102 S.Ct. 252, 70 L.Ed.2d 419 (1981)

Justice MARSHALL delivered the opinion of the Court.

[Five Scottish citizens perished in an air crash in Scotland. Reyno, the legal secretary for the decedents' survivors' attorney brought wrongful-death actions against aircraft and propeller manufacturers from Pennsylvania and Ohio in a California state court. The case was removed to California federal court, and then transferred to United States District Court for the Middle District of Pennsylvania, where the defendants moved to dismiss on the ground of *forum non conveniens*. The District Court granted their motions, noting that an alternative forum existed in Scotland.

The trial court relied on the balancing test from *Gulf Oil Corp. v. Gilbert,* 330 U.S. 501 (1947). There, "to guide trial court discretion, the Court provided a list of 'private interest factors' affecting the convenience of the litigants, and a list of 'public interest factors' affecting the convenience of the forum."

The factors pertaining to the private interests of the litigants included the "relative ease of access to sources of proof; availability of compulsory process for attendance of unwilling, and the cost of obtaining attendance of willing, witnesses; possibility of view of premises, if view would be appropriate to the action; and all other practical problems that make trial of a case easy, expeditious and inexpensive." The public factors bearing on the question included the administrative difficulties flowing from court congestion; the "local interest in having localized controversies decided at home"; the interest in having the trial of a diversity case in a forum that is at home with the law that must govern the action; the avoidance of unnecessary problems in conflict of laws, or in the application of foreign law; and the unfairness of burdening citizens in an unrelated forum with jury duty.]

After describing our decisions in *Gilbert*, the District Court analyzed the facts of these cases. It began by observing that an alternative forum existed in Scotland; Piper and Hartzell had agreed to submit to the jurisdiction of the Scottish courts and to waive any statute of limitations defense that might be available. It then stated that plaintiff's choice of forum was entitled to little weight. The court recognized that a plaintiff's choice ordinarily deserves substantial deference. It noted, however, that Reyno "is a representative of foreign citizens and residents seeking a forum in the United States because of the more liberal rules concerning products liability law," and that "the courts have been less solicitous when the plaintiff is not an American citizen or resident, and particularly when the foreign citizens seek to benefit from the more liberal tort rules provided for the protection of citizens and residents of the United States."

The District Court next examined several factors relating to the private interests of the litigants, and determined that these factors strongly pointed towards Scotland as the appropriate forum. Although evidence concerning the design, manufacture, and testing of the plane and propeller is located in the United States, the connections with Scotland are otherwise "overwhelming." The real parties in interest are citizens of Scotland, as were all the decedents. Witnesses who could testify regarding the maintenance of the aircraft, the training of the pilot, and the investigation of the accident—all essential to the defense—are in Great Britain. Moreover, all witnesses to damages are located in Scotland. Trial would be aided by familiarity with Scottish topography, and by easy access to the wreckage.

The District Court reasoned that because crucial witnesses and evidence were beyond the reach of compulsory process, and because the defendants would not be able to implead potential Scottish third-party defendants, it would be "unfair to make Piper and Hartzell proceed to trial in this forum." The survivors had brought separate actions in Scotland against the pilot, McDonald, and Air Navigation. "[I]t would be fairer to all parties and less costly if the entire case was presented to one jury with available testimony from all relevant witnesses." Ibid. Although the court recognized that if trial were held in the United States, Piper and Hartzell could file indemnity or contribution actions against the Scottish defendants, it believed that there was a significant risk of inconsistent verdicts.

The District Court concluded that the relevant public interests also pointed strongly towards dismissal. The court determined that Pennsylvania law would apply to Piper and Scottish law to Hartzell if the case were tried in the Middle District of Pennsylvania. As a result, "trial in this forum would be hopelessly complex and confusing for a jury." In addition, the court noted that it was unfamiliar with Scottish law and thus would have to rely upon experts from that country. The court also found that the trial would be enormously costly and time-consuming; that it would be unfair to burden citizens with jury duty when the Middle District of Pennsylvania has little connection with the controversy; and that Scotland has a substantial interest in the outcome of the litigation.

In opposing the motions to dismiss, respondent contended that dismissal would be unfair because Scottish law was less favorable. The District Court explicitly rejected this claim. It reasoned that the possibility that dismissal might lead to an unfavorable change in the law did not deserve significant weight; any deficiency in the foreign law was a "matter to be dealt with in the foreign forum."

On appeal, the United States Court of Appeals for the Third Circuit reversed and remanded for trial. The decision to reverse appears to be based on two alternative grounds. First, the Court held that the District Court abused its discretion in conducting the *Gilbert* analysis. Second, the Court held that dismissal is never appropriate where the law of the alternative forum is less favorable to the plaintiff.

The Court of Appeals began its review of the District Court's Gilbert analysis by noting that the plaintiff's choice of forum deserved substantial weight, even though the real parties in interest are nonresidents. It then rejected the District Court's balancing of the private interests. It found that Piper and Hartzell had failed adequately to support their claim that key witnesses would be unavailable if trial were held in the United States: they had never specified the witnesses they would call and the testimony these witnesses would provide. The Court of Appeals gave little weight to the fact that Piper and Hartzell would not be able to implead potential Scottish third-party defendants, reasoning that this difficulty would be "burdensome" but not "unfair," 639 F.2d, at 162. Finally, the court stated that resolution of the suit would not be significantly aided by familiarity with Scottish topography, or by viewing the wreckage.

The Court of Appeals also rejected the District Court's analysis of the public interest factors. It found that the District Court gave undue emphasis to the application of Scottish law: " 'the mere fact that the court is called upon to determine and apply foreign law does not present a legal problem of the sort which would justify the dismissal of a case otherwise properly before the court.' " In any event, it believed that Scottish law need not be applied. After conducting its own choice-of-law analysis, the Court of Appeals determined that American law would govern the actions against both Piper and Hartzell. The same choice-of-law analysis apparently led it to conclude that Pennsylvania and Ohio, rather than Scotland, are the jurisdictions with the greatest policy interests in the dispute, and that all other public interest factors favored trial in the United States.

II

The Court of Appeals erred in holding that plaintiffs may defeat a motion to dismiss on the ground of *forum non conveniens* merely by showing that the substantive law that would be applied in the alternative forum is less favorable to the plaintiffs than that of the present forum. The possibility of a change in substantive law should ordinarily not be given conclusive or even substantial weight in the *forum non conveniens* inquiry.

* * * The Court of Appeals' decision is inconsistent with this Court's earlier *forum non conveniens* decisions in another respect. Those decisions have repeatedly emphasized the need to retain flexibility. * * *

In fact, if conclusive or substantial weight were given to the possibility of a change in law, the *forum non conveniens* doctrine would become virtually useless. Jurisdiction and venue requirements are often easily satisfied. As a result, many plaintiffs are able to choose from among several forums. Ordinarily, these plaintiffs will select that forum whose choice-of-law rules are most advantageous. Thus, if the possibility of an unfavorable change in substantive law is given substantial weight in the *forum non conveniens* inquiry, dismissal would rarely be proper. * * *

The Court of Appeals' approach is not only inconsistent with the purpose of the forum non conveniens doctrine, but also poses substantial practical problems. If the possibility of a change in law were given substantial weight, deciding motions to dismiss on the ground of *forum non conveniens* would become quite difficult. Choice-of-law analysis would become extremely important, and the courts would frequently be required to interpret the law of foreign jurisdictions. * * * The doctrine of *forum non conveniens*, however, is designed in part to help courts avoid conducting complex exercises in comparative law. As we stated in Gilbert, the public interest factors point towards dismissal where the court would be required to "untangle problems in conflict of laws, and in law foreign to itself."

Upholding the decision of the Court of Appeals would result in other practical problems. At least where the foreign plaintiff named an American manufacturer as defendant, a court could not dismiss the case on grounds of *forum non conveniens* where dismissal might lead to an unfavorable change in law. The American courts, which are already extremely attractive to foreign plaintiffs, would become even more attractive. The flow of litigation into the United States would increase and further congest already crowded courts. * * *

We do not hold that the possibility of an unfavorable change in law should never be a relevant consideration in a *forum non conveniens* inquiry. Of course, if the remedy provided by the alternative forum is so clearly inadequate or unsatisfactory that it is no remedy at all, the unfavorable change in law may be given substantial weight; the district court may conclude that dismissal would not be in the interests of justice. In these cases, however, the remedies that would be provided by the Scottish courts do not fall within this category. Although the relatives of the decedents may not be able to rely on a strict liability theory, and although their potential damages award may be smaller, there is no danger that they will be deprived of any remedy or treated unfairly.

III

The Court of Appeals also erred in rejecting the District Court's *Gilbert* analysis. * * *

A

The District Court acknowledged that there is ordinarily a strong presumption in favor of the plaintiff's choice of forum, which may be overcome only when the private and public interest factors clearly point towards trial in the alternative forum. It held, however, that the presumption applies with less force when the plaintiff or real parties in interest are foreign.

The District Court's distinction between resident or citizen plaintiffs and foreign plaintiffs is fully justified. * * * When the home forum has been chosen, it is reasonable to assume that this choice is convenient. When the plaintiff is foreign, however, this assumption is much less reasonable. Because the central purpose of any *forum non conveniens* inquiry is to ensure that the trial is convenient, a foreign plaintiff's choice deserves less deference.

B

The *forum non conveniens* determination is committed to the sound discretion of the trial court. * * * In examining the District Court's analysis of the public and private interests, however, the Court of Appeals seems to have lost sight of this rule, and substituted its own judgment for that of the District Court.

(1)

In analyzing the private interest factors, the District Court stated that the connections with Scotland are "overwhelming." This characterization may be somewhat exaggerated. Particularly with respect to the question of relative ease of access to sources of proof, the private interests point in both directions. As respondent emphasizes, records concerning the design, manufacture, and testing of the propeller and plane are located in the United States. She would have greater access to sources of proof relevant to her strict liability and negligence theories if trial were held here. However, the District Court did not act unreasonably in concluding that fewer evidentiary problems would be posed if the trial were held in Scotland. A large proportion of the relevant evidence is located in Great Britain. * * *

The District Court correctly concluded that the problems posed by the inability to implead potential third-party defendants clearly supported holding the trial in Scotland. * * * The Court of Appeals rejected this argument. Forcing petitioners to rely on actions for indemnity or contributions would be "burdensome" but not "unfair." Finding that trial in the plaintiff's chosen forum would be burdensome, however, is sufficient to support dismissal on grounds of *forum non conveniens*.

(2)

The District Court's review of the factors relating to the public interest was also reasonable. * * *

Scotland has a very strong interest in this litigation. The accident occurred in its airspace. All of the decedents were Scottish. Apart from Piper and Hartzell, all potential plaintiffs and defendants are either Scottish or English. As we stated in Gilbert, there is "a local interest in having localized controversies decided at home." Respondent argues that American citizens have an interest in ensuring that American manufacturers are deterred from producing defective products, and that additional deterrence might be obtained if Piper and Hartzell were tried in the United States, where they could be sued on the basis of both negligence and strict liability. However, the incremental deterrence that would be gained if this trial were held in an American court is likely to be insignificant. The American interest in this accident is simply not sufficient to justify the enormous commitment of judicial time and resources that would inevitably be required if the case were to be tried here.

IV

The District Court * * * did not act unreasonably in deciding that the private interests pointed towards trial in Scotland. Nor did it act unreasonably in deciding that the public interests favored trial in Scotland. Thus, the judgment of the Court of Appeals is reversed.

Notes and Questions

1. In the federal system, intra-system transfer provisions like § 1404(a) supersede the common law notion of *forum non conveniens*. However, it is still a tool for dismissal and deference 1) by the courts of one state to another state, e.g., a New York court might dismiss a claim so that it can brought in Colorado; or 2) by a federal or state court to a foreign court, as in *Piper*. The premise for using *forum non conveniens* is that the current venue and jurisdiction of a case are proper, but the only remedy for a finding of *forum non conveniens* is dismissal. Compare that remedy with the motions to transfer under § 1404(a) and § 1406(a).

2. A common rationale for *forum non conveniens* is a concern that foreign cases will flood American courts. As one British judge has stated:

> As a moth is drawn to light, so is a litigant drawn to the United States. If he can only get his case into their courts, he stands to win a fortune. At no cost to himself, and at no risk of having to pay anything to the other side. The lawyers there will conduct the case ... on a "contingency fee" ... There is also in the United States a right to trial by jury. These are prone to award fabulous damages. They are notoriously sympathetic and know that the lawyers will take their 40 per cent. All this means that the defendant can readily be forced into a settlement. The plaintiff holds all the cards.

Smith Kline & French Laboratories Ltd. v. Bloch, 1 W.L.R. 730 (C.A. 1982).

3. Invoking *forum non conveniens* requires that there is in fact an adequate and alternative court in which the lawsuit can be maintained. What is an "adequate" forum? As you read, *Piper* emphasized that less

favorable foreign substantive law does not make the alternative forum "inadequate." An adequate remedy exists when the parties have a remedy available elsewhere, even though it may be less than an American court would grant the plaintiff.

The court will not dismiss a claim unless it lacks the authority to transfer the claim to an alternative forum, e.g., another state court or a foreign court. That alternative court may be the result of the trial court making the defendant's agreement to being subject to personal jurisdiction elsewhere a condition for the dismissal. If the alternative court refuses to take the claim, the original trial court will set aside its order dismissing because it erroneously assumed that another court was willing to adjudicate the case.

4. Not only must there be an adequate alternative forum, there must be an "available" alternative forum where the parties can be within the jurisdiction of a foreign court. *In re Union Carbide Corp. Gas Plant Disaster at Bhopal, India*, 634 F.Supp. 842 (S.D.N.Y. 1986) denied plaintiffs' argument that the legal system of India, which included filing fees of nearly 5% of the damages sought, heavy backlogs, and less favorable tort damages, was inadequate and unavailable. By contrast, the corrupt nature of a foreign court may persuade a federal court that there is no available forum. See, e.g., *Eastman Kodak Co. v. Kavlin*, 978 F.Supp. 1078 (S.D.Fla. 1997) (Bolivian courts deemed "too corrupt to permit fair adjudication of plaintiffs' claims").

5. A court may condition a dismissal on *forum non conveniens* grounds to insure that the lawsuit can be filed in another court, i.e., to be sure that the alternative forum is adequate. For example, if a claim is barred by the statute of limitations under foreign law, the American court will require the defendants to waive any limitations defense in order to make the forum adequate. See *Bank of Credit and Commerce International Ltd. v. State Bank of Pakistan*, 273 F.3d 241 (2d Cir. 2001). Of course, the more certain a court is that a foreign court will hear the case, the fewer conditions if any that need to be imposed.

6. Assuming that there is an adequate, available forum, the balancing of the *Gilbert* private and public factors must strongly favor dismissal. You probably noticed that the *Gilbert* factors overlap with the "fair play" factors from personal jurisdiction, leaving you with the impression that if personal jurisdiction is reasonable a court also is unlikely to find that the convenience factors favor dismissal.

Likewise, the balancing of public and private factors for *forum non conveniens* is similar to the considerations in evaluating a change of venue motion under § 1404(a). However, the Court has predictably held that less inconvenience is necessary to obtain a transfer than is necessary to support a dismissal under *forum non conveniens*. *Norwood v. Kirkpatrick*, 349 U.S. 29, 75 S.Ct. 544, 99 L.Ed. 789 (1955).

7. The defendant has the burden of proof, because as *Gilbert* stated, "the plaintiff's choice of forum should rarely be disturbed." On the other hand, when the plaintiff is not American, courts accord less deference to the plaintiff's choice of forum. The choice of forum then is presumed to be less convenient than when an American plaintiff files the claim.

8. If a defendant forgets/neglects to file a timely Rule 12(b)(3) motion to dismiss for improper venue, can she nevertheless file a motion to dismiss based on *forum non conveniens*? One premise for seeking a dismissal under *forum non conveniens* is that venue is currently proper, validating dismissal on *forum non conveniens* in favor of an alternative court. (On the other hand, if venue is *improper*, a court can dismiss the case under a Rule 12(b)(3) motion or can transfer the case under § 1406(a).) While a belated motion is likely to be denied, the fairness and convenience related to the *forum non conveniens* motion inquiry may suggest that a delay could be justified due to the need to investigate alternative jurisdictions, foreign and domestic, in which the case could be heard. See *Jacobs v. Felix Bloch Erben Verlag fur Buhne Film*, 160 F.Supp.2d 722 (S.D.N.Y. 2001).

Problems

In the following problems, identify which transfer mechanism (§ 1404(a), § 1406(a), § 1441, or *forum non conveniens*), without analyzing the transfer under the provision or concept you select, would be proper to transfer the lawsuit.

1. Shelton, a resident of the Central District of California, sues William, a resident of the Southern District of New York, for injuries suffered in an automobile accident. William owned the vehicle at the time of the accident in the Eastern District of North Carolina. The lawsuit was filed in the Central District of California. The defendant wants to transfer the case, and he asks you for your advice on the feasibility of moving the case to:

    A. The Eastern District of North Carolina;

    B. The Southern District of New York; or

    C. A New York state court.

2. Shelton, a resident of the Central District of California, sues William, a resident of the Southern District of New York, and Samuel, a resident of Wales who is in the United States on a student visa, for injuries suffered in a automobile accident. William owned the vehicle which was driven by Samuel at the time of the accident in the Eastern District of North Carolina. The lawsuit was filed in a North Carolina state court which is located in the Eastern District of North Carolina . The defendants want to transfer the case, and they ask you for your advice on the feasibility of moving the case to:

    A. The Eastern District of North Carolina;

    B. The Southern District of New York;

    C. A New York state court; or

    D. A court in Wales.

3. Shelton, a resident of the Central District of California, sues William, a resident of the Southern District of New York, for injuries suffered in an automobile accident. William currently attends graduate school in Wales. William drove and owned the vehicle at the time of the accident in the Southern District of New York. The lawsuit was filed in a New York state court which is located in the Southern District of New York. The defendants

want to transfer the case, and they ask you for your advice on the feasibility of moving the case to:

    A.   The Southern District of New York;

    B.   A California state court; or

    C.   A court in Wales.

    4.   Shelton, a resident of the Central District of California, sues William and Samuel, both police officers and both residents of the Southern District of New York, for violation of his federal civil rights which resulted in injuries suffered from a beating during a routine traffic stop. William has retired from the police department and is currently enrolled in graduate school in New Hampshire. William owned the vehicle which was driven by Samuel at the time of the stop in the Northern District of New York. The lawsuit was filed in a New York state court which is located in the Northern District of New York. The defendants want to transfer the case, and they ask you for your advice on the feasibility of moving the case to:

    A.   The Northern District of New York;

    B.   The Southern District of New York; or

    C.   A New Hampshire state court.

D.   RULE 12(b) PROCEDURAL CHALLENGES

If a defendant moves to dismiss under Rule 12(b), per Rule 12(g) the motion must include all defenses and objections then available that Rule 12 permits to be raised by motion. The defendant cannot make a second pre-answer motion raising other defenses or objections. For example, a defendant who makes a motion to dismiss a complaint for failure to state a claim on which relief can be granted cannot thereafter raise, either by motion or in its answer, defenses such as lack of personal jurisdiction, improper venue, insufficiency of process, or insufficiency of service of process. Rule 12(h) contains several exceptions to the rule that a defense of objection is waived if it not made by answer or by motion. As you learned in Chapter 3, an objection that a lack of subject matter jurisdiction is never waived, per Rule 12(h)(3).

The defenses of 1) failure to state a claim for relief on which relief can be granted, 2) failure to join an indispensable party, and 3) failure to state a legal defense to a claim do not have to be asserted at the earliest opportunity. Under Rule 12(h)(2), they may be made later in a pleading, a post-answer motion, or at the trial. After trial, the three objections cannot be raised.

A defendant choosing to assert defenses and objections in an answer rather than by raising them in a Rule 12(b) motion waives most defenses or objections that are not included in the answer. If a subsequent judgment in a case is taken to another jurisdiction to be enforced, i.e., to be collected, the latter jurisdiction's viewpoint about whether to permit the judgment-loser in the first state to raise a jurisdictional issue in the enforcement action depends on what happened in the first jurisdiction's case. For example, if an objection to personal jurisdiction was raised in the first case, the court where the judgment is taken to be enforced will not permit the issue to be retried.

In brief, Rule 12(g) bars successive pre-answer Rule 12 motions. Rule 12(h)(1)(A) bars successive Rule 12 pre-answer motions and/or successive Rule 12 motions in the answer. Rule 12(h)(1)(B) prohibits a Rule 12 objection altogether if it is not made either as a pre-answer motion or as a Rule 12 motion in the answer. All of these timing rules are subject to the explicit exceptions in Rule 12(h)(2) and 12(h)(3).

Problems

1. Letterman sues Leno for defamation. Leno files a timely motion to dismiss the complaint for insufficient process. The judge denies the motion. Can Leno then move to dismiss for lack of personal jurisdiction?

2. Letterman sues Leno for defamation. Leno files a timely motion to dismiss the complaint for lack of subject matter jurisdiction. The judge denies the motion. Can Leno then move to dismiss for lack of personal jurisdiction?

3. Letterman sues Leno for defamation. Leno files a timely motion to dismiss the complaint for insufficient process. The judge denies the motion. Can Leno then move to dismiss for lack of subject matter jurisdiction?

4. Letterman sues Leno for defamation. Leno files a timely motion to dismiss the complaint for insufficient process. The judge denies the motion. Can Leno answer, raising the defense of lack of personal jurisdiction?

5. Letterman sues Leno for defamation. If Leno decides to answer the complaint rather than filing a Rule 12(b) motion to dismiss, can Leno include a defense of insufficient process in the answer?

6. Letterman sues Leno for defamation. If Leno moves to dismiss the complaint for insufficiency of service of process, may or must Leno move at the same time to dismiss for lack of personal jurisdiction?

7. Letterman sues Leno for defamation in Missouri. Leno files a timely motion to dismiss the complaint for lack of personal jurisdiction. The judge grants the motion. What is the effect of granting the motion?

8. Letterman sues Leno for defamation in Missouri. Leno answers the complaint and defends the case on its merits. Before trial begins Leno files a motion to dismiss the complaint for lack of personal jurisdiction. How should the court react?

9. Letterman sues Leno for defamation in Missouri. Leno answers the complaint and defends the case on its merits and loses. Letterman files suit in Illinois to enforce the Missouri judgment. Leno moves to dismiss the Illinois action, saying that the Missouri court lacked personal jurisdiction over him. How should the court react?

10. Letterman sues Leno for defamation in Missouri. Leno ignores the complaint and the Missouri court issues a default judgment for Letterman. Letterman takes the Missouri judgment to Illinois to enforce. Leno defends

against the enforcement action on the ground that Missouri lacked personal jurisdiction over him. How should the court react?

11.   Letterman sues Leno for defamation in Missouri. Leno files a timely motion to dismiss the complaint for lack of personal jurisdiction. The judge denies the motion. Leno does nothing else in the lawsuit and the court awards Letterman a default judgment. Letterman takes the Missouri judgment to Illinois for enforcement. How should the Illinois court react to any motion by Leno to dismiss the Illinois enforcement action?

Chapter 5

PLEADING

Pleading is the process by which the litigants advise each other and the court of the claims and defenses they intend to present at trial. Although the governing rules have been considerably relaxed over the years, there is still a certain formalism to the pleading process. The Federal Rules of Civil Procedure, for example, require pleadings to be in writing, dictate a certain basic form, and limit the parties' ability to amend their pleadings. The Rules likewise limit the number of pleadings that may be filed and give each pleading a separate and distinct name.

This chapter explores the rules that govern pleading. The main focus is pleading in the federal courts. Nevertheless, the chapter begins with a brief discussion of how pleading developed in the Anglo–American legal system. That historical overview is important for several reasons. First, and most practically, not all states follow the Federal Rules. Although the pleading rules in most states closely mirror the Federal Rules, some states use a different system. As you will see, there are a number of important differences between the Federal Rules and the rules that apply in these other courts. If you plan to practice in a state that does not follow the Federal Rules, some of what you read in this Chapter will not apply in your state court system.

Second, and perhaps more importantly, you cannot really appreciate the pleading system created by the Federal Rules without understanding the systems it was intended to replace. Although the federal pleading rules are by no means a panacea, they were adopted to cure perceived deficiencies in the pleading systems that predated them. The Federal Rules did much more than change the technical rules of pleading. They instead represent a quantum shift in the philosophy underlying pleading. Pleading under the Federal Rules is different than it was under the older systems mainly because the function of pleadings has changed. In the early 1800s pleading was a very important, if not the most important, aspect of procedure, at least in the common-law courts. Cases were often won or lost based on technical mistakes in pleading. Even if a party survived the pleading stage, strict pleading rules could force a party into a difficult tactical position by requiring him to adopt one strategy over another. Today, by contrast, pleading does not play nearly as significant a role in litigation as it did in the past. Modern courts are much more lenient about allowing a party to fix mistakes in her pleadings. Most cases are won or lost on the facts and law, not on the technical rules of pleading.

Nevertheless, it would be a fundamental mistake to conclude that pleadings are not important today. Although the pleading rules have been relaxed, courts still take pleading seriously. As the *Roe* and *Vess* cases in Part B of this chapter demonstrate, cases can still be won or lost solely on the pleadings. Therefore, a thorough understanding of the rules governing pleading is a crucial part of the arsenal of skills of every attorney.

A. PHILOSOPHY AND HISTORY OF PLEADING

There is no *a priori* reason why a legal system should require formal pleading of claims. In fact, outside the Anglo–American systems pleadings play a much less significant role. In many nations the pleadings merely serve to give the adjudicator a general idea of what happened. Those pleadings do not necessarily limit the course of the proceedings in the case. The adjudicator is not bound by the claims or defenses—or even the version of the facts—set forth in the pleadings, but may instead decide what matters bear looking into and what legal theories might apply to the case.

In Anglo–American systems, by contrast, the pleadings serve two basic functions. First, as in other systems, they provide information for both the court and the other side. Second, however, pleadings also serve a constraining function. Even if a plaintiff could, under the facts, have recovered under theory X, the parties may through the pleadings prevent the court from deciding for plaintiff under theory X. Therefore, pleading gives the parties a degree of control over their case that does not exist in other systems. But with that control comes a degree of responsibility. It is up to the parties to make sure that they do not overlook crucial facts or viable claims or defenses.

The history of pleadings in the Anglo–American systems in large part reflects a shift from the constraining function of pleadings to the notice function. Historically, the pleadings provided very little in the way of factual information to the other side. Their role was instead to narrow the case down to a single issue for trial. Today, the pleading rules focus on the facts, and do not necessarily limit the party to one issue or legal theory.

Generally speaking, the rules that have governed pleading in Anglo–American lay* courts since the eleventh century fall into one into one of

---

* The ecclesiastical courts, which applied church or canon law, used their own method of pleading.

three paradigms: historical English pleading, Code pleading, and Federal or "notice" pleading. Each of these will be discussed in turn.

1. Historical English Pleading

Following independence, courts in the United States quite naturally borrowed extensively from the rules and customs of English civil practice. Key among these rules were those governing pleading. Starting in the eleventh century, England developed over several centuries a complex, if not Byzantine, set of rules governing pleading. These rules were transplanted across the Atlantic Ocean, and dominated pleading in the United States courts until the latter part of the 19th century.

Today, no court in the United States uses rules that are anywhere close to the historical English rules. Nevertheless, study of the old pleading rules is of much more than historical interest. Although the historical rules no longer apply directly, they established a basic paradigm of pleading that still dominates our thought today. First, pleadings in the Anglo–American systems follow a certain prescribed order, with each step serving a different role. Plaintiff must commence the action. Plaintiff's pleading must do more than merely advise the court as to what happened to give rise to a dispute. It must also both show that plaintiff is entitled to recover under the law, and demonstrate that the court has the authority to hear the case. Defendant's response must deal with all of the allegations of the complaint. Moreover, defendant is limited in the ways in which it can respond.

Second, the historical pleading system established our modern view of the substantive law. Consider your courses in Contracts and Torts. As you know, there are wide differences between the rules that govern a breach of contract claim and a tort claim, including differences in the defendant's state of mind and damages that can be recovered. And yet, reduced to their essence, contracts and torts are both concerned with whether defendant breached a duty to plaintiff. The only core difference between the claims is that while in tort the law establishes and defines the duty, in contract the parties agree on the scope of any duty. The wide differences that exist between tort and contract today are attributable in large part to historical procedural rules. The English courts used a different type of pleading for tort and contract claims. Because the differences in pleading were also accompanied by differences in the procedure used in the case, litigation of what we would today call a tort claim differed tremendously from litigation of a case involving an agreed-upon duty. Over the years, these differences in procedure led judges and attorneys to view tort and contract as completely separate areas of law.

There is a great deal of discussion of historical pleading in the case law and literature. Unfortunately, there is considerably more chaff than wheat. Many discussions of the old pleading rules are little more than a caricature. The historical rules are portrayed in these discussions as the work of some sort of mad scientist, a hopelessly complex system with myriad arbitrary rules, filled with traps for the unwary. What these discussions fail to point out is that there was a method to the madness. The historical pleading rules reflected certain basic principles and assumptions about the proper role of pleading. Although the rules are admittedly complex—and yes, at times seemingly arbitrary—they make more sense when viewed in light of the basic principles. The following excerpts illustrate how the core principles and assumptions evolved into the historical system.

CHARLES E. CLARK, HANDBOOK OF THE LAW OF CODE PLEADING 10–14 (1928)

COMMON-LAW PLEADING

The two great characteristics of common-law pleading were the issue-forming process and the system of forms of action. The parties by successive steps of affirmation or denial were expected eventually to reach an issue which formed the sole point to be tried in the case. Under the system of forms of action a party seeking judicial relief was compelled to bring his claim within the limits of one of the existing forms or he was denied relief.

The common-law system of pleading came into vogue in England after the Norman Conquest. It developed as a more or less gradual process; the beginnings of most of the common-law actions cannot be stated with absolute precision. By the time of Edward I it had become a science to be formulated and cultivated. From that time until the time of the reforms of the nineteenth century the "science of special pleading" was of the utmost importance and among its devotees are included the great legal names of all but the most recent English lawyers.

Since the facts were passed upon by a body of laymen, not by a trained judge, it was felt necessary to ascertain clearly the points of dispute between the parties before the trial was begun. The institution of trial by jury, which meant so much to our ancestors in their efforts to secure a free and impartial justice, is therefore responsible for this striking characteristic of common-law pleading—the development of an issue. Unlike the Roman formulary system the issue was to be made by the parties themselves, not by a judicial officer of the government. Hence under the original idea of common-law pleading each party must in turn answer the previous pleading of his adversary by either denying, or affirming and adding new matter (*confessing and avoiding*) until there is ultimately reached a stage where one side has affirmed and the other has denied a single material point in the case. This was the issue, and, except as modified by later rules, provision was made for only one such issue. It was thought to be the glory of the system that the parties themselves would thus in advance of the trial single out and disclose the one material point as to which they were in dispute, thus eliminating all extraneous or agreed matter. The highly technical rules so characteristic of the system of common-law pleading were in the main designed either to aid or to force the parties in this matter to formulate the issue.

The other great characteristic feature of common-law pleading—the forms of action—had a close connection with the triumph of the king's courts over the local courts, a history too long to be traced in detail here. Whenever a litigant desired to sue in the king's court, he was required to procure a writ from the king through the office of the chancellor; that is, from the clerks in chancery. The writ was the king's command, directing the sheriff to summon the defendant before one of the king's courts. It served the further important purpose of giving jurisdiction to the court named in it. The process of issuing writs came to be strictly limited to cases where precedents existed, so that a litigant had to bring his claim within the limits set by some former precedent. Many writs were developed in reference to land, but because of the cumbersome nature of the procedure gradually fell into disuse. Actions for money damages— called personal actions—were the actions in general use under this system of pleading. At its later development, due to the restrictions on the issuance of new writs, these were limited to the famous forms of action—trespass, trespass on the case, trover, replevin, and detinue, in tort; and covenant, debt, account, and assumpsit in contract. The action of ejectment came to be practically a substitute for all the actions concerning land.

The practice of the clerks in chancery of *forming* new writs had ceased by the middle of the thirteenth century. * * * Hence the common-law system was limited in the extent of the relief which it could grant and the manner of granting it to the arbitrary units comprising the forms of action. Coupled with this were the refinements enforced to induce the production of an issue, resulting in a highly technical system which afforded none too complete relief. The rise of the courts of equity served, however, to postpone the necessity of reform for some time.

Equity Pleading

Pleadings in the equity courts consisted of detailed statements of the contentions of the parties. There were no formed actions in equity and little emphasis on the formation of an issue. The proceedings were more flexible than those at law in such matters as the joining of parties and the rendering of split judgments. Many of the principles of equity were later incorporated in the codes.

The equity courts developed from the exercise by the king of his royal prerogative through the chancellor to do justice where the courts failed to do so. Since the first chancellors were churchmen, they followed the ecclesiastical law. In this way equity pleading goes back through the canon law to the later period of the Roman law, although the connection is not so direct as to have been completely controlling. But we do find a general similarity between the English equity system and the Roman libellary procedure in the absence of a separate body for the trial of facts and hence the absence of emphasis upon the formation of an issue. Likewise there were no forms of action in equity, the complainant stated his case at large in the form of a petition to the chancellor. The pleadings in equity were, however, quite detailed, since, being sworn to, they gave the facts upon which the case was decided. No formal trial with witnesses was ordinarily had, at least until modern times. The equity procedure was much more flexible in many respects, particularly as to joinder of parties and of actions, and as to the form and kind of judgment which might be rendered.

. . . The equity procedure itself was designed as a flexible system to meet varying claims and hence was of a kind to appeal to those who were attempting to change the harshness and inflexibility of the common law. But equity jurisprudence too had tended to become rigid; the procedure seems to have aggravated the delays apparently natural in all systems of law, and hence it also came to the point where it was not fulfilling the needs of a growing and developing system of law. The division of remedial justice into two systems with two courts entirely distinct from each other intensified the defects inherent in each system. A litigant not infrequently would have to be sent out of court to bring his action in another tribunal simply because he had chosen the wrong one. Since the rules governing the choice of tribunal were not always clear and easy of application, the harm to innocent seekers for justice was great.

ROBERT WYNESS MILLAR, CIVIL PROCEDURE OF THE TRIAL COURT IN HISTORICAL PERSPECTIVE 33–35 (1952)

Here, too, flourishes uniquely that recondite method of preparatory allegation which we call common-law pleading. Allegation in the systems of other lands is a humble servitor, dismissed when it has discharged its purely informative function; here it is lord and master, tyrannizing over the substantive law, at times trampling it under foot. The roots of its prepotence are to be found in its lineage. Alone of the Germanic nations, England has preserved the Germanic idea that the parties themselves, by their mutual averments, shall formulate in concrete terms the theme of decision. Out of the crudity of the old *thwert-ut-nay*, through coalescence of Romano-canonical borrowings with the German rule that whatever is not denied stands admitted, there has long ago emerged the principle requiring the parties to plead either by way of traverse or by way of confession and avoidance. . . .

The very language of allegation is strange. Pleading talks with a Latin accent, barbarian not Ciceronian. When, as a result of the statute of 1731, English was substituted for Latin as a medium of averment, what the practitioners largely did was to adopt as nearly literal a translation as possible of the forms of allegation theretofore employed. Hence it is that we have such expressions as "force and arms" and "breaking the close"; hence it is that there appears such an un-English locution as that "with feet in walking" (*pedibus calcando*) the defendant wasted the plaintiff's grass. Witness the common counts in assumpsit solemnly averring the making and breaking of promises inexistent save in juristic metaphor; the losing and finding which every declaration in trover must charge, be the circumstances of conversion what they may or its subject a paper of pins or a thousand tons of coal; and the lease, entry, and ouster which in ejectment give impulse to the marionette figures of John Doe and Richard Roe. Fiction, indeed, is the constant substitute for what rationally should be alternative allegation, looking to the avoidance of accidents of proof; the plaintiff may state his claim in different ways, but for each variant statement is compelled to suppose a distinct happening, contrary to the fact.

Moreover, as part of its Germanic legacy, England has inherited something of the Germanic notion that in litigation the parties are acting at peril. *Ein Mann, ein Wort* has had here its echoes. ... The possibilities of recovery from a false step were always restricted; after the change from oral to written allegation this restriction had become intensified.

Notes

1. As the first excerpt makes clear, you cannot understand English pleading without understanding the English court system. A defining feature of that system was that judicial authority was spread among several different courts. The most important of these systems were the "common law" or "law" courts, and the "Chancery" or courts of "equity." A large majority of civil disputes involving private parties would be heard in one of these two courts. However, there were important differences between the procedure in these courts, including fundamental differences in the process of pleading. Most discussion of historical pleading focuses on the rules that applied in the common law courts. The complexity and seeming arbitrariness of these rules, as compared to the relative flexibility of pleading in equity, was a major impetus for development of the modern pleading regimes.

2. The readings also illustrate that three historical features of the common-law courts played a crucial role in the development of the complex pleading rules that applied in those courts. The first was the use of *lay juries*. Only the common law courts used juries. Because important issues in the case would be decided by people untrained in the law, the pleading system in the common law courts tried to keep the case in a form that could be managed by the jury. Thus, one overriding goal of pleading in the common-law courts was to "form the issue"—to reduce the case to a single issue that the jury could both fathom and decide.

The second feature was the *writ system*. A party could not sue in the king's courts without obtaining a writ. At first, the writ system was designed to make the claimant show why the king's courts, rather than local courts, should hear the case. As one of the king's main roles was to preserve peace in the realm, obtaining a writ often required the claimant to show how the dispute threatened breach of the peace. Thus, much of the language in the traditional writs speaks of acts done "with force of arms." Often, this allegation had nothing to do with what actually happened, but was merely a talismanic statement designed to fit the case into the writ.

As the first excerpt indicates, the writ system soon became highly rigid. The number of writs was fixed. If a party could not make his case fit into one of the writs, he could not obtain relief from the common-law courts. In that situation, only equity could afford relief.

The final distinguishing feature—the *forms of action*—relates directly to the fixing of the writs. The writs did more than define the situations in which a party could obtain relief. Each writ also had its own unique procedure and remedies. Under some writs, for example, a party was required to produce twelve "oath helpers" who would swear that his allegations were true. If all of the oath helpers recited the oath in precisely the prescribed form, the party automatically won. Because procedures under some writs were more advantageous, claimants would often try to bend their case to fit it into a certain writ. Writs with more cumbersome or onerous procedures would then fall into disuse.

Similarly, courts of law were extremely limited with respect to the remedies they could provide. Depending on the writ, the primary remedies available in law were damages, ejectment, replevin, mandamus, and prohibition. The court could not grant other remedies, such as an injunction or specific performance.

3. At first, the overlapping jurisdiction of common law and equity caused a power struggle between the two systems. During the reign of James I, however, the English lawmakers reached a compromise that gave the common law courts primacy over private disputes. From that point forward, a party could sue in equity only if he could demonstrate that he could not obtain adequate relief in the common-law courts. How could a party make such a showing? Often, the plea to equity turned on one of the constraining features of common-law pleading and procedure.

a. **Remedy**. The first situation was where the party sought a remedy that was unavailable in law. Suppose, for example, that A wants to sue B for breach of a contract to sell a rare painting. A does not want damages; she wants B to deliver the painting itself. Because a court of law could not grant the remedy of specific performance, A could not obtain the relief she wanted in law. Courts of equity, by contrast, had considerable discretion in fashioning a remedy to fit the needs of the parties. Specific performance was one of the many remedies available in equity but not in common law.

Similarly, suppose C wants to sue D, a large factory, for nuisance based on D's continued emission of noxious fumes. C would prefer an injunction to damages because a damages award would require C to keep suing every time D emits more fumes. As injunctions were not available in law, C could only obtain proper relief in equity.

b. **Substantive Rights**. A second situation where a party would sue in equity is where the case did not fit within one of the writs. The writs, as eventually fixed, did not begin to cover all of the situations where a party should be able to recover. However, a party could go to equity—which was not constrained by the writ system—in order to obtain recovery. Several causes of action, including the actions for cancellation of a contract based on fraud and for breach of fiduciary duty, originated in this fashion in the courts of equity.

c. **Procedure**. The procedural facets of the writs could also prove unduly restraining. For example, a party who sued in common law could not force the other side to divulge information that might be useful in preparing the case. The modern concept of discovery owes its origins to the bill of discovery, a form of relief available in equity that allowed a party to obtain information. Similarly, modern procedural devices such as the class action originated in the courts of equity.

4. Courts in the United States did not slavishly mirror the English system. United States courts were never as rigidly compartmentalized as their English forerunners. For example, although most states originally had separate courts of law and equity, the United States federal courts assigned the same judges to hear both cases at law and in equity. Nor did United States courts necessarily follow all of the pleading rules and limitations on the writs applied in the English courts. Nevertheless, the English rules did establish a basic model that applied in varying degrees in the early United States courts.

5. Most jurisdictions in the United States have merged common law and equity into a single system. In the federal courts, this merger occurred in 1938. Federal Rule 1 indicates that the rules apply with equal force in all cases, regardless of whether they would historically have been heard in law or in equity. Federal Rule 2 provides for a unitary action known simply as a "civil action." As a result, many of the procedural tools traditionally available only in equity, such as the class action and discovery, are now available in any type of action.

However, the procedural merger of common law and equity did not entirely erase the distinctions between the two systems. Vestigial remnants of the old division remain to this day. For example, although a party may obtain either legal or equitable relief from a single court, most courts still require a party to show that his legal remedy (typically damages) is inadequate before he may obtain an equitable remedy such as an injunction or specific performance. Another area where the distinction between law and equity remains important is in the constitutional right to a jury trial in civil cases in federal court. As discussed in greater depth in Chapter 9, this right exists only if the action is by nature a suit at common law. If the action is in equity, there is no right to a jury.

2. Code Pleading

The historical system only grew more complex—and foreign to the layperson—as it developed. This increased complexity led to increased discontent. In the common-law courts, cases were too often resolved on technicalities instead of the merits. Although equity involved fewer technicalities, proceedings in equity were so flexible and fact oriented that they proved inordinately time-consuming and expensive. There developed a real sense that the traditional system was failing in its calling to be a system of administering justice.

As the system grew more cumbersome and arcane, courts, attorneys, and eventually legislatures began to push for reform. William Blackstone, a noted British jurist, published a work in 1765 entitled "Commentaries on the Law of England." This work severely criticized several aspects of the English system, including the complex pleading system. Blackstone's work strongly influenced the philosopher Jeremy Bentham, who was at that time Blackstone's pupil. Bentham spearheaded a movement to change the English legal system so that it was more just. Bentham's efforts were to bear fruit on both sides of the Atlantic. In England, a series of promulgations beginning in 1834 effected significant changes in that system. The American states began their reform process shortly thereafter, but in some important ways the American reforms were more notable than the English reforms.

CHARLES E. CLARK, HANDBOOK OF THE LAW OF CODE PLEADING 17–19 (1928)

In this country the movement for pleading reform resulted in the adoption of the New York Code of 1848, the model and forerunner of all the practice codes in states which have adopted code pleading. By this act a single combined system of law and equity administered through the form of the one civil action was substituted for the two separate law and equity systems previously existing, and the forms of action at law and the separate suit in equity were abolished. It was further provided that the pleadings should state the facts, and the forming of the issue was less stressed. In addition to the fusion of law and equity and the substitution of fact pleading for issue pleading, the code adopted for all actions various equity principles such as freer joinder of parties and the split judgment, in part for plaintiff, in part for defendant.

The New York Code of 1848

In New York the movement for reform which had been making some real strides in England, became especially strong just prior to the middle of the nineteenth century. By a new constitution, adopted in that state in 1846, the court of chancery was abolished, and there was created in its place a court having general jurisdiction in law and equity. Further, the next legislature was directed to provide for the appointment of three commissioners "to revise, reform, simplify, and abridge" the practice and pleadings of courts of record of the state. The following year the legislature instructed the commissioners more explicitly, directing them "to provide for the abolition of the present forms of actions and pleadings in cases at common law; for a uniform course of proceeding in all cases whether of legal or equitable cognizance, and for the abandonment of all Latin and other foreign tongues, so far as the same shall by them be deemed practicable, and of any form and proceeding not necessary to ascertain or preserve the rights of the parties." The commission speedily went to its task and the following year reported a code which with some amendments was passed on April 12, 1848, and became operative on the following first of July. The code was in large measure the work of David Dudley Field, one of the commissioners, and is generally referred to as the "Field Code." Though so expeditiously prepared and enacted, it has served as the model of all succeeding codes in this country.

Characteristics of the Code

Probably the most important characteristics of the code were the one form of action and the system of pleading the facts. The first still remains as the crowning achievement of the codes .... The forms of action were abolished, the separation of law and equity was done away with, and in its place the codifiers planned a *blended* system of law and equity with only a single form of action to be known as the *civil action*. As to the second characteristic, it was planned that the parties should in their pleadings state the facts in simple and concise form. Instead of the *issue pleading* of the common law there was to be *fact pleading*. * * * [However,] this part of the plan has worked least successfully of all the reforms made, since the codifiers and the courts failed to appreciate that the difference between statements of facts and statements of law is almost entirely one of degree only.

Among other important changes may be noted the adoption of the equity principles of greater freedom of joining parties and of rendering judgments in part for or against the various parties as the justice of the case may require (the *split judgment* of equity).

Notes and Questions

1. "Code" pleading caught on quickly, in part because of a perception that it made the pleading process much simpler and less technical. Missouri followed New York in 1849, and California in 1850. Within 25 years of adoption of the Field Code, twenty four states had adopted code pleading. Moreover, although the federal courts did not abolish the distinction between law and equity until 1938, the rules used in federal equity cases were amended in 1912 to borrow many of the principles of the codes.

Most of the jurisdictions that originally adopted Code pleading eventually replaced it with the notice pleading system of the Federal Rules. Nevertheless, Code pleading remains in force in a few states, most notably California and Nebraska. Although these states have borrowed other aspects of the Federal Rules, they still require a claimant to follow the fact pleading standards of the Field Code.

Because this book deals primarily with *federal* procedure, it will not deal with Code pleading in any depth. Should you find the need to study the topic further, there are a number of detailed books on the subject. An excellent start is Walter Heiser, Rex Perschbacher, and Margaret Johns, *California Civil Procedure* (2d ed. 2004).

2. The basic standard of pleading under the Codes was the polar opposite of that employed in common-law pleading. Pleadings in the common-law courts focused on stating a claim in a particular preordained form. Because these forms were created to fit exactly the elements of the limited number of causes of action, the pleadings provided very little real information about the underlying event. Code pleading, by contrast, required the party to focus on the actual facts. In fact, a pleading under the Codes would be deemed insufficient if it contained "legal conclusions" instead of facts. As the excerpt points out, however, the line between law and facts is not always

clear. As just one example, is a statement that "plaintiff and defendant entered into a contract" a statement of fact or one of law?

3. Code pleading also distinguished between "ultimate" and "evidentiary" facts. A pleading was supposed to contain only ultimate facts. If the pleader included too much detail, the pleading was deemed insufficient because it pled evidentiary facts. Of course, if you find it hard to distinguish between statements of fact and statements of law, you will find it even harder to tell what is an ultimate fact and what is merely evidentiary. Nevertheless, the system proved remarkably workable in practice. As precedent expounded on the meanings of the terms "legal conclusion," "ultimate fact," and "evidentiary fact," and as courts continued to prove fairly accommodating when applying the rules, the percentage of cases dismissed for purely technical problems with the pleadings decreased.

4. Even though the Codes required the parties to plead facts rather than law, a party could not simply file a complaint that detailed everything that happened. Instead, the Codes required a complaint to contain "a statement of facts *constituting a cause of action*." The attorney therefore had to pick and choose among the facts, focusing on those that were most pertinent to the theory under which the plaintiff hoped to recover.

This feature is a crucial feature of both Code pleading and notice pleading, but one that is often not apparent to the newcomer. Code and notice pleading purport to focus on the facts rather than the law. But the law always lurks just beneath the surface. Unless the facts fit into a recognized theory of recovery, a plaintiff cannot prevail even if she can set out the most compelling facts. Therefore, notwithstanding their genesis and stated standards, Code and notice pleading still require a claimant to plead the facts in a way that tracks the elements of the claim or claims she is bringing.

B. PLEADING A CLAIM UNDER THE FEDERAL RULES

The Federal Rules of Civil Procedure, adopted in 1938, represent the third main theory of pleading in United States history. The Federal Rules' system of "notice" pleading is in force not only in the federal courts, but also in the vast majority of state courts. Even states like Illinois, New York, and Texas, which have retained other elements of the Codes, have basically adopted this form of pleading, primarily because it is even more forgiving than the Codes. Notice pleading is somewhat similar to Code pleading insofar as it concentrates on the facts rather than the underlying legal claim. Nevertheless, there are significant differences between the two, especially in the extent to which a party may include legal conclusions in her pleading.

INTRODUCTORY PROBLEM

Van Gogh, a painter, is known to be very impetuous. One morning, van Gogh suddenly decides to give up his career in painting. He strikes a deal with Rembrandt under which Rembrandt will buy van Gogh's studio. After Rembrandt pays, van Gogh departs in great haste, leaving a number of his paintings behind.

Several months later, van Gogh decides to visit an outdoor art fair. Stopping by Rembrandt's booth, van Gogh is shocked to see a painting that looks almost exactly like a work entitled "Starry Night" that van Gogh painted two years earlier. Van Gogh left Starry Night in the studio when he departed. The only noticeable difference between the work on display and Starry Night is that the painting on display has the name "Rembrandt" painted in the exact location where van Gogh's name appeared on Starry Night.

The very next day, while reading the newspaper, van Gogh learns that the gargantuan Halliburton Company has offered Rembrandt $10,000,000 for the studio. It seems that Rembrandt discovered a large oil reserve underneath the studio. Although van Gogh had mentioned in his negotiations with Rembrandt that there might be "quite a bit of oil on this property," both he and Rembrandt thought this was a reference to left-over oil paint, not raw petroleum.

Van Gogh has had enough, and decides to sue Rembrandt. His complaint contains three separate counts. Count One is for copyright infringement. The operative language that Van Gogh's complaint uses for this count reads:

4. In May, 2003, Plaintiff van Gogh completed an original oil painting entitled "Starry Night."

5. Plaintiff owns the copyright in this painting.

6. On or before November, 2005, Defendant Rembrandt painted a painting that was identical to Starry Night.

7. By producing a painting that is identical to Plaintiff's copyrighted work, Defendant infringed Plaintiff's copyright.

Count Two is for breach of the common-law right of attribution. This portion of the complaint reads as follows:

10. Plaintiff readopts and realleges the language in paragraph 4 of this Complaint.

11. In June, 2005, Defendant acquired title to and possession of Starry Night when Plaintiff sold his studio and its contents to Defendant.

12. Sometime before November, 2005, Defendant altered Starry Night by removing Plaintiff's name from the surface of the painting and substituting the name of Defendant.

13. In November, 2005, and possibly earlier, Defendant offered the altered painting to the public for sale.

14. By displaying the painting without any reference to Plaintiff as the original artist, Defendant violated Plaintiff's common-law right of attribution.

Van Gogh's third count deals with the sale of the studio itself. In this count, van Gogh claims:

17. In June, 2005, Plaintiff and Defendant entered into a contract in which Defendant agreed to purchase Plaintiff's studio and its contents for the price of $100,000.

18. The sale was completed on June 22, 2005, and Defendant took possession immediately thereafter.

19. Said contract is void for a mutual mistake of fact concerning the value of the property that was sold. Both parties thought the property sold was worth approximately $100,000, while in actuality its value was at least $10,000,000.

20. Because of this mutual mistake of fact, Plaintiff is entitled either to have the contract declared null and void, or for judgment against Defendant in an amount equal to the difference between the actual value of the property and the $100,000 that Defendant paid.

Rembrandt files a timely objection to the complaint. First, he argues that van Gogh has not provided enough detail in any of his counts. For example, he claims that van Gogh needs to provide more detail of how the paintings are similar in Count One, and more details about the nature of the mistake in Count Three. Rembrandt also claims that van Gogh needs to provide cites to the statutes and cases that support his claims. Finally, Rembrandt argues that Counts One and Two are fatally defective because they are logically inconsistent; Count One presupposes that Rembrandt painted the work on display, while Count Two presupposes that van Gogh painted it.

Did van Gogh properly allege his claims?

Governing Rules: Federal Rules of Civil Procedure 8 and 9.

1. General Rule

As discussed in the prior section, the Federal Rules of Civil Procedure simplified pleading even more than had the Codes. For most claims, the Federal Rules require only what is commonly called "notice pleading." This basic standard is reflected in Federal Rule 8(a), which provides:

(a) Claims for Relief. A pleading which sets forth a claim for relief, whether an original claim, counterclaim, cross-claim, or third-party claim, shall contain (1) a short and plain statement of the grounds upon which the court's jurisdiction depends, unless the court already has jurisdiction and the claim needs no new grounds of jurisdiction to support it, (2) a short and plain statement of the claim showing that the pleader is entitled to relief, and (3) a demand for judgment for the relief that the pleader seeks. Relief in the alternative or of several different types may be demanded.

Note that Rule 8(a) by its very terms applies not only to complaints by plaintiffs, but to *all* claims for relief. Therefore, the basic notice pleading standard also applies to counterclaims, cross-claims, and claims by and against third-party defendants. Although most of the case law and literature focuses on the plaintiff's claim, do not forget that other claims are analyzed the same way.

The first element of a proper claim, a statement about jurisdiction, actually deals only with subject-matter jurisdiction. A claimant is not technically required to plead how the court can exercise personal jurisdiction over the party against whom the claim is alleged. Nevertheless, most plaintiffs include in their complaint some language about how the court has personal jurisdiction (and often venue). Because these issues are likely to come up at a fairly early stage in the case anyway, as a practical matter it makes sense to include them in the complaint.

Many of the state versions of Rule 8(a) do not require the claimant to plead the basis for jurisdiction. The reasons for this difference will be apparent if you think back to Chapter 3. Federal courts are courts of limited subject-matter jurisdiction. Federal jurisdiction, which by its very nature comes at the expense of state authority, is meant to be the exception rather than the rule. Because federal judges respect the constitutional and statutory limits on their authority, any attempt to invoke federal jurisdiction must be made clear at the outset.

Most of the disputes involving Rule 8(a) turn on the second criterion, the "short and plain statement of the claim." At first glance, this may not seem appreciably different than the standard used in the Codes, which required the pleader to state facts constituting a cause of action. Nevertheless, there is an important difference, although one that is admittedly difficult to appreciate in the abstract. Code pleading required the claimant to "show his cards" by divulging what facts he had to support his claim. Federal notice pleading, by contrast, requires the claimant to reveal very few of the facts she has to support her claim. Instead, the claimant must only give the other side a rough idea—that is, put the other side "on notice"—of why he is being sued. This standard requires the claimant to disclose not only the legal claim or claims, but also give the defendant some clue as to the events that gave rise to that claim. Armed with that information, the other side can decide how to respond. The party against whom the claim is alleged can either deny that the incident occurred, or argue that even if it did occur, she is not liable. *See* Part E of this Chapter.

One way to understand how Rule 8(a) works is to look at the Supreme Court approved forms for pleading jurisdiction and a simple negligence claim.

Form 2.

ALLEGATION OF JURISDICTION

(a) Jurisdiction founded on diversity of citizenship and amount.

Plaintiff is a [citizen of the State of Connecticut][2] [corporation incorporated under laws of the State of Connecticut having its principal place of business in the State of Connecticut] and defendant is a corporation incorporated under the laws of the State of New York having its principal place of business in a State other than the State of Connecticut. The matter in controversy exceeds, exclusive of interest and costs, the sum specified by 28 U.S.C. § 1332.

(b) Jurisdiction founded on the existence of a Federal question.

The action arises under [the Constitution of the United States, Article ___, Section ___]; [the ___ Amendment to the Constitution of the United States, Section ___]; [the Act of ___, ___ Stat. ___; U.S.C., Title ___, § ___]; [the Treaty of the United States (here describe the treaty)][3] as hereinafter more fully appears.

(c) Jurisdiction founded on the existence of a question arising under particular statutes.

The action arises under the Act of ___, ___] Stat. ___; U.S.C., Title ___, § ___]; as hereinafter more fully appears.

(d) Jurisdiction founded on the admiralty or maritime character of the claim.

This is a case of admiralty and maritime jurisdiction, as hereinafter more fully appears. [If the pleader wishes to invoke the distinctively maritime procedures referred to in Rule 9(h), add the following or its substantial equivalent: This is an admiralty or maritime claim within the meaning of Rule 9(h).]

Form 9.

COMPLAINT FOR NEGLIGENCE

1. Allegation of jurisdiction.

2. On June 1, 1936, in a public highway called Boylston Street in Boston, Massachusetts, defendant negligently drove a motor vehicle against plaintiff who was then crossing said highway.

3. As a result plaintiff was thrown down and had his leg broken and was otherwise injured, was prevented from transacting his business, suffered great pain of body and mind, and incurred expenses for medical attention and hospitalization in the sum of one thousand dollars.

Wherefore plaintiff demands judgment against defendant in the sum of ___ dollars and costs.

Another way to understand the low threshold established by Rule 8(a) is to see how it applies in practice. The following three cases give a

---

2. Form for natural person.

3. Use the appropriate phrase or phrases. The general allegation of the existence of a Federal question is ineffective unless the matters constituting the claim for relief as set forth in the complaint raise a Federal question.

good idea of the general principles. Nevertheless, because the results in the case are arguably inconsistent, be sure to read the opinions in light of both the language of, and the policy underlying, Rule 8(a). The notes following the third case compare the results and provide clues into why the courts decided the way they did.

SWIERKIEWICZ v. SOREMA, N.A.

534 U.S. 506, 122 S.Ct. 992, 152 L.Ed.2d 1 (2002)

JUSTICE THOMAS delivered the opinion of the Court.

This case presents the question whether a complaint in an employment discrimination lawsuit must contain specific facts establishing a prima facie case of discrimination under the framework set forth by this Court in *McDonnell Douglas Corp.* v. *Green,* 411 U.S. 792 (1973). We hold that an employment discrimination complaint need not include such facts and instead must contain only "a short and plain statement of the claim showing that the pleader is entitled to relief." Fed. Rule Civ. Proc. 8(a)(2).

Petitioner Akos Swierkiewicz is a native of Hungary, who at the time of his complaint was 53 years old.[1] In April 1989, petitioner began working for respondent Sorema N. A., a reinsurance company headquartered in New York and principally owned and controlled by a French parent corporation. Petitioner was initially employed in the position of senior vice president and chief underwriting officer (CUO). Nearly six years later, Francois M. Chavel, respondent's Chief Executive Officer, demoted petitioner to a marketing and services position and transferred the bulk of his underwriting responsibilities to Nicholas Papadopoulo, a 32–year-old who, like Mr. Chavel, is a French national. About a year later, Mr. Chavel stated that he wanted to "energize" the underwriting department and appointed Mr. Papadopoulo as CUO. Petitioner claims that Mr. Papadopoulo had only one year of underwriting experience at the time he was promoted, and therefore was less experienced and less qualified to be CUO than he, since at that point he had 26 years of experience in the insurance industry.

Following his demotion, petitioner contends that he "was isolated by Mr. Chavel ... excluded from business decisions and meetings and denied the opportunity to reach his true potential at SOREMA." Petitioner unsuccessfully attempted to meet with Mr. Chavel to discuss his discontent. Finally, in April 1997, petitioner sent a memo to Mr. Chavel outlining his grievances and requesting a severance package. Two weeks later, respondent's general counsel presented petitioner with two options: He could either resign without a severance package or be dismissed. Mr. Chavel fired petitioner after he refused to resign.

Petitioner filed a lawsuit alleging that he had been terminated on account of his national origin in violation of Title VII of the Civil Rights

---

1. Because we review here a decision granting respondent's motion to dismiss, we must accept as true all of the factual allegations contained in the complaint.

Act of 1964, as amended, 42 U.S.C. § 2000e *et seq*, and on account of his age in violation of the Age Discrimination in Employment Act of 1967 (ADEA), as amended, 29 U.S.C. § 621 *et seq*. The United States District Court for the Southern District of New York dismissed petitioner's complaint because it found that he "had not adequately alleged a prima facie case, in that he had not adequately alleged circumstances that support an inference of discrimination." The United States Court of Appeals for the Second Circuit affirmed the dismissal . . . .

Applying Circuit precedent, the Court of Appeals required petitioner to plead a prima facie case of discrimination in order to survive respondent's motion to dismiss. In the Court of Appeals' view, petitioner was thus required to allege in his complaint: (1) membership in a protected group; (2) qualification for the job in question; (3) an adverse employment action; and (4) circumstances that support an inference of discrimination.

The prima facie case under *McDonnell Douglas*, however, is an evidentiary standard, not a pleading requirement. . . .

This Court has never indicated that the requirements for establishing a prima facie case under *McDonnell Douglas* also apply to the pleading standard that plaintiffs must satisfy in order to survive a motion to dismiss. . . . Consequently, the ordinary rules for assessing the sufficiency of a complaint apply. See, *e.g.*, *Scheuer* v. *Rhodes,* 416 U.S. 232, 236 (1974) ("When a federal court reviews the sufficiency of a complaint, before the reception of any evidence either by affidavit or admissions, its task is necessarily a limited one. The issue is not whether a plaintiff will ultimately prevail but whether the claimant is entitled to offer evidence to support the claims").

In addition, under a notice pleading system, it is not appropriate to require a plaintiff to plead facts establishing a prima facie case because the *McDonnell Douglas* framework does not apply in every employment discrimination case. For instance, if a plaintiff is able to produce direct evidence of discrimination, he may prevail without proving all the elements of a prima facie case. Under the Second Circuit's heightened pleading standard, a plaintiff without direct evidence of discrimination at the time of his complaint must plead a prima facie case of discrimination, even though discovery might uncover such direct evidence. It thus seems incongruous to require a plaintiff, in order to survive a motion to dismiss, to plead more facts than he may ultimately need to prove to succeed on the merits if direct evidence of discrimination is discovered. . . .

Furthermore, imposing the Court of Appeals' heightened pleading standard in employment discrimination cases conflicts with Federal Rule of Civil Procedure 8(a)(2), which provides that a complaint must include only "a short and plain statement of the claim showing that the pleader is entitled to relief." Such a statement must simply "give the defendant fair notice of what the plaintiff's claim is and the grounds upon which it rests." *Conley* v. *Gibson,* 355 U.S. 41, 47 (1957). This simplified notice pleading standard relies on liberal discovery rules and summary judgment motions to define disputed facts and issues and to dispose of unmeritorious claims. ...

Rule 8(a)'s simplified pleading standard applies to all civil actions, with limited exceptions. Rule 9(b), for example, provides for greater particularity in all averments of fraud or mistake. This Court, however, has declined to extend such exceptions to other contexts. ... Thus, complaints in these cases, as in most others, must satisfy only the simple requirements of Rule 8(a).

Other provisions of the Federal Rules of Civil Procedure are inextricably linked to Rule 8(a)'s simplified notice pleading standard. Rule 8(e)(1) states that "no technical forms of pleading or motions are required," and Rule 8(f) provides that "all pleadings shall be so construed as to do substantial justice." Given the Federal Rules' simplified standard for pleading, "[a] court may dismiss a complaint only if it is clear that no relief could be granted under any set of facts that could be proved consistent with the allegations." *Hishon* v. *King & Spalding,* 467 U.S. 69, 73 (1984). If a pleading fails to specify the allegations in a manner that provides sufficient notice, a defendant can move for a more definite statement under Rule 12(e) before responding. Moreover, claims lacking merit may be dealt with through summary judgment under Rule 56. The liberal notice pleading of Rule 8(a) is the starting point of a simplified pleading system, which was adopted to focus litigation on the merits of a claim. See *Conley, supra,* at 48 ("The Federal Rules reject the approach that pleading is a game of skill in which one misstep by counsel may be decisive to the outcome and accept the principle that the purpose of pleading is to facilitate a proper decision on the merits").

Applying the relevant standard, petitioner's complaint easily satisfies the requirements of Rule 8(a) because it gives respondent fair notice of the basis for petitioner's claims. Petitioner alleged that he had been terminated on account of his national origin in violation of Title VII and on account of his age in violation of the ADEA. His complaint detailed the events leading to his termination, provided relevant dates, and included the ages and nationalities of at least some of the relevant persons involved with his termination. These allegations give respondent fair notice of what petitioner's claims are and the grounds upon which they rest. In addition, they state claims upon which relief could be granted under Title VII and the ADEA.

Respondent argues that allowing lawsuits based on conclusory allegations of discrimination to go forward will burden the courts and encourage disgruntled employees to bring unsubstantiated suits. Whatever the practical merits of this argument, the Federal Rules do not contain a heightened pleading standard for employment discrimination suits. A requirement of greater specificity for particular claims is a result that "must be obtained by the process of amending the Federal Rules, and not by judicial interpretation." *Leatherman* [v. *Tarrant County Narcotics Intelligence and Coordination Unit,* 507 U.S. 163, 164 (1993)] at 168. Furthermore, Rule 8(a) establishes a pleading standard without regard to whether a claim will succeed on the merits. "Indeed it may appear on the face of the pleadings that a recovery is very remote and unlikely but that is not the test." *Scheuer*, 416 U.S. at 236.

For the foregoing reasons, we hold that an employment discrimination plaintiff need not plead a prima facie case of discrimination and that petitioner's complaint is sufficient to survive respondent's motion to dismiss. Accordingly, the judgment of the Court of Appeals is reversed, and the case is remanded for further proceedings consistent with this opinion. . . .

Notes and Questions

1. It is easier to understand the Court's reasoning in *Swierkiewicz* if you understand something about the substantive law that applies in employment discrimination cases. Generally speaking, discrimination law is designed to protect negative treatment of people based on their race, religion, sex, national origin, or age. However, a claimant bringing a discrimination claim cannot prevail merely by showing he is a member of a protected group who suffered negative treatment. Instead, he must show *causation*: that his race, religion, gender, national origin, or age was a factor behind the negative treatment.

Of course, the best way to prove causation is with direct proof: a statement or memorandum from a defendant directly showing that the decision was made on an improper basis. But such direct evidence is rarely available, especially at the early stage in the dispute when the complaint is filed. Most employers are savvy enough not to tell employees that they have been treated a particular way because of their race or gender. Without the coercive force of the discovery rules—rules that come into play only once a proper complaint is filed—the employee who has suffered negative treatment will have no access to such direct proof. To counteract this situation, the courts also allow a discrimination plaintiff to establish a "prima facie" case of discrimination through the use of indirect or circumstantial evidence.

The issue in *Swierkiewicz* is whether the complaint must state facts that show an indirect or prima facie case of discrimination. The Court places some weight, however, on the fact that establishing a prima facie case is only one way to prevail in such a case. Do you understand how requiring the plaintiff to include facts sufficient to demonstrate a prima facie case would constitute an undue burden in certain cases?

2. Suppose that the Court had decided the case the other way. What more would plaintiff need to allege to state a claim?

3. The Federal Forms are a set of sample pleadings and motions that accompany the Federal Rules of Civil Procedure. Forms 2 and 9 were set out earlier. Review a few of the other forms. As you can see, they are extremely "bare bones," proving little more than a quick reference to the underlying event and the claimant's theory of recovery. Nevertheless, Federal Rule 84 provides that pleadings and motions that comply with the Forms automatically meet the pleading standards of the Federal Rules.

In actual practice, very few attorneys file pleadings as brief as the Forms allow. Nevertheless, the Forms do illustrate how little the federal "notice pleading" standard really requires. Given that low threshold, you may wonder how a complaint could ever fail to meet the standards of Rule 8(a). The following two cases explore the limits.

DANIELS v. USS AGRI–CHEMICALS

965 F.2d 376 (7th Cir. 1992)

CUDAHY, Circuit Judge.

Pamela Daniels is a resident of Indiana. So was her late husband, who died in 1986 as a result of injuries he sustained in an accident that occurred in Indiana. In spite of these Indiana connections, Daniels filed suit seeking compensation for the wrongful death of her husband in Illinois state court, stating her theory of the case as one based on Illinois law. The defendants removed the case to federal court based on diversity of citizenship. During the course of discovery, the parties concluded that the applicable law was not that of Illinois, but of Indiana. By the time Daniels amended her complaint to reflect that conclusion, however, Indiana's two-year time limit for filing wrongful death actions had expired. The district court found that the suit was therefore barred and granted summary judgment for the defendants. Daniels appeals.

I

On May 9, 1986, Anthony K. Daniels was severely injured when the container of anhydrous ammonia with which he was working exploded. He sustained burns to approximately 80% of his body, resulting in his death on May 18, 1986. On January 16, 1987, his wife Pamela Daniels filed an ex parte petition in the Circuit Court of Cook County, Illinois, requesting appointment as a "Special Administrator" of her husband's estate for purposes of asserting an action under the Illinois Wrongful Death Act (Illinois Act). Daniels believed that the Illinois Act would apply to her claim because the ammonia cylinder had been filled in Illinois and her husband's death actually had occurred there. Daniels stated in her petition that she was "competent to act in the capacity of special administrator pursuant to Chapter 110 1/2, § 9–1 of the Illinois Revised Statutes." As it later turned out, Daniels did not in fact meet the requirements of that provision because she was not a resident of Illinois. The Circuit Court, however, was not aware of this fact and granted Daniels' petition.

Following her appointment, Daniels filed a complaint in the Circuit Court of Cook County against USX Corporation, the manufacturer of the ammonia cylinder, and several affiliated companies (collectively, USX). Count I of the two-count complaint alleged that the ammonia cylinder had been "unreasonably dangerous" due to design defects, manufacturing defects and inadequate warnings to consumers, and that as a direct and proximate result of its unreasonably dangerous condition the cylinder had exploded, causing the death of Daniels' husband. The complaint alleged that these facts gave rise to a cause of action under the Illinois Wrongful Death Act and demanded judgment against the defendants in the amount of $2,000,000. The complaint also contained a count for Daniels' loss of consortium, which is not at issue here.

On February 15, 1987, USX petitioned for removal of the case to the Northern District of Illinois on the basis of diversity of citizenship. Approximately one year later, on February 24, 1988, Daniels filed her first amended complaint, adding Union Carbide, the distributor of the ammonia cylinder, and affiliated companies (collectively, Union Carbide) as defendants. The first amended complaint contained the same counts as the original complaint, although the factual allegations as to the defendants' wrongful conduct were significantly more specific.

On March 4, 1988, USX filed its answer and affirmative defenses to the amended complaint. The affirmative defenses included the allegation that the Illinois Wrongful Death Act had no application to the case and that Daniels was not competent to act as special administrator under chapter 110 1/2, § 9-1 of the Illinois Revised Statutes because she was not an Illinois resident. Union Carbide raised the same defenses in its answer to the amended complaint, filed on April 8, 1988.

On September 22, 1988, Daniels petitioned the district court to appoint her as personal representative of her husband's estate under section 29-1-10-15 of the Indiana code for the purpose of asserting a claim under the Indiana Wrongful Death Act, Ind. Code Ann. § 34-1-1-2 (Indiana Act). She also sought leave to file a second amended complaint deleting her Illinois Wrongful Death Act claim and substituting a claim under Indiana law. The court granted both motions on September 28. A month later, the district court vacated Daniels' earlier appointment as special administrator under Illinois law on motion of the defendants. On November 2, 1988, Daniels filed a third amended complaint containing two counts under the Indiana Wrongful Death Act and two counts of loss of consortium.

On March 2, 1989, Union Carbide moved for summary judgment on Daniels' claims under the Indiana Act. Union Carbide argued that it was entitled to summary judgment because Daniels had failed to comply with the two conditions precedent to maintaining a wrongful death action under the Indiana statute: (1) that she be appointed as her husband's personal representative to assert a claim within two years of his death; and (2) that she actually file the action within that two years. The district court agreed and granted summary judgment for the defendants on the wrongful death claims. . . .

II

. . . There are . . . two conditions precedent to a cause of action under the Indiana Act: (1) the plaintiff must be appointed "personal representative" of the decedent within two years of the death; and (2) the suit must be brought within that same two years. The district court found that Daniels had not fulfilled either of these conditions because she had neither been validly appointed as her husband's personal representative nor brought suit under the Indiana Act until more than two years after her husband's death. The court rejected Daniels' argument that her September, 1988 appointment as personal representative under Indiana law and her third amended complaint alleging a cause of action under the Indiana Act related back to the date of the original complaint under Federal Rule 15(c)* and were therefore timely. . . .

Although the applicability of Rule 15(c) to the facts of this case is an interesting question, we see no need to reach it because Daniels makes an alternative argument for reversal which we find persuasive. Daniels contends that her suit, as *originally filed,* fulfilled the two conditions precedent to suit under the Indiana statute. We address the two conditions separately.

A. Commencement of the Action

. . . Indiana, like the federal courts, employs a system of "notice" pleading.[1]

Under notice pleading, "a plaintiff essentially need only plead the operative facts in the litigation." *State v. Rankin,* 260 Ind. 228, 294 N.E.2d 604, 606 (1973). Neither federal nor Indiana pleading rules require the complaint to include even a theory of the case, much less the statutory basis for recovery. *Id.*; *Bartholet v. Reishauer A.G.,* 953 F.2d 1073 (7th Cir. 1992). Moreover, "specifying an incorrect theory is not fatal." *Bartholet,* 953 F.2d at 1078; *see also* 5 Charles Wright & Arthur Miller, *Federal Practice and Procedure* § 1219 at 191–94 (1990). Complaints are to be construed liberally; the court "should ask whether relief is possible under any set of facts that could be established consistent with the allegations." *Bartholet,* 953 F.2d at 1078; *see also Rankin,* 294 N.E.2d at 606. This approach is consistent with the purpose of the complaint under a notice pleading system, which is "to advise the other party of the event being sued upon." Wright & Miller, *supra* § 1202 at 69.

There is no question that the defendants in this case were so advised within the statutory period. The substantive allegations in Count I of Daniel's third amended complaint were identical to those contained in both the first and second amended complaints, both of which were filed well within two years of her husband's death; the third amended complaint merely deleted the Illinois Wrongful Death Act and substituted the Indiana Wrongful Death Act. The defendants have never argued that the substantive allegations in the third amended complaint were insufficient to state a claim under the Indiana Act, and we see no basis on which they could do so. Clearly, then, both the first and second amended complaints *also* stated a claim under Indiana law, although

---

* Rule 15(c) is discussed in section G of this chapter. *Eds*

1. Because the Indiana rules are modeled closely on the federal rules, Indiana courts often look to federal cases for guid-ance in applying the Indiana rules. Therefore, we need not decide whether federal or state procedural rules apply in construing the pleadings in this case. . . .

they *cited* Illinois law. What Daniels did, in essence, was specify the wrong legal basis for her claim. That error was not unreasonable given the tendency of Illinois courts to interpret the applicability of the Illinois Wrongful Death Act broadly. Nor did it affect the gravamen of her complaint. Had defendants made a motion to dismiss the first amended complaint under Federal Rule 12(b)(6) once they realized that Illinois law was inapplicable to the case, the district court would have been obliged to deny it. Under either Indiana or federal pleading rules, the court would have had to conclude that the complaint stated a claim for relief under Indiana law. Therefore, the complaint fulfilled the two-year condition precedent of the Indiana Act. Daniels' later amendment was of no more legal significance than the correction of a typographical error. *Cf. Bartholet,* 953 F.2d at 1075 ("An effort to invoke nonexistent state law is no different from a spelling error.").

B.   Personal Representative

The Indiana Wrongful Death Act also requires that the wrongful death action be brought by the "personal representative" of the decedent. Daniels had in fact been appointed her husband's representative by the Cook County Circuit Court at the time she filed her initial complaint against USX. It is clear that a foreign personal representative may maintain an action under the Indiana Wrongful Death Act. Although the district court later vacated Daniels' appointment on the ground that it was invalid, that vacation did not retroactively render the appointment a nullity. ... Daniels was in fact the personal representative of her husband at the time she filed her suit and thus fulfilled the condition precedent of the Indiana Act. ...

Although Daniels (or, more realistically, her lawyer) made technical mistakes, she nevertheless managed to fulfill both conditions of suit under the Indiana Act, and she clearly "advised the other parties of the event being sued upon." Wright & Miller, *supra* § 1202 at 69. Therefore, the judgment of the district court is REVERSED and the case is REMANDED for further proceedings consistent with this opinion.

ROE v. AWARE WOMAN CENTER FOR CHOICE, INC.

253 F.3d 678 (11th Cir. 2001)

CARNES, Circuit Judge.

A woman seeking to proceed in this lawsuit under the name Jane Roe alleges that she was injured during the course of an abortion procedure performed by Dr. William P. Egherman at the Aware Woman Center for Choice, which is operated by a Florida corporation controlled by Edward and Patricia Windle. Roe sued Egherman, the Windles, and the corporation under the Freedom of Access to Clinic Entrances Act ("FACE"), 18 U.S.C. § 248. That statute provides civil remedies for anyone whose ability to obtain reproductive health services has been intentionally interfered with. This is Roe's appeal from the district court's dismissal of her complaint under Federal Rule of Civil Procedure 12(b)(6) and from its denial of her motion to proceed anonymously.

I. BACKGROUND

Of course, in reviewing the dismissal of a complaint under Fed. R.Civ.P. 12(b)(6), we, like the district court, "must accept the allegations set forth in the complaint as true." *See United States v. Pemco Aeroplex, Inc.*, 195 F.3d 1234, 1236 (11th Cir. 1999). Accepting the allegations of the complaint in this case as true, the facts are that on March 29, 1997, Roe entered the defendants' clinic for what was to be her third abortion procedure. Soon after the procedure began, she felt "extreme, excessive pain in her abdomen" that she had not experienced during her previous two abortion procedures. Roe demanded that Dr. Egherman stop the procedure and call an ambulance for her. He refused and, instead, instructed four assistants to restrain Roe while he continued to perform the procedure. Roe was eventually taken by ambulance to an emergency room where it was discovered that during the procedure at the clinic she had suffered both a perforated uterus and a colon laceration. At the hospital, the dead fetus was removed from Roe's uterus and she underwent surgery to repair her organs.

On July 9, 1999, Roe filed suit against the defendants pursuant to FACE, 18 U.S.C. § 248 (c)(1). Alleging the facts we have just summarized, Roe's complaint claimed that defendants "interfered with' . . . 'intimidated' . . . and used 'physical obstruction' . . . to restrain Plaintiff and render impassable her desired egress from the clinic," in violation of 18 U.S.C.§ 248 (a)(1). In response, the defendants filed Rule 12(b)(6) motions to dismiss, arguing that Roe was attempting to use FACE in a manner contrary to both the language and purpose of the statute. Along with her opposition to the motions to dismiss, Roe filed a motion to proceed anonymously. The district court granted the motions to dismiss, explaining that in its view the complaint failed to allege the defendants had acted "in order to prevent Roe from obtaining reproductive health services. "The dismissal was without prejudice, the court giving Roe leave to amend her complaint within ten days of the dismissal. In the same order, the district court also denied Roe's request to proceed anonymously, concluding that the "presumption of openness in judicial proceedings" was not outweighed by any substantial privacy right of Roe's.

II. DISCUSSION

In order to decide whether the complaint made the necessary allegations, we first look at the elements of a cause of action under FACE, an inquiry which requires us to construe the statute. The statute itself sets out the three elements of a FACE claim:

1) that a defendant, by "force or threat of force or by physical obstruction";

2) "intentionally injures, intimidates or interferes with or attempts to injure, intimidate or interfere with any person";

3) "because that person is or has been, or in order to intimidate such person or any other person or any class of persons from, obtaining or providing reproductive health services."

18 U.S.C. § 248 (a)(1).

The defendants do not contest that the first element is met by the allegations, and it clearly is. Regarding the second element, the statute provides that "the term 'interfere with' means to restrict a person's freedom of movement." 18 U.S.C. § 248(e)(2). Thus, the second element is satisfied if the defendants, in restraining Roe, intended to restrict her freedom of movement. Dr. Egherman concedes that Roe has alleged sufficient facts to satisfy the second element. While the other defendants do not concede as much, the allegation that the defendants held Roe down sufficiently implies that in doing so they intended to restrict her freedom of movement.

It is the third element, that of the defendants' motive, which is primarily at issue in this case. The district court determined that in order to satisfy the third element, Roe's complaint must contain allegations that the defendants, in restraining her, were motivated by a desire to "prevent Roe from obtaining reproductive health services." The parties agree on that much. They disagree, however, about whether the complaint can be fairly read as alleging that element. Included in their disagreement is a difference about the nature of "reproductive health services."

The statute defines "reproductive health services" to include "medical, surgical, counseling or referral services relating to the human reproductive system, including services relating to pregnancy or the termination of a pregnancy." *Id.* § 248(e)(5). The defendants attempt to limit the "reproductive health services" at issue in this case to Roe's abortion procedure, arguing that "Roe has failed to allege the defendants' acts were intended to interfere with Roe's egress from the clinic in order to prevent her from obtaining an abortion." However, the complaint, properly construed, alleges that Roe was denied a type of "reproductive health service" other than the termination of her pregnancy. . . .

Viewed in the light most favorable to her, Roe's complaint alleges that she wanted to go to the hospital to obtain some kind of "medical" or "surgical" services "relating to" either her "reproductive system" or "the termination of her pregnancy." *Id.* § 248(e)(5). For purposes of FACE, it matters not whether the reason Roe wanted to leave the clinic immediately and go to a hospital emergency room was so that she could have the damage done to her uterus repaired, or because she had changed her mind and wanted to save the pregnancy, or because she wanted to have the abortion completed at a hospital instead of at the clinic. If the defendants restrained Roe for the purpose of preventing her from obtaining any of those services, then she has adequately pleaded a violation of FACE because all of those services fall within the statutory definition of "reproductive health services."

The next question then is whether Roe's complaint can be construed as alleging that defendants, in restraining Roe, were motivated by a desire to prevent her from obtaining those services. Defendants contend that it is unreasonable to assume that they restrained Roe in order to prevent her from obtaining reproductive health services. They argue that if they did restrain Roe, the only reason they did so was to protect her life and health and prevent further injury from the complications that had arisen during the course of the abortion procedure. Roe concedes that if that were the defendants' motive, there was no violation of FACE.

A complaint cannot be dismissed unless "it is clear that no relief could be granted under any set of facts that could be proved consistent with the allegations." *Shands Teaching Hosp. and Clinics, Inc. v. Beech St. Corp.*, 208 F.3d 1308, 1310 (11th Cir. 2000). And that is true even where "it may appear on the face of the pleadings that a recovery is very remote and unlikely." *Scheuer v. Rhodes*, 416 U.S. 232, 236 (1974). The possibility that defendants were motivated by considerations other than protecting Roe's life and health may be "remote and unlikely," but it is not a possibility that is inconsistent with the allegations of the complaint.

The reasonableness of that assumption aside, the defendants correctly point out that Roe failed to allege anything at all regarding defendants' motive. Defendants argue that the motive requirement is the load-bearing element of a FACE claim and that Roe's failure to plead motive should result in the dismissal of her complaint. As observed by the Eighth Circuit:

> FACE's motive requirement accomplishes . . . the perfectly constitutional task of filtering out conduct that Congress believes need not be covered by a federal statute. Congress enacted FACE to prohibit conduct that interferes with the ability of women to obtain abortions. FACE's motive requirement targets this conduct while ensuring that FACE does not federalize a slew of random crimes that might occur in the vicinity of an abortion clinic.

United States v. Dinwiddie, 76 F.3d 913, 923 (8th Cir. 1996). Thus, it is clear that the motive requirement is an essential element of a FACE claim. The question then, is whether Roe's failure to specifically plead motive, or to include any allegations at all that would establish motive, is fatal to her claim.

Rule 8(a) requires only "a short and plain statement of the claim showing that the pleader is entitled to relief." Fed.R.Civ.P. 8(a)(2). As this Court has previously observed, the liberal "notice pleading" standards embodied in Federal Rule of Civil Procedure 8(a)(2) do not require that a plaintiff specifically plead every element of a cause of action.

However, while notice pleading may not require that the pleader allege a "specific fact" to cover every element or allege "with precision" each element of a claim, it is still necessary that a complaint "contain either direct or inferential allegations respecting all the material elements necessary to sustain a recovery under some viable legal theory." *In re Plywood Antitrust Litigation*, 655 F.2d 627, 641 (5th Cir. Unit A Sept.8, 1981). See also *St. Joseph's Hosp. [v. Hospital Corp. of America*, 795 F.2d 948, 954 (11th Cir. 1986)] ("The pleading must contain either direct allegations on every material point necessary to sustain a recovery on any legal theory . . . or contain allegations from which an inference fairly may be drawn that evidence on these material points will be introduced at trial.") (internal quotation and citation omitted); *Quality Foods v. Latin Am. Agribusiness Dev. Corp.*, 711 F.2d 989, 995 (11th Cir. 1983) (stating, "enough data must be pleaded so that each element of the alleged . . . violation can be properly identified").

Thus, at a minimum, notice pleading requires that a complaint contain inferential allegations from which we can identify each of the material elements necessary to sustain a recovery under some viable legal theory. Here, Roe's complaint contains no allegations, inferential or otherwise, regarding defendants' motive, and Roe will ultimately have to prove that defendants acted with the proscribed motive if she is to prevail on the merits. Accordingly, the district court correctly dismissed Roe's complaint.

In dismissing Roe's complaint, the district court expressly granted Roe ten days to amend her complaint. However, in the same order, the district court also denied Roe's motion to proceed anonymously, thereby presenting her with a Hobson's choice—amend her complaint under her real name, or elect to treat the dismissal as final and stand on her complaint as written. Seeking to preserve her anonymity, Roe elected the latter option. Although we conclude that her complaint as currently fashioned does not state a claim under FACE, for reasons that we will discuss below, the district court erred in denying Roe's motion to proceed anonymously. Accordingly, on remand Roe should again be afforded a reasonable opportunity to amend her complaint and to do so while proceeding anonymously.

If Roe chooses to amend her complaint to include allegations regarding defendants' motive, it will not be a difficult matter for her to draft allegations that would satisfy Rule 9(b). The second sentence of Rule 9(b) provides that "malice, intent, knowledge, and other conditions of mind of a person may be averred generally." Of course, every complaint is a good faith representation to the court that, "to the best of the person's knowledge, information, and belief, formed after an inquiry reasonable under the circumstances," there is evidentiary support for the allegations contained therein. Fed.R.Civ.P. 11(b). If, for whatever reason, Roe fails or refuses to properly amend her complaint, the district court should reinstate its order of dismissal. If she does amend her complaint to allege, based on information and belief, the requisite motive, the complaint cannot be dismissed for failure to state a claim.
. . .

Notes and Questions

1. Before comparing the three cases in this section, recreate the defendants' arguments in each case. Were the defendants alleging that the complaints were all deficient in the same way? According to the defendants, what was wrong with the complaint in each case?

2. Now, focus on the situation in *Swierkiewicz*. Do you agree with the Court that the plaintiff put the defendant "on notice" of what the plaintiff was claiming? If the complaint is proper, defendant's next step will be to file an answer, in which it admits or denies the claim against it. Did the plaintiff provide the defendant enough information to allow it honestly to admit or deny the claim?

3. How does the logic of the prior note apply to *Daniels*? The complaint in that case argued that plaintiff was entitled to recover under Illinois law, whereas in truth Illinois law did not give any rights to plaintiff. However, plaintiff could recover under Indiana law. Did that complaint really put defendant on notice of plaintiff's claim? If you represented defendant in that case, how would you respond to a complaint that cites Illinois law? More particularly, suppose you had concluded that your client was liable under Indiana law, but not under Illinois law (because Illinois law did not govern). After reading *Daniels*, would you feel confident simply denying liability? Doesn't the court conclude that the complaint actually states a claim, although not under the cited law?

On the other hand, suppose that, as in the case itself, you were confident that your client was not negligent. In that case you would be free to file an answer denying liability, because without negligence your client would not be liable under either Illinois or Indiana law.

Rethink this issue after you have studied the rules governing the answer in Part E of this chapter. A defendant may well be under an obligation to explain exactly *why* she is denying liability.

In *Daniels*, was there any question whether the plaintiff had included enough *facts* when stating its claim?

4. Of the three cases above, the two that are most difficult to reconcile are *Swierkiewicz* and *Roe*. Is the result in *Roe* consistent with the Supreme Court's interpretation of Rule 8(a)? Is there any question whether the defendant in *Roe* knew exactly the incident that gave rise to the suit, as well as the plaintiff's theory of recovery?

5. The result in *Roe* hinges on the court's conclusion that the element of motive is a "load bearing element" of a claim under the Freedom of Access to Clinic Entrances Act. Therefore, the court concludes, a complaint is not proper unless plaintiff specifically alleges that defendant meant to prevent her from obtaining medical services. Do you understand why the court is singling out motive as a crucial element of a FACE claim?

Consider another claim—a common-law claim for negligence. As you have learned or will learn in Torts, the elements of a negligence claim are (a) that the defendant owed a duty to the plaintiff, (b) that the duty was breached (usually by a careless act or failure to act), (c) that the carelessness caused the plaintiff's injury, and (d) damages. Which, if any, of these are "load bearing elements?" What about carelessness? In one respect, the notion of carelessness is the heart and soul of a negligence claim. Therefore, shouldn't a plaintiff in a negligence case at least be required to state specifically that the defendant acted carelessly, and possibly even state *how* the defendant was careless?

Now test your reasoning of what are the load bearing elements of a negligence claim with Federal Form 9 set out above. According to Form 9—which because of Federal Rule 84 is *per se* sufficient—a plaintiff claiming negligence may simply describe the event, and state in the most conclusory fashion that the defendant acted "negligently." The complaint does not have to say anything in particular about duty or breach, and barely needs to touch upon causation.

In light of Form 9, do you think that the court reached the right result in *Roe*?

6. What is the penalty for filing an insufficient complaint? *Roe* reflects the overwhelming consensus on this issue. If a court determines that plaintiff's complaint is insufficient, the remedy is not to dismiss outright, but to give plaintiff at least one additional opportunity to remedy the situation. Viewed in that light, is the result in *Roe* that draconian? True, the court requires plaintiff specifically to allege that defendant acted with improper motive. However, it does not require plaintiff to include detailed facts demonstrating that motive. The plaintiff need only reveal what facts it has in its possession that might allow the factfinder to find, or even infer, motive.

Therefore, even if the court in *Roe* is technically wrong, is the result all that big a deal? Consider the issue over which the parties are fighting. Is there something special about an issue such as motive that makes it unfair to require the plaintiff to allege it specifically? Who best knows why the defendant acted the way it did?

2. Heightened Pleading Standards

The "notice pleading" standard of Rule 8(a) sets a very low threshold on a party seeking to file a claim. Although that standard applies to the vast majority of civil claims filed with a federal court, it is not universal. In a few situations, a party is required to plead a claim with greater specificity. The following cases describe two such situations.

ALTERNATIVE SYSTEM CONCEPTS, INC. v. SYNOPSYS, INC.

374 F.3d 23 (1st Cir. 2004)

SELYA, Circuit Judge.

This is a case of a suitor scorned. Plaintiff-appellant Alternative System Concepts, Inc. (ASC) courted Language for Design Automation, Inc. (LEDA) and forged a short-term distribution relationship. As the couple moved toward a more durable bond, defendant-appellee Synopsys, Inc. acquired LEDA and dashed ASC's hopes.

The jilted suitor responded aggressively, haling Synopsys into court and claiming, inter alia, misrepresentation and breach of promise. The district court dismissed the former claim early in the proceedings and subsequently granted summary judgment for Synopsys on the latter. ASC appeals. . . .

I. BACKGROUND

We rehearse the facts in the light most favorable to the nonmoving party (here, ASC) and draw all reasonable inferences in that party's favor. . . .

ASC is a New Hampshire corporation involved in the design and marketing of programs used in the production of computer chips. On March 29, 1999, it entered into a letter of understanding (the LOU) with LEDA, a French software designer. In the LOU, LEDA appointed ASC as the exclusive distributor of its Proton product line in the United States for a six-month term commencing April 1, 1999. The parties further declared that they would attempt to "negotiate in good faith a permanent agreement based on experiences during the term of the LOU." That declaration was purely aspirational; the LOU stated expressly that neither party had any obligation to enter such a permanent agreement.

During the next six months, the two firms engaged in sporadic negotiations. On September 1, 1999, their representatives met in France in hopes of hammering out the details of a permanent arrangement. Although LEDA's managing director assured ASC that "all was satisfactory with regard to a permanent agreement," the parties neither developed nor signed a written contract. Later that month, the parties exchanged e-mails that apparently extended the geographic coverage of the LOU to Canada.

Talks continued past the LOU's expiration date (September 30, 1999). On October 5, representatives of the two companies met in Florida. LEDA agreed to extend the LOU for a reasonable time pending the completion of negotiations. It also notified a prospective customer that ASC remained the exclusive distributor of LEDA products in the United States and Canada. ASC claims that the parties had by then substantially agreed on the key terms of a permanent distribution relationship, but the fact remains that LEDA balked at signing such an agreement.

In January of 2000, Synopsys (a California-based competitor of ASC) acquired LEDA. It promptly terminated the interim distribution agreement and broke off the negotiations for a permanent relationship. ASC was left out in the cold.

ASC lost little time in bringing this diversity action against Synopsys in New Hampshire's federal district court. Its first amended complaint charged that LEDA had been derelict in its duty to negotiate a permanent distribution agreement in good faith; that LEDA had intentionally misrepresented the nature of its interactions with Synopsys; that LEDA had flouted an implied covenant of good faith and fair dealing; and that Synopsys bore responsibility for these transgressions as LEDA's successor in interest. Finally, the first amended complaint charged Synopsys, in its own right, with having interfered with ASC's advantageous contractual relations.

Synopsys moved to jettison the complaint for failure to state claims upon which relief could be granted. See Fed. R. Civ. P. 12(b)(6). On August 2, 2001, the district court dismissed the misrepresentation claim on the ground that ASC had not pleaded misrepresentation with the requisite particularity. ...

On appeal, ASC contends that the lower court erred in (i) dismissing its misrepresentation claim ...

ASC assigns error to both the district court's dismissal of its misrepresentation claim and to the court's subsequent "failure" to allow a curative amendment. These remonstrances need not occupy us for long.

A. Applicable Legal Standards.

We review *de novo* a trial court's allowance of a Rule 12(b)(6) motion to dismiss. In that process, we take as true the factual averments contained in the complaint, but "eschew any reliance on bald assertions, unsupportable conclusions, and opprobrious epithets." *Chongris [v. Board of Appeals*, 811 F.2d 36, 37 (1st Cir. 1987)]. From this plaintiff-friendly coign of vantage, we may affirm an order for dismissal only if no well-pleaded set of facts supports recovery. *Conley v. Gibson*, 355 U.S. 41, 45–46 (1957).

Federal civil practice is based on notice pleading. Thus, "great specificity is ordinarily not required to survive a Rule 12(b)(6) motion." *Garita Hotel Ltd. P'ship v. Ponce Fed. Bank*, 958 F.2d 15, 17 (1st Cir. 1992). Cases alleging fraud—and for this purpose, misrepresentation is considered a species of fraud—constitute an exception to this general proposition. The Civil Rules explicitly require that "in all averments of fraud ... the circumstances constituting fraud ... shall be stated with particularity." Fed. R. Civ. P. 9(b). In such cases, the pleader usually is expected to specify the who, what, where, and when of the allegedly false or fraudulent representation.[4]

B. The Original Claim.

ASC's first amended complaint alleged in substance that LEDA failed to disclose that merger talks were ongoing between it and Synopsys, but, rather, downplayed the discussions and characterized the contemplated relationship as merely a "technical partnership" that would not affect the outcome of the ASC–LEDA negotiations. ASC further alleged that it relied on these knowingly false representations to its detriment. Despite the fervor with which ASC denounced this treachery,

---

4. We say "usually" because there may be occasional exceptions, owing to extraordinary circumstances. See, e.g., *Corley v.* *Rosewood Care Ctr., Inc.*, 142 F.3d 1041, 1050–51 (7th Cir. 1998). No such circumstances are extant here.

it did not provide any details as to who allegedly uttered the misleading statements, to whom they were made, where they were made, when they occurred, and what actions they engendered. In short, ASC's misrepresentation claim was wholly conclusory and lacking any semblance of specific detail. Given the strictures of Rule 9(b), the district court's dismissal of that barebones claim was entirely proper.

C. The Curative Amendment.

ASC's fallback position is as insubstantial as a house built upon the shifting sands. It notes that, after the district court had dismissed the misrepresentation claim for want of specificity, it moved for leave to refile, in a further amended complaint, a more particularized version of the claim. The district court denied this request on February 14, 2003, and ASC now calumnizes that order.

This challenge is based on a half-truth. Although ASC did seek leave to file a curative amendment, it unilaterally withdrew that motion before the court reached the matter. A party who voluntarily withdraws a motion prior to judicial consideration cannot later claim that the court's pro forma denial of the withdrawn motion constitutes reversible error. See *Baty v. United States*, 275 F.2d 310, 311 (9th Cir. 1960) (per curiam); cf. *United States v. Tierney*, 760 F.2d 382, 388 (1st Cir. 1985) ("Having one's cake and eating it, too, is not in fashion in this circuit.").

[Affirmed.]

Notes and Questions

1. Do you understand how the heightened pleading standard of Rule 9(b) actually differs in practice from the notice pleading standard of 8(a)? To help you understand the difference, try to rewrite the form complaint in Federal Form 9 as if negligence were subject to the 9(b) heightened standard. How much more would a plaintiff need to say to satisfy 9(b)?

2. Rule 9(b) indicates that the heightened pleading standard applies to fraud and to mistake. Why, then, is the court applying it to a claim for misrepresentation?

3. Unlike the basic standard of Rule 8(a), Rule 9(b) applies not only to claims for relief, but to all assertions of fraud or mistake. In actual practice, claims of fraud or mistake are often asserted by defendants as defenses to contract claims. If the plaintiff induced the defendant to enter into the contract by fraud, or if the parties were mistaken as to a core underlying fact, the contract is void, which means that plaintiff cannot sue for breach.

4. Why does Rule 9(b) single out certain claims for a higher pleading standard? Many courts and commentators state that the purpose is to protect reputation. Because an allegation of fraud could damage defendant's reputation (and because any judgment exonerating the defendant would not occur for some time, and not receive as much media coverage), a complaint alleging fraud must show that it is well-grounded in fact before plaintiff will even be allowed in court.

If protecting reputation is the rationale behind the rule, why does the heightened pleading standard also apply to *mistake*? Allegations that one has made a mistake, after all, are not likely to besmirch one's good name. And why are other damning accusations such as the intentional torts of battery and conversion of property governed by mere notice pleading? In truth, Rule 9(b) is a historical accident; a carryover from pre-Federal Rules pleading regimes. An excellent discussion of the evolution of the Rule can be found in William M. Richman, Donald E. Lively, and Patricia Mell, "The Pleading of Fraud: Rhymes Without Reason," 60 S. Cal. L. Rev. 959 (1987). Although the reputation argument may not be historically correct, it does provide some *post hoc* justification for keeping the rule the way it is.

5. In many cases the facts necessary to prove fraud are under the control of the defendant. Some courts have proven willing to relax the standards of Rule 9(b) when the plaintiff has no access to the facts. In addition to footnote 4 in *Alternative System Concepts*, see *In re Rockefeller Center Properties, Inc. Securities Litigation*, 311 F.3d 198 (3d Cir. 2002). By allowing plaintiff to file the complaint, the court makes it possible for plaintiff to avail itself of discovery to unearth the necessary facts.

6. Are there other areas in which courts subject claims to a heightened pleading standard? For a number of years, some courts held civil rights claims to a heightened standard, perhaps because of the disproportionately high percentage of such claims found to be frivolous. The Supreme Court ended this practice in *Leatherman v. Tarrant County Narcotics Intelligence and Coordination Unit*, 507 U.S. 163, 113 S.Ct. 1160, 122 L.Ed.2d 517 (1993). The Court in *Leatherman* held that Rules 8(a) and 9(b) mean what they say, and that lower courts had no authority to export Rule 9(b)'s higher standards to claims other than fraud and mistake. Therefore, civil rights claims, like others, must only afford the defendant notice of the underlying events and the claim.

Although the Court's rationale technically applied only to claims against units of government, not individual officials, post-*Leatherman* decisions have generally applied it to all civil rights claims. However, in cases in which an official claims that she is protected by a qualified immunity, plaintiff is required to plead additional facts. These facts are usually set out in the reply, after defendant has filed an answer claiming the immunity. This unique feature of civil rights law is discussed below in the section dealing with the reply.

Notwithstanding *Leatherman*, some scholars have argued that courts routinely impose heightened pleading standards on certain types of claims. *See, e.g.*, Christopher M. Fairman, "The Myth of Notice Pleading," 45 Ariz. L. Rev. 987 (2003).

———————————

The prior case and notes show how Rule 9(b) requires a party to provide more detail than would otherwise be required by Rule 8(a). The following case discusses another subsection of Rule 9 that similarly requires a party to be more specific.

BROWNING v. CLINTON

292 F.3d 235 (D.C. Cir. 2002)

TATEL, Circuit Judge:

In this appeal, we review the district court's Rule 12(b)(6) dismissal of eight common and federal law claims against former President Clinton, two of his lawyers, one of his aides, *The New Yorker*, and a journalist. Construing the complaint liberally and giving appellant the "benefit of all inferences that can be derived from the facts alleged," *Kowal v. MCI Communications Corp.*, 16 F.3d 1271, 1276 (D.C. Cir. 1994), we affirm as to all appellees except Mr. Clinton; with respect to Mr. Clinton, we affirm the dismissal of six claims and reverse two.

This case involves appellant Dolly Kyle Browning's "longstanding friendship" with former President Clinton—a friendship she alleges "included an extramarital, sexual relationship"—and her "semi-autobiographical novel" in which the female protagonist has a long-standing extramarital affair with the governor of a southern state. Browning copyrighted her novel in 1988 and sent it to Warner Books, where an editor "encouraged [her] to continue to work on [it]." Thereafter, Browning charges, Clinton and the other appellees engaged in a scheme to prevent publication of her book and defame her. According to the amended complaint, the scheme involved the following:

In 1992, Browning's own brother, allegedly at Clinton's direction, telephoned to "warn[ ] [Browning], 'if you cooperate with the media we will destroy you.' " Clinton's brother also "threatened [her]" by phone. The following year, appellee Bruce Lindsey, then serving as Deputy White House Counsel, "threatened [ ] Browning by telling her sister[,] 'we've read your sister's book and we don't want it published.' "

In 1994, Browning and Clinton met at their thirtieth high school reunion where, according to Browning, Clinton "apologized to [her] for the threat that had been made against her." Shortly thereafter, Browning's sister and Lindsey, acting as intermediaries, reached an "understanding" about what Browning could say: She "was permitted to say publicly that she and Clinton had a thirty-three year relationship that from time to time included sex," but "agreed not to tell the true story" and "not to use ... the 'A words' ... adultery and affair"; Clinton agreed "not [to] tell any lies about [her]."

Browning retained a literary agent in the summer of 1995. Later that year, *Esquire* magazine published an article about Browning and her book, and in early 1996, *Publisher's Weekly* reported that Browning was "ready to go public in a big way via the book business[,] ... assuming, that is, that a publisher bites. This month, [Browning's literary agent] will begin shopping around a bombshell *roman a clef* that could knock *Primary Colors* right out of the headlines." In the end, however, Browning received no "positive responses, offers to publish, or contracts from any of the publishers that she contacted." Appellant

Direct Outstanding Creations Corporation, a business created by Browning's husband, subsequently "acquired . . . rights to . . . the manuscript . . . [but] has not been able to sell [those] rights to . . . any publisher[ ]."

Appellee *The New Yorker* ran an article in 1997 by appellee Jane Mayer attributing comments to publisher Alfred S. Regnery about "a memoir by a putative Presidential mistress." According to the article, although "it seemed plausible . . . that [such] a memoir . . . would find a home at Regnery [Publishing Co.][,]" Regnery said he "wouldn't touch [the book] with a ten-foot pole" because it wasn't "particularly newsworthy" and was "far below [Regnery's] standards." Browning claims that she never sent her manuscript to Regnery, and that Regnery never made these statements. . . .

Based on the foregoing, Browning asserts eight common and federal law claims: (1) tortious interference with prospective business opportunity (against all appellees); (2) disparagement of property (against *The New Yorker* and Mayer); . . . Concluding that Browning failed to state a claim with respect to each count and denying leave to amend, the district court dismissed the complaint with prejudice under Federal Rules of Civil Procedure 12(b)(6) and 15(a). Browning appeals. . . .

[Discussion of other claims omitted.]

As support for her disparagement of property claim against *The New Yorker* and Mayer, Browning relies on the article reporting Regnery's negative comments. A disparagement of property claim requires that the plaintiff plead "special damages," *Fowler v. Curtis Publ'g Co.*, 182 F.2d 377, 378 (D.C. Cir. 1950), that is, "pecuniary harm resulting from the defendant's unprivileged publication of false statements, with knowledge or reckless disregard of the falsity, concerning the plaintiff's property or product," *Art Metal–U.S.A., Inc. v. United States*, 753 F.2d 1151, 1155 n.6 (D.C. Cir. 1985). Federal Rule of Civil Procedure 9(g) requires that special damages be "specifically stated," i.e., the plaintiff must allege actual damages with "particularity" and specify " 'facts showing that such special damages were the natural and direct result' "of the defendant's conduct (here, the alleged false and disparaging article). *Fowler*, 182 F.2d at 379. This heightened pleading standard applies because "special damages," unlike general damages, are "not the necessary consequence of [the] defendant's conduct, [but] stem from the particular circumstances of the case." 5 Charles Wright & Arthur Miller, *Federal Practice and Procedure* § 1310, at 700. A plaintiff can satisfy this pleading obligation by identifying either particular customers whose business has been lost or facts showing an established business and the amount of sales before and after the disparaging publication, along with evidence of causation.

Browning's amended complaint states that "as a proximate result of the publication of [Mayer's article], . . . neither [ ] Browning nor Direct Outstanding Creations Corporation were [sic] able to sell the publishing and other rights in the manuscript," and therefore that they suffered damages "including but not limited to marketing and other business expenses incurred ... , loss of goodwill, [and] emotional distress and mental anguish." According to Browning, these allegations satisfy Rule 9(g) because they "notify the defendant as to the nature of the claimed damages." Amplifying this point at oral argument, counsel insisted that "the standard of pleading special damages has been relegated to notice pleading." We find no support for this proposition. Indeed, it runs counter to the very case Browning cites, *Schoen v. Washington Post*, which expressly requires that disparagement of property claims set forth "the precise nature of the losses as well as the way in which the special damages resulted from the allegedly false publication." 246 F.2d 670, 672 (D.C. Cir. 1957). The plaintiff in *Schoen* specified his business receipts before and after defendant's disparaging publication, alleged that the publication caused "many customers to withdraw their custom," and identified three such customers. Browning's amended complaint contains no allegations remotely like those in *Schoen*. She neither quantifies her loss nor identifies any lost business relationships. She alleges no facts suggesting causation. While it may not be "necessary ... to provide ... the *maximum* degree of detail that plaintiff might be capable of providing," Browning merely asserts in general terms that *The New Yorker* article cost her financially. We agree with the district court that Rule 9(g) requires more. ...

Notes and Questions

1. In *Browning*, a showing of special damages was an element of the claim itself. Plaintiff could not recover for disparagement of property unless she could prove actual pecuniary loss. Because of Rule 9(g), she must not only be able to prove that loss at trial, but she must also include specific information about that loss in her complaint. Ordinary damages, by contrast, may be alleged in general terms.

2. Very few legal claims require a showing of special damages as an element. Most of these are claims that evolved from libel and slander. However, this does not mean that Rule 9(g) issues rarely arise. Courts have interpreted the term "special damages" in a way that is not limited to a handful of cases. Today, courts interpret special damages to mean any injury that would not be expected to flow from the underlying event. As a result, Rule 9(g) can apply to any substantive claim.

For example, consider an automobile accident in which plaintiff suffered whiplash and a heart attack. Whiplash would constitute general damages, as it is easily foreseeable. Therefore, the complaint would not have to mention the whiplash specifically. However, courts would interpret Rule 9(g) to require the plaintiff to mention the heart attack in the complaint. Failure to include special damages precludes plaintiff from introducing evidence of that injury at trial, although courts may allow the plaintiff to amend. Under this broader interpretation, special damages can more accurately be thought of as special *injury*—any injury that would come as a surprise to the defendant.

Rules 9(b) and (g) require more of a claimant for certain issues. Other provisions in Rule 9, however, have just the opposite effect. Rule 9(a), for example, provides that a party need not allege either her or the other side's capacity to sue or be sued. Rules 9(c), (d), and (e) allow a party to allege conditions precedent (such as conditions to performance of a contract), official documents and acts, and judgments in very general terms. When attempting to recover on a judgment from one state in a different state, for example, the judgment victor does not have to allege that the rendering court had jurisdiction. If defendant wants to argue that the judgment is void because of lack of jurisdiction, he must raise that issue in his answer.

3.   The Prayer for Relief

In addition to the jurisdictional statement and statement of the claim, Rule 8(a) requires a party to include "a demand for judgment for the relief the pleader seeks." This gives the pleader the opportunity to inform the court what she hopes to gain from the case, whether it be an award of damages or an injunction. The Rule specifically allows a pleader to seek several different remedies, or even to plead for alternative, inconsistent remedies. Therefore, a plaintiff in a breach of contract case could ask the court for both an order of specific performance and damages for nonperformance. Although it would constitute double recovery for a court to grant both, plaintiff can make its preferences as to remedy known.

A party who asks for damages must include a specific figure in the request. If the party also seeks punitive damages, the prayer usually lists the figures for compensatory and punitive damages separately. Note that the specific damages figure is not the same as an allegation of special damages, discussed just above. Special damages are essentially part of the statement of the claim itself. The damages request in the prayer for relief is usually merely a specific dollar figure, with little if any explanation of how it is calculated.

Many states do not allow a claimant to state a damages figure, because of a fear that exaggerated damages requests might unduly influence the jury. This difference between state and federal practice can prove to be an issue in cases that are removed from the state to the federal courts based on diversity, as the court cannot immediately determine the amount in controversy. The federal court in a removal case will often ask for additional information on the damages being sought. Others will treat defendant's removal as an admission that the amount in controversy exceeds $75,000.

The prayer for relief mainly serves as a rough guide. Under Federal Rule 54(c), the court is not limited by the prayer for relief when awarding judgment for a party. Therefore, the court can grant damages even when the claimant sought only an injunction. By the same token, if the court or jury determines that plaintiff suffered one million dollars of damage, the court can enter judgment for that amount even though plaintiff asked for only eighty thousand. (For an example from pop culture that drives this point home, watch the film "The Verdict" with Paul Newman.)

There is, however, one situation where the prayer for relief is binding. If defendant chooses not to defend the case and thereby defaults, the default judgment cannot exceed, or be different in kind from, the relief requested in the prayer. Therefore, it is important for a plaintiff to ask for enough to satisfy the claim.

4. The Form of the Complaint

The discussion to this point has concentrated on the language a party uses to state a claim. The Federal Rules, however, also contain some requirements concerning the *form* of the complaint. Most of these requirements can be found in Rule 10.

Before reviewing these requirements, make sure you understand the difference between a *pleading* and *motion*. Although attorneys and judges understand the difference intuitively, it can be difficult for a first-year student to see the difference. Like pleadings, most motions are in writing. Both must also meet most of the rules governing form set out in Federal Rule 10. Both ask the court to do something. So what is the difference?

A case in federal court will involve a very limited number of pleadings. If there is a single plaintiff and a single defendant, the only pleadings will be a complaint, an answer, and possibly a reply. Additional pleadings may occur in a case involving multiple parties, as there may be pleadings for the cross-claims and third-party claims. Even so, the number of pleadings is strictly limited by Rule 7(a). All other requests to the court are made by motion, as provided in Rule 7(b).

Motions are best thought of as a "silver bullet." They are both more specific and more immediate than a pleading. A pleading is a comprehensive instrument in which a party lays out all of its claims, defenses, and/or objections. In some respects, a pleading sets out a roadmap for the entire trial. A motion seizes on one or more issues in that case, and attempts to convince the court to resolve them immediately. Of course, the same issues can appear in both a pleading and a motion. For example, a defendant may assert lack of personal jurisdiction as one of the defenses in her answer, a pleading. After filing that answer, that defendant will probably file a motion asking the court to dismiss the case for that very reason.

Rule 10 sets out a certain basic form that all pleadings must follow. The following hypothetical complaint illustrates how Rule 10 applies in practice. This complaint will also serve as the basis for further discussion.

UNITED STATES DISTRICT COURT
WESTERN DISTRICT OF KENTUCKY
AT LOUISVILLE

GEORGE W. KERRY, Plaintiff
101 Oak Street
Political City, Kentucky 45000

COMPLAINT

v.   Case No. _____

FLY–BY–NIGHT INSURANCE CO.
Premium City, Montana 90000

_____

Plaintiff for his Complaint against Defendant states as follows:

PARTIES

1.   Plaintiff, George W. Kerry, is a citizen of the Commonwealth of Kentucky.

2.   Defendant, Fly–By–Night Insurance Company ["Fly–By–Night"] is a Delaware corporation with its principal place of business in Premium City, Montana.

JURISDICTION AND VENUE

3.   This Court has subject matter jurisdiction pursuant to 28 United States Code § 1332. Plaintiff is a citizen of the Commonwealth of Kentucky. Defendant is a citizen of the States of Delaware and Montana. The amount of controversy, excluding interest and costs, exceeds $75,000.

4.   Defendant has transacted business within the Commonwealth of Kentucky as hereinafter more particularly described, and is therefore subject to the personal jurisdiction of this Court pursuant to Kentucky Revised Statutes § 454.210.

5.   Venue is proper in this Court pursuant to 28 United States Code § 1391 because a substantial portion of the activities giving rise to this action occurred in the Western District of Kentucky.

FACTUAL BACKGROUND

6.   On November 1, 2004, Plaintiff made an application for a policy of electability insurance, Policy No. 007, through Defendant's agent, Ralph Raider.

7.   On November 1, 2004, Plaintiff issued a check to Defendant for $76,000 for the premium on the policy. In exchange for the premium, Ralph Raider, as agent for Defendant, issued a Receipt to Plaintiff on November 1, 2004.

8. On November 3, 2004, Defendant notified Plaintiff that there is a variance between his statements to the media and statements made in his application concerning his prior use of facts. Defendant further notified Plaintiff that this variance precludes coverage for electability insurance.

9. At all times referred to in this Complaint, Defendant was acting by and through its agents and employees, who were at all times acting within the scope of their agency or employment with Defendant.

FIRST CLAIM FOR RELIEF—BREACH OF CONTRACT

10. Plaintiff readopts and realleges the allegations previously set forth in paragraphs 1 to 9 of this Complaint.

11. Defendant has failed and refused to perform its obligations under its contract of insurance with Plaintiff in that it refused to insure Plaintiff.

12. By refusing to perform its obligations, Defendant has breached the terms of the insurance contract.

13. As a result of Defendant's breach of contract, Plaintiff has suffered damages of at least $76,000.

SECOND CLAIM FOR RELIEF—BREACH OF GOOD FAITH

14. Plaintiff readopts and realleges the allegations previously set forth in paragraphs 1 to 9 of this Complaint.

15. Defendant's denial of insurance coverage for Plaintiff on the grounds of Plaintiff's fact abuse is not a valid ground for denial and constitutes a breach of Defendant's obligation to act in good faith.

16. As a result of the wanton or reckless disregard by Defendant of its duties toward Plaintiff, Defendant is liable for punitive damages in an amount to be determined at trial.

WHEREFORE, Plaintiff demands:

1. A judgment and order of this Court that Defendant continue to insure Plaintiff;

2. In the alternative, a judgment and order of this Court against Defendant for ordinary damages in the amount of $200,000;

3. A judgment and order of this Court against Defendant for punitive damages in the amount of $4,000,000; and

4. All other relief, in law and in equity, as may be found proper.

Ash Johncroft
Atty License No. 12345
Smith and Johncroft
200 North Water Street
River City, Kentucky 40001
Counsel for George W. Gore

DEMAND FOR JURY TRIAL

Pursuant to Federal Rule of Civil Procedure 38(b), Plaintiff demands a trial by jury on all claims raised in this Complaint which are so triable.

_____

Counsel for Plaintiff

DATE: January 3, 2005

Notes and Questions

1.   The above complaint really merges two separate documents into one. First, the complaint sets out plaintiff's claims and asks the court to grant recovery. Second, the plaintiff demands a jury trial. A plaintiff does not have to demand a jury in the complaint to preserve his right to a jury trial. Instead, Federal Rule 38(b) allows any party to demand a jury on an issue as late as ten days following the *last* pleading directed to that particular issue. Therefore, a plaintiff could wait to file its demand until after the defendant's answer. Nevertheless, as there is no reason to delay the request, most parties file the demand with their original pleading. At the very least the party saves the additional filing fee.

Note that the plaintiff's attorney signs twice; once after the complaint, and again after the demand for a jury. This seeming redundancy reflects Rule 11, which you will discuss in greater detail later in the chapter. Rule 11 requires that every pleading and motion be signed by an attorney of record. Because the plaintiff is using a single document to serve two functions, the attorney signs twice, as if it were two documents.

2.   Rule 10(a) requires a caption setting out the name of the court, the title of the action, the nature of the pleading (that is, complaint, answer, or reply), and the file number. The heading of the above complaint contains the required information. The "title of the action" is simply the name of the plaintiff and the defendant. If a case involves more than one plaintiff or defendant, all must be named in the complaint, but subsequent pleadings and motions need only state the first named plaintiff and defendant. In other words, if A, B, and C sue X and Y, the complaint would list all five parties, but in all other pleadings and motions the title of the action would be simply "A v. X."

3.   Rule 10(b) requires that the paragraphs in the complaint be numbered. In addition, it indicates that the pleader should limit each paragraph "as far as practicable to a statement of a single set of circumstances." Note that using narrow, numbered fact allegations allows a pleader to incorporate earlier statements by reference, as the drafter of this hypothetical complaint has done.

4.   The description of the parties in Paragraphs One and Two is not technically required. Nevertheless, it is very commonly included. This information provides the court a quick "who's who" in the case. Given that most judges do not immediately review the pleadings when the case is assigned to them, the information provided in this overview is very useful when the

court is called upon to deal with preliminary challenges to jurisdiction and venue.

5. Federal Rule 17(a) requires that all actions "be prosecuted in the name of the real party in interest." Although located outside the portion of the Rules dealing with pleadings, this Rule directly affects how a party drafts its complaint. In essence, Rule 17(a) requires the complaint to name the person who will actually benefit from any judgment for the plaintiff. To see how the Rule applies, consider a situation where an insurance company has fully compensated its insured for a tortious injury caused by another. By law, the insurance company is *subrogated* to the rights of the insured, and can bring an action against the tortfeasor. Under Rule 17, the action must be brought in the name of the insurance company rather than the insured, as any judgment would be paid to the insurance company. Similarly, where the insured has been compensated for part of the injury, the case should be brought in the names of both the insured and the insurance company. Can you see why the insurance company would prefer to leave its name off of the complaint?

Failure to name the real party in interest is rarely fatal to a case. The Rule explicitly provides that a case will not be dismissed for failure to name the real party in interest until the plaintiff has been given a reasonable time to join or substitute the real party in interest.

Note that Rule 17(a) does not require that the action be prosecuted *by* the real party in interest. In the insurance example discussed above, the insurance company may well control litigation of the case. Rule 17 only deals with how the case is captioned.

6. Paragraphs Three to Five comprise the statement of jurisdiction, the first of Rule 8(a)'s three basic elements. As noted earlier, although a statement of subject-matter jurisdiction is required for most claims (including counterclaims, cross-claims, and third-party claims) filed in federal court, allegations concerning personal jurisdiction and venue are not required. Again, however, such allegations are often included as a convenience to the court.

7. Rule 10(b) requires that different claims be stated in separate "counts." The hypothetical complaint uses the more recognizable phrase "claims for relief." Technically, two claims must be phrased as two counts only when they arise from different underlying transactions or occurrences. Therefore, the plaintiff in the hypothetical complaint was not required to list his claims separately. As a matter of convenience, however, most attorneys treat each claim as a separate count or claim for relief.

8. What is the sanction for failing to comply with Rule 10's form requirements? As you may already have guessed, it is extremely rare for a case to be dismissed for failure to number the paragraphs or divide the claims into separate counts. Nor is a court likely to impose sanctions on the attorney. A court may require that the pleading be amended, but even that is rare.

Problems

1. P sues D for breach of contract. The operative language of plaintiff's complaint reads simply, "D owes P $100,000 for goods that P delivered to D

on August 9, 2005.'' D objects to this language, arguing that it does not meet the standards of Rules 8 and 9. Will D prevail on her objection?

2. Same as Problem 1, except that D received several large shipments of different goods from P on the date in question.

3. P sues D, a car dealer, for rescission of a contract for the sale of a used car. P's complaint states that ''D's salesman purposefully lied to P about the condition of the car in question.'' D objects to this language, arguing that it does not meet the standards of Rules 8 and 9. Will D prevail on her objection?

4. P sues D, a car dealer, for rescission of a contract for the sale of a used car. P's complaint goes into great detail about how D's salesman lied about the condition of the car, providing not only the dates upon which the representations occurred, but also the gist of what the salesman said and how it was false. However, because P is suing D rather than the salesman, P also includes the following language in the complaint, ''Because D knew of the salesman's activities, D is also liable.'' D objects to the quoted language, arguing that it fails to provide enough detail about what D knew and how she learned of it. Will D prevail on her objection?

5. Same as Problem 4, except assume that the language set out in that paragraph is sufficient. When the car in question would not start, P could not make it to the local convenience store to buy his weekly lottery ticket, and accordingly did not win the lottery. In his prayer for relief, P does not mention anything about the lottery ticket, but does state that ''as a consequence of the false statement, P suffered $10,000,000 in damages.'' D objects to the quoted language, arguing that it does not meet the standards of Rules 8 and 9. Will D prevail on her objection?

6. P sues D for conversion of P's personal property. In her prayer for relief, P asks the court both to order D to return the property, and to pay P the market value of the property. D objects, pointing out that plaintiff is not entitled to both the property and its value in damages. Will D prevail on his objection?

C. OBJECTING TO THE STATEMENT OF A CLAIM

INTRODUCTORY PROBLEM

ACME, Inc. and Fisk's Disks are engaged in a life-and-death struggle. Both companies sell floppy disks for use in computers. Because demand for floppy disks has fallen off dramatically during the past few years, both companies have had difficulties eking out a profit. ACME and Fisk's both need to divert business from the other in order to survive.

Over the past few months, ACME's sales have fallen precipitously. When ACME discovers that Fisk's has been engaged in some arguably shady activities to win over ACME's customers, ACME sues Fisk's in a federal district court. ACME's complaint contains three claims for relief. The first is a false advertising claim under federal law. ACME alleges that Fisk's sales staff has been making false and derogatory statements about ACME's product to customers, therefore convincing them to switch brands. Claim number two is a common-law tortious interference with contract claim. The third claim alleges "sales below cost," arguing that Fisk's sold its product at a price below its total production costs, thereby winning over additional customers. Jurisdiction is based on federal question, coupled with supplemental jurisdiction.

Fisk's immediately files a pre-answer motion to dismiss for lack of personal jurisdiction and venue. The court denies the motion to dismiss. Fisk's then files an answer. In this answer, Fisk's argues that the second and third claims should be dismissed because they do not state claims on which relief can be granted. With respect to the tortious interference claim, Fisk's argues that the complaint is insufficient. ACME alleged only that "Fisk's intentionally contacted some of ACME's regular customers to convince them to buy Fisk's products." The tort of tortious interference with contract, however, requires proof that the defendant caused someone *who had a binding contract* with the plaintiff to breach that contract. Because ACME did not allege the existence of a contract between the customers and ACME, Fisk's argues that the complaint is deficient.

With respect to the sales below cost claim, Fisk's acknowledges that the complaint contains plenty of background facts. However, Fisk's points out that under governing law, a competitor cannot be held liable for selling its products on the retail level at a price below the cost of production. Therefore, Fisk's claims, ACME cannot prevail on this claim. Fisk's follows its answer with a motion to dismiss the tortious interference and sales below cost claims.

Before the court rules on Fisk's request to dismiss the second and third claims, the parties conduct discovery. In the discovery process, Fisk's learns that ACME has no evidence whatsoever that Fisk's sales personnel made any false statements to ACME's customers. Fisk's then files a new motion to dismiss for failure to state a claim. Although Fisk's acknowledges that the wording of the false advertising claim meets the notice pleading requirements of Rule 8(a), Fisk's argues that the court should dismiss the false advertising claim because ACME is bound to lose.

ACME objects to both the timing and substance of the motions. First, ACME argues that Fisk waived the defense of failure to state a claim by failing to include it along with its personal jurisdiction and venue challenges, and, in the case of the post-answer motion, by failing to include it in the answer. Second, ACME argues that even if the challenges were timely, all three of its claims do state claims upon which relief can be granted.

How will the court rule?

Governing Law: Federal Rules 12(b)(6), 12(e), (g), and (h).

In most of the cases set out to this point in this Chapter, the defendant or defendants moved to dismiss the plaintiff's complaint for failure to state a claim upon which relief can be granted. (*Daniels*, the sole exception, dealt with a motion for summary judgment. The defendant's challenge in that case dealt not with the wording of the complaint, but instead with whether it had been filed on time.) Each of the defendants claimed that the respective complaints were so inadequate that plaintiff should not be allowed to proceed any further with its case. In footnote 1 of *Swierkiewicz*, however, the Supreme Court states that the Court will "accept as true all of the factual allegations contained in the complaint." If a court must accept everything the plaintiff says as true, how can it ever dismiss a complaint for failure to state a claim?

The answer lies in the nature of the motion to dismiss for failure to state a claim. This motion, often called a "12(b)(6)" motion to reflect its location in the Federal Rules, tests only whether the plaintiff has drafted a legally and technically proper complaint. It does not ask whether the claimant is telling the truth or whether it has evidence to support its claim. Nor does it consider any defenses or denials that defendant may include in its answer. As long as the complaint seeks recovery under a theory recognized by governing law, and provides enough detail to comply with Federal Rules 8 and 9, it will survive a 12(b)(6) challenge.

1.   When a Pleading "Fails to State a Claim"

Logically, there are two basic forms that a 12(b)(6) challenge can take. First, the pleading being challenged may be missing some key language. The claimant may not have provided enough detail, or failed specifically to allege a crucial element of a claim. Second, the pleading may contain ample facts, but those facts do not state a claim recognized at law. Although in both of these situations the pleading fails to state a claim, courts treat these two situations quite differently. In the former, the court rarely dismisses. Instead, it will give the claimant at least one opportunity to amend the pleading to add the missing details. In the latter, however, the court is more likely to dismiss. Unless the plaintiff can show that the complaint can be modified to allow recovery under a different legal theory, it would waste both the court's and the defendant's time to allow plaintiff to amend when she simply has no chance of recovery under even the most prolix complaint.

In some situations, a defendant will need to add a fact or two in order to prove that plaintiff cannot prevail. For example, plaintiff's breach of contract claim might be based on an oral contract that violates the statute of frauds. Similarly, if plaintiff sues on a claim that arises from the same basic event as a claim that plaintiff litigated in a prior action against defendant, it may be barred by the doctrine of claim preclusion. In some of these cases, the plaintiff's complaint will supply the missing fact; *e.g.*, plaintiff could specify that the contract was oral. If plaintiff does not provide the crucial fact, however, the complaint is sufficient on its own, and will survive a 12(b)(6) challenge. Defendant's proper recourse in this situation is to file a motion for summary judgment under Federal Rule 56, a topic covered in Chapter 10. Nevertheless, many defendants will file a 12(b)(6), but attach affidavits or other proof of the missing facts to the motion. In these situations, Rule 12(b)(6) provides that the 12(b)(6) motion will be converted into a motion for summary judgment, and treated under the provisions of Rule 56.

2. Procedural Aspects of the 12(b)(6) Motion

The Federal Rules are quite flexible concerning how a party raises the defense of failure to state a claim. The defense can be raised by pre-answer motion just like a motion to dismiss for lack of subject matter jurisdiction or improper service. The defendant can combine the 12(b)(6) motion with any other defenses it can raise by pre-answer motion.

Moreover, unlike the personal jurisdiction, service, and venue defenses, a party does not waive the defense of failure to state a claim by failing to include it in a pre-answer motion. The second sentence of 12(g), which requires many Rule 12(b) defenses to be raised in certain pre-answer motions, makes an exception for those defenses listed in Rule 12(h)(2). Failure to state a claim is listed in Rule 12(h)(2). Rule 12(h)(2) allows the defense of failure to state a claim to be raised at any point in the case, including at the trial itself. The defense cannot be waived by any other motion (except, of course, a previous unsuccessful motion to dismiss for failure to state a claim). Note, however, that Rule 12(h)(2) also dictates how the defense must be raised. Therefore, a defendant who makes a pre-answer motion based on some other ground, and then later decides to challenge the sufficiency of the complaint, does not make a second pre-answer motion. Instead, he raises the defense of failure to state a claim in his answer, by a Rule 12(c) motion for judgment on the pleadings (which occurs after pleading is complete), or by motion at the trial itself.

This flexibility in the timing of the 12(b)(6) motion stands in stark contrast to the rules that applied under the common-law pleading regime. Common-law pleading's counterpart to the 12(b)(6) was the *demurrer*. Raising a demurrer, however, required the defendant to make a difficult choice. The demurrer served to form the issue. If the defendant demurred, it was deemed to have admitted that all the factual allegations of the complaint were true. Thus, if defendant lost the demurrer, it had essentially lost the case. A 12(b)(6) motion, by contrast, does not operate as an admission of any facts. If the court finds that the complaint properly states a claim, the defendant can then deny one or more of plaintiff's facts in her answer, and force plaintiff to prove those facts at trial.

Cases involving multiple claims have at times caused courts some concern. Suppose that plaintiff alleges two claims against defendant. One of the claims is not recognized under governing law, but the other is. Should a court grant a 12(b)(6) dismissal in this situation? Most courts will simply dismiss the improper claim, leaving the other in place. A few, however, interpret Rule 12(b)(6) to require dismissal of the entire case. These courts typically turn to the 12(f) motion to strike (discussed immediately below) when they need to get rid of one or more, but fewer than all, claims.

3.   Motion for a More Definite Statement and Motion to Strike

Rules 12(e) and (f) give a defendant additional options. Rule 12(e) allows a party against whom a claim has been asserted to move for a more definite statement if the pleading "is so vague or ambiguous that a party cannot reasonably be required to frame a responsive pleading . . . ." If the motion is granted, the plaintiff has ten days to amend the complaint to make it more clear. In theory, this provision gives the defendant an alternative in that category of cases where the facts set out in the complaint are so sparse that defendant cannot determine exactly what plaintiff is actually claiming. In practice, however, Rule 12(e) is rarely invoked. If a complaint is indeed so vague or ambiguous that it does not fairly apprise defendant of what plaintiff is claiming, defendant will succeed on a 12(b)(6) motion to dismiss for failure to state a claim. A vague or ambiguous complaint, after all, does not comply with Rule 8(a)'s notice pleading requirements. The 12(b)(6) motion is preferable from the defendant's standpoint because it tests both the wording and the underlying law, and can result in outright dismissal. At the very worst, the court will give the plaintiff the opportunity to amend the complaint, leaving defendant no worse off than it would have been had it filed a 12(e) motion.

The 12(f) motion to strike serves two basic purposes. First, as discussed above, it allows a party to strike specific claims or allegations in a pleading. The most common situation in which this occurs is when the *plaintiff* wants to strike portions of the defendant's answer.

Second, the Rule also mentions striking "redundant, immaterial, impertinent, or scandalous matter." Mere redundancy or immateriality by itself rarely supports a motion to strike. However, in a few cases courts have struck particularly inflammatory allegations, or those that intrude too greatly on a party's privacy. Note, however, that a court will usually strike an allegation as "scandalous" only if it is both beyond the pale and of little relevance to the dispute. Scandalous allegations that are highly relevant are rarely struck.

Problems

1.   P sues D for personal injuries sustained in an automobile accident. P's complaint fails to mention that P previously sued D for property damage suffered in the same accident. Because P's claim is barred by claim preclusion, D moves to dismiss for failure to state a claim. How will the court rule?

2.   Same as Problem 1, except that P's complaint discusses the prior case, and the fact that the court found D liable. Because P's claim

is barred by claim preclusion, D moves to dismiss for failure to state a claim. How will the court rule?

3. P sues D for fraud. D moves to dismiss the case for lack of subject-matter jurisdiction. The court denies the motion. D files an answer denying liability. Later, before the trial commences, D then moves to dismiss the case for failure to plead fraud with particularity. Assuming that D is correct that P's complaint is insufficient, how should the court rule?

4. Same as Problem 3, except that D titles his motion a "motion for judgment on the pleadings."

5. P sues D for fraud. D files an answer. D's answer contains a counterclaim in which D alleges that P libeled D by accusing D of fraud in the complaint. Under governing law, statements in a court pleading cannot give rise to a cause of action for libel or slander. What should P do?

Exercise

For the state a) where you intend to practice after graduation, b) where your law school is located, and/or c) your professor assigns, go to that state's annotated rules and research the procedural rules by which service of process is made. Based on your research, print the rule and bring it to class for discussion. In addition, answer the following questions.

1. Identify the minimum requirements for stating a claim.
2. Identify the topics which are required to be pled with specificity.
3. Identify the requirement for demanding judgment.
4. Do the rules prescribe the format for a pleading?
5. Is pleading in the alternative permitted?

D. DETERMINING THE APPLICABLE LAW

INTRODUCTORY PROBLEM

Corky, a citizen of Connecticut, purchases a purebred Pembroke Welsh Corgi puppy. Corky strongly suspects that the puppy will eventually prove to be a champion in the show ring. While vacationing in upstate New York, Corky takes the dog to a local veterinary clinic for routine vaccinations. When he returns later in the day, Corky is horrified to find that his puppy was accidentally neutered. Neutering greatly reduces a dog's value, for in addition to the obvious loss of stud fees, a neutered dog cannot compete in dog shows. Corky is emotionally devastated that his little friend underwent unnecessary surgery.

Corky's demands for compensation go unanswered. Thirteen months after the incident, Corky sues Violet, the veterinarian who performed the operation, for veterinary malpractice. Although the clinic is located in upstate New York, Violet resides just across the border in Vermont. Corky names only Violet, not the clinic, as defendant. Corky sues Violet in Vermont to prevent any personal jurisdiction challenges. Because the parties are diverse, and because Corky claims damages in excess of $200,000 ($1500 for the diminution in value of the puppy and $200,000 for Corky's personal emotional distress), Corky avails himself of diversity jurisdiction and sues in federal court.

Violet immediately moves to dismiss, based on three separate arguments. First, Violet points out that under Vermont law, the owner of an animal that is harmed or killed can recover only the decrease in value. Vermont does not allow recovery for any emotional trauma to the owner. Second, a recently-enacted Vermont law requires all plaintiffs who want to sue for any form of professional malpractice, including veterinary, to submit their claims to a panel of three experts who will provide their honest, but non-binding, evaluation of the merits of the claim. If a party files a claim in state court without first submitting it to the panel, the case will be dismissed. Third, Violet notes that the Vermont statute of limitations is one year. Because Corky waited 13 months to file his claim, Violet argues that it is time-barred.

Corky counters Violet's motion with two separate lines of attack. First, he notes that the laws of Connecticut and New York differ from those of Vermont. Both Connecticut and New York would allow recovery for emotional distress. Neither state would require the malpractice claim to be vetted before experts as a precondition to suit. And the statute of limitations on veterinary malpractice claims in Connecticut is two years, while in New York it is three years.

In the alternative, Corky argues that the laws of Vermont, New York, and Connecticut do not matter. After all, Corky filed his case in a *federal* court. Therefore because nothing in federal statutes or the Federal Rules of Procedure indicates to the contrary, he argues that the federal court is free to craft its own rules on damages for emotional distress, whether a claim must be submitted to a panel, and the limitations period.

How should the court resolve Violet's motion?

———————

So far, this Chapter has focused on how a party files a pleading that will survive a motion to dismiss for failure to state a claim. A proper pleading takes the background facts and presents them in a way that makes them fit one or more theories of recovery under governing law. To this point, however, our discussion has glossed over one complicating factor. The United States is a federal nation. Unlike most nations, there is not a single unitary "law" on a given subject, but at least fifty different laws. In many cases these rules will lead to significantly different outcomes for the dispute.

How does a court determine which of fifty or more governing rules applies? The easiest solution would be for every state simply to apply its own law. However, in order to afford the parties some predictability in how they organize their daily activities, no court automatically applies forum law to every case that comes before it. Indeed, the Supreme Court has held that it would violate the United States Constitution for a state to apply its own law to a case that has no significant connection with the state. *Phillips Petroleum Co. v. Shutts*, 472 U.S. 797, 105 S.Ct. 2965, 86 L.Ed.2d 628 (1985).

Because a court does not always apply its own law to multistate disputes, states have been forced to develop rules to deal with selecting a governing law. In the vast majority of states this task of developing rules has fallen on the courts rather than the legislatures. A body of case law called "Conflicts of Law" has developed, which provides rules and considerations for courts to use in determining which law applies.

In many cases the choice is obvious. If plaintiff, defendant, and all significant events giving rise to the claim are situated in the same state, the law of that state will usually govern, regardless of where the case is litigated. But in many other cases, the choice is not immediately clear. The *Daniels* case on p. 282 provides a good example. As the dispute in *Daniels* had connections with both Illinois and Indiana, a case could be made for applying the law of either of those two states. Similarly, solid arguments can be made for applying different states' laws in the Introductory Problem.

Further complicating the problem is the existence of federal law. Although the legislative authority of the federal government is limited by the Constitution, Congress nevertheless has broad authority, especially in matters of national and interstate concern. Federal law today covers a wide range of primary activity, sometimes complementing, but at other times replacing, state law. Federal courts work alongside their state counterparts, and many cases can be tried in either system.

The federal nature of the United States system gives rise to two legal doctrines. The first, called *choice of law*, comprises the set of rules that dictate how a court selects which state's law will govern a particular case. Choice of law is a complicated field that in most law schools is the subject of an entire upper level course. The first case in this section provides a brief overview of this area of the law, and provides a flavor of how choice of law considerations must enter into an attorney's planning process as she selects a forum and frames the complaint. As you will see in *Paul*, different states use different rules to deal with choice of law problems.

Note that choice of law almost always deals with clashes between the laws of different states, or, in the case of international disputes, nations. Clashes between state and federal law are subject to an entirely different set of principles. In fact, the United States Constitution itself governs how clashes between federal statutes and state law are resolved. Unlike the laws of different states, it is often possible for federal and state laws to stand side by side, with both governing a given case. You have already seen an example of this in the materials on supplemental jurisdiction, in which a party could bring claims under both state and federal law for the same injury. This concept of parallel laws is a unique feature of a federal nation. In some situations, however, federal law will displace, or *preempt*, state law. Preemption typically occurs where the rule of state law conflicts with or impairs federal law. In some cases, however, preemption can occur even when there is no clash between the laws.

Preemption does not completely resolve the federal-state choice of law issues that can arise. Another feature of the United States is its common-law heritage, where courts as well as legislatures play a key role in defining the law. This feature gives rise to the second main legal doctrine, which is called the "*Erie* doctrine" after the case that spawned the debate. The *Erie* doctrine deals with the extent to which a federal court may ignore state law and instead fashion its own judge-made rule to apply to a dispute. Chapter 13 of this book explores this doctrine in depth. Nevertheless, the last three cases in this section provide a brief glimpse into the *Erie* doctrine, especially how it affects parties at the pleading stage of a case.

1. Choice of Law

PAUL v. NATIONAL LIFE

177 W.Va. 427, 352 S.E.2d 550 (1986)

NEELY, J.

In September of 1977 Eliza Vickers and Aloha Jane Paul, both West Virginia residents, took a weekend trip to Indiana. The two women were involved in a one-car collision on Interstate 65 in Indiana when Mrs. Vickers lost control of the car. That collision took both women's lives. The administrator of Mrs. Paul's estate brought a wrongful death action against Ms. Vickers' estate and the National Life Accident Company in the Circuit Court of Kanawha County. Upon completion of discovery, the defendants below moved for summary judgment. Defendants' motion contended that: (1) the Indiana guest statute, which grants to a gratuitous host immunity from liability for the injury or death of a passenger unless that host was guilty of willful and wanton misconduct at the time of the accident, was applicable; and (2) that the record was devoid of any evidence of willful or wanton misconduct on the part of Ms. Vickers. By order dated 29 October 1984, the Circuit Court of Kanawha County entered summary judgment for the defendants below. The order of the circuit court held that our conflicts doctrine of *lex loci delicti* required that the law of the place of the injury, namely, Indiana, apply to the case, and that the record contained no evidence of willful or wanton misconduct on the part of Ms. Vickers. It is from this order that the plaintiffs below appeal.

The sole question presented in this case is whether the law of Indiana or of West Virginia shall apply. The appellees urge us to adhere to our traditional conflicts doctrine of *lex loci delicti,* while the appellants urge us to reject our traditional doctrine and to adopt one of the "modern" approaches to conflicts questions. Although we stand by *lex loci delicti* as our general conflicts rule, we nevertheless reverse the judgment of the court below.

I

Unlike other areas of the law, such as contracts, torts and property, "conflicts of law" as a body of common law is of relatively recent origin. Professor Dicey has written that he knew of no decisions in England considering conflicts of law points before the accession of James I, and it is generally acknowledged that the first authoritative work on conflicts did not appear until the publication of Joseph Story's *Conflict of Laws* in 1834. Accordingly, no conflicts of law doctrine has ever had any credible pretense to being "natural law" emergent from the murky mists of medieval mysticism. Indeed, the mention of conflicts of law and the *jus naturale* in the same breath would evoke a power guffaw in even the sternest scholastic. In our post-Realist legal world, it is the received wisdom that judges, like their counterparts in the legislative branch, are political agents embodying social policy in law. Nowhere is the received wisdom more accurate than in the domain of conflict of laws.

Conflicts of law has become a veritable playpen for judicial policymakers. The last twenty years have seen a remarkable shift from the doctrine of *lex loci delicti* to more "modern" doctrines, such as the more flexible, manipulable *Restatement* "center of gravity" test. Of the twenty-five landmark cases cited by appellants in which a state supreme court rejected *lex loci delicti* and adopted one of the modern approaches, the great majority of them involved the application to an automobile accident case of a foreign state's guest statute, doctrine of interspousal or intrafamily immunity, or doctrine of contributory negligence. All but one of these landmark cases was decided in the decade between 1963 and 1973, when many jurisdictions still retained guest statutes, the doctrine of interspousal immunity, and the doctrine of contributory negligence. However, in the years since 1970, these statutes and doctrines have all but disappeared from the American legal landscape. . . .

Thus nearly half of the state supreme courts of this country have wrought a radical transformation of their procedural law of conflicts in order to sidestep perceived substantive evils, only to discover later that those evils had been exorcised from American law by other means. Now these courts are saddled with a cumbersome and unwieldy body of conflicts law that creates confusion, uncertainty and inconsistency, as well as complication of the judicial task. This approach has been like that of the misguided physician who treated a case of dandruff with nitric acid, only to discover later that the malady could have been remedied with medicated shampoo. Neither the doctor nor the patient need have lost his head.

The *Restatement* approach has been criticized for its indeterminate language and lack of concrete guidelines. *Restatement (Second) of Conflicts of Law,* Sec. 145–146 (1971)* provides:

§ 145. *The General Principle*

(1) The rights and liabilities of the parties with respect to an issue in tort are determined by the local law of the state which, with respect to that issue, has the most significant relationship to the occurrence and the parties under the principle stated in § 6.

(2) Contacts being taken into account in applying the principle of § 6 to determine the law applicable to an issue include:

(a) the place where the injury occurred,

(b) the place where the conduct causing injury occurred,

(c) the domicile, residence, nationality, place of incorporation, and place of business of the parties, and

(d) the place where the relationship, if any, between the parties, is centered.

These contacts should be evaluated according to their relative importance with respect to the particular issues.

§ 146. *Personal Injuries.*

In an action for a personal injury, the local law of the state where the injury occurred determines the *rights and liabilities* of the parties, unless, with respect to the particular issue, some other state has a more significant relationship under the principles stated in § 6 to the occurrence and the parties, in which event the local law of the other state will be applied.

Section 6 of the *Restatement* lists the following factors as important choice of law considerations in all areas of law.

(a) The needs of the interstate and international systems;

(b) The relevant policies of the forum;

(c) The relevant policies of other interested states and relative interest of those states in the determination of the particular issue;

(d) The protection of justified expectations;

(e) The basic policies underlying the particular field of law;

(f) Certainty, predictability, and uniformity of results; and

(g) Ease in the determination and application of the law to be applied.

As Javolenus once said to Julian, *res ipsa loquitur.* The appellant cites with approval the description of the *Restatement* approach set forth in *Conklin v. Horner,* 38 Wis.2d 468, 473, 157 N.W.2d 579, 581 (1968):

We emphasized that what we adopted was not a rule, but a method of analysis that permitted dissection of the jural bundle constituting a tort and its environment to determine what elements therein were relevant to a reasonable choice of law.

That sounds pretty intellectual, but we still prefer a rule. The lesson of history is that methods of analysis that permit dissection of the jural bundle constituting a tort and its environment produce protracted litigation and voluminous, inscrutable appellate opinions, while rules get cases settled quickly and cheaply.

The manipulability inherent in the *Restatement* approach is nicely illustrated by two cases from New York, the first jurisdiction to make a clean break with *lex loci delicti*. The cases of *Babcock v. Jackson*, 12 N.Y.2d 473, 191 N.E.2d 279 (1963), and *Kell v. Henderson*, 47 Misc.2d 992, 263 N.Y.S.2d 647 (1965), *aff'd*, 26 App. Div.2d 595, 270 N.Y.S.2d 552 (1966), are aptly discussed by the Supreme Court of Virginia:

> In *Babcock,* an automobile guest sued her host in New York for injuries sustained in Ontario caused by the defendant's ordinary negligence. Under New York law, the guest could recover for injuries caused by the host's lack of ordinary care, but the Ontario guest statute barred such a recovery. The court abandoned its adherence to the place-of-the-wrong rule and permitted recovery. It decided that, on the guest-host issue, New York had the "dominant contacts" because the parties were domiciled in New York, were on a trip which began in New York, and were traveling in a vehicle registered and regularly garaged in New York. The court noted that Ontario had no connection with the cause of action except that the accident happened to take place there.
>
> *Kell* presented the converse of *Babcock.* There, the question was also whether the New York ordinary negligence rule applied or whether the Ontario guest statute controlled. The guest was injured by the host's ordinary negligence while the parties, both residents of Ontario, were on a trip in New York which was to begin and end in Ontario. The New York court purported to follow *Babcock* but held that Ontario law would not apply.

McMillan v. McMillan, 219 Va. 1127, 253 S.E.2d 662, 664 (1979). It was perhaps recognition of just such gross disparities in result that prompted the Court of Appeals of New York to remark, in a towering achievement in the art of understatement, "candor requires the admission that our past decisions have lacked a precise consistency." *Miller v. Miller,* 22 N.Y.2d 12, 237 N.E.2d 877, 879, 290 N.Y.S.2d 734 (1968).

II

The appellant urges us in the alternative to adopt the "choice-influencing considerations approach" set forth by Professor Leflar in "Choice–Influencing Considerations and Conflicts of Law", 41 N.Y.U.L. Rev. 267 (1966). Professor Leflar has narrowed the list of considerations in conflicts cases to five:

(1) Predictability of results;

(2) Maintenance of interstate or international order;

(3) Simplification of the judicial task;

(4) Advancement of the forum's governmental interests;

(5) Application of the better rule of law.

Professor Leflar's approach has been adopted in the guest statute context in the landmark cases of *Clark v. Clark,* 107 N.H. 351, 222 A.2d 205 (1966); *Milkovich v. Saari,* 295 Minn. 155, 203 N.W.2d 408 (1973); and *Conklin v. Horner,* 38 Wis.2d 468, 157 N.W.2d 579 (1968). In practice the cases tend to focus more on the fourth and fifth considerations than the first three, and the upshot is that the courts of New Hampshire, Minnesota and Wisconsin simply will not apply guest statutes. This seems to us a perfectly intelligible and sensible bright-line rule. However, it seems unnecessary to scrap an entire body of law and dress this rule up in a newfangled five-factor costume when the same concerns can be addressed and the same result achieved through judicious employment of the traditional public policy exception to *lex loci delicti.*

III

Lex loci delicti has long been the cornerstone of our conflict of laws doctrine. The consistency, predictability, and ease of application provided by the traditional doctrine are not to be discarded lightly, and we are not persuaded that we should discard them today. The appellant contends that the various exceptions that have been engrafted onto the traditional rule have made it manipulable and have undermined the predictability and uniformity that were considered its primary virtues. There is certainly some truth in this, and we generally eschew the more strained escape devices employed to avoid the sometimes harsh effects of the traditional rule. Nevertheless, we remain convinced that the traditional rule, for all of its faults, remains superior to any of its modern competitors. Moreover, if we are going to manipulate conflicts doctrine in order to achieve substantive results, we might as well manipulate something we understand. Having mastered marble, we decline an apprenticeship in bronze. We therefore reaffirm our adherence to the doctrine of *lex loci delicti* today.

However, we have long recognized that comity does not require the application of the substantive law of a foreign state when that law contravenes the public policy of this State. West Virginia has never had an automobile guest passenger statute. It is the strong public policy of this State that persons injured by the negligence of another should be able to recover in tort. ... Today we declare that automobile guest passenger statutes violate the strong public policy of this State in favor of compensating persons injured by the negligence of others. Accordingly, we will no longer enforce the automobile guest passenger statutes of foreign jurisdictions in our courts.[14]

For the foregoing reasons, the order of the circuit granting summary judgment in favor of the appellees is hereby vacated, and the cause remanded for further proceedings not inconsistent with this opinion. . . .

Notes and Questions

1. The *lex loci delicti* rule was applied by all states in negligence cases from the late 1800s to the 1950s. Translating to "the law of the place of the wrong," the rule required courts to determine the outcome of a negligence case by applying the law of the place where the injury occurred. Dissatisfaction with the rule, especially as it applied in certain cases where the parties both lived in one state but the injury occurred in another, led to the development of the alternate choice-of-law regimes discussed in *Paul*.

2. One feature shared by the modern approaches is that they seek to move away from the strict territoriality of the traditional rules. Of course, choice of law cannot escape being territorial, as laws differ from state to state. But the traditional rules isolated one single event—the injury in the case of a tort, the place a contract was made or to be performed in the case of a contract—and made the choice turn on that single event, without considering other factors. The modern approaches consider a greater number of relevant factors, especially the residence of the parties.

3. The modern approaches to choice of law bear some similarity to the analysis used in the constitutional part of personal jurisdiction analysis, insofar as both consider the connections a given state has with the case. Nevertheless, there are crucial differences. For example, modern choice of law doctrines consider all parties' connections, while personal jurisdiction focuses primarily on the defendant. In addition, a contact need not be purposeful to count in choice of law analysis. Because of these differences and others, it is often true that a forum has jurisdiction, but will not apply its own law. Conversely, a state's law may govern a case even though that state's courts do not have jurisdiction over the defendant.

4. *Paul* is a tort case. Of all the areas of the law, choice of law rules in tort have undergone perhaps the most radical revision during the past fifty years. Although many states employ a similar contact-based analysis in contract cases, see, e.g., *Restatement (Second) of Conflicts of Law* § 188, the choice of law analysis in property cases is not all that different than it was in the early 1900's. Most issues governing ownership of property, for example, are still governed by the law of the place where the property is situated.

14. Although we intended this to be a rule of general application, we do not intend it as an invitation to flagrant forum shopping. For example, were a resident of a guest statute jurisdiction to sue another resident of a guest statute jurisdiction over an accident occurring in a guest statute jurisdiction, the simple fact that the plaintiff was able to serve process on the defendant within our State borders would not compel us to resist application of any relevant guest statute. This State must have some connection with the controversy above and beyond mere service of process before the rule we announce today will be applied. In other words, venue must be proper under some provision other than W.Va. Code 56–1–1(a)(4) [1986].

Similarly, the validity of marriages are still usually governed by the law of the place where the marriage was celebrated.

5. *Procedure.* A decision to apply the law of another state does not mean that that other state's law will govern every aspect of the case. Instead, a court only borrows the other state's substantive law. A forum will almost always apply its own procedural law to a case. Although it is difficult to draw a bright line between substance and procedure, procedural rules, generally speaking, are those rules that deal with the steps a party must take to litigate his claims or defenses in court. Rules governing pleading, joinder, costs, and the like are clearly procedural. Other issues, however, are less obvious. One particular issue that falls on the line between substance and procedure is the statute of limitations. For purposes of choice of law analysis, however, most states consider statutes of limitations procedural. As a result, State X will apply the State X limitations period even when it hears a tort or contract claim governed by the law of State Y.

6. As *Paul* points out, choice of law rules differ tremendously between states. Does a forum making a choice of law decision consider the choice of law rules in force in other states when making its decision? In other words, should the court in *Paul* have considered not only Indiana tort law, but also Indiana choice of law rules? If your head is spinning at this point, you will be glad to hear that the answer is no. Choice of law rules are "procedural." A court making a choice of law almost always applies its own choice of law rules, and considers only other states' substantive rules.

2.   An Introduction to *Erie*

The *Erie* doctrine is the second important doctrine that determines what law a court will apply in deciding a case. As the introductory materials note, the doctrine applies almost exclusively in federal court. Although *Erie* is in one sense a choice of law doctrine, it differs significantly from the type of choice of law decision involved in *Paul*. Instead of choosing among the laws of various states, *Erie* involves a clash between state and federal law.

Erie is rarely much of an issue when there is federal statute law on point. If the federal statute truly covers the situation, the federal court will apply it either along with or in lieu of state law. But not all federal law is statutory. You have already encountered the Federal Rules of Civil Procedure, a body of law promulgated by the United States Supreme Court. Similarly, federal courts, like their state counterparts, have authority to create rules to govern certain issues that may arise in cases before them. Because the authority of the federal government in the United States federal system is limited, however, there are significant constraints on federal judge-made law. The *Erie* doctrine is the set of rules that define the limits on this "federal common law."

Like choice of law, the *Erie* doctrine has been developed almost exclusively in the courts. The major Supreme Court cases are set out in Chapter 13, which explores *Erie* in greater depth, along with other issues unique to the federal courts. However, the following cases retrace the genesis of the doctrine, and set out the basic analysis used in *Erie* questions today. The second and third cases focus in particular on how *Erie* affects the pleading process in federal court.

HOUBEN v. TELULAR CORPORATION

309 F.3d 1028 (7th Cir. 2002)

WOOD, Circuit Judge.

... Although the *Erie* doctrine is a familiar one, it is notorious for the subtle distinctions it requires courts to draw between matters that are "substantive" (a conclusory term that means that state law will be used in cases where the rule of decision is derived from state law) and matters that are "procedural" (a similarly conclusory term that means the law of the forum will apply, and thus the same case will be handled differently depending on whether it is being pursued in a state court or a federal court). It is therefore useful to take a quick look at the development of the doctrine and the approach the current Supreme Court appears to be taking to this central issue of judicial federalism.

Erie itself presented a very broad question: whether, for purposes of the Rules of Decision Act, which was part of the First Judiciary Act and is now codified at 28 U.S.C. § 1652, federal courts sitting in diversity or otherwise applying state law as the rule of decision are obliged to follow only positive laws of the state as announced in statutes, or if the idea of "state law" also encompassed state decisional law. The Act itself, at the time *Erie* was decided, read simply:

> The laws of the several states, except where the Constitution, treaties or statutes of the United States shall otherwise require or provide, shall be regarded as rules of decision in trials at common law in the courts of the United States in cases where they apply.

[Today the reference to "trials at common law" is to "civil actions," but the statute is otherwise unchanged.] In the case of *Swift v. Tyson*, 16 Pet. (41 U.S.) 1 (1842), the Court had opted for the narrower construction of the statute, under which the decisions of courts did not generally have the status of "laws" that had to be followed. The Court overruled *Swift* in *Erie*, noting that the *Swift* doctrine had led to a lack of uniformity between state and federal courts and was dubious from a constitutional standpoint. *Erie*, 304 U.S. at 74–75, 77–78. Thus, *Erie* established the rule that the federal courts were obliged to follow state decisional law, as well as all other state law, in cases governed by the Rules of Decision Act. (While *Erie* questions arise most frequently in diversity cases, the Supreme Court has made clear that the doctrine applies equally to state law claims like Houben's that are brought to the federal courts through supplemental jurisdiction under 28 U.S.C. § 1367. See *Felder v. Casey*, 487 U.S. 131, 151 (1988).)

Questions soon arose over the full reach of the *Erie* ruling, however, because in the very same year that *Erie* was decided, 1938, the Supreme Court promulgated the Federal Rules of Civil Procedure. The new rules replaced the old Conformity Act, which had been enacted in 1789 almost contemporaneously with the First Judiciary Act. The Conformity Act provided that the procedure in actions at law in the federal courts was to be the same as the procedure used in the state in which the federal court sat. Had the Federal Rules not appeared at almost the same moment as the *Erie* decision, life would have been easy for federal courts: both state rules of procedure and the full body of state substantive law would have been applicable, and there would have been no need to worry about categorizing any particular law. But for a variety of reasons, Congress had passed the Rules Enabling Act, the successor to which can be found at 28 U.S.C. § 2072, in 1934. That Act empowered the Supreme Court to unify the systems of law and equity and to issue a single set of civil procedure rules to be used in the federal district courts. The rules that were developed under the authority of the Enabling Act were adopted by the Supreme Court on December 20, 1937, and took effect on September 1, 1938, less than five months after *Erie* was handed down.

Erie may have solved one problem, and the Rules Enabling Act may have solved another one, but in a small but significant set of cases they combined to create a new one. For cases involving obvious rules of substance (*e.g.*, whether a person walking beside a railroad track is a "trespasser" or an "invitee" under state land law; whether a tort plaintiff's claim is defeated if she was contributorily negligent, or if she loses only if her negligence was more than 50% responsible for the tort; whether the holder in due course rule applies to certain endorsers of commercial paper), it was easy for the federal courts to conclude that they were now to apply state law. (Ascertaining the content of state law poses its own problems, but we need not consider that aspect of *Erie* here.) For cases involving obvious rules of procedure (*e.g.*, which documents must be served formally and which must be filed with the court, see Fed. R. Civ. P. 5; when is the earliest time a motion for summary judgment may be filed, see Fed. R. Civ. P. 56(a), (b); what kinds of discovery devices are available, see Fed. R. Civ. P. 26–37), federal courts knew that they were required to follow the Federal Rules, even if those rules were different from the rules applicable in state court. But there was a middle ground for rules that might be seen as "substantive," or might be seen as "procedural," and it was difficult both to define what those terms might mean, and to decide the box in which to put different rules.

The Court's first effort to grapple with the middle ground came in *Guaranty Trust Co. v. York*, 326 U.S. 99 (1945), in which it had to decide whether a state statute of limitations barred a claim brought for breach of trust by certain noteholders of a corporation against the trustee, or if the fact that the suit had been brought on the "equity" side of the federal court meant that the state statute of limitations governing "law" actions did not apply. The Court summarized the question before it as follows:

> Whether, when no recovery could be had in a State court because the action is barred by the statute of limitations, a federal court in equity can take cognizance of the suit because there is diversity of

citizenship between the parties. Is the outlawry, according to State law, of a claim created by the States a matter of "substantive rights" to be respected by a federal court of equity when that court's jurisdiction is dependent on the fact that there is a State-created right, or is such statute of "a mere remedial character," ... which a federal court may disregard?

326 U.S. at 107–08. After commenting on the slippery nature of the distinction between substance and procedure, the Court reformulated the question as:

Whether [the statute under review] concerns merely the manner and the means by which a right to recover, as recognized by the State, is enforced, or whether such statutory limitation is a matter of substance in the aspect that alone is relevant to our problem, namely, does it significantly affect the result of a litigation for a federal court to disregard a law of a State that would be controlling in an action upon the same claim by the same parties in a State court?

Id. at 109. Applying this test, which came to be known as the "outcome-determinative" test, the Court concluded that the state statute of limitations was one of those laws that the federal court was obliged to apply, even if a different rule would have prevailed in a claim arising under federal law.

Not long after *York* was decided, however, the Court came to realize that the outcome-determinative test swept too much under state law. As it observed in *Hanna v. Plumer*, 380 U.S. 460 (1965), in a certain sense

every procedural variation is "outcome-determinative." For example, having brought suit in a federal court, a plaintiff cannot then insist on the right to file subsequent pleadings in accord with the time limits applicable in state courts, even though enforcement of the federal timetable will, if he continues to insist that he must meet only the state time limit, result in determination of the controversy against him.

Id. at 468–69 (emphasis in original). Instead, it began to look at the issue in a broader way. Thus, in *Byrd v. Blue Ridge Rural Elec. Coop., Inc.,* 356 U.S. 525 (1958), the Court decided that the "manner in which, in civil common law actions, [the federal system] distributes trial functions between judge and jury" is a question governed solely by federal law. As the *Hanna* Court put it, the " 'outcome-determination' test ... cannot be read without reference to the twin aims of the *Erie* rule: discouragement of forum-shopping and avoidance of inequitable administration of the laws." 380 U.S. at 468.

Hanna went further than this, however. It held that *Erie* was never intended to cover cases where a federal rule of procedure covers the point at issue. In those cases, the proper questions are only (1) whether the rule clearly applies, (2) whether the rule falls within the scope of the Rules Enabling Act, and (3) whether the application of the rule would be constitutional. If the rule applies and is "rationally capable of classification" as procedural, then (in the absence of other constitutional problems, of course) the federal court must apply it.

The Supreme Court has revisited the *Erie* issue many times since those early years, but it is enough for us to look at the Court's two most recent decisions in order to complete our background review. We turn, then, to *Gasperini v. Center for Humanities, Inc.*, 518 U.S. 415 (1996), and *Semtek Int'l, Inc. v. Lockheed Martin Corp.*, 531 U.S. 497 (2001). In *Gasperini*, the Court considered the question whether a New York rule of procedure, NYCPLR § 5501(c), which empowers state appellate courts to review the size of jury verdicts and to order new trials when the award "deviates materially from what would be reasonable compensation," could be applied in federal court consistently with the re-examination clause of the Seventh Amendment to the U.S. Constitution. . . . The Court of Appeals for the Second Circuit concluded that it had to apply § 5501(c); after reviewing the [$450,000 jury] verdict, it decided that it was indeed excessive and it vacated the judgment unless Gasperini would agree to a reduced award of $100,000.

The Supreme Court took the case to decide whether, in a case where New York law governed the claims for relief, New York law also supplied the test for federal court review of the size of the verdict. At the outset, it stated that "the dispositive question, therefore, is whether federal courts can give effect to the substantive thrust of § 5501(c) without untoward alteration of the federal scheme for the trial and decision of civil cases." *Id.* The Court then asked whether NYCPLR § 5501(c) was "outcome affective" in the sense that application of its standard would be so significant to one or both of the litigants that failure to apply it would either unfairly discriminate against citizens of the forum state or would be likely to cause the plaintiff to choose federal court. *Id.* at 428. It was common ground among the parties and the Court that if New York had instead enacted a statutory cap on damages, that would have been a "substantive" rule binding on the federal court in a diversity case. But, the Court thought, § 5501(c) was not the equivalent of a damages cap. Nevertheless, it did implicate the "twin aims" of *Erie*.

What the Court did in the end was to find a middle ground. First, it decided that appellate review in the federal system of a trial judge's denial of a motion to set aside a jury verdict as excessive was compatible with the Seventh Amendment. Second, it found a way to accommodate the state and the federal interests, consistently with the Seventh Amendment's clause forbidding appellate re-examination of jury verdicts other than according to the rules of the common law. It allocated to the district court (not the appellate court, as would have been the case in the state system) the primary duty to apply New York's substantive standard forbidding verdicts that "deviate materially" from a reasonable compensation. The federal courts of appeals could then review the district court's decision under the normal abuse of discretion standard. Thus, at the end of the day the Court found a way to implement the substantive elements of the state statute within the framework of federal procedures.

The *Semtek* decision also involved a delicate balancing of federal and state interests, but as in *Gasperini*, the Court ultimately affirmed the applicability of federal procedures. The question there was "whether the claim-preclusive effect of a federal judgment dismissing a diversity action on statute-of-limitations grounds is determined by the law of the State in which the federal court sits." 531 U.S. at 499. After deciding that neither precedent, nor Fed. R. Civ. P. 41(b), nor the Full Faith and Credit Clause of the Constitution, Art. IV, § 1, nor the full faith and credit statute, 28 U.S.C. § 1738, dictated the answer to the question, the Court went back to first principles. It was already established that the effect of a federal court judgment in a federal question case was whatever the Supreme Court prescribed. By extension, it then concluded that the Supreme Court had "the last word on the claim-preclusive effect of *all* federal judgments." *Id.* (emphasis in original). "In short, federal common law governs the claim-preclusive effect of a dismissal by a federal court sitting in diversity." *Id.* at 508. It then turned around and decided that for this purpose, the rule of federal common law would be to adopt the claim-preclusion rule of the state where the federal court was sitting, since there was no particular need for national uniformity in this set of cases. Finally, however, it created an exception to its adoption of state law as the federal rule for "situations in which the state law is incompatible with federal interests." *Id.* at 509. No such incompatibility was present in the case before it, and so it decided to give the federal judgment the same effect a California court would have given an analogous California judgment. . . .

Notes and Questions

1. As the opinion indicates, the *Erie* doctrine applies primarily in diversity cases and the state-law claims in a supplemental jurisdiction case. Can you see why *Erie* is less of a factor in a federal question case? What is the source of the substantive law in a federal question case?

2. Although *Erie* is mainly a judge-made doctrine, two statutes play a significant role in the analysis. The Rules of Decision Act, 28 U.S.C. § 1652 ["RODA"], requires federal courts to follow state law "except where the Constitution, treaties, or statutes of the United States shall otherwise require or provide." The second influential statute is the Rules Enabling Act, 28 U.S.C. § 2072, ["REA"] which gives the Supreme Court the authority to enact rules of procedure and evidence.

3. The Supreme Court's *Guaranty Trust* decision, discussed in *Houben*, significantly tempered the language of RODA and the Court's earlier *Erie* decision. While RODA and *Erie* can be read to preclude a federal court from making any binding rules whatsoever, *Guaranty Trust* held that federal courts had the authority to create rules to regulate their internal procedure. Many *Erie* cases turn on whether the rule the federal court wants to apply is a rule of procedure or a rule of substantive law.

4. *Houben* states that there are actually two separate analyses used to determine if a rule is "procedural"—one for the Federal Rules of Civil

Procedure and similar written rules, and another for all other judge-made law. Restate the tests that courts use in each of these two situations. Under which of the tests is a given federal judge-made rule more likely to be applied?

5. Why should there be two separate tests? Regardless of whether the rule is a Federal Rule or ordinary judge-made law, the question is the same: is the rule "procedural?" Why should the analysis differ? The Supreme Court's analysis in *Hanna*, which created the two tests, relied on the fact that the Federal Rules were created pursuant to the REA. To understand why that matters, consider who enacted the REA. Does Congress have the authority to enact substantive law? On the other hand, doesn't the REA explicitly provide that the Supreme Court may enact only rules of "procedure and evidence?"

6. *Statutes of limitation.* Suppose the federal courts decide to adopt a uniform limitations period of one year for all claims filed in federal court. Is that statute of limitations a valid procedural rule under *Erie*? Would it matter whether the rule was created by precedent or pursuant to the REA? Under either analysis, would it matter what the limitations period would otherwise be under state law?

Recall that for purposes of choice of law, statutes of limitation are deemed procedural. A forum usually applies its own limitations period even when it borrows another state's law to decide the merits. However, in *Guaranty Trust*, the Supreme Court held that statutes of limitations were substantive for purposes of *Erie*, which meant that state law must be applied. Although *Guaranty Trust* did not deal with a Federal Rule of Civil Procedure, most courts have assumed that the same result would obtain even if the Federal Rules were amended to impose some sort of limitations period on state-law claims.

How can statutes of limitations be both procedural (for choice of law purposes) and substantive (for *Erie* purposes)? To resolve this seeming paradox, consider the underlying goals of choice of law and *Erie*. Although the two areas use the same basic terms, do they really deal with the same sort of issue?

7. *Erie and Choice of Law Rules.* Suppose that a court applies the *Erie* analysis and concludes that it must apply state law on a particular issue. Which state's law will it use? We already saw that *Erie* issues arise predominantly in diversity cases, where by definition two or more states have a connection with the parties. Does a federal court decide for itself which of the connected states' laws apply, or does it look to state choice of law rules? But if it looks to state choice of law rules, which state?

The Supreme Court answered this question in *Klaxon Co. v. Stentor Elec. Mfg. Co.*, 313 U.S. 487, 61 S.Ct. 1020, 85 L.Ed. 1477 (1941). It held that state choice of law rules are substantive, so that they must be applied in federal court. The Court also indicated that the federal court should apply the choice of law rules of the state in which the federal court sits. Therefore, a federal court in Iowa will apply Iowa choice of law rules to determine what state's laws govern the case.

Note that yet again the *Erie* and choice of law analyses differ on which rules are substantive and which are procedural. Recall that under choice of law, a state always applies its own choice of law rules. What *Klaxon* holds, in essence, is that there *are* no federal choice of law rules.

CHAMBERLAIN v. GIAMPAPA

210 F.3d 154 (3d Cir. 2000)

STAPLETON, Circuit Judge.

Robin Chamberlain appeals from the dismissal of her medical malpractice complaint filed in the United States District Court of New Jersey. Count I of the complaint alleged negligent medical treatment and care by the defendant physician, and Count II alleged a failure to properly advise and inform the plaintiff of the nature and extent of a surgical procedure the defendant performed on her. Jurisdiction was based on the diversity of the citizenship of the parties. The District Court dismissed both counts of Chamberlain's complaint with prejudice for failure to file a timely affidavit of merit pursuant to N.J. Stat. Ann. §§ 2A:53A–26 to–29 (West 1987) ("the New Jersey affidavit of merit statute").[1]

We address five distinct issues in the disposition of this appeal:

1) Whether the New Jersey affidavit of merit statute can properly be applied by a federal court sitting in diversity; . . .

4) Whether the District Court erred in dismissing the entire complaint, when one or more of the alleged acts of negligence may have occurred before the effective date of the New Jersey affidavit of merit statute; . . .

We hold that the New Jersey affidavit of merit statute does not conflict with the Federal Rules of Civil Procedure and must be applied by federal courts sitting in diversity; the District Court did not plainly err in applying the affidavit of merit statute to the lack of informed consent cause of action; there are no extraordinary circumstances that would warrant dismissal without prejudice; and the denial of a default judgment was not an abuse of discretion. However, we further conclude that the District Court erred in dismissing the plaintiff's case when the record indicates that one or more of the alleged negligent acts occurred before the effective date of the affidavit of merit statute. Accordingly, we

---

1. Section 2A:53A–27 provides:

In any action for damages for personal injuries, wrongful death or property damage resulting from an alleged act of malpractice or negligence by a licensed person in his profession or occupation, the plaintiff shall, within 60 days following the date of filing of the answer to the complaint by the defendant, provide each defendant with an affidavit of an appropriate licensed person that there exists a reasonable probability that the care, skill or knowledge exercised or exhibited in the treatment, practice or work that is the subject of the complaint, fell outside acceptable professional or occupational standards or treatment practices. The court may grant no more than one additional period, not to exceed 60 days, to file the affidavit pursuant to this section, upon a finding of good cause.

will reverse the judgment of the District Court and remand for further proceedings consistent with the opinion.

The New Jersey affidavit of merit statute applies to medical malpractice causes of action that "occur" on or after June 29, 1995, the effective date of the statute. It requires that the plaintiff file an affidavit of a licensed physician within 60 days of the date the answer is filed or face dismissal of the complaint. In the affidavit, the physician must state that a "reasonable probability" exists that the care that is the subject of the complaint falls outside acceptable professional standards. In lieu of an affidavit, the plaintiff may provide a sworn statement that, after written request, the defendant failed to provide the plaintiff with records that have a substantial bearing on preparation of the affidavit. Failure to provide either the affidavit or the sworn statement within 60 days, or 120 days if the court grants an extension for good cause, results in dismissal for "failure to state a cause of action."

In January of 1994, Dr. Vincent C. Giampapa performed plastic surgery on the plaintiff's nose. Thereafter, he injected cortisone in her nose on several occasions. On August 20, 1995, the plaintiff visited Dr. Giampapa for a checkup and, at his suggestion, she allowed him to perform a second plastic surgery, which she expected to be minor. The plaintiff claims Dr. Giampapa instead performed extensive surgery without properly advising her about, and obtaining consent for, the procedure. The plaintiff experienced problems after the August 20 surgery, and, as a result, Dr. Giampapa performed additional plastic surgery on March 20, 1996. When the plaintiff continued to experience problems, she sought medical care and treatment from another plastic surgeon and underwent extensive reconstructive surgery.

The plaintiff sued Dr. Giampapa on March 10, 1998, alleging negligence with respect to her medical care and treatment. The defendant's answer, filed on May 8th, responded to the complaint in full but did not include a demand for an affidavit of merit from the plaintiff. ...

The defendant thereafter filed a motion to dismiss based on the plaintiff's failure to file an affidavit of merit. ... Both counts of the complaint were dismissed with prejudice. ...

A.   THE CHOICE OF LAW ISSUE

A federal court sitting in diversity must apply state substantive law and federal procedural law. See *Erie R.R. v. Tompkins*, 304 U.S. 64, 78 (1938). This substantive/procedural dichotomy of the "Erie rule" must be applied with the objective that "in all cases where a federal court is exercising jurisdiction solely because of the diversity of citizenship of the parties, the outcome of the litigation in the federal court [will] be substantially the same, so far as legal rules determine the outcome of a litigation, as it would be if tried in a State court." *Guaranty Trust Co. v. York*, 326 U.S. 99, 109 (1945). This focus on whether application of a state rule will or may affect the outcome is intended to serve "twin aims": "discouragement of forum shopping and avoidance of inequitable administration of the laws." *Hanna v. Plumer*, 380 U.S. 460, 468 (1965). Accordingly, the outcome determinative test should not produce a decision favoring application of the state rule unless one of these aims will be furthered:

> *Erie* and its progeny make clear that when a federal court sitting in a diversity case is faced with a question of whether or not to apply state law, the importance of a state rule is indeed relevant, but only in the context of asking whether application of the rule would make so important a difference to the character or result of the litigation that failure to enforce it would unfairly discriminate against citizens of the forum State, or whether application of the rule would have so important an effect upon the fortunes of one or both of the litigants that failure to enforce it would be likely to cause a plaintiff to choose the federal court.

Hanna, 380 U.S. at 468 n. 9.

The Supreme Court has added two caveats to these *Erie* principles. First, even though application of the state rule may hold some potential for affecting the outcome, a strong countervailing federal interest will dictate recourse to the federal rule. *Byrd v. Blue Ridge Rural Electric Coop, Inc.*, 356 U.S. 525 (1958). Second, the *Erie* rule may not be "invoked to void a Federal Rule" of Civil Procedure. *Hanna v. Plumer*, 380 U.S. 460, 470 (1965). Where a Federal Rule of Civil Procedure provides a resolution of an issue, that rule must be applied by a federal court sitting in diversity to the exclusion of a conflicting state rule so long as the federal rule is authorized by the Rules Enabling Act and consistent with the Constitution.

Under *Hanna*, a federal court sitting in diversity first must determine whether a Federal Rule directly "collides" with the state law it is being urged to apply. If there is such a direct conflict, the Federal Rule must be applied if it is constitutional and within the scope of the Rules Enabling Act. If a "direct collision" does not exist, then the court applies the *Erie* rule to determine if state law should be applied.

In deciding whether a Federal Rule "directly collides" with a state law, the federal court sitting in diversity must consider whether the scope of the Federal Rule is "sufficiently broad to control the issue before the Court," *Walker v. Armco Steel Corp.*, 446 U.S. 740, 749–50 (1980), "thereby leaving no room for the operation of [the state] law," *Burlington Northern R.R. Co. v. Woods*, 480 U.S. 1, 4–5 (1987). Although the Rules should be given their plain meaning and are not to be construed narrowly in order to avoid a direct collision, "a broad reading that would create significant disuniformity between state and federal courts should be avoided if the text permits." *Stewart Org., Inc. v. Ricoh*, 487 U.S. 22, 37–38 (1988). "Federal courts have interpreted the Federal Rules, however, with sensitivity to important state interests and regulatory policies." *Gasperini*, 518 U.S. at 427 n.7.

In the case at hand, the plaintiff argues the New Jersey affidavit of merit statute conflicts with Federal Rules 8 and 9, which govern the content of pleadings in federal actions. Rule 8 requires only "a short and plain statement of the claim showing that the pleader is entitled to relief." Fed. R. Civ. P. 8(a). The only situations that require pleading with particularity are specified in Fed. R. Civ. P. 9, and a malpractice claim is not one of the situations listed in that rule. There is, of course, no contention that Federal Rules 8 and 9 are beyond the scope of the Rules Enabling Act or inconsistent with the Constitution.

We find no direct conflict between the New Jersey affidavit of merit statute and Federal Rules 8 and 9. Rules 8 and 9 dictate the content of the pleadings and the degree of specificity that is required. The rules' overall purpose is to provide notice of the claims and defenses of the parties. The affidavit of merit statute has no effect on what is included in the pleadings of a case or the specificity thereof. The required affidavit is not a pleading, is not filed until after the pleadings are closed, and does not contain a statement of the factual basis for the claim. Its purpose is not to give notice of the plaintiff's claim, but rather to assure that malpractice claims for which there is no expert support will be terminated at an early stage in the proceedings. This state policy can be effectuated without compromising any of the policy choices reflected in Federal Rules 8 and 9. In short, these Federal Rules and the New Jersey Statute can exist side by side, "each controlling its own intended sphere of coverage without conflict." *Walker v. Armco Steel Corp.*, 446 U.S. 740, 752 (1980).

In reaching our conclusion that there is no direct collision here, we are not unmindful of the stipulation in the New Jersey statute that a failure to file the required affidavit "shall be deemed a failure to state a cause of action." N.J. Stat. Ann. 2A:53A–29. Contrary to the plaintiff's suggestion, we do not read this stipulation as implying that a failure to file the required affidavit somehow renders pleadings insufficient that would otherwise be sufficient. We read the "deeming" language to be no more than the New Jersey legislature's way of saying that the consequences of a failure to file shall be the same as those of a failure to state a claim.

Finding no direct collision, we proceed to the second part of the Hanna analysis. Applying traditional Erie principles, we conclude that the New Jersey affidavit of merit statute is substantive state law that must be applied by federal courts sitting in diversity. The state statute is outcome determinative on its face, and failure to apply it would encourage forum shopping and lead to the inequitable administration of the law. Further, we perceive no overriding federal interest here that would prevent application of the state law by the federal courts.

By requiring dismissal for failure to adhere to the statute, the New Jersey legislature clearly intended to influence substantive outcomes. It sought early dismissal of meritless lawsuits, not merely to apply a new procedural rule. Clearly, failure to apply the statute in a federal diversity action where no affidavit of merit has been filed would produce a different outcome than that mandated in a state proceeding.

In addition to undercutting the state's interest in early dismissal of meritless lawsuits, failure to apply the state statute in federal courts could promote forum-shopping, despite the relatively low hurdle the New Jersey affidavit requirement presents to a legitimate claimant. Plaintiffs who have been unable to secure expert support for their claims and face dismissal under the statute in state court may, by filing in the federal court, be able to survive beyond the pleading stage and secure discovery. The resulting opportunity for a "fishing expedition," which would hold the hope of turning up evidence of a meritorious claim or of a settlement to save defense litigation costs, can reasonably be expected to affect the forum choice of these plaintiffs.

Failure to apply the New Jersey affidavit of merit statute also implicates the second of the "twin aims" of Erie, avoiding inequitable administration of the laws. A defendant in a federal court that refused to apply the affidavit requirement would be unfairly exposed to additional litigation time and expense before the dismissal of a non-meritorious lawsuit could be secured, merely because the plaintiff is a citizen of a different state. Perhaps more importantly, the reputation of the professional involved would be more likely to suffer the longer the lawsuit went on, putting added pressure on the defendant to settle rather than endure extensive discovery.

Finally, we must also consider whether any countervailing federal interests prevent the state law from being applied in federal court. The only relevant federal interest that has been suggested is an interest in maintaining the integrity of the federal system of pleading embodied in the Federal Rules of Civil Procedure. We have previously concluded, however, that the New Jersey statute can be applied without compromising the federal system of pleading. Accordingly, we hold that the District Court did not err in applying the New Jersey affidavit of merit statute. . . .

[The court determined that the affidavit of merit requirement only applied to acts of negligence occurring on or after June 29, 1995, the effective date of the state statute.]

We will reverse the judgment of the District Court and remand for further proceedings on the plaintiff's claim that the defendant was guilty of malpractice with respect to cortisone injections occurring before June 29, 1995.

In VESS v. CIBA–GEIGY CORP. USA, 317 F.3d 1097 (9th Cir. 2003), plaintiff Vess sued three defendants for fraud, alleging a conspiracy to increase sales of the drug Ritalin for hyperactive children. Defendants argued that plaintiff did not allege fraud with the particularity required by Rule 9(b). Plaintiff Vess argued that Rule 9(b) did not apply to the state law fraud claim. The court disagreed with plaintiff's argument. Noting that the Federal Rules stem from the Rules Enabling Act,

28 U.S.C. § 2072, the court applied the "second part" of the *Hanna* analysis:

> The Federal Rules of Civil Procedure apply irrespective of the source of subject matter jurisdiction, and irrespective of whether the substantive law at issue is state or federal. The Constitution and the Rules Enabling Act authorize and, at the same time, limit the scope of the federal rules. The "constitutional provision for a federal court system" confers power on Congress to regulate the procedures in the federal courts, but limited to "a power to regulate matters which, though falling within the uncertain area between substance and procedure, are rationally capable of classification as either." The Enabling Act similarly implements the constitutional power and limits the scope of its implementation. The Enabling Act authorizes the adoption of federal rules, but provides that "such rules shall not abridge, enlarge or modify any substantive right." 28 U.S.C. § 2072. A federal district court can refuse to apply a Federal Rule of Civil Procedure in a civil case "only if the Advisory Committee, [the Supreme] Court, and Congress erred in their prima facie judgment that the Rule in question transgresses neither the terms of the Enabling Act nor constitutional restrictions." *Hanna*, 380 U.S. at 471. In other words, if a Federal Rule of Civil Procedure is valid under the Constitution and the Enabling Act, it applies according to its terms in all civil cases in federal district court.

To the court, there was no real question as to whether Rule 9(b) was a valid procedural rule within the meaning of the Rules Enabling Act.

> It is established law, in this circuit and elsewhere, that Rule 9(b)'s particularity requirement applies to state-law causes of action. "While a federal court will examine state law to determine whether the elements of fraud have been pled sufficiently to state a cause of action, the Rule 9(b) requirement that the *circumstances* of the fraud must be stated with particularity is a federally imposed rule." *Hayduk v. Lanna*, 775 F.2d 441, 443 (1st Cir. 1985) (emphasis in original). We therefore reject Vess's argument that we should refuse to apply Rule 9(b) to his state-law causes of action in this diversity case. . . .

Notes and Questions

1. In both *Chamberlain* and *Vess*, the courts noted a tension between state law and the pleading requirements of Federal Rules 8 and 9. However, in *Chamberlain* the court applied the "likely to cause forum shopping" analysis that courts use when dealing with rules that are not promulgated under the Rules Enabling Act. Is the court applying the wrong test?

2. How would refusing to apply the state law in *Chamberlain* promote forum shopping? The state law tries to weed out meritless claims at a very

early stage. Even if a plaintiff with a weak claim can "get in the door" by filing in federal court, shouldn't it still lose the case on the merits? Will a plaintiff really shop for federal court merely to have the opportunity to sink a great deal of time and money into a case that it will eventually lose anyway?

3.   Do you agree with the *Vess* court that Rule 9(b) is a procedural rule under the Rules Enabling Act? By requiring specific and detailed facts—facts that may not be available to the plaintiff when he files his complaint—doesn't the Rule abridge the right to recover for fraud? Or is there a difference between abridging the right and making it more difficult to recover for that right?

4.   The Supreme Court applies one Federal Rule differently in diversity and federal question cases. In a federal question case, Rule 3 dictates when a case commences for purposes of the statute of limitations. In cases governed by state law, however, the federal court borrows state law. *Burlington Northern Railroad v. Woods*, 480 U.S. 1, 107 S.Ct. 967, 94 L.Ed.2d 1 (1987). The difference is important in those states that require a plaintiff to serve the defendant, not merely file the complaint, in order to beat out the statute of limitations. The differing treatment of Rule 3 is likely due to the fact that that rule directly affects the statute of limitations. Because the Supreme Court held in *Guaranty Trust* that statutes of limitation are substantive, the Court may be hesitant to interpret Rule 3 in a way that affects how state statutes of limitation apply.

If Rule 3 does not apply to the statute of limitations, what purpose does it serve? Why else do we care when a case "commences?" Are there any other Federal Rules that turn on when a case commences?

Problems

1.   P sues D in a state court in State X for injuries arising out of an automobile accident in State Y. P and D are both domiciled in State Z. P chose state X because neither Y nor Z would allow him to recover. D files a Rule 12(b)(6) motion, arguing that State X should not apply its own law. Who is correct?

2.   P sues D in a state court in State A for injuries arising out of an automobile accident occurring at an intersection in State A. P and D are both domiciled in State B, and work for the same company in that state. State A has a "fellow servant rule" that prevents one employee from recovering against another. State B has no such rule. Assuming she has evidence to support her claim, can P recover from D?

3.   Same as Problem 2, except that neither State has a fellow servant rule. However, State A requires all drivers to stop whenever they approach an unmarked intersection. State B only requires the driver on the left to yield. At the time of the accident, D was on P's right. P argues that D was negligent for failing to follow the law of State A. Is P correct?

4.   Landlord leased certain commercial premises to Tenant. As a condition to signing the lease, however, Landlord required Guarantor to sign a guarantee of Tenant's obligations. When Tenant fails to pay its rent, Landlord sues Guarantor in federal court. Guarantor impleads Tenant under

Rule 14. Tenant objects to the impleader. Tenant notes that in state court, impleader of third-party defendants is not allowed. Instead, in the state system Guarantor would need to bring a separate action against Tenant. May Guarantor implead Tenant?

5.   P sues D in federal court for medical malpractice. D prevails at trial. D asks the court to award her the attorneys' fees she incurred in defending the case. Under a recently enacted "tort reform" law in the state, a doctor who is sued for medical malpractice is entitled to receive attorneys' fees if she successfully defends the case. No such law exists at the federal level. Is D entitled to her attorneys' fees?

6.   P sues D for trespass in a federal court in State X. D argues that P's claim is barred by the statute of limitations. Under the law of State X, the claim would be barred. However, the land upon which D allegedly trespassed is located in State Y. Under the law of State Y, P's claim is not barred. Is P's claim barred?

E.   RESPONDING TO THE COMPLAINT

INTRODUCTORY PROBLEM

The National Park Service has sued four Virginia defendants (Jefferson, Madison, Monroe, and Washington) in a Virginia federal court for civil trespass at Shenandoah National Park in Luray, Virginia on or about July 4, 2005. (A trespasser is a person who enters or remains upon or in possession of the land of another without the possessor's consent.) Jefferson answered the federal complaint by stating that he was in the Park on July 4, 2005. Madison's Answer to the complaint contains no reference to his whereabouts on or about July 4, 2005. Monroe responds to the United States' complaint by stating that he celebrated the Fourth of July holiday energetically by getting a lot of exercise and by drinking alcoholic beverages heavily, but he does not believe that he has enough information to know whether he was at the Park on or about that day. In his Answer, Washington admits that he was at the Park on July 4, 2005, but only because someone intentionally and falsely misrepresented to him that Bono was having a concert there on that evening. Assess the effect of each defendant's Answer to the Plaintiff's Complaint.

Governing law: Federal Rule 8(b)-(d).

———

After a plaintiff has filed a complaint, it seems only fair for the person sued to have the opportunity to respond to that complaint. After a defendant has had the chance to digest the allegations of the complaint, to take a few deep breaths to try and relax, and to contact an attorney, the defendant and counsel can determine how to respond to the complaint. The defendant's response may serve multiple purposes: to admit certain allegations, to deny allegations, to accompany the response with a defendant's counterclaim, and/or to bring in other parties to the lawsuit. The defendant's response to the complaint is called the "answer." The response to the defendant's answer is called a "reply" and is discussed later in this chapter. This portion of the chapter will focus on the methods available to the defendant in responding to the plaintiff's complaint.

Federal Rule 8(b) informs a defendant how to challenge and require a plaintiff to prove some or all of the allegations in the complaint. The defendant is to state in short and plain terms defenses to each claim and to admit or deny the plaintiff's allegations. Failure to deny an allegation when an answer is required results in the allegation being treated as admitted, per Rule 8(d). Read together, Rules 8(b) and 8(e) inform a defendant that the answer to the complaint should notify the plaintiff of the allegations in the complaint that the defendant admits and will not be in issue at trial. They also alert the plaintiff about which allegations are denied and therefore will require proof to be established at trial to enable the plaintiff to succeed. Pleading of affirmative defenses, as opposed to denials, is governed by Rule 8(c) and will be discussed in the next section. As previously discussed for claims for relief in a complaint, the answer should notify the plaintiff of the issues contested by the defendant. Later discovery and pretrial procedures provide factual development of the facts applicable to the claims and defenses.

1. Menu of Responses

The defendant has a variety of devices to use in answering a complaint. An obvious alternative is for the defendant to *admit* each and every allegation in the complaint. Any defendant in that position is probably better off to begin a course of negotiations with the plaintiff to settle the case for less than the plaintiff has sought in the complaint. Negotiation is preferable to admitting all the allegations immediately, which subjects the defendant to a judgment for all the relief sought by the plaintiff.

A more likely and preferred alternative is for the defendant to *deny all or part* of the allegations in the complaint. Rule 8(b) requires that denials fairly meet the substance of the statements they purport to deny. This standard potentially applies to any type of denial, whether it is a general denial, a specific denial, or a qualified denial. How can an answer fail to meet the substance of what is being denied? Suppose the defendant states in the answer, "Prove whatever you alleged" or "Your allegations do not even justify a response." Even though Rule 8(b) does not prescribe a proper model to deny allegations and even though these statements may characterize the defendant's initial reaction to the complaint, they neither admit nor deny the plaintiff's allegations and therefore cannot be said to meet fairly the substance of the allegation. A denial that does not meet the substance of the statements being denied is treated under Rule 8(d) as admitted.

General denial. What happens if the defendant selects the responsive alternative of denying every one of the complaint's allegations, also known as a general denial and recognized in the last sentence of Rule 8(b)? How does the defendant say this? While there is no set formula for making a general denial, it would be typical for the defendant to state simply, "Defendant denies each and every allegation of the complaint." The tactical advantage of a general denial is that it forces the plaintiff to prove every matter of fact alleged in the complaint.

Can a defendant justify this response? Even though the rules allow a defendant to make a general denial, its use is limited. First, because the complaint included jurisdictional statements as well as the claims for relief, it is unlikely that a plaintiff incorrectly stated all matters relating to the matters such as the parties' identities and addresses. Situations are rare when a defendant can completely deny the complaint's allegations. In the language of Rule 8(b), can a general denial "fairly meet the substance of all averments denied"?

Second, as Rule 8(b) notes, the general denial is "subject to the obligations set forth in Rule 11" (discussed later in this chapter). If a plaintiff moves under Rule 12(f) to strike the defendant's answer because the defendant has failed to meet the Rule 8(b) obligation, all the plaintiff has to show is one defect in order for the entire answer to be stricken. True, the grant of the motion is likely to permit the defendant to file another answer, but it may be questionable how the court regards the defendant's credibility. A more specific answer will compel the defendant to admit some matters, which means that the plaintiff will not have so many things to prove at trial. Third, issues relating to a party's capacity or the performance or occurrence of a condition precedent require specific denials.

Specific denials. Because it is unlikely that a defendant can make a general denial in good faith, Rule 8(b) permits the defendant to "make denials as specific denials of designated averments or paragraphs." A specific denial is the most common method of answering a complaint when all allegations in a complaint's paragraph can be controverted. There is no magic formula for making a specific denial, other than for the defendant to be clear about which allegations are being denied and which are not, e.g., "Defendant denies all the allegations in Paragraph 3."

Qualified denials. A defendant may prefer to admit some of the allegations in a paragraph but deny others. A general or specific denial is inappropriate because some allegations are being admitted. Rule 8(b) authorizes the defendant to "generally deny all the averments except such designated averments or paragraphs as the pleader expressly admits." This denial often is called a qualified denial, because it has the effect of a specific denial but is subject to express qualifications, e.g., "Defendant denies all the allegations in Paragraph 5, except those relating to identity and residential address."

Denial based on lack of knowledge or information to form a belief. Rule 8(b) states that if a party is without knowledge or information sufficient to form a belief as to the truth of an allegation, the defendant shall so state and this statement has the effect of a denial. Who can use this denial? A defendant can use this type of denial when there is insufficient data to justify either an honest admission or a denial of the plaintiff's allegation. When can the denial be used? Within the time for a defendant to answer the complaint (usually 20 days unless service of process was waived), the defendant lacks both first-hand knowledge of important facts and the ability to find out about those facts in order to form a belief, e.g., "For lack of knowledge or information sufficient to form a belief, Defendant can neither affirm nor deny the Plaintiff's domicile."

Denial based upon information and belief. A defendant who lacks first-hand or personal knowledge about the validity of one or more of the allegations in the complaint, *but* has sufficient information to form a belief about the truth or falsity of the allegations may assert a denial upon "information and belief." This type of denial is not explicitly authorized by Rule 8(b), as is the denial based upon a lack of knowledge or information sufficient to form a belief. However, federal courts have permitted allegations on information and belief, presumably because of the language in Rule 11 stating that an attorney's signature on a pleading certifies "that to the best of the person's knowledge, information, and belief formed after an inquiry reasonable under the circumstances" it is well grounded in fact and warranted by existing law.

A denial upon information and belief is most appropriate when the denial is based upon information from a third person, such as the party's attorney. Denials by corporate defendants are typical examples, because the corporation lacks first-hand or personal knowledge. A denial upon information and belief is not available if the statements in the complaint address matters within the defendant's personal knowledge, matters within the general knowledge of the community, or matters of public record. Any use of a denial on information and belief in this context is subject to a motion to strike under Rule 12(f).

Negative pregnant. Sometimes, a denial, if read literally and interpreted against the defendant, actually denies only an immaterial part of the complaint and leaves admitted the key allegations by the plaintiff. At common law this pleading defect was called a negative pregnant, i.e., the "negative" was said to be "pregnant" with an admission. Although the answer was in the form of a denial, it was uncertain whether the defendant intended to deny all the elements of the allegation or to deny only some elements. An example of one form of a negative pregnant occurs when a plaintiff claims that the value of a car exceeds $15,000, and the defendant denies that the value exceeded that sum. Taken literally, the defendant denied only the immaterial word "exceeded" but admitted that the value of the car at least equaled $15,000.

A negative pregnant may be the result of the defendant framing the denial in exactly the same language as the plaintiff's affirmative allegation, e.g., a defendant attempts to deny an allegation that he "negligently drove his automobile causing injury to plaintiff" with the statement that he "did not negligently drive his automobile causing injury to the plaintiff." At common law, the defendant only denied that he acted negligently but admitted having driven the car when it struck and injured the plaintiff.

Failure to deny. Under the first sentence of Rule 8(d), a failure to deny allegations in the complaint constitutes an admission of the facts alleged in those averments. The sentence applies when an answer has not been filed. There are two limitations on the application of the basic rule. First, allegations of damages specifically are exempted from the effect of Rule 8(d) and are not admitted by a failure to deny. Second, the rule makes it clear that an admission by failure to deny only applies to allegations in those pleadings to which a responsive pleading is required. According to the second sentence of Rule 8(d), allegations contained in a pleading (like an answer) to which no response is required or permitted are deemed denied and thus contested automatically without the necessity of a denial.

To avoid the effect of the first sentence of Rule 8(d), a pleader must do more than make a passing reference to the allegations in the preceding pleading or interpose an ambiguous response to them. As discussed under Rule 8(b) a denial must meet the substance of the averments denied; otherwise the response will be treated as an admission under Rule 8(d). Rule 8(d) should be read in conjunction with Rule 7(a), which lists those pleadings that are required or permitted to be interposed under the federal rules. For example, any affirmative defense raised in an answer automatically is deemed denied and at issue because no reply is permitted to an affirmative defense in the absence of a court order. Similarly, because no responsive pleading to an answer is permitted, facts raised for the first time in an answer are considered denied. However, if the trial court orders a reply to the answer, which is permitted by Rule 7(a), an allegation in the answer that is not denied in the reply is deemed admitted under Rule 8(d).

KING VISION PAY PER VIEW, LTD. v. J.C. DIMITRI'S RESTAURANT, INC.

180 F.R.D. 332 (N.D. Ill. 1998)

SHADUR, Senior District Judge.

J.C. Dimitri's Restaurant, Inc. ("Dimitri's") and James Chelios ("Chelios") have filed what purports to be a Response to Complaint that addresses the Complaint filed against them by King Vision Pay Per View, Ltd. This *sua sponte* opinion is triggered by the Response's pervasive and impermissible flouting of the crystal-clear directive of Fed.R.Civ.P. ("Rule") 8(b) as to how any responsive pleading to a federal complaint must be drafted.[1]

---

1. "Drafted" is really too fancy a label for a task that, in this respect, requires no drafting skills at all—merely the ability to read and to comply with instructions that the Rule's drafters have set out in plain and simple English.

This is it. For too many years and in too many hundreds of cases this Court has been reading, and has been compelled to order the correction of, allegedly responsive pleadings that are written by lawyers who are either unaware of or who choose to depart from Rule 8(b)'s plain roadmap. It identifies only three alternatives as available for use in an answer to the allegations of a complaint: to admit those allegations, to deny them or to state a disclaimer (if it can be made in the objective and subjective good faith demanded by Rule 11) in the express terms of the second sentence of Rule 8(b), which then entitles the pleader to the benefit of a deemed denial.

Here Dimitri's' and Chelios' counsel has engaged in a particularly vexatious violation of that most fundamental aspect of federal pleading. It is hard to imagine, but fully 30 of the Response's 35 paragraphs (its express statements in Response ¶¶ 6–12, 17, 25–26 and 33–34, plus the incorporation by reference of such earlier paragraphs in Response ¶¶ 19 and 28) contain this nonresponse, in direct violation of Rule 8(b)'s express teaching: Neither admit nor deny the allegations of said Paragraph—, but demand strict proof thereof.

* * * [A] a host of this Court's unpublished opinions ... speak not only of the unacceptability of any such Rule 8(b) violation but also to the equally unacceptable "demand" for "strict proof," a concept that to this Court's knowledge is unknown to the federal practice or to any other system of modern pleading.

This Court's efforts at lawyer education through the issuance of repeated brief opinions or oral rulings, or through faculty participation in seminars and symposia on federal pleading and practice,[4] have proved unavailing. It is time for this Court to follow the Rules itself, in this instance Rule 8(d):

> Averments in a pleading to which a responsive pleading is required, other than those as to the amount of damage, are admitted when not denied in the responsive pleading.

Accordingly all of the allegations of Complaint ¶¶ 6–12, 17, 25–26 and 33–34 are held to have been admitted by Dimitri's and Chelios, and this action will proceed on that basis. And although the same phenomenon referred to in n. 4 probably makes it quite unlikely that the lawyers who are most prone to commit the same offense will be lawyers who are regular (or even sporadic) readers of F.Supp. or F.R.D., this opinion is being sent to West Publishing Company for publication. Future Rule 8(b) violators are hereby placed on constructive notice that their similarly defective pleadings will encounter like treatment.

Problems

1. Constant sues Mocerf for breach of contract. In his Answer, the defendant in ¶¶ 3 through 7 responds to corresponding allegations in the

---

4. Unfortunately those seminars and symposia usually turn out to involve preaching to the converted. Lawyers who really need such continuing legal education rarely attend (they must be too busy making mistakes).

Complaint that allege the terms of provisions in documents. Instead of providing direct responses to the allegations, Mocerf asserts that the documents "speak for themselves." Is this a proper response under Rule 8?

2. In addressing later paragraphs of the same Complaint, for his Answer, Mocerf states: "Defendant is without sufficient knowledge to admit the allegations contained in paragraphs 8–12, and therefore denies same." Is this a proper response under Rule 8?

3. Podoll's Complaint stated that on July 1, 2004, the insured property was completely destroyed by fire. Defendant Singlust answers that "on July 1, 2004, the insured property was not completely destroyed by fire." Is this a proper response under Rule 8? How can you improve the response?

4. Podoll's Complaint also stated that "Defendant Singlust made, executed and delivered" an insurance contract. Singlust's Answer denied that he had "made, executed and delivered" an insurance contract. Is there a problem with that response?

Exercise

In response to the complaint filed, Fly-by-Night Insurance Company filed the following Answer. After reading the Answer, determine which of its paragraphs are illustrative of the textual material discussed above. Specifically, do any parts of the Answer illustrate a general denial, specific denial, qualified denial, denial based on lack of information or belief, denial based on information and belief, negative pregnant, or a failure to deny?

UNITED STATES DISTRICT COURT
WESTERN DISTRICT OF KENTUCKY
AT LOUISVILLE
Civil Action 2004–1

GEORGE W. KERRY   Plaintiff

v.   ANSWER

FLY–BY–NIGHT INSURANCE CO.   Defendant

Defendant for its Answer to Plaintiff's Complaint states as follows:

1. The Defendant admits the allegations contained in Paragraphs 1, 2, 5, and 8.

2. The Defendant denies the allegations contained in Paragraphs 10,-11, 12, 14, and 15.

3. With respect to the allegations contained in Paragraphs 3 and 4 of the Complaint, Defendant admits that this Court has subject matter jurisdiction and that venue is proper in this Court, but denies that the cited

statutory provisions support the subject matter jurisdiction and venue of this Court.

4. With respect to the allegations contained in Paragraph 6 of the Complaint, Defendant admits that on November 1, 2004, George W. Gore issued a check for $75,500 for the premium on a policy of confirmation insurance. Defendant denies all remaining allegations of Paragraph 6.

5. Defendant is without knowledge or information sufficient to form a belief as to the truth of the allegations contained in Paragraph 7 of the Complaint and therefore denies all of the allegations in Paragraph 7.

6. With respect to the allegations contained in Paragraphs 9 and 13 of the Complaint, Defendant incorporates to the same force and effect its answers to Paragraphs 1–8 of the Complaint as set forth above admits.

7. Defendant denies all allegations of the Complaint not specifically admitted in this Answer.

8. Plaintiff's claim fails to state a claim upon which relief can be granted.

9. If Defendant had any obligation under the insurance contract, Plaintiff waived the performance of that obligation by withdrawing his candidacy for United States President.

WHEREFORE, Defendant, Fly-by-Night Insurance Co., demands that the Plaintiff's Complaint be dismissed with prejudice, that it recover its costs from this case, and that it be granted all further relief to which it may be entitled.

Howdy Doody
Bar Wars, P.S.C.
6000 Seventh National Tower
Passivity, KY 44444
COUNSEL FOR DEFENDANT

CERTIFICATE OF SERVICE

I certify that on the 20th day of January, 2005, a copy of the foregoing Answer was mailed to Robert Cork, 5000 Second Hemp Tower, Privacy, KY 40007, Counsel for Plaintiff.

Counsel for Defendant

2. Affirmative Defenses

An affirmative defense is usually described as an avoidance of the plaintiff's allegations in the complaint. Information contained in an affirmative defense does not necessarily negate any allegations in the complaint, but it avoids those allegations by adding new information. The purpose of requiring an affirmative defense under Rule 8(c) is to give the plaintiff notice of the defendant's intent to introduce new matter as a defense.

Access of the parties to the facts, types of defenses, mere convenience, and the nature of the substantive law involved are all factors for consideration on the issue of whether a defendant must plead a matter as an affirmative defense. The usual test for whether matter should be pleaded as an affirmative defense is whether the matter is directly inconsistent or contrary to allegations in the complaint. If so, it is not a matter to be pleaded affirmatively.

When in doubt about whether a certain defense not listed in Rule 8(c) should be pleaded as an affirmative defense, the safe course is to plead it affirmatively, and in addition, any relevant allegations in the complaint should be denied. It is relatively common to plead affirmative defenses generally, but the particularity provisions of Rule 9 concerning the pleading of fraud, denials of capacity, and denials of occurrence of conditions should be noted. What happens if a defendant fails to plead an affirmative defense? Because Rule 8(c) is mandatory, principles of statutory construction suggest that failure to raise the defense results in a waiver and exclusion of the defense from the case.

RED DEER v. CHEROKEE COUNTY, IOWA

183 F.R.D. 642 (N.D. Iowa 1999)

BENNETT, District Judge.

[Plaintiff is a female, Native American who unsuccessfully applied for a deputy sheriff's job and then sued the county alleging age, race, and sex discrimination and retaliation. She filed a motion to exclude "after-acquired" evidence of her prior employment records. The court addressed the issue of whether such "after-acquired evidence" constitutes an affirmative defense.]

* * * The plaintiff ... seeks to exclude evidence from her prior employment records, because she contends those records were not considered by the county at the time it decided not to hire her, but the county contends those records are admissible "after-acquired evidence" of misrepresentations in the plaintiff's job application. Although the court must resolve these evidentiary questions, they have been overshadowed by pleading and trial readiness questions that have arisen as a consequence of the motions in limine. Those questions include whether "after-acquired evidence" is an affirmative defense that must be pleaded and proved by the defendant, and if the defense is an affirmative one....

* * * The County contends that Red Deer misrepresented the reasons for her departures from two of her previous jobs, and characterizes her termination from one of those jobs as a discharge for "dishonest conduct." Dishonest conduct, the County points out, is a ground for termination of a deputy sheriff and prior dishonest conduct would have constituted a ground not to hire Red Deer at all. Thus, the County asserts that, had it known about Red Deer's misrepresentations on her job application at the time of its decision not to hire her, the County would not have hired Red Deer regardless of her race, sex, or age. * * *

The court finds that Red Deer's motion in limine, which seeks to exclude evidence of her prior employment records on the ground that such records were not considered by the County in making its decision not to hire her, must ... be denied. In *McKennon v. Nashville Banner Pub. Co.*, 513 U.S. 352 (1995), the Supreme Court considered the impact of "after-acquired evidence" of an employee's wrong-doing upon the relief the employee may obtain for discrimination by the employer. * * *

The one black letter rule established in *McKennon* is that where an employer seeks to rely upon after-acquired evidence of wrongdoing by the employee during his or her employment—and this court concludes where the employer seeks to rely on evidence of wrongdoing in the application process—the employer "must first establish that the wrong-doing was of such severity that the employee in fact would have been terminated on those grounds alone if the employer had known of it at the time of the discharge." *Id.* at 362–63. In the circumstances of the case now before the court, a failure-to-hire case not a discharge case, this court reads the rule to be that the County must first establish that the wrongdoing was of such severity that Red Deer in fact would not have been hired on those grounds alone if the County had known of the wrongdoing at the time of the decision not to hire her. * * *

The question under *McKennon* is not whether the County actually relied on the evidence in making its decision, but what the County would have done had the evidence come to light at the time of Red Deer's applications. Indeed, the Supreme Court was aware of Red Deer's concern, because it specifically noted that "[t]he employer could not have been motivated by knowledge it did not have and it cannot now claim that the employee was fired [or not hired] for the nondiscriminatory reason." *Id.* at 360. * * *

In these circumstances, the evidence of Red Deer's past employment is relevant to the availability and success of the County's after-acquired evidence defense, and is not unfairly prejudicial. . . .

* * * Scant case law considers whether "after-acquired evidence" is an affirmative defense that must be pleaded as well as proved by the defendant. Indeed, no court appears to have considered the question directly. * * *

In *McKennon*, the Supreme Court clearly placed the burden of proving the "after-acquired evidence" defense upon the defendant. For example, the Court stated that "[w]here an employer seeks to rely upon after-acquired evidence of wrongdoing, *it must first establish* that the wrongdoing was of such severity that the employee in fact would have been terminated [or not hired] on those grounds alone if the employer had known of it at the time of the discharge." *McKennon*, 513 U.S. at 362–63 (emphasis added). The Court did not, however, specifically identify the defense as an "affirmative" one, and said nothing whatever about the defendant's obligation to plead the defense. Unfortunately, more general guidance on what constitutes an affirmative defense is also sparse, but what suggestions this court has discovered are discussed in the next subsection.

* * * The purpose of the pleading requirement for affirmative defenses in Rule 8(c) "is to give the opposing party notice of the plea of [the affirmative defense] and a chance to argue, if he can, why the imposition of [the affirmative defense] would be inappropriate." *Blonder–Tongue Lab. v. University of Illinois Found.*, 402 U.S. 313, 350 (1971). * * *

"[A]fter-acquired evidence" plainly is not among the affirmative defenses specifically enumerated in Rule 8(c). Where a defense is not one of the enumerated defenses, whether or not it comes within the ambit of Rule 8(c) depends upon whether it falls within the "catchall" for "any other" defenses. * * *

In *Sayre v. Musicland Group, Inc.*, 850 F.2d 350 (8th Cir.1988), a diversity case, the Eighth Circuit Court of Appeals stated that "[t]he pleading of affirmative defenses is a procedural matter" to which federal rules of procedure apply. *Sayre*, 850 F.2d at 352. Therefore, in determining whether mitigation of damages was an affirmative defense that must be pleaded and proved, the Eighth Circuit Court of Appeals looked first to federal decisions, which had uniformly found mitigation of damages to be an affirmative defense that must be pleaded and proved. Id. Such guidance from federal decisions is lacking here.

* * * The case now before the court is not a diversity case, but a federal question case. However, this court can think of no reason why allocation of the burden of proof, if it is the pertinent factor to be drawn from state decisions for determining what is an affirmative defense within the meaning of Fed.R.Civ.P. 8(c) in a diversity case, should not also be a pertinent factor for determining what is an affirmative defense in a federal question case. Thus, to the extent federal cases establish the burden of proof for the defense in question here, the allocation of that burden of proof is relevant to the determination of what is an affirmative defense.

* * * The test in the First Circuit is "whether the defense 'shares the common characteristic of a bar to the right of recovery even if the general complaint were more or less admitted to.'" *Wolf v. Reliance Standard Life Ins. Co.*, 71 F.3d 444, 449 (1st Cir.1995) (quoting *Jakobsen v. Massachusetts Port Auth.*, 520 F.2d 810, 813 (1st Cir.1975).

* * * [T]he various authorities considered so far do suggest a number of factors that may be pertinent to the question of whether a particular defense is an affirmative one within the meaning of Rule 8(c). This court finds it unnecessary to select any one test of what constitutes an affirmative defense over another or to consider one suggested factor to the exclusion of others. This is so, because—at least in the absence of a definitive test from the Eighth Circuit Court of Appeals—perhaps the best manner in which the court can analyze the question of what

constitutes an affirmative defense within the meaning of Rule 8(c) is to consider each of the suggested factors or tests.

Therefore the court will consider here each of the following factors. First, the court will consider the allocation of the burden of proof, reasoning that if the defendant bears the burden of proof on the defense, it is an affirmative defense. Second, the court will consider whether the defense simply controverts the plaintiff's proof, or instead "avoids" the plaintiff's claim. To put it another way, the court will consider "whether the defense 'shares the common characteristic of a bar to the right of recovery even if the general complaint were more or less admitted to,' " not simply controverted. *Wolf*, 71 F.3d at 449 (quoting *Jakobsen*, 520 F.2d at 813). If so, the defense is an affirmative one. Third, the specific purposes of Rule 8(c) must not be overlooked. Thus, the court should consider the need for notice of the defense to avoid surprise and undue prejudice to the plaintiff. * * *

The court now turns to application of these factors or analyses to the defense in question here. As to allocation of the burden of proof, the Supreme Court has made clear that the burden of proof on the "after-acquired evidence" defense is allocated to the defendant. *McKennon*, 513 U.S. at 362–63. Thus, under this test, the defense is an affirmative one that must also be pleaded pursuant to Rule 8(c). The "after-acquired evidence" defense is also one that does not controvert the plaintiff's proof, but instead "avoids" the plaintiff's claim, or at least part of the plaintiff's potential relief. As the Supreme Court explained in *McKennon*, the defense, if proved, limits the plaintiff's relief, generally precluding frontpay or reinstatement, and limiting backpay to the period from the date of the unlawful discharge or failure to hire to the date the new information was discovered. *McKennon*, 513 U.S. at 361–62. * * * In other words, the "after-acquired evidence" defense " 'shares the common characteristic of a bar to the right of recovery even if the general complaint were more or less admitted to,' " *Wolf*, 71 F.3d at 449 (emphasis added) (quoting *Jakobsen*, 520 F.2d at 813), or the claim was otherwise in fact proved.

Treating the "after-acquired evidence" defense as an affirmative one that must be pleaded and proved also is consonant with the purposes of Rule 8(c), because it is a defense for which the need for notice to avoid surprise and undue prejudice to the plaintiff is particularly apparent. * * * For example, here, Red Deer must frame legal arguments concerning what constitutes a "misrepresentation" and what constitutes "misconduct" of sufficient gravity that it meets the *McKennon* standard of misconduct for which the County would not have hired her on those grounds alone. She must also establish relevant facts concerning the applicability of the defense, including whether she did indeed make any "misrepresentations" and what were the actual circumstances under which she left the two jobs that are at the focus of the County's assertion of the defense.

Therefore, the court concludes that "after-acquired evidence" is an affirmative defense that must indeed be pleaded and proved pursuant to Rule 8(c). [The court proceeded to permit the County to amend its answer to include the affirmative defense.]

Notes and Questions

1. What is an affirmative defense? Instead of being regarded as denials, the defenses listed in Rule 8(c) are analogous to confessions or avoidances that exonerate the defendant because of circumstances that occurred before, during, or after the alleged wrong. However, the rule provides no help in identifying the essential characteristics of an affirmative defense. By asserting an affirmative defense, the defendant introduces new matter that constitutes an excuse or justification if the defense is valid.

Rule 8(c) does not specifically define what is meant by an "affirmative defense." Instead, it provides an illustrative list of defenses that is interpreted to be a nonexhaustive listing of affirmative defenses. In addition to the listed affirmative defenses, Rule 8(c) provides that "any other matter constituting an avoidance or affirmative defense" is to be pleaded as an affirmative defense. Some recognized affirmative defenses that are not listed in Rule 8(c) are alteration of an instrument, condition subsequent, impossibility of performance, infancy, insanity, mistake, novation, privilege in defamation actions, rescission, and breach of warranty.

2. The assertion of an affirmative defense may involve three related burdens: the burden of pleading, the burden of production, or going forward with the evidence, and the burden of persuasion, or risk of nonpersuasion. The rule does not state which, if any, of the three burdens are essential characteristics for describing an affirmative defense.

In *Gomez v. Toledo*, 446 U.S. 635, 639–40, 100 S.Ct. 1920, 64 L.Ed.2d 572 (1980), the Court held that a defendant has the burden of pleading an affirmative defense, because whether an affirmative defense exists depends on facts peculiarly within the knowledge and control of the defendant. For example, the applicable test for immunity focuses on whether he has an objectively reasonable basis for his belief that his conduct was lawful and whether he has a subjective belief.

Burdens of production may shift between the parties. For example, once the plaintiff produces sufficient evidence to establish a prima facie case, the burden of production shifts to the defendant to produce evidence either conclusively rebutting one or more elements of plaintiff's prima facie case, or establishing an affirmative defense.

Finally, the defendant has the burden of proof on an affirmative defense to establish every essential element of the defense so that he would be entitled to a directed verdict if the evidence went unchallenged at trial. For example for the affirmative defense of a statute of limitation, the defendant has the burden of demonstrating by prima facie proof that the limitations period has expired since the plaintiff's claims accrued.

3. The last sentence of Rule 8(c) provides that "When a party has mistakenly designated a defense as a counterclaim or a counterclaim as a

defense, the court on terms, if justice so requires, shall treat the pleading as if there had been a proper designation.'' The purpose of the rule is to protect a defendant against designation errors in pleading matters such as fraud and mistake leading to reformation or cancellation of a written instrument like a contract. The question is one primarily of name and form, and the rule is designed to protect a party who has made a wrong choice in that respect.

4. *Motion to strike.* When the merits or lack of merits of the defendant's affirmative defense depends on a legal question, the Rule 12(f) motion to strike tests the legal sufficiency of the defense. After the plaintiff has asserted a claim and the defendant has raised an affirmative defense by answer, the plaintiff may move for the defense to be stricken from the pleadings. A motion to strike a defense which is insufficient in law has the same function with respect to an affirmative defense that a motion to dismiss for failure to state a claim performs with respect to the complaint. Thus a motion to strike an insufficient defense assumes the truth of the allegations of the defense. The test for a motion to strike on this ground is similar to the test for a motion to dismiss on the ground that the complaint does not state a claim entitling the plaintiff to relief: do the allegations of the defense authorize the defendant to prove any state of facts which would constitute an affirmative defense?

Because it may be used as a delaying tactic, courts generally disapprove of a Rule 12(f) motion. Especially when there has been no opportunity to conduct discovery, courts are unlikely to grant the motion because of the reluctance to make a decision based on only hypothetical facts. On the other hand, the procedure can be a useful device for limiting the issues. Before the court will order a defense stricken, however, it must ''be convinced that there are no questions of fact, that any questions of law are clear and not in dispute, and that under no set of circumstances could the defense succeed.''

---

3. Responding to the Answer

The terms of Federal Rule 7(a) require a court order authorizing a reply to any part of an answer other than a counterclaim. Without a court order, a reply to a counterclaim is the only reply authorized. That reply is in effect an answer to the claim stated in the counterclaim. Assuming that there is a complaint and an answer containing affirmative defenses, the case law indicates that an affirmative defense in the answer does not generally merit a reply. Thus, ordinarily, some unusual reason must be urged, e.g., the complaint and answer with new matter do not cover the issues in the case, or the availability or expense of discovery procedures or the possibility of summary judgment justify a reply.

REYES v. SAZAN
168 F.3d 158 (5th Cir. 1999)

PATRICK E. HIGGINBOTHAM, Circuit Judge.

This lawsuit alleges that various officials violated the plaintiffs' constitutional rights by conspiring to enforce selectively the traffic laws and damaging a pickup truck in a fruitless search for contraband. We conclude the district court abused its discretion by not requiring a Rule 7 reply to the defense of qualified immunity. * * *

As we must, we assume the plaintiffs' story: Florentino and Elizabeth Martinez, brother and sister, were driving with Elizabeth's minor daughter in Ramiro Reyes's pickup truck on Interstate 12 in St. Tammany Parish, Louisiana, en route to Alabama. The truck had Texas plates. When they passed a marked Louisiana State Police vehicle, Carl Sazan, a Louisiana State Trooper, pulled them over. They were driving under the speed limit. [Everyone got out of the truck. A police dog arrived with another trooper, but no drugs were found. Nevertheless, Sazan ordered the plaintiffs to follow him to headquarters where a more thorough search occurred which damaged the vehicle at a cost exceeding $2,000. Again the police found no drugs and brought no charges against any of the vehicles occupants. During the search, plaintiffs were forced to stand in a cold rain. The plaintiffs sued Sazan and the supervisory officers for federal civil rights violations and state damage claims. All defendants asserted qualified immunity as an affirmative defense.]

The plaintiffs replied that their suits were against the defendants in their individual capacities and that these defendants were not entitled to qualified immunity. They explained that [the supervising officers] conspired with Sazan to enforce traffic laws selectively against Hispanics and out-of-state residents.

While the district court agreed that Reyes could not maintain his claims under §§ 1983 and 1985(3), it denied the motion to dismiss in other respects. It also decided that it had supplemental jurisdiction over plaintiffs' state law claims. * * *

The complaint alleges specific facts detailing plaintiffs' personal experience with Sazan. It offers no similar detail for the claim that [the supervising officers] conspired to deny them and other Hispanic drivers their civil rights. The district court concluded that the plaintiffs had "plead with particularity that this was part of a policy to stop and search those of Hispanic origin and/or that the supervisors failed to adequately train and/or monitor the Troopers." The court did not dismiss the suit, suggesting that it would grant summary judgment to the supervisors absent evidence raising a genuine issue of material fact. As we will explain, we do not agree that the claim was plead with particularity against the supervisory officers, and we conclude that the district court moved too quickly.

Faced with sparse details of claimed wrongdoing by officials, trial courts ought routinely require plaintiffs to file a reply under Federal Rule of Civil Procedure 7(a) to qualified immunity defenses. See *Schultea v. Wood*, 47 F.3d 1427, 1430, 1432 (5th Cir.1995) (en banc). The *Schultea* court held that "the [district] court may, in its discretion, insist that a plaintiff file a reply tailored to an answer pleading the defense of qualified immunity." *Id.* at 1433–44. The district court need not allow any discovery at this point unless the "plaintiff has supported his claim with sufficient precision and factual specificity to raise a genuine issue as to the illegality of defendant's conduct at the time of the alleged acts." *Id.* at 1434.

Plaintiffs did not allege their claims against the supervisory defendants with particularity. Their pleading was little more than a bare conclusion, and the district court erred in finding the complaint to be sufficient. Rather, it should first have ordered a reply, and if the required detail was not forthcoming, dismiss the complaint. The *Schultea* rule governing the Rule 7(a) reply is an instantiation of the more general principle that "heightened pleading" is needed in qualified immunity cases. See *id.* at 1430. Heightened pleading requires allegations of fact focusing specifically on the conduct of the individual who caused the plaintiffs' injury.

The district court abused its discretion in failing to require a Rule 7 reply. As the *Schultea* court made clear, "Vindicating the immunity doctrine will ordinarily require such a reply, and a district court's discretion not to do so is narrow indeed when greater detail might assist." *Id.* at 1434.

The Supreme Court since *Schultea* has attempted to clarify the jurisdiction of the courts of appeal to review a denial of qualified immunity. At present, the rule of jurisdiction comes to this: Legal conclusions are immediately appealable, but not the sufficiency of the evidence to support the denial. The appellate court can consider the materiality of disputed issues of fact, but not contentions that there are factual disputes.

The Supreme Court's refinement of qualified immunity jurisdiction has only made the more important *Schultea*'s emphasis upon the reply as a tool of the trial court insisting on particularity in pleading. Indeed, the Court's vigorous adherence to the distinction between fact and law— or genuine issues and material issues—underscores the strength of the *Schultea* approach. Whether the complaint is insufficiently particular, and thus a reply to the defense of qualified immunity is needed, is a question of law. Similarly, we can examine afresh whether a reply is "tailored to the assertion of qualified immunity and fairly engage[s] its allegations," *Schultea*, 47 F.3d at 1433, a look that does not require reviewing the record to determine if the reply's factual assertions are true.

We vacate the district court's denial of qualified immunity to [the supervising officers], and remand with instructions to require that the plaintiffs file a reply to the defense. * * *

Notes and Questions

1. *Reyes* and *Schultea* state that a reply can be useful to test the sufficiency of an affirmative defense. *Schultea* noted that its rule creates an

incentive for a defendant "to plead his defense with some particularity because it has the practical effect of requiring particularity in the reply."

How does the language of Rules 7(a), 8(a), and 8(e) require a particularized reply?

> The Federal Rules of Civil Procedure permit the use of Rule 7 in this manner. The only Civil Rule that governs the content of Rule 7 replies is Rule 8(e)(1), which demands that "[e]ach averment of a pleading shall be simple, concise, and direct." We do not read Rule 8(e)(1) as a relevant limitation upon the content of a Rule 7 reply. Indeed, a party pleading fraud or mistake with particularity under Rule 9(b) is also required to do so in a simple, concise and direct manner. Nor is Rule 8(a)(2)'s "short and plain" standard a limitation on the content of a Rule 7 reply. Rule 8 applies only to the subset of pleadings that "set[ ] forth a claim for relief, whether an original claim, counterclaim, cross-claim, or third-party claim." Rule 8(a) does not encompass pleadings that it does not list, including Rule 7 replies. * * * [W]e hold that because Rule 8(a) does not list Rule 7 replies, Rule 8(a)'s "short and plain" standard does not govern Rule 7 replies.

Schultea, 47 F.3d at 1433.

In a special concurrence in *Schultea*, Judge Garza expressed two concerns:

> Any minimum requirement on the content of the reply will depend on (1) the district court's discretionary decision to require detailed averments in the reply; and (2) the practical effect of the particularity of the defendant's answer. The majority has thus abandoned an independent pleading requirement for a system that depends on the district court's discretion and the litigants' incentives.
>
> The majority's limitation on the district court's discretion to order a reply is also troubling. * * * Rule 7(a) . . . simply states that "the court may order a reply." On one hand, the opinion states that the "court *may, in its discretion*, insist that a plaintiff file a reply. . . ." (emphasis added). On the other hand, it states: "Vindicating the immunity doctrine will ordinarily require such a reply, and a district court's discretion to do so is narrow indeed when greater detail might assist." Such a limitation on the district court's discretion is not contained in Rule 7(a), and in my view the majority has not explained why the application of Rule 7(a) to qualified immunity cases requires reading such a limitation into the rule.

Schultea, 47 F.3d at 1437.

2. The three-step pleading process recommended in *Reyes* is that 1) the plaintiff files a short and plain statement asserting a civil rights claim; 2) the defendant then pleads qualified immunity as an affirmative defense in its answer; and 3) the trial judge has the discretion to insist that the plaintiff file a reply responding to the affirmative defense.

3. Following the filing of the defendant's answer, are there any strategic or financial reasons why a defendant would try to obtain a court order directing the plaintiff to reply? If indeed there are good reasons for a

defendant to seek a reply by the plaintiff, are there valid reasons for Rule 7(a) being so restrictive when the defendant asserts an affirmative defense?

4. When should a plaintiff be denied a court order to file a reply to the defendant's answer and affirmative defense? In *Beckstrom v. Coastwise Line*, 13 F.R.D. 480 (D. Alaska 1953), the plaintiff sought permission to reply to an answer containing a number of affirmative defenses. Although it denied the plaintiff's request, the court responded to the contention that a motion of this type was impermissible in the following manner:

> Defendants suggest that the plaintiff may not be ordered to file a reply upon its own motion because Rule 7(a) gives the power to order a reply to the defendants' answer and it would be inappropriate for a plaintiff to ask the Court to order him to reply, and that if the rule had been intended to permit the plaintiff to seek leave to reply, the rule would not have contained its present phraseology.
>
> That conclusion is not inevitable. It is usually the defendant who requests the reply but * * * the Court, in each instance, denied plaintiff's motion for leave to file a reply * * * without questioning the right of the plaintiff to make such a motion or to have the motion granted in the proper case. The liberal construction required of the rules would permit the granting of plaintiff's motion for leave to file a reply, and an order accordingly.

In *Beckstrom*, the plaintiff was attempting to revive his right to demand a jury trial, which had been lost by his failure to file a timely demand, by obtaining permission to interpose a reply and then demanding a jury trial within ten days thereafter. Was the court correct to deny the motion to file a reply?

Exercise

For the state a) where you intend to practice after graduation, b) where your law school is located, and/or c) your professor assigns, go to that state's annotated rules and research the procedural rules for answering complaints, asserting affirmative defenses, and filing replies. Based on your research, print the rules and bring them to class for discussion. In addition, answer the following questions.

1. Identify the types of responses (e.g., denials) that are:

    A. Recognized explicitly in the rules; and

    B. Recognized by the courts as methods for responding to a complaint.

2. Identify whether affirmative defenses (e.g., statute of limitations) are:

    A. Recognized explicitly in the rules; and

    B. Recognized by the courts as valid affirmative defenses.

3. Identify whether a motion to strike a pleading is recognized, and if so, how it compares to Federal Rule 12(f).

4. Identify whether a reply to an answer is recognized, and if so, how it compares to Federal Rule 7(a).

F. VERACITY STANDARDS FOR FILED DOCUMENTS

While a court has inherent authority to impose sanctions, *Chambers v. NASCO*, 501 U.S. 32, 111 S.Ct. 2123, 115 L.Ed.2d 27 (1991), in federal courts Federal Rule 11 is the primary source of power for sanctioning attorneys and their clients. Under the federal rules, an attorney's signature originally constituted a certification that "good grounds" existed for a pleading. Sweeping changes to Rule 11 were made in 1983 and again in 1993. The certification of a signer under the 1983 version of the rule guaranteed that the signer had read the paper to be filed and that to the best of the signer's knowledge, information and belief it was "well grounded in fact and warranted by existing law or a good faith argument" for changing existing law. Sanctions for violations were mandatory.

The 1993 (and current) version of Rule 11 was a response to the widespread criticism of the 1983 rule. The 1983 version apparently affected plaintiffs more severely than defendants, created problems for the party who alleged a novel legal theory, rarely was enforced with non-monetary sanctions, provided little incentive to discontinue a legal or factual position after it had lost its legal or factual support, and created conflicts between the attorney and client. Despite the view of Justices Scalia and Thomas, dissenting from the order transmitting rule amendments to Congress, that the "proposed revision [of Rule 11] would render the Rule toothless," the amended rule took effect on December 1, 1993.

The federal rule has a dual purpose: it 1) establishes the standards for attorneys and parties who file pleadings, motions or other documents in court; and 2) regulates the situations in which court may impose sanctions for rule violations. State procedural systems follow their own versions of Rule 11 for filed documents, and every jurisdiction maintains ethical standards for attorneys who take frivolous positions.

Rule 11 requires that a document must be signed by an attorney or by the party, if there is no attorney. Unless preserved by statute or rule, the Rule 11 signature requirement eliminates verification requirements, by which the client had to co-sign certain documents along with the attorney. If the document is not signed, by Rule 11(a) the court must strike the paper unless the paper is signed promptly after the attorney or party becomes aware of the problem. The following paragraphs summarize the significance of the Rule 11 signature requirement and the sanctions that may be imposed for its violation.

The duty of candor. Litigants are subject to sanctions for advocating a position after it is no longer tenable. The rule protects litigants against sanctions if they withdraw or correct contentions after being notified about a potential violation.

When does the duty of candor apply? It applies only to assertions in papers filed with the court, but does not cover matters arising for the first time during oral presentations to the court when an attorney may make a statement that would not have been made had there been more time for research and thought. A litigant's obligations regarding contents of filed papers include continuing to advocate positions contained in pleadings and motions after learning that the positions no longer are meritorious.

What happens when a litigant realizes the lack of merit in a position already taken in writing? Sometimes a litigant may have good reason to believe that a fact is true, but may need time to develop the facts from the opposition or third parties to confirm the basis for the allegation. Even if support for the fact does not exist after reasonable investigation, it is unnecessary to amend the pleading. However, the attorney can no longer advocate the fact as part of the claim or defense.

Are sanctions mandatory? Under Rule 11, the trial court has discretion to determine whether to apply sanctions. It also has significant discretion to decide what sanctions should be imposed for a Rule 11 violation. However, the rule states that the sanctions should be no more severe than reasonably necessary to deter repetition of the conduct by the offending attorney or party or comparable conduct by similarly situated persons.

How does the Rule indicate that its primary purpose is to deter counsel from advocating meritless positions? If a court imposes a monetary sanction, it is ordinarily to be paid to the court as a penalty. If requested, monetary sanctions may be awarded to another party. Any sanction may be imposed on attorneys, law firms, or parties who violate the rule or are deemed to be responsible for the rule violation. A person who signs, files, submits, or advocates a document has a nondelegable responsibility to the court.

Are sanctions imposed automatically? Before sanctions are imposed, litigants must receive notice about an alleged violation and a chance to respond. If the court imposes sanctions, it generally must express its reasons for the sanction in a written order or on the record.

What is a "safe harbor" provision and how is it expressed in Rule 11? A motion for sanctions is not to be filed until at least 21 days after the motion is served on the offending person. During that period, if the violation is corrected by for example withdrawing an allegation, the motion should not be filed with the court. A court can act on its own initiative, but only through a show cause order, thereby providing the person with notice and an opportunity to be heard.

Are any writings exempt from the Rule's coverage? Rule 11 explicitly is inapplicable to discovery and disclosure requests, responses, objections and motions under the discovery provisions in Rules 26–37.

RUSZALA v. WALT DISNEY WORLD CO.

132 F.Supp.2d 1347 (M.D. Fla. 2000)

GLAZEBROOK, United States Magistrate Judge.

* * * On January 16, 1996, Corporal Robert Stephens, of the Orange County Sheriff's Office, responded to a request for service from Walt Disney World Company ("Walt Disney"). Upon his arrival at the Walt Disney offices, Corporal Stephens obtained the following information. Walt Disney was investigating possible employee theft at Walt Disney's Ohana restaurant. Plaintiff Bill R. Ruszala was a server at Walt Disney's Ohana restaurant. A documented analysis of the restaurant's computerized transaction log revealed a discrepancy between the number of guests that Ruszala "rung up" on the register and the number of guests actually served by Ruszala. Walt Disney security investigators, Phillip McNab and Dennis J. Ramos, interviewed Ruszala at the Walt Disney security offices. During the interview, Ruszala confessed to stealing money from Walt Disney's Ohana Restaurant.

After obtaining the foregoing information, Corporal Stephens entered the room where Ruszala was located. Before asking Ruszala any questions, Corporal Stephens advised Ruszala of his right to an attorney. When Ruszala asked for an attorney, Corporal Stephens ceased questioning him and placed Ruszala under arrest on the charge of employee theft.

On June 29, 1998, Ruszala brought this action against defendants Walt Disney, Dennis Ramos, and Kevin Beary as Sheriff of Orange County, Florida, in connection with his arrest on January 16, 1996. In total, Ruszala alleged six causes of action including: false imprisonment, false arrest, malicious prosecution, defamation, violating of civil rights, and conspiracy to violate civil rights. Specific to Sheriff Beary, Ruszala alleged false arrest and conspiracy to violate civil rights in violation of 42 U.S.C. § 1983. The only basis for adding Sheriff Beary as a defendant was that Corporal Stephens purportedly did not have personal knowledge of the facts purporting to constitute probable cause for Ruszala's arrest. Ruszala claimed that Corporal Stephens impermissibly relied solely on Walt Disney's private security personnel to provide him information to support Ruszala's arrest.

On March 20, 2000, Sheriff Beary moved for summary judgment on Ruszala's claims of false arrest and conspiracy to violate civil rights. On April 25, 2000, the Honorable G. Kendall Sharp granted Sheriff Beary's motion for summary judgment as against Ruszala. On that same date, the Court ordered Ruszala and his attorney, Scott Sterling, to show cause within 2 days why they should not be held jointly liable for Sheriff Beary's attorney's fees and costs incurred in defending this action. On May 4, 2000, Beary filed a motion to tax costs and entitlement to attorneys' fees, together with his bill of costs. On May 5, 2000, the Clerk of Court taxed costs in the amount of $726.02. On May 10, 2000, Ruszala filed a response to this Court's show cause order and defendant Kevin Beary's motion to tax costs and entitlement to attorney's fees. Ruszala did not object to the costs requested by Sheriff Beary and previously taxed by the Clerk of Court.

* * *

Rule 11(b) of the Federal Rules of Civil Procedure imposes a duty upon attorneys and parties to refrain from filing or pursuing frivolous claims. Fed.R.Civ.P. 11(b). Rule 11 sanctions are proper: (1) when a party files a pleading that has no reasonable factual basis; (2) when the party files a pleading that is based on a legal theory that has no reasonable chance of success and that cannot be advanced as a reasonable argument to change existing law; and (3) when the party files a pleading in bad faith for an improper purpose. Rule 11(c) allows a court to "impose an appropriate sanction upon the attorneys, law firms, or parties that have violated subdivision (b) or are responsible for the violation," which may include "some or all of the reasonable attorneys' fees and other expenses incurred as a direct result of the violation." Fed.R.Civ.P. 11(c)(2).

The objective standard for testing conduct under Rule 11 is "reasonableness under the circumstances" and "what was reasonable to believe at the time" the pleading was submitted. This court requires a two-step inquiry as to: 1) whether the party's claims are objectively frivolous; and 2) whether the person who signed the pleadings should have been aware that they were frivolous. Although sanctions are warranted when the claimant exhibits a "deliberate indifference to obvious facts," they are not warranted when the claimant's evidence is merely weak but appears sufficient, after a reasonable inquiry, to support a claim under existing law. The purpose of Rule 11 is to deter frivolous lawsuits and not to deter novel legal arguments or cases of first impression. The grant of summary judgment, in and of itself, does not mean that an action is frivolous or warrants the imposition of sanctions.

As amended in December 1993, Rule 11 makes clear the continuing nature of a litigant's responsibility under Rule 11. Under the 1993 amendment:

> It [Rule 11] also, however, emphasizes the duty of candor by subjecting litigants to potential sanctions for insisting upon a position after it is no longer tenable. . . .
>
> . . . .
>
> [A] litigant's obligations with respect to the contents of these papers are not measured solely of the time they are filed with or submitted to the court, but include reaffirming to the court and advocating positions contained in those pleadings and motions after learning that they cease to have any merit.

Fed.R.Civ.P. 11, advisory committee's note. Thus, Rule 11 sanctions are appropriate when a party pursues a claim after it is no longer tenable in fact or law. * * *

This Court carefully evaluates Sheriff Beary's claim of frivolity given that the Court granted summary judgment before trial on the ground that no genuine issue of material fact remains as to whether Corporal Stephens had probable cause to arrest Ruszala. Finding that Ruszala's arrest was made pursuant to probable cause, the district court decided the action in Ruszala's favor on a dispositive motion rather than at a trial on the merits. Sheriff Beary is clearly a prevailing defendant.

Nevertheless, Congress has determined that success on summary judgment is not alone sufficient to require an assessment of attorney's fees. Congress could have enacted legislation mandating an award of attorney's fees to all prevailing parties, but instead opted to leave such an award to the Court's discretion.

The undersigned is unable to determine from the record whether Ruszala brought the claim in subjective bad faith, and therefore presumes that he did not. Nevertheless, in applying the stringent standard established by current case law, defendant Sheriff Beary has established that as of Ruszala's February 26, 1999 deposition, Ruszala's and his counsel's actions in litigating through summary judgment was frivolous, unreasonable, and without foundation. * * *

At the February 26, 1999 deposition, Ruszala admitted that he previously confessed to stealing money from Walt Disney's Ohana Restaurant. Ruszala also said that Corporal Stephens acted in a very professional manner and that Corporal Stephens "wouldn't violate my civil rights." Ruszala further admitted that Corporal Stephens had no reason not to believe the Walt Disney security people when they advised Corporal Stephens that Ruszala had confessed to committing a theft. Additionally, Ruszala stated that Corporal Stephens "arrested me because I confessed to something. Like I said, I knew he had a job to do, so apparently I believed he was doing his job as he though he was suppose to." By Ruszala's own admissions, Corporal Stevens had probable cause to arrest Ruszala.

Subsequent to Ruszala's February 26, 1999 deposition, Sheriff Beary's counsel, Bruce R. Bogan, sent two letters to Ruszala's counsel on June 24, 1999 and on December 28, 1999. In those letters, Bogan asked Ruszala to withdraw his claims against Sheriff Beary. In the December 28, 1999 letter, Bogan warned counsel that if Sheriff Beary was not voluntarily dismissed from this suit, Sheriff Beary would seek attorney's fees and costs on the basis that the action was frivolous.

In light of these factors, the Court finds that the false arrest claim and the conspiracy to violate civil rights claim stemming from an arrest without probable cause were unreasonable and without foundation. * * *

It is clear to the undersigned that after Ruszala's deposition Ruszala and his attorney were clearly on notice that Ruszala's claims lacked any basis in fact or law. Yet, it is equally clear that Ruszala and his attorney continued the pursuit of their claims against Sheriff Beary even when it became patently clear that Ruszala's claims had no chance of success. In applying the objective standard of reasonableness test, the Court finds that Ruszala and his counsel violated Rule 11 by pursuing claims that were not tenable despite overwhelming evidence of probable cause—an absolute defense to the claims asserted in the complaint.

In considering the nature of sanctions to be imposed, the Court finds that monetary penalty in the form of attorney's fees is the minimum necessary to deter such future conduct. As already discussed, Ruszala's claims against Sheriff Beary lacked any merit. The primary evidence presented in support of this conclusion was Ruszala's own testimony. This action did not turn on subtle, unsettled issues of law, nor did it involve close questions of facts. Under these circumstances, Sheriff Beary is entitled to attorney's fees expended in the defense of this case under Rule 11.

Notes and Questions

1. Since the 1980s, politicians have tried to use the issue of frivolous lawsuits for political gain. For example, in 1995, the Congress adopted the Private Securities Litigation Reform Act of 1995, which in part cross-referenced parts of Rule 11 and amended Rule 11 *exclusively* for securities cases. See 15 U.S.C. § 78u. According to the Conference Committee:

> Existing Rule 11 has not deterred abusive securities litigation. Courts often fail to impose Rule 11 sanctions even where such sanctions are warranted. When sanctions are awarded, they are generally insufficient to make whole the victim of a Rule 11 violation: the amount of the sanction is limited to an amount that the court deems sufficient to deter repetition of the sanctioned conduct, rather than imposing a sanction that equals the costs imposed on the victim by the violation. Finally, courts have been unable to apply Rule 11 to the complaint in such a way that the victim of the ensuing lawsuit is compensated for all attorneys' fees and costs incurred in the entire action.

The Act made sanctions mandatory and presumed that the opposing party's attorneys' fees would be the sanction, rejecting the deterrence rationale in Rule 11. Upon final adjudication of each securities case, the trial court is required to make specific findings on the parties' compliance with Rule 11. This requirement thereby dispenses with the filing of a motion, as well as the safe harbor provision.

Two other subject-specific areas of litigation have recently inspired federal statutes. First, the Prison Litigation Reform Act was signed into law in 1996 to limit frivolous inmate litigation by requiring the inmates to prepay the initial filing costs and to pay other costs associated with the lawsuit. 28 U.S.C. § 1915. It also prohibits lawsuits by inmates who on three or more prior occasions have brought a case which was dismissed as frivolous, malicious, or because it failed to state a claim upon which relief could be granted. Second, President Clinton signed the 1999 Y2K Act, which expressed a concern about the number of frivolous lawsuits expected to be filed relating to the year 2000 computer date-change problem (which you may recall never materialized). See 15 U.S.C. § 6601 et seq.

Other litigation proposals associated with the House Republican majority's "Contract with America" during the mid–1990s did not become law. In 1996, President Clinton vetoed the Common Sense Product Liability Legal Reform Act of 1996, which attempted to impose federal limits on product liability cases in state and federal courts, and punitive damages in all civil cases. The "Attorney Accountability Act" of 1995 passed the House but was never brought to a vote in the Senate. Among other things, it would have eliminated Rule 11's safe harbor provision and made sanctions mandatory.

2. All filed pleadings, motions and other papers must be signed by the individual attorney of record or by the party who is unrepresented. In either situation, the signer's address must be included. When a team of attorneys is conducting the litigation, the attorney who signs the paper may not necessarily be the one responsible for either the decision to file it or its preparation. For example, an associate in a law firm may prepare, sign, and file a paper at the direction of a partner. The rule's emphasis on the responsibility of the attorney suggests that the potential scope of the obligation under the rule might extend to attorneys who share responsibility for the filing of a paper even though they may not have signed the document in question.

When is a represented party responsible for problems with a filed document? Does it matter whether the party signs the document? In *Business Guides, Inc. v. Chromatic Communications, Enters., Inc.*, 498 U.S. 533, 111 S.Ct. 922, 112 L.Ed.2d 1140 (1991), the Court applied the reasonable inquiry standard to a represented party who signed a document along with counsel. Because the rule concentrates on the person who signs the document, a represented party who does not sign a document does not appear to be subject to Rule 11. *Aetna Ins. Co. v. Meeker*, 953 F.2d 1328 (11th Cir. 1992). Even if a party does not sign the document, should the party nevertheless be liable for providing false facts to the attorney?

"Absent exceptional circumstances, a law firm shall be held jointly responsible for violations committed by its partners, associates, and employees." That language from Rule 11(c)(1)(A) overruled *Pavelic & LeFlore v. Marvel Entertainment Group*, 493 U.S. 120, 110 S.Ct. 456, 107 L.Ed.2d 438 (1989), which had held that sanctions could be imposed only on the signing attorney.

3. Like the warranties in Rule 11(b), the American Bar Association Model Rules of Professional Conduct require analogous guarantees for attorneys in civil litigation. Consistent with Rule 11(b)(1), Rule 3.2 requires a lawyer to "make reasonable efforts to expedite litigation consistent with the interests of the client." Also, Rule 4.4 prohibits actions when the "means ... have no substantial purpose other than to embarrass, delay, or burden a third person..." The analogous ethical standards for Rule 11(b)(2)-(4) are found in Rule 3.1, which addresses the issue of nonfrivolous legal and factual assertions. "A lawyer shall not bring or defend a proceeding, or assert or controvert an issue therein, unless there is a basis for doing so that is not frivolous, which includes a good faith argument for an extension, modification or reversal of existing law." Having devoted so much attention to concerns about frivolous lawsuits, notice that neither the procedural nor the ethical standards are willing or able to define the term "nonfrivolous."

Which is more demanding of attorneys, the ethical standard or the legal standard?

Exercise

For the state a) where you intend to practice after graduation, b) where your law school is located, and/or c) your professor assigns, go to that state's annotated rules and research the procedural rules for veracity standards relating to documents filed with the court. Based on your research, print the portion of the rule and bring it to class for discussion. In addition, answer the following questions.

1. What is the scope of the standard, e.g., documents only, exempting discovery documents?

2. What does an attorney's signature certify?

3. Define the scope of the attorney's obligation, i.e., is it a continuing duty or is it restricted to the attorney's knowledge at the time the document is filed?

4. Who may be responsible for violations, e.g., the signing attorney, the attorney's law firm, the client?

5. Regarding sanctions:

    A. What does the moving party have to prove in order for sanctions to be imposed?

    B. Are sanctions mandatory or discretionary?

    C. What types of sanctions are available?

    D. What ordinarily happens to collected sanctions, e.g., paid to the court?

    E. Can the court initiate sanctions, without a motion from a party?

6. Are the tests for a violation objective or subjective?

CHRISTIAN v. MATTEL, INC.

286 F.3d 1118 (9th Cir. 2002)

McKEOWN, Circuit Judge.

It is difficult to imagine that the Barbie doll, so perfect in her sculpture and presentation, and so comfortable in every setting, from "California girl" to "Chief Executive Officer Barbie," could spawn such acrimonious litigation and such egregious conduct on the part of her challenger. In her wildest dreams, Barbie could not have imagined herself in the middle of Rule 11 proceedings. But the intersection of copyrights on Barbie sculptures and the scope of Rule 11 is precisely what defines this case.

James Hicks appeals from a district court order requiring him, pursuant to Federal Rule of Civil Procedure 11, to pay Mattel, Inc. $501,565 in attorneys' fees that it incurred in defending against what the district court determined to be a frivolous action. Hicks brought suit on behalf of Harry Christian, claiming that Mattel's Barbie dolls infringed Christian's Claudene doll sculpture copyright. In its sanctions orders, the district court found that Hicks should have discovered prior to commencing the civil action that Mattel's dolls could not have infringed Christian's copyright because, among other things, the Mattel dolls had been created well prior to the Claudene doll and the Mattel dolls had clearly visible copyright notices on their heads. After determining that Hicks had behaved "boorishly" during discovery and had a lengthy rap sheet of prior litigation misconduct, the district court imposed sanctions.

We hold that the district court did not abuse its discretion in determining that the complaint filed by Hicks was frivolous under Rule 11. In parsing the language of the district court's sanctions orders, however, we cannot determine with any degree of certainty whether the district court grounded its Rule 11 decision on Hicks' misconduct that occurred outside the pleadings, such as in oral argument, at a meeting of counsel, and at a key deposition. This is an important distinction because Rule 11 sanctions are limited to misconduct regarding signed pleadings, motions, and other filings. Consequently, we vacate the district court's orders and remand for further proceedings consistent with this opinion. In so doing, we do not condone Hicks' conduct or suggest that the district court did not have a firm basis for awarding sanctions. Indeed, the district court undertook a careful and exhaustive examination of the facts and the legal underpinnings of the copyright challenge. Rather, the remand is to assure that any Rule 11 sanctions are grounded in conduct covered by Rule 11 and to ensure adequate findings for the sizeable fee award.

As context for examining the district court's determination that the underlying copyright action was frivolous, we begin by discussing the long history of litigation between Mattel and Hicks' past and current clients: Harry Christian; Christian's daughter, Claudene; and the Collegiate Doll Company ("CDC"), Claudene's proprietorship.

Mattel is a toy company that is perhaps best recognized as the manufacturer of the world-famous Barbie doll. Since Barbie's creation in 1959, Mattel has outfitted her in fashions and accessories that have evolved over time. In perhaps the most classic embodiment, Barbie is depicted as a slender-figured doll with long blonde hair and blue eyes. Mattel has sought to protect its intellectual property by registering various Barbie-related copyrights, including copyrights protecting the doll's head sculpture. Mattel has vigorously litigated against putative infringers.

In 1990, Claudene Christian, then an undergraduate student at the University of Southern California ("USC"), decided to create and market a collegiate cheerleader doll. The doll, which the parties refer to throughout their papers as "Claudene," had blonde hair and blue eyes and was outfitted to resemble a USC cheerleader.

Mattel soon learned about the Claudene doll. After concluding that it infringed certain Barbie copyrights, Mattel brought an administrative action before the United States Customs Service in 1996 in which it alleged that the Claudene doll, manufactured abroad, had pirated the head sculpture of the "Teen Talk" and "SuperStar" Barbies. The Customs Service ruled in CDC's favor and subsequently released a shipment of Claudene dolls. Undaunted, Mattel commenced a federal court action in 1997 in which it once again alleged that CDC infringed various of Mattel's copyrights. At the time, Claudene Christian was president of CDC and Harry Christian was listed as co-founder of the company and chief financial officer. CDC retained Hicks as its counsel.

After the court dismissed CDC's multiple counterclaims, the case was settled. Mattel released CDC from any copyright infringement liability in exchange for, among other things, a stipulation that Mattel was free to challenge CDC's alleged copyright of the Claudene doll should CDC "or any successor in interest" challenge Mattel's right to market its Barbie dolls.

Seizing on a loophole in the parties' settlement agreement, within weeks of the agreement, Harry Christian, who was not a signatory to the agreement, retained Hicks as his counsel and filed a federal court action against Mattel. In the complaint, which Hicks signed, Christian alleged that Mattel obtained a copy of the copyrighted Claudene doll in 1996, the year of its creation, and then infringed its overall appearance, including its face paint, by developing a new Barbie line called "Cool Blue" that was substantially similar to Claudene. Christian sought damages in the amount of $2.4 billion and various forms of injunctive relief. * * *

Two months after the complaint was filed, Mattel moved for summary judgment. In support of its motion, Mattel proffered evidence that the Cool Blue Barbie doll contained a 1991 copyright notice on the back of its head, indicating that it predated Claudene's head sculpture copyright by approximately six years. Mattel therefore argued that Cool Blue Barbie could not as a matter of law infringe Claudene's head sculpture copyright. * * *

At a follow-up counsel meeting required by a local rule, Mattel's counsel attempted to convince Hicks that his complaint was frivolous. During the videotaped meeting, they presented Hicks with copies of various Barbie dolls that not only had been created prior to 1996 (the date of Claudene's creation), but also had copyright designations on their heads that pre-dated Claudene's creation. Additionally, Mattel's counsel noted that the face paint on some of the earlier-created Barbie dolls was virtually identical to that used on Claudene. Hicks declined Mattel's invitation to inspect the dolls and, later during the meeting, hurled them in disgust from a conference table.

Having been unsuccessful in convincing Hicks to dismiss Christian's action voluntarily, Mattel served Hicks with a motion for Rule 11 sanctions. In its motion papers, Mattel argued, among other things, that Hicks had signed and filed a frivolous complaint based on a legally meritless theory that Mattel's prior-created head sculptures infringed Claudene's 1997 copyright. Hicks declined to withdraw the complaint during the 21–day safe harbor period provided by Rule 11, and Mattel filed its motion.

Seemingly unfazed by Mattel's Rule 11 motion, Hicks * * * sought information regarding the face painting on certain Barbie dolls and the face paint/head sculpture combinations used by Mattel after 1996. The district court summarily denied the motion. It later noted, in the context of its summary judgment order, that "it is unclear what [Christian] is requesting when he seeks access to post–1996 Barbies." * * *

The district court granted Mattel's motions for summary judgment and Rule 11 sanctions. * * *

As for Mattel's Rule 11 motion, the district court found that Hicks had "filed a meritless claim against defendant Mattel. A reasonable investigation by Mr. Hicks would have revealed that there was no factual foundation for [Christian's] copyright claim." Indeed, the district court noted that Hicks needed to do little more than examine "the back of the heads of the Barbie dolls he claims were infringing, . . ."

The district court awarded Mattel $501,565 in attorneys' fees. At the outset of its order, the court summarized the findings in its earlier order, namely that it had "predicated its [Rule 11] decision" on Hicks' filing a frivolous complaint and "further found" that he had " 'behaved boorishly, misrepresented the facts and misstated the law.' " * * *

The district court next considered various arguments that Hicks had advanced in opposition to Mattel's fee application. Hicks first contended, without much elaboration, that a fee award would have a "ruinous" effect on his finances and ability to practice law. The district court held, however, that "repeated reprimands and sanctions" imposed in prior litigations "clearly have not had the desired deterrent effect on his behavior," and it concluded that Hicks would not be punished sufficiently if the court were to impose mere "non-monetary sanctions." Hicks also argued (somewhat ironically) that Mattel's fees request was excessive in light of how simplistic it should have been to defend against Christian's action. The district court disagreed, reasoning that like the court in *Brandt v. Schal Assocs., Inc.*, 960 F.2d 640, 648 (7th Cir.1992), the judiciary has " 'little sympathy for the litigant who fires a big gun, and when the adversary returns fire, complains because he was firing blanks.' "

* * *

The court is satisfied that the other attorneys' fees Mattel has claimed are both reasonable and proximately caused by Mr. Hicks' pursuit of this frivolous action. [T]he Court grants Mattel its attorneys' fees in the amount of $501,565.00.

* * * We review the district court's decision to impose Rule 11 sanctions—and, if they are warranted, the reasonableness of the actual

amount imposed—for abuse of discretion. *Cooter & Gell v. Hartmarx Corp.*, 496 U.S. 384, 401, 405 (1990). In conducting our review of the district court's factual findings in support of the sanctions, we "would be justified in concluding that [the court] had abused its discretion in making [the findings] only if [they] were clearly erroneous." The district court's legal findings must be affirmed unless they result from a "materially incorrect view of the relevant law."

The district court found that Hicks "filed a meritless claim against defendant Mattel. A reasonable investigation by Mr. Hicks would have revealed that there was no factual foundation for plaintiff's copyright claim." Hicks challenges these findings, arguing that the issues were "more complex" than the district court recognized. Before considering this operative issue, we first consider Rule 11 principles that guide our review.

Filing a complaint in federal court is no trifling undertaking. An attorney's signature on a complaint is tantamount to a warranty that the complaint is well grounded in fact and "existing law" (or proposes a good faith extension of the existing law) and that it is not filed for an improper purpose.

The attorney has a duty prior to filing a complaint not only to conduct a reasonable factual investigation, but also to perform adequate legal research that confirms whether the theoretical underpinnings of the complaint are "warranted by existing law or a good faith argument for an extension, modification or reversal of existing law." *Golden Eagle Distrib. Corp. v. Burroughs Corp.*, 801 F.2d 1531, 1537 (9th Cir. 1986). One of the fundamental purposes of Rule 11 is to "reduce frivolous claims, defenses or motions and to deter costly meritless maneuvers, ... [thereby] avoid[ing] delay and unnecessary expense in litigation." Nonetheless, a finding of significant delay or expense is not required under Rule 11. Where, as here, the complaint is the primary focus of Rule 11 proceedings, a district court must conduct a two-prong inquiry to determine (1) whether the complaint is legally or factually "baseless" from an objective perspective, and (2) if the attorney has conducted "a reasonable and competent inquiry" before signing and filing it.

Hicks filed a single claim of copyright infringement against Mattel. The complaint charges that the Cool Blue Barbie infringed the copyright in the Claudene doll head. In addition, in a subsequent letter to Mattel's counsel, he claimed that Virginia Tech Barbie also infringed Claudene. Hicks cannot seriously dispute the district court's conclusions that, assuming the applicability of the doctrine of prior creation, Christian's complaint was legally and factually frivolous. Indeed, as a matter of copyright law, it is well established that a prior-created work cannot infringe a later-created one. See *Grubb v. KMS Patriots, L.P.*, 88 F.3d 1, 5 (1st Cir.1996) (noting that "prior creation renders any conclusion of access or inference of copying illogical."). * * *

Recognizing the futility of attacking prior creation, Hicks argues that the paint on the Claudene doll's face features a light makeup that is distinctive and that the two Barbie dolls thus infringe Claudene's overall appearance and presentation. This argument fails because, among other things, Mattel used the light face paint on the Pioneer Barbie, which was created two years before the Claudene doll, thus defeating once again any claim of copying. It also bears noting that Mattel has been repainting various doll heads for decades. * * *

The district court concluded that Hicks "filed a case without factual foundation." Hicks, having argued unsuccessfully that his failure to perform even minimal due diligence was irrelevant as a matter of copyright law, does not contest that he would have been able to discover the copyright information simply by examining the doll heads. Instead he argues that the district court did not understand certain "complex" issues. Simply saying so does not make it so. The district court well understood the legal and factual background of the case. It was Hicks' absence of investigation, not the district court's absence of analysis, that brought about his downfall.

The district court did not abuse its discretion in concluding that Hicks' failure to investigate fell below the requisite standard established by Rule 11.

Hicks argues that even if the district court were justified in sanctioning him under Rule 11 based on Christian's complaint and the follow-on motions, its conclusion was tainted because it impermissibly considered other misconduct that cannot be sanctioned under Rule 11, such as discovery abuses, misstatements made during oral argument, and conduct in other litigation.

Hicks' argument has merit. * * *

The laundry list of Hicks' outlandish conduct is a long one and raises serious questions as to his respect for the judicial process. Nonetheless, Rule 11 sanctions are limited to "paper[s]" signed in violation of the rule. Conduct in depositions, discovery meetings of counsel, oral representations at hearings, and behavior in prior proceedings do not fall within the ambit of Rule 11. Because we do not know for certain whether the district court granted Mattel's Rule 11 motion as a result of an impermissible intertwining of its conclusion about the complaint's frivolity and Hicks' extrinsic misconduct, we must vacate the district court's Rule 11 orders.

We decline Mattel's suggestion that the district court's sanctions orders could be supported in their entirety under the court's inherent authority. To impose sanctions under its inherent authority, the district court must "make an explicit finding [which it did not do here] that counsel's conduct constituted or was tantamount to bad faith." *Primus Auto. Fin. Serv., Inc. v. Batarse*, 115 F.3d 644, 648 (9th Cir.1997). We acknowledge that the district court has a broad array of sanctions options at its disposal: Rule 11, 28 U.S.C. § 1927, and the court's inherent authority. Each of these sanctions alternatives has its own particular requirements, and it is important that the grounds be separately articulated to assure that the conduct at issue falls within the scope of the sanctions remedy. On remand, the district court will have an opportunity to delineate the factual and legal basis for its sanctions orders.

Hicks raises various challenges to the quantum of attorneys' fees. Because we are vacating the district court's Rule 11 orders on other legal grounds, we express no opinion at this stage about the particular reasonableness of any of the fees the district court elected to award Mattel. We do, however, encourage the district court on remand to ensure that the time spent by Mattel's attorneys was reasonably and appropriately spent in relation to both the patent frivolousness of Christian's complaint and the services directly caused by the sanctionable conduct.[12] See Fed.R.Civ.P. 11, advisory committee notes, 1993 Amendments, Subdivisions (b) and (c) (noting that attorneys' fees may only be awarded under Rule 11 for those "services directly and unavoidably caused" by the sanctionable conduct).

We vacate the district court's Rule 11 orders and remand for further proceedings consistent with this opinion.

Notes and Questions

1. Use of the words "reasonable under the circumstances" in Rule 11 codifies the previous judicial conclusion that the thoroughness of the inquiry required by Rule 11 depends in part upon the time available for investigation. Rule 11(b). The Supreme Court held under the 1983 rule, that "[a]n inquiry that is unreasonable when an attorney has months to prepare a complaint may be reasonable when he has only a few days before the statute of limitations runs." *Cooter & Gell v. Hartmarx Corp.*, 496 U.S. 384, 401–2, 110 S.Ct. 2447, 110 L.Ed.2d 359 (1990).

2. Absent time pressures, what should a reasonable factual inquiry include? For example, must counsel interview the available witnesses? May counsel rely on a document reciting the state of incorporation of a party to a lease? Or, must counsel review the relevant "original source" documents that are available to the client? See, e.g., *Belleville Catering Co. v. Champaign Market Place, L.L.C.*, 350 F.3d 691 (counsel's reliance on lease's erroneous description of state of incorporation does not satisfy reasonable inquiry requirement when document showing certificate of incorporation is available).

On the other hand, because Rule 11 does not require the impossible, what if the evidence to prove or disprove a claim is in an opponent's exclusive possession? Rule 11 permits a claim or answer to be based on

---

12. For example, because the action was frivolous on its face, why would Mattel's attorneys need to spend 700 hours ($173,151.50 in fees) for the summary judgment motion and response? Although Hicks clearly complicated the proceedings through multiple filings, Mattel's theory and approach was stunningly simple and required little explication: (1) Mattel's Barbie dolls and face paint were prior copyright creations that could not infringe the after-created Claudene doll and (2) Christian was neither a contributor to nor owner of the copyright. This is not to say that Hicks' defense of the motion necessarily called for a timid response, but neither does it compel a bazooka approach.

information and belief. However, Rule 11(b)(3) requires a party to state when their factual contentions depend on an opportunity for further investigation or discovery.

Can counsel rely upon a client's statements to show a reasonable factual inquiry? In *Hadges v. Yonkers Racing Corp.*, 48 F.3d 1320, 1329–30 (2d Cir. 1995), the court stated that, in deciding whether an attorney may be sanctioned for relying on a client's statements, courts must determine whether there was "evidentiary support" corroborating factual misrepresentations. By contrast, is it unreasonable to file a paper based on the client's knowledge if the client is relying on second-hand assertions?

3. Does an attorney's inexperience in a particular area of law reduce the Rule 11 obligations? In *Zuk v. Eastern Pa. Psychiatric Inst. of the Med. College of Pa.*, 103 F.3d 294 (3d Cir. 1996), the attorney claimed that the case at bar was the first copyright case which he had handled, pointing out that a practitioner has to begin somewhere. The court responded that,

> [w]hile we are sympathetic to this argument, its thrust is more toward the nature of the sanctions to be imposed rather than to the initial decision whether sanctions should be imposed. Regrettably, the reality of appellant's weak grasp of copyright law is that it caused him to pursue a course of conduct which was not warranted by existing law and compelled the defendant to expend time and money in needless litigation.

4. When is a claim warranted by existing law per rule 11(b)(2) (i.e., must the law clearly support the attorney's position on behalf of the client)? In *Anderson v. Smithfield Foods, Inc.*, 353 F.3d 912 (11th Cir. 2003), a group of landowners sued the world's largest hog producer and pork processor, alleging that the defendants "polluted land and water in violation of numerous laws and regulations, and lied about and profited from these environmental transgressions. Plaintiffs alleged that this conduct gives rise to liability under" the Racketeer Influenced and Corrupt Organizations Act for business practices amounting to racketeering because it constituted a pattern of money laundering and wire and mail fraud. The appellate court reversed the award of Rule 11 sanctions, noting that

> there is scant on-point authority to guide the reasonable lawyer to the conclusion that, with the RICO claims . . , he either had no reasonable chance of success or was advancing an unreasonable argument to change existing law. Though we have concluded that the ... Amended Complaint does not state viable RICO claims, we are unable to conclude that only an unreasonable lawyer would have made these claims.

Similarly, what happens when the state of the law is unsettled or involves a case of first impression? Sanctions are unlikely to be imposed, i.e., a court is not going to conclude that the claim is unwarranted by existing law.

5. When do you know that a paper you filed is warranted by existing law? To be warranted under existing law, does an argument contained in the paper have to ultimately prevail? No, what is relevant is whether the attorney presented an objectively reasonable argument in support of the view of what the law is or should be. Rule 11 sanctions are not merited on

the grounds of frivolousness merely because the court disagrees with an attorney's position on behalf of a client and rules for the opposing side.

Should a dismissal for failure to state a claim for relief automatically justify Rule 11 sanctions for filing a paper that is unwarranted under existing law? *Tahfs v. Proctor*, 316 F.3d 584 (6th Cir. 2003) found that:

> At the pleading stage in the litigation, ordinarily there is little or no evidence before the court at all, and such facts as are alleged, must be interpreted in favor of the nonmovant. While a party is bound by Rule 11 to refrain from filing a complaint "for any improper purpose," from making claims "[un]warranted by existing law," or from making "allegations and other factual contentions [without] evidentiary support," making those determinations is difficult when there is nothing before the court except the challenged complaint. * * * "Rule [11] must be read in light of concerns that it will spawn satellite litigation and chill vigorous advocacy." [*Cooter & Gill*] Rule 11 "is not intended to chill an attorney's enthusiasm or creativity in pursuing factual or legal theories." * * * While we agree that the magistrate judge's Report and Recommendation provides a forceful argument for dismissal of Tahfs's complaint pursuant to Rule 12(b)(6) for lack of factual specificity, it does not follow, therefrom, that "the claims . . . therein are [un]warranted by existing law," as the expression is used in Rule 11(b)(2). If that were so, almost any complaint dismissed under Rule 12(b)(6) would warrant the imposition of sanctions. Had the district court read Tahfs's complaint in a light most favorable to her, as it was obligated to do, we are convinced it would have seen that the filing of a federal complaint was not "unreasonable" under the circumstances. Tahf's complaint was dismissed because it failed to provide the defendants sufficient notice regarding the actors who allegedly were corrupt and their allegedly corrupt actions. A complaint alleging conspiracy, whose essential deficiency is that it is lacking in sufficient factual detail and specificity, is not, perforce, "[un]warranted by existing law" or frivolous. A complaint does not merit sanctions under Rule 11 simply because it merits dismissal pursuant to Rule 12(b)(6).

On the other hand, is a legal position unwarranted by existing law if it is contrary to clear precedent? When the attorney knew or should have known that the position taken on behalf of a client has no chance of success under the existing case law, sanctions are likely. But where does that leave the pleader who seeks to overturn long-standing precedents on an issue? How do you argue that Rule 11 would have permitted you to attack public school segregation in 1950? Wouldn't Rule 11 have chilled your enthusiasm for pursuing a novel legal theory like desegregation?

Rule 11 permits you to argue for an extension or modification of existing law. Under what circumstance is that argument likely to be most successful? Suppose that you have raised an issue of first impression in your jurisdiction. Even if courts elsewhere have ruled against your position, it would appear unreasonable to sanction you assuming that you have made a good faith argument for a change in the law. The important question is how to resolve the apparent conflict between the duty to represent your client zealously and Rule 11's purpose of reducing frivolous claims. Can you accommodate both goals?

6. Rule 11 explicitly requires notice and an opportunity to respond to allegations of a Rule 11 violation. In addition, it contains a 21–day "safe harbor" provision. By sending a Rule 11 motion to the opposition, those attorneys and parties opposing sanctions have 21 days in which to correct or withdraw a challenged paper. Under Rule 11(c)(1)(A) after the 21 days expire, a separate Rule 11 motion must be filed describing the specific conduct that allegedly violated the rule. Most courts require strict compliance with safe harbor provision and deny Rule 11 motions which fail to comply. The safe harbor provision is inapplicable to the court's imposition of sanctions on its own initiative.

You have already learned that the federal rules typically require an answer to be filed within 20 days of service. In *Religious Tech. Ctr. v. Gerbode*, 1994 WL 228607 (C.D. Cal. 1994), the court in fn. 6 raised the following conflict between the time within which to answer and the safe harbor provision:

> It would appear to be problematical to comply with the "safe harbor" provision in any case involving a challenge to a complaint. Even if the frivolousness is immediately apparent on the face of the pleading at the time of service, does service of a motion for sanctions under Rule 11 toll the 20–day period to answer under Rule 12(a)(1)(A)? If not, what purpose does compliance with the "safe harbor" provision serve if the complaint must be responded to before the 21–day waiting period expires? If the frivolousness is not immediately apparent and the Rule 11 motion is not made until after the complaint is dismissed, what useful purpose is served by compliance with the "safe harbor" provision at that point? Certainly, by that juncture, it is too late for the complaint to be "withdrawn or appropriately corrected."

7. Does the safe harbor provision encourage a "threat and retreat" behavior whereby a plaintiff could file a series of complaints, and then withdraws them when faced with possible Rule 11 sanctions? Dissenting from adoption of the 1993 safe harbor amendment to Rule 11, Justice Scalia expected parties to "file thoughtless, reckless, and harassing pleadings, secure in the knowledge that they have nothing to lose." 146 F.R.D. 507, 508 (1993). See Carl Tobias, "Civil Rights Plaintiffs and the Proposed Revision of Rule 11," 77 Iowa L. Rev. 1775 (1992).

Problems

1. Prior to filing a Rule 11 motion for sanctions against Chumbley and Associates, plaintiff Boyer sent an e-mail to Chumbley warning her that he would file a Rule 11 motion against her unless she withdrew her "obviously groundless motion to dismiss his complaint." How should Chumbley respond?

2. Defendant Chumbley responds to plaintiff Boyer's complaint by filing one document with the court, containing an answer, a motion to dismiss, and a motion for sanctions under Rule 11. How should Boyer respond?

3. After Carrell Corp.'s motion to dismiss Lerner's good faith complaint was denied for the first time for failure to state a claim for relief, Carrell notified Lerner about its intent to seek sanctions and three weeks later moved for sanctions under Federal Rule 11. Should the court grant or deny the motion for sanctions?

4. Same as #3, except that Carrell Corp. filed its Rule 11 motion for sanctions when Lerner's identical complaint was dismissed for the third time within a ten-month period under Rule 12(b)(6), based on the current law. Should the court grant or deny the motion for sanctions?

5. The Waldman Partnership sued Davis, Inc. for breach of contract. After two years of discovery and an unsuccessful motion to dispose of the case on its merits, the parties settled the case. A month later, the judge in the case issued an order for Davis, Inc. to pay the plaintiffs more than $40,000 in attorney fees and court costs for Rule 11 violations. Was the order proper?

6. Abramson is serving as local counsel for the firm of Cross and Deason, a law partnership with forty partners and sixty associates located in another federal district. Cross is the plaintiffs' lead counsel in *The Waldman Partnership v. Davis, Inc.*, a breach of contract action. Three associates are working on the case with Cross. Cross and the three associates work on a pretrial motion to dismiss for lack of subject matter jurisdiction, and one of the associates signs it and sends it to Abramson to file it. The motion can only be termed a legally groundless motion. Assuming that the defendant has followed the Rule 11 procedures, who is liable for sanctions if the court agrees that monetary sanctions are appropriate in reaction to the subject matter motion?

7. Same as #6, except that the motion is not only legally deficient. It also reflects numerous factual misstatements by the clients who were in a position to investigate and report accurately the facts supporting the motion. Can the client now be sanctioned?

8. In #6, the court is inclined to impose monetary sanctions against the attorneys, instead of other sanctions. What criteria determine when monetary sanctions are appropriate? What alternative non-monetary sanctions are available?

G. AMENDED AND SUPPLEMENTAL PLEADINGS

What is the purpose of a rule allowing pleadings to be amended? Given the relative flexibility of the federal rules, the purpose seems to be to provide a maximum opportunity for each claim to be decided on its merits rather than on procedural technicalities. Generally, Rule 15 emphasizes a permissive approach that courts are to approve amendment requests regardless of their nature. The rule also reflects the fact that the federal rules assign the pleadings a limited role of providing notice of both the nature of the pleader's claim or defense and the transaction or event that has been called into question. The purpose of the later discovery process is to develop the factual and legal issues.

Rule 15 relates to amended and supplemental pleadings. There are four sub-rules which set forth when and under what circumstances pleadings may be amended, and provide for amendments to conform to the evidence, the relation back of amendments, and the presentation of supplemental matters.

INTRODUCTORY PROBLEM

There are two Stan's Stereo Stores in Champaign–Urbana, Illinois— Stan's Stereo, Inc. (Champaign) and Stan's Stereo Corp. (Urbana). Stock in each separate corporation is owned by the same persons in the same proportion. Kelly slipped in the Champaign store while shopping for a stereo and brought suit mistakenly against Stan's Stereo Corp. (the Urbana store). Service was made upon Stan's brother, Bill, who managed the Urbana store, at Bill's home. After the statute of limitations had run, Kelly's counsel moved to amend the complaint to name Stan's Stereo, Inc. as the defendant. As the judge, what additional information do you need before ruling on Kelly's motion?

Governing law: Rule 15.

1. Amending Pleadings With (or Without) the Court's Permission

Rule 15(a) enables a party to assert new information that was overlooked or unknown to the pleader at the time the complaint or answer was filed. It also establishes a time period during which the pleadings may be amended automatically and by granting the court broad discretion to allow amendments to be made after that period has expired.

BEECK v. AQUASLIDE 'N' DIVE CORP.

562 F.2d 537 (8th Cir. 1977)

BENSON, District Judge.

This case is an appeal from the trial court's exercise of discretion on procedural matters in a diversity personal injury action.

Jerry A. Beeck was severely injured on July 15, 1972, while using a water slide. He and his wife, Judy A. Beeck, sued Aquaslide 'N' Dive Corporation (Aquaslide), a Texas corporation, alleging it manufactured the slide involved in the accident, and sought to recover substantial damages on theories of negligence, strict liability and breach of implied warranty.

Aquaslide initially admitted manufacture of the slide, but later moved to amend its answer to deny manufacture; the motion was resisted. The district court granted leave to amend. On motion of the defendant, a separate trial was held on the issue of "whether the defendant designed, manufactured or sold the slide in question." This motion was also resisted by the plaintiffs. The issue was tried to a jury, which returned a verdict for the defendant, after which the trial court entered summary judgment of dismissal of the case. Plaintiffs took this appeal, [arguing that the trial court abused its discretion in permitting an amendment that denied manufacture after the statute of limitations had run].

I. FACTS.

* * * In 1971 Kimberly Village Home Association of Davenport, Iowa, ordered an Aquaslide product from one George Boldt, who was a local distributor handling defendant's products. The order was forwarded by Boldt to Sentry Pool and Chemical Supply Co. in Rock Island, Illinois, and Sentry forwarded the order to Purity Swimming Pool Supply in Hammond, Indiana. A slide was delivered from a Purity warehouse to Kimberly Village, and was installed by Kimberly employees. On July 15, 1972, Jerry A. Beeck was injured while using the slide at a social gathering sponsored at Kimberly Village by his employer, Harker Wholesale Meats, Inc. Soon after the accident investigations were undertaken by representatives of the separate insurers of Harker and Kimberly Village. On October 31, 1972, Aquaslide first learned of the accident through a letter sent by a representative of Kimberly's insurer to Aquaslide, advising that "one of your Queen Model #Q–3D slides" was involved in the accident. Aquaslide forwarded this notification to its insurer. Aquaslide's insurance adjuster made an on-site investigation of the slide in May, 1973, and also interviewed persons connected with the ordering and assembly of the slide. An inter-office letter dated September 23, 1973, indicates that Aquaslide's insurer was of the opinion the "Aquaslide in question was definitely manufactured by our insured." The complaint was filed October 15, 1973. Investigators for three different insurance companies, representing Harker, Kimberly and the defendant, had concluded that the slide had been manufactured by Aquaslide, and the defendant, with no information to the contrary, answered the complaint on December 12, 1973, and admitted that it "designed, manufactured, assembled and sold" the slide in question.

The statute of limitations on plaintiff's personal injury claim expired on July 15, 1974. About six and one-half months later Carl Meyer, president and owner of Aquaslide, visited the site of the accident prior to the taking of his deposition by the plaintiff. From his on-site inspection of the slide, he determined it was not a product of the defendant. Thereafter, Aquaslide moved the court for leave to amend its answer to deny manufacture of the slide.

II. LEAVE TO AMEND.

Amendment of pleadings in civil actions is governed by Rule 15(a), F.R.Civ.P., which provides in part that once issue is joined in a lawsuit, a party may amend his pleading "only by leave of court or by written consent of the adverse party; and leave shall be freely given when justice so requires."

In *Foman v. Davis*, 371 U.S. 178 (1962), the Supreme Court had occasion to construe that portion of Rule 15(a) set out above:

> Rule 15(a) declares that leave to amend "shall be freely given when justice so requires," this mandate is to be heeded. . . . If the underlying facts or circumstances relied upon by a plaintiff may be a proper subject of relief, he ought to be afforded an opportunity to test his claim on the merits. In the absence of any apparent or declared reason such as undue delay, bad faith or dilatory motive on the part of the movant, repeated failure to cure deficiencies by amendments previously allowed, undue prejudice to the opposing party by virtue of allowance of the amendment, futility of amendment, etc. the leave sought should, as the rules require, be "freely given." Of course, the grant or denial of an opportunity to amend is within the discretion of the District Court, ...

This Court in *Hanson v. Hunt Oil Co.*, 398 F.2d 578, 582 (8th Cir. 1968), held that "(p)rejudice must be shown." (Emphasis added). The burden is on the party opposing the amendment to show such prejudice. In ruling on a motion for leave to amend, the trial court must inquire into the issue of prejudice to the opposing party, in light of the particular facts of the case. * * *

It is evident from the order of the district court that in the exercise of its discretion in ruling on defendant's motion for leave to amend, it searched the record for evidence of bad faith, prejudice and undue delay which might be sufficient to overbalance the mandate of Rule 15(a), F.R.Civ.P., and *Foman v. Davis*, that leave to amend should be "freely given." Plaintiffs had not at any time conceded that the slide in question had not been manufactured by the defendant, and at the time the motion for leave to amend was at issue, the court had to decide whether the defendant should be permitted to litigate a material factual issue on its merits.

[The Defendant's] reliance upon investigations of three insurance companies, and the fact that "no contention has been made by anyone that the defendant influenced this possibly erroneous conclusion," persuaded the court that "defendant has not acted in such bad faith as to be precluded from contesting the issue of manufacture at trial." The court further found "(t)o the extent that 'blame' is to be spread regarding the original identification, the record indicates that it should be shared equally."

In considering the issue of prejudice that might result to the plaintiffs from the granting of the motion for leave to amend, the trial court held that the facts presented to it did not support plaintiffs' assertion that, because of the running of the two year Iowa statute of limitations on personal injury claims, the allowance of the amendment would sound the "death knell" of the litigation. In order to accept plaintiffs' argument, the court would have had to assume that the defendant would prevail at trial on the factual issue of manufacture of the slide, and further that plaintiffs would be foreclosed, should the amendment be allowed, from proceeding against other parties if they were unsuccessful in pressing their claim against Aquaslide. On the state of the record before it, the trial court was unwilling to make such assumptions, and concluded "[u]nder these circumstances, the Court deems that the possible prejudice to the plaintiffs is an insufficient basis on which to deny the proposed amendment." The court reasoned that the amendment would merely allow the defendant to contest a disputed factual issue at trial, and further that it would be prejudicial to the defendant to deny the amendment.

The court also held that defendant and its insurance carrier, in investigating the circumstances surrounding the accident, had not been so lacking in diligence as to dictate a denial of the right to litigate the factual issue of manufacture of the slide.

On this record we hold that the trial court did not abuse its discretion in allowing the defendant to amend its answer. * * *

Notes and Questions

1. As indicated by Federal Rule 15(a), a pleading may be amended once without leave of court (as a matter of course) at any time before a responsive pleading is served, or, if the pleading is one to which no responsive pleading is permitted and the action has not been placed upon the trial calendar, within twenty days after the pleading to be amended is served. What is the policy of Rule 15(a)'s liberal approach to early amendments? Why does the rule permit only one amendment without the court's permission?

According to the rule, when no responsive pleading is permitted (as in the case of an answer if no reply is required or ordered) the right of amendment as a matter of course may be cut off prior to the end of twenty days after the pleading is served (e.g., the serving of the answer) if the action is set for trial before the end of the twenty days. Do you sense that plaintiffs and defendants are treated differently under the rule?

2. A party may amend once as a matter of course, as long as no responsive pleading has been filed. What constitutes a responsive pleading? A Rule 12(b)(6) motion to dismiss is not a responsive pleading, according to Rule 7(a) which defines pleadings. Therefore, if the only paper that has been filed is a motion to dismiss, the plaintiff may amend the pleading once as a matter of course without the need to seek the trial court's permission. See, e.g., *Shaver v. Operating Engineers Local 428 Pension Trust Fund*, 332 F.3d 1198 (9th Cir. 2003).

3. What is the relation between Rule 15(a) and Rule 12(h)(1)? The latter refers to "matter of course" amendments. Does that mean that, when no responsive pleading is necessary, a defendant has twenty additional days in which to insert omitted Rule 12 motions? How can the plaintiff take away the additional twenty-day period from the defendant?

4. Except for amendments as a matter of course, all amendments require leave of court or consent of the adverse party. Rule 15(a) provides that leave to amend shall be freely given when justice so requires. The motion to amend may be stated with some generality. For example, it could

be stated "justice requires the amendment in order that the actual issues between the parties be tried" or "the amendment is necessary to clarify and simplify the issues", or "the proposed amendment was inadvertently omitted", etc.

In *Beeck*, what arguments could be made that the plaintiff would be prejudiced by allowing the amendment? What does prejudice mean in this case? Why was there no bad faith in *Beeck*? If the court had rejected the amendment, how could the defendant have defended the lawsuit?

The decision as to whether justice requires the amendment is within the court's discretion, and is liberally construed. In *Dennis v. Dillard Dept. Stores, Inc.*, 207 F.3d 523 (8th Cir. 2000), the appellate court found that the trial court had abused its discretion by denying defendant employer's motion for permission to amend its answer under Rule 15(a). The defendant employer claimed that "it inadvertently omitted the 'factor other than sex' defense [to an employee's Equal Pay Claim], and that the omission was an oversight, unrealized until Dennis pointed it out in her response to Dillards' summary judgment motion." Dillards argued that granting its motion for leave to amend would not have unfairly prejudiced Dennis. While discovery had closed when the employer sought to amend, the trial court could reopen discovery for the limited purpose of exploring the added defense. Moreover, almost three months remained until trial when the employer filed its motion to amend, and the Eighth Circuit found that the defendant did not omit the defense in bad faith.

5. Likewise, Rule 15(a) allows a party to amend a pleading "by written consent of the adverse party," even after the time for amending as a matter of course has passed. If the parties consent, the usual motion procedure need not be followed. The right to amend is not subject to the court's discretion and the court must permit the amendment to be filed. See, e.g., *American States Insurance Company v. Dastar Corp.*, 318 F.3d 881 (9th Cir. 2003).

6. A court may impose conditions when granting leave to amend. The statement in Rule 15(a) that "leave shall be freely given when justice so requires" presupposes that the court may use its discretion to impose conditions on the grant of a proposed amendment as an appropriate way of balancing the interests of the party seeking the amendment and those of the objecting party. The most common condition imposed on the amending party is costs for other parties to assume additional preparation in order to meet the new issues or theories that are asserted in the amended pleading. The trial court also may grant a continuance to provide additional time for the opposing party to prepare for trial. On the other hand, a trial court may deny permission to amend when the amendment would cause the opposing party to bear additional costs litigating a new issue and the moving party does not offer to reimburse the nonmoving party for its expenses. See, e.g., *Campania Management Co. v. Rooks, Pitts & Poust*, 290 F.3d 843 (7th Cir. 2002).

7. There is no fixed time limit for making a motion for permission to amend a pleading. That matter too is within the discretion of the court. What are the relevant considerations in deciding the timeliness of a motion to amend a pleading? Prejudice to the other party? Mistake or excusable neglect?

8. Rule 15 does not require that an amended pleading be made by restatement of the entire original pleading as proposed to be amended. The amendment may be accomplished by service of the amendment itself, or, if leave is granted, even by interlineation or by striking a part of the pleading to be amended. However, the better way to request a court for leave to amend under Rule 15 is to attach a copy of the amended pleading to the motion so that it becomes part of the record at that time, regardless of what action the trial court takes or fails to take on it. This ensures that the appellate courts know exactly what amendment the trial court was asked to allow. It is only with such knowledge that the trial court's decision can be reviewed.

9. A pleading that has been amended under Rule 15(a) supersedes the pleading it modifies. The superceded pleading has no legal effect unless its successor pleading specifically refers to it and adopts or incorporates it by reference. Per Rule 15(a), when a complaint is amended, the defendant is entitled to amend the answer to meet the content of the new complaint.

2. Amendments to Add Issues at Trial

OTNESS v. UNITED STATES

23 F.R.D. 279 (D. Alaska Terr. 1959)

KELLY, District Judge.

Plaintiff brought suit against the United States of America under the Federal Tort Claims Act for damages suffered to his vessel while navigating in the Wrangell Narrows south of Petersburg, Alaska, as a result of an alleged collision with a navigation aid maintained by the United States Coast Guard. During the course of the trial evidence was introduced showing that the navigation aid, of great dimensions in size and weight, submerged and disappeared beneath the surface of the channel waters leading into Petersburg. Plaintiff in his complaint alleged that the Coast Guard was negligent in its operations to locate the submerged navigation structure, and that the Coast Guard negligently issued a bulletin to mariners to the effect that dragging operations revealed that the structure was not present above the contour of the natural bottom of the Wrangell Narrows. The plaintiff further alleged that these acts of negligence of the Coast Guard proximately caused injury to the plaintiff, who collided with the submerged navigation aid while navigating in the area where the structure disappeared.

After the presentation of all testimony in the case and while the court still had the decision under advisement, plaintiff filed a motion for leave to file a second amended complaint wherein he seeks to amend his complaint under Rule 15(b) of the Federal Rules of Civil Procedure, raising the additional claim to relief based on the "willful, wanton, or reckless conduct" of the Coast Guard in the circumstances surrounding its efforts to locate the submerged structure. Before decision can be made in the case itself, this motion must be disposed of.

Rule 15(b) provides that:

When issues not raised by the pleadings are tried by express or implied consent of the parties, they shall be treated in all respects as if they had been raised in the pleadings. Such amendment of the pleadings as may be necessary to cause them to conform to the evidence and to raise these issues may be made upon motion of any party at any time, even after judgment; but failure so to amend does not affect the result of the trial of these issues * * *

The plaintiff contends that "the amendment goes to matters which have already been in proof and the defendant cannot possibly be prejudiced by this amendment, since any effort which it would make to show lack of willful, wanton or reckless care would be no different than its efforts already made to show lack of negligence on the part of the defendant." While the contention of the plaintiff may have some merit if the issues of the case were limited solely to the negligence of the defendant, the prejudicial effect of granting such a motion would be underscored in the defendant's selection of affirmative defenses. The plaintiff by his pleadings confined the issues solely to negligence, and it is to be presumed that the defendant planned his defense of ordinary care and contributory negligence in reliance on the plaintiff's complaint. If the requested amendment were allowed and the issue thereunder were now to be resolved in plaintiff's favor, defendant's affirmative defense would be of no avail, since contributory negligence is not generally regarded as a defense to wanton or willful conduct. To overcome the motion it would be necessary for the defendant to have proved willful or wanton contributory conduct by the plaintiff. However, in the trial of the case, the defendant had no duty to go further than to allege and prove ordinary care or contributory negligence as a bar to recovery by the plaintiff under the plaintiff's complaint. Since the defendant had no notice of plaintiff's intention to request an amendment, and since a different defense would be required under the amendment, which the defendant may or may not have been capable of proving, the defendant cannot be said to have had a fair opportunity to defend against the issue raised by the motion.

In filing his motion under Rule 15(b), the plaintiff has apparently assumed that the issue of willful or wanton conduct was tried by the implied consent of the parties. There is no authorization within the above rule to allow an amendment to the pleadings to conform to proof merely because evidence presented which is competent and relevant to the issue created by the pleadings may incidentally tend to prove another fact not in issue. Where proof is taken only under the claim of the complaint, there is no proper case for amendment even though the proof may prove another issue. The plaintiff gave no indication of, or intention to claim, additional grounds for relief during the course of the trial. The line of demarcation as to what evidence might go no further than proving mere negligence and that which may tend to prove willful or wanton conduct is not so clear and capable of recognition as to warrant a holding that if evidence submitted under a complaint of negligence may also tend to prove willful, wanton or reckless conduct by the defendant, the defendant impliedly consents to its introduction for that purpose if he had made no objection, even though the plaintiff has not made his additional purpose clear during the trial. No consent to the trial of the issue created by the motion has been shown.

Furthermore, this case was fully tried and the evidence was quite complete, and it appears to this court that as a matter of fact there was no evidence in the case which would indicate that there was any 'willful, wanton or reckless conduct' on the part of the Coast Guard or any of its personnel in any particular whatsoever.

It follows, therefore, that the motion of the plaintiff must be denied.

Notes and Questions

1. Why did the court deny the plaintiff's motion? Do you believe that the plaintiff's counsel was acting deviously in not raising the willful claim until the defendant could not respond? (A court in a bench trial can reopen the proof to hear additional proof.) Was the issue proposed relevant to an issue already in the case? Was there any indication at trial that the plaintiff was seeking to raise a new issue?

2. Rule 15(b) provides for amendments necessary to cause the pleadings to conform to the evidence. One of the reasons for permitting such amendments is to insure that the pleadings support the judgment. Another is to take cognizance of the issues that were actually tried. The Rule goes further than authorizing amendments to conform to the evidence. It provides that if issues not raised by the pleadings are tried by express or implied consent, they are treated as if they had been raised.

Rule 15(b) applies to defenses as well as to affirmative claims and the criteria for allowing the amendment is the same. Thus, if evidence of an unpleaded affirmative defense is introduced without objection, it is treated as if it had been raised by the pleadings. The test for allowing an amendment to conform pleadings to issues impliedly tried is whether the opposing party would be prejudiced by the implied amendment. The focus is on whether evidence was introduced without objection even though introduced on a different theory.

During trial, when an objection to evidence is made on the ground that it is not within the issues presented by the pleadings, the court may permit amendments freely if the presentation of the merits of the action will be served and the objecting party will not be actually prejudiced or seriously disadvantaged. Under such circumstances the court is authorized to grant a continuance of the trial to enable the objecting party to meet such evidence.

Problems

1. Hillary files her complaint against Bill. Before Bill answers, Hillary files an amended complaint adding new claims and seeking an additional $10 million in damages. Why did Hillary have a right to do this?

2. Hillary files her complaint against Bill, who files a motion to dismiss under Rule 12(b)(6). Hillary realizes that Bill is correct because she omitted

important allegations of her claims. Before the hearing on Bill's motion, Hillary files an amended complaint fixing the problem raised by Bill's motion (thereby mooting the motion). Why did Hillary have a right to do this?

3. Hillary files her complaint against Bill, who is served on September 15. Bill files his answer to the complaint and has it served on Hillary on October 3. His answer contains no counterclaims. On October 20, Bill files an amended answer, correcting some errors in the original answer. Why does Bill have a right to do this?

4. If Hillary in #1 or Bill in #3 had waited too long to take advantage of filing an amendment as a matter of right, what showing would either have to make to be allowed to amend?

5. Hillary sues for breach of Contract #1 and at trial introduces evidence regarding Bill's breach of both Contract #1 and Contract #2. If the trial court finds implied consent by Bill to have tried the second contract claim, how should the court treat the proof relating to the second contract?

6. Hillary sues for breach of Contract #1 and at trial introduces evidence regarding Bill's breach of both Contract #1 and Contract #2. Bill objects to introduction of evidence on the Contract #2 claim. What is the basis of the objection?

7. In #6, how should Hillary respond to Bill's objection?

3. Amendments Filed After the Limitations Period Has Expired

SINGLETARY v. PENNSYLVANIA DEPT. OF CORRECTIONS

266 F.3d 186 (3d Cir. 2001)

BECKER, Chief Judge.

[The mother of an inmate at the State Correctional Institution at Rockview, who committed suicide, brought a civil rights claim against several Pennsylvania corrections officials, along with several defendant "Unknown Corrections Officers." Following the grant of summary judgment for the defendants, the inmate's mother appealed].

In her original complaint, the plaintiff also included as defendants "Unknown Corrections Officers." The only chance for the plaintiff to prevail depends on her ability to succeed in: (1) amending her original complaint to add as a defendant Robert Regan, a psychologist at SCI–Rockview, against whom the plaintiff has her only potentially viable case; and (2) having this amended complaint relate back to her original complaint under Federal Rule of Civil Procedure 15(c)(3) so that she overcomes the defense of the statute of limitations. Rule 15(c)(3) provides for the "relation back" of amended complaints that add or change parties if certain conditions are met, in which case the amended complaint is treated, for statute of limitations purposes, as if it had been filed at the time of the original complaint.

* * * Regan was working as a "psychological service specialist" at SCI–Rockview * * *; his duties included the psychological testing and

assessment of inmates, parole evaluations, group therapy, mental health intervention, and suicide risk evaluation and prevention. Regan did not have any administrative or supervisory duties at the prison. [Beginning in late 1994, Regan met with and evaluated Singletary on a weekly basis, but he and others saw no reason to take precautions with Singletary, who "vehemently denied" that he was suicidal] Just after midnight on October 6, 1996, Singletary committed suicide by hanging himself with a bedsheet.

* * * The parties agree that the statute of limitations for this action is two years, which expired on October 6, 1998, the day that Singletary filed her original complaint. The plaintiff then moved to amend her complaint by adding Regan as a defendant on July 28, 2000, almost two years after the statute of limitations had run. The plaintiff argues that this proposed amendment did not violate the statute of limitations because the amendment would relate back to the original, timely filed complaint under Federal Rule of Civil Procedure 15(c)(3). Rule 15(c) can ameliorate the running of the statute of limitations on a claim by making the amended claim relate back to the original, timely filed complaint. * * *

The issue in the case is whether the plaintiff can use 15(c)(3) to have her amended complaint substituting Regan as a defendant in place of "Unknown Corrections Officers" relate back to her original complaint. The Rule is written in the conjunctive, and courts interpret 15(c)(3) as imposing three conditions, all of which must be met for a successful relation back of an amended complaint that seeks to substitute newly named defendants. The parties do not dispute that the first condition— that the claim against the newly named defendants must have arisen "out of the conduct, transaction, or occurrence set forth or attempted to be set forth in the original pleading"—is met. The second and third conditions are set out in 15(c)(3)(A) & (B), respectively, and must be met "within the period provided by Rule 4(m) for service of the summons and complaint," Fed.R.Civ.P. 15(c)(3), which is "120 days after the filing of the complaint," Fed.R.Civ.P. 4(m). The second condition is that the newly named party must have "received such notice of the institution of the action [within the 120 day period] that the party will not be prejudiced in maintaining a defense on the merits." Fed.R.Civ.P. 15(c)(3)(A). [T]his condition "has two requirements, notice and the absence of prejudice, each of which must be satisfied." The third condition is that the newly named party must have known, or should have known, (again, within the 120 day period) that "but for a mistake" made by the plaintiff concerning the newly named party's identity, "the action would have been brought against" the newly named party in the first place. Fed.R.Civ.P. 15(c)(3)(B).

* * * The District Court concluded that Regan did not receive any notice of the litigation or of his role in that litigation during the 120 day period. The court also concluded that Regan would be unfairly prejudiced by having to mount his defense at this late date, and that he neither

knew nor should have known that, but for a mistake, he would have been named in the original complaint.

Notice is the main issue, and we will address that first. For reasons that we set forth in the margin, the unfair prejudice issue is closely dependent on the outcome of our notice inquiry; because we agree with the District Court that Regan did not receive notice within the 120 day period (and because the District Court based its decision on notice and mentioned prejudice only in passing), we will not address prejudice.[3]

This court has seldom spoken on the meaning of "notice" in the context of Rule 15(c)(3). Still, we can glean some general instruction from the few cases that address the issue. First, Rule 15(c)(3) notice does not require actual service of process on the party sought to be added; notice may be deemed to have occurred when a party who has some reason to expect his potential involvement as a defendant hears of the commencement of litigation through some informal means. At the same time, the notice received must be more than notice of the event that gave rise to the cause of action; it must be notice that the plaintiff has instituted the action. * * *

The "shared attorney" method of imputing Rule 15(c)(3) notice is based on the notion that, when an originally named party and the party who is sought to be added are represented by the same attorney, the attorney is likely to have communicated to the latter party that he may very well be joined in the action. This method has been accepted by other Courts of Appeals and by district courts within this Circuit. We endorse this method of imputing notice under Rule 15(c)(3).

The relevant inquiry under this method is whether notice of the institution of this action can be imputed to Regan within the relevant 120 day period, i.e., by February 3, 1999, by virtue of representation Regan shared with a defendant originally named in the lawsuit. The plaintiff contends that Regan shared an attorney with all of the originally named defendants; more precisely, she submits that appellees' attorney, Deputy (State) Attorney General Gregory R. Neuhauser, entered an appearance as "Counsel for Defendants" in the original lawsuit, and hence that Neuhauser represented the "several Unknown Corrections Officers" defendants, one of whom turned out to be Regan. The plaintiff submits that Neuhauser's investigation for this lawsuit must have included interviewing Regan (as he was one of the last counselors to evaluate Edward Singletary's mental state), so that Regan would have gotten notice of the institution of the lawsuit at that time. * * *

In this case, however, the record is clear that Neuhauser did not become the attorney for the defendants until well after the relevant 120 day period had run. The plaintiff originally filed this action in the

3. Prejudice and notice are closely intertwined in the context of Rule 15(c)(3), as the amount of prejudice a defendant suffers under 15(c)(3) is a direct effect of the type of notice he receives. That is, once it is established that the newly named defendant received some sort of notice within the relevant time period, the issue becomes whether that notice was sufficient to allay any prejudice the defendant might have suffered by not being named in the original complaint. * * *

Eastern District of Pennsylvania on October 6, 1998. * * * Neuhauser was substituted as counsel for the defendants on February 24, 1999, replacing John O.J. Shellenberger. The relevant 120 day period ended on February 3, 1999, so any representation and investigation (and contact with Regan) by Neuhauser did not begin until at least three weeks after the 120 day period ended. * * *

The "identity of interest" method of imputing Rule 15(c)(3) notice to a newly named party is closely related to the shared attorney method. Identity of interest is explained by one commentator as follows: "Identity of interest generally means that the parties are so closely related in their business operations or other activities that the institution of an action against one serves to provide notice of the litigation to the other." 6A Charles A. Wright et al., Federal Practice And Procedure § 1499, at 146 (2d ed.1990). * * *

The plaintiff does not substantially develop her identity of interest argument (she concentrates mainly on the shared attorney method of imputing notice), but she does advance the argument that Regan shared an identity of interest with SCI–Rockview because he was employed by SCI–Rockview. The question before us is therefore whether an employee in Regan's position (staff psychologist) is so closely related to his employer for the purposes of this type of litigation that these two parties have a sufficient identity of interest so that the institution of litigation against the employer serves to provide notice of the litigation to the employee.

There is not a clear answer to this question in the case law. * * * We believe, however, that Regan does not share sufficient identity of interest with SCI–Rockview so that notice given to SCI–Rockview can be imputed to Regan for Rule 15(c)(3) purposes. Regan was a staff level employee at SCI–Rockview with no administrative or supervisory duties at the prison. Thus, Regan's position at SCI–Rockview cannot alone serve as a basis for finding an identity of interest, because Regan was clearly not highly enough placed in the prison hierarchy for us to conclude that his interests as an employee are identical to the prison's interests. That is, Regan and SCI–Rockview are not "so closely related in their business operations or other activities that the institution of an action against one serves to provide notice of the litigation to the other."

* * * [A]bsent other circumstances that permit the inference that notice was actually received, a non-management employee like Regan does not share a sufficient nexus of interests with his or her employer so that notice given to the employer can be imputed to the employee for Rule 15(c)(3) purposes. For this reason, we reject the plaintiff's identity of interest argument, and conclude that the District Court did not err in denying the plaintiff leave to amend her complaint to add Regan as a defendant.

Rule 15(c)(3)(B) provides a further requirement for relating back an amended complaint that adds or changes a party: the newly added party knew or should have known that "but for a mistake concerning the identity of the proper party, the action would have been brought against the party." Fed.R.Civ.P. 15(c)(3)(B). The plaintiff argues that this condition is met in her proposed amended complaint, but the District Court found otherwise. The defendants also contend that (1) the plaintiff did not make a mistake as to Regan's identity, and (2) Regan did not know, nor should he have known, that the action would have been brought against him had his identity been known, because the original complaint named "Unknown Corrections Officers" and Regan is not a corrections officer but a staff psychologist.

The issue whether the requirements of Rule 15(c)(3)(B) are met in this case is a close one. We begin by noting that the bulk of authority from other Courts of Appeals takes the position that the amendment of a "John Doe" complaint—i.e., the substituting of real names for "John Does" or "Unknown Persons" named in an original complaint—does not meet the "but for a mistake" requirement in 15(c)(3)(B), because not knowing the identity of a defendant is not a mistake concerning the defendant's identity. This is, of course, a plausible theory, but in terms of both epistemology and semantics it is subject to challenge.

In *Varlack v. SWC Caribbean, Inc.*, 550 F.2d 171, 175 (3d Cir.1977), this Court appeared to have reached the opposite conclusion insofar as we held that the amendment of a "John Doe" complaint met all of the conditions for Rule 15(c)(3) relation back, including the "but for a mistake" requirement. In *Varlack*, the plaintiff had filed a complaint against, inter alia, an "unknown employee" of a branch of the Orange Julius restaurant chain, alleging that this employee had hit him with a two-by-four in a fight, which caused him to fall through a plate glass window, injuring his arm so severely that it had to be amputated. After the statute of limitations had run, the plaintiff sought to amend his complaint to change "unknown employee" to the employee's real name, using Rule 15(c)(3) to have the amended complaint relate back to the original. The newly named defendant testified that he had coincidentally seen a copy of the complaint naming both Orange Julius and an "unknown employee" as defendants, and that he had known at that time that he was the "unknown employee" referred to. This Court affirmed the district court's grant of the 15(c)(3) motion, holding that the plaintiff met all the requirements of 15(c)(3), including the requirement that the newly named defendant "knew or should have known but for a mistake concerning the identity of the proper party." See *id.* at 175.

* * * [E]very other Court of Appeals that has considered this issue (specifically, the First, Second, Fourth, Fifth, Sixth, Seventh, and Eleventh Circuits) has come out contrary to *Varlack*; generally speaking, the analysis in these other cases centers on the linguistic argument that a lack of knowledge of a defendant's identity is not a "mistake" concerning that identity. However, even assuming that *Varlack* allows for amended "John Doe" complaints to meet Rule 15(c)(3)(B)'s "mistake" requirement, it is questionable whether the other parts of 15(c)(3)(B) are met in this case, namely, whether Regan knew or should have known that he would have been named in the complaint if his identity were

known. Because the original complaint named "Unknown Corrections Officers," it is surely arguable that psychologist Regan would have no way of knowing that the plaintiff meant to name him.

These are sticky issues. Because, as we explained above, the plaintiff's argument on the applicability of Rule 15(c)(3) to her case fails on notice grounds, we do not need to decide these questions here. We do, however, take this opportunity to express in the margin our concern over the state of the law on Rule 15(c)(3) (in particular the other Circuits' interpretation of the "mistake" requirement) and to recommend to the Advisory Rules Committee a modification of Rule 15(c)(3) to bring the Rule into accord with the weight of the commentary about it.[5]

For the above reasons, the District Court's * * * order denying the plaintiff's motion to amend her complaint will be affirmed. * * *

Notes and Questions

1. Relation back is a legal fiction. If an amendment can be said to "relate back," it is treated as if it were filed along with the original pleading even though it was actually filed after the limitations period.

Rule 15(c)(1) provides that if the statute of limitations governing a claim for relief allows relation back of amended pleadings, relation back is permitted. If a statute of limitations is more generous to the amended pleading, the point of Rule 15(c)(1) is to ensure that Rule 15 cannot be used to contravene statutes of limitations specifically allowing relation back. Rule 15(c)(1) defers to a statute of limitations only when it is more generous on relation back, but it is inapplicable if the statute is *more* restrictive. When that happens, Rule 15(c)(2) or 15(c)(3) governs whether an amended pleading relates back.

2. Rule 15(c)(3) applies when an amendment adds a party or changes a party's name. The rule is satisfied if the amendment both fulfills Rule 15(c)(2) ("if the foregoing provision is satisfied") and meets the language in Rule 15(c)(3)(A) and (B). First, it must relate to the same factual transaction as the original, timely-filed claim, per Rule 15(c)(2). (By contrast, a new claim, e.g., breach of a different contract, negligence by the defendant at a different time, is subject to the defense of statute of limitations.) If the plaintiff amends to A) expand or modify the facts alleged in an earlier pleading, B) cure a defective statement of jurisdiction, C) reassert a claim that was deficiently stated and dismissed under Rule 12(b)(6), or D) change the legal theory based on the factual transaction, the amendment may relate back because it satisfies the Rule 15(c)(2) standard.

---

5. * * * In his manuscript "Rule 15(c)(3) Puzzles," Professor Edward H. Cooper of the University of Michigan Law School suggests the following alteration (in italics) in subsection 15(c)(3)(B) of the Rule in order to make it clear that the relation back of "John Doe" amended complaints is allowed: "the party to be brought in by amendment ... knew or should have known that, but for a mistake *or lack of information* concerning the identity of the proper party...." We believe that a change in Rule 15(c)(3) along the lines advocated by Professor Cooper would fix the lack of fairness to plaintiffs with "John Doe" complaints that currently inheres in the other Circuits' interpretation of the Rule, and would bring the Rule more clearly into alignment with the liberal pleading practice policy of the Federal Rules of Civil Procedure. * * *

4. As discussed in *Singletary*, under Rule 15(c)(3)(A) the notice received by the party to be added must ensure that no prejudice will result in presenting a defense on the merits. The focus of the prejudice requirement is on the proposed defendant's ability to obtain sufficient evidence that he may properly prepare his case to defendant against the plaintiff's allegations. The case law is split about whether the notice received by the party to be added may be formal or informal. How is the fact pattern in *Varlack*, cited by the court, consistent with the notice requirement?

In addition, under Rule 15(c)(3)(B), a proposed defendant must also know or be expected to know that but for a mistake regarding his identity, the original claim would have been instituted against him. Does the absence of knowledge constitute a mistake? See, e.g., *Garrett v. Fleming*, 362 F.3d 692 (10th Cir. 2004) (no).

Singletary discusses the various methods by which the plaintiff can prove knowledge. Did *Varlack* really involve a lack of knowledge by the newly named defendant?

4. Supplemental Pleadings

STEWART v. SHELBY TISSUE, INC.

189 F.R.D. 357 (W.D. Tenn. 1999)

DONALD, District Judge.

Before the court is the plaintiff's, Dennis Stewart (hereinafter "Stewart"), motion for leave to file counts VII and VIII of his First Amended Verified Complaint. The defendants, Shelby Tissue, Inc. (hereinafter "Shelby") and General Electric Capital Corporation (hereinafter "GE") have filed a joint response opposing the motion.

Stewart was employed by Shelby and its parent, GE, starting in November of 1997, as Chief Executive Officer. A contract of employment was entered into between the parties. In November of 1998, apparently disagreements started to arise between the parties, resulting in Stewart's demotion to Sales Manager. Stewart resigned from Shelby/GE on January 8, 1999. Subsequently, he began work with Kruger, Inc., which, at some point in time, became associated with Global Tissue, LLC. On January 8, 1999, Stewart filed this complaint.

On or about January 22, 1999, Shelby/GE sent a letter to Kruger concerning Stewart claiming that he could not compete with Shelby based upon an alleged employment agreement. Further, Shelby/GE wrote Stewart and advised him he was in violation of that alleged employment agreement. Stewart was terminated from Kruger/Global Tissue in March 1999. Stewart alleges that Shelby/GE's efforts resulted in his termination from Kruger/Global Tissue.

On April 26, 1999, Stewart filed his First Amended Verified Complaint. This complaint included Count VII, alleging unlawful inducement of breach of contract, and Count VIII, alleging tortious interference with contractual relations. At the time Stewart filed his First Amended

Verified Complaint, neither Shelby nor GE had filed an answer. Both of these counts are based on the actions of Shelby/GE subsequent to Stewart's initial filing of his complaint.

On May 6, 1999, Stewart filed a Motion for Leave to File Counts VII and VIII. Shelby/GE have filed a response in opposition.

Fed.R.Civ.P. 15 permits a party to either amend or supplement a pleading. There are two fundamental purposes for permitting a party to amend or supplement a pleading. The first is the policy of deciding a complaint on its merits rather than dismissing it on technical reasons. The second is that pleadings, in the federal system, generally serve the limited purpose of notice to the opposing party.

[The court's discussion of amendment principles under Rule 15(a) and 15(c) is omitted.]

Amendment of a pleading only applies concerning facts and circumstances which occurred prior to the date of filing of the original complaint. For transactions, occurrences or events arising after the date of filing a complaint, a supplemental pleading must be filed. Thus, a supplemental pleading may include new facts, new claims, new defenses, and new parties. Supplemental pleadings may be used to bring in additional parties when the subsequent events alleged in the new pleadings make it necessary. However, a supplemental pleading will only be allowed upon reasonable notice and terms that are just.

The granting of a motion to file a supplemental pleading is within the discretion of the trial court. Factors such as undue delay, trial inconvenience, and prejudice to the parties should be considered when evaluating a motion to file a supplemental pleading. Even if the original pleading is defective, the court may permit a supplemental pleading. However, as a general rule, applications for leave to file a supplemental pleading are normally granted.

Like motions to amend under Fed.R.Civ.P. 15(a), motions to supplement under Fed.R.Civ.P. 15(d) must be presented within a reasonable period of time. See *McHenry v. Ford Motor Co.*, 269 F.2d 18, 24 (6th Cir.1959) (denying a motion to amend which was brought four years after the commencement of the case). Generally, they can be brought at any time the action is before the trial court.

Although Fed.R.Civ.P. 15 does not provide for the application of the "relation back" provision under Fed.R.Civ.P. 15(c) to Fed.R.Civ.P. 15(d), the courts have generally recognized that it does apply. Thus, there is protection for supplemental pleadings against responses claiming statutes of limitations.

In his brief, Stewart claims that the factual bases for Counts VII and VIII are of a continuing nature since the filing of his initial complaint and, as such, amendment of his complaint concerning these two counts should fall within the scope of Fed.R.Civ.P. 15(a). It is evident from the record that the factual bases for these claims, unlawful inducement of breach of contract and tortious interference with contractual relations, only arose after the filing of the initial complaint. Thus, Fed.R.Civ.P. 15(d) applies.

Stewart acknowledges in his motion that Fed.R.Civ.P. 15(d) may apply and argues for leave to file a supplemental pleading for the two claims in question, after the fact. In support, Stewart claims that Shelby/GE will not be prejudiced by the granting of such leave and that because of the early filing of this request to file a supplemental pleading, there will be no undue delay or inconvenience. Further, Stewart argues that these two additional counts involve a common nucleus of facts with the other claims which would promote the speedy and economic disposition of the entire controversy. Stewart's arguments have merit.

In response, Shelby/GE argues that Stewart is actually bringing these additional claims to protract the litigation and complicate the defense. Shelby/GE, however, presents precious little in support of these arguments. Shelby/GE does not refer to any evidence or facts which would support the contention that Stewart is attempting to protract the litigation or complicate the defense. Indeed, a brief review of Stewart's allegations concerning Shelby/GE's activities since Stewart filed his original complaint indicates that his claim may very well have merit.

Shelby/GE also argues that because Stewart's claim is without merit, as discussed in Shelby/GE's motion to dismiss filed March 26, 1999, Stewart should not be permitted to file a supplemental pleading. However, Shelby/GE's motion was filed well before Stewart's First Amended Verified Complaint and the motion does not directly address Counts VII and VIII. Further, this court has already addressed Shelby/GE's motion to dismiss by order dated June 9, 1999, and found that the majority of the claims raised in Stewart's complaint should not be dismissed. Thus, this argument of Shelby/GE is also without merit.

The court is not unmindful of the fact that Stewart has filed his supplemental pleading before asking the court's leave, in violation of Fed.R.Civ.P. 15(d). However, the court finds that Shelby/GE had reasonably timely notice of the facts and circumstances underlying the supplemental pleading and that no prejudice will result.

Shelby/GE has not demonstrated that any undue delay, trial inconvenience, or prejudice would result if Stewart's motion was granted. Further, not granting Stewart's motion would require him to file a separate action, which would be a waste of judicial resources. Thus, the court finds that the motion should be granted.

Notes and Questions

1. Rule 15(d) allows a supplemental pleading to set forth transaction or events which have occurred *since* the filing of the original pleading, thereby bringing the case up to date. The supplemental pleading may set forth new facts in order to update the earlier pleading or change the amount or nature of the relief sought in the original pleading.

2. As *Stewart* indicates, amended and supplemental pleadings differ. Amended pleadings relate to matters that occurred prior to the filing of the

original pleading and replace them entirely. A supplemental pleading relates to events which have occurred subsequent to the pleading to be altered. The discretion exercised by the court in deciding to grant leave to file a supplemental pleading is similar to that applied in passing on a motion to amend. Unlike an amendment pursuant to Rule 15(a), a supplemental pleading is never allowed as a matter of right, but only by leave of court.

3. Why did Stewart believe that Counts VII and VIII could be filed as amendments to the original complaint? Did Stewart's counsel err by filing the First Amended Verified Complaint without obtaining the court's permission?

4. As stated previously, leave of court is required before filing a supplemental pleading. If a supplemental pleading is filed without obtaining a court order, the opposing party may file a Rule 12(f) motion to strike. Before ruling on the motion to strike the court determines if any prejudice has occurred. If there is none, the court orders the supplemental pleading filed as though a proper petition for leave had been filed.

Exercise

For the state a) where you intend to practice after graduation, b) where your law school is located, and/or c) your professor assigns, go to that state's annotated rules and research the procedural rules for amending and supplementing pleadings. Based on your research, print the portion of the rules and bring them to class for discussion. In addition, answer the following questions.

1. Identify whether, and if so under what circumstances, the following types of amendments are recognized in the rules:

A. Amendments "as a matter of course," which do not require the court's approval;

B. Amendments with consent of the court;

C. Amendments conforming to the evidence at trial, or tried by express or implied consent; and

D. Amendments which are filed after the limitations period has expired, but are allowed to relate back.

2. Identify whether, and if so when, supplemental pleadings are permitted.

CHAPTER 6

ADVANCED JOINDER

A. INTERVENTION

INTRODUCTORY PROBLEM

Pat has a patent on the world's best mousetrap, which uses a computer chip to ensure that no mouse can escape. Jealous of Pat's success, Diane begins to produce and sell a similar mousetrap. Pat immediately sues Diane in federal court for patent infringement.

Diane obtains the computer chips that she uses in her trap from Interel, Inc. Interel produces only one style of chip, which was custom-designed for Diane's trap. Interel sells its entire output of chips to Diane. Therefore, Interel is justifiably concerned with Pat's suit against Diane. Although Interel is not liable directly to Pat—Pat's patent covers a trap that uses a chip, not the chip itself—Interel fears that if Diane is held liable the demand for its product will disappear.

Is there any way that Interel can become a party in Pat's lawsuit?

Governing Rule: Rule 24(a) and (b).

A plaintiff has considerable autonomy over who will be a party to a case. The plaintiff names the defendants, and as we saw in Chapter 2, may elect to sue fewer than all potentially liable parties. Moreover, even though plaintiffs with closely aligned interests *may* join as co-plaintiffs, nothing requires one plaintiff to allow another person to join his case.

Rule 24 is an exception to the basic principle of plaintiff autonomy. In some situations, a party may join a pending case even though the plaintiff would rather that person not be in the case. Of course, it would be inefficient to allow anyone to join in a case merely because he wants to have a say in the outcome. Instead, Rule 24 limits intervention to people who are genuinely interested in the outcome of the case. If the person can convince the court that her interest is genuine, and that there is an overlap between her case and the one before the court, she may be able to *intervene by permission* under Rule 24(b). In some

387

situations, however, a person's interest is so directly threatened that she can *intervene of right* under Rule 24(a). If a person satisfies Rule 24(a), she can join the case even if the parties and the court all agree that they would prefer not to have her as a party.

CHILES v. THORNBURGH

865 F.2d 1197 (11th Cir. 1989)

CLARK, Circuit Judge.

In November of 1985, Lawton Chiles, a United States Senator from Florida, filed an action against the Attorney General of the United States and several other Department of Justice (DOJ) officials, and the Secretary of the Department of Defense (DOD), alleging that the federal government was operating Krome Detention Center (Krome), a federal facility located in Dade County, Florida, illegally. After Senator Chiles' complaint was filed, Dade County and Bob Martinez, the Governor of Florida, were granted leave to intervene and filed complaints. Several Krome detainees, individual homeowners living near Krome, and a Homeowners' Association (the proposed intervenors) were not granted leave to intervene.

The district court dismissed the complaints, holding that all the plaintiffs and most of the proposed intervenors lacked standing and that the issues raised by the complaints presented nonjusticiable political questions. For the reasons which follow, we affirm in part, reverse in part, and remand the case to the district court. * * *

I

Krome is a minimum-security, short-term Bureau of Prisons (BOP) facility. Since the Mariel Boatlift of 1980, DOJ officials have used Krome to detain aliens awaiting processing, exclusion, or asylum. In 1981, several high-ranking DOJ officials, including the Attorney General and the Commissioner of the Immigration and Naturalization Service (INS), testified before Congress that Krome was not a long-term detention facility for aliens. * * *

When he questioned DOJ officials about the status of Krome in 1983, Senator Chiles was assured that Krome remained a temporary detention facility and that a permanent long-term detention facility would be ready by 1985.

Despite their assurances, DOJ officials used Krome as a long-term detention facility to hold large numbers of aliens, including convicted felons, indefinitely. Many of the felons held at Krome were aliens who had finished serving jail sentences for state and federal offenses committed in the United States and were waiting determination of their status by INS. In October of 1985, over forty alien felons rioted and escaped from Krome. Soon afterwards, the INS District Director stated publicly that the alien felons had to be removed from Krome for the protection of the other aliens. Although DOJ officials recognized that events such as the 1985 escape were the result of their policy of housing felons with nonviolent aliens, they did not transfer most of the felons from Krome. By 1986, the felons at Krome had formed gangs which preyed upon nonviolent aliens and regularly assaulted guards. DOJ officials hired improperly trained private security guards to protect the nonviolent aliens and maintain control of Krome.

The procedural history of this case is important to an accurate understanding of what is at issue on appeal. In 1985, Senator Chiles filed his complaint. Alleging the facts above, the complaint sought several forms of relief: (1) a declaratory judgment that the government's affirmative misrepresentations estopped the government from operating Krome as other than a minimum security, short term facility with a cap of 525 persons, none of whom would be felons ("the estoppel claim"); (2) declaratory and injunctive relief relating to the responsibilities and duties of DOJ, BOP, and INS with respect to Krome; and (3) a writ of mandamus ordering the government to (a) remove all alien felons from Krome and transfer them to medium security or maximum security federal facilities; (b) obey the cap on the number of aliens which can be detained at Krome; and (c) limit detention of aliens at Krome to short-term minimum security processing stays.

Dade County and Governor Martinez sought to intervene. Their complaints alleged the same facts and sought similar relief as Senator Chiles except that they did not assert a separate and distinct equitable estoppel claim. The district court allowed them to intervene. Subsequently, three additional groups sought to intervene: detainees X and Y individually and as representatives of a class of non-felon detainees, the Kendall Federation Homeowners Association, and two individual homeowners, David Lowry and Dorothy Cissel. The intervenors sought the same relief as Senator Chiles. In an order of dismissal, the district court ended the lawsuit. The court found that Senator Chiles, the Governor, and Dade County did not have standing. He also denied the proposed intervenors right to intervene on the grounds that the detainees had adequate recourse through habeas corpus and that the homeowners and Homeowners Association had failed to allege an injury from the operation of Krome. Finally, the district court held that the case presented a nonjusticiable political question because it involved policy decisions which were entrusted to the Executive branch.

All plaintiffs and proposed intervenors appealed. * * *

II

The Constitution limits the "judicial power" of federal courts to the resolution of "cases" and "controversies." U.S. Const. Art. III, § 2. "As an incident to the elaboration of this bedrock requirement, [the Supreme Court] has always required that a [plaintiff] have 'standing' to challenge the action sought to be adjudicated in the lawsuit." *Valley Forge Chris-*

tian College v. Americans United for Separation of Church and State, 454 U.S. 464, 471 (1982). In essence, the question of standing is whether the plaintiff has a "personal stake in the outcome of the controversy as to assure that concrete adverseness which sharpens the presentation of issues upon which [a] court so largely depends for illumination of difficult . . . questions[.]" *Baker v. Carr*, 369 U.S. 186 (1962). To have standing a plaintiff must allege, at "an irreducible minimum," that he has suffered some actual or threatened injury as a result of the putatively illegal conduct of the defendants and that the injury can fairly be traced to the challenged conduct and is likely to be redressed by a favorable decision. In addition to meeting these constitutional requirements, a plaintiff may have to satisfy several prudential principles in order to have his claim heard. For example, he must generally assert his own rights and not the rights of third parties, he must be within the zone of interests protected by the provisions at issue, and he cannot raise abstract questions of wide public significance which amount to "generalized grievances" and are best left to the representative branches. * * *

[The court held that Dade County had standing to bring the claims, but that neither Senator Chiles nor Governor Martinez had standing. Therefore, it upheld the lower court's dismissal of the Senator's and Governor's claims.]

III

In their motions to intervene pursuant to Rule 24 of the Federal Rules of Civil Procedure, the proposed intervenors alleged that their liberty and property interests were violated by the government's operation of Krome. The district court denied the motions, holding that the detainees had adequate recourse through writs of habeas corpus and that the homeowners and the Homeowners' Association lacked standing.

Under the "anomalous" rule we have provisional jurisdiction [over the appeal] to determine whether the district court erred in concluding that the proposed intervenors were not entitled to intervene under Rule 24. If we find that the district court's disposition of the motions to intervene was correct, "then our jurisdiction evaporates because the proper denial of leave to intervene is not a final decision, and we must dismiss [the] appeals for want of jurisdiction. But if we find that the district court was mistaken, then we retain jurisdiction and must reverse. In either event, we are authorized to decide whether the [motions] to intervene [were] properly denied." *EEOC v. Eastern Airlines, Inc.*, 736 F.2d 635, 637 (11th Cir.1984).

A

The Supreme Court has held that an interest under Rule 24(a)(2) means a "significantly protectable interest," *Donaldson v. United States*, 400 U.S. 517, 531 (1971), but it has never articulated the precise relationship between that interest and the Article III standing requirements. *See Diamond v. Charles*, 476 U.S. 54, 68–70 (declining to address whether a party seeking to intervene must satisfy not only the requirements of Rule 24 but also the requirements of Article III). Indeed the lower courts have rendered anomalous decisions on this issue. *See United States v. 36.96 Acres of Land*, 754 F.2d 855, 859 (7th Cir.1985) (interest of proposed intervenor must be greater than the interest sufficient to satisfy standing requirements of APA); *SCLC v. Kelley*, 241 U.S.App.D.C. 340, 747 F.2d 777, 779 (D.C.Cir.1984) (interest necessary to intervene is equivalent to interest necessary to confer standing); *United States v. Imperial Irrigation Distr.*, 559 F.2d 509, 521 (9th Cir.1977) (party seeking to intervene need not possess standing necessary to initiate lawsuit), *vacated on other grounds*, 447 U.S. 352 (1980); *Indian River Recovery Co. v. The China*, 108 F.R.D. 383, 386 (D.Del. 1985) (intervenor need not have standing required to initiate lawsuit).

The reason for this confusion stems from the fact that standing concerns the subject matter jurisdiction of the court. The standing doctrine ensures that a justiciable case and controversy exists between the parties. Intervention under Rule 24 presumes that there is a justiciable case into which an individual wants to intervene. The focus therefore of a Rule 24 inquiry is whether the intervenor has a legally protectable interest in the litigation.[1] It is in this context that the standing cases are relevant, for an intervenor's interest must be a particularized interest rather than a general grievance. *See Howard v. McLucas*, 782 F.2d 956, 959 (11th Cir.1986) (using standing cases to determine that intervenors with only generalized grievance could not intervene); *Athens Lumber Co., Inc. v. Federal Election Commission*, 690 F.2d 1364, 1366 (11th Cir.1982) (citing standing cases to determine that intervenor's claimed interest that unions would be financially overwhelmed in federal elections too generalized to support claim for intervention of right). We therefore hold that a party seeking to intervene need not demonstrate that he has standing in addition to meeting the requirements of Rule 24 as long as there exists a justiciable case and controversy between the parties already in the lawsuit. The standing cases, however, are relevant to help define the type of interest that the intervenor must assert.[2]

B

A party seeking to intervene as of right under Rule 24(a)(2) must show that: (1) his application to intervene is timely; (2) he has an

---

1. "There is a difference between the question whether one is a proper plaintiff or defendant in an initial action and the question whether one is entitled to intervene.... When one seeks to intervene in an ongoing lawsuit, [justiciability] questions have presumably been resolved.... A may not have a dispute with C that could qualify as a case or controversy, but he may have a sufficient interest in B's dispute with C to warrant his participation in the case once it has begun, and the case or controversy limitation should impose no barrier to his admission [as an intervenor]." Shapiro, *Some Thought on Intervention Before Courts, Agencies and Arbitrators*, 81 Harv.L.Rev. 721, 726 (1968) (footnote omitted); *see also*

Weinstein, *Litigations Seeking Changes in Public Behavior and Institutions—Some Views on Participation*, 13 U.C.Davis L.Rev. 231, 241 (1980) ("Since the litigation is already pending there is less reason to be as finicky about [the intervenor's] standing than there would be if the intervenor was commencing the suit.")

2. We need not address the issue of whether an intervenor who seeks to raise a claim unrelated to a case or controversy that already exists must have standing with respect to that claim. In this case, the detainees' claims are related to the underlying suit and the detainees clearly would have standing.

interest relating to the property or transaction which is the subject of the action; (3) he is so situated that disposition of the action, as a practical matter, may impede or impair his ability to protect that interest; and (4) his interest is represented inadequately by the existing parties to the suit. If he establishes each of the four requirements, the district court must allow him to intervene.

A party seeking to intervene under Rule 24(b)(2) must show that: (1) his application to intervene is timely; and (2) his claim or defense and the main action have a question of law or fact in common. The district court has the discretion to deny intervention even if both of those requirements are met, and its decision is reviewed for an abuse of discretion.

1.

In determining whether the detainees' motion to intervene was timely, we must consider the length of time during which the detainees knew or reasonably should have known of their interest in the case before moving to intervene, the extent of prejudice to the existing parties as a result of the detainees' failure to move for intervention as soon as they knew or reasonably should have known of their interest, the extent of prejudice to the detainees if their motion is denied, and the existence of unusual circumstances militating either for or against a determination that their motion was timely. We must also keep in mind that "timeliness is not a word of exactitude or of precisely measurable dimensions. * * * We believe that the detainees' motion to intervene was timely. It was filed only seven months after Senator Chiles filed his original complaint, three months after the government filed its motion to dismiss, and before any discovery had begun. None of the parties already in the lawsuit could have been prejudiced by the detainees' intervention.

Under Rule 24(a)(2), the detainees' intervention must be supported by a " 'direct, substantial, legally protectable interest in the proceeding.' ... In essence, the [detainees] must be at least ... real part[ies] in interest in the transaction which is the subject of the proceeding." *Athens Lumber*, 690 F.2d at 1366 (citations omitted). The detainees' interest need not, however, "be of a legal nature identical to that of the claims asserted in the main action." *Diaz*, 427 F.2d at 1124. Our inquiry on this issue "is 'a flexible one, which focuses on the particular facts and circumstances surrounding each [motion for intervention].' " *United States v. Perry County Board of Education*, 567 F.2d 277, 279 (5th Cir.1978) (quoting *United States v. Allegheny–Ludlum Indus., Inc.*, 517 F.2d 826, 841 (5th Cir.1975), *cert. denied*, 425 U.S. 944, 96 S. Ct. 1684, 48 L. Ed. 2d 187 (1976)).

There is no doubt that the detainees satisfy the interest requirement of Rule 24(a)(2). The detainees are being held at Krome, the axis on which the lawsuit turns. They claim that the government's operation of Krome—e.g., its practice of keeping alien felons along with nonviolent alien detainees and its hiring of untrained security personnel—is in violation of minimum federal and state prison standards and threatens them with an imminent risk of harm. The detainees are analogous to prisoners who have standing to sue over the conditions of the institution where they are detained. By any imaginable yardstick, the detainees have a "direct, substantial, legally protectable interest" in the lawsuit challenging the operation of Krome and are asserting legal rights of their own.

The nature of the detainees' interest and the effect that the disposition of the lawsuit will have on their ability to protect that interest are closely related issues. "The second cannot be answered without reference to the first." *Hobson v. Hansen*, 44 F.R.D. 18, 30 (D.D.C.1968). We think the detainees are so situated that the disposition of the lawsuit will, as a practical matter, impair their ability to protect their interests. As we have already discussed, the detainees are confined in the institution whose operation is being challenged. There is therefore a conjunction of a claim to and an interest in the very transaction which is the subject of the main action, and the *stare decisis* effect of a decision suggests the practical disadvantage requisite for intervention. Where a party seeking to intervene in an action claims an interest in the very property and very transaction that is the subject of the main action, the potential *stare decisis* effect may supply that practical disadvantage which warrants intervention as of right. The detainees' ability to litigate the government's operation of Krome in a separate lawsuit might be an exercise in futility if the instant lawsuit was decided in favor of the government.

Because the detainees' interest is similar to, but not identical with, that of Dade County, we must determine whether the detainees' interest is adequately represented. The Supreme Court has held that the inadequate representation requirement "is satisfied if the [proposed intervenor] shows that representation of his interest 'may be' inadequate" and that "the burden of making that showing should be treated as minimal." *Trbovich v. United Mine Workers of America*, 404 U.S. 528, 538 n. 10 (1972). Thus, the detainees "should be allowed to intervene unless it is clear that [Dade County] will provide adequate representation." 7C C. Wright, A. Miller, & M. Kane, *Federal Practice and Procedure* § 1909, at 319 (2d ed. 1986). The fact that the interests are similar does not mean that approaches to litigation will be the same. Dade County may decide not to emphasize the plight of the aliens held at Krome but focus instead on the effect that Krome has on those who live outside its walls. After all, Dade County is mainly concerned with the expenditures that have to be made because of Krome. We conclude that this possibility sufficiently demonstrates that the detainees' interests are not adequately represented.

Our foregoing discussion indicates that the district court erred in not allowing the detainees to intervene as of right under Rule 24(a)(2). We therefore reverse its ruling. On remand, the detainees are to be treated as original parties and stand on equal footing with the original parties.

2.

We need address only one of the requirements of Rule 24—inadequate representation—to dispose of the argument of the homeowners and the Homeowners' Association that they were entitled to intervene as of right. Unlike the detainees, the homeowners and the Homeowners' Association have an interest which is *identical* to Dade County: the prevention of riots and escapes from Krome and the protection of nearby residents. There is no indication whatsoever that the representation rendered by Dade County would be inadequate. *See Athens Lumber*, 690 F.2d at 1366 (where interest of proposed intervenor is the same as that of one of the parties, court can presume that the interest is adequately represented).

As to permissive intervention under Rule 24(b)(2), we cannot say that the district court abused its discretion with regard to the homeowners and the Homeowners' Association. The duplicative nature of the claims and interests they asserted threatens to unduly delay the adjudication of the rights of the parties in the lawsuit and makes it unlikely that any new light will be shed on the issues to be adjudicated. Having concluded that the homeowners and the Homeowners' Association were not entitled to intervene as of right, and that the district court did not abuse its discretion with regard to permissive intervention under the anomalous rule, we find that we are without jurisdiction. We therefore dismiss the appeals of the homeowners and the Homeowners' Association. * * *

Notes and Questions

1.   Read literally, Rule 24 provides for what appear to be two distinct types of intervention: *intervention of right* under Rule 24(a) and *permissive intervention* under Rule 24(b). In practice, however, a person seeking to intervene need not choose between intervention of right and permissive intervention. Under Rule 24(c), the person files a motion to intervene. Nothing in this Rule requires the movant to specify whether she is relying on Rule 24(a) or (b) as a basis for intervention. If the court decides to permit intervention under the fairly easy standard of Rule 24(b), it is irrelevant whether the intervention was permissive or of right–the person is now a party. It is only when the court refuses permission that the distinction between Rule 24(a) and (b) becomes important. If the movant meets the Rule 24(a) standard for intervention of right, the court abuses its authority if it denies the motion to intervene.

2.   *Permissive intervention.* Rule 24(b) allows a court to approve a timely motion to intervene whenever the intervenor's claim or defense shares a common question of law or fact with the pending action. As you saw in Chapter 2 when you studied Rule 20, the "common question" standard is very easy to satisfy. Therefore, there are few cases involving challenges to a judge's decision allowing intervention under Rule 24(b). For a discussion of the factors courts consider, compare *Security Insurance Co. v. Hartford*, 69 F.3d 1377 (7th Cir. 1995) (permissive intervention allowed) with *Donnelly v.*

Glickman, 159 F.3d 405 (9th Cir. 1998) (permissive intervention denied because no common facts).

Even if the standards of Rule 24(b) are met, a court has the discretion to deny intervention. Are there limits on that discretion? An appellate court will overturn a trial court's denial of permissive intervention only if it finds an abuse of discretion. *League of United Latin Amer. Citizens v. Wilson*, 131 F.3d 1297, 1307–07 (9th Cir. 1997). Because the trial judge is in the best position to evaluate whether allowing intervention will unduly complicate or bog down the case, denials of motions to intervene by permission are rarely overturned.

3. *Timeliness.* Both Rule 24(a) and 24(b) require a "timely" motion to intervene. As the court in *Chiles* indicates, there is no precise standard for determining timeliness. Courts consider all relevant factors. In *Smith v. Marsh*, 194 F.3d 1045 (9th Cir. 1999), for example, intervenors filed a motion to intervene fifteen months after the case was commenced. During those fifteen months, the parties had conducted substantial discovery, filed and argued motions for summary judgment and jury trial (which the court had ruled on), and set a trial date six months following the motion to intervene. The court considered three factors in determining whether the motion to intervene was timely:

(a) the "stage of the proceeding" at which intervenor files the motion,

(b) whether the other parties would be prejudiced by the late intervention, and

(c) any reasons justifying the delay.

Applying these factors to the case, the court upheld the trial court's decision that the motion to intervene was not timely.

In practice, timeliness is more likely to be a disputed issue in a case of intervention of right. A judge dealing with a request for permissive intervention has discretion to deny intervention for reasons other than timeliness. In intervention by right, by contrast, timeliness is the *only* issue on which the judge may exercise any meaningful discretion in denying intervention.

4. *Intervention of right.* The threshold standard for intervention of right is that the intervenor have an "interest" that could be "impaired" by the pending dispute. Courts sometimes conflate these two issues, finding an interest whenever the party can show a significant potential detriment. However, although they may overlap to some extent, interest and impairment are two separate issues, involving separate considerations.

5. *Interest.* The intervening detainees in *Chiles* clearly had an "interest" within the meaning of Rule 24(a). By law, they were entitled to be confined in a facility meeting certain basic standards. If the government was violating that law, the detainees could bring an action to force compliance.

But what about the homeowners and the Homeowner's Association? Because the court found that their interest was adequately represented by Dade County, it did not have to reach the issue of whether they had a sufficient interest. If the County had not already been a party, the court would have had to reach that question. Would the homeowners and the association have had enough of an interest to satisfy Rule 24? Although they might be "interested" in the outcome of the case, did they have an interest on par with that of the detainees? Is it necessary that an interest be something protected by law?

In *Donaldson v. United States*, 400 U.S. 517, 91 S.Ct. 534, 27 L.Ed.2d 580 (1971) (a case briefly discussed in *Chiles*), the Supreme Court held that Rule 24 requires an intervenor to have "a significantly protectable interest." A number of lower courts have had to interpret this somewhat ambiguous phrase. As you might expect, the results in these cases are sometimes hard to reconcile. Two recent cases from the Eighth and Ninth Circuits illustrate how difficult this phrase can be to apply.

In *Curry v. Regents of the University of Minnesota*, 167 F.3d 420 (8th Cir. 1999), a number of students sued the University of Minnesota, claiming that the University had violated their constitutional right to free speech by using the mandatory student fee to fund campus organizations that espoused views that the plaintiff students did not support. Three of the campus organizations sought to intervene of right in the case. The organizations argued that if the students were to prevail, the organizations would lose a significant portion of their funding, which would affect their ability to operate. The court denied intervention, finding that the organizations did not have an "interest" within the meaning of Rule 24(a):

> Although the Movants' motion was timely, they have not established that they possess a recognized interest in this action's subject matter. The Movants merely have asserted an economic interest, maintaining the quantum of their funding, in the outcome of this litigation. The Movants' economic interest in upholding the current fee system simply does not rise to the level of a legally protectable interest necessary for mandatory intervention. See *Greene v. United States*, 996 F.2d 973, 976 (9th Cir.1993) (stating that an economic stake in the outcome of an action is not sufficient to demonstrate a "significantly protectable interest").

Arakaki v. Cayetano, 324 F.3d 1078 (9th Cir. 2003) also dealt with an economic interest. That case dealt with Hawaii's program of providing significant economic benefits, such as low-cost leases, to Native Hawaiians. A number of non-Native Hawaiians sued the state and various state agencies, alleging (among other things) that the policy violated the United States Constitution's equal protection clause because it discriminated based on national origin. Several Native Hawaiians sought to intervene as of right in the case. The intervenors claimed that they had an "interest" in continuing to receive benefits under the state program. The court agreed with the intervenors (who it collectively called "Hoohuli", the name of one of the people seeking to intervene):

> The district court observed that Hoohuli had a significantly protectable interest in the manner in which its tax dollars are used. A ruling in Plaintiffs' favor would impair Hoohuli's interest in the continued receipt of homestead leases. * * *
>
> We agree with the district court that Hoohuli has a significantly protectable interest in the manner in which its tax dollars are used, specifically a continued receipt of benefits. Hoohuli, as lessees of Hawaiian homestead lands or applicants for such leases, have a stake in the

outcome of Plaintiffs' equal protection challenge. Consequently, Hoohuli's protectable interest in the continued receipt of benefits supports intervention.

However, because the existing defendants adequately protected the intervenors' interests, the court ultimately held that the intervenors could not intervene as of right.

Is there any appreciable difference in the nature of the intervenors' interests in *Curry* and *Arakaki*? Does it matter that the Native Hawaiians were also taxpayers, and that their tax dollars helped fund the state program? Weren't the students in *Curry* also similar to taxpayers, in that they had paid a mandatory student fee?

Other recent cases discussing the interest factor in intervention include *United States v. Alisal Water Corp.*, 370 F.3d 915 (9th Cir. 2004) (United States brought action against city water company to force company to comply with environmental laws; creditor with a lien on the water company's property did not have a sufficient interest to intervene as of right even though the value of its collateral might decrease); *Public Service Co. of New Hampshire v. Patch*, 136 F.3d 197 (1st Cir. 1998) (ratepayers did not have a sufficient interest to intervene as of right in action that certain electrical utilities had filed against state public utilities commission to challenge commission's plan to require competition in electrical market); and *Sierra Club v. U.S. Environmental Protection Agency*, 995 F.2d 1478 (9th Cir. 1993) (city could intervene in action by environmental group against EPA seeking to force the EPA to change the terms of city's existing license). For a case with a more macabre twist, see *Fierro v. Grant*, 1995 WL 242312 (9th Cir.) (unpublished) (prisoner on death row could not intervene of right in case challenging the constitutionality of California's method of execution; prisoner had no legally protectable interest in any particular method of execution).

6. *Impairment.* A person seeking to intervene must also show that her interest could be impaired. Note that the person need not demonstrate that the impairment is certain to occur. Indeed, in most cases impairment will exist only if the case is decided in favor of one of the existing parties.

The most obvious situation in which an interest is impaired is when the court decision could result in actual, irrevocable harm to the intervenor. Suppose, for example, that a builder wants to tear down a historic structure in order to build a new building. When the city denies a permit to raze the building, the builder sues the city. Several citizens interested in historic preservation seek to intervene. If the builder prevails in his case against city, any interest these citizens have is bound to be impaired, as the building will then be torn down.

The impairment in a case like *Chiles* is less apparent. If the governor were to lose the case, conditions would not be improved. However, the detainees at Krome could then file their own action challenging the conditions. Because the detainees were not parties to the prior case, they would not be bound by claim or issue preclusion from bringing their own action.

Nevertheless, a victory for the federal government in *Chiles* would have some effect on a later suit by the detainees. Once one court finds that the conditions at Krome did not violate any legal norms, other courts would tend to respect that decision. The impairment in *Chiles*, then, is the *stare decisis* effect of the judgment.

How far does this sort of reasoning extend? Consider a twist on the historic preservation example set out just above. City designates several areas historic zones, and imposes severe building limits in those zones. X, who owns land in Zone A, sues City, claiming that the restrictions constitute a taking for which X should be compensated. Y and Z seek to intervene in the case of right. Y and Z are both landowners, and like X seek compensation for a taking. However, Y's land is in Zone A, while Z's is in Zone B, located a few miles away. Are Y and Z equally impaired by the *stare decisis* effect of X v. City? Does it matter that Y's claim involves the same zone, while Z's involves a different zone?

Generally speaking, *stare decisis* will be a sufficient impairment only in cases like *Chiles*, where the parties and the intervenors are all fighting over the same place or thing. *See, e.g., Atlantis Development Corp. v. United States*, 379 F.2d 818 (5th Cir. 1967) (one party sued the United States to allow development of an artificial island, another person interested in developing the same island allowed to intervene of right).

7.   Recall that Rules 20(b) and 42(b) allow a court to sever one or more claims from a pending case if trying all the claims together would prove unwieldy or confusing. A decision to sever is ordinarily within the discretion of the trial court, and will not be disturbed on appeal. Should a court have the discretion to sever a claim involving a party who has intervened as of right?

8.   *Adequate representation.* Even if a person has a legally recognized interest that is impaired, she cannot intervene of right if the existing parties adequately look out for that interest. As the court in *Chiles* indicates, it is relatively easy to show that representation is inadequate. As long as the intervenor can show that the party's interests *may* diverge from her interests, this requirement is satisfied. For another case demonstrating the minimal burden of showing adequate representation, consider *Natural Resources Defense Council v. United States Nuclear Regulatory Comm.*, 578 F.2d 1341 (10th Cir. 1978) (challenge to a government requirement for uranium licenses, a party with an existing license held not to provide adequate representation for another person with a pending application for a license).

9.   *Intervention and jurisdiction.* A person who intervenes becomes a full party to the action. As a result, intervention raises potential issues of jurisdiction and venue. However, personal jurisdiction and venue are not bars to intervention. By voluntarily joining the case, the intervenor consents to the court's exercise of jurisdiction over it. Similarly, courts ignore the residence and claims of the intervenor when determining venue. *Commonwealth Edison Co. v. Train*, 71 F.R.D. 391 (N.D. Ill. 1976).

Subject matter jurisdiction limitations, however, can prevent a person from intervening in a case. Of course, subject matter jurisdiction is mainly an issue in federal court. The intervening party will become a plaintiff or defendant in the action, according to her interest. As discussed in Chapter 3, a federal court must have jurisdiction over every claim presented to it in a case, including claims by or against intervenors. The court must therefore consider §§ 1331, 1332, and 1367 to determine if the new composition of parties and claims destroys the court's jurisdiction.

In some cases, claims by or against an intervenor will independently qualify for federal subject matter jurisdiction because they are federal questions, or because the case satisfies the requirements of § 1332 for diversity. Even if a claim does not itself qualify for federal jurisdiction, the court may have authority to hear it by exercising its supplemental jurisdiction under § 1367. The court in *Chiles* never discusses the question of jurisdiction. Can you nevertheless deduce why the court had jurisdiction to hear the claims of the intervening detainees?

Test your understanding of subject matter jurisdiction in intervention by solving a simple scenario loosely based on *Chiles*. P, a citizen of Florida, sues D, a citizen of the District of Columbia, based on D's operation of Krome detention center. X, a detainee, is intervening as of right in the case. X is a citizen of Florida. Would the court have jurisdiction over the claim involving X in the following situations?

   a.   P claims that D is running the prison in violation of federal law; X is also asserting a violation of that same federal law.

   b.   P claims that D's operation of the prison is a public nuisance, X claims that the conditions involve intentional infliction of emotional distress.

   c.   P sues to cut off water and power to Krome because D has not paid the utility bills, X is intervening because the conditions would become unbearable if water and power were cut off.

10.   *Standing*. The *Chiles* court also discusses whether the intervenors have "standing" to bring the claims they hope to bring. Standing is a fundamental limitation on a court's power to decide a case presented to it. The doctrine applies in the federal system, as well as in many states. In the federal system, the standing requirement stems from the language of Article III of the Constitution, which provides that the federal courts may hear only "cases" and "controversies." In some ways, then, standing is a cousin to the doctrine of jurisdiction, for if the party bringing the claim has no standing to bring it, the court must dismiss the claim for lack of jurisdiction.

A comprehensive study of standing is far beyond the scope of a first-year Procedure course. You will study standing in depth in upper-level courses such as Constitutional Law and Federal Courts. Basically, however, the analysis asks whether the plaintiff is the proper person to present a particular claim to the court for adjudication. Several factors enter into the analysis. For example, it is essential that the plaintiff have suffered an injury due to the complained-of conduct. Moreover, the plaintiff must assert her own legal rights when seeking to redress that injury, not the legal rights of someone else.

As *Chiles* recognizes, there is a potential clash between intervention, which allows a party to join a dispute between two or more other people, and the standing requirement. In Part III.A. of the opinion, however, the court concludes that standing is not a concern, at least in this case. Can you restate the court's basic argument in your own words? Do you understand the court's concern in footnote 17?

11. The *Chiles* court's conclusion that the order denying intervention by right is immediately appealable is not followed by all courts. See *Rhode Island v. United States Environmental Protection Agency*, 378 F.3d 19 (1st Cir. 2004).

Problems

1. X, Y, and Z are involved in a three-car accident. X sues Y for his injuries. Z also feels that Y is at fault, and would accordingly like to join with X in his suit. However, X steadfastly refuses to allow Z to join as a co-plaintiff. The judge recognizes the potential savings in time, and would like to allow Z to join the case. May the judge allow Z to join the case notwithstanding X's protestations?

2. A recent scientific experiment showed that BSE, or "Mad Cow Disease," can mutate and affect chickens. To protect the large numbers of chicken-eating Americans, Congress enacts the Mad Chicken Disease Act. This Act prevents anyone from selling chickens or eggs unless that person can provide documentary proof that the chicken in question was never fed animal proteins (it is thought that BSE is passed through the consumption of certain animal parts). The Act is administered by the United States Department of Agriculture ["USDA"].

X, a chicken rancher, immediately sues the USDA in federal court. X argues that the Act is unconstitutional because it applies retroactively to chickens that a rancher acquired before the Act was passed. X argues that prior to the Act, no rancher thought it was necessary to keep records of what they fed their chickens.

Y, another chicken rancher, seeks to intervene in the case. The court denies permissive intervention. Y, however, claims that he can intervene as of right. Like X, Y sells his chickens to a large processing plant, which in turn distributes them to grocery stores. May Y intervene as of right?

3. Same facts as Problem 2, except that X sells to a different processor that produces only dog food.

B. NECESSARY PARTIES

INTRODUCTORY PROBLEM

At the end of every semester, Professor Bohrene awards the coveted "Golden Rules Award" in his Civil Procedure class. The award earns the recipient a $100 cash prize, paid by the law school. In addition, the recipient is honored at the law school's prestigious and swanky Honors Banquet. According to the stated criteria, the award goes to the student with the "highest final grade" in the course. This past semester, however, a dispute arose concerning who ought to receive the award. Campbell received the highest grade on her final exam. However, Professor Bohrene also decided to award extra credit for class participation. Because Hartley spoke out more often, her grade in the course is actually higher than Campbell's. Nevertheless, Professor Bohrene exercises his professorial discretion and awards the Golden Rules Award to Campbell, under the reasoning that "highest final grade" means highest grade on the final exam. Bohrene has Associate Dean Penny Wise pay $100 to Campbell, and begins to prepare his speech honoring Campbell for the upcoming Honors Banquet.

Professor Bohrene's discretion lands him in the middle of a lawsuit, as Hartley immediately sues him in federal court. Hartley asks the court to issue an order barring Bohrene from awarding the Golden Rule Award to Campbell, and requiring him to give it to her instead. Hartley also seeks $100 in damages for failure to receive the award.

Professor Bohrene is worried about the implications of the lawsuit. First, he thinks that Campbell should also be a party to the case. After all, if Hartley should prevail in the case, Bohrene is sure that Campbell will bring her own suit against him for either damages or a conflicting injunction. In addition, Bohrene feels that Associate Dean Wise should be in the case. According to law school rules, only Wise has the authority to pay out law school funds.

Is there any way that Bohrene may join Campbell and Wise to this suit? Failing that, is there any way he can object to Hartley's failure to join Campbell and Wise?

Governing Rule: Federal Rule 19

In some situations, litigation can have collateral effects. Take a case in which X sues Y. Although only X and Y are legally bound by the court's decision, the consequences of that decision may spill over and affect others. For example, suppose that Y is a factory, and X is suing to force Y to install expensive scrubbers. If X prevails, the decision will have a legal effect only on Y, but will also have a practical effect on Y's employees (certainly an economic effect; possibly also health effects) and perhaps others who live in the community.

Intervention under Rule 24 responds to these concerns by allowing a party threatened with collateral effects to join the case and protect her interest. But intervention is not a panacea. In many cases, a party may choose not to intervene because of cost or other considerations. Or, as discussed in note 9 on p. 398, a party may not be able to intervene because it would destroy federal subject matter jurisdiction. What should a court do in a case where an interested person is not in the case? Should the threat to the third person's interest cause the court to refuse to hear the case?

DAWAVENDEWA v. SALT RIVER PROJECT AGRICULTURAL IMPROVEMENT AND POWER DISTRICT

276 F.3d 1150 (9th Cir. 2002)

TROTT, Circuit Judge.

OVERVIEW

Harold Dawavendewa ("Dawavendewa") sued the Salt River Project Agricultural Improvement and Power District ("SRP") for employing a hiring preference policy in violation of Title VII of the Civil Rights Act of 1964. In particular, he alleged that SRP's lease with the Navajo Nation ("Nation") required it to preferentially hire Navajos at the Navajo Generating Station ("NGS"). The district court dismissed Dawavendewa's complaint for failure to join the Nation as an indispensable party.

Pursuant to 28 U.S.C. § 1291, we have jurisdiction over Dawavendewa's timely appeal. As a signatory to the lease, we conclude the Nation is a necessary party that cannot be joined because it enjoys tribal sovereign immunity. We further conclude that tribal officials cannot be joined to replace the immune Nation; rather, the Nation itself is indispensable to this suit. Accordingly, we affirm the district court's dismissal of Dawavendewa's complaint without prejudice.

BACKGROUND

SRP operates NGS on reservation lands leased directly from the Navajo Nation. As required by its lease, SRP extends employment preferences to qualified local Navajos at NGS.[3]

Dawavendewa, a member of the Hopi Tribe, lives less than three miles from the Navajo reservation. Dawavendewa applied for employment as an Operator Trainee at NGS. After a qualifications test, Dawavendewa ranked ninth out of twenty applicants. Yet, because Dawavendewa is not affiliated with the Nation, he was never interviewed for the Operator Trainee position.

Dawavendewa filed a complaint in district court accusing SRP of discriminating against him on the basis of his national origin in violation of Title VII. Dawavendewa's complaint asserted no causes of action against the Nation or tribal officials, and they are not parties to this litigation. * * *

SRP moved to dismiss Dawavendewa's complaint for failure to join the Nation as an indispensable party. The district court ruled that the Nation was an indispensable party and granted SRP's motion.

---

3. The lease provision at issue reads as follows: Lessees agree to give preference in employment to qualified local Navajos, it being understood that "local Navajos" means members of the Navajo Tribe living on land within the jurisdiction of the Navajo Tribe. * * * In the event sufficient quali-fied unskilled, semi-skilled and skilled local Navajo labor is not available, or the quality of work of available skilled or semi-skilled workmen is not acceptable to Lessees, Lessees may then employ, in order of preference, first, qualified non-local Navajos, and second, non-Navajos.

Dawavendewa appeals that determination.

STANDARD OF REVIEW

We review a district court's decision to dismiss for failure to join an indispensable party for abuse of discretion.

DISCUSSION

Application of Federal Rule of Civil Procedure 19 determines whether a party is indispensable. The inquiry is a practical, fact-specific one, designed to avoid the harsh results of rigid application. We must determine: (1) whether an absent party is necessary to the action; and then, (2) if the party is necessary, but cannot be joined, whether the party is indispensable such that in "equity and good conscience" the suit should be dismissed.

I. Necessary Party

In determining whether the Nation is necessary under Rule 19, we consider whether, in the absence of the Nation, complete relief can be accorded to Dawavendewa. In the alternative, we consider whether the Nation claims a legally protected interest in the subject of the suit such that a decision in its absence will (1) impair or impede its ability to protect that interest; or (2) expose SRP and Dawavendewa to the risk of multiple or inconsistent obligations by reason of that interest. See Fed. R. Civ. P. 19(a)(2). If the Nation satisfies either of these alternative tests, it is necessary to the instant litigation.

A. In the Absence of the Navajo Nation, Complete Relief Cannot Be Accorded To Dawavendewa

Even if ultimately victorious in federal court, Dawavendewa cannot be accorded complete relief in the absence of the Nation. Dawavendewa seeks injunctive relief to ensure his employment at SRP and to prevent SRP from employing the Navajo hiring preference policy required by its lease with the Nation. Yet only SRP and Dawavendewa—and not the Nation—would be bound by such an injunction. The Nation could still attempt to enforce the lease provision in tribal court and ultimately, even attempt to terminate SRP's rights on the reservation. The district court correctly observed that "if SRP were to ignore [the] injunction, [Dawavendewa] and others like him would not receive the employment they seek," whereas "if SRP were to comply with the injunction, the Navajo Nation would be likely to take action against SRP under its lease."

We faced a similar situation in *Confederated Tribes* [*v. Lujan*, 928 F.2d 1496 (9th Cir. 1991)], where we addressed an action brought by various Indian Tribes against federal officials challenging the United States' continued recognition of the Quinault Indian Nation as the sole governing authority of the Quinault Indian Reservation. In affirming the district court's dismissal of the case for failure to join the Quinault Nation as an indispensable party, we held that "success by the plaintiffs

. . . would not afford complete relief to them" because "judgment against the federal officials would not be binding on the Quinault Nation, which could continue to assert sovereign powers and management responsibilities over the reservation." 928 F.2d at 1498.

Dawavendewa stands in the same position as the * * * various Indian Tribes in *Confederated Tribes*: he is not assured complete relief even if victorious. Indeed, if the federal court granted Dawavendewa's requested injunctive relief, SRP would be between the proverbial rock and a hard place—comply with the injunction prohibiting the hiring preference policy or comply with the lease requiring it. If, in resolving this quandary, SRP declines to abide by the injunction and instead continues to comply with its lease obligations, Dawavendewa would not be accorded complete relief. Thus, under Rule 19(a)(1), the Nation is a necessary party.

B. Impairment of the Nation's Legally Protected Interest

The Nation is also a necessary party to Dawavendewa's action against SRP under the second prong of Rule 19(a). Under Rule 19(a)(2), an absent party is necessary if it claims "an interest relating to the subject of the action," and disposition of the action in its absence may "as a practical matter impair or impede [its] ability to protect that interest." Fed. R. Civ. P. 19(a)(2)(I).

Here, the Nation claims a legally protected interest in its contract rights with SRP. In *Lomayaktewa v. Hathaway*, 520 F.2d 1324, 1325 (9th Cir. 1975), we observed that, "no procedural principle is more deeply imbedded in the common law than that, in an action to set aside a lease or a contract, all parties who may be affected by the determination of the action are indispensable." Accordingly, we held unequivocally that the Hopi Tribe was a necessary (and indispensable) party to a suit by an individual challenging a lease between the Hopi Tribe and the Peabody Coal Company simply by virtue of being a signatory to the lease.

Quite similar to * * * *Lomayaktewa*, the instant litigation threatens to impair the Nation's contractual interests, and thus, its fundamental economic relationship with SRP. The Nation strenuously emphasizes the importance of the hiring preference policy to its economic well-being. In fact, the Nation asserts that "[without the hiring preference provision], the Navajo Nation leadership would never have approved this lease agreement." * * *

In addition, a judgment rendered in the Nation's absence will impair its sovereign capacity to negotiate contracts and, in general, to govern the Navajo reservation. * * * [T]he Nation has an interest in determining the appropriate balance between alternative lease terms. Nation Amicus Br. at 7 ("[The lease] has cost Navajo water, Navajo coal, Navajo prime land, and the inevitable pollution of the Navajo homeland. It is a bargained for price that the Navajo Nation alone paid in return for jobs for the Navajo people.").

Undermining the Nation's ability to negotiate contracts also undermines the Nation's ability to govern the reservation effectively and efficiently. Thus, as a result of its multiple economic and sovereign interests, the Nation sufficiently asserts claims relating to this litigation which may be impaired in its absence. Under Rule 19(a)(2)(I) the Nation is, therefore, a necessary party.

C. The Substantial Risk of Inconsistent or Multiple Obligations by Virtue of the Nation's Legally Protected Interests

Any disposition in the Nation's absence threatens to leave SRP subject to substantial risk of incurring multiple or inconsistent obligations. As explained above, although an injunction may compel SRP to stop its hiring preference policy and to hire Dawavendewa, an injunction would not bind the Nation, which could continue to enforce the hiring preference policy required by the lease. This scenario leaves SRP facing intractable, mutually exclusive alternatives and thus, subjects SRP to the substantial risk of facing multiple, inconsistent obligations. Thus, we determine that the Nation is also a necessary party under Rule 19(a)(2)(ii). * * *

II. Tribal Sovereign Immunity

Having determined that the Nation is thrice over a necessary party to the instant litigation, we next consider whether it can feasibly be joined as a party. We hold it cannot. Federally recognized Indian tribes enjoy sovereign immunity from suit, and may not be sued absent an express and unequivocal waiver of immunity by the tribe or abrogation of tribal immunity by Congress. See *Santa Clara Pueblo v. Martinez*, 436 U.S. 49, 58–59 (1978).

In this case, the Nation has not waived its tribal sovereign immunity and Congress has not clearly abrogated tribal sovereign immunity in Title VII cases. Dawavendewa, undaunted, argues that tribal sovereign immunity does not exist because the suit could be sustained against tribal officials. We disagree. * * *

Undoubtedly many actions of a sovereign are performed by individuals. Yet even if Dawavendewa alleged some wrongdoing on the part of Nation officials, his real claim is against the Nation itself. At bottom, the lease at issue is between SRP and the Nation, and the relief Dawavendewa seeks would operate against the Nation as signatory to the lease. As such, we reject Dawavendewa's attempt to circumvent the Nation's sovereign immunity by joining tribal officials in its stead.

III. Indispensable Party

The Nation is a necessary party that cannot be joined due to its tribal sovereign immunity. Accordingly, we consider whether the Nation is indispensable such that Dawavendewa's action must be dismissed. See Fed. R. Civ. P. 19(b). A party is indispensable if in "equity and good conscience," the court should not allow the action to proceed in its absence. To make this determination, we must balance four factors: (1) the prejudice to any party or to the absent party; (2) whether relief can be shaped to lessen prejudice; (3) whether an adequate remedy, even if not complete, can be awarded without the absent party; and (4) whether there exists an alternative forum. If no alternative forum exists, we should be "extra cautious" before dismissing the suit.

If the necessary party enjoys sovereign immunity from suit, some courts have noted that there may be very little need for balancing Rule 19(b) factors because immunity itself may be viewed as "one of those interests 'compelling by themselves,' " which requires dismissing the suit. *Wichita & Affiliated Tribes v. Hodel*, 788 F.2d 765, 777 (D.C. Cir. 1986); see also *Enterprise Mgmt. Consultants, Inc. v. United States*, 883 F.2d 890, 894 (10th Cir. 1989). Cognizant of these out-of-circuit decisions, the Ninth Circuit has, nonetheless, consistently applied the four part balancing test to determine whether Indian tribes are indispensable parties.

A. Prejudice—The prejudice to the Nation stems from the same impairment of legal interests that makes the Nation a necessary party under Rule 19(a)(2)(I). A decision rendered in this case prejudices the Nation's economic interests in the lease with SRP, namely its ability to provide employment and income for the reservation. A decision so rendered would also prejudice the Nation's sovereign interests in negotiating contractual obligations and governing the reservation.

Furthermore, the absence of the Nation prejudices SRP by preventing the resolution of its lease obligations. As explained by the district court, "SRP could be faced with an irreconcilable conflict between SRP's obligations to Dawavendewa and others similarly situated and SRP's obligations to the Navajo Nation under the lease." * * *

B. Shaping Relief—No relief mitigates the prejudice. Any decision mollifying Dawavendewa would prejudice the Nation in its contract with SRP and its governance of the tribe. This factor weighs in favor of dismissal.

C. Adequate Relief—No partial relief is adequate. Any type of injunctive relief necessarily results in the above-described prejudice to SRP and the Nation. An award of damages would not resolve SRP's potential liability to other plaintiffs or address the Nation's contention that Title VII does not apply on the reservation.

D. Alternative Forum—Finally, we note that in *Lomayaktewa* * * * we determined that the plaintiff would be without an alternative forum to air his grievances. Nevertheless, * * * we determined that the absent Indian Tribe was indispensable and dismissed the case.

Dawavendewa, on the other hand, may have a viable alternative forum in which to seek redress. Sovereign immunity does not apply in a suit brought by the United States. Moreover, recently, in *EEOC v. Karuk Tribe Hous. Auth.*, 260 F.3d 1071, 1075 (9th Cir. 2001), we held that because no principle of law "differentiates a federal agency such as the

EEOC from 'the United States itself,' " tribal sovereign immunity does not apply in suits brought by the EEOC.

At the eleventh hour, the EEOC moved to intervene in an effort to salvage Dawavendewa's case and possibly combine it with other pending litigation. Although we denied that motion, we note that nothing precludes Dawavendewa from refiling his suit in conjunction with the EEOC.[4]

Recognizing the resources and aggravation consumed in relitigating, however, we determine that factor four remains in equipoise. Balancing these four factors, we find the Nation is indispensable, and in "equity and good conscience," this action should not proceed in its absence. Dawavendewa is not entitled to attorney's fees.

CONCLUSION

We affirm the district court's decision to dismiss Dawavendewa's complaint for failure to join the Nation as an indispensable party.

Notes and Questions

1. You may have been surprised to see that the plaintiff in *Dawavendewa* was claiming discrimination on the basis of national origin rather than discrimination based on race. That claim reflects the somewhat unique status of Indians in United States law. Federally-recognized Indian tribes are treated as sovereign, with limited rights of self-governance. The employment preference at issue in *Dawavendewa* turned on membership in the tribe, not ethnicity. Although membership in a tribe may turn in part on a person's heritage, one's status as an "Indian" (that is, a member of a recognized tribe) is considered a political, rather than racial, classification. *Cf. Morton v. Mancari*, 417 U.S. 535, 94 S.Ct. 2474, 41 L.Ed.2d 290 (1974).

The sovereign status of Indian tribes also plays a part in another significant aspect of the case. Indian tribes have a form of sovereign immunity that shields them from any suits in state court, and virtually all suits in federal court. Because of the tribe's immunity, the parties could not force the tribe into the case. The court accordingly had to decide whether the case could proceed without the tribe as a party.

2. *Necessary party as a defense.* Who invoked Rule 19 in *Dawavendewa*, and how did they invoke it? Unlike almost every other joinder rule, Rule 19 arises as a **defense** in the case. Like the defenses of subject matter jurisdiction or failure to state a claim, a party invokes Rule 19 to object to the claim brought against it. The party is objecting because that claim also involves the rights of third persons who have not been made parties to the suit. Because of the collateral effects of the case, the party who raises the defense of failure to join a necessary party is asking the court to order that the third persons be joined to the case—and if such joinder cannot be

---

4. Moreover, Dawavendewa may * * * bring suit in tribal court and after an adverse decision, Dawavendewa could allege sufficient actions by tribal officials, i.e., Navajo Supreme Court Justices, to sustain his action. See also *National Farmers Union Ins. v. Crow Tribe of Indians*, 471 U.S. 845, 856–57, 105 S.Ct. 2447 (1985).

effected, that the case be dismissed. In most cases the actual joinder of the person will occur not under Rule 19, but under some other rule, usually Rules 20 or 24.

However, as discussed below in note 8, Rule 19 also provides a way to join a party to the case in situations not covered by any other joinder rule. Thus, although primarily a defense, Rule 19 also serves as a joinder rule in some cases.

3. Rule 19 uses a functional three-part test. First, the court asks whether a person should be joined to the case. If the person should be joined, he is considered necessary and should be made a party to the case. Second, the court determines if the party can be joined. Third, and only if the necessary party is not joined, the court considers whether it should dismiss the case, applying the factors used in Rule 19(b). If the court decides that it cannot proceed without the party, the party is deemed indispensable. Note that under the Rule 19 analysis, the terms "necessary" and "indispensable" are little more than conclusory labels. In fact, you might be better off leaving the word "indispensable" out of your analysis altogether.

A necessary party problem has something of a jurisdictional flavor under the Federal Rules. Under Rule 12(h)(2), a party cannot waive a necessary parties problem by raising other defenses. In addition, the party can raise the necessary party defense as late as the trial. Therefore, as far as timing is concerned, a necessary party defense is more like the defense of failure to state a claim than it is like the defense of improper venue. Is there any justification to allow a party to wait until trial to raise a defense of failure to join a necessary party?

4. *Step 1: Rule 19(a).* Rule 19(a) specifies three different tests for determining if a party should be joined. The court in *Dawavadewena* analyzes all three. Was that analysis necessary? Does the rule require that the missing person meet all three tests, or will meeting one of the three suffice?

5. *Intervention of Right and Rule 19(a).* Compare Rule 19(a)(2)(i) to Rule 24(a)(2), which governs intervention of right. The similarity is striking. Moreover, both rules were revamped in 1966 to include this similar language. Does this symmetry mean that the two rules are interpreted the same way? The Advisory Committee that drafted the amendments certainly thought so:

> The amendment provides that an applicant is entitled to intervene in an action when his position is comparable to that of a person under Rule 19(a)(2)(i), as amended, unless his interest is already adequately represented in the action by existing parties.

Advisory Committee Notes to 1966 Amendments to Rule 24. Most courts also interpret the two rules in the same way. *See, e.g., Atlantis Development Corp. v. United States,* 379 F.2d 818, 825 (5th Cir. 1967) ("Although this is question-begging and therefore not a real test, this approach shows that the question of whether an intervention as a matter of right exists often turns on the unstated question of whether joinder of the intervenor was called for under new Rule 19."); *Metropolitan Life Ins. Co. v. Ditmore,* 729 F.2d 1, 9 (1st Cir. 1984); *Taco Bell Corp. v. Continental Casualty Co.,* 2003 WL 124454

*8 (N.D. IL); *UNI Storebrand Ins. Co. v. Star Terminal Corp.*, 1997 WL 391125 (S.D. NY) *c.f. International Brotherhood of Teamsters v. Keystone Freight Lines, Inc.*, 123 F.2d 326, 329 (10th Cir. 1941) (similar analysis under pre–1966 version of Rules).

However, as the Advisory Committee notes indicate, there is one significant difference between the two rules. Although a party who can intervene of right is always necessary under Rule 19(a)(2)(i), the converse is not true. A party who is necessary under Rule 19(a)(2)(i) cannot intervene of right if her interests are adequately represented by one or more existing parties. Does that difference make sense? Why should the parties be forced to add that person to the case, which can raise personal jurisdiction and venue problems, when the person is willing to intervene and thereby waive any personal jurisdiction and venue objections?

Note that even though Rule 19 does not mention adequate representation, some courts will consider whether a necessary party's interests are adequately represented when applying the rule. However, it is unclear whether adequate representation factors into the issue of whether the party is necessary under Rule 19(a), or whether it only affects whether the court should dismiss under Rule 19(b). For an excellent discussion of this issue, see *Glancy v. Taubman Centers*, 373 F.3d 656, 666–70 (6th Cir. 2004) (after surveying practice in other circuits, considers representation for purposes of Rule 19(b)).

Incidentally, there is a third Federal Rule that uses language similar to Rules 19(a)(2)(i) and 24(a)(2). Rule 23(a) lists various situations in which a case may be certified as a class action. One of these situations, covered by Rule 23(a)(1)(B), is when "the prosecution of separate actions by or against individual members of the class would create a risk of * * * adjudications with respect to individual members of the class which would * * * substantially impede their ability to protect their interests." In essence, this Rule allows for use of the class action device when the case involves so many necessary parties that joinder of all of them as individual parties is impracticable. Class actions are covered in Part D of this chapter. Is there a difference between Rule 23(a)(1)(B)'s requirement of *substantial* impairment and the requirement of Rules 19(a) and 24(a)?

6. Is there something facile about the way the court in *Dawavendewa* deals with the issue of impairment of the Nation's interest? In Part I.A, the court notes that because the Navajo Nation would not be bound by a judgment rendered in its absence, Dawavendewa could not obtain the relief he wanted. In Part I.B, however, the court notes that the suit affects the Nation's interest in enforcing its contract. If the Nation is not bound by the judgment, would it not be free to sue SRP for enforcement of the lease? Does the impairment arise from the simple fact that the Nation may now have to go to court to enforce its contractual rights? Or is this another example of how *stare decisis* can be enough to impair someone's interest?

7. The plaintiff in *Dawavendewa* sought injunctive relief. What if plaintiff had instead sought only damages? Would the Navajo Nation still have been a necessary party? Is the presence of the Nation required for defendant to pay damages? Would a judgment for damages leave defendant exposed to double liability?

If you understand why the Navajo Nation would not have been a necessary party in a suit for damages, can you ever conceive of a situation where a party would be necessary in a suit seeking only damages?

8. *Step 2: Joining the necessary party.* If a person is deemed necessary under any of the three criteria set out in Rule 19(a), that person must be made a party if possible. When would it *not* be possible to join the person? The joinder rules are rarely the issue. If the missing person should be a defendant, the plaintiff can use Rule 20 to join her. Do you see why a person who is a necessary defendant will always meet the requirements of Rule 20?

If the necessary party should be a plaintiff, things are slightly more difficult. Admittedly, nothing in the other joinder rules allows a current plaintiff unilaterally to add another plaintiff. However, the plaintiff can offer to allow the person to join as co-plaintiff under Rule 20. Similarly, as discussed above in Note 5, the person will normally be able to intervene of right, or the court may invite the person to intervene by permission under Rule 24(b). Because the case will affect the person's rights, the person may well accept the invitation. Even if the necessary party refuses to join as a plaintiff, Rule 19 allows the court to make the person an "involuntary plaintiff." This provision is the one exception to the basic principle, set out in note 2 above, that Rule 19 is a defense rather than a joinder rule. The involuntary plaintiff language of Rule 19 provides for a form of joinder not contemplated under any other joinder rule.

The more likely obstacles to joinder of the necessary party are jurisdiction and venue.* Subject matter jurisdiction problems arise mainly in federal court, especially when jurisdiction over the pending case is based on diversity. Adding the necessary party may destroy complete diversity. Moreover, supplemental jurisdiction may not be an option because of the § 1367(b) diversity exception to supplemental jurisdiction. That exception, as you recall, prohibits the use of supplemental jurisdiction over certain claims involving joinder under listed rules. Section 1367(b) specifically includes Rule 19 among that list ("claims by plaintiffs against persons made parties under Rule 14, *19*, 20, or 24 * * * or over claims *by persons proposed to be joined as plaintiffs under Rule 19 * * * *"*).

Personal jurisdiction problems are also relatively commonplace. If the necessary party voluntarily intervenes or joins the complaint as a co-plaintiff, she waives any personal jurisdiction problems. However, personal jurisdiction is an issue if the necessary party is joined as a defendant or an involuntary plaintiff. In these situations, if the necessary party does not have contacts with the chosen forum, the court cannot effectively join her to the case either as a new defendant or as an involuntary plaintiff.

---

* *Eds.* Note that subject matter jurisdiction and personal jurisdiction are issues notwithstanding some ambiguous language in the introductory clause of Rule 19(a). That clause seems to say that a person is not necessary if the court cannot assert jurisdiction over the person or the subject matter. Courts simply ignore this language. If a party otherwise meets the standard of Rule 19(a), the party should be joined. If subject matter and/or personal jurisdiction are not present, the court then considers whether to dismiss under Rule 19(b). Indeed, a contrary reading would suggest that a court could always keep a case if it could not exercise subject matter jurisdiction or personal jurisdiction after joinder, and would only consider dismissing if the person could not be joined because of venue.

Rule 19 specifically deals with venue. If the addition of the necessary party destroys venue, and the necessary party thereby objects, the last sentence of Rule 19(a) provides that the court will dismiss the party from the action. However, because the necessary party is not in the case, the court must then turn to the third part of the analysis, and determine whether to keep the remainder of the case.

9. *Failure to intervene.* As the prior note demonstrates, nothing in the joinder rules allows a court to force someone to intervene. Could a court nevertheless provide a strong incentive to intervene by use of the doctrine of claim preclusion? In other words, could a court rule that if a party is offered a chance to intervene but refuses to do so, she cannot bring her claim to court in a subsequent proceeding?

In *Martin v. Wilks*, 490 U.S. 755, 109 S.Ct. 2180, 104 L.Ed.2d 835 (1989), the Supreme Court held that it would violate a person's right to due process for a court to bar that person from litigating his rights merely because he did not intervene in a prior case that affected those rights. After *Martin*, then, a necessary party who refuses to intervene is entitled to his day in court.

10. *Step 3: Deciding whether to dismiss.* If a person should be joined, but cannot be joined because of lack of jurisdiction or venue, Rule 19(b) provides that the court must decide whether it can continue to hear the remainder of the case. That rule also lists four factors that the court considers in making that determination. Review the *Dawavendewa* court's discussion of the four factors, and see if you understand what each involves.

Note that although the second factor—altering the nature of the judgment—did not solve the problem in *Dawavendewa*, in other cases it can prove quite useful. For example, suppose that P sues D for an order requiring D to deliver a valuable jewel. The jewel, however, has already been conveyed to X. X is a necessary party to this suit. However, if damages would fully compensate P for her loss, the court can alter the form of relief and obviate the necessary party problem.

Another option under this second factor would be for the court to order the party raising the Rule 19 objection to *interplead* the existing and missing parties. As you will see in Part C of this chapter, interpleader is a useful joinder device that can solve many necessary party problems. For some reason, however, courts rarely force parties to interplead.

11. *Other compulsory joinder provisions.* Note that Rule 19 is not the only law requiring joinder of nonparties to a case. In some situations, a legislature may recognize that a proceeding will affect outsiders, and require joinder of those outsiders by statute. See, for example, the Kentucky champerty statute, KRS § 372.070. Under that statute, a creditor who seeks to bring proceedings to foreclose or execute on land owned by a debtor must join to that action anyone in actual possession of the property. Would a person in possession be necessary under either the common-law approach or Rule 19? What if the person was in adverse possession of the land?

Problems

1. P is seriously burned when his toaster malfunctions. P sues D Corp., the company that manufactured the toaster. D argues that R, the retailer

who sold the toaster to P, should be joined to the case as an additional defendant. D's defense rests entirely on its assertion that R stored the toaster in a damp storeroom, leading to excess condensation that caused the toaster to short circuit in P's home. Is R a necessary party? If R is necessary and cannot be joined, should the case be dismissed?

2.   Same facts as Problem 1, except that the suit occurs in a jurisdiction that uses comparative fault. D realizes that the jury may find it partially at fault for designing a toaster that was susceptible to condensation. However, D argues that it is necessary to join R to the case in order for the jury accurately to apportion fault. D correctly points out that if the jury in this case found D, for example, 80% negligent, the jury in a separate case against R might find R only 10% at fault. D argues that the possibility of inconsistency makes it necessary for P to sue both defendants simultaneously. Is R a necessary party? If R is necessary and cannot be joined, should the case be dismissed?

3.   D Corp. is involved in another case. For many years, D has sold toasters by phone order. D holds the toll-free number 800–TOASTER for use in its phone order operations. D has advertised its phone order service extensively for many years, with most of its ads prominently displaying the 800 number.

Earlier this year, Kitchens Online, an internet seller, registered a number of domain names. One of the domain names it registered was www.800toaster.com. A number of D Corp.'s customers happened onto this site, thinking that it was operated by D Corp. Customer confusion is exacerbated by the fact that D Corp. and Kitchens Online are citizens of the same state. To stop the confusion, D has sued Network Solutions, Inc. ("NSI"), the company that allocates domain names, in federal court for an injunction requiring NSI to cancel Kitchen Online's 800toaster.com domain name, and assign it instead to D Corp. D relies solely on state law for its claim. NSI moves to dismiss for failure to join Kitchens Online. Is Kitchens Online a necessary party? If Kitchens Online is necessary, how would it be joined to the case? If Kitchens Online is necessary and cannot be joined, should the case be dismissed?

4.   Same as Problem 3, except that D Corp. sues for damages rather than an injunction.

C.   INTERPLEADER

INTRODUCTORY PROBLEM

Truth is sometimes stranger than fiction. Consider the following facts from the actual case of *Republican National Committee v. Taylor*, 299 F.3d 887 (D.C. Cir. 2002):

In December 1995, the Republican National Committee ran an advertisement in the newspapers *USA Today* and *Roll Call*. * * * Prominently featured at the top of the ad is a photograph of Haley Barbour, then chair of the RNC, holding an oversized check for one million dollars, payable to "your name here." Next to and below Barbour's image, the following text appears:

Heard the one about Republicans 'cutting' Medicare? The fact is Republicans are increasing Medicare spending by more than half. I'm Haley Barbour, and I'm so sure of that fact I'm willing to give you this check for a million dollars if you can prove me wrong.

The advertisement goes on to assert that under the Republican plan, the government would increase Medicare spending over the next seven fiscal years, culminating in a 2002 expenditure 62% higher than that in 1995. * * *

The ad then invites readers who disagree with the [statement] to check a box labeled "I don't believe you, Haley" and return the coupon with their analyses of "why you are wrong" to the RNC's Washington, D.C. address.

Approximately eighty people across the country did not believe Haley and mailed in claims for the million-dollar prize. The RNC responded to each claimant by sending him or her a form letter rejecting the claim as incorrect, and enclosing a Congressional Budget Office report. * * * [O]ne rejected claimant filed a breach of contract suit in the Superior Court of the District of Columbia * * *.

The RNC * * * [claims]: (1) that the advertisement was merely a "parody" and not binding on the RNC; and (2) that even if the ad were an offer to contract, the Challenge Statement was not false.

In this situation, the RNC quite rightly fears that multiple lawsuits will be filed against it all over the country. Is there anything the RNC can do to force all claimants to litigate their claims in the same action? Does it matter that there is no single state that could exercise personal jurisdiction over all of the claimants?

Governing Rules: Federal Rule 22; 28 U.S.C. §§ 1335, 1397, 2361. *Note*: Although the RNC invoked these rules in the actual case, the court does not discuss the issue of whether the case satisfied those rules.

STAR INSURANCE CO. v. CEDAR VALLEY EXPRESS, LLC

273 F.Supp.2d 38 (D.D.C. 2002)

SULLIVAN, District Judge.

Pending before the Court are plaintiff's motion to interplead defendants pursuant to 28 U.S.C. § 1335 and deposit the interpleaded funds into the registry of the Court, as well as plaintiff's motion for a preliminary injunction. * * *

I. BACKGROUND

Plaintiff, Star Insurance Company, a Michigan corporation, alleges that on September 20th, 2000, * * * it issued Property Broker's Surety

Bond No. SA3158428 to defendant Cedar Valley Express, LLC, an Iowa corporation. It further alleges that approximately 35 parties, consisting of corporations located in at least 13 different states, have asserted adverse and conflicting claims against the bond, which, in the aggregate, exceed the bond's penal sum of $10,000. Asserting that it is unable to adjudicate the parties' claimed interests in the proceeds of the bond, and that it will therefore be exposed to unnecessarily vexatious and duplicative litigation, plaintiff has filed this action pursuant to the Federal Interpleader Act, 28 U.S.C. § 1335.

II. PLAINTIFF'S MOTION TO FILE INTERPLEADER

* * * An action in the nature of interpleader is proper where a party is exposed to multiple claims on a single obligation, and wishes to obtain adjudication of such claims and its obligation in a single proceeding. Interpleader is an equitable remedy that may be used to achieve an orderly distribution of a limited fund, usually on a ratable basis. Such an action may be brought in a U.S. District Court under the Federal Interpleader Act, 28 U.S.C. § 1335, provided the jurisdictional requirements set out therein are established.[1]

Generally speaking, there are two stages in an interpleader action. The first stage involves a determination of whether the plaintiff has met the statutory prerequisites for the invocation of the interpleader remedy.[2] The District Court's exercise of jurisdiction over a statutory interpleader action requires that: (1) the plaintiff have custody of the disputed property, which must exceed $500 in value; (2) the plaintiff deposit the disputed property into the registry of the court; and (3) two or more adverse claimants of diverse citizenship claim or may claim an interest in the disputed property. 28 U.S.C. § 1335.

The District Court's jurisdiction in a statutory interpleader action is premised on diversity of citizenship. However, complete diversity is not required, and the courts have adopted a standard of "minimal diversity," under which it is sufficient that at least two opposing claimants be of diverse citizenship. *State Farm Fire & Casualty Co. v. Tashire*, 386 U.S. 523, 530 (1967). Therefore, jurisdiction is proper in a case where, as here, some claimants share citizenship with each other, the plaintiff, or both, so long as at least two of the claimants are citizens of different states.

Additionally, the statute requires that claimants be "adverse" to each other, although their claims need only be independent of each

---

1. Such an action is known as "statutory interpleader," to distinguish it from "rule interpleader," an action brought pursuant to Fed.R.Civ.P. 22, which implicates different jurisdictional requirements.

2. The second stage of an interpleader action consists of a determination of the respective rights of the claimants to the disputed property. * * * Once a court determines that interpleader is appropriate, it may discharge the stakeholder-plaintiff from the action if it is disinterested in the distribution of the subject matter, permanently enjoin the parties from prosecuting any other claim relating to the subject matter, and make any other order it deems appropriate to the resolution of the issues. 28 U.S.C. § 2361.

other, and need not have a common origin or be identical. 28 U.S.C. § 1335(b). Claimants need not have obtained a judgment with respect to the subject matter of the interpleader action, nor does it appear that they need to have actually initiated legal action against the stakeholder with respect to the disputed property. The adversity requirement is met so long as the stakeholder has a " 'bona fide' fear of adverse claims arising with respect to the res." *New Jersey Sports Prod., Inc. [v. Don King Prod., Inc.* 15 F.Supp.2d 534 (D. N.J. 1998)] at 541.

Although the party seeking to institute an interpleader action bears the burden of demonstrating that the statutory requirements are satisfied, there is no set procedure governing how the court is to decide the jurisdictional question. * * * All parties must receive notice and an opportunity to be heard on the issue of the appropriateness of an interpleader action before a court's final determination with respect to jurisdiction.

Even if all of the jurisdictional requirements are established, acceptance of jurisdiction over a statutory interpleader action is by no means mandatory: "the mere fact that [a court] possesses jurisdiction over the subject matter of an equitable action of interpleader does not require that the [c]ourt should exercise that jurisdiction ... some courts have, in their discretion, dismissed interpleader actions for want of equity because an adequate remedy at law existed, even though the required jurisdictional facts were proven." *Prudential Ins. Co. of Am. v. Shawver,* 208 F.Supp. 464, 469 (W.D.Mo.1962).

However, a court may provisionally accept jurisdiction over an action in the nature of interpleader where the plaintiff has alleged that the jurisdictional requirements of Section 1335 are met, and the plaintiff has deposited an appropriate sum with the registry of the court. The court may then issue nationwide service of process for all claimants to the disputed property pursuant to 28 U.S.C. § 2361.[4] Where potential claimants are unknown, notice by publication may be required. The court may subsequently require the parties to brief any jurisdictional issues before it renders its final decision with respect to whether plaintiff has met the statutory requirements for bringing an action in the nature of interpleader, and whether it chooses to exercise that jurisdiction.

Plaintiff in this case has requested permission to deposit with the court registry the full penal value of a $10,000 bond, against which it alleges the putative defendants, at least two of whom appear to be citizens of different states, have asserted adverse claims. The complaint therefore appears, on its face, to meet the jurisdictional requirements of Section 1335, rendering it proper for this Court to provisionally accept jurisdiction over the action, order the plaintiff to deposit $10,000 into

---

4. Although 28 U.S.C. § 2361 provides for issuance of process addressed to and served by the United States marshals for the respective districts where the claimants reside or may be found, it appears to be the practice of plaintiffs in interpleader actions to directly serve process on claimants, without burdening the U.S. marshals.

the court registry, and issue summons to all claimants named in the complaint.

The Court is permitting plaintiff to proceed with an action in the nature of interpleader pursuant to 28 U.S.C. § 1335 on a provisional basis only. The Court will make a final determination with respect to whether the jurisdictional requirements of 28 U.S.C. § 1335 have been met once all parties have been afforded notice of the action and an opportunity to be heard on the jurisdictional issues.

III. PLAINTIFF'S MOTION FOR PRELIMINARY INJUNCTION

* * * The Federal Interpleader Act authorizes a U.S. District Court to enter both preliminary and permanent injunctions restraining claimants from instituting or prosecuting any proceeding in any state or federal court affecting the subject matter of an interpleader action. 28 U.S.C. § 2361. The Court has "extensive discretion under Section 2361 with respect to the issuance and scope of the order." 7 Wright, Miller & Kane, *Federal Practice & Procedure: Civil* § 1717.

A preliminary injunction may be issued without notice to the putative defendants in the action, for Fed.R.Civ.P. 65 does not modify Section 2361, which in turn provides for entry and of a preliminary injunction order at the same time as summons are issued by the court.

However, "[t]his does not mean ... that the practice under Section 2361 should be without any notice or provision for hearing in all cases. The practice in actions under the Interpleader Act is still governed by principles of equity practice." *Shawver*, 208 F.Supp. at 470. Therefore, courts are urged to exercise judicial discretion and restraint when issuing such orders, balancing equitable considerations against temporal and spatial constraints which may weigh against notice and a hearing. "A request for an injunction may be refused if there is no real threat of litigation relating to the subject matter of the interpleader suit or if a previously commenced action will afford the parties effective relief." 7 Wright, Miller & Kane, *Federal Practice & Procedure: Civil* § 1717. * * *

A number of policy considerations underlying the adoption of the interpleader statute weigh in favor of immediately granting a provisional preliminary injunction without notice to the claimants, as requested by plaintiff in this case. The Supreme Court has emphasized that the difficulties posed in a case where an earlier claimant may appropriate all, or a disproportionate slice, of a fund before fellow claimants are able to establish their claims, potentially leading to a "race to judgment" and unfairness to some claimants, "were among the principal evils the interpleader device was intended to remedy." *Tashire*, 386 U.S. at 533. This Circuit has stated that "the interpleader statute is liberally construed to protect the stakeholder from the expense of defending twice, as well a to protect him from double liability." *New York Life Ins. Co. v. Welch*, 297 F.2d 787, 790 (D.C.Cir.1961). * * * Maintenance of the status quo while jurisdictional questions are resolved through issuance of a provisional preliminary injunction is one means of vindicating the policy considerations underlying the Federal Interpleader Act.

Courts have also considered the counterbalancing policy in favor of vindicating of claimants' interest in pursuing claims in the forum of their choice. This interest carries greater weight once a claimant has already instituted an action, or when the plaintiff seeks an injunction extending to suits against an insured party, stakeholder, or both, rather than one restricted to potential actions regarding the disputed *res*.[5]

The plaintiff in this case does not seek to preclude actions unrelated to the bond against itself or Cedar Valley Express, the bond principal. Therefore, any factors that would counsel against the use of the Court's "extraordinary powers" under Section 2361 do not carry substantial weight in the determination of whether a preliminary injunction should issue in this case.

* * * [T]he Court reiterates that this preliminary injunction is issued on a provisional basis only, and will remain in effect only until jurisdictional questions are resolved. At that point, the injunction's continued operation will be revisited upon proper motion of counsel or of this Court. * * *

ORDER

Upon careful consideration of plaintiff's motion to file interpleader action and motion for preliminary injunction and the applicable statutory and case law, it is hereby ORDERED that plaintiff's motion to file interpleader action, and to deposit funds into the registry of the court is GRANTED until further order of this Court; and it is FURTHER ORDERED that and plaintiff's motion for a preliminary injunction is GRANTED until further order of this Court; and it is FURTHER ORDERED that plaintiff shall deposit into the registry of the Court funds equivalent to $10,000 penal value of Property Broker's Surety Bond No. SA3158428 issued by the plaintiff to defendant Cedar Valley Express, LLC; and it is FURTHER ORDERED that the Clerk of the Court shall receive and invest these funds so that interest may accrue, for ultimate disposition by order of this Court in the above-captioned case; and it is FURTHER ORDERED that plaintiff shall serve a copy of this order on all defendants named in this action; and it is FURTHER ORDERED that all defendants named in this action are hereby ENJOINED from instituting or prosecuting any action in any state or federal district court affecting plaintiff's surety obligations under Property Broker's Surety Bond No. SA3158428 until further order of this Court; and it is FURTHER ORDERED that all parties to this matter

---

5. Finally, courts have also weighed considerations of comity and deference to state courts when determining whether a preliminary injunction should issue in interpleader actions. In light of these concerns, some have held that, where a state action commenced prior to the interpleader action provides an adequate remedy, an interpleader action, and by extension, a preliminary injunction, is not appropriate. See *New Jersey Sports Prod.*, 15 F.Supp.2d at 542. However, there is no indication that any of the alleged claimants in this case have instituted any actions affecting the bond at issue in either state or federal court.

shall file submissions addressing the basis for this Court's jurisdiction under 28 U.S.C. § 1335, as well as the necessity and propriety of the continued operation of the preliminary injunction hereby issued, by no later than NOVEMBER 1, 2002.

Overview of Interpleader

If you feel at this juncture that interpleader is hopelessly complex, rest assured you are not alone. Many first-year law students find interpleader somewhat daunting at first. Part of the confusion stems from the fact that interpleader has several different facets. First, interpleader has its own *language*, with the courts referring to the parties as "claimants" and "stakeholders" rather than the typical plaintiff and defendant. Second, it can be difficult for the novice to figure out exactly when the joinder device of interpleader is proper. Finally, as if matters were not complicated enough, there are special rules that govern jurisdiction and venue in interpleader cases.

Notwithstanding these idiosyncrasies, interpleader is no more difficult than any of the other devices covered in this chapter. Before delving into the nuances, it may be helpful to view the big picture with a few basic observations.

Conceptually, interpleader is designed to deal with situations where more than one person claims the same "thing," but by law only one (or at least fewer than all) of those people is entitled to receive that thing. In this respect, interpleader is a corollary to the necessary party and intervention of right rules, which can also cover this situation. If each of the people claiming the thing is allowed to proceed in a separate action, then the person who possesses that thing might be exposed to multiple liability.

That basic nature of interpleader gives rise to the special language. The *stake* is the thing over which the parties are fighting. The *stakeholder* is the party who possesses the stake. The *claimants* are those who claim to be entitled to the stake.

Historically, the stakeholder could not use interpleader if he also claimed any interest in the stake. In modern practice, this requirement has been relaxed. Now, the stakeholder can claim that none of the claimants is entitled to the stake, and that he should be able to keep it.

As a joinder device, interpleader allows the stakeholder to join all the claimants into a single action, allowing one court to determine who owns that stake. In cases where the stakeholder admits that she owes the stake to *someone*, the stakeholder then drops out of the suit and the claimants fight among themselves for the stake. In cases where the stakeholder claims it should get to keep the stake, the stakeholder remains in the suit and asserts its claim.

In many cases, however, the claimants may be scattered all across the United States, or in other nations. This feature of interpleader raises potentially difficult problems of subject-matter jurisdiction, personal jurisdiction, and venue. Because interpleader can prove to be a very useful device in the proper case, Congress responded by enacting special jurisdiction and venue laws for interpleader actions in the federal courts. As you will see later, these laws make it much easier to bring a diversity-based interpleader action in federal court.

Rule 22 of the Federal Rules also deals with interpleader. However, as alluded to in footnote 1 in *Star Insurance*, Rule 22 is *independent* of the federal statutes. In other words, there are two distinct types of interpleader, "statutory" and "Rule." Statutory interpleader, which is available only in federal court, is authorized by 28 U.S.C. § 1335. That statute, along with §§ 1397 and 2361, contain the special jurisdiction and venue rules enacted by Congress to make interpleader easier. Rule interpleader, governed by Rule 22, is subject to the usual rules governing jurisdiction and venue. Because of these differences, it will often be much easier for a stakeholder to bring a particular action as one of statutory interpleader rather than Rule interpleader.

With these basic principles in mind, it is best to divide any question of interpleader into three distinct sub-questions. First, is the dispute a proper one for use of interpleader? Second, if interpleader is proper, can the action be heard in the selected court given subject matter jurisdiction, personal jurisdiction, and venue limitations? And third, if the court can hear the interpleader action, what does it do? May it prevent parallel cases involving one or more of the claimants from proceeding? How does it decide who receives the stake? The following discussion deals with each of these issues in turn.

1. When a Party May Use Interpleader

As discussed above, interpleader deals with situations where several people have filed inconsistent claims to the same "thing." This basic principle applies with equal force to both statutory and Rule interpleader cases. In fact, the question of whether a case is a proper interpleader case is dealt with exactly the same way under both types of interpleader.

If multiple claims to the same stake are litigated in separate cases, the piecemeal litigation poses a threat to both the stakeholder and one or more claimants. The threat to the stakeholder is that both courts will require that the stake be paid or turned over to the respective claimants, resulting in double liability. The threat to the claimants is that a victory for one claimant will effectively bar other claimant's claims to the stake. By allowing all claims to be litigated in a single action, interpleader both prevents inconsistent results and offers the promise of greater efficiency. However, as the following cases demonstrate, efficiency alone will not suffice. It is not enough for the stakeholder to show that she is subject to "multiple claims." Instead, she must demonstrate that those multiple claims lead to legally unacceptable results.

INDIANAPOLIS COLTS V. MAYOR AND CITY COUNCIL OF BALTIMORE, 741 F.2d 954 (7th Cir. 1984). In 1984, the Baltimore Colts, a National Football League team, began negotiations with Indianapolis to move the team to that city. The team signed a lease with CIB, the firm that ran the Hoosier Dome in Indianapolis. Shortly thereafter, the City of Baltimore began eminent domain proceedings against the team, seeking to take over ownership and thereby keep the team in Baltimore. The Colts then filed an interpleader action in the Southern District of Indiana. The Colts argued that they faced multiple liability, for if the eminent domain proceedings were successful, the team would be forced to breach its lease with CIB. The court of appeals disagreed:

> A basic jurisdictional requirement of statutory interpleader is that there be adverse claimants to a particular fund. The CIB and Baltimore are not claimants to the same stake. Baltimore seeks ownership of the Colts franchise, whereas the CIB has no claim to ownership of the franchise. Instead, the CIB has a lease with the Colts that requires the team to play its games in the Hoosier Dome and imposes other obligations to ensure the success of the enterprise. * * *

> Interpleader is a suit in equity. Because the sole basis for equitable relief to the stakeholder is the danger of exposure to double liability or the vexation of conflicting claims, the stakeholder must have a real and reasonable fear of double liability or vexatious, conflicting claims to justify interpleader.

FIRST INTERSTATE BANK OF OREGON, N.A. V. HOYT & SONS RANCH PROPERTIES NEVADA, LTD., 891 F.Supp. 543 (D. Or. 1995). Hoyt maintained a checking account at First Interstate Bank of Oregon ("FIOR"). The Internal Revenue Service levied on the account, claiming that Hoyt owed over a million dollars in overdue taxes. When FIOR notified Hoyt that it planned to honor the levy, Hoyt threatened to sue FIOR. FIOR then attempted to interplead the United States and Hoyt. The federal government objected to use of the interpleader device. It pointed out that a federal statute, 26 U.S.C. § 6332(e), would shield FIOR from any liability to Hoyt if it honored the levy. Therefore, the government claimed, FIOR could not be held liable to both the IRS and Hoyt. The court disagreed, holding that interpleader was proper:

> [I]nterpleader is to be granted in instances where a stakeholder faces a legitimate fear of multiple litigation, irrespective of the merits of the competing claims. See generally 3A James Wm. Moore & Jo D. Lucas, Moore's Federal Practice §§ 22.02[1] (2d ed. 1994) (typically, one or more of the claims will be void of merit, "but that alone may not relieve the stakeholder of a substantial risk of vexatious litigation"). The record before this court clearly reflects that FIOR faced a real possibility of defending an unwanted lawsuit had it simply remitted the disputed funds to the IRS. Indeed, Hoyt explicitly informed FIOR that by honoring the levy it would be inviting litigation. * * *

In sum, because FIOR legitimately feared that the competing claims to the disputed funds might expose it to multiple liability or multiple litigation, and because FIOR instituted this interpleader action in good faith to resolve the competing claims, it is entitled to be discharged from liability.

Notes and Questions

1. The *Star Insurance* opinion does not address whether interpleader was proper. Do you see why there was no real question as to whether interpleader was available in that case?

2. While carelessly careening down a city street one day, Reckless Rex causes a multiple vehicle pileup. Total damages exceed $1,000,000, and it is clear that Rex is solely at fault. Rex has only $5,000 in assets to his name. In addition, Rex has a liability insurance policy with NeverPay, Inc., with a policy limit of $10,000 per person and $30,000 per incident. Based on the discussion in *Indianapolis Colts* and *First Interstate Bank*, may Rex and/or NeverPay interplead all of the victims of the accident, in order to avoid paying out more than $5,000 and $30,000, respectively?

3. If you recognized that the insurance company has a much stronger argument for interpleader in the prior note than the insured, you are well on the way to understanding interpleader. But before you conclude that interpleader will be available in all types of insurance cases, consider another feature of liability insurance. When you purchase a policy of liability insurance, you are purchasing much more than a right to indemnity for any liability you may incur. In addition, the insurance company agrees to defend you from any lawsuits, including paying your attorneys' fees. In many cases this duty to defend is far more valuable than the amount of indemnity. Should the insurance company be able to avoid this important obligation under the policy by turning over the policy limits to the court and washing its hands of the whole mess? See *Emcasco Insurance Co. v. Davis*, 753 F.Supp. 1458 (W.D. Ark. 1990).

4. Note that not all courts agree with *First Interstate Bank* that a threat of multiple inconsistent litigation is enough to invoke interpleader. Some only allow interpleader if there is a chance that the stakeholder might actually be subjected to multiple liability. *See, e.g., Alfa Financial Corp. v. Key*, 927 F.Supp. 423 (M.D. Ala. 1996); *Mt. Hawley Ins. Co. v. Federal Savings & Loan Insurance Corp.*, 695 F.Supp. 469 (C.D. Cal. 1987).

5. As the *Star Insurance* case indicates, a party who desires to use interpleader need not wait until all the claimants have actually filed suit. As long as the stakeholder has a reasonable apprehension of multiple suits, she may use interpleader.

6. How does the stakeholder actually effect interpleader? If the stakeholder has been sued by one or more claimants, Rule 22 makes it clear that she may file the interpleader as a counterclaim or cross-claim in that suit. In the alternative, the stakeholder may initiate a new action of interpleader in a court of her choosing. The latter option is available even if the stakeholder has already been sued in one or more separate actions.

In addition, the stakeholder may be required to deposit the stake with the court. On this issue, there is a slight, but potentially important, difference between statutory and rule interpleader. Deposit of the stake is explicitly required by § 1335(a)(2) in statutory interpleader cases. In Rule interpleader, by contrast, it is up to the discretion of the court whether to require deposit. This difference might prove important to a stakeholder who is fairly certain that he is entitled to keep the stake, and wants to use it during the pendency of the case.

7. *Interpleader evolved in equity.* Because of concerns about overreaching its authority, the courts of equity imposed certain strict requirements on use of the device:

> Historically, a bill of interpleader was an equitable device whose purpose was "the avoidance of the burden of unnecessary litigation or the risk of loss by the establishment of multiple liability when only a single obligation is owing." *Texas v. Florida*, 306 U.S. 398, 412 (1939). As "strict" interpleader evolved, it was available to a plaintiff when (1) the same debt or duty was demanded by all of the defendants, (2) all of the defendants' adverse titles or claims were derived from or dependent upon a common source, (3) the plaintiff was a neutral stakeholder, asserting no claim of its own to the fund or property against which the defendants made claims, and (4) the plaintiff had no independent liability to any of the defendants.

> As "equity extended its jurisdiction," the third of these requirements was relaxed, and a bill "in the nature of interpleader" became available in order to "guard against the risks of loss from the prosecution in independent suits of rival claims where the plaintiff himself claimed an interest in the property or fund which was subjected to the risk." *Texas v. Florida*, 306 U.S. at 406–07. Whether "strict" or merely "in the nature of," however, in each instance the goal of interpleader was to protect the plaintiff from "the risk of multiple suits when the liability was single." Id. at 406.

> Since the 1930's, interpleader has been authorized both by statute, see 28 U.S.C. § 1335 (1988), and by Fed. R. Civ. P. 22. Both the statute and the Rule further relax some of the classic prerequisites for interpleader. To the extent pertinent here, Rule 22 provides as follows:

>> Persons having claims against the plaintiff may be joined as defendants and required to interplead when their claims are such that the plaintiff is or may be exposed to double or multiple liability. It is not ground for objection to the joinder that the claims of the several claimants or the titles on which their claims depend do not have a common origin or are not identical but are adverse to and independent of one another.

Bradley v. Kochenash, 44 F.3d 166, 168 (2d Cir. 1995). Because the historical requirements have largely been abandoned in federal court, it is no longer necessary to distinguish between "strict" interpleader actions and actions "in the nature of interpleader." Most states have likewise dispensed with the historical requirements.

2. Jurisdiction and Venue

The most important differences between Rule and statutory interpleader relate to subject matter jurisdiction, personal jurisdiction, and venue. In a Rule interpleader case, the usual rules apply. Therefore, for example, a plaintiff may bring a Rule interpleader case in federal court only if the case either arises under federal law (which is rare) or if diversity exists. Because of the $75,000 amount in controversy requirement and the complete diversity requirement, however, satisfying the requirements for diversity can be difficult. Under the complete diversity rule, diversity jurisdiction is unavailable if even one claimant is a citizen of the same state as the stakeholder.

Personal jurisdiction can prove an even more formidable obstacle, at least where the claimants are from different states. At first glance, it would seem that a court located in the state in which the stake is situated could use *in rem* jurisdiction in interpleader, given that the court is being called upon to determine competing rights in a single stake. However, courts have rejected the use of *in rem* jurisdiction in interpleader, concluding that the action is personal in nature. *Metropolitan Property and Casualty Ins. Co. v. Shan Trac, Inc.*, 324 F.3d 20 (1st Cir. 2003); *Humble Oil & Refining Co. v. Copeland*, 398 F.2d 364, 368 (4th Cir. 1968). Therefore, regardless of whether the stakeholder brings a Rule interpleader case in state or federal court, there must be minimum contacts between every claimant and the chosen forum. To make matters even more difficult, many ''laundry list'' state long-arm statutes contain no specific provisions authorizing service in interpleader cases.

Venue can also pose serious problems in a Rule interpleader case. If the stakeholder is the plaintiff, venue would be proper only in a district where all the claimants reside or a significant portion of the events or omissions giving rise to the claims occurred.

Now carefully read §§ 1335, 1397, and 2361, the provisions governing statutory interpleader. These sections significantly relax the requirements for diversity jurisdiction, personal jurisdiction, and venue in statutory interpleader actions brought in federal court. The *Star Insurance* case contains a good discussion of how the statutes modify the ordinary rules of jurisdiction and venue. You may also find the following chart helpful.

Attribute	*Rule interpleader*	*Statutory interpleader*
Determining diversity	Complete diversity between the stakeholder and all claimants	Minimal diversity among claimants; satisfied if any one claimant is diverse from any other claimant
Amount in controversy (value of stake)	greater than $75,000	at least $500
Personal Jurisdiction	all claimants must have minimum contacts with	nationwide service (§ 2361), not bound by

	state, and state must allow service	state limits (Rule 4(k)(1)(c))
Venue based on residence	where *all* defendants reside	where *any* claimant resides

AMERICAN FAMILY MUTUAL INS. CO. V. ROCHE, 830 F.Supp. 1241 (E.D. Wis. 1993). Roche, an individual, was involved in an automobile accident with four other people (the "Grimms"). Roche had a liability insurance policy with American Family Mutual Insurance Company. Because the Grimms' claims exceed the policy limits, American Family brought a statutory interpleader action against Roche (a Wisconsin citizen) and the Grimms (all Illinois citizens) in federal court. The Grimms challenged subject-matter jurisdiction, arguing that the case did not satisfy § 1335. The court agreed:

> As for diversity, the statute "has been uniformly construed to require only 'minimal diversity,' that is, diversity of citizenship between two or more claimants, without regard to the circumstance that other rival claimants may be co-citizens." *State Farm Fire & Casualty Co. v. Tashire*, 386 U.S. 523, 530, 87 S.Ct. 1199 (1967). "Minimal diversity" is also determined without regard to the stakeholder's citizenship; that is, without regard to the circumstance that the stakeholder and one of the claimants may be co-citizens. * * *

> The foregoing principles narrow the possible bases for the Court's jurisdiction. Assuming for purposes of the motion that the combined value of the Grimms' claims exceeds the policy limits of $300,000, each Grimm would be adverse to the others because each would be competing for portions of a fund that is not large enough to satisfy them all. But while each would be adverse, they would not be diverse, because all of the Grimms reside in Illinois. * * * Thus, jurisdiction is proper only if American Family and the Grimms (who are diverse) can be considered adverse to each other, or if Roche and the Grimms (who are also diverse) can be considered adverse to each other. Neither group can be so considered.

> Since the interpleader statute was amended to expressly include "bills in the nature of interpleader", it is clear that the fact that American Family denies any liability whatsoever, and is therefore not a neutral or disinterested stakeholder, cannot destroy this Court's jurisdiction. * * * [It is also] clear that the citizenship of American Family, as a stakeholder, cannot destroy jurisdiction. What remains unclear, however, is whether the citizenship of American Family, as an interested stakeholder, can create jurisdiction under the statute. American Family claims it can. It reasons that by denying liability it has become a "claimant" to the fund both adverse and diverse to the Grimms. The Supreme Court has not yet answered this interesting question * * *.

> The few courts that have addressed the issue favor letting an interested stakeholder's citizenship create jurisdiction under the statute. * * *

The judicial tendency to expand the jurisdiction of federal interpleader relief when issues such as these arise is somewhat understandable. Because § 1335 developed in equity and is a piece of "remedial legislation," courts generally construe it liberally with an eye towards doing justice. Nevertheless, this Court disagrees with other courts and commentators who would hold that American Family's citizenship can be used to create interpleader jurisdiction. * * *

[O]ur first consideration must be the language of the statute itself. The statute requires "two or more adverse claimants, of diverse citizenship. . . ." 28 U.S.C. § 1335(a)(1). What is a claimant? In the insurance context, a claimant is one who is "claiming or may claim to be entitled to . . . any one or more of the benefits arising by virtue of . . . [the] policy. . . ." Can American Family truly be said to claim an entitlement to the benefits of its own policy? Such a position might be defensible if American Family was exercising its subrogation rights or some other "benefit" inuring to itself. But liability coverage? That is a benefit inuring to its insured and those injured by the insured. As such, Roche may claim an entitlement to the benefit. The Grimms may claim an entitlement to the benefit. But American Family cannot. American Family denies the existence of the benefit. The same applies if we focus, as American Family does, on the "fund" at issue, i.e., the $300,000 proceeds of the policy. As stated earlier, "to satisfy the adversity requirement for an interpleader action, the interpleader claims must be adverse to the fund and adverse to each other." *Industrial Bank*, 763 F.Supp. at 634. By denying that coverage exists American Family has clearly stated a claim that is adverse to the Grimms, but how is it adverse to "the fund"? American Family owns "the fund". It seeks to preserve its ownership of "the fund". Indeed, from American Family's perspective, "the fund" does not even exist. It is simply a fiction used as an analytical reference for its potential liability to the real claimants, a liability which American Family denies, and which would in any event be paid out of its general assets. There is no separate, distinguishable "fund" of dollars which American Family now seeks to obtain and add to its own general fund of dollars. The two are the same.

* * * While there are those who might view the foregoing considerations as "metaphysical objections at best", 7 Wright, Miller & Kane at 547, it is a metaphysics compelled by the language of the statute itself, which is the sole source of this Court's jurisdiction. It is also a metaphysics which has (as does all good metaphysics) sound practical consequences. The federal interpleader statute is best viewed as a unique exception to the federalist notion, rooted in exceedingly good policy, that federal courts are courts of limited jurisdiction. That is, the interpleader statute allows a federal court to provide a federal remedy in a dispute which is almost always going to be governed by state law and which is often based on

nothing more than a "minimal diversity" between the disputing parties. This unique exception can be justified in those situations where the only way for the dispute to be finally decided by a single decision emanating from a single court is to allow a federal forum with nationwide service of process. But because alternatives exist, allowing federal interpleader relief based solely on the stakeholder's citizenship sets a dangerous precedent. It would permit a Rule 22 interpleader action absent the necessary jurisdictional amount and thereby alter the prerequisites of federal jurisdiction by judicial decision.

The court also refused to consider Roche's Wisconsin citizenship in determining whether diversity existed, concluding that Roche's interest was not adverse to those of the Grimms.

However, the court noted that jurisdiction might be available if the case had been brought as a Rule interpleader case, as American Family was diverse from all of the Grimms and Roche and the policy limits of $300,000 met the amount in controversy requirement.

Notes and Questions

1. In most other types of joinder, Congress has refrained from tinkering with the complete diversity rule, the limitations on service, and the requirements for venue. Why did Congress make such a significant exception in the case of interpleader? Is there any compelling reason not to relegate these cases to state courts, as often occurs in intervention cases where complete diversity is lacking?

2. As *American Family* indicates, many courts hold that for purposes of determining diversity under § 1335, a stakeholder who has a claim to the stake is also treated as a claimant. Does the same rule apply when determining venue? If so, an interested stakeholder could always bring an interpleader action in the state where he resides, as § 1397 provides that venue is proper in a statutory interpleader action wherever any claimant resides.

In *New Jersey Sports Prod., Inc. v. Don King Prod., Inc.*, 15 F.Supp.2d 534 (D. N.J. 1998), the court held that an interested stakeholder would not be considered a claimant for purposes of § 1397. Can these rulings be reconciled? Does it matter that § 1335 speaks in terms of *adverse* claimants, while § 1397 merely mentions claimants? What about the fact that subject-matter jurisdiction is ultimately limited by the United States Constitution, while venue is a limit that Congress created purely as a convenience to the litigants?

3. So far, our discussion of subject-matter jurisdiction in interpleader has concentrated only on diversity. In ordinary cases, however, federal question jurisdiction also provides a way to get a case into federal court. Can a party use federal question jurisdiction in an interpleader case? The question is more difficult than it may seem at first glance. First, although federal laws such as ERISA (the law that governs employee retirement plans) may determine the claimants' rights to the stake, in a technical sense those federal laws do not give rise to the stakeholder's "claim"–its request

for interpleader relief. Nevertheless, some courts have allowed for federal question jurisdiction when federal law controls who is entitled to the stake. In *Commercial Union Insurance Company v. United States*, 999 F.2d 581 (D.C. Cir. 1993), for example, the court held that interpleader should be treated like a declaratory judgment for purposes of determining federal question jurisdiction. As discussed in Chapter 3, in declaratory judgment cases a court ignores the declaratory relief, and instead tries to determine what action would have eventually have been brought. If that later action would be a federal question, the declaratory judgment is also treated as a federal question. By analogy, if federal law controls the rights of the claimants in an interpleader case, the case presents a federal question, because those claimants could eventually bring a federal question case against the stakeholder.

Federal question jurisdiction is clearly available in Rule interpleader cases. However, *Commercial Union* also suggests that it is not available in statutory interpleader cases. The court's rationale is that § 1335 is itself a jurisdictional statute, which as written ignores whether the claims arise under federal or state law. If that suggestion is correct, it means that the advantageous personal jurisdiction and venue rules are unavailable in cases where the minimum diversity or amount in controversy requirements of § 1335 are not met, even if that case arises under federal law.

4. Recall that under the probate exception to diversity, federal courts will not hear probate cases brought under their diversity jurisdiction. Probate, however, is a fertile breeding ground for conflicting claims, and therefore a common situation in which interpleader may arise. Does the probate exception also apply to cases under the "minimal" diversity standard of § 1335? At least one court has held that interpleader is an exception to the probate exception. *American Financial Life Ins. and Annuity Co. v. Youn*, 7 Fed.Appx. 913, 2001 WL 369826 (10th Cir.) (unpublished).

3. Enjoining Other Litigation

The primary aim of interpleader is to protect the stakeholder from inconsistent judgments. If two or more courts are allowed, in separate proceedings, to determine who owns the stake, there is no guarantee they will reach the same result. Filing the interpleader action allows the stakeholder to submit all of the claims in orderly fashion to a single factfinder.

However, merely filing the interpleader action does not by itself halt any other proceedings that may affect the stakeholder's liability concerning the stake. Even if the stake is deposited with the court hearing the interpleader action, other courts may continue to adjudicate the stakeholder's liability to one or more of the claimants. Ideally, then, the stakeholder needs a mechanism to stop all of the other courts from proceeding any further. The most obvious way to accomplish this goal would be for the interpleader court to enjoin the filing or continued prosecution of other actions. When another action is already pending in *state* court, however, the Anti–Injunction Act, 28 U.S.C. § 2283, poses a potential problem. As a general rule, the Anti–Injunction Act prohibits a federal court from issuing an injunction against a pending state proceeding.

On the other hand, the Anti–Injunction Act does contain certain exceptions. First, the statute allows for an injunction when expressly authorized by some other federal statute. Congress made use of this exception in § 2361. Read that statute and identify the language that allows a court to evade the strictures of the Anti–Injunction Act.

Of course, § 2361 applies only to statutory interpleader. What about *Rule* interpleader cases? Although no statute expressly authorizes an injunction in Rule interpleader cases, many courts allow such injunctions based on the "where necessary in aid of its jurisdiction" exception in § 2283. Is enjoining a state-court proceeding really necessary to preserve a federal court's jurisdiction over a Rule interpleader case?

Finally, as *Star Insurance* indicates, merely because a federal court has the power to enjoin state proceedings does not mean that the stakeholder is entitled to an injunction. Instead, the court will determine whether parallel litigation poses a real threat to the stakeholder's rights. If no parallel litigation is likely, or if that parallel litigation contains adequate safeguards for the stakeholder's interests, the court may well deny the injunction.

4. The Subsequent Proceeding

Rule 22 and the statutes governing interpleader go into considerable detail on the issues of when interpleader is available, what a party must do to commence an interpleader case, and which court may hear the case. But what happens after that? Somewhat surprisingly, neither Rule 22 nor the statutes specify what a court is supposed to do in order to resolve the interpleader case. As a result, the courts have been forced to fill in the gaps by themselves.

In some situations, the court's task is obvious. Suppose for example, that an elderly woman with three sons dies and her will leaves her entire estate to "my favorite son." If the executor interpleads the three sons, the court's task is to determine which son was her favorite at the time she signed the will. That determination controls who gets the entire estate.

Now consider a variation on that theme. Suppose that the same executor faces claims in the amount of $200,000, but the total value of the estate is only $50,000. Clearly, the court's first task is to determine whether all the claims are valid. If the court finds that the total liability is actually less than $50,000, every creditor gets paid in full. But what if the court finds that all the claims are valid, so the estate owes the full $200,000? How should it distribute the limited funds?

Most courts distribute the funds *pro rata*, so that in our hypothetical situation each creditor would get twenty five cents for every dollar it claims. *See, e.g., Heller Financial, Inc. v. Prudential Ins. Co. of America,* 371 F.3d 944 (7th Cir. 2004); *Commercial Union Ins. Co. v. United*

States, 999 F.2d 581 (D.C. Cir. 1993). However, if one creditor would have a priority under state law, courts will respect that priority in interpleader, which means the party with the priority is paid in full before any junior creditor receives anything. *Texaco, Inc. v. Ponsoldt*, 118 F.3d 1367 (9th Cir. 1997). Some courts hold that if one or more creditors has obtained a judgment that can be levied against the fund, the creditors should be paid in the order in which they obtained their judgments. *Great American Ins. Co. v. Spraycraft, Inc.*, 844 F.Supp. 1188 (S.D. Ohio 1994).

If the stakeholder is truly disinterested, many courts will allow it to recover its costs and attorneys fees. *Estate of Ellington v. EMI Music Publishing*, 282 F.Supp.2d 192 (S.D.N.Y. 2003); *Unum Life Ins. Co. of America v. Kelling*, 170 F.Supp.2d 792 (M.D. Tenn. 2001). The rationale is that the stakeholder saved the claimants considerable time and expense by bringing the interpleader action.

Problems

1. Landlord and X enter into a lease agreement under which X will lease an apartment commencing in September. The lease is conditioned on X "submitting a security deposit by August 15." On August 20, Landlord has still not received the security deposit. Landlord therefore enters into another lease agreement under which she leases the same apartment to Y.

On September 1, both X and Y show up with their possessions, ready to move into the apartment. X claims that he "submitted" the check to Landlord by mailing it well before August 15. Although Landlord feels that the lease was not effective unless Landlord received the check, he is nevertheless unsure who is entitled to the apartment. May Landlord interplead X and Y?

2. Landlord leases an apartment to X. After the lease is complete, Landlord is prepared to return the security deposit to X. Before he returns the deposit, however, Landlord is sued by Y. Y claims to be one of X's creditors, and claims that he has a court order garnishing all debts owed to X. If Y is telling the truth, Landlord must pay him the security deposit. However, Landlord is sure that Y is lying. May Landlord interplead X and Y? Assuming for a moment that interpleader is proper, must Landlord file a new action, or can he file a claim in Y's suit?

3. While walking in a mall in Des Moines, Iowa, Brown finds a CD–ROM lying on the floor. Because the CD–ROM has no visible identifying information, Brown puts it into his computer to see what it contains. Brown is quite surprised to discover that the CD–ROM contains a database of the buying habits of everyone in the city. Although the physical CD–ROM has a value of only thirty cents, any marketing firm would be willing to pay $50,000 for the database.

Brown takes out a newspaper advertisement to try to discover the true owner of the database. Three people respond; Abramson, a citizen of Kentucky, Cross, a citizen of Minnesota, and Deason, a citizen of Ohio. Each claims to be the sole owner of the database.

Brown, a citizen of Illinois, would like to file an interpleader action against Abramson, Cross, and Deason in a Minnesota federal court. May the Minnesota federal court hear this case?

4.   Same as Problem 3, except that (a) Brown did not find the CD–ROM on the ground, but instead had it handed to him by a stranger, and (b) Brown wants to bring his action in a federal district court in the Central District of Illinois, where he resides. Brown claims that the person who handed him the CD was the actual owner, and that he therefore now owns the CD as a gift. May Brown bring his interpleader action in the chosen court?

D.   CLASS ACTIONS

INTRODUCTORY PROBLEM

Dash Communications, Inc. is the newest mobile phone provider in the United States. In order to compete against the more established companies, Dash offers rates that are significantly lower than the industry leaders. In addition, however, Dash decides to take advantage of the renewed sense of patriotism in the United States. Dash's advertisements proclaim that "all of our phones are assembled right here in the United States." That statement is only partly true. The components of Dash's phones are manufactured by sweatshop labor in several impoverished nations. However, when a customer buys a phone in the United States, a Dash employee takes the phone apart, programs it, and then replaces the back cover—thereby "assembling" the phone for the final time, as Dash would have it.

In time, truth wins out, and the deception in Dash's marketing scheme is brought to light. Pat Riot is a mobile phone user who maintains an account with Dash. Pat bought from Dash primarily because he thought that Dash's phones were produced entirely in the United States. Infuriated to learn the truth, Pat wants to cancel his contract with Dash. However, Pat signed Dash's standard three-year contract. Moreover, like all of Dash's contracts, Pat's contract provides that he must pay a $500 fee for early termination of the contract.

To get around these draconian terms, Pat sues Dash in state court. Although federal law provides no cause of action, state law would allow a buyer such as Pat to sue for misrepresentation. Prevailing on a claim of misrepresentation requires Pat to prove that he both knew of and relied on the "Assembled in America" statement. In his prayer for relief, Pat asks the state court to rescind the contract. Under the remedy of rescission, Pat would not only be relieved of paying the termination fee, but would also be entitled to a refund of any payments already submitted, less the "reasonable value" of any calls Pat had made.

Pat is also an avid online chatter. After Pat files his case, he talks to a number of other Dash customers who were similarly upset to find out where Dash's phones are made. These customers are located all across the country. When Pat suggest that they sue Dash too, some of the people respond that the amount involved is too small to justify suing. Others indicate that under the law of their state, a false statement about where a product is made would not qualify as a misrepresentation.

Pat begins to wonder whether there is any way he can join the claims of all Dash customers in the United States into his case. Is there any way that Pat can arrange to litigate not only his rights, but also the rights of all other Dash customers? What about the fact that many, if not most, of these customers have no connection whatsoever with Pat's state? Thinking practically rather than logically, would this be a good case to allow one person to litigate the rights of others?

Governing (and guiding) Rule: Federal Rule 23.

Before you took Civil Procedure, you may never have heard of impleader, intervention, and interpleader. But the odds are quite good that you have heard of class actions. Over the past quarter century, class actions have gained a great deal of notoriety. The media devotes considerable coverage to certain class actions, either because of the incredible damages sought or the novel legal theory of recovery. Advocates of "tort reform" cite some of the more spectacular uses of the class action as evidence of how the tort system has run amok. These same advocates blame class actions for driving up the cost of health care, insurance, automobiles, and a host of other products. Some even accuse class actions of serving as a back-door way to achieve mass income redistribution in society.

On the other hand, supporters of the class action would argue that the device is an invaluable tool for achieving justice, especially in certain types of cases. Consolidating all claims as a group may be the only practical way to remedy a situation in which government or a large private firm is engaged in widespread discrimination, or in which a company lies in connection with its issue of stock. In these situations, few individuals have the inventive, much less the financial wherewithal, to hire an attorney and pursue what may prove to be a long and arduous case. The class action not only allows the costs of litigation to be spread among all claimants, but also gives the plaintiff's side considerably more clout in negotiating a favorable settlement.

In truth, there is some merit to both sides of the debate. It is unquestioned that class actions have made it feasible to challenge in court certain actions by government and large companies that might otherwise have gone unchecked. Without the class action, the nation would not have made as much progress in the area of school desegregation and securities fraud, as well as combating various illegal practices by record companies and airlines. On the other hand, it is equally clear that the class action has at times been abused. In some cases, a plaintiff will bring a legally questionable claim as a class action in the hope that the sheer weight of the claim will pressure the defendant in to a quick settlement.* The merits of the claim sometimes take a back seat to the fight over whether the case may proceed as a class action. If the case is allowed to be a class action, the defendant immediately settles, while if the judge denies class status, the case is usually dismissed.

Understanding the debate about class actions requires an understanding of the ways in which class actions are unique. In one sense, a class action is nothing more than a collection of dozens, hundreds, or perhaps thousands of individual claims. However, there is a fundamental difference between a case in which one hundred plaintiffs join under Rule 20, and a class action involving those same hundred people. In a case of ordinary joinder, everyone looks out for her own interests. In a class action, one or a few of the interested parties represents the rights of everyone. That basic feature—representational litigation—is a two-edged sword. It offers tremendous opportunities for economies of scale, but at the same time presents *sui generis* problems. The following case and notes explore the problems with representational litigation.

1. Problems with Representational Litigation

HANSBERRY v. LEE

311 U.S. 32, 61 S.Ct. 115, 85 L.Ed. 22 (1940)

Mr. Justice STONE delivered the opinion of the Court. * * *

[Hundreds of landowners in a particular area negotiated a restrictive covenant, under which each signer agreed that his lot could not be sold to or used by a black person. However, the covenant specifically provided that it was not binding unless signed by owners owning at least 95% of the street frontage of land in the area.

After the covenant had been signed, Burke, a landowner, sued Kleinman and others in an Illinois state court. Although the record is not entirely clear, the United States Supreme Court's opinion suggests that this case may have been brought to obtain a judicial declaration that the covenant was legally enforceable against all who had signed. The plaintiff and defendants had all signed the covenant. Burke specified that she was bringing the action not only on her own behalf, but also on behalf of all other property owners who had signed. The parties in *Burke v. Kleinman* stipulated that owners of 95 percent of the frontage had signed. The court found the covenant to be legally binding, and held for Burke.

Later, Lee, another landowner who had signed the covenant, sued the Hansberrys, a black family seeking to purchase a lot from someone else who had signed the covenant. The Hansberrys proved that only owners of 54 percent of frontage in the area had signed the covenant. The state courts, although agreeing that the 95 percent requirement was

---

* For an interesting take on class actions and tort litigation in general, read   John Grisham, "The King of Torts".

not in fact satisfied, held that the Hansberrys could not challenge the *Burke* court's ruling that owners of 95 percent had signed, even if that finding was based on a fraudulent stipulation. On appeal, the Illinois Supreme Court justifying this result by holding that *Burke* was by nature a class action, brought by Burke on behalf of those who had signed the covenant. Because the Hansberrys' seller had signed the covenant, the court found that he was a member of this class. And as the Hansberrys would be successors in interest to their seller, they too were bound by the judgment in *Burke*.]

It is a principle of general application in Anglo–American jurisprudence that one is not bound by a judgment *in personam* in a litigation in which he is not designated as a party or to which he has not been made a party by service of process. *Pennoyer* v. *Neff*, 95 U.S. 714. A judgment rendered in such circumstances is not entitled to the full faith and credit which the Constitution and statute of the United States prescribe, and judicial action enforcing it against the person or property of the absent party is not that due process which the Fifth and Fourteenth Amendments require.

To these general rules there is a recognized exception that, to an extent not precisely defined by judicial opinion, the judgment in a "class" or "representative" suit, to which some members of the class are parties, may bind members of the class or those represented who were not made parties to it.

The class suit was an invention of equity to enable it to proceed to a decree in suits where the number of those interested in the subject of the litigation is so great that their joinder as parties in conformity to the usual rules of procedure is impracticable. Courts are not infrequently called upon to proceed with causes in which the number of those interested in the litigation is so great as to make difficult or impossible the joinder of all because some are not within the jurisdiction or because their whereabouts is unknown or where if all were made parties to the suit its continued abatement by the death of some would prevent or unduly delay a decree. In such cases where the interests of those not joined are of the same class as the interests of those who are, and where it is considered that the latter fairly represent the former in the prosecution of the litigation of the issues in which all have a common interest, the court will proceed to a decree.

It is evident that the considerations which may induce a court thus to proceed, despite a technical defect of parties, may differ from those which must be taken into account in determining whether the absent parties are bound by the decree or, if it is adjudged that they are, in ascertaining whether such an adjudication satisfies the requirements of due process and of full faith and credit. Nevertheless, there is scope within the framework of the Constitution for holding in appropriate cases that a judgment rendered in a class suit is *res judicata* as to members of the class who are not formal parties to the suit. Here, as elsewhere, the Fourteenth Amendment does not compel state courts or legislatures to adopt any particular rule for establishing the conclusive-ness of judgments in class suits, nor does it compel the adoption of the particular rules thought by this Court to be appropriate for the federal courts. With a proper regard for divergent local institutions and inter-ests, this Court is justified in saying that there has been a failure of due process only in those cases where it cannot be said that the procedure adopted, fairly insures the protection of the interests of absent parties who are to be bound by it.

It is familiar doctrine of the federal courts that members of a class not present as parties to the litigation may be bound by the judgment where they are in fact adequately represented by parties who are present, or where they actually participate in the conduct of the litiga-tion in which members of the class are present as parties, or where the interest of the members of the class, some of whom are present as parties, is joint, or where for any other reason the relationship between the parties present and those who are absent is such as legally to entitle the former to stand in judgment for the latter.

In all such cases, so far as it can be said that the members of the class who are present are, by generally recognized rules of law, entitled to stand in judgment for those who are not, we may assume for present purposes that such procedure affords a protection to the parties who are represented, though absent, which would satisfy the requirements of due process and full faith and credit. Nor do we find it necessary for the decision of this case to say that, when the only circumstance defining the class is that the determination of the rights of its members turns upon a single issue of fact or law, a state could not constitutionally adopt a procedure whereby some of the members of the class could stand in judgment for all, provided that the procedure were so devised and applied as to insure that those present are of the same class as those absent and that the litigation is so conducted as to insure the full and fair consideration of the common issue. We decide only that the proce-dure and the course of litigation sustained here by the plea of *res judicata* do not satisfy these requirements.

The restrictive agreement did not purport to create a joint obligation or liability. If valid and effective its promises were the several obligations of the signers and those claiming under them. The promises ran several-ly to every other signer. It is plain that in such circumstances all those alleged to be bound by the agreement would not constitute a single class in any litigation brought to enforce it. Those who sought to secure its benefits by enforcing it could not be said to be in the same class with or represent those whose interest was in resisting performance, for the agreement by its terms imposes obligations and confers rights on the owner of each plot of land who signs it. If those who thus seek to secure the benefits of the agreement were rightly regarded by the state Su-preme Court as constituting a class, it is evident that those signers or their successors who are interested in challenging the validity of the agreement and resisting its performance are not of the same class in the sense that their interests are identical so that any group who had elected to enforce rights conferred by the agreement could be said to be acting in the interest of any others who were free to deny its obligation.

Because of the dual and potentially conflicting interests of those who are putative parties to the agreement in compelling or resisting its performance, it is impossible to say, solely because they are parties to it, that any two of them are of the same class. Nor without more, and with the due regard for the protection of the rights of absent parties which due process exacts, can some be permitted to stand in judgment for all.

It is one thing to say that some members of a class may represent other members in a litigation where the sole and common interest of the class in the litigation, is either to assert a common right or to challenge an asserted obligation. It is quite another to hold that all those who are free alternatively either to assert rights or to challenge them are of a single class, so that any group, merely because it is of the class so constituted, may be deemed adequately to represent any others of the class in litigating their interests in either alternative. Such a selection of representatives for purposes of litigation, whose substantial interests are not necessarily or even probably the same as those whom they are deemed to represent, does not afford that protection to absent parties which due process requires. * * *

The plaintiffs in the *Burke* case sought to compel performance of the agreement in behalf of themselves and all others similarly situated. They did not designate the defendants in the suit as a class or seek any injunction or other relief against others than the named defendants, and the decree which was entered did not purport to bind others. In seeking to enforce the agreement the plaintiffs in that suit were not representing the petitioners here whose substantial interest is in resisting performance. The defendants in the first suit were not treated by the pleadings or decree as representing others or as foreclosing by their defense the rights of others; and, even though nominal defendants, it does not appear that their interest in defeating the contract outweighed their interest in establishing its validity. For a court in this situation to ascribe to either the plaintiffs or defendants the performance of such functions on behalf of petitioners here, is to attribute to them a power that it cannot be said that they had assumed to exercise, and a responsibility which, in view of their dual interests it does not appear that they could rightly discharge.

Reversed.

Notes and Questions

1. Racially restrictive covenants were fairly common in residential housing in the first half of the twentieth century. Indeed, the title to the house owned by at least one of your authors contains such a restriction. For many years, courts enforced the covenants, albeit sometimes hesitantly. A few years after *Hansberry*, however, the United States Supreme Court held that enforcement of racially (and by implication religiously) restrictive

covenants violated the Equal Protection clause of the Fourteenth Amendment to the United States Constitution. *Shelley v. Kraemer*, 334 U.S. 1, 68 S.Ct. 836, 92 L.Ed. 1161 (1948).

2. The Hansberrys did not sign the covenant at issue in the case. Can you nevertheless reconstruct the Illinois Supreme Court's argument as to why the Hansberrys were not only bound, but were precluded from arguing in court that the covenant was invalid?

3. Why does the United States Supreme Court reject the Illinois court's conclusions?

4. The Court in *Hansberry* is careful to limit its holding to the specific facts before it. But does the decision as a practical matter completely destroy the class action device? Can we ever be sure that the ostensible members of the class—who, after all, sit silently on the sidelines while the case is being litigated—truly share interests with the representative?

Suppose that Alpha brings a class action against City on behalf of himself and everyone who resides in or near the downtown in City. The action challenges City's decision to build a new downtown stadium in the hope of luring one of Major League Baseball's increasingly peregrine teams to City. City plans to finance the stadium by raising taxes on City residents. Alpha argues that the noise, light, and increased traffic from the stadium will constitute a public nuisance, seriously reducing property values in the area. Alpha asks the court to compensate all owners for the decrease in value of their property. Although Alpha diligently prosecutes the case, he eventually loses on the merits. Are any or all of the following people bound by the decision?

Beta:	Beta is a rabid baseball fan who wants the stadium at any cost.
Gamma:	Gamma argues that had *she* been the representative, she would not have sued for a public nuisance, but instead would have argued that City's plan violated state environmental statutes dealing with large construction projects.
Delta:	Delta agrees that the public nuisance theory was the best bet. However, Delta argues that *he* would have preferred the court to enjoin City from building the stadium.
Epsilon:	Epsilon, a baseball fan, feels that a reduction in property values is a fair trade for the benefits of having a new stadium. Epsilon nevertheless objects to City's proposal. Her objection is based on the City's plan to use tax revenues to pay for the stadium. Epsilon feels that the proposal violates a provision of the state constitution that prevents municipal taxes from being used for private projects.

5. Consider again the hypothetical situation posed in the prior note, but now suppose that Alpha *won* the suit. Can any of the other people take advantage of Alpha's victory?

6. Most class actions involve a class of plaintiffs suing one or more named defendants. However, the opposite is also possible. In some cases, a plaintiff may sue one or more people as representatives of a class of *defendants*. These "defendant class actions" can present serious problems of adequate representation, especially in situations where there is an incentive

for one party to "point the finger" at others. Nevertheless, courts have allowed defendant class actions in the proper case. For an example of a defendant class action, see *In re Integra Realty Resources, Inc.*, 262 F.3d 1089 (10th Cir. 2001). *Integra* is a massive, complicated case. The caption alone for the case is over one and one-half pages long.

Would a *defendant* class action have helped in *Hansberry*? When answering this question, ask yourself whether the plaintiff in *Burke* gained anything by suing on behalf of a class, rather than suing as an individual.

7. The Court's opinion in *Hansberry* indicates that a person may be barred by the results of a case not only when she is a party to the case or a member of a properly-constituted class, but also when she "controls" the litigation of the case. For an example of control of a case by a non-party, see *Montana v. United States*, 440 U.S. 147, 99 S.Ct. 970, 59 L.Ed.2d 210 (1979).

Problem

Marvel Windows makes high quality wood-frame windows for residences. Water is a window frame's main enemy. From 1985 to 1988, Marvel used a chemical called SHED to waterproof its frames. SHED proved to be almost completely ineffective against water. As a result, Marvel windows would rot out after ten to twenty years.

In 1999, Scarlett O'Hara brought a class action in the District of Minnesota against Marvel Windows, on behalf of everyone who had bought a Marvel SHED-treated window between 1985 and 1988. O'Hara sought recovery for breach of contract and breach of warranty. The case was settled in 2001 for $300,000. The court issued judgment in that amount. Pursuant to this judgment, Marvel paid $300,000 into a fund. Members of the class could obtain compensation from the fund by filing a claim. Notice of the settlement and the fund was both sent to the known members and published in mainstream newspapers across the nation. The fund was depleted by the summer of 2002.

Rhett Butler bought SHED-treated windows from Marvin in 1988. Butler thought his windows were fine. In October of 2002, however, Butler discovered that his window frames were rotting. Rhett sued Marvel in a Massachusetts federal court for replacement of his windows. Unlike O'Hara's action, Butler sought recovery for failure to warn after the sale. Marvel filed a Rule 12(b)(6) motion, asserting that the judgment in the *O'Hara* class action barred Butler because he was a member of the class. Butler argued that he could not be a member because he had not yet experienced any problems while the *O'Hara* case was pending. In addition, Butler argued that because of his different legal theory, he was not adequately represented.

How will the court rule? *See Reppert v. Marvin Lumber and Cedar Co.*, 359 F.3d 53 (1st Cir. 2004).

---

2. The Protection Afforded by Rule 23

In *Hansberry*, the Illinois courts determined that the *Burke* case was a class action after that action was complete. The Supreme Court, of course, disagreed. That hindsight-based approach presents obvious problems to the parties to a class action. Take a situation where one plaintiff sues on behalf of a class of one thousand members. Because the stakes are so high, the defendant will defend the suit vigorously. The defendant may well offer evidence to show why some of the class members are not entitled to recovery. That defendant would be quite frustrated if a court stepped in later and declared that the only party bound by the judgment was the representative, and the other class members could bring their own individual suits.

Federal Rule 23 deals with class actions in the federal courts. That rule was completely revamped in 1966, in part to answer many of the concerns raised by *Hansberry*. Read Rule 23 carefully. In what ways does the Rule attempt to deal with the representation issues raised by *Hansberry*? In what way does it seek to avoid the practical problems with judging whether these requirements were met in hindsight, as occurred in *Hansberry*? In particular, consider the roles that the following features of Rule 23 play:

- certification of the class by the trial court
- the general requirements of 23(a)
- the three different types of class action contemplated by 23(b)
- notice to the class members
- the "opt-out" provisions of Rule 23(c)(2)(B)
- the provisions governing settlement of a class action

Although states are free to adopt their own methods of meeting the requirements of *Hansberry*, many have opted for an approach much along the lines of Rule 23.

SZABO v. BRIDGEPORT MACHINES, INC.

199 F.R.D. 280 (N.D. Ind. 2001)

William C. Lee, Chief Judge.

This matter is before the court on a motion for class certification filed by the plaintiff, John D. Szabo, d/b/a Zatron ("Szabo"), on August 16, 2000. * * *

FACTUAL BACKGROUND

The pertinent introductory facts of this case are as follows. Szabo, operating as Zatron (a machine shop), provides 3–D design services, CAD/CAM and CNC (computer numerically controlled) programming, the building of precision tool, dies and mold-tooling and production machining. Szabo resides in Indiana. Bridgeport, a Delaware corporation with its principal place of business in Connecticut, is in the business of manufacturing and distributing machine tools. Szabo's complaint arises out of his purchase in July 1997 of a Bridgeport 800/22 vertical machining center with a DX–32 Control Unit from Bridgeport. Szabo alleges that the machine did not perform up to and in accordance with certain technical specifications and performance characteristics allegedly contained in promotional material and an offer letter that Bridgeport's alleged agent, Advance Machinery Company, Inc. ("Advance Machinery"), purportedly gave to Szabo. According to Szabo, the Bridgeport Machine was unable to meet the technical specifications and performance characteristics due to defects inherent in the Bridgeport DX–32 Control Unit. Szabo alleges that Bridgeport had knowledge of these defects and that Bridgeport's brochure and written offer letter contained numerous fraudulent statements and omissions and that Bridgeport acted knowingly or recklessly in making these alleged false and misleading representations and omissions of fact. Szabo asserts claims of negligent misrepresentation, fraud and breach of warranties.

Motion to Certify Class

Szabo seeks certification of a class of all persons who purchased a machining center or a CNC milling machine from Bridgeport that included a Bridgeport DX–32 Control Unit between January 1, 1996 and the present (the "Class Period") and were damaged thereby (the "Class"). * * * Szabo notes that the thrust of this action is that the DX–32 Control Unit incorporated into the machine he bought was inherently defective, which prevented the machine from operating in accordance with its specifications. Therefore, because the Class members all purchased computer numerically controlled machines with the same defective Control Unit, on the basis of standardized performance representations, Szabo argues that this action should be certified as a class action. Certification is sought under Rule 23(a) and Rule 23(b)(3) of the Federal Rules of Civil Procedure.

Under Rule 23 of the Federal Rules of Civil Procedure, this court undertakes a two-step analysis in determining whether class certification is proper. First, the court determines whether the four threshold requirements of subsection (a) of Rule 23 have been met. These requirements are as follows:

> One or more members of a class may sue or be sued as representative parties on behalf of all only if (1) the class is so numerous that joinder of all members is impracticable; (2) there are questions of law or fact common to the class; (3) the claims or defenses of the representative parties are typical of the claims or defenses of the class; and (4) the representative parties will fairly and adequately protect the interest of the class.

These four factors are often referred to as: "numerosity", "commonality", "typicality", and "adequate representation".

Secondly, the court determines whether the action qualifies for class treatment under at least one of the subdivisions of Rule 23(b). Szabo is proceeding under Rule 23(b)(3), which provides in relevant part as follows:

(b) An action may be maintained as a class action if the prerequisites of subdivision (a) are satisfied, and in addition:

* * *

(3) the court finds that the questions of law or fact common to the members of the class predominate over any questions affecting only individual members, and that a class action is superior to other available methods for the fair and efficient adjudication of the controversy.

These two factors are commonly referred to as: "predominance" and "superiority".

Szabo bears the initial burden of advancing reasons why this action meets the requirements of Rule 23. In ruling on a motion for class certification the focus is simply on whether the prerequisites of Rule 23 have been met. The court does not conduct a hearing on the merits when deciding upon certification of a class. * * * Rule 23 is to be construed liberally.

NUMEROSITY

The first requirement of Rule 23 is that "the class is so numerous that joinder of all members is impracticable. This rule does not require that joinder be impossible, but impracticable. Courts may make "common sense assumptions" in order to support the finding of numerosity.

Szabo estimates that hundreds of individuals fall within the parameters of the class definition. Szabo claims that members of the Class can be identified by reference to objective criteria such as Bridgeport's sales records which will reveal who purchased CNC milling machines or vertical machining centers that incorporated the DX–32 Control Unit. Szabo indicates that the proposed class consists of all persons, nationwide, who purchased these machines and that, although the exact number of jurisdictions in which the class members reside is not yet known, it would be impracticable to join hundreds of class members from different states. Therefore, Szabo concludes that the numerosity requirement is satisfied.

Bridgeport, however, argues that Szabo has not met the numerosity requirement because he has not sufficiently put forth evidence of the number of the class members. Nevertheless, Bridgeport, which presumably knows the exact number of purchasers who would fit within the proposed class, has not attempted to make any showing that there are not hundreds of potential class members. Additionally, as Szabo points out in detail in his reply brief, Bridgeport's annual report clearly supports an estimate of domestic sales of machining centers in 1998 of over 600 machining centers. In any event, the law is clear that precise enumeration of the members of a class is not necessary for an action to proceed as a class action, and it is permissible to estimate class size. Consequently, the court finds that Szabo has met the numerosity requirement.

Commonality, Predominance, Typicality

The next issue is whether there are "questions of law or fact common to the class" and whether the commons questions predominate. This is not a demanding requirement. The rule does not require that all questions be common. In fact, a single common question is sufficient to satisfy the requirements of Rule 23(a)(2), at least in some circumstances.

A common question is one which "arises from 'a common nucleus of operative facts'" regardless of whether the underlying facts change over the class period and vary as to individual claimants.

Szabo claims that he has alleged a variety of common questions concerning the defects in the DX–32 Control Unit, Bridgeport's dealings with the members of the Class, and the Class members' potential remedies. * * *

Bridgeport, in response, argues that where, as here, the plaintiff moves for certification under Rule 23(b)(3), "Rule 23(a)(2)'s 'commonality' requirement is subsumed under, or superseded by, the more stringent Rule 23(b)(3) requirement that questions common to the class 'predominate over' other questions." *Amchem Prods., Inc. v. Windsor*, 521 U.S. 591, 609, 117 S. Ct. 2231 (1997). Bridgeport claims that Szabo cannot meet the requirement that the common questions predominate because, according to Bridgeport multiple individualized issues permeate both Szabo's particular claim and the class claims he alleges. The issue raised by Bridgeport will be discussed below, in connection with typicality. ("The commonality and typicality requirements of Rule 23(a) tend to merge. Both serve as guideposts for determining whether under the particular circumstances maintenance of a class action is economical and whether the named plaintiff's claim and the class claims are so interrelated that the interests of the class members will be fairly and adequately represented in their absence." *General Tel. Co. v. Falcon*, 457 U.S. 147, 157 n. 13, 102 S. Ct. 2364 (1982)).

A plaintiff's claim is typical if it arises from the same event or practice or course of conduct that gives rise to the claims of the other class members and his or her claims are based on the same legal theory. The typicality requirement is satisfied when all plaintiffs have the same theory of recovery against the defendant based on the same set of facts. For class certification purposes, "a named plaintiff need not have suffered precisely the same injury as every member of the class, so long as he has been adversely affected by the same practice or policy, therefore the court must focus on the nature of the class claims and whether they are 'fairly encompassed by the named plaintiff's claims.'" *Koski v. Gainer* [sic], 1993 WL 153828 (N.D. IL).

Szabo argues that he is a typical victim of the defendant's practices and that his claims arise out of the same course of conduct and are based on the same legal theories as those of the putative Class members. Szabo notes that the gravamen of his claims is that the DX–32 Control Unit was defective. * * * Szabo alleges in his complaint that the defects in the DX–32 were inherent, and therefore present in every CNC milling machine and vertical machining center that incorporated that unit. * * * The complaint describes numerous complaints by other purchasers of the DX–32 who experienced the same problems as Szabo with their machines. In light of all the above allegations, Szabo concludes that the common issues in this case are central to his claim and that by litigating the liability issues he can reasonably be expected to advance the interests of all putative Class members in a favorable determination on each common issue.

Bridgeport, in response, contends that Szabo's claim is inherently dependent upon his unique factual circumstances and, therefore, common factual issues do not predominate. Bridgeport relies on Szabo's deposition, wherein he indicated that numerous oral representations were made to him by Bridgeport's alleged agent (Advanced Machinery), as well as a demonstration of the product. Bridgeport then concludes that Szabo's claim is one based on oral misrepresentations, which oral misrepresentations would be different for each potential Class member, and, therefore, class certification is not permissible.

Clearly, Bridgeport is forgetting that this court must accept the substantive allegations of Szabo's complaint as true. While Bridgeport is free to argue during the merits phase of the case that Szabo cannot base his claim on written materials he received, such an argument has no place in response to a motion to certify class. In any event, the law is clear that the presence of some oral misrepresentations does not preclude class treatment.

Bridgeport also presents the argument that where class members have differing degrees of reliance on promotional materials, class issues do not predominate. Szabo, however, strongly contends that the existence of reliance issues does not preclude class certification. Szabo points out that he has alleged that the representations and performance specification in the contracts for sale were uniformly given to all class members.

As Szabo points out there is an ample body of federal decisional law holding that reliance may be presumed where common representations are directed at class members. "When the fraud was perpetrated in a uniform manner against every member of the class, such as when all plaintiffs received virtually identical written materials from the defendants, courts typically hold that individual reliance questions do not predominate." *Rohlfing v. Manor Care, Inc.,* 172 F.R.D. 330, 338 (N.D. Ill. 1997). * * *

Szabo reiterates the fact that the four causes of action asserted here are based on the uniform written representations. The available brochures discuss the DX–32 Control Unit in similar terms and Bridgeport used standardized form quotations for the sale of its machines. * * * Szabo further maintains that it is "logical" to presume that because the Class members contracted for, paid for and received the machines, they relied on the uniform written representations made in connection with the sale. Szabo concludes that Bridgeport's use of uniform and standardized written documents obviates the need to demonstrate reliance on an individual basis and, therefore, reliance can be established on a class-wide basis and common issues predominate. * * *

[I]t is clear that (contrary to Bridgeport's arguments) the fact that Szabo seeks to represent class members who purchased different models of Bridgeport's machines that incorporated the DX–32 Control Unit does not render him atypical. Typicality is satisfied even where there are factual differences between the claims of the named plaintiff and the claims of class members. * * *

In conclusion, the court finds that Szabo has met Rule 23's requirements with respect to commonality, predominance, and typicality.

ADEQUATE REPRESENTATION

The adequacy of representation requirement of Rule 23(a)(4) consists of two parts: (1) the adequacy of the named plaintiff's counsel and (2) the adequacy of representation provided in protecting the different, separate and distinct interest of the class members. The requirement is met if it appears that the plaintiff's interests are not antagonistic to those of other members of the class he or she seeks to represent, that the representative has a sufficient interest in the outcome to ensure vigorous advocacy, and the plaintiff's attorneys are qualified, experienced and generally able to conduct the litigation.

Bridgeport does not take issue with the qualifications of Szabo's counsel to adequately represent the class. However, Bridgeport claims that Szabo's interests (doing 3D mold work) are incompatible with other Bridgeport machine owners who were not using their machines for the same type of work as the plaintiff. Clearly, however, as the underlying claim is that the allegedly defective DX–32 Control Unit caused the machines at issue to not meet their specifications, whether Szabo intended to perform the exact type of work with his machine as other potential plaintiffs is totally immaterial. * * *

For a court to deny class certification based on a conflict with the potential class members, there must be real and substantial conflict, not merely a speculative or conjectural one, and it must go to the subject matter of the controversy. It is abundantly clear that none of Bridgeport's arguments meet this standard. * * *

Therefore, as Szabo's counsel is qualified to adequately represent the class and Szabo's interests are not antagonistic to those of other class members, the court finds Rule 23's "adequate representation" requirement to have been met.

SUPERIORITY

Rule 23(b)(3) requires the consideration of the following factors in determining whether a class action is "superior to other available methods for the fair and efficient adjudication of the controversy": (1) the interest of the members of the class in individually controlling the prosecution or defense of separate actions; (2) the extent and nature of any litigation concerning the controversy already commenced by or against members of the class; (3) the desirability or undesirability of concentrating the litigation of the claims in the particular forum; and (4) the difficulties likely to be encountered in the management of a class action. As Szabo notes, it has been widely recognized that a class action is superior to other available methods for the fair and efficient adjudication of a suit that affects a large number of persons injured by violations of a common law. See *Paper Sys., Inc. v. Mitsubishi*, 193 F.R.D. 601, 616 (class action superior where repeatedly litigating the same issues in individual suits would consume more judicial resources than addressing them in a single blow in consolidated actions).

Szabo argues that Bridgeport has inflicted economic injury on a large number of geographically dispersed persons to such an extent that the cost of pursuing individual litigation to seek recovery against a well-financed adversary is not feasible and, thus, the alternatives to a class action are either no recourse for hundreds of small businesses, or a multiplicity of scattered suits resulting in the inefficient administration of litigation. Szabo further argues that, given the complex nature of the technology at issue and the need for extensive experts, the cost of pursuing individual claims by Class members could effectively preclude their ability to recover.

Bridgeport, however, argues that there is no need for class certification because the potential class members are business people who have spent over $70,000 for a machine. Bridgeport hypothesizes that any such class member would likely be capable of protecting his own rights. * * *

Szabo asserts that this is a complex case, and that developing the evidence of defect and presenting it in a way that a jury can comprehend will require significant time and effort. Szabo also informs the court that the possibility of pursuing the case on an individual basis was initially considered by counsel and rejected because of the complex subject matter. Szabo further points out that to the extent that a member of the proposed class has a claim that it wishes to pursue individually, it will remain free to do so by opting out. Fed.R.Civ.P. 23(c)(2). Similarly, class members will be given the option of entering an appearance through counsel should they wish to do so. The court finds that Szabo has the better argument on this point and holds that the mere fact that the machines at issue cost approximately $70,000 does not preclude class certification.

Bridgeport has also claimed that differing state laws militate against a finding of superiority. The court will discuss the issue of choice of law below.

CHOICE OF LAW

* * * The parties agree that Indiana's choice of law rules are to be used to determine what law applies to the proposed class' claims. The application of choice of law principles will vary slightly for the different claims raised in the amended complaint. The warranty claims are

contractual, while the remaining claims (negligent misrepresentation and fraud) are based upon tort theories. * * * [Indiana's choice of law rules require] an assessment of which jurisdiction has the most significant relationship with the particular tort. * * * [T]he place where the harm occurred will frequently have the most significant relationship with the dispute, but other factors are to be considered when the place where the harm occurred is an insignificant contact.

Szabo argues that the law of Connecticut is the most appropriate source of substantive law whereas, of course, Indiana law would still govern matters of procedure. With respect to the tort claim of negligent misrepresentation, there are significant differences between Indiana and Connecticut law. The Connecticut Supreme Court has "long recognized liability for negligent misrepresentation...." *Citino v. Redevelopment Agency*, 51 Conn.App. 262, 721 A.2d 1197, 1206 (App. Ct. 1998). Indiana, however, does not recognize negligent misrepresentation, except in limited circumstances focused on the area of employment. * * *

While it is true that Szabo is an Indiana resident and the machine he purchased is located in Indiana, the court finds these to be insignificant contacts with respect to the current action. Szabo's allegations against Bridgeport concentrate on Bridgeport's action and representations made in Connecticut. Therefore, Indiana's contacts are of inconsequential significance. * * *

As Szabo has shown that Indiana does not have significant contacts with the cause of action, and Connecticut does have significant contacts, the law of Connecticut will be applied to Szabo's negligent misrepresentation and fraud claims.

With respect to the warranty claims, this court agrees with Szabo that under Indiana choice of law principles for contract actions, Connecticut law should apply to both the express and implied warranty claims. Indiana's choice of law rule for contract actions directs that the court should apply the substantive law of the state with "the most intimate contact to the facts." *Travelers Indem. Co. v. Summit Corporation of America*, 715 N.E.2d 926, 931 (Ind. App. 1999). Clearly, Connecticut is the state with the "most intimate contacts" to the warranty claims.

Szabo claims that he was injured because the DX–32 Control Unit incorporated into his machining center is defective. The shipment of the defective machining center is the conduct that caused Bridgeport to breach its express and implied warranties. The brochures and sales contract containing the specifications that form the basis of the express warranty claim came from Connecticut. Bridgeport is based in Connecticut, which is where the machine was shipped from and where the decision to sell under the faulty specifications was made. Finally, the contract that Szabo signed was F.O.B. Bridgeport Connecticut, which means that title to the machine and risk of loss passed to him at that location, not in Indiana.

In sum, the court finds that Connecticut law applies to the claims in this cause of action. As the substantive law of a single state is applicable to all of the claims with respect to Szabo and all putative class members, Bridgeport's argument that the case is unmanageable as a class action fails. The court finds that Szabo has shown that all of Rule 23's requirements have been met. Accordingly, the court will grant Szabo's motion to certify a class. * * *

Notes and Questions

1. As *Szabo* demonstrates, Rule 23 requires a party to move to certify the case as a class action. Although that motion is usually made by the party or parties seeking to be class representative, it may also be made by the opposing side. Why might a defendant being sued by one plaintiff want to turn the case into a class action involving hundreds or thousands of claims?

2. *Timing and appeal.* A motion to certify the case is usually filed at a very early stage in the case. Rule 23(c)(1)(A) also requires the court to rule on that motion "at an early practicable time." In many cases, the court's ruling on certification effectively ends the case. If the court certifies the class, the defendant will have a great incentive to settle. If the court denies certification, the plaintiff will often dismiss the case rather than go it alone.

Because of the importance of the certification decision, a losing party would like to file an immediate appeal. However, as discussed in Chapter 12, the federal courts, and many states, generally only allow appeals from final judgments. A decision granting or denying class certification is not final because it does not resolve the merits of the case.

In 1998, Rule 23 was amended by adding new Rule 23(f). This new rule allows an immediate appeal of a decision granting or denying class certification. However, the court of appeals has discretion as to whether to hear the appeal.

3. Suppose a defendant fails to respond to plaintiff's motion to certify the case. In other situations, a party who fails to respond waives any objections to the request made by motion. By analogy, may a court certify a case "by default" where the defendant fails to respond to the certification motion? *See Davis v. Hutchins*, 321 F.3d 641 (7th Cir. 2003).

4. *The Certification Process. Szabo* does a good job of separating the complex requirements of Rule 23, and dealing with each in turn. At the risk of overgeneralization, the certification process involves three basic steps. First, the court considers the factors set out in Rule 23(a). Second, it determines whether the case fits any of the three allowable categories of class actions described in Rule 23(b). Third, if both 23(a) and (b) are satisfied, the court considers whether the class members receive notice and the right to "opt out." Rule 23(a) is discussed in Notes 5–11; Rule 23(b) in Notes 12–20; and notice and opt out in Notes 21–25.

5. *Rule 23(a).* Rule 23(a) sets out four basic requirements that all class actions must satisfy in order to be certified. These four requirements are often referred to as numerosity, commonality, typicality, and adequate representation.

6. *Numerosity* was not really an issue in *Szabo*. The case involved hundreds of potential claimants, making it impracticable to join all of them

as individual plaintiffs. Imagine the chaos that would result if each of these parties was represented by separate counsel. How could discovery ever be coordinated? Where would everyone sit in the courtroom once the case went to trial?

7. How small may a class be before it will fail numerosity? Although the number varies somewhat based on the type of case, 40 seems to be a threshold. *Basco v. Wal–Mart Stores, Inc.*, 216 F.Supp.2d 592 (E.D La. 2002). If there are 40 or more members, courts presume that joinder would be impracticable.

8. As *Szabo* indicates, the party seeking class certification does not have to be able to identify the potential class members by name. It need only have an approximate number. In many cases, additional discovery—often from the opposing party's files—will be needed to ascertain who the class members are. In some cases, it will never be possible to identify the members. Nevertheless, a class action can proceed even if the identify of many members cannot be determined. Ironically, inability to determine who the members are makes certification even more likely.

9. *Commonality* asks whether the claims to be joined in the class share common issues of law or fact. Note that even a single common issue may satisfy this requirement. Do not confuse this factor with Rule 23(b)(3)'s requirement that the common issues *predominate* over the individual questions of law or fact. There must be at least one common question in all class actions. Only in 23(b)(3) class actions must the common questions predominate.

10. Turning to the fourth requirement for a moment, the requirement of *adequate representation* acknowledges the concerns raised in *Hansberry*. Although Rule 23(a) requires the court to make a threshold determination of adequate representation, that issue can be revisited at any point in the case. Therefore, if circumstances change and a conflict arises between the representative and one or more class members, the court can remove people from the class or even de-certify the class.

There are also other provisions in Rule 23 designed to ensure adequate representation. Rule 23(d) allows a judge to issue orders that, for example, give class members the opportunity "to signify whether they consider the representation fair and adequate." Similarly, Rule 23(e), governing settlement, contains extensive protections for the class members.

11. *Typicality*, the third requirement, is designed to deal with the same sorts of concerns as adequate representation. If a representative's claim is significantly different than those of the class, there is a greater chance that the interests of the representative may diverge from the interests of those being represented. However, given that Rule 23(a) already requires adequate representation, it is not entirely clear what additional function typicality serves. In fact, the requirement may operate to prevent someone from serving as representative even though she might be a completely adequate representative.

12. *Rule 23(b)* describes three types of class actions. Unless the case at bar fits into one of these three classes, it cannot be certified as a class action. Rule 23(a) and 23(b) must both be satisfied for certification to occur.

13. You may have found the language of *Rule 23(b)(1)* vaguely familiar. That should come as no surprise. The language of Rule 23(b)(1) closely tracks the language of Rule 19 (necessary parties) and 24(a) (intervention of right). In essence, Rule 23(b)(1) provides that a class action is appropriate when the dispute involves a large number of people who should be in the case because their interests will likely be affected, or because their claims expose one of the existing parties to a risk of inconsistent judgments. Suppose a defendant faces lawsuits by thousands of different plaintiffs who were all injured by defendant's allegedly defective product. If the suits are prosecuted individually, defendant may win some and lose some. Does that defendant face a risk of "incompatible standards of conduct" within the meaning of Rule 23(b)(1)(A)? *See Zinser v. Accufix Research Institute, Inc.*, 253 F.3d 1180, 1193–94 (9th Cir. 2000).

14. Rule 23(b)(1)(B) class actions can raise serious problems of adequacy and typicality under Rule 23(a). Can you see why? Because certification may occur only if both Rule 23(a) and (b) are satisfied, do not assume that a class comprising hundreds of necessary parties with competing claims will automatically be certified.

15. *Rule 23(b)(2).* The Rule 23(b)(2) class action is in some ways the most intuitively obvious type of class action. Suppose a part-time law student sues his law school to prevent the school from carrying out its decision to terminate its part-time division. If the student wins, all other students who want to continue the part-time division will automatically benefit. Rule 23(b)(2), then, merely allows the plaintiff to spread the costs of obtaining the injunction among all parties who will benefit. The party opposing the class (the law school in our example) also benefits from knowing that a single case can finally resolve this issue, as the judgment in the class action would bind all members of the class.

16. *Rule 23(b)(3).* The Rule 23(b)(3) class action, the type at issue in *Szabo*, is the most complex and controversial form of class action. In this sort of case, the claims are neither logically intertwined as they are under 23(b)(1), nor practically intertwined as under 23(b)(2). Instead, Rule 23(b)(3) class actions exist mainly because of the potential savings due to economies of scale. It is much more efficient if a single court decides a particular issue once and for all, rather than having many different courts decide that exact same question time and time again in separate cases. In addition, allowing a single court to decide the issue prevents inconsistent judgments.

However, because the class action introduces a new set of complexities (both legal and practical), those savings can be realized only if there is a high degree of overlap between the claims. This concern is reflected in Rule 23(b)(3)'s requirement that the common issues of law or fact *predominate* over the individual issues. Predominance is measured not simply by counting the number of shared and individual issues, but instead by evaluating how much time the court will have to spend on each issue.

17. Apply the Rule 23(b)(3) standard to a typical case. Several thousand people are injured by the air bags installed in a particular make of car. These injuries range from broken noses to death. One of the injured brings a claim, alleging that the airbags were defectively designed to deploy prematurely. The manufacturer denies the product is defective. Assuming Rule

23(a) is met, is the court likely to certify this case as a class action? What are the common issues of law and fact? The individual issues?

18. *Szabo* raises another issue that often arises in nationwide class actions: differences in the governing law. In that case, the court found that all claims would be governed by the same state's law. However, if different states' laws govern the various claims, a court is extremely unlikely to certify all the claims as part of a single class action. *In the Matter of Bridgestone/Firestone, Inc., Tires Products Liability Litigation*, 288 F.3d 1012, 1014 (7th Cir. 2002) ("No class action is proper unless all litigants are governed by the same legal rules.")

Of course, if the claims are governed by *federal* law, this problem does not arise. Similarly, the problem does not arise if the substantive rules of all governing state laws are the same. *See, e.g., In the Matter of Mexico Money Transfer Litigation*, 267 F.3d 743 (7th Cir. 2001) (certification of nationwide class granted because plaintiffs alleged only federal law claims and state claims where the law of all involved states was the same.)

19. *Limited certification.* Even when the individual issues predominate when the case is viewed as a whole, a court may be able to make limited use of the class action by certifying a class only on the *common issue.* For example, in the airbag situation described in note 17, the court could certify a class solely on the issue of whether the airbags were defectively designed. If the court determines that there was no defect, the claims would be dismissed. If the court determines that there was a defect, each of the individual plaintiffs could then file an individual claim for damages. The manufacturer in these later cases would be precluded by the doctrine of issue preclusion from arguing that the airbag was not defective. For two examples of partial certification, *see Mejdrech v. Met–Coil Systems Corp.*, 319 F.3d 910 (7th Cir. 2003) *and Rink v. Cheminova, Inc.*, 203 F.R.D. 648 (M.D. Fla. 2001).

20. *Superiority.* Predominance is not the only requirement for a proper Rule 23(b)(3) class action. The court must also find that a class action is superior to other methods of resolving the entire controversy. This "superiority" factor compares the class action to both individual lawsuits and joinder of the claims under Rule 20. A major consideration in determining whether a class action is superior is whether each claimant has a sufficient *incentive* to litigate her own rights. Other things equal, a court is more likely to certify a class made up a number of small claims than one in which the claimants all suffered serious injuries. If each claimant only suffered a few dollars in damages, it is quite likely that many would not bother with the time and expense of an individual lawsuit, or even with joining as a co-plaintiff in an existing case.

Apply that reasoning to *Szabo*. The plaintiff in *Szabo* was seeking damages in excess of $70,000. Why does he want the case to be a class action? After all, the class action certification process is complicated and expensive. Does Szabo gain any advantages by having to represent not only his own rights, but also the rights of other purchasers of the part?

At the opposite end of the spectrum are securities fraud cases. Victims in these cases typically have fairly small claims. Moreover, because they can sue under federal law, the choice of law problem is not a factor. However, fraud class actions have problems of their own. The issue on which a fraud class action is most likely to fail is *reliance*. Even if the victims all saw the same information (for example, a written prospectus), the representative must demonstrate that everyone relied on the statement, and that such reliance was reasonable.

21. *Certification order; Notice and opt-out.* If the court decides to grant the motion to certify, Rule 23(c) requires it to issue an order defining the composition of the class, and setting out the claims, issues, and defenses that will be considered in the class action. The court must also appoint an attorney for the class. Furthermore, depending on the type of class, the representative may be required to notify all the members of the class and give them the right to "opt out."

Note that the order does not have to describe the class members by name. In many cases, it is impossible to determine who is in a class, either because of lack of records or because the particular trait that applies to the members has not yet manifested itself. In these situations, a court could define the class as "Every person who purchased a sound recording under the *XYZ* label between 2001 and 2005," or "Every person who took the medication commonly called 'Placebo,' and who subsequently developed, or will develop, any form of skin rash." Note that in the latter case, it may be many years before the class can be identified with certainty. In fact, a person's rights may be adjudicated by a class action even though she does not realize she is in the class. In such a case, a court will typically order the creation of a fund against which future claimants can file claims.

The class attorney is typically someone with experience with class actions, ideally someone who also has experience with the type of claim involved in this case.

22. Rule 23(c)(2) covers notice and opt-out. Read that rule carefully, noting how it distinguishes between the three types of class actions listed in Rule 23(b).

23. *Notice.* Although Rule 23(c)(2)(A) makes notice optional in Rule 23(b)(1) and (b)(2) class actions, many courts require notice. Part of the motivation for requiring notice is a concern that notice may be constitutionally required. See *Richards v. Jefferson County*, 517 U.S. 793, 116 S.Ct. 1761, 135 L.Ed.2d 76 (1996) (see page 763); *Phillips Petroleum v. Shutts*, 472 U.S. 797, 105 S.Ct. 2965, 86 L.Ed.2d 628 (1985).

Rule 23 requires individual notice to all class members whose name and location can be identified. This requirement cannot be waived through the use of other means such as notice by publication. *Eisen v. Carlisle and Jacquelin*, 417 U.S. 156, 94 S.Ct. 2140, 40 L.Ed.2d 732 (1974). As you might imagine, the cost of providing this notice can be quite high, especially in a large class action. Although the costs of notice can be deducted from the recovery if the class should ultimately prevail, the Supreme Court has held that the class representative must initially bear the costs of notice. *Oppenheimer Fund, Inc. v. Sanders*, 437 U.S. 340, 98 S.Ct. 2380, 57 L.Ed.2d 253 (1978).

24. *Opt out.* The rules allowing a member to opt out are a direct response to the representation concerns raised in *Hansberry*. A party himself

is the ultimate judge of whether his rights will be adequately represented. If the party feels, for whatever reason, that he would rather try his own luck, he may withdraw his claim from the class action.

Why is opt-out not required in Rule 23(b)(1) and (b)(2) class actions? Aren't the concerns for adequate representation and party autonomy at least as great in those cases? Think again about the nature of those two types of class actions. In Rule 23(b)(1), the members would all be necessary parties under Rule 19. If they are necessary, does it make sense to allow them to opt out? Under Rule 23(b)(2), by contrast, allowing for opt-out would create a more practical problem. Consider a situation where X is a member of a class in a case seeking to enjoin pollution from a nearby factory. A rational person in X's shoes would almost always choose to opt out. Can you see why? Consider what happens if X opts out and the class wins the case. Compare that to what happens if X opts out and the class loses.

25. In class actions brought under the Age Discrimination in Employment Act, courts use an "opt-in" mechanism rather than the opt-out system provided in Federal Rule 23. *Hipp v. Liberty Nat'l Life Ins.*, 252 F.3d 1208, 1216 (11th Cir. 2001).

26. What happens if the notice and opt-out form cannot be served on one or more members? Rule 23 allows the court to keep these members in the class. However, out of a concern for fairness many courts will exclude from the class any member who did not receive the notice.

3. Other Issues in Class Actions

a. Personal Jurisdiction

Rule 23(c)(3) provides that a judgment in a class action binds all members of the class who do not opt out, regardless of whether it is favorable. As you saw in Chapter 4, a court must have personal jurisdiction over someone in order to issue an order that binds them in any way. As in the *Szabo* case, however, many class actions include members scattered all across the nation. How can a court in one state bind people who have no minimum contacts with that state? Is jurisdiction somehow based on "consent," as with ordinary plaintiffs?

In *Phillips Petroleum v. Shutts*, 472 U.S. 797, 105 S.Ct. 2965, 86 L.Ed.2d 628 (1985), the Supreme Court held that a state court could adjudicate the rights of all members of a plaintiff class action even though there were not minimum contacts between those members and the state. The Court indicated that the protections of Rule 23 were enough to satisfy due process. However, the Court was careful to point out that its reasoning only applied to *plaintiff* class actions certified under *Rule 23(b)(3)*. Should the analysis be different for defendant class actions, or for actions under Rule 23(b)(1) or (2)? What about the fact that notice is not required by Rule 23 in 23(b)(1) and (2) actions?

b. Federal Subject Matter Jurisdiction

As in the case of interpleader, there is a special statute that expands federal subject-matter jurisdiction in certain class action cases. In 2005,

Congress amended the general diversity statute, 28 U.S.C. § 1332, to add a new subsection (d). This subsection applies to any plaintiff class action where the total amount in controversy exceeds $5,000,000. Thus, unlike previous law, the statute allows plaintiffs to aggregate their claims to meet the amount in controversy requirement. Moreover, § 1332(d) requires only "minimal diversity;" that is, only one member of the plaintiff class needs to be diverse from any one defendant. However, if more than one-third of the class members are from the same state as the "primary defendants," the action is filed in the state where those parties reside, and the claim arose in that same state, the court may decline to exercise jurisdiction based on factors listed in § 1332(d)(3). If more than two-thirds of the plaintiff class resides in the same state as any significant defendant, the action is filed in that state, and the claims arose in that state, the court must refuse to exercise jurisdiction. Can you guess Congress's motives in expanding federal jurisdiction to cover these cases? The bill was strongly supported by the Bush administration.

In plaintiff class actions involving less than $5,000,000, and in defendant class actions, a class representative who sues in federal court must demonstrate that the case meets the requirements of the general federal question or diversity statutes (§§ 1331 and 1332 respectively), or that the particular claim fits under one of the more specialized federal question statutes, such as § 1343 (civil rights claims). As long as every member of the class has a claim arising under federal law, subject matter jurisdiction presents no special issues in class action cases. Courts determine whether the claims arise under federal law in exactly the same way they analyze claims in ordinary cases.

When some of the class members' claims arise under *state* law, however, the plaintiff may need to make use of diversity and/or supplemental jurisdiction. In these situations, additional unique rules apply to class actions.

1. Diversity

Under the complete diversity rule that applies under § 1332, diversity is proper only if no plaintiff is from the same state as any defendant. However, in class actions, the court considers *only the citizenship of the named representative(s). Supreme Tribe of Ben–Hur v. Cauble*, 255 U.S. 356, 41 S.Ct. 338, 65 L.Ed. 673 (1921). Therefore, diversity jurisdiction can still exist even if a number of the class members are from the same state as one or more of the defendants. Should this rule still apply when 90 percent of the class members are from the same state as the opposing party, but the attorney purposefully picked a representative who was diverse?

Conversely, when applying the amount in controversy requirement, courts historically considered the claims of *all* members. According to the Supreme Court's decision in *Zahn v. International Paper Co.*, 414 U.S. 291, 94 S.Ct. 505, 38 L.Ed.2d 511 (1973), every member's claim must be greater than the amount in controversy. Aggregation of the members' claims will rarely be an option. Note that this requirement does not necessarily force a particular class action into state court. As long as the class is defined to include only those members whose claims exceed the amount in controversy, the class action can proceed under diversity jurisdiction.

2. Supplemental Jurisdiction

EXXON MOBIL CORP. v. ALLAPATTAH SERVICES, INC.

___ U.S. ___, 125 S.Ct. 2611, 162 L.Ed.2d 502 (2005)

[This case is set out in Chapter 3, Part D.]

Notes and Questions

1. *Exxon Mobil* largely overturns the holding in *Zahn*. Now, members of a plaintiff class have a limited ability to aggregate their claims to meet the amount in controversy requirement.

2. Note, however, that supplemental jurisdiction is available only if at least one of the members of the plaintiff class has a claim exceeding $75,000.

3. Would the rule of *Exxon Mobil* apply to a *defendant* class action? Why or why not?

4. What effect, if any, does *Exxon Mobil* have on the citizenship requirements for diversity jurisdiction? What if some members of the plaintiff class are not diverse from the defendant? What if one of the named representatives is not diverse?

5. *Exxon Mobil* has no effect on the expanded federal jurisdiction granted by 28 U.S.C. § 1332(d). That statute, discussed above, applies in cases where the total amount in controversy exceeds $5,000,000.

---

c. *Resolving the Class Action*

Many, if not most, cases brought as a class action are settled. Settlement often occurs after the court's decision whether to certify the case as a class action. If the court denies class certification, settlement presents no special issues. If the court does certify the class, however, settlement becomes a trickier issue. As you have seen throughout this discussion, Rule 23 is designed to protect the interests of the class members. One of these protections is set out in Rule 23(e). Under this rule, the court must approve any settlement of the class action. (Courts do not usually concern themselves with the terms of a settlement.) Rule 23 allows the court to scrutinize the settlement carefully to ensure that it is not a "sweetheart deal" benefitting the representative at the expense of the members. Moreover, the parties must provide notice of the proposed settlement to the class members. The class members may then challenge the settlement if they feel it is not in their best interests.

Plaintiffs sometimes delay seeking class action certification until *after* the general terms of a settlement have been reached. In these cases, the parties ask the court to certify a "settlement class action." Class certification is as beneficial to the defendant in these cases as it is to the plaintiff, as it allows defendant to deal in one fell swoop with all claims arising out of a particular transaction or occurrence. Plaintiff also stands to benefit, as if the case is settled he need not conduct any more litigation. Nevertheless, these settlement class actions create a real possibility of abuse. In *Anchem Products, Inc. v. Windsor*, 521 U.S. 591, 117 S.Ct. 2231, 138 L.Ed.2d 689 (1997), the Supreme Court set out significant limits on the use of settlement class actions. These limits seek to ensure that the interests of the class members—who played no role whatsoever in the negotiation of the settlement—are fully and fairly represented.

If a class action proceeds to trial, courts continue to be solicitous of the interests of the absent members. Class members do not have the right to hire their own counsel to litigate their individual claims. However, the class members may challenge the adequacy of the representation at any time during the course of the proceedings. Even in the middle of trial, the court may de-certify the class, or exclude a certain subset of the members, if representation is not adequate.

Problems

1. A union declares a labor strike against a certain employer. According to the union agreement, all union members agree, as a condition of membership, to co-operate in a strike. Nevertheless, X, a union member, declares that she will cross the picket line. R, a union official, sues X for an injunction. R gets the case certified as a class action, in which R represents all union members. X defends by claiming that the provision in the union agreement preventing her from working is illegal under federal law. R prevails, and the court renders judgment.

Later, Y declares that he will cross the picket line. When R sues Y, Y also raises the defense that the term in the union agreement is illegal. R argues that Y is barred by the judgment in *R v. X* from arguing that the agreement is illegal. Is Y barred?

2. Same facts as Problem 1, except that suppose that the court gave all class members notice and the chance to opt out. Y received notice, but did not opt out. Is Y barred?

3. Same as Problem 1, except suppose that R *lost* his case against X. When Y declares his intention, Z, another member of the union, sues Y. Y argues that Z is barred from arguing that the agreement *is* enforceable. Is Z barred?

4. Same as Problem 3, except that the reason R lost the first case was because he refused to allow the attorney to call a crucial witness who would have testified in favor of enforceability.

5. In Problem 1, if the court were to certify the case as a class action, into which Rule 23(b) category(ies) would it fit?

6. Professor X teaches an upper-level law school class in which 15 students are enrolled. When Professor X unilaterally changes the date of the final, student R sues Professor X. Student R wants to have the case certified as a class action. Is the case likely to satisfy Rule 23(a)?

7. Same as Problem 6, except suppose that the Rule 23(a) requirements of numerosity and adequacy are satisfied. Student R's reason for wanting to prevent a change in the date of the exam is that he is to be married on the date that Professor X has selected. Is the case likely to satisfy Rule 23(a)?

8. Skinflint Corp. insists that when its employees are on a business trip, they all eat together. Of course, Skinflint picks up the tab. However, company policy strictly forbids employees from leaving a tip. Skinflint has learned that many restaurants have adopted a policy of automatically adding in a 15 to 20 percent gratuity for groups of six or more diners. Company auditors calculate that as a result of this policy, the company has been forced to pay gratuities to hundreds of restaurants all over the nation. Skinflint therefore sues Ginny's Diner, one of the offending restaurants, for reimbursement of the amount it paid as a gratuity to Ginny's. Skinflint claims that under state law, an automatic fee added to a bill is not a "gratuity." Skinflint seeks to have Ginny's Diner named as representative of a defendant class of all restaurants that have charged such a fee to Skinflint employees. Is the case likely to satisfy Rule 23(a)?

9. Same as Problem 8. Assuming that the case meets Rule 23(a), into which Rule 23(b) category does it fit best? Would the class action satisfy the requirements of that subpart of Rule 23(b)?

10. Same as Problem 8. Skinflint brings its action in federal court. Skinflint is diverse from Ginny's Diner. Moreover, because its employees love Ginny's fried pickles, Skinflint seeks well over $100,000 in damages from Ginny's. However, Skinflint is not diverse from some of the other restaurants. Moreover, in many cases the forced gratuity was $500 or less. Will a federal court have subject-matter jurisdiction over the class action?

11. R sues D for damages. The court certifies R as the representative of a Rule 23(b)(1) class action. Must R pay for notice to be sent to all members of the class?

12. Same as Problem 11. X, a member of the class, asks the court to be excluded from the class. The court refuses to exclude X, reasoning that he is not entitled to "opt out" in this sort of case. Is the court correct?

13. Same as Problem 11, except that the court certifies R as the representative of a Rule 23(b)(3) class. R sends notice to all of the class members. R and D eventually settle the case. The court approves the settlement. Later, X, a member of the class who received notice of class certification and did not opt out, sues D for the same claim as that litigated in the class action. D argues that the settlement agreement bars X from suing. X disagrees, arguing that he should have received a second, separate notice of the proposed settlement. Assuming that no second notice was sent, who will win?

CHAPTER 7

DISCOVERY

———————

In Chapter 5, we noted that the primary function of modern pleading rules is to provide notice to the opposing party about the nature of the claim or answer. The general requirements for pleading, though, postpone the development of the claims' and defenses' underlying facts. The discovery rules thus play a vital role in trial preparation. The Supreme Court in *United States v. Procter & Gamble Company,* 356 U.S. 677, 78 S.Ct. 983, 2 L.Ed.2d 1077 (1958) stated that discovery devices "together with pretrial procedures make a trial less a game of blind man's bluff and more a fair contest with the basic issues and facts disclosed to the fullest practicable extent."

At a minimum, the purposes of the discovery rules are:

- to narrow the issues, so that it may be unnecessary to produce evidence at trial for issues that are not disputed;

- to obtain evidence for use at trial;

- to learn about the existence of evidence that may be used at the trial and to determine how and from whom it may be obtained. e.g., the existence, custody, and location of documents or the names and addresses of persons having knowledge of relevant facts;

- to promote negotiated settlements through observation of the demeanor and responses of witnesses and through verification of documents which facilitate a practical assessment of the value of a case;

- to further trial verdicts based upon accurate presentations, instead of surprise; and

- to provide an economical method of resolving disputes, presuming that attorneys use the rules appropriately.

The rationale for discovery is that every party to a civil action is entitled to pretrial disclosure of all relevant information in the control of any person, unless the information is privileged. Pretrial discovery is not bound by the evidentiary rules of admissibility applicable at trial. The discovery rules provide several devices for use under varying circumstances to acquire information. Federal Rules 30 and 32 govern depositions; Rule 33 authorizes interrogatories to parties; Rule 34 provides for the production of documents and things and entry upon land for inspection and other purposes; Rule 35 permits physical and mental examination of persons; Rule 36 governs requests for admissions.

Rule 26 is the basic device applicable to all the federal discovery devices. It contains the principal provisions on the scope of discovery that regulate all discovery devices. By the use of one or more of the discovery mechanisms, a party can prepare for trial in a manner that promotes the just, speedy, and inexpensive determination of the case as prescribed in Rule 1. Courts recognize the value of the discovery rules and generally construe them liberally. The goal of flexible discovery is to end the "sporting theory of justice," by which the result depends on the fortuitous availability of evidence or the skill and strategy of counsel. Concerns about discovery abuse, e.g., excessive discovery, have produced specific rules mandating exchange of certain information, as well as Rule 26(g), which is analogous to Federal Rule 11.

A. THE SCOPE OF DISCOVERY

1. Mandatory Disclosure

INTRODUCTORY PROBLEM

Grant and Hayes (doing business as City Cycle) sue Harding Cycle in an Ohio federal court over a contract dispute involving a bicycle franchise agreement. The legal basis of the plaintiffs' claim is a violation of the Federal Franchisee Protection Act of 1962. Plaintiffs for several years sold more bicycles in the United States than any other retailer. Harding Cycle was plaintiffs' wholesaler, renting the store to the plaintiffs and supplying the bikes for the plaintiffs' retail operation. The plaintiffs allege that Harding Cycle became jealous of their success, broke the rental agreement for leasing the store, and persuaded the manufacturer not to renew the franchise agreement with them because it told the manufacturer that it could sell even more bicycles than City Cycle.

Following the filing of the pleadings, what information must the parties exchange with each other under the Federal Rules?

Governing Rule: Rule 26(a).

———————

In 1993, following years of controversy about discovery abuses such as the failure to turn over even the most basic of information, the Supreme Court drafted Rule 26(a), mandating the disclosure by each party of certain types of information that otherwise would and should be exchanged by the parties in any civil litigation. Rule 26(a) requires disclosure of certain information at three periods during litigation, without the need for a discovery request from an opposing party. First, following a discovery meeting under Rule 26(f), the parties must make broad initial disclosures under Rule 26(a)(1). Second, 90 days before trial, the parties must disclose information about expert testimony, pursuant to Rule 26(a)(2). Finally, 30 days before trial, the parties must make specific pretrial disclosures, under Rule 26(a)(3).

What is the normal order of initial discovery events in federal litigation? First, the court schedules a Rule 26(f) scheduling conference, before which the parties conduct a discovery meeting to explore the possibility of a settlement, arrange for the Rule 26(a) mandatory disclosures, and develop a proposal for a discovery plan. Second, the parties make their mandatory disclosures and then meet with the trial judge for the scheduling conference at which a discovery timetable is established.

Rule 26(a) requires automatic, initial disclosure, without the need for a request, of four categories of information that are then "reasonably available": 1) names of witnesses "likely to have discoverable information that the disclosing party may use to support its claims or defenses" and the subjects of such information; 2) copies (or at least categories and locations) of "documents, data compilations, and tangible things that are in the possession, custody, or control of the party" which the disclosing party may use in support of its claims or defenses; 3) damage computations of any category of damage claimed by the disclosing party, including non-privileged documents supporting the computation and the nature and extent of injuries; and 4) all insurance policies that may provide coverage for all or part of a later judgment in the case. Disclosure of information or documents to be used exclusively for impeachment is unnecessary at this point. (Impeachment refers to questioning which discredits a witness by showing that the witness is not telling the truth or does not have a reliable basis for the offered testimony.) Failing to disclose the information can result in the exclusion of the witness's testimony or the document from evidence. A party can object to making the disclosures at the conference, because they "are not appropriate in the circumstances of the action...." By stipulation or court order, the initial disclosure process may be modified or eliminated.

Unless otherwise ordered or stipulated, ninety days before trial the parties must disclose information about expert testimony, per Rule 26(a)(2). The content of the disclosure is the identity of any person who "may" testify as an expert witness, along with the disclosure of a report for each expert witness. The written report must be signed by the expert, and state: 1) all of the expert's opinions as well as the grounds for the opinions; 2) any information considered by the expert in reaching those opinions; 3) any exhibits which support or summarize the opinions; and 4) the expert's qualifications, publications, compensations and cases during the past four years where she testified or was deposed. See Section A.4 of this Chapter, *infra*.

Unless otherwise ordered by the trial court under Rule 26(a)(3), thirty days before trial every party must make a written disclosure of the identity of each witness who may testify, as well as deposition testimony and exhibits that may be offered at trial. Again, impeachment witnesses and other information do not have to be disclosed. Any opponent objecting to a deposition or exhibit must express an objection within two weeks of the disclosure of the intent to use it.

2. Discovery of Relevant and Non–Privileged Information

INTRODUCTORY PROBLEM #1

In *Grant and Hayes v. Harding Cycle* (referred to in part 1, *supra*), the defendant sent interrogatories and a request for production of documents to the plaintiffs. Defendant seeks information for the previous five years about plaintiffs' business income, business and personal expenses, financial worth, tax returns, the identities of all legal counsel employed, the advice sought from them, and any oral and written statements about this litigation made to legal counsel by plaintiffs or anyone else.

Upon defendant's request, what is the obligation of plaintiffs to disclose the information to the defendant?

Governing Rule: Rule 26(b).

INTRODUCTORY PROBLEM #2

Pete Lilly sits forlornly in his prison dormitory, thinking of happier days in Las Vegas or selling his wares on cable television. Lilly misses playing baseball, too, and he contacts attorney Ruben Feline about whether a lawsuit can be filed to install a baseball diamond at the prison. Feline files a civil rights claim in federal court in Indianapolis against the United States Bureau of Prisons, seeking to require prison officials to institute a baseball rehabilitation training program at Lilly's prison. Feline has a letter from Lilly outlining the benefits of such a program as well as the logistical difficulties of installing a diamond at the prison. Pretrial discovery ensues.

Ned Mice is the attorney for the U.S. Bureau of Prisons. He serves a timely request upon Lilly for production of copies of "all information in your files pertaining to the justification for this lawsuit." Must Lilly or Feline produce a copy of the letter or provide this information to Mice?

Governing Rule: Federal Rule 26(b)-(c).

––––––––––

Federal Rule 26(b)(1) states that discovery is appropriate when it is "reasonably calculated to lead to the discovery of admissible evidence." Thus, for purposes of discovery, "relevant" information is broader than the information that would be admissible at trial, as long as it can be said that the information sought satisfies the "reasonably calculated" language.

Without judicial intervention using Rule 26(b)(1), a party may discover information "relevant to the claims or defenses of any party." In addition, the trial judge may order discovery of information that is "relevant" to the subject matter on a showing of "good cause."

THOMPSON v. DEPARTMENT OF HOUSING AND URBAN DEVEL.

199 F.R.D. 168 (D. Md. 2001)

GRIMM, United States Magistrate Judge.

Plaintiffs are class representatives of African American residents of Baltimore's public housing developments. They filed suit in January, 1995 against the U.S. Department of Housing and Urban Development and its secretary (the "federal defendants") and the Housing Authority of Baltimore City ("HABC"), its executive director and the Mayor and City Council of Baltimore (the "local defendants"). The class action lawsuit alleged that the defendants and their predecessors, from 1933 through the present, established and perpetuated *de jure* racial segregation in Baltimore's public housing, in violation of the 5th, 13th, and 14th Amendments to the United States Constitution, as well as Title VI of the Civil Rights Act of 1964, Title VIII of the Civil Rights Act of 1968, 42 U.S.C. Sections 1981, 1982, and 1983, the U.S. Housing Act of 1937 and the Housing and Community Development Act of 1974. Plaintiffs seek declaratory, injunctive, and equitable relief, and attorneys' fees.

* * * [I]n mid–2000 the plaintiffs initiated discovery against the defendants, and the undersigned was referred the case for resolution of discovery disputes. Pending is the motion by the plaintiffs to compel the local defendants to provide responsive answers to Rule 33 and 34 discovery requests.

* * * The combined effect of the changes to Rule 26(b)(1) and (2) [between 1993 and 2000] was to create a procedural syllogism of sorts, which defined the contours of the scope of discovery. Under it, facts were discoverable if: (1) relevant to the subject matter of the litigation; and (2) not privileged; and (3) if not themselves admissible, then reasonably calculated to lead to admissible evidence, unless the court, *sua sponte*, or at the request of a party, determined that the discovery sought was: (a) unreasonably cumulative, duplicative, or obtainable from another more convenient, less burdensome or less expensive source; or (b) the party seeking the discovery had had sufficient opportunity by discovery in the pending action to obtain it; or, (c) following a costs-benefits analysis that balanced (i) the burden or expense associated with the requested discovery; (ii) the likely benefit to the requesting party of the challenged discovery; (iii) taking into account the following factors: (aa) the needs of the case; (bb) the amount in controversy, (cc) the parties resources, (dd)

the importance of the issues at stake in the litigation, and (ee) the importance of the proposed discovery in resolving the issues, the court determined that the requested discovery should not be allowed.

For purposes of applying the above test the definition of relevance in Fed.R.Evid. 401 was most helpful; Rule 26(b)(5) and Discovery Guidelines 5 and 9 of this court required that privileges be identified with particularity in order to justify a refusal to disclose requested information, and courts were quick to add that unparticularized claims of burden or expense were insufficient. Moreover, application of the cost-benefit factors identified in Rule 26(b)(2) enabled the court to allocate the costs of discovery between the parties, thereby, in appropriate cases, requiring a party seeking contested discovery to pay all or part of the expenses of obtaining it.

Despite the obvious utility of the Rule 26(b)(2) factors in tailoring discovery to accommodate fair disclosure without imposing undue burden or expense, they have tended largely to be ignored by litigants, and, less frequently than desirable, used by the courts, *sua sponte,* to manage discovery. Instead, particularly with respect to disputes involving Rule 33 and Rule 34 discovery, the focus of the litigants tends to be the party seeking discovery's perceived "right" to all information relating to the broad "subject matter" of the litigation, without any reflection as to the real usefulness of the information sought, or the burden or expense required to produce it, countered by the party resisting the discovery's unparticularized claims of burden, expense, irrelevance, and privilege. Further, despite the requirements of Local Rule 104.7 and Discovery Guideline 1(d) of this court, the efforts of the litigants to resolve their disputes before seeking court intervention infrequently demonstrated that, during their discussions, the parties themselves attempted to evaluate the Rule 26(b)(2) factors to reach a common ground.

The most recent revisions to the discovery rules imposed changes intended to reach lingering concerns about the overbreadth and expense of discovery, and remind the courts and litigants of the fact that in determining what discovery should take place in a particular case, Rule 26(b)(1) is but the first step, necessarily followed by balancing the Rule 26(b)(2) factors. Accordingly, the December 1, 2000 changes to Rule 26(b)(1) restricted the scope of discovery to unprivileged facts relevant to "the claim or defense of any party", unless the court determines that there is "good cause" to permit broader discovery relevant to the subject matter of the action, but not more directly connected to the particular claims and defenses. They additionally required that discovery of inadmissible facts that appear reasonably calculated to lead to the discovery of admissible evidence also must be within the scope of permissible discovery. Furthermore, they emphasize that "all discovery is subject to the limitations imposed by Rule 26(b)(2)(i), (ii), and (iii)", the cost-benefit balancing factors.

The commentary to the rule changes clarifies that the amendment to the scope of discovery provisions of Rule 26(b)(1) "is designed to involve the court more actively in regulating the breadth of sweeping or contentious discovery", so that, if there is "an objection that discovery goes beyond material relevant to the parties' claims or defenses, the court would become involved to determine whether the discovery is relevant to the claims or defenses and, if not, whether good cause exists for authorizing it so long as it is relevant to the subject matter of the action." "Commentary to Rules Changes, Court Rules," 192 F.R.D. 340, 389. It also emphasizes the desirability of courts more vigorously applying the Rule 26(b)(2) cost-benefit factors in determining allowable discovery. *Id.* at 390.

Although the rule changes do not specifically explain the difference in scope between discovery relevant to "claims and defenses" in the litigation, and discovery relevant to the "subject matter," it is clear that the former is intended to be narrower than the latter, and that the broader discovery is only to be allowed for "good cause". Further, it seems clear that the most valuable reference to use in implementing the new change in the scope of discovery is the pleadings that have been filed, as that is where the claims and defenses are stated. However, the pleadings are only the starting place, as:

> [a] variety of types of information not directly pertinent to the incident in suit could be relevant to the claims or defenses raised in a given action. For example, other incidents of the same type, or involving the same product could be properly discoverable under the revised standard. Information about organizational arrangements or filing systems of a party could be discoverable if likely to yield or lead to the discovery of admissible information. Similarly, information that could be used to impeach a likely witness, although not otherwise relevant to the claims or defenses, might be properly discoverable. In each instance, the determination whether such information is discoverable because it is relevant to the claims or defenses depends on the circumstances of the pending action.

Id. at 389.

* * * Lest litigants and the court become consumed with the philosophical exercise of debating the difference between discovery relevant to the "claims and defenses" as opposed to the "subject matter" of the pending action—the juridical equivalent to debating the number of angels that can dance on the head of a pin—the practical solution to implementing the new rule changes may be to focus more on whether the requested discovery makes sense in light of the Rule 26(b)(2) factors, than to attempt to divine some bright line difference between the old and new rule. Under this approach, when confronted with a difficult scope of discovery dispute, the parties themselves should confer, and discuss the Rule 26(b)(2) factors, in an effort to reach an acceptable compromise, or narrow the scope of their disagreement.

For example, if the plaintiff seeks discovery of information going back 20 years, and the defendant objects on the grounds of burden, a possible solution may be to agree first to produce information going back

5 years. Then, depending on the results of a review of the more recent information, if more extensive disclosure can be justified, based on the results of the initial, more limited, less burdensome, examination, it should be produced. Similarly, if the burden and expense of searching for and producing all documents that fall within the scope of a broad Rule 34 request is objected to, the party objecting might agree to spend up to a stated amount of time looking for the records, and producing them for inspection, with the understanding that if, following review of the documents produced, the requesting party can justify a request for more, under the Rule 26(b)(2) factors, it would be produced, perhaps under a cost sharing, or shifting agreement. The court, too, if called upon to resolve discovery disputes, may find such an incremental, phased approach useful, as a result of evaluating the Rule 26(b)(2) factors.

The pending discovery dispute illustrates the points raised above. The plaintiffs have filed a sweeping lawsuit alleging discriminatory action by the defendants covering three-quarters of a century, and involving all aspects of the public housing programs in Baltimore. Within a year or so of suit being filed, the parties entered into a comprehensive partial consent decree, itself broad in scope, which settled many, but by no means all, of the claims originally filed. After a hiatus in discovery of several years, plaintiffs initiated renewed discovery requests, under Rules 33 and 34. The local defendants objected to certain of these requests, asserting: overbreadth and burden, without giving particulars to permit either plaintiffs or the court meaningfully to evaluate this claim; and that the challenged requests exceeded the scope of permissible discovery as they were not tailored to the existing "claims and defenses" remaining in the litigation following the consent decree. Plaintiffs, justifying their discovery requests, argue their broad entitlement to discovery relating to the whole of the dispute that is the basis for the litigation, without once attempting to identify which claims that survived the partial consent decree will be furthered by the requested information, or addressing the burden to the local defendants to produce it. Both parties seem content to leave it to the court to sift through the 56–page complaint and the 74–page partial consent decree to determine what discovery should be allowed. Moreover, although counsel for the parties undoubtedly have conferred in an effort to resolve or narrow the dispute, they have provided the court with nothing to show whether they have attempted to apply the Rule 26(b)(2) balancing factors to try to reach common ground, at least as to some of the areas of dispute. This will not do.

I am returning this dispute to the parties with guidance as to how they should meet and confer to attempt to resolve or narrow their differences. * * * In this regard, it seems clear that the challenged requests are too broad as stated, and need to be narrowed by a good faith analysis of which claims that survived the partial consent decree will be furthered by the discovery sought. Additionally, the local defendants are cautioned that, provided the plaintiffs accommodate legitimate concerns of the local defendants regarding burden and expense, it is likely that for each of the discovery requests challenged on the basis of scope or burden, some discovery will be appropriate. However, unparticularized claims of burden or expense . . . will not suffice. If the local defendants claim that they cannot produce requested information because of burden, they must justify this claim with specific details that can be evaluated by the plaintiffs, and, if necessary, the court.

This means that the parties must set aside their differences as adversaries and make a good faith effort to reach common ground on the disputes. It strikes me that this case is a perfect example of how creative counsel can employ the phasing methods [described] by the Court . . . to permit the plaintiffs to have access to some, but less than all, of the information they seek, with the understanding that if, following the initial, limited review, additional discovery would make sense under the Rule 26(b)(2) factors, it will be provided. Cost shifting or sharing also should be considered.

If, following their consultations, counsel find that there still are differences that cannot be overcome by negotiation, as likely will be the case, they will contact me, and a discovery conference will be set promptly. While I am mindful of the fact that the commentary to the recent rule changes emphasizes the need for the court actively to be involved in applying the Rule 26(b)(2) factors, this involvement necessarily must follow, not precede, the parties own good faith efforts to do so. Therefore, if there is to be a discovery conference, the court will expect counsel to demonstrate that they have fully considered the cost/benefit factors, and made reasonable modifications of their positions to accommodate them.

Accordingly, it is . . . ordered that the plaintiffs' motion to compel discovery from the local defendants is denied, without prejudice, and the parties are to take further action in accordance with this order.

Notes and Questions

1. *Any matter . . . relevant to the claim or defense.* Rule 26(b)(1) begins with a general statement that "[p]arties may obtain discovery regarding any matter." What is a "matter"? Does it include information about the party's own case? About the opponent's case?

What is the practical significance of the 2000 amendment to rule 26(b)(1) changing the phrase "relevant to the subject matter" to "relevant to the claim or defense"? Is information about a similar incident or product still discoverable without the court's intervention? What about information about how a party operates its business? What about impeachment information?

What is information that is not "relevant to the claim or defense" but *is* "relevant to the subject matter," and thereby discoverable after a showing of "good cause"?

2. *What can be discovered.* Rule 26(b)(1) states which types of information are discoverable: "the existence, description, nature, custody, condition,

and location of any books, documents, or other tangible things and the identity and location of persons having knowledge of any discoverable matter." This portion of the rule clarifies that tangible things are discoverable, as are the names of individuals as sources of information. Indeed, those people do not have to have first-hand information. It is permissible to learn their identities if they have knowledge of any discoverable information, including inadmissible sources such as hearsay.

Even for information that is privileged and thus is not itself discoverable, it is still proper to request whether, for example, documents which may contain such privileged information exist or the identities of persons who may have privileged information. An example of such discovery could be phrased: "State whether documents were written to plaintiff's counsel by the plaintiff." *or* "State the identity of any person from whom a statement was taken."

As Rule 26(b)(1) states, evidence does not have to be admissible at a judicial proceeding in order to be relevant for discovery purposes. Relevant *in*admissible evidence is discoverable as long as it is "reasonably calculated to lead to the discovery of admissible evidence." Conversely, admissible evidence is generally discoverable.

3. *Attorney-client privilege.* Generally, the attorney-client privilege applies to communications between an attorney and the client, to whom the privilege belongs. The privilege protects communications made in confidence to an attorney (or the attorney's agent) whose legal advice is sought by a person who is or is attempting to become a client. The purpose of the privilege is to encourage complete and honest communication between the attorney and client. In response to a discovery request, a person claiming the privilege must raise it in response to a discovery request and will have the burden of proving that the privilege applies. For corporations, the privilege applies to all corporate employees (not just upper-level managers) who seek or receive legal advice from an attorney. *Upjohn Co. v. United States*, 449 U.S. 383, 101 S.Ct. 677, 66 L.Ed.2d 584 (1981).

If correctly stated, a request for discovery should not create an issue that privileged information is being sought by a party. For example, in a personal injury case, an interrogatory that asks, "What color was the traffic signal when you went through the intersection?" properly seeks relevant information and ordinarily must be answered. However, an interrogatory which asks, "What did you tell your attorney about the color of the traffic signal at the intersection?" seeks information that was the subject of an exchange between the party and the party's attorney. The party receiving the interrogatory should object to answering this interrogatory because it seeks privileged information. If the party answers the interrogatory, she has voluntarily waived the claim of privilege.

4. *Rule 26(b)(5)'s requirements.* An attorney withholding information based on a claim of privilege or based on attorney work product protection is supposed to maintain a document index, or "privilege log," which expressly states the basis of her claim and describes in detail the nature of the information of the document withheld so that the opposing party can evaluate the claim. Specifically, a party objecting to discovery must describe the documents without having to disclose the information that is privileged

and provide "precise reasons" for the objection to the discovery. The information provided in the privilege log also must be sufficient to enable the court to determine whether each element of the asserted privilege is satisfied. See, e.g., *McCoo v. Denny's Inc.*, 192 F.R.D. 675 (D. Kan. 2000).

Maintaining a privilege log operates as a sufficient assertion of a privilege. What is the effect on the assertion of a privilege if a responding party raises a Rule 26(b)(5) objection but fails to keep a privilege log? Is the privilege waived? *Burlington Northern & Santa Fe Ry. Co. v. U.S. Dist. Court for Dist. of Mont.*, 408 F.3d 1142, 1149 (9th Cir. 2005) addressed the issue.

> [W]e . . . reject a per se waiver rule that deems a privilege waived if a privilege log is not produced within Rule 34's 30–day time limit. Instead, using the 30–day period as a default guideline, a district court should make a case-by-case determination, taking into account the following factors: the degree to which the objection or assertion of privilege enables the litigant seeking discovery and the court to evaluate whether each of the withheld documents is privileged (where providing particulars typically contained in a privilege log is presumptively sufficient and boilerplate objections are presumptively insufficient); the timeliness of the objection and accompanying information about the withheld documents (where service within 30 days, as a default guideline, is sufficient); the magnitude of the document production; and other particular circumstances of the litigation that make responding to discovery unusually easy (such as, here, the fact that many of the same documents were the subject of discovery in an earlier action) or unusually hard.

5. *Protective orders.* Does a party or witness have a remedy when she has a problem with the type or manner of discovery? Rule 26(c) governs protective orders, which are intended to protect parties and witnesses during discovery from having to disclose information under the requested circumstances. A protective order may be sought because either 1) the information sought falls outside the rules, or 2) though the information can be discovered under the rules, some aspect of the discovery of that information is troubling to the responding party. Prior to seeking a protective order, a party must in good faith confer or attempt to confer with the other party to try to resolve the discovery dispute without the trial court's intervention.

Either a party or a witness may file a motion for a protective order, which issues only on a showing of "good cause" to shield her "from annoyance, embarrassment, oppression, or undue burden or expense." For example, when the frequency or extent of discovery sought violates the proportionality rules of Rule 26(b)(2), the court has the discretion to grant a motion for a protective order. Courts may also issue protective orders to address automatic disclosure or other types of requested discovery.

Rule 26(c) specifies eight examples of protective orders, but the list is not exhaustive. Specific categories are that disclosure or discovery:

- not occur (rarely granted for depositions);
- occur only under specific terms and conditions, e.g., time to respond;
- occur using a different method than the discovery method selected, e.g., no depositions;

- not occur about certain matters or that it be limited to certain matters, e.g., limits on scope or time;

- occur with only certain persons present, e.g., exclude the public or other witnesses;

- occur as a sealed deposition, to be opened only by court order, i.e., no disclosure to third parties;

- of a trade secret not occur or be revealed by a specific method; and

- occur simultaneously and opened at the court's direction.

6. *Proportionality of discovery requests.* Courts presume that the responding party must pay for the expenses of discovery compliance. However, Rule 26(b)(2)'s proportionality principle may subject the requesting party to a protective order under Rule 26(c) for the cost of compliance to shift "for good cause shown." For example, in *Zubulake v. UBS Warburg LLC,* 216 F.R.D. 280 (S.D.N.Y. 2003), an employment gender discrimination suit, the court considered whether cost-shifting is appropriate for discovery of inaccessible e-mail data, using the following factors as "a guide":

1. The extent to which the request is specifically tailored to discover relevant information;

2. The availability of such information from other sources;

3. The total cost of production, compared to the amount in controversy;

4. The total cost of production, compared to the resources available to each party;

5. The relative ability of each party to control costs and its incentive to do so;

6. The importance of the issues at stake in the litigation; and

7. The relative benefits to the parties of obtaining the information

* * *

The more likely it is that the backup tape contains information that is relevant to a claim or defense, the fairer it is that the [responding party] search at its own expense.

* * *

Because some of the factors cut against cost shifting, but only *slightly so*—in particular, the possibility that the continued production will produce valuable new information—some cost-shifting is appropriate in this case, although UBS should pay the majority of the costs. There is plainly relevant evidence that is only available on UBS's backup tapes. At the same time, Zubulake has not been able to show that there is indispensable evidence on those backup tapes (although the fact the [the UBS employee accused of the discrimination] apparently deleted certain e-mails indicates that such evidence may exist).

* * *

Because the seven factor test requires that UBS pay the lion's share, the percentage assigned to Zubulake must be less than fifty percent. A share that is too costly may chill the rights of litigants to pursue meritorious claims. However, because the success of this search is somewhat speculative, any cost that fairly can be assigned to Zubulake is appropriate and ensures that UBS's expenses will not be unduly burdensome. A twenty-five percent assignment to Zubulake meets these goals.

Id. at 284, 289. [emphasis in original]

7. *Supplementing disclosure or discovery.* Under the conditions described in Rule 26(e), parties have a duty to supplement automatic disclosure and discovery responses when the information has not already been provided. "At appropriate intervals," a party must supplement initial, expert and pretrial disclosures in interrogatories, requests for production, and requests for admission that a party learns are incomplete or incorrect in a material way. Why does the rule not require a duty to supplement depositions?

Supplementation is also necessary "seasonably" for requested discovery which becomes incomplete or incorrect in a material respect. For example, in *United States v. Boyce*, 148 F.Supp.2d 1069 (S.D.Cal. 2001), the court suggested that a party cannot wait until just before trial to supplement a discovery response.

8. *Stipulations about discovery procedures.* Despite what may appear to be much rigidity in the discovery rules, Rule 29 generally permits the parties to agree to conduct discovery outside the rules. As long as an agreement is in writing and the trial court has not directed them otherwise, the parties may stipulate to modify discovery procedures provided the agreements do not interfere with hearing or trial dates or a discovery deadline. The 1970 Advisory Committee Notes to Rule 29 state that the trial court can override any stipulation by the parties.

Problems

1.   Paulin and Vesely witnessed an intersection vehicle collision at the corner of Third Street and Eastern Parkway. In the subsequent case of *Smith v. Jones*, Jones takes Paulin's deposition and asks, "Based on your observations at the time of the accident, who was at fault—the driver of the VW Beetle or the driver of the Jaguar convertible?" Under Rule 26(b)(1), is that information discoverable?

2.   Same facts as #1, and the next question at Paulin's deposition is, "Did you hear Vesely express an opinion about whom she believed was at fault?" Paulin's answer would constitute hearsay, and would not be admissible at a trial. Is the information sought discoverable?

3.   In the same *Smith v. Jones* case, Smith sends Jones an interrogatory asking, "State whether you have automobile insurance." Is the information sought discoverable?

4.   In *Smith v. Jones*, plaintiff Smith is seeking both compensatory damages for lost wages and for punitive damages. Can Smith send an interrogatory to Jones seeking his tax returns and other information about his assets, to prepare for the punitive damages claim? Can Jones send an interrogatory to Smith seeking his tax returns and other information about his assets, to prepare for the lost wages claim?

5. Again, in *Smith v. Jones*, Jones wants to file a motion to dismiss Smith's complaint because it fails to state a claim upon which relief can be granted. Jones has a copy of a statement from Smith that directly contradicts one of Smith's claims. Can Jones send Smith an interrogatory asking, "State all facts which you have disclosed to your attorney and to all other persons about your claim." How should Smith respond?

6. In a product liability case, *Abadu v. National Motors*, the plaintiff sends the following interrogatory: "State whether defendant has made any subsequent changes in the product after the accident which gave rise to this litigation." Is the information sought discoverable?

7. In a Title VII employment discrimination case, law student Greenidge claims that he suffered racial discrimination when he did not receive an offer of employment from Dewey, Cheatham and Howe, a law firm he clerked for during the summer between his second and third years of law school. As his attorney, what is the scope of discoverable relevant information about the hiring practices at Dewey and other law firms?

3. Discovery of Attorney Work Product

INTRODUCTORY PROBLEM

When the purchaser of a recreational vehicle (RV) returned it to the seller (Dixie RV) because of alleged defects and breaches of warranties, the seller sued the buyer for breach of contract. During discovery, the defendant-buyer sent several requests for information to Dixie RV.

A. All written statements made by the buyer to any employee of Dixie RV preceding and following the buyer's purchase of the RV.

B. The law that governs Dixie's view that it is entitled to recover damages from the buyer.

C. Memoranda by any Dixie employee to any other Dixie employee about the buyer's problems with the RV purchased by the buyer.

Is the buyer entitled to discover any of the preceding information?

Governing law: Federal Rule 26(b).

HICKMAN v. TAYLOR

329 U.S. 495, 67 S.Ct. 385, 91 L.Ed. 451 (1947)

Mr. Justice MURPHY delivered the opinion of the Court.

[The tugboat "J.M. Taylor" sank in 1943, drowning five of the nine crew members. Several days later, the tug boat owners and their insurers hired a law firm to investigate and defend against future claims. One of the lawyers, Fortenbaugh, interviewed the four survivors and took statements from them. He also interviewed others who knew about the accident; he wrote memoranda of his interviews in some cases. At a later public hearing, all the witnesses testified and their testimony was made available to the general public. A representative of one of the drowning victims sued and requested "copies of all [written] statements" of the [witnesses] along with the "exact provisions" of the oral statements. The defendants refused to produce or summarize the materials on the grounds that the requests were for "privileged matter obtained in preparation for litigation." After the trial court ordered discovery, and the Third Circuit reversed, the Supreme Court granted certiorari.]

In urging that he has a right to inquire into the materials secured and prepared by Fortenbaugh, petitioner emphasizes that the deposition-discovery portions of the Federal Rules of Civil Procedure are designed to enable the parties to discover the true facts and to compel their disclosure wherever they may be found. It is said that inquiry may be made under these rules, epitomized by Rule 26, as to any relevant matter which is not privileged; and since the discovery provisions are to be applied as broadly and liberally as possible, the privilege limitation must be restricted to its narrowest bounds. On the premise that the attorney-client privilege is the one involved in this case, petitioner argues that it must be strictly confined to confidential communications made by a client to his attorney. And since the materials here in issue were secured by Fortenbaugh from third persons rather than from his clients, the tug owners, the conclusion is reached that these materials are proper subjects for discovery under Rule 26.

* * * We agree, of course, that the deposition-discovery rules are to be accorded a broad and liberal treatment. No longer can the time-honored cry of 'fishing expedition' serve to preclude a party from inquiring into the facts underlying his opponent's case. Mutual knowledge of all the relevant facts gathered by both parties is essential to proper litigation. To that end, either party may compel the other to disgorge whatever facts he has in his possession. The deposition-discovery procedure simply advances the stage at which the disclosure can be compelled from the time of trial to the period preceding it, thus reducing the possibility of surprise. But discovery, like all matters of procedure, has ultimate and necessary boundaries. * * *

We also agree that the memoranda, statements and mental impressions in issue in this case fall outside the scope of the attorney-client privilege and hence are not protected from discovery on that basis. * * * [T]his privilege does not extend to information which an attorney secures from a witness while acting for his client in anticipation of litigation. Nor does this privilege concern the memoranda, briefs, communications and other writings prepared by counsel for his own use in prosecuting his client's case; and it is equally unrelated to writings which reflect an attorney's mental impressions, conclusions, opinions or legal theories.

But the impropriety of invoking that privilege does not provide an answer to the problem before us. Petitioner has made more than an ordinary request for relevant, non-privileged facts in the possession of his adversaries or their counsel. He has sought discovery as of right of oral and written statements of witnesses whose identity is well known and whose availability to petitioner appears unimpaired. He has sought production of these matters after making the most searching inquiries of his opponents as to the circumstances surrounding the fatal accident, which inquiries were sworn to have been answered to the best of their information and belief. Interrogatories were directed toward all the events prior to, during and subsequent to the sinking of the tug. Full and honest answers to such broad inquiries would necessarily have included all pertinent information gleaned by Fortenbaugh through his interviews with the witnesses. Petitioner makes no suggestion, and we cannot assume, that the tug owners or Fortenbaugh were incomplete or dishonest in the framing of their answers. In addition, petitioner was free to examine the public testimony of the witnesses taken before the United States Steamboat Inspectors. We are thus dealing with an attempt to secure the production of written statements and mental impressions contained in the files and the mind of the attorney Fortenbaugh without any showing of necessity or any indication or claim that denial of such production would unduly prejudice the preparation of petitioner's case or cause him any hardship or injustice. For aught that appears, the essence of what petitioner seeks either has been revealed to him already through the interrogatories or is readily available to him direct from the witnesses for the asking.

The District Court, after hearing objections to petitioner's request, commanded Fortenbaugh to produce all written statements of witnesses and to state in substance any facts learned through oral statements of witnesses to him. Fortenbaugh was to submit any memoranda he had made of the oral statements so that the court might determine what portions should be revealed to petitioner. All of this was ordered without any showing by petitioner, or any requirement that he make a proper showing, of the necessity for the production of any of this material or any demonstration that denial of production would cause hardship or injustice. The court simply ordered production on the theory that the facts sought were material and were not privileged as constituting attorney-client communications.

In our opinion, neither Rule 26 nor any other rule dealing with discovery contemplates production under such circumstances. That is not because the subject matter is privileged or irrelevant, as those concepts are used in these rules. Here is simply an attempt, without purported necessity or justification, to secure written statements, private memoranda and personal recollections prepared or formed by an adverse party's counsel in the course of his legal duties. As such, it falls outside the arena of discovery and contravenes the public policy underlying the orderly prosecution and defense of legal claims. Not even the most liberal of discovery theories can justify unwarranted inquiries into the files and the mental impressions of an attorney.

Historically, a lawyer is an officer of the court and is bound to work for the advancement of justice while faithfully protecting the rightful interests of his clients. In performing his various duties, however, it is essential that a lawyer work with a certain degree of privacy, free from unnecessary intrusion by opposing parties and their counsel. * * * This work is reflected, of course, in interviews, statements, memoranda, correspondence, briefs, mental impressions, personal beliefs, and countless other tangible and intangible ways—aptly though roughly termed by the Circuit Court of Appeals in this case as the "Work product of the lawyer." Were such materials open to opposing counsel on mere demand, much of what is now put down in writing would remain unwritten. An attorney's thoughts, heretofore inviolate, would not be his own. Inefficiency, unfairness and sharp practices would inevitably develop in the giving of legal advice and in the preparation of cases for trial. The effect on the legal profession would be demoralizing. And the interests of the clients and the cause of justice would be poorly served.

We do not mean to say that all written materials obtained or prepared by an adversary's counsel with an eye toward litigation are necessarily free from discovery in all cases. Where relevant and non-privileged facts remain hidden in an attorney's file and where production of those facts is essential to the preparation of one's case, discovery may properly be had. Such written statements and documents might, under certain circumstances, be admissible in evidence or give clues as to the existence or location of relevant facts. Or they might be useful for purposes of impeachment or corroboration. And production might be justified where the witnesses are no longer available or can be reached only with difficulty. * * * But the general policy against invading the privacy of an attorney's course of preparation is so well recognized and so essential to an orderly working of our system of legal procedure that a burden rests on the one who would invade that privacy to establish adequate reasons to justify production through a subpoena or court order. * * *

No attempt was made to establish any reason why Fortenbaugh should be forced to produce the written statements. There was only a naked, general demand for these materials as of right and a finding by the District Court that no recognizable privilege was involved. That was insufficient to justify discovery under these circumstances and the court should have sustained the refusal of the tug owners and Fortenbaugh to produce.

But as to oral statements made by witnesses to Fortenbaugh, whether presently in the form of his mental impressions or memoranda, we do not believe that any showing of necessity can be made under the circumstances of this case so as to justify production. Under ordinary conditions, forcing an attorney to repeat or write out all that witnesses have told him and to deliver the account to his adversary gives rise to grave dangers of inaccuracy and untrustworthiness. No legitimate purpose is served by such production. The practice forces the attorney to testify as to what he remembers or what he saw fit to write down regarding witnesses' remarks. Such testimony could not qualify as evidence; and to use it for impeachment or corroborative purposes would make the attorney much less an officer of the court and much more an ordinary witness. The standards of the profession would thereby suffer.

Denial of production of this nature does not mean that any material, non-privileged facts can be hidden from the petitioner in this case. * * * Searching interrogatories directed to Fortenbaugh and the tug owners, production of written documents and statements upon a proper showing and direct interviews with the witnesses themselves all serve to reveal the facts in Fortenbaugh's possession to the fullest possible extent consistent with public policy. Petitioner's counsel frankly admits that he wants the oral statements only to help prepare himself to examine witnesses and to make sure that he has overlooked nothing. That is insufficient under the circumstances to permit him an exception to the policy underlying the privacy of Fortenbaugh's professional activities. * * *

We therefore affirm the judgment of the Circuit Court of Appeals.

Notes and Questions

1. What are the justifications for the work product doctrine? After you read the first paragraph of current Rule 26(b)(3), compare it with the holding in *Hickman*. Which is broader? If you find that the scope of the federal rule is broader, why does the rule cover more issues than *Hickman*?

2. *Prepared in Anticipation of Litigation or for Trial.* A document or thing is defined as work product only if it was "prepared in anticipation of litigation or for trial." A document or thing that existed before the claim or defense in your case was asserted is outside that definition, although it is possible that it may have constituted work product in a prior case. Several courts have adopted the test enunciated in Wright, Miller & Marcus, 8 *Fed. Practice & Procedure,* § 2024 at 343 (1994): documents are "prepared for litigation" and therefore within the scope of the work product rule if, "in light of the nature of the document and the factual situation in the particular case, the document can be fairly said to have been prepared or obtained because of the prospect of litigation." See, e.g., *United States v. Adlman,* 134 F.3d 1194, 1197–1198 (2d Cir. 1998):

> It is universally agreed that a document whose purpose is to assist in preparation for litigation is within the scope of the Rule and thus eligible to receive protection if the other conditions of protection prescribed by the Rule are met. The issue is less clear, however, as to documents which, although prepared because of expected litigation, are intended to inform a business decision influenced by the prospects of the litigation. The formulation applied by some courts in determining whether documents are protected by work-product privilege is whether they are prepared "primarily or exclusively to assist in litigation"—a

formulation that would potentially exclude documents containing analysis of expected litigation, if their primary, ultimate, or exclusive purpose is to assist in making the business decision. Others ask whether the documents were prepared "because of" existing or expected litigation—a formulation that would include such documents, despite the fact that their purpose is not to "assist in" litigation.

In *E.E.O.C. v. Lutheran Social Services*, 186 F.3d 959 (D.C. Cir. 1999), the Equal Employment Opportunity Commission sought access to a report prepared by the attorneys for the defendant summarizing the results of an investigation into alleged gender discrimination violations of federal law. Concluding that the report was protected as work product, the court stated:

> In *In re Sealed Case*, [146 F.3d 881(D.C. Cir.1998)], we held that for a document to meet this standard, "the lawyer must at least have had a subjective belief that litigation was a real possibility, and that belief must have been objectively reasonable." 146 F.3d at 884. Applying that test to the facts of that case, we found that documents prepared by counsel for the Republican National Committee in response to news reports questioning the legality of its relationship with another organization, the National Policy Forum, had been prepared in anticipation of litigation even though the Federal Election Commission had yet to file a formal complaint. We relied on an affidavit from an RNC lawyer that stated, "I was . . . aware that the chairman of the FEC had announced that the FEC was investigating cases involving allegations of illegal contributions in U.S. elections. . . . I was further aware that the [National Policy Forum] had been criticized in the press as an organization used by the RNC to evade federal campaign finance laws, and thus I had a significant concern that litigation over this issue was probable." *Id.* at 886. Another RNC lawyer stated, "[F]rom the time the NPF was formed, I and the RNC were concerned about the substantial likelihood of potential litigation. . . ." *Id.* at 886.
>
> Lutheran faced a virtually identical situation. Like the RNC, it had not been sued at the time it hired outside counsel. Also like the RNC, Lutheran hired counsel because it feared litigation. In her affidavit, a Lutheran board member stated, "To prepare for the possibility of a lawsuit by the president, the Board wanted a careful investigation and legal analysis of the allegations against him. . . ." She further "agreed" with Williams & Connolly that the investigation "should also be conducted in anticipation of a suit being brought on grounds of a hostile work environment for women." The Williams & Connolly lawyer to whom the Board first spoke said he advised the Board that "the investigation [into hostile work environment] should also be conducted in preparation for a discrimination suit brought by a disgruntled current or former employee." In terms of demonstrating a genuine fear of litigation, we see no significant difference between these affidavits and the affidavits in *In re Sealed Case*.
>
> Offering no evidence to counter Lutheran's affidavits, the EEOC hypothesizes that Lutheran undertook its investigation in the "ordinary course of business," which, the Commission says, includes looking into whether the organization was complying with the relevant laws regard-

ing discrimination in the workplace. Even if accurate, the Commission's recharacterization of Lutheran's motivation does nothing to undermine Lutheran's contention that it genuinely feared litigation. Indeed, fear of EEOC or employee-initiated litigation may well be the very reason why an employer hires outside counsel to determine whether it is complying with Title VII.

Turning to the objective prong of the work product test, the EEOC argues that Williams & Connolly could not have prepared its report "in anticipation of litigation" because the litigation Lutheran feared was "too remote and speculative." But the prospect of litigation in this case was no less speculative than in *In re Sealed Case*. There, we found that news reports hinting at illegal behavior coupled with the RNC's fear of litigation provided sufficient objective support for the lawyers' assertion that they had prepared the documents "in anticipation of litigation." *See* 146 F.3d at 885–86, 888. Here, too, evidence suggests that litigation lay just over the horizon. Lutheran had documents in which its own employees (perhaps future plaintiffs) directly accused the president of creating a hostile work environment. That those documents were anonymous and the charges nonspecific does nothing to undermine the objective reasonableness of Lutheran's fear of litigation. And just as in *In re Sealed Case,* where the RNC's fear of litigation was eventually confirmed when the FEC filed suit, Lutheran's fear was confirmed when two of its employees filed EEOC charges based on allegations contained in the anonymous memoranda.

Is the standard described in *Lutheran Social Services* too easy to satisfy? Is the subjective part always going to be satisfied by a self-serving argument about the expectation and/or fear of being sued? Does the fact that a party ultimately was sued contribute to what the thoughts of the party were at the time of the material's preparation?

Does work product protection apply to documents prepared in anticipation of other litigation, rather than only the pending claims? See *In re Ford Motor Co.*, 110 F.3d 954 (3d Cir. 1997) (Rule 26(b)(3) "requires that the material be prepared in anticipation of some litigation, not necessarily in anticipation of the particular litigation in which it is being sought").

3. *By or for Another Party, etc.* Rule 26(b)(3) qualifies the definition of a work product as a document or thing prepared in anticipation of litigation by the requirement that such a document or thing was prepared "by or for another party or by or for that other party's representative." The rule lists examples of a party's representative as "including the other party's attorney, consultant, surety, indemnitor, insurer, or agent."

4. *Obtaining Statements of Parties and Witnesses.* Would you like to have copies of all the statements that the opposing party has taken, both before and after the claim was filed? The problem is that statements obtained by attorneys from party-opponents and witnesses qualify as trial preparation materials. After a plaintiff files a claim, the work product doctrine in Rule 26(b)(3) can shield a diligent attorney from having to disclose all statements taken by the diligent attorney.

Two types of existing statements are discoverable under Rule 26(b)(3) merely for the asking. First, a party can obtain a copy of her own statement from another party. As counsel for that person, you definitely want to read anything that your client already has told the opposing party's attorney or agents. Second, a witness also can obtain her own statement from any party. The witness can authorize you to request her statement and have it mailed to the witness, in care of your office, i.e., address the envelope to Wally Witness, c/o Clarence Darrow.

The definition of a "statement" in Rule 26(b)(3) is broad, applying to any written statement or technological recording or transcript thereof, regardless of who writes, prepares, or records the statement. A statement also includes a "substantially verbatim recital of an oral statement by the person making it" that was "contemporaneously recorded." The person whose statement is sought need only to have signed, adopted, or approved it as her own.

What about all other statements? Assuming that there is no voluntary disclosure, they can be obtained from the party-opponent only upon a showing of substantial need and undue hardship. Otherwise, a party may ask in an interrogatory: "Name any person from whom you have taken a statement." That request is legitimate; work product prohibits the disclosure of the statement itself. With the person's identity, the party's attorney can attempt to talk to that person or depose her. In addition, a party may ask for the identity of the custodian of the statement and/or its location.

5. *Attorney's mental impressions and legal evaluations.* Why do an attorney's mental impressions have almost absolute protection from disclosure? An attorney's notes or memoranda from a meeting or an interview reveal her mental processes. Notes also indicate her legal conclusions. Why? When she is taking notes, an attorney (any person, for that matter) focuses on the facts and the documents that she deems legally significant. In the case of documents, the work product historically applies. It may also apply, though, to an attorney or her agent being asked in a deposition to recall conversations with witnesses, because what she recalls is likely to be what she regards as important. See, e.g., *Baker v. General Motors Corp.*, 209 F.3d 1051 (8th Cir. 2000) (interviews of GM's employees were protected as opinion work product). Of course, even the opinion work product concept does not prevent an attorney from learning the identities of who has been interviewed and later deposing those persons. Other than a fraud exception for opinion work product, it cannot be overcome by a showing of substantial need and undue hardship to obtain a substantial equivalent document, as is possible with ordinary work product—the topic of the next case.

GUTSHALL v. NEW PRIME, INC.
196 F.R.D. 43 (W.D. Va. 2000)

MICHAEL, Senior District Judge.

This case presents the questions of whether surveillance evidence conducted by a defendant in a personal injury case is discoverable if the defendant only intends to use the evidence for impeachment purposes, and whether such evidence is protected by the attorney work product doctrine. Finding that the federal discovery rules require discovery of such evidence, and that it is not protected by the work product doctrine, the court shall grant the plaintiff's motion to compel.

On June 10, 1998, the plaintiff was operating a tractor-trailer on Interstate 80 in Lake County, Indiana, when he allegedly was rear-ended by another tractor-trailer, owned by defendant New Prime, Inc. ("New Prime"), and operated by defendant Robert Tapper ("Tapper"). The plaintiff sued on April 8, 1999, claiming that Tapper was operating his tractor-trailer within the course and scope of employment with New Prime, that Tapper's negligence caused back injuries the plaintiff suffered as a result of the accident, and that New Prime is liable under the doctrine of *respondeat superior*.

On April 15, 1999, the plaintiff served the following interrogatory on New Prime: "Please state whether or not you have conducted and/or obtained any surveillance of the plaintiff." On November 17, 1999, the plaintiff requested production of: "Documents and things . . . relating to any . . . visual depiction . . . of . . . any person involved in the collision, which is in your possession, to which you have access or of which you have knowledge." An accompanying interrogatory contains the same language.

As of the date of New Prime's initial responses to these requests, New Prime had not conducted any surveillance, and properly responded that it had not. New Prime subsequently arranged for surveillance of the plaintiff from May 1 to June 1, 2000. The plaintiff noticed the surveillance on May 26, and so informed his attorney. Claiming that New Prime failed to supplement its discovery responses in compliance with Federal Rule of Civil Procedure 26(e)(2) by not producing the surveillance evidence, the plaintiff filed a "Motion to Compel Discovery Responses" on June 30, and a motion to exclude that evidence. Trial was scheduled to begin less than a month later, on July 26.

* * * New Prime argues that because Rule 26(a)(3) excludes information that will be used solely for impeachment purposes, which is the only purpose for which New Prime claims it intends to use the surveillance evidence, it was not required to produce that evidence pursuant to the document requests.

Rule 26(a)(3) does not describe the scope of discovery or exclude impeachment evidence therefrom; it describes the scope of automatic initial disclosure requirements. The plaintiff does not assert that the evidence should have been produced because it fell within automatic initial disclosure requirements, but because it was responsive to two interrogatories and a request for production of documents. Therefore, New Prime's reliance on Rule 26(a)(3) is misplaced. The scope of discovery is described in Rule 26(b). * * *

Unlike subsection (a), subsection (b) does not distinguish between substantive and impeachment evidence. Rule 26(b) defines discoverable evidence as that which "appears reasonably calculated to lead to the discovery of admissible evidence." * * *

As evidence that bears directly on the plaintiff's physical condition, the surveillance evidence is relevant to the subject matter of the case. Even though New Prime only intends to use such evidence at trial for impeachment purposes, the evidence falls within the broad scope of Rule 26(b)(1). * * *

New Prime prepared, or commissioned the preparation of, the surveillance materials in anticipation of trial in this case. Consequently, those materials constitute "work product" that New Prime ordinarily would not be compelled to produce. However, even work product materials are discoverable if the plaintiff "has substantial need of the materials in the preparation of [his] . . . case and that [he] . . . is unable without undue hardship to obtain the substantial equivalent of the materials by other means." Fed.R.Civ.P. 26(b)(3). * * * Most other federal courts have not found surveillance tapes to be protected work product. *See, e.g., Smith v. Diamond Offshore Drilling, Inc.,* 168 F.R.D. 582 (S.D.Tex.1996) (surveillance evidence must be produced notwithstanding its work product status); *Snead v. American Export–Isbrandtsen Lines, Inc.,* 59 F.R.D. 148, 151 (E.D.Pa.1973) (observing that even though the plaintiff may be unable to bend without pain, "under some particular circumstances he may have done so and this may be the very incident the camera recorded. . . . there is substantial need to have knowledge of the films for the preparation of the plaintiff's case").

The court agrees with the majority of courts that considered the issue, and finds that a plaintiff alleging claims for personal injury has a substantial need for surveillance evidence in preparing his case for trial, due to the relevance and importance of such evidence, and the substantial impact it may have at trial. Further, it is impossible to procure the substantial equivalent of such evidence without undue hardship, as videotape "fixes information available at a particular time and a particular place under particular circumstances, and therefore cannot be duplicated." *Smith,* 168 F.R.D. at 586. Notwithstanding the work product status of the surveillance evidence, it therefore must be produced by New Prime pursuant to Federal Rule of Civil Procedure 26(e)(2). The plaintiff's motion to compel shall be granted. However, the plaintiff having cited no legal basis for excluding the surveillance evidence, his motion to exclude shall be denied. * * *

Problems

1. Long before one of Paulin Electronics's drills malfunctioned in Vesely's hand in 2003, other Paulin drills had injured consumers in 2001. Several months after they were injured but before Vesely was injured, Paulin's President asked the production supervisor (Prewitt) and the product designer (Christian) to send her memoranda detailing the decision making process by which the specific drill design was selected and the drill was produced. Each of them drafted a long memorandum detailing the meetings with employees and outside consultants.

Vesely's counsel now sends interrogatories to Paulin seeking all "notes, records, letters, memoranda, or other communications concerning the Paulin

Deluxe electric drill in issue." May Paulin use Rule 26(b)(3) to avoid producing Prewitt's and Christian's memoranda?

2. Prewitt's first assistant, Henn, actually drafted the memo attributed to Prewitt. Henn no longer works for Paulin and cannot be located. Vesely's attorney sends an interrogatory to Paulin's President asking her to "relate the substance of any interviews you and/or your counsel conducted with Henn concerning the Paulin Deluxe electric drill in issue." Paulin's lawyer, Prizant, in fact had interviewed Henn before she left, but he did not record the meeting or take notes. Must Prizant provide the requested information?

3. Assume that Prizant met with Henn after Vesely's attorney had filed a lawsuit against Paulin Electronics. Prizant took extensive notes during the interview with Henn. The notes include factual statements made by Henn about the drill, Prizant's evaluative notes about the credibility of Henn's statements, other evidence that might contradict what Henn said, and problems with admissibility of the evidence. Vesely's interrogatories seek production of "any notes, memoranda, recordings, or other records of discussions with Henn concerning the Paulin Deluxe electric drill." Are the notes protected under Rule 26(b)(3)?

4. Vesely sends the following interrogatory to Paulin Electronics: "During the time President Paulin sought the Prewitt and Christian memos, did Prewitt, Christian, or Henn give oral or written assurances that the Paulin Deluxe electric drill was free of any defects?" In fact, Henn had told Prizant and Christian that the drill was free of defects. Prizant refuses to answer, on the ground that the information is protected by the work product privilege. Does Rule 26(b)(3) apply?

5. Assume that in #1 above, the memoranda are ordinary work product. Can work product be overcome if:

    A. Vesely's counsel proves to the court that she wants the memoranda to ensure that she has overlooked anything of value in preparing her case?

    B. Neither Prewitt nor Christian can be found?

    C. Vesely did not hire an attorney until two years after he was injured, i.e., 2005, and both Prewitt and Christian have retired from Paulin Electronics, relocating in a distant state?

    D. Vesely's counsel tried unsuccessfully to speak personally to Prewitt and Christian but both refused to answer her questions?

    E. Vesely's counsel tried unsuccessfully to speak personally to Prewitt and Christian after their retirements but neither could remember anything about the time period surrounding the writing of the memos?

6. Consider whether any of the following meets the definition of a "statement" under Rule 26(b)(3), and must be provided on request to the person who made the statement.

    A. An attorney's two-page memorandum, contemporaneously summarizing a one-hour interview with a witness to a vehicle collision.

    B. Same as A, except that the witness signed the page on which the attorney had taken notes of the interview.

C. A ten-minute tape recording, by an attorney, memorializing a one-hour interview with a witness. The attorney's recording was made the day after the witness interview.

4. Discovery About Experts

INTRODUCTORY PROBLEM

Vicki Victim was seriously hurt when a lawnmower manufactured by Lucky Lawnmower, Inc. and operated by Vicki, exploded. Vicki contacted Arnold Attorney who began an investigation of the case. Lucky Lawnmower's investigation consists of the following:

1. A report of a design engineer who was hired to determine the cause of the accident. She was the first person to look at the lawnmower after the accident. She disassembled the lawnmower and concluded that the accident was probably caused by an improperly installed carburetor. Being a kind soul, she reassembled the lawnmower correctly. The report itself was inconclusive as to the cause of the accident and Lucky does not plan to use the design engineer at trial. Somehow, Arnold found out about the disassembly process, even though he does not know the engineer's identity.

2. A report of a products safety engineer/expert who works for Lucky in the quality control department. The report states that there have been two other reported explosions of the model involved in the lawsuit but, in his opinion, the other explosions were caused by improper consumer use of the lawnmower. The products safety expert will testify at trial.

A. May Arnold take the deposition of the design engineer to find out about both the opinions of the engineer and the re-assembly of the lawnmower?

B. Arnold wants to know about all prior complaints regarding the particular lawnmower model in controversy. May Arnold require the products safety engineer/expert to appear for a deposition and being with him all prior complaints and any reports he has prepared concerning other accidents?

Governing rule: Rule 26(b).

As noted earlier in this chapter, the Federal Rules address the mandatory pretrial (ninety days before trial, unless otherwise ordered or agreed) disclosure of expert witnesses who "may be used at trial to present evidence." Every party must disclose the identity of its experts and present an expert report for each expert witness, per Rule 26(a)(2) which also describes the contents of the expert report. In addition, those experts may be deposed about their opinions. The disclosure is subject to the Rule 26(e) duty to supplement, also discussed earlier.

Based on the expert's special knowledge, skill, experience or training, parties offer expert testimony to assist the fact finder in comprehending information about the case and reaching conclusions about the issues. Having just studied work product, you may be wondering about the nature of the identity of an expert and the expert's report. Is the identity of an expert work product? The person's name and the report prepared by the expert surely was assembled for the party in anticipation of trial. Indeed, the first phrase of the work product rule, Rule 26(b)(3), states the it is "[s]ubject to the provisions of subdivision (b)(4)." Therefore, discovery about experts is recognized as work product but discoverable nonetheless.

LEHAN v. AMBASSADOR PROGRAMS, INC.

190 F.R.D. 670 (E.D. Wash. 2000)

SHEA, District Judge.

* * * This action is brought by Michael Lehan against his former employer, Contrarian Group, Inc., doing business as Ambassador Programs International, Inc. ("Ambassador"), alleging that he was unlawfully terminated as a result of his employer's policies and practices of discrimination on the basis of age in violation of the Age Discrimination in Employment Act ("ADEA"). Mr. Lehan claimed he continues to suffer humiliation and emotional damages due to his termination.

On October 19, 1999, the Court ordered a mental exam pursuant to Federal Rules of Civil Procedure 35 ("Rule 35") upon the stipulation of the parties. As stipulated by the parties, Dr. Ronald Klein was the Rule 35 examiner defense retained to conduct an independent examination of Mr. Lehan's mental state. The Court presumes that Defendant identified Dr. Klein as an expert witness by October 4, 1999, the date specified in the Amended Scheduling Order. On November 5, 1999, Dr. Ronald Klein performed the Rule 35 exam. It is undisputed that the Plaintiff received Dr. Klein's report based on the Rule 35 exam. It is unknown whether or not Defendant served a Rule 26(a)(2)(B) report of Dr. Klein.

In Defendant's Witness and Exhibit List filed December 30, 1999, Defendant names as a witness its Rule 35 expert Dr. Ronald Klein. Since emotional distress damages are not recoverable under the claims brought by Mr. Lehan, Defendant has represented to the Court that it does not intend to call Dr. Klein as a witness at trial even though he was named on Defendant's expert witness list.

In Plaintiff's List of Witnesses and Exhibits for Trial, untimely filed on January 14, 2000, Plaintiff also names Defendant's Rule 35 expert Dr. Ronald Klein as his own expert witness. Plaintiff did not identify either Dr. Dennis Twigg or Dr. Michal Wilson, the two psychiatrists who had examined or treated Plaintiff after his termination, although their records had been given to Defendant and Dr. Klein prior to the Rule 35 exam. Plaintiff's purpose in calling Dr. Klein as a witness in his case is to counter Defendant's affirmative defense of failure to mitigate. Plaintiff also seeks to introduce at trial through Dr. Klein's testimony the treating records of Dr. Twigg and Dr. Wilson as records which Dr. Klein reviewed and arguably relied upon in forming opinions expressed in his report. Defendant Ambassador Programs, Inc. objects to Plaintiff's use of Dr. Klein and the admission into evidence of the medical records of Dr. Twigg and Dr. Wilson.

The presumption underlying litigation is that the trier of fact will be able to decide the "truth" and render a fair verdict based on the evidence produced at trial by parties with competing interests in the outcome. A correlative presumption in litigation is that each party interested in the outcome will make strategic determinations to produce that evidence which will best persuade the trier of fact to rule in its favor. The trier of fact seldom knows the reasoning of the party in determining which witnesses will be called at trial. In the matter of expert witnesses, each party has the opportunity and right to retain and call experts in an effort to increase the potential for success at trial. The corresponding duty is to disclose the identity of the expert witness to the other party and to provide related material. See Fed.R.Civ.P. 26(a)(2). The other party then has adequate notice and can undertake discovery as well as select an expert to testify on the same subject or issue. In cases where the physical or mental health of one of the parties may be a relevant factor on the issue of liability or damages, treating physicians are often called to provide evidence on this issue in addition to experts retained specifically for the litigation. See Fed.R.Civ.P. 35. The latter are often Rule 35 examiners, as is true of Dr. Klein in this case.

A party also has the right to consult with experts without designating them as expert witnesses and without calling them at trial. The opposing party may discover the opinions of that expert only in two situations: 1) as provided in Rule 35, and 2) only "upon a showing of exceptional circumstances under which it is impracticable for the party seeking discovery to obtain facts or opinions on the same subject by other means." Fed.R.Civ.P. 26(b)(4)(B).

Here, Mr. Lehan was given a copy of the Rule 35 report of Dr. Klein. Some courts have found that by submitting to a Rule 35 exam, the party has an "entitlement" not only to the Rule 35 report but also "to call an opposing party's Rule 35 expert, despite the opposing party's desire not to have the expert testify." *House v. Combined Ins. Co. of Am.*, 168 F.R.D. 236, 240 (N.D.Iowa 1996). The rationale for such an approach is that this "entitlement" is the corresponding right that accompanies the surrender of a right of privacy upon the duty to submit to the Rule 35 exam. * * *

Another approach adopted by courts calls for a " 'discretionary' or 'balancing' standard, involving a balancing of the interests of the party and the court against the potential for prejudice to the party who hired the expert, but who does not wish to use that expert at trial." *House*, 168 F.R.D. at 240. These courts have reasoned that the trial is to determine the truth and if the examined party determines that the testimony of a

Rule 35 examiner will advance the examined party's advocacy of the truth of the issue, then pursuit of the truth requires that he be allowed to call that witness.

Still other courts have adopted the "exceptional circumstances" approach founded on Fed.R.Civ.P. 26(b)(4)(B). Relying on a combination of Rule 26(b)(4)(B) and Rule 26(b)(4)(A), courts have recognized interests weighing against allowing an opposing party to depose or to call at trial a consultative, non-testifying expert witness and will only allow such testimony in "exceptional circumstances."

This Court is persuaded that the "exceptional circumstances" approach is the proper one to be applied. It recognizes certain underlying principles of litigation: that each party is free to choose its expert witnesses to consult with and to exercise its judgment on whether or not to call the expert witness at trial; that expert witnesses once retained remain the witness of the retaining party; that fair opportunity to evaluate the merits of the case and to conduct discovery to prepare for trial require designation of expert witnesses, delivery of the Rule 26(a)(2) expert report, and identification of expert witnesses to be called at trial; that, correspondingly, each party has the duty in preparing the case for trial to identify its expert witnesses who might be called at trial; and, that the court has the discretion to permit one party to call as a witness at trial the opposing party's expert witness when there has been a showing of "exceptional circumstances."

The benefit to the party subjected to a Rule 35 exam is the right to obtain a report of the Rule 35 examiner and discover the opinions expressed therein in order to prepare for trial. See Fed.R.Civ.P. 35(b)(1). That is all that Rule 35 guarantees, and that is confirmed by Rule 26(b)(2)(B). An additional benefit is the possibility that the Rule 35 examiner will agree with the opinion of the examined party's experts or treating physicians thereby increasing the potential for settlement of the case. In practice, the Rule 35 exam may occur after the time set in the scheduling order for designating expert witnesses and providing the related Rule 26(a)(2) report.

Often, the Rule 35 report will be the Rule 26(b)(2)(B) report. This appears to be what occurred here. The Rule 35 exam was conducted and Dr. Klein's report was issued after the date for designation of Defendant's expert witnesses but before the November 16, 1999, discovery cutoff date as set out in the Amended Scheduling Order. Mr. Lehan, armed with the report, was then able to consult with his expert witnesses and treating physicians to prepare for a deposition of the Rule 35 examiner and his cross-examination at trial.

What is unusual about this case is that Mr. Lehan identified no treating physician or expert witness on his psychological condition. Neither Dr. Twigg, a psychiatrist who treated him after the termination of employment, nor Dr. Wilson, who took over Dr. Twigg's practice, was identified as a witness for trial by Mr. Lehan. Perhaps that is because he cannot recover damages for emotional distress in an ADEA case. Perhaps it is for other reasons. The report of Dr. Klein contains the following:

> He [Mr. Lehan] did see Dr. Twigg a few times for psychiatric consultation. He has seen Dr. Michal Wilson who assumed Dr. Twigg's psychiatric practice after Dr. Twigg left the state and Mr. Lehan has been getting medication from Dr. Wilson. He also noted that Dr. Wilson told him he would not be of much help to Mr. Lehan regarding the legal aspects of his case and did not understand why he should have to provide information to Mr. Lehan's attorney in this case. * * *

The Court cannot know if this is factually accurate or whether this is the underlying reason for Mr. Lehan's effort to call Defendant's Rule 35 expert. What is known is that Mr. Lehan had originally indicated that he wanted to call Dr. Klein to get the records of Drs. Twigg and Wilson into evidence in order to show that his psychological condition after termination prevented him from seeking and obtaining employment; this evidence would then rebut the affirmative defense that Mr. Lehan failed to mitigate his damages. That produced Defendant's original objections. However, in his brief on the Rule 35 issue, Mr. Lehan stated that "[i]t is plaintiff's intention to present the testifying expert's opinions and only those facts (including statements by the plaintiff duly recorded by the other examiners and reviewed by the witness) upon which he relies for his opinions." This intended use is typical of the use of such witnesses made by the party retaining them and yet, this is Defendant's retained expert witness and remains so whether or not it intends to call Dr. Klein at trial.

The Court believes that this case is factually dissimilar to *House v. Combined Insurance Co. of America*, 168 F.R.D. 236 (N.D.Iowa 1996), where the court, without benefit of the Rule 35 report, apparently inferred that the Rule 35 examiner would express an opinion favorable to the examined party on a material issue and then emphasized that plaintiff's expert witness was a counselor while the Rule 35 examiner was a psychologist. Unlike the *House* court, this Court has reviewed the Rule 35 report of Dr. Klein and does not have to speculate as to its support for [Mr.] Lehan's position on mitigation of damages. The report reveals Dr. Klein reviewed the records of both Dr. Twigg and Dr. Wilson. There is nothing in Dr. Klein's report of the Rule 35 exam that indicated any reliance by him upon those records in the formation of any opinions expressed by him in the Rule 35 report. Dr. Klein's opinions are found in the Rule 35 report under "CLINICAL IMPRESSIONS" where he states in pertinent part:

> But his [Mr. Lehan's] being terminated from his job did not create new damage nor change old symptoms. He is able to work right now. . . . His history would indicate that psychological stress associated with his war time experience and more recently with the break up of his ten year girlfriend relationship are clearly the driving factors in his current daily function.

Recalling that the basis for Mr. Lehan's effort to call Dr. Klein is to rebut the defense of failure to mitigate and also recalling that there is no recovery in an ADEA case for emotional damages, those observations by Dr. Klein do not lead to the inference that Defendant is declining to call Dr. Klein as a witness to prevent testimony supporting Mr. Lehan on any issue including failure to mitigate damages. Additionally, *House's* preference for psychologists over counselors is an unreliable basis for granting Mr. Lehan the right to call the Rule 35 examiner. To apply the *House* preference here would presumably require denial of Mr. Lehan's request to call Dr. Klein, a psychologist, when Mr. Lehan could have identified as witnesses either Dr. Twigg or Dr. Wilson, both treating psychiatrists. However, this Court believes that applying the *House* preference would be unreliable stereotyping of the professionals and no basis for a decision on Defendant's objections. On the issue of whether Mr. Lehan's termination caused him such a mental or emotional condition which prevented him from seeking employment, psychologists, psychiatrists and also mental health counselors are equally qualified to express an opinion.

In sum, adoption of the "exceptional circumstances" test preserves the fundamental principles governing litigation while enabling the court to exercise its discretion to permit the calling of the Rule 35 examiner by the examined party upon the proper showing when justice requires. The Court finds Mr. Lehan has not indicated any exceptional circumstances warranting the Court's discretion to allow him to call the Defendant's Rule 35 examiner. * * *

Notes and Questions

1. Testifying experts' depositions may be taken before trial but after the preparation of the expert's report has been provided to opposing counsel. While the 1993 Advisory Committee's Notes suggested that detailed expert reports may eliminate the need for depositions or reduce their length, it is unlikely that a litigator should be satisfied with the report's information which is likely to have been prepared in close consultation with the counsel hiring the expert and which may contain less than satisfactory explanations of the expert's qualifications, experience, conclusions, or reasons in support of the conclusions.

2. Can you obtain discovery about an opponent's experts who will not be testifying at trial? The rules deal with non-testifying experts differently and categorically, explicitly and implicitly. If an expert is retained or specially employed, by Rule 26(b)(4)(B), information about her identity or opinion is treated as though it constitutes work product; it is subject to discovery only "upon a showing of exceptional circumstances under which it is impracticable for the party seeking discovery to obtain the facts or opinions on the same subject by other means." The meaning of "retained or specially employed" matters, because of another implicit category of experts. For an expert who is merely informally consulted (as opposed to retained or specially employed), nothing about her identity or opinion is subject to discovery, no matter how badly the adversary party needs the information.

3.   Is the information about non-testifying experts qualified work product or opinion work product? Do "decisions by lawyers about which people to use for confidential pretrial consultation fall into that almost sacrosanct category recognized in the last sentence of the first paragraph of Rule 23(b)(3), namely 'the mental impressions, conclusions, opinions or legal theories of an attorney' "? Isn't a decision "about which people to use in confidence for which purposes in preparing a case for trial . . . as central to lawyering strategy as one can get"? See *In re Pizza Time Theatre Securities Litigation*, 113 F.R.D. 94 (N.D.Cal.1986).

4.   *Discovery of experts' reports sent to counsel.* In *Taylor v. Anderson–Tully Co.*, 151 F.R.D. 295, 296–7 (W.D. Tenn. 1993), the defendants moved to compel the plaintiffs to produce all experts' reports and investigative data prepared on the plaintiffs' behalf, apart from the reports produced for disclosure to the defendants.

> Although liberal discovery is generally encouraged by the Federal Rules of Civil Procedure, parties involved in litigation or acting in anticipation of litigation are entitled to hire experts, consultants, investigators, etc. for the purpose of aiding them in preparation for trial. In order to make full use of such agents, including those who are anticipated to testify at trial, the party and that party's attorney must have free communication with such agents. It is the opinion of this court that routine disclosure of reports prepared by experts in anticipation of litigation or in preparation for trial would substantially impede such communications and lead to the practice of avoiding the preparation of written reports in favor of oral communications to make certain that such written reports do not fall into the hands of the opposing parties. That is not a practice to be encouraged.

> On balance, the court concludes that, where there is no showing of any particularized need for such reports, such as might be the case in a particularly complex expert dispute, parties should not be required to produce their expert witness' reports which have been prepared in anticipation of litigation.

Problems

1.   McCoy is a university expert in evaluating the effect of heat on various metal wiring. He consults for Paulin Electronics occasionally, analyzing the effects of heat on the wire used in Paulin Electronics's product line. Before Vesely's accident, McCoy had performed tests on the wires used in the Paulin Deluxe electric drill. Vesely's attorney sends a notice to Paulin to take McCoy's deposition, but Prizant objects that McCoy's deposition cannot be taken because he is a non-testifying expert. Evaluate the validity of the objection under Rule 26(b)(4)(B)?

2.   Before suing Paulin Electronics, Vesely's attorney contacts Dr. Friedrich von Dufus, a renowned expert on metallurgy to ask for a preliminary opinion about whether the quality of metals used in the wires for Paulin Deluxe electric drills was adequate. Von Dufus reviews the information about Vesely's accident and finds that the drill wiring did not malfunction. Vesely's attorney decides not to hire von Dufus and looks elsewhere for

an expert with "better" views. In his interrogatories to Vesely, Ashcroft seeks the names of all experts who have been consulted or retained. Evaluate Vesely's obligation to disclose information about von Dufus.

3.   On behalf of Paulin, Ashcroft learned that there are only five known metal wiring experts—Dr. Dufus, Dr. McCoy, two from the West Coast, and one other person who makes a terrible impression as a trial witness. Prizant hires one of the West Coast experts to testify at trial, and he hires the other only as a non-testifying expert. Meanwhile, as Vesely's attorney begins his preparation of the case he has the same five names as Ashcroft. He contacts the West Coast experts, who both decline his employment offer. Is Vesely's attorney out of luck on locating an expert to consult?

Exercise

For the state where a) you intend to practice after graduation, b) your law school is located, and/or c) your professor assigns, go to that state's annotated statutes and research the procedural rules by which discovery is governed. Based on your research, print the rule and bring it to class for discussion. In addition, answer the following questions.

1.   Is discovery of certain information mandatory? Is discovery conducted by informal request between counsel or must the trial court approve all discovery?

2.   Identify the standards for determining relevancy, privileged information, protective orders, and work product. How are the state standards narrower or broader than the discovery standards in the federal rules?

3.   For discovery of expert witnesses, evaluate how the standards of your state are similar or dissimilar from the federal rules.

B.   DISCOVERY DEVICES

1.   Depositions

Federal Rule 30 is one of the few discovery rules that applies equally to parties and non-parties. A party may take any person's deposition, per Rule 30(a). Even a party's attorney's deposition may be taken, but the attorney-client privilege may limit the scope of questioning. Recent amendments to Rule 30 limit the number of depositions to ten by plaintiffs or by defendants as a group, subject to expansion by the court or by stipulation. Rule 30(d) provides for a time limit of one day of seven hours for each deposition, which can be extended by court order. Similarly, the court's permission is necessary in order to repeat a person's deposition or to take any deposition before the court conducts a discovery conference. Why does the rule impose these limitations?

As the next case shows, the rules enable a party to describe the information sought, while placing the burden on the opposing party to designate a specific person for deposition.

ALEXANDER v. F.B.I.

186 F.R.D. 148 (D.D.C. 1999)

LAMBERTH, District Judge.

This matter comes before the Court on Plaintiffs' Motion to Compel Re–Designation of Witness on Surveillance Systems Under Fed.R.Civ.P. 30(b)(6) and for Attorneys' Fees and Costs. Upon consideration of plaintiffs' motion, defendant Executive Office of the President's opposition, and plaintiffs' reply thereto, the Court will DENY plaintiffs' motion without prejudice, as discussed and ordered below.

The underlying allegations in this case arise from what has become popularly known as "Filegate." Plaintiffs allege that their privacy interests were violated when the FBI improperly handed over to the White House hundreds of FBI files of former political appointees and government employees under the Reagan and Bush Administrations. The instant dispute revolves around the deposition of John Dankowski, Director of White House Operations.

Dankowski was designated by defendant EOP to testify pursuant to Fed.R.Civ.P. 30(b)(6) Rule 30(b)(6) states, in pertinent part, that:

> A party may in the party's notice and in a subpoena name as the deponent a ... governmental agency and describe with reasonable particularity the matters on which examination is requested. In that event, the organization so named shall designate one or more officers, directors, or managing agents, or other persons who consent to testify on its behalf, and may set forth, for each person designated, the matters on which the person will testify.... This subdivision (b)(6) does not preclude taking a deposition by any other procedure authorized in these rules.

The reasonableness of the testimony sought by plaintiffs is not in dispute. Thus, defendant EOP's duty to designate a suitable witness (or suitable witnesses) was triggered.

Although not disputed, the scope of the testimony sought merits some discussion, as it will bear upon the adequacy of defendant EOP's Rule 30(b)(6) designation. The Court addressed the proper scope of plaintiffs' Rule 30(b)(6) deposition notice in its April 13, 1998 Memorandum and Order denying defendant EOP's motion to quash. In that opinion, the Court described plaintiffs' deposition notice, in pertinent part, as follows:

> Deposition request 3 seeks to have a deponent testify regarding "the system of recording devices, whether audio or video, used to record sounds or pictures in any of the office, common, residential, and/or other areas of the White House and the entirety of the [EOP], including the Office of White House Counsel and the Office of the First Lady." ... Deposition request 8 seeks to have a deponent testify regarding "any recording, transcription, communi-

cation, printing, filing, and any and all recordation devices used by Hillary Rodham Clinton and others in the White House in their governmental, official, and/or allegedly private capacities.''

* * * Plaintiffs seek to elicit testimony on these audio or visual recordation devices because, in their view, evidence gleaned from such devices could be ''highly probative of the partisan misuse of the FBI and government files'' at issue in this case. The theory behind this assertion appears to be that ''traffic to and from [Craig] Livingstone's office is one of the likely ways to definitively trace what was done with information read and copied out of the physical FBI files.''

Defendant EOP designated Dankowski as their Rule 30(b)(6) witness with regard to audio and video recordation systems, also referred to as ''surveillance systems.'' His deposition was taken on June 23, 1998. The dispute currently before the Court involves whether defendant EOP complied with its duties under Fed.R.Civ.P. 30(b)(6) and, if not, what the consequences of that dereliction should be.

* * * [D]efendant EOP does not dispute that plaintiffs have described the matter upon which testimony is sought with reasonable particularity, as required by Rule 30(b)(6). Once it is established that plaintiffs have met this initial burden, a number of duties were triggered that must be met by defendant EOP, as the party named in the notice. At the outset, and most obviously, defendant EOP must designate one or more persons to testify on the subject matter designated by plaintiffs. Defendant EOP met this burden by designating Dankowski. The dispute, however, centers around a number of concomitant duties involved in the preparation and proper designation of the witness.

The Court recently addressed the topic of a party's duties in designating and preparing a witness under Rule 30(b)(6). First, the deponent has a duty of being knowledgeable on the subject matter identified as the area of inquiry. Clearly, a deponent that does not know about the relevant subject matter is useless as a deponent at all. Second, the designating party is under the duty to designate more than one deponent if it would be necessary to do so in order to respond to the relevant areas of inquiry that are specified with reasonable particularity by the plaintiffs. Third, the designating party has a duty to prepare the witness to testify on matters not only known by the deponent, but those that should be reasonably known by the designating party. Obviously, the purpose of a Rule 30(b)(6) deposition is to get answers on the subject matter described with reasonable particularity by the noticing party, not to simply get answers limited to what the deponent happens to know. Fourth, the designating party has a duty to substitute an appropriate deponent when it becomes apparent that the previous deponent is unable to respond to certain relevant areas of inquiry. All of these duties correspond to the ultimate underlying purposes of Rule 30(b)(6)—namely, preventing serial depositions of various witnesses without knowledge within an organization and eliminating ''bandying,'' which is the name given to the practice in which people are deposed in turn but each disclaims knowledge of facts that are clearly known to persons in the organization and thereby to the organization itself.

Plaintiffs assert four arguments on why Dankowski was an inappropriate or non-exhaustive Rule 30(b)(6) witness with regard to the relevant non-Secret Service operated surveillance systems. First, plaintiffs contend that Dankowski is not qualified to testify on the relevant subject matter because he has no expertise in surveillance systems. Second, plaintiffs argue that Dankowski did not adequately prepare for his deposition because, for example, he did not inspect certain premises for surveillance equipment. Third, plaintiffs assert that Dankowski is not knowledgeable about surveillance systems because he doesn't "know whether or not there's a department of the White House ... that's kept secret from other personnel that's in charge of surveillance." Dankowski Depo. at 47. Fourth, plaintiffs claim that defendant EOP must designate another Rule 30(b)(6) witness on the topic of voice mail recordation because, in their view, Dankowski could not answer adequately the questions posed to him in that regard at the deposition. Upon review of the parties' memoranda and the deposition transcript, the Court rejects plaintiffs' first three arguments in full and plaintiffs' fourth argument in part.

First, Dankowski appears to be the appropriate person for defendant EOP to have designated on the topic of surveillance systems. Dankowski is the Director of White House Operations and is responsible for the purchases of all goods and services for the White House Office. If any non-Secret Service surveillance system was maintained in the White House Office, money, equipment, and services would be required for its use and upkeep. Plaintiffs adduce no evidence that any other person would be more qualified than Dankowski on the relevant subject matter. Therefore, plaintiffs' first argument must be rejected.

Second, the Court finds that Dankowski did adequately prepare for his deposition. In short, he had twelve years of experience in the White House Office, reviewed all of the spending obligation records for the White House Office dating back to 1992, and consulted with three separate individuals to obtain even more information with regard to matters such as staffing for potential surveillance systems. Although some of his preparations involved conversations with political appointees, a point that plaintiffs are fond of making, this fact does not belie Dankowski's proper designation. Dankowski appears to have asked questions of the proper people in order to receive answers; their political affiliation cannot be construed as making his testimony inherently incredible simply because some of these people are, of course, the same political affiliation as the President. Plaintiffs point to no other evidence that would cast doubt upon Dankowski's preparation or testimony. Therefore, plaintiffs' contention that Dankowski was inadequately prepared fails.

Third, the Court expressly rejects plaintiffs' conjecture that a "secret department" may exist within the White House Office independently of the Secret Service that monitors employee activity. Plaintiffs point to absolutely no evidence to support such a claim, aside from the Nixon Presidential tapes incident. When this assertion is combined with plaintiffs' claim that they "are entitled to obtain testimony under oath ... stating categorically that there is no audio or visual surveillance system at the White House other than what may be operated by the Secret Service," defendant EOP's burden becomes insurmountable. Defendant EOP cannot be expected or required to prove the non-existence of surveillance equipment to an absolute certainty. Dankowski testified repeatedly that he has no personal knowledge of any such systems, has never seen anything that would indicate the existence of such systems, and has never heard anything to indicate that such systems exist. Defendant EOP has met its Rule 30(b)(6) burden in this regard by designating Dankowski to testify about matters known or reasonably known to defendant EOP. Fed.R.Civ.P. 30(b)(6).

The plaintiffs' fourth argument—that Dankowski could not testify fully as to the voice mail system—merits closer attention. Although plaintiffs attempt to dismiss Dankowski's testimony with regard to voice mail in full, they clearly overstate their case in this regard. Dankowski testified competently that the White House Office has a voice mail system. He stated that no other telephone recording devices existed. The voice mail comes into individual mailboxes and accumulates up to a certain limit. Once that limit is reached, the mailbox will not accept further messages. Unopened mail is erased from the system in ten days and opened mail is erased after fifteen. That voice mail system was set up in 1994. Thus, Dankowski has a good understanding of the current voice mail system in the White House Office, and he testified fully in that regard.

The one area, however, to which Dankowski could not testify was pre–1994 voice mail. In this context, the following exchange occurred:

[Plaintiffs' counsel:] When were you first cognizant of the fact that there was a voice mail system at the White House?

[Dankowski:] I believe it came in '94, if I recall correctly.

[Plaintiffs' counsel:] Was there a voice mail system in the White House before that?

[Dankowski:] Not that I recall.

[Plaintiffs' counsel:] You don't know one way or the other?

[Dankowski:] I do not.

. . .

[Plaintiffs' counsel:] So, consequently, you don't really know whether or not a prior system had a permanent voice mail retention system?

[Dankowski:] I do not know that.

As stated above, the relevancy on this area of discovery is limited to the time period beginning in 1992. Thus, Dankowski could not testify as to the status of a certain type of audio recording system from the time period 1992–1994 (although he did state at one point that he does not believe one existed). This information, however unlikely to be helpful to plaintiffs, would be within the realm of discoverable evidence in this case. Thus, plaintiffs are entitled to answers to this limited subject matter.

As was the case with plaintiffs' motion to compel the re-designation of a witness on the White House Office Database (WhoDB), however, plaintiffs' need for answers to these questions does not warrant a new oral deposition at this juncture. Instead, as set out in the Court's Order below, plaintiffs shall be allowed to pose specific interrogatories and requests for production to defendant EOP on the limited subject matter of voice mail systems during the period 1992–1994. If, after they have received written discovery responses on this issue, a new Rule 30(b)(6) oral deposition is warranted, plaintiffs may again move to compel such a deposition at that time. Until then, however, plaintiffs' motion to compel defendant EOP to re-designate a Rule 30(b)(6) witness on the topic of White House Office audio and video recordation devices must be denied without prejudice.

Because the Court will deny plaintiffs' requested relief in all respects except to the extent they are allowed to pose certain limited discovery requests, the only plausible ground for sanctions appears to be Dankowski's inability to testify as to the voice mail systems before 1994. As is clear from the discussion above, Dankowski was thoroughly prepared and testified fully on nearly all of plaintiffs' inquiries. He did have a duty to find out about the existence of voice mail from the period 1992–1994, since this would fall within the plain meaning of an audio recording device and be within the other limits imposed by the Court. But Dankowski's failure to be prepared in this limited aspect cannot be said to be a result of bad faith conduct. Dankowski did consult with the Deputy Assistant for Management and Administration on the general topic of voice mail and the more specific topic of potential voice mail backup systems. Based upon this preparation, the Court does not believe that Dankowski's inability to testify on one narrow issue rises to the level of being sanctionable. Therefore, plaintiffs' request for sanctions will be denied. * * *

Notes and Questions

1. *Notice about the deposition.* A party must give reasonable written notice about the deposition to the deponent and to all other parties. Unless otherwise agreed by all parties and the deponent, a notice of less than one week is likely to be deemed unreasonable. When the parties cannot agree on a date and location for a deposition, the notice is subject to challenge by a motion for a protective order under Rule 26(c). A notice to take a deposition may look like the following:

UNITED STATES DISTRICT COURT
WESTERN DISTRICT OF KENTUCKY
AT LOUISVILLE

GEORGE W. KERRY   Plaintiff

v.   Case No. 05–007

FLY–BY–NIGHT INSURANCE CO.   Defendant

NOTICE TO TAKE DEPOSITION

To: Ash Johncroft
     Smith and Johncroft
     200 North Water Street
     River City, Kentucky 40001

Please take notice that the defendant in the above-styled action will take the oral deposition by stenographic means of George W. Kerry at the office of the undersigned on February 28, 2006.

The deposition will be taken pursuant to and for all purposes allowed by the Federal Rules of Civil Procedure.

Respectfully submitted,

_____
Howdy Doody
Bar Wars, P.S.C.
6000 Seventh National Tower
Passivity, KY 44444
COUNSEL FOR DEFENDANT

CERTIFICATE OF SERVICE

I certify that on the 12th day of February, 2006, a copy of the foregoing Notice was mailed to Ash Johncroft, Smith and Johncroft, 200 North Water Street, River City, Kentucky 40001, Counsel for Plaintiff.

_____
Counsel for Defendant

A non-party witness is not required to travel more than 100 miles from where she works, lives or regularly transacts business to be deposed, per Rule 45(c)(3)(A). However, the parties may agree with the deponent to compensate the non-party witness to travel a longer distance. If a party fails to serve a non-party witness with a subpoena for a deposition and that non-party witness fails to show up, the party noticing the deposition may have to pay the expenses of other parties for preparing and appearing for the deposition. Rule 30(g)(2)

2. *Methods for recording the deposition.* Under Rule 30(b)(2), the notice also specifies the method for recording the deposition testimony, e.g., audio tape, videotape, stenographic means, and the party noticing the deposition is

responsible for the costs of the recording method. Rule 30(b)(7) permits the parties to stipulate to a deposition by telephone or to seek a court order for such a deposition, with a court reporter in the presence of the deponent. The other parties, at their expense, may also arrange to record the deposition by additional means with prior notice. If the party taking the deposition wants the deponent to bring documents to a deposition, the rules permit the party either to describe the documents in the notice of deposition for a party-witness or issue a subpoena under Rule 45 for a non-party witness.

3. *"Deposing" an organization.* As *Alexander* indicates, per Rule 30(b)(6), when a party sues an organization, she may not know who within the entity has knowledge relating to the claim for relief. The notice to take the deposition of a private corporation or a public agency is sufficient if it merely specifies the areas of inquiry with particularity, without naming a specific person to be deposed. The organization then is responsible for designating one or more representatives to appear and answer questions about the areas of inquiry. Assuming that the entity has acted in good faith to identify person(s) who can testify about the areas specified in the deposition notice, the entity is bound by the designee's deposition testimony. If the entity's witness cannot answer questions reflecting those areas, the entity is subject to sanctions. See, e.g., *In re Vitamins Antitrust Litigation*, 216 F.R.D. 168 (D.D.C. 2003).

4. *What happens at the deposition?* At the beginning of a deposition, the person recording the deposition must put on the record a statement about her name and address, the time, place and date of the deposition, the deponent's name, the administration of an oath, and the identity of all persons present. Rule 30(c) indicates that the deposition questioning is similar to a trial, although most objections (e.g., relevancy) are reserved until the deposition testimony is offered in evidence at trial. An attorney can instruct a witness not to answer a question only to 1) claim a privilege such as the attorney client privilege, 2) enforce a court order limiting the scope of questioning, or 3) stop the deposition for the purpose of making a motion relating to improper harassing conduct.

5. *After the deposition.* On a timely request per Rule 30(e), a deponent has the opportunity to review and correct a deposition transcript in a timely manner, i.e., failure to submit changes within the allowable period waives the right to correct the transcript. If a deponent changes the substance of her answers, the transcript must reflect the reason for the change and later the deponent is subject to impeachment with her earlier answers.

6. *Pre-filing discovery.* When it is important to perpetuate testimony *before* a lawsuit is filed, Federal Rule 27(a) provides an opportunity for conducting discovery by taking a deposition to avoid losing the deponent's information, e.g., a person's memory may be fading. Why is a putative plaintiff unable to conduct discovery for other reasons, e.g., in order to ensure that the complaint she plans to file is accurate and complete? Why is the rule restricted to taking depositions, without the chance to obtain documents?

Under Rule 27, the putative party must file a verified petition for permission to take the deposition. The contents of the petition must include a statement about 1) the petitioner's anticipation of being a party in a federal lawsuit but she cannot yet file the suit or cause it to be filed, 2) the petitioner's role in that lawsuit as well as a description of the case, 3) the deponent's identity and the information to be gained from the deposition, and 4) the petitioner's need for perpetuating that information. If the petitioner satisfies the court that justice requires the perpetuation of the information, it will order the deposition.

2. Interrogatories

O'CONNOR v. BOEING NORTH AMERICAN, INC.

185 F.R.D. 272 (C.D. Cal. 1999)

CHAPMAN, United States Magistrate Judge.

* * * [P]laintiffs allege that, beginning in approximately 1946, the defendants researched, developed, manufactured and tested various missile and rocket engines, as well as propellants, lasers and nuclear reactors at four facilities located in the greater Simi Valley and San Fernando Valley. * * *

The plaintiffs allege that the activities of the defendants at the Rocketdyne Facilities involved the use and release of certain chemicals, including, among others, trichloroethene (TCE) and hexavalent chromium, as well as the use, storage, generation and disposal of certain radioactive materials. The plaintiffs allege that they were personally exposed to and/or that their properties were contaminated by certain radioactive and/or chemical substances which were released from one or more of the Rocketdyne Facilities [also known as the Hughes, Canoga or DeSoto facilities] and which were dispersed through the contamination area by means of air currents, surface water runoff and/or subsurface ground water.

The plaintiffs further allege that their exposure to these substances has placed them at an increased risk of developing cancer or some other serious illness or disease. As a result, plaintiffs seek the implementation of a court-supervised program of medical monitoring designed to detect early signs of such illness or disease.

The plaintiffs also allege that the defendants' release of these substances has resulted in the contamination of their properties and has diminished the value of their properties, and they have incurred certain necessary expenses in response to the contamination of their properties for which they seek reimbursement under federal law.

The defendants maintain that plaintiffs have not been exposed to any substances released from the Rocketdyne Facilities that place them at an increased risk of illness or disease. The defendants also maintain that plaintiffs' properties are not contaminated by any releases from the Rocketdyne Facilities and that, consequently, plaintiffs are not entitled to recover damages for any harm caused to their properties.

[The court had already certified three classes, and in addition 71 plaintiffs sued for personal injury and wrongful death.]

PLAINTIFFS' MOTION TO COMPEL

I

The plaintiffs served interrogatory nos. 1 through 20 on defendants on November 11, 1997.[3] The defendants filed multiple objections, including relevancy and definitional objections to the interrogatories; however, without waiving their objections, defendants generally responded to the interrogatories under Rule 33(d), stating that the answers to these interrogatories may be derived or ascertained from defendants' business records previously produced to plaintiffs. The plaintiffs argue that defendants' responses are improper in that defendants have not complied with Rule 33(d), and, when answering narratively, have not completely and responsively answered.

* * * The Court, prior to addressing plaintiffs' motion and its several issues, notes that due to the complex nature of the pending class action, written interrogatories to the defendants are not likely to be particularly helpful or useful to plaintiffs and, more likely than not, will only lead to unnecessary discovery disputes. Rather, the depositions of knowledgeable corporate witnesses under Rule 30(b)(6), or the individually noticed depositions of defendants' employees, will ultimately be more productive.

The nature of the inquiries made by plaintiffs in their interrogatories was sufficiently broad for defendants to answer under Rule 33(d). However, Rule 33(d) is not satisfied by the wholesale dumping of documents. Rather, under Rule 33(d), the responding party chooses to produce business records in answer to the interrogatories—not to avoid answering them. To answer an interrogatory, "a responding party has the duty to specify, by category and location, the records from which answers to interrogatories can be derived." *Rainbow Pioneer No. 44–18–04A v. Hawaii–Nevada Investment Corp.*, 711 F.2d 902, 906 (9th Cir. 1983).[7] Thus, when voluminous documents are produced under Rule 33(d), they must be accompanied by indices designed to guide the searcher to the documents responsive to the interrogatories.

Interrogatory no. 18 asks defendants to: IDENTIFY the date and location of your first discovery of CONTAMINATION in the SURROUNDING AREA. The defendants, in their Supplemental Further Responses to interrogatory no. 18, state that:

3. These interrogatories generally seek information regarding the identities, quantities, and time periods of hazardous substances used and released at each of defendants' facilities, as well as the locations, dates and results of offsite testing of hazardous substances. Additionally, plaintiffs seek information identifying the locations, nature of, and results from tests on substances in the surrounding area, groundwater, surface water, air, and soil.

7. The defendants, in response to interrogatory nos. 1 through 5, responded that, because the volume of responsive documents is "huge, and listing all the responsive documents would be an overly burdensome endeavor," defendants have identified only a "representative sampling" of some of the documents containing responsive information. Such a response clearly shows lack of compliance with Rule 33(d).

BNA first became aware that releases from its SSFL [Santa Susana Field Laboratory] operations in concentrations above normal background had migrated offsite in August or September 1991. Water from a monitoring well approximately one hundred feet north of SSFL on property then owned by the Brandeis–Bardin Institute measured above background for tritium, but below the drinking water standard.

The plaintiffs object that this response is inadequate under Rule 33(d) and that defendants have provided no information with regard to the Hughes, Canoga or DeSoto facilities. However, defendants have narratively answered the interrogatory, rather than rely on Rule 33(d). Additionally, interrogatory no. 18 only requests information regarding defendants' first discovery of contamination, not the first discovery of contamination in the surrounding areas of each of the Rocketdyne Facilities; thus, defendants answered the interrogatory.

Interrogatory no. 20 asks defendants to: IDENTIFY all allegations, reports, or claims of OFFSITE CONTAMINATION YOU have received. In their Supplemental Further Responses to interrogatory no. 20, defendants list sixteen lawsuits, including the instant action, and further responded that they "are not aware of specific complaints of contamination of offsite property other than these lawsuits."

The plaintiffs object that this response is inadequate under Rule 33(d), that defendants have provided no information regarding the Hughes, Canoga or DeSoto facilities, and that the response should also list informal complaints. Here again, defendants have narratively answered the interrogatory, rather than rely on Rule 33(d), and defendants have answered the interrogatory, albeit not to plaintiffs' satisfaction.

II

The Court would like to take this opportunity to provide guidance to the parties regarding the use of Rule 33(d), so that, when properly used, both sides will be able to easily find for trial the documents produced during discovery. For trial purposes, it is best to have all documents placed on CD–ROM, which affords a method by which the storage of voluminous documents is less burdensome to the parties. This is not possible, however, without two things: One, a general index describing by topic and subtopic the information in the documents and, two, a locator index identifying the location of each document on CD–ROM. Since the Fourth Amended Complaint spans five decades, the descriptive index should also provide the decade (date) in which the document was created. Because both the descriptive and locator indices must meet the needs of both sides, the Court believes the parties should jointly create these indices. Thus, the parties must meet and confer regarding the indices, and such meeting or meetings shall take place no later than fourteen (14) days from the date of this Order.

Under Rule 33(d), certain documents which would otherwise be responsive may be withheld based on privilege, provided the exercise of the privilege does not prevent the interrogating party from ascertaining or deriving complete answers to the interrogatories and the withheld documents are listed on a privilege log. *Ampex Corp. v. Mitsubishi Elec. Corp.*, 937 F.Supp. 352, 355 (D.Del.1996). For purposes of this action, when defendants choose to answer an interrogatory under Rule 33(d), they may claim only the attorney-client privilege and work product doctrine and they must set forth the purportedly privileged documents on a privilege log. Other privileges, such as the patient-physician privilege and third party privacy rights, are not to be claimed on the privilege log; rather, the protective order, coupled with the redaction of selected information (when necessary), is sufficient to safeguard the interests protected by such privileges and rights. By these limitations, defendants' claims of privilege should not prevent the plaintiffs from ascertaining the complete answers to the interrogatories that are the subject of the pending motion, thereby permitting defendants to answer the interrogatories under Rule 33(d).

As to documents subject to the attorney-client privilege or work product doctrine, the plaintiffs are correct in contending that not all attachments to, or enclosures with, such documents are necessarily protected by the privilege. Rather, to claim the attorney-client privilege or work product doctrine for an attachment to, or enclosure with, another privileged document, the attachment or enclosure must be listed as a separate document on the privilege log; otherwise, such attachment or enclosure must be disclosed. * * *

DEFENDANTS' MOTION TO COMPEL

IV

Rule 33(c) of the Federal Rules of Civil Procedure provides, in part, for the serving of an interrogatory the answer to which involves "an opinion or contention that relates to fact or the application of law to fact...." Fed.R.Civ.P. 33(c). Here, defendants seek to compel responses to several interrogatories that are essentially contention interrogatories. Such interrogatories are permissible and acceptable under Rule 33(c). * * *

The defendants served the following interrogatory (which the Court will call interrogatory no. 1) on Class I representatives, the Samuels, Class II representatives, the O'Connors, Rueger, and Vroman, and Class III representative, Grandinetti:

> DESCRIBE FULLY EACH ALLEGED EXPOSURE TO YOU TO ALLEGED TOXIC SUBSTANCES WHICH YOU CONTEND WAS CAUSED BY DEFENDANTS' CONDUCT.

Class I representatives initially objected to the interrogatory as being compound, and then answered that they "may have been exposed" through ingestion of airborne releases, soil and surface water contamination. Finally, the Samuels stated that "the amount of toxic substances to which [plaintiff] has been exposed is unknown." The response was supplemented by the Samuels stating, upon information and belief, that additional information regarding their exposure may be determined from documents produced by defendants and these documents show, among other things, that toxic substances have traveled through the air, water or soil in patterns causing them to come in contact with plaintiffs.

The defendants argue that these responses are "evasive or incomplete" and should, thus, be treated as a failure to respond. There is no merit to defendants' argument. The plaintiffs' response to interrogatory no. 1 is sufficient since the clear inference from the response is that plaintiffs do not yet know exactly how they were exposed to contaminants, but exposure occurred. When additional information is known to plaintiffs, they must supplement their response under Rule 26(e). Thus, defendants' motion regarding interrogatory no. 1 is DENIED as to the Class I representatives. * * *

The defendants served the following interrogatory (which the Court will call interrogatory no. 2) on Class I representatives, the Samuels, Class II representatives, the O'Connors, Rueger, and Vroman, and Class III representative Grandinetti:

> For each of YOUR properties allegedly contaminated by DEFEN- DANTS' conduct, DESCRIBE FULLY THE NATURE AND SCOPE OF THE ALLEGED CONTAMINATION BY TOXIC SUBSTANCES caused by DEFENDANTS' conduct.

All class representatives initially objected to the form of the interrogatory and then answered, stating that their residency is within proximity of one of defendants' facilities and providing general information regarding the use of certain chemicals at the facility. The class representatives also filed a supplemental response identifying specific chemicals and noting that documents produced by defendants show the release of these chemicals into the environment. Finally, plaintiffs argue that they were in the process of further supplementing their responses based upon the documentary evidence provided to them, and defendants knew that these responses would be available by March 15, 1999.

The defendants complain that plaintiffs' responses are inadequate in that they do not identify the substances that could actually be found on plaintiffs' properties, and, further, complain that since some plaintiffs want reimbursement for cleaning up their property they surely must know of the contamination to it. There is no merit to defendants' argument since interrogatory no. 2 does not specifically ask the plaintiffs to identify the toxic substances found on the plaintiffs' properties, nor does the defendants' definition of the phrase "DESCRIBE FULLY THE NATURE AND SCOPE OF THE ALLEGED CONTAMINATION BY TOXIC SUBSTANCES" ask the plaintiffs to identify such substances. Thus, defendants' motion to compel further responses to interrogatory no. 2 is DENIED. * * *

The Court would like to take this opportunity to address the parties and their counsel, to stress that

[t]he discovery system depends absolutely on good faith and common sense from counsel. The courts, sorely pressed by demands to try cases promptly and to rule thoughtfully on potentially case dispositive motions, simply do not have the resources to police closely the operation of the discovery process. The whole system of [c]ivil adjudication would be ground to a virtual halt if the courts were forced to intervene in even a modest percentage of discovery transactions. That fact should impose on counsel an acute sense of responsibility about how they handle discovery matters. They should strive to be cooperative, practical and sensible, and should turn to the courts (or take positions that force others to turn to the courts) only in extraordinary situations that implicate truly significant interests.

In re Convergent Technologies Securities Litigation, 108 F.R.D [328, 331 (N.D.Cal.1985)]. ** *

Notes and Questions

1. *Asking.* Parties can send interrogatories only to other parties, under Rule 33(a), who must respond in writing within thirty days. Only parties are required to answer interrogatories. How soon can interrogatories be used? Generally, a party sends interrogatories after the Rule 26(f) discovery conference, but the trial court may permit them earlier. How late can they be sent? While the rules prescribe no deadline for sending them, most trial courts use case management orders to set discovery schedules which establish the deadline for sending interrogatories.

Is there a limit to the number of interrogatories a party can send? Rule 33(a) sets a limit of twenty-five questions, unless the trial court orders otherwise or the parties agree on another number. When trial courts apply the limits, the limit often is twenty-five *per interrogatory set*, rather than a total of twenty-five interrogatories. Why? Even after mandatory disclosures under Rule 26(a), many fact patterns underlying claims for relief suggest a need for a variety of types of information.

2. *Opinions or Contentions.* Despite the fact that work product may be involved, Rule 33(c) states that an interrogatory may seek "an opinion or contention that relates to fact or the application of law to fact." For example, even though it may reveal something about the answering attorney's mental impressions, an interrogatory is proper if it asks, "In Paragraph 10 of the Complaint, you state that the Defendant drove his vehicle negligently. State the facts supporting your contention that the Defendant drove his vehicle negligently."

3. *Types of interrogatories.*

a. *Factual request:* "Mr. Horner, did you pull a plum from a Christmas pie on December 25, 2005?"

b. *Factual opinion or conclusion:* "Did the person who first advised you to put your thumb in a Christmas pie on December 25, 2005, appear to be laughing?"

c. *Application of law to fact:* "What acts of negligence were committed by defendant?" OR "Upon what factual grounds does plaintiff base the claim asserted in Paragraph 3 of the Complaint that defendant was negligent?"

d. *Legal opinion or conclusion (an objectionable interrogatory, because it constitutes opinion work product):* "What is the constitutional, statutory, common law, or intergalactic basis for your claim?"

4. *Answering.* When a party answers, Rule 33(b) requires that each interrogatory be answered separately and fully in writing, within thirty days of service, unless there is an objection. The scope of information attributable to a party reaches information within the control of the party as well as the party's agents. The reach of that coverage includes facts known by the party's attorney as well as factual information provided to the party by other persons. An individual party must sign the answers, verifying their accuracy. For a party-entity, a representative of the entity verifies the answers.

As discussed previously, a party can object to discovery on a variety of grounds. For interrogatories, typical objections are that an interrogatory or a portion of an interrogatory is overly broad, vague, or ambiguous. For example, the interrogatory may be overbroad—asking for information covering a time period that is not included within the events described in the complaint of answer. One method for avoiding objections based on vagueness or ambiguity is to include a clearly expressed glossary of terms used repeatedly in the interrogatories at the beginning of the interrogatories. Other common objections were discussed previously—asking for A) privileged or work product information, B) non-discoverable expert information, C) irrelevant information not calculated to lead to the discovery of admissible evidence, or D) information the production of which is burdensome and oppressive. An objecting party may file a motion for a protective order under Rule 26(c); the party sending the interrogatories may respond to an objection by filing a motion to compel under Rule 37(a). Regardless, the trial court has broad discretion in ruling on objections to interrogatories. As a result, the parties may first try to resolve their interrogatory disagreement in order to avoid judicial intervention in the discovery process.

5. *Rule 33(d)'s Option to Produce Business Records.* Suppose the responding party does not feel like expending the resources necessary to find the information sought by the requesting party. Instead of answering an interrogatory, Rule 33(d) allows a party to produce business records. Unlike a Rule 34 request for production for the documents themselves, the purpose of Rule 33(d) is for the requesting party to discover requested information which happens to be located in the responding party's business records. The rule contains several limitations on a broad application.

- The rule is restricted to business records, rather than personal records or litigation documents such as transcripts.

- The responding party must be able to state that the documents contain the requested information. The party also must provide adequate detail so that the requesting party can identify *which* documents contain the requested information.

- The burden of locating the answer must be "substantially the same" for the requesting and the responding party, who has the burden of proof. If the requesting party believes that the burdens are not "substantially the same," she can file a Rule 37(a) motion to compel an answer to the interrogatory from the responding party.

Does the use of Rule 33(d) pose any risks for the responding party? Would you want an adversary party rummaging for information in your client's business files? Before using the Rule 33(d) technique, what questions would you ask your client about the contents of his business files?

Exercise

For one of the Introductory Problems from earlier in the chapter, draft at least ten interrogatories which you as plaintiff's counsel or defense counsel would want to sent the opposing party to discover factual information about the case.

3. Request for Production of Documents

PLAYBOY ENTERPRISES, INC. v. WELLES

60 F.Supp.2d 1050 (S.D. Cal. 1999)

STIVEN, United States Magistrate Judge.

* * * Plaintiff, Playboy Enterprises Incorporated, owns and utilizes the trademarks Playboy, Playmate, Playmate of the Month, and Playmate of the Year, in connection with Playboy Magazine and various goods and services sold by Plaintiff and/or its licensees. Defendant, Terri Welles, posed in Playboy magazine as a Playmate of the Month model in 1980 and was designated Playmate of the Year in 1981. Defendant has established and is operating a personal website on the Internet. Plaintiff alleges that Defendant has used and continues to use Plaintiff's Playboy and Playmate trademarks throughout her website, without authorization from Playboy. Plaintiff claims that Defendant is infringing on its trademarks, diluting its trademarks, and is unfairly competing with Plaintiff. Defendant has counterclaimed for damages due to defamation, interference with prospective business advantage, intentional infliction of emotional distress, and unfair competition.

The discovery conference was requested by Plaintiff when Plaintiff learned that Defendant Welles may have in the past deleted, or continues to presently delete, e-mail communications which have been requested for production by Plaintiff. In response to a request for production of documents, Co–Defendant Huntington produced two e-mail communications between Defendant Welles and Janey Huntington that Defendant Welles had not produced herself. Plaintiff contacted Defense counsel to inquire why these e-mails had not been produced by Defendant. It appears to the Court that during meet and confer attempts between counsel during May and June 1999, Plaintiff learned from Defendant's counsel that Defendant has had a custom and practice of deleting electronic mail soon after sending or receiving e-mail. Plaintiff asserts that Defendant has continued this practice throughout the litigation, irrespective of whether the e-mail is responsive to Plaintiff's request for production of documents. Plaintiff requests access to Defendant's personal computer hard drive to make a "mirror image" of the hard drive, and then have Defense counsel review the recovered e-mails to produce relevant and responsive documents.

Plaintiff also requests that Defendant produce her personal and corporate income tax statements. Plaintiff has requested financial information from Welles, but alleges that Welles has failed to provide sufficient information for Plaintiff to determine the damages it has allegedly suffered due to Defendant's use of Plaintiff's trademarks. Plaintiff also asserts that such financial information is relevant to claims raised by Defendants' counterclaims. * * *

Plaintiff requests that it be able to access Defendant's hard drive to attempt to recover deleted files which may be stored on the hard drive of Defendant's personal computer. * * *

Federal Rule of Civil Procedure 34 governs the scope and procedure for the production of documents. This rule allows a party to ask another party "to produce and permit the party making the request . . . to inspect and copy, any designated documents, . . . or to inspect and copy, test, or sample any tangible things which constitute or contain matters within the scope of Rule 26(b) and which are in the possession, custody or control of the party upon whom the request is served." Fed.R.Civ.P. 34(a)(1). The Advisory Committee Notes for Fed.R.Civ.P. 34 address how information stored as electronic data is discoverable.

> The inclusive description of "documents" is revised to accord with changing technology. It makes clear that Rule 34 applies to electronics data compilations from which information can be obtained only with the use of detection devices, and that when the data can as a practical matter be made usable by the discovering party only through respondent's devices, respondent may be required to use his devices to translate the data into usable form. In many instances, *this means that respondent will have to supply a print-out of computer data.* The burden thus placed on respondent will vary from case to case, and the courts have ample power under Rule 26(c) to protect respondent against undue burden or expense, either by restricting discovery or requiring that the discovering party pay costs. Similarly, if the discovering party needs to check the electronic source itself, the court may protect respondent with respect to preservation of his records, confidentiality of nondiscoverable matters, and costs.

(Emphasis added.)

The Court finds that by requesting "documents" under Fed.R.Civ.P. 34, Plaintiff also effectively requested production of information stored in electronic form. Had Defendant printed any relevant e-mails, as is directed by the Advisory Notes to Fed.R.Civ.P. 34, such e-mails would have been produced as a "document". Plaintiff needs to access the hard drive of Defendant's computer only because Defendant's actions in deleting those e-mails made it currently impossible to produce the information as a "document". This Court finds that Plaintiff's prior discovery request satisfies any procedural requirement under Fed. R.Civ.P. 34.

* * * The Court finds it likely that relevant information is stored on the hard drive of Defendant's personal computer. Defendant uses her e-mail system for both business and personal communications. In Defendant's July 9, 1999 Declaration, she stated, "Since first acquiring the computer, I have routinely used it for personal as well as business matters." This business use is further illustrated by the April 2, 1999, e-mail sent by Defendant Welles to Co–Defendant Mihalko, when Defendant Welles asked Mihalko to place "one of Doria's banners on my home page when you get the chance."

The Advisory Committee Notes to Fed.R.Civ.P. 34 referenced above makes it clear that information stored in computer format is discoverable. Defendant has cited no cases finding that electronically stored data is exempt from discovery. The only restriction in this discovery is that the producing party be protected against undue burden and expense and/or invasion of privileged matter. In determining whether a request for discovery will be unduly burdensome to the responding party, the court weighs the benefit and burden of the discovery. Fed.R.Civ.P. 26(b)(2). This balance requires a court to consider the needs of the case, the amount in controversy, the importance of the issues at stake, the potential for finding relevant material and the importance of the proposed discovery in resolving the issues. Fed.R.Civ.P. 26(b)(2).

Plaintiff asserts that these e-mails may provide evidence in support of its trademark infringement and dilution claims, as well as a defense to Defendant's claim for emotional distress. Plaintiff believes that these e-mails may reflect Defendant's knowledge of the "Playmate of the Year" contract, and imply that she knew the contract required her to obtain written approval from Plaintiff before she could use the "Playmate of the Year" designation. Plaintiff also believes these e-mails may negate Defendant's emotional distress claim because they will indicate her state of mind regarding issues addressed in the lawsuit. Finally, Plaintiff believes that the e-mails may support Plaintiff's position that visitors to Defendant's website will view the website as associated with hard core pornography.

Defendant contends that her business will suffer financial losses due to the approximate four to eight hour shutdown required to recover information from the hard drive. Defendant also contends that any recovered e-mails between her and her attorneys are protected by attorney-client privilege. Lastly, Defendant contends that the copying of her hard drive would be an invasion of her privacy.

Considering these factors, the Court determines that the need for the requested information outweighs the burden on Defendant. Defendant's privacy and attorney-client privilege will be protected pursuant to the protocol outlined below, and Defendant's counsel will have an opportunity to control and review all of the recovered e-mails, and produce to Plaintiff only those documents that are relevant, responsive, and non-privileged. Any outside expert retained to produce the "mirror image" will sign a protective order and will be acting as an Officer of the Court pursuant to this Order. Thus, this Court finds that Defendant's privacy and attorney-client communications will be sufficiently protected. Further, Plaintiff will pay the costs associated with the information recovery. Lastly, if the work, which will take approximately four to eight hours, is coordinated to accommodate Defendant's schedule as much as possible, the Court finds that the "down time" for Defendant's computer will result in minimal business interruption. * * *

Plaintiff seeks to discover Defendant's personal and corporate income tax returns. Plaintiff has requested financial information from the Defendant, but alleges it has failed to receive sufficient information to determine the damages it has allegedly suffered due to Defendant's use of Plaintiff's trademarks. Plaintiff also asserts that this financial information is important to defend against Defendant's claims of damages from economic loss and/or emotional distress based on Plaintiff's actions and this litigation.

Plaintiff claims that the income tax returns are necessary to determine its damages suffered under their federal claims of trademark infringement and dilution, as well as to defend against Defendant's state claims of economic loss and emotional distress. Specifically, this Court notes that the financial information in Defendant's tax returns are related to Plaintiff's damages sought under § 43(a) of the Lanham Act. * * *

In *ALPO Petfoods, Inc. v. Ralston Purina Co.*, 913 F.2d 958, 969 (D.C.Cir.1990) (citations omitted), the court stated that actual damages in false advertising cases under § 35(a) can include: 1) profits lost by the plaintiff on the sales actually diverted to the false advertiser; 2) profits lost by the plaintiff on sales made at prices reduced as a demonstrated result of the false advertising; 3) the costs of the completed advertising that actually and reasonably responds to the defendant's offering ads; and 4) quantifiable harm to the plaintiff's good will, to the extent that completed corrective advertising has . . . repaired that harm. Thus, at a minimum, information from Defendant's tax returns establishing Defendant's profits are relevant to this action.

* * * Under federal law, tax returns are not privileged. Tax returns are generally discoverable where necessary in private civil litigation. In *St. Regis Paper Company v. United States*, the United States Supreme Court found that although tax returns are made confidential within the government bureau, copies in the hands of the tax payer are subject to discover[y]. *St. Regis Paper Company v. United States*, 368 U.S. 208, 217 (1961).

This Court ORDERS Defendant to produce to Plaintiff the 1997 Corporate Income Tax Return for Terri Welles Inc., and to submit her 1996, 1997, and 1998 Personal Income Tax Returns to the Court for in camera review. Defendant must produce these documents by August 13,

1999. The Court will determine which, if any, business related information contained in the tax returns should be produced to Plaintiff. Defendant shall also produce to Plaintiff the 1998 Corporate Income Tax Return for Terri Welles Inc., when filed, even if this date is beyond the discovery cut-off set for this litigation. * * *

Plaintiff shall submit a declaration supporting its assertions that deleted e-mail recovery is feasible from a computer's hard drive. Presuming that Plaintiff can provide such a declaration, the Court orders that a "mirror image" of Defendant's hard drive will be made by a computer specialist trained in the area of data recovery. This Court appointed specialist will act as an Officer of the Court. The "mirror image" copy will be given to Defendant's attorney to print, review, and produce to Plaintiff all relevant, requested, and non-privileged documents. Plaintiff will pay for the costs associated with the production of the "mirror image." * * *

Notes and Questions

1. *Asking.* Parties can request inspection of documents and things only from other parties under Rule 34(a), who also must respond in writing within thirty days. However, requests can be served on non-parties by the issuance of a subpoena *duces tecum* under Rule 45.

How soon can a request for production be used? Again, a party usually sends such requests after the Rule 26(f) discovery conference, or sooner with the trial court's permission. Rule 34 fails to prescribe a deadline for sending requests, but trial courts often use case management orders to set discovery schedules which establish the deadline for responding to the request. Unlike Rule 33, though, there is no limit on the number of requests for production that are submitted.

2. *What is a document?* An important aspect of a request for production is for the requesting party to define the term "document," for the scope of that definition is determinative of how much effort the answering party must exert to satisfy the request. With newer forms of technology constantly emerging, the Rule 34(a) reference to designated documents is subject to nitpicking as far too narrow. Instead, given the diverse methods of data compilation, the following definition may be used as a starting point but even it is not necessarily exhaustive.

The term "documents" means all writings of any kind, including the originals and all non-identical copies, whether different from the originals by reason of any notation made on such copies or otherwise, including without limitation, correspondence, memoranda, notes, e-mail messages, diaries, statistics, letters, telegrams, minutes, contracts, reports, studies, checks, statements, receipts, returns, summaries, pamphlets, books, interoffice and intra-office communications, internet communications, notations of any sort of conversations, telephone calls, meetings or other communications, bulletins, printed matter, computer print-outs, teletypes, telefax, invoices, worksheets, all drafts, alterations, modifications, changes, and amendments of any of the foregoing, graphic or oral records or representations of any kind (including, without limitation, photographs, charts, graphs, microfiche, microfilm, video-tapes, recordings, motion pictures), and any electronic, mechanical, or electric records or representations of any kind (including, without limi-tation, tapes, cassettes, discs, recordings, CDs, and computer memories).

By contrast, a request to enter another party's land for "inspection and measuring, surveying, photographing, testing, or sampling" is relatively simple to make because the address and/or location of the property is relatively fixed.

The requesting party must seek the documents individually or categori-cally and describe them "with reasonable particularity." As you might expect, the particularity requirement is often a disputed issue. The request-ing party wants the request to be construed as broadly as possible so that maximum disclosure is made, while the responding party wants the request rendered narrowly so that a limited number of documents must be turned over. Why does that matter? Often the requesting party is uncertain about exactly what the other party has in the way of documents. By the permitted breadth of its request, the requesting party is trying to "guess" what documents the other side has in its possession, custody or control. The requesting party also must "specify a reasonable time, place , and manner" of complying with the request.

3. *Answering.* Rule 34(b) also requires the responding party to produce all documents within its "possession, custody or control." The case law has interpreted the term "control" so that the responder must turn over documents she has the legal right to demand from others (e.g., her attorney or accountant) as well as those of which she has actual possession (even if they belong to another person).

Besides the objections already mentioned for interrogatories, a respond-ing party may refuse compliance by claiming that the documents can be procured by the adversary party from another source, e.g., a public record. See, e.g., *Bleecker v. Standard Fire Ins. Co.*, 130 F.Supp.2d 726 (E.D.N.C. 2000). As you might have suspected, the basis for the objection is that it is an undue burden to produce the documents due to the accessibility of an alternative source.

The responding party must produce the documents "as they are kept in the usual course of business or shall organize and label them to correspond with the categories in the request." Why does Rule 34(b) state that princi-ple? An attorney may not use a system of record-keeping that effectively conceals relevant documents instead of disclosing them. It is also impermissi-ble for a responding attorney to react to a request by handing over the requested documents as part of a much larger (and unresponsive) produc-tion, i.e., response by avalanche.

4. *Electronic discovery.* The Administrative Office of the United States Courts has released draft amendments to the Federal Rules addressing reform for the disclosure and discovery of electronically stored information, which one study estimated constitutes over 90% of all information. *In re Bristol–Myers Squibb Securities Litigation*, 205 F.R.D. 437 (D.N.J. 2002). They are not effective until December 1, 2006. The fear of discovery expenses often forces parties to settle their cases.

- Rule 26(b)(2): Relevant, reasonably accessible electronically stored information must be provided without a court order, subject to objection that the information is not reasonably accessible.

- Rule 26(b)(5): Inadvertent production of privileged information may be raised, and could result in the return, sequestration, or destruction of the material.

- Rule 26(f): Parties must address issues regarding the discovery or disclosure of electronically stored information, including the form of production as well as its preservation.

- Rule 33: Answers to interrogatories relating to the review of business records should include a search of electronically stored information.

- Rule 34: Parties must frame discovery requests to specify whether discovery documents, electronically stored information, or both, is being sought.

- Rule 37: A safe harbor would protect a party from sanctions for failing to provide electronically stored information lost due to the routine operation of the party's computer system. (This proposal was the only amendment not to be submitted by the Civil Rules Advisory Committee to the United States Judicial Conference's Standing Committee on Rules for the latter's consideration in June 2005.)

5. After *Welles*, how do you advise your client about recording and retaining information? If clients have a duty to disinter electronic data in order to respond to a discovery request, such as "deleted" e-mail, what advice do you give your client about communicating in any form (even orally)?

Exercise

For one of the Introductory Problems from earlier in the chapter, draft at least ten requests for production of documents which you as plaintiff's counsel or defense counsel would want to sent the opposing party to discover factual information about the case.

4. Request for Admissions

ASEA, INC. v. SOUTHERN PAC. TRANSP. CO.
669 F.2d 1242 (9th Cir. 1981)

WALLACE, Circuit Judge

Southern Pacific Transportation Co. and Harbor Belt Line (the railroads) appeal from a judgment entered in favor of Asea, Inc. (Asea) and from the denial of their motion for a new trial. The railroads' principal contention in this appeal is that the district court erred in ordering admitted certain matters the railroads failed to admit or deny in response to requests for admissions served by Asea. We affirm in part and vacate and remand in part.

Asea, a New York corporation, is the sole United States distributor of electrical transformers manufactured in Sweden by Asea A/B, a

Swedish corporation. Asea sold a transformer to the Los Angeles Department of Water & Power. The transformer was transported by merchant vessel from Sweden to the Los Angeles harbor. Pursuant to their contract with Asea, the railroads then took custody of the transformer and shipped it to North Hollywood, California. Upon its arrival, the transformer was inspected by representatives of the railroads and Asea. It was found that the transformer had shifted on the railroad car during transit despite being shored and braced. An electrical check revealed the transformer had shorted. Asea had installed an "impact recorder" on the transformer to measure any impact that might occur during rail carriage. Inspection of the impact recorder tape indicated that, while the transformer was in the custody of the railroads, it had suffered an impact measured at 1.8 on the recorder scale, equivalent to an impact at a speed in excess of 5 miles per hour. Internal inspection of the transformer revealed that it had sustained substantial damage during transit.

On July 10, 1978, Asea filed an action for damages in the district court, invoking its diversity jurisdiction pursuant to 28 U.S.C. § 1332(a), relying on theories of negligence, breach of implied warranty, and violation of California Civil Code § 2194 (inland carrier's liability for loss). The parties engaged in extensive discovery for over one year. On January 22, 1979, Asea served a series of requests for admissions pursuant to Fed.R.Civ.P. 36(a). Those of primary importance in this appeal related essentially to the condition of the transformer at the time the railroads took custody of it, the impact revealed on the impact recorder tape, the location of the transformer at the time the impact occurred, the short discovered in the transformer after its arrival and the reasonable cost of repairing the transformer and returning it to the Los Angeles Department of Water & Power. The district court allowed additional time to reply. To eighteen of these requests, the railroads responded on May 24, 1979:

> Answering party cannot admit or deny. Said party has made reasonable inquiry. Information known or readily obtainable to this date is not complete. Investigation continues.

Each of the requests for admissions was accompanied by an interrogatory which asked that if the railroads' response was anything other than an unqualified admission, they should state the facts, documents and witnesses upon which the response was based. The railroads answered these interrogatories by insisting they were "(n)ot applicable."

Discovery continued following a pretrial conference held in June, 1979. As a result of further depositions of certain railroad employees, Asea became convinced that the railroads had known the actual cause of the impact on the transformer for many months, and therefore could have admitted or denied the requests for admissions. On December 3, 1979, five weeks prior to trial, Asea moved to have the requests ordered admitted. At the hearing on the motion, the railroads claimed that their responses were proper by authority of Rule 36(a) because they did not have any firsthand information. The district court inquired whether the railroads had "subsequently come into more information that (would) enable (them) to supply more appropriate answers?" Counsel for the railroads responded, "We may possibly, Your Honor," but insisted that "the answers still stand." The railroads claimed the information relevant to the requests for admissions was "wholly within the hands of (Asea)." The court replied:

> (T)hat's what I hear all the time. . . . (T)his case has been here so many times, and you are a constant complainer about the inadequacy of the other side. Now it appears that you're standing behind that same shield yourself saying that you just don't have the information to provide.

The district court took the matter under submission and subsequently granted Asea's motion to order the matters admitted. The railroads' later motion to have these admissions withdrawn was denied.

The railroads contend their responses to the requests for admissions satisfied the requirements of Fed.R.Civ.P. 36(a). In the alternative, they argue that the sanction for failure of a party to make reasonable inquiry prior to answering a request for admission lies in an award of the expenses incurred in proving the fact at trial, pursuant to Fed.R.Civ.P. 37(c), and not in deeming the matter admitted. We have considered this issue carefully because it apparently is a question of first impression. We conclude, however, that a district court may, under proper circumstances and in its discretion, order admitted matters which an answering party has failed to admit or deny, where the information known or readily obtainable after reasonable inquiry was sufficient to enable the answering party to admit or deny.

* * * The Rule provides that a party may not give lack of information as a reason for failure to admit or deny "unless he states that he has made reasonable inquiry and that the information known or readily obtainable by him is insufficient to enable him to admit or deny." The railroads cite in support of this construction *Adley Express Co. v. Highway Truck Drivers & Helpers, Local No. 107*, 349 F.Supp. 436 (E.D.Pa.1972), where the district court observed that "it would appear that a mere statement in the answer that the answering party has made reasonable inquiry and that the information solicited was insufficient to enable him to admit or deny the requested matter will suffice." *Id.* at 451–52. Their position is further supported by the Advisory Committee's Note, which states:

> The revised rule requires only that the answering party make reasonable inquiry and secure such knowledge and information as are readily obtainable by him. In most instances, the investigation will be necessary either to his own case or to preparation for rebuttal. Even when it is not, the information may be close enough at hand to be "readily obtainable." Rule 36 requires only that the party state that he has taken these steps. The sanction for failure of

a party to inform himself before he answers lies in the award of costs after trial, as provided in Rule 37(c).

* * * We are not persuaded that an answer to a request for admission necessarily complies with Rule 36(a) merely because it includes a statement that the party has made reasonable inquiry and that the information necessary to admit or deny the matter is not readily obtainable by him. The discovery process is subject to the overriding limitation of good faith. Callous disregard of discovery responsibilities cannot be condoned. The abuses of the current discovery rules are well documented. In our view, permitting a party to avoid admitting or denying a proper request for admission simply by tracking the language of Rule 36(a) would encourage additional abuse of the discovery process. Instead of making an evasive or meritless denial, which clearly would result in the matter being deemed admitted, a party could comply with the Rule merely by having his attorney submit the language of the Rule in response to the request. * * * .

We hold, therefore, that a response which fails to admit or deny a proper request for admission does not comply with the requirements of Rule 36(a) if the answering party has not, in fact, made "reasonable inquiry," or if information "readily obtainable" is sufficient to enable him to admit or deny the matter. A party requesting an admission may, if he feels these requirements have not been met, move to determine the sufficiency of the answer, to compel a proper response, or to have the matter ordered admitted. Although the district court should ordinarily first order an amended answer, and deem the matter admitted only if a sufficient answer is not timely filed, this determination, like most involved in the oversight of discovery, is left to the sound discretion of the district judge. The general power of the district court to control the discovery process allows for the severe sanction of ordering a matter admitted when it has been demonstrated that a party has intentionally disregarded the obligations imposed by Rule 36(a).

Here, the district judge decided not to require an amended response. Although counsel for the railroads asserted that they would stand pat on the prior responses, she did state that additional answers would be filed if the court required it. But this was not the first discovery problem presented to the court. Far from it. A year of volatile and acrimonious fighting, during which many discovery disputes were placed before the judge as referee, had preceded it. Thus, we cannot say the district judge abused his wide discretion in not requiring amended responses. * * *

The more difficult question is whether that discretion was abused when he imposed the severe sanction of deeming admitted certain key matters described in the requests. This is answered by determining whether the district judge properly found that the railroads did not make reasonable inquiry or that the information readily obtainable was sufficient to allow them to admit or deny the particular requests. The order of the district judge, however, does not state the basis upon which he concluded that the matters should be ordered admitted. There is evidence in the record suggesting that the railroads in fact had sufficient information to admit or deny the requested admissions at the time they submitted their answers to Asea, or that they subsequently discovered sufficient information to require them to amend their answers. It is less clear whether a finding could be made that the railroads failed to make reasonable inquiry. With a sanction as severe as the one imposed, we conclude that a finding by the district court is necessary for proper appellate review. We therefore vacate the judgment and remand for the limited purpose of reconsideration of the order deeming the requests admitted and the filing of appropriate findings of fact. What that reconsideration entails shall be determined by the district court, but we do not exclude an evidentiary hearing if one is determined to be necessary. * * *

Notes and Questions

1. *Asking.* Under Rule 36, each party can require other parties to admit relevant facts and/or authenticate documents that are not in controversy. The procedure can eliminate the necessity of producing witnesses and evidence to support those facts. As with interrogatories and requests for production, a party usually sends such requests after the Rule 26(f) discovery conference, or sooner with the trial court's permission. The federal rules have no limitation on the number of requests for admission, although local rules may limit the number. To simplify this process, the requesting party should follow Rule 36(a) and set forth each fact or document for which admission or authenticity is requested in a separate paragraph.

2. *Opinions or Contentions.* Rule 36(a) states that a request for admission may seek "statements or opinions of fact or the application of law to fact." On the other hand, the rule does not authorize a request that requires a purely legal conclusion, without also applying the law to the facts. For example, in *Tulip Computers Intern., B.V. v. Dell Computer Corp.* 210 F.R.D. 100 (D. Del. 2002), the court ruled that a request for an admission that a patent was valid is an inappropriate use of Rule 36: "whether a patent is valid would call for a legal conclusion although dependant on factual inquiries." *Id.* at 107.

3. *Answering.* The responding party has an obligation to investigate the requests, and in good faith partially or fully admit, partially or fully deny, state the reasons for the inability to admit or deny, or object to each requested admission, within thirty days of receiving the requests. As the *Asea* court stated, a party cannot avoid the request by being evasive, and the requesting party can move the court to determine the sufficiency of a denial. When a party believes that part of a request is true and part is untrue, the proper response is to admit the factual portion and deny the incorrect part. If a responding party cannot admit or deny the requested information after a reasonable inquiry, she needs to describe her inability in detail. Why? She risks the court treating her response as insufficient and instead treating the answer as an admission. The objections previously discussed for interrogatories and requests for production also apply to requests for admission.

Rule 36(b) states that an admission is conclusively established unless the trial court permits the admission's withdrawal or amendment. Unlike work product, which applies to cases beyond which it is first raised, the effect of the admission is for the instant case only. At trial, the requesting party can introduce the admission, although it is subject to evidentiary objections.

Exercise

For one of the Introductory Problems from earlier in the chapter, draft at least ten requests for admission which you as plaintiff's counsel or defense counsel would want to sent the opposing party to discover factual information about the case.

5. Physical and Mental Examinations

ALI v. WANG LABORATORIES, INC.

162 F.R.D. 165 (M.D. Fla. 1995)

STEELE, United States Magistrate Judge.

This cause is before the Court on Defendant's Motion To Compel Physical and Mental Examinations of Plaintiff, filed March 22, 1995. Plaintiff's Response and Memorandum in Opposition to Motion To Compel Physical and Mental Examinations of Plaintiff was filed April 3, 1995. On April 18, 1995 the Court heard oral argument on the motion.

Plaintiff's Complaint alleges he was employed by defendant Wang Laboratories, Inc. (Wang) from 1978 until terminated in May, 1993. Plaintiff alleges that during his employment he suffered a work-related injury which caused medical problems involving sclerosis of the cervical joints and bone-spurring, which in turn resulted in his becoming an individual with a "disability" under the American with Disabilities Act (ADA). Plaintiff asserts his termination violated various federal and state statutes because it was caused by unlawful consideration of his age (over 40), an alleged disability, and his national origin. Plaintiff further alleges that he could have and can perform the essential functions of his employment with defendant. Plaintiff claims defendant's actions caused "severe emotional and mental distress", and his requested relief includes compensatory damages "for emotional pain and suffering" and reinstatement to his previous employment position. Defendant denies plaintiff is an individual with a "disability" and denies plaintiff could have performed and can still perform the essential functions of his employment.
* * *

Both parties agree that defendant's motion is governed by Fed. R.Civ.P. 35(a). The general principles under Rule 35(a) have been articulated in *Schlagenhauf v. Holder*, 379 U.S. 104 (1964). Defendant must establish that plaintiff's mental condition or physical condition is "in controversy" and must show "good cause" for the mental or physical examination(s). This requires an affirmative showing that the mental or physical condition is "really and genuinely" in controversy and that good cause exists for each particular examination. The Court must decide, by making a "discriminating application", whether the "in controversy" and "good cause" requirements have been adequately demonstrated by the production of sufficient information which allows the Court to perform its function under Rule 35(a). *Schlagenhauf v. Holder*, 379 U.S. at 118–122. This requires a greater showing than for other types of discovery under Rule 26, Fed.R.Civ.P.

The Court need not resolve defendant's assertion that its burden has been satisfied by the pleadings alone. The Court has considered the pleadings and other documents in the court file, the documents submitted at the hearing, and the information from and argument of counsel. The Court finds that this combination provides sufficient information by which the Court can fulfill its function under Rule 35(a). *Schlagenhauf v. Holder*, 379 U.S. at 119.

Defendant claims that plaintiff's mental condition has been placed in controversy because plaintiff claims he suffers continuing emotional and mental distress for which he seeks substantial damages. Defendant seeks the mental examination to determine the existence and extent of plaintiff's mental distress.

The Court agrees with those cases which hold that plaintiff's "mental condition" within the meaning of Rule 35 is not necessarily placed in controversy merely because plaintiff seeks recovery for "emotional distress". A person with no "mental condition" may still suffer emotional distress which is compensable. Plaintiff, however, has gone beyond a mere claim for emotional distress. In answers to interrogatories, plaintiff stated his "personal character and performance were severely and permanently damaged"; he "lost his self esteem and was embarrassed to call on his former customers" and others; he and his wife and son suffered "severe and permanent psychological damage"; his "humiliation and embarrassment" "created a great deal of anger and hatred within him" as well as family problems; he "suffered extreme emotional distress"; he "has been very depressed and remains depressed", and he has had an outbreak of skin and scalp rash attributed to the "ordeal" of his termination. This is clearly sufficient to place plaintiff's mental condition in controversy.

The Court also finds that good cause has been shown for a mental examination. Plaintiff is seeking substantial damages for his alleged emotional injuries. While plaintiff may be content to offer only his own testimony to a jury, defendant is not compelled to limit its case to mere cross examination. Since plaintiff's mental condition is in controversy and substantial damages are asserted, it is essential for defendant to have the reasonable opportunity to challenge plaintiff's claim and testimony. The testimony of an expert is a well recognized and reasonable way of doing so, and an examination of plaintiff by that expert is necessary for the expert to form a meaningful opinion.

The Court finds that plaintiff's physical condition has been placed in controversy. In answers to interrogatories, plaintiff stated he suffered whiplash in a 1979 automobile accident which caused spurs on vertebrae C5, C6, and C7 which indent the thecal sac in his spine. This is asserted to have resulted in chronic cervical pain syndrome, chronic severe neck pains and headaches, chest pains, and muscular pains and spasms in his neck and shoulder area. Plaintiff asserted that his injuries caused permanent restrictions to his lifting, range of motion and ability to work overhead.

Plaintiff also asserted that a physician anticipates his condition will continue to deteriorate and will require surgery in the future. Plaintiff alleges he was and is disabled under the Americans with Disabilities Act, seeks damages under the Act, and seeks reinstatement to his employment. Both plaintiff's current physical condition and his past physical condition have therefore been placed in controversy.

Good cause exists for a physical examination. The expert must conduct such an examination to form a meaningful opinion. In the social security disability context, *Spencer ex rel. Spencer v. Heckler,* 765 F.2d 1090, 1094 (11th Cir.1985) quoted an Eighth Circuit case noting that evaluation in absentia was "medical sophistry at its best." Additionally, a physician is able to provide a retrospective opinion of plaintiff's condition even though he did not examine plaintiff until after the relevant date. * * *

Plaintiff requests that if either or both examinations are permitted, the Court set certain conditions. These include the presence of a court reporter, the presence of plaintiff's wife, or the recording of the examinations. The Court is satisfied that it has the discretionary authority to impose a variety of conditions which, balancing the factors in each individual case, ensure that the interests of justice are obtained. After considering all the circumstances of this case, the Court can find no special need which requires the presence of a court reporter, plaintiff's wife, or other recording equipment. The conditions set forth below are adequate under the circumstances of this case. Accordingly, it is now ORDERED:

1. Defendant's Motion To Compel Physical and Mental Examinations of Plaintiff is GRANTED to the extent set forth below.

2. Plaintiff shall submit to a mental examination by Dr. Ernest C. Miller and a physical examination by Dr. Michael B. Scharf. Each examination will be conducted at the respective business office of Dr. Miller and Dr. Scharf in Jacksonville, Florida during normal business hours.

3. The examinations will be conducted within 20 days after the completion of plaintiff's deposition, unless the parties otherwise mutually agree.

4. The mental examination will focus upon the matters alleged by plaintiff in his Complaint and/or deposition and the mental and emotion-

al injury and damages resulting from the misconduct alleged of defendant. Defendant shall provide Dr. Miller with the appropriate portion of plaintiff's answers to interrogatories, deposition, and such other documents as it deems appropriate.

The examination will include the routine procedures for such an examination. Plaintiff has requested that it also include the Minnesota Multiphasic Personality Inventory examination. Dr. Miller may administer this test, but the Court will not require it. A copy of any resulting report will be provided to plaintiff's counsel.

5. The physical examination will focus upon the injuries alleged by plaintiff in his Complaint and/or deposition and the existence and severity of the injuries and plaintiff's physical capabilities. Defendant shall provide Dr. Scharf with the appropriate portion of plaintiff's answers to interrogatories, deposition, and such other documents as it deems appropriate. The examination will include the routine procedures for such an examination. A copy of any resulting report will be provided to plaintiff's counsel. * * *

Notes and Questions

1. Unless the parties agree, Rule 35 requires a court order before a party must submit to a physical or mental examination. Before a court will order the examination, the moving party must show that 1) there is "good cause" for the testing, and 2) another party's physical or mental condition is "in controversy." Courts are split as to whether a plaintiff's claim for damages due to emotional harm puts her mental condition "in controversy." Compare *Bowen v. Parking Authority of City of Camden*, 214 F.R.D. 188 (D.N.J. 2003) (plaintiff's mental condition not at issue) with *Cauley v. Ingram Micro, Inc.*, 216 F.R.D. 241 (W.D.N.Y. 2003) (mental examination justified).

2. Sometimes a person is named as a party, in order to effectively put the person's condition "in controversy." For example, in *Schlagenhauf v. Holder*, 379 U.S. 104, 85 S.Ct. 234, 13 L.Ed.2d 152 (1964), the plaintiff class named not only the defendant corporation (with the "deep pocket") as a defendant, but also named as a defendant the corporate employee whose negligence damaged members of the class. Why? In order to enable the plaintiff-class to seek an order for his eyesight to be examined.

Schlagenhauf also addressed the issue of whether "good cause" exists requires a balancing of the need for the information with the party's right to privacy and safety. The "easy" cases for good cause are tort claims in which the plaintiff seeks damages for her personal injuries. On the other hand, as *Ali* indicated, good cause is not as obvious when the a person has not placed her mental or physical condition in dispute.

3. The court order for the examination must "specify the time, place, manner, conditions, and scope of the examination," as well as the person conducting the exam. Testing may be for blood, x-rays, EKG, or any other medically accepted test that is both indicated by the condition "in controversy" and is safe for the party. The examiner must be licensed or certified and

is often selected by the moving party unless there is an objection. Mental tests are conducted by a psychologist or psychiatrist. The judicial decisions are split about 1) who may be present or observe the testing, and 2) whether observers include attorneys of record.

4. Rule 35(b) provides that by request of the party examined, the moving party must provide a detailed written report by the examiner. In return, the examined party must provide reports of other examinations for the same condition, regardless of when they were conducted. At trial, the examiner may testify as an expert witness.

C. DISCOVERY SANCTIONS

LEE v. WALTERS

172 F.R.D. 421 (D.Or. 1997)

STEWART, United States Magistrate Judge.

On June 18, 1996, plaintiff Vickie Lee filed a Motion for Sanctions based upon defendants' failure to cooperate in scheduling depositions, to timely file an Answer, and to timely and completely respond to plaintiffs' request for production of documents. On June 24, 1996, when defendants failed to appear for duly noticed depositions, both plaintiffs filed Motions to Compel and for Sanctions. On June 25, 1996, this court granted the Motion to Compel in part and set both motions for sanctions for decision on July 15, 1996, after the close of discovery.

* * * For the reasons set forth below, this court recommends that plaintiffs' motions for sanctions be granted.

Plaintiffs seeks monetary sanctions against defendants in the sum of $10,000.00 pursuant to FRCP 37(a)(4)(A), (b), and (d), FRCP 26(g), and the court's inherent authority. Because each of the subsections of FRCP 37 and FRCP 26(g) targets a particular form of misconduct for which sanctions may be awarded, each must be analyzed separately.

I. FRCP 37(D)

A. *Standard*

FRCP 37(d) authorizes the court to impose sanctions against a party who fails: (1) to attend a duly noticed deposition, (2) to serve answers or objections to interrogatories properly submitted under FRCP 33, or (3) to serve a written response to a request for inspection properly submitted under FRCP 34. Sanctions are mandatory for failure to attend a noticed deposition or to respond to a request for production of documents unless the court finds that the failure was "substantially justified or that other circumstances make an award of expenses unjust." FRCP 37(d).

"The burden of establishing substantial justification is on the party being sanctioned." *Telluride Mgmt. Solutions, Inc. v. Telluride Inv. Group*, 55 F.3d 463, 466 (9th Cir.1995). The phrase "substantially justified" does not mean " 'justified to a high degree,' but rather has been said to be satisfied if there is a 'genuine dispute,' or 'if reasonable people could differ as to [the appropriateness of the contested action.]' " *Pierce v. Underwood*, 487 U.S. 552, 565 (1988) (brackets in original; citations deleted). However, FRCP 37(d) explicitly eliminates the excuse that "the discovery sought is objectionable unless the party failing to act has a pending motion for a protective order as provided by Rule 26(c)." * * *

B. *Violations*

* * * [D]efendants have committed two violations of FRCP 37(d). It is undisputed that defendants failed to attend depositions duly noticed by plaintiffs on June 24 and 25, 1996. In addition, despite repeated requests, defendants still have not submitted a written response to Plaintiffs' First Request for Production of Documents ("First Request") dated April 19, 1996.

The record reveals that plaintiffs have satisfied the prerequisite to an award of sanctions under FRCP 37(d) in that they attempted to first resolve the issues without judicial intervention.

C. *Defendants' Excuses*

1. *Belated Compliance*

Defendants argue that sanctions are inappropriate because they belatedly appeared for depositions and produced most (though not all) of the requested documents, blaming plaintiffs' motion for sanctions on "obvious impatience." This excuse has repeatedly been rejected by the Ninth Circuit. "Belated compliance with discovery orders does not preclude the imposition of sanctions." *North Am. Watch Corp. v. Princess Ermine Jewels*, 786 F.2d 1447, 1451 (9th Cir.1986).

2. *Substantial Justification*

(a) Document Production

Mr. Barnes does not dispute any of the material facts regarding his failure to timely produce documents. Instead, he states only that he provided all documents "with one minor exception" for "copies of all documents generated around March of 1993 now in the possession of any of the defendants, even if they are duplicates of documents plaintiffs have already seen in the Racing Commission files."

This explanation is deficient for several reasons. First, it entirely fails to address the fact that he has not yet served a written response to the First Request, despite the pendency of these sanction motions. Second, even if a written response to the First Request is unnecessary, given that most of the responsive documents have now been produced, defendants' explanation does not substantially justify the belated production of responsive documents.

Mr. Barnes may have initially believed that producing the Oregon Racing Commission's files would provide plaintiffs with all of the documents requested in the First Request. However, this does not explain why he did not produce any documents until after plaintiffs were forced to seek the assistance of the court at the June 6, 1996 scheduling conference. * * *

(b) Depositions

Mr. Barnes now claims that Mr. Sanders should have understood that he would not be appearing for depositions on June 24, 1996, even though he did not clearly say so. This explanation directly contradicts Mr. Sanders' recollection that just before terminating their last telephone conversation on June 21, 1996, Mr. Barnes said he would seek a protective order. That statement of Mr. Barnes' intention, which Mr. Barnes has not specifically denied, would lead Mr. Sanders to reasonably conclude that Mr. Barnes would not simply ignore the deposition notices. * * *

In sum, Mr. Barnes's failure to appear for the noticed depositions was not substantially justified in the absence of a protective order or, at the very least, a clear and unambiguous agreement by Mr. Sanders to postpone the depositions. As a result, FRCP 37(d) requires the court to order defendants, Mr. Barnes, or both, to pay the reasonable expenses, including attorney's fees, caused by that failure.

II.   FRCP 37(A)(4)(A)

A.   Standards

In contrast to FRCP 37(d), FRCP 37(a)(4)(A) targets motions to compel discovery. It awards reasonable expenses incurred, including attorney fees, not only when the court grants a motion to compel, but also if the opposing party provides the requested discovery after the motion to compel is filed. FRCP 37(a)(4)(A). An award of expenses is mandated unless the motion to compel was filed without "first making a good faith effort to obtain the disclosure of discovery without court action," the "nondisclosure, response, or objection was substantially justified," or "other circumstances make an award of expenses unjust." FRCP 37(a)(4)(A).

B.   Violations

As set forth above, plaintiffs were obliged to file three motions to compel as a result of Mr. Barnes' conduct. * * *

The record reveals that plaintiffs have satisfied the prerequisite to an award of sanctions under FRCP 37(a)(4) because they first attempted to resolve the issues without judicial intervention.

C.   Defendants' Excuses

Defendants offer virtually no excuse for forcing plaintiffs to file the motions to compel, other than Mr. Barnes' busy schedule. He proffers several reasons that made it difficult for him to schedule depositions in this case. First, in the Torts and Employment Group of the Trial

Division, the area of the Department of Justice in which he works, two of the eight attorneys left during the first part of 1996. Because Mr. Barnes handles between 40 and 50 active litigation files and must travel extensively throughout the Pacific Northwest, he "was required to spend a minimum of twenty-nine days in deposition and attend hearings or trial on 15 different days." This court does not doubt that Mr. Barnes has been very busy and perhaps more so than usual during the first five months of 1996. Nevertheless, the fact remains that he never advised the court that his schedule prevented him from complying with the court's orders. The problem is not when depositions were set, but that Mr. Barnes repeatedly ignored inquiries from opposing counsel, which required plaintiffs to file motions to compel. Mr. Barnes may have been able to avoid these motions had he (or someone else in his office) simply returned Mr. Sanders' telephone calls or responded to Mr. Sanders' letters.

Second, Mr. Barnes notes that scheduling depositions of defendants, who are retired or are employed in the private sector, was more difficult than scheduling depositions of state employees. * * *

This court finds no substantial justification or other circumstances for avoiding the mandatory award under FRCP 37(a)(4)(A) to plaintiffs of their reasonable expenses, including attorney fees, for filing the three motions to compel.

III.   FRCP 37(B)

A.   Standards

Whereas FRCP 37(d) addresses the failure to attend a deposition and FRCP 37(a)(4)(A) addresses motions to compel, FRCP 37(b) targets a party's failure to obey an order to provide or permit discovery. It allows the court to make such orders "as are just," and in lieu or in addition, requires the offending party, its attorney or both "to pay the reasonable expenses, including attorney's fees, caused by the failure" unless it "was substantially justified" or "other circumstances make an award of expenses unjust." *Id.*

A prerequisite for imposing sanctions under FRCP 37(b) is the existence of an "order." However, the term "order" is broadly construed for purposes of imposing sanctions. The "order" need not be in writing. It is a violation of an "order" for purposes of FRCP 37(b) when a party fails to deliver documents it had promised by a certain date. It is not even necessary for the opposing party to move for this order, only that it be issued and disobeyed. * * *

B.   Violations

The record reveals that defendants disobeyed four orders that fall within the scope of FRCP 37(b). * * *

C.   Defendants' Excuses

Defendants offer the same excuses for repeated violations of this court's orders as for their other violations of FRCP 37. As discussed above, this court finds that defendants' failure to comply with the court's orders was not substantially justified. Therefore, the court finds that sanctions are appropriate.

IV. FRCP 26(G)

A. Standards

FRCP 26(g) mandates the imposition of sanctions for conducting discovery irresponsibly. It adopts the certification requirements of FRCP 11 and applies them to "[e]very discovery request, response or objection." FRCP 26(g)(2). Like FRCP 11, its requirements are strict; the standard of care is objective; and the sanctions are mandatory. Due to the similarity, courts have applied the case law applicable to the 1983 version of FRCP 11 to the sanctions language in FRCP 26(g). In fact, sanctions inappropriately imposed under FRCP 11 or 37 have been converted to FRCP 26(g) sanctions.

B. Violation

Although noting that Mr. Barnes has repeatedly failed to comply with the discovery rules, plaintiffs concede that he has managed to avoid sanctions under FRCP 26(g) by filing no discovery responses at all. The imposition of sanctions under FRCP 26(g) rests upon the signing of a discovery document that violates the rule. If the wrongdoing does not involve a violative signature on a discovery request, response or objection, then FRCP 26(g) does not apply. Until defendants file an improper discovery response or objection, plaintiffs must seek sanctions under other rules.

V. AMOUNT OF SANCTIONS * * *

C. Appropriate Sanctions

The decision to impose sanctions under FRCP 37 is left to the court's discretion. *National Hockey League v. Metropolitan Hockey Club, Inc.*, 427 U.S. 639 (1976). * * *

This court may impose even the "most severe" sanction to fulfill the purpose "not merely to penalize those whose conduct may be deemed to warrant such a sanction, but to deter those who might be tempted to such conduct in the absence of such a deterrent." *National Hockey League*, 427 U.S. at 643 (affirming extreme sanction of dismissal for violation of FRCP 37).

In fixing the amount of the sanction, the court may consider a party's entire course of conduct during the proceedings.

For at least the past six months defendants' attorney, Mr. Barnes, has repeatedly failed to cooperate with plaintiffs in good faith in the discovery process, employed dilatory tactics, and repeatedly ignored the rules and this court's orders. He offers no satisfactory explanation for his complete indifference to his professional obligations both to the court and opposing counsel. His egregious dilatory conduct not only has unnecessarily delayed the completion of discovery and the filing of dispositive motions, but also has increased the time and expense of this litigation to plaintiffs and unnecessarily and repeatedly involved the court in resolving ongoing discovery problems.

Mr. Barnes is not a novice attorney, but is a veteran trial lawyer who is or should be aware of the conduct expected of him by this court. Unacceptable conduct by him [has occurred in other cases.] * * * Unless remedial action is taken by this court, Mr. Barnes' pattern of conduct may continue unabated.

* * * At an hourly rate of $120.00, which defendants have not contested, the total award of attorney's fees based on recorded hours is $7,026.00. Although plaintiffs seek an award for additional unrecorded hours and costs, this court is reluctant to do so without supporting documentation.

* * * In addition to an award of expenses, FRCP 37 authorizes the court to make orders "as are just." Federal courts have a number of weapons in their armory of non-monetary sanctions. For example, courts may remove attorneys from cases, order the attorney to attend ethics seminars at the attorney's own expense, dispatch the attorney to the employer's internal disciplinary office, or issue a public reprimand. FRCP 37(b)(2) also authorizes a variety of non-monetary sanctions against the party who fails to obey a court order * * * .

Although not specifically requested by plaintiffs, this court has carefully considered these other types of sanctions in lieu of, or in addition to, an award of expenses. This court is concerned by the fact that other judges and opposing counsel have experienced difficulties with Mr. Barnes in other cases at other times. Furthermore, any sanction that adversely impacts the defendants' ability to present a defense is aimed in the wrong direction: it is Mr. Barnes, and not his clients, who is the offender. Thus, in order to ensure that Mr. Barnes takes appropriate remedial action, this court recommends the issuance of a public reprimand in addition to the award of expenses. A public reprimand will serve the purpose of notifying other attorneys and judges of conduct that this court finds unacceptable, and of ensuring that any such future conduct by Mr. Barnes will be brought to the court's attention and, if appropriate, will subject Mr. Barnes to the imposition of more severe sanctions.

For the foregoing reasons, this court recommends that plaintiffs' motions for sanctions be granted as follows: (1) defendant's attorney, Assistant Attorney General Kendall M. Barnes, be ordered to pay to plaintiffs their expenses in the sum of $7,026.00, and (2) this court publicly reprimand Mr. Barnes by publishing its order.

Notes and Questions

1. *Sources of sanctions.* Rule 37 serves as the primary source for imposing discovery sanctions. In *Societe Internationale Pour Participations Industrielles Et Commerciales, S.A. v. Rogers, Attorney General*, 357 U.S. 197, 78 S.Ct. 1087, 2 L.Ed.2d 1255 (1958), the Court stated:

In our opinion, whether a court has power to dismiss a complaint because of noncompliance with a production order depends exclusively upon Rule 37, which addresses itself with particularity to the consequences of a failure to make discovery by listing a variety of remedies which a court may employ as well as by authorizing any order which is "just." There is no need to resort to Rule 41(b) [regarding involuntary dismissals], which appears in that part of the Rules concerned with trials and which lacks such specific references to discovery. * * * Reliance upon Rule 41, which cannot easily be interpreted to afford a court more expansive powers than does Rule 37, or upon "inherent power," can only obscure analysis of the problem before us.

Despite the Court's statement that it is ordinarily inappropriate to go beyond Rule 37 for discovery sanctions, other sources may be necessary. For example, Rule 45(e) authorizes contempt proceedings for a witness failing to obey a subpoena to appear for the taking of her deposition. Rule 26(g) prescribes sanctions similar to Rule 11 against a party, an attorney, or both, if the certification that accompanies a discovery request or response violates that rule.

2. *Sanctions rules.* Rule 37 describes the consequences for failing to make discovery. Usually, sanctions are applied for failing to comply with a court order. For example, when Rule 35 requires a court order or when the court issues a protective order under Rule 26(c), failure to obey the order is punishable immediately using the sanctions listed in Rule 37(b). By contrast, when the parties conduct discovery *without* a court order, the party seeking discovery first must obtain a court order under Rule 37(a). The effect of the order is to require the opposing party to make the discovery sought. A violation of that order is punishable under Rule 37(b). Both a motion to compel (Rule 37(a)(2)(A)) and most motions for sanctions for complete failure to disclose, answer or respond (Rule 37(d)) must include a certification by the aggrieved party that she has attempted to confer with the unresponsive party in an effort to obtain the desired material without court action.

In addition to the federal rules, the Constitution is relevant to whether a sanction is "just." For example, *Societe Internationale* involved the dismissal with prejudice of a complaint in a civil action when the plaintiff had failed to comply with a pretrial production order. The Court held that it would be a denial of due process for a court to dismiss a complaint because of petitioner's noncompliance with a discovery order when it has been established that failure to comply was due to inability and not to willfulness, bad faith, or any fault of the party.

3. *Judicial discretion to impose sanctions.* The appropriateness of imposing sanctions against a party for noncompliance with the discovery rules, if a sanction is to be imposed at all, is within the trial judge's discretion. Rule 37(b)(2) contains two standards limiting a court's discretion. Any sanction must be "just," and it must specifically relate to the particular "claim" which was at issue in the order to provide discovery.

Although the list of sanctions in Rule 37(b)(2) is not exclusive, the listed penalties are the sanctions usually imposed. A court may deem facts established, prohibit evidence from being introduced, strike pleadings, issue a stay of the proceedings until the order is obeyed, dismiss all or a part of the claims, and generally hold a disobedient party in contempt. In addition, the court may impose payment of all expenses including attorneys' fees incurred by the moving party as a result of the failure to comply.

How should a court decide whether sanctions should be imposed? When any noncompliance occurs? When the noncompliance with the discovery order is unreasonable? According to the Supreme Court, the conduct of the offending party should be characterized by a deliberate and pronounced disregard for the order. In *National Hockey League v. Metropolitan Hockey Club, Inc.*, 427 U.S. 639, 96 S.Ct. 2778, 49 L.Ed.2d 747 (1976), the Court reinstated a trial court dismissal for failure to comply with a discovery order, reasoning that

> here, as in other areas of the law, the most severe in the spectrum of sanctions provided by statute or rule must be available to the district court in appropriate cases, not merely to penalize those whose conduct may be deemed to warrant such a sanction, but to deter those who might be tempted to such conduct in the absence of such a deterrent.

Sanctions, then, may be imposed for their deterrent effect in other cases in addition to being a remedy for the wrong committed in the instant case.

Most appellate courts have developed criteria for the imposition of sanctions. For example, in *Wanderer v. Johnston*, 910 F.2d 652, 656 (9th Cir. 1990) the court identified five factors to be applied in considering whether a dismissal or default is appropriate as a Rule 37 sanction: (1) the public's interest in expeditious resolution of litigation; (2) the court's need to manage its dockets; (3) the risk of prejudice to the party seeking sanctions; (4) the public policy favoring disposition of cases on their merits; and (5) the availability of less drastic sanctions. *Mutual Federal Savings & Loan Ass'n v. Richards & Assoc.*, 872 F.2d 88, 92 (4th Cir. 1989) applied a four-factor test: (1) whether the noncomplying party acted in good faith: (2) the amount of prejudice its noncompliance caused its adversary; (3) the need for deterrence of the particular sort of noncompliance; and (4) the effectiveness of less drastic sanctions.

Chapter 8

ALTERNATIVE DISPUTE RESOLUTION AND SETTLEMENT

A. INTRODUCTION

Much of the focus in law school curricula is on published appellate cases. This can give the false impression that most cases are pursued to a decision in a trial court and then appealed. In popular culture, television shows and movies reenforce this image of the trial as the central event in legal disputes. In fact, civil trials and, to an even greater extent, appeals are exceptional events that occur only in a small minority of cases.

This chapter explores some of the processes that are used to resolve disputes without a trial. Collectively, these processes are often called "alternative dispute resolution" or ADR. They are "alternative" in two senses. In some situations parties end their dispute using an ADR procedure without ever filing suit; in these instances, the process serves as an alternative to engaging in litigation. Parties also use ADR processes in conjunction with litigation to reach a settlement in their case; then ADR provides a method for disposing of litigation as an alternative to trial or a pre-trial judicial decision.

First, this chapter examines two of the basic ADR processes: arbitration and mediation. Parties choose arbitration as a complete substitute for litigation, while they use mediation either as a substitute dispute resolution method or as a way to settle a filed case. There often is confusion over the differences between these two processes, probably due to lack of familiarity and misapplication of the labels "arbitration" and "mediation." For lawyers to advise their clients adequately about the processes available to them, they need to understand the differences between arbitration and mediation.

Second, we introduce the role of the courts in settling litigation. Judges often preside over settlement conferences or suggest that parties use an ADR process. Many courts provide parties access to one or more ADR processes and, as you will see, judges even have the power to order unwilling parties to participate. Finally, the chapter discusses how the

American system for allotting attorneys fees and the federal rules encourage parties to settle cases.

B.   ALTERNATIVE DISPUTE RESOLUTION PROCESSES

1.   Arbitration

Arbitration is a process in which a third-party neutral arbitrator, or a panel of arbitrators, decides the outcome of a dispute. The decision, called an arbitral award, is usually regarded as final, with only a very narrow opportunity for court review. The process and the arbitrator(s) are selected by the agreement of the parties either before or after they have a dispute. This agreement is the source of the arbitrator's power to decide the dispute.

Arbitration is commonly designated as the resolution process for disputes in labor relations, commercial relationships, individual employment contracts, and many consumer transactions. The parties may negotiate their own terms to govern their arbitration or select a set of procedural rules provided by organizations such as the American Arbitration Association or the International Chamber of Commerce. In addition, parties may opt to have their proceeding administered by one of these organizations.

An advantage of arbitration is that traditional arbitral procedures can make the process quicker and less expensive than litigation. The format for the process depends on the ground rules agreed to by the parties, but it is typically more informal than a court proceeding. There may be discovery, but it is usually limited. At the hearing, evidence is frequently considered without strict adherence to evidentiary rules. The parties may require an arbitrator to observe a strict deadline for delivering the award, which is often provided without any written explanation. The arbitrator can be anyone agreed upon by the parties, who may prefer a business person or an expert to a generalist judge. The parties may agree to keep the arbitration process private, which provides an important reason to choose this process for disputes they would like to keep out of the public eye. Unlike mediation or other consensual processes, arbitration assures the parties that there will be a resolution to their dispute.

In recent years, critics have objected that arbitration is taking on so many of the attributes of litigation that the process is losing some of its advantages. The following case contains some examples of this migration toward litigation procedures, including an agreement for expanded judicial review of the arbitral award.

BOWEN v. AMOCO PIPELINE COMPANY

254 F.3d 925 (10th Cir. 2001)

TACHA, Chief Judge.

Defendant Amoco Pipeline Company appeals from the district court's confirmation of an arbitration award. We exercise jurisdiction pursuant to 28 U.S.C. § 1291 and affirm.

I. BACKGROUND

I. Facts

In 1993, Ernest Bowen noticed an oily sheen in Flag Branch Creek, which is located on his property. * * * [H]e notified the Pollution Control Division of the OCC [Oklahoma Corporate Commission], as well as Amoco Pipeline Company (Amoco) and Koch Gathering Systems, Inc. (Koch). Both Amoco and Koch own oil pipelines that cross the creek; Koch owns two idled lines and Amoco owns two idled lines and two active lines. * * *

In a memorandum dated September 1996, the OCC summarized the information available regarding the contamination in Flag Branch Creek and reached some conclusions. * * * Because wells and documented leaks were not the source, the OCC concluded the source of the hydrocarbon contamination must be an undocumented leak from one of the six pipelines. * * * In order to determine the source, the OCC recommended Koch and Amoco uncover their lines in order to expose any visual evidence of historic or current leaks.

Despite Amoco's repeated assertions of its good corporate citizenship and willingness to follow all rules and regulations, it refused to follow the OCC's recommendation and uncover its pipelines, arguing uncovering the lines would be unnecessary and jeopardize the lines' safety. * * *

Displeased with Amoco's continued denial of any responsibility, Mr. and Mrs. Bowen filed a lawsuit in May 1998 in federal district court, asserting a cause of action for damages to real property, nuisance, trespass, unjust enrichment, breach of contract, and exemplary damages. In July, Amoco asked the district court to stay the proceeding and order the dispute to arbitration pursuant to an enforceable arbitration agreement.[1] In arguing their motion to compel arbitration, Amoco contended the arbitration panel would have the power to decide *all* claims, an assertion they now refute. The Bowens objected to arbitration, challenging the arbitration agreement as unenforceable. In October 1998, the district court granted Amoco's motion and entered an order compelling arbitration.

In July 1998, Amoco responded to the Bowens' interrogatories, continuing to deny its lines were the source of hydrocarbon contamina-

---

1. In 1918, the predecessors in interest of both parties entered into a right-of-way agreement, which contained an arbitration provision. This agreement, which governed the grant of a pipeline easement, was ratified in 1943 by a second agreement.

tion in the creek. In addition, Amoco explicitly denied that any leaks or spills attributable to its pipeline operation had occurred on the Bowens' property and even denied the existence of pollution in the soil. * * *

In June and July of 1999, three years after the OCC recommended that Amoco uncover its pipelines, Amoco exposed limited portions of its lines on the Bowens' property and admitted the existence of contaminants next to the lines. Significantly, the stripping of the lines revealed a pipeline replacement in the contaminated area. Less than two months before the arbitration hearing, the Bowens discovered that Amoco had replaced approximately 1,000 feet of pipeline on the east side of the creek. According to the Bowens' expert, the 1,000 feet of replaced pipeline corresponds almost exactly with the contaminated creek area. * * *

* * * Although Amoco's employees and experts argued the line replacement could have been a preventative measure, they admitted a leak in the line would be one explanation for the line replacement and for the concentration of crude oil in the soil in that exact location. Moreover, after years of denying any connection to the contaminated soil, [an Amoco environmental safety official] finally testified that the hydrocarbon-contaminated soil under the replaced pipelines was probably from Amoco's line. Testing by Amoco's own expert confirmed the oil around the replaced line—as well as the oil in the creek—was at least twenty years old, further evidence that the more recent leaks from Koch's pipelines were not the source. * * *

Although Amoco changed its initial theory and admitted its lines might be the source of contamination in the soil, it continued to claim no responsibility for the hydrocarbon contamination in the creek. Admitting a small two-barrel leak may have occurred in 1952, Amoco continued to deny any connection to the contamination in the creek. Amoco contended that, despite the contamination in the soil around its pipelines, the hydrocarbon levels in the groundwater did not exceed EPA standards, and because the pollution in the soil was not reaching the water table, it was not reaching the creek. * * *

II. The Arbitration

The Bowens' case was tried to a panel of three arbitrators in August 1999. The parties agreed to use the Rules for Non–Administered Arbitration of Business Disputes (NABD), but they also agreed to modify these rules to expand the scope of judicial review. Specifically, the parties agreed that both would have the right to appeal any arbitration award to the district court within thirty days "on the grounds that the award is not supported by the evidence." They also agreed that the district court's ruling "shall be final."

On October 18, 1999, the arbitration panel granted the following relief: (1) $3,032,000 to be deposited in an escrow fund for the use and benefit of a special master responsible for supervising the abatement of the contamination on the Bowens' property; (2) $100,000 for the diminution in property value; (3) $1,200,000 for annoyance, inconvenience, and aggravation; (4) $1,000,000 in punitive damages; and (5) $41,000 for the costs of investigation and mitigation. One panel member dissented, objecting to the escrow fund for abatement and punitive damages award. Under the Federal Arbitration Act (FAA), 9 U.S.C. § 9, the Bowens then filed a motion for confirmation of the arbitration award in district court. Amoco responded by filing an objection to the confirmation and a motion to vacate the award. In addition, Amoco filed a notice of appeal of the arbitration award pursuant to the modified arbitration rules. Limiting its review to that provided under the FAA, the district court did not apply the parties' expanded judicial standard of review and declined to vacate the award. The court granted the Bowens' motion to confirm the award and affirmed the arbitrators' order awarding the Bowens attorneys fees, costs, and arbitrators' fees. Amoco appeals the district court's order, urging us to vacate the entire award and remand for a new arbitration, or alternatively to vacate the remediation award and remand the case to district court for review based on the expanded standard of review.

* * *

III.   STANDARD OF REVIEW

* * * [The FAA] applies to a written arbitration clause in "a contract evidencing a transaction involving commerce," a requirement broadly interpreted to correspond with Congress's power under the Commerce Clause. The district court ordered the arbitration in the case before us pursuant to a right-of-way agreement, a transaction involving pipelines for the interstate transportation of crude oil. The FAA therefore applies to the parties' dispute.

Our review of the arbitration panel's decision under the FAA is strictly limited; this highly deferential standard has been described as "among the narrowest known to the law." In consenting to arbitration, "a party trades the procedures and opportunity for review of the courtroom for the simplicity, informality, and expedition of arbitration." We employ this limited standard of review and exercise caution in setting aside arbitration awards because one "purpose behind arbitration agreements is to avoid the expense and delay of court proceedings." A court may not, therefore, independently judge an arbitration award.

Mindful of the strong federal policy favoring arbitration, a court may grant a motion to vacate an arbitration award only in the limited circumstances provided in § 10 of the FAA, or in accordance with a few judicially created exceptions. Under the FAA, vacation is proper in certain instances of fraud or corruption, arbitrator misconduct, or "[w]here the arbitrators exceeded their powers, or so imperfectly executed them that a mutual, final, definite award upon the subject matter submitted was not made." Although Amoco does not allege fraud or misconduct, it does argue that the arbitrators exceeded their powers. In addition, Amoco argues the arbitration panel's decision is in "manifest disregard of the law," a judicially crafted exception to the general rule that arbitrators' "erroneous interpretations or applications of law are not reversible." We have interpreted manifest disregard of the law to mean "willful inattentiveness to the governing law." Requiring more than error or misunderstanding of the law, a finding of manifest disregard means the record will show the arbitrators knew the law and explicitly disregarded it. Under traditional standards of review, we would, therefore, review Amoco's claims to determine whether the arbitrators exceeded their powers or rendered a decision in manifest disregard of the law.

Amoco argues, however, that the parties in this case contracted for expanded judicial review in agreeing that the arbitration award would be appealable if "not supported by the evidence." The district court did not apply this expanded standard, deciding instead that parties may not alter the traditional standards of review by contract. Emphasizing the policies behind the FAA, Amoco argues the district court erred and we should apply the contractually created standard. Although Amoco presents a difficult question, we conclude the purposes behind the FAA, as well as the principles announced in various Supreme Cases, do not support a rule allowing parties to alter the judicial process by private contract.

The only two circuits to definitively decide this issue have, however, held that private parties may agree to expand the judicial standard of review. *Lapine Tech. Corp. v. Kyocera Corp.,* 130 F.3d 884, 887–890 (9th Cir.1997); *Gateway Tech., Inc. v. MCI Telecomms. Corp.,* 64 F.3d 993, 996–97 (5th Cir.1995). Both the Fifth and the Ninth Circuits were persuaded by language in Supreme Court decisions emphasizing, in particular, the FAA's purpose of " 'ensuring that private agreements to arbitrate are enforced according to their terms.' " Although, as the Ninth Circuit acknowledged, agreeing to the judicial standard of review is not the same as agreeing to the rules governing the scope of arbitration, the court concluded the two are "inexorably intertwined" and could find "no sufficient reason to pay less respect to the review provision than . . . to the myriad of other agreements which the parties have been pleased to make." In a splintered decision, the court decided the opposite result would be contrary to Congress's intent in enacting the FAA "under the guise of deference to the arbitration concept."

In resolving conflicts among the FAA, state law, and parties' agreements, the Supreme Court has repeatedly acknowledged that Congress's intent in enacting the FAA was to ensure judicial enforcement of private arbitration agreements. *See, e.g., Mastrobuono v. Shearson Lehman Hutton, Inc.,* 514 U.S. 52, 57 (1995) ("[C]ourts are bound to interpret contracts in accordance with the expressed intentions of the parties. . . ."); *Volt Info. Sciences, Inc. v. Bd. of Trustees,* 489 U.S. 468, 479 (1989) ("Just as [parties] may limit by contract the issues which they will arbitrate, so too may they specify by contract the rules under which the arbitration will be conducted."); *Dean Witter Reynolds, Inc.,* 470 U.S. at 219–20 (observing the FAA's legislative history "makes clear that its purpose was to place an arbitration agreement upon the same footing as other contracts, where it belongs, and to overrule the judiciary's long-standing refusal to enforce agreements to arbitrate"). When Congress passed the Act in 1925, it did so with the primary goal of changing the judiciary's refusal to enforce arbitration clauses in private contracts. With the passage of the FAA, Congress intended to "make arbitration agreements as enforceable as other contracts, but not more so."

Guided by the FAA's underlying purpose and the essentially contractual nature of arbitration, the Court has held, for example, that parties may agree to conduct arbitration under procedural rules different from the FAA. The Court has also held district courts must compel arbitration even if arbitrable and nonarbitrable claims are pleaded in the same complaint despite the potential negative effects on efficient dispute resolution. Parties may even agree to submit questions concerning arbitrability to the arbitrators. The contractual nature of arbitration is, therefore, well established. Parties are free to structure their arbitration agreements as they wish, and our decision today must further the FAA's primary policy ensuring judicial enforcement of private agreements to arbitrate.

We disagree, however, with the Fifth and Ninth Circuits' conclusion that the Supreme Court precedent emphasizing the FAA's primary purpose compels enforcement of contractual modifications of judicial review. Although the Court has emphasized that parties may "specify by contract the rules under which [ ] arbitration will be conducted," *Volt Info. Sciences, Inc.*, 489 U.S. at 479, it has never said parties are free to interfere with the judicial process. As both the concurring and dissenting opinions in *Lapine* acknowledge, parties may determine by contract what issues to arbitrate and what rules will govern arbitration, but no authority clearly allows private parties to determine how federal courts review arbitration awards. To the contrary, through the FAA Congress has provided explicit guidance regarding judicial standards of review of arbitration awards. Moreover, if parties desire broader appellate review, "they can contract for an appellate arbitration panel to review the arbitrator's award." The decisions directing courts to honor parties' agreements and to resolve close questions in favor of arbitration simply do not dictate that courts submit to varying standards of review imposed by private contract.

* * *

Unlike the contract clause at issue in *Volt*, the contract clause in this case threatens to undermine the policies behind the FAA. We would reach an illogical result if we concluded that the FAA's policy of ensuring judicial enforcement of arbitration agreements is well served by allowing for expansive judicial review after the matter is arbitrated. The FAA's limited review ensures judicial respect for the arbitration process and prevents courts from enforcing parties' agreements to arbitrate only to refuse to respect the results of the arbitration. These limited standards manifest a legislative intent to further the federal policy favoring arbitration by preserving the independence of the arbitration process. * * *

Not surprisingly, the FAA's narrow standards reflect the Supreme Court's well-established view of the relationship between arbitration and judicial review: "[B]y agreeing to arbitrate, a party 'trades the procedures and opportunity for review of the courtroom for the simplicity, informality, and expedition of arbitration.'" Contractually expanded standards, particularly those that allow for factual review, clearly threaten to undermine the independence of the arbitration process and dilute the finality of arbitration awards because, in order for arbitration awards to be effective, courts must not only enforce the agreements to arbitrate but also enforce the resulting arbitration awards.

Moreover, expanded judicial review places federal courts in the awkward position of reviewing proceedings conducted under potentially unfamiliar rules and procedures. Under either expanded legal or expanded factual standards, the reviewing court would be engaging in work different from what it would do if it had simply heard the case itself. The Eighth Circuit has also recognized this potential problem: "We have served notice that where arbitration is contemplated the courts are not equipped to provide the same judicial review given to structured judgments defined by procedural rules and legal principles. Parties should be aware that they get what they bargain for and that arbitration is far different from adjudication." Because parties may not force reviewing courts to apply unfamiliar rules and procedures, expanded judicial review would threaten the independence of arbitration and weaken the distinction between arbitration and adjudication. Arbitrators are chosen for their specialized experience and knowledge, which enable them to fashion creative remedies and solutions that courts may be less likely to endorse. Expanded judicial review therefore places a court in the position of reviewing that which it would not do and reduces arbitrators' willingness to create particularized solutions for fear the decision will be vacated by a reviewing court.

* * * We * * * hold that parties may not contract for expanded judicial review of arbitration awards. We therefore proceed to review the arbitration award in the case before us under the FAA and "manifest disregard of justice" standards.

* * *

V. DOUBLE RECOVERY: DAMAGES AND ABATEMENT

* * * Amoco argues the three-million-dollar escrow fund is in manifest disregard of Oklahoma law, which prohibits double recovery for the same injury and limits monetary damages to the diminished value of the land. Although a nuisance action may include claims for both permanent and temporary damages, double recovery for the same damage is not allowed. If a plaintiff alleges both kinds of damage, "a defendant can in no event be held liable for more than the total diminution in reasonable market value assuming the temporary injuries were left standing or unrestored."

In addition to awarding $100,000 in damages for the diminished value of the Bowens' land, the arbitrators also set up a three-million-dollar escrow fund for the abatement of the nuisance. Amoco argues that the two awards constitute double recovery in manifest disregard of state law. Conversely, the Bowens argue the escrow fund is an equitable remedy facilitating cleanup rather than an award of damages constituting double recovery under Oklahoma law. We agree that the escrow fund is an equitable remedy, rather than a legal award of damages. The arbitration panel appointed a special master to administer the funds and oversee the abatement plan, which must be submitted to the OCC for approval. Should the abatement cost less than expected, Amoco will receive any remaining funds. Because Oklahoma cases precluding double recovery do not explicitly address equitable remedies, the arbitration panel did not act in manifest disregard of state law.

Although Amoco's legal arguments are not without merit, the written order for the arbitration award does not reveal that the arbitrators deliberately disregarded Oklahoma law. Short of some evidence of "willful inattentiveness to the governing law," we may not question their conclusions. Our limited standard of review requires more than error or misunderstanding in legal reasoning.

In addition, we have observed that "courts favor the arbitrator's exercise of [ ] broad discretion in fashioning remedies." We have also acknowledged that arbitrators have broad equity powers provided the rules governing the arbitration allow equitable relief. Both parties, as well as the district court judge, concluded the arbitration panel had the power to order injunctive relief and remediation. We will not second-guess their judgment.

VI.   Punitive Damages

Amoco also contends the arbitration panel lacked the authority to award punitive damages and, alternatively, awarded punitive damages in manifest disregard of Oklahoma law. In addition, Amoco argues the limited judicial review of the punitive damages awarded by the arbitration panel violates due process. We disagree with all three arguments.

The first argument, that the panel exceeded its powers in awarding punitive damages, is without merit in light of the Supreme Court's decision in *Mastrobuono v. Shearson Lehman Hutton, Inc.*, 514 U.S. 52 (1995). In *Mastrobuono*, the Court resolved a conflict between state law preventing arbitrators from awarding punitive damages and the parties' arbitration agreement, which adopted arbitration rules allowing arbitrators to award "damages and other relief." Noting the federal policy favoring arbitration, the Court concluded the arbitration agreement and rules contemplated punitive damages as a remedy and the award should be enforced despite contrary state law. In the case before us, the parties agreed to be governed by rules that authorize "any remedy or relief which the Tribunal deems just and equitable and within the scope of the agreement of the parties." Given the broad scope of this rule, the arbitrators did not exceed their powers in awarding punitive damages. Indeed, the language "any remedy or relief" is even broader than the language interpreted by the Supreme Court and clearly contemplates punitive damages.

Amoco's contention that the arbitrators acted in manifest disregard of Oklahoma law in awarding punitive damages is also without merit. First, state statutory law provides limitations on exemplary damages awarded by a *jury* and does not clearly address arbitration awards. Second, one subsection of the statute allows a jury to award exemplary damages beyond the limitations provided in other subsections when the jury concludes the "defendant has acted intentionally and with malice toward others." As the panel's written order reflects, the arbitrators awarded punitive damages based on several factors, including Amoco's egregious conduct prior to and after the discovery of contamination, Amoco's awareness and blatant disregard of the pollution, and Amoco's *concealment* of the pollution from the Bowens and the OCC. In light of these findings, we conclude the arbitration panel did not act in manifest disregard of the law in awarding punitive damages.

Finally, we disagree with Amoco's contention that the limited judicial review of punitive damage awards by arbitrators violates due process. As we have already discussed at length, Amoco not only voluntarily entered into arbitration, but also petitioned the district court to compel arbitration. Before asking the district court to compel arbitration, Amoco was aware that the Bowens' cause of action included a claim for exemplary damages. In addition, Amoco agreed to be governed by the broad language in the arbitration rules authorizing the granting of "any remedy or relief." Amoco may not now oppose the very process it advocated and to which it voluntarily submitted. Because we conclude that Amoco is essentially foreclosed from arguing a due process violation, we need not decide whether arbitration constitutes state action.

We recognize, of course, that this case presents the unique situation in which the parties contracted for an expanded judicial standard of review, which was later invalidated. When the parties agreed to arbitrate all claims, including the punitive damages claim, they also agreed to the added security of a broader scope of judicial review. Our response to this concern is twofold. First, Amoco petitioned the district court to compel all claims to arbitration *before* agreeing to an expanded judicial standard of review; the Bowens' claim for exemplary damages did not therefore deter Amoco from arguing the entire matter should be submitted to arbitration. Second, because the arbitration rules adopted by the parties required the arbitration panel to detail the reasoning behind the award, even our limited review has produced ample evidence in support of the panel's award of punitive damages.

We therefore AFFIRM the district court's confirmation of the arbitration award.

Notes and Questions

1. As this case makes obvious, although arbitration is intended to substitute for litigation, not all arbitrations proceed without court involvement. First, a party may need to invoke the power of the courts to enforce the agreement to arbitrate the dispute. Under the Federal Arbitration Act (FAA), a party can file suit seeking an order for the uncooperative party to arbitrate or, if the other party tries to litigate, can file a motion to stay the court proceedings while the case is arbitrated according to the agreement.

Second, a winning party may need a court's help to enforce the arbitral award. Under the FAA, a party may "confirm" an award in court within one year of the decision. Once confirmed, the award is regarded as a court judgment and may be enforced in the same manner as any judgment. A losing party may seek to block confirmation and have the court vacate or modify the award. *Bowen* lists the circumstances under which the FAA authorizes a court to vacate an arbitral award. How do these standards compare to appellate review of a trial court judgment? Do you think that arbitral awards are vacated frequently under these standards? Are there policy reasons for the FAA's limited grounds to vacate awards?

2. The U.S. Supreme Court has emphasized the narrow scope of judicial review of arbitral awards: "Because the parties have contracted to have disputes settled by an arbitrator chosen by them rather than by a judge, it is the arbitrators' view of the facts and of the meaning of the contract that they have agreed to accept. Courts thus do not sit to hear claims of factual or legal error by an arbitrator as an appellate court does in reviewing decisions of lower courts." *United Paperworkers Int'l Union, AFL– CIO v. Misco, Inc.*, 484 U.S. 29, 37–38, 108 S.Ct. 364, 98 L.Ed.2d 286 (1987). *Misco* involves arbitration of collective bargaining agreements, but this explanation for limited judicial review applies to arbitration in general and has been accepted by the lower courts.

3. Do you think that this same hands-off approach to judicial review is justified when arbitrators are deciding legal issues? As discussed in *Bowen*, the courts have fashioned a non-statutory basis for vacating an award if it is in "manifest disregard of the law." The courts have articulated differing interpretations of this standard, but all are narrow. What would a party need to establish in court to vacate an award on this ground in the Tenth Circuit?

4. Are typical arbitral procedures consistent with in-depth court review? In *Bowen*, the parties' arbitration agreement required a written explanation for the award. Arbitrators usually provide written opinions in labor and international commercial arbitrations, but in other arenas the award is often limited to a single sentence designating the outcome. The *Bowen* court commented that "expanded judicial review would require arbitrators to issue written opinions with conclusions of law and findings of fact, further sacrificing the simplicity, expediency, and cost-effectiveness of arbitration. Rather than providing a single instance of dispute resolution with limited review, arbitration would become yet another step on the ladder of litigation." 254 F.3d at 936, n.7.

5.   Arbitration is treated as a creature of contract. Unless a party can prove a contract law defense such as fraud or duress, courts will enforce agreements to arbitrate even when there is an imbalance of power between the parties and the agreement is a take-it-or-leave-it adhesion contract. In addition, the parties not only determine the decision to arbitrate, they have complete control over the topics they wish the arbitrator to decide and the procedures for the process. As indicated in *Bowen*, parties can even specify that an award can include punitive damages when such damages would be contrary to state law. Given this broad ability to define arbitration to suit their needs, should the parties be able to incorporate judicial review beyond the narrow standards of the FAA and "manifest injustice" into their version of arbitration?

6.   The federal courts of appeal continue to send mixed signals on whether parties can contract for expanded judicial review of arbitral awards. Since the *Bowen* case, the Third Circuit has joined the Fifth in holding that parties may expand the grounds for judicial review. *Roadway Package Sys., Inc. v. Kayser*, 257 F.3d 287 (3d Cir. 2001). But the Ninth Circuit has abandoned that position and joined the Tenth by overruling en banc the decision cited in the *Bowen* case. *Kyocera Corp. v. Prudential–Bache Trade Serv., Inc.*, 341 F.3d 987 (9th Cir. 2003). The Seventh and the Eighth Circuits have not ruled on the question directly, but have indicated in dicta that parties may not contract for special judicial review. Given this split in authority, how would you counsel a client considering an agreement with an arbitration clause that provides for expanded judicial review?

Exercise

Check the terms of a consumer agreement you've entered into, such as a credit card agreement, cellular telephone agreement or computer purchase agreement. If you don't have an actual agreement, assume you've just bought a Gateway Computer and check the terms and conditions for the product and the warranty (available on-line). You may find that you have agreed to arbitrate disputes arising out of your agreement. Use the internet to find the arbitration rules designated in the agreement or, if none are designated, the American Arbitration Association rules for consumer disputes. How do the rules compare in scope and specificity to the Federal Rules of Civil Procedure? How is the arbitrator chosen? How much will arbitration cost you? Would you prefer to litigate or arbitrate disputes of the sort covered by your agreement?

2.   Mediation

A mediation session is an informal meeting of a mediator with the parties and, when the disputants are represented, often the parties' lawyers. Mediation is perhaps best described as "facilitated negotiation." The presiding neutral is not a decisionmaker like a judge or arbitrator, and has no power to resolve the dispute for the parties. Instead, the parties attempt to reach their own agreement with the assistance of the mediator. That agreement may depart from the legal remedy that a court deciding the case would impose. The parties' outcome is not necessarily a result of applying the law, but ideally responds to their particular circumstances and interests.

The mediation process is flexible and can be adapted to many different circumstances. Following pre-mediation preparation and selection of a mediator, the mediation session typically begins in a joint session with all the participants present. The mediator starts with an introductory statement reviewing and explaining the process. Then each side presents its view of the dispute in an initial statement. This is often followed by a discussion in joint session moderated by the mediator. The mediator may break the group up and meet separately for private discussions called caucuses. The full group may reconvene, or the mediator may shuttle between caucus meetings. If an agreement is reached, it is reviewed with all present and often recorded in a memorandum of understanding that is signed by the parties. If the parties do not reach an accord, the mediation is terminated and the parties may proceed to other dispute resolution procedures or continue with litigation.

In order for the mediation process to work effectively, the parties need to be assured that they can participate freely and discuss their interests without fear that their statements will be used against them if settlement is unsuccessful and the case ends up in adjudication. Consequently, many state laws provide a privilege or other protection against disclosure of mediation communications in discovery, at trial, or in an arbitral hearing.

As with arbitration, sometimes a court needs to be brought into the process to enforce a mediated outcome. Instead of the confirmation process established for arbitral awards by the FAA, mediated agreements are enforced as a matter of contract law.

The following excerpts explore the characteristics of mediation and the role of effective mediators.

MEDIATION—ITS FORMS AND FUNCTIONS

Lon L. Fuller
44 S. Cal. L. Rev. 305, 307–308, 318, 325–326 (1971)

* * * [O]f mediation one is tempted to say that it is all process and no structure.

Casual treatments of the subject in the literature of sociology tend to assume that the object of mediation is to make the parties aware of the "social norms" applicable to their relationship and to persuade them to accommodate themselves to the "structure" imposed by these norms. From this point of view the difference between a judge and a mediator is simply that the judge orders the parties to conform themselves to the rules, while the mediator persuades them to do so. But mediation is commonly directed, not toward achieving conformity to norms, but toward the creation of the relevant norms themselves. This is true, for example, in the very common case where the mediator assists the parties in working out the terms of a contract defining their rights and duties toward one another. In such a case there is no pre-existing structure that can guide mediation; it is the mediational process that produces the structure.

It may be suggested that mediation is always, in any event, directed toward bringing about a more harmonious relationship between the parties, whether this be achieved through explicit agreement, through a reciprocal acceptance of the "social norms" relevant to their relationship, or simply because the parties have been helped to a new and more perceptive understanding of one another's problems. The fact that in ordinary usage the terms "mediation" and "conciliation" are largely interchangeable tends to reinforce this view of the matter.

* * * Where the bargaining process proceeds without the aid of a mediator the usual course pursued by experienced negotiators is something like this: the parties begin by simply talking about the various proposals, explaining in general terms why they want this and why they are opposed to that. During this exploratory or "sounding out" process, which proceeds without any clearcut offers of settlement, each party conveys—sometimes explicitly, sometimes tacitly, sometimes intentionally, sometimes inadvertently—something about his relative evaluations of the various items under discussion. After these discussions have proceeded for some time, one party is likely to offer a "package deal," proposing in general terms a contract that will settle all the issues under discussion. This offer may be accepted by the other party or he may accept it subject to certain stipulated changes.

Now it is obvious that the process just described can often be greatly facilitated through the services of a skillful mediator. His assistance can speed the negotiations, reduce the likelihood of miscalculation, and generally help the parties to reach a sounder agreement, an adjustment of their divergent valuations that will produce something like an optimum yield of the gains of reciprocity. These things the mediator can accomplish by holding separate confidential meetings with the parties, where each party gives the mediator a relatively full and candid account of the internal posture of his own interests. Armed with this information, but without making a premature disclosure of its details, the mediator can then help to shape the negotiations in such a way that they will proceed most directly to their goal, with a minimum of waste and friction.

* * * [T]he central quality of mediation * * * [is] its capacity to reorient the parties toward each other, not by imposing rules on them, but by helping them to achieve a new and shared perception of their relationship, a perception that will redirect their attitudes and dispositions toward one another.

This quality of mediation becomes most visible when the proper function of the mediator turns out to be, not that of inducing the parties to accept formal rules for the governance of their future relations, but that of helping them to free themselves from the encumbrance of rules and of accepting, instead, a relationship of mutual respect, trust and understanding that will enable them to meet shared contingencies without the aid of formal prescriptions laid down in advance.

THE THEORY AND PRACTICE OF MEDIATION: A REPLY TO PROFESSOR SUSSKIND

Joseph B. Stulberg
6 Vt. L. Rev. 85, 91–97, 115–116 (1981)

[Professor Susskind's article advocates that mediators of environmental disputes must ensure that agreements are fair, a role that "may make it difficult to retain the appearance of neutrality and the trust of the active parties." Lawrence Susskind, *Environmental Mediation and the Accountability Problem*, 6 Vt. L. Rev. 1, 47 (1981). In responding, Professor Stulberg discusses the functions and desirable characteristics of a mediator.]

A mediator is a catalyst. Succinctly stated, the mediator's presence affects how the parties interact. His presence should lend a constructive posture to the discussions rather than cause further misunderstanding and polarization, although there are no guarantees that the latter condition will not result. It seems elementary, but many persons equate a mediator's neutrality with his being a non-entity at the negotiations. Nothing could be further from the truth.* * * Much as the chemical term catalyst connotes the mediator's presence alone creates a special reaction between the parties. Any mediator, therefore, takes on a unique responsibility for the continued integrity of the discussions.

A mediator is also an educator. He must know the desires, aspirations, working procedures, political limitations, and business constraints of the parties. He must immerse himself in the dynamics of the controversy to enable him to explain (although not necessarily justify) the reasons for a party's specific proposal or its refusal to yield in its demands. He may have to explain, for example, the meaning of certain statutory provisions that bear on the dispute, the technology of machinery that is the focus of discussion, or simply the principles by which the negotiation process goes forward.

Third, the mediator must be a translator. The mediator's role is to convey each party's proposals in a language that is both faithful to the desired objectives of the party and formulated to insure the highest degree of receptivity by the listener. The proposal of an angry neighbor that the "young hoodlum" not play his stereo from 11:00 p.m. to 7:00 a.m. every day becomes, through the intervention and guidance of a mediator, a proposal to the youth that he be able to play his stereo on a daily basis from 7:00 a.m. to 11:00 p.m.

Fourth, the mediator may also expand the resources available to the parties. Persons are occasionally frustrated in their discussions because of a lack of information or support services. The mediator, by his personal presence and with the integrity of his office, can frequently gain access for the parties to needed personnel or data. This service can range from securing research or computer facilities to arranging meetings with the governor or President.

Fifth, the mediator often becomes the bearer of bad news. Concessions do not always come readily; parties frequently reject a proposal in whole or in part. The mediator can cushion the expected negative reaction to such a rejection by preparing the parties for it in private conversations. Negotiations are not sanitized. They can be extremely emotional. Persons can react honestly and indignantly, frequently launching personal attacks on those representatives refusing to display flexibility. Those who are the focus of such an attack will, quite understandably, react defensively. The mediator's function is to create a context in which such an emotional, cathartic response can occur without causing an escalation of hostilities or further polarization.

Sixth, the mediator is an agent of reality. Persons frequently become committed to advocating one and only one solution to a problem. There are a variety of explanations for this common phenomenon, ranging from pride of authorship in a proposal to the mistaken belief that compromising means acting without principles. The mediator is in the best position to inform a party, as directly and as candidly as possible, that its objective is simply not obtainable through those specific negotiations. He does not argue that the proposal is undesirable and therefore not obtainable. Rather, as an impartial participant in the discussions, he may suggest that the positions the party advances will not be realized, either because they are beyond the resource capacity of the other parties to fulfill or that, for reasons of administrative efficiency or matters of principle, the other parties will not concede. If the proposing party persists in its belief that the other parties will relent, the question is reduced to a perception of power. The mediator's role at that time is to force the proposing party to reassess the degree of power that it perceives it possesses.

The last function of a mediator is to be a scapegoat. No one ever enters into an agreement without thinking he might have done better had he waited a little longer or demanded a little more. A party can conveniently suggest to its constituents when it presents the settlement terms that the decision was forced upon it. In the context of negotiation and mediation, that focus of blame—the scapegoat—can be the mediator.

* * * One way to generate a list of the desirable qualities and abilities a mediator should possess is to adopt the posture of a potential party to a mediation session and analyze the type of person that it would want in the role. The following qualities and abilities would probably be included: capable of appreciating the dynamics of the environment in which the dispute is occurring, intelligent, effective listener, articulate, patient, non-judgmental, flexible, forceful and persuasive, imaginative, resourceful, a person of professional standing or reputation, reliable, capable of gaining access to necessary resources, non-defensive, person of

integrity, humble, objective, and neutral with regard to the outcome.
* * *

* * *

[A] mediator must be neutral with regard to outcome. Parties negotiate because they lack the power to achieve their objectives unilaterally. They negotiate with those persons or representatives of groups whose cooperation they need to achieve their objective. If the mediator is neutral and remains so, then he and his office invite a bond of trust to develop between him and the parties. If the mediator's job is to assist the parties to reach a resolution, and his commitment to neutrality ensures confidentiality, then, in an important sense, the parties have nothing to lose and everything to gain by the mediator's intervention. In these two bases of assistance and neutrality there is no way the mediator could jeopardize or abridge the substantive interests of the respective parties.
* * *

There is a variety of information that parties will entrust to a neutral mediator, including a statement of their priorities, acceptable trade-offs, and their desired timing for demonstrating movement and flexibility. All of these postures are aimed to achieve a resolution without fear that such information will be carelessly shared or that it will surface in public forums in a manner calculated to embarrass or exploit the parties into undesired movement. This type of trust is secured and reinforced only if the mediator is neutral, has no power to insist upon a particular outcome, and honors the confidences placed in him. If any of these characteristics is absent, then the parties must calculate what information they will share with the mediator, just as they do in communicating with any of the parties to the controversy.

Notes and Questions

1. Professor Fuller argues that pre-existing structures are not applied to disputes in mediation, but instead the parties produce their own structure through the process. Do you think, however, that disputants in a mediation are likely to ignore completely what they would be entitled to under applicable legal structures? If your client sued for divorce in a state with a rule that each spouse receives half the marital assets, would you advise her to disregard that allocation in mediation if her spouse argues he is entitled to a larger share? What if her spouse wants to keep the family home (their major asset) and your client has other priorities? Under these circumstances, how could she use the allocation rule in mediation? Despite the flexibility to create their own norms in mediation, parties often "bargain in the shadow of the law." *See* Robert H. Mnookin & Lewis Kornhauser, *Bargaining in the Shadow of the Law: The Case of Divorce*, 88 Yale L.J. 950 (1979).

2. Many of the mediator functions described by Professor Stulberg involve facilitating communication. Often this happens without direct disclosures between the parties. One of the keys to a successful mediation is the willingness of the parties to reveal information that a mediator can use to assist them in developing options for a mutually acceptable resolution.

Confidentiality, which can take three separate forms in mediation, is a crucial aspect of the proceeding because it encourages the parties to be candid and forthcoming. First, the mediator is ethically bound not to reveal communications to the other side without the consent of the party who revealed the information. Second, under many statutes and court rules, communications made in mediation are privileged or otherwise protected from disclosure in court proceedings. And third, the parties can contract to keep their communications confidential from others, such as the public, press, fellow employees, etc.

3. The form of mediation practiced in the United States places great emphasis on the neutrality of the mediator. This neutrality incorporates the same type of impartiality—freedom from favoritism, bias, or self-interest—that we expect from judges in the adversary system. In addition, a mediator is supposed to be neutral as to the outcome of the dispute. This is different from the role of a judge, who cares very much about the outcome and tries to make her decision consistent with the law. A mediator, in contrast, relies on the parties for the outcome. An important aspect of not favoring either side means not influencing the content of the agreement. Thus the mediator is supposed to be indifferent to the substantive outcome reached by the parties. Does this mean that a mediator should stand by and let parties reach an agreement the mediator thinks is unfair or unjust? What if one of the parties has an attorney and the other does not?

Exercise

This is a role play simulation that contrasts the processes of arbitration and mediation. Your professor will divide you into groups of three with two designated as disputants and one as the neutral. The disputants will receive a short set of instructions for their roles. After they read the instructions, the neutral will preside over two proceedings. First, the neutral will conduct an arbitration. Each disputant will have a short period of time to present their case and argue why they should prevail, followed by questions from the arbitrator and rebuttals by each side. The arbitrator then decides who wins and records the decision, but does not share the result with the parties. Second, the neutral will conduct a mediation. The disputants will be able to discuss their situation with the help of the mediator and try to reach a resolution of their disagreement. When time is called, your professor will ask the neutrals to report the decisions they made as arbitrators and the parties to describe the agreements they reached, if any. As you conduct the exercise, monitor your reactions. Which process do you prefer and why? Which do you think is better suited to this dispute between these parties?

C. CASE SETTLEMENT

INTRODUCTORY PROBLEM

Your new client, Ms. Patsy Parker, is employed in the transportation industry as a local truck driver for Rising Sun Delivery, an international express service headquartered in Japan that specializes in delivering fragile shipments for the electronics and computer industries. Ms.

Parker has worked for the company for five years, advancing from a part-time substitute to a full-time driver with seniority. She has been attending night school to earn a degree in business and her dream is to advance to a management position within the company. She has been encouraged by Rising Sun Delivery's policy of promoting workers from within its ranks, which it believes will foster employee loyalty and productivity.

Six months ago, Mr. Dan DuPont began work as the new dispatcher and supervisor for the delivery district. There was immediate friction. According to Ms. Parker, DuPont attempted to fondle her and she rebuffed him. Since then, he has ignored her seniority in assigning routes, insulted and taunted her constantly and given her an unfavorable evaluation. She complained to Mr. DuPont about this treatment, but he merely laughed at her. She also wrote a letter to DuPont's immediate superior, the division delivery director, but never received a response to her complaint. Parker says she doesn't know what else to do; the company is hierarchical and she doesn't know of any other complaint procedure. She can no longer tolerate the stress caused by DuPont's retaliation and decided to consult you about filing some sort of claim against him. She is extremely angry at him and thinks he should be made to "pay for his conduct." When you asked what she meant, Parker said she would like to see him fired or demoted. At a minimum, she doesn't want him to continue as her supervisor.

You could recommend suing Rising Sun for maintaining a hostile workplace environment, but Ms. Parker seems very hesitant to think about suing her employer. Her experience at the company was entirely positive until Mr. DuPont became her supervisor. She is frustrated with the company's seeming lack of concern for her situation, but the top executives in the U.S. division of the company are of Japanese descent and she fears they do not approve of what they probably see as a penchant for lawsuits in the United States. She is afraid of ruining her prospects for advancement or that she might even lose her job. As the sole supporter of two sons, she needs a good job. Moreover, after two more years at Rising Sun, she would be vested in an excellent pension plan.

Your legal research reveals that while most courts have held that supervisors are not subject to individual liability under Title VII and the other federal employment civil rights statutes, some have found supervisors liable for monetary damages under state employment discrimination statutes. This would be an issue of first impression in your jurisdiction. The senior partner in the firm is enthusiastic about the prospect of a ground-breaking case and has authorized you to offer to represent Ms. Parker at half your normal litigation rates. If she decides to sue either Rising Sun or Mr. DuPont (or both) under the state statute, the first step would be to file a claim with the state civil rights agency to exhaust administrative remedies. That agency has a voluntary mediation program that could be used to try to settle the dispute without filing suit.

You have an upcoming meeting with Ms. Parker to discuss her litigation and mediation options. What factors weigh in favor of pursuing litigation? What other factors weigh in favor of initiating settlement discussions through the mediation program?

---

1. Trends in Judicial Activity

THE VANISHING TRIAL: AN EXAMINATION OF TRIALS AND RELATED MATTERS IN FEDERAL AND STATE COURTS

Marc Galanter
1 J. Empirical Stud. 459, 460–61, 464–65, 477–78, 481–84 (2004)

I. THE NUMBER OF CIVIL TRIALS

This project reflects the growing awareness of a phenomenon that runs counter to the prevailing image of litigation in the United States. Over the past generation or more, the legal world has been growing vigorously. On almost any measure—the number of lawyers, the amount spent on law, the amount of authoritative legal material, the size of the legal literature, the prominence of law in public consciousness—law has flourished and grown. It seems curious, then, to find a contrary pattern in one central legal phenomenon, indeed one that lies at the very heart of our image of our system—trials. The number of trials has not increased in proportion to these other measures. In some, perhaps most, forums, the absolute number of trials has undergone a sharp decline.
* * *

[Between 1962 and 2002] dispositions [of civil cases in the federal courts per year] increased by a factor of five—from 50,000 to 258,000 cases. But [as indicated in Figure 1,] the number of civil trials in 2002 was more than 20 percent lower than the number in 1962—some 4,569 now to 5,802 then. So [as shown in Figure 2] the portion of dispositions that were by trial was less than one-sixth of what it was in 1962—1.8 percent now as opposed to 11.5 percent in 1962.

Figure 1
Number of Civil Trials, U.S. District Courts, by Bench or Jury, 1962–2002

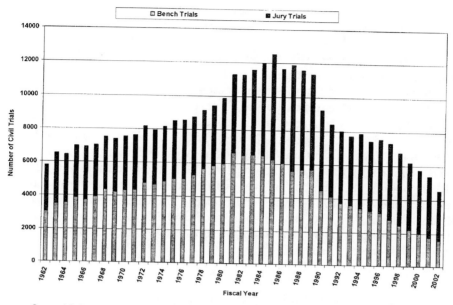

Source: Administrative Office of the United States Courts, Annual Report of the Director, Table C-4 (1962-2002)

Figure 2
Percentage of Civil Terminations During/ After Trial in U.S. District Courts, 1962–2002

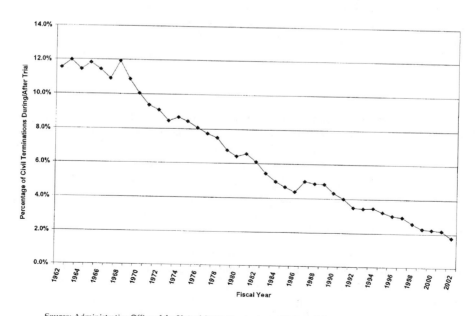

Source: Administrative Office of the United States Courts, Annual Report of the Director, Table C-4 (1962-2002)

* * *

II.   THE CHANGING CHARACTER OF TRIALS: TIME AND COMPLEXITY

As we busy ourselves counting trials, we should not overlook the possibility that what constitutes a trial may have changed over the years. * * * [I]n earlier eras trials were often brief and perfunctory. The elaboration of procedure, the enlargement of evidentiary possibilities, and the increased participation of lawyers have made the trial more complex and refined than its remote ancestors. It is widely believed that within the period covered here, the cases that are tried have become more complex and consume larger investments of resources. * * * Studies of [state] courts suggest that complexity, investment, and length of trial are connected. In their study of Los Angeles Superior Court, Selvin and Ebener note that from their earlier (1915–1949) to their later (1950–1979) period, the number of events in filed cases increased as did the portion of cases with discovery and that the length of trials "dramatically increased." "In the earlier sample of civil filings, 60 percent of the trials lasted no longer than one day. Since 1950, only 20 percent of all trials took one day or less."

* * *

Few measures of complexity are available for cases in federal courts. There is data on the length of trials in federal courts. A larger portion of trials take longer. Civil trials that lasted four days or more were 15 percent of trials in 1965 and 29 percent of trials in 2002; trials of three days or more rose from 27 percent to 42 percent over the same amount of time. * * * [T]his shift to longer trials is produced by an increase in the number of the longest trials combined with a shrinking of the number of short trials.

* * *

III.   FROM FILING TO TRIAL

Interestingly, although the number and rate of trials has fallen, judicial involvement in case activity—at least on some level—has increased. Although the portion of cases that terminate "during or after pretrial" has fallen only slightly from 15 percent in 1963 to 11 percent in 2002, the number of cases that terminated "before pretrial" (but with some type of court action) rose from 20 percent in 1963 to 68 percent in 2002. Clearly, courts are more involved in the early resolution of cases than they used to be.

Figure 15 shows the portion of cases that terminated at each stage of the process. In 1963, more than half (55 percent) terminated before the occurrence of any "court action." By 2002, only 19 percent terminated at this stage. The big change came in the late 1980s, when the number of cases moving into the "before pretrial" stage began a dramatic increase, so that today nearly 70 percent of cases terminate at this stage as opposed to some 20 percent in 1962.

Figure 15
Percentage of Civil Cases Terminating at Each Stage,
U.S. District Courts, 1963–2002

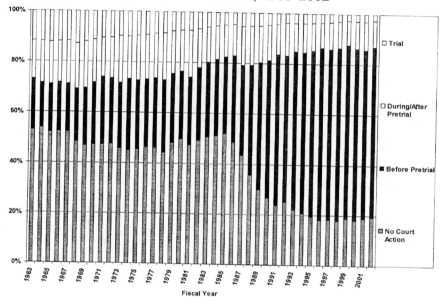

Source: Administrative Office of the United States Courts, Annual Report of the Director, Table C-4 (1962-2002)

This tells us that cases are departing the court at an earlier stage, but not how. Both popular speech and a great deal of scholarly discourse proceed as if the universe of disposition is made up of trial and settlement, so that a decline in trials must mean an increase in settlements. Analyzing dispositions in federal courts from 1970 to 2000, Gillian Hadfield concludes that settlements were actually "a smaller percentage of cases were disposed of through settlement in 2000 than was the case in 1970." What increased as trials disappeared was not settlement, but nontrial adjudication. This is consistent with a documented increase in the prevalence of summary judgment. * * * [The data] suggest that we have moved from a world in which dispositions by summary judgment were equal to a small fraction of dispositions by trial into a new era in which dispositions by summary judgment are a magnitude several times greater than the number of trials.

'THE VANISHING TRIAL' REPORT:
AN ALTERNATIVE VIEW OF
THE DATA

John Lande

Disp. Resol. Mag., Summer 2004, at 19–21

The title of the report and emphasis on [the data showing a decline in the civil trial rate] imply that something has gone wrong with the legal system. Like Mark Twain's reported death, however, accounts of the demise of the trial may be exaggerated.

* * * Galanter's report could just as well have been titled, "The Amazing Success of Judicial Case Management." Relying primarily on data cited in his report, this article shows that (a) there are many trials in the state courts, which have substantially higher trial rates than federal courts, (b) the expansion of pretrial activity and the increased complexity of cases have added reasons for litigants to settle, (c) courts have shifted some of their efforts from trials to pretrial work, and (d) declining trial rates have not reduced the production of case law. * * *

CHANGES IN LITIGATION PATTERNS

Comparing trial rates in state courts. Although trial rates in state courts have declined in recent decades, state courts still resolve a substantial number of cases by trial. Galanter's report focuses primarily on federal courts, though it also presents data on trials in the state courts, where the vast majority of litigation occurs. A recent analysis by the National Center for State Courts (NCSC) shows that in 1999, for example, "state courts of general jurisdiction resolved nearly 28 times as many civil cases * * * as federal district courts."

The NCSC study analyzes data from 22 states between 1976 and 2002 and shows that the civil trial rate dropped by more than half, primarily because the number of filings more than doubled during that period. * * * [T]he trial rate dropped from 36.1 percent to 15.8 percent. Even so, the lowest state court civil trial rate is substantially higher than the highest federal court civil trial rate since 1962, which is 11.5 percent. Similarly, the number of state court trials dwarfs the largest number of federal civil trials shown in Galanter's report. * * *

Increasing size and complexity of cases. Cases are bigger and more complex than they used to be. Before litigants can get to trial, they often have to deal with the increased use of discovery, expert testimony, legal research and pretrial conferences and hearings. * * * Galanter presents data indicting that, on average, court files are fatter and trials are longer than they used to be. As a result, there is an apples-and-oranges phenomenon when comparing 1960s-era trials with their modern counterparts. Thus, contrasting trial statistics from different eras can be misleading.

Some cases settle these days because each side knows more about the case before trial than it would have known in earlier eras. Moreover, litigation costs are higher, which increases incentive to settle. Thus, it should not be surprising—or particularly disturbing—if litigants use litigation to help resolve disputes short of trial.

Judges doing more pretrial work. Galanter's report indicates that federal judges continue to work hard and have shifted some of their efforts from trials to pretrial work. The workload of federal district court judges has grown substantially as the caseload of district judges "more than doubled, from 196 in 1962 to 443 in 2002." * * * A recent major study found that federal judges are actively involved in holding pretrial conferences, setting pretrial schedules and trial dates, setting limits on discovery and ruling on motions. In more than half the cases, the judges described their level of pretrial management as moderate or intensive. * * *

Increasing case law. Although Galanter argues that trials have been vanishing, he does not find a problem of vanishing case law. He reports that the number of pages of federal opinions published yearly has more than doubled since 1962. If there is too little precedent to guide lawyers and judges, presumably it would be more appropriate to increase the publication rate of appellate decisions than to increase the number of trials.

Smaller numbers of trials do, however, reduce the number of trial judgments that provide legal "signals" for lawyers or judges to use in settling and adjudicating future cases. But it is not clear that lawyers or judges suffer from a lack of such signals in most cases or that additional trial judgments would help them. Indeed, further proliferation of legal signals could aggravate problems of legal complexity and information overload.

VILLAINS OR HEROES?

Rhetoric of "vanishing trials" feeds the fears of "litigation romanticists" who lament the passing of an era when it was easier to get to trial, and a judge's primary role was to try cases with little thought of "managing" cases. Such critics argue that by settling cases without court adjudication, ADR impedes the development of public norms and vindication of public values.

* * *

All the changes in the litigation environment in recent decades that reduced the trial rate probably also increased ADR use. Given the increases in many aspects of the legal system, such as judicial caseloads and the complexity of litigation, courts are quite prudent to devote more resources to pretrial case management and ADR.

Telling this story as a success would cast ADR as one of the heroes rather than a possible villain. Similarly, judges would be applauded as wise managers of public institutions rather than suspected of shirking their duty and letting trials vanish.

Notes and Questions

1. Professor Galanter's study provoked some strong reactions: " 'What's documented here,' William G. Young, the chief judge of the Federal District Court in Boston, said in an interview, 'is nothing less than the passing of the common law adversarial system that is uniquely American.' * * * 'This is a cultural shift of enormous significance,' said Arthur Miller, a law professor at Harvard." Adam Lipak, *U.S. Suits Multiply, but Fewer Ever Get to Trial, Study Says*, N.Y. Times, Dec. 14, 2003. Based on the data in the articles, do you agree?

2. For years, the number of federal civil trials did not decline but instead, over time, a lower percentage of cases went to trial (as shown in Figure 2) because the number of filings increased faster than the number of trials. Now the actual number of trials is falling off as well as the percentage. Is there a some minimum number or proportion of cases that should be decided by trial each year? How should we decide the appropriate level of adjudication?

3. The numerical trends are very important, but so are the characteristics of the cases that reach trial. What would be the consequences if parties were routinely encouraged to settle cases raising issues of privacy and First Amendment rights on the Internet? Would you have the same reaction if you discovered that parties typically settle contract cases about sales of goods between merchants when the disputes do not raise novel issues?

4. Professor Lande argues that if the development of precedent is inadequate, the courts could publish more of their opinions. Studies have shown that 60 to 90 percent of appellate decisions are unpublished. Does Lande's solution adequately address the issues raised by ADR procedures that enable parties to resolve cases as a private matter between the settling parties?

5. Other concerns are also raised by the trend toward fewer trials. The following excerpt describes a settlement in which the parties agreed to keep the documents they shared in discovery confidential. What are the consequences of the private dispute resolution settlement in this case?

> As Wall Street sex discrimination suits go, last week's $54 million deal between Morgan Stanley and the Equal Employment Opportunity Commission wasn't a bad one for women. Allison Schieffelin, the 43-year-old former saleswoman whose problems led to the E.E.O.C. suit in 2001, gets $12 million. As many as 340 current and former Morgan Stanley women share $40 million. And women who continue to work at Morgan Stanley—which denies having presided over any discrimination—get the benefit of a brand-new $2 million diversity program.

> So what's not to like?

> An honest lawyer might say it's always good to avoid the risk of losing a trial. Government lawyers up against Morgan Stanley's deep pockets and blue-chip legal army got the investment bank to agree to write a big, fat check just minutes before opening arguments.

But Morgan Stanley, and all of Wall Street, scored an even bigger win: the statistics remain under wraps. No matter how generous a dollar settlement the Commission garnered, it is still an important step short. Wall Street will make changes only when its culture, and the hard numbers of compensation and promotion, are exposed in open court. But don't hold your breath.

Susan Anitlla, *Money Talks, Women Don't*, N.Y. Times, July 21, 2004.

6. You might wonder why it is necessary to study civil procedure when federal courts try only 1.8 percent of the civil cases filed. In addition to the litigation of cases to judicial dispositions short of trial, litigation is often intertwined with the process of reaching a settlement. Based on earlier studies, Professor Galanter coined the term "litigotiation" to describe cases in which litigation is combined with negotiation to reach a negotiated settlement before trial. Can you think of some benefits of proceeding with litigation before attempting to settle a case? Many cases, however, settle just before trial "on the courthouse steps." Are there detriments to delaying settlement until this late stage of the case?

Often a key procedural step or outcome can influence a party's decision to consider settlement during the course of litigation. What settlement considerations would you discuss with your client in the following situations?

a. You represent a defendant against a plaintiff's claim for damages that exceeds your client's insurance coverage. You filed a pre-answer motion to dismiss the plaintiff's complaint under Federal Rule of Civil Procedure 12(b)(6) and the judge denied the motion.

b. You represent a plaintiff in a product liability suit who is besieged with medical bills he has no way to pay. The judge has granted extension of time after extension of time to the defendants and you anticipate that trial is about a year away at the earliest.

c. You represent a plaintiff in an antitrust suit who will be entitled to treble damages if he prevails. Discovery yielded an exceedingly incriminating document that will embarrass the defendants if it is made public.

d. You represent a defendant employer in an employment discrimination suit that you think is frivolous. You filed a motion for summary judgment, but the judge has not yet issued a decision. The plaintiff's attorney has suggested mediation.

2. Court-annexed ADR

As part of the courts' role in encouraging settlement, judges have long held settlement conferences with the parties and this common step in litigation is not usually regarded as falling within the rubric of ADR. In addition, judges often encourage parties to use an ADR process on a private voluntary basis to attempt settlement.

Many jurisdictions have now established court-based programs that provide ADR processes for litigants. The following case and notes describe the development of court-annexed ADR in the federal district courts. In addition, the federal courts of appeals have mediation programs as authorized by Federal Rule of Appellate Procedure 33, and many bankruptcy courts have ADR programs as well. In state courts, the availability of ADR programs varies greatly depending on legislation and state court rules. In some states, such as Florida, mediation is fully institutionalized and routine. Courts must refer certain cases to mediation on the motion of one of the parties and may refer them on the judge's initiative. FLA. STAT. ANN. § 44.102(2). In other states, such as Minnesota, mediation has become an important part of the litigation culture through rules that require attorneys to discuss ADR with their clients. MINN. GEN. R. PRAC. 114.

Some of the federal district court programs established by local rule authorize judges to require parties to participate in certain ADR processes whether they are willing or not. The following case considers whether there is also a broader judicial power to require parties to mediate.

IN RE ATLANTIC PIPE CORPORATION

304 F.3d 135 (1st Cir. 2002)

SELYA, Circuit Judge.

This mandamus proceeding requires us to resolve an issue of importance to judges and practitioners alike: Does a district court possess the authority to compel an unwilling party to participate in, and share the costs of, non-binding mediation conducted by a private mediator? We hold that a court may order mandatory mediation pursuant to an explicit statutory provision or local rule. We further hold that where, as here, no such authorizing medium exists, a court nonetheless may order mandatory mediation through the use of its inherent powers as long as the case is an appropriate one and the order contains adequate safeguards. Because the mediation order here at issue lacks such safeguards (although it does not fall far short), we vacate it and remand the matter for further proceedings.

I. BACKGROUND

In January 1996, Thames–Dick Superaqueduct Partners (Thames–Dick) entered into a master agreement with the Puerto Rico Aqueduct and Sewer Authority (PRASA) to construct, operate, and maintain the North Coast Superaqueduct Project (the Project). Thames–Dick granted subcontracts for various portions of the work, including a subcontract for construction management to Dick Corp. of Puerto Rico (Dick–PR), a subcontract for the operation and maintenance of the Project to Thames Water International, Ltd. (Thames Water), and a subcontract for the fabrication of pipe to Atlantic Pipe Corp. (APC). After the Project had been built, a segment of the pipeline burst. Thames–Dick incurred significant costs in repairing the damage. Not surprisingly, it sought to recover those costs from other parties. In response, one of PRASA's insurers filed a declaratory judgment action in a local court to determine whether Thames–Dick's claims were covered under its policy. The litigation ballooned, soon involving a number of parties and a myriad of issues above and beyond insurance coverage.

On April 25, 2001, the hostilities spilled over into federal court. Two entities beneficially interested in the master agreement—CPA Group International and Chiang, Patel & Yerby, Inc. (collectively CPA)—sued Thames–Dick, Dick–PR, Thames Water, and various insurers in the United States District Court for the District of Puerto Rico, seeking remuneration for consulting services rendered in connection with repairs to the Project. A googol of claims, counterclaims, cross-claims, and third-party complaints followed. Some of these were brought against APC (the petitioner here). To complicate matters, one of the defendants moved to dismiss on grounds that, inter alia, (1) CPA had failed to join an indispensable party whose presence would destroy diversity jurisdiction, and (2) the existence of the parallel proceeding in the local court counseled in favor of abstention.

While this motion was pending before the district court, Thames–Dick asked that the case be referred to mediation and suggested Professor Eric Green as a suitable mediator. The district court granted the motion over APC's objection and ordered non-binding mediation to proceed before Professor Green. The court pronounced mediation likely to conserve judicial resources; directed all parties to undertake mediation in good faith; stayed discovery pending completion of the mediation; and declared that participation in the mediation would not prejudice the parties' positions vis-à-vis the pending motion or the litigation as a whole. The court also stated that if mediation failed to produce a global settlement, the case would proceed to trial.

After moving unsuccessfully for reconsideration of the mediation order, APC sought relief by way of mandamus. Its petition alleged that the district court did not have the authority to require mediation (especially in light of unresolved questions as to the court's subject-matter jurisdiction) and, in all events, could not force APC to pay a share of the expenses of the mediation. * * *

Prior to argument in this court, * * * the district court considered and rejected the challenges to its exercise of jurisdiction. * * *

      * * *

III. THE MERITS

There are four potential sources of judicial authority for ordering mandatory non-binding mediation of pending cases, namely, (a) the court's local rules, (b) an applicable statute, (c) the Federal Rules of Civil Procedure, and (d) the court's inherent powers. Because the district court did not identify the basis of its assumed authority, we consider each of these sources.

A. *The Local Rules*

A district court's local rules may provide an appropriate source of authority for ordering parties to participate in mediation. In Puerto Rico, however, the local rules contain only a single reference to any form of alternative dispute resolution (ADR). That reference is embodied in the district court's Amended Civil Justice Expense and Delay Reduction Plan (CJR Plan).

The district court adopted the CJR Plan on June 14, 1993, in response to the directive contained in the Civil Justice Reform Act of 1990 (CJRA), 28 U.S.C. §§ 471–482. Rule V of the CJR Plan states:

> Pursuant to 28 U.S.C. § 473(b)(4), this Court shall adopt a method of Alternative Dispute Resolution ("ADR") through mediation by a judicial officer.
>
> Such a program would allow litigants to obtain from an impartial third party—the judicial officer as mediator—a flexible nonbinding, dispute resolution process to facilitate negotiations among the parties to help them reach settlement.

D.P.R. R. app. III (R. V.). In addition to specifying who may act as a mediator, Rule V also limits the proper procedure for mediation sessions and assures confidentiality.

The respondents concede that the mediation order in this case falls outside the boundaries of the mediation program envisioned by Rule V. It does so most noticeably because it involves mediation before a private mediator, not a judicial officer. Seizing upon this discrepancy, APC argues that the local rules limit the district court in this respect, and that the court exceeded its authority thereunder by issuing a nonconforming mediation order (i.e., one that contemplates the intervention of a private mediator). The respondents counter by arguing that the rule does not bind the district court because, notwithstanding the unambiguous promise of the CJR Plan (which declares that the district court "shall adopt a method of Alternative Dispute Resolution"), no such program has been adopted to date.

This is a powerful argument. APC does not contradict the respondents' assurance that the relevant portion of the CJR Plan has remained unimplemented, and we take judicial notice that there is no formal, ongoing ADR program in the Puerto Rico federal district court. Because that is so, we conclude that the District of Puerto Rico has no local rule in force that dictates the permissible characteristics of mediation orders. Consequently, APC's argument founders.

B.   The ADR Act

There is only one potential source of statutory authority for ordering mandatory non-binding mediation here: the Alternative Dispute Resolution Act of 1998 (ADR Act), 28 U.S.C. §§ 651–658. Congress passed the ADR Act to promote the utilization of alternative dispute resolution methods in the federal courts and to set appropriate guidelines for their use. The Act lists mediation as an appropriate ADR process. Moreover, it sanctions the participation of "professional neutrals from the private sector" as mediators. Finally, the Act requires district courts to obtain litigants' consent only when they order arbitration, not when they order the use of other ADR mechanisms (such as non-binding mediation).

Despite the broad sweep of these provisions, the Act is quite clear that some form of the ADR procedures it endorses must be adopted in each judicial district by local rule. *See id.* § 651(b) (directing each district court to "devise and implement its own alternative dispute resolution program, by local rule adopted under [28 U.S.C.] section 2071(a), to encourage and promote the use of alternative dispute resolution in its district"). In the absence of such local rules, the ADR Act itself does not authorize any specific court to use a particular ADR mechanism. Because the District of Puerto Rico has not yet complied with the Act's mandate, the mediation order here at issue cannot be justified under the ADR Act.

* * *

Although the ADR Act was designed to promote the use of ADR techniques, Congress chose a very well-defined path: it granted each judicial district, rather than each individual judge, the authority to craft an appropriate ADR program. In other words, Congress permitted experimentation, but only within the disciplining format of district-wide local rules adopted with notice and a full opportunity for public comment. To say that the Act authorized each district judge to disregard a district-wide ADR plan (or the absence of one) and fashion innovative procedures for use in specific cases is simply too much of a stretch.

We add, however, that although the respondents cannot use the ADR Act as a justification, neither can APC use it as a nullification. Noting that the Act requires the adoption of local rules establishing a formal ADR program, APC equates the absence of such rules with the absence of power to employ an ADR procedure (say, mediation) in a specific case. But that is wishful thinking: if one assumes that district judges possessed the power to require mediation prior to the passage of the ADR Act, there is nothing in the Act that strips them of that power. After all, even the adoption of a federal procedural rule does not implicitly abrogate a district court's inherent power to act merely because the rule touches upon the same subject matter.

* * * Even though Congress may cabin the district courts' inherent powers, its intention to do so must be clear and unmistakable. Not so here: we know of nothing in either the ADR Act or the policies that undergird it that can be said to restrict the district courts' authority to engage in the case-by-case deployment of ADR procedures. Hence, we conclude that where, as here, there are no implementing local rules, the ADR Act neither authorizes nor prohibits the entry of a mandatory mediation order.

C. The Civil Rules

The respondents next argue that the district court possessed the authority to require mediation by virtue of the Federal Rules of Civil Procedure. They concentrate their attention on Fed.R.Civ.P. 16, which states in pertinent part that "the court may take appropriate action[ ] with respect to ... (9) settlement and the use of special procedures to assist in resolving the dispute when authorized by statute or local rule...." Fed.R.Civ.P. 16(c)(9). But the words "when authorized by statute or local rule" are a frank limitation on the district courts' authority to order mediation thereunder, and we must adhere to that circumscription. Because there is no statute or local rule authorizing mandatory private mediation in the District of Puerto Rico, Rule 16(c)(9) does not assist the respondents' cause.

D. Inherent Powers

Even apart from positive law, district courts have substantial inherent power to manage and control their calendars. This inherent power takes many forms. See Fed.R.Civ.P. 83(b) (providing that judges may regulate practice in any manner consistent with federal law and applicable rules). By way of illustration, a district court may use its inherent power to compel represented clients to attend pretrial settlement conferences, even though such a practice is not specifically authorized in the Civil Rules.

Of course, a district court's inherent powers are not infinite. There are at least four limiting principles. First, inherent powers must be used in a way reasonably suited to the enhancement of the court's processes, including the orderly and expeditious disposition of pending cases. Second, inherent powers cannot be exercised in a manner that contradicts an applicable statute or rule. Third, the use of inherent powers must comport with procedural fairness. And, finally, inherent powers "must be exercised with restraint and discretion."

* * *

We begin our inquiry by examining the case law. In *Strandell v. Jackson County,* 838 F.2d 884 (7th Cir.1987), the Seventh Circuit held that a district court does not possess inherent power to compel participation in a summary jury trial.[5] In the court's view, Fed.R.Civ.P. 16 occupied the field and prevented a district court from forcing "an unwilling litigant [to] be sidetracked from the normal course of litigation." But the group that spearheaded the subsequent revision of Rule 16 explicitly rejected that interpretation. See Fed.R.Civ.P. 16, advisory committee's note (1993 Amendment) ("The [amended] rule does not attempt to resolve questions as to the extent a court would be authorized to require [ADR] proceedings as an exercise of its inherent powers."). Thus, we do not find *Strandell* persuasive on this point.

The *Strandell* court also expressed concern that summary jury trials would undermine traditional discovery and privilege rules by requiring certain disclosures prior to an actual trial. We find this concern unwarranted. Because a summary jury trial (like a non-binding mediation) does

---

5. A summary jury trial is an ADR technique in which the opposing attorneys present their case, in abbreviated form, to a mock jury, which proceeds to render a non-binding verdict.

not require any disclosures beyond what would be required in the ordinary course of discovery, its principal disadvantage to the litigants is that it may prevent them from saving surprises for the time of trial. Since trial by ambush is no longer in vogue, that interest does not deserve protection.

Relying on policy arguments, the Sixth Circuit also has found that district courts do not possess inherent power to compel participation in summary jury trials. *See In re NLO, Inc.,* 5 F.3d 154, 157–58 (6th Cir.1993). The court thought the value of a summary jury trial questionable when parties do not engage in the process voluntarily, and it worried that "too broad an interpretation of the federal courts' inherent power to regulate their procedure ... encourages judicial high-handedness...."

The concerns articulated by these two respected courts plainly apply to mandatory mediation orders. When mediation is forced upon unwilling litigants, it stands to reason that the likelihood of settlement is diminished. Requiring parties to invest substantial amounts of time and money in mediation under such circumstances may well be inefficient.

The fact remains, however, that none of these considerations establishes that mandatory mediation is always inappropriate. There may well be specific cases in which such a protocol is likely to conserve judicial resources without significantly burdening the objectors' rights to a full, fair, and speedy trial. Much depends on the idiosyncracies of the particular case and the details of the mediation order.

In some cases, a court may be warranted in believing that compulsory mediation could yield significant benefits even if one or more parties object. After all, a party may resist mediation simply out of unfamiliarity with the process or out of fear that a willingness to submit would be perceived as a lack of confidence in her legal position. In such an instance, the party's initial reservations are likely to evaporate as the mediation progresses, and negotiations could well produce a beneficial outcome, at reduced cost and greater speed, than would a trial. While the possibility that parties will fail to reach agreement remains ever present, the boon of settlement can be worth the risk.

This is particularly true in complex cases involving multiple claims and parties. The fair and expeditious resolution of such cases often is helped along by creative solutions—solutions that simply are not available in the binary framework of traditional adversarial litigation. Mediation with the assistance of a skilled facilitator gives parties an opportunity to explore a much wider range of options, including those that go beyond conventional zero-sum resolutions. Mindful of these potential advantages, we hold that it is within a district court's inherent power to order non-consensual mediation in those cases in which that step seems reasonably likely to serve the interests of justice.

E. The Mediation Order

Our determination that the district courts have inherent power to refer cases to non-binding mediation is made with a recognition that any such order must be crafted in a manner that preserves procedural fairness and shields objecting parties from undue burdens. We thus turn to the specifics of the mediation order entered in this case. As with any exercise of a district court's inherent powers, we review the entry of that order for abuse of discretion.

As an initial matter, we agree with the lower court that the complexity of this case militates in favor of ordering mediation. At last count, the suit involves twelve parties, asserting a welter of claims, counterclaims, cross-claims, and third-party claims predicated on a wide variety of theories. The pendency of nearly parallel litigation in the Puerto Rican courts, which features a slightly different cast of characters and claims that are related to but not completely congruent with those asserted here, further complicates the matter. Untangling the intricate web of relationships among the parties, along with the difficult and fact-intensive arguments made by each, will be time-consuming and will impose significant costs on the parties and the court. Against this backdrop, mediation holds out the dual prospect of advantaging the litigants and conserving scarce judicial resources.

In an effort to parry this thrust, APC raises a series of objections. * * *

＊ ＊ ＊

* * * APC posits that the appointment of a private mediator proposed by one of the parties is per se improper (and, thus, invalidates the order). We do not agree. The district court has inherent power to "appoint persons unconnected with the court to aid judges in the performance of specific judicial duties." In the context of non-binding mediation, the mediator does not decide the merits of the case and has no authority to coerce settlement. Thus, in the absence of a contrary statute or rule, it is perfectly acceptable for the district court to appoint a qualified and neutral private party as a mediator. The mere fact that the mediator was proposed by one of the parties is insufficient to establish bias in favor of that party.

We hasten to add that the litigants are free to challenge the qualifications or neutrality of any suggested mediator (whether or not nominated by a party to the case). APC, for example, had a full opportunity to present its views about the suggested mediator both in its opposition to the motion for mediation and in its motion for reconsideration of the mediation order. Despite these opportunities, APC offered no convincing reason to spark a belief that Professor Green, a nationally recognized mediator with significant experience in sprawling cases, is an unacceptable choice. When a court enters a mediation order, it necessarily makes an independent determination that the mediator it appoints is both qualified and neutral. Because the court made that implicit determination here in a manner that was procedurally fair (if not ideal), we find no abuse of discretion in its selection of Professor Green.[7]

---

7. We say "not ideal" because, in an ideal world, it would be preferable for the district court, before naming a mediator, to solicit the names of potential nominees

APC also grouses that it should not be forced to share the costs of an unwanted mediation. We have held, however, that courts have the power under Fed.R.Civ.P. 26(f) to issue pretrial cost-sharing orders in complex litigation. Given the difficulties facing trial courts in cases involving multiple parties and multiple claims, we are hesitant to limit that power to the traditional discovery context. This is especially true in complicated cases, where the potential value of mediation lies not only in promoting settlement but also in clarifying the issues remaining for trial.

The short of the matter is that, without default cost-sharing rules, the use of valuable ADR techniques (like mediation) becomes hostage to the parties' ability to agree on the concomitant financial arrangements. This means that the district court's inherent power to order private mediation in appropriate cases would be rendered nugatory absent the corollary power to order the sharing of reasonable mediation costs. To avoid this pitfall, we hold that the district court, in an appropriate case, is empowered to order the sharing of reasonable costs and expenses associated with mandatory non-binding mediation.

The remainder of APC's arguments are not so easily dispatched. Even when generically appropriate, a mediation order must contain procedural and substantive safeguards to ensure fairness to all parties involved. The mediation order in this case does not quite meet that test. In particular, the order does not set limits on the duration of the mediation or the expense associated therewith.

We need not wax longiloquent. As entered, the order simply requires the parties to mediate; it does not set forth either a timetable for the mediation or a cap on the fees that the mediator may charge. The figures that have been bandied about in the briefs—$900 per hour or $9,000 per mediation day—are quite large and should not be left to the mediator's whim. Relatedly, because the mediator is to be paid an hourly rate, the court should have set an outside limit on the number of hours to be devoted to mediation. Equally as important, it is trite but often true that justice delayed is justice denied. An unsuccessful mediation will postpone the ultimate resolution of the case—indeed, the district court has stayed all discovery pending the completion of the mediation—and, thus, prolong the litigation. For these reasons, the district court should have set a definite time frame for the mediation.

The respondents suggest that the district court did not need to articulate any limitations in its mediation order because the mediation process will remain under the district court's ultimate supervision; the court retains the ability to curtail any excessive expenditures of time or money; and a dissatisfied party can easily return to the court at any time. While this might be enough of a safeguard in many instances, the instant litigation is sufficiently complicated and the mediation efforts are

from all parties and to provide an opportunity for the parties to comment upon each others' proposed nominees.

likely to be sufficiently expensive that, here, reasonable time limits and fee constraints, set in advance, are appropriate.

A court intent on ordering non-consensual mediation should take other precautions as well. For example, the court should make it clear (as did the able district court in this case) that participation in mediation will not be taken as a waiver of any litigation position. The important point is that the protections we have mentioned are not intended to comprise an exhaustive list, but, rather, to illustrate that when a district court orders a party to participate in mediation, it should take care to assuage legitimate concerns about the possible negative consequences of such an order.

To recapitulate, we rule that a mandatory mediation order issued under the district court's inherent power is valid in an appropriate case. We also rule that this is an appropriate case. We hold, however, that the district court's failure to set reasonable limits on the duration of the mediation and on the mediator's fees dooms the decree.

IV.   CONCLUSION

We admire the district court's pragmatic and innovative approach to this massive litigation. Our core holding—that ordering mandatory mediation is a proper exercise of a district court's inherent power, subject, however, to a variety of terms and conditions—validates that approach. We are mindful that this holding is in tension with the opinions of the Sixth and Seventh Circuits in *NLO* and *Strandell*, respectively, but we believe it is justified by the important goal of promoting flexibility and creative problem-solving in the handling of complex litigation.

That said, the need of the district judge in this case to construct his own mediation regime ad hoc underscores the greater need of the district court as an institution to adopt an ADR program and memorialize it in its local rules. In the ADR Act, Congress directed that "[e]ach United States district court shall authorize, by local rule under section 2071(a), the use of alternative dispute resolution processes in all civil actions...." 28 U.S.C. § 651(b). While Congress did not set a firm deadline for compliance with this directive, the statute was enacted four years ago. This omission having been noted, we are confident that the district court will move expediently to bring the District of Puerto Rico into compliance.

We need go no further. For the reasons set forth above, we vacate the district court's mediation order and remand for further proceedings consistent with this opinion. The district court is free to order mediation if it continues to believe that such a course is advisable or, in the alternative, to proceed with discovery and trial.

Notes and Questions

1.   Federal Rule of Civil Procedure 16 is discussed in *Atlantic Pipe* as one possible source of authority for the court to order the parties to

participate in mediation. As originally adopted, Rule 16 contemplated pretrial conferences as an important step in trial preparation, but did not mention any role for the court in encouraging settlement. It has evolved over the years to provide authority for settlement activities.

In 1983, the Rule was amended to recognize courts' increasingly common practice of using pretrial conferences as judicial settlement conferences or as a forum to discuss other settlement procedures for use in a case. The new Rule 16(c)(7) stated: "the parties at any conference under this rule may consider and take action with respect to * * * the possibility of settlement or the use of extrajudicial procedures to resolve the dispute."

After further amendment in 1993, Rule 16 now contains the language quoted in *Atlantic Pipe* authorizing courts to use pretrial conferences to consider and to "take appropriate action, with respect to * * * (9) settlement and the use of special procedures to assist in resolving the dispute when authorized by statute or local rule." Fed.R.Civ.P. 16(c)(9). According to the advisory committee that recommended the change, its primary purpose was to "eliminate questions that have occasionally been raised regarding the authority of the court to make appropriate orders designed either to facilitate settlement or to provide for an efficient and economical trial. The prefatory language * * * is revised to clarify the court's power to enter appropriate orders at a conference notwithstanding the objection of a party." Fed. R. Civ. P. 16(c) advisory committee's notes.

2. The District of Puerto Rico local rule discussed in *Atlantic Pipe* was adopted pursuant to the Civil Justice Reform Act of 1990 (CJRA), which was an attempt by Congress to reduce litigation costs and delay in civil cases. The legislation required the district courts to form local advisory groups to evaluate the docket and make proposals. The districts then formulated individualized civil expense and delay reduction plans. Under the plans, many districts implemented case management techniques or alternative dispute resolution programs. By 1996, over half the federal district courts offered mediation pursuant to the CJRA, making it the primary federal court ADR process. Elizabeth Plapinger & Donna Stienstra, ADR and Settlement in the Federal District Courts 4 (1996).

3. Congress further encouraged the development of ADR in the federal courts with the Alternative Dispute Resolution Act of 1998 (ADR Act), which directed *all* district courts to establish ADR programs by local rule that offer at least one ADR process. The offerings depend on the district and include mediation, non-binding arbitration, early neutral evaluation, minitrial, and summary jury trial. The Act itself does not require litigants to participate in ADR, but it requires the courts to "encourage and promote" the use of ADR, 28 U.S.C. § 651(b), and to adopt local rules to "require that litigants in all civil cases consider the use of an alternative dispute resolution process at an appropriate stage in the litigation," *id.* § 652(a). If authorized by the local rules, a district court judge may require the use of mediation or early neutral evaluation. *Id.*

4. The Supreme Court has defined inherent powers as those which " 'must necessarily result to our courts of justice from the nature of their institution,' powers 'which cannot be dispensed with in a Court, because they are necessary to the exercise of all others.' " *Chambers v. NASCO, Inc.*,

501 U.S. 32, 43, 111 S.Ct. 2123, 115 L.Ed.2d 27 (1991) (quoting *United States v. Hudson*, 11 U.S. (7 Cranch) 32, 34, 3 L.Ed. 259 (1812). These powers are to be "exercised with restraint and discretion," *id.* at 44, but their scope has proved malleable, with courts relying on them in many contexts. For example, courts have recognized inherent powers to assess attorneys fees as a sanction for misconduct, to dismiss a suit for failure to prosecute, to dismiss an action on grounds of forum non conveniens, to appoint an expert as an advisor to the judge, and to order represented parties to appear at a pretrial settlement conference, all in contexts where the Federal Rules of Civil Procedure did not provide authority. When there is a rule that governs a particular situation, however, a court should ordinarily use the rule rather than its inherent powers.

In the case of Rule 16, the advisory committee's notes explicitly leave open the question of inherent power, stating "[t]he rule does not attempt to resolve questions as to the extent a court would be authorized to require [ADR procedures] as an exercise of its inherent powers." Do you think requiring ADR procedures over the objection of a party is a matter that *should* be left to a judge's discretion as a matter of inherent power? Are there instead advantages to adopting local rules to govern ADR, as directed by Congress in the ADR Act? Do you agree that the need for flexibility in handling complex litigation justified the district court judge's use of inherent powers in *Atlantic Pipe*?

5. At the beginning of its opinion, the First Circuit states that a court may use its inherent powers to order mandatory mediation if the case is "appropriate" and "the order contains adequate safeguards." Are there desirable procedural safeguards in addition to those the court required in *Atlantic Pipe*? What types of cases might not be appropriate? *See, e.g., Bouchard Transportation Co. v. Florida Dept. of Environmental Protection*, 91 F.3d 1445, 1448–49 (11th Cir. 1996) (finding an abuse of discretion when the district court exercised its inherent power to order the State of Florida to mediate without first deciding the State's claim that it was immune from suit). Would *Atlantic Pipe* have been an appropriate case for court-ordered mediation if the district court had not yet resolved the question of its subject matter jurisdiction?

6. As indicated in *Atlantic Pipe*, with an appropriate local rule adopted pursuant to the CJRA or the ADR Act, a district court may have the authority to order unwilling parties to participate in an ADR procedure pursuant to Federal Rule of Civil Procedure 16. Without a local rule, a court may be able to rely on its inherent power. Do these powers mean that a court should exercise this authority? Is it likely that an unwilling party who participates in ADR under court order will agree to settle the case?

7. What constitutes compliance with a court's order to mediate? Is a party "mediating" if it attends the session with the mediator and opposing party and listens politely, but does not make any settlement offers and rejects the other party's offers without discussion? Some local court rules require "good faith participation" or "meaningful participation" by the parties. What does that entail and how should courts enforce such rules? *See Nick v. Morgan's Foods, Inc.*, 270 F.3d 590 (8th Cir. 2001) (upholding district court's imposition of fines for a party's minimal participation in

court-ordered mediation under a local rule that authorizes "sanctions the judge deems appropriate" if a party fails to appear, is substantially unprepared to mediate, or fails to participate in good faith). What effect is enforcement likely to have on the confidentiality of the mediation process?

8. The district court in *Atlantic Pipe* appointed a private mediator suggested by one of the parties, which the court of appeals described as "procedurally fair (if not ideal)." What effect might this appointment process have on the mediation? Some courts employ mediators, others rely on volunteer lawyers trained to mediate, and yet others provide the parties a list of mediators who meet requirements for education and experience established by the court. Do you think courts should routinely provide mediators in the way they provide judges? Should the Court or the parties pay the mediator? If a court orders mediation, does it bear responsibility for the quality of the mediator?

Exercise

The Federal Rules of Civil Procedure provide a uniform set of procedures in all the federal district courts. At the same time, however, Rule 83 authorizes courts to adopt local rules, so long as they are "consistent with—but not duplicative of—Acts of Congress" and the Federal Rules of Civil Procedure. Local rules provide flexibility in tailoring procedures to local conditions and litigation practices, but they also introduce inconsistencies among the districts that can pose challenges for attorneys who do not practice regularly in a particular district. The CJRA's "grass roots" approach to reform expanded the role of local rules and contributed significantly to district-to-district procedural variation. The ADR Act continued this trend.

For the district a) where you plan to practice after graduation, b) where your law school is located, or c) assigned by your professor, use the court's web site or an online research database to find the local rules. Scan the rules to get a sense of their subject matter and find the rule that governs ADR. Print the rule and bring it to class for discussion. In addition, answer the following questions.

1. What processes are included in the district's ADR program?

2. Are the processes voluntary or does the court have the authority to require parties to participate?

3. Does the rule contain procedural safeguards that you think will help ensure a fair ADR process?

D.   LEGAL RULES THAT SUPPORT SETTLEMENT

Litigation involves transaction costs that are not reflected in the remedies available in court and the desire to avoid these transaction costs creates an incentive to settle cases. In the United States, the largest component of the monetary cost of litigation is attorney's fees. In the absence of a statutory provision to the contrary, fees are allocated according to the "American Rule": each side bears its own fees. This practice is in contrast to the allocation in Great Britain where, according to the "English Rule," the loser pays the fees of the prevailing party.

How does the American Rule affect settlement? Assume a plaintiff anticipates a jury award of $500,000 that would be reduced by $100,000 in attorney's fees. The plaintiff's net recovery after trial would be $400,000. If the defendant also values the case at $500,000 and would spend $125,000 to litigate through trial, the cost to the defendant will total $625,000. In considering settlement, each party would like to do as well as they would if the case went to trial. Assume that the plaintiff's attorney has billed $15,000 at this stage of the case and the defendant's accrued bill is $10,000. That means if the plaintiff can recover $415,000 in settlement now, she would avoid the need to expend $85,000 in attorney's fees and would be in a position equivalent to the estimated result of a trial. Making a payment of $615,000 would accomplish the same for the defendant. At any settlement amount greater than $415,000 for the plaintiff or less than $615,000 for the defendant, the parties would be better off than if they proceeded to trial, creating a bargaining zone of possible settlement outcomes. Thus, assuming the parties agree roughly on the outcome of their suit, they have an incentive to settle the litigation to avoid incurring the cost of attorney's fees.

Some of the other costs of litigation are allocated according to Rule 54(d). These costs, enumerated in 28 U.S.C. § 1920, include court filing fees, jury and witness fees, photocopying costs, and expenses for a court reporter. Unless the court orders otherwise, the prevailing party submits these costs and they are charged to the losing party. Rule 68 is designed to promote settlement further by altering this default allocation of costs.

Problems

1.   Patrick sues Denise for $100,000 in damages due to an automobile accident. The case is in federal court under diversity jurisdiction. The jury awards only $25,000 and there is no order regarding costs. How much money will Patrick receive if his attorney's fees are $15,000 and his costs under § 1920 are $2,000?

2.   The case is the same except that Denise makes an offer of judgment pursuant to Rule 68 for $30,000. Patrick declines the offer and the case proceeds to trial. The jury awards Patrick $25,000. This time how much will he recover? (Assume $1,500 of his § 1920 costs were incurred after the Rule 68 offer and Denise's costs after the offer totaled $2,000.)

3.   Does your answer change if Denise's lawyer made the settlement offer during a phone call with Patrick's lawyer?

4.   Can Patrick make an offer of settlement under Rule 68?

5.   The case is the same as in problem 2, except that the jury finds Denise not liable. Who pays what amount in costs?

In cases brought under certain U.S. statutes, fee shifting changes the normal allocation of attorney's fees through provisions that require the losing party to pay the prevailing party's fees. This is typically done in circumstances when Congress decides to encourage meritorious claims. For example, under Title VII of the Civil Rights Act, a successful plaintiff in an employment discrimination suit is awarded not only damages but also attorney's fees on the theory that such suits help eliminate discriminatory practices and thus the plaintiff is serving public purposes by acting as a "private attorney general." Another statute, the Equal Access to Justice Act, provides for awards of attorneys' fees to plaintiffs who prevail in suits against the federal government "unless the position of the United States was substantially justified." This provision is designed to help level the playing field for a party opposing the vast resource of the government and to deter agencies from fighting claims when the government's position is weak.

What happens when an offer of settlement is made in a case subject to a fee shifting statute? Rule 68 is designed to encourage settlement, while fee shifting statutes are intended to encourage certain types of litigation. The Supreme Court considered the conflicting policy incentives in the following case. Chesny, the plaintiff, filed suit under 28 U.S.C.A. § 1983, a statute that provides remedies for violations of federal law by state officials, other persons "acting under the color of state law," and local governments. The prevailing party in a § 1983 suit may be awarded attorney's fees under 28 U.S.C.A. § 1988.

MAREK v. CHESNY

473 U.S. 1, 105 S.Ct. 3012, 87 L.Ed.2d 1 (1985)

Chief Justice BURGER delivered the opinion of the Court. We granted certiorari to decide whether attorney's fees incurred by a plaintiff subsequent to an offer of settlement under Federal Rule of Civil Procedure 68 must be paid by the defendant under 42 U.S.C. § 1988, when the plaintiff recovers a judgment less than the offer.

I

Petitioners, three police officers, in answering a call on a domestic disturbance, shot and killed respondent's adult son. Respondent, in his own behalf and as administrator of his son's estate, filed suit against the officers in the United States District Court under 42 U.S.C. § 1983 and state tort law.

Prior to trial, petitioners made a timely offer of settlement "for a sum, including costs now accrued and attorney's fees, ONE HUNDRED THOUSAND ($100,000) DOLLARS." Respondent did not accept the offer. The case went to trial and respondent was awarded $5,000 on the state-law "wrongful death" claim, $52,000 for the § 1983 violation, and $3,000 in punitive damages.

Respondent filed a request for $171,692.47 in costs, including attorney's fees. This amount included costs incurred after the settlement offer. Petitioners opposed the claim for postoffer costs, relying on Federal Rule of Civil Procedure 68, which shifts to the plaintiff all "costs" incurred subsequent to an offer of judgment not exceeded by the ultimate recovery at trial. Petitioners argued that attorney's fees are part of the "costs" covered by Rule 68. The District Court agreed with petitioners and declined to award respondent "costs, including attorney's fees, incurred after the offer of judgment." 547 F.Supp. 542, 547 (N.D. Ill. 1982). The parties subsequently agreed that $32,000 fairly represented the allowable costs, including attorney's fees, accrued prior to petitioners' offer of settlement. Respondent appealed the denial of postoffer costs.

The Court of Appeals reversed. 720 F.2d 474 (CA7 1983). The court rejected what it termed the "rather mechanical linking up of Rule 68 and section 1988." *Id.,* at 478. It stated that the District Court's reading of Rule 68 and § 1988, while "in a sense logical," would put civil rights plaintiffs and counsel in a "predicament" that "cuts against the grain of section 1988." *Id.,* at 478, 479. Plaintiffs' attorneys, the court reasoned, would be forced to "think very hard" before rejecting even an inadequate offer, and would be deterred from bringing good-faith actions because of the prospect of losing the right to attorney's fees if a settlement offer more favorable than the ultimate recovery were rejected. *Id.,* at 478–479. The court concluded that "[t]he legislators who enacted section 1988 would not have wanted its effectiveness blunted because of a little known rule of court." *Id.,* at 479.

* * * We reverse.

II

Rule 68 provides that if a timely pretrial offer of settlement is not accepted and "the judgment finally obtained by the offeree is not more favorable than the offer, the offeree must pay *the costs incurred after the making of the offer.*" (Emphasis added.) The plain purpose of Rule 68 is to encourage settlement and avoid litigation. The Rule prompts both parties to a suit to evaluate the risks and costs of litigation, and to balance them against the likelihood of success upon trial on the merits. This case requires us to decide whether the offer in this case was a proper one under Rule 68, and whether the term "costs" as used in Rule 68 includes attorney's fees awardable under 42 U.S.C. § 1988.

A

The first question we address is whether petitioners' offer was valid under Rule 68. Respondent contends that the offer was invalid because it lumped petitioners' proposal for damages with their proposal for costs. Respondent argues that Rule 68 requires that an offer must separately recite the amount that the defendant is offering in settlement of the substantive claim and the amount he is offering to cover accrued costs. Only if the offer is bifurcated, he contends, so that it is clear how much the defendant is offering for the substantive claim, can a plaintiff possibly assess whether it would be wise to accept the offer. He apparently bases this argument on the language of the Rule providing that the defendant "may serve upon the adverse party an offer to allow judgment to be taken against him for the money or property or to the effect specified in his offer, *with costs then accrued*" (emphasis added).

The Court of Appeals rejected respondent's claim * * *. We, too, reject respondent's argument. We do not read Rule 68 to require that a defendant's offer itemize the respective amounts being tendered for settlement of the underlying substantive claim and for costs.

The critical feature of this portion of the Rule is that the offer be one that *allows judgment to be taken against the defendant for both the damages caused by the challenged conduct and the costs then accrued.* In other words, the drafters' concern was not so much with the particular components of offers, but with the *judgments* to be allowed against defendants. If an offer recites that costs are included or specifies an amount for costs, and the plaintiff accepts the offer, the judgment will necessarily include costs; if the offer does not state that costs are included and an amount for costs is not specified, the court will be obliged by the terms of the Rule to include in its judgment an additional amount which in its discretion it determines to be sufficient to cover the costs. In either case, however, the offer has *allowed* judgment to be entered against the defendant both for damages caused by the challenged conduct and for costs. Accordingly, it is immaterial whether the offer recites that costs are included, whether it specifies the amount the defendant is allowing for costs, or, for that matter, whether it refers to costs at all. As long as the offer does not implicitly or explicitly provide that the judgment *not* include costs, a timely offer will be valid.

This construction of the Rule best furthers the objective of the Rule, which is to encourage settlements. If defendants are not allowed to make lump-sum offers that would, if accepted, represent their total liability, they would understandably be reluctant to make settlement offers. As the Court of Appeals observed, "many a defendant would be unwilling to make a binding settlement offer on terms that left it exposed to liability for attorney's fees in whatever amount the court might fix on motion of the plaintiff." 720 F.2d, at 477.

Contrary to respondent's suggestion, reading the Rule in this way does not frustrate plaintiffs' efforts to determine whether defendants' offers are adequate. At the time an offer is made, the plaintiff knows the amount in damages caused by the challenged conduct. The plaintiff also knows, or can ascertain, the costs then accrued. A reasonable determination whether to accept the offer can be made by simply adding these two figures and comparing the sum to the amount offered. Respondent is troubled that a plaintiff will not know whether the offer on the substantive claim would be exceeded at trial, but this is so whenever an offer of settlement is made. In any event, requiring itemization of damages separate from costs would not in any way help plaintiffs know in advance whether the judgment at trial will exceed a defendant's offer.

Curiously, respondent also maintains that petitioners' settlement offer did not exceed the judgment obtained by respondent. In this regard, respondent notes that the $100,000 offer is not as great as the sum of the $60,000 in damages, $32,000 in preoffer costs, and $139,692.47 in claimed postoffer costs. This argument assumes, however, that postoffer costs should be included in the comparison. The Court of Appeals correctly recognized that postoffer costs merely offset part of the expense of continuing the litigation to trial, and should not be included in the calculus.

B

The second question we address is whether the term "costs" in Rule 68 includes attorney's fees awardable under 42 U.S.C. § 1988. By the time the Federal Rules of Civil Procedure were adopted in 1938, federal statutes had authorized and defined awards of costs to prevailing parties for more than 85 years. Unlike in England, such "costs" generally had not included attorney's fees; under the "American Rule," each party had been required to bear its own attorney's fees. The "American Rule" as applied in federal courts, however, had become subject to certain exceptions by the late 1930's. Some of these exceptions had evolved as a product of the "inherent power in the courts to allow attorney's fees in particular situations." But most of the exceptions were found in federal statutes that directed courts to award attorney's fees as part of costs in particular cases.

Section 407 of the Communications Act of 1934, for example, provided in relevant part that, "[i]f the petitioner shall finally prevail, he shall be allowed a reasonable attorney's fee, to be taxed and collected as a part of the costs of the suit." 47 U.S.C. § 407. There was identical language in § 3(p) of the Railway Labor Act, 45 U.S.C. § 153(p) (1934 ed.). Section 40 of the Copyright Act of 1909, 17 U.S.C. § 40 (1934 ed.), allowed a court to "award to the prevailing party a reasonable attorney's fee as part of the costs." And other statutes contained similar provisions that included attorney's fees as part of awardable "costs." See, *e.g.*, the Clayton Act, 15 U.S.C. § 15 (1934 ed.); the Securities Act of 1933, 15 U.S.C. § 77k(e) (1934 ed.); the Securities Exchange Act of 1934, 15 U.S.C. §§ 78i(e), 78r(a) (1934 ed.).

The authors of Federal Rule of Civil Procedure 68 were fully aware of these exceptions to the American Rule. The Advisory Committee's Note to Rule 54(d), 28 U.S.C.App., contains an extensive list of the federal statutes which allowed for costs in particular cases; of the 35 "statutes as to costs" set forth in the final paragraph of the Note, no fewer than 11 allowed for attorney's fees as part of costs. Against this background of varying definitions of "costs," the drafters of Rule 68 did not define the term; nor is there any explanation whatever as to its intended meaning in the history of the Rule.

In this setting, given the importance of "costs" to the Rule, it is very unlikely that this omission was mere oversight; on the contrary, the most reasonable inference is that the term "costs" in Rule 68 was intended to refer to all costs properly awardable under the relevant substantive statute or other authority. In other words, all costs properly awardable in an action are to be considered within the scope of Rule 68 "costs." Thus, absent congressional expressions to the contrary, where the underlying statute defines "costs" to include attorney's fees, we are satisfied such fees are to be included as costs for purposes of Rule 68.

Here, respondent sued under 42 U.S.C. § 1983. Pursuant to the Civil Rights Attorney's Fees Awards Act of 1976, 90 Stat. 2641, as amended, 42 U.S.C. § 1988, a prevailing party in a § 1983 action may be awarded attorney's fees "as part of the costs." Since Congress expressly included attorney's fees as "costs" available to a plaintiff in a § 1983 suit, such fees are subject to the cost-shifting provision of Rule 68. This "plain meaning" interpretation of the interplay between Rule 68 and § 1988 is the only construction that gives meaning to each word in both Rule 68 and § 1988.

Unlike the Court of Appeals, we do not believe that this "plain meaning" construction of the statute and the Rule will frustrate Congress' objective in § 1988 of ensuring that civil rights plaintiffs obtain "'effective access to the judicial process.'" *Hensley v. Eckerhart,* 461 U.S. 424, 429 (1983), quoting H.R.Rep. No. 94–1558, p. 1 (1976). Merely subjecting civil rights plaintiffs to the settlement provision of Rule 68 does not curtail their access to the courts, or significantly deter them from bringing suit. Application of Rule 68 will serve as a disincentive for the plaintiff's attorney to continue litigation after the defendant makes a settlement offer. There is no evidence, however, that Congress, in considering § 1988, had any thought that civil rights claims were to be on any different footing from other civil claims insofar as settlement is concerned. Indeed, Congress made clear its concern that civil rights plaintiffs not be penalized for "helping to lessen docket congestion" by settling their cases out of court. See H.R.Rep. No. 94–1588, *supra,* at 7.

Moreover, Rule 68's policy of encouraging settlements is neutral, favoring neither plaintiffs nor defendants; it expresses a clear policy of favoring settlement of all lawsuits. Civil rights plaintiffs—along with other plaintiffs—who reject an offer more favorable than what is thereafter recovered at trial will not recover attorney's fees for services performed after the offer is rejected. But, since the Rule is neutral, many civil rights plaintiffs will benefit from the offers of settlement encouraged by Rule 68. Some plaintiffs will receive compensation in settlement where, on trial, they might not have recovered, or would have recovered less than what was offered. And, even for those who would prevail at trial, settlement will provide them with compensation at an earlier date without the burdens, stress, and time of litigation. In short, settlements rather than litigation will serve the interests of plaintiffs as well as defendants.

To be sure, application of Rule 68 will require plaintiffs to "think very hard" about whether continued litigation is worthwhile; that is precisely what Rule 68 contemplates. This effect of Rule 68, however, is in no sense inconsistent with the congressional policies underlying

§ 1983 and § 1988. Section 1988 authorizes courts to award only "reasonable" attorney's fees to prevailing parties. In *Hensley v. Eckerhart, supra,* we held that "the most critical factor" in determining a reasonable fee "is the degree of success obtained." *Id.,* at 436, 103 S.Ct., at 1941. We specifically noted that prevailing at trial "may say little about whether the expenditure of counsel's time was reasonable in relation to the success achieved." *Ibid.* In a case where a rejected settlement offer exceeds the ultimate recovery, the plaintiff—although technically the prevailing party—has not received any monetary benefits from the postoffer services of his attorney. This case presents a good example: the $139,692 in postoffer legal services resulted in a recovery $8,000 less than petitioners' settlement offer. Given Congress' focus on the success achieved, we are not persuaded that shifting the postoffer costs to respondent in these circumstances would in any sense thwart its intent under § 1988.

Rather than "cutting against the grain" of § 1988, as the Court of Appeals held, we are convinced that applying Rule 68 in the context of a § 1983 action is consistent with the policies and objectives of § 1988. Section 1988 encourages plaintiffs to bring meritorious civil rights suits; Rule 68 simply encourages settlements. There is nothing incompatible in these two objectives.

III

Congress, of course, was well aware of Rule 68 when it enacted § 1988, and included attorney's fees as part of recoverable costs. The plain language of Rule 68 and § 1988 subjects such fees to the cost-shifting provision of Rule 68. Nothing revealed in our review of the policies underlying § 1988 constitutes "the necessary clear expression of congressional intent" required "to exempt ... [the] statute from the operation of" Rule 68. We hold that petitioners are not liable for costs of $139,692 incurred by respondent after petitioners' offer of settlement.

The judgment of the Court of Appeals is *Reversed.*

[The concurring opinions of Justice POWELL and Justice REHNQUIST are omitted.]

Justice BRENNAN, with whom Justice MARSHALL and Justice BLACKMUN join, dissenting. The question presented by this case is whether the term "costs" as it is used in Rule 68 of the Federal Rules of Civil Procedure and elsewhere throughout the Rules refers simply to those taxable costs defined in 28 U.S.C. § 1920 and traditionally understood as "costs"—court fees, printing expenses, and the like—or instead includes attorney's fees when an underlying fees-award statute happens to refer to fees "as part of" the awardable costs. Relying on what it recurrently emphasizes is the "plain language" of one such statute, 42 U.S.C. § 1988,[3] the Court today holds that a prevailing civil rights

---

3. Civil Rights Attorney's Fees Awards Act of 1976, 90 Stat. 2641, as amended, 42 U.S.C. § 1988. That section provides in relevant part that "[i]n any action or proceed-

litigant entitled to fees under that statute is *per se* barred by Rule 68 from recovering any fees for work performed after rejecting a settlement offer where he ultimately recovers less than the proffered amount in settlement.

I dissent. The Court's reasoning is wholly inconsistent with the history and structure of the Federal Rules, and its application to the over 100 attorney's fees statutes enacted by Congress will produce absurd variations in Rule 68's operation based on nothing more than picayune differences in statutory phraseology. Neither Congress nor the drafters of the Rules could possibly have intended such inexplicable variations in settlement incentives. Moreover, the Court's interpretation will "seriously undermine the purposes behind the attorney's fees provisions" of the civil rights laws, *Delta Air Lines, Inc. v. August,* 450 U.S. 346, 378 (1981) (REHNQUIST, J., dissenting)—provisions imposed by Congress pursuant to § 5 of the Fourteenth Amendment. * * * Finally, both Congress and the Judicial Conference of the United States have been engaged for years in considering possible amendments to Rule 68 that would bring attorney's fees within the operation of the Rule. That process strongly suggests that Rule 68 has not previously been viewed as governing fee awards, and it illustrates the wisdom of deferring to other avenues of amending Rule 68 rather than ourselves engaging in "standardless judicial lawmaking." *Delta Air Lines, Inc. v. August, supra* 450 U.S., at 378, 101 S.Ct., at 1163 (REHNQUIST, J., dissenting).

I

The Court's "plain language" analysis goes as follows: Section 1988 provides that a "prevailing party" may recover "a reasonable attorney's fee as part of the costs." Rule 68 in turn provides that, where an offeree obtains a judgment for less than the amount of a previous settlement offer, "the offeree must pay the costs incurred after the making of the offer." Because "attorney's fees" are "costs," the Court concludes, the "plain meaning" of Rule 68 *per se* prohibits a prevailing civil rights plaintiff from recovering fees incurred after he rejected the proposed out-of-court settlement.

* * *

For a number of reasons, "costs" as that term is used in the Federal Rules should be interpreted uniformly in accordance with the definition of costs set forth in § 1920:

First. The limited history of the costs provisions in the Federal Rules suggests that the drafters intended "costs" to mean only taxable costs traditionally allowed under the common law or pursuant to the statutory predecessor of § 1920. Nowhere was it suggested that the meaning of taxable "costs" might vary from case to case depending on

ing to enforce a provision of sections 1981, 1982, 1983, 1985, and 1986 of this title, title IX of Public Law 92–318, or title VI of the Civil Rights Act of 1964, the court, in its discretion, may allow the prevailing party, other than the United States, a reasonable attorney's fee as part of the costs."

the language of the substantive statute involved—a practice that would have cut against the drafters' intent to create uniform procedures applicable to *"every* action" in federal court. Fed.Rule Civ.Proc. 1.

Second. The Rules provide that "costs" may automatically be taxed by the clerk of the court on one day's notice, Fed.Rule Civ.Proc. 54(d)—strongly suggesting that "costs" were intended to refer only to those routine, readily determinable charges that could appropriately be left to a clerk, and as to which a single day's notice of settlement would be appropriate. Attorney's fees, which are awardable only by the *court* and which frequently entail lengthy disputes and hearings, obviously do not fall within that category.

Third. When particular provisions of the Federal Rules are *intended* to encompass attorney's fees, they do so *explicitly.* Eleven different provisions of the Rules authorize a court to award attorney's fees as "expenses" in particular circumstances, demonstrating that the drafters knew the difference, and intended a difference, between "costs," "expenses," and "attorney's fees."

Fourth. With the exception of one recent Court of Appeals opinion and two recent District Court opinions, the Court can point to no authority suggesting that courts or attorneys have ever viewed the cost-shifting provisions of Rule 68 as including attorney's fees. * * *

Fifth. We previously have held that words and phrases in the Federal Rules must be given a consistent usage and be read *in pari materia,* reasoning that to do otherwise would "attribute a schizophrenic intent to the drafters." *Id.,* at 353, 101 S.Ct., at 1150. Applying the Court's "plain language" approach consistently throughout the Rules, however, would produce absurd results that would turn statutes like § 1988 on their heads and plainly violate the restraints imposed on judicial rulemaking by the Rules Enabling Act. * * *

Sixth. As with all of the Federal Rules, the drafters intended Rule 68 to have a uniform, consistent application in *all* proceedings in federal court. In accordance with this intent, Rule 68 should be interpreted to provide uniform, consistent incentives "to encourage the settlement of litigation." *Delta Air Lines, Inc. v. August, supra,* 450 U.S., at 352, 101 S.Ct., at 1150. Yet today's decision will lead to dramatically different settlement incentives depending on minor variations in the phraseology of the underlying fees-award statutes—distinctions that would appear to be nothing short of irrational and for which the Court has no plausible explanation.

Congress has enacted well over 100 attorney's fees statutes, many of which would appear to be affected by today's decision. As the Appendix to this dissent illustrates, Congress has employed a variety of slightly different wordings in these statutes. It sometimes has referred to the awarding of "attorney's fees *as part of* the costs," to "costs *including* attorney's fees," and to "attorney's fees and *other* litigation costs." Under the "plain language" approach of today's decision, Rule 68 will operate to *include* the potential loss of otherwise recoverable attorney's fees as an incentive to settlement in litigation under these statutes. But Congress frequently has referred in other statutes to the awarding of "costs *and* a reasonable attorney's fee," of "costs *together* with a reasonable attorney's fee," or simply of "attorney's fees" without reference to costs. Under the Court's "plain language" analysis, Rule 68 obviously will *not* include the potential loss of otherwise recoverable attorney's fees as a settlement incentive in litigation under these statutes because they do not refer to fees "as" costs.

The result is to sanction a senseless patchwork of fee shifting that flies in the face of the fundamental purpose of the Federal Rules—the provision of uniform and consistent procedure in federal courts. * * * [M]any statutes contain several fees-award provisions governing actions arising under different subsections, and the phraseology of these provisions sometimes differs slightly from section to section. It is simply preposterous to think that Congress or the drafters of the Rules intended to sanction differing applications of Rule 68 depending on which particular subsection of, *inter alia,* the Privacy Act of 1974, the Home Owners' Loan Act of 1933, the Outer Continental Shelf Lands Act Amendments of 1978, or the Interstate Commerce Act the plaintiff happened to invoke.

II

A

Although the Court's opinion fails to discuss any of the problems reviewed above, it does devote some space to arguing that its interpretation of Rule 68 "is in no sense inconsistent with the congressional policies underlying § 1983 and § 1988." * * *

The Court is wrong. Congress has instructed that attorney's fee entitlement under § 1988 be governed by a *reasonableness* standard. Until today the Court always has recognized that this standard precludes reliance on any mechanical "bright-line" rules automatically denying a portion of fees, acknowledging that such "mathematical approach[es]" provide "little aid in determining what is a reasonable fee in light of all the relevant factors." [*Hensley v. Eckerhart,*] 461 U.S., at 435–436, n. 11, 103 S.Ct., at 1040–1041, n. 11. * * * Section 1988's reasonableness standard is, in sum, "acutely sensitive to the merits of an action and to antidiscrimination policy." *Roadway Express, Inc. v. Piper,* 447 U.S., at 762, 100 S.Ct., at 2462.

Rule 68, on the other hand, is not "sensitive" at all to the merits of an action and to antidiscrimination policy. It is a mechanical *per se* provision automatically shifting "costs" incurred after an offer is rejected, and it deprives a district court of *all* discretion with respect to the matter by using "the strongest verb of its type known to the English language—'must.' " The potential for conflict between § 1988 and Rule 68 could not be more apparent.

Of course, a civil rights plaintiff who *unreasonably* fails to accept a settlement offer, and who thereafter recovers less than the proffered amount in settlement, is barred under § 1988 itself from recovering fees for unproductive work performed in the wake of the rejection. This is because "the extent of a plaintiff's success is *a* crucial factor in determining the proper amount of an award of attorney's fees"; hours that are "excessive, redundant, or otherwise unnecessary" must be excluded from that calculus. To this extent, the results might sometimes be the same under either § 1988's reasonableness inquiry or the Court's wooden application of Rule 68. Had the Court allowed the Seventh Circuit's remand in the instant case to stand, for example, the District Court after conducting the appropriate inquiry might well have determined that much or even all of the respondent's postoffer fees were unreasonably incurred and therefore not properly awardable.

But the results under § 1988 and Rule 68 will *not* always be congruent, because § 1988 mandates the careful consideration of a broad range of other factors and accords appropriate leeway to the district court's informed discretion. * * *

The Court argues * * * that its interpretation of Rule 68 "is neutral, favoring neither plaintiffs nor defendants." This contention is also plainly wrong. As the Judicial Conference Advisory Committee on the Federal Rules of Civil Procedure has noted twice in recent years, Rule 68 "is a 'one-way street,' available only to those defending against claims and not to claimants." Interpreting Rule 68 in its current version to include attorney's fees will lead to a number of skewed settlement incentives that squarely conflict with Congress' intent. To discuss but one example, Rule 68 allows an offer to be made any time after the complaint is filed and gives the plaintiff only 10 days to accept or reject. The Court's decision inevitably will encourage defendants who know they have violated the law to make "low-ball" offers immediately after suit is filed and before plaintiffs have been able to obtain the information they are entitled to by way of discovery to assess the strength of their claims and the reasonableness of the offers. The result will put severe pressure on plaintiffs to settle on the basis of inadequate information in order to avoid the risk of bearing all of their fees even if reasonable discovery might reveal that the defendants were subject to far greater liability. Indeed, because Rule 68 offers may be made recurrently without limitation, defendants will be well advised to make ever-slightly larger offers throughout the discovery process and before plaintiffs have conducted all reasonably necessary discovery.

This sort of so-called "incentive" is fundamentally incompatible with Congress' goals. Congress intended for "private citizens . . . to be able to assert their civil rights" and for "those who violate the Nation's fundamental laws" not to be able "to proceed with impunity." Accordingly, civil rights plaintiffs " 'appear before the court cloaked in a mantle of public interest' "; to promote the "*vigorous* enforcement of modern civil rights legislation," Congress has directed that such "private attorneys general" shall not "be deterred from bringing good faith actions to vindicate the fundamental rights here involved." Yet requiring plaintiffs to make wholly uninformed decisions on settlement offers, at the risk of *automatically* losing all of their postoffer fees no matter what the circumstances and notwithstanding the "excellent" results they might achieve after the full picture emerges, will work just such a deterrent effect.

Other difficulties will follow from the Court's decision. For example, if a plaintiff recovers less money than was offered before trial but obtains potentially far-reaching injunctive or declaratory relief, it is altogether unclear how the Court intends judges to go about quantifying the "value" of the plaintiff's success. And the Court's decision raises additional problems concerning representation and conflicts of interest in the context of civil rights class actions. These are difficult policy questions, and I do not mean to suggest that stronger settlement incentives would necessarily conflict with the effective enforcement of the civil rights laws. But contrary to the Court's 4–paragraph discussion, the policy considerations do not all point in one direction, and the question of whether and to what extent attorney's fees should be included within Rule 68 has provoked sharp debate in Congress, in the Advisory Committee on the Federal Rules, and among commentators. The Court has offered some interesting arguments based on an economic analysis of settlement incentives and aggregate results. But I believe Judge Posner had the better of this argument in concluding that the incentives created by interpreting Rule 68 in its current form to include attorney's fees would "cu[t] against the grain of section 1988," and that in any event a modification of Rule 68 to encompass fees is for Congress, not the courts.

Notes and Questions

1. Calculate what Chesny, the plaintiff, might have received if the Court had affirmed the Seventh Circuit and the District Court had granted an award of full attorneys fees. Compare it to what he received under the Court's holding.

2. Under Rule 68, what was Chesny obligated to pay in costs? The Court interprets the plaintiff's "costs" for purposes of Rule 68 as including attorney's fees because it imports the definition of costs from § 1988. Does this mean that Chesny had to pay the defendants' post-offer attorney's fees? Read § 1988 (in footnote 3 of Justice Brennan's dissent) again carefully. How is it different from the English Rule?

3. Rule 68 has been described as "the defendant's best friend." Why?

4. *Marek v. Chesny* describes Rule 68 as establishing a "clear policy of favoring settlement of all lawsuits" and some scholars claim that the whole structure of the litigation system reveals a "preference for private ordering." Samuel R. Gross & Kent D. Syverud, *Don't Try: Civil Jury Verdicts in a System Geared to Settlement*, 44 UCLA L. Rev. 1, 4 (1996). As you proceed through the course, try to think how each procedural rule affects settlement incentives and strategy.

CHAPTER 9

JURY TRIAL

When our civilization wants a library catalogued or the solar system discovered, or any trifle of that kind, it uses up its specialists. But when our civilization wishes anything done which is really serious, it collects 12 ordinary people standing around.

—G.K. Chesterton, *Alarms and Discussions* 212–13 (1911)

Many view trial by lay jury as one of the defining characteristics of the Anglo–American legal system. This is not to say that no other system uses juries. Many nations use some form of jury in criminal cases. A few non Anglo–American nations even allow juries in certain civil cases.[1] But while juries are not unique to the Anglo–American system, it is probably fair to say that in no other system has the jury played so significant a role in defining the nature of an institution. The jury originated in England prior to the Magna Carta. It has served over the centuries as a populist check on government, offsetting the power of the wealthier and often more elitist judges. In this fashion, the jury gave "12 ordinary people standing around" a limited role in government.

Given the crucial role that juries have played in Anglo–American legal history, you may be surprised to learn that the use of juries in civil cases has been steadily decreasing in most nations with an Anglo–American legal system. The lone exception is the United States. While jury trials in civil cases in the United Kingdom and Canada, for example, are increasingly rare, they remain commonplace in the United States.[2] Juries are widely used in both state and federal courts, and in a wide array of civil cases. Indeed, in the federal courts and most state systems, a party may even have a constitutional right to have her case heard by a jury. That the framers thought the right to a jury trial in a civil case was important enough to enshrine in the United States Constitution speaks volumes about the historic view of the jury in American legal history.

---

1. Sweden, for example, allows for jury trial in defamation cases involving the press.

2. The United Kingdom allows for juries only in certain types of civil cases. In Cana-

da, use of the jury varies from province to province. Throughout Canada, however, juries are used far less frequently than in the United States.

576

In the United States, then, it seems that juries are here to stay, at least for the foreseeable future. However, a jury trial presents a number of unique issues that do not arise in cases tried before a judge. This chapter explores these unique questions. Part A discusses the constitutional right to a jury in federal civil litigation. Part B discusses how a party demands a jury. Part C deals with the rules governing jury selection and deliberation.

A. THE CONSTITUTIONAL RIGHT TO A JURY TRIAL IN CIVIL CASES

The Seventh Amendment to the United States Constitution provides:

> In Suits at common law, where the value in controversy shall exceed twenty dollars, the right of trial by jury shall be preserved, and no fact tried by a jury, shall be otherwise reexamined in any Court of the United States, than according to the rules of the common law.

The Seventh Amendment is actually one of three separate provisions in the Constitution dealing with juries. Article III, § 2 and the Sixth Amendment both require a jury in criminal cases. The Seventh Amendment, by contrast, applies only to *civil* cases. Because there are a number of significant differences between the Seventh Amendment and these two other provisions, you should be careful not to confuse them. Precedent decided under the Sixth Amendment, for example, may or may not apply to the Seventh. You will learn more about the criminal trial jury provisions in courses such as Criminal Procedure.

One of the most important differences between the Seventh Amendment and these other provisions is that the Seventh Amendment applies only to cases being tried in *federal* court. The right to a jury trial in civil cases is one of the few provisions in the Bill of Rights that has been interpreted not to apply to the states. There is accordingly no Seventh Amendment right to a jury in state courts, even when those state courts are hearing federal or constitutional claims. However, that the Seventh Amendment does not apply does not mean that state courts operate without juries. Most state constitutions contain their own right to a jury trial (although not necessarily in the same situations as the Seventh Amendment). If a state constitution requires a jury, courts of that state will provide a jury in all covered cases regardless of whether the claim arises under state or federal law.

In addition to state constitutions, statutes may also afford litigants the right to a jury trial. Congress in particular has created a statutory right to juries in connection with several federal claims. When a federal statute requires a jury, the Seventh Amendment is not a factor. A party can demand a jury in such a case regardless of whether the case is being litigated in state or federal court.

Merely because a statute or constitutional provision provides a right to a jury in certain cases does not guarantee that a jury will be empanelled in a particular case. As discussed in part B of this Chapter, a party must file a timely demand for a jury. In addition, even if there is a timely demand, a court will empanel a jury only if there are contested factual issues in the case. *Garvie v. City of Fort Walton Beach*, 366 F.3d 1186 (11th Cir. 2004); *Harris v. Interstate Brands Corp.*, 348 F.3d 761 (8th Cir. 2003). The role of the jury, after all, is to determine the facts, not the law.

1. Applying the Seventh Amendment: A Historical Analysis

A careful reading of the Seventh Amendment reveals two unusual features. First, unlike most of the other civil rights set out in the Constitution, the Seventh Amendment does not *create* a right. Rather, it *preserves* the right to a jury as it existed in 1791, the year in which the amendment was ratified. Second, the Seventh Amendment does not require a jury in all civil cases, but only in "Suits at common law" involving more than $20. Those two restrictions are actually related. In the late 1700s, a litigant in the English courts was entitled to a jury only if he was litigating a "suit at common law." The amendment preserves that right. Therefore, to the extent federal courts would now be hearing suits at common law, they would continue to provide a jury.

But what is a suit at common law? In your other courses, you probably use the term "common law" as a synonym for judge-made rules of law, as opposed to "positive" law that comes from statutes, regulations, or a constitution. In the Seventh Amendment, however, the term has a very different meaning. The term "Suits at common law" is in fact a *jurisdictional* term rather than a distinction between legislation and judge-made law. A case is a suit at common law for purposes of the Seventh Amendment if it would be heard by a certain court, which historically was referred to as a "Law" or "Common Law" court. Note that a Law court could hear not only claims involving judge-made law, but also claims arising under statutes.

Unfortunately, one cannot understand which cases would be heard in the Law courts without a basic grounding in the English legal system in the eighteenth century. Actually, you have been exposed to some aspects of that system before, in the discussion of common-law pleading in Chapter 5. As you will recall, one key feature of the English system was that it was divided into several different court systems. In actual practice, there was a mind-numbing array of judicial and quasi-judicial bodies.[3] For our purposes, however, we need to focus on only three of these courts, and of these one needs only brief mention. Three of the most important royal courts were the courts of Law, Chancery (or Equity), and Admiralty. Of these three, only Law made use of juries.

---

3. History buffs may enjoy the colorful description of bodies such as the "sewer courts" in William Blackstone, *Commentaries on the Laws of England* 30 (1771), and the comprehensive organizational chart in the Introduction to Harold Potter, *A Short Outline of English Legal History* (3d ed. 1933, 2004 reprint).

Therefore, interpreting the Seventh Amendment requires knowledge of what sorts of cases would be heard in these three courts.[4]

Determining whether a case would be heard in Admiralty is relatively simple. Although admiralty jurisdiction in the United States is significantly broader than it was in England, the courts' jurisdiction is defined along geographic lines. Admiralty courts deals with claims (including both tort and contract) that occur on the high seas and navigable rivers and lakes. To this day, it is true that the Seventh Amendment does not give a party a right to a jury for admiralty claims. *Curtis v. Loether*, 415 U.S. 189, 193, 94 S.Ct. 1005, 39 L.Ed.2d 260 (1974); *Parsons v. Bedford*, 28 U.S. (3 Pet.) 474, 7 L.Ed. 732 (1807). However, several federal statutes that govern admiralty cases provide a *statutory* right to a jury.[5]

The more difficult question—and the one that has proven most troubling to the courts—is determining whether a given claim would be heard in Law or Equity. Unlike Admiralty, courts of Law and Equity had a jurisdiction that overlapped to a significant degree. At first, this overlapping jurisdiction caused a sort of power struggle between the two systems. During the reign of James I, however, English lawmakers reached a compromise that gave the Law courts primacy over private disputes. From that date on, a party could sue in Equity only if he could demonstrate that he could not obtain adequate relief in Law. In other words, although the same disputes could potentially be heard in Law or Equity, a party suing in Equity had to demonstrate that Equity afforded him some advantage not available in Law.

As you saw in Chapter 5, the writ system that applied in the Law courts placed a number of technical restrictions on that system. At the risk of oversimplification, we can group these differences into three categories: differences in remedies, procedures, and underlying substantive rights.

Remedy. Perhaps the most important difference between Law and Equity concerned what remedies were available in the two systems. The writ system limited what remedies a Law court could provide. Law's main remedy was *compensatory damages*. However, certain specific remedies were also available in Law, including *ejectment* (removing someone wrongfully occupying land) and *replevin* (return of personal property to the rightful owner).

A hallmark of Equity, by contrast, was its ability to devise a remedy to fit the situation. Many of the specific remedies you may have encountered in your other courses were devised in Equity. Although an exhaus-

---

4. As noted in Chapter 5, the North American colonies, and the states after independence, did not slavishly imitate the English system. It is especially noteworthy that in the federal system there were not separate courts of Law, Equity, and Admiralty. Instead, the same federal court would hear different sorts of cases at different times. However, because the purpose of the Seventh Amendment was to preserve the tradition established in the English courts, the historical practice in the United States is not controlling.

5. See the Jones Act, 46 U.S.C. § 688, the "saving to suitors" provision in the admiralty jurisdiction statute, 28 U.S.C. § 1333, and the Great Lakes Act, 28 U.S.C. § 1873.

tive list of equitable remedies is beyond the scope of this book, the main remedies available only in Equity included:

- *injunction* (which was probably the most important)
- *specific performance* of a contract
- *accounting* of profits from defendant's wrongful use of plaintiff's property
- *restitution* (often used in cases of unjust enrichment)
- *rescission* of a contract because of fraud, mistake, or other defect in formation
- *reformation* of a contract or conveyancing instrument such as a deed
- *constructive trust*, under which defendant is ordered to hold property for plaintiff's benefit

Although damages were usually the province of Law, in some situations Equity could also award damages. For example, under the *Equity clean-up doctrine* a court of Equity could award compensatory damages if such damages were incidental to equitable relief. Therefore, if P sued D for an injunction based on nuisance, the court of Equity could both grant the injunction and award L damages for the period prior to the injunction. No jury would be involved. Similarly, if a party sued based on a substantive right recognized only in Equity (as discussed below), the court could award damages.

To check your understanding of these differences, determine whether a jury would hear the following cases in 1791.

1. L leases the upstairs of her home to T. T plays his trombone quite loudly at odd hours, which clearly violates the lease. L sues T for damages for the noise.

2. Same, except that L sues T not for damages, but for an order requiring T to stop playing his trombone at odd hours.

3. Same as #1, except that L wants the court to order T to vacate the premises because of breach of the lease.

4. Same as #1, except that L wants the court to declare the lease null and void because T lied to L about T's plans to use the space as a practice room.

5. L leases the upstairs of her home to T. T holds trombone concerts in the leased space at odd hours, which clearly violates the lease. L sues T to recover the profits that T has earned from this wrongful use of the space.

Procedure. A second problem with suing in Law was that the writs also limited the procedure available in Law. One of the most significant limitations was that no discovery was available in Law. The modern concept of discovery, as well as related procedures such as the "creditor's bill," evolved in Equity as ways to ameliorate these limitations in Law. Equity was also much more liberal than Law when it came to the joinder of claims and parties. Certain joinder devices such as the class action and interpleader were originally available only in Equity.

Substantive Rights. Finally, the writ system that governed the Law courts only allowed for recovery if certain predicate facts existed. In some cases, a party had a claim that fell between two or more writs. If that party's case was nevertheless appealing, he could sue in Equity and hope that that court, in its discretion, would find in his favor. Some modern causes of action, such as cancellation of a contract because of fraud or mistake, and for breach of fiduciary duty, originated in Equity. If a party sued upon a claim cognizable only in Equity, Equity could award damages even though it tried the case without a jury.

2. Problems in Applying the Historical Approach to a Modern Procedural System

Until the mid–1800s, applying the Seventh Amendment was relatively straightforward. Following the Civil War, however, the American legal system began to change in various ways that made it increasingly difficult to apply the historical test. The first change was the increasing tendency for legislatures to create new *statutory* rights. If Congress or a state legislature creates a claim that did not exist in 1791, application of the historical test is indeterminate, as such as a claim was obviously not traditionally heard in either Law or Equity. Can a claim that did not exist in 1791 nevertheless qualify as a "Suit at common law?"

The second change was the merger of Law and Equity, which occurred in the federal courts in 1938 with the enactment of the Federal Rules. After merger, a party could combine both legal and equitable claims and defenses in the same proceeding. The Federal Rules also provided a uniform procedure, including many of the historically equitable procedural devices such as discovery, for all cases. Does merger create a right to a jury on equitable claims, and/or take away the right to a jury on legal claims? This section discusses how courts have adapted the Seventh Amendment to these changes.

a. *Statutory Claims*

INTRODUCTORY PROBLEM

Notwithstanding harsh criticism of the existing law from a variety of sources, Congress decides to expand its "No Child Left Behind" ["NCLB"] law. The new provisions seize on the act's ostensible theme of "accountability," and extend the statute to high schools and colleges. To ensure that schools and parents take an active role in ensuring quality education for America's youth, the modified law provides a number of statutory claims to students who think they have been shortchanged by the educational process.

Rocky recently was denied admission to the Northern Minnesota State University Law School. Sure that this denial was due to a deficiency in his undergraduate education, Rocky brings two separate cases under the NCLB statute. First, Rocky sues Whatsammata U, his undergraduate *alma mater*, under NCLB § 21. Section 21 allows a student to recover against any school that provides the student a "defective education." The statute allows the student to recover the difference between the value of a proper education and the value of the education he or she actually received. Rocky seeks one million dollars in this first case.

Rocky's second case is against Boris Badenov. Rocky lost his parents at a young age, and Boris was appointed Rocky's legal guardian until Rocky turned 21. In a money-saving move, when Rocky was 18 Boris decided to send him to Whatsamatta U instead of the academically stronger University of Frostbite Falls. Because Rocky blames Whatsamatta U for all his troubles, he sues Boris under NCLB § 22 for $500,000 in damages. Section 22 creates a statutory claim against "parents or legal guardians" who fail to satisfy their "fiduciary duty" to ensure that their wards receive a good education. Although state-law precedent would also afford Rocky a right to sue for breach of fiduciary duty, Rocky sues under NCLB to obtain a federal forum.

Rocky asks for a jury in both cases, but both defendants object. Whatsamatta U claims that Rocky's case against it cannot be a "Suit at common law" because no such claim existed in 1791. Boris, although recognizing that every jurisdiction in 1791 allowed a claim against a legal guardian for breach of fiduciary duty, nevertheless argues that Rocky is not entitled to a jury in his statutory action. Will the court empanel a jury in either (or both) cases?

CITY OF MONTEREY v. DEL MONTE DUNES AT MONTEREY, LTD.

526 U.S. 687, 119 S.Ct. 1624, 143 L.Ed.2d 882 (1999)

JUSTICE KENNEDY delivered the opinion of the Court, except as to Part IV–A–2.

This case began with attempts by the respondent, Del Monte Dunes, and its predecessor in interest to develop a parcel of land within the jurisdiction of the petitioner, the city of Monterey. The city, in a series of repeated rejections, denied proposals to develop the property, each time imposing more rigorous demands on the developers. Del Monte Dunes brought suit in the United States District Court for the Northern District of California, under Rev. Stat. § 1979, 42 U.S.C. § 1983. After protracted litigation, the case was submitted to the jury on Del Monte Dunes' theory that the city effected a regulatory taking or otherwise injured the property by unlawful acts, without paying compensation or providing an adequate postdeprivation remedy for the loss. The jury found for Del Monte Dunes, and the Court of Appeals affirmed.

The petitioner contends that the regulatory takings claim should not have been decided by the jury and that the Court of Appeals adopted an erroneous standard for regulatory takings liability. * * *

IV

* * * [T]he answer [to whether a jury should have been empaneled] depends on whether Del Monte Dunes had a statutory or constitutional right to a jury trial, and, if it did, the nature and extent of the right. Del Monte Dunes asserts the right to a jury trial is conferred by § 1983 and by the Seventh Amendment.

Under our precedents, "before inquiring into the applicability of the Seventh Amendment, we must 'first ascertain whether a construction of the statute is fairly possible by which the [constitutional] question may be avoided.' " *Feltner* v. *Columbia Pictures Television, Inc.,* 523 U.S. 340, 345, 118 S. Ct. 1279, 140 L. Ed. 2d 438 (1998).

The character of § 1983 is vital to our Seventh Amendment analysis, but the statute does not itself confer the jury right. Section 1983 authorizes a party who has been deprived of a federal right under the color of state law to seek relief through "an action at law, suit in equity, or other proper proceeding for redress." Del Monte Dunes contends that the phrase "action at law" is a term of art implying a right to a jury trial. We disagree, for this is not a necessary implication.

In *Lorillard* v. *Pons,* 434 U.S. 575, 583, 98 S. Ct. 866, 55 L. Ed. 2d 40 (1978), we found a statutory right to a jury trial in part because the statute authorized "legal ... relief." Our decision, however, did not rest solely on the statute's use of the phrase but relied as well on the statute's explicit incorporation of the procedures of the Fair Labor Standards Act, which had been interpreted to guarantee trial by jury in private actions. We decline, accordingly, to find a statutory jury right under § 1983 based solely on the authorization of "an action at law."

As a consequence, we must reach the constitutional question. The Seventh Amendment provides that "in Suits at common law, where the value in controversy shall exceed twenty dollars, the right of trial by jury shall be preserved...." Consistent with the textual mandate that the jury right be preserved, our interpretation of the Amendment has been guided by historical analysis comprising two principal inquiries. "We ask, first, whether we are dealing with a cause of action that either was tried at law at the time of the founding or is at least analogous to one that was." *Markman* v. *Westview Instruments, Inc.,* 517 U.S. 370, 376, 134 L. Ed. 2d 577, 116 S. Ct. 1384 (1996). "If the action in question belongs in the law category, we then ask whether the particular trial decision must fall to the jury in order to preserve the substance of the common-law right as it existed in 1791." *Ibid.*

A

With respect to the first inquiry, we have recognized that "suits at common law" include "not merely suits, which the common law recognized among its old and settled proceedings, but [also] suits in which *legal* rights were to be ascertained and determined, in contradistinction to those where equitable rights alone were recognized, and equitable remedies were administered." *Parsons* v. *Bedford,* 3 Peters 433, 447

(1830). The Seventh Amendment thus applies not only to common-law causes of action but also to statutory causes of action " 'analogous to common-law causes of action ordinarily decided in English law courts in the late 18th century, as opposed to those customarily heard by courts of equity or admiralty.' " *Feltner, supra,* at 348 (quoting *Granfinanciera, S. A.* v. *Nordberg,* 492 U.S. 33, 42 (1989)).

1.

* * * It is undisputed that when the Seventh Amendment was adopted there was no action equivalent to § 1983, framed in specific terms for vindicating constitutional rights. It is settled law, however, that the Seventh Amendment jury guarantee extends to statutory claims unknown to the common law, so long as the claims can be said to "sound basically in tort," and seek legal relief. *Curtis [v. Loether,* 415 U.S. 189, 195–96, 94 S. Ct. 1005, 39 L. Ed. 2d 260 (1974)].

As Justice Scalia explains, there can be no doubt that claims brought pursuant to § 1983 sound in tort. Just as common-law tort actions provide redress for interference with protected personal or property interests, § 1983 provides relief for invasions of rights protected under federal law. Recognizing the essential character of the statute, " 'we have repeatedly noted that 42 U.S.C. § 1983 creates a species of tort liability,' " *Heck v. Humphrey,* 512 U.S. 477, 483, 114 S. Ct. 2364, 129 L. Ed. 2d 383 (1994) (quoting *Memphis Community School Dist.* v. *Stachura,* 477 U.S. 299, 305 (1986)), and have interpreted the statute in light of the "background of tort liability," *Monroe* v. *Pape,* 365 U.S. 167, 187 (1961). Our settled understanding of § 1983 and the Seventh Amendment thus compel [*sic*] the conclusion that a suit for legal relief brought under the statute is an action at law.

Here Del Monte Dunes sought legal relief. It was entitled to proceed in federal court under § 1983 because, at the time of the city's actions, the State of California did not provide a compensatory remedy for temporary regulatory takings. The constitutional injury alleged, therefore, is not that property was taken but that it was taken without just compensation. Had the city paid for the property or had an adequate postdeprivation remedy been available, Del Monte Dunes would have suffered no constitutional injury from the taking alone. Because its statutory action did not accrue until it was denied just compensation, in a strict sense Del Monte Dunes sought not just compensation *per se* but rather damages for the unconstitutional denial of such compensation. Damages for a constitutional violation are a legal remedy. See, *e.g., Teamsters* v. *Terry,* 494 U.S. 558, 570, 108 L. Ed. 2d 519, 110 S. Ct. 1339 (1990) ("Generally, an action for money damages was 'the traditional form of relief offered in the courts of law' ") (quoting *Curtis, supra,* at 196).

Even when viewed as a simple suit for just compensation, we believe Del Monte Dunes' action sought essentially legal relief. "We have recognized the 'general rule' that monetary relief is legal." *Feltner,* 523 U.S.

at 352 (quoting *Teamsters* v. *Terry, supra,* at 570). Just compensation, moreover, differs from equitable restitution and other monetary remedies available in equity, for in determining just compensation, "the question is what has the owner lost, not what has the taker gained." *Boston Chamber of Commerce* v. *Boston,* 217 U.S. 189, 195 (1910). As its name suggests, then, just compensation is, like ordinary money damages, a compensatory remedy. The Court has recognized that compensation is a purpose "traditionally associated with legal relief." *Feltner, supra,* at 352. Because Del Monte Dunes' statutory suit sounded in tort and sought legal relief, it was an action at law.

2.

In attempt to avoid the force of this conclusion, the city urges us to look not to the statutory basis of Del Monte Dunes' claim but rather to the underlying constitutional right asserted. At the very least, the city asks us to create an exception to the general Seventh Amendment rule governing § 1983 actions for claims alleging violations of the Takings Clause of the Fifth Amendment. Because the jury's role in estimating just compensation in condemnation proceedings was inconsistent and unclear at the time the Seventh Amendment was adopted, this Court has said "that there is no constitutional right to a jury in eminent domain proceedings." *United States* v. *Reynolds,* 397 U.S. 14, 18 (1970). The city submits that the analogy to formal condemnation proceedings is controlling, so that there is no jury right here. * * *

Although condemnation proceedings spring from the same Fifth Amendment right to compensation which, as incorporated by the Fourteenth Amendment, is applicable here, a condemnation action differs in important respects from a § 1983 action to redress an uncompensated taking. Most important, when the government initiates condemnation proceedings, it concedes the landowner's right to receive just compensation and seeks a mere determination of the amount of compensation due. Liability simply is not an issue. As a result, even if condemnation proceedings were an appropriate analogy, condemnation practice would provide little guidance on the specific question whether Del Monte Dunes was entitled to a jury determination of liability. * * *

Our conclusion is confirmed by precedent. Early authority finding no jury right in a condemnation proceeding did so on the ground that condemnation did not involve the determination of legal rights because liability was undisputed * * *.

In these circumstances, we conclude the cause of action sounds in tort and is most analogous to the various actions that lay at common law to recover damages for interference with property interests. Our conclusion is consistent with the original understanding of the Takings Clause and with historical practice. * * *

B.

Having decided Del Monte Dunes' § 1983 suit was an action at law, we must determine whether the particular issues of liability were proper for determination by the jury. See *Markman* v. *Westview Instruments, Inc.,* 517 U.S. 370 (1996). In actions at law, issues that are proper for the jury must be submitted to it "to preserve the right to a jury's resolution of the ultimate dispute," as guaranteed by the Seventh Amendment. 517 U.S. at 377. We determine whether issues are proper for the jury, when possible, "by using the historical method, much as we do in characterizing the suits and actions within which [the issues] arise." *Id.* at 378. We look to history to determine whether the particular issues, or analogous ones, were decided by judge or by jury in suits at common law at the time the Seventh Amendment was adopted. Where history does not provide a clear answer, we look to precedent and functional considerations.

1.

Just as no exact analogue of Del Monte Dunes' § 1983 suit can be identified at common law, so also can we find no precise analogue for the specific test of liability submitted to the jury in this case. We do know that in suits sounding in tort for money damages, questions of liability were decided by the jury, rather than the judge, in most cases. This allocation preserved the jury's role in resolving what was often the heart of the dispute between plaintiff and defendant. Although these general observations provide some guidance on the proper allocation between judge and jury of the liability issues in this case, they do not establish a definitive answer.

2.

We look next to our existing precedents. Although this Court has decided many regulatory takings cases, none of our decisions has addressed the proper allocation of liability determinations between judge and jury in explicit terms. This is not surprising. Most of our regulatory takings decisions have reviewed suits against the United States, suits decided by state courts, or suits seeking only injunctive relief. It is settled law that the Seventh Amendment does not apply in these contexts. * * *

3.

In actions at law predominantly factual issues are in most cases allocated to the jury. The allocation rests on a firm historical foundation, see, *e.g.,* 1 E. Coke, Institutes 155b (1628) *("ad quaestionem facti non respondent judices; ad quaestionem juris non respondent juratores"),* and serves "to preserve the right to a jury's resolution of the ultimate dispute."

Almost from the inception of our regulatory takings doctrine, we have held that whether a regulation of property goes so far that "there must be an exercise of eminent domain and compensation to sustain the act . . . depends upon the particular facts." *Pennsylvania Coal Co.* v. *Mahon,* 260 U.S. 393, 413 (1922). Consistent with this understanding, we have described determinations of liability in regulatory takings cases as " 'essentially ad hoc, factual inquiries,' " *Lucas [v. South Carolina Coastal Council*, 505 U.S. 1003, 1015 (1992) (quoting *Penn Central Transp. Co.* v. *New York City*, 438 U.S. 104, 124 (1978)), requiring "complex factual assessments of the purposes and economic effects of government actions."

In accordance with these pronouncements, we hold that the issue whether a landowner has been deprived of all economically viable use of his property is a predominantly factual question. * * * [I]n actions at law otherwise within the purview of the Seventh Amendment, this question is for the jury.

The jury's role in determining whether a land-use decision substantially advances legitimate public interests within the meaning of our regulatory takings doctrine presents a more difficult question. Although our cases make clear that this inquiry involves an essential factual component, it no doubt has a legal aspect as well, and is probably best understood as a mixed question of fact and law.

In this case, the narrow question submitted to the jury was whether, when viewed in light of the context and protracted history of the development application process, the city's decision to reject a particular development plan bore a reasonable relationship to its proffered justifications. As the Court of Appeals recognized, this question was "essentially fact-bound [in] nature." 95 F.3d at 1430. Under these circumstances, we hold that it was proper to submit this narrow, factbound question to the jury. * * *

JUSTICE SCALIA, concurring in part and concurring in the judgment.

I join all except Part IV–A–2 of JUSTICE KENNEDY's opinion. In my view, all § 1983 actions must be treated alike insofar as the Seventh Amendment right to jury trial is concerned; that right exists when monetary damages are sought; and the issues submitted to the jury in the present case were properly sent there. * * *

The Seventh Amendment inquiry looks first to the "nature of the statutory action." *Feltner* v. *Columbia Pictures Television, Inc.*, 523 U.S. 340, 348, (1998). The only "statutory action" here is a § 1983 suit. The question before us, therefore, is not what common-law action is most analogous to some generic suit seeking compensation for a Fifth Amendment taking, but what common-law action is most analogous *to a § 1983 claim*. The fact that the breach of duty which underlies the particular § 1983 claim at issue here—a Fifth Amendment takings violation—may give rise to *another* cause of action besides a § 1983 claim, namely a so-called inverse condemnation suit, which is (according to Part IV–A–2 of JUSTICE KENNEDY's opinion) or is not (according to JUSTICE SOUTER's opinion) entitled to be tried before a jury, seems to me irrelevant. The central question remains whether a *§ 1983 suit* is entitled to a jury. * * *

JUSTICE SOUTER, with whom JUSTICE O'CONNOR, JUSTICE GINSBURG, and JUSTICE BREYER join, concurring in part and dissenting in part.

* * * Respondents had no right to a jury trial either by statute or under the Constitution; the District Court thus erred in submitting their claim to a jury. In holding to the contrary, that such a right does exist under the Seventh Amendment, the Court misconceives a taking claim under § 1983 and draws a false analogy between such a claim and a tort action. I respectfully dissent from the erroneous Parts III and IV of the Court's opinion. * * *

[Justice Souter first argued that the closest historic analogy was a condemnation proceeding.]

The reason that direct condemnation proceedings carry no jury right is not that they fail to qualify as "Suits at common-law" within the meaning of the Seventh Amendment's guarantee, for we may assume that they are indeed common law proceedings. The reason there is no right to jury trial, rather, is that the Seventh Amendment "preserves" the common law right where it existed at the time of the framing, but does not create a right where none existed then. There is no jury right, then, because condemnation proceedings carried "no uniform and established right to a common law jury trial in England or the colonies at the time . . . the Seventh Amendment was adopted." 5 J. Moore, J. Lucas, & J. Wicker, *Moore's Federal Practice* P38.32[1], p. 38–268 (2d ed. 1996). See, *e.g.*, *Atlas Roofing Co.* v. *Occupational Safety and Health Review Comm'n,* 430 U.S. 442, 458 (1977) ("Condemnation was a suit at common law but constitutionally could be tried without a jury"). * * *

Notes and Questions

1. As discussed above, Congress can—and sometimes has—created a right to a jury trial in connection with a new statutory claim. Therefore, before turning to the constitutional issue, the Court first considers whether § 1983, the statute creating the underlying claim, also provides for a jury trial. The Court concludes that the statute does not. And yet, the statute explicitly allows aggrieved parties to bring an "action at law." Do you understand why the Court concludes that this language—which is virtually identical to the language in the Seventh Amendment—is not enough to guarantee a jury trial?

2. After concluding that § 1983 did not itself require a jury, the Court turns to the issue of whether the Seventh Amendment requires a jury in an action arising under that statute. As *City of Monterey* and several other Supreme Court cases have concluded, the simple fact that a claim is based on a statute rather than judge-made law is not controlling. Instead, the Court looks to the *nature* of the statutory cause of action. In your own words, restate the two-part test that the Court uses when dealing with a statute.

3. The first part of the test attempts to analogize the statutory claim to an action that existed in 1791. If the analogous action would have been heard in Law, the statutory claim falls under the Seventh Amendment.

Where Justices Kennedy and Souter differ is whether a traditional eminent domain proceeding is the closest analogue. Government exercises its power of eminent domain when it takes private property. In *City of Monterey*, the plaintiff was claiming that the City for all practical purposes condemned its property by refusing to allow development. Given this basic similarity, how can Justice Kennedy conclude that eminent domain is not the best analogue?

4. The eminent domain proceeding was in some respects a historic anomaly. Although such actions were tried in Law, they were tried *without a jury*. Therefore, as there was no right to a jury in such a case in 1791, no jury is required by the Seventh Amendment.

5. Justice Kennedy found that the more appropriate analogy was a tort claim. However, that finding alone did not determine the question. Do you see why not? In 1791, where would a party sue to recover for a tort? Why did Justice Kennedy take such pains to point out that the plaintiff was in essence seeking damages?

6. In earlier opinions, the Supreme Court has indicated that when applying the test for statutory claims, the nature of the relief is "more important" than the historical analogue. *See, e.g., Chauffers, Teamsters & Helpers, Local No. 391 v. Terry*, 494 U.S. 558, 565, 110 S.Ct. 1339, 108 L.Ed.2d 519 (1990). Does Justice Kennedy's opinion reject that view?

One problem with focusing exclusively on the type of relief sought is that in some situations the same remedy could be provided in both systems. As discussed above, for example, Equity could award damages when hearing a claim, such as breach of fiduciary duty, that was recognized only in Equity. Suppose that Congress passed a statute simply codifying the historic action for breach of fiduciary duty. If plaintiff sued for damages under that statute, would the claim be heard with a jury because the "nature of the relief"— damages—was legal? *See In re Hutchinson*, 5 F.3d 750 (4th Cir. 1993).

7. *Restitution.* One of the most persistent and vexing problems that arises in the first part of the test is distinguishing damages from the equitable remedy of restitution. Damages and restitution both involve the payment of money to plaintiff because of harm that defendant caused to plaintiff. Although the precedent on this issue is complex and often inconsistent, the Supreme Court has held that a claim involves restitution when it requires defendant to disgorge property *in its possession or control* that should rightly go to plaintiff. *See generally Chauffers*, 494 U.S. at 571 (money that union members failed to receive because of union's breach of duty of fair representation is damages rather than restitution because it was not "money wrongfully held by the Union"); *Porter v. Warner Holding Co.*, 328 U.S. 395, 402, 66 S.Ct. 1086, 90 L.Ed. 1332 (1946) (restitution involves "restoring the status quo and ordering return of that which rightfully belongs to" plaintiff). The most difficult issue seems to be when a party seeks backpay in a discrimination case. Depending on the statute in question, the lower courts have held backpay awards to be either legal or equitable. *Compare Sullivan v. School Board of Pinellas County*, 773 F.2d 1182, 1187 (11th Cir. 1985) (backpay under 42 U.S.C. §§ 1981 and 1983 is equitable) *with Sailor v. Hubbell, Inc.*, 4 F.3d 323, 325 (4th Cir. 1993) (back pay under Age Discrimination in Employment Act, 29 U.S.C. §§ 621–634, is legal).

8. The second part of the test, discussed in Part IV.B of the majority opinion, considers whether use of a jury to decide the question is "proper." Like the first part, this part also looks to history and custom. If there is a history of having juries decide analogous questions, then it is more likely to be proper to have a jury decide the question at hand. Why did the Court conclude that this part of the test was satisfied? Given that juries historically did *not* decide compensation in eminent domain proceedings, doesn't history suggest that this sort of issue is not a proper one for the jury?

Is the majority's ruling on the second part of the test based on the simple fact that the jury is deciding facts rather than law? But deciding facts is what juries *do*. Can you conceive of a situation where it would *not* be proper to have the jury decide facts? Consider *Markman v. Westview Instruments, Inc.*, 517 U.S. 370, 116 S.Ct. 1384, 134 L.Ed.2d 577 (1996). In that case, plaintiff sued defendant for damages for patent infringement. To recover for infringement, plaintiff had to show that defendant made, used, or sold something that fell within plaintiff's rights under the patent. The Supreme Court held that while the jury could determine damages, the *judge* would determine the scope of the plaintiff's patent. In reaching this conclusion, the Court noted that in 1791 there was nothing analogous to the modern process by which a court determines the scope of a patent. That lack of historical tradition, coupled with the complex scientific questions involved in determining the scope of a patent, led the Court to conclude that it would not be proper for the jury to decide the question of scope. Note, however, that the Court did not suggest that an issue could be taken from a jury simply because it is complex. Instead, it is also necessary that the issue be of a type that was not historically allocated to a jury.

b. Problems Arising from the Merger of Law and Equity

INTRODUCTORY PROBLEM

Candid Cameras operates a camera shop in the local shopping mall. Candid leases its space from Molly, the mall's owner. The lease between Molly and Candid provides that Candid may use the space only for the "sale of cameras and/or photographic equipment." However, the lease also provides that Molly cannot recover damages if Candid violates the use restriction. Instead, her remedy is limited to declaring the lease terminated, and taking the space back from Candid. In return for including the use restriction, Molly agreed in the lease not to rent any other space in the mall to a tenant who sells goods "similar to" those sold by Candid.

The Molly–Candid lease is several years old, predating the advent of digital photography. When digital cameras first started to become popular, Candid began to stock photo-editing computer software and computer add-ons specifically designed for photo editing. Now that digital photography is all the rage, Candid has decided to quit carrying cameras altogether, and concentrate on the sale of photo-editing software and computer add-ons. However, Candid has two concerns. First, Candid is worried that this change in the nature of its store might put it in violation of the use restrictions in its lease. Although the only remedy for such a violation would be loss of its space, Candid would rather keep its lucrative location in the mall. Second, Candid has learned that Molly is negotiating with a prospective tenant who plans to open a store selling computer software (including photo-editing software) and accessories. In Candid's opinion, Molly would violate the exclusivity provision in the Molly–Candid lease should she enter into a lease with this prospective tenant.

Because of these concerns, Candid sues Molly in federal court, based on diversity jurisdiction. Candid files two claims. First, it asks for a declaratory judgment stating that because photo-editing software and related computer accessories qualify as "photographic equipment," Candid would not violate the use restrictions in the lease if it quits selling cameras and sells only such software and accessories. Second, Candid asks for an injunction barring Molly from entering into a lease with the prospective tenant. Molly files a counterclaim in the action, in which she claims that Candid violated its obligation, explicitly set out in the lease, to participate in the mall's annual sidewalk sale. Molly seeks damages under this counterclaim.

Molly files a timely demand for a jury. The case has boiled down to the following issues:

1) Would Candid breach the use restriction in the lease if it quit selling cameras and sold only photo-editing software and computer accessories for photo-editing?

2) Would Molly violate the exclusivity provision in the lease if she entered into a lease with the prospective tenant?

3) If Molly would violate the exclusivity provision in the lease by leasing space to the prospective tenant, is Candid entitled to an injunction?

4) Did Candid violate the terms of its lease by refusing to participate in the sidewalk sale?

5) If Candid did violate its lease by refusing to participate, what are Molly's damages?

Will a jury decide any or all of these issues?

The historical test for applying the Seventh Amendment assumes a clear line between Law and Equity. Although the federal system and some states did not maintain separate *courts* of Law and Equity in the eighteenth century, they did usually require that legal and equitable claims be presented in separate *cases*. Even if a person's legal and equitable claims arose from the same event, they had to be tried in different proceedings, one with a jury and the other without. The main exception—a fairly limited one at that—was the Equity clean-up doctrine, which allowed a party to bring legal claims as an incident to a case that was predominantly equitable. Even under this doctrine, however, the entire case was tried in Equity without a jury.

Today, most system have "merged" Law and Equity, and allow for all legal and equitable claims and defenses to be tried together. In the federal courts, this merger occurred in 1938, when the Federal Rules came into force. Federal Rule 2 provides, "There shall be one form of action to be known as 'civil action.' " Federal Rule 18 makes it clear that a party may join "as many claims, legal, equitable, or maritime, as the party has against an opposing party." In the unitary civil action, a wide array of traditional equitable procedural devices, such as class actions and discovery, are available.

The unitary civil action, however, presents a real problem for a court trying to apply the Seventh Amendment. What should a court do if only part of a case would traditionally have been tried by a jury? Should the court try to determine if the legal or equitable portion of the case predominates, and grant or deny a jury accordingly? Or is a more discriminating approach possible?

MARSEILLES HYDRO POWER, LLC v. MARSEILLES LAND AND WATER COMPANY

299 F.3d 643 (7th Cir. 2002)

POSNER, Circuit Judge.

The plaintiff ("the power company") owns a disused hydroelectric plant built in 1912. When functional the plant was powered by water from a canal, owned by the defendant ("the canal company"), that connects the plant to the Illinois River. A contract between the parties' predecessors required the owner of the plant to pay rent to the owner of the canal and required the latter to keep the canal in good repair. The requirement had no practical significance when the plant was not being used. But the current owner of the plant, that is, the power company, decided to put the plant back into service and so it became concerned about the state of the canal and in particular feared that the canal's wall was about to collapse. The canal company refused to repair it, and so the power company brought this suit to enforce the canal company's duty under the contract and moved for a preliminary injunction; but before the motion could be heard, the canal wall collapsed. [The power company brought three claims. First, it sought an injunction to keep the canal company from preventing the power company from entering the canal company's land to repair the canal. Second, it asked the court to grant it a lien on the canal company's land to pay for these repairs. Finally, it asked the court for a declaratory judgment that the power company was relieved of its obligation to pay rent to the canal company because of the latter's failure to keep the canal in repair.] The canal company counterclaimed for the rent due under the contract, rent that the power company refused to pay until the canal was repaired. After a bench trial, the judge awarded judgment for the power company both on its complaint and on the canal company's counterclaim. The judgment seems (the reason for this hedge will appear momentarily) to include an order injunctive in character that entitles the power company to enter upon the canal company's property for the purpose of repairing the canal wall and to obtain a lien on the property for the cost of the repair. * * *

[T]he canal company's principal argument, and the only one we strictly need to consider, is that it was entitled to a jury trial. Rule 38(b) of the civil rules gives a party only ten days "after the service of the last pleading directed to the issue" (that is, "any issue triable of right by a jury," *id.*) to demand a jury trial on that issue. The canal company filed its demand within ten days after serving on the power company its counterclaim demanding payment of the rent specified in the contract for the use of the canal, which the power company had decided to withhold until the canal was repaired. The district judge thought the demand had come too late, because the rent issue was clearly flagged in the power company's complaint; part of the declaratory judgment sought was a declaration that the power company owed no rent until the canal was back in working order.

The power company and the judge were confused by the word "issue" in Rule 38(b). They think it means that if an issue *could* give rise to a claim for damages, either party can demand that it be tried to a jury. That is not correct. If the only relief sought is equitable, such as an injunction or specific performance (a type of affirmative injunction), neither the party seeking that relief nor the party opposing it is entitled to a jury trial. Rule 38(a), so far as applicable to this case, creates a right to a jury trial merely coextensive with the Seventh Amendment, which in turn confines that right to "Suits at common law." A suit seeking only equitable relief is not a suit at common law, regardless of the nature of the issues likely or even certain to arise in the case, most of which indeed might be legal, such as whether the canal company broke its contract with the power company, an issue normally determined by the common law of contracts rather than by some principle of equity jurisprudence. * * *

The complaint in this case sought an injunction against the canal company's preventing the power company from going on the canal company's land to repair the canal at the latter's expense, as well as specific performance (the granting of a lien), also a form of equitable relief. If that were all, it would be clear there was no right to a jury trial. But declaratory relief was also sought. Despite the equitable origins of such relief, the Supreme Court has said that actions for declaratory judgments are "neither legal nor equitable." *Gulfstream Aerospace Corp. v. Mayacamas Corp.*, 485 U.S. 271, 284 (1988). (So much for the historical test for Seventh Amendment rights.) Rule 57 of the civil rules provides that "the procedure for obtaining a declaratory judgment pursuant to [the Declaratory Judgment Act, 28 U.S.C. § 2201] shall be in accordance with these rules, and the right to trial by jury may be demanded under the circumstances and in the manner provided in Rules 38 and 39." In other words, casting one's suit in the form of a suit for a declaratory judgment, or adding a claim for a declaratory judgment to one's other claim or claims for relief, does not create a right to a jury trial. Rather, as the Third Circuit put it nicely in *Owens–Illinois, Inc. v. Lake Shore Land Co.*, 610 F.2d 1185, 1189 (3d Cir. 1979), "If the declaratory judgment action does not fit into one of the existing equitable patterns but is essentially an inverted law suit—an action brought by one who would have been a defendant at common law—then the parties have a right to a jury. But if the action is the counterpart of a suit in equity, there is no such right." See also *Beacon Theatres, Inc. v. Westover*, 359 U.S. 500, 504 (1959). We prefer the formulation that we just quoted from *Owens-Illinois* to that in *Petition of Rosenman & Colin*, 850 F.2d 57, 60 (2d Cir. 1988): "the nature of the underlying dispute determines whether a jury trial is available." The "nature of the underlying dispute" here is breach of contract, but a plaintiff who is seeking equitable relief and not damages cannot wrest an entitlement to a jury trial by the facile expedient of attaching a claim for declaratory judgment. Otherwise anyone seeking an injunction could obtain a jury trial.

So neither the power company nor the canal company had a right to demand a jury trial on the basis of the complaint. Any such right would have had to arise later. It did arise later; it arose when the canal company counter-claimed for the withheld rent. Founded on an alleged breach of contract by the power company, the counter-claim was a claim for damages and hence—despite its being a counterclaim rather than a free-standing lawsuit, since a counterclaim *is* a suit, only joined for economy with an existing suit—it was a suit at common law within the meaning of the Seventh Amendment. The canal company's demand for a jury, filed within ten days after the counterclaim, was the earliest either party could have demanded a jury trial. At that point the fact that there was a common issue underlying both the equitable and the legal claims, namely the duty if any of the power company to pay rent, and under that issue perhaps the deeper issue of which party had actually broken the contract, became significant. Common issues, if triable at all in the sense that their resolution requires resolving a material dispute of fact, as was the case here, must be tried to a jury in order to prevent a judge's determination from foreclosing a party's right to have the issues in a common law suit tried by a jury. So the demand for a jury trial was timely and its rejection error; and until the jury trial to which the canal company is entitled is completed issuance of an injunction is premature.
* * *

Reversed and remanded.

Notes and Questions

1. Note that a right to a jury can arise because of a claim in the complaint, or, as in *Marseilles Hydro*, from a counterclaim asserted in the answer. The right may similarly stem from a cross-claim or third-party claim.

2. In *City of Monterey* on p. 582, the plaintiff sought a jury based on a claim in its complaint. In *Marseilles Hydro*, the defendant sought a jury based on a counterclaim in its answer. Does this mean that only the party stating a legal claim has the right to insist on a jury trial? Suppose the demand for a jury in *Marseilles Hydro* had been filed by the plaintiff and opposed by the defendant. Same result? *See* Federal Rule 38(b).

3. *Marseilles Hydro* also illustrates how a court deals with a case involving a mixture of legal and equitable claims. This analysis is often called the *Beacon Theatres* test, after the 1959 Supreme Court case of *Beacon Theatres, Inc. v. Westover*, 359 U.S. 500, 79 S.Ct. 948, 3 L.Ed.2d 988 (1959), that established the basic approach. Prior to *Beacon Theatres,* a court would attempt to determine whether the case, as a whole, was "essentially" legal or equitable, and would either deny or grant a jury for the entire case accordingly. The *Beacon Theatres* rejects this all-or-nothing approach, and instead requires the court to divide the case into its various claims. Under this analysis, the jury will decide all issues relating to the legal claims, while the judge will decide the equitable issues. That rule seems at first glance to be eminently logical and relatively simple. The problem, however, is that in many cases the legal and equitable claims will share one or more factual issues. In *Marseilles Hydro*, for example, plaintiff's equitable claim for an injunction and defendant's legal counterclaim shared the issue of whether the plaintiff was required to pay rent. Does the judge or the jury decide these shared issues?

4. Courts applying the *Beacon Theatres* test sometimes state that the jury must decide all issues relevant to the legal claims "first," after which the judge decides any remaining, purely equitable, issues. But technically the case need not proceed in that order. A judge could decide all the purely equitable questions first, and then let the jury decide the solely legal and shared issues. 3 James W. Moore, Allan D. Vestal, and Philip B. Kurland, *Moore's Manual: Federal Practice and Procedure* 2–40 (2001). Regardless of whether the judge or the jury decides first, the judge is bound by the jury's findings on the legal and shared issues. The findings on the shared issues often will dictate whether a party succeeds on its equitable claims.

5. *Declaratory Judgments.* The first steps in the *Beacon Theatres* test are to determine exactly what claims have been filed in the lawsuit and to label those claims as legal or equitable (or maritime, which fall within admiralty jurisdiction). In *Marseilles Hydro*, applying that analysis to the plaintiff's injunction and specific performance claims, and to defendant's damages counterclaim, is easy. Plaintiff's claims are equitable, while the counterclaim is legal.

But plaintiff had also presented a third claim: a request for a declaratory judgment. Declaratory judgments did not exist in 1791, and thus cannot automatically be classified as legal or equitable. The court's opinion sets out the accepted approach for dealing with these claims. This approach recognizes that declaratory judgments exist mainly to allow a party who anticipates being sued on a claim to "accelerate" that dispute and have it decided now rather than later. Therefore, the analysis of declaratory judgment looks beyond the form of the case, and instead asks what suit would have occurred at some later date if the party had not sought the declaration. If the later suit would involve a legal claim, the declaratory judgment will also be treated as legal; while if the later suit would have been equitable, no jury will be used on the declaratory judgment claim. Do you agree with Judge Posner's conclusion that the declaratory judgment in this case is equitable? Had plaintiff not sought the declaration, what would eventually have happened?

Note that you encountered a similar test for declaratory judgments when you studied subject matter jurisdiction in Chapter 3. When determining whether a declaratory judgment presents a federal question, courts look past the declaratory judgment and ask if the suit that would eventually have occurred would have been a federal question. See Note 6, p. 60.

6. A federal statute, 28 U.S.C. § 2201, gives a person the right to seek a declaratory judgment. Given that the right to seek a declaratory judgment arises under a federal statute, do you understand why the court eschews the two-part test for statutory claims that was discussed in the prior section?

7. Rule 39(c) also allows a federal court to use an *advisory jury* to decide claims that cannot be tried as of right to a jury. Unlike a jury's findings on legal issues, findings by an advisory jury are merely recommendations that the judge can accept or reject as he sees fit. In *Marseilles Hydro*, the court could have assigned all factual determinations to the jury. Although the findings on the legal issues would be binding, the findings on the solely equitable issues would have been recommendations.

c. The Effect of the Federal Rules on Historically Equitable Claims

In 1791, the English Law courts were bound by a number of technical restrictions that could cause serious practical problems for litigants. A party who needed to use discovery, or who wanted to file the case as a class action or interpleader case, could only find relief in Equity, as those procedures were not available in Law. The Federal Rules, however, borrowed many of the more useful features of Equity practice and made them available in all cases. Does the fact that discovery, class actions, and the like are now available in traditionally legal cases affect the right to a jury trial?

ROSS v. BERNHARD

396 U.S. 531, 90 S.Ct. 733, 24 L.Ed.2d 729 (1970)

Mr. Justice WHITE delivered the opinion of the Court.

[Plaintiffs, stockholders of an investment company, brought a shareholders derivative action against the directors of the company, alleging that the directors harmed the company by violating certain federal laws. Plaintiffs sought damages and asked for a jury. The Court held that the Seventh Amendment required a jury, even though a shareholder's derivative action could historically be brought only in Equity.]

However difficult it may have been to define with precision the line between actions at law dealing with legal rights and suits in equity dealing with equitable matters, some proceedings were unmistakably actions at law triable to a jury. * * * [A] corporation's suit to enforce a legal right was an action at common law carrying the right to jury trial at the time the Seventh Amendment was adopted.

The common law refused, however, to permit stockholders to call corporate managers to account in actions at law. * * * Early in the 19th century, equity provided relief both in this country and in England. * * * The remedy made available in equity was the derivative suit, viewed in this country as a suit to enforce a corporate cause of action against officers, directors, and third parties. * * *

Derivative suits posed no Seventh Amendment problems where the action against the directors and third parties would have been by a bill in equity had the corporation brought the suit. Our concern is with cases based upon a legal claim of the corporation against directors or third parties. Does the trial of such claims at the suit of a stockholder and without a jury violate the Seventh Amendment?

* * * The Seventh Amendment question depends on the nature of the issue to be tried rather than the character of the overall action. * * *

We have noted that the derivative suit has dual aspects: first, the stockholder's right to sue on behalf of the corporation, historically an equitable matter; second, the claim of the corporation against directors or third parties on which, if the corporation had sued and the claim presented legal issues, the company could demand a jury trial. * * * The heart of the action is the corporate claim. If it presents a legal issue, one entitling the corporation to a jury trial under the Seventh Amendment, the right to a jury is not forfeited merely because the stockholder's right to sue must first be adjudicated as an equitable issue triable to the court. * * *

If under older procedures, now discarded, a court of equity could properly try the legal claims of the corporation presented in a derivative suit, it was because irreparable injury was threatened and no remedy at law existed as long as the stockholder was without standing to sue and the corporation itself refused to pursue its own remedies. * * *

Actions are no longer brought as actions at law or suits in equity. Under the Rules there is only one action—a "civil action"—in which all claims may be joined and all remedies are available. Purely procedural impediments to the presentation of any issue by any party, based on the difference between law and equity, were destroyed. In a civil action presenting a stockholder's derivative claim, the court after passing upon the plaintiff's right to sue on behalf of the corporation is now able to try the corporate claim for damages with the aid of a jury. * * * Under the rules, law and equity are procedurally combined; nothing turns now upon the form of the action or the procedural devices by which the parties happen to come before the court. * * *

Thus, for example, before-merger class actions were largely a device of equity, and there was no right to a jury even on issues that might, under other circumstances, have been tried to a jury. * * * [I]t now seems settled in the lower federal courts that class action plaintiffs may obtain a jury trial on any legal issues they present. * * *

After adoption of the rules there is no longer any procedural obstacle to the assertion of legal rights before juries, however the party may have acquired standing to assert those rights. Given the availability in a derivative action of both legal and equitable remedies, we think the Seventh Amendment preserves to the parties in a stockholder's suit the same right to a jury trial that historically belonged to the corporation and to those against whom the corporation pressed its legal claims.

[Justice STEWART's dissent is omitted.]

———

DAIRY QUEEN, INC. v. WOOD, 369 U.S. 469, 82 S.Ct. 894, 8 L.Ed.2d 44 (1962). Plaintiff, owner of the trademark DAIRY QUEEN, had given Dairy Queen, Inc. a license to use the mark. The license agreement required Dairy Queen to pay royalties based on its sales using the mark. When Dairy Queen stopped paying, plaintiff sued for (i) an injunction preventing Dairy Queen from using the mark, (ii) an injunction barring Dairy Queen from collecting money from "Dairy Queen" stores in the area where Dairy Queen did business, and (iii) an accounting to determine exactly how much Dairy Queen owed to plaintiff for breaching the agreement. If granted, the accounting would require Dairy Queen to examine its own records to determine the sales it had made. The court would then enter judgment for plaintiff in that amount. Like an injunction, an accounting was a remedy that in 1791 was available only in Equity.

Although all three of plaintiff's claims were on their face equitable, Dairy Queen nevertheless demanded a jury. When the trial court denied the jury, the corporation brought a writ of mandamus against Wood, the trial judge. The court of appeals denied the writ, and Dairy Queen appealed to the Supreme Court. The Supreme Court held that a jury should have been empanelled to hear the accounting claim, although not any issues unique to the injunctions:

> Petitioner's contention, as set forth in its petition for mandamus to the Court of Appeals and reiterated in its briefs before this Court, is that insofar as the complaint requests a money judgment it presents a claim which is unquestionably legal. We agree with that contention. * * * [W]e think it plain that their claim for a money judgment is a claim wholly legal in its nature however the complaint is construed. As an action on a debt allegedly due under a contract, it would be difficult to conceive of an action of a more traditionally legal character. * * *
>
> The respondents' contention that this money claim is "purely equitable" is based primarily upon the fact that their complaint is cast in terms of an "accounting," rather than in terms of an action for

"debt" or "damages." But the constitutional right to trial by jury cannot be made to depend upon the choice of words used in the pleadings. The necessary prerequisite to the right to maintain a suit for an equitable accounting, like all other equitable remedies, is * * * the absence of an adequate remedy at law. Consequently, in order to maintain such a suit on a cause of action cognizable at law, as this one is, the plaintiff must be able to show that the "accounts between the parties" are of such a "complicated nature" that only a court of equity can satisfactorily unravel them. In view of the powers given to District Courts by Federal Rule of Civil Procedure 53 (b) to appoint masters to assist the jury in those exceptional cases where the legal issues are too complicated for the jury adequately to handle alone, the burden of such a showing is considerably increased and it will indeed be a rare case in which it can be met. But be that as it may, this is certainly not such a case. A jury, under proper instructions from the court, could readily determine the recovery, if any, to be had here, whether the theory finally settled upon is that of breach of contract, that of trademark infringement, or any combination of the two. The legal remedy cannot be characterized as inadequate merely because the measure of damages may necessitate a look into petitioner's business records. * * *

Notes and Questions

1. *Ross* is fundamentally different than a case like *Marseilles Hydro*. In *Marseilles Hydro*, the court was dealing with a combination of legal and equitable claims. In *Ross*, by contrast, the court was faced with one claim—which everyone agrees would have been heard in Equity in 1791. The Court nevertheless concludes that a jury is required. In *Ross*, as in the *Beacon Theatres* test applied in *Marseilles Hydro*, that conclusion stems in large part from the Federal Rules. In *Beacon Theatres*, the result stems from the simple fact that the Federal Rules allow legal and equitable claims to be brought in the same case. What feature or features of the Federal Rules support the Court's ruling in *Ross*?

2. The Court in *Ross* does not hold that a jury will be used in every shareholder's derivative action. What else must be true before a party has a Seventh Amendment right to a jury in such a case?

3. The *Ross* Court strongly intimates that a jury would also be available in a class action asserting a legal claim, even though class actions were traditionally available only in Equity. The lower courts uniformly agree with this conclusion.

4. Although decided prior to *Ross*, in some respects *Dairy Queen* presents a more difficult logical question. Whereas *Ross* involved an equitable procedural device, *Dairy Queen* involved an equitable remedy. *Ross* held that for purposes of the Seventh Amendment, it was no longer necessary to distinguish between equitable and legal procedural devices, because the Federal Rules make those procedural devices available in all types of cases. Is the Court in *Dairy Queen* saying that it is likewise no longer necessary to think in terms of equitable and legal *remedies*? Is a party now entitled to a

jury in a case seeking a purely equitable remedy involving the payment of money, like specific performance?

Dairy Queen clearly does not abolish all distinctions between legal and equitable remedies. Note that the Court held that a jury was required for the accounting, but not for the two injunction claims. Why is there a difference? Consider the nature of the accounting in *Dairy Queen*. If granted, the accounting would require defendant to examine its records to ascertain its total sales. Recall, however, that the contract between the parties called for payment of royalties based on sales. What are plaintiff's legal damages for breach of that contract? Does the accounting change what plaintiff will receive if it wins, or simply provide an easier way to determine that amount? Is it really accurate to call the accounting in *Dairy Queen* an equitable "remedy"? Moreover, given the various tools provided plaintiffs under the Federal Rules, such as discovery and special masters, is the equitable remedy of accounting really necessary?

5. Although one could argue that *Dairy Queen* requires that accountings be treated as legal remedies only when the amount being calculated is equivalent to damages, most courts apply the *Dairy Queen* rule to any request for an accounting, at least in trademark cases. 5 J. Thomas McCarthy, *McCarthy on Trademarks and Unfair Competition* § 32:124 (4th ed. 2004).

6. As discussed above in note 7, p. 589, it is often difficult to distinguish the equitable remedy of restitution from damages. However, *Dairy Queen* has no effect on restitution. If the remedy being sought meets the Court's definition of restitution, it is equitable and tried without a jury.

7. Review the list of equitable remedies in Part 1 of this section. Are any of the other listed remedies really legal actions in equitable garb? What about the action for specific performance? Suppose a seller seeks specific performance of a contract in which a buyer agreed to buy real property. Is there any real difference between that remedy and damages?

d. Public Rights

INTRODUCTORY PROBLEM

For the past decade, members of Congress have been flooded with letters from irate law students complaining about differences in the grading curves used at various law schools. Because many schools have succumbed to "grade inflation," students at schools with lower grade curves feel they are unfairly disadvantaged in the hiring process. Congress's response to this dire threat to national security is to enact the Grading Practices Act, which sets strict standards for law school grades. As part of this comprehensive statutory scheme, Congress also establishes the Grading Practices Administration, or "GPA", a new federal agency charged with enacting regulations on technical grading matters and policing law school compliance with the Act. The GPA is also given the authority to adjudicate claims involving law school grading practices, regardless of whether those claims arise under the Act or under some other law.

Within six months of its creation, the GPA decides to bring two test cases against two of the worst offenders. The first case, which is filed in a federal district court, is against the University of Carolina College of Law. Agency regulations establish a mandatory curve to be used in all Civil Procedure courses. In an attempt to make its students more competitive in the job market, the University of Carolina used a higher curve. The GPA asks the court to impose a civil penalty of $10,000 on the University, as provided by the Grading Practices Act.

The GPA's second case is against the University of Dakota Law School. The GPA brings this case before the GPA administrative tribunal. The action charges that Dakota's grading practices are so random that they constitute a common-law public nuisance, as they result in unqualified graduates being unleashed on an unsuspecting public. The GPA seeks $100,000 in damages for this public nuisance.

Although the Grading Practices Act does not mention jury trials, both law schools demand a jury trial in their respective cases. Is there a Seventh Amendment right to a jury in either or both of these cases?

The Seventh Amendment does not require a jury in a case brought against the United States or a federal official. *Lehman v. Nakshian*, 453 U.S. 156, 101 S.Ct. 2698, 69 L.Ed.2d 548 (1981). Such actions are not considered "suits at common law" within the meaning of the Seventh Amendment because of the historic principle of sovereign immunity. A suit against the sovereign has traditionally been considered to be not a matter of right, but instead something that exists solely at the pleasure of the sovereign. A sovereign may refuse to allow itself to be sued in its own courts, or may place restrictions on a party's ability to bring such a suit. Therefore, when a person sues the United States or a federal official today, the case will be tried by a jury only if the statute creating the claim also provides for jury trials. *See, e.g.*, 28 U.S.C. § 2402 (right to a jury when suing the United States for wrongful assessment of taxes). By the same token, because a person cannot sue a *foreign* government without Congressional authorization, a suit against a foreign government or official does not qualify for a jury under the Seventh Amendment. *In re Air Crash Disaster Near Roselawn, Indiana*, 96 F.3d 932 (7th Cir. 1996); *Wilmington Trust v. District Court*, 934 F.2d 1026 (9th Cir. 1991).*

But what happens when the federal government is the *plaintiff* in a case? Because sovereign immunity is no longer an issue, a suit by the federal government would fall under the command of the Seventh Amendment, at least to the extent that the government is bringing a legal claim. Jury trials present no major concerns in many cases, such as when the government sues for damages for breach of contract. In other

* Whether the same rule applies to suits against *state* governments is unclear. The Seventh Amendment applies only to suits in federal court. Because the Eleventh Amendment to the United States Constitution places significant limits on a party's ability to sue a state or state official in federal court, there is little precedent dealing with the issue.

situations, however, jury trials might interfere with the efficient operation of government. The federal government often relies on *administrative agencies* to oversee specialized areas. These agencies may perform a
mix of quasi-legislative, executive, and sometimes even judicial functions.
If jury trials were required as a matter of course in areas assigned to
agencies, it could significantly impede the operations of some agencies.
Do these efficiency concerns outweigh a party's Seventh Amendment
rights?

ATLAS ROOFING CO., INC. v. OCCUPATIONAL SAFETY AND HEALTH REVIEW
COMMISSION, 430 U.S. 442, 97 S.Ct. 1261, 51 L.Ed.2d 464 (1977). When an
OSHA inspection of Atlas Roofing's workplace revealed a serious violation, the agency imposed civil penalties on the company. Atlas appealed
to the Occupational Safety and Health Review Commission, which upheld the penalty in a hearing conducted without a jury. Atlas sought
judicial review in the federal courts, claiming that it was entitled to a
jury trial on the question of civil penalties. Arguing that it would have
been entitled to a jury had the government sought civil penalties in an
action in federal court, Atlas argued that Congress should not be able to
strip it of its constitutional right by the expediency of assigning the
dispute to an administrative agency rather than a court. The Supreme
Court disagreed, finding that Atlas had no right to a jury trial:

> At least in cases in which "public rights" are being litigated—e.g.,
> cases in which the Government sues in its sovereign capacity to
> enforce public rights created by statutes within the power of Con-
> gress to enact—the Seventh Amendment does not prohibit Congress
> from assigning the factfinding function and initial adjudication to an
> administrative forum with which the jury would be incompatible.
> * * *
>
> Congress is not required by the Seventh Amendment to choke the
> already crowded federal courts with new types of litigation or
> prevented from committing some new types of litigation to adminis-
> trative agencies with special competence in the relevant field. This is
> the case even if the Seventh Amendment would have required a jury
> where the adjudication of those rights is assigned to a federal court
> of law instead of an administrative agency. * * *
>
> [Atlas asserts] that the right to jury trial was never intended to
> depend on the identity of the forum to which Congress has chosen to
> submit a dispute; otherwise, it is said, Congress could utterly de-
> stroy the right to a jury trial by always providing for administrative
> rather than judicial resolution of the vast range of cases that now
> arise in the courts. The argument is well put, but it overstates the
> holdings of our prior cases and is in any event unpersuasive. Our
> prior cases support administrative factfinding in only those situa-
> tions involving "public rights," e.g., where the Government is in-
> volved in its sovereign capacity under an otherwise valid statute
> creating enforceable public rights. Wholly private tort, contract, and

property cases, as well as a vast range of other cases, are not at all implicated.

GRANFINANCIERA, S.A. v. NORDBERG

492 U.S. 33, 109 S.Ct. 2782, 106 L.Ed.2d 26 (1989)

JUSTICE BRENNAN delivered the opinion of the Court.

[Chase & Sanborn Corporation filed for bankruptcy in 1983. Nordberg was appointed to serve as "bankruptcy trustee," the official who oversees marshalling the debtor's assets and deals with the claims of the creditors against the estate. One of the trustee's duties is to recover "fraudulent conveyances": transfers of the debtor's assets to others on the eve of bankruptcy in an attempt to keep those assets from one or more creditors. Nordberg sued Granfinanciera in the United States District Court for the Southern District of Florida, claiming that the transfers to Granfinanciera were fraudulent under 11 U.S.C. § 548.

The case was assigned to Bankruptcy Court. The Bankruptcy Court is a specialized federal tribunal that hears certain matters connected to bankruptcy cases. Granfinanciera demanded a jury trial, but the Bankruptcy Court refused. Granfinanciera appealed to the District Court, which affirmed the decision without discussing the jury trial issue.]
* * *

The Court of Appeals for the Eleventh Circuit also affirmed. The court found that petitioners lacked a statutory right to a jury trial, because the constructive fraud provision under which suit was brought— 11 U.S.C. § 548(a)(2)—contains no mention of a right to a jury trial, and 28 U.S.C. § 1411 "affords jury trials only in personal injury or wrongful death suits." The Court of Appeals further ruled that the Seventh Amendment supplied no right to a jury trial, because actions to recover fraudulent conveyances are equitable in nature, even when a plaintiff seeks only monetary relief, and because "bankruptcy itself is equitable in nature and thus bankruptcy proceedings are inherently equitable."

We granted certiorari to decide whether petitioners were entitled to a jury trial, and now reverse. * * *

[The Court first applied the two-part test for determining whether a statutory claim is entitled to a jury trial. It found that the common-law courts could and did hear closely analogous actions to recover fraudulent transfers, and used juries to decide such matters. The nature of the relief—payment of the money—was also held to be legal. The Court then turned to the issue of whether the fact that the claim was tried by an "agency"—the Bankruptcy Court—meant that the claim could be tried without a jury.]

In *Atlas Roofing*, we noted that "when Congress creates new statutory 'public rights,' it may assign their adjudication to an administrative agency with which a jury trial would be incompatible, without violating the Seventh Amendment's injunction that jury trial is to be 'preserved' in 'suits at common law.'" [*Atlas Roofing Co., Inc. v. Occupational Safety and Health Review Commission*, 430 U.S. 442 (1977).] We emphasized, however, that Congress' power to block application of the Seventh Amendment to a cause of action has limits. Congress may only deny trials by jury in actions at law, we said, in cases where "public rights" are litigated: "Our prior cases support administrative factfinding in only those situations involving 'public rights,' e. g., where the Government is involved in its sovereign capacity under an otherwise valid statute creating enforceable public rights. Wholly private tort, contract, and property cases, as well as a vast range of other cases, are not at all implicated." *Id.*, at 458.[8] * * *

Congress may devise novel causes of action involving public rights free from the strictures of the Seventh Amendment if it assigns their adjudication to tribunals without statutory authority to employ juries as factfinders. But it lacks the power to strip parties contesting matters of private right of their constitutional right to a trial by jury. * * *

In certain situations, of course, Congress may fashion causes of action that are closely analogous to common-law claims and place them beyond the ambit of the Seventh Amendment by assigning their resolution to a forum in which jury trials are unavailable. Congress' power to do so is limited, however, just as its power to place adjudicative authority in non-Article III tribunals is circumscribed. Unless a legal cause of action involves "public rights," Congress may not deprive parties litigating over such a right of the Seventh Amendment's guarantee to a jury trial.

In *Atlas Roofing*, we noted that Congress may effectively supplant a common-law cause of action carrying with it a right to a jury trial with a statutory cause of action shorn of a jury trial right if that statutory cause of action inheres in, or lies against, the Federal Government in its sovereign capacity. Our case law makes plain, however, that the class of "public rights" whose adjudication Congress may assign to administrative agencies or courts of equity sitting without juries is more expansive than *Atlas Roofing*'s discussion suggests. Indeed, our decisions point to the conclusion that, if a statutory cause of action is legal in nature, the question whether the Seventh Amendment permits Congress to assign its adjudication to a tribunal that does not employ juries as factfinders requires the same answer as the question whether Article III allows Congress to assign adjudication of that cause of action to a non-Article III tribunal. For if a statutory cause of action, such as respondent's right to recover a fraudulent conveyance under 11 U.S.C. § 548(a)(2), is not a "public right" for Article III purposes, then Congress may not assign its adjudication to a specialized non-Article III court lacking "the essential

---

8. Although we left the term "public rights" undefined in *Atlas Roofing Co. v. Occupational Safety and Health Review Comm'n*, 430 U.S., at 450, 458, we cited *Crowell v. Benson*, 285 U.S. 22 (1932), approvingly. In *Crowell*, we defined "private right" as "the liability of one individual to another under the law as defined," *id.*, at 51, in contrast to cases that "arise between the Government and persons subject to its authority in connection with the performance of the constitutional functions of the executive or legislative departments." *Id.*, at 50.

attributes of the judicial power." *Crowell v. Benson*, supra, at 51. And if the action must be tried under the auspices of an Article III court, then the Seventh Amendment affords the parties a right to a jury trial whenever the cause of action is legal in nature. Conversely, if Congress may assign the adjudication of a statutory cause of action to a non-Article III tribunal, then the Seventh Amendment poses no independent bar to the adjudication of that action by a nonjury factfinder. In addition to our Seventh Amendment precedents, we therefore rely on our decisions exploring the restrictions Article III places on Congress' choice of adjudicative bodies to resolve disputes over statutory rights to determine whether petitioners are entitled to a jury trial.

In our most recent discussion of the "public rights" doctrine as it bears on Congress' power to commit adjudication of a statutory cause of action to a non-Article III tribunal, we rejected the view that "a matter of public rights must at a minimum arise 'between the government and others.'" *Northern Pipeline Construction Co.* [*v. Marathon Pipe Line Co.*], 458 U.S. 50, 69 (1982) (opinion of Brennan, J.), quoting *Ex parte Bakelite Corp.*, 279 U.S. 438, 451 (1929). We held, instead, that the Federal Government need not be a party for a case to revolve around "public rights." *Thomas v. Union Carbide Agricultural Products Co.*, 473 U.S. 568, 586; *id.*, at 596–599 (1985) (Brennan, J., concurring in judgment). The crucial question, in cases not involving the Federal Government, is whether "Congress, acting for a valid legislative purpose pursuant to its constitutional powers under Article I, [has] create[d] a seemingly 'private' right that is so closely integrated into a public regulatory scheme as to be a matter appropriate for agency resolution with limited involvement by the Article III judiciary." *Id.*, at 593–594. If a statutory right is not closely intertwined with a federal regulatory program Congress has power to enact, and if that right neither belongs to nor exists against the Federal Government, then it must be adjudicated by an Article III court. If the right is legal in nature, then it carries with it the Seventh Amendment's guarantee of a jury trial.

Although the issue admits of some debate, a bankruptcy trustee's right to recover a fraudulent conveyance under 11 U.S.C. § 548(a)(2) seems to us more accurately characterized as a private rather than a public right as we have used those terms in our Article III decisions. In *Northern Pipeline Construction Co.*, 458 U.S., at 71, the plurality noted that the restructuring of debtor-creditor relations in bankruptcy "may well be a 'public right.'" But the plurality also emphasized that state-law causes of action for breach of contract or warranty are paradigmatic private rights, even when asserted by an insolvent corporation in the midst of Chapter 11 reorganization proceedings. * * * There can be little doubt that fraudulent conveyance actions by bankruptcy trustees—suits which * * * "constitute no part of the proceedings in bankruptcy but concern controversies arising out of it"—are quintessentially suits at common law that more nearly resemble state-law contract claims brought by a bankrupt corporation to augment the bankruptcy estate than they do creditors' hierarchically ordered claims to a pro rata share of the bankruptcy *res*. They therefore appear matters of private rather than public right. * * *

Nor can Congress' assignment be justified on the ground that jury trials of fraudulent conveyance actions would "go far to dismantle the statutory scheme," *Atlas Roofing*, 430 U.S., at 454, n. 11, or that bankruptcy proceedings have been placed in "an administrative forum with which the jury would be incompatible." *Id.*, at 450. * * *

It may be that providing jury trials in some fraudulent conveyance actions * * * would impede swift resolution of bankruptcy proceedings and increase the expense of Chapter 11 reorganizations. But "these considerations are insufficient to overcome the clear command of the Seventh Amendment." *Curtis v. Loether*, 415 U.S. 189, 198 (1974). See also *Bowsher v. Synar*, 478 U.S. 714, 736, (1986) (" '[T]he fact that a given law or procedure is efficient, convenient, and useful in facilitating functions of government, standing alone, will not save it if it is contrary to the Constitution' "), quoting *INS v. Chadha*, 462 U.S. 919, 944 (1983); *Pernell v. Southall Realty*, 416 U.S. 363, 383–384 (1974) (discounting arguments that jury trials would be unduly burdensome and rejecting "the notion that there is some necessary inconsistency between the desire for speedy justice and the right to jury trial"). * * *

We do not decide today whether the current jury trial provision—28 U.S.C. § 1411 (1982 ed., Supp. V)—permits bankruptcy courts to conduct jury trials in fraudulent conveyance actions like the one respondent initiated. Nor do we express any view as to whether the Seventh Amendment or Article III allows jury trials in such actions to be held before non-Article III bankruptcy judges subject to the oversight provided by the district courts pursuant to the 1984 Amendments. We leave those issues for future decisions. We do hold, however, that whatever the answers to these questions, the Seventh Amendment entitles petitioners to the jury trial they requested. Accordingly, the judgment of the Court of Appeals is reversed, and the case is remanded for further proceedings consistent with this opinion.

[The concurring and dissenting opinions are omitted.]

Notes and Questions

1. As the *Atlas* and *Granfinanciera* opinions indicate, the question of jury trials in administrative proceedings is actually merely a part of a broader separation of powers issue. One of the unique features of the United States Constitution was to establish the federal courts as an independent third branch of government, as opposed to a ministerial organ that carries out the wishes of the other branches, as is the norm in many other nations. To ensure this independence, Article III of the Constitution provides certain protections to federal judges, including life tenure. The broader issue underlying cases like *Atlas* and *Granfinanciera* is the extent to which Congress may assign adjudication of cases to tribunals that do not have the same protections (Bankruptcy judges, for example, do not enjoy life tenure, but

serve for a limited term). You will address this broader issue if you take the upper-level course in Federal Courts. Nevertheless, as the Court in *Granfinanciera* indicates at the end of its opinion, the broader issue intersects the jury trial question in another way. Even if Congress may assign a particular dispute to an agency, it is not clear that an agency has the authority to conduct a jury trial. If it does not, Congress would have no choice but to assign cases in which a jury trial is required to a "normal" Article III court.

2. If Congress wants to avoid a jury trial, does it really need to assign cases to agencies? What about the *state* courts? Recall that the Seventh Amendment does not apply to the state courts, even when they litigate claims arising under federal law. Would assigning disputes like those in *Atlas* and *Granfinanciera* to the state courts be a viable option?

3. *Granfinanciera* indicates that considerations of convenience and complexity of the dispute are not by themselves sufficient reasons to deprive a party of a jury trial. However, such considerations are not completely irrelevant. As indicated in the *City of Monterey* case in Part A.2.a of this Chapter, a court will consider the complexity of the case when determining whether a jury trial is required for a statutory claim without a clear historic analogue.

4. Does the Court in either opinion ever adequately explain why the Seventh Amendment does not require a jury trial in cases involving "public rights?" Is the Court somehow making an analogy to the historic notion of sovereign immunity, which applied only in cases brought *against* government?

5. *Atlas* indicates that a claim involving a public right is one "in which the Government sues in its sovereign capacity." *Granfinanciera* suggests that language is too confining, stating that a case could involve a public right even when it involves a claim brought by a private party. And yet, the Court in *Granfinanciera* holds that the right in that case was a private right. Can you think of a claim that would be a public right even though filed by one private party against another?

6. As the prior note indicates, having the government as a party is not a necessary condition to finding a public right. Is it even a sufficient condition? Are there ever situations where government brings a suit to enforce purely private rights?

7. Test your knowledge of the public rights exception by answering the following three questions:

a. Suppose that Congress decides to give the Environmental Protection Agency the authority to adjudicate all cases involving pollution. The United States sues a large factory for damages, under a theory of common-law public nuisance. The government brings this action before the new EPA tribunal. Why does the Seventh Amendment require a jury in this action?

b. The Federal Communications Commission brings an action in federal district court against CBS and Janet Jackson to levy civil penalties for a "wardrobe malfunction" that occurred during a Super Bowl halftime performance. Why does the Seventh Amendment require a jury in this case?

c. Suppose that the United States enters into a contract to buy pencils for use in government offices. The seller falsely represented that the pencils were "Made in the U.S.A." When the United States learns the truth, it sues in federal district court to rescind the contract based on the false representation. Why will there *not* be a jury in this case?

3. The Reexamination Clause

As you have seen, the Seventh Amendment gives parties a right to a jury in certain types of cases. However, the amendment also provides, "no fact tried by a jury, shall be otherwise reexamined in any Court of the United States, than according to the rules of the common law." This "Reexamination Clause" prevents judges from undercutting the right to a jury trial by letting the jury decide the case, but then overturning the jury verdict.

The Reexamination Clause does not completely bar a judge from second-guessing a jury. It allows a judge to overturn a verdict, but only to the extent that a judge could do so at common law. Like the basic right to a jury trial, then, the Reexamination Clause requires a historical analysis.

At common law, a judge's authority to take a case away from the jury was fairly limited. First, a judge could decide the case on the pleadings if the pleadings established that one side should prevail as a matter of law. Therefore, the modern Federal Rule 12(b)(6) dismissal and Federal Rule 12(c) judgment on the pleadings clearly pass constitutional muster. Second, because the role of the jury is to decide disputed facts, a party is entitled to a jury only if there is a genuine dispute as to one or more relevant facts. Under this reasoning, the modern device of summary judgment does not violate the Seventh Amendment. Third, even if the case went to trial, the trial judge at common law could direct the jury to find for one side if the evidence was so completely one-sided that no reasonable jury could fail to find for that side. That practice continues in modern courts as the "directed verdict" or "judgment as a matter of law" (although the trial judge today simply decides the case herself, rather than telling the jury how to decide). Finally, once the case was submitted to the jury and a verdict was returned, the judge could grant a new trial if there was a serious procedural error or the verdict was against the great weight of the evidence. The Federal Rule 59 new trial carries forward this practice. Aside from these devices, however, the trial judge could not upset a jury verdict. Nor could the court of appeals question the merits of the jury verdict.

Modern procedure provides a few other checks on the jury in addition to those mentioned above. Today, a federal trial judge can grant a judgment as a matter of law not only before the case is submitted to the jury, but also after the jury reports its verdict. Because of the Seventh Amendment, however, the Federal Rules require a pre-verdict motion for judgment as a matter of law as a prerequisite to a post-verdict motion. This process is described in greater detail in Chapter 10.

Some states also give their courts of appeal the authority to overturn juries. When cases involving these state laws are heard in federal court, there is a potential clash between the Reexamination Clause and the federal court's obligations under the *Erie* doctrine to follow state law. The United States Supreme Court dealt with this problem in *Gasperini v. Center for Humanities, Inc.*, 518 U.S. 415, 116 S.Ct. 2211, 135 L.Ed.2d 659 (1996), which is discussed in greater detail in Chapter 13. In *Gasperini*, the Court was faced with a New York state law that gave the appellate court the authority to overturn jury verdicts if they deviated materially from the results in similar cases. Although the Court held that the federal court could meet its *Erie* obligations and apply the state standard of review without violating the Seventh Amendment, concerns about the Reexamination Clause led it to hold that the standard should be applied in the federal system by the trial court rather than the Court of Appeals.

Problems

1. P sues D in federal court for damages for injuries sustained when P and D's yachts collided during a regatta held on Lake Huron. D files a timely demand for a jury trial. Does the Seventh Amendment afford a right to a jury in this case?

2. P leases a notebook computer to D pursuant to a written lease. When D fails to make the required payments for several months, P terminates the lease and orders D to return the computer. D refuses to return the computer. P therefore sues D for an order requiring D to return the computer. P files a timely demand for a jury. Does the Seventh Amendment afford a right to a jury in this case?

3. Same as Problem 2, except that D is the United States government. P files a timely demand for a jury. Does the Seventh Amendment afford a right to a jury in this case?

4. P, a painter, sells a painting of a nude subject to D. D modifies the work by painting fig leaves over certain private parts. In P's opinion, these changes ruin the painting. P accordingly sues D under § 106A of the federal Copyright Act. Section 106A provides artists a cause of action against anyone who damages or defaces their works, even if the defacer owns the work. This statute, which was enacted in 1990, represents a first for Anglo–American law. Traditionally, an artist lost all rights in a physical painting once the painting was sold to another. P files a timely demand for a jury trial. Does the Seventh Amendment afford a right to a jury in this case?

5. S and B have a contract under which S agrees to supply a rare mineral to B. The only source for this mineral is a small nation in Africa. When civil war breaks out in this nation, S is temporarily unable to meet B's demand. Later, however, S is able to resume mining, although at a much higher cost of production.

S sues B in state court. S asks the court to reform the contract by increasing the price that B must pay to reflect S's higher costs. B counterclaims, seeking damages for the shipments that S failed to make, as well as an order requiring S to continue to supply the mineral at the agreed-upon price. S files a timely demand for a jury trial. Does the Seventh Amendment afford a right to a jury on any or all of the issues in this case?

6. Same as Problem 5, except that P sues in federal district court. Does the Seventh Amendment afford a right to a jury on any or all of the issues in this case?

7. The owner of the Springfield Isotopes, a minor league baseball team, has indicated that he would like to move the team to another city. In response, the City of Springfield threatens to use its powers of eminent domain to condemn the team and then sell it to a private owner. Owner, worried that this threat will deter potential buyers, sues Springfield in federal court. Owner asks the federal court for a declaratory judgment that any attempted condemnation would exceed the City's constitutional powers. Owner files a timely demand for a jury trial. Does the Seventh Amendment afford a right to a jury on any or all of the issues in this case?

8. When B's lawn mower dies, L loans B his riding mower. After several weeks, L asks B several times to return the mower. B refuses. L later learns that B has set up a lawn mowing service using L's mower. When L confronts B with this information, B returns the mower. L then sues B for an order requiring B to pay to L all the profits B earned from her wrongful use of the mower. L also asks the court for an order of accounting requiring B to examine her records and reveal how much money she made using the mower.

B files a timely request for a jury trial. Does the Seventh Amendment afford a right to a jury on any or all of the issues in this case?

9. The federal Environmental Protection Agency sues X–Off, Inc. in federal court, after one of X–Off's tankers leaks a large amount of toxic waste. The EPA's action asks the court to impose civil penalties on X–Off, as authorized by the federal Superfund statute. X–Off files a timely demand for a jury in the case, even though the Superfund law is silent on the subject of jury trials. Does the Seventh Amendment afford a right to a jury on any or all of the issues in this case?

B. DEMANDING A JURY TRIAL

As we have just seen, the Seventh Amendment gives parties a constitutional right to a jury trial for certain claims. How do the parties exercise this right? Can a party waive its right to have a case tried by a jury?

MARSEILLES HYDRO POWER, LLC v. MARSEILLES LAND AND WATER COMPANY

299 F.3d 643 (7th Cir. 2002)

[This case is set out at page 592 above.]

Notes and Questions

1. As *Marseilles Hydro* demonstrates, a party can lose its right to a jury trial by failing to request a jury in timely fashion. Should constitutional rights be waived merely because a party forgets to insist that government honor them? In this context, think back to the question of personal jurisdiction in Chapter 4. The due process clause of the Constitution protects a person from being sued in a state that lacks minimum contacts with that person. Can a party waive this due process protection by failing to assert it in a timely fashion? Review Federal Rule 12(h)(1).

2. Rule 38(c) provides that a party may request a jury trial for specific issues. Of course, as the prior section showed, in cases involving a mix of legal and equitable claims the right to a jury trial may not apply to all of the issues. However, a party may also limit its demand for a jury to fewer than all of the claims that qualify for a jury under the Seventh Amendment or governing law. If the demand is limited, any other party who desires a jury trial of other issues triable by a jury must also file a timely demand for those issues or waive its rights.

3. If a demand for jury is made without specifying any issues, it is deemed to be a demand for a jury trial on all issues in the case. What if the demand includes issues on which there is no right to a jury trial? The court will limit the jury trial to those issues which qualify for a jury trial.

4. Rule 38(b) requires that a demand for a jury trial of any issue be served within ten days after service of the "last pleading directed to such issue." When the legal issue first appears in a counterclaim, as in *Marseilles Hydro*, this period begins to run when the reply is served. If the complaint includes a legal claim, either party may request a jury prior to the answer. Plaintiffs often demand a jury trial in the complaint itself. However, if a party includes a demand for a jury in a pleading, the demand must be set off from the main body of the pleading.

5. The court in *Marseilles Hydro* is attempting to determine whether the complaint or the answer was the first pleading raising a legal issue. Why? Does it matter when the issue was *first* raised?

6. In cases filed in state court, the rules governing availability of and demand for a jury may differ significantly. What happens when a case is removed from state to federal court? Rule 81(c) give a party at least ten days following removal to demand a jury.

7. Rule 38(d) provides that once a party files a demand for a jury, she cannot withdraw it without the consent of all parties. Why should the consent of the other parties be required?

8. *Challenging the Trial Judge's Ruling on the Jury Request.* Suppose a party disagrees with how the judge rules on a demand for a jury. May the party seek immediate appeal by an appellate court, or must she wait until after the trial is complete? As a general rule, 28 U.S.C. § 1291 only allows appeals from "final judgments" of the district court. A ruling on whether to use a jury is clearly not a final judgment under § 1291 because it does not resolve any of the substantive issues in the case.

As discussed in Chapter 12, however, there are certain exceptions to the final judgment rule of § 1291. One of these exceptions is the writ of *mandamus*, in which the aggrieved party files what is technically a new action against the trial judge in the Court of Appeals. In most situations, *mandamus* is an extraordinary writ, available only when the party presents a compelling case as to why he needs immediate relief. However, because the right to a jury is enshrined in the Constitution, a party need not present a compelling case to file for *mandamus* based on a trial judge's denial of a jury. Note that this special rule applies only to a *denial* of a jury. Because there is no constitutional right to a bench trial, a party must ordinarily wait until after final judgment to challenge a judge's decision to *grant* a jury trial.

9. Even if no party demands a jury, Rule 39(b) allows the court, in its discretion, to order a jury trial for any or all issues that could have been tried as of right to a jury. That rule gives the court a limited ability to relieve a party of the strict timing rules of Federal Rule 38. The main factors the court considers are whether the demand was made within a reasonable time after the time for demanding a jury expired, whether the failure to make a timely demand was the result of inadvertence, mistake, or excusable neglect, and whether a late motion for a jury trial will prejudice the other parties.

Problems

1. P is about to sue D for damages for trespass. What is the earliest point at which P may request a jury? May P include a request along with her complaint?

2. P and D are embroiled in a dispute concerning a contract. On February 1, P serves D with a complaint seeking specific performance of the contract. On February 8, D files an answer, denying that it breached the contract and counterclaiming against P for damages, alleging that P breached the contract. D serves that answer on February 11. On February 19th, P files and serves its reply, denying liability on the counterclaim. Can P and/or D still file a timely request for a jury trial? What is the latest date on which P or D may file and serve this request?

C. SELECTING A GROUP OF PROSPECTIVE JURORS

In federal courts, the Jury Selection and Service Act of 1968 (28 U.S.C. § 1861 et seq.) provides a uniform method for selecting jurors in federal civil cases. Each district court has a plan for jury selection consistent with the statute, which includes two important general principles: (1) random selection of jurors from voter lists; and (2) determination of juror disqualifications, excuses, exemptions, and exclusions on the basis of objective criteria. The statute also provides that no citizen shall be excluded from jury service "on account of race, color, religion, sex, national origin, or economic status."

Jurors do not have to be drawn from an entire federal district. The local plan must prescribe a method for putting into the master jury wheel at least 1,000 names chosen at random from voter registration lists or lists of actual voters within the district or division. Each county, parish, or similar political subdivision must be substantially proportionally represented in the master jury wheel. Periodically, names are drawn at random from the master jury wheel, and each person whose name is drawn is sent a juror qualification form to complete and return. A judge then determines on the basis of the information provided on the juror qualification form and other competent evidence whether a person is unqualified for, exempt from, or excused from jury service. The remaining names are then put into the qualified jury wheel, from which names are drawn at random as needed for assignment to jury panels.

Any United States citizen who is 18 or over, who has resided for one year within the judicial district, and is able to read, write, speak, and understand the English language is qualified to serve as a juror unless she is incapable, by reason of mental or physical infirmity, to render satisfactory jury service, or has been convicted of or charged with a felony in federal or state court and her civil rights have not been restored. The local plan specifies groups of persons or occupational classes whose members are barred from jury service on the ground that they are exempt. The plan must provide exemption for persons on active service in the armed forces, firemen and policemen, and federal or state public officials actively engaged in the performance of official duties. The plan may also specify groups of persons or occupational classes whose members shall, on individual request, be excused from jury service.

A person chosen for a jury panel from the qualified jury wheel and summoned for service may be excused by the court upon a showing 1) of undue hardship or extreme inconvenience, for a period as the court deems necessary; 2) of an inability to render impartial jury service; 3) that her service as a juror would be likely to disrupt the proceedings; or 4) that her service as a juror would be likely to threaten the secrecy of the proceedings or otherwise adversely affect the integrity of jury deliberations.

A party must challenge compliance with the jury selection procedures within seven days after the moving party discovered or, in the exercise of diligence, could have discovered the grounds for challenge, and in any event before the voir dire examination begins. A party also has an unqualified right to inspect jury lists in order to determine whether there is a basis for challenge. The challenge can prevail only if there has been "a substantial failure to comply with the provisions" of the federal statute.

A defendant may challenge underrepresentation of particular groups in his jury pool as a violation of the "fair cross-section" requirement. The qualifications of jurors and the selection of jury panels as prescribed in the Jury Selection and Service Act of 1968, are intended to ensure that litigants have their disputes decided by juries chosen from a fair cross section of the community and that all citizens have the opportunity to be considered for service on juries. This requirement applies only to the jury *panel* from which the petit jury is selected. The petit jury, the jury which actually decides the case does not have to reflect a cross-section of the community. *Holland v. Illinois*, 493 U.S. 474, 110 S.Ct. 803, 107 L.Ed.2d 905 (1990). Imagine the difficulties in applying a cross-section requirement to the petit jury, as well as its impact on the voir dire process.

Relief requires a showing that the group alleged to have been excluded is a "distinctive" group in the community, that the representation of this group in the venire from which the jury is selected was not fair and reasonable in relation to the number of such persons in the community, and that this underrepresentation was due to systematic exclusion of the group in the jury selection process. The party claiming discrimination by the systematic exclusion of a particular group has the burden of establishing the exclusion. A sufficiently large disparity between the representation of a group in the population and its representation on jury panels is sufficient to show a prima facie case. The opposing party may rebut a prima facie case by showing that "a significant state interest [is] manifestly and primarily advanced by those aspects of the jury-selection process . . . that result in the disproportionate exclusion of a distinctive group."

FLOYD v. GARRISON

996 F.2d 947 (8th Cir. 1993)

FAGG, Circuit Judge.

Mattie Ruth Floyd, a black, brought this civil rights action alleging officer Marty Garrison, a white, used unreasonable and unlawful deadly force by shooting and killing Jason L.C. Floyd. Floyd moved to dissolve the jury pool before trial, and moved for a new trial after the jury returned a verdict for Garrison, because only one of the forty prospective jurors was black. The district court denied the motions. Floyd appeals contending the use of voter registration lists as the sole source for selecting jury pools violates the fair-cross-section requirement of the Jury Selection and Service Act of 1968 (Act) and the Fifth Amendment guarantee of equal protection. We affirm.

The Act requires that jury pools be chosen at random from a fair cross section of the community. 28 U.S.C. § 1861 (1988). To establish a prima facie violation of the fair-cross-section requirement, Floyd must show: (1) blacks are a distinctive group in the community; (2) the representation of blacks in jury pools is not "fair and reasonable in relation to the number of [blacks] in the community;" and (3) "this underrepresentation is due to systematic exclusion of [blacks] in the jury-selection process." *Duren v. Missouri*, 439 U.S. 357, 364 (1979) (Sixth Amendment fair-cross-section requirement); see *United States v. Clifford*, 640 F.2d 150, 154–55 (8th Cir.1981) (*Duren* elements apply to § 1861).

Floyd has failed to establish the third prong of the fair-cross-section test by showing underrepresentation of blacks in jury pools is inherent in the jury-selection process. Floyd merely asserts the use of voter registration lists as the sole source for selecting jury pools does not provide a fair cross section of the community because blacks do not register to vote in the same proportion as other persons. We have consistently approved the use of voter registration lists to select jury pools. The use of voter registration lists is required by the Act and was designed to give qualified citizens an equal chance to be selected for jury pools. Even if proportionally fewer blacks register to vote, "[t]he mere fact that one identifiable group of individuals votes in a lower proportion than the rest of the population does not make a jury selection system illegal or unconstitutional." Absent proof that obstacles are placed in the path of blacks attempting to register to vote, voter registration lists may be used as the sole source for selecting jury pools. *United States v. Freeman*, 514 F.2d 171, 173 (8th Cir.1975).

The Fifth Amendment guarantee of equal protection requires that the procedures used to select jury pools be racially nondiscriminatory. To establish a prima facie equal protection violation, Floyd must show (1) blacks are "a recognizable, distinct class, singled out for different treatment;" (2) blacks were substantially underrepresented in jury pools over a significant period of time; and (3) the jury-selection process is "susceptible of abuse or is not racially neutral." *Castaneda v. Partida*, 430 U.S. 482, 494 (1977).

Floyd has failed to establish the third prong of the equal protection test by showing a discriminatory purpose in the jury-selection process. Floyd concedes there was no intentional discrimination in the random selection of jurors from the voter registration lists, but again contends proportionately fewer blacks register to vote. The use of voter registration lists was intended to eliminate discriminatory and arbitrary selection practices, and Floyd has not shown that blacks are prevented from registering to vote. Thus, the sole use of voter registration lists to select jury pools does not violate equal protection.

Even if Floyd had established the third prongs of the fair-cross-section and equal protection tests, Floyd failed to show blacks were substantially underrepresented on jury pools. Over a thirteen month period, 10.335% of the jurors called for service in the Western Division of the Eastern District of Arkansas were blacks, and 13.8% of the general population in that Division were blacks. The absolute disparity between blacks on jury pools and blacks in the general population was less than 4% (13.8%–10.335%). This underrepresentation is not substantial and does not constitute evidence of a fair-cross-section violation. *Clifford*, 640 F.2d at 155 (absolute disparity of 7.2% is not substantial underrepresentation). The disparity also is not significant enough to prove purposeful discrimination against blacks. Although Floyd contends we should apply a comparative disparity analysis, we decline to adopt that concept as a better means of calculating underrepresentation. We affirm the district court's rulings.

Notes and Questions

1. *Floyd* refers to *Duren v. Missouri,* 439 U.S. 357, 99 S.Ct. 664, 58 L.Ed.2d 579 (1979), in which Missouri "provided an automatic exemption from jury service for any women requesting not to serve." The Supreme Court found the automatic exemption to be a violation of the federal *constitutional* cross-section requirement. Note that *Floyd* involved a violation of the *statutory* cross-section requirement which applies to civil as well as criminal cases. In *Duren,* the Court held that "systematic exclusion of women that results in jury venires averaging less than 15% female violates the Constitution's fair-cross-section requirement."

If the percentage of women appearing on jury pools in Jackson County had precisely mirrored the percentage of women in the population, more than one of every two prospective jurors would have been female. In fact, less than one of every six prospective jurors was female; 85% of the average jury was male. Such a gross discrepancy between the percentage of women in jury venires and the percentage of women in the community requires the conclusion that women were not fairly represented in the source from which petit juries were drawn in Jackson County.

Finally, in order to establish a prima facie case, it was necessary for petitioner to show that the underrepresentation of women, generally and on his venire, was due to their systematic exclusion in the jury-selection process. Petitioner's proof met this requirement. His undisputed demonstration that a large discrepancy occurred not just occasionally but in every weekly venire for a period of nearly a year manifestly indicates that the cause of the underrepresentation was systematic— that is, inherent in the particular jury-selection process utilized. * * *

The resulting disproportionate and consistent exclusion of women from the jury wheel and at the venire stage was quite obviously due to the system by which juries were selected. Petitioner demonstrated that the underrepresentation of women in the final pool of prospective jurors was due to the operation of Missouri's exemption criteria—whether the automatic exemption for women or other statutory exemptions—as implemented in Jackson County. Women were therefore systematically underrepresented . . . * * *

We recognize that a State may have an important interest in assuring that those members of the family responsible for the care of children are available to do so. An exemption appropriately tailored to this interest would, we think, survive a fair-cross-section challenge. We stress, however, that the constitutional guarantee to a jury drawn from a fair cross section of the community requires that States exercise proper caution in exempting broad categories of persons from jury service.

The Court noted that "reasonable exemptions, such as those based on special hardship, incapacity, or community needs," could produce a pool of jurors that was representative of the community.

2.   What other groups are "distinctive" for purposes of a cross-section requirement? Young adults and college students are not a distinctive group. Likewise, the exclusion of young people which results from the intermittent recompiling of the jury lists has been justified in the interest of judicial economy. *See Hamling v. United States*, 418 U.S. 87, 94 S.Ct. 2887, 41 L.Ed.2d 590 (1974), rehearing denied 419 U.S. 885, 95 S.Ct. 157, 42 L.Ed.2d 129 (1974). What about other groups? Social Security recipients? Military veterans? Members of large religious groups within a community? Are there more specific ways to decide whether a group is "distinctive"?

3.   *Jury Size.* Federal Rule 48 prescribes a jury of no fewer than six and no more than twelve members. In *Colgrove v. Battin*, 413 U.S. 149, 93 S.Ct. 2448, 37 L.Ed.2d 522 (1973), the Supreme Court upheld the propriety of a local rule prescribing a six-person jury. The Court distinguished the constitutional right of trial by jury in civil actions from the "various incidents of trial by jury," reasoning that effective jury performance is not a function of jury size. Do you agree?

Federal district local rules vary from district to district in the number of jurors prescribed. Individual districts' rules set the jury size at six, eight, or twelve. Some local rules follow Rule 48 and provide a range between six and twelve from which the district court can choose. Many local rules also provide the court with discretion to seat a number of jurors different from the rule.

Exercise

For the state where a) you intend to practice after graduation, b) your law school is located, and/or c) your professor assigns, go to that state's annotated statutes and research the statutes and procedural rules by which the right to a jury trial and the jury selection process is governed. Based on your research, print the statute or rule and bring it to class for discussion. In addition, answer the following questions.

1.   Is the right to a jury trial in civil cases governed by the state constitution or by statute? How many persons are prescribed by law to sit on a jury in a civil case?

2.   What is the method for selecting an array or a panel of jurors? Drivers' licenses? Personal property tax rolls? Another method?

D.   CHALLENGING INDIVIDUAL PROSPECTIVE JURORS

INTRODUCTORY PROBLEM

Garner sued the Swell Computer Corp. in local federal court for a product defect. She is seeking more than $10 million in compensatory and punitive damages suffered when her computer's hard drive "crashed," causing Garner to lose her Ph.D. dissertation that she had been writing for two years. At the time of jury selection, forty-eight prospective jurors completed jury questionnaires which included information about the panel member's address, occupation, group affiliations, and prior litigation. The questionnaires disclosed that two jurors worked for the defendant, two worked at the university where Garner is seeking her doctorate, three live in her neighborhood, four belong to a local "Bloggers" club, and one has sued Swell in the past for employment discrimination. In addition, the questionnaires sought information about the prospective juror's spouses. One spouse works for the state consumer protection agency, another works in telephone sales for one of Swell's competitors, and two other spouses are computer science majors at Garner's university.

Assuming that the prospective jurors confirm their questionnaire answers during voir dire, is any juror subject to a successful challenge for cause by either party? If such a challenge is denied by the trial judge, would you advise either counsel to use a peremptory challenge to exclude any of the jurors based on the questionnaire?

Governing Law: 28 U.S.C. §§ 1866(c)(4); 1870.

Under Federal Rule 47(a) the trial court has broad discretion to conduct the examination of prospective jurors or to permit the parties to ask questions. If the court conducts the voir dire examination exclusively, the parties may submit proposed questions, which the court may ask if it deems the questions to be proper. Sufficient questioning is necessary to ensure that the selection process is meaningful.

Usually, voir dire occurs by the court or counsel questioning all prospective jurors simultaneously. However, the court has the authority to conduct individual voir dire, which consumes a lot more time, if there is a concern about answers given by one juror "poisoning" the views of other jurors, e.g., knowledge about the case.

The purpose of voir dire examination is to determine any possible basis for challenging jurors for cause (when the challenging party must establish the prospective juror's explicit or implicit bias) and to develop background information to be considered in the intelligent exercise of peremptory challenges (when the challenging party generally need not offer a reason for the challenge).

Because of its central role in the selection of a fair and impartial jury, the voir dire examination is one of the most important parts of the trial. It is the first opportunity afforded to counsel to address the jury in connection with the case. The impressions which the jurors have about the case and about counsel at the conclusion of the examination may last throughout the trial.

If there are reasonable grounds to believe that a juror cannot render a fair and impartial verdict, the juror should be excused for cause. However, disqualification is not required merely because a juror does not understand or immediately accept every legal concept presented during voir dire. The test is not whether a juror agrees with the law when it is presented; it is whether, after having heard all of the evidence, the prospective juror can adjust his views to the requirements of the law and render a fair and impartial verdict.

The court may exercise considerable discretion in deciding whether to excuse an individual juror for cause. Even if the parties fail to make a challenge for cause, the court has an affirmative duty to explore undisclosed information of which it is aware affecting the qualification of an individual juror.

THOMPSON v. ALTHEIMER & GRAY

248 F.3d 621 (7th Cir. 2001)

POSNER, Circuit Judge.

The plaintiff brought suit against her employer under Title VII of the Civil Rights Act of 1964, charging racial discrimination. The case was tried, the jury returned a verdict for the defendant, and the plaintiff appeals, arguing that a juror named Leiter should have been struck for cause. If the plaintiff is right, she is entitled to a new trial without having to show that Leiter's presence on the jury caused the jury to side with the defendant. Denial of the right to an unbiased tribunal is one of those trial errors that is not excused by being shown to have been harmless.

But what of the plaintiff's failure to use any of her three peremptory challenges to strike Leiter? She says that she used up her peremptory challenges on jurors whom she considered even less likely to favor her cause than Leiter was. This acknowledgment might seem to imply—since the plaintiff is not contending that any of those jurors had to be stricken for cause—that she can't really think that Leiter was biased; for if Leiter was biased and those other three were not, surely the plaintiff would have used a peremptory challenge to get rid of Leiter first. That doesn't follow. Bias is only one factor in deciding whether to challenge a juror. A lawyer might be utterly convinced that a member of the jury venire would vote against his client no matter what the evidence showed, and yet his belief might be based on a hunch that he could not articulate as a ground for a challenge for cause. He might be more eager to strike that juror than one who had an evident bias (though the judge hadn't been convinced of this), for he might think he could overcome the hurdle posed by that bias more readily than he could persuade the stubborn but not demonstrably biased juror.

* * * [C]ould a defendant preserve the issue of bias simply by failing to use his peremptory challenge to remove the biased juror? Since the use of a peremptory challenge to remove that juror would cure the judge's error, the defendant's failure to use a peremptory challenge to do this might well be thought to make the error a self-inflicted wound, as argued in a concurring opinion in [*United States v.*] *Martinez-Salazar,* 528 U.S. 304, 318–19 (2000). The majority opinion, however, suggests a

different view—that the litigant can let the biased juror be seated and seek to reverse the adverse judgment (if one results) on appeal on grounds of bias. The suggestion is dictum, and can be questioned as putting the litigant in a heads-I-win-tails-you-lose position: if he wins a jury verdict, he can pocket his victory, and if he loses, he can get a new trial.

* * * The important question is whether the plaintiff's constitutional right to an impartial tribunal was infringed. Let us see.

During the voir dire of the jury, the judge asked the members of the venire whether "there is something about this kind of lawsuit for money damages that would start any of you leaning for or against a particular party?" Leiter raised her hand and explained that she has "been an owner of a couple of businesses and am currently an owner of a business, and I feel that as an employer and owner of a business that will definitely sway my judgment in this case." The judge asked her whether "if I instructed you as to what the law is that you would be able to apply the law recognizing that you are a business owner?" To which she replied, "I think my experience will cloud my judgment, but I can do my best." The judge permitted the lawyers also to ask questions of the prospective jurors and Thompson's lawyer asked Leiter, "And you said earlier that you were concerned that your position as a business owner may cloud your judgment. Can you tell me how?" And she replied, "I am constantly faced with people that want various benefits or different positions in the company [what Thompson was seeking from her employer, the defendant, Altheimer & Gray] or better contacts or, you know, a myriad of issues that employers face on a regular basis, and I have to decide whether or not that person should get them." The lawyer then asked Leiter whether she was concerned "that if somebody doesn't get them [benefits sought from their employer] they're going to sue you," and she answered, "Of course." Asked then whether "you believe that people file lawsuits just because they don't get something they want?", she answered, "I believe there are some people that do." In answer to the next and last question, "Are you concerned that that might cloud your judgment in this case?" she said, "I think I bring a lot of background to this case, and I can't say that it's not going to cloud my judgment. I can try to be as fair as I can, as I do every day."

That was the end of the voir dire of Leiter. After refusing to strike her for cause (though urged to do so by the plaintiff's lawyer), and releasing the jurors who had not been selected for the jury (the defendant had also exercised its three peremptory challenges, none overlapping with the plaintiff's), the judge asked the eight remaining jurors, that is, the jurors selected to hear the case, whether they would follow his instructions on the law even if they didn't agree with them and whether they would be able to suspend judgment until they had heard all the evidence. The question was asked to the jurors at large and all either nodded their heads or said yes. The defendant, again perhaps dropping the ball, makes nothing of Leiter's failure at this stage to reiterate her doubts about her ability to exercise an unclouded judgment.

The defendant is content to argue that the answers that Leiter gave to the earlier questions by the judge, and the questions by Thompson's lawyer, did not require that Leiter be struck for cause.

Our review of the trial judge's ruling with respect to a challenge for cause is deferential, but not completely supine, and it is pertinent to note that no issue of credibility is presented. There is no argument that Leiter was not telling the truth. The issue is interpretive: did what she say manifest a degree of bias such that the judge abused his discretion in failing to strike her for cause?

* * * When Leiter said that she believed that some people sue their employer just because they haven't gotten a promotion or a raise or some other benefit, she was not manifesting bias. She was expressing a prior belief (prior, that is, to hearing any evidence in this case) that was not only not irrational, but was undoubtedly true—there are indeed some people who will sue their employer just because of disappointment over the failure of the employer to give them something they want. In other words, there are spurious suits, in the employment domain as elsewhere. Leiter could not be thought biased for holding a true belief, or even for holding it unshakably if it is indubitably true. The belief that some employees make bogus claims against employers is so obviously true that it could not be shaken; but inability to set aside a clearly sound belief does not make for a biased juror. It makes for a realistic one. * * *

The question in this case was not whether Leiter's belief that some claims against employers are spurious was true or false (it was, as we have noted, true), but whether this belief would somehow impede her in giving due weight to the evidence and following the judge's instructions. That question was not adequately explored. The last thing Leiter said before the judge refused to strike her for cause was that she couldn't say the "background" she brought to this case wasn't going to "cloud" her judgment. She said she would try to be fair, but she expressed no confidence in being able to succeed in the attempt. She may have realized that because of bad experiences in the past, she might have difficulty separating the logically distinct propositions that some claims against employers are bogus and that this claim must be bogus because it is a claim against an employer.

Had she said she could not be fair, the judge would of course have had to strike her for cause. She did not say that, and so the judge (the defendant ... does not argue that the plaintiff's lawyer was at fault in failing to follow up his question whether Leiter's background would cloud her judgment) should have followed up by asking her, as he later asked the jury en masse, whether she would follow his instructions on the law and suspend judgment until she had heard all the evidence.

Instead the matter was left dangling, just as it had been in *Martinez–Salazar*. That juror whom the defendant in that case used a peremptory challenge to excuse after the judge refused to excuse him for cause, when asked "whether, if he were a defendant facing jurors with backgrounds and opinions similar to his own, he thought he would get a fair trial," answered: "I think that's a difficult question. I don't think I know the answer to that." 528 U.S. at 308. And when asked whether he "would feel more comfortable erring on the side of the prosecution or the defense," he said he "would probably be more favorable to the prosecution." *Id.* When the judge then scolded him for reversing the presumption of innocence, the juror said, "I understand that in theory." *Id.* The judge nevertheless refused to excuse the juror for cause because "he said ... he could follow the instructions, and he said ... 'I don't think I know what I would do,' et cetera." *Id.* at 309. The Supreme Court held that in these circumstances the judge had erred in not allowing the challenge for cause. It is just like our case. The judge didn't push hard enough to determine whether Leiter could relinquish her prior beliefs for purposes of deciding the case.

Had the judge pushed Leiter and had she finally given unequivocal assurances that he deemed credible, his ruling could not be disturbed. But he failed to do that. The venire contained 20 prospective jurors, and more than enough were left to make up a full jury of 8 when he refused to excuse her. A candid and thoughtful person, if one may judge from the transcript, Leiter would probably have made an excellent juror—in another case.

When a prospective juror manifests a prior belief that is both material and contestable (for, to repeat an earlier point, it is not bias to cling to a belief that no rational person would question), it is the judge's duty to determine whether the juror is capable of suspending that belief for the duration of the trial. When as in this case the record contains no assurances that the belief is "shakable," that the prospective juror can exercise a judgment unclouded by that belief, the verdict cannot stand. "When a juror is unable to state that she will serve fairly and impartially despite being asked repeatedly for such assurances, we can have no confidence that the juror will 'lay aside' her biases or her prejudicial personal experiences and render a fair and impartial verdict." *United States v. Gonzalez*, 214 F.3d 1109, 1114 (9th Cir. 2000). That's this case. Missing are those "unwavering affirmations of impartiality" that permitted the district judge in *United States v. Garcia*, 936 F.2d 648, 653 (2d Cir.1991), to find the challenged juror unbiased. Reversed and remanded.

Notes and Questions

1. *Thompson* states that the judge has the "duty to determine whether the juror is capable of suspending that belief for the duration of the trial." How does the court become aware of any information relating to bias, i.e., who has the duty of raising bias issues?

Did Leiter indicate an automatic or absolute viewpoint, regardless of what the evidence might later show? What is the problem with seating someone with Leiter's views on the jury? Aren't those views part of the perspective of a cross-section of the community where the trial is held? What else should the judge have asked Leiter to resolve any confusion about Leiter's views?

2.   The term "challenge for cause" is used to include both a juror who fails to meet one or more of the statutory qualifications for jury duty as well as a juror who is biased as between the parties or as to the substance of the dispute. Challenges for cause are determined by the trial judge who exercises considerable discretion in ruling on such challenges. The challenger has the burden of persuading the judge that the prospective juror is not impartial, and the standard of review on appeal is abuse of discretion. There is no limit to the number of jurors who may be struck for cause.

3.   As a former law professor, Judge Posner posed another hypothetical in *Thompson*.

> Suppose a member of the venire in a case involving alleged sex discrimination by a fire department stated his belief that men on average have greater upper-body strength than women. Suppose he added that this belief was unshakable in the sense that if some social scientist testified otherwise, he would conclude that he was being fed junk science. Should this juror be disqualified? Not automatically, surely. The relevant questions would be whether he could distinguish averages from individuals, and thus recognize the possibility that a given woman might have greater upper-body strength than a given man, and whether he was so fixated on the average sex difference in upper-body strength that he was not open to the possibility that a woman whose upper-body strength was indeed less than that of the least strong firefighter in the fire department could nevertheless be as good a firefighter, or even a better one.

Thompson v. Altheimer & Gray, 248 F.3d 621, 625 (7th Cir. 2001).

4.   As Judge Posner stated in *Thompson*, appellate courts are highly deferential to the trial judge's exercise of discretion in ruling on challenges for cause. For example, two jurors were challenged for cause in a medical malpractice case. One was a patient of the doctor-defendant in the case, and the other worked in a physician's office and had been named as a defendant in a malpractice case. After each prospective juror stated that she could be impartial in hearing the case, the trial judge denied the challenges for cause which were upheld on appeal. *Poynter v. Ratcliff*, 874 F.2d 219 (4th Cir. 1989). Does the case suggest the possibility of *excessive* deference?

5.   What happens if a juror gives false information during voir dire, or simply remains silent and does not answer a question which applied to him? As to the issue of false information, a trial court has the discretion to decide whether a post-verdict hearing is necessary to determine juror bias or in exceptional circumstances whether such bias is to be inferred. It must be proved both that the juror failed to answer honestly a material question on voir dire, and that a correct answer would have provided a valid basis for a challenge for cause. *McDonough Power Equip., Inc. v. Greenwood*, 464 U.S. 548, 104 S.Ct. 845, 78 L.Ed.2d 663 (1984). As for a failure to answer at all, the concern is that the information the juror should have revealed may have justified a challenge for cause or at least would have enabled a party to exercise a peremptory challenge intelligently. Does a prospective juror's failure to answer an applicable question carry as much potential for deception as an affirmative statement of false information?

Exercise

As you read the following examples of voir dire questions, consider the propriety and the strategic purpose for each category of questions as well as for individual inquiries being asked of prospective jurors. The question for voir dire is in italics; queries and case law follow the question.

1. **Knowledge and opinions**. Ordinarily, the court will ask prospective jurors whether they have any prior knowledge or opinions about the case. However, the questions may be too general to elicit accurate responses. If the court rules permit counsel to address prospective jurors directly, counsel may wish to give a capsule summary of the facts to stimulate the memory of the jurors and then to ask the jurors questions about their knowledge about the case or the parties. Consider the following illustrative comments and voir dire examination. What answers to these questions may form the basis for a successful challenge for cause? If a trial judge denies the challenge for cause, will an appellate court deem the denial to be an abuse of discretion? The judge might make introductory remarks to the jurors preceding the questioning.

> JUDGE: This case involves an argument at the intersection of Third Street and Eastern Parkway last August between Jane Doe and Officer Ron Roe. Because liability and monetary damages must be judged solely on the basis of the evidence from the witness stand, there are several questions which must be asked to find out whether you already have knowledge or opinions about this case:

> (A) *Have you seen or heard anything about this accident in the news media?* Should exposure to pretrial publicity alone result in the disqualification of jurors for cause? *See Murphy v. Florida*, 421 U.S. 794, 95 S.Ct. 2031, 44 L.Ed.2d 589 (1975); *Irvin v. Dowd*, 366 U.S. 717, 81 S.Ct. 1639, 6 L.Ed.2d 751 (1961). The interrogation of jurors about pretrial publicity is obviously necessary to determine this basis for disqualification.

> (B) *Do you have any knowledge or information about the case from any other source?* Is it relevant that one or more of the jurors served on previous juries involving the same party? Is hearsay information obtained from discussions with persons interested in the case also relevant? For example, is it a valid basis for a challenge for cause if a prospective juror drove to the scene of the event on the evening it occurred and talked to bystanders?

> (C) *Have you ever formed or expressed an opinion of any kind about this incident?* Does the formation of an opinion prior to trial create an inference that the juror cannot be fair and impartial?

2. **Relationships and Associations**. Normally, the court will identify the parties and will ask the prospective jurors whether they are related by blood or marriage to either of them. The court ordinarily identifies counsel for the parties at the same time and inquires whether the jurors have had any prior associations with counsel. The court may also ask the jurors whether they are acquainted with the persons identified or know anything about them. A related line of inquiry is identification of potential witnesses

and the relationships and associations between the jurors and these witnesses. Consider the propriety of the following questions. Is the connection between a juror and any of the following a proper subject for inquiry?

> JUDGE: The law recognizes that previous relationships and associations with various people may naturally influence your judgment about the case. For this reason, all of the people who are connected with the trial will now be identified so that these relationships and associations may be explored:
>
> (1) The plaintiff in this case is Jane Doe.
>
> (2) The defendants are the City of Metroville and Officer Ron Roe.
>
> (3) The witnesses who may testify in this case include Detective Paul Poe, Donna Doe, Charlie Coe and Nina Noe.
>
> (4) The attorneys involved in the case are Peter Plaintiff and Donald Defense.
>
> (5) The trial judge is James Justice.

(A) *Are you related to any of these people by blood or marriage?* Once a close relationship is established, without regard to protestations of lack of bias, should the court sustain a challenge for cause and excuse the juror? How would you respond as the judge if the challenge was based upon a relationship when the prospective juror was:

> (1) The third cousin of the plaintiff?
>
> (2) The first cousin of the defense counsel?
>
> (3) The first cousin by marriage of a plaintiff's witness?
>
> (4) The spouse of the plaintiff's second cousin who knew the plaintiff for a long time?

(B) *Do you know any of these people personally?* Does acquaintance alone constitute grounds for a challenge for cause? Does information about any of them based upon rumor or gossip?

(C) *Have you had any business or social dealings with any of them?* Should a prospective juror be excused if a key witness is employed by the same organization? Is the number of persons employed by the organization relevant? See, e.g., *Getter v. Wal–Mart Stores, Inc.*, 66 F.3d 1119 (10th Cir. 1995) (juror owned stock in defendant corporation and juror's spouse was employed by defendant; juror's "financial well-being was to some extent dependent upon defendant's"; juror's assertions of impartiality must be discounted; bias is presumed; reversible error).

(D) *Have any of you ever sat on a trial jury involving any of these people before?* Should jurors who have served in previous trials of the same party or co-party arising out of the same transaction be excused for cause? What about jurors who have previously served in cases involving similar testimony from the same witness?

(E) *As a result of any prior information or dealings of any kind, are you inclined to give more or less weight to what any of these people say or do than you would if you knew nothing about them?* This question goes to the heart of implied bias.

(F) *Do you or any of your close friends or relatives belong to any organization or group which has any interest in the outcome of this case?*

(G) *Have you or any of your close friends or relatives ever been a member of a law enforcement agency in military or civilian life?* If a juror is connected with a law enforcement official who is actively involved in the case, should the juror be excused for cause?

(H) *Do you have any information or opinions about law enforcement from any source which might influence your judgment about the activities or conclusions of the officers involved in the investigation of this case?* Does this question explore the background of the jurors relative to law enforcement in the same way as questions concerning their direct connection with law enforcement agencies?

(I) *Have you or any of your close friends or relatives ever been employed by a governmental agency?*

3. **Attitudes and Prejudices**. Jurors who know nothing about the case or the persons involved in it may nevertheless have fixed attitudes or strong prejudices which would seriously affect their ability to render a fair and impartial verdict. Courts generally permit the exploration of attitudes and prejudices which bear some reasonable relationship to the issues to be decided by the jury. Since the parties are in a better position to determine what attitudes and prejudices may prove to be crucial as the issues are joined during the trial, the voir dire examination in this area is best left to them. See e.g., *Art Press, Ltd. v. Western Printing Mach. Co.*, 791 F.2d 616 (10th Cir. 1991) (trial judge's questioning restrictions "undermined voir dire's purpose of eliciting information that shows the biases of a venireperson or provides counsel with a basis for exercising peremptory challenges").

To be effective, an examination in this area must expose the jurors to the issues which they will be asked to decide and to the law and facts upon which the issues will be decided. Because questions in this area tend to preview critical aspects of the trial, they are extremely sensitive and must be drawn with great care. Moreover, the jurors have a limited capacity to absorb lengthy voir dire examination. Therefore, a few selective questions which go directly to the theory of the case are much more effective than a laundry list of factors affecting the trial of cases in general. Consider the propriety of the following questions.

JUDGE: The plaintiff will attempt to prove that Ron Roe, who is African–American, wrongfully caused the death of a white man, John Doe. On the other hand, the defendant may show that the death resulted from a racial incident started by John Doe. Therefore, there are several questions which must be asked about your attitudes in racial matters:

(A) *Do any of you have any conscious prejudice for or against African–Americans?*

(B) *Have you or your close friends or relatives had any experiences with African–Americans which might influence your judgment one way or the other in deciding this case?*

(C) *Do any of you feel that African–Americans are more likely to commit crime than other people?*

(D) *Do any of you feel that African–American persons are more prone to violence than other people and are thus more likely to be at fault in a violent incident such as the one involved in this case?*

(E) *Would the fact that the case for the plaintiff will depend largely on the testimony of a white law enforcement official affect your decision one way or the other?*

(F) *Can you follow the law and judge the decision which Ron Roe made based on what he believed instead of what you feel that you or some other person might have done in that situation?* How is this question relevant to jury selection?

JUDGE: There will be evidence that Ron Roe was drinking at the time of the accident. Because these matters relate to the issues before you, there are several questions which must be asked about your attitudes in this regard.

(G) *Do any of you believe that the consumption of alcohol, even in moderate quantities, is wrong?*

(H) *Do any of you belong to any group or organization which has taken a position on the consumption of alcohol?*

4. **The Juror's Background**. In addition to matters specifically related to the case to be tried, the prospective jurors may have various items in their backgrounds which could have some bearing on their decision in the case. Although some inquiry into these general matters is undoubtedly proper, the questions frequently appear to the jurors to be prying into their personal lives. Moreover, extensive general questions soon reach the point of diminishing returns, particularly in the area of courtroom procedure.

JUDGE: Unfortunately, some of you may have had some previous exposure to this type of civil case in some fashion or another. There are several questions which must be asked about your experiences and attitudes in this regard.

(A) *Have you or any of your close friends or relatives ever been a victim of a traffic accident?*

(B) *Have you or any of your close friends or relatives ever been a party or a witness to a traffic accident?*

(C) *Have you ever testified in court?*

(D) *Would any experiences which you may have had or may have heard about the courts influence your decision in this case?*

(E) *In light of any experiences which you or your close friends or relatives may have had, would you rather not serve on a jury in this case?*

It is relevant to establish whether a person had sat as a juror in a similar case. However, should the juror's deliberative processes be explored? Even an inquiry into the verdict in an earlier case may be misleading. A juror who held out for a verdict in a previous case may have been waiting for years for a second chance to correct that error. By the same token, a juror who found someone liable may have had second thoughts about the verdict, resulting in reluctance to return another plaintiff's verdict. Consider the following questions.

JUDGE: Some of you may have previous experience as jurors which might affect your decision in this case. There are several questions which must be asked in this regard.

(G) *Have any of you ever served on a jury panel in any court?*

(H) *Have any of you ever actually served on a jury which tried a civil or a criminal case?*

(I) *Do you feel that any experience which you may have had as a juror would influence you in any way in deciding the issues in this case?*

(J) *Do you understand the difference between the burden of proof in a civil case and a criminal case?* In other words, in a civil case, you may decide in favor of either party if you believe that the evidence is even slightly stronger or better or more believable than the evidence on the other side. In a criminal case, it is your duty to find the defendant not guilty unless the prosecution proves guilt beyond a reasonable doubt. Do you understand and agree with those principles?

(K) *Do you believe that a blameless person is not likely to be sued and accused of causing the wrongful death of another person?*

(L) *Do you understand that the lawsuit which brings the claim to trial is not evidence at all?*

(M) *Do you realize that a trial is the only opportunity which the law gives the parties to present the full facts of this case?*

(N) *If you were asked to render a verdict right now, how would you vote?*

(O) *Would any of you require the defendant to prove that she is blameless to you in some way?*

(P) *Do you agree that witnesses belong to no one, and will you consider everything the witnesses say, regardless of who calls them or who is asking questions at the time?*

(Q) *Will you withhold your judgment until you have heard all of the evidence and the case has been submitted to you for a decision?*

(R) *Do you understand that the law limits the evidence which you may hear, and that it is my duty to object whenever I believe that evidence is being introduced in violation of the law?*

(S) *Do you promise not to draw any conclusions from my objections and not to hold anything I may do in performing my duty against my client?*

In addition to challenges for cause, each party in federal court has a statutory right to three peremptory challenges. The use of peremptory challenges protects each party's interest in a fair and impartial jury. Generally, no reason is necessary for the use of a peremptory challenge. However, a party in a civil case cannot use peremptory challenges to exclude jurors on account of their race or gender. Several defendants or several plaintiffs may be regarded as a single party for making challenges. Alternatively, the trial court may grant additional peremptory challenges, to be exercised separately or jointly. The procedure by which the parties are required to use their peremptory challenges varies widely from district to district and is regulated by local rule or local custom.

ALVERIO v. SAM'S WAREHOUSE CLUB, INC.

253 F.3d 933 (7th Cir. 2001)

TERENCE T. EVANS, Circuit Judge.

Carmen Alverio worked as a food demonstrator at Sam's Warehouse Club. There, she encountered assistant manager Terrence Lloyd who, she claimed, had the disconcerting habit of laterally adjusting his groin while wandering the aisles of the store. Lloyd allegedly began harassing Alverio, and eventually, after matters worsened, she filed suit and went to trial. Sam's Club argued that Lloyd's behavior was not harassing. Alternatively, it asserted the *Ellerth/Faragher* affirmative defense alleging that Alverio failed to take advantage of the store's harassment policy by not telling management of the situation. A jury found in favor of Sam's Club. Alverio then filed a post-trial motion for judgment notwithstanding the verdict or in the alternative for a new trial. The motions were denied. On appeal, Alverio renews her prior objections, asserting that peremptory challenges were used by Sam's Club to exclude females from the jury panel and that admissible testimony was improperly kept from the jury. * * *

Alverio bases her request for a new trial on two arguments— improper jury selection and the exclusion of evidence. We begin with jury selection. The venire consisted of 3 women and 11 men. Judge Cleland conducted voir dire and asked each attorney to exercise three peremptory challenges. Alverio struck three men and Sam's Club struck all three women. Alverio raised a *Batson* challenge, requiring Sam's Club to explain each strike. After reviewing these justifications, Judge Cleland determined that the strikes were not motivated by invidious discrimination.

The rule in *Batson v. Kentucky*, 476 U.S. 79 (1986), that prohibited the use of peremptory challenges based on race has been extended to the exercise of peremptory challenges that are the result of intentional gender discrimination, see *J.E.B. v. Alabama ex rel. T.B.*, 511 U.S. 127 (1994). The right to have jury members selected based on nondiscriminatory criteria also applies in the civil context. See *Edmonson v. Leesville Concrete Co.*, 500 U.S. 614 (1991).

Under *Batson*, allegations of discriminatory peremptory challenges are evaluated via a three-part mini-hearing: (1) the opponent of the strike must make a prima facie showing that the striking party exercised the challenge because of a discriminatory reason; (2) the striking party must next proceed to articulate a gender-neutral reason for the challenge; and then (3) the court must determine whether the opponent of the strike has carried his burden of proving purposeful discrimination.

"[T]he ultimate burden of persuasion regarding racial (or gender-based) motivation rests with and never shifts from, the opponent of the strike." *Purkett v. Elem*, 514 U.S. 765, 768 (1995) (per curiam).

The parties do not contest the first step. So, we focus on Sam's Club's proffered reasons and the judge's acceptance of these justifications. However, we keep in mind that "[t]he trial court's determination about the ultimate question of discriminatory intent is a finding of fact, which will be overturned only if clearly erroneous." *United States v. Evans*, 192 F.3d 698, 700 (7th Cir.1999). "Once the trial judge has been persuaded of the neutrality of the . . . reason for striking a juror, we have 'no basis for reversal on appeal unless the reason given is completely outlandish or there is other evidence which demonstrated its falsity.' " *United States v. Griffin*, 194 F.3d 808, 826 (7th Cir.1999) (quoting *Morse v. Hanks*, 172 F.3d 983, 985 (7th Cir.1999)).

Alverio argues that Sam's Club used its peremptory challenges to systematically remove women from the jury pool. She contends that the justification for its strikes—the lack of business experience and knowledge—was pretextual and invalid and argues that this is evidenced by the fact that the challenged female jurors had educational backgrounds that were greater than or equal to that of several of the empaneled male jurors. Finally, she asserts that an all-male jury was particularly unjust, given that the case involved sexual harassment claims which are "women's issues."

Sam's Club, as we said, struck the three females: (1) Nancy Kiec, a 38–year-old, married, unemployed woman with no children; (2) Robin Braxton, a 38–year-old mother of three who had worked as a hospital housekeeper for 3 years; and (3) Patricia Knorps, a secretary for an insurance agent, who had completed some college.[1] The attorney for Sam's Club, William Holloway, explained that he struck Kiec because she was unemployed. He challenged Braxton because she was the only prospective juror who had been a plaintiff in a lawsuit and she was reluctant to discuss the outcome of that case. As for Knorps, Holloway said he was concerned that her job put her in contact with insurance companies and their lawyers. Since Holloway's firm was active in insurance litigation, he was concerned that she might be familiar with his law firm, although she did not claim to have heard of it. In addition, he thought Knorps had given equivocal answers about her level of education, stating only that she completed "some college."

In addition to these particular objections, Holloway stated that his overall objection to all three prospective jurors was their limited work experience. He stated that he was looking for jurors with a level of "sophistication about business and how it is conducted in the work-a-day

---

1. Although at oral argument Alverio bemoaned the rough and tumble nature of the remaining male jurors, she struck the three most educated potential jurors, all of whom held managerial positions. One, Hetrick, was college-educated and served as a business director for a food supplier. Another, Chana, was a public school assistant principal who held a master's degree, and the last, Vaseloff, who had an MBA, served as an electronic engineering manager.

world." While he considered each juror's education level, his primary concern was work-force participation.

As to the second step of the *Batson* analysis, lawyers are given considerable leeway in formulating a gender-neutral rationale for jury strikes. *United States v. Evans*, 192 F.3d at 701 ("Any neutral reason, no matter how 'implausible or fantastic,' even if it is 'silly or superstitious,' is sufficient to rebut a prima facie case of discrimination.") (quoting *Purkett v. Elem*, 514 U.S. at 768). Here, in addition to identifying unique factors that only affected the three struck jurors—unemployment, participation as a plaintiff in a lawsuit, and employment in an insurance company—Holloway also identified an overarching concern, extensive work-force participation, which he applied consistently to the entire array. All remaining empaneled jurors were employed, and many had considerable work experience.

We have approved the exclusion of potential jurors because of their professions, see *Griffin*, 194 F.3d at 826, and their lack of a profession. *United States v. Jones*, 224 F.3d 621, 624 (7th Cir.2000) (affirming peremptory strike, where prospective juror was unemployed, watched soap operas, and was inactive in her community). We have also held that inadequate education and business experience are nondiscriminatory justifications for excluding prospective jurors. Moreover, where a party gives multiple reasons for striking a juror, it is not enough for the other side to assert that the empaneled juror shares one attribute with the struck juror. Several of the empaneled jurors may have had less formal education than the three female jurors, but Holloway's decision to strike was not based on this factor alone.

Because all the women were removed from the panel, Alverio contends that Sam's Club's proffered reason was pretextual and rested on a stereotype that women have less business experience. First, the exclusion of all members of a specific minority group does not, on its own, establish that the peremptory strikes were discriminatory. Second, we doubt that at this point in time, women can be said to have less work experience than their male counterparts; thus, it is unlikely that "having business experience" can serve as a proxy for "male juror." Even were this true, and Mr. Holloway's stated reason had a disparate impact on female jurors, this would still be irrelevant. The question here is whether Mr. Holloway had a gender-neutral reason for striking these jurors. According to Judge Cleland, he did, and we give great deference to the judge's determination of discriminatory intent. The third step of the Batson jig requires the judge to make a factual determination based on Mr. Holloway's demeanor and credibility. This is a judgment call which the trial judge is in a much better position to make than we are. Even were we to find his decision to be dubious, we would not reverse unless we were left with a "definite and firm conviction that a mistake had been made." Here, we find that Judge Cleland did not err in allowing Sam's Club to strike the three female jurors from the pool.

Finally, we decline Alverio's invitation to find that sexual harassment trials must necessarily include female jurors. The idea that one gender is better suited to hear a class of cases than another, is itself a sexist concept. Alverio contends that this trial involved "women's issues." We disagree. This trial concerned an allegedly hostile work environment created by sexually explicit comments and gestures. Productive work environments, free of harassment, are not merely a woman's worry, they are a national concern. Alverio's assumption that women, by virtue of their gender, are better suited to adjudicate these cases falls prey to the very stereotypical generalizations that the Court sought to eradicate in *J.E.B. v. Alabama ex rel. T.B.*, 511 U.S. at 132–33 (documenting "romantic paternalism" that justified exclusion of women from polluted atmosphere of courtrooms). Moreover, protection from gender-based discriminatory strikes is not a one-way street. It is a right that extends to both genders. * * *

For all these reasons, the judgment of the district court is Affirmed.

Notes and Questions

1. As the Seventh Circuit noted, *Batson*'s analytical structure is in three parts. First, a party may show a prima facie case of purposeful racial or gender discrimination by showing that the facts and any other relevant circumstances raise an inference that the party opposing the peremptory challenges excluded the veniremen from the petit jury on account of their race or gender. For example, a "pattern" of strikes (e.g., 60% of African–Americans were excluded using the challenges but only 30% of panels undergoing voir dire are African–American) or the questions and statements during voir dire examination and in exercising his challenges may support or refute an inference of discriminatory purpose. If the first step is satisfied, the second step shifts the burden to the opposing party to show a neutral explanation for challenging the jurors, although the explanation need not satisfy the proof justifying exercise of a challenge for cause. Finally, the trial court then will have the duty to determine if the challenging party has established purposeful discrimination.

2. Intentional discrimination in jury selection is prohibited on the basis of both race and gender. For example, in *Hernandez v. New York*, 500 U.S. 352, 111 S.Ct. 1859, 114 L.Ed.2d 395 (1991), the Court found that Hispanics have a right to be free from discrimination in jury selection. Then, in *J.E.B. v. Alabama ex rel. T.B.*, 511 U.S. 127, 114 S.Ct. 1419, 128 L.Ed.2d 89 (1994), the Court extended *Batson* and held that the Equal Protection Clause forbids the exercise of a peremptory challenge based upon the gender of a prospective juror. "Striking individuals on the assumption that they hold particular views simply because of their gender is practically a brand upon them, affixed by law, an assertion of their inferiority."

Does the Batson analysis apply to other "groups"? Ethnic groups? Religious groups? Is the immutability concept the same for *Batson* as it is for a challenge to the array, discussed *supra*?

3. If the chosen race-neutral reasons for the strikes "are so far at odds with the evidence that pretext is the fair conclusion," those explanations

may indicate "the very discrimination the explanations were meant to deny." In *Miller–El v. Dretke,* ___ U.S. ___, 125 S.Ct. 2317, 162 L.Ed.2d 196 (2005), the Court found reversible error when the trial court accepted offered race-neutral explanation which were pretextual. Peremptory challenges were used to strike ten of eleven qualified black venire panel members, when at last two of them were "ostensibly acceptable" to a prosecutor seeking the death penalty, and there were strong similarities between struck black venire members and retained white venire members.

Does *Batson* require the neutral explanation for peremptorily striking a potential juror to be derived from voir dire? Most decisions have answered in the negative. A party may use her own personal knowledge concerning a juror and information supplied from outside sources. The test is not whether the information is true or false; it is whether she has a good-faith belief in the information and whether she can articulate the reason to the trial court in a race-neutral or gender-neutral way which does not violate the defendant's constitutional rights. The trial court then decides whether the party has acted with a prohibited intent.

Problems

1. Evaluate the "reasonableness" of the explanation offered for the following peremptory challenges in a breach of contract case involving the sale of a home.

A. African–American female struck because the mortgage on her son's home was recently foreclosed.

B. African–American male struck because he never owned a home.

C. White female struck because her stepfather is a real estate broker.

D. White female struck because her mother is a loan officer at a bank.

2. What result when the only African–American on the venire is struck by the plaintiff with a peremptory challenge "because he absolutely failed to establish eye contact with the plaintiff during questioning, and in plaintiff counsel's amateur psychological opinion, seemed not to be possessed of a certain degree of assertiveness which the plaintiff prefers to have in jurors."

3. In *Davey v. Lockheed Martin Corp.,* 301 F.3d 1204 (10th Cir.2002), a gender-based employment discrimination case, the court found that a prima facie case of discrimination in the exercise of peremptory challenges had occurred after three women were removed from the jury. The court then asked the party exercising the challenges for a neutral explanation.

Counsel for defendant: There's a common basis for striking actually all three of those people. And that is none of them work in a workplace setting. This is a case of discrimination, alleged discrimination in the workplace. They need to understand concepts such as performance evaluations, rankings, what supervisors are confronted with on a day-to-day basis is something that would be useful to the jurors' understanding of the case. [Ms. Elder] is not working outside of the home. Miss Whitely is not working outside of the home, and Miss Murley is not working for an employer but works for herself selling Mary Kay cosmetics. So frankly, the major basis for striking each one of them is that they do not have current employers and so they would not have that perspective to bring to their deliberations.

Counsel for plaintiff responded: Your Honor, that's clearly pretexual. Let's take Ms. Elder. Ms. Elder worked for ten years as a nurse. She was a head nurse. Had responsibilities for other individuals whom she was supervising as a nurse. She clearly was someone who was aware of policies and procedures. Nurses have to follow those policies, and clearly she knew about personnel policies because that was her job.

As judge, how would you respond to the proffer of a neutral explanation for the exercise of a peremptory challenge? Does *Alverio* help you reach a conclusion?

4. On April 13, the Ku Klux Klan held a rally on the steps of the local courthouse. Although the rally itself occurred without incidents leading to arrests, a member of the Klan, Karl Kody, a 25-year-old unemployed Caucasian, swung his uniform at a crowd of people who were protesting the Klan's presence. Several persons in the crowd sued Kody for common law battery. At trial, Karl's attorney, Kalvin Cline, used all three of the defense's available peremptory challenges to remove the following African–Americans from the jury. (Cline's reasons for striking each of the three jurors, though undisclosed to anyone other than Kody at this time, are listed.)

A. Juror A is Gerald Jones, a 72-year-old retired accountant. Cline felt that Mr. Jones would be antagonistic toward Kody because Kody is unemployed.

B. Juror B is Victoria Chandler, a 35-year-old garment worker. Cline believed that Ms. Chandler would be hostile toward Kody because of the way he dresses.

C. Juror C is Stokely Jackson, a 41-year-old salesman who is the President of the local chapter of the NAACP. Cline believed that Jackson would be hostile to Kody because of his political views.

After the defense used its peremptory challenges, no African–American jurors remained on the jury. Prior to swearing in the jurors, is there any motion that you as plaintiff's counsel can present to the judge to question Cline's actions?

Exercise

For the state where a) you intend to practice after graduation, b) your law school is located, and/or c) your professor assigns, go to that state's annotated statutes and research the statutes and procedural rules by which the jury selection process is governed. Based on your research, print the statute or rule and bring it to class for discussion. In addition, answer the following questions.

1. What are the rules governing the conduct of voir dire? Must the judge permit counsel for the parties to address the jurors personally?

2. Are any jurors in excess of the statutory number permitted to be selected during jury selection, in case another juror must be excused? If so, how many others may be selected? What is their role, i.e., are they

regarded as alternate jurors from the beginning or is the actual jury which will decide the case selected from the remaining jurors as of the time the jurors retire to deliberate? How late may jurors be substituted, at the time the jurors retire to deliberate or later?

3. How many peremptory challenges do the rules permit? Can the number be expanded? If so, by what standard?

4. Must a jury verdict be unanimous or may it be a simple or supermajority?

5. After the judge announces the jury's verdict, may the jury be polled so that each juror may be asked whether she agrees with the jury verdict in open court?

E. JURY INSTRUCTIONS AND JURY VERDICTS

1. Requesting and Objecting to Jury Instructions

Before a jury leaves the courtroom to deliberate, the judge must instruct them about the applicable law. Prior to the jury instructions, the parties can request that the judge instruct the jury about certain topics, as well as certain versions of topical instructions. (Even if no party submits requested instructions, the judge still must instruct the jury.) By Federal Rule 51(a), the parties submit proposed jury instructions to the court, no later than the close of the evidence and at an earlier time if the court chooses. Local rules for that trial court also may set time limits for making jury instruction requests. Court may consider late submissions, especially for issues that were unanticipated when the parties submitted their requests.

Before instructing the jury and before the parties' closing arguments to the jury, the trial court informs the parties about the instructions it intends to use. A party may object to a proposed instruction, regardless of whether it was requested by the party. Besides enabling the parties to object to the instructions the trial court intends to give, informing them also permits them to adjust their closing arguments to "fit" the instructions. For example, if the defendant requested an instruction on the defense of assumption of risk but the court declined to instruct the jury about that defense, in the closing argument to the jury the defendant is better off concentrating on arguing the facts to the jury that parallel the actual jury instructions rather than emphasizing the plaintiff's assumption of a risk.

What should the jury instructions include? They should cover every important issue in the case and communicate the applicable principles of law. What follows is a sample jury instruction for the defense of assumption of risk in a tort case.

I instruct you that the defendant is not liable for the harm caused to the plaintiff in this case if you find from the evidence that the following conditions exist:

1) That the plaintiff was aware that [his or her] use of the
_____ [name of product] created an unreasonable risk of personal
injury;

2) That the plaintiff voluntarily exposed [himself or herself] to
that risk; and

3) That the risk which the plaintiff exposed [himself or herself]
to was the proximate cause of the plaintiff's injury.

If the defendant proves all three of these elements, your verdict
will be for the defendant. If the defendant does not prove all three
elements, your verdict will be for the plaintiff.

Mich. Nonstan Jury Inst Civ § 17:05 (1999).

Merely tendering proposed jury instructions to a court does not
preserve an objection to those instructions. Rule 51(c) requires a party to
object in a timely manner to the instructions on the record, stating
"distinctly" both the instruction objected to and the grounds for the
objection. An objection to the failure to instruct on an issue or to a
particular instruction is not preserved simply by tendering a proposed
instruction to the trial court.

JARVIS v. FORD MOTOR CO.

283 F.3d 33 (2d Cir. 2002)

SOTOMAYOR, Circuit Judge.

[Plaintiff-driver sued Ford Motor for negligence and strict liability,
claiming that a Ford Aerostar minivan's design defect caused sudden
acceleration. A jury returned a verdict for the plaintiff on the negligence
claim but not on the strict products liability claim, and awarded damages
to the plaintiff.]

Immediately after the jury returned its verdict but before the jury
was excused, Ford moved for relief on the basis of an inconsistent
verdict. The district court agreed with Ford that the jury verdict was
"irreconcilable," but did not reach the issue of what relief would be
appropriate because, as discussed above, it found the evidence insufficient to sustain a verdict for Jarvis and granted Ford's motion for
judgment as a matter of law.

We find that any potential error related to the jury instructions and
verdict sheet, and not to the jury's general verdicts and that, therefore,
Ford's objection needed to conform to the strictures of Fed.R.Civ.P. 51.
We hold that the district court, in finding that Ford had not waived its
objection, erred, as a matter of law, in not applying the Fed.R.Civ.P. 51
requirements that any objection must "stat[e] distinctly the matter
objected to and the grounds of the objection." Applying this legal
standard, we find that Ford's pre-trial statement that the court should
charge either negligence or strict liability, but not both, failed to alert
the court to the precise nature of Ford's objection and its legal ground-

ing. Finding no "fundamental error" in the instructions, we order the district court to reinstate the jury verdict. * * *

[The jury instructions make it] abundantly clear that the jury was instructed that it could find Ford liable under theories of either negligence or strict liability or both. The verdict sheet given to the jury accurately reflected this by indicating, after question 1(a) concerning strict liability, "IF YOUR ANSWER TO QUESTION 1(a) IS 'NO', THEN PROCEED TO QUESTION 2(a)." Question 2(a), concerning negligence, asked, "Do you find by a preponderance of the evidence that the defendant Ford Motor Company was negligent in the design of the cruise control system in the 1991 Ford Aerostar? (Plaintiff's Burden of Proof)," followed by blanks to check either "yes" or "no." The jury checked the "no" blank in response to question 1(a), and "yes" in answer to question 2(a).

* * * In reviewing de novo the district court's choice of legal standard, we hold that it did not apply the correct standard in ruling that Ford was relieved from the obligation of presenting a more explicit, precise, and reasoned objection before the jury deliberated. Applying the correct standard, we find that Ford did not satisfy the requirements of Fed.R.Civ.P. 51. * * *

Ford claims that once the district court, knowing Ford's preference for charging one but not both theories of liability, decided to send the case to the jury under theories of both negligence and strict liability, Ford was not required to object to the jury instructions or the verdict sheet because it was reasonable to conclude that further objection would be unavailing, echoing the district court's finding that no further objection was necessary. We disagree. At no point in its ruling on Ford's preservation of its objection did the district court consider whether Ford had satisfied the appropriate legal standard that Ford "stat[e] distinctly the matter objected to and the grounds of the objection." Fed.R.Civ.P. 51. We find that Ford did not, and note that the district court's own comments lead to the same conclusion.

In their proposed jury instructions submitted prior to trial, both Ford and Jarvis requested that the court charge the jury on both negligence and strict products liability. After receiving the parties' proposed requests to charge, the judge wrote to the parties asking them to "clarify their positions with respect to the appropriate causes of action in this case." Letter from Judge Buchwald to the parties, July 6, 1999, at 2. The court inquired, *inter alia*, whether "it would be sensible" to follow the approach taken in *Pahuta v. Massey–Ferguson, Inc.*, 170 F.3d 125, 134–35 (2d Cir.1999), "in which the plaintiff withdrew his negligence cause of action as duplicative of his strict liability claim," stating that the court's research "indicates a substantial overlap in the elements of negligence and strict liability claims for defective design." Letter from Judge Buchwald to the parties, July 6, 1999, at 1–2.

Counsel for Jarvis responded that "we do not regard the negligence claim and the strict liability claim as duplicative but, rather, we regard them as distinct, unlike the apparent factual situation referenced in Pahuta v. Massey–Ferguson, Inc." Letter of George N. Tompkins, Jr. to Judge Buchwald, July 6, 1999, at 2. The letter explained that "[t]his claim raises the question whether the defendant Ford acted reasonably in selecting the design for the Aerostar cruise control system, whereas the strict liability claim focuses upon the question whether the Aerostar cruise control system itself was unreasonably dangerous." *Id.*

Counsel for Ford, in its letter to the district court, responded only that "[w]e have read the *Pahuta* case and agree with the Court that the Court should charge either negligence or strict products liability, but not both." Letter of Brian P. Crosby to Judge Buchwald, July 7, 1999, at 1. The letter offered no legal argument or citation to any other authority as to why both theories could not be charged. The *Pahuta* case itself does not state that the two causes of action are necessarily duplicative. There, we mentioned in a footnote merely that "[a]t the charging conference, *Pahuta* abandoned a negligence cause of action as duplicative of his strict liability claim." *Pahuta*, 170 F.3d at 134 n. 7. The parties appear to agree, with good reason, that our footnote in *Pahuta* did not decide the issue of the potential overlap of the two theories of liability for all future design defect claims brought under New York law. Tellingly, in arguing on appeal that the causes of action are duplicative as a matter of law, Ford makes no mention of *Pahuta.* * * *

After the charge to the jury, Ford did not object to instructing the jury on both theories of liability or to the instruction in the jury charge and on the verdict sheet that the jury could find Ford negligent but not strictly liable. * * *

We review de novo the district court's interpretation of the legal standard for waiver under Fed.R.Civ.P. 51. We hold that the district court failed to apply the correct legal standard in ruling that the expression of Ford's "fundamental position" sufficed to preserve its objection to the jury instruction and verdict sheet. The district court neither mentioned Fed.R.Civ.P. 51 or its requirements nor applied them in substance. Applying the requirements of Fed.R.Civ.P. 51 de novo, we find that Ford waived any objection.

Under Rule 51, an objection must "stat[e] distinctly the matter objected to and the grounds of the objection." Fed.R.Civ.P. 51. "The purpose of the Rule is to allow the trial court an opportunity to cure any defects in the instructions before sending the jury to deliberate." *Fogarty v. Near N. Ins. Brokerage, Inc.,* 162 F.3d 74, 79 (2d Cir.1998). The "objections to a charge must be sufficiently specific to bring into focus the precise nature of the alleged error." *Palmer v. Hoffman,* 318 U.S. 109, 119 (1943). * * *

The statement by Ford that "[w]e have read the *Pahuta* case and agree with the Court that the Court should charge either negligence or strict products liability, but not both," failed to state distinctly either "the matter objected to" or "the grounds of the objection." Fed.R.Civ.P. 51. The specific objection that Ford asks this Court to read into its pretrial correspondence is that the jury's finding that the cruise control system of the 1991 Ford Aerostar was not designed in a defective manner presumes that Ford was not negligent in the design of the cruise control system. Ford's statement that either negligence or strict liability, but not both, should be charged, does not distinctly state this objection. Ford's current contention is not that it was error to charge two theories of liability but rather that, after determining that Ford was not strictly liable, the jury should not have considered whether Ford was negligent. Ford's conduct at the pre-trial conference, if anything, obscured any objection it might have made in its correspondence with the court. At the conference, the speaker identified by Jarvis as "counsel for Ford" explained that "it seems that the claim of the plaintiff here is one of negligence and certain product liability." After the court later asked, "[s]o you don't want me to charge negligence?" the speaker, identified again by Jarvis as a counsel for Ford, responded, "Well, we're going to reserve on that. We want you to leave negligence in for now." Pre-trial tr. at 36. Accordingly, Ford did not distinctly state "the matter objected to." In fact, it appears to have asked the court to leave both causes of action in the jury charge.

Neither did Ford state distinctly "the grounds of its objection." In the pre-trial correspondence and conference, Ford made no legal argument for charging only one cause of action outside of the passing reference to our footnote in the *Pahuta* case. In that footnote, we mentioned merely that the plaintiff had voluntarily withdrawn a negligence charge. *Pahuta*, 170 F.3d at 134 n. 7. Ford cited no authority to show why the district court should find the negligence cause of action duplicative of the strict liability claim in this case. In recalling how it came to charge the jury under both theories, the district court remarked simply that the plaintiff had asked for the charge and that in one case, presumably *Pahuta*, "the plaintiff[ ] had agreed to drop one of the claims." After the verdict, in ruling on Ford's motions, the district court rebuked counsel for not calling its attention earlier to the relevant legal authority in New York regarding the similarities between negligence and strict liability for product defects, indicating its suspicion that it appeared that this failure was "a tactical decision" made "for strategic reasons to refrain from informing us of the overlap and potential for inconsistent verdicts." *Jarvis*, 69 F.Supp.2d at 587 n. 8. In this regard, it appears that the district court agreed that Ford did not distinctly state "the grounds of its objection." Fed.R.Civ.P. 51.

* * * For the reasons stated, under the principles of Rule 51 Ford has waived its objection to verdict inconsistency. * * * In this ten-year litigation, the issue of the jury charge was litigated extensively. Ford asked for this jury charge, presumably for strategic reasons, and was well apprised of the law of waiver. To excuse Ford from the well-established rules of waiver would permit precisely the sort of "sandbagging" that the rules are designed to prevent, while undermining the ideal of judicial economy that the rules are meant to serve.

Although Ford has not requested that we do so, this Court may review jury instructions and verdict sheets for "fundamental" error even when a litigant has not complied with the Fed.R.Civ.P. 51 objection requirements. * * * We have found relief from fundamental error to be warranted when the jury charge "deprived the jury of adequate legal guidance to reach a rational decision." *Werbungs v. Collectors' Guild, Ltd.*, 930 F.2d 1021, 1026 (2d Cir.1991). Because the degree of overlap between negligence and strict liability for design defects is unsettled under New York law, the integrity of the trial was not endangered by the jury instructions and verdict sheet in this case. * * *

Notes and Questions

1. Does the court's opinion exalt form over substance? What is the court's point about the rule's purpose being the avoidance of "sandbagging"?

2. The instructions must include direction to the jurors about the number of jurors required for a verdict. In criminal cases, unanimity is required for a conviction or an acquittal under the federal constitution and most state constitutions. In federal civil cases, Federal Rule 48 states that a verdict must be unanimous. By contrast, in many states the minimum number of jurors who must agree to a verdict is less than unanimity, e.g., 9 of 12 jurors must agree, or 5 of 6 jurors must agree. What is the effect of the distinction? Is a jury more likely to reach a verdict sooner when a supermajority is required rather than unanimity? What is the likely effect of the distinction on jury deliberations?

2. Jury Verdicts

Trial courts in most civil jury cases instruct the jury to return what is known as a "general verdict," which in a single statement reflects the jury's conclusion about which party wins the case. The essence of a general verdict is "We find in favor of the plaintiff" or "We find in favor of the defendant." Federal Rule 49 describes two alternate methods to a general verdict: a special verdict and a general verdict with interrogatories.

LAVOIE v. PACIFIC PRESS & SHEAR CO.

975 F.2d 48 (2d Cir. 1992)

CARDAMONE, Circuit Judge:

This appeal presents a question of waiver. After a young industrial worker suffered a severe injury caused by the equipment she was operating, she sued and obtained a substantial verdict at the hands of a jury. The equipment maker asserts for the first time on appeal that written questions and a verdict form submitted by the trial judge and responded to by the jury resulted in an inconsistency that entitles it to a new trial. Because defendant had ample opportunity—as well as notice of the possible inconsistency to which it presently objects—throughout the entire trial proceedings from pre-trial conference to judgment, yet failed to speak, it must now be ruled that it should hold its peace. * * *

Plaintiff filed suit in the District of Vermont in February 1989 alleging defendants were liable in strict liability for selling a product that was unreasonably dangerous, for breach of implied warranty of merchantability and breach of implied warranty of fitness for a particular purpose, and for negligence. A trial on the merits was held from May 14–25, 1991. At the conclusion of the trial, following a precharge conference, the jury was instructed on the law pertaining to these four alternative theories of liability. The trial court instructed the jury specifically on the theory of negligence as separate and independent from the strict liability and the two warranty theories. No objection was made by defendant at the charging conference or during the charge itself regarding any inconsistency between the different theories of liability, nor did defendant interpose an objection respecting the submission of separate interrogatories and separate general verdict forms to the jury pertaining to each theory.

Although the jury found Pacific not liable for breach of either warranty or on grounds of strict liability, it found both plaintiff and defendant negligent and assigned 85 percent of the liability, or $412,250 in damages, against defendant. Subsequent to the verdict, the jurors were individually polled, and a bench conference was held with counsel. Again, inconsistency of the verdicts was not raised on any of these occasions.

After the jury was discharged and before the judgment was entered, defendant moved on May 30, 1991 for judgment notwithstanding the verdict or, in the alternative, for a new trial. Pacific declared that insufficient evidence supported the jury's finding of negligence on defendant's part, the evidence plainly showed the conduct of GE's employees was an efficient intervening proximate cause, and the verdict was the product of jury sympathy. Once again, no objection on the ground of inconsistency was noted. The trial court denied these motions.

On defendant's appeal from the $422,536.35 judgment, it challenges for the first time the verdicts the jury handed down as irreconcilably inconsistent. It contends, therefore, negligence is entirely subsumed by breach of warranty and strict liability. Findings of no liability under either of those theories require, as a matter of law, a finding of no negligence on its part as the seller. Defendant alternatively contends the evidence adduced at trial is insufficient as a matter of law to support a finding of negligence.

The parties disagree whether the forms submitted to the jury called for special verdicts, as contemplated by Fed.R.Civ.P. 49(a), or a general verdict accompanied by written answers to interrogatories, as contemplated by Fed.R.Civ.P. 49(b). The trial court submitted two sets of forms to the jurors for their use in reporting their decisions. First, on a form with "Special Verdict" printed across the top, the jury was asked whether defendant breached either of the two implied warranties, whether it was strictly liable, whether it or plaintiff was negligent, whether any of these findings were a proximate cause of plaintiff's injuries, and what percentage of contribution and amount of damages was attributable to each cause of the injuries. The trial court also requested the jury to complete a second form labeled "Verdicts" that asked whether defendant was liable to plaintiff under each of the four alternative theories and for what amount.

Rule 49 of the Federal Rule of Civil Procedure states that a trial court may request from a jury a special verdict or a general verdict accompanied by answers to interrogatories. Under Rule 49(a) special verdicts are described as "a special written finding upon each issue of fact." A general verdict accompanied by answers to interrogatories, provided for in Rule 49(b), permits a jury to make written findings of fact and to enter a general verdict. The distinction between the two provisions is that under Rule 49(a) the jury answers primarily factual questions for the benefit of the trial court which then applies the law to those answers. Under Rule 49(b), the jury after being fully instructed answers the interrogatories, renders a general verdict and the trial court enters judgment on the jury's verdict.

In this case, the trial court's first set of forms called for answers to specific questions that would have served as either special verdicts, as contemplated by Rule 49(a), or answers to interrogatories, as contemplated by Rule 49(b). But the second set of forms was a hybrid; it did not offer the jurors only the ultimate choice normally called for by a general verdict—the defendant is liable to the plaintiff for a specified amount of damages, or the defendant is not liable to the plaintiff. Instead, it purported to ask for general verdicts on different theories of liability. Since the jury's fact-finding with respect to the different theories of liability was already properly elicited by the first set of detailed questions, the jurors should have been asked on the general verdict form only whether the defendant was liable to the plaintiff, and, if so, what damages are awarded. Despite the somewhat unusual nature of the general verdict forms submitted to the jury, it is apparent that the trial judge was endeavoring to use the provisions of Rule 49(b) and was seeking a general verdict accompanied by answers to interrogatories.

Although Rule 49(a) provides no instructions to the trial court for resolving jury inconsistencies in its special verdicts, we have held that judgment may not be entered pursuant to inconsistent special verdicts. Rule 49(b) instructs the trial court how to proceed when there are inconsistencies between the answers to the interrogatories and the general verdict. "When the answers are inconsistent with each other and one or more is likewise inconsistent with the general verdict, judgment shall not be entered, but the court shall return the jury for further consideration of its answers and verdict or shall order a new trial." Fed.R.Civ.P. 49(b).

Where there are seeming inconsistencies between interrogatory responses and a general verdict, a trial court should normally attempt to reconcile them. When the verdicts are not capable of reconciliation and resubmission of the determinations for reconsideration or clarification is not possible because the jury has been discharged, a new trial may be—but is not always—required.

The charge to the present jury required that it consider the necessary legal principles given to it by the trial court and make determinations of ultimate liability. In such case, the answers to the questions submitted to the jury are not special verdicts, despite the use of those words in the title appended to the form, and Rule 49(a) therefore does not apply. Further, the alleged inconsistency to which defendant points is between two general verdicts on different legal theories and not between a general verdict and responses to interrogatories. Hence, the instruction given to trial courts under Rule 49(b) has no application.

In any event, we think defendant waived its challenge to the jury verdict as inconsistent. It had ample opportunity to raise its objection to the alleged inconsistency and the course of the trial proceedings put it on notice that an inconsistency might arise. At a bench conference before the parties made their opening statements, Judge Coffrin noted the potential for inconsistencies between the four theories of recovery plaintiff alleged. He commented on the overlapping nature of the alternative theories again on the last day of trial. The instructions he gave the jury were discussed in detail with counsel at a precharge conference and at the bench just prior to the actual charge. Counsel were well aware of the content of the verdict forms submitted to the jury, including the separate questions relating to the four alternative theories.

After the jury returned its verdict, the district court polled the jurors individually and held a brief conference at the bench prior to the jury's discharge during which aspects of the verdict were discussed with counsel. Post trial motions were filed on May 30, 1991 and a hearing held on them on July 15, 1991. At no time throughout all these proceedings did defendant's counsel suggest the possibility that the verdicts rendered were inconsistent. * * *

Judgment affirmed.

Notes and Questions

1. Rule 49(b) describes a process by which the trial court may ask the jury to return a general verdict, but to accompany that general verdict with answers to certain interrogatories about particular issues in the case. A general verdict with interrogatories under Rule 49(b) requires the jury to give close attention to the more important fact issues and the jury's answers serve to check the propriety of the general verdict. One benefit of using this type of verdict is that if some legal error requires setting aside the general verdict and the answer to some of the interrogatories, it may be unnecessary to relitigate other issues already decided under properly submitted questions. For example, with no error on the issue of liability and causation, a new trial may be confined to damage issues.

The disadvantage of a general verdict with interrogatories is that the interrogatory answers may be inconsistent with each other *and* with the general verdict. The last part of Rule 49(b) addresses these issues. If the general verdict and the answers to specific questions are compatible, the court enters a judgment on the verdict and the answers. If the answers are consistent with each other but one or more of them is inconsistent with the general verdict, the trial court has three options: order the jury to deliberate further, order a new trial, or disregard the general verdict and order a judgment on the basis of the interrogatory answers (on the theory that special findings prevail over a general verdict). Finally, if the answers are inconsistent with each other and one or more of them is also inconsistent with the general verdict, the court can either order further deliberations or order a new trial.

2. Under Rule 49(a), the trial court has the authority to dispense with a general verdict altogether, and instead to submit various fact issues in the case to the jury in the form of individual fact questions, on each of which the jury is to return a special verdict. From the special verdict answers, the judge constructs the equivalent of a general verdict. A special verdict asks the jury to decide specific factual questions such as "At the time of the accident, was the plaintiff wearing her seat belt?" Because Rule 49(a) does not address the issue of inconsistency between answers, courts have had to improvise rules on inconsistency. Answers should be consistent with each other, and it is the duty of the trial court to harmonize them if possible. When the answers are inconsistent, a new trial is likely unless the judge asks the jury to reconsider its verdict in an attempt to remove the inconsistency.

3. In *Bills v. Aseltine*, 52 F.3d 596 (6th Cir. 1995), plaintiff brought a civil rights action against police officers for allowing a private security agent to participate in a search of her residence. After the court submitted special verdict interrogatories to a jury, it entered judgment for the officer who invited private security agent into plaintiff's home during execution of search warrant. The plaintiff appealed.

[Plaintiff] Bills argues that a special interrogatory on the verdict form did not state all the issues, was inaccurate, and consequently misled the jury. The verdict form provided to the jury stated: "Was it unreasonable under the circumstances for the defendant to invite [private security guard] William Meisling to enter plaintiff's home on August 20, 1987?" The court submitted questions asking if [police officer] Aseltine had a "reasonable and good faith belief" that he was not violating Bills's rights, and if his conduct proximately caused injury to Bills. The court also asked the jury to assess damages if appropriate. Bills contends that the court should have submitted her proposed special interrogatory: "Did Sgt. Aseltine unreasonably exceed the scope of the search warrant for the generator by permitting William Meisling, the Chief of Security at the Milford Proving Grounds, to enter the plaintiff's premises and conduct a general inspection for the suspected stolen GM property?"

Whether a court uses a special or general verdict rests in its discretion, as does the content and form of any interrogatories it chooses to submit. *Portage II v. Bryant Petroleum Corp.*, 899 F.2d 1514, 1520 (6th Cir.1990). Therefore, an appellate court reviews for an abuse of discretion. Federal Rule of Civil Procedure 49 governs the use of special verdicts and general verdicts with interrogatories. A special verdict is used where the jury finds only issues of fact and the court applies the law, as opposed to a general verdict with interrogatories, which is used to give close attention to certain factual matters.

The court below clearly used the latter. "Where special verdicts are involved, the jury's sole function is to determine the facts; therefore, neither an instruction on the law nor a summary concerning their role in relation to the law was necessary." *Id.* at 1521. The court's twenty-four jury instructions discussed legal matters in detail, and also required the jury to apply the law to the facts. The verdict form served only to direct the jury's attention to the most important issues: reasonableness, good faith, proximate cause, and damages.

Bills's proposed interrogatory is admittedly more detailed, but asks a question that is only slightly different. The plaintiff emphasizes whether Aseltine unreasonably exceeded the scope of the search warrant, while the court focuses on whether Aseltine's invitation was unreasonable. Undoubtedly, Bills would have preferred to remind the jury through the interrogatory that Meisling's presence was beyond the scope of the search warrant for the generator. However, that is the job of Bills's attorney at closing argument.

Bills cites several cases for the obvious proposition that special interrogatories must fairly present the relevant issues to the jury. Yet reasonableness, good faith, proximate cause and damage are the relevant issues. Further, the interrogatories must be considered in the context of the entire jury charge. In light of the court's detailed jury instructions, the interrogatories were neither inaccurate, misleading nor confusing.

4. Why do trial courts not favor special verdicts or general verdicts with interrogatories under Rule 49? First, as with discovery requests, it may be difficult for a judge to frame precise and accurate questions, leading to a corresponding increase in the chance for error. Second, jurors may misunderstand the relationship between the questions and give inconsistent answers. It is not surprising, then, that trial courts generally exercise their discretion not to use these "different" types of verdicts.

Problems

1. In a products liability case, the trial court submits a general verdict with interrogatories. The interrogatories address such fundamental issues as negligence, proximate cause, and the complete defense of assumption of risk. The jury returns with a general verdict for the plaintiff, and answers to the following interrogatories:

Was the defendant negligent?	Answer: Yes
Did the plaintiff assume the risk of injury?	Answer: Yes

Is there a problem with this verdict? If not, what should the court do? If so, what remedy is available to fix any problem?

2. Same as #1, except that the jury returns with a general verdict for the plaintiff, and answers to the following interrogatories:

Was there a defect in the product?   Answer: No
Was the defect the proximate cause
of the plaintiff's injury?   Answer: Yes

Is there a problem with this verdict? If not, what should the court do? If so, what remedy is available to fix any problem?

3.   Same as #1, except that the jury returns with a general verdict for the plaintiff, and answers to the following interrogatories:

Was there a defect in the product?   Answer: Yes
Was the defect the proximate cause
of the plaintiff's injury?   Answer: Yes

Is there a problem with this verdict? If not, what should the court do? If so, what remedy is available to fix any problem?

4.   Same as #1, except that the jury reports to the court that it has agreed on a general verdict but cannot agree on the answer to one or more of the interrogatories. Can the trial judge withdraw all of the interrogatories and enter a general verdict?

Exercise

For the state where a) you intend to practice after graduation, b) your law school is located, and/or c) your professor assigns, go to that state's annotated statutes and research the procedural rules by which jury instructions and jury verdicts are governed. Based on your research, print the rule and bring it to class for discussion. In addition, answer the following questions.

1.   As for jury instructions,

A.   Are standard jury instructions used?

B.   Must proposed instructions be in writing?

C.   Are there any circumstances, e.g., plain error, when an instruction will be reviewed on appeal, without the need for an objection having been made?

D.   Is the jury instructed before or after counsel's closing arguments?

2.   As for jury verdicts,

A.   Do the rules provide alternatives to a general verdict? If so, what types of alternative verdicts are used?

B.   If the answer to the first part of 2.A is yes, what remedies are available when alternative verdict answers are inconsistent with each other and/or with the general verdict?

CHAPTER 10

DISPOSITIVE AND POST-TRIAL MOTIONS

A. DISMISSALS

INTRODUCTORY PROBLEM

In *Grant and Hayes v. Harding Cycle*, following the pleadings and discovery, plaintiff Grant became concerned about the bills for attorney's fees and for court costs that he already had incurred. He concluded that by the end of trial the cost of the litigation would approach the level of compensatory damages that he and Hayes were seeking from the defendant. Grant decided that he needed to move on with his personal and business life, because there was no guarantee that he and Hayes would prevail at trial. Meanwhile, Hayes who had incurred the same bills as Grant had not been able to pay his share of the attorney's fees. As a result, plaintiffs' counsel stopped his preparation for trial and did nothing to pursue the case for eight months.

Coincidentally, on the same day, two motions were filed in the case. First, against the advice of his counsel and his co-plaintiff Hayes, Grant voluntarily dismissed his complaint against Harding Cycle. Second, sensing that the plaintiffs had overextended themselves financially in the case, the defendant moved to dismiss the case because the plaintiffs seemed to have lost their nerve to prosecute their claim.

Is either Grant or Harding Cycle entitled to relief from the trial court?

Governing Rule: Rule 41(a)-(b)

The Federal Rules control the procedural considerations and the effects of dismissals. Rule 41(a) deals with voluntary dismissals, which are essentially a plaintiff's remedy. For example, if a plaintiff decides that, upon further reflection, she does not want her claim to go forward, she may have the case dismissed by the trial court. Rule 41(b) concerns involuntary dismissals, which constitute a defendant's remedy. The involuntary dismissal may occur as a result of the plaintiff's failure to comply with rules like Rule 12(b)(6) or a failure to move the case at a pace satisfactory to the court, which may assume that the lack of progress in the case indicates the plaintiff's lack of interest in pursuing it.

1. Voluntary Dismissals

MARQUES v. FEDERAL RESERVE BANK OF CHICAGO

286 F.3d 1014 (7th Cir. 2002)

Posner, Circuit Judge.

The plaintiffs brought suit against the Federal Reserve Bank of Chicago and the Federal Deposit Insurance Corporation, plus the shareholders of the federal reserve bank (the other national banks in the bank's federal reserve district), which are individually liable for the bank's debts "to the extent of the amount of their subscriptions to [the bank's] stock at the par value thereof in addition to the amount subscribed." 12 U.S.C. § 502. The plaintiffs claim to be the agents for the owners of $25 billion in bearer bonds that the bank had issued back in 1934 in exchange for 1665 metric tons of gold. They want the bank ordered to redeem the bonds for face value plus simple interest at 4 percent since 1934 (although the bonds matured in 1965); the total amount of money they are seeking is thus close to $100 billion.

The suit is preposterous. There is no record of any such bond issue, and as the national debt of the United States was only $28 billion in 1934, as a year later the entire stock of gold owned by the United States had a value of only $9 billion, and as no securities issue by a U.S. government entity exceeded $100 million before 1940, the claim that in 1934 a federal reserve bank issued bonds that virtually doubled the national debt and added $25 billion in gold to the government's gold holdings can only cause one to laugh. What is more (not that more is needed), although the price at which the government bought gold was fixed at $35 an ounce effective at the beginning of that year, the plaintiffs are claiming that the federal reserve bank bought gold from their predecessors at a price of $467.02 an ounce. The plaintiffs further undermine their case by arguing that there is an international conspiracy to deny the validity of these bonds, a conspiracy pursuant to which the plaintiffs' documents expert, who certified the genuineness of the bonds (in an unsworn and evasive report), has been repeatedly arrested and then released without charges being filed.

The bank's lawyer told us without being contradicted that the Department of Justice has declined to prosecute the persons involved in the fraud because no one could possibly be deceived by such obvious nonsense. We are puzzled by this suggestion. The Treasury has established a Website warning the public against the class of frauds (called "Morgenthaus," after Henry Morgenthau, Jr., the Secretary of the

Treasury in 1934) of which the bond issue alleged in this suit is one (the others also involve supposed $25 billion bond issues). See http://www.publicdebt.treas.gov/cc/ ccphony3.htm. There is no ceiling on gullibility. Mr. Portman, the plaintiff who argued the appeal pro se, is one of the deceived—if he is not one of the deceivers, another and perhaps more plausible possibility, Portman having recently submitted a demand to the Federal Reserve Bank of Cleveland that it pay him $125 billion to redeem a similar set of fictitious 1934 vintage "Federal Reserve Bonds." We are sending this opinion to the Justice Department for whatever further consideration the Department may wish to give the fraud.

* * * The plaintiffs attempted to dismiss their suit voluntarily under Fed.R.Civ.P. 41(a)(1). Had they succeeded in their attempt, the dismissal would have been without prejudice, and so they could reinstate the suit without facing the bar of res judicata. They can't do that if the judgment granting the bank's motion for summary judgment—a judgment on the merits and therefore with prejudice—stands.

The reason they give for having wanted to dismiss their suit is, naturally, preposterous—that they were in serious negotiations in Spain with the U.S. Government and hoped that the government would acknowledge the legitimacy of their claim so that they could sell the bonds to Russia. But one doesn't need a good reason, or even a sane or any reason, to dismiss a suit voluntarily. The right is absolute, as Rule 41(a)(1) and the cases interpreting it make clear, until, as the rule states, the defendant serves an answer or a motion for summary judgment. The plaintiffs filed their notice of voluntary dismissal, and the bank served a motion to dismiss the suit under Rule 12(b)(6), on the same day. A motion under Rule 12(b)(6) becomes a motion for summary judgment when the defendant attaches materials outside the complaint, as the bank did, and the court "actually considers" some or all of those materials. But the judge did not convert the bank's motion to a motion for summary judgment until later.

And anyway we do not know which document, the plaintiffs' notice of voluntary dismissal or the defendant's motion to dismiss, came first. The plaintiffs argue that the bank acknowledged in the district court that the notice of voluntary dismissal was filed before the motion to dismiss was served, but the only record of this acknowledgment is a transcript that the parties neglected to make a part of the appellate record. However, the district judge, rather than make a finding on which document came first, appears to have believed that as long as they were on the same day, it didn't matter. (It is unquestioned that the plaintiffs did succeed in dismissing the FDIC as a defendant under Rule 41(a)(1), and it is not a party to this appeal.) We cannot find an appellate case on who has the burden of proving the sequence of the submissions, but *Keal v. Monarch Life Ins. Co.*, 126 F.R.D. 567 (D.Kan.1989), places the burden on the defendant, sensibly, as it seems to us, since it is the defendant that is asserting the right to prevent the plaintiff from dismissing the suit.

* * * There is ... considerable and unchallenged case authority (including decisions by this court) that a judgment on the merits that is entered after the plaintiff has filed a proper Rule 41(a)(1) notice of dismissal is indeed void. * * *

We are therefore compelled to reverse the judgment and direct the dismissal of the suit, without prejudice, under Rule 41(a)(1). Should the plaintiffs attempt to bring a new suit similar to the one they are dismissing, namely a fraudulent and possibly a criminal suit, they will be subject to appropriate sanctions. Reversed.

Notes and Questions

1. Federal Rule 41(a) addresses the circumstances by which a plaintiff can voluntarily dismiss a claim prior to adjudication. The purpose of the rule is to give the plaintiff the right to take a case out of court if no other party will be prejudiced by the dismissal. Why *should* a plaintiff be allowed to dismiss her claim before it is resolved on the merits? Why *would* a plaintiff voluntarily dismiss her own case? One possibility may be that the plaintiff has identified a more convenient forum, but why did that not occur to the plaintiff when she first filed her claim? Can you think of other reasons?

2. Rule 41(a)(1) provides two methods by which a plaintiff has an "absolute right" to dismiss a claim without having to obtain the consent of the trial court. First, prior to service of an answer or a motion for summary judgment, a plaintiff by her own unilateral act can dismiss her claim merely by filing a notice (not a motion, which invites a response by the opposing side) that informs the court and all other parties that she is dismissing her claim. The rule's application is automatic, without regard to the effort already expended by the court and/or the defendant on the case. See *American Soccer Co., Inc. v. Score First Enterprises*, 187 F.3d 1108 (9th Cir. 1999).

3. What is the effect of a voluntary dismissal by notice? A corollary point to the *Marques* holding is that once a notice of dismissal is filed, the trial court loses jurisdiction over the case. See, e.g., *Commercial Space Management Co., Inc. v. The Boeing Co., Inc.*, 193 F.3d 1074 (9th Cir. 1999). Filing the notice

> closes the file. There is nothing the defendant can do to fan the ashes of that action into life and the court has no role to play. This is a matter of right running to the plaintiff and may not be extinguished or circum-scribed by adversary or court. There is not even a perfunctory order of court closing the file. Its alpha and omega was the doing of the plaintiff alone. He suffers no impairment beyond his fee for filing.

American Cyanamid Co. v. McGhee, 317 F.2d 295 (5th Cir.1963).

4. The notice rule is explicitly subject to the provision of Rule 23(e), whereby a plaintiff cannot voluntarily dismiss a class action by this notice procedure. What is the purpose of that provision? What effect would a voluntary dismissal have on the absent members of a class that has already been certified by the court? Courts commonly are willing to approve class

action dismissals under Rule 23(e) that have been settled between the parties.

5. Unilateral dismissals by the plaintiff are subject to the so-called "Two Dismissal Rule." The first voluntary dismissal of a claim is without prejudice to bringing the claim again. However, as you read in Rule 41(a)(1), a notice dismissal operates as an adjudication on the merits when the plaintiff already had dismissed the claim (with or without the consent of the court) in any state or federal court. The effect of the "Two Dismissal Rule" is that when the plaintiff tries to file the claim a *third* time, the defendant can refer to Rule 41(a)(1) in support of his assertion that the third filing is precluded.

6. The second type of voluntary dismissal has no time restriction. Under Rule 41(a)(1)(ii), a case may be dismissed *at any time* by a signed agreement of all the parties. Dismissals by stipulation are presumed to be without prejudice unless they specify otherwise.

Under Rule 41(a)(2) if a party cannot dismiss unilaterally or with the consent of the opposing party, a plaintiff must file a motion to obtain the court's consent to dismiss. Whether a trial court grants or denies the motion is within the court's discretion, and some courts have suggested relevant factors for the exercise of that discretion. In addition, a dismissal granted by the court is without prejudice to the case being filed again.

HINFIN REALTY CORP. v. PITTSTON CO.

206 F.R.D. 350 (E.D.N.Y. 2002)

SPATT, Judge.

[Landowners brought a claim to recover the costs of environmental cleanup. During discovery, the landowners moved to voluntarily dismiss action without prejudice and the defendant opposed the motion.]

The Second Circuit has delineated a number of factors that courts should consider when determining whether a defendant will be prejudiced by a voluntary dismissal. See *Zagano v. Fordham Univ.*, 900 F.2d 12 (2d Cir. 1990). These factors include: (1) the plaintiff's diligence in bringing the motion; (2) any "undue vexatiousness" on the plaintiff's part; (3) the extent to which the suit has progressed, including the defendant's efforts and expense in preparation for trial; (4) the duplicative expense of relitigation; and (5) the adequacy of the plaintiff's explanation for a need to dismiss.

The Court finds that the plaintiffs were diligent in bringing their motion to dismiss the action without prejudice because they filed it immediately after the events that led to their decision not to pursue the action at this time. The complaint was initially filed on July 24, 2000, but no proceedings occurred during the remainder of that year. The plaintiffs filed their amended complaint on February 1, 2001, and Judge Orenstein held an initial conference four days later. The plaintiffs litigated the action throughout 2001, responding to Pittston's motion to stay the proceeding and to Pittston's discovery demands.

In early January 2002, the plaintiffs determined that they no longer wished to proceed with the action. First, they had begun responding to Pittston's discovery demands and realized that they wished to conserve their limited finances rather than pursue this action. In addition, Donald Death, Sr., had fallen ill, his prognosis was not good, and he was the individual who knew the most about the history of the premises, which goes back many years. In this kind of environmental case, the so-called "ancient" history is extremely important in determining the source of pollution. Therefore, in a letter dated January 11, 2002, the plaintiffs informed the Court that they wished to withdraw their opposition to the defendant's motion to stay the proceedings because the defendant had presented them with documentary evidence showing that Pittston was the incorrect defendant. The plaintiffs also advised the Court that they had asked Pittston to stipulate to a dismissal without prejudice so that the plaintiffs could investigate whether Pittston was the proper defendant, but Pittston declined to consent to the dismissal.

Had the plaintiffs prosecuted this case more vigorously, they might have reached this conclusion earlier in the action. Nevertheless, the Court finds that as soon as the plaintiffs made the decision to dismiss the action without prejudice, they informed Pittston. In addition, immediately after Pittston declined to consent to the withdrawal, the plaintiffs' withdrew their opposition to Pittston's motion to stay the action. When that tactic failed to halt the proceedings, the plaintiffs promptly filed the present motion. Accordingly, the Court finds that the plaintiffs were diligent in moving to dismiss the action without prejudice, and thus, the first *Zagano* factor weighs in their favor.

In addition, the Court finds no evidence of vexatiousness on the part of the plaintiff. Although the plaintiff could have pursued the action with more vigor, there is no evidence to suggest that the case was brought to harass the defendant. To the contrary, the plaintiffs have made few, if any, requests of the defendant after filing this lawsuit. Therefore, the Court finds that this factor also weighs in favor of granting the plaintiffs' motion.

The Court finds that the third *Zagano* factor, the extent to which the suit has progressed, is neutral. The fact that the case is approximately 21–months old weighs against granting the motion to dismiss without prejudice. However, when the plaintiffs first asked Pittston to agree to a dismissal without prejudice in January 2002, virtually no discovery had been conducted. Indeed, in an order dated November 2, 2001, Judge Orenstein stated, "Little or no discovery done." In the two months following that order, Pittston served extensive interrogatories, a notice to admit 188 facts, and a request for documents. On the other hand, the plaintiffs have not made any discovery requests. Importantly, as of the date of this order, no depositions have been conducted. Further, the Court notes that the defendant chose not to move to dismiss the case, and neither party has moved for summary judgment. In addition, a trial date has not been set. Thus, in light of the fact that the case is now 21–months old, but little action has been taken, the Court finds the third *Zagano* factor to be neutral.

In their memorandum in opposition, Pittston claims that absent the plaintiffs' conduct, the case would be ready for summary disposition. The Court finds this argument unpersuasive in light of the fact that Pittston seeks to file a third-party action, which would require additional trial preparation. Accordingly, the defendants' argument does not alter the Court's conclusion that the third *Zagano* factor is neutral.

Pittston contends that if it is forced to relitigate this case, it faces the prospect of duplicative expenses. The defendant states that it has spent significant sums propounding and compelling discovery in this case and avers that if the plaintiffs re-file the lawsuit, Pittston will be required to "re-answer the complaint, re-exchange Rule 26(a) disclosures, re-retain its environmental experts, attend status hearings, and re-issue discovery." If the plaintiffs choose to file another lawsuit against Pittston, the grounds likely will be the same, and much of the work already done by Pittston will be easy to duplicate. Certainly, Pittston can use some of the material discovered and the legal work already done, if the case is renewed in the future. Further, this is not a case in which substantial discovery has been conducted, and the Court does not perceive a large amount of duplicative expenditures. As such, the fourth *Zagano* factor does not weigh against dismissal without prejudice.

The Court finds that the explanations for the plaintiffs' application are sufficient to support the motion. Donald Death, Jr., the president of the plaintiff corporations, needs time to settle his late father's affairs. He also requires time to review the companies' documents, some of which are over 40 years old. In addition, the plaintiffs' environmental consultant must devise a remediation plan to be approved by the DEC. Donald Death, Jr., wishes to gather all of this relevant information before deciding whether to recoup the cost of remediation through litigation. While he investigates this matter, he does not want to spend additional money to continue an action that he might find to be unnecessary. In doing so, he is sparing the defendants from expending additional monies in the defense of this lawsuit. The plaintiffs have limited assets and, apparently, wish to spend the money they have remediating their land, rather than litigating this matter.

Economic concerns, such as those raised by the plaintiff, almost always dictate the course of litigation, and this case is no exception. The Court is not persuaded by Pittston's argument that the plaintiffs' motion is an attempt to avoid the discovery cutoff date. Accordingly, the Court finds that the plaintiffs' explanation for their request weighs heavily in favor of dismissing this action without prejudice.

Thus, an application of the *Zagano* factors leads the Court to conclude that the plaintiffs' motion to dismiss the action without prejudice should be granted. However, Pittston argues that it will suffer prejudice if the plaintiffs are permitted to refile this case at a later date because the witnesses will die, such as Donald Death, Sr., for example, memories will continue to fade, and the land may be sold. The defendant is not the only party who may suffer the consequences of the passage of time. The memories of witnesses for both sides may fade and the witnesses for both sides might become unavailable. Indeed, the unavailability of Donald Death, Sr., who was an important witness for the plaintiffs, is a main reason that the plaintiffs seek to discontinue this action. As both parties could suffer due to the passage of time, the Court finds that the defendant's argument against dismissing the action is not determinative. Indeed, the prospect of "starting a litigation all over again does not constitute legal prejudice." *D'Alto v. Dahon Cal., Inc.*, 100 F.3d 281 (2d Cir. 1996). As such, the Court grants the plaintiffs' motion to dismiss the action without prejudice.

However, this does not end the inquiry. Pittston asks the Court to condition the dismissal upon an award of its costs, including attorney's fees, in the amount of $135,000. Where a plaintiff successfully dismisses a suit without prejudice under Rule 41(a)(2), courts often grant the defendant an award of costs or fees. See *Colombrito v. Kelly*, 764 F.2d 122, 133 (2d Cir.1985) ("Fee awards are often made when a plaintiff dismisses a suit without prejudice."). "The purpose of such awards is generally to reimburse the defendant for the litigation costs incurred, in view of the risk (often the certainty) faced by the defendant that the same suit will be refiled and will impose duplicative expenses upon him." *Colombrito*, 764 F.2d at 133. By contrast, courts rarely award fees and costs when an action is dismissed voluntarily with prejudice.

Applying these guidelines, the Court must seriously consider the application to award reasonable attorney's fees and costs to the defendant. Of course, if the plaintiffs were to agree to dismiss the action with prejudice, the Court would deny the defendant's motion for attorney's fees and costs because the risk of duplicative expenses will be moot. However, even if the Court were to grant this application, Pittston has not submitted billing time sheets or affidavits in support of its claim that it has incurred over $135,000 in attorney's fees and costs defending this suit since July 24, 2000. In addition, the plaintiffs have not had an opportunity to respond to a detailed accounting of Pittston's claim. Accordingly, the Court denies the defendant's motion for attorney's fees and costs, without prejudice and with leave to renew with the proper documentation and in accordance with the Court's Individual Rules.

By making this decision, the Court is not indicating that it has, as yet, decided to grant this application for attorney's fees and costs. Indeed, if the plaintiffs submit a notice to the Court, within ten days of the date of this decision, indicating that they are dismissing the action with prejudice, the Court will deny an application for attorney's fees and costs, because Pittston will no longer bear the risk of duplicative litigation and expense. However, if the plaintiffs decide not to submit a notice indicating that they are dismissing the action with prejudice, the defendant is permitted to file an application for attorney's fees and costs and is instructed to submit the appropriate documentation in support of its application. The Court notes that with reasonable certainty, it will reduce the defendant's fee application by the amount of work the defendant will be able to use in a subsequent litigation. * * *

Notes and Questions

1. Can you explain the meaning of each *Zagano* factor and how each contributes to the overall exercise of the court's discretion? Without the benefit of the *Zagano* list of factors, a court typically will grant a Rule 41(a)(2) motion for voluntary dismissal unless the defendant can show that the dismissal will result in some legal prejudice to him other than the prospect of a second lawsuit. The purpose of requiring a court order to dismiss is to prevent voluntary dismissals which unfairly affect the opposing party. Can you explain how examining a list of factors is preferable to deciding merely whether the defendant will experience prejudice from the dismissal?

2. Because dismissals under Rule 41(a)(1) are by notice or stipulation, the court does not set any conditions on that type of dismissal. However, Rule 41(a)(2) explains that a court may grant a motion for voluntary dismissal "upon such terms and conditions as the court deems proper." What is the purpose of imposing such conditions? In *Hinfin Realty*, the defendant sought payment of its attorney's fees and costs as a condition for the dismissal. What are some other conditions that could be attached to a dismissal? As you might expect, the plaintiff can decline the dismissal if it is dissatisfied with the conditions imposed by the court. If a plaintiff accepts a dismissal but fails to meet the condition, the court's order of dismissal may be modified so that the claim is dismissed "with prejudice."

3. What happens to a defendant's counterclaim after the plaintiff seeks voluntary dismissal of her claim? The second sentence of Rule 41(a)(2) precludes the court from dismissing the plaintiff's claim unless the defendant's counterclaim can remain pending for independent adjudication. By itself, a compulsory counterclaim may or may not have an independent basis for subject matter jurisdiction. If it does have an independent basis, dismissal of the plaintiff's claim has no effect on the counterclaim's continued viability. If it does not have an independent basis, it is likely that the court is hearing the compulsory counterclaim because of supplemental jurisdiction. When the dismissal occurs, the trial court has to decide whether it wants to exercise its discretion to continue to hear the claim under the criteria in 28 U.S.C. § 1367(c), one of which relates to the dismissal of all claims which had an independent basis for subject matter jurisdiction. See, e.g., *Piedra v. Mentor Graphics Corp.*, 979 F.Supp. 1297 (D. Or 1997) (court dismisses compulsory counterclaim as well as the plaintiff's claim).

2. Involuntary Dismissals

Rule 41(b) codifies the inherent authority to dismiss a claim against the wishes of the plaintiff and with prejudice to the plaintiff bringing the claim again. The rule is often used to authorize dismissals for failure to prosecute, but the rule also governs involuntary dismissals for failing to comply with other rules or with a court order. Thus, involuntary dismissal is an available sanction for such rule violations such as a discovery violation (Rule 37) or a failure to state a claim upon which relief can be granted (Rule 12(b)(6)). In *LeSane v. Hall's Security Analyst*, 239 F.3d 206 (2d Cir. 2001), the court identified several criteria for deciding whether to grant an involuntary dismissal for violating a court order:

> the duration of the plaintiff's failures, whether plaintiff had received notice that further delays would result in dismissal, whether the defendant is likely to be prejudiced by further delay, whether the district judge has take[n] care to strik[e] the balance between alleviating court calendar congestion and protecting a party's right to due process and a fair chance to be heard ... and whether the judge has adequately assessed the efficacy of lesser sanctions.

LaSane, 239 F.3d at 209. Rule 41(b), providing for involuntary dismissals, is a defendant's remedy. What is meant by an involuntary dismissal for "failure to prosecute"?

AURA LAMP & LIGHTING INC. v. INTERNATIONAL TRADING CORP.

325 F.3d 903 (7th Cir. 2003)

ILANA DIAMOND ROVNER, Circuit Judge.

The district court dismissed this case for want of prosecution and the plaintiff, Aura Lamp & Lighting Inc. ("Aura Lamp"), appeals. * * *

I

Because the district court dismissed the case for want of prosecution and for violations of discovery orders, the salient facts are few. Aura Lamp and International Trading Corporation ("ITC") allegedly entered into a number of contracts relating to lighting products and their components. The details of these agreements are unnecessary to the resolution of this appeal. Aura Lamp sued ITC in a six-count complaint. Five of the counts allege breach of contract. The sixth claim seeks to invalidate a patent held by ITC. Aura Lamp filed the complaint on April 6, 2000. A few weeks later, the district court ordered Aura Lamp to amend its complaint by May 19, 2000 to cure jurisdictional defects related to certain diversity jurisdiction allegations in the complaint. That date came and went without any amendment to the complaint by Aura Lamp. ITC then moved to dismiss the complaint or in the alternative to transfer the case. The district court set a briefing schedule, ordering Aura Lamp to reply by July 5, 2000. Again the date passed without any action by Aura Lamp. ITC complied with the district court's scheduling order by filing its reply brief even though no responsive brief had been filed by Aura Lamp. Aura Lamp then belatedly filed a response brief which the district court accepted over ITC's objection. The district court denied the motion to dismiss, ordered Aura Lamp once again to amend its complaint to cure the jurisdictional defect and threatened dismissal if Aura Lamp continued to ignore the court's orders. Aura Lamp then amended the complaint.

On December 21, 2000, the court ordered the close of written discovery by March 21, 2001 and the close of all other discovery by August 1, 2001. Approximately one week later, ITC served interrogatories, document requests and requests for admission on Aura Lamp. Under the Federal Rules of Civil Procedure, Aura Lamp was to respond to this discovery within thirty days. The thirty days passed without a response from Aura Lamp and without any request for an extension of time to respond. Numerous calls and letters from ITC's counsel followed, and Aura Lamp failed to meet two agreed extension dates. ITC then moved to compel discovery, asking that the requests for admission be deemed admitted, and also seeking sanctions. The case was scheduled for a status conference on March 22, 2001, and the court took up the motion to compel at that time. When asked to explain the delays in responding to discovery, Aura Lamp's counsel replied that he was solely responsible for the case, stating, "I wish I had somebody else to go through this stuff." [Transcript references are deleted.] He explained that his client was a "one-man operation" that did not have the resources to sort through the documents requested. Over ITC's objection, the district court elected to grant one final extension to Aura Lamp, allowing counsel for Aura Lamp to pick the date on which all discovery was to be produced. Several times during the status conference, the court threatened dismissal of the case if Aura Lamp failed to meet the deadline. ("I'll set a deadline, if the case [sic] isn't met, the case is going away."); ("I want to set a date that is going to be real so that if it isn't met, I'm going to take severe action in this case."); ("Due to the amount of time it's taken the plaintiff to respond to these discovery requests, and given the enormous amount of time I'm giving you to respond over the objection of the defendants, if there is not good faith compliance by that date, I am going to seriously consider a motion to dismiss for want of prosecution."). *See also* ("I'm going to have to take some severe action."); ("[I]f I set a deadline, given all that's transpired, it's going to have to be it."); ("I'm setting a deadline, and I want it to be a real deadline, and I want there to be consequences if it isn't followed."). Aura Lamp's counsel asked to set the deadline to the last working day in April, amounting to an additional one and a half month extension. Shortly thereafter, ITC served a second set of document requests on Aura Lamp.

On the very last day of April 2001, Aura Lamp served ITC with responses that ITC characterized as incomplete and defective. According to ITC, Aura Lamp failed to produce a single page of documents and filed specious objections to both the document and interrogatory requests. Aura Lamp filed no response to ITC's second request for the production of documents. ITC's counsel again tried to resolve the matter with a letter requesting compliance. When Aura Lamp did not respond, ITC moved to dismiss the case for repeated violations of court orders, failure to comply with discovery, and failure to prosecute. On June 15, 2001, the court held a status hearing on the motion. Counsel for Aura Lamp informed the court he wanted to reply to the motion in writing and that he intended to file two motions of his own. Remarkably (given the tenor of the prior hearing), he intended to move to extend time to propound the plaintiff's discovery requests and also for additional time to respond to ITC's request for the production of documents. After setting out a deadline for Aura Lamp to file these new motions and briefing schedules for all pending motions, the court set a hearing date of July 11, 2001.

At the July 11 hearing, the court learned that, in addition to missing several other deadlines, Aura Lamp had failed to comply with the briefing schedule set on June 15. Counsel for Aura Lamp explained that the most recent delays were due to secretarial difficulties, computer problems, and scheduling challenges posed by an ongoing trial in chancery court. He insisted that his conduct was not wilful and wanton but rather due to unforeseen circumstances beyond his control. The district court replied, "I don't think I have to find wilful and wanton." Ultimately, the court found that Aura Lamp repeatedly missed court-ordered deadlines and failed to prosecute the case. She noted that Aura Lamp had been granted numerous extensions both by the court and by counsel for ITC to no avail. Aura Lamp had also failed to follow basic court procedures by failing to sign many of the documents filed with the court. The court concluded, "[Y]ou brought the case, and the plaintiff has to prosecute a case when they bring it, and the plaintiff hasn't. And I think to allow this to go on anymore would just compound all the problems that have occurred by really doing something that's unfair to the defendants." The court then dismissed the case for want of prosecution and denied all other motions as moot. Aura Lamp appeals.

II

On appeal, Aura Lamp maintains that the district court erred in dismissing the case under Federal Rule of Civil Procedure 37 because that rule requires a finding of wilful and wanton misconduct, and the court thus applied the wrong standard. Aura Lamp also contends that dismissal under Rule 37 or Rule 41 requires specific warnings prior to dismissal and also requires that the court consider lesser sanctions before dismissing. Aura Lamp argues that the court's warnings were inadequate and that no lesser sanctions were considered before the court dismissed the case. * * *

B

ITC moved to dismiss the complaint with prejudice "pursuant to Fed.R.Civ.Proc.... 41(b)." The district judge ultimately dismissed the case for want of prosecution pursuant to Rule 41(b) but she also discussed and may have relied upon Aura Lamp's violations of orders related to discovery. * * * In our Circuit, we review for abuse of discretion the district court's decision to sanction a plaintiff by dismissing a suit. Our review of a dismissal for want of prosecution is highly deferential. *Ball v. City of Chicago*, 2 F.3d 752, 760 (7th Cir.1993). In order to find an abuse of discretion, the district court's decision must strike us as fundamentally wrong.

Certain principles guide the district court in determining whether to dismiss a case for want of prosecution pursuant to Rule 41. Ideally, the district court should consider the frequency and magnitude of the plaintiff's failure to comply with deadlines for the prosecution of the suit, the apportionment of responsibility for those failures between the plaintiff and his counsel, the effect of those failures on the judge's calendar and time, the prejudice if any to the defendant caused by the plaintiff's dilatory conduct, the probable merits of the suit, and the consequences of dismissal for the social objectives of the type of litigation that the suit represents. *Ball,* 2 F.3d at 759–60. "There is no 'grace period' before dismissal for failure to prosecute is permissible and no requirement of graduated sanctions, but there must be an explicit warning before the case is dismissed." *Ball,* 2 F.3d at 760. Aura Lamp asks us to find the district court abused its discretion in dismissing the case because (1) the court did not adequately warn Aura Lamp that the case would be dismissed; (2) the court failed to consider whether lesser sanctions would be effective; (3) Aura Lamp's violations were not of sufficient frequency or magnitude to warrant dismissal; (4) in apportioning the fault between the parties, the district court should have found that ITC's conduct was responsible for more egregious delays than Aura Lamp's; (5) neither the court nor the defendant suffered prejudice due to Aura Lamp; (6) Aura Lamp's claims are meritorious.

We begin with the issue of warning. The district judge is not obliged to warn the plaintiff repeatedly nor is the court required to issue a formal rule to show cause before dismissing a case. *Ball,* 2 F.3d at 755. "A judge is not obliged to treat lawyers like children" *Ball,* 2 F.3d at 755. All that is required is explicit warning. Here, the court repeatedly and expressly warned Aura Lamp that it was contemplating dismissal during the March 22 status conference. ("I'll set a deadline, if the case [sic] isn't met, the case is going away."); ("I want to set a date that is going to be real so that if it isn't met, I'm going to take severe action in this case."); ("Due to the amount of time it's taken the plaintiff to respond to these discovery requests, and given the enormous amount of time I'm giving you to respond over the objection of the defendants, if there is not good faith compliance by that date, I am going to seriously consider a motion to dismiss for want of prosecution."). This is by no means a complete list of the court's warnings but is merely a representative sample. These warnings are more than adequate. Aura Lamp was on notice of the consequences of further failures to respond to the court's orders.

Aura Lamp also faults the court for failing to consider the efficacy of lesser sanctions first. Although we recommend that courts consider sanctioning a misbehaving lawyer before the sanction of dismissal is imposed on a possibly faultless plaintiff, we do not require that courts do so. *Ball,* 2 F.3d at 758. At the July 11 hearing, as the court was ruling on the motion to dismiss, counsel for Aura Lamp asked the court to allow him to resign from the case and find someone else who could handle the case properly. The court replied that it was too late for such a maneuver. The district judge acknowledged that both counsel and his client had difficulties in prosecuting the case but that ultimately the plaintiff was responsible for prosecuting the case and had failed to do so. Clearly the court believed this was the only effective sanction at the time. Especially in light of counsel's earlier admission that his client was a "one-man operation" without the resources to respond to discovery, it would appear that the court did not abuse its discretion in refusing to impose lesser sanctions. See also *Dickerson v. Board of Educ. of Ford Heights, Ill.*, 32 F.3d 1114, 1117 (7th Cir.1994) (where a pattern of dilatory conduct is clear, dismissal need not be preceded by the imposition of less severe sanctions).

Aura Lamp next argues that its violations were not sufficiently egregious and were too infrequent to warrant such a harsh sanction. This claim is easily answered by merely listing the violations. In addition to failing to sign pleadings filed with the court, Aura Lamp repeatedly missed court-imposed deadlines for both discovery and motion practice, ignored agreed extensions, and failed to amend its complaint to cure a jurisdictional defect for several months after the court ordered it do so. Moreover, Aura Lamp asked permission to propound discovery on the defendant after the court-ordered discovery cut-off date, a date that Aura Lamp's counsel had himself selected at the court's invitation. We have upheld dismissals in cases where the violations were comparable to or less severe than they are here, and no court would find an abuse of discretion in these circumstances.

Aura Lamp maintains that ITC caused at least some of the delay. But in apportioning the fault between Aura Lamp and ITC, Aura Lamp offers no valid evidence of dilatory conduct by ITC that contributed to any of Aura Lamp's failures. The sum and substance of Aura Lamp's argument on this point is that ITC did not tell Aura Lamp's counsel that his extraordinarily late responses to discovery were evasive and incomplete. Aura Lamp also complains that ITC did not contact its counsel concerning responses to ITC's request for production of documents. Aura Lamp claims it made the documents available for inspection and ITC did not take advantage of the opportunity to review them. However, Aura Lamp fails to mention that ITC specifically requested that Aura Lamp photocopy the documents and forward them to ITC. This argument is frivolous. So too is Aura Lamp's claim that neither the court nor the defendant suffered any prejudice at its hands. The district court specifically listed the motions that ITC was forced to bring to protect its interests in the case, adding needless expense to the case and clogging the court's docket. We conclude that this is not a close question. On the Rule 41 issues, the appeal is doomed. . . .

Notes and Questions

1. The Supreme Court reviewed a dismissal for want of prosecution in *Link v. Wabash Railroad Company*, 370 U.S. 626, 82 S.Ct. 1386, 8 L.Ed.2d 734 (1962). There, in a train-automobile collision claim, after the case had been pending for six years, the court set a date for a pretrial conference. Two hours before the time for the conference, plaintiff's attorney called the judge's office to say that he could not attend the pretrial conference. When the lawyer did fail to appear at the conference, the judge exercised his inherent power to dismiss the case for want of prosecution. The Supreme Court affirmed the dismissal.

> Neither the permissive language of the Rule which merely authorizes a motion by the defendant nor its policy requires us to conclude that it was the purpose of the Rule to abrogate the power of courts, acting on their own initiative, to clear their calendars of cases that have remained dormant because of the inaction or dilatoriness of the parties seeking relief. The authority of a court to dismiss *sua sponte* for lack of prosecution has generally been considered an "inherent power," governed not by rule or statute but by the control necessarily vested in courts to manage their own affairs so as to achieve the orderly and expeditious disposition of cases. * * * It would require a much clearer expression of purpose than Rule 41(b) provides for us to assume that it was intended to abrogate so well-acknowledged a proposition.

Link, 370 U.S. at 630–31. The Court then concluded that the judge's exercise of inherent power was not an abuse of discretion. Counsel's absence at the pretrial conference, in the light of the whole history of the litigation, supported a reasonable inference that the plaintiff deliberately had been intentionally trying to delay the progress of the case. The Court also rejected the argument that counsel's absence would penalize his client.

> There is certainly no merit to the contention that dismissal of petitioner's claim because of his counsel's unexcused conduct imposes an unjust penalty on the client. Petitioner voluntarily chose this attorney as his representative in the action, and he cannot now avoid the consequences of the acts or omissions of this freely selected agent. Any other notion would be wholly inconsistent with our system of representative litigation, in which each party is deemed bound by the acts of his lawyer-agent and is considered to have "notice of all facts, notice of which can be charged upon the attorney."

Link, 370 U.S. at 633–34. *Link* is clear that a trial court has the inherent authority to dismiss for want of prosecution. Rule 41(b) codifies that authority in part. Even though the rule speaks of a motion by the defendant, the cases make it clear that the court may act on its own without a motion.

2. As the *Aura Lamp* court noted, the appellate standard of review for an involuntary dismissal due to delay is abuse of discretion. While that is a difficult burden for an appellant to satisfy, involuntary dismissals are sometimes set aside because the dismissal under Rule 41(b) is with prejudice to the plaintiff refiling the claim. Contrary to *Aura Lamp*, though, some appellate courts may be concerned about whether the trial court could have

imposed less severe sanctions to move the case to trial. See, e.g., *Mann v. Lewis*, 108 F.3d 145 (8th Cir. 1997) (dismissal with prejudice excessive when dilatory conduct of counsel was not attributable to plaintiff). What are some examples of less serious sanctions?

3.   No fixed time limits control involuntary dismissals. A court should examine the totality of the circumstances in each case in deciding whether failure to pursue the case is serious enough to require dismissal under Rule 41(b). A lengthy period of inaction may justify a dismissal for failure to prosecute if it is the plaintiff who appears to be at fault, e.g., failing to follow an earlier warning to act with more diligence.

4.   Most trial courts maintain a set of local rules, which often include a provision about the failure to prosecute. The typical local rule provides that if a case has been pending for a given length of time, or if no action has been taken in the case for a particular period, the case must be reviewed to determine whether there is an adequate excuse for past delays.

Problems

1.   Peter sues Donald in federal court, but before Donald is even served with process, Peter wants to withdraw his complaint. How could you as Peter's attorney accomplish his goal?

2.   Same facts as Problem 1. In addition, Peter tells you that last year he filed the same claim against Donald in a state court and also withdrew that claim almost as soon as he filed it. Does this change the situation for Peter seeking a dismissal with this second lawsuit?

3.   Same facts as Problem 1, except that by the time Peter wants to withdraw his claim Donald has filed an answer as well as a motion for summary judgment. Is Peter's goal of dismissal less likely to be met?

4.   Same facts as Problem 3, except that Donald has filed a counterclaim against Peter. What happens to Donald's counterclaim if the court grants Peter's motion to dismiss his claim?

5.   Same facts as Problem 3, except that Donald wants Peter to pay for the money he's spent to pay his attorney. Is Peter's goal of dismissal still likely to be met?

6.   Peter sues Donald in a federal court. For the next two years, Peter obtains a series of continuances. The trial judge grants the last continuance, saying that it will dismiss Peter's claim if he is not ready for trial in sixty days. At the end of the sixty-day period, Peter requests another continuance. What can Donald do?

Exercise

For the state where a) you intend to practice after graduation, b) your law school is located, and/or c) your professor assigns, go to that state's annotated statutes and research the procedural rules by which dismissals are governed. Based on your research, print the rule and bring it to class for discussion. In addition, answer the following questions.

1.   Can voluntary dismissals be made by notice?

2. Identify whether there is a point in time beyond which notice dismissals are disallowed.

3. Is there a limitation on the number of dismissals that may occur before a dismissal is deemed to be an adjudication on the merits?

4. Do certain types of cases require a court's consent before dismissing?

5. If a court must approve at least some types of voluntary dismissals, what are the criteria for the court to follow in granting such dismissals?

6. What are the stated grounds for involuntary dismissals?

7. Are there stated criteria for determining whether a dismissal (voluntary or involuntary) is with prejudice or without prejudice?

B. DEFAULT JUDGMENTS

INTRODUCTORY PROBLEM

Carter, a citizen of Georgia, loaned Clinton, a citizen of New York, approximately $1,000,000 for one year at five percent interest. Clinton signed a promissory note to signify her debt to Carter. At the end of the one-year period, Clinton refuses to pay and Carter immediately sues Clinton in a New York federal court requesting $1,050,000 in damages. Clinton does not answer Carter's summons and complaint, appear in court, or otherwise defend the claim against her. The court clerk enters Clinton's default and subsequently enters a default judgment against Clinton, awarding Carter $1,050,000.

May a court clerk enter a judgment with such serious consequences to a defendant?

Governing Rule: Rule 55(a)-(b).

KPS & ASSOCIATES, INC. v. DESIGNS BY FMC, INC.

318 F.3d 1 (1st Cir. 2003)

LIPEZ, Circuit Judge.

[A sales agent, KPS & Associates, Inc. ("KPS"), sued in September, 1999, to recover commissions owing from a vendor, Designs by FMC, Inc. ("Designs"), whose products the agent promoted. The trial court entered a default judgment based on the defendant's failure to answer the complaint. Thereafter, the court refused to set aside the default judgment and entered a damage award for $367,154 against the defendant, which it doubled pursuant to Massachusetts unfair trade practices law (Chapter 93A).] * * *

For the reasons stated below, we affirm the district court in all respects save one—the computation of the base quantum of damages after the entry of default. In fixing that amount, the district court erred in its application of Rule 55(b)(2) of the Federal Rules of Civil Procedure (dealing with the determination of damages after an entry of default).

Following the filing of the complaint in this case, the litigation quickly bogged down in a messy motion practice. Both parties and their attorneys accused each other of misconduct and filed numerous motions for sanctions, to strike, to quash, to compel, and to disqualify.

* * * [O]n March 1, 2000, [KPS's counsel] Hurvitz submitted to the court a request for an entry of default since Designs had yet to file its answer. This request was served on Designs' New York and local counsel. On March 10, 2000, the clerk entered a notice of default against Designs pursuant to Rule 55(a) of the Federal Rules of Civil Procedure. Copies of the notice were served on all counsel. On March 17, 2000, KPS filed a request for the entry of default judgment, which was likewise served on all counsel.

On March 21, 2000, [Designs' counsel] Schrader finally took action, faxing a letter to the court in which he asserted that he had sent a timely answer on March 1, 2000, by Federal Express. Shortly thereafter, Designs filed a motion to set aside the default, and the district court conducted a hearing on May 17, 2000. At the close of the hearing, the district court ruled from the bench, denying Designs' motion to set aside the entry of default. The court characterized Schrader's behavior over the course of the litigation as "stonewalling" and explicitly disbelieved Schrader's proffered explanation with regard to the filing of the answer. She told Schrader: "We have had trouble with you from the very beginning." She concluded: "And because I do not credit these stories, because I do not find there to be good cause to remove the default, the motion to remove the default is denied." * * *

Subsequently, on July 27, 2000, the court issued a brief written order on damages which stated, in part:

> No further hearing is necessary to ascertain the compensatory damages claimed as the verified complaint and plaintiff's affidavit attached thereto set forth a sum certain based on sales and commission figures there detailed, and, a default having been entered, each of plaintiff's allegations of fact are established as a matter of law. [citations omitted]

The district court then referred the matter to a magistrate judge for the sole purpose of determining whether Designs should be held liable for double or treble damages under Chapter 93A—i.e., to determine whether Designs' unlawful conduct was "willful or knowing." The magistrate judge permitted no evidence on the base quantum of damages, which the court had fixed as the "sum certain" contained in the complaint and a supporting affidavit.

Following the hearing on 93A liability, the magistrate judge issued a Report and Recommendation finding that Designs had willfully and knowingly engaged in conduct prohibited by Chapter 93A and that KPS should be awarded double damages. Designs filed its objections to the Report and Recommendation with the district judge, who overruled those objections. Judgment was entered on September 28, 2001, for $367,154—twice the $183,577 recited in the *ad damnum* clause of KPS's complaint—plus prejudgment interest. On October 23, 2001, Designs filed a timely notice of appeal. * * *

Designs argues that the district court erred in denying its motion to set aside the entry of default. *See* Fed.R.Civ.P. 55(c). * * *

Rule 55(c) provides that a court may set aside an entry of default "for good cause shown." We review the district court's denial of a Rule 55(c) motion for abuse of discretion, while we review any factual findings underlying that decision for clear error. *Conetta v. Nat'l Hair Care Ctrs., Inc.,* 236 F.3d 67, 75 (1st Cir.2001); *Gen. Contracting & Trading Co. v. Interpole, Inc.,* 899 F.2d 109, 112 (1st Cir.1990). We will not disturb the district court's decision unless it is "clearly wrong." *Bond Leather Co. v. Q.T. Shoe Mfg. Co.,* 764 F.2d 928, 938 (1st Cir.1985).

* * * In *McKinnon v. Kwong Wah Restaurant,* 83 F.3d 498 (1st Cir.1996), we identified no fewer than seven factors a district court may consider:

> (1) whether the default was willful; (2) whether setting it aside would prejudice the adversary; (3) whether a meritorious defense is presented; (4) the nature of the defendant's explanation for the default; (5) the good faith of the parties; (6) the amount of money involved; (7) the timing of the motion [to set aside entry of default].

Id. at 503. Thus Rule 55(c), as an "express[ion of] the traditional inherent equity power of the federal courts," 10A Wright, Miller & Kane, Federal Practice and Procedure: Civil 3d § 2692 (1998), permits the consideration of a panoply of "relevant equitable factors." *Enron Oil Corp. v. Diakuhara,* 10 F.3d 90, 96 (2d Cir.1993). The "Rule 55(c) determinations are case-specific" and "must, therefore, be made in a practical, commonsense manner, without rigid adherence to, or undue reliance upon, a mechanical formula." *Gen. Contracting & Trading,* 899 F.2d at 112. * * * [T]he decision of the district court to accord dispositive weight to one of the familiar factors or other relevant equitable factors does not necessarily mean an abuse of discretion.

This flexibility is necessitated by the competing policies and values that underlie the concept of default. On the one hand, it "provide[s] a useful remedy when a litigant is confronted by an obstructionist adversary," and "play[s] a constructive role in maintaining the orderly and efficient administration of justice." *Enron,* 10 F.3d at 96. It furnishes an invaluable incentive for parties to comply with court orders and rules of procedure. *See* Fed.R.Civ.P. 37(b)(2)(C). It encourages the expeditious resolution of litigation and promotes finality. *See* Wright, Miller & Kane, *supra,* § 2693. On the other hand, countervailing considerations include the goals of "resol[ving] cases on the merits," *Key Bank of Me. v. Tablecloth Textile Co.,* 74 F.3d 349, 356 (1st Cir.1996), and avoiding "harsh or unfair result[s]." *Enron,* 10 F.3d at 96. Since "default judgments implicate sharply conflicting policies ... the trial judge, who is usually the person most familiar with the circumstances of the case and is in the best position to evaluate the good faith and credibility of the parties, is entrusted with the task of balancing these competing considerations." *Eagle Assocs. v. Bank of Montreal,* 926 F.2d 1305, 1307 (2d Cir.1991) (internal quotation marks omitted).

Eleven days after the clerk had entered the default against Designs, Schrader faxed a letter to the court in which he asserted that he had submitted a timely answer via Federal Express. In that letter, Schrader stated that the answer had been sent by a "temporary secretary" and that he had been told by Federal Express that "the packages were likely rejected because the federal express [sic] slip filled out was an **International** Air Waybill" (original emphasis). Schrader indicated that he had been trying to get an affidavit from the temporary secretary who had been working that day. He also told the court that he would submit to the clerk that same day a motion to vacate the default, along with an explanatory affidavit. The motion and affidavit were not filed until one week later.

* * * The district court held a hearing on May 17, 2000, on Designs' motion to remove the default. * * * At the hearing, Schrader argued that the default should be set aside because (a) the default was not willful, (b) Designs had a meritorious defense, and (c) KPS could not show any prejudice. Schrader focused on the willfulness factor.* * * .

The district court was not impressed. First, commenting on the procedural history to that point, the court characterized Schrader's behavior as "stonewalling," and she admonished him in open court: "We have had trouble with you from the beginning." She noted his previous failures to meet deadlines and remarked on his duplicitousness, referencing his earlier representation that he could not attend the hearing and then his sudden appearance. She noted inconsistencies and implausibilities in Schrader's representations during the hearing about the late answer, and she found other representations he had made in affidavits to be incredible. * * * These findings led to the dispositive ruling from the bench: "And because I do not credit these stories, because I do not find there to be good cause to remove the default, the motion to remove the default is denied."

* * * By the time the district court denied Designs' motion to set aside the default, it had become well acquainted with the parties and circumstances in this case. It had conducted two motion hearings and one pretrial conference. It had received numerous written communications from counsel and had taken several motions (with supporting materials) under advisement. Given the district court's familiarity with the case, and on the record developed in connection with the hearing, we cannot say that the district court clearly erred in its assessment of Schrader's credibility, nor did it clearly err in rejecting his proffered explanation for the default.

The burden of demonstrating good cause for the removal of a default rested with Designs. *See Bond Leather,* 764 F.2d at 938. Thus, Designs had the burden to demonstrate a lack of willfulness. When the district court rejected Schrader's explanation, Designs was effectively left with *no* explanation for the default. Hence Designs' argument that the default was not willful lacked any factual predicate and was properly disregarded by the district court.

At the default hearing, Schrader also argued that Designs had a meritorious defense which weighed in favor of setting aside the default. The district court, however, had once before taken a dim view of Designs' asserted defenses ..... Thus we take the district court's comment on "stonewalling" to imply that it adhered to its prior skepticism about the defenses, and that it felt that Designs was merely trying to postpone the inevitable. We cannot say that the court erred in its evaluation of Designs' defense. All of the materials offered by Designs in support of its defense were internally generated balance sheets, reports, and the like. KPS, on the other hand, attached copies of actual customer invoices and purchase orders to its complaint. Moreover, over the course of this dispute, the amount Designs claims it is due from KPS has varied wildly: at one time nothing ("a wash"), at another $6,000, at another $30,000, at another $60,000, and finally over $74,000 (not including the $10 million claimed in the New York lawsuit).

Schrader also argued before the district court that KPS would suffer no prejudice if the default were to be set aside. Schrader was correct on this point. * * * We have stated elsewhere that in the context of a Rule 55(c) motion, delay in and of itself does not constitute prejudice. "The issue is not mere delay, but rather its accompanying dangers: loss of evidence, increased difficulties of discovery, or an enhanced opportunity for fraud or collusion." *FDIC v. Francisco Inv. Corp.,* 873 F.2d 474, 479 (1st Cir.1989). There is no indication that any of these dangers were present or considered by the district judge when she ruled on the Rule 55(c) motion.

The district court, however, correctly gave significant weight to two other factors—the nature of Designs' explanation for the default, and the good faith of the parties. *See McKinnon,* 83 F.3d at 503. The district court determined that Schrader had fabricated his explanation regarding the filing of an answer—a finding that goes to the nature of the explanation as well as to Designs' good faith. * * * In light of these determinations of fabrication and bad faith, and its consideration of other salient factors, the district court did not abuse its discretion in refusing to set aside the default.

* * * In its order of July 27, 2000, the district court indicated that no hearing was necessary to determine the base quantum of damages since "the verified complaint and plaintiff's affidavit attached thereto set forth a sum certain based on sales and commission figures there detailed." The order also referred the matter to the magistrate judge for a hearing on Chapter 93A liability. The order did not, however, identify

the amount of this "sum certain." The district court subsequently clarified the amount of damages on September 28, 2001, when it overruled Designs' objections to the magistrate judge's Report and Recommendation on the doubling of damages under Chapter 93A: "Judgment may be entered for plaintiff in double the amount of its damages of $183,577." The district court apparently arrived at this sum by looking to the *ad damnum* clause of the complaint.

Designs argues two related points with respect to the district court's calculation of damages. First, Designs argues that KPS's claim was not for a "sum certain" and that the district court erred in thereby fixing the base quantum of damages on the basis of the complaint, without a hearing. Second, Designs argues that the district court erred in limiting the scope of the hearing before the magistrate judge to the issue of liability for multiple damages under Chapter 93A. Designs maintains that it was entitled to an evidentiary hearing to determine the base quantum of damages, notwithstanding any admissions made as result of its default or the amount claimed in the *ad damnum* clause.

The district court's order of July 27, 2000, as clarified by its memorandum and order of September 28, 2001, was entered pursuant to Rule 55(b). . . .

On the basis of its conclusion that "the verified complaint and plaintiff's affidavit attached thereto set forth a sum certain," the district court determined that no evidentiary inquiry was necessary to calculate the amount of damages to be set forth in the default judgment. We review the district court's refusal to inquire further for abuse of discretion.

We conclude that the district court abused its discretion in failing to conduct further inquiry before fixing the base quantum of damages. There are two reasons why further inquiry was required. First, there are obvious discrepancies between the damages claimed in the body of the complaint and the damages requested in the *ad damnum* clause, as well as serious arithmetical errors in the affidavit filed with the complaint. Second, even without these errors and discrepancies, there would still be a need for further inquiry given the nature of KPS's claim.

According to the face of the complaint, KPS claims that it is entitled to $67,238 in base commissions and $63,795 in "sales price differentials," i.e., price mark-ups beyond cost. Adding these two figures results in a total of $131,033. However, in the enumerated counts and *ad damnum* clause, the complaint states that KPS is entitled to judgment against Designs in the amount of $183,577—an unexplained difference of over $50,000. Likewise, KPS's affidavit filed in support of its complaint contains several computational errors. * * * Moreover, many of the accountings and purchase orders attached as exhibits to the complaint's supporting affidavit are illegible or incomprehensible. Given these inconsistencies and errors, the district court erred in simply fixing the base quantum of damages at the amount stated in the complaint's *ad damnum* clause.

Even if KPS's complaint and affidavit were free from the discrepancies and errors detailed above, the district court could not have determined damages without a further evidentiary inquiry. Following the entry of default, a district court can enter a final judgment without requiring further proof of damages only in limited situations. For example, no evidentiary inquiry is necessary if the claim is for a "sum certain."

Contrary to the district court's statement, this is not a sum certain case. In the Rule 55 context, a claim is not a sum certain unless there is no doubt as to the amount to which a plaintiff is entitled as a result of the defendant's default. * * *

As with a "sum certain," a hearing is not normally required if the claim is "liquidated." " 'Liquidated' means adjusted, certain, settled with respect to amount, fixed. A claim is liquidated when the amount thereof has been ascertained and agreed upon by the parties or fixed by operation of law." *Hallett Constr. Co. v. Iowa State Highway Comm'n*, 258 Iowa 520, 139 N.W.2d 421, 426 (1966). The classic example is an enforceable liquidated damages clause in a contract. Another example would be a delinquent tax assessment. KPS and Designs, however, vigorously dispute the issue of damages. Likewise, KPS's damages have not been fixed by operation of law. Finally, as the inconsistencies and inaccuracies in the complaint and the supporting affidavit amply demonstrate, KPS's claims are not capable of simple mathematical computation. Thus, KPS's complaint and its supporting affidavit do not state a liquidated claim.

Relying on the erroneous conclusion that KPS's claim stated a claim for a sum certain, the district court did not look beyond the complaint's *ad damnum* clause and an internally inconsistent supporting affidavit in fixing the base quantum of damages. For the reasons explained above, this limited approach was an abuse of discretion requiring that we remand the matter to the district court for further consideration of the damages issue. * * *

Notes and Questions

1. Federal Rule 55 establishes the process for default judgments, as well as setting aside those judgments. Before a default or a default judgment can be entered, the court must have jurisdiction over the party against whom the judgment is sought, which means that the party was effectively served with process. See *Peralta v. Heights Medical Center*, 485 U.S. 80, 108 S.Ct. 896, 99 L.Ed.2d 75 (1988) ("a judgment entered without notice or service is constitutionally infirm"). Rule 55(a) permits a party to file a motion asking the clerk of the court to enter a default against an opposing party who "failed to plead or otherwise defend" against the moving party's claim. "Otherwise defend" refers to attacks on service of process, motions to dismiss, or Rule 12(e) motions for more specificity, any of which may prevent entry of a default without having to answer on the merits.

Is the entry of a default limited to complaints, or may defaults be entered on other claims for relief? The entry of a default for failure "to plead or otherwise defend" is not limited to situations involving a failure to answer a complaint, but instead applies to any pleading. For example, a plaintiff's failure to answer a counterclaim may entitle the defendant to an entry of default on the counterclaim.

When the requirements of Rule 55(a) are satisfied, an entry of default is made by the court clerk without any action by the court. An entry of default is simply a notation of the fact of default, and cuts off the party's right to further notice about the proceedings unless the party has appeared. The entry of a default serves as an intermediate step in anticipation of a final judgment by default by the clerk under Rule 55(b)(1). Thus, compliance with Rule 55(a) is always a prerequisite to a default judgment under Rule 55(b)(1), but it is not necessarily required as a prerequisite for a default judgment under Rule 55(b)(2). For example, when a default is entered as a sanction, the judge, not the clerk, will enter the default.

After a default is entered under Rule 55(a) and upon request of the party seeking the default judgment, the clerk may enter a default judgment under Rule 55(b)(1) when the claim "is for a sum certain." and the defaulting party has not made any appearance in the case. Rule 55(b)(1) applies only when a party has never appeared in the case to defend; it does not apply when a party appears and then merely fails to participate further. Rule 55(b)(1) gives the court clerk authority to enter a default judgment only when the defendant has clearly defaulted by showing no interest in participating in the case.

Under Rule 55(b)(1), the plaintiff submits an affidavit to establish that the amount due is certain or easily can be computed and is reasonable under the circumstances. By contrast, if the relief sought is for an unliquidated sum of money or if some other relief (e.g., injunctive relief, specific performance) is sought, the judge must decide whether that relief is appropriate following a hearing.

2. Any situation not covered by Rule 55(b)(1) falls within Rule 55(b)((2) and must be examined by a judge. Rule 55(b)(2) applies to a defendant who has filed a procedural or legal challenge to the complaint that does not address the merits of the plaintiff's claim. For a default judgment, the defaulting party's appearance must be unrelated to the merits of the case. Conversely, if a defendant has been served and appeared on the merits by, for example, filing an answer, the court cannot grant a default judgment and a trial proceeds in the defendant's absence.

The trial judge has the discretion about whether to enter a default judgment, and the judge may hold hearings to aid in the exercise of that discretion. The judge's ability to exercise discretion is made effective by the requirement that the motion for a default judgment be sent to the defaulting party, enabling that party to appear and show cause why a default judgment should not be entered. At a hearing, the judge can require proof of the facts that must be proved to establish liability. If the sum of damages is not certain or capable of easy computation, the hearing may include that issue. Once the judge determines that a default judgment should be entered, he or she determines the amount and character of the recovery that should be awarded. Rule 54(c) limits the amount of relief to the amount sought in the plaintiff's demand for judgment.

3. Rule 55(c) provides relief from either an entry of default or a default judgment. A court may set aside an entry of default for "good cause." A default judgment is set aside for the same reasons as a motion for relief from a judgment found in Rule 60(b). See Chapter 11, part E, *infra*. In either situation, it is within the trial court's discretion to set aside the entry of default or the default judgment. A court is more likely to grant a motion under Rule 55(c) after a showing that if relief is granted the outcome of the lawsuit may be different than if the default judgment is allowed to stand, i.e., the potential injustice of allowing the case to be disposed of by default. The trial judge will often require the party in default to show a meritorious defense to the claim as a prerequisite to vacating the judgment.

Problems

1. For problems a.-d., decide who enters the default and who enters the default judgment.

a. Paul (from a different state than the defendant) sues the City of Davenport in federal court for trespass for an uncertain amount of damages. The city is served with process.

b. Same as a., except that the amount of damages is a sum certain.

c. Same as a., except that the city moves to dismiss for improper service of process, but after losing the motion does nothing in the case, which involves a sum certain.

d. Same as a., except that the city answers the complaint, and then does nothing else in the case, which involves a sum certain.

2. Paul sues the City of Davenport in federal court for a federal civil rights violation. Inexplicably, the city is never served with process and Paul moves for a default judgment a month after filing his claim. Can a default judgment be granted?

3. Pam sues Daphne Temporary Employees, Inc. in federal court for a Fair Labor Standards violation, which is valued for a sum certain. The defendant is served with process, but never files an answer or any motions in the case. Can Pam seek a default judgment? If so, how?

4. Pat sues Dan in federal court in a diversity action for breach of a contract that clearly states a sum certain in case a court finds a breach. The trial court denies Dan's motion to dismiss the complaint for improper venue, and Dan fails to file an answer or any other motions. Pat wants to file a motion for a default judgment. Can she, and if so, by what method under Federal Rule 55?

5. Six months ago, Pablo sued Doris and obtained a default judgment. Doris recently learned that the default judgment had been granted, because her wages were being garnished (as often happens after a default judgment). She is mad about the situation, and wants your help. What, is anything, can you do under Rule 55 to stop Doris's wages from being garnished?

Exercise

For the state where a) you intend to practice after graduation, b) your law school is located, and/or c) your professor assigns, go to that state's annotated statutes and research the procedural rules by which default judgments are governed. Based on your research, print the rule and bring it to class for discussion. In addition, answer the following questions.

1. Can a court clerk enter a default? If so, on what grounds?

2. When can a court clerk enter a default judgment?

3. When can a judge grant a default judgment?

4. Under what circumstances, if any, can a default judgment be set aside?

C.   RESOLVING THE CASE BASED ON THE PLEADINGS ALONE

INTRODUCTORY PROBLEM

Bailey and Givens are first-year law students who sit together in every class. One day, Givens has a job interview scheduled immediately following Civil Procedure. However, Professor Droan is waxing particularly eloquent that day, and keeps the class well past the scheduled dismissal time. Worried that she will be late—and not wanting to lug her notebook computer to the interview—Givens asks Bailey if he will keep her notebook for the afternoon as a "favor." Bailey agrees.

Later that day, Bailey and friends decide to use the notebook as a substitute Frisbee. The non-aerodynamic notebook crashes to the ground and is ruined. Understandably furious, Givens sues Bailey for the cost of replacing the notebook. Givens's complaint argues that Bailey was a "bailee" of the notebook, and that Bailey's gross negligence caused the damage to the notebook.

Bailey files a timely answer. Although he admits all the facts alleged by Givens in her complaint (including Givens's assertion that he acted with gross negligence), Bailey denies that he is liable. Bailey asserts in his answer that he received no consideration for acting as a bailee. Therefore, he claims, he owed no duty whatsoever to Givens to care for her notebook.

It is no wonder that Givens had an interview and Bailey didn't . . . for under governing law, no consideration is required to establish a bailment. Although a bailee who receives no benefit from the bailment is held to a lesser standard of care, such a bailee can be held liable if he acted in a grossly negligent fashion.

Givens would like to resolve this case without the time and expense of discovery and trial. What motion should she bring? Is she likely to prevail on that motion?

Governing Law: Federal Rules 12(b)(6) and (c).

In Chapter 5, you discussed the motion to dismiss for failure to state a claim. The materials in that chapter focused mainly on how a defendant uses that motion to deal with an insufficient complaint. If the complaint is insufficient, and plaintiff cannot cure the defects, the obvious solution is for the court to dismiss the case. A 12(b)(6) dismissal operates as an adjudication on the merits unless the court specifies otherwise, preventing the plaintiff from suing again on the same claim or any other claim arising from the same basic set of facts. Federal Rule 41(b); *Federated Department Stores v. Moitie*, 452 U.S. 394, 101 S.Ct. 2424, 69 L.Ed.2d 103 (1981). Therefore, from the defendant's perspective, a 12(b)(6) dismissal effectively ends the case.

In situations like that posed in the Introductory Problem, however, a 12(b)(6) motion does not produce the desired result. Now it is plaintiff who should prevail. Dismissing the case, however, leaves the plaintiff with nothing. What plaintiff wants is a way for the court to decide the case on the pleadings alone, granting judgment to plaintiff for the relief requested. The Federal Rule 12(c) motion for judgment on the pleadings is one way for plaintiff to achieve this goal.

Notwithstanding this difference in outcome, a 12(c) motion is conceptually similar to a 12(b)(6). In both cases, the court *does not consider the evidence*, but looks only at one or more pleadings. A court dealing with a defendant's motion to dismiss for failure to state a claim looks only at the complaint. In a 12(c) motion, by contrast, the court looks at *all* the pleadings. If the pleadings, taken together, indicate that one party should prevail, the court can grant judgment without considering the actual evidence.

Note that plaintiff is not the only party who can use the Federal Rule 12(c) motion. Suppose plaintiff sues defendant for alienation of affection. Defendant files an answer in which she denies that she committed the facts alleged by plaintiff. Later, however—perhaps because the higher courts cleared up the law—defendant realizes that the law in that jurisdiction does not allow recovery for alienation of affection. Defendant in such a case can file a Federal Rule 12(c) motion for judgment on the pleadings. In this situation, the Rule 12(c) motion serves basically as a delayed motion to dismiss for failure to state a claim. See also Federal Rule 12(h)(2), which requires a party who wants to raise the defense of failure to state a claim after the pleadings are closed to use a Federal Rule 12(c) motion for judgment on the pleadings.

A judgment on the pleadings is a final judgment. If plaintiff is the judgment winner, it may collect on that judgment once 10 days have elapsed following entry of the judgment. Federal Rule 69(a). The party who loses the judgment may appeal immediately.

D. SUMMARY JUDGMENT

Most cases cannot be resolved on the pleadings alone. If defendant denies any of the essential facts alleged by plaintiff, for example, the case cannot be resolved by a Federal Rule 12(b)(6) or 12(c) motion. However, the existence of a factual dispute in the pleadings does not necessarily mean that the case must go to trial. The device of summary judgment gives a court a limited opportunity to look beyond the pleadings themselves and determine whether a factual dispute that appears in the pleadings is actually supported by evidence.

INTRODUCTORY PROBLEM

Arriving at his home after a grueling day at the office, Forrest Green is shocked to discover that several trees have been removed from his yard. After some investigation, Green sues Lon's Lawn Service. Green claims that Lon's employees removed the trees without Green's permission. Lon denies liability.

Discovery reveals the following facts. Green has several witnesses who say they saw a crew of men wearing identical light blue shirts removing trees from Green's yard on the date in question. Although the shirts had writing on them, none of the witnesses could make out the writing. In his answers to interrogatories that Green served upon him, Lon admits that his employees wear shirts of that color. Green also obtained affidavits from the owners of all the lawn and tree service companies listed in the yellow pages. All of these owners swear that their employees do not wear shirts of that color. Finally, one of Green's neighbors testified in her deposition that she had arranged with Lon's to have several trees removed from *her* yard that day, but that Lon's employees never showed up to do the work.

Lon has comparatively little testimony to back up his story. Turnover in the lawn service industry is high, and all of the workers who worked for Lon on the date in question have moved on to other positions. Neither Lon nor Green has been unable to track down any of the employees who worked for him at that time. Lon nevertheless sticks by his original story: although he does not deny that the trees were removed, he claims that neither he nor anyone who worked for him is responsible.

Both Green and Lon are confident they would prevail at trial. Green feels that not only is his evidence overwhelming, but Lon has nothing that contradicts it. Lon, by contrast, feels that Green has no direct evidence that it was Lon's employees who removed the trees.

Is there a motion that either or both parties may make to have the judge decide the case, thereby obviating the need for a trial? If both parties file that motion, will either of them prevail?

Governing Rule: Rule 56.

CELOTEX CORP. v. CATRETT

477 U.S. 317, 106 S.Ct. 2548, 91 L.Ed.2d 265 (1986)

JUSTICE REHNQUIST delivered the opinion of the Court.

* * * Respondent commenced this lawsuit in September 1980, alleging that the death in 1979 of her husband, Louis H. Catrett, resulted from his exposure to products containing asbestos manufactured or distributed by 15 named corporations. Respondent's complaint sounded in negligence, breach of warranty, and strict liability. Two of the defendants filed motions challenging the District Court's *in personam* jurisdiction, and the remaining 13, including petitioner, filed motions for summary judgment. Petitioner's motion, which was first filed in September 1981, argued that summary judgment was proper because respondent had "failed to produce evidence that any [Celotex] product ... was the proximate cause of the injuries alleged * * *." In particular, petitioner noted that respondent had failed to identify, in answering interrogatories specifically requesting such information, any witnesses who could testify about the decedent's exposure to petitioner's asbestos products. In response to petitioner's summary judgment motion, respondent then produced three documents which she claimed "demonstrate that there is a genuine material factual dispute" as to whether the decedent had ever been exposed to petitioner's asbestos products. The three documents included a transcript of a deposition of the decedent, a letter from an official of one of the decedent's former employers whom petitioner planned to call as a trial witness, and a letter from an insurance company to respondent's attorney, all tending to establish that the decedent had been exposed to petitioner's asbestos products in Chicago during 1970–1971. Petitioner, in turn, argued that the three documents were inadmissible hearsay and thus could not be considered in opposition to the summary judgment motion.

In July 1982, almost two years after the commencement of the lawsuit, the District Court granted all of the motions filed by the various defendants. The court explained that it was granting petitioner's summary judgment motion because "there [was] no showing that the plaintiff was exposed to the defendant Celotex's product in the District of Columbia or elsewhere within the statutory period." Respondent appealed only the grant of summary judgment in favor of petitioner, and a divided panel of the District of Columbia Circuit reversed. The majority of the Court of Appeals held that petitioner's summary judgment motion was rendered "fatally defective" by the fact that petitioner "made no effort to adduce *any* evidence, in the form of affidavits or otherwise, to support its motion." * * *

We think that the position taken by the majority of the Court of Appeals is inconsistent with the standard for summary judgment set forth in Rule 56(c) of the Federal Rules of Civil Procedure. Under Rule 56(c), summary judgment is proper "if the pleadings, depositions, answers to interrogatories, and admissions on file, together with the affidavits, if any, show that there is no genuine issue as to any material fact and that the moving party is entitled to a judgment as a matter of law." In our view, the plain language of Rule 56(c) mandates the entry of summary judgment, after adequate time for discovery and upon motion, against a party who fails to make a showing sufficient to establish the existence of an element essential to that party's case, and on which that party will bear the burden of proof at trial. In such a situation, there can be "no genuine issue as to any material fact," since a complete failure of proof concerning an essential element of the nonmoving party's case necessarily renders all other facts immaterial. The moving party is "entitled to a judgment as a matter of law" because the nonmoving party has failed to make a sufficient showing on an essential element of her case with respect to which she has the burden of proof. "[The] standard [for granting summary judgment] mirrors the standard for a directed verdict under Federal Rule of Civil Procedure 50(a)...." *Anderson* v. *Liberty Lobby, Inc.* [477 U.S. 242 (1986)] at 250.

Of course, a party seeking summary judgment always bears the initial responsibility of informing the district court of the basis for its motion, and identifying those portions of "the pleadings, depositions, answers to interrogatories, and admissions on file, together with the affidavits, if any," which it believes demonstrate the absence of a genuine issue of material fact. But unlike the Court of Appeals, we find no express or implied requirement in Rule 56 that the moving party support its motion with affidavits or other similar materials *negating* the opponent's claim. On the contrary, Rule 56(c), which refers to "the affidavits, *if any*" (emphasis added), suggests the absence of such a requirement. And if there were any doubt about the meaning of Rule 56(c) in this regard, such doubt is clearly removed by Rules 56(a) and (b), which provide that claimants and defendants, respectively, may move for summary judgment *"with or without supporting affidavits"* (emphasis added). * * *

Respondent argues, however, that Rule 56(e), by its terms, places on the nonmoving party the burden of coming forward with rebuttal affidavits, or other specified kinds of materials, only in response to a motion for summary judgment "made and supported as provided in this rule." According to respondent's argument, since petitioner did not "support" its motion with affidavits, summary judgment was improper in this case. But as we have already explained, a motion for summary judgment may be made pursuant to Rule 56 "with or without supporting affidavits." In cases like the instant one, where the nonmoving party will bear the burden of proof at trial on a dispositive issue, a summary judgment motion may properly be made in reliance solely on the "pleadings, depositions, answers to interrogatories, and admissions on file." Such a motion, whether or not accompanied by affidavits, will be "made and supported as provided in this rule," and Rule 56(e) therefore requires the nonmoving party to go beyond the pleadings and by her own affidavits, or by the "depositions, answers to interrogatories, and admissions on file," designate "specific facts showing that there is a genuine issue for trial."

We do not mean that the nonmoving party must produce evidence in a form that would be admissible at trial in order to avoid summary judgment. Obviously, Rule 56 does not require the nonmoving party to depose her own witnesses. Rule 56(e) permits a proper summary judgment motion to be opposed by any of the kinds of evidentiary materials listed in Rule 56(c), except the mere pleadings themselves, and it is from this list that one would normally expect the nonmoving party to make the showing to which we have referred. * * *

The last two sentences of Rule 56(e) were added * * * [in 1963] to disapprove a line of cases allowing a party opposing summary judgment to resist a properly made motion by reference only to its pleadings. While * * * these two sentences were not intended to *reduce* the burden of the moving party, it is also obvious that they were not adopted to *add to* that burden. Yet that is exactly the result which the reasoning of the Court of Appeals would produce; in effect, an amendment to Rule 56(e) designed to *facilitate* the granting of motions for summary judgment would be interpreted to make it *more difficult* to grant such motions. Nothing in the two sentences themselves requires this result, for the reasons we have previously indicated, and we now put to rest any inference that they do so. * * *

Respondent commenced this action in September 1980, and petitioner's motion was filed in September 1981. The parties had conducted discovery, and no serious claim can be made that respondent was in any sense "railroaded" by a premature motion for summary judgment. Any potential problem with such premature motions can be adequately dealt with under Rule 56(f), which allows a summary judgment motion to be denied, or the hearing on the motion to be continued, if the nonmoving party has not had an opportunity to make full discovery.

In this Court, respondent's brief and oral argument have been devoted as much to the proposition that an adequate showing of exposure to petitioner's asbestos products was made as to the proposition that no such showing should have been required. But the Court of Appeals declined to address either the adequacy of the showing made by respondent in opposition to petitioner's motion for summary judgment, or the question whether such a showing, if reduced to admissible evidence, would be sufficient to carry respondent's burden of proof at trial. We think the Court of Appeals with its superior knowledge of local law is better suited than we are to make these determinations in the first instance.

The Federal Rules of Civil Procedure have for almost 50 years authorized motions for summary judgment upon proper showings of the lack of a genuine, triable issue of material fact. Summary judgment procedure is properly regarded not as a disfavored procedural shortcut, but rather as an integral part of the Federal Rules as a whole, which are designed "to secure the just, speedy and inexpensive determination of every action." Fed. Rule Civ. Proc. 1. Before the shift to "notice pleading" accomplished by the Federal Rules, motions to dismiss a complaint or to strike a defense were the principal tools by which factually insufficient claims or defenses could be isolated and prevented from going to trial with the attendant unwarranted consumption of public and private resources. But with the advent of "notice pleading," the motion to dismiss seldom fulfills this function any more, and its place has been taken by the motion for summary judgment. Rule 56 must be construed with due regard not only for the rights of persons asserting claims and defenses that are adequately based in fact to have those claims and defenses tried to a jury, but also for the rights of persons opposing such claims and defenses to demonstrate in the manner provided by the Rule, prior to trial, that the claims and defenses have no factual basis.

The judgment of the Court of Appeals is accordingly reversed, and the case is remanded for further proceedings consistent with this opinion.

JUSTICE WHITE, concurring.

I agree that the Court of Appeals was wrong in holding that the moving defendant must always support his motion with evidence or affidavits showing the absence of a genuine dispute about a material fact. I also agree that the movant may rely on depositions, answers to interrogatories, and the like, to demonstrate that the plaintiff has no evidence to prove his case and hence that there can be no factual dispute. But the movant must discharge the burden the Rules place upon him: It is not enough to move for summary judgment without supporting the motion in any way or with a conclusory assertion that the plaintiff has no evidence to prove his case. * * *

JUSTICE BRENNAN, with whom THE CHIEF JUSTICE and JUSTICE BLACKMUN join, dissenting.

This case requires the Court to determine whether Celotex satisfied its initial burden of production in moving for summary judgment on the ground that the plaintiff lacked evidence to establish an essential element of her case at trial. I do not disagree with the Court's legal analysis. The Court clearly rejects the ruling of the Court of Appeals that the defendant must provide affirmative evidence disproving the plaintiff's case. Beyond this, however, the Court has not clearly explained what is required of a moving party seeking summary judgment on the ground that the nonmoving party cannot prove its case. This lack of clarity is unfortunate: district courts must routinely decide summary judgment motions, and the Court's opinion will very likely create confusion. For this reason, even if I agreed with the Court's result, I would have written separately to explain more clearly the law in this area. However, because I believe that Celotex did not meet its burden of production under Federal Rule of Civil Procedure 56, I respectfully dissent from the Court's judgment.

Summary judgment is appropriate where the court is satisfied "that there is no genuine issue as to any material fact and that the moving party is entitled to a judgment as a matter of law." Fed. Rule Civ. Proc. 56(c). The burden of establishing the nonexistence of a "genuine issue" is on the party moving for summary judgment. This burden has two distinct components: an initial burden of production, which shifts to the nonmoving party if satisfied by the moving party; and an ultimate burden of persuasion, which always remains on the moving party. The court need not decide whether the moving party has satisfied its ultimate burden of persuasion unless and until the court finds that the moving party has discharged its initial burden of production.

The burden of production imposed by Rule 56 requires the moving party to make a prima facie showing that it is entitled to summary judgment. The manner in which this showing can be made depends upon which party will bear the burden of persuasion on the challenged claim at trial. If the *moving* party will bear the burden of persuasion at trial, that party must support its motion with credible evidence—using any of the materials specified in Rule 56(c)—that would entitle it to a directed verdict if not controverted at trial. Such an affirmative showing shifts the burden of production to the party opposing the motion and requires that party either to produce evidentiary materials that demonstrate the existence of a "genuine issue" for trial or to submit an affidavit requesting additional time for discovery.

If the burden of persuasion at trial would be on the *nonmoving* party, the party moving for summary judgment may satisfy Rule 56's burden of production in either of two ways. First, the moving party may submit affirmative evidence that negates an essential element of the nonmoving party's claim. Second, the moving party may demonstrate to the court that the nonmoving party's evidence is insufficient to establish an essential element of the nonmoving party's claim. If the nonmoving party cannot muster sufficient evidence to make out its claim, a trial would be useless and the moving party is entitled to summary judgment as a matter of law.

Where the moving party adopts this second option and seeks summary judgment on the ground that the nonmoving party * * * has no evidence, the mechanics of discharging Rule 56's burden of production are somewhat trickier. Plainly, a conclusory assertion that the nonmoving party has no evidence is insufficient. Such a "burden" of production is no burden at all and would simply permit summary judgment procedure to be converted into a tool for harassment. Rather, as the Court confirms, a party who moves for summary judgment on the ground that the nonmoving party has no evidence must affirmatively show the absence of evidence in the record. This may require the moving party to depose the nonmoving party's witnesses or to establish the inadequacy of documentary evidence. If there is literally no evidence in the record, the moving party may demonstrate this by reviewing for the court the admissions, interrogatories, and other exchanges between the parties that are in the record. Either way, however, the moving party must affirmatively demonstrate that there is no evidence in the record to support a judgment for the nonmoving party.

* * * [T]he nonmoving party may defeat a motion for summary judgment that asserts that the nonmoving party has no evidence by calling the court's attention to supporting evidence already in the record that was overlooked or ignored by the moving party. In that event, the moving party must respond by making an attempt to demonstrate the inadequacy of this evidence, for it is only by attacking all the record evidence allegedly supporting the nonmoving party that a party seeking summary judgment satisfies Rule 56's burden of production. Thus, if the record disclosed that the moving party had overlooked a witness who would provide relevant testimony for the nonmoving party at trial, the court could not find that the moving party had discharged its initial burden of production unless the moving party sought to demonstrate the inadequacy of this witness' testimony. Absent such a demonstration, summary judgment would have to be denied on the ground that the moving party had failed to meet its burden of production under Rule 56. * * *

I do not read the Court's opinion to say anything inconsistent with or different than the preceding discussion. My disagreement with the Court concerns the application of these principles to the facts of this case.

Defendant Celotex sought summary judgment on the ground that plaintiff had "failed to produce" any evidence that her decedent had ever been exposed to Celotex asbestos. Celotex supported this motion with a two-page "Statement of Material Facts as to Which There is No Genuine Issue" and a three-page "Memorandum of Points and Authorities" which asserted that the plaintiff had failed to identify any evidence in responding to two sets of interrogatories propounded by Celotex and that therefore the record was "totally devoid" of evidence to support plaintiff's claim.

Approximately three months earlier, Celotex had filed an essentially identical motion. Plaintiff responded to this earlier motion by producing three pieces of evidence which she claimed "[at] the very least . . . demonstrate that there is a genuine factual dispute for trial," (1) a letter from an insurance representative of another defendant describing asbestos products to which plaintiff's decedent had been exposed, (2) a letter from T. R. Hoff, a former supervisor of decedent, describing asbestos products to which decedent had been exposed, and (3) a copy of decedent's deposition from earlier workmen's compensation proceedings. Plaintiff also apparently indicated at that time that she intended to call Mr. Hoff as a witness at trial.

Celotex subsequently withdrew its first motion for summary judgment. However, as a result of this motion, when Celotex filed its second summary judgment motion, the record *did* contain evidence—including at least one witness—supporting plaintiff's claim. Indeed, counsel for Celotex admitted to this Court at oral argument that Celotex was aware of this evidence and of plaintiff's intention to call Mr. Hoff as a witness at trial when the second summary judgment motion was filed. Moreover, plaintiff's response to Celotex' second motion pointed to this evidence—noting that it had already been provided to counsel for Celotex in connection with the first motion—and argued that Celotex had failed to "meet its burden of proving that there is no genuine factual dispute for trial."

On these facts, there is simply no question that Celotex failed to discharge its initial burden of production. Having chosen to base its motion on the argument that there was no evidence in the record to support plaintiff's claim, Celotex was not free to ignore supporting evidence that the record clearly contained. Rather, Celotex was required, as an initial matter, to attack the adequacy of this evidence. Celotex' failure to fulfill this simple requirement constituted a failure to discharge its initial burden of production under Rule 56, and thereby rendered summary judgment improper. * * *

[JUSTICE STEVENS'S dissent is omitted.]

Notes and Questions

1. In your own words, explain what the majority in *Celotex* requires a party moving for summary judgment to demonstrate in order to prevail. Do the dissenters disagree as to the rule, or as to how the rule is being applied to the facts of the case?

2. The Court in *Celotex* holds that the party moving for summary judgment has the initial burden of establishing that there is no genuine issue of material fact. But what happens if the other side does not contest the motion? Rule 56(e) states that in such a case summary judgment may be entered against the adverse party "if appropriate." May the court enter a sort of "default" summary judgment, sparing the moving party the trouble of proving the absence of an issue? See *Vermont Teddy Bear Co., Inc. v. 1–800 BEARGRAM Co.*, 373 F.3d 241 (2d Cir. 2004).

3. In *Celotex*, the party moving for summary judgment was the defendant. Would a court analyze the evidence in the same way if the *plaintiff* had moved for summary judgment?

4. *Burdens.* The reason why the standard differs for plaintiffs and defendants is because of the *burden of production*. Justice Brennan's dissent discusses how the burden affects what a party must show in order to obtain a summary judgment. But what *is* a burden of production, and why is everyone on the Court assuming it falls on the plaintiff?

The term burden of production may be new to you. On the other hand, you have probably heard of the "burden of proof." The burden of proof in a case is actually made up of three separate burdens: the burdens of *pleading, production* and *persuasion*. Although summary judgment is primarily concerned with the burden of production, an explanation of all three burdens may be helpful.

a. *Pleading.* You have studied the burden of pleading before, in Chapter 5. That burden determines who is responsible for bringing up an issue in her pleadings. If neither party includes the issue in his pleadings, the party with the burden may not offer evidence on that issue at trial (although the liberal amendment policy in the federal courts will often allow the party with the burden to correct her oversight when she tries to introduce evidence). A claimant—that is, a plaintiff on its claim, and a defendant on a counterclaim—has the burden of informing the court and the opposing party of the claims he wants to bring. A party defending against a claim has the burden of pleading any affirmative defenses. Thus, for example, in the *Red Deer* case in Chapter 5, the court refused to hear evidence on the affirmative defense of after-acquired evidence because the defendant failed to plead that defense in its answer.

b. *Production.* The burden of production—which is sometimes called the burden of "going forth with the evidence"—applies after the pleading stage. This burden controls who bears the onus of offering evidence on a particular issue. The party with the burden must offer enough evidence that a reasonable jury could find for that party. If the party with the burden offers no evidence on that issue, or so little evidence that no reasonable jury could find for the party, that party *loses* on that issue. In *Celotex*, the plaintiff had the burden of production on the issue of causation. To meet that burden, she had to offer evidence showing that her husband had been exposed to defendant's asbestos. Defendant—who did not have the burden— was not required to offer any evidence on that point. Because the plaintiff had no evidence tending to show such exposure, the Supreme Court held that it was proper to render summary judgment for the defendant.

Note that some states would require less of the plaintiff in *Celotex*. Rather than requiring the plaintiff to offer enough evidence to allow a reasonable jury to decide in her favor, these states would deny summary judgment as long as the plaintiff had a "mere scintilla" of supporting evidence. Although some older federal cases also applied the mere scintilla standard, the Supreme Court has made it clear in cases like *Celotex* that more is required to defeat summary judgment in federal court.

The burden of production usually (but not always) follows the burden of pleading. Consider, for example, a defendant defending a breach of contract claim by arguing the defense of insanity. Defendant would have the burden of pleading insanity, as well as the burden of offering evidence on her mental state to the court.

It is also possible for the burden of production to *switch* to the other side. In *Celotex*, suppose that the plaintiff had the testimony of ten disinterested OSHA inspectors, all of whom testified that on separate occasions they saw decedent working with asbestos bearing a Celotex label. At that point, plaintiff has offered evidence so compelling that the burden of production would switch to the defendant. Although Celotex would not otherwise be required to offer evidence on whether plaintiff's husband had been exposed to its asbestos, if it fails to offset plaintiff's evidence with its own evidence disproving exposure to its asbestos, it would have failed to satisfy the burden of production, and summary judgment for the plaintiff would be appropriate.

c. *Persuasion.* The burden of persuasion applies only once the case reaches trial. Basically, it is the standard that the jury considers when deciding the case. In a normal civil case, the standard is "a preponderance of the evidence." Under this standard, if neither party offers evidence, or if both parties offer evidence that is equally persuasive, the jury must find for the party who does not have the burden. The burden of persuasion usually falls upon the party with the burden of production, but again there are exceptions.

In some cases, courts apply a burden of persuasion that is more demanding than the preponderance standard. In criminal cases, for example, the prosecution must prove every element of the crime "beyond a reasonable doubt." The defense, by contrast, must only prove its defenses by a preponderance of the evidence. In civil fraud cases, the party alleging fraud must prove the fraud by "clear and convincing evidence," a standard that is also considerably more rigorous than the preponderance standard.

5. Does the burden of persuasion affect the burden of production? Suppose P sues D for negligent misrepresentation based on an advertisement. If P has one witness who testifies unequivocally that the advertisement is false, most courts would hold that P has met his burden of production. Now suppose P sues D for fraud (a claim governed by the stricter "clear and convincing evidence" burden of persuasion) based on the same advertisement. Will one witness still be enough to meet P's burden of production, or is something more required?

In *Anderson v. Liberty Lobby, Inc.,* 477 U.S. 242, 106 S.Ct. 2505, 91 L.Ed.2d 202 (1986) (cited in *Celotex*), the Court held that the burden of production did change along with the ultimate burden of persuasion. But does that make sense? Consider the example set out immediately above. If one person testifies unequivocally that an advertisement is false, and that witness is neither impeached nor rebutted by other witnesses, won't that evidence meet both the preponderance and clear and convincing standards?

6. *Presumptions.* Presumptions further complicate the burden of production. In certain circumstances, the law provides that one or more parties is entitled to a presumption that a certain fact is true. As just one example, a party who has registered his trademark with the United States Patent and Trademark Office is entitled to a presumption that the mark is valid, and that she is the owner. 15 U.S.C. § 1115(a). A presumption switches the burden of production to the other side. Therefore, if our registered trademark owner sues someone for trademark infringement, the owner would merely offer the certificate of registration. If defendant wants to challenge the validity of the mark or claim that plaintiff is not the owner, defendant would have the burden of offering evidence tending to show invalidity or lack of ownership.

7. *Celotex* makes it clear that a motion for summary judgment introduces what is in essence a *new* "burden of production." The party moving for summary judgment has an initial burden of showing to the court that the "no genuine issue of material fact" standard of Rule 56 is satisfied. How the movant goes about meeting that burden depends in turn on the burden of production for the substantive claims and defenses.

To make sure you understand how these different burdens of production play out, consider the following situations. In each case, who has the burden of showing that there is no genuine issue? How can that party satisfy that burden?

a.   P sues D for breach of contract. D denies that there was a contract. D moves for summary judgment.

b.   Same as (a), except that P moves for summary judgment.

c.   P sues D for breach of contract. D admits that there was a contract and that D did not perform as stipulated, but argues that a flood made D's performance impossible. P moves for summary judgment, asserting that no flood occurred.

8.   In *Celotex*, the Court indicates that a party seeking to avoid summary judgment need not offer admissible evidence, but may use whatever information may be at his disposal, including inadmissible evidence such as hearsay. That statement at first glance seems at least partially at odds with Rule 56(e), which provides that *affidavits* offered to support or oppose a summary judgment motion "set forth such facts as would be admissible in evidence." However, there is no contradiction. Rule 56(e) does not require that the affidavit itself be admissible evidence. It merely requires that the information contained in the affidavit be of a type that *could* be admissible.

To illustrate, suppose that the plaintiff in *Celotex* opposed the summary judgment with an affidavit of witness W. W states in her affidavit that "E, a Celotex employee, told me that he saw plaintiff's husband working with Celotex-brand asbestos." If E is available to testify, W's affidavit is inadmissible because it is hearsay evidence. Nevertheless, because the underlying information (what E saw) would be admissible if offered in the proper way (by E testifying as to what he saw), the affidavit may be used for the limited purpose of opposing the summary judgment motion.

9.   *Timing.* According to Rule 56, what is the *earliest* point at which a party may move for summary judgment? Note that the answer varies depending on whether the plaintiff or defendant is moving. Why is there a difference?

Is there a point in the proceedings *after* which a party may no longer move for summary judgment? Could a party move for summary judgment in the middle of the trial?

10.   Given that a motion for summary judgment may be filed very early in the case, it is entirely possible—and probably common—for one side to lack evidence on one or more crucial issues in the case. Why, then, would a defendant served with a complaint not always file immediately for summary judgment? Given that the plaintiff has the burden of production on every element of its claim, wouldn't such a motion often catch the plaintiff without evidence to back up one or more elements of its claim—especially when the claim requires proof of defendant's state of mind or other facts available only to defendant? If the defendant does file a motion immediately, must the court resolve it expeditiously?

11.   In Chapter 5 and Section C of this chapter, you discussed the Rule 12(b) motion to dismiss for failure to state a claim and the Rule 12(c) motion for judgment on the pleadings. Like the motion for summary judgment,

these motions can be brought very early in the case. Moreover, although a motion for judgment on the pleadings must be brought "within such time as not to delay the trial," Rule 12(c), a motion to dismiss for failure to state a claim may be brought at the trial itself. Rule 12(h)(2). Finally, in the federal courts, a dismissal for failure to state a claim and a judgment on the pleadings operate as a final judgment on the issues presented.

What is the difference between a summary judgment motion and these other motions? Review Rule 12(b)(6) and 12(c), and determine which motion is *best* suited to the following situations:

> a. P sues D for trespass. D's answer does not deny liability, but claims that P's property was an attractive nuisance. P feels that he should prevail because attractive nuisance is not a defense to a trespass claim.

> b. P sues D for trespass. P's complaint specifically states that the trespass occurred on August 9, 2004. P files his complaint on August 31, 2005, and that date is stamped on the pleading. The statute of limitations for trespass claims is one year. Under governing law, the statute of limitations is tolled at the point the complaint is filed. D wants to get rid of the case based on the statute of limitations.

> c. Same as b, except that (i) P filed his complaint on August 1, 2005, and (ii) under governing law, the statute of limitation is tolled only when the complaint is *served*. D was not served until August 31, 2005. P has not yet made proof of service. D wants to get rid of the case based on the statute of limitations.

12. In part (c) of the prior problem, there are actually *two* procedural options. If you concluded that D should move for summary judgment, you are correct; for D cannot prevail without proving a fact that is not asserted in the pleadings. But suppose that D files a 12(b)(6) motion, and attaches to it an affidavit stating that he was not served until August 31. In these situations, Rule 12(b)(6) states that the 12(b)(6) motion will be converted into a motion for summary judgment. Similarly, a Rule 12(c) motion is converted into a motion for summary judgment if supporting materials are attached.

13. P sues D for a civil rights violation, seeking $1,000,000 in compensatory and punitive damages. D denies that she violated any of P's rights, and in the alternative argues that even if P's rights were violated, P suffered no damages. During discovery, P acquires incontrovertible evidence (including D's admission in a deposition) that D violated civil rights laws. D has no evidence to the contrary. However, the evidence concerning P's damages is less persuasive, with each side having some evidence to support its claims. In this situation, it may be possible for P to obtain a *partial* summary judgment, limited to the question of liability. See Rules 56(c) and (d). As a practical matter, a partial summary judgment operates like an amendment of the pleadings. If the court grants summary judgment to P on the question of liability, the trial will be limited to damages, just as if D had admitted liability in his answer.

Can you conceive of a situation where it would be inappropriate to grant partial summary judgment on fewer than all the issues? Could a court grant summary judgment on damages without determining liability? What if the case involves a request for punitive damages?

The battle over summary judgment turns on whether a party has introduced sufficient evidence to satisfy its burden of production. In some cases, that issue will be clear-cut. Take a case in which X and Y are involved in a two-car accident at an intersection with a stoplight. Both X and Y die in the accident. P, the executor of X's estate, sues D, the executor of Y's estate, for wrongful death. P would have the burden of production of showing that the light facing Y was red. However, dead men can't talk. Unless P has some other witnesses who can testify as to the color of the light, a court would grant D's motion for summary judgment.

Many cases, however, are not so cut-and-dried. Suppose P can muster thirty witnesses who will testify in his favor. All thirty testify that the light facing X was green. D moves for summary judgment. Has P met his burden of production? Although he has thirty witnesses, none of them testify directly that the light facing Y was red. Instead, their testimony calls for an *inference*, namely, that the light in question was working properly on the date in question.

The problem of inferences arises quite frequently not only in summary judgment motions, but also in motions for judgments as a matter of law and a new trial. What does a court do when faced with evidence that calls for an inference? The following case explores the issue.

JORGENSEN v. EPIC/SONY RECORDS

351 F.3d 46 (2d Cir. 2003)

STRAUB, Circuit Judge.

* * * Jorgensen, a musician and songwriter, wrote and copyrighted a song entitled "Long Lost Lover" ("Lover") that he claims has been infringed upon by the songs "My Heart Will Go On" ("Heart") and "Amazed." Written by James Horner and Will Jennings, and sung by Celine Dion, "Heart" was the Academy Award-winning theme song for the 1997 blockbuster movie *Titanic*. Defendants Famous Music Corporation, Fox Film Music Corp. and Blue Sky Rider Songs are the three co-publishers of "Heart," and Defendant Sony Music Entertainment Inc. ("Sony") manufactured and distributed the *Titanic* soundtrack. These defendants are collectively referred to as 'the "Heart" defendants' in this opinion.

"Amazed," a song written by Chris Lindsey, Aimee Mayo and Marv Green, was recorded by the country music group Lonestar and released on their multi-platinum album "Lonely Grill." Defendants Careers BMG Music Publishing ("BMG"), Songs of Nashville Dreamworks, and Warner–Tamerlane Publishing Corp. (collectively 'the "Amazed" defendants') are music publishing companies that administer the publishing rights to "Amazed."

Jorgensen asserts two primary theories by which he hypothesizes that the writers of "Heart" and "Amazed" had access to, and copied his song, "Lover": (i) through his unsolicited mass mailings of "Lover" to a multitude of entertainment companies listed in industry songwriter market books, including the defendants; and (ii) through actual receipt of his mailings by two executives at two of the defendant companies, BMG and Sony. Jorgensen has not named the writers of either song as defendants in this suit.

After discovery, the defendants moved for summary judgment on the ground that Jorgensen had failed to adduce any evidence to support these theories of access. In particular, the defendants argued that, with the two exceptions noted below, Jorgensen had made no showing that any of the defendants ever actually received his submission. Even where Jorgensen established actual receipt, the defendants asserted that there was no evidence that Jorgensen's song had been forwarded to the writers of "Amazed" or "Heart," or to any other third party. In addition, the defendants argued that Jorgensen never had any contact with the writers of either "Amazed" or "Heart," and that Jorgensen had no evidence that the writers of either song would ever have received any tapes of unsolicited material from any of the companies to which Jorgensen sent copies of "Lover."

Bruce Pollock, a managing producer at a BMG division that has no connection with the music publishing company, submitted a sworn declaration in which he admitted having received a compact disc copy of "Lover" from Jorgensen. Pollock stated, however, that he did not give the CD to anyone at any time, including the writers of "Amazed" whom he did not know and had never met.

Harvey Leeds, a Vice President at Sony responsible for reviewing touring budgets for Sony artists, also admitted during his deposition that he had received a few tapes from Jorgensen but stated that he did not listen to them, and had assumed they were thrown away. Leeds also testified that he did not know the "Heart" songwriters.

Based on this evidence from Pollock and Leeds and because Jorgensen did not produce any cover letters or other correspondence to the defendants indicating to whom (or when) he sent his other mailings of "Lover," the District Court held that Jorgensen could not establish that the authors of either "Amazed" or "Heart" had a reasonable opportunity to hear his unpublished work. The court held that "bare corporate receipt" of Jorgensen's work by those defendants who may have received Jorgensen's mass mailings did "not create a prima facie case of access sufficient to defeat summary judgment." And, according to the District Court, with respect to BMG and Sony, the fact that Pollock and Leeds, respectively, admitted receiving Jorgensen's songs, without further evidence that they had forwarded the tapes to the songwriters or anyone else, was similarly inadequate to show access.

The District Court's summary of the evidence regarding Jorgensen's interactions with Leeds and Sony, however, was incomplete. During his deposition, Jorgensen testified at length about multiple conversations that he'd had with both Leeds and Leeds's assistants over the course of three or more years regarding several tapes that Jorgensen sent to Leeds, including at least one tape that contained a recording of "Lover." According to Jorgensen, during every one of these conversations, Leeds or his assistants confirmed that Leeds had received Jorgensen's tapes (including, in particular, the "Lover" tape) and told Jorgensen that his tapes had been forwarded to Sony's Artist and Repertoire ("A & R") Department, the department responsible for helping the company "find, sign and guide new talent." In addition, in response to Jorgensen's Requests for Admissions, Sony indicated that "on limited occasions, writers, producers or musicians affiliated with Sony may have been shown some material solicited by the A & R Dept. at some point during 1995, 1996 and 1997. . . ." This evidence—which the District Court does not appear to have considered—undercuts the defendants' claim that "Jorgensen failed to adduce even a scintilla of evidence" that Leeds "provided [Jorgensen's] song to anyone else. . . ."

DISCUSSION

We review the District Court's grant of summary judgment *de novo*, construing the evidence in the light most favorable to Jorgensen, the non-moving party. Moreover, because Jorgensen is proceeding *pro se*, we read his pleadings "liberally and interpret them to raise the strongest arguments that they suggest." *McPherson v. Coombe*, 174 F.3d 276, 280 (2d Cir. 1999). As the District Court observed, however, our "application of this different standard does not relieve plaintiff of his duty to meet the requirements necessary to defeat a motion for summary judgment."

To prevail on a motion for summary judgment, the defendants must demonstrate the absence of material evidence supporting an essential element of Jorgensen's copyright infringement claim. Jorgensen, to avoid summary judgment, "may not rely simply on conclusory allegations or speculation . . ., but instead must offer evidence to show that [his] version of the events is not wholly fanciful." *Morris v. Lindau*, 196 F.3d 102, 109 (2d Cir. 1999).

In a copyright infringement case, the plaintiff must show: (i) ownership of a valid copyright; and (ii) unauthorized copying of the copyrighted work. A certificate of registration from the United States Register of Copyrights constitutes *prima facie* evidence of the valid ownership of a copyright. Jorgensen secured such registration for "Lover," and the defendants do not dispute the validity of that copyright. Thus, Jorgensen has met the first element of an infringement claim.

To satisfy the second element of an infringement claim—the "unauthorized copying" element—a plaintiff must show both that his work was "actually copied" and that the portion copied amounts to an "improper or unlawful appropriation." "Actual copying may be established by direct or indirect evidence." *Boisson v. Banian, Ltd.*, 273 F.3d 262, 267 (2d Cir. 2001). Because direct evidence of copying is seldom available, a plaintiff may establish copying circumstantially "by demonstrating that the person who composed the defendant's work had access to the copyrighted material," *Herzog v. Castle Rock Entm't*, 193 F.3d 1241, 1249 (11th Cir. 1999), and that there are similarities between the two works that are "probative of copying," *Repp* [*v. Webber*, 132 F.3d 882 (2d Cir. 1997), *cert. denied*, 525 U.S. 815 (1998)] at 889.

Access means that an alleged infringer had a "reasonable possibility"—not simply a "bare possibility"—of hearing the prior work; access cannot be based on mere "speculation or conjecture." *Gaste v. Kaiserman*, 863 F.2d 1061, 1066 (2d Cir. 1988); *see also* 4 MELVILLE B. NIMMER & DAVID NIMMER, NIMMER ON COPYRIGHT § 13.02[A], at 13–19 to 13–20 (2002) ("Reasonable opportunity ... does not encompass any bare possibility in the sense that anything is possible. Access may not be inferred through mere speculation or conjecture."); *but cf. id.* at § 13.02[A], at 13–22 (noting that "at times, distinguishing a 'bare' possibility from a 'reasonable' possibility will present a close question"). In order to support a claim of access, a plaintiff must offer "significant, affirmative and probative evidence." *Scott v. Paramount Pictures Corp.*, 449 F. Supp. 518, 520 (D.D.C. 1978), *aff'd*, 607 F.2d 494 (D.C. Cir. 1979) (table), *cert. denied*, 449 U.S. 849, 101 S. Ct. 137 (1980).

1. *The mass mailings of "Lover"*

Jorgensen argues, first, that his act of mailing unsolicited tapes of "Lover" to scores of record and music publishing companies, including the corporate defendants, constituted access because the corporate employees who allegedly received the mailing could have provided the "Heart" and "Amazed" songwriters with a copy of "Lover." With two exceptions reviewed below, however, Jorgensen has not provided *any* reasonable documentation that he actually mailed such tapes (or when or to whom these tapes were purportedly sent). Jorgensen's mass-mailing allegation was, thus, properly rejected by the District Court as legally insufficient proof of access. 2002 WL 31119377, at *5 (noting that Jorgensen "did not maintain a log of where and when he sent his work, or keep receipts from certified mailings to establish a chain of access"); *see also Dimmie v. Carey*, 88 F. Supp. 2d 142, 146 (S.D.N.Y. 2000) (rejecting plaintiff's claim that the mailing of tapes to a corporation could "be equated with access" where there was no evidence that the tapes were ever received or forwarded to the alleged infringers); *Jorgensen v. Careers BMG Music Publ'g*, No. 01 Civ. 0357, 2002 WL 1492123, at *4–5 (S.D.N.Y. July 11, 2002) (Preska, J.) ("*Jorgensen I*").[4]

2. *The submissions to Pollock and Leeds*

Jorgensen's second and more narrow theory of access, predicated on Pollock's and Leeds's admissions that they received Jorgensen's submissions, was also rejected by the District Court. * * *

---

4. In *Jorgensen I*, a separate action filed the same day as this action, Jorgensen alleged copyright infringement of another of his songs by Eric Clapton's Grammy Award-winning song, "Change the World." The district court granted summary judgment for defendants, finding that Jorgensen's "evidence of access was speculative and/or legally insufficient [such that] no rational fact finder could find in favor of [him]." Jorgensen has not appealed in *Jorgensen I*.

a. Pollock and the "Amazed" defendants

In his sworn declaration, Pollock stated that his job as a managing producer in BMG's Special Products division "has nothing to do with the publishing company, Careers BMG Music Publishing, Inc., or working creatively with songwriters at all." Although he conceded that he had received a CD recording of "Lover," Pollock denied that he had ever listened to the song and asserted that he never conveyed the CD "to anyone at any time," much less anyone who "contributed creative ideas or material" to "Amazed" or "Heart." In fact, Jorgensen conceded at his deposition that he had no knowledge that Pollock did anything with the CD that Jorgensen sent to him. Pollock stated that he did not have *any* relationship with the writers of "Amazed," and Jorgensen has submitted no evidence to the contrary. *Cf. Towler v. Sayles*, 76 F.3d 579, 583 (4th Cir. 1996) ("A court may infer that the alleged infringer had a reasonable possibility of access if the author sent the copyrighted work to a third party intermediary who has a *close relationship* with the infringer. An intermediary will fall within this category, for example, if she supervises or works in the same department as the infringer or contributes creative ideas to him."); *Moore v. Columbia Pictures Indus., Inc.*, 972 F.2d 939, 944 (8th Cir. 1992) (finding access where intermediary was "in a position to provide suggestions" to the alleged copiers).

Jorgensen's claim against the "Amazed" defendants was properly dismissed because he has not offered any evidence to rebut Pollock's assertions. The most that Jorgensen offers to show a nexus between Pollock and the "Amazed" songwriters is his global assertion that "anything and everything can very well happen." Such speculation does not give rise to a triable issue of access. Jorgensen has not adduced proof of a reasonable possibility that "the paths of [the "Amazed" songwriters] and the infringed work crossed." *Towler*, 76 F.3d at 582. Bare corporate receipt of Jorgensen's work, without any allegation of a nexus between the recipients and the alleged infringers, is insufficient to raise a triable issue of access.

b. Leeds and the "Heart" defendants

At his deposition, Leeds admitted that he had received tapes from Jorgensen but stated that he did not listen to them and he believed that they had been discarded. Leeds testified that his job as a Sony vice president involved reviewing promotional touring budgets and that he was "not involved in the A & R process." Leeds also stated that he did not know the "Heart" songwriters.

Citing this evidence (and echoing their arguments with respect to Pollock), the defendants assert that the mere fact that Leeds had received a copy of Jorgensen's song does not mean that the "Heart" songwriters had a reasonable opportunity to hear it. Defendants argue that it is "undisputed" that Leeds did not forward Jorgensen's tape to the "Heart" songwriters, but they do not address the evidence introduced by Jorgensen that Leeds and his assistants repeatedly told Jorgensen that his tapes—including, in particular, one containing the song "Lover"—were being sent to Sony's A & R department. Leeds, at his deposition, disputed Jorgensen's version of events, testifying that he did not recall ever making such a promise to Jorgensen and that he likely threw Jorgensen's tapes away. Leeds also conceded, though, that it was possible that if there was a tape that he received that he found interesting he might "pass it on" to one of his "friends in the A & R department."

To draw a connection between Sony's A & R department and Horner and Jennings, the creators of "Heart," Jorgensen relied on Sony's admission, in its response to his Request for Admissions, that during the relevant time period, "on limited occasions, writers, producers or musicians affiliated with Sony may have been shown some material solicited by the A & R Dept ..." In concluding that Leeds "did not forward Jorgensen's package," the District Court made no mention of (i) Jorgensen's deposition testimony to the contrary or (ii) Sony's admission regarding the practices of it's A & R Department.

Although the defendants accurately note that Jorgensen has put forth no evidence that the "Heart" songwriters *actually* heard his song, that argument misapprehends Jorgensen's burden. Jorgensen must show a "reasonable possibility of access" by the alleged infringer. He is not required to establish *actual* access.

* * * What is not clear from the record before us is whether Horner and Jennings were songwriters "affiliated" with Sony in the period between when Jorgensen sent his tapes to Sony and when "Heart" was published. Absent some evidence on this issue, a jury could not reasonably infer simply from Sony's access to Jorgensen's work that Horner and Jennings also had such access.

As already noted, it is the defendant seeking summary judgment who must demonstrate a lack of evidence supporting an essential element of plaintiff's claim. The "Heart" defendants, who undoubtedly possess information about the time frame of Sony's affiliation with Horner and Jennings, failed to support their summary judgment motion with any evidence showing the lack of a relationship during the relevant period.[8] Because Jorgensen, appearing *pro se*, may not have appreciated the need to develop this particular evidence in discovery, summary judgment should not have been granted to defendants until the timing of any affiliation was clarified. Viewing the evidence adduced thus far in the light most favorable to Jorgensen and drawing all justifiable inferences in his favor, as we must at the summary judgment stage, we find

---

8. The most that the "Heart" defendants offer to challenge the connection between Sony's A & R Department and the alleged infringers is defense counsel's claim in his affidavit that *"upon information and belief,* neither Horner nor Jennings are associated as songwriters with Sony." (emphasis added). That supposition, however, is too tentative to qualify as evidence warranting summary judgment. *See* Fed. R. Civ. P. 56(e) ("Supporting ... affidavits shall be made on personal knowledge, shall set forth such facts as would be admissible in evidence, and shall show affirmatively that the affiant is competent to testify to the matters stated therein.")

that the District Court erred in granting summary judgment to the "Heart" defendants. Of course, it would be well within the District Court's discretion to permit limited discovery into the question of the timing of the songwriters' affiliation with Sony and to entertain a renewed motion for summary judgment, as may be appropriate. * * *

CONCLUSION

We have reviewed the record and considered all of Jorgensen's remaining contentions and find them to be without merit. We therefore AFFIRM the District Court's grant of summary judgment in favor of Defendants Careers BMG Music Publishing, Songs of Nashville Dreamworks, and Warner–Tamerlane Publishing Corporation. With respect to Defendants Famous Music Corporation, Fox Film Music Corporation, Blue Sky Rider Songs, and Sony Music Entertainment Inc., however, we VACATE the District Court's grant of summary judgment and remand the case for further proceedings not inconsistent with this opinion. Each party shall bear its own costs in regard to this appeal.

Notes and Questions

1. *Jorgenson* involves both a presumption and an inference. It can be difficult for a copyright owner suing for infringement to prove that defendant actually copied his work. To get around this practical problem, courts will allow plaintiff a presumption: they will presume defendant copied if plaintiff can show that defendant had access to the work, and that defendant's work was substantially similar to plaintiff's. Had Jorgenson been able to show access and substantial similarity, the burden would switch to defendants to prove that they had *not* copied the work in question.

In the case itself, however, Jorgenson had no evidence that defendants had access to his work. He was instead asking the court to infer access based on the fact that he had sent copies of his work to some of the defendants.

2. Is the *Jorgenson* court saying that inferences are never allowed? Can a plaintiff ever prevail if it has only circumstantial evidence? If circumstantial evidence is allowed, what test does the court suggest to determine what inferences are possible?

3. There is an important difference between a presumption and an inference. As noted above, a presumption switches the burden of production. If the court agrees to allow an inference, by contrast, there is no change in the burden. Allowing the inference only means that the issue goes the jury. In most cases, the jury can determine for itself whether the inference is the most likely version of the story.

4. Conversely, in some situations an inference can be so likely that the jury *must* believe it. Be prepared to offer a hypothetical example of an inference meeting this standard.

5. Consider the following statement: "Negligence cases by their very nature do not usually lend themselves to summary judgment, since often, even if all parties are in agreement as to the underlying facts, the very question of negligence is itself a question for jury determination." *Ugarriza*

v. Schmieder, 46 N.Y.2d 471, 474, 386 N.E.2d 1324, 1325, 414 N.Y.S.2d 304, 305 (1979). Do you understand what the court is saying? Is a finding of negligence a finding of fact, or an inference to be drawn from the facts? See *Borden v. CSX Transportation, Inc.*, 843 F.Supp. 1410 (M.D. Ala. 1993) (even when facts are undisputed, whether a particular act constitutes negligence is a jury question); *Roy v. Inhabitants of City of Lewiston*, 42 F.3d 691 (1st Cir. 1994) (judgments about whether a party acted reasonably are made by the jury).

Nevertheless, do not conclude that courts will not grant summary judgment in negligence cases. A quick search will reveal many cases in which summary judgment was granted. For one instructive example, see *Sharpe v. United States*, 936 F.2d 1178 (11th Cir. 1991) (summary judgment for plaintiff). Some of these cases involve proof that the defendant was negligent *per se* because he violated a statutory standard. In others, the facts were such that the court concluded that no reasonable jury could conclude that the defendant's acts were reasonable.

Are there any other issues that are exclusively within the province of the jury? How about the question of whether two parties have a contract? What about the issue of whether a written contract was ambiguous? On this latter issue, *see ESI, Inc. v. Coastal Power Prod. Co.*, 13 F.Supp.2d 495 (S.D.N.Y. 1998).

6. A summary judgment is a final judgment. If one party is held liable to the other, the winner can collect on the judgment. Similarly, the loser can appeal the judgment to a higher court. However, neither the *denial* of a summary judgment nor the grant of a *partial* summary judgment on fewer than all the issues relevant to a party's claim are considered final judgments. The parties must wait until the remainder of the case is resolved before they can collect and/or appeal.

Problems

1. P sues D for trespass. D's answer admits that she intentionally was on P's property on the date in question. However, D also claims in her answer that at the time she had a good-faith belief that *she* owned the property instead of P. Although D admits she now knows that the property belongs to P, she claims that her good faith belief shields her from liability for trespass. P disagrees. As P understands the law, a person is liable for trespass whenever he is intentionally on property that belongs to another, even if the person was mistaken as to who owned the property. What motion—12(b)(6), 12(c), or summary judgment—will allow P to test whether his knowledge of the law is correct, and if so, avoid a trial?

2. P sues D for trespass. D's answer asserts that she owns the land on which she allegedly trespassed. P has incontrovertible proof that the land belongs to him rather than D. D has no proof other than her conclusory statement in her answer. What motion—12(b)(6), 12(c), or summary judgment—will allow P to avoid a trial?

3. Same as Problem 2, except that D's answer specifies that she owns the land "pursuant to an oral conveyance from P, which occurred before the date on which D is alleged to have trespassed." Under governing law, a

conveyance of real property is not valid unless it is in writing. What motion—12(b)(6), 12(c), or summary judgment—will allow P to avoid a trial?

4.   P sues D for fraud in connection with the sale of corporate stock, based on D's glowing representations concerning the future prospects of the corporation. Before filing his answer, D moves for summary judgment. D's motion claims that P has no evidence whatsoever tending to show that D knew that his statements were false. Under governing law, a claim for fraud requires proof that the defendant knew the statements were false. Is D's motion timely? Assuming that D is correct that P has no evidence that D knew the statements were false, is a court likely to grant summary judgment for D at this juncture?

5.   Same as Problem 4, except that D makes its motion after discovery is complete. D's motion simply states that "After extensive discovery, it is clear that P has no evidence of a crucial element of a fraud claim; namely, D's knowledge that the statements concerning the corporation were false." Is D's motion sufficient?

6.   Same as Problem 4, except that D makes its motion after discovery is complete. P's evidence of D's knowledge consists of a statement that D made to one of his colleagues. This statement makes it clear that D knew the corporation did not have a rosy future. However, this statement was made two weeks *after* D made the representations to P. Will the court grant D's motion?

7.   P and D sell very similar products. P sues D for false advertising, based on D's advertising campaign. After discovery, both P and D move for summary judgment. P has evidence that the claims in the advertisement were false, and that D intended to deceive consumers. However, a false advertising claim requires proof that consumers were deceived to their detriment. Because P has been unable to track down any of the people who bought D's product, P has no evidence whatsoever that anyone actually relied on the advertisement. On the other hand, governing law also creates a presumption: if a plaintiff can show that its competitor intended to deceive consumers, courts will presume that consumers were in fact deceived. Are either P or D entitled to summary judgment? Does it depend on what evidence D has on the question of reliance?

8.   P sues D for defamation, claiming that D is falsely accusing P of infringing D's patented process for preparing lutefisk (cod cured in lye, which is definitely an acquired taste). D counterclaims for patent infringement. In order to prevail on the patent infringement claim, the patent holder must show that the infringing party "made, used, or sold" a product using the patented process. After discovery, P learns that D has no evidence that P made, used, or sold lutefisk using D's process. Can P move for summary judgment? If the motion succeeds, will the court also throw out P's claim?

E.   JUDGMENT AS A MATTER OF LAW

INTRODUCTORY PROBLEM ONE

Same basic scenario as the Introductory Problem to Part D of this chapter, except assume that summary judgment was denied.

The parties conduct some additional discovery, and the case goes to trial before a jury. At trial, Green calls Driver to the stand. Driver is one of Lon's employees. Driver testifies that on the date in question, Lon asked him to take certain equipment out to a crew working at a certain address. Driver could not find a crew at that address. However, he saw a crew working at Green's house. When Driver informed the crew boss that he had a delivery, the crew boss said, "Thanks, we were expecting Lon to send that stuff." (You should assume that this testimony is not barred by the hearsay evidence rule.)

Later in the case, Lon himself takes the stand. Lon cannot remember whether he sent Driver anywhere on the date in question. However, Lon then claims that he also had a contract with Green, under which Lon was to remove Green's trees. Lon introduces a written contract with a signature that looks like Green's on it.

Green, however, anticipated this ploy. After Lon steps down, Green calls several witnesses to impeach Lon's testimony. First, these witnesses testify that Lon has three convictions for forgery, all arising out of situations where Lon forged customers' signatures on contracts. Second, Green calls Lon's secretary to the stand. The secretary testifies that, soon after Green filed suit against Lon, she saw Lon writing Green's name on a piece of paper. On this same paper, Lon also wrote a date that was two weeks prior to the date on which Green's trees were removed— the exact same date as the contract that Lon is now using to prove his case at trial. However, because of the lighting and the angle, the secretary cannot say whether the paper that Lon was writing on was the same as the contract that he is now introducing.

At the close of all the evidence, Green moves for judgment as a matter of law. Lon protests, arguing that the jury should decide the case.

Governing Rule: Federal Rule 50.

INTRODUCTORY PROBLEM TWO

Same as Introductory Problem One, except that the court denies the motion. The case goes to the jury, which renders a verdict for Lon. Green asks the judge to ignore the jury verdict, and enter judgment for him instead. May the judge enter judgment for Green?

Governing Rule: Federal Rule 50(b).

—————

Summary judgment prevents a trial from occurring. If a case survives summary judgment and makes it to trial, each party is entitled to present its evidence to the factfinder. However, what if the evidence presented at trial makes it clear that one side will prevail? In this situation, a party may move for "judgment as a matter of law" under Rule 50. Under that Rule, a court will grant a party's motion for judgment as a matter of law if "there is no legally sufficient evidentiary basis for a reasonable jury to find for" the opposing side.

For all practical purposes, judgment as a matter of law keeps the case from the jury. However, as the Introductory Problems demonstrate, a court can grant judgment as a matter of law either before the case is submitted to the jury under Rule 50(a), or after the jury returns with a verdict under Rule 50(b). If judgment is granted pre-verdict, the case is truly "kept from" the jury, as the jury does not get to deliberate and decide the matter. If judgment is granted post-verdict, the jury does deliberate and render a verdict, but the judge disregards the verdict and enters a judgment for the verdict loser. Either way, the judge, not the jury, decides the issue.

The phrase "judgment as a matter of law" is of relatively recent vintage. Historically, courts used the term "directed verdict" to refer to the situation where the judge rendered judgment before the case was submitted to the jury.* After the jury returned with a verdict, the court could set aside the jury's findings and enter a "judgment notwithstanding the verdict"—often referred to by the Latin equivalent "judgment *non obstante veredicto*," or simply "JNOV." Although the Rule was amended in 1991 to adopt a uniform terminology, many courts still prefer the old terminology, as opposed to the somewhat more cumbersome "pre-verdict judgment as a matter of law" and "post-verdict judgment as a matter of law."

When is it appropriate for a court to render judgment as a matter of law? How does the Rule 50 standard compare with the standard for rendering summary judgment? The following case discusses how the Rule 50 standard apples.

KINSERLOW v. CMI CORP., BID–WELL DIV.

217 F.3d 1021 (8th Cir. 2000)

BATAILLON, District Judge* * *

I. BACKGROUND

Kinserlow, a cement mason working for Fred Weber, Inc. (FWI), brought this action for personal injuries against CMI Corporation, Bid–Well Division (Bid–Well), after he fell from a bridge over a highway in St. Louis County, Missouri. At the time he fell, Kinserlow was operating a bull float, walking backwards and forward on a mini workbridge behind a Bid–Well paving machine, smoothing out concrete. The workbridge had tapered end sections, but no written or painted warnings or guard rails to alert workers that they were coming to the end of the workbridge. Kinserlow, walking backwards, fell from the end of the workbridge to the

---

* The phrase "directed verdict" stems from the historic practice of having the judge submit the case to the jury with strict instructions to decide the case in favor of one party. Today, courts have dispensed with that formality, and simply render judgment for the prevailing party.

ground 18' below. He was severely hurt, and his injuries still cause him debilitating pain. His suit against Bid–Well alleged strict liability and negligence.

The primary issue in the suit was the identity of the company that had manufactured the workbridge and then sold or supplied it to FWI. According to the testimony of Kinserlow's witnesses, Bid–Well and another company, Gomaco, both manufacture steel workbridges similar to the one from which Kinserlow fell. Kinserlow's workbridge had lost any identifying markings or labels it might have once had, having apparently been in FWI's inventory since before 1977. The primary evidentiary hurdle for Kinserlow was to establish that Bid–Well manufactured and then sold or supplied the workbridge to FWI. An FWI employee testified that at the time of Kinserlow's accident, FWI had two types of workbridges in inventory, one with filled-in metal triangles placed in the frame and another without filled-in metal triangles but with tapered end sections. Kinserlow's workbridge was one of the latter, and he alleged that Bid–Well had manufactured and sold or supplied it to FWI.

Two FWI employees testified that in their experience, once a concrete company purchased a workbridge and a paving machine, from whatever source, the two pieces of equipment are generally kept together as a set. Kinserlow himself testified that when he worked with a Bid–Well paving machine, he always used a workbridge identical to the one from which he fell. He also testified that when he worked for a different concrete company, he saw Bid–Well paving machines used with workbridges with tapered end sections like the one from which he fell. On the day of his accident, his workbridge was paired with a Bid–Well paving machine. The two pieces of equipment had been in FWI's inventory since at least 1977.

Kinserlow's witnesses offered no direct documentary evidence that Bid–Well had ever sold or supplied a workbridge to FWI prior to the date of the accident, and the FWI employee who would have been responsible for buying the workbridge is deceased. Kinserlow therefore attempted to establish through inference that Bid–Well had sold FWI the workbridge in question. For example, Thomas Held, the president of Allied Construction Company, Bid–Well's primary competitor in the steel workbridge market, testified during Kinserlow's case in chief that Allied Construction was the exclusive distributor of Gomaco paving machines and workbridges in the St. Louis area. Held testified that he could find but one invoice recording a sale of a Gomaco workbridge to FWI; that sale occurred in 1980 and did not involve the sale of a paving machine. He also testified that the Gomaco workbridges he was familiar with— those manufactured and sold after 1984, the year he began working for Allied Construction—all had metal triangles inserted in their frames, unlike the workbridge from which Kinserlow fell.

On cross-examination, however, Held testified that he could not say whether Gomaco workbridges manufactured and sold before 1984 had such triangles. He also did not know what types of workbridges FWI had in inventory on the day of the accident, whether FWI had purchased a Gomaco workbridge from a source other than Allied Construction, or whether Bid–Well had ever sold workbridges with tapered end sections. Kinserlow and his other witnesses made similar admissions on cross-examination: they did not know whether Bid–Well had ever manufactured or sold a workbridge with tapered end sections, or whether Bid–Well had ever sold or supplied a workbridge to FWI prior to the accident.

In contrast, Bid–Well's witness Daniel Napierala, a long-time Gomaco employee, testified that since 1968 when it began building workbridges, Gomaco alone had been making workbridges with tapered end sections. Napierala said that he had never seen a tapered end section built by Bid–Well or by any other competitor in his seventeen years in the industry. He also testified that beginning in 1984, Gomaco began to put metal triangles on the frame of its workbridges so that warning labels could be attached to the workbridge. He further testified that as an exclusive Gomaco distributor, Allied Construction would have sold only new Gomaco equipment. FWI nevertheless could have acquired its inventory of Gomaco workbridges from a source other than Allied. Bid–Well's only other witness, Jack Lease, has been a Bid–Well employee since 1970. He was originally hired as a design draftsman, and is now Bid–Well's vice president and sales manager. He testified that Bid–Well began manufacturing and selling workbridges in 1975, but had never manufactured or sold workbridges with tapered end sections.

Kinserlow appeals the decision of the trial court to grant Bid–Well's motion, renewed at the close of evidence, for judgment as a matter of law under Federal Rule of Civil Procedure 50(a). The trial court found that Kinserlow failed to establish by a preponderance that Bid–Well—rather than some other manufacturer—had manufactured, sold, or distributed the tapered end section of the workbridge from which Kinserlow fell. Kinserlow argues that the trial court's decision to grant judgment as a matter of law was incorrect because the court improperly weighed the facts presented by the plaintiff against the facts presented by the defendant. Kinserlow contends that the court should have given him the benefit of all beneficial inferences and not considered any of Bid–Well's evidence except as it might have helped his case.

II. DISCUSSION

In both Rule 56 motions for summary judgment and Rule 50 motions for judgment as a matter of law, the inquiry is the same: "Whether the evidence presents a sufficient disagreement to require submission to a jury or whether it is so one-sided that one party must prevail as a matter of law." *Anderson v. Liberty Lobby, Inc.*, 477 U.S. 242, 251–52 (1986). Rule 50(a) allows the judge in a jury trial to enter judgment against a party with respect to a claim or defense "that cannot under the controlling law be maintained or defeated without a favorable finding on that issue," when the party has been fully heard on the issue and "there is no legally sufficient evidentiary basis for a reasonable jury to find for that party on the issue." Fed. R. Civ. P. 50(a).

Our review of the district court's decision is de novo, using the same standards as the district court. The court views the evidence "in the light most favorable to the [nonmoving] party and must not engage in a weighing or evaluation of the evidence or consider questions of credibility." *Smith v. World Ins. Co.*, 38 F.3d 1456, 1460 (8th Cir. 1994). The court should grant judgment as a matter of law "only when all of the evidence points one way and is 'susceptible of no reasonable inference sustaining the position of the nonmoving party.' " *Id.*

In a recent age-based employment discrimination case in which an employer appealed the district court's decision to deny its motion for judgment as a matter of law, the United States Supreme Court clarified the standard of review dictated by Rule 50. *Reeves v. Sanderson Plumbing Prods., Inc.*, 530 U.S. 133 (2000). * * *

The Court stated that when entertaining a motion for judgment as a matter of law, a trial court "should review all of the evidence in the record." 530 U.S. at 150.

> In doing so, however, the court must draw all reasonable inferences in favor of the nonmoving party, and it may not make credibility determinations or weigh the evidence. 'Credibility determinations, the weighing of evidence, and the drawing of legitimate inferences from the facts are jury functions, not those of a judge. Thus, although the court should review the records as a whole, it must disregard all evidence favorable to the moving party that the jury is not required to believe. That is, the court should give credence to the evidence favoring the nonmovant as well as that 'evidence supporting the moving party that is uncontradicted and unimpeached, at least to the extent that that evidence comes from disinterested witnesses.'

Id. at 150–51 (citations omitted).

Kinserlow argues that the evidence he presented at trial, if taken in the light most favorable to him, established by a preponderance that Bid–Well supplied the tapered-end workbridge to FWI. He contends that had the trial court properly drawn all inferences in his favor and avoided weighing his evidence against Bid–Well's, the court would have submitted his case to the jury. Kinserlow argues that he was entitled to the inference that he was on a Bid–Well workbridge when he fell because Gomaco workbridges have metal triangles inserted in their frames; his did not. Moreover, he contends that a Bid–Well sales brochure that showed a Bid–Well paving machine paired with a Gomaco workbridge created an inference that Bid–Well would not have advertised an item in its brochure so substantially similar to the workbridge from which Kinserlow fell unless Bid–Well itself also manufactured or sold such a workbridge.

In a motion for judgment as a matter of law, the nonmoving party is only entitled to the benefit of reasonable inferences. *Fought v. Hayes Wheels Int'l, Inc.*, 101 F.3d 1275, 1277 (8th Cir. 1996). A "reasonable inference is one 'which may be drawn from the evidence without resort to speculation. When the record contains no proof beyond speculation to support the verdict, judgment as a matter of law is appropriate.' " *Id.* (citations omitted). The record is not clear whether the district court rejected as unreasonable the inferences urged on it by Kinserlow or allowed them as reasonable but found them unpersuasive on the issue of product identification. What is clear, however, is that the court evaluated all the evidence in the record in reaching its decision to grant Bid–Well's motion for judgment as a matter of law. The court stated that

> the burden is on the Plaintiff to prove by a preponderance of the evidence that—its case, and I have reached the conclusion in this case that he has not done so and that I will not submit the case to the Jury. I don't believe that there is a legally sufficient evidentiary basis for a reasonable jury to find for the party on the issue of product identification. And in a preponderance of the evidence case, it's—if it's equally divided between the parties, then the party that has the burden—in this case, the Plaintiff—I must rule against them. There's just not enough evidence, in the Court's view, to show that the Defendant CMI, the Bid–Well Division, manufactured, sold, distributed, or placed in the stream of commerce the workbridge tapered end section.

Although the trial court mentions "equally divided" proof, suggesting a weighing of evidence, the court also indicates that Kinserlow failed to meet his burden of production. The evidence as outlined above does not support a reasonable inference that the only Gomaco workbridge in FWI's inventory was acquired in the single sale evidenced by the 1980 Allied Construction invoice. The evidence does not support an inference that Bid–Well paving machines are always paired with Bid–Well workbridges, or that FWI acquired the workbridge from which Kinserlow fell at the same time it acquired the Bid–Well paving machine with which it was paired. Nor does the evidence support an inference that because the workbridge from which Kinserlow fell lacked metal triangle inserts, it was therefore manufactured by Bid–Well. Kinserlow's witnesses could not establish that he fell from a Bid–Well workbridge because they could not testify that Bid–Well had ever manufactured or sold a workbridge with tapered end sections, or that Bid–Well had ever sold or supplied a workbridge to FWI prior to the accident. The trial court did not weigh Kinserlow's evidence against Bid–Well's or make credibility determinations. The trial court simply found that Kinserlow had not offered enough evidence to tie Bid–Well to the workbridge from which Kinserlow fell.

In reaching this conclusion, the court was entitled to give credence to any of Bid–Well's evidence that was " 'uncontradicted and unimpeached, at least to the extent that that evidence [came] from disinterested witnesses.' " *Reeves v. Sanderson Plumbing Prods., Inc.*, at 150–51.

Kinserlow does not appear to have contradicted or impeached the testimony of Bid–Well's disinterested witness, Gomaco employee Daniel Napierala, that 1) only Gomaco had ever made workbridges with tapered end sections, and 2) Gomaco did not insert metal triangles into the frames of its workbridges until 1984. A strong inference to be drawn from this testimony is that the workbridge from which Kinserlow fell was in fact not manufactured by Bid–Well but by Gomaco prior to 1984. This inference is consistent with the testimony of Kinserlow's own disinterested witness, Thomas Held of Allied Construction, that the Gomaco workbridges with which he was familiar—only those manufactured and sold after 1984, the year he began working for Allied Construction—all had metal triangle inserts. Finally, the inference is consistent with the testimony of Bid–Well's interested witness, Jack Lease, that Bid–Well had never sold or manufactured a tapered end workbridge during his nearly thirty year tenure with the company. * * *

III. CONCLUSION

For the foregoing reasons, the decision of the district court is affirmed.

Notes and Questions

1. The plaintiff in *Kinserlow* claimed that judgment as a matter of law was improper because the judge had "weighed the evidence" in the case. Does that argument correctly reflect the standard set out in Rule 50? Is a court considering a motion for judgment as a matter of law supposed to determine which side has presented a stronger case?

2. The court indicates that plaintiff has no direct evidence which shows that the workbridge on which he was injured was manufactured by defendant. Therefore, this case involves an *inference*, much like the *Jorgenson* case in the prior section. But does the defendant in *Kinserlow* really have any direct evidence showing that it did *not* manufacture the workbridge? Indeed, isn't the defendant also asking the court to make an inference in its favor?

Does defendant need any evidence as to who manufactured the workbridge? Would the court have issued judgment as a matter of law if defendant had not introduced the testimony of the Gomaco employee?

3. *Burden of production.* Like summary judgment, judgment as a matter of law turns on the burden of production. If the party without the burden moves for judgment as a matter of law (*e.g.*, a defendant moving for judgment on plaintiff's claim), it can prevail merely by showing that no reasonable jury could find for the other party on one or more elements of the claim or defense. Given the importance of the burden of production, can a court ever grant judgment as a matter of law *for* the party with the burden of production on an issue?

To illustrate, suppose that plaintiff sues defendant for breach of an oral contract. Defendant denies that there is a contract. At trial, plaintiff offers 20 witnesses who testify that they heard defendant agree to the terms of the contract. Defendant offers no testimony whatsoever, but moves for judgment as a matter of law. Even though plaintiff is the only party who has offered evidence, isn't the jury entitled to disbelieve all that evidence? Re-read carefully the quote from the Supreme Court's *Reeves* case set out in *Kinserlow*. Are plaintiff's 20 witnesses interested or disinterested? What if the witnesses are plaintiff's employees? Plaintiff's neighbors?

Although it is fairly uncommon, courts on occasion will grant judgment as a matter of law for plaintiffs. See, e.g., *Hurd v. American Hoist and Derrick Co.*, 734 F.2d 495 (10th Cir. 1984) (judgment as matter of law for plaintiff in products liability case); *United States v. Kwoczak*, 210 F.Supp.2d 638 (E.D. Pa. 2002) (judgment as a matter of law for United States in deportation proceeding was appropriate even though the government has the burden of showing grounds for deportation by "clear, unequivocal, and convincing evidence"—a higher burden than that which applies in most civil cases).

4. *Bench trials*. Rule 50 applies only in cases tried before a jury. However, Rule 52(c) provides for a similar mechanism in bench trials. Is the standard under the two rules the same? When determining whether to grant judgment as a matter of law in a bench trial, may the judge weigh conflicting evidence? Does the judge have to draw all reasonable inferences in favor of the nonmoving party?

5. *Summary judgment and judgment as a matter of law compared.* Rule 50 provides that judgment as a matter of law is appropriate when "there is no legally sufficient basis for a reasonable jury to find for" the nonmoving party. How does that standard compare to the "no genuine issue of material fact" standard for summary judgment set out in Rule 56? After comparing the standards, are you surprised by the statement in *Kinserlow* that the standard for granting judgment as a matter of law is the same as the standard for summary judgment? In fact, you can find hundreds of other decisions containing similar statements. See, e.g., *Schnabel v. Abramson*, 232 F.3d 83 (2d Cir. 2000); *Appelbaum v. Milwaukee Metro. Sewerage Dist.*, 340 F.3d 573 (7th Cir. 2003); *Computer Access Tech. Corp. v. Catalyst Enters., Inc.*, 273 F.Supp.2d 1063 (N.D. Cal. 2003); *Mohr v. Chicago Sch. Reform Bd. of Trs. of the Bd. of Educ.*, 155 F.Supp.2d 923 (N.D. Ill. 2001).

In actual practice, however, there is a small, but real, difference between how willing courts are to keep cases from the jury under the two rules. Generally speaking, it is slightly easier for a party to win a judgment as a matter of law than it is a summary judgment. Why might this be so? Is it attributable to the different wording of the two rules? Or is the difference caused by more practical factors? To what extent could the difference be due to the fact that a judge hearing a motion for summary judgment usually considers only documentary evidence such as affidavits and deposition transcripts, while the judge hearing a Rule 50 motion has heard live witnesses who have been cross-examined in the courtroom? On the other hand, if the judge is not to determine credibility under either Rule, should this difference matter?

6. Some have also suggested that there is a difference in the way judges evaluate pre-verdict and post-verdict motions for judgment as a matter of law. *See, e.g., EEOC v. Kohler Co.*, 335 F.3d 766 (8th Cir. 2003).

Can you think of any practical reasons why this might be the case? The standard for granting judgment as a matter of law is that "no reasonable jury" could find for the nonmoving party. Put yourself in the shoes of a judge who is considering a post-verdict motion for judgment as a matter of law. If you grant the motion, what are you saying?

7.   Read Rule 50 carefully and answer the following questions:

a.   D is confident that P has failed to prove her case. D is accordingly surprised when the jury returns a verdict for P. D therefore first files for judgment as a matter of law following the jury verdict. May the court grant the motion?

b.   D moves for judgment as a matter of law at the close of P's case. The court denies the motion. D then presents his evidence and the case is submitted to the jury. When the jury returns a verdict for P, D again files a motion for judgment as a matter of law. May the court grant the motion?

Why does Rule 50 require a pre-verdict motion for judgment as a matter of law as a precondition to filing a post-verdict motion? Somewhat surprisingly, the answer has to do with the constitutional right to a jury trial. Recall that the seventh amendment merely "preserves" the right to a jury trial as it existed in 1792. In 1792, the common-law courts allowed a court to render judgment as a matter of law before the case was submitted to the jury. Because a party was entitled to a jury only in cases in which there were disputed facts, the court could keep the case from the jury in cases where the facts were completely clear. However, at common law there was no way the court could overturn the jury once it had rendered its verdict (although the judge could grant a new trial). This historical practice, especially when viewed in light of the seventh amendment's language providing that "no fact tried by a jury, shall be otherwise reexamined in any Court of the United States, than according to the rules of the common law," would seem to prevent federal courts from granting a post-verdict judgment as a matter of law.

To get around this constitutional problem, Rule 50 engages in some definitional sleight of hand. Rule 50(a)(2) states that a motion for judgment as a matter of law can only be made before the case is submitted the jury (in other words, the party must move for a pre-verdict judgment as a matter of law). If the judge denies the pre-verdict motion, the rule states that that denial "is considered to be" a decision to *delay* ruling. If the moving party "reasserts" the motion after the jury verdict (that is, moves for a post-verdict judgment), the judge can then make a "delayed" ruling. Of course, the rule is merely a legal fiction. If the party who moved pre-verdict does not move again after the verdict, the judge will not issue a delayed ruling.

A proposed amendment to Rule 50(a) would change the result in Problem 6 above. Under this proposal, which will take effect on December 1, 2006 unless rejected by Congress, a post-verdict motion is proper as long as the party had made *any* pre-verdict motion for judgment as a matter of law.

8.   There are many cases in which a judge has denied a motion for judgment as a matter of law at the close of all the evidence, only to grant the "renewed" motion after the jury has returned with the verdict. Given that

no additional evidence has been offered, what could possibly cause the judge to change her mind? Again, the explanation for this phenomenon is practical. First, if the judge honestly feels that no reasonable jury could find for the nonmoving side, then she may think the odds are quite high that the jury will agree with her and rule for the moving side. Courts of appeal will overturn a judgment as a matter of law if there was any chance the nonmoving side could have won. A jury verdict, by comparison, is virtually unassailable on appeal. Therefore, the judge would rather have the jury render the decision.

Second, consider what happens if the judge is *wrong* in granting judgment as a matter of law. If the judge grants a pre-verdict motion for judgment as a matter of law, and the court of appeals reverses, what happens? What happens if the judge overturns the jury verdict by rendering a post-verdict judgment as a matter of law and the court of appeals reverses?

9.   Suppose the court submits the case to the jury, and the jury deadlocks. Can the court nevertheless grant a timely motion for judgment as a matter of law? Does the fact that this jury could not agree on a verdict mean that reasonable minds could differ? *See Headwaters Forest Defense v. County of Humboldt*, 240 F.3d 1185 (9th Cir. 2000), *judgment vacated on other grounds* 534 U.S. 801, 122 S.Ct. 24, 151 L.Ed.2d 1 (2001).

Problems

1.   P owns a beachfront lot. Although the beach in this area is only 25 feet deep, P's lot is 300 feet deep. Under state law, a party owns the beach, and can prevent others from using it. P sues D for trespassing on his beachfront lot. D denies that she trespassed. At trial, P's evidence consists of the testimony of two witnesses, W1 and W2. Neither W1 nor W2 actually saw D on P's beach. W1 saw D at 8:00 p.m. on the beach of the lot immediately south of P's land. W1 testifies that D was walking north. W2 saw D at 8:15 p.m., standing on the beach of the lot immediately to the *north* of P's lot. D was completely dry when W2 saw her. Because no one saw D actually *on* P's lot, D moves for judgment as a matter of law at the close of P's case. Will the court grant the motion?

2.   Same as Problem 1, except that *P* moves for judgment as a matter of law at the close of his case. Will P prevail?

3.   Same as Problem 1, except that D does not move for judgment as a matter of law. D instead presents her evidence. D herself does not testify, and none of D's other evidence touches upon the issue of whether D was on P's land. P moves for judgment as a matter of law at the close of all the evidence. Will the court grant P's motion?

4.   Same as Problem 1, where D moves for judgment as a matter of law. The court denies D's motion. Is D precluded from raising the same challenge again at a later point in the trial, or after the jury returns with a verdict?

5.   Same as Problem 1, except that P does not call W1 and W2. Instead, P calls a different witness, X. X testifies that he saw D walking across P's beach at 8:10 p.m. X states that he was standing east of the eastern edge of P's lot, five hundred feet inland from the beach. On cross-examination, X admits that the sun was setting directly to the west at the moment that he

observed D. Nevertheless, X insists that the person he saw was D. At the close of P's case, D moves for judgment as a matter of law. Will the court grant D's motion?

6. Same basic facts as Problem 1, except that P has considerably more evidence. A group of a dozen bishops was vacationing on the beach. All twelve of these bishops state that they saw D walking across P's beach. P also has a photograph of D, taken while D was on P's beach. Finally, D left behind footprints in the sand on P's beach. P had the folks from CSI make plaster casts of these footprints, noting the location and date.

After P rests, D offers her testimony. D has only one witness–herself. While on the stand, D flatly denies that she walked across P's land. However, on cross-examination, D admits that she has a prior perjury conviction.

P moves for judgment as a matter of law at the close of the evidence. Will the court grant P's motion?

F. NEW TRIAL

INTRODUCTORY PROBLEM

Lincoln sued Kennedy Railroad Corp. for damages incurred from a train derailment which spilled toxic substances on Lincoln's farm causing damage to his soil and animals. At the conclusion of the four-day trial, the jury returned a verdict in favor of the defendant. After the verdict, Lincoln's counsel decided to file a motion for a new trial, in which Lincoln alleged several trial errors. After the second day of trial, without asking the trial judge's permission, two jurors visited the site of the derailment and reported their observations to the other jurors. During the jury's deliberations, the deputy bailiff told the jurors that they needed to find in favor of the railroad; otherwise the railroad company could relocate its headquarters to another community. In addition to the allegations of jury tampering and misconduct, Lincoln's counsel renewed objections she had made during trial to three of the court's rulings on the admissibility of evidence and to one of the trial court's instructions to the jury. Each of the court's decisions on evidentiary issues and on the jury instruction appeared to help Kennedy Railroad defend against Lincoln's allegations of negligence.

Are the allegations raised by Lincoln in the motion for new trial proper subjects for seeking a new trial?

Governing Rule: Rule 59(a).

––––––––––––

The governing principle for Federal Rule 59(a) is that a court has the authority and the duty to order a new trial whenever it is necessary to prevent injustice. The federal standard is stated in broad terms, due to the impracticality of listing all the possible grounds for a new trial. (Some states in their rules do indeed enumerate specific grounds for a new trial.) The appellate standard of review is for abuse of the trial judge's discretion.

New trials may be granted in bench trials and jury trials. Rule 59(a)(2) allows a new trial to be granted in a bench trial "for any of the reasons for which rehearings have heretofore been granted" in federal courts. The trial court may take "additional testimony, amend findings of fact and conclusions of law or make new findings and conclusions, and direct the entry of a new judgment.

In effect, the federal rule prescribes any ground for a new trial that has already been the basis for granting a new trial in another jury trial. The typical grounds for a new trial are that procedural errors at trial tainted the jury's decision-making process, e.g., improper admission or exclusion of evidence or improper jury instructions. The rationale for these grounds is that the errors led the jury to consider inappropriate information in reaching its verdict or to use the wrong rules of law in assessing liability or damages.

A trial court also can grant a new trial on the ground that the verdict was against the great weight of the evidence. What does that mean? The trial judge believes that there was sufficient evidence for the case to be submitted to the jury, and that a rational jury could decide in favor of the verdict-winner. Nevertheless, the great weight of the evidence favors the verdict-loser. The judge is not required to view the evidence in the light most favorable to the verdict-winner, i.e., she is free to weigh the evidence for herself including an assessment of credibility. In other words, the judge can sit as a "13th juror." If the judge believes that the jury made a mistake in its verdict, she can grant a new trial.

PIESCO v. KOCH

12 F.3d 332 (2d Cir. 1993)

KEARSE, Circuit Judge.

This case, previously before this Court on appeal from the granting of summary judgment in favor of defendants, returns to us following the entry of judgment in favor of plaintiff after trial. Defendants City of New York (the "City"), its Department of Personnel (DOP), Juan Ortiz, and Nicholas LaPorte, Jr., appeal from a judgment entered in the United States District Court for the Southern District of New York after a jury trial before John S. Martin, Jr., Judge, awarding plaintiff Dr. Judith Piesco $1,800,000 in compensatory damages against all defendants, $50,000 in punitive damages against Ortiz, and $50,000 in punitive damages against LaPorte, on her claim under 42 U.S.C. § 1983 (1988) for termination of her employment in retaliation for the exercise of her speech rights under the First Amendment to the Constitution. * * * For the reasons below, we ... vacate the denial of a new trial and remand for consideration of the new-trial motion under the proper legal standard.

[Piesco was hired to develop and administer employment examinations for various City jobs.] By all accounts, Piesco's tenure at DOP began well. For the period September 20, 1982, to June 30, 1983, both [of Piesco's supervisors] Ortiz and LaPorte rated her work "outstanding," concluding that Piesco had "proven to be a valuable asset to this agency." [H]owever, there is substantial dispute as to the quality of her performance thereafter.

In December 1984, DOP administered Examination Number 4061 ("No. 4061"), a test for whose development Piesco's bureau had responsibility, for the position of entry-level police officer. The test was modeled after the previous test for that position, Examination Number 1175 ("No. 1175"), but apparently was simplified by the removal of several complex questions. In February 1985, representatives from DOP and the Police Department met to set the "pass mark" for No. 4061, i.e., the score deemed to be the minimum passing grade. The pass mark for No. 1175 had been 82 (115 correct answers out of 140), but Piesco, arguing that No. 4061 should have a higher pass mark to compensate for its reduced complexity, pressed for a pass mark of 89 (125 correct out of 140). She argued that anything less would pass unqualified candidates. Eventually, the matter was compromised, and the pass mark was set at 85. Piesco testified that she had viewed that mark as inappropriate but had essentially thrown up her hands, stating, "You do what you want to do." In contrast, one participant at the meeting testified that Piesco did not express any disagreement with setting the mark at 85 when that compromise was reached. Ortiz testified that Piesco told him that though a pass mark of 89 was preferable, 85 was acceptable, and "she could live with an 85."

In early 1985, the New York State Senate Committee on Investigation, Taxation, and Government Operations, chaired by Senator Roy M. Goodman, established a committee to review the City's Police Department ("Goodman Committee"). Representatives of the Goodman Committee met with Piesco, Ortiz, and LaPorte at the DOP offices in June 1985. At that meeting, Piesco told them that, in her view, given the pass mark of 85, any moron could pass No. 4061.

Ortiz testified that he was surprised to hear this view because he had met with Piesco at least once every two weeks and she had never complained to him that the pass mark was too low. He also testified that after that initial meeting with the Goodman Committee representatives, Piesco recanted and agreed with him that 85 was an acceptable pass mark. In the wake of that meeting, Laporte suggested to Piesco that she needed to "learn to tell the truth more creatively," in light of the potential for negative publicity from use of terms such as "moron." During the following month, Piesco twice went to meet with representatives of the committee but did not disclose those meetings to Ortiz or Laporte.

On July 11, 1985, Piesco testified at a hearing of the Goodman Committee. At that hearing, Senator Goodman asked Piesco, "Would a functional illiterate pass the entrance examination to the Police Academy?" Piesco answered, "At the pass mark set, I would say that it is possible." There was apparently no attempt during the hearing to define either "functional illiterate" or "possible" with any specificity. At trial, in response to questioning from the court, Piesco clarified that by "functional illiterate" she meant "people who may not be able to appropriately read and write and understand," or "who could read words but could not draw enough inference from what they were reading to apply the concepts, particularly within the context of a given function, such as to be a police officer you have to understand concepts such as illegal search and seizure"; by saying that it was "possible" that such persons could pass if the pass mark were 85, she meant "likely."

Ortiz sent a letter to the Mayor on the day after Piesco's committee testimony, calling that testimony "irresponsible." He testified at trial that his first opportunity to try to discuss in detail with Piesco why she felt the 85 pass mark was unacceptable was a meeting on July 31, 1985. He began by asking her whether she had read the exam, but she stood up and said, "You don't know a f* * ** * * thing about testing. I am fed up with your bull* * ** and ineptitude." When Ortiz asked Piesco to calm down, she responded, "I don't have to do a f* * ** * * thing, why don't you fire me?" Ortiz promptly terminated the meeting and placed a letter of reprimand in Piesco's personnel file.

As indicated above, Piesco's performance for the first nine months of her tenure was rated "outstanding." For the following year, 1983–84, her performance was rated "very good," and in March 1983, July 1983, and May 1984 she received the maximum permissible merit raises in salary. For the year ending June 30, 1985, however, Ortiz and Laporte rated Piesco's performance "marginal." Both testified that the ratings were indicative solely of the continual decline they had observed in Piesco's performance, and that they had scrupulously avoided considering Piesco's remarks to the Goodman Committee because those remarks occurred after June 30, the end of the evaluation period. LaPorte informed Piesco of the 1984–85 evaluations personally on August 13, 1985. * * *

On December 27, 1985, Ortiz terminated Piesco's employment.

In the meantime, on December 19, 1985, Piesco commenced the present action under 42 U.S.C. § 1983, alleging principally that defendants' unfavorable personnel actions had been taken in retaliation for her testimony to the Goodman Committee, in violation of her First Amendment rights. The complaint was amended shortly thereafter to allege that the dismissal of Piesco on December 27 was a further act of retaliation. The amended complaint sought more than $8 million in compensatory and punitive damages.

[After trial,] [t]he jury, with appropriate instructions as to the burdens of proof, was asked to return a special verdict determining, as to liability, (1) whether Piesco's statements before the Goodman Committee were constitutionally protected, (2) whether the fact that she made those statements was a substantial or motivating factor in defendants' decision to terminate her employment, and (3) whether defendants would have dismissed her even if she had not made those statements. As to the first question, the jury was instructed that it must find that Piesco's statements were protected if it found that her testimony before the committee was truthful and responsive to the questions asked.

The jury answered the first two liability questions in the affirmative, finding that Piesco had established by a preponderance of the evidence that her statements to the Goodman Committee were constitutionally protected and that the fact that she made those statements was a substantial or motivating factor in defendants' decision to discharge her. The jury found that defendants had not established by a preponderance that they would have dismissed Piesco regardless of her statements. In response to questions addressed to damages, the jury found that Piesco should receive $1,800,000 as compensatory damages, and that she should receive $50,000 each from Ortiz and Laporte as punitive damages. [The trial court denied defendants' post-trial motions for judgment as a matter of law and for a new trial. After ruling that the trial court properly denied the post-trial motion for a judgment as a matter of law, the court turned its attention to the motion for a new trial.]

Defendants' alternative motion for a new trial was based on their contention that the jury's findings were against the weight of the evidence. In ruling on this motion, the district judge stated that if he had been the factfinder he "clearly would have reached a different result," however, he viewed this Court's then-recent decision in *Dunlap–McCuller v. Riese Organization*, 980 F.2d 153, 158 (2d Cir.1992) ("*Dunlap-McCuller*"), as holding that such a motion could not be granted unless the jury's verdict could be characterized as "egregious," a standard that he felt was not met here:

> If I were the factfinder, I clearly would have reached a different result. The uncontradicted facts on the record indicate that plaintiff was a difficult employee who went out of her way to antagonize those with whom she worked. It is hard to believe that any employee could reasonably expect to remain in her position for any substantial time after telling her immediate supervisor "I am fed up with your bull* * **. . . . I don't have to do a f* * ** * * thing. Why don't you fire me?" * * *
>
> In addition, the evidence that plaintiff met secretly with the staff of the State Senate committee and lied about these meetings when she was subsequently questioned also suggests that she would not have remained in her position long even if her superiors fully respected her right to exercise her First Amendment freedoms. In addition, Judith Levitt testified that she would not have retained plaintiff in her position after Ms. Levitt succeeded Ortiz as personnel director in February 1986.
>
> Yet all of these facts were before the jury which apparently found that, but for her exercise of her First Amendment rights,

plaintiff would have continued in the City's employ until her retirement and would have received regular pay increases during her remaining years as a City employee. Clearly, I believe this conclusion is wrong and appears to ignore the uncontradicted testimony of Judith Levitt that she would have fired Dr. Piesco for reasons unrelated to her State Senate testimony. Thus, I would be prepared to find that the jury's result was seriously erroneous which, according to the Second Circuit's decision in *Smith v. Lightning Bolt Productions*, 861 F.2d 363, 370 (2d Cir.1988), could justify the grant of a new trial. More recently, however, the Second Circuit has cautioned that "the grant of a new trial on weight of the evidence should be reserve[d] for those occasions where the jury's verdict was *egregious*." *Dunlap–McCuller v. The Riese Organization*, [980 F.2d at 158] (emphasis added). Because I do not believe the jury's verdict can be characterized as egregious, the motion for a new trial is denied.

Defendants contend that the court erred in applying an "egregious" standard, rather than the "seriously erroneous" standard, in ruling on their motion. Piesco contends that a district court's denial of a motion for a new trial is not reviewable. Though there is support for the proposition that the denial of a new trial is unreviewable in some circumstances, such a decision is plainly reviewable to the extent that the challenge is that the district court applied the wrong legal standard. We agree with defendants that the court did not apply the proper standard.

In numerous cases prior to *Dunlap-McCuller*, this Court had described the power of the district court to grant a new trial based on the weight of the evidence as one that could properly be exercised only if the court viewed the jury's verdict as "seriously erroneous." This formulation was adopted in *Bevevino v. Saydjari*, 574 F.2d 676, 684 (2d Cir. 1978), to standardize the conceptual framework within which such motions should be decided. In the ensuing years, the "seriously erroneous" formulation was used in at least a dozen cases, including several in the same year in which *Dunlap–McCuller* was decided. In *Dunlap–McCuller*, a majority of the panel stated that "the grant of a new trial on weight of the evidence grounds should be reserved for those occasions where the jury's verdict was egregious." 980 F.2d at 158. For several reasons, we do not view this statement as having changed the legal landscape.

First, the *Dunlap–McCuller* statement was dictum. The panel had ruled that as to the contention that the district court erred in assessing the weight of the evidence, the panel had no authority to review the grant of a new trial. Second, a panel of the Court lacks the authority to overrule the prevailing law of the Circuit. Third, there is no suggestion in either of the *Dunlap–McCuller* opinions that the panel believed a new standard was being established. The concurring opinion, for example, described the majority as "not[ing]" that a new trial should not be granted unless the verdict was egregious, a description that treats the majority as recognizing an existing standard rather than adopting a new standard. Further, the majority opinion itself took explicit pains to follow the procedural law of this Circuit, stating, for example, "we are constrained by prior precedent in this Circuit, and consequently must hold that the district court's grant of a new trial is not reviewable," 980 F.2d at 157, and "[t]his panel is ... not empowered to overturn a longstanding precedent in this Circuit that has recently been reaffirmed by another panel," *id.* at 158. Given these statements, we think it inconceivable that the *Dunlap–McCuller* panel meant, sub silentio, to change the substantive standard that had been reaffirmed in four of our cases just months earlier.

In sum, the *Dunlap–McCuller* majority's obiter use of the word "egregious" was not meant to represent a change in circuit law. We construe its use of that term as an intended equivalent of "seriously erroneous," and we conclude that "seriously erroneous" remains the general standard that the district court should apply in ruling on a motion for a new trial on the ground that the jury's verdict is against the weight of the evidence, bearing in mind, as always, that [w]here the resolution of the issues depended on assessment of the credibility of the witnesses, it is proper for the court to refrain from setting aside the verdict and granting a new trial.

Accordingly, we reverse the order denying a new trial and remand for consideration under the proper standard.

Notes and Questions

1. Most new trial motions seek a retrial on all fact and law issues. However, Rule 59(a) enables a party to obtain a trial on "part" of the issues. If an error at trial requires a new trial on one issue which is separate from other issues in the case, and the error did not affect the determination of other issues, the scope of the new trial may be limited to the single issue. For example, a court can grant a new trial motion for damages only when the liability issues were properly determined. A new trial on damages only is improper, though, if there is a reason to think that an alleged error about damages may also have affected the liability issue. (A court will not grant a partial new trial on an issue that was not litigated at the first trial.)

2. *Erroneous evidentiary rulings.* A common ground for seeking a new trial is that the trial court committed reversible error in its evidentiary rulings. For example, in *Ruvalcaba v. City of Los Angeles*, 64 F.3d 1323 (9th Cir. 1995), a vehicle passenger brought a civil rights claim for excessive force during a traffic stop. After a jury verdict for the city and the officers, plaintiff moved for a new trial on the ground that the court had permitted the defendant officers "to testify about their knowledge of Ruvalcaba's criminal history." Citing the trial court's broad discretion, the Ninth Circuit affirmed the denial of plaintiff's new trial motion.

> The district court permitted the police officers to testify in a limited manner about their prior contacts with Ruvalcaba. This testimony was relevant to establish the facts and circumstances known to the officers

during their confrontation with Ruvalcaba. In addressing an excessive force case under the Fourth Amendment, "the question is whether the officers' actions are 'objectively reasonable' in light of the facts and circumstances confronting them, without regard to their underlying intent or motivation." *Graham v. Connor*, 490 U.S. 386, 397 (1989).

Keeping in mind that this trial involved the officers' alleged use of excessive force during the entire confrontation with Ruvalcaba, we conclude that the district court properly allowed the officers to testify about the facts known to them regarding Enrique Ruvalcaba's criminal past. The district court also properly admonished the jury to consider Ruvalcaba's prior bad conduct only in determining whether the officers' actions were reasonable under the circumstances. There was no abuse of discretion in admitting this evidence.

3. *Remittitur.* When a trial court determines that a jury award is excessive, it may offer the verdict-winner a reduction, known as remittitur, in exchange for the court's denial of a motion for a new trial. The verdict-winner's acceptance of the court's offer is a waiver of the right to appeal and the jury's verdict will be reduced to the maximum amount the jury could have awarded without being excessive. In *Eiland v. Westinghouse Elec. Corp.* 58 F.3d 176 (5th Cir. 1995), the jury responded to plaintiff's product liability claim by awarding $5,000,000.

Of the $5 million in compensatory damages awarded to Eiland, approximately $3.6 is noneconomic loss, including pain and suffering, disfigurement, and impairment not accounted for in lost wages. Westinghouse made a post-trial motion for new trial or for remittitur, which the district court denied.

Mississippi law provides that a court may grant a remittitur if it finds that the damages are excessive "for the reason that the jury or trier of the facts was influenced by bias, prejudice, or passion, or that the damages awarded were contrary to the overwhelming weight of credible evidence. If such ... remittitur be not accepted then the court may direct a new trial on damages only." Miss.Code Ann. § 11–1–55 (1972). Likewise, this circuit's case law provides for remittitur if the award is excessive, and new trial on damages alone if the plaintiff declines the remitted award.

There is a strong presumption in favor of affirming a jury award of damages. The damage award may be overturned only upon a clear showing of excessiveness or upon a showing that the jury was influenced by passion or prejudice. The decision to grant or deny a motion for new trial or remittitur rests in the sound discretion of the trial judge; that exercise of discretion can be set aside only upon a clear showing of abuse. *Id.* However, when this court is left with the perception that the verdict is clearly excessive, deference must be abandoned.

A verdict is excessive if it is "contrary to right reason" or "entirely disproportionate to the injury sustained." *Caldarera v. Eastern Airlines, Inc.*, 705 F.2d 778 (5th Cir.1983). While pain and suffering is not easily susceptible to monetary quantification, and the jury has broad leeway, "the sky is simply not the limit for jury verdicts, even those that have been once reviewed." *Simeon v. T. Smith & Son, Inc.*, 852 F.2d 1421

(5th Cir.1988). Eiland no doubt experienced intense pain during his initial treatment, and was left with a lifetime of disfigurement and some degree of disability. However, he was able to return to work part time within a few months, and full time by the end of two years. After a review of the record, we have concluded that the $5 million verdict was excessive and the district court abused its discretion in denying Westinghouse's motion for remittitur.

Our power to grant a remittitur is the same as the district court's. We determine the size of the remittitur in accordance with this circuit's "maximum recovery rule" by reducing the verdict to the maximum amount the jury could properly have awarded. Of course, our reassessment of damages cannot be supported entirely by rational analysis, but involves an inherently subjective component. *Id.* In our view, $3 million is the maximum the jury could properly have awarded in this case.

4. *Additur.* When a trial court finds that a jury award is inadequate, it cannot offer the verdict-winner an increase in the size of the verdict, known as additur, in exchange for the court's denial of a motion for new trial. The court's only option is to order a new trial. In *Dimick v. Schiedt*, 293 U.S. 474, 55 S.Ct. 296, 79 L.Ed. 603 (1935), Supreme Court held that additur violates the Seventh Amendment right to a jury verdict. It invades the province of the jury by granting an amount in excess of the jury's award. By contrast, remittitur results in an amount that is within the amount that the jury awarded.

5. *Judge's own initiative.* Rule 59(d) permits a court to grant a new trial on its own initiative, without the need for a party to file a motion. The court's *sua sponte* order may be for any of the reasons that a party could request a new trial by motion. See, e.g., *Pryer v. C.O. 3 Slavic*, 251 F.3d 448 (3d Cir. 2001) (new trial granted when the verdict was against the great weight of the evidence). In *Pryer*, the jury awarded nominal damages of $1.00. Because of the additur principle, the trial court lacked the authority to increase the damage amount. Thus, the trial court's only way to express its displeasure with the jury's verdict for the plaintiff was to grant a new trial.

6. *Newly discovered evidence.* Courts have the authority to grant new trial based on newly discovered evidence. However, few new trials are sought on this basis because a party must file a motion for new trial within ten days after the entry of judgment. Because that time frame is usually too short for newly discovered evidence to have been "discovered," newly discovered evidence is relied on as a remedy under Rule 60(b)(2) for vacating the judgment with a longer time to make that motion. See Part E of this Chapter, *infra*.

7. *Altering or amending the judgment.* Rule 59(e) permits a party to file a motion asking the court to alter or amend its judgment, instead of granting a new trial. As with a motion for new trial, the appellate standard of review is abuse of discretion. The common grounds for a motion to alter or amend include an intervening change in the law, newly discovered evidence, correction of a clear error, and prevention of manifest injustice.

8. *The relationship between motions for judgment as a matter of law with motions for new trial.* At the same time a motion for judgment as a

matter of law is filed, Rule 50 offers the option that a Rule 59 motion for new trial can (indeed must) be filed within the same time frame. One rationale for the simultaneous filing is that if an appellate court reverses the grant of a judgment as a matter of law, it also can review the trial court's ruling on the new trial motion.

In *Weisgram v. Marley*, 528 U.S. 440, 120 S.Ct. 1011, 145 L.Ed.2d 958 (2000), a baseboard heater built by defendant caught fire and plaintiff's mother died. Over defendant's objections, plaintiff's experts testified the heater was defective and caused the fire. After the jury returned a verdict for the plaintiff, the defendant argued that without the expert testimony the plaintiff had not proved a defect or causation and moved for judgment as a matter of law under Federal Rule 50, which was denied.

The Eighth Circuit disagreed, struck plaintiff's expert testimony, weighed the evidence, found that the case was "not close," and entered judgment as a matter of law for the defendant. The Supreme Court ruled on whether an appellate court of appeals could enter judgment as a matter of law for defendant, or whether it had to remand the case to the trial court's discretion to choose between final judgment for defendant or a new trial. The Court concluded that the Eighth Circuit did not abuse its discretion under Rule 50. Without the inadmissible expert testimony, plaintiff's evidence was insufficient. The plaintiff had argued that the appellate court unfairly deprived him of arguing for a new trial before the trial judge and that if given a new trial, he would offer admissible evidence. The Court found a plaintiff who fails to offer admissible evidence for elements necessary to sustain a claim does so at its own risk. Should an appellate court have the discretion to review the entire record and make a ruling instead of remanding it to a trial court to rule on a new trial motion?

9. When only a motion for a new trial is filed, an order granting a new trial is generally not immediately appealable because there is no final judgment from which to appeal. That ruling can be appealed, but not until *after* the new trial. An order denying a new trial is appealable immediately, because the trial court already has or soon will enter a judgment on the verdict.

When the verdict-loser files *both* a motion for a judgment as a matter of law and a motion for a new trial, the appealability issue depends on the court's disposition of the motions. Rules 50(c) and (d) govern.

- Trial court grants the JML motion and conditionally rules on the new trial motion. Rule 50(c)(1) permits the immediate appeal of the JML grant, regardless of the ruling on the new trial motion. Why? If the appellate court reverses the grant of the JML motion, it already knows the trial court's attitude toward a new trial and can evaluate that conditional ruling as well.

- Trial court denies the JML motion and grants the new trial motion. That ruling is not immediately appealable because there is no final judgment.

- Trial court denies both the JML motion and the new trial motion. The trial court's ruling is immediately appealable, because the trial court has entered a judgment on the verdict.

Problems

1. Abbott sues Costello. After a bench trial, the judge finds for Abbott and enters judgment for Abbott. Costello believes that the judge improperly excluded important evidence. What post-trial motion should Costello make to the trial court?

2. In Problem #1, if the judge grants the motion, what relief can she provide to Costello?

3. Abbott sues Costello, who moves for a judgment as a matter of law after all the proof is presented but prior to the jury instructions. The court denies Costello's motion, and the jury finds for Abbott. Costello moves for a judgment as a matter of law within three days after the judgment. The judge denies the motion five weeks later. Costello then moves for a new trial, on the ground that the judge improperly excluded important evidence. What should the judge do?

4. Abbott sues Costello, who moves for a judgment as a matter of law after all the proof is presented. The court denies Costello's motion, and the jury finds for Abbott. Costello believes that the judge should have granted the judgment as a matter of law motion. What motion(s) should Costello file?

5. In Problem #4, Abbott is satisfied with the verdict but is also convinced that his case would have been stronger if the judge had not excluded important evidence that he offered at trial. What should Abbott do about his objection to the exclusion of evidence?

6. After a jury verdict for Abbott, Costello moves for a new trial on the ground of improper jury instructions. The judge grants the motion. Can Abbott appeal?

7. Same facts as Problem #6, except that Costello's motion for new trial is denied. Can Costello appeal?

8. Same facts as Problem #6, except that in addition to a new trial motion Costello moves for judgment as a matter of law. The judge grants that motion and conditionally grants the new trial motion as well. Can Abbott appeal?

9. Same facts as Problem #6, except that the judge denies the judgment as a matter of law motion but grants the new trial motion. Can Abbott appeal?

Exercise

For the state where a) you intend to practice after graduation, b) your law school is located, and/or c) your professor assigns, go to that state's annotated statutes and research the procedural rules by which new trial motions are evaluated. Based on your research, print the rule and bring it to class for discussion. In addition, answer the following questions.

1. Is the state rule for new trial motions a "laundry list" of grounds for granting a new trial, or is it similar to the federal rule which simply incorporates case law by reference?

2. Describe whether the state rule establishes standards for the appealability of new trial grants.

3. Does the case law in your state follow *Weisgram*?

G. RELIEF FROM JUDGMENT

A motion for relief from a judgment under Federal Rule 60 requires a court to balance two important considerations: the finality of a judgment versus the justice of the outcome signified by the judgment. Usually, finality prevails, with the rationale being that in order to encourage parties to prepare fully for trial, a judgment-winner ought to rely on a resulting judgment. If a party believes that a trial court made a judicial error, the proper remedy is to file a timely motion for a new trial and/or appeal the judgment.

Given the policy importance of final judgments, Rule 60 relief is seldom granted; however Rule 60 is often used successfully as a device for setting aside default judgments under Rule 55(c).

TATE v. RIVERBOAT SERVICES, INC.

305 F.Supp.2d 916 (N.D. Ind. 2004)

MOODY, District Judge.

[Plaintiffs filed a claim for overtime wages under federal maritime laws. After being served with the complaint, defendant failed to file an answer or respond to the complaint in a timely manner. After the plaintiffs demanded judgment for over $1,000,000 on the clerk of the court, the clerk entered a default and a default judgment was entered for the plaintiffs. Six weeks later, the defendant filed a motion to vacate the entry of default and the default judgment under Rule 60(b).]

III. DEFENDANT'S MOTION TO VACATE

Defendant seeks to set aside the default and judgment entered against it on September 11, 2003, pursuant to Fed.R.Civ.P. 60(b). Relief under F ed.R.Civ.P. 60(b) is an "extraordinary remedy and is granted only in exceptional circumstances." *McCormick v. City of Chicago*, 230 F.3d 319, 327 (7th Cir.2000) (internal quotation marks and citation omitted). However, because "the philosophy of modern federal procedure favors trials on the merits," *A.F. Dormeyer Co. v. M.J. Sales & Distrib. Co.*, 461 F.2d 40, 43 (7th Cir.1972) (internal quotation marks and citation omitted), Rule 60(b) relief is granted more liberally in those cases where the relief is sought to vacate a default judgment, *C.K.S. Engineers, Inc. v. White Mountain Gypsum Co.*, 726 F.2d 1202, 1205 (7th Cir.1984).

It is in the context of a default judgment that defendant seeks relief under Rule 60(b). In particular, defendant seeks relief pursuant to Rule 60(b)(1) which authorizes courts to free a party from the constraints of a final judgment against it for reasons of "mistake, inadvertence, surprise, or excusable neglect." Fed.R.Civ.P. 60(b)(1). To prevail on its Rule 60(b)(1) motion to vacate the default judgment against it, defendant must show: (1) good cause for the default; (2) quick action to correct the default; and, (3) the existence of a meritorious defense to the original action.

A. Good Cause

Federal Rule of Civil Procedure 60(b)(1) provides that good cause can consist of "mistake, inadvertence, surprise, or excusable neglect." It is the latter—"excusable neglect"—which defendant asserts was the cause of its failure to respond to plaintiffs' complaint in a timely manner, and thus, the cause of the default judgment entered against it.

The Supreme Court has adopted a "flexible understanding" of "excusable neglect," *Pioneer Inv. Services Co. v. Brunswick Associates Ltd. P'ship*, 507 U.S. 380 (1993), which "encompass[es] situations in which the failure to comply with a filing deadline is attributable to negligence." *Id.* at 394. Defendant admits that it was negligent in responding to plaintiffs' complaint, and plaintiffs seem to agree that ordinary negligence caused defendant to miss the deadline for filing an answer to their claims for seamen's wages. However, plaintiffs argue that ordinary negligence cannot constitute excusable neglect, and therefore, a showing of such negligence is not enough to warrant relief under Rule 60(b)(1). * * * Yet, as already stated above, with its 1993 decision in *Pioneer*, the Supreme Court made it quite clear that "for purposes of Rule 60(b), 'excusable neglect'" does indeed "encompass situations in which the failure to comply with a filing deadline is attributable to negligence." 507 U.S. at 394. Thus, the fact that defendant's failure to respond to plaintiffs' complaint was caused by ordinary negligence, rather than some extraordinary circumstance over which the defendant did not have control, does not preclude this court from finding that defendant's actions constitute excusable neglect and therefore warrant relief under Rule 60(b)(1).

Ultimately, the important question here is whether or not defendant's "neglect" is "excusable." See *id.* at 395. In determining whether defendant's neglect is excusable, this court must take account of "all relevant circumstances" surrounding defendant's failure to timely respond to plaintiffs' complaint, including: (1) defendant's reason for failing to comply with its filing deadline; (2) the potential impact of defendant's neglect upon judicial proceedings; (3) the danger of prejudice to plaintiffs should defendant's neglect be deemed excusable; and, (4) whether defendant acted in good faith. *Id.* Accordingly, this court shall now review the "relevant circumstances" of this case in order to determine whether defendant's failure to timely respond to plaintiffs' complaint is, in fact, "excusable."

First, defendant argues that the delay in responding to plaintiffs' complaint was the result of confusion over several lawsuits pending, or recently dismissed against defendant, all involving the same overtime wage claims presented by the same groups of plaintiffs who are, (or were), all represented by the same attorney. In particular, defendant points to confusion caused by the nearly identical-styled captions of the instant action and the Illinois Tate case, and the nearly identical list of plaintiffs involved in both lawsuits. Accordingly, defendant argues that confusion over "which claims were proceeding, which claims were resolved and whether there were, in fact, new lawsuits being filed" against defendant, caused defendant's attorney to neglect her obligation to respond to plaintiff's complaint, and this negligence resulted in the default judgment against defendant.

Plaintiffs admit that there were, and are a number of cases pending against defendant involving the same issues, the same or similar plaintiffs, and the same plaintiffs' attorney. Nevertheless, plaintiffs argue that these other cases are "of no moment," as any confusion caused by them cannot excuse defendant's default. (" 'Confusion' has never been a reason under Rule 60(b)(1) FRCP for relief from a judgment or default order."). However, plaintiffs do not cite to any law to support this argument, nor can this court find any cases stating that confusion over multiple cases involving the same plaintiffs and claims is not a factor that courts may consider when determining whether a party's neglect in complying with filing deadlines is excusable. Perhaps confusion alone cannot excuse a party's default, but the court must review "all [the] relevant circumstances" surrounding a default. See *Pioneer*, 507 U.S. at 395. Therefore, this court fails to see why a genuine confusion over multiple similar cases involving the same plaintiffs and defendant may not, in combination with all of the other relevant circumstances this court must look at, aid in excusing a defaulting party's neglect of deadlines. And, it seems to this court, that defendant's confusion was in fact genuine as, after all, even this court was, at first, a bit confused over "which claims were proceeding [and] which claims were resolved" against defendant. Moreover, this court's general experience confirms that multiple lawsuits in multiple venues involving the same claims by the same parties can cause a certain amount of confusion which sometimes (unfortunately) results in missed filing deadlines.

Second, defendant argues that because it acted promptly in seeking to vacate the default judgment against it, neither plaintiffs nor any proceedings have been prejudiced by defendant's neglect, and neither plaintiffs nor any proceeding would be prejudiced should this court vacate the default judgment in this case. The court agrees. First, as this matter did not progress past the complaint, vacating the judgment in this case would not prejudice any judicial proceedings. Second, as this case is relatively young, (it was instituted in this court less than a year ago), it is improbable that any necessary and/or important information concerning this case would have been lost or would be prejudicially difficult to retrieve. In addition, plaintiffs' attorney is engaged in at least two other currently-active cases in the Northern District of Indiana involving the same overtime wage claims thus making it likely that little additional work would be needed to pursue this lawsuit should the default judgment be vacated.

Ultimately, should this court vacate the default and judgment against defendant, plaintiffs would merely be required to pursue their case on the merits of their claims, or rather, do what they were (presumably) prepared and capable of doing before default judgment was entered. Certainly, assuming plaintiffs are indeed entitled to overtime wages from defendant, vacating the default judgment against defendant may delay the receipt of those wages from sometime in the near-future to sometime in the less-near-future, but such a delay seems relatively minor in comparison to the cost suffered by defendant—a judgment against it of over one million dollars—should the default judgment be allowed to stand. Moreover, any prejudice suffered by a minor delay in receiving their overtime wages—should plaintiffs even be entitled to those wages—waxes thin against the Seventh Circuit's "well-established policy favoring a trial on the merits over a default judgment," *C.K.S. Engineers*, 726 F.2d at 1205; a policy which helps to promote a fair system of justice by ensuring that decisions made by the administrators of that system are generally based upon a full presentation of the evidence. Therefore, were this court to vacate the default judgment against defendant, it would be very unlikely that plaintiffs or any proceedings would suffer prejudice.

Finally, there is not any evidence to suggest that defendant acted in any other manner than in good faith while dealing with (or neglecting to deal with) this lawsuit; even plaintiffs do not argue that defendant acted in bad faith. Ultimately, since 1999, defendant's attorney, Ms. Mannix, has been actively involved in defending RSI in other related actions. Indeed, the day after plaintiffs' attorney moved for entry of default in this case, Ms. Mannix was engaged in defending RSI in the Harkins matter. The fact that defendant and Ms. Mannix have been actively involved in litigating other similar suits involving different combinations of the same plaintiffs and the same overtime wage claims strongly suggests, at least to this court, that neither defendant nor its attorney have acted willfully in neglecting to timely respond to plaintiffs' complaint in this case.

Therefore, as neither the plaintiffs nor any judicial proceeding would be appreciably prejudiced by this court's decision to vacate the default judgment against defendant, and as the default judgment rendered against defendant is attributable to a genuine confusion and was not caused willfully, this court believes the circumstances of this case excuse defendant's negligence in failing to respond to plaintiffs' complaint in a timely manner. Accordingly, this court finds that the circumstances of this case constitute "excusable neglect" within the meaning of Rule 60(b)(1). Defendant has therefore demonstrated "good cause" for its default.

B. *Quick Action to Correct the Default*

Rule 60(b) provides that a motion for relief from a judgment by reason of mistake, inadvertence, excusable neglect, etc., "shall be made within a reasonable time," but "not more than one year after the judgment, order, or proceeding was entered or taken." The defendant filed its motion for relief under Rule 60(b)(1) on October 29, 2003, approximately one-and-a-half months after learning of the entry of a default judgment against it. Thus, defendant was well within the one-year period prescribed by Fed.R.Civ.P. 60(b). However, in some cases, even a Rule 60(b)(1) motion filed within one year may be rejected as untimely if not made within a reasonable time. "What constitutes a 'reasonable time' ultimately depends on the facts of each case including the reason for delay, the practical ability of the litigant to have learned about the grounds of the judgment earlier, and the degree of prejudice to the other parties." *Kagan v. Caterpillar Tractor Co.*, 795 F.2d 601, 610 (7th Cir.1986).

The delay between the filing of defendant's motion and the entry of default judgment was approximately fifty (50) days. Defendant claims that this delay was ultimately due to "scheduling difficulties." Generally, "scheduling difficulties" alone, (without further explanation), would not be enough to convince this court to excuse such a delay. However, considering such scheduling difficulties in combination with the Seventh Circuit's preference for litigating claims on the merits rather than letting harsh sanctions, like a default judgment, stand, see *C.K.S. Engineers*, 726 F.2d at 1205, and considering the other relevant circumstance of this case, such as the fact that the delay is unlikely to prejudice plaintiffs' position or claims, it seems that fifty days is not so tardy as to compel denial of defendant's motion. More importantly, neither defendant nor its attorney have shown any disrespect for, or have a history of demonstrating disrespect for the court or its processes, and, where such is the case, "courts have been inclined towards leniency," *Palmer v. City of Decatur*, 814 F.2d 426, 430 n. 6 (7th Cir.1987); this is especially true in the context of vacating a default judgment, see *C.K.S. Engineers*, 726 F.2d at 1205. Accordingly, this court finds that defendant has filed its Rule 60(b)(1) motion within a reasonable time after default judgment was entered against it.

C. *Meritorious Defenses*

Not only must defendant show that it had good cause for the default and that it acted quickly in attempt to cure the default in order to prevail on its Rule 60(b)(1) motion, but, defendant must also demonstrate that it has a "meritorious defense" to plaintiffs' claims. This does not mean that defendant needs to prove that its defense would, beyond a doubt, succeed in defeating the default judgment against it. Rather, defendant need only present a defense "which at least raises a serious question regarding the propriety of [the] default judgment and which is supported by a developed legal and factual basis."

In its motion to vacate the default judgment against it, defendant asserts that the claims of several of the plaintiffs in this action are barred by res judicata. Defendant argues that several of the plaintiffs involved in this action have sued defendant at least twice before, each time voluntarily dismissing their claims pursuant to Fed.R.Civ.P.

41(a)(1), which "only allows the plaintiff [sic] the right to dismiss their claims, without prejudice, once in order to refile." ("Unless otherwise stated in the notice of dismissal or stipulation, the dismissal is without prejudice, except that a notice of dismissal operates as an adjudication upon the merits when filed by a plaintiff who has once dismissed in any court of the United States. . . ."). Therefore, defendant asserts that the claims of these plaintiffs have already been adjudicated on the merits, and such plaintiffs are thus barred from litigating this suit against defendant. Plaintiffs readily admit that at least one of them—plaintiff Ringbauer—has filed more than one suit against defendant in which he voluntarily dismissed his claims pursuant to Fed.R.Civ.P. 41(a)(1); and, therefore, plaintiffs allow that Ringbauer may be dismissed, if need be, from the instant action. This admission alone certainly "raises a serious question regarding the propriety of [the] default judgment" against defendant. See *Phipps*, 39 F.3d at 165. Indeed, if Ringbauer is barred from bringing his claim against defendant, then the default judgment against defendant is wholly inappropriate as it includes plaintiff Ringbauer's claim.

Even without plaintiffs' admission however, defendant nevertheless still has a meritorious defense based upon res judicata. The docket reports for both the Ringbauer and Harkins cases, (provided to this court by defendant), and plaintiffs' Notice of Dismissal in the Illinois Tate case, (of which this court has taken judicial notice), demonstrate that many of the plaintiffs involved in this case have indeed dismissed their claims twice (and even three times in some instances) against defendant pursuant to Fed.R.Civ.P. 41(a)(1). Plaintiffs, nevertheless, are adamant that this court ought not to consider the voluntary dismissal of plaintiffs' claims in the Illinois Tate case as counting toward the number of Rule 41(a)(1) dismissals they have filed against defendant. According to plaintiffs, defendant "consented" to its dismissal in the Illinois Tate case, and the "two dismissal rule" does not apply to dismissals by "consent." Yet, nowhere in any case discussing the "two dismissal rule" can this court find anything about "consent." It is true that the "two dismissal rule" does not apply to cases where dismissal is by "stipulation," see *Sutton Place*, 826 F.2d at 640, but plaintiffs' voluntary dismissal of defendant in the Illinois Tate case was not by stipulation; the Notice of Dismissal in that case is signed by plaintiffs only, and a stipulation to dismissal would have required the signatures of all parties appearing in the action.

In any event, even if "consent" were important to the "two dismissal rule," there is not any evidence that defendant "consented" to its dismissal in the Illinois Tate case. Ultimately, plaintiffs' Notice of Dismissal indicates that they dismissed their claims against defendant pursuant to Rule 41(a)(1)(i), and, indeed, dismissal under Rule 41(a)(1)(i) seems to have been the most appropriate form of dismissal as defendant had not yet filed an answer or a motion for summary judgment so as to require a court order dismissing defendant from the action. Thus, defendant's argument that the claims of many of the plaintiffs in this action are barred by res judicata is sufficiently supported by a developed legal and factual basis, and therefore, the court finds this defense meritorious.

* * *

Accordingly, as defendant has demonstrated good cause for the default, has shown quick action, (given the circumstances of this case), to correct the default, and has clearly presented a meritorious defense to this action, this court hereby grants defendant's Motion to Vacate Entry of Default and Entry of Default Judgment.

JONES v. LINCOLN ELEC. CO.

188 F.3d 709 (7th Cir. 1999)

KANNE, Circuit Judge.

[Plaintiff-welder sued manufacturers and distributors of welding rods for neurological injuries sustained from exposure to manganese present in fumes emitted from welding rods. His claims were for negligence and strict liability. After entering jury verdict for defendants, the trial court denied plaintiff's motions for new trial and for relief from final judgment.]

We ... turn to address Jones's challenge that the district court erred in denying his Rule 60(b)(2) motion in which he claimed that "newly discovered" evidence showed that Dr. Eager testified falsely at trial and that evidence of this false testimony was sufficient to warrant granting him a new trial. Pursuant to Federal Rule of Civil Procedure 60(b)(2), a party may be entitled to relief from the entry of final judgment if that party presents "newly discovered evidence which by due diligence could not have been discovered in time to move for a new trial under Rule 59(b)." Relief under Rule 60(b)(2) "is an extraordinary remedy that is to be granted only in exceptional circumstances." *Provident Sav. Bank v. Popovich*, 71 F.3d 696, 698 (7th Cir.1995). We have held that the grant of a new trial on the ground of newly discovered evidence requires proof of the following five prerequisites:

1. The evidence was discovered following trial;

2. Due diligence on the part of the movant to discover the new evidence is shown or may be inferred;

3. The evidence is not merely cumulative or impeaching;

4. The evidence is material; and

5. The evidence is such that a new trial would probably produce a new result.

If any one of these prerequisites is not satisfied, the movant's Rule 60(b)(2) motion for a new trial must fail.

Jones's "newly discovered" evidence consisted of allegations that Dr. Eager's trial testimony concerning the Joint Research and the Caterpillar Study were false. Specifically, Jones pointed to three areas in which he submitted that Dr. Eager gave false testimony. First, Jones alleged that Dr. Eager falsely testified to the "facts" that formed the basis for the district court's ruling that he had the necessary qualifications to offer an opinion regarding the ability of the body to absorb manganese contained in welding fumes and the toxicity of manganese in mild steel welding fumes. Jones argued that in order to qualify himself to offer an opinion as to these matters, Dr. Eager testified that he had conducted "joint research" with Professors Brain and Ulrich on the effects of welding fumes on animal lungs (the Joint Research) and that he and Professor Brain "had published papers together." Jones submits that the district court relied on that testimony as the basis for its ruling that Dr. Eager was qualified to testify as to the conclusions reached by the Joint Research regarding absorption and toxicity.

In his Rule 60(b) motion, Jones contended this testimony was false because Dr. Brain testified in a subsequent unrelated case that he had never conducted any "joint research" with Dr. Eager, nor had he published any papers with him. Moreover, Jones relied on Dr. Eager's deposition testimony from that same litigation in which Dr. Eager testified that he was not an author of the article that eventually published the results of the Joint Research ("Welding Article"), that he specifically requested to have his name removed from an earlier draft of that article because he felt that he had not made a significant contribution to the underlying research, and that his role in the Joint Research had been limited to attending researcher's meetings and providing advice on welding.

Second, having hoodwinked the court into allowing him to testify, Jones contends that Dr. Eager materially mischaracterized the conclusions reached by the Joint Research. Jones submits that Dr. Eager falsely testified that their "joint research" reached conclusions regarding the ability of the body to absorb manganese contained in welding rod fumes and toxicity of the manganese in that form. * * *

Jones argued that his "newly discovered" evidence showed that the Joint Research, or more specifically, Dr. Brain, never studied or reached any conclusions with respect to these two issues. In support of his argument, Jones once again relied on Dr. Brain's deposition testimony in the subsequent unrelated case. * * *

Jones contended that this testimony was also false because the Caterpillar Study did not address the potential neurological effects of manganese in welding fumes. Instead, the Study compared causes of death among Caterpillar workers focusing primarily on lung cancer death rates. It did not, Jones submitted, address any non-fatal health effects from welding. Moreover, Jones alleged that Dr. Eager testified in subsequent unrelated proceedings that the Caterpillar Study did not examine the effects of manganese in mild steel welding fumes on welders.

After conducting two hearings and reviewing the substantial amount of evidence submitted by both parties on the veracity of Dr. Eager's trial testimony, the district court issued an order denying Jones's Rule

60(b)(2) motion. The court cited four grounds in support of its ruling. First, the district court concluded that Eager did not materially mischaracterize his participation in the Joint Research. The court found that Jones read too much into Dr. Brain's deposition testimony that he never conducted "joint research" with Dr. Eager. Placing Dr. Brain's testimony into context revealed that he has an extremely narrow personal view of what it means to conduct "joint research" with another person. * * * Dr. Brain did acknowledge that he had a working research relationship with Dr. Eager, that he consulted with Dr. Eager as a welding expert in connection with the Joint Research, and that Dr. Eager participated in meetings and provided advice on welding in connection with that research. * * * Based on this evidence, the district court found that Dr. Eager's trial testimony was not materially false.

Second, the court determined that Dr. Eager did not testify falsely regarding the results of research underlying the Joint Research. The district court concluded that Jones, at best, showed that Dr. Eager and Dr. Brain had a difference of opinion as to the results generated by the research on exposing animal lungs to welding fumes and that such a scholarly and subjective disagreement was not a sound basis for finding that Dr. Eager lied on the witness stand. In essence, the district court found that the evidence adduced in the Rule 60(b)(2) proceedings could colorably be construed to support the conclusions Dr. Eager ascribed to the Joint Research, and, therefore, Dr. Eager's testimony could not be said to be materially false.

Third, the court concluded that any Rule 60(b)(2) challenge concerning Dr. Eager's testimony with regard to the Caterpillar Study failed because Jones did not exercise due diligence in discovering the alleged falsity of Dr. Eager's trial testimony. The court found that the "new" evidence raised by Jones in his Rule 60(b)(2) motion purporting to show that Dr. Eager testified falsely was the Caterpillar article summarizing the Caterpillar Study's conclusions. However, the district court concluded that statements made by Jones during closing argument indicated that he was aware of the article and the conclusions reported therein. Specifically, during his closing, counsel stated that the Caterpillar Study was a cancer study involving welders and that it did not, as Dr. Eager testified, evaluate the effects of welding fumes on welders. * * * Accordingly, the court concluded that the Caterpillar article was either known to Jones and his counsel at trial or could have been obtained, in the exercise of due diligence, in time to file a Rule 59 motion.

Finally, and most importantly, the district court concluded that a new trial without Dr. Eager's allegedly "false testimony" testimony would probably not produce a new result. The court first noted that Jones took much of the force away from Dr. Eager's testimony when he pointed out to the jury that Dr. Eager was neither a toxicologist nor an expert on matters of physiology. The court also found that Jones undermined Dr. Eager's testimony by reminding the jury that whatever findings Dr. Eager testified to regarding the toxic effect of welding fumes on lungs, it bore little relevance to Jones's claim of brain damage.

Moreover, Jones's medical expert, Dr. Klawans, undercut the weight of Dr. Eager's testimony by testifying that medical research showed that manganese in welding fumes could lead to the onset of manganism by entering a welder's respiratory tract, being absorbed into the bloodstream, and traveling to the brain where it causes neurological damage. But most fundamentally, the district court found that the weakness in Jones's medical causation evidence was absolutely fatal to his claim against Defendants. The court noted that at least four physicians diagnosed Jones with idiopathic Parkinson's disease; whereas only Jones's expert determined that Jones suffered from manganism, and the court found that his testimony was "significantly undermined on cross-examination." Accordingly, the court concluded that Jones failed to prove that subtracting Dr. Eager's challenged testimony would probably change the outcome of the trial in light of what the physicians said at trial concerning the cause of Jones's condition.

On appeal, Jones contends that the district court abused its discretion in reaching each of these conclusions and, as a result, abused its discretion in denying his motion for a new trial. We review a district court's denial of a Rule 60(b)(2) motion for abuse of discretion. In the context of a motion for a new trial, we employ a highly deferential abuse of discretion standard under which we affirm the decision of the district court unless the movant can show that no reasonable person could agree with the court. "We especially are disinclined to substitute our judgment for that of the district court when the record affirmatively manifests that the matter received careful, thorough consideration by the district judge." *Gomez v. Chody*, 867 F.2d 395, 405 (7th Cir.1989). After reviewing the district court's denial of Jones's Rule 60(b)(2) motion, we find no indication that the district court abused its discretion in denying Jones a new trial.

* * * [W]e ultimately agree with the final and dispositive ground the court articulated as a basis for denying relief—the newly discovered evidence was not significantly material to the ultimate outcome of this case and Jones failed to show that subtracting this testimony from the trial would have probably resulted in a verdict in his favor. As we set forth above, in order to have a successful Rule 60(b)(2) motion, Jones had to prove that the newly discovered evidence "is such that a new trial would probably produce a new result." *In re Chicago, Milwaukee, St. Paul & Pacific R.R. Co.*, 78 F.3d 285, 294 (7th Cir. 1996). The district court concluded that Jones failed to satisfy this requirement, and Jones offers no convincing argument on appeal that the district court abused its discretion in reaching this conclusion.

* * * Simply put, the outcome of this case turned on the issue of whether Jones suffered from idiopathic Parkinson's disease or manganism. The medical evidence introduced at trial showed that he suffered from idiopathic Parkinson's disease, and, therefore, evidence suggesting that welding fumes either could or could not lead to the onset of manganism was not terribly material nor relevant to the ultimate determination of Defendants' liability for Jones's neurological disorder.

And since we have already concluded that the admission into evidence of the testimony that Jones now challenges as being false was harmless error, it would make little sense for us now to conclude that subtracting this testimony from trial would probably result in a verdict in Jones's favor in the context of Jones's Rule 60(b)(2) motion for a new trial.

Thus, given the weakness of Jones's case, we cannot say that the outcome of a retrial without Dr. Eager's testimony would probably produce a different result. Therefore, Jones's "newly discovered" evidence fails to satisfy all the necessary requirements under Rule 60(b)(2) to warrant the grant of a new trial. Accordingly, we conclude that the district court did not abuse its discretion in denying Jones's Rule 60(b) motion.

Notes and Questions

1.   Was *Tate*'s analysis consistent with *Pioneer*? Is the *Tate* court too flexible in its interpretation of what constitutes "excusable neglect"? How is the presence of prejudice, quick action, or a meritorious defense relevant to the justification for the neglect? Should any of those elements discussed in *Tate* be limited to Rule 55(c) motions to set aside default judgments using Rule 60(b) grounds, or are they applicable to all Rule 60 motions?

Why are courts so reluctant to grant relief for newly discovered evidence, as in *Jones*? Are courts attempting to encourage more complete trial preparation?

2.   *Clerical errors.* Rule 60(a) allows a trial court, on its own or by motion, to correct clerical errors in judgments, orders or other parts of the record. What is meant by a "clerical mistake"? The classic example is the "slip of the pen," where a judge erroneously added three zeros to a $1,000 judgment, converting it to a $1,000,000. That clerical error can be corrected at any time.

3.   *Fraud, misrepresentation, and other misconduct of an adversary.* Through the case law, a distinction has developed between Rule 60(b)(3) fraud and fraud on the court, which is said to be governed by Rule 60(b)(6). Not every fraud connected with presentation of a case is regarded as a fraud on the court. An example of fraud involves a nondisclosure by a party or attorney. Any wrong was between the parties only, rather than a fraud on the court, which involve a direct assault on the integrity of the judicial process, i.e., far more than an injury to a single litigant. *Hazel–Atlas Glass Co. v. Hartford–Empire Co.*, 322 U.S. 238, 64 S.Ct. 997, 88 L.Ed. 1250 (1944). Examples of fraud on the court include misrepresentations, bribery of a judge, perjury where the attorney is involved, or employment of a particular lawyer in order to improperly influence the court. If these examples appear to draw blurred lines, you are not alone, as some courts also experience difficulty making the distinction. However, the distinction may be important given the absence of a time limit for Rule 60(b)(6) fraud on the court. If you are in doubt about which provision is applicable, argue that both parts of the rule apply and let the court pick the applicable provision.

4. *Void judgment.* Rule 60(b)(4) simply states that relief from a judgment is available because the judgment is void. A judgment is void if the court lacked jurisdiction 1) over the subject matter; or 2) over the parties, when the motion is made to vacate a default judgment. Unlike most decisions under Rule 60(b), the issue of void judgments is a matter of law, rather than being discretionary with the court.

5. *Change of circumstances.* Rule 60(b)(5) provides relief from a judgment when the judgment is satisfied, released or discharged, when a prior judgment on which the current judgment is based has been reversed or vacated, or any other time when continued enforcement of the judgment would be unfair. Rule 60(b)(5) is available when Rule 59(e)'s ten-day limit for modifying or amending a judgment has lapsed.

The first reason is used rarely. The second basis is limited to cases where the current judgment is based on a prior judgment, e.g., a judgment in a suit to enforce a prior judgment which has been reversed. This basis is inapplicable merely because a case relied on as precedent by a court in rendering the current judgment has been reversed, because otherwise so-called final judgments would lose much of their "finality."

The third application of Rule 60(b)(5) occurs when it is no longer equitable that the current judgment should have prospective application, i.e., the trial court can modify a decree with prospective effects in light of changed circumstances. The "prospective effect" aspect limits Rule 60(b)(5) to judgments providing injunctive relief, rather than to judgments for damages. The operative rationale is that it is no longer fair to enforce a judgment as a result of legislation or a change in the operative facts. In *Frew v. Hawkins*, 540 U.S. 431, 124 S.Ct. 899, 157 L.Ed.2d 855 (2004) noted this purpose of Rule 60(b)(5) as applied to consent decrees.

> The Rule encompasses the traditional power of a court of equity to modify its decree in light of changed circumstances. In *Rufo v. Inmates of Suffolk County Jail*, 502 U.S. 367, 112 S.Ct. 748, 116 L.Ed.2d 867 (1992), the Court explored the application of the Rule to consent decrees involving institutional reform. The Court noted that district courts should apply a "flexible standard" to the modification of consent decrees when a significant change in facts or law warrants their amendment.

> *Rufo* rejected the idea that the institutional concerns of government officials were "only marginally relevant" when officials moved to amend a consent decree, and noted that "principles of federalism and simple common sense require the [district] court to give significant weight" to the views of government officials.

> The federal court must exercise its equitable powers to ensure that when the objects of the decree have been attained, responsibility for discharging the State's obligations is returned promptly to the State and its officials.

6. *"Any other reason."* The catchall provision is Rule 60(b)(6), which permits motion to be filed relieving a judgment-loser from the judgment for "any other reason justifying relief." *Pioneer Inv. Services Co. v. Brunswick Associates Ltd. P'ship*, 507 U.S. 380, 394–95, 113 S.Ct. 1489, 123 L.Ed.2d 74

(1993), relied on by *Tate*, also discussed the scope of Rule 60(b)(6) relative to Rule 60(b)(1).

> Rule 60(b)(6) ... empowers the court to reopen a judgment even after one year has passed for "any other reason justifying relief from the operation of the judgment." These provisions [Rule 60(b)(1) and 60(b)(6)] are mutually exclusive, and thus a party who failed to take timely action due to "excusable neglect" may not seek relief more than a year after the judgment by resorting to subsection (6). To justify relief under subsection (6), a party must show "extraordinary circumstances" suggesting that the party is faultless in the delay. If a party is partly to blame for the delay, relief must be sought within one year under subsection (1) and the party's neglect must be excusable.

On a broader scale, the policy of Rule 60(b)(6) was stated in *Liljeberg v. Health Services Acquisition Corp.*, 486 U.S. 847, 108 S.Ct. 2194, 100 L.Ed.2d 855 (1988). The rule gives federal courts broad authority to grant relief from a final judgment "upon such terms as are just," provided that the motion is made within a reasonable time. It is appropriate to consider the risk of injustice to the particular parties, the risk that the denial of relief will produce injustice in other cases, and the risk of undermining the public's confidence in the judicial process.

7. *Meritorious defenses.* As *Tate* indicates, generally a federal court will grant a motion to set aside a default judgment under Rule 55(c) only after the party in default demonstrates a meritorious defense to the action. On the other hand, when the judgment is void, no other defense is necessary. In *Peralta v. Heights Medical Center, Inc.*, 485 U.S. 80, 108 S.Ct. 896, 99 L.Ed.2d 75 (1988), the Court held that "under our cases, a judgment entered without notice or service is constitutionally infirm." The defendant was entitled to set aside a default judgment, although he did not have a meritorious defense. Why? He had not been properly served with process which could have provided him notice about the case so that he could have avoided the adverse consequences of a judicial sale.

8. *Independent actions to seek relief from judgments.* Rule 60(b) also permits litigants to file an "independent action" to prevent miscarriages of justice. The time limits of Rule 60(b) are inapplicable to these separate lawsuits. An example of an appropriate independent action occurs when the judgment was obtained through a fraud on the court, which provides a court with the inherent authority to set aside a judgment. See note 2.

Exercise

For the state where a) you intend to practice after graduation, b) your law school is located, and/or c) your professor assigns, go to that state's annotated statutes and research the procedural rules by which motions for relief from a judgment are evaluated. Based on your research, print the rule and bring it to class for discussion. Is the state rule for granting relief from judgments a "laundry list" of grounds for granting relief? Are the grounds narrower or broader than the Federal Rule 60?

Chapter 11

THE EFFECT OF A JUDGMENT

A. ENFORCING A JUDGMENT

In your very first case after being sworn in as an attorney, you represent a party who writes custom computer software for business clients. Your client claims that it wrote a special program for D, designed to meet D's specific needs. D, however, has refused to pay for the software, prompting your suit. After a hard-fought trial, you are delighted when the court enters judgment in your favor.

So what happens next? The answer turns in part on the nature of the judgment. If the court entered an order of specific performance, or any other form of equitable remedy, there is little you need to do. An equitable order is a direct command to the defendant to do or refrain from doing something. If the defendant fails to comply, you can ask the court to hold the defendant in contempt for failing to abide by the court order.

But what if the judgment is for money damages? Unlike an equitable order, an adjudication of damages is not an order to the defendant to pay. Instead, it simply represents a finding by the court that, in our example, D owes your client $100,000. But you already *knew* that when you brought the case. What good does it do you to have the judge agree with your assessment?

The value of a money judgment lies in the fact that it enables you to enlist the power of government to help you collect the debt. Most states provide a number of ways in which a judgment victor can enlist the help of the state to collect what he or she is owed. The three most important methods of collection are execution, garnishment, and the judgment lien.

Execution involves a state official—typically the sheriff—seizing certain property of the defendant and selling it at a judicial sale. The proceeds of that sale are then paid first to creditors with mortgages, security interests, or other priority claims on the property, and then to the judgment victor in satisfaction of the judgment. The excess, if any, is returned to the judgment loser. Note, however, that not all of the defendant's property is subject to execution. State law provides for certain *exemptions*. For example, in most states the debtor is entitled to keep a certain amount of personal clothing, and may be entitled to keep all or part of the value of her car and principal residence.

Garnishment is in some ways analogous to execution. The main difference is that the property being seized is not tangible, but is a debt owed to the defendant. A judgment victor can use garnishment to obtain the defendant's wages, as well as bank and other accounts. The victor effects the garnishment by serving it on the person who owes the debt, after which the person served is obligated to pay the debt to the victor rather than the judgment loser. As with execution, however, there are limits on what the judgment victor can obtain. Federal law, for example, places strict limits on how much of the defendant's wages may be garnished.

In most states, entry of a judgment creates a *judgment lien* on all real property located in the county where the rendering court sits. The judgment lien is not a collection device in and of itself, but works in conjunction with the process of execution. This lien gives the judgment victor an interest analogous to a mortgage in that property. Therefore, if the defendant tries to convey or mortgage that real property to someone else, the judgment victor can demand that his claim be satisfied. Similarly, if the judgment victor later executes on that real property, the victor is entitled to have his claim satisfied from the proceeds of the sale prior to the claims of any creditors who acquired an interest in the property after the judgment lien was created. However, mortgagees and other secured creditors who recorded their interests prior to the judgment generally get paid before the judgment victor.

Note that Federal Rule 62(a) generally requires a judgment victor to wait ten days until she attempts to enforce her judgment. This delay gives the losing party a chance to move for a new trial or judgment as a matter of law (recall that the Rules give the losing party only ten days to make these motions) or to appeal. Rule 62(a) applies not only to execution and garnishment, but also to attempts to enforce equitable orders such as specific performance.

What happens if the judgment victor wants to use a judgment to execute on or garnish property located in a different state? That situation presents additional complications, and is discussed in part F of this chapter.

B. PRECLUSIVE EFFECT OF A JUDGMENT: AN OVERVIEW

A judgment resolves a given dispute. However, that same judgment may also affect how *other* legal disputes are resolved. After all, judges do not like to "reinvent the wheel." If a question decided in one case is presented again in a later case, the court hearing the second case will naturally give some deference to the earlier decision. There are two compelling reasons for this deference. The first is *efficiency*. Resolving a dispute is expensive and time-consuming. To the extent that a court can avoid some of this cost by relying on the results in an earlier case, it helps reduce the cost of maintaining a court system.

The second concern is *consistency*. If two judges are both called upon to decide the same question in two separate cases, there is a real chance that they might decide the question differently. Such inconsistency not only diminishes people's perceptions of the legal system, but also can leave parties not knowing how they should act in the future.

The desire for efficiency and consistency has spawned a number of separate, but ultimately related, doctrines, pursuant to which the results in one case may affect the outcome of later litigation. The first, *stare decisis*, is a doctrine with which you should already be quite familiar. *Stare decisis* applies to questions of law. Once a legal question has been decided in one case, later courts faced with that same legal question will consider the earlier ruling in their own determination. The strength of a case as precedent depends on several factors, including its age and whether it was issued by the same court system.

The remainder of this chapter does not deal with *stare decisis*. Instead, it deals with several other doctrines under which a judgment can have an effect on later litigation. The main focus will be the doctrines of *claim preclusion* and *issue preclusion*. You briefly encountered claim preclusion, the focus of Section C, in the *Huffey v. Lea* case in Chapter 2. Under that doctrine, a party may be barred from presenting claims or defenses that were, or should have been, litigated by that party in an earlier case. Section D deals with the related doctrine of *issue preclusion*, which prevents the relitigation not of entire claims, but instead of particular issues that were actually decided by the court in the prior case. Sections E and F deal with other issues affecting both claim and issue preclusion, namely, which parties are bound by preclusion, and how claim and issue preclusion apply when the first and second courts are located in different states. Finally, Section G explores two other doctrines—law of the case and judicial estoppel—that are of the same basic *genre* as claim and issue preclusion, but have their own unique considerations.

Although you may see some basic similarities between *stare decisis* and claim and issue preclusion, it is important to realize that there are fundamental differences. First, *stare decisis* applies to all prior cases, even if the litigants are completely different. In the doctrines discussed in this chapter, by contrast, the parties in the first and second cases will either be the same or closely related. Second, *stare decisis* applies to questions of law. Claim and issue preclusion, by contrast, do not apply to pure questions of law, but instead to the application of law to fact. To illustrate, imagine a case in which plaintiff, a trespasser, sues defendant for injuries that plaintiff sustained when he ran into defendant's electric fence. The court will use *stare decisis* to determine the purely legal questions of whether a landowner owes a trespasser a duty, and if so what the standard of care is. However, if there is another case in which a court found that that same landowner was negligent for maintaining that same electric fence, it may apply the doctrine of issue preclusion to preclude the landowner from arguing that he was not negligent.

The third difference between *stare decisis* and claim and issue preclusion is the *degree* to which the first judgment binds the second court. In *stare decisis*, the court may refuse to follow any decision except that of a higher court. A court is especially likely to ignore precedent rendered by courts in other states. Under claim and issue preclusion, by contrast, the prior decision is binding on the second court. If preclusion applies, the second court must prevent relitigation of the claim or issue even if the court disagrees with the result or the analysis in the earlier case. Moreover, claim and issue preclusion apply even if the first decision is rendered by a trial court—and, generally speaking, even if that court is situated in another state.

One *caveat* before embarking on our tour of preclusion: the terminology in this area can be quite confusing. Many cases (including some of those in this chapter) use the older terms *res judicata* to refer to claim preclusion, and *collateral estoppel* to refer to issue preclusion. To make matters even more ambiguous, many courts also use the term *res judicata* as a collective term to refer to both forms of preclusion. Still others use the phrase estoppel by bar to refer to one type of claim preclusion. Although we have attempted to use the modern and more descriptive terms claim and issue preclusion throughout this chapter, not all courts and commentators are so accommodating.

C. CLAIM PRECLUSION

INTRODUCTORY PROBLEM

While riding the Tilt–A–Whirl at a county fair, plaintiff hits her head on a protruding metal bar. Plaintiff sues the fair operator. After discovery is complete, the court enters a summary judgment for plaintiff for $5,000. Defendant pays the judgment in full.

Five years later, plaintiff suffers a *grand mal* epileptic seizure. Plaintiff's physician determines that the earlier accident was the proximate cause of this condition. Plaintiff accordingly sues the fair operator again, this time seeking $200,000 in damages.

Defendant moves to dismiss the case, arguing that plaintiff has already litigated this claim. Is plaintiff's claim barred? *See Faulkner v. Caledonia County Fair Ass'n*, 869 A.2d 103 (Vt. 2004)

Variation #1: What if defendant had not paid the prior judgment?

Variation #2: What if defendant had evidence—perhaps the result of a Rule 35 physical examination—that made it clear to defendant that plaintiff would develop epilepsy? What if defendant not only had such evidence, but wrongly refused to disclose it in discovery?

1. The Basics of Claim Preclusion

Claim preclusion prevents a party from litigating a claim that was or should have been litigated in a prior case. It stems from the sensible notion that a party should have only "one bite at the apple." Once the party has litigated a particular legal wrong, she should not be able to litigate that same wrong again in a different case. The issue, however, is determining what we mean by a single legal wrong. Courts have adopted different approaches to the problem. The next case discusses the two leading approaches.

RODGERS v. ST. MARY'S HOSPITAL

149 Ill.2d 302, 597 N.E.2d 616 (1992)

CHIEF JUSTICE MILLER delivered the opinion of the court:

* * *

FACTS

Rodgers filed a medical malpractice action in the circuit court of Macon County on May 27, 1986, alleging the wrongful death of his wife, Brenda, who died at the hospital two days after giving birth to their son. Named as defendants in the medical malpractice action were Brenda's obstetricians, her radiologists, and the hospital. The circuit court entered summary judgment in favor of the hospital on May 13, 1988. Rodgers did not appeal the summary judgment in favor of the hospital.

Rodgers proceeded to trial against the obstetricians and radiologists. On June 10, 1988, the jury found in favor of Rodgers on his claims against the obstetricians and assessed damages at $1.2 million. The jury found the radiologists not liable and Rodgers did not appeal that finding. The obstetricians appealed, but the appeal was dismissed by stipulation of the parties on May 24, 1989, when Rodgers and the obstetricians agreed to settle the medical malpractice claim for $800,000.

In the meantime, on September 25, 1987, Rodgers had filed a separate complaint for damages against the hospital alleging that the hospital breached its statutory duty to preserve for five years all of the X rays taken of Brenda (see Ill. Rev. Stat. 1987, ch. 111 1/2, par. 157–11 (X–Ray Retention Act)). He claimed that the X rays were crucial to proving his case against the obstetricians and radiologists. On April 12, 1988, on motion of the hospital, the circuit court dismissed that complaint without prejudice.

Rodgers amended his complaint and brought the present action against the hospital on May 25, 1989, the day after he reached the $800,000 settlement with the obstetricians. In his complaint, Rodgers alleged that Brenda's death was caused by a sigmoid colonic volvulus, and that the condition appeared on an X ray that the hospital had a duty to preserve. Rodgers alleged that the hospital's failure to preserve the X ray was a breach of its duty arising from the X–Ray Retention Act and from the hospital's internal regulations. Rodgers asserted that because the hospital failed to preserve the X ray, Rodgers was unable to prove his case against the radiologists. He further alleged that had he recovered against the radiologists and the obstetricians jointly and severally, the verdict would have been paid in full and would not have been appealed. He thus sought $400,000 in damages from the hospital, the difference between the $1.2 million verdict and the $800,000 settlement. The trial court dismissed the amended complaint on the grounds that Rodgers' settlement with the obstetricians and failure to appeal the judgment in favor of the radiologists barred his loss-of-evidence claim against the hospital. Rodgers appealed.

The appellate court reversed the judgment of the circuit court. The appellate court held that Rodgers' amended complaint stated a statutory cause of action that was not barred by *res judicata* or waived by Rodgers' post-judgment settlement with the obstetricians. We granted the hospital's petition for leave to appeal. The issues presented are whether there is a statutory cause of action under the X–Ray Retention Act and whether Rodgers' suit is barred by his earlier settlement with the obstetricians or by res judicata.

Discussion

We first address whether the statute grants Rodgers a private cause of action by implication. [The court held that the statute created a cause of action.] * * *

The hospital next contends that Rodgers' settlement with the obstetricians operated as a waiver of any subsequent claims against the parties in the original malpractice case and that Rodgers' claimed damages of $400,000 were self-imposed when Rodgers voluntarily settled for less than the amount of the judgment. We find nothing to support the hospital's waiver argument.

As the appellate court pointed out, a rule that a post-judgment settlement bars an action for loss of evidence in this situation would be contrary to well-established principles of joint liability. When a plaintiff settles with one party, the remaining tortfeasors remain jointly and severally liable for the full amount of the judgment, minus the amount of the settlement. Additionally, such a rule would discourage settlement of disputed claims. Accordingly, we believe that the present claim against the hospital must remain intact, despite Rodgers' settlement with the obstetricians. * * *

Finally, the hospital argues that even if Rodgers' amended complaint states a cause of action, the action is barred by the summary judgment rendered on May 13, 1988, in favor of the hospital in the malpractice case. The doctrine of res judicata provides that a final judgment on the merits is conclusive as to the rights of the parties, constituting an absolute bar to a subsequent action involving the same claim, demand, or cause of action.

To determine whether causes of action are the same for *res judicata* purposes, Illinois courts have adopted two tests. The first is called the "same evidence" test. Under that test, *res judicata* bars a second suit if the evidence needed to sustain the second suit would have sustained the first, or if the same facts were essential to maintain both actions. The second test is the "transactional" approach, which considers whether both suits arise from the same transaction, incident, or factual situation. The transactional approach provides that " 'the assertion of different kinds or theories of relief still constitutes a single cause of action if a single group of operative facts give rise to the assertion of relief.' " *Pfeiffer [v. William Wrigley Jr. Co.* 139 Ill. App. 3d 320, 323, 484 N.E.2d 1187 (1985), quoting *Baird & Warner Inc. v. Addison Industrial Park, Inc.* (1979), 70 Ill. App. 3d 59, 64, 387 N.E.2d 831.

We conclude that under either test, res judicata does not bar the present action. Here, Rodgers' amended complaint against the hospital is based on a different cause of action than that underlying his prior claim against the hospital, obstetricians, and radiologists. The present action is for loss of evidence; the first was for medical malpractice. The same evidence would not sustain both verdicts, and the facts essential to each suit did not arise from the same transactions or incidents.

To obtain a favorable verdict on the present cause of action, Rodgers must show that but for the hospital's failure to preserve all X rays of Brenda, he would have prevailed against the radiologists and that in so doing he would have recovered more than $800,000 of the damages awarded by the jury in the medical malpractice suit. These facts would not have sustained a verdict in the medical malpractice action. There the issue was whether the doctors or hospital negligently caused Brenda's death. The X ray was lost after Brenda died and could therefore not have affected the defendants' exercise of care in treating Brenda. Furthermore the existence of the duty to preserve the X ray, the incidents causing the X ray to be missing at trial, and the facts surrounding the potential evidentiary value of the missing X ray are circumstances unrelated to determining medical malpractice liability in the first cause of action. Thus, under either test for identical causes of action, res judicata does not bar the present action. * * *

In sum, Rodgers' amended complaint states a cause of action implied by statute. It is for the trier of fact to determine whether the hospital's failure to preserve the X ray proximately caused Rodgers to lose his malpractice case against the radiologists, and if so, to what damages Rodgers is entitled. The present action is not barred by Rodgers' settlement with the obstetricians in the earlier medical malpractice suit, or by res judicata.

Accordingly, we affirm the judgment of the appellate court.

Notes and Questions

1. Unlike many of the doctrines discussed in Civil Procedure, preclusion began as—and to this date largely remains—a court-created doctrine. Therefore, our discussion will focus more heavily on case law and the *Restatement* than the discussion in the other chapters.

2. Illinois is somewhat unique in that it purports to follow *both* of the leading tests for determining whether a particular claim is barred by claim preclusion. *See also Whitaker v. Ameritech Corp.*, 129 F.3d 952 (7th Cir. 1997). Most states follow only the "same transaction" approach. That approach is also favored by the authors of the *Restatement of Judgments*, as evidenced by sections 24 and 25:

RESTATEMENT OF THE LAW (SECOND): JUDGMENTS*

§ 24. Dimensions of "Claim" for Purposes of Merger or Bar— General Rule Concerning "Splitting"

(1) When a valid and final judgment rendered in an action extinguishes the plaintiff's claim pursuant to the rules of merger or bar (see §§ 18, 19), the claim extinguished includes all rights of the plaintiff to remedies against the defendant with respect to all or any part of the transaction, or series of connected transactions, out of which the claim arose.

(2) What factual grouping constitutes a "transaction", and what groupings constitute a "series", are to be determined pragmatically, giving weight to such considerations as whether the facts are related in time, space, origin, or motivation, whether they form a convenient trial unit, and whether their treatment as a unit conforms to the parties' expectations or business understanding or usage.

§ 25. Exemplifications of General Rule Concerning Splitting

The rule of § 24 applies to extinguish a claim by the plaintiff against the defendant even though the plaintiff is prepared in the second action

(1) To present evidence or grounds or theories of the case not presented in the first action, or

(2) To seek remedies or forms of relief not demanded in the first action.

3. In a state like Illinois that has adopted both tests, does the "same evidence" approach have any real practical significance? Can you ever think of a case where two claims would be supported by much of the same evidence, and yet do not arise from the same transaction or related series of transactions?

4. California follows a different approach to claim preclusion called the "primary rights" test. Under that approach, two claims comprise the same cause of action if they involve "1) a primary right possessed by the plaintiff, 2) a corresponding primary duty devolving upon the defendant, and 3) a delict or wrong done by the defendant which consists in a breach of such primary right and duty." *Citizens for Open Access to Sand and Tide, Inc. v. Seadrift Ass'n*, 60 Cal.App.4th 1053, 1067, 71 Cal.Rptr.2d 77, 86 (1998) (citations omitted). What is a "primary right?" Suppose that P was involved in an automobile accident with D, in which P suffered both personal injury and damage to his automobile. Could P sue for personal injury and property damage in separate actions, under the theory that two different "primary rights" (bodily integrity and property rights) were involved?

5. *Splitting*. The main goal of claim preclusion is to prevent a plaintiff from "splitting" a single dispute into multiple claims and litigating those claims in two or more cases. Plaintiff may try to split a single transaction in several different ways, including (a) splitting the injury (for example, suing for medical expenses and pain and suffering in separate cases), (b) using separate legal theories (for example, products liability and breach of warranty) and (c) splitting the relief (for example, suing separately for damages for past harm and for an injunction to prevent threatened future harm).

6. The different approaches discussed in the main case and these notes are really nothing more than different views as to how broadly we should define a dispute. As noted in Section B of this chapter, all forms of preclusion are concerned with efficiency and consistency. Given that all of the tests for preclusion require some connection between the claims in the first and second cases, all will help prevent inefficient duplicative litigation. But do all of the tests really further consistency? If two claims arise out of the same transaction, but do not involve the same evidence, is there a risk of inconsistent judgments?

7. When the first case is litigated in federal court, the claim preclusive effect of the judgment is measured by a *federal* standard, at least in cases involving federal and constitutional claims. The federal courts standard is the "same transaction" approach of the Restatement (Second). *Massachusetts School of Law at Andover, Inc. v. American Bar Ass'n*, 142 F.3d 26, 38 (1st Cir. 1998).

8. *Series of transactions*. What does the Restatement mean by a "series of transactions?" Suppose that Andre Preneur, an aspiring businessman, wants to open up a dozen Moondoe Coffee Shops. Andre enters into a dozen franchise agreements with Moondoe Corp. All of these agreements are identical except for the information about location of the coffee shop. When Andre's business acumen proves to be less acute than he thought, he is unable to make the minimum payments under all twelve of these agreements. Must Moondoe sue under all twelve agreements in the same suit? Most courts would hold no: the different contracts are different transactions, notwithstanding their similarity.

What about installment payments under a single contract? Suppose that Andre fails to make both the January and February payments under the agreement relating to his Main Street coffee shop. Under the so-called "Rule of Accumulated Breaches," if Moondoe sued Andre in March for only the January installment, claim preclusion would prevent it from bringing a separate action for the February installment. However, Moondoe could sue separately for any additional installments that came due after it filed its case on the January installment. For example, suppose Moondoe sued for the January installment on February 28. Although it could not sue for the overdue February installment, it could bring a separate action for the March and any later installments that came due after the case was filed. Of course, Moondoe might also be able to use Federal Rule 15(d) to supplement its complaint in the original case to add the later-occurring installments.

The Rule of Accumulated Breaches is subject to a limited, but important exception. If the installments are paid using separate instruments—such as a note, check, or coupon on a bond—the Rule of Accumulated Breaches does not apply. Suppose that Andre paid the rent on his Main Street store in advance, delivering separate post-dated checks for each month's rent. After the January, February, and March checks bounce, Landlord sues, but only for the January check. Landlord could bring separate suits for the other two checks. The rationale for this seemingly odd rule lies in the policy of ensuring that these sorts of instruments remain freely assignable. If someone buying a note or coupons from a bond had to worry that her right to recover might be barred by claim preclusion, she would give far less than full value for the instrument.

9.   How should a defendant raise claim preclusion? Can the defendant move to dismiss for failure to state claim? Or is summary judgment the proper way to raise the issue?

10.   Generally speaking, claim preclusion only applies to a single plaintiff and defendant. Suppose that while crossing a street, Walker and Jogger are both struck and injured by a car driven by Driver. Driver swears that the crossing light was malfunctioning. Walker sues Driver, but loses at trial. Walker now wants to sue City for failing properly to maintain the crossing light. Because Walker's claim against City is considered legally distinct, claim preclusion will not bar Walker's suit against City. Similarly, Jogger's rights are legally distinct, and so claim preclusion will have no effect on Jogger's suit(s) against Driver and City.

This general principle is subject to some qualifications. First, as you will see in Part E of this chapter, in some cases two people with a legal relationship will be treated as one person for preclusion purposes under the doctrine of *privity*. Second, as Part D of this chapter demonstrates, although claim preclusion may not bar Walker's suit against City, *issue preclusion* may prevent Walker from relitigating certain key questions in the case.

11.   Even though a single plaintiff may ordinarily sue two defendants for the same injury, that plaintiff can collect only once. If P obtains separate $10,000 judgments against D1 and D2, and collects $10,000 from D1, he cannot recover anything from D2. D2's defense in this situation is not claim preclusion, but instead the substantive defense that the judgment has been satisfied.

2.   Precluding Counterclaims, Cross-claims, and Defenses

The prior section dealt with how a plaintiff is forced to litigate in a single case all transactionally-related claims she has against a single defendant. But what about other claims that parties have against each other? Does claim preclusion also apply to claims other than those by a plaintiff against a defendant? The answer turns both on judge-made rules of claim preclusion and the applicable rules of procedure.

RESTATEMENT OF THE LAW (SECOND): JUDGMENTS*

§ 22.   Effect of Failure to Interpose Counterclaim

(1) Where the defendant may interpose a claim as a counterclaim but he fails to do so, he is not thereby precluded from subsequently maintaining an action on that claim, except as stated in Subsection (2).

(2) A defendant who may interpose a claim as a counterclaim in an action but fails to do so is precluded, after the rendition of judgment in that action, from maintaining an action on the claim if:

> (a) The counterclaim is required to be interposed by a compulsory counterclaim statute or rule of court, or

> (b) The relationship between the counterclaim and the plaintiff's claim is such that successful prosecution of the second action would nullify the initial judgment or would impair rights established in the initial action.

Counterclaims. As you learned in Chapter 2, the Federal Rules and most state procedural rules contain a compulsory counterclaim provision. Federal Rule 13(a), for example, requires a defendant to file any counterclaims that he has against the plaintiff arising from the same transaction or occurrence as the plaintiff's claim against the defendant, unless one of the narrow exceptions apply. *Restatement* § 22(2)(a) explicitly acknowledges these compulsory counterclaim rules. In the vast majority of cases, then, you need look no further than Rule 13(a) or its state-court counterpart to determine if a claim is barred by the party's failure to raise it as a counterclaim in the prior case.

If one of the Rule 13(a) exceptions applies, most courts follow an approach similar to that set out in § 22(b)(2). Under this rule, it is not enough that the counterclaim arises from the same transaction or occurrence as the claim. Instead, the counterclaim is barred only if allowing it might "nullify the initial judgment" or "impair rights established in the initial action." Some of the Illustrations set out in the comments to § 22 help elucidate this principle:

1. A brings an action against B for the negligent driving of an automobile by B resulting in a collision with an automobile driven by A. B fails to plead and judgment by default is given against him. B is not precluded from subsequently maintaining an action against A for his own injuries on the ground that those injuries were the result of A's negligence.

3. A brings an action against B for the purchase price of a boiler sold by A to B. B defends on the sole ground that the price has been paid, and judgment is given for A. B is not precluded from subsequently maintaining an action against A, in which he alleges that A was guilty of breach of warranty and that the boiler was defective and exploded, causing damage to B. (B is precluded, however, from seeking restitution of any amount paid pursuant to the judgment. * * *)

9. A brings an action against B for failure to pay the contract price for goods sold and delivered and recovers judgment by default. After

entry of final judgment and payment of the price, B brings an action against A to rescind the contract for mutual mistake, seeking restitution of the contract price and offering to return the goods. The action is precluded.*

In Illustration 9, do you see how the second case threatens to "nullify the judgment" in the first? Why does that same reasoning not apply in the other two Illustrations? In Illustration 1, for example, B's counterclaim asserts that A was negligent. But if A was negligent, then B should have prevailed because of contributory negligence (or at least reduced A's recovery under comparative fault). Would allowing B to recover against A nullify the judgment in Case One? Would it impair A's rights?

Why is the "common-law compulsory counterclaim rule" so narrow? After all, isn't one of the justifications for claim preclusion that we want to avoid inconsistent results? In both Illustrations 1 and 3, isn't it inconsistent to allow A to recover in Case One—an outcome that presupposes that A was not negligent (Illustration 1) or that A's goods conformed to the contract requirements (Illustration 3)—and then to turn around and allow B to recover for that same negligence or defect? Does it matter that P has chosen the forum for Case One? *See* RESTATEMENT OF THE LAW (SECOND): JUDGMENTS § 22, comment a. Note, however, that the rule applies even if B sues in the same court that heard the first case.

Three additional points are worth stressing. First, unlike Rule 13(a), the common-law compulsory counterclaim rule applies only if the plaintiff *prevails* in the first case. If the defendant prevails, he is free to assert his claim in the second case. If plaintiff lost Case One, there is no risk of inconsistency by allowing the defendant to bring Case Two. Second, the common-law rule applies only if defendant did not assert the issue in question as a defense in Case One. If defendant litigated the issue and lost, it will be barred by *issue* preclusion from relitigating that same issue as part of a claim in Case Two. Issue preclusion is discussed in Part D of this chapter.

Finally, do not forget the point made at the outset of this discussion: If the forum has a compulsory counterclaim rule like Federal Rule 13, that rule takes precedence over the common-law rule. Federal Rule 13(a) is grounded in efficiency, not consistency. Under Federal Rule 13(a) it is irrelevant whether allowing the counterclaim would nullify the first suit, or even if there is a risk of logical inconsistency.

Cross-claims. Neither Federal Rule 13(a) nor *Restatement* § 22 apply to cross-claims. Generally speaking, cross-claims are always optional. A party is free to assert a claim in Case Two even if she could have asserted it as a cross-claim in Case One. This general rule even applies when the party was a plaintiff in Case One. Thus, if P1 and P2 sue D in

Case One, P1 is free to sue P2 in a separate case, even though the case arises from the same transaction or occurrence as Case One.

Remember, however, that once one co-party files a claim against the other, Federal Rule 13(a) comes into play. In the prior example, if P2 had filed a cross-claim against P1, P1's claim would be a compulsory counterclaim, and therefore barred by Federal Rule 13(a) if not filed in Case One.

Pure Defenses. A defense is not a claim. Pure defenses are never compulsory. Suppose L sues T for failing to pay rent in January. T defends by arguing that he paid the rent. L prevails. L now sues for failure to pay the February rent. T now defends by arguing that the lease is invalid because L lied about the premises. Even though allowing T to prevail on that defense creates a risk of logical inconsistency (do you see how?), T is free to assert the defense in Case Two.

Note, however, that if T *does* litigate the defense in Case One and loses, he will be barred by *issue* preclusion from asserting the defense again in Case Two.

3. Final Judgment on the Merits

A court ruling is not entitled to claim preclusion effect unless it constitutes a final judgment on the merits. This phrase is unfortunately not as clear as it may seem.* Basically, a judgment is considered "final" with respect to a given claim if the trial judge is finished dealing with the claim, other than ordering entry of final judgment. A judgment after a full trial clearly meets this test. Similarly, a summary judgment—even a summary judgment on fewer than all the claims—is considered final. Default and consent judgments likewise are entitled to claim preclusion effect.

What does it mean for a judgment to be "on the merits?" A judgment is on the merits if it is based on the substance of plaintiff's claim and any defenses, rather than on a procedural ground. Therefore, a dismissal for lack of subject matter jurisdiction, personal jurisdiction, or venue is not a judgment on the merits. *See also* Federal Rule 41(b), which specifies that such dismissals are not an "adjudication on the merits." What about a 12(b)(6) dismissal for failure to state a claim? In the federal courts, a dismissal for failure to state a claim (and by implication a 12(c) judgment on the pleadings) is "on the merits" unless the judge explicitly states otherwise in the order of dismissal. *Federated Department Stores v. Moitie*, 452 U.S. 394, 399 n.3, 101 S.Ct. 2424, 69 L.Ed.2d 103 (1981). Many states disagree, even if their rules are based on the Federal Rules.

Dismissals and judgments based on the statute of limitations are a special case. In most situations, a forum will apply its own statute of limitations, even when the claim arises under the law of another state.

---

* Compounding the confusion is that 28 U.S.C. § 1291, the statute governing appeals, also speaks in terms of "final judg-ments"—but is interpreted differently. See page 802 (Chapter 12).

RESTATEMENT OF THE LAW (SECOND): CONFLICT OF LAWS § 142. Therefore, while a dismissal based on the statute of limitations in the courts of State A will prevent the plaintiff from suing again in State A, it will generally not bar a suit on that claim in State B, as long as the limitations period in State B is longer.

Note that finality turns on whether the *trial* court is finished with the claim. That a judgment may have been appealed does not affect its finality. If an appellate court overturns Case One while Case Two is pending, the court in Case Two will base its rulings on the appellate decision. If the court in Case Two enters judgment before the appeal of Case One is complete, however, the plaintiff faces a potential quandary. In that situation, plaintiff's only recourse is to reopen Case Two pursuant to a rule like Federal Rule 60(b)(5) (allowing a judgment to be reopened when " * * * a prior judgment on which it is based has been reversed or otherwise vacated * * * ").

4. Exceptions to Claim Preclusion

Claim preclusion is a strict doctrine. Nevertheless, there are certain exceptions that lessen its sting. Under these exceptions, a party may be able to allege a claim in Case Two even if it arises from the same transaction as the claim in Case One.

Some of the exceptions are relatively obvious. For example, if the parties agree or the court in Case One expressly states that plaintiff's right to bring a second case is reserved, claim preclusion does not apply. Similarly, if a plaintiff actually does file a particular claim in Case One, but the court dismisses it for lack of jurisdiction, pursuant to its discretion under 28 U.S.C. § 1367(c), or for some other procedural reason, plaintiff is free to refile it in a later case.

Other exceptions are more technical in nature. If the first action is *in rem* rather than *in personam*, counterclaims by the defendant are never compulsory. *See also* Federal Rule 13(a), which incorporates the same exception. Because we still maintain the myth that an *in rem* action is a suit against the property rather than the owner, as a technical matter only the property is bound.

Finally, there are exceptions to claim preclusion that are based on substantive policy. The negotiable instruments exception to the Rule of Accumulated Breaches is one example. Beyond this situation, courts split concerning what sorts of substantive policies are significant enough to warrant relieving the parties of the effects of claim preclusion.

Problems

1. After P and D are involved in an automobile accident, P sues D for the injuries that P suffered. The court enters judgment for D. P then sues D for the damage to P's automobile. How should D raise the defense of claim preclusion? Assuming that D raises the issue in the proper fashion, will D prevail?

2. Same facts as Problem 1, except assume that P prevails in the first trial. Does this change in facts affect D's chances of prevailing on claim preclusion?

3. P recently purchased an office suite software package from D. When D demonstrated the software prior to the sale, P thought it looked highly similar to another office suite sold by the software giant Gil Bates. Accordingly, at P's insistence, the contract between P and D contained a clause in which D warranted that the software does not infringe any copyright or violate any other rights of third parties.

Shortly after the sale, Gil Bates sued P for one million dollars for copyright infringement. Bates obtained a $600,000 judgment in this case. One week after P paid the judgment to Bates, a design defect in the office suite program causes the computers in P's headquarters to malfunction. P loses all of his data, including irreplaceable customer lists and tax records.

P sues D for breach of the contractual warranty, seeking reimbursement for the money it paid to Bates. After a long and acrimonious trial, the court entered judgment for P for $600,000. P then brings a products liability action against D, seeking to recover the value of the lost data. D argues that this action is barred by claim preclusion. Is D correct?

4. Same facts as Problem 3, except that the court in the first case (the case involving the contractual warranty) enters a default judgment for P.

5. Same facts as Problem 3, except that D did not pay the first judgment. P accordingly brings an action on the judgment in a different court, hoping to obtain a new judgment that he can use to execute on property owned by D in that area. D argues that the second action is barred by claim preclusion. Assuming the majority "same transaction" test applies, is D correct?

6. Because of soaring tuition costs, P, a law school, implements a program that allows students to pay tuition in monthly installments. D, a law student, takes advantage of this program. D makes the payment due on January 1, but cannot pay the February 1 and March 1 installments. On March 5th, P sues D for the February installment. In D's answer, she admits that she did not pay. Therefore, on April 7th, the court enters judgment on the pleadings for P.

P now sues D for the March and April installments. D argues that the claims for both months are barred by claim preclusion. Is D correct?

7. Same facts as Problem 6, except assume that claim preclusion bars neither claim. D files an answer in which she admits not making the payments, but argues that the tuition contract is invalid under state usury law. Under state law, a borrower such as D who enters into a usurious contract is relieved of the obligation to pay all amounts owed under the contract. Thus, if D is correct, she could attend school without paying tuition. P counters by arguing that because D's usury argument would also have applied to the *February* installment, D is barred by claim preclusion from making the argument in this later case. Is P correct?

8. P sues D for a tort in State Alpha. The court grants summary judgment to D based on the one-year Alpha statute of limitations. P then brings the exact same claim before a court in State Beta, where the statute

of limitations has not yet expired. D argues that the claim is barred by claim preclusion. Is D correct?

D. ISSUE PRECLUSION

In some ways, issue preclusion can be thought of as a "backup" to claim preclusion. Claim preclusion is a sword that cuts with a broad swath, barring one or more complete claims from a case. When claim preclusion does not apply, however, a party still may be barred from litigating one of more *issues* involved in a case by the doctrine of issue preclusion. Compared to claim preclusion, issue preclusion is more like a surgical scalpel, with a narrower and more precise cut. Nevertheless, like a sword, a scalpel can also prove fatal. To the extent that a barred issue is a crucial element in a claim presented in Case Two, issue preclusion can control the outcome of an entire claim.

INTRODUCTORY PROBLEM

Tenant leases space from Landlord in a "strip" shopping center (a center where each store has its own entrance, but shares parking). The lease gives Tenant the right to "make such use of the common areas, including the parking lot, as reasonably necessary."

In early August, Tenant holds a two-day "Dog Days" sale. Because the air conditioning unit in the center is not cooling his store sufficiently, Tenant decides to hold the sale outdoors. Tenant accordingly moves much of its inventory into the parking lot, placing it under large tents.

When Landlord learns of this, he sues Tenant for damages for breaching the lease. Tenant admits holding the sale, but denies liability based on two arguments. First, Tenant argues that holding a two-day sale in the parking lot is not an unreasonable use of the lot. Second, Tenant argues that even if such a sale is unreasonable, Landlord failed to provide Tenant the notice of breach called for by the lease. The case is submitted to the jury, which returns a general verdict for Tenant.

In late October, Tenant advertises its one-day "Columbus Day Sale," which, given the lovely weather, Tenant wants to hold in the parking lot. This time, however, Landlord is prepared. Landlord gives Tenant notice that holding a sale in the parking lot would breach the lease. Tenant ignores the notice, and holds the sale anyway. Landlord therefore sues Tenant a second time for damages for breach of lease.

Tenant realizes that claim preclusion does not bar this new action. Tenant nevertheless argues that the earlier case established that holding a one-day or two-day sale in the parking lot is a "reasonable use" within the meaning of the lease. Is Tenant correct in arguing that Landlord is precluded from relitigating this issue?

Variation: Suppose the jury in the first case had rendered a special verdict finding that the August sale was not unreasonable, and that Landlord had failed to provide the required notice.

———————

The test for claim preclusion asks if the same basic event or transaction is involved in two cases. Similarly, issue preclusion focuses on whether the same issue is before the court in the two cases. Aside from this parallel, however, there is a fundamental difference in the way the two doctrines operate. In claim preclusion, it is irrelevant whether the particular claim in question was actually presented to or decided by the court in Case One. In issue preclusion, by contrast, it is crucial not only that the issue have been presented to the court in Case One, but that it was fully litigated and decided by the court in a way that affected the outcome of that case. This difference makes the analysis of issue preclusion more technical in several ways.

Issue preclusion has four basic "elements." First, the two cases must involve the same issue. Second, that issue must have been actually litigated in Case One. Third, the court in that case must actually decide that question. Finally, the ruling on the question must have been necessary to the judgment rendered by the court in Case One. Each of these elements presents its own special difficulties, and will be discussed in turn.

The more complicated analysis in issue preclusion gives you a strong incentive to treat issue preclusion as a backup to claim preclusion. If the entire claim is barred, it is largely irrelevant whether particular issues relevant to that claim are barred. Therefore, to save yourself time and trouble, always consider claim preclusion before diving headlong into issue preclusion.

1. Same Issue

WILLIAMS v. CITY OF JACKSONVILLE POLICE DEPT.

599 S.E.2d 422 (N.C. App. 2004)

TYSON, Judge.

The City of Jacksonville Police Department ("Jacksonville Police Department"), Officer Billy J. Houston ("Officer Houston"), and Officer Earl K. Burkhart ("Officer Burkhart") (collectively, "defendants") appeal from an order denying their Motion for Summary Judgment. We reverse.

I. BACKGROUND

Plaintiff originally filed this action on 2 March 2000 in Onslow County Superior Court from incidents that arose during a traffic stop of plaintiff by defendants. Plaintiff asserted claims for: (1) "personal injuries, pain and suffering, humiliation, loss of liberty and emotional distress" that he suffered as a result of defendants' "negligence, malicious and wanton conduct;" (2) "the action of Defendants violated the 4th and/or the 14th Amendments to the U.S. Constitution, protecting against unlawful seizures;" (3) "the acts and conduct of the Defendants ... constitutes [sic] false arrest and negligence under the laws of the State of North Carolina;" and (4) "The City of Jacksonville intentionally or negligently failed to properly train its officers...."

Defendants removed the action to the United States District Court for the Eastern District of North Carolina ("the U.S. District Court") pursuant to plaintiff's assertion of a violation of the Civil Rights Act, Title 42 U.S.C. § 1983 and moved for summary judgment. By Order entered 29 May 2001, the Honorable James C. Fox, Senior U.S. District Court Judge, granted defendants' motion. Judge Fox found, as a matter of law: (1) defendants had probable cause to stop and detain plaintiff; (2) defendants acted reasonably in conducting a pat-down search and in using "threat of force;" and (3) defendants did not use excessive force. Judge Fox also concluded, "Because the officers [Houston and Burkhart] did not commit any constitutional violation, summary judgment is also appropriate as to the plaintiff's claims against the City of Jacksonville." Judge Fox's Order stated, "To the extent that the plaintiff's complaint alleges state law causes of action, the court, pursuant to 28 U.S.C. § 1367(c)(3), declines to exercise supplemental jurisdiction over such pendent claims, and ORDERS these claims DISMISSED without prejudice."

Plaintiff timely filed a new complaint on 16 November 2001 asserting the causes of action stated in his earlier complaint, except for deleting his claim for violations of the Fourth and Fourteenth Amendments of the United States Constitution. Defendants filed an answer and asserted thirty defenses, including governmental immunity, public duty doctrine, and *res judicata*/collateral estoppel. Defendants moved for summary judgment and asserted, "Plaintiff's pendant [sic] state tort claims are premised on either the lack of probable cause or the unreasonableness of Defendants' conduct ... [and] are barred under the doctrines of *res judicata* and collateral estoppel in that the necessary elements of Plaintiff's claims have been previously adjudicated in favor of Defendants." The trial court denied defendants' motion. Defendants appeal.

II. Issues

The issues presented are whether: (1) this appeal is interlocutory; and (2) the trial court erred in denying defendants' Motion for Summary Judgment because the doctrines of *res judicata* and collateral estoppel bar plaintiff's claims.

[The court first held that the appeal was timely.] * * *

V. *Res Judicata* and Collateral Estoppel

The trial court concluded neither *res judicata* nor collateral estoppel precluded plaintiff's claims and denied defendants' Motion for Summary Judgment.

"The companion doctrines of *res judicata* (claim preclusion) and collateral estoppel (issue preclusion) have been developed by the courts for the dual purposes of protecting litigants from the burden of relitigating previously decided matters and promoting judicial economy by preventing needless litigation." *Bockweg [v. Anderson*, 333 N.C. 486, 428 S.E.2d 161 (1993)], 333 N.C. at 491, 428 S.E.2d at 161.

> Where the second action between two parties is upon the same claim, the prior judgment serves as a bar to the relitigation of all matters that were or should have been adjudicated in the prior action. Where the second action between the same parties is upon a different claim, the prior judgment serves as a bar only as to issues actually litigated and determined in the original action.

Id. at 492, 428 S.E.2d at 161 (citations omitted). Our Supreme Court has distinguished between these two doctrines:

> Under the doctrine of res judicata or "claim preclusion," a final judgment on the merits in one action precludes a second suit based on the same cause of action between the same parties or their privies. The doctrine prevents the relitigation of all matters ... that were or should have been adjudicated in the prior action. Under the companion doctrine of collateral estoppel, also known as "estoppel by judgment" or "issue preclusion," the determination of an issue in a prior judicial or administrative proceeding precludes the relitigation of that issue in a later action, provided the party against whom the estoppel is asserted enjoyed a full and fair opportunity to litigate that issue in the earlier proceeding.

Whitacre P'ship v. Biosignia, Inc., 358 N.C. 1, 15, 591 S.E.2d 870, 880 (2004) (internal citations and quotations omitted). *Res judicata* precludes a party from "bringing a subsequent action based on the 'same claim' ... litigated in an earlier action...." *Id.* Collateral estoppel bars "the subsequent adjudication of a previously determined issue, even if the subsequent action is based on an entirely different claim." *Id.*

VI. *Res Judicata*

In *City–Wide Asphalt Paving, Inc. v. Alamance County*, we held the doctrines of *res judicata* and collateral estoppel did not bar the plaintiff's claims under the North Carolina Constitution, although the federal court had already ruled on the same issues under the United States Constitution. 132 N.C.App. 533, 536, 513 S.E.2d 335, 338, *appeal dismissed and disc. rev. denied*, 350 N.C. 826, 537 S.E.2d 815 (1999).

> After careful review of the record, briefs and contentions of both parties, we hold that plaintiff's claims are not barred by *res judicata* or collateral estoppel. The federal court expressly stated that it

"declined to exercise supplemental jurisdiction over Plaintiff's state law claims," and dismissed them without prejudice. While the federal court did review federal due process and equal protection claims, this Court has stated that "our courts ... when construing provisions of the North Carolina Constitution, are not bound by the opinions of the federal courts 'construing even identical provisions in the Constitution of the United States ...'" and that "an independent determination of plaintiff's constitutional rights under the state constitution is required."

Id. at 536, 513 S.E.2d at 338.

Here, Judge Fox expressly declined to review plaintiff's state claims, and stated in his Order, "To the extent that the plaintiff's complaint alleges state law causes of action, the court, pursuant to 28 U.S.C. § 1367(c)(3), declines to exercise supplemental jurisdiction over such pendent claims, and ORDERS these claims DISMISSED without prejudice." Plaintiff's complaint, filed after the U.S. District Court's ruling, alleged causes of action under state law for negligence, false arrest, and assault. By dismissing these claims without prejudice, plaintiff's "subsequent action" is not "based on the 'same claim' as that litigated in an earlier action." *Whitacre P'ship*, 358 N.C. at 15, 591 S.E.2d at 880.

We hold that plaintiff's claims are not barred by *res judicata* as Judge Fox's Order addressed only plaintiff's claims under federal law and the United States Constitution. Judge Fox expressly declined to rule on plaintiff's causes of action controlled by state law.

VII. COLLATERAL ESTOPPEL

Defendants assert that the doctrine of collateral estoppel precludes plaintiff's suit in state court. "Under the doctrine of collateral estoppel, when an issue has been fully litigated and decided, it cannot be contested again between the same parties, even if the first adjudication is conducted in federal court and the second in state court." *McCallum [v. N.C. Coop. Extension Serv.*, 142 N.C.App. 48, 542 S.E.2d 227 (2001)], 142 N.C.App. at 52, 542 S.E.2d at 231 (citation omitted). * * * For collateral estoppel to bar a party's subsequent claim:

> (1) the issues to be concluded must be the same as those involved in the prior action; (2) in the prior action, the issues must have been raised and actually litigated; (3) the issues must have been material and relevant to the disposition of the prior action; and (4) the determination made of those issues in the prior action must have been necessary and essential to the resulting judgment.

Id. at 54, 542 S.E.2d at 233.

Here, the federal court's Order addressed the issue of whether "Defendant Billy Houston and Defendant Earl K. Burkhart violated [plaintiff's] Fourth and Fourteenth Amendment rights during a traffic stop...." In granting summary judgment for defendants on the issues of unlawful seizure and excessive force under the United States Constitution, Judge Fox ruled, among other things, Officer Houston and Officer Burkhart: (1) did not "expand[] the permissible scope of the stop;" (2) did not use excessive force because "the threat of force displayed by Houston in order to persuade the driver not to leave the scene was not unreasonable;" (3) "did not violate the plaintiff's Fourth Amendment rights" by asking the plaintiff to step out of his vehicle; and (4) "a pat-down search was not unreasonable under the circumstances...." The U.S. District Court held, "Because the officers did not commit any constitutional violation, summary judgment is also appropriate as to the plaintiff's claims against the City of Jacksonville [Police]."

Following entry of the U.S. District Court's Order, plaintiff filed a new complaint in state court and asserted claims for negligence, false arrest, and assault. Plaintiff also asserted the Jacksonville Police Department negligently trained its officers. While the U.S. District Court's Order did not rule on defendants' ultimate liability for these claims, the Order ruled on several underlying issues and identical elements of these claims. To the extent the U.S. District Court ruled on these issues, plaintiff is barred from relitigating the issues in state court.

A. Negligence

Plaintiff's complaint alleges Officer Houston and Officer Burkhart acted negligently in their official and individual capacity. * * * A law enforcement officer may be held liable for use of "unreasonable or excessive force" upon another person. N.C. Gen. Stat. § 15A–01(d)(2)(2003).

In the U.S. District Court's Order, Judge Fox held, "Viewed from the perspective of an objectively reasonable police officer, the court concludes that the threat of force displayed by Houston ... was not unreasonable." Additionally, the officers' actions did "not amount to an unreasonable seizure," and the "pat-down search was not unreasonable under the circumstances...." The issues regarding the reasonableness of Officer Houston and Officer Burkhart's actions were litigated in federal court. Plaintiff is precluded from relitigating the issue of whether the officers acted reasonably in performing their official duties. The trial court erred in failing to grant summary judgment for defendants in their official capacity on the issue of negligence.

"To withstand a law enforcement officer's motion for summary judgment on the issue of individual capacity, plaintiff must allege and forecast evidence demonstrating the officers acted maliciously, corruptly, or beyond the scope of duty." *Prior[v. Pruett*, 143 N.C.App. 612, 550 S.E.2d 166 (2001), *disc. rev. denied*, 355 N.C.493, 563 S.E.2d 572 (2002)], 143 N.C.App. at 623, 550 S.E.2d at 173–74. "State governmental officials can be sued in their individual capacities for damages under section 1983." *Corum v. University of North Carolina*, 330 N.C. 761, 772, 413 S.E.2d 276, 283, *reh'g denied*, 331 N.C. 558, 418 S.E.2d 664, *cert. denied*, 506 U.S. 985, 121 L.Ed.2d 431, 113 S.Ct. 493 (1992) (citing *Kentucky v. Graham*, 473 U.S. 159, 87 L.Ed.2d 114, 105 S.Ct. 3099 (1985)).

Unlike a suit against a state official in his official capacity, which is basically a suit against the official office and therefore against the State itself, a suit against an individual who happens to be a governmental official but is not acting in his official capacity is not imputed to the State. Such individuals are sued as individuals, not as governmental employees.

Corum, 330 N.C. at 772, 413 S.E.2d at 283.

In support of his claim that defendants acted negligently in their individual capacity, plaintiff asserts that Officer Houston "intentionally," "negligently[,] and maliciously pointed a loaded weapon" at plaintiff. Other than this broad assertion, plaintiff presents no other allegation or forecast of evidence to show that defendants acted "maliciously, corruptly, or beyond the scope of duty." *Prior*, 143 N.C.App. at 623, 550 S.E.2d at 174. The U.S. District Court ruled that Officer Houston acted reasonably in pointing his service weapon at plaintiff. Plaintiff is collaterally estopped from relitigating this issue.

Plaintiff's complaint also alleges that defendants "intentionally destroyed dispatch tapes" and "conspired to unnecessarily call the plaintiff's supervisor to the scene...." Judge Fox's Order recites these allegations and indicates that he considered these actions in ruling on plaintiff's claim under 42 U.S.C. § 1983. The U.S. District Court's Order does not rule on the ultimate issue of defendants' *negligence* in their individual capacity. However, Judge Fox's award of summary judgment to defendants essentially ruled both officers' actions were reasonable; neither officer violated plaintiff's constitutional rights; and their actions did not extend "beyond the scope of duty." *Id.* Collateral estoppel precludes plaintiff's suit on the issue of negligence for Officer Houston and Officer Burkhart in their individual capacity. The trial court erred in denying defendants' Motion for Summary Judgment on the issue of negligence.

B. *False Arrest*

"Under state law, a cause of action in tort will lie for false imprisonment, based upon the 'illegal restraint of one's person against his will.' A false arrest, *i.e.*, one without proper legal authority, is one means of committing a false imprisonment." *Myrick v. Cooley*, 91 N.C.App. 209, 212, 371 S.E.2d 492, 494, *disc. rev. denied*, 323 N.C. 477, 373 S.E.2d 865 (1988) (quoting *Mobley v. Broome*, 248 N.C. 54, 56, 102 S.E.2d 407, 409 (1958)). Probable cause is an absolute bar to a claim for false arrest. *Burton v. City of Durham*, 118 N.C.App. 676, 682, 457 S.E.2d 329, 333, *disc. rev. denied and cert. denied*, 341 N.C. 419, 461 S.E.2d 756 (1995).

In the prior federal court action, Judge Fox ruled that Officer Burkhart had probable cause to detain plaintiff because "plaintiff admittedly drove his vehicle in excess of the speed limit." Further, Judge Fox ruled that defendants did not unreasonably expand the permissible scope of the stop. As probable cause is an absolute bar to plaintiff's claim, he is collaterally estopped from relitigating this issue. Plaintiff's claim for false arrest fails. *Burton*, 118 N.C.App. at 682, 457 S.E.2d at 333. The trial court erred in failing to grant summary judgment on plaintiff's claim of false arrest.

C. Assault

" '[A] civil action for damages for assault . . . is available at common law against one who, for the accomplishment of a legitimate purpose, such as justifiable arrest, uses force which is excessive under the given circumstances.' " *Thomas v. Sellers*, 142 N.C.App. 310, 315, 542 S.E.2d 283, 287 (2001) (quoting *Myrick*, 91 N.C.App. at 215, 371 S.E.2d at 496. * * *

In the prior federal court action, Judge Fox held that defendants' display of force and the subsequent pat-down search of plaintiff were reasonable under the circumstances. Collateral estoppel bars plaintiff from relitigating these issues and bars plaintiff's assault claim in state court. The trial court erred in failing to grant summary judgment in favor of defendants on plaintiff's assault claim.

D. Jacksonville Police Department

"Without an underlying negligence charge against the [law enforcement officers], a claim of negligence against the [department] can not [sic] be supported." *Prior*, 143 N.C.App. at 622, 550 S.E.2d at 172–73. To the extent collateral estoppel bars plaintiff's claims against defendants' in their official governmental capacity, plaintiff is precluded from asserting a negligence action against the Jacksonville Police Department.

VII. CONCLUSION

Plaintiff's claims are not barred by *res judicata*. However, the trial court erred in failing to grant summary judgment in favor of defendants based on collateral estoppel. Essential elements of plaintiff's claims for false arrest and assault were raised, litigated, and ruled upon in the U.S. District Court's Order. * * *

Reversed and remanded.

Judges BRYANT and STEELMAN concur.

Notes and Questions

1. The court's ruling on *res judicata*, or claim preclusion, is based on one of the exceptions discussed in Part C.4 of this Chapter. Which exception is the court using?

2. What are the issues that are common to the constitutional and state-law claims?

3. Do you agree that these common questions are really the "same issue?" What about the fact that the claims in Case One and Case Two have different origins? Might the question of what is "reasonable" behavior by the officers be determined differently under state tort law as compared to

the Constitution? Indeed, isn't the purpose of the fourth and fourteenth amendments to hold state officials to a *higher*—or at least different—standard than they would be held to anyway under tort law?

4.   P sues D for negligence, based on injuries that P sustained in an automobile accident. P sues in a court that has no compulsory counterclaim rule. After a full trial, P obtains a judgment for $10,000.

After judgment is entered, D now sues P to recover for the injuries that D sustained in the same accident. Because the first court had no compulsory counterclaim rule, claim preclusion does not bar the suit. Will issue preclusion nevertheless apply? If P alleges that D was contributorily negligent, will D be barred from relitigating the issue of D's negligence? Is negligence the same as contributory negligence? While negligence is acting unreasonably toward someone else, isn't contributory negligence acting unreasonably toward *yourself*? What if D's negligence in Case One consisted of carrying a surfboard on top of the car without adequately tying it down?

5.   *Burden of persuasion.* Differences in the burden of persuasion can also affect whether two cases involve the same issue. A party who lost on an issue in Case One will not be barred from relitigating that issue if the burden of persuasion is lower in Case Two, or if the burden has switched from that party to the other side. Apply this basic principle to the following scenarios. In each of the scenarios, assume that claim preclusion does not bar Case Two.

a.   X and Y are neighbors. A dirt road lies near the border between their properties. X sues Y for trespass, alleging that the road lies on X's land, and that Y is using it without permission. The court enters judgment for Y, specifically finding that X failed to prove that she owned the road.

Later, Y sues X for trespass, alleging that X has been using the road since entry of judgment in the first case. X denies that Y owns the road. Y argues that issue preclusion applies to the question of ownership. The two cases do not involve the same issue.

b.   State prosecutes C for assault, arguing that C assaulted victim. C is convicted. Later, V brings a tort action against C for assault. Victim claims that C cannot relitigate the question of whether he committed the assault. The two cases involve the same issue.

c.   Same as b, except that State *lost* the first case. When V sues C, C argues that the issue of whether the assault occurred has already been litigated. The two cases do not involve the same issue.*

2.   Actually Litigated

The requirement that the issue be actually litigated in Case One is one of the most significant differences between claim and issue preclusion. Claim preclusion usually applies to claims that were not themselves presented in Case One, but are grounded in the same event as claims that were presented. By contrast, if an issue was not actually litigated,

---

* In Part E of this Chapter, you will learn that regardless of whether the cases involve the same issue, C cannot use issue preclusion against V because V was not a party to the first case.

issue preclusion can never apply to that issue. Therefore, a default judgment or involuntary dismissal for failure to prosecute will never have issue preclusion effect, even though both may have claim preclusion effect. Consent judgments likewise do not bar relitigation of the issues relevant to the claims.

Judgments or dismissals based on procedural grounds present a variation on this theme. A dismissal based on lack of subject matter jurisdiction, or a summary judgment based on the statute of limitations, does have issue preclusion effect, but only on the narrow issue of, respectively, whether the first court had subject matter jurisdiction, or whether Case One was filed in timely fashion in the chosen forum. If plaintiff sues again in that court, the action will be dismissed on the same ground. However, if plaintiff files in a *different* jurisdiction, the underlying questions of jurisdiction and statute of limitations may be governed by a different law, and issue preclusion accordingly may not apply.

How do you prove whether an issue was (or was not) actually litigated in an earlier proceeding? If the earlier court issued a written opinion, the discussion in that opinion may make it clear that a particular issue was contested. In the absence of a written opinion, the parties may introduce extrinsic evidence as to what issues were actually litigated in Case One.

Unlike claim preclusion, issue preclusion applies the same way regardless of the status of the party as plaintiff, defendant, or third-party defendant in Cases One and Two. As long as that party actually litigated the issue, and provided the other elements are met, issue preclusion will prevent that party from relitigating the question in Case Two, even if her party status has changed.

3. Actually Decided

Suppose P sues D for breach of contract. D counters by invoking the affirmative defense of waiver of the breach. If P wins the case at trial, we are sure of what the factfinder decided. In order to prevail, P must demonstrate that there was a contract, and that D breached the contract. Similarly, P would not prevail unless the court found that P did not waive the breach. Should P later sue D for another breach of the same agreement, D will be precluded from arguing that there was no contract. (Do you see why the other issues will *not* be precluded?)

But what if P loses Case One? Can we be sure of *why* P lost the case? The analysis of this question turns in large part on whether the first decision was rendered by a jury using a general verdict or by a judge, or jury using a special verdict. If the case was decided by a judge or by special verdict, the judge or jury must make specific findings on every issue. In this case, we know what the factfinder found. The only issue is whether all of those findings are necessary to the judgment, which is an issue explored in the next section. This section, by contrast, discusses how issue preclusion applies in the case of general jury verdicts, where the basis for the holding may not be clear.

Take the breach of contract case hypothesized above. If P loses a general verdict, we have no way of knowing whether P lost because the jury found there was no contract, or because of issues peculiar to the first case; namely, that there was at that time no breach by D, because P suffered no damages, or because P waived the earlier breach. Because there is no way to be sure of the reason(s) for the holding, courts do not give *any* of the issues issue preclusion effect in later litigation (except in the rare situation where all the issues in Case One and Case Two are exactly the same, in which claim preclusion is likely to apply anyway).

4. Necessary to the Judgment

As discussed in the prior section, the question of whether an issue is necessary to the judgment arises primarily in bench trials and cases utilizing a special verdict. In these situations, we know what the factfinder found. Depending on the claims and defenses asserted, however, it may have been logically possible for the factfinder to reach the same result without addressing one or more issues. In that case, do the unnecessary findings have issue preclusion effect?

STEMLER v. FLORENCE

350 F.3d 578 (6th Cir. 2003)

BOGGS, Chief Judge.

Appellant/cross-appellee William Chipman, administrator of the estate of Conni Black, * * * [appeals] the district court's order granting summary judgment for the defendants in this civil action arising out of an encounter between Conni Black and Susan Stemler, on the one hand, and police officers from the City of Florence, Kentucky and Boone County, Kentucky. * * *

This case arises out of an incident that occurred on February 19, 1994. We have reviewed this case on a previous appeal. Briefly, Black was killed in a car accident shortly after police officers allegedly removed her from Stemler's car and placed her in the truck of her boyfriend, Steve Kritis. Both Black and Kritis had been drinking heavily, and after an altercation between them at a bar, Black left with Stemler in Stemler's car. Kritis then began to chase the women on the streets of Florence before both the car and the truck were stopped by the police after a concerned citizen alerted them to the situation. Stemler was arrested for driving under the influence. Witnesses say that all the police officers present repeated Kritis's assertion that Stemler was a lesbian to each other and to others present. No police officer ever checked Kritis for intoxication or asked him to leave his truck. Black was either escorted or carried from Stemler's car to the passenger seat of Kritis's truck. Kritis then drove away and turned onto the northbound lanes of I–75. According to Kritis, Black, who had passed out, woke up and began to hit Kritis. He began to hit back and lost control of the truck. The truck swerved and collided with the guardrail. Black was partially ejected from the passenger-side window [and killed] * * *.

I. THE CLAIMS

* * *

On March 7, 1994, William Chipman, the administrator of the estate of Conni Black, filed a wrongful death action in the Boone County Circuit Court against Florence police officers Dusing, Dolan, and Wince; Boone County police officers Rob Reuthe and Chris Alsip; the City of Florence; and Ron Kenner, the Boone County Sheriff. [The court refers to this state-court litigation as the *Chipman* case.] The Boone County Circuit Court entered summary judgment on behalf of the defendants on Chipman's wrongful death claim. The Kentucky Court of Appeals reversed the Circuit Court. The Kentucky Supreme Court then reversed the Court of Appeals and reinstated the summary judgment ordered by the Boone County Circuit Court. *City of Florence v. Chipman*, 38 S.W.3d 387 (Ky. 2001). [In this ruling, the Kentucky Supreme Court stated, "Black was never in custody or otherwise restrained so as to give rise to a special relationship between the police officers and Black." 38 S.W.3d at 392. Absent this special relationship, the officers owed no duty to Black.]

Chipman also filed a complaint in federal court against the same defendants on March 31, 1994. [The court refers to this case as *Stemler*.] The complaint alleged that the defendants were liable under 42 U.S.C. § 1983 for Black's wrongful death because they had displayed deliberate indifference by forcing her into Kritis's car.

Chipman's federal claims were dismissed by the district court in 1994. The district court granted the individual officers' motions to dismiss under Federal Rule of Civil Procedure 12(b)(6), for failure to state a claim, on the ground of qualified immunity. The district court also granted the motions for summary judgment of Florence and Boone County.

On appeal, we upheld the district court's order granting summary judgment to the municipal defendants, Florence and Boone County. [*Stemler v. Florence*, 126 F.3d 856 (6th Cir. 1997)] at 866. However, we reversed the district court's dismissal of Chipman's claims against the individual officers. We held that Chipman had pled facts sufficient to maintain her substantive due process claim against the individual officers. The only state court decision prior to our decision was the Boone County Circuit Court decision awarding judgment to the defendant officers, holding that Black was not in custody when the pickup struck the guardrail and that none of the state actors were the direct cause of her death on the highway. We stated in *Stemler* that "while these findings are entitled to preclusive effect, they are irrelevant to the merits of her substantive due process claim." *Id.* at 870 n.12. [The earlier decision also discussed the meaning of the term "in custody," and concluded by stating, "Under any definition of the term, Black was in the defendant officers' custody at the time she was forced into Kritis's truck. *Id.* at 868–69.] The case was remanded to the district court for further proceedings consistent with the opinion.

* * * [On remand, the] district court found that the decision of the Kentucky Supreme Court barred their claims under the doctrine of issue preclusion. The issue that the district court found could not be relitigated was whether Black was in "custody" when she got into Kritis's car because, according to the district court, the Kentucky Supreme Court had held that Black was never in custody. * * *

II. Chipman's substantive due process claim

Chipman argues that our resolution of the custody issue in his favor in Stemler should have had preclusive effect on the Kentucky state courts. He argues that our opinion's holdings constituted the "law of the case" and the district court erred in applying the doctrine of issue preclusion based on the state court proceedings. The officers argue that the district court was correct in deciding that issue preclusion barred the relitigation of the issue of custody. * * *

A. *Issue Preclusion*

In order for issue preclusion to apply in Kentucky, (1) the issue in the second case must be the same as the issue in the first case, (2) the issue must have been actually litigated, (3) the issue must have been actually decided, and (4) the decision on the issue in the prior action must have been necessary to the court's judgment. The district court found that all four factors were met when the Kentucky Supreme Court resolved Chipman's state claims.

In order for Chipman to prevail in the Kentucky state courts, the Kentucky Supreme Court stated that he had to show "the existence of a duty and unless a special relationship was present, there is no duty owing from any of the police officers. . . ." *Chipman,* 38 S.W.3d at 392. The court went on, stating that "in order for the special relationship to exist, two conditions are required: 1) the victim must have been in state custody or otherwise restrained by the state at the time the injury producing act occurred, and 2) the violence or other offensive conduct must have been committed by a state actor." *Ibid.* The court held that "there is no evidence from which it can be ascertained that Black was in state custody or otherwise restrained by the police at the time the pickup truck struck the guardrail with the fatal result. In addition, there is no evidence to support a claim that the conduct which caused the pickup truck to leave the roadway and strike the guardrail was the result of the actions of the police officers." *Ibid.*

The Kentucky Supreme Court also stated that Black was *never* in custody. This is precisely the issue that is relevant in a § 1983 action. In order to prevail on the § 1983 claim, Chipman needs to show that the defendant officers "violated substantive due process by placing [Black] at risk of harm from a third party...." *Stemler*, 126 F.3d at 867. The court must first determine whether "the plaintiff and the state actors had a sufficiently direct relationship such that the defendants owed [Black] a duty not to subject her to danger," and then "the court must also conclude that the officers were sufficiently culpable to be liable under a substantive due process theory." *Ibid.* As to the first part, the relevant inquiry is whether Black was in custody at the time the officers allegedly forced her into Kritis's truck.

First, the Kentucky Supreme Court stated that there was no evidence in the record to support a finding that Black was ever in custody, the same issue that is necessary to Chipman's federal claim. Second, the custody issue was actually litigated in the state courts: in the Boone County Circuit Court, the Kentucky Court of Appeals and the Kentucky Supreme Court. The Kentucky Supreme Court found that there was no evidence to support a finding that Black was ever in custody in the context of deciding the appeal of a summary judgment motion. A summary judgment order is a decision on the merits. Third, the issue was actually decided by the Kentucky Supreme Court. The court made an explicit statement that there was insufficient evidence to support a finding that Black was in custody.

However, the Kentucky Supreme Court's statement that she was never in custody was not necessary to its judgment. The Boone County Circuit Court held that there was no genuine issue of material fact regarding whether Black was in custody at the time the pickup struck the guardrail—the point at which the injury-producing act occurred. Specifically, it stated she was not in custody at this point. This was the only holding necessary for the affirmance of the Boone County Circuit Court's judgment. As we noted in discussing this lower court decision in *Stemler*, the holdings of the state court on this issue are entitled to preclusive effect. Nonetheless, this precise issue is irrelevant to the substantive due process claim.

As the Kentucky Court of Appeals (now the Kentucky Supreme Court) stated in *Sedley v. City of West Buechel*, 461 S.W.2d 556, 558 (Ky. 1971):

> The general rule is that a judgment in a former action operates as an estoppel only as to matters which were necessarily involved and determined in the former action, and is *not conclusive as to matters* which were immaterial or *unessential to the determination* of the prior action or which were not necessary to uphold the judgment.

(Emphasis added).

As the Kentucky Supreme Court correctly stated, our statements in *Stemler* regarding whether Black was in custody were dicta, as the only issue before us at that point was the sufficiency of the allegations in the complaint. Similarly, the statements of the Kentucky Supreme Court regarding whether Black was *ever* in custody are dicta, as they are not necessary to the state courts' disposition of the case. The actual holding of the Kentucky Supreme Court reads:

In order for a claim to be actionable in negligence, there must be the existence of a duty and unless a special relationship was present, there is no duty owing from any of the police officers to Black to protect her from crime or accident. In order for the special relationship to exist, two conditions are required: 1) the victim must have been in state custody or otherwise restrained by the state at the time the injury producing act occurred, and 2) the violence or other offensive conduct must have been committed by a state actor. Neither of these factors can be found from the undisputed material facts in this case. There is no evidence from which it can be ascertained that Black was in state custody or otherwise restrained by the police at the time the pickup truck struck the guardrail with the fatal result. In addition, there is no evidence to support a claim that the conduct which caused the pickup truck to leave the roadway and strike the guardrail was the result of the actions of the police officers.

City of Florence v. Chipman, 38 S.W.3d 387, 392 (Ky. 2001) (emphasis added and citations omitted).

The Kentucky Supreme Court would have reached the same result if it had found that Black was in custody at the time she entered Kritis's truck, so long as it found she was not in custody at the time the truck hit the guardrail.

The district court erred in finding that issue preclusion barred Chipman's substantive due process claim.

B. Claim Preclusion

The defendant officers also argue that claim preclusion should bar Chipman's claim against them. [The court held, applying Kentucky law, that claim preclusion did not apply.]

[Reversed and remanded on the due process claim.]

Notes and Questions

1. In *Stemler*, the court considers whether two earlier statements—one by the Sixth Circuit, the other by the Kentucky Supreme Court—are entitled to issue preclusion effect. Why does the court refuse to afford issue preclusion effect to either statement? Are the concerns the same for each statement?

2. Why does issue preclusion only apply when a statement in an opinion is necessary to the judgment? As long as the factfinder specifically indicates its finding, why should that finding not be entitled to issue preclusion effect?

3. The Kentucky courts conducted a full and, from all appearances, fair trial in the first case. Isn't it somewhat insulting for the Sixth Circuit to ignore all the Kentucky's court's efforts, and refuse to apply issue preclusion?

4. *Alternate reasons*. Cases in which a court gives two or more alternate reasons for a holding also present questions as to whether an issue is necessary to the judgment. To illustrate, suppose P buys accounting software from D, a computer programmer. The parties negotiate a detailed contract, in which D warrants that the software will perform in certain ways. When the software fails to perform, P sues D both for breach of express warranty (the specific provision in the contract) and the implied warranty of fitness for a particular purpose (a warranty imposed by law whenever a party indicates that he is buying goods for a particular purpose). After a bench trial, the judge finds for P. The judge's opinion explicitly states that the software violated both the express warranty and the implied warranty of fitness.

Later, X, another purchaser of the software who is engaged in the same line of business as P, sues D. Although the contract between X and D contains no express warranty, X claims a violation of the implied warranty of fitness for a particular purpose. Will the finding in *P v. D* that the software violated the implied warranty have issue preclusion effect in *X v. D*?

Note that this situation differs from that in the main case. Because P won his case against D, we know that *one* of the alternate findings (express or implied warranty) was necessary to the judgment. The other finding could be dictum. But can we be sure which is which? Because of these concerns, the *Restatement* takes the position that *none* of the alternate grounds for a holding are entitled to issue preclusion:

RESTATEMENT OF THE LAW (SECOND): JUDGMENTS*

§ 27. Issue Preclusion—General Rule

* * *

Comment:

i. Alternative determinations by court of first instance. If a judgment of a court of first instance is based on determinations of two issues, either of which standing independently would be sufficient to support the result, the judgment is not conclusive with respect to either issue standing alone. * * *

There are * * * persuasive reasons for analogizing the case to that of the nonessential determination * * *. First, a determination in the alternative may not have been as carefully or rigorously considered as it would have if it had been necessary to the result, and in that sense it has some of the characteristics of dicta. Second, and of critical importance, the losing party, although entitled to appeal from both determinations, might be dissuaded from doing so because of the likelihood that at least one of them would be upheld and the other not even reached. * * *

5. Isn't the *Restatement*'s approach to the alternate holdings problem especially insulting to the earlier court? Given that at least one of the alternate holdings is absolutely necessary, should the first court's efforts be overlooked merely because it took the time and trouble to address *all* of the

relevant claims? Doesn't the Restatement's approach assume that the first court acted carelessly in all but one of its findings? Is the lack of incentive to appeal really "of critical importance", as the comment suggests?

5. Exceptions

Courts have recognized more exceptions to issue preclusion than they have to claim preclusion. The *Restatement* provides a list of commonly-recognized exceptions:

RESTATEMENT OF THE LAW (SECOND): JUDGMENTS**

§ 28. Exceptions to the General Rule of Issue Preclusion

Although an issue is actually litigated and determined by a valid and final judgment, and the determination is essential to the judgment, relitigation of the issue in a subsequent action between the parties is not precluded in the following circumstances:

(1) The party against whom preclusion is sought could not, as a matter of law, have obtained review of the judgment in the initial action; or

(2) The issue is one of law and (a) the two actions involve claims that are substantially unrelated, or (b) a new determination is warranted in order to take account of an intervening change in the applicable legal context or otherwise to avoid inequitable administration of the laws; or

(3) A new determination of the issue is warranted by differences in the quality or extensiveness of the procedures followed in the two courts or by factors relating to the allocation of jurisdiction between them; or

(4) The party against whom preclusion is sought had a significantly heavier burden of persuasion with respect to the issue in the initial action than in the subsequent action; the burden has shifted to his adversary; or the adversary has a significantly heavier burden than he had in the first action; or

(5) There is a clear and convincing need for a new determination of the issue (a) because of the potential adverse impact of the determination on the public interest or the interests of persons not themselves parties in the initial action, (b) because it was not sufficiently foreseeable at the time of the initial action that the issue would arise in the context of a subsequent action, or (c) because the party sought to be precluded, as a result of the conduct of his adversary or other special circumstances, did not have an adequate opportunity or incentive to obtain a full and fair adjudication in the initial action.

Note that some of the situations addressed by § 28 can be viewed either as exceptions or simply as situations in which the threshold requirements of issue preclusion are not satisfied. For example, the fourth exception, where the burden of persuasion differs, could be resolved by concluding that the cases do not involve the "same issue." See Note 5, p. 752 above. Similarly, exceptions 5(b) and (c) arguably involve situations where the issue in question was not actually litigated. Whether these cases are treated as exceptions or as part of the basic issue preclusion analysis has no effect on the outcome.

Problems

1. P sues D for products liability, seeking damages for injuries P suffered when using D's product. D counters with the affirmative defense of assumption of the risk. P prevails in a general verdict. When the product again injures P a few months later, P sues D again. Which of the following issues (if any) will be subject to issue preclusion?

    a. Whether the product was defective

    b. Whether P suffered injury

    c. Whether P assumed the risk

2. Same as Problem 1, except that P lost the case in a general verdict. Which of the issues (if any) will be subject to issue preclusion?

3. D is prosecuted for assaulting P. D is convicted after a full trial. P then brings a civil assault case against D. The elements of civil and criminal assault are identical. P argues that issue preclusion bars D from arguing that he did not assault P. Is P correct?

4. Same as Problem 3, except that D was acquitted in the criminal action. D argues that issue preclusion bars P from arguing that D assaulted P. Is D correct?

5. P sues D for damages for breach of contract. D's answer admits that there was a contract, but denies breach. P wins a general verdict at trial.

P now sues D again, arguing another breach of the same contract. This time, D denies that there was a contract. Will issue preclusion bar D from making this assertion?

6. P and D are competitors. P sues D for defamation in state court based on a statement that D made about P's product. D denies liability using a general denial. At trial, P offers extensive evidence that the statement was false, and of P's damages, none of which was contradicted by D. The parties contest only one issue: whether D knew the statement was false. The jury renders a general verdict for D.

P then sues D in federal court under a new federal false advertising statute. Because federal jurisdiction under this new statute is exclusive, claim preclusion does not apply. Unlike state defamation law, this federal statute makes a competitor liable for a false statement regardless of whether the party knew the statement was false. P therefore moves for summary judgment on the basis of issue preclusion. Will issue preclusion apply?

7. P, a "frequent flyer" with D airlines, suffers from a serious allergy to peanuts. Two years ago, P had a serious allergic reaction to a dish containing ground peanuts that he ate on one of D's flights. P sued D for negligence. In a bench trial, the judge entered judgment for D, specifically finding that D did not act negligently in serving a dish containing peanuts to P.

Last month, P suffered another peanut reaction on a flight operated by D. P again sues D for negligence. D moves for summary judgment, arguing that issue preclusion controls on the issue of whether it is negligent to serve peanuts on an airline. Is D correct?

8. D, a large nationwide fast food corporation, uses P, a shipping company, to deliver supplies to its many locations. P and D enter into separate contracts in each state in which P performs services. The wording of all these contracts is identical. Every contract contains a clause providing that it is "governed by the law of the state where P performs shipping services under this contract."

Rising fuel costs lead P to ask for an increase in its compensation under these contracts. D is sympathetic to P's plight, and agrees to amend all the contracts to increase the price paid to P. P provides no additional consideration for these amendments.

Several months after the amendments, P discovers that D has been paying only the old price under the contracts. P therefore sues D in Alabama, under the Alabama contract. D argues that the amendment is invalid because D received no additional consideration. P argues that under the provisions of the Uniform Commercial Code, which is in force in Alabama, no additional consideration is needed to amend a contract "between merchants." The court rules that P is not a merchant because it does not sell goods, and accordingly enters judgment for D.

P then brings another suit against D, also in Alabama. This time, however, the claim seeks compensation under all the *other* contracts. All of the states in question have adopted the Uniform Commercial Code provision that applied in the earlier case. D argues that issue preclusion controls on the question of whether P is a merchant. Is D correct?

9. P sues D for negligence. D argues both that she was not negligent, and that plaintiff's contributory negligence bars recovery. The case is submitted to the jury under a special verdict. The jury finds both that D was not negligent, and that P was negligent. The court therefore enters judgment for D. Which, if either, of these two rulings—D's negligence, or P's contributory negligence—will have issue preclusion effect in later litigation?

E.   PARTIES AFFECTED BY CLAIM AND ISSUE PRECLUSION

To this juncture, our discussion of claim preclusion and issue preclusion has assumed that the parties in Case One and Case Two are exactly the same. This section abandons that assumption, and explores the extent to which preclusion can apply when at least one of the parties has changed. The analysis differs significantly depending on whether the non-party in Case One is the person to be *bound* by preclusion, or whether that non-party is trying to take advantage of a victory in Case One.

INTRODUCTORY PROBLEM

Greasy Spoon operates a restaurant in the Southpark Mall. The lease for the store allows the Landlord to charge Greasy for the cost of all "maintenance" made necessary by Greasy's operations. Because Greasy specializes in high-fat, deep-fried food, its kitchen emits a great deal of smoke and grease spatters. Several customers have complained about the cloud of smoke and the slippery floors. Landlord therefore finds that it must undertake a major cleaning of the mall space near Greasy's store at least once a week.

When Landlord sends Greasy a bill for this cleanup, however, Greasy refuses to pay. Landlord therefore sues Greasy in state court for the cleanup costs. Greasy argues that because cleaning is not "maintenance," the maintenance cost clause does not apply. The jury renders a general verdict for Landlord.

Shortly after this lawsuit, Greasy assigns the lease to Splatterin' Suet, a national chain of restaurants. Splatterin' commences operations in the space. Because Splatterin's cooking methods are remarkably like those employed by Greasy, Landlord finds that the weekly cleanups are still necessary. When Splatterin' refuses to pay, however, Landlord commences another lawsuit against the new tenant.

Like Greasy before it, Splatterin' argues that cleaning is not maintenance. Landlord argues that Splatterin' is precluded by the earlier case from making this argument. Who is correct?

1.   Who is Bound by an Adverse Judgment?

The discussion of intervention, necessary parties, and interpleader in Chapter 6 demonstrated that litigation between two people can affect the rights of third parties. That Chapter focused on practical impairment of rights. Is it also possible for a judgment to effect a *legal* impairment of a non-party's rights, by precluding that party from litigating claims or issues resolved in the first case? As the following case indicates, the answer is "no" ... with one important, but somewhat amorphous, exception.

RICHARDS v. JEFFERSON COUNTY

517 U.S. 793, 116 S.Ct. 1761, 135 L.Ed.2d 76 (1996)

Justice STEVENS delivered the opinion of the Court. * * *

I

Jason Richards and Fannie Hill (petitioners) are privately employed in Jefferson County, Alabama. In 1991 they filed a complaint in the Federal District Court challenging the validity of the occupation tax imposed by Jefferson County Ordinance 1120, which had been adopted in 1987. That action was dismissed as barred by the Tax Injunction Act, 28 U.S.C. § 1341. They then commenced this action in the Circuit Court of Jefferson County.

Petitioners represent a class of all nonfederal employees subject to the county's tax. Petitioners alleged that the tax, which contains a lengthy list of exemptions, violates the Due Process and Equal Protection Clauses of the Fourteenth Amendment and similar provisions of the Alabama Constitution. * * *

The county moved for summary judgment on the ground that petitioners' claims were barred by a prior adjudication of the tax in an earlier action brought by the acting director of finance for the city of Birmingham and the city itself. That earlier action had been consolidated for trial with a separate suit brought by three county taxpayers, and the Supreme Court of Alabama upheld the tax in the resulting appeal. See *Bedingfield v. Jefferson County*, 527 So.2d 1270 (1988). After examining the course of this prior litigation, the trial court granted the county's motion for summary judgment as to the state constitutional claims, but refused to do so as to the federal claims because they had not been decided by either the trial court or the Alabama Supreme Court in *Bedingfield*.

On appeal, the county argued that the federal claims as well as the state claims were barred by the adjudication in *Bedingfield*. The Alabama Supreme Court agreed. The majority opinion noted that in Alabama, as in most States, a prior judgment on the merits rendered by a court of competent jurisdiction precludes the relitigation of a claim if there is a "substantial identity of the parties" and if the "same cause of action" is presented in both suits. 662 So.2d 1127, 1128 (1995). Moreover, the court explained, the prior judgment is generally " 'res judicata not only as to all matters litigated and decided by it, but as to all relevant issues which could have been but were not raised and litigated in the suit.' " *Ibid.* (quoting *Heiser v. Woodruff*, 327 U.S. 726, 735 (1946)).

The Alabama Supreme Court concluded that even though the opinion in *Bedingfield* did not mention any federal issue, the judgment in that case met these requirements. The court gave three reasons for this conclusion: (1) The complaints in the earlier case had alleged that the county tax violated the Equal Protection Clause of the Fourteenth Amendment and an equal protection issue had been argued in the appellate briefs; (2) the taxpayers in *Bedingfield* adequately represented petitioners because their respective interests were "essentially identical"; and (3) in pledging tax revenues and issuing bonds in 1989, the county and the intervenor "could have relied on *Bedingfield* as authoritatively establishing that the county occupational tax was not unconstitutional for the reasons asserted by the *Bedingfield plaintiffs*," 662 So.2d, at 1130. * * *

We now conclude that the State Supreme Court's holding that petitioners are bound by the adjudication in *Bedingfield* deprived them of the due process of law guaranteed by the Fourteenth Amendment.

II

State courts are generally free to develop their own rules for protecting against the relitigation of common issues or the piecemeal resolution of disputes. *Postal Telegraph Cable Co. v. Newport*, 247 U.S. 464, 475 (1918). We have long held, however, that extreme applications of the doctrine of res judicata may be inconsistent with a federal right that is "fundamental in character." *Id.*, at 476.

The limits on a state court's power to develop estoppel rules reflect the general consensus " 'in Anglo–American jurisprudence that one is not bound by a judgment in personam in a litigation in which he is not designated as a party or to which he has not been made a party by service of process.' *Hansberry v. Lee*, 311 U.S. 32, 40 (1940).... This rule is part of our 'deep-rooted historic tradition that everyone should have his own day in court.' 18 C. Wright, A. Miller, & E. Cooper, Federal Practice and Procedure § 4449, p. 417 (1981)." *Martin v. Wilks*, 490 U.S. 755, 761–762 (1989). As a consequence, "[a] judgment or decree among parties to a lawsuit resolves issues as among them, but it does not conclude the rights of strangers to those proceedings." *Id.*, at 762; *Blonder-Tongue Laboratories, Inc. v. University of Ill. Foundation*, 402 U.S. 313, 329 (1971).

Of course, these principles do not always require one to have been a party to a judgment in order to be bound by it. Most notably, there is an exception when it can be said that there is "privity" between a party to the second case and a party who is bound by an earlier judgment. For example, a judgment that is binding on a guardian or trustee may also bind the ward or the beneficiaries of a trust. Moreover, although there are clearly constitutional limits on the "privity" exception, the term "privity" is now used to describe various relationships between litigants that would not have come within the traditional definition of that term.

In addition, as we explained in *Wilks*:

"We have recognized an exception to the general rule when, in certain limited circumstances, a person, although not a party, has his interests adequately represented by someone with the same interests who is a party. See *Hansberry v. Lee*, 311 U.S. 32 (1940) 'class' or 'representative' suits); Fed. Rule Civ. Proc. 23 (same); *Montana v. United States*, 440 U.S. 147, 154–155 (1979) (control of litigation on behalf of one of the parties in the litigation). * * *

Here, the Alabama Supreme Court concluded that res judicata applied because petitioners were adequately represented in the *Bedingfield* action. We now consider the propriety of that determination.

III

We begin by noting that the parties to the *Bedingfield* case failed to provide petitioners with any notice that a suit was pending which would conclusively resolve their legal rights. That failure is troubling because, as we explained in *Mullane v. Central Hanover Bank & Trust Co.*, 339

U.S. 306 (1950), the right to be heard ensured by the guarantee of due process "has little reality or worth unless one is informed that the matter is pending and can choose for himself whether to appear or default, acquiesce or contest." *Id.*, at 314. Nevertheless, respondents ask us to excuse the lack of notice on the ground that petitioners, as the Alabama Supreme Court concluded, were adequately represented in *Bedingfield*.[5]

Our answer is informed by our decision in *Hansberry v. Lee*, 311 U.S., at 40–41. [As *Hansberry* is set out on page 432 of this book, the Court's discussion of the case is omitted.] * * * [We concluded] that because the interests of those class members who had been a party to the prior litigation were in conflict with the absent members who were the defendants in the subsequent action, the doctrine of representation of absent parties in a class suit could not support the decree.

Even assuming that our opinion in *Hansberry* may be read to leave open the possibility that in some class suits adequate representation might cure a lack of notice, it may not be read to permit the application of res judicata here. Our opinion explained that a prior proceeding, to have binding effect on absent parties, would at least have to be "so devised and applied as to insure that those present are of the same class as those absent and that the litigation is so conducted as to insure the full and fair consideration of the common issue." 311 U.S., at 43. It is plain that the *Bedingfield* action, like the prior proceeding in *Hansberry* itself, does not fit such a description.

The Alabama Supreme Court concluded that the "*taxpayers* in the *Bedingfield* action adequately represented the interests of the taxpayers here," 662 So.2d, at 1130 (emphasis added), but the three county taxpayers who were parties in *Bedingfield* did not sue on behalf of a class; their pleadings did not purport to assert any claim against or on behalf of any nonparties; and the judgment they received did not purport to bind any county taxpayers who were nonparties. That the acting director of finance for the city of Birmingham also sued in his capacity as both an individual taxpayer and a public official does not change the analysis. Even if we were to assume, as the Alabama Supreme Court did not, that by suing in his official capacity, the finance director intended to represent the pecuniary interests of all city taxpayers, and not simply the corporate interests of the city itself, he did not purport to represent the pecuniary interests of county taxpayers like petitioners.[6]

As a result, there is no reason to suppose that the *Bedingfield* court took care to protect the interests of petitioners in the manner suggested

---

5. Of course, mere notice may not suffice to preserve one's right to be heard in a case such as the one before us. The general rule is that "[t]he law does not impose upon any person absolutely entitled to a hearing the burden of voluntary intervention in a suit to which he is a stranger." *Chase Nat. Bank v. Norwalk*, 291 U.S. 431, 441 (1934); but *cf. Penn–Central Merger and N & W*

Inclusion Cases, 389 U.S. 486, 505, n. 4 (1968) (noting that absent parties were invited to intervene by the court).

6. We need not decide here whether public officials are always constitutionally adequate representatives of all persons over whom they have jurisdiction when, as here, the underlying right is personal in nature.

in *Hansberry*. Nor is there any reason to suppose that the individual taxpayers in *Bedingfield* understood their suit to be on behalf of absent county taxpayers. Thus, to contend that the plaintiffs in *Bedingfield* somehow represented petitioners, let alone represented them in a constitutionally adequate manner, would be "to attribute to them a power that it cannot be said that they had assumed to exercise." *Hansberry*, 311 U.S., at 46.

Because petitioners and the *Bedingfield* litigants are best described as mere "strangers" to one another, *Martin v. Wilks*, 490 U.S., at 762, we are unable to conclude that the *Bedingfield* plaintiffs provided representation sufficient to make up for the fact that petitioners neither participated in, see *Montana v. United States*, 440 U.S. 147 (1979), nor had the opportunity to participate in, the *Bedingfield* action. Accordingly, due process prevents the former from being bound by the latter's judgment. * * *

V

Because petitioners received neither notice of, nor sufficient representation in, the *Bedingfield* litigation, that adjudication, as a matter of federal due process, may not bind them and thus cannot bar them from challenging an allegedly unconstitutional deprivation of their property. Accordingly, the judgment of the Alabama Supreme Court is reversed, and the case is remanded to that court for further proceedings not inconsistent with this opinion.

Privity

As the Court in *Richards* acknowledges, it has long been recognized that a judgment in a case may bind a non-party who is in privity with one of the named parties to that case. If a person is in privity, both claim and issue preclusion apply in full, just as if the person had been a party to Case One. Privity survives the sort of due process challenge involved in *Richards* as long as the person's interests were adequately represented by one of the parties in the earlier case.

But what does the Court mean by "interest" and "adequate representation?" In a proper class action, it is easy to see how the parties are in privity. The legal claims of all members of the class are actually presented to the court, and the court makes a ruling with respect to each specific claim. What other sorts of relationships can result in privity? On this question there are basically two camps: courts that adhere to the *traditional* view, and those that follow a *functional* view.

Traditional view. The traditional view recognizes privity only when the party in Case Two is litigating essentially the same legal right as was litigated in Case One. At a minimum, there must be a legal relationship between the parties, such as a contract or guardianship. However, not all legal relationships will satisfy the test. Two people are in privity under the traditional approach only if they have *mutual* or *successive* interests in the same legal right.

Successive interests are relatively easy to identify. Suppose X sues Y for a missed payment on a note. X loses. If X conveys the note to Z, Z will also be bound by claim preclusion from suing Y on that payment, as X and Z have successive interests. Moreover, although Z is not barred by claim preclusion from suing for later payments, any issues decided by the court in the first case that are also relevant in the second (for example, a finding that the note is invalid) will also be binding on Z. In fact, the real property concept of easements and other interests "running with the land" is at its core grounded in notions of "successive interest" privity.

Mutual interests are more difficult to define. Here, the key is to look for a shared interest in the same thing. A landlord and a tenant have a mutual interest in the leased premises, and will therefore be in privity with respect to two cases involving that leased premises. Co-owners of property, however, do *not* have a mutual interest. Each co-owner owns a specific (even if undivided) separate share of the property. Similarly, partners in a partnership do not have a mutual interest in partnership property.

The Eighth Circuit's opinion in *Williams v. Marlar*, 267 F.3d 749 (8th Cir. 2001), provides a good example of how the traditional rule operates. In that case, a debtor transferred real estate to his son for ten dollars plus the "love and affection" between the two. During divorce proceedings, the debtor's soon-to-be ex-wife challenged the sale as a fraudulent conveyance (a fraudulent conveyance is a transfer of property by a debtor with the intent to prevent creditors from obtaining the property). The court found for the debtor. After this judgment, the debtor was forced into bankruptcy. The debtor owed money to several creditors, including his ex-wife. The trustee in bankruptcy sought to recover the same property, arguing that the conveyance to the son was a fraudulent conveyance.

Applying Arkansas law, the court held that the trustee in bankruptcy and the ex-wife had a *successive* relationship. The trustee serves as agent of the creditors, and succeeds to the debtor's rights to recover property. Had the ex-wife been the only creditor, the fraudulent conveyance claim would have been precluded. However, the debtor had two other creditors—a lender and the debtor's divorce attorney. The court held that the ex-wife (Davis) was *not* in privity with these other creditors (Farm Credit Services and Bradshaw):

> "Privity of parties within the meaning of res judicata means a person so identified in interest with another than he represents the same legal right." "[P]rivity denotes mutual or successive relationship to the same right of property." *Curry v. Hanna*, 228 Ark. 280, 307 S.W.2d 77, 79 (Ark. 1957). Although the three creditors may now share a common interest in setting aside the transfer, the unsecured claims of Bradshaw and Farm Credit Services derive from completely different transactions. They had no interest in the di-

vorce proceedings that gave rise to Davis's claim, and the reason Davis lost her state court action—her prior notice of the transfer to [the son] * * * in 1986—does not apply to subsequent creditors such as Bradshaw and Farm Credit Services.

Id. at 754. Because the trustee took over the claim of these creditors too, he could exercise their rights and recover the transferred property.

Functional view. Many courts have abandoned the traditional view in favor of the more modern and flexible functional view. Unlike the highly formalistic traditional view, which asks whether the "same legal right" is at stake in both cases, the functional view asks if the rights of the non-party were "fully and fairly represented" in the first action. The Ninth Circuit's decision in *Tahoe–Sierra Preservation Council, Inc. v. Tahoe Regional Planning Agency,* 322 F.3d 1064 (9th Cir. 2003) illustrates the modern approach. In this case, the court held that under federal preclusion law, a prior suit by an association barred later suits against the same defendant by members of the association:

> Even when the parties are not identical, privity may exist if "there is 'substantial identity' between parties, that is, when there is sufficient commonality of interest." *In re Gottheiner,* 703 F.2d 1136, 1140 (9th Cir.1983) (citation omitted). We made clear, in *In re Schimmels* [127 F.3d 875 (9th Cir. 1997)], that privity is a flexible concept dependent on the particular relationship between the parties in each individual set of cases:
>
> > Federal courts have deemed several relationships "sufficiently close" to justify a finding of "privity" and, therefore, preclusion under the doctrine of res judicata: "First, a non-party who has succeeded to a party's interest in property is bound by any prior judgment against the party. Second, a non-party who controlled the original suit will be bound by the resulting judgment. Third, federal courts will bind a non-party whose interests were represented adequately by a party in the original suit." In addition, "privity" has been found where there is a "substantial identity" between the party and nonparty, where the nonparty "had a significant interest and participated in the prior action," and where the interests of the nonparty and party are "so closely aligned as to be virtually representative." Finally, a relationship of privity can be said to exist when there is an "express or implied legal relationship by which parties to the first suit are accountable to non-parties who file a subsequent suit with identical issues."

Schimmels, 127 F.3d at 881 (citations omitted); *see also Alpert's Newspaper Delivery Inc. v. N.Y. Times Co.,* 876 F.2d 266, 270 (2d Cir.1989) ("The issue is one of substance rather than the names in the caption of the case; the inquiry is not limited to a traditional privity analysis."); *ITT Rayonier,* 627 F.2d at 1003 ("Courts are no longer bound by rigid definitions of parties or their privies for purposes of applying collateral estoppel or res judicata.").

One of the relationships that has been deemed "sufficiently close" to justify a finding of privity is that of an organization or unincorporated association filing suit on behalf of its members. Of course, the organization must adequately represent the interests of its individual members if its representation is to satisfy the due process concerns articulated in *Hansberry v. Lee*, 311 U.S. 32, 40–43 (1940).
* * *

In this case, all of the remaining individual plaintiffs are members of the Association, and given the history and nature of this litigation, their membership in and close relationship with the Association is sufficient to bind them as parties in privity for res judicata purposes.
* * *

322 F.2d at 1081–82.

Another way to view the functional approach is to ask whether the party in Case One, by looking out for her own personal interests, also by default fully protected the interests of the non-party.

Notes and Questions

1. In *Andrews v. Daw*, 201 F.3d 521 (4th Cir. 2000), a driver sued a state police officer in the officer's official capacity. By suing the officer in his official capacity, the driver hoped that the state would be liable to pay any judgment rendered in the case. However, the court dismissed the action based on the officer's Eleventh Amendment immunity. The driver then brought an action against the same officer, this time suing the officer in his *individual* capacity. Although the driver could not recover against the state by suing the officer individually, the case would not be barred by the Eleventh Amendment. The court of appeals held that claim preclusion did not apply because there was no privity between the defendants in the two cases. How can someone not be in privity with *himself*? Or is that question too simplistic?

2. Now turn to *Richards*. Before considering the finer details of the Supreme Court's opinion, try to reconstruct the argument of the Alabama courts. Why did the state courts consider it proper to bar the plaintiffs' claims with a judgment in a suit in which they were not named parties? Is the Alabama court applying one of the privity tests described above? Or was its reasoning based on general notions of fairness?

3. What effect does *Richards* have on the functional view of privity?

4. Might *Richards* even pose a threat to some situations in which the courts would find privity under the traditional rule? Consider the case of successive interests in land. Is a buyer of land bound by an earlier judgment concerning that land? Note that *Richards* focuses on *notice* to the non-party. How can you give notice to everyone who might later decide to buy the land?

5. The *Restatement* does not attempt to define privity. Instead, eschewing that term altogether, the *Restatement* simply lists a number of situations in which non-parties may be bound by the judgment in a case. *See* RESTATE-

MENT OF THE LAW (SECOND): JUDGMENTS §§ 36 to 61. Overall, however, the *Restatement* approach closely resembles the functional view.

6. *Control.* Even absent any sort of formal legal relationship between a non-party and a party, a non-party can be bound by a judgment if she effectively controlled how one party litigated Case One. *Montana v. United States*, 440 U.S. 147, 99 S.Ct. 970, 59 L.Ed.2d 210 (1979) (United States bound by issue preclusion where it both financed and directed course of litigation on behalf of a private party); RESTATEMENT OF THE LAW (SECOND): JUDGMENTS § 39.

2. Who Can Take Advantage of a Judgment?

As the prior section indicates, the due process clause places significant limits on a state's ability to use a judgment to preclude a non-party from later litigating a claim or issue. But does anything preclude a non-party from taking *advantage* of a favorable ruling in an earlier case? For example, suppose Diner recovers a judgment against Restaurant for food poisoning. Can Diner 2, who ate at the same restaurant the same evening, take advantage of that judgment in her own suit against Restaurant? Due process is not a bar, because the party to be bound— Restaurant—has already had a full and fair opportunity to protect itself. Nevertheless, is there something unfair about letting Diner 2 ride on Diner 1's coattails?

PARKLANE HOSIERY CO., INC. v. SHORE

439 U.S. 322, 99 S.Ct. 645, 58 L.Ed.2d 552 (1979)

Mr. Justice SWEWART delivered the opinion of the Court.

This case presents the question whether a party who has had issues of fact adjudicated adversely to it in an equitable action may be collaterally estopped from relitigating the same issues before a jury in a subsequent legal action brought against it by a new party.

The respondent brought this stockholder's class action against the petitioners in a Federal District Court. The complaint alleged that the petitioners, Parklane Hosiery Co., Inc. (Parklane), and 13 of its officers, directors, and stockholders, had issued a materially false and misleading proxy statement in connection with a merger. * * * The complaint sought damages, rescission of the merger, and recovery of costs.

Before this action came to trial, the SEC filed suit against the same defendants in the Federal District Court, alleging that the proxy statement that had been issued by Parklane was materially false and misleading in essentially the same respects as those that had been alleged in the respondent's complaint. Injunctive relief was requested. After a 4–day trial, the District Court found that the proxy statement was materially false and misleading in the respects alleged, and entered a declaratory judgment to that effect. The Court of Appeals for the Second Circuit affirmed this judgment.

The respondent in the present case then moved for partial summary judgment against the petitioners, asserting that the petitioners were collaterally estopped from relitigating the issues that had been resolved against them in the action brought by the SEC. The District Court denied the motion on the ground that such an application of collateral estoppel would deny the petitioners their Seventh Amendment right to a jury trial. The Court of Appeals for the Second Circuit reversed, holding that a party who has had issues of fact determined against him after a full and fair opportunity to litigate in a nonjury trial is collaterally estopped from obtaining a subsequent jury trial of these same issues of fact. The appellate court concluded that "the Seventh Amendment preserves the right to jury trial only with respect to issues of fact, [and] once those issues have been fully and fairly adjudicated in a prior proceeding, nothing remains for trial, either with or without a jury."
* * *

I

The threshold question to be considered is whether, quite apart from the right to a jury trial under the Seventh Amendment, the petitioners can be precluded from relitigating facts resolved adversely to them in a prior equitable proceeding with another party under the general law of collateral estoppel. Specifically, we must determine whether a litigant who was not a party to a prior judgment may nevertheless use that judgment "offensively" to prevent a defendant from relitigating issues resolved in the earlier proceeding.[4]

A

Collateral estoppel, like the related doctrine of res judicata, has the dual purpose of protecting litigants from the burden of relitigating an identical issue with the same party or his privy and of promoting judicial economy by preventing needless litigation. *Blonder-Tongue Laboratories, Inc. v. University of Illinois Foundation,* 402 U.S. 313, 328–329. Until relatively recently, however, the scope of collateral estoppel was limited by the doctrine of mutuality of parties. Under this mutuality doctrine, neither party could use a prior judgment as an estoppel against the other unless both parties were bound by the judgment. Based on the premise that it is somehow unfair to allow a party to use a prior judgment when he himself would not be so bound,[7] the mutuality requirement provided a party who had litigated and lost in a previous action an opportunity to relitigate identical issues with new parties.

---

4. In this context, offensive use of collateral estoppel occurs when the plaintiff seeks to foreclose the defendant from litigating an issue the defendant has previously litigated unsuccessfully in an action with another party. Defensive use occurs when a defendant seeks to prevent a plaintiff from asserting a claim the plaintiff has previously litigated and lost against another defendant.

7. It is a violation of due process for a judgment to be binding on a litigant who was not a party or a privy and therefore has never had an opportunity to be heard. *Blonder-Tongue Laboratories, Inc. v. University of Illinois Foundation,* 402 U.S. 313, 329; *Hansberry v. Lee,* 311 U. S. 32, 40.

By failing to recognize the obvious difference in position between a party who has never litigated an issue and one who has fully litigated and lost, the mutuality requirement was criticized almost from its inception. Recognizing the validity of this criticism, the Court in *Blonder–Tongue Laboratories, Inc. v. University of Illinois Foundation, supra*, abandoned the mutuality requirement, at least in cases where a patentee seeks to relitigate the validity of a patent after a federal court in a previous lawsuit has already declared it invalid. The "broader question" before the Court, however, was "whether it is any longer tenable to afford a litigant more than one full and fair opportunity for judicial resolution of the same issue." 402 U.S., at 328. The Court strongly suggested a negative answer to that question:

> "In any lawsuit where a defendant, because of the mutuality principle, is forced to present a complete defense on the merits to a claim which the plaintiff has fully litigated and lost in a prior action, there is an arguable misallocation of resources. * * * Permitting repeated litigation of the same issue as long as the supply of unrelated defendants holds out reflects either the aura of the gaming table or 'a lack of discipline and of disinterestedness on the part of the lower courts, hardly a worthy or wise basis for fashioning rules of procedure.' *Kerotest Mfg. Co. v. C–O–Two Co.*, 342 U.S. 180, 185 (1952). Although neither judges, the parties, nor the adversary system performs perfectly in all cases, the requirement of determining whether the party against whom an estoppel is asserted had a full and fair opportunity to litigate is a most significant safeguard." *Id.*, at 329.

B

The *Blonder–Tongue* case involved defensive use of collateral estoppel—a plaintiff was estopped from asserting a claim that the plaintiff had previously litigated and lost against another defendant. The present case, by contrast, involves offensive use of collateral estoppel—a plaintiff is seeking to estop a defendant from relitigating the issues which the defendant previously litigated and lost against another plaintiff. In both the offensive and defensive use situations, the party against whom estoppel is asserted has litigated and lost in an earlier action. Nevertheless, several reasons have been advanced why the two situations should be treated differently.

First, offensive use of collateral estoppel does not promote judicial economy in the same manner as defensive use does. Defensive use of collateral estoppel precludes a plaintiff from relitigating identical issues by merely "switching adversaries." Thus defensive collateral estoppel gives a plaintiff a strong incentive to join all potential defendants in the first action if possible. Offensive use of collateral estoppel, on the other hand, creates precisely the opposite incentive. Since a plaintiff will be able to rely on a previous judgment against a defendant but will not be bound by that judgment if the defendant wins, the plaintiff has every incentive to adopt a "wait and see" attitude, in the hope that the first action by another plaintiff will result in a favorable judgment. Thus offensive use of collateral estoppel will likely increase rather than decrease the total amount of litigation, since potential plaintiffs will have everything to gain and nothing to lose by not intervening in the first action.

A second argument against offensive use of collateral estoppel is that it may be unfair to a defendant. If a defendant in the first action is sued for small or nominal damages, he may have little incentive to defend vigorously, particularly if future suits are not foreseeable. Allowing offensive collateral estoppel may also be unfair to a defendant if the judgment relied upon as a basis for the estoppel is itself inconsistent with one or more previous judgments in favor of the defendant.[14] Still another situation where it might be unfair to apply offensive estoppel is where the second action affords the defendant procedural opportunities unavailable in the first action that could readily cause a different result.[15]

C

We have concluded that the preferable approach for dealing with these problems in the federal courts is not to preclude the use of offensive collateral estoppel, but to grant trial courts broad discretion to determine when it should be applied. The general rule should be that in cases where a plaintiff could easily have joined in the earlier action or where, either for the reasons discussed above or for other reasons, the application of offensive estoppel would be unfair to a defendant, a trial judge should not allow the use of offensive collateral estoppel.

In the present case, however, none of the circumstances that might justify reluctance to allow the offensive use of collateral estoppel is present. The application of offensive collateral estoppel will not here reward a private plaintiff who could have joined in the previous action, since the respondent probably could not have joined in the injunctive action brought by the SEC even had he so desired. Similarly, there is no unfairness to the petitioners in applying offensive collateral estoppel in this case. First, in light of the serious allegations made in the SEC's complaint against the petitioners, as well as the foreseeability of subsequent private suits that typically follow a successful Government judgment, the petitioners had every incentive to litigate the SEC lawsuit

---

14. In Professor Currie's familiar example, a railroad collision injures 50 passengers all of whom bring separate actions against the railroad. After the railroad wins the first 25 suits, a plaintiff wins in suit 26. Professor Currie argues that offensive use of collateral estoppel should not be applied so as to allow plaintiffs 27 through 50 automatically to recover.

15. If, for example, the defendant in the first action was forced to defend in an inconvenient forum and therefore was unable to engage in full scale discovery or call witnesses, application of offensive collateral estoppel may be unwarranted. Indeed, differences in available procedures may sometimes justify not allowing a prior judgment to have estoppel effect in a subsequent action even between the same parties, or where defensive estoppel is asserted against a plaintiff who has litigated and lost. The problem of unfairness is particularly acute in cases of offensive estoppel, however, because the defendant against whom estoppel is asserted typically will not have chosen the forum in the first action.

fully and vigorously. Second, the judgment in the SEC action was not inconsistent with any previous decision. Finally, there will in the respondent's action be no procedural opportunities available to the petitioners that were unavailable in the first action of a kind that might be likely to cause a different result.[19]

We conclude, therefore, that none of the considerations that would justify a refusal to allow the use of offensive collateral estoppel is present in this case. Since the petitioners received a "full and fair" opportunity to litigate their claims in the SEC action, the contemporary law of collateral estoppel leads inescapably to the conclusion that the petitioners are collaterally estopped from relitigating the question of whether the proxy statement was materially false and misleading. * * *

[The Court also held that giving issue preclusion effect to the SEC proceeding—where there was no right to a jury—did not violate the Seventh Amendment, even though in the case at bar the defendant would otherwise have been entitled to a jury on the precluded issues.]

[The dissenting opinion of Justice REHNQUIST is omitted.]

Notes and Questions

1. Historically, courts required full mutuality for both claim and issue preclusion. The trend to relax the mutuality requirement has mainly affected only issue preclusion. Although courts have occasionally suggested that mutuality should be abandoned for all types of preclusion, most courts still require mutuality in claim preclusion. Do you see why?

2. Privity is an exception to the mutuality rule. If X and Y are in privity, Y is not only bound by any judgment against X, but can also take advantage of any victory for X.

3. Most courts allow defensive use of non-mutual issue preclusion with few limits. However, like the court in *Parklane*, they are more wary of offensive use. There are two basic arguments against offensive use. What are these arguments? Do you find them convincing? Why do these arguments not also apply to defensive use?

4. Note that the labels "offensive" and "defensive" are important only where *non-mutual* use of issue preclusion is involved. If the same parties (or their privies) are involved in both cases, it makes no difference whether the person is trying to use issue preclusion offensively or defensively.

5. Although *Parklane* technically only established the federal law governing mutuality, the Court's reasoning has had a tremendous influence on the state courts. Most states allow offensive non-mutual use along the lines established in *Parklane. See, e.g., Hossler v. Barry*, 403 A.2d 762 (Me. 1979) (adopts similar rule for Maine, relying heavily on *Parklane.*)

---

19. It is true, of course, that the petitioners in the present action would be entitled to a jury trial of the issues bearing on whether the proxy statement was materially false and misleading had the SEC action never been brought * * *. But the presence or absence of a jury as factfinder is basically neutral, quite unlike, for example, the necessity of defending the first lawsuit in an inconvenient forum.

6. Non-mutual issue preclusion may not be used against the United States government. *United States v. Mendoza*, 464 U.S. 154, 104 S.Ct. 568, 78 L.Ed.2d 379 (1984). Because the federal government deals with the public at large, and litigates a large number of cases every year, the Court in *Mendoza* indicated that applying the normal rules allowing non-mutual use would force the government to seek appellate review of every unfavorable decision. 464 U.S. at 163.

7. The marriage of two modern doctrines—the abandonment of mutuality and the tort doctrine of comparative fault—creates some interesting problems. Suppose that several passengers are injured in a bus crash. P1, one of the passengers, sues D, the bus operator, for her injuries. The court finds D 30 percent at fault, and the manufacturer of the bus 70 percent at fault. Then another passenger, P2, sues D. Can D argue that it is less than 30 percent at fault? Is P2 precluded from trying to prove that D is *more* than 30 percent at fault? Can D argue that P2 was also responsible for his injuries, thereby rendering D's percentage less than 30?

Problems

1. P is injured in an automobile accident. The other vehicle was driven by D and owned by O. P sues D for negligence. In a bench trial, the court enters judgment for D, specifically finding that P was 100% at fault. P then sues O for the same injuries, arguing that O failed to maintain the brakes on the vehicle. O argues that the claim is barred by claim preclusion. Is O correct?

2. Same facts as Problem 1, except that O argues that issue preclusion, not claim preclusion, applies. Is O correct?

3. Same facts as Problem 1, except that D is O's employee. In P's suit against O, P argues that O is vicariously liable for D's careless driving. If the court does not apply preclusion, what problem may arise?

4. P1 and P2 are partners in a general partnership. P1 sues D, alleging that D misappropriated valuable partnership trade secrets. D prevails. P2 then sues D, alleging the same claim. D argues that P2's case is barred by claim and issue preclusion. P2 argues that she cannot be barred because she was not a party in the first case. Who is correct?

5. Same facts as Problem 4, except assume that P1 prevailed in his action against D. When P2 sues D, D alleges that the case is barred by claim preclusion. P2 argues both that claim preclusion does not apply, and that issue preclusion bars *D* from arguing that he did not misappropriate the secrets. Who is correct?

F. APPLYING PRECLUSION ACROSS STATE LINES

INTRODUCTORY PROBLEM

Dan Debtor deeply regrets his recent purchase of aluminum siding. Dan was pressured into buying the siding from Carol Creditor, a door-to-door aluminum siding salesperson. Carol stopped by unannounced at Dan's house in the state of Dakota, and won Dan over with her high-pressure sales techniques. Dan eventually signed a contract to purchase siding and pay for it in installments. As soon as Carol left with the signed contract, however, Dan wanted out of the deal. Unfortunately for Dan, the contract did not allow for cancellation.

Two months later, Dan regrets his decision even more. The aluminum siding that Carol installed blocks all radio and television signals into Dan's home. Deprived of his daily dose of soap operas, Dan refuses to pay the remaining installments.

Carol immediately sues Dan in a state court in the state of Carolina, Carol's home state. Dan's answer denies liability, invoking the Dakota Consumer Protection Act. The Dakota act reflects Dakota's strong public policy of protecting innocent consumers, especially in their own home. Under the act, all contracts made pursuant to door-to-door sales are void unless they contain a clause explicitly giving the buyer a right to cancel the contract for 10 days. Because the Carol–Dan contract contained no such clause, it is clearly invalid under the Dakota act.

The Carolina court, however, rejects Dan's defense. It instead concludes that *Carolina* law governs the contract between Carol and Dan. This ruling is clearly incorrect as a matter of Carolina choice of law rules, and may even be unconstitutional. Nevertheless, because Carolina law does not have a consumer protection statute, the court enters summary judgment for Carol on her breach of contract claim.

Of course, Dan has no assets in Carolina. Carol therefore brings a new suit in a Dakota court, hoping to obtain a judgment and thereby seize Dan's Dakota assets. In this second action, Carol argues that claim and issue preclusion bar Dan from relitigating the merits of the case in the Dakota court. Is Carol correct?

Governing law: United States Constitution, art. IV, sec. 1; 28 U.S.C. § 1738.

––––––––––––

To this point we have been dealing with how preclusion applies within a given court system. Do the same rules apply when Case One and Case Two are in different jurisdictions? If a state was free to ignore judgments rendered by the courts of other states, the resulting multiplicity of cases would not only be inefficient, but would also threaten to weaken the United States federal system. Anticipating the possibility that states might choose to ignore judgments of other states, the framers of the Constitution included Article IV, § 1:

> Full Faith and Credit shall be given in each State to the public Acts, Records, and judicial Proceedings of every other State. And the Congress may by general Laws prescribe the Manner in which such

Acts, Records, and Proceedings shall be proved, and the Effect thereof.

There is some debate as to exactly what this clause was meant to accomplish. One scholar, in an exhaustive historical study, concluded that it was simply a rule of *evidence* requiring courts to admit written judgments as evidence without further authentication. Ralph U. Whitten, *The Constitutional Limitations on State–Court Jurisdiction: A Historical–Interpretative Reexamination of the Full Faith and Credit and Due Process Clauses (Part One)*, 14 CREIGHTON L. REV. 499 (1981); Ralph U. Whitten, *The Constitutional Limitations on State–Court Jurisdiction: A Historical–Interpretative Reexamination of the Full Faith and Credit and Due Process Clauses (Part Two)*, 14 CREIGHTON L. REV. 735 (1981). Although Professor Whitten may well be correct, the courts have uniformly interpreted the "full faith and credit" clause as a command to give a certain degree of preclusive effect to sister-state judgments, as the following case demonstrates.

SENTINEL ACCEPTANCE LTD., L.P. v. HODSON AUTO SALES & LEASING, INC.

45 S.W.3d 464 (Mo. App. 2001)

BRECKENRIDGE, Judge.

Sentinel Acceptance, Ltd., L.P., appeals the trial court's judgment quashing the registration of its California judgment against Janet R. Hodson. On appeal, Sentinel argues that the trial court quashed the registration of its judgment on an improper ground. * * *

FACTUAL AND PROCEDURAL BACKGROUND

On March 8, 1999, the Superior Court for the State of California, County of San Diego, entered a judgment confirming an arbitration award in the amount of $16,052.11 in favor of Sentinel and against Hodson Auto Sales & Leasing, Inc., and Ms. Hodson, who was president of Hodson Auto Sales. In June 1999, the attorney for Sentinel filed an affidavit for registration of the California judgment in the Circuit Court of Clay County, Missouri. On April 6, 2000, Sentinel requested that a garnishment order be issued against Hodson Auto Sales and Ms. Hodson to satisfy the judgment.

Ms. Hodson's bank notified Ms. Hodson of the garnishment order on April 14, 2000. On April 20, 2000, Ms. Hodson filed a motion to quash registration of the foreign judgment, executions, and garnishments. Ms. Hodson alleged in her motion that the California judgment was not entitled to full faith and credit because the California court lacked personal jurisdiction over her, and she received no notice of the California proceedings. * * * Ms. Hodson later filed a motion for relief from the California judgment in which she argued that the registration of the California judgment should be set aside under Rule 74.06(b)(1) on the basis of surprise. Specifically, Ms. Hodson alleged that the arbitration and confirmation proceedings in California were a "complete and total surprise" to her, as was the registration of the California judgment in Clay County. Alternatively, Ms. Hodson argued that the judgment should be set aside under Rule 74.06(b)(1) on the basis of excusable neglect, because her California counsel abandoned her.

At the subsequent hearing on Ms. Hodson's motions, she testified that she was the president of Hodson Auto Sales. Ms. Hodson allowed her husband, William E. Hodson, to handle the day-to-day details of running the corporation. Ms. Hodson was employed as a realtor, and maintained an office at a different location than Hodson Auto Sales.

Ms. Hodson testified that she was never personally served with any documents relating to the California arbitration or confirmation proceedings. In fact, she testified that she was completely unaware of both proceedings, despite the fact that attorneys in California entered their appearance on her behalf and filed a response to Sentinel's petition to confirm the arbitration award, which contained a supporting affidavit from Ms. Hodson's husband. Ms. Hodson testified that her husband never told her she had been named in a lawsuit in California. She claimed that she never hired the attorneys in California to represent her, nor did she have any knowledge that the attorneys had been retained to represent her. In support of her testimony, Ms. Hodson offered the affidavit of one of the California attorneys, in which he averred that his only contact regarding the proceedings in California was with Mr. Hodson and Mr. Hodson's Kansas City attorney, and that his first contact with Ms. Hodson was on April 21, 2000.

On May 9, 2000, the trial court entered a judgment sustaining Ms. Hodson's motion to quash the registration of the California judgment. The court found that Rule 74.14, which pertains to the uniform enforcement of foreign judgments, provides that once a foreign judgment is filed in Missouri, it "has the same effect and is subject to the same procedures, defenses, and proceedings for reopening, vacating, or staying" as a judgment entered in Missouri. The court then ruled that a party could obtain relief from the judgment on one of the grounds set forth in Rule 74.06(b), which was surprise.

On the issue of surprise, the court found that although the filing of the foreign judgment complied with the requirements of Rule 74.14, the underlying claim was unknown to Ms. Hodson because she was not served with process in the California confirmation proceeding, and all actions purportedly taken on her behalf and in her name in California were "wholly undertaken without her knowledge, consent or authority." Because it found that Ms. Hodson suffered a legal injury as to which she was totally free of neglect or lack of prudence, the court quashed the registration of the California judgment against her. Sentinel filed this appeal. * * *

SURPRISE IS IMPROPER GROUND FOR REFUSING TO REGISTER A FOREIGN JUDGMENT

In its sole point on appeal, Sentinel argues that the trial court erred in quashing registration of the California judgment because surprise is not a proper ground for refusing to give full faith and credit to a foreign judgment. To qualify for registration in Missouri, a foreign judgment must be "entitled to full faith and credit under the Full Faith and Credit Clause of the Federal Constitution, Art. 4, § 1." *Campbell v. Campbell*, 780 S.W.2d 89, 91 (Mo.App.1989). The Full Faith and Credit Clause provides that, "Full Faith and Credit shall be given in each State to the Public Acts, Records, and Judicial Proceedings of every other State." U.S. CONST. art. IV, § 1. Legal historians have inferred that the Constitutional Framers' purpose of including the Full Faith and Credit Clause in the Constitution was to "impose [ ] mandatory comity on the states in the hope that treating the judicial proceedings of other states with appropriate deference would lessen friction among the states in the new and fragile union." William L. Reynolds, *The Iron Law of Full Faith and Credit*, 53 MD. L.REV. 412, 413 (1994) (footnotes omitted). Indeed, the United States Supreme Court "has held that the Full Faith and Credit Clause demands rigorous obedience." *Id.* (citing *Fauntleroy v. Lum*, 210 U.S. 230, 237 (1908)).

There are only a few recognized exceptions to this long-standing Constitutional requirement of according full faith and credit to judgments of sister states. * * * [T]he Missouri Supreme Court recently reiterated those exceptions. In *Phillips v. Fallen*, 6 S.W.3d 862, 864 (Mo. banc 1999), the Court stated that "Missouri is obligated to give full faith and credit to a judgment of a sister state unless that judgment is void for lack of jurisdiction over the person or over the subject matter, or is obtained by fraud."

Rather than denying full faith and credit on any of these recognized exceptions, however, the trial court in this case quashed registration of the California judgment on the basis of surprise under Rule 74.06(b). To do so, the trial court relied on the statement in Rule 74.14(b) that a foreign judgment registered in Missouri "is subject to the same procedures, defenses, and proceedings for reopening, vacating, or staying as a judgment of a circuit court of this state." The trial court reasoned that since parties may obtain relief from Missouri judgments on any of the grounds listed in Rule 74.06, parties can also obtain relief from foreign judgments on any of these grounds.

The statement in Rule 74.14 that a foreign judgment registered in Missouri is subject to the same defenses as a judgment entered in Missouri refers only to the Missouri judgment registering the foreign judgment, however, and not to the actual judgment entered in the foreign state. To find otherwise, as the trial court did, would significantly broaden the exceptions to the Full Faith and Credit Clause. Under the trial court's interpretation of Rule 74.14, a Missouri court could refuse to register a foreign judgment if it finds mistake, inadvertence, surprise, excusable neglect, intrinsic or extrinsic fraud, misrepresentation, or misconduct of an adverse party; or that the judgment is irregular, void, or has been satisfied, released, or discharged, or that a prior judgment upon which it is based has been reversed or vacated; or it is no longer equitable that the judgment remain in force. Rule 74.06(b).

Broadening the exceptions to the registering of a foreign judgment to include all of the grounds for obtaining relief under Rule 74.06 is not compatible with Missouri Supreme Court case law applying the deeply-rooted Constitutional principle that courts of this state are obligated to give full faith and credit to a foreign judgment unless the judgment is void for lack of personal or subject matter jurisdiction, or it was obtained by fraud. Furthermore, this court notes that Phillips, the Missouri Supreme Court's most recent pronouncement of the exceptions to giving full faith and credit to foreign judgments, was decided eleven years after the effective date of Rules 74.06 and 74.14. The Court in *Phillips* did not recognize surprise, or any of the grounds listed in Rule 74.06, as a basis for refusing to register a foreign judgment. Therefore, this court finds that the trial court erred in quashing registration of the California judgment on the basis of surprise.

In her brief, however, Ms. Hodson contends that this court should affirm the trial court's judgment anyway because she was not properly served with process in the California proceeding and, therefore, the California judgment was void for lack of personal jurisdiction over her. * * *

At trial, however, the only theory upon which Ms. Hodson's counsel proceeded was whether registration of the California judgment should be quashed on the basis of surprise. * * * Ms. Hodson abandoned her personal jurisdiction claim in favor of her claim of surprise. Ms. Hodson's failure to obtain a ruling from the trial court regarding her claim that the California judgment was void for lack of personal jurisdiction precludes appellate review of the issue.* * *

Moreover, even if this court were to find that Ms. Hodson did not abandon her claim that the California judgment was void for lack of personal jurisdiction, the issue of personal jurisdiction was adjudicated in the California proceeding. "However, when the party litigates the issue of jurisdiction in the initial court proceedings, that court's determination on the issue, right or wrong, is conclusive upon that party and entitled to full faith and credit." [*Williams v. Williams*, 997 S.W.2d 80, 83 (Mo.App. 1999)].

Notes and Questions

1. *Sentinel Acceptance* deals with the situation where a party attempts to use a judgment from one forum (F1) in order to reach assets in another forum (F2). The F1 judgment is not itself enforceable in F2. Instead, the judgment victor must "domesticate" the judgment. Domestication involves using the F1 judgment as the basis for obtaining a new judgment from the courts of F2.

Historically, the only way to domesticate a judgment was to bring a new action in the courts of F2. Because this new action is a suit on the judgment rather than the underlying claim, it is not barred by claim preclusion. Moreover, to the extent that full faith and credit applies, the judgment victor may use issue preclusion to avoid having to relitigate the case. The F2 case can often be resolved on the pleadings or by summary judgment.

Today, most states have enacted the Uniform Enforcement of Foreign Judgments Act. This act provides a process by which a judgment of one Uniform Act state can simply be registered in any other Uniform Act state. Assuming the person complies with the filing and notice requirements, the registered judgment is treated as a new F2 judgment, and can be enforced accordingly in F2. This process saves the time and expense of prosecuting a new action in F2.

2.   Nothing in the facts of *Sentinel Acceptance* suggests that Ms Hodson received any sort of notice of the California proceeding. Nevertheless, the Missouri court holds that it is bound by full faith and credit to enforce the California judgment. Is the command of full faith and credit so powerful that it overrides the fairness concerns inherent in due process? Is there *anything* that Ms Hodson can do to avoid having her assets garnished? Did she file her motion to reopen the judgment in the wrong court?

3.   In *Sentinel Acceptance*, what if the judgment of the California court was patently incorrect? Could the Missouri court refuse to recognize it?

4.   *Fauntleroy v. Lum*, 210 U.S. 230, 28 S.Ct. 641, 52 L.Ed. 1039 (1908), which is cited in *Sentinel Acceptance*, demonstrates how powerful the command of full faith and credit to judgments is. In that case, a party brought suit in a Missouri state court based on a gambling contract that had arisen in Mississippi. Under Mississippi law, the contract was illegal and therefore unenforceable. The Missouri court, however, refused to apply Mississippi law, and entered judgment for the plaintiff. When plaintiff took that judgment to Mississippi to enforce it against defendant, the Mississippi courts refused to enforce it. The Supreme Court reversed, holding that full faith and credit required Mississippi to honor the judgment even though the Missouri court had refused to apply Mississippi law. As a result, the Mississippi courts had to allow plaintiff to use their courts to collect a debt that was clearly illegal in Mississippi.

5.   If all this discussion of "enforcing judgments" sounds vaguely familiar, you should not be surprised. Full faith and credit also lies at the heart of the doctrine of personal jurisdiction in Chapter 4. In the watershed case of *Pennoyer v. Neff* on page 122, the issue was whether one court had to enforce an earlier judgment of a court that did not have personal jurisdiction.

6.   In *Sentinel Acceptance*, the plaintiff won in F1. Full faith and credit also applies if a plaintiff loses the first action. Thus, a plaintiff who loses a case in F1 is barred by full faith and credit and claim preclusion from filing that claim, or another claim arising from the same transaction or occurrence, in another state. In addition, because a plaintiff consents to jurisdiction by choosing the court, a plaintiff who loses in F1 will usually be unable to escape full faith and credit by arguing that F1 lacked personal jurisdiction.

7.   *"Last in time" rule.* Suppose X sues Y for a tort in F1. X loses. X then sues Y for that same tort in F2. The F2 court wrongfully denies full faith and credit to the F1 judgment, and grants X a money judgment. X

seeks to enforce that judgment against property in F3 by bringing a new action in that forum. Which judgment is entitled to full faith and credit in F3—the first or second? Under the "last in time" rule, it is the *F2* judgment that receives full faith and credit. Although the F2 court clearly erred in failing to afford full faith and credit, Y's remedy is to appeal the judgment, not to attack it collaterally in the F3 action. Robert A. Leflar, Luther L. McDougal III, & Robert L. Felix, *American Conflicts Law* 242 (4th ed. 1986).

8. In the situation posed in the prior note, suppose that X takes his F2 judgment back to *F1* for enforcement. Is F1 relieved of its full faith and credit obligation when F2 ignored a F1 judgment? *Treinies v. Sunshine Mining Co.*, 308 U.S. 66, 60 S.Ct. 44, 84 L.Ed. 85 (1939) indicates that there is no exception. Technically, *Treinies* is not controlling on the question posed in this note, for in that case the F2 courts held that the F1 courts lacked jurisdiction to render the first judgment. Nevertheless, it is generally accepted that the last in time rule applies even when the second court flatly refused to apply full faith and credit. Again, Y's remedy is to appeal the F2 judgment.

9. *Federal judgments.* Review the full faith and credit clause, set out at the outset of this section. Does the mandate apply to federal courts that are asked to enforce state judgments? Conversely, does the clause require state courts to enforce judgments rendered by federal courts? Because the clause as written applies only to state courts and state judgments, Congress enacted 28 U.S.C. § 1738. That statute extends the full faith and credit obligation to the federal courts. Congress's authority to enact the statute comes from Article IV itself, which gives Congress the power to legislate as to the "effect" of judgments.

Section 1738, however, does not deal with federal judgments. Although nothing in either Article IV or § 1738 requires state courts to enforce federal judgments, it is generally assumed that federal judgments are entitled to full faith and credit. When pressed for a reason, most courts cite the Supremacy Clause of Article VI of the Constitution. Read Article VI. Do you see why this argument is not particularly convincing?

10. The Canadian Constitution contains no full faith and credit provision. Nevertheless, in *De Savoye v. Morguard Investments Ltd.*, [1990] 3 S.C.R. 1077, 76 D.L.R. (4th) 256, the Supreme Court of Canada held that basic principles of federalism required one province to honor the judgments of another. Absent a certain level of co-operation between provinces, the Court reasoned, a federal state cannot survive. Are these federalism arguments a better way to deal with the problem of state courts enforcing federal judgments than the Supremacy Clause argument set out in the prior note?

While we are looking abroad, note that Article 26 of the Brussels–Lugano Convention (*EC EFTA Convention on Jurisdiction and the Enforcement of Judgements in Civil and Commercial Matters*, Lugano, 16 September 1988) requires member states of the European Union to enforce judgments rendered by other member states. However, under Article 27, one state need not recognize a judgment of another if that judgment is "contrary to public policy" in the enforcing state.

11. The preclusive effect of a judgment is measured initially by the law of the court that rendered the judgment, not the court that is asked to

enforce that judgment. Therefore, F2 may be required to give claim or issue preclusion effect to an F1 judgment even if the law of F2 would not give any preclusive effect to a similar judgment from an F2 court. On the other hand, the law of the rendering state is only a floor, not a ceiling. F2 is free to apply claim or issue preclusion effect to a sister-state or federal judgment under the preclusion law of F2 even if the law of F1 would not give the judgment preclusive effect in F1 courts.

The rule differs when a state judgment is enforced in federal court. Although a federal court must give as much preclusive effect as the rendering state would give, it cannot give more. *Migra v. Warren City School Dist.*, 465 U.S. 75, 104 S.Ct. 892, 79 L.Ed.2d 56 (1984); *Marrese v. American Academy of Orthopedic Surgeons*, 470 U.S. 373, 384, 105 S.Ct. 1327, 84 L.Ed.2d 274 (1984). In other words, if the state's own courts would not apply claim or issue preclusion, neither will the federal courts.

12.   The law that governs the preclusive effect of a *federal* judgment differs depending on the source of the claim being adjudicated. When a federal court hears a federal or constitutional claim, there is a uniform federal judge-made law of claim and issue preclusion. *Parklane Hosiery* represents an example of this federal preclusion law. When a federal court hears a state-law claim, by contrast, it will generally "borrow" the law of the state in which it sits. *Semtek Int'l Inc. v. Lockheed Martin Corp.*, 531 U.S. 497, 121 S.Ct. 1021, 149 L.Ed.2d 32 (2001). The governing rule in these cases is technically still federal, but the *content* of the rule may vary from state to state. However, if a particular state's preclusion law is not compatible with a federal interest, federal preclusion law may not incorporate the state rule, and the preclusive effect will be governed by the uniform standard that applies in federal question cases.

13.   Full faith and credit does not apply to judgments rendered by courts outside the United States. However, under the doctrine of "comity," United States courts will enforce foreign judgments, provided the procedure comports with basic notions of fairness and justice. *Hilton v. Guyot*, 159 U.S. 113, 16 S.Ct. 139, 40 L.Ed. 95 (1895). Unlike full faith and credit, comity is not a binding doctrine, and states are free to enforce foreign judgments as they see fit. A few states apply a rule of reciprocity, under which they will enforce judgments from nation *X* only if *X* will generally enforce United States judgments. Most states no longer require reciprocity.

14.   *The Rooker–Feldman doctrine.* The Rooker–Feldman doctrine is a special rule that applies only if Case One is in state court and Case Two is in federal court. The doctrine is quite complex—and often misapplied by the courts. Although the nuances of the doctrine are best left to a course in Federal Courts, the gist of the rule is that a federal court cannot revisit questions decided in the state courts if the federal case could end up nullifying rights established by the state court. Courts applying the doctrine look to see if the state and federal claims are "inextricably intertwined." As one court explained the analysis:

> the federal claim is inextricably intertwined with the state-court judg-
> ment if the federal claim succeeds only to the extent that the state court
> wrongly decided the issues before it. Where federal relief can only be
> predicated upon a conviction that the state court was wrong, it is

difficult to conceive the federal proceeding as, in substance, anything other than a prohibited appeal of the state-court judgment.

Peterson Novelties, Inc. v. Berkley, 305 F.3d 386, 391 (6th Cir. 2002).

Note that a court applying *Rooker–Feldman* dismisses the case for lack of subject matter jurisdiction, not because of preclusion. Nevertheless, the effect of the doctrine is to prevent relitigation of the state case.

––––––––––

As the *Sentinel* case indicates, a court is not required to afford full faith and credit to a judgment if the court that rendered the judgment did not have jurisdiction. How broad is that exception? The next case explores the limits.

To understand *Durfee v. Duke*, you must understand the concept of a *quiet title* action in Property law. If you have taken the course in Property, you know that a quiet title action is a suit that adjudicates the rights of everyone in the world to a given parcel of property. The suit will name everyone who has a known claim to the property. However, the judgment ostensibly binds everyone, even those parties whose claim or identity is unknown.

DURFEE v. DUKE

375 U.S. 106, 84 S.Ct. 242, 11 L.Ed.2d 186 (1963)

Mr. Justice STEWART delivered the opinion of the Court.

* * * In 1956 the petitioners brought an action against the respondent in a Nebraska court to quiet title to certain bottom land situated on the Missouri River. The main channel of that river forms the boundary between the States of Nebraska and Missouri. The Nebraska court had jurisdiction over the subject matter of the controversy only if the land in question was in Nebraska. Whether the land was Nebraska land depended entirely upon a factual question—whether a shift in the river's course had been caused by avulsion or accretion. The respondent appeared in the Nebraska court and through counsel fully litigated the issues, explicitly contesting the court's jurisdiction over the subject matter of the controversy.[4] After a hearing the court found the issues in favor of the petitioners and ordered that title to the land be quieted in them. The respondent appealed, and the Supreme Court of Nebraska affirmed the judgment after a trial *de novo* on the record made in the lower court. The State Supreme Court specifically found that the rule of avulsion was applicable, that the land in question was in Nebraska, that the Nebraska courts therefore had jurisdiction of the subject matter of the litigation, and that title to the land was in the petitioners. *Durfee v. Keiffer*, 168 Neb. 272, 95 N.W.2d 618. The respondent did not petition this Court for a writ of certiorari to review that judgment.

––––––––––

4. This is, therefore, not a case in which a party, although afforded an opportunity to contest subject-matter jurisdiction, did not litigate the issue. Cf. *Chicot County Drainage Dist. v. Baxter State Bank*, 308 U.S. 371.

Two months later the respondent filed a suit against the petitioners in a Missouri court to quiet title to the same land. Her complaint alleged that the land was in Missouri. The suit was removed to a Federal District Court by reason of diversity of citizenship. The District Court after hearing evidence expressed the view that the land was in Missouri, but held that all the issues had been adjudicated and determined in the Nebraska litigation, and that the judgment of the Nebraska Supreme Court was res judicata and 'is now binding upon this court.' The Court of Appeals reversed, holding that the District Court was not required to give full faith and credit to the Nebraska judgment, and that normal res judicata principles were not applicable because the controversy involved land and a court in Missouri was therefore free to retry the question of the Nebraska court's jurisdiction over the subject matter. We granted certiorari to consider a question important to the administration of justice in our federal system. * * *

The constitutional command of full faith and credit, as implemented by Congress, requires that 'judicial proceedings * * * shall have the same full faith and credit in every court within the United States * * * as they have by law or usage in the courts of such State * * * from which they are taken.' Full faith and credit thus generally requires every State to give to a judgment at least the *res judicata* effect which the judgment would be accorded in the State which rendered it. * * *

It is not questioned that the Nebraska courts would give full *res judicata* effect to the Nebraska judgment quieting title in the petitioners. It is the respondent's position, however, that whatever effect the Nebraska courts might give to the Nebraska judgment, the federal court in Missouri was free independently to determine whether the Nebraska court in fact had jurisdiction over the subject matter, i.e., whether the land in question was actually in Nebraska.

In support of this position the respondent relies upon the many decisions of this Court which have held that a judgment of a court in one State is conclusive upon the merits in a court in another State only if the court in the first State had power to pass on the merits—had jurisdiction, that is, to render the judgment. * * *

However, while it is established that a court in one State, when asked to give effect to the judgment of a court in another State, may constitutionally inquire into the foreign court's jurisdiction to render that judgment, the modern decisions of this Court have carefully delineated the permissible scope of such an inquiry. From these decisions there emerges the general rule that a judgment is entitled to full faith and credit—even as to questions of jurisdiction—when the second court's inquiry discloses that those questions have been fully and fairly litigated and finally decided in the court which rendered the original judgment.

With respect to questions of jurisdiction over the person, this principle was unambiguously established in *Baldwin v. Iowa State Traveling Men's Ass'n*, 283 U.S. 522. There it was held that a federal court in Iowa must give binding effect to the judgment of a federal court in

Missouri despite the claim that the original court did not have jurisdiction over the defendant's person, once it was shown to the court in Iowa that that question had been fully litigated in the Missouri forum. 'Public policy,' said the Court, 'dictates that there be an end of litigation; that those who have contested an issue shall be bound by the result of the contest; and that matters once tried shall be considered forever settled as between the parties. We see no reason why this doctrine should not apply in every case where one voluntarily appears, presents his case and is fully heard, and why he should not, in the absence of fraud, be thereafter concluded by the judgment of the tribunal to which he has submitted his cause.' 283 U.S., at 525–526.

Following the *Baldwin* case, this Court soon made clear in a series of decisions that the general rule is no different when the claim is made that the original forum did not have jurisdiction over the subject matter. In each of these cases the claim was made that a court, when asked to enforce the judgment of another forum, was free to retry the question of that forum's jurisdiction over the subject matter. In each case this Court held that since the question of subject-matter jurisdiction had been fully litigated in the original forum, the issue could not be retried in a subsequent action between the parties. * * *

To be sure, the general rule of finality of jurisdictional determinations is not without exceptions. Doctrines of federal pre-emption or sovereign immunity may in some contexts be controlling. But no such overriding considerations are present here. While this Court has not before had occasion to consider the applicability of the rule * * * to a case involving real property, we can discern no reason why the rule should not be fully applicable.

It is argued that an exception to this rule of jurisdictional finality should be made with respect to cases involving real property because of this Court's emphatic expressions of the doctrine that courts of one State are completely without jurisdiction directly to affect title to land in other States. This argument is wide of the mark. Courts of one State are equally without jurisdiction to dissolve the marriages of those domiciled in other States. But the location of land, like the domicile of a party to a divorce action, is a matter 'to be resolved by judicial determination.' *Sherrer v. Sherrer*, 334 U.S., at 349. The question remains whether, once the matter has been fully litigated and judicially determined, it can be retried in another State in litigation between the same parties. Upon the reason and authority of the cases we have discussed, it is clear that the answer must be in the negative.

It is to be emphasized that all that was ultimately determined in the Nebraska litigation was title to the land in question as between the parties to the litigation there. Nothing there decided, and nothing that could be decided in litigation between the same parties or their privies in Missouri, could bind either Missouri or Nebraska with respect to any controversy they might have, now or in the future, as to the location of the boundary between them, or as to their respective sovereignty over the land in question. Either State may at any time protect its interest by initiating independent judicial proceedings here.

For the reasons stated, we hold in this case that the federal court in Missouri had the power and, upon proper averments, the duty to inquire into the jurisdiction of the Nebraska courts to render the decree quieting title to the land in the petitioners. We further hold that when that inquiry disclosed, as it did, that the jurisdictional issues had been fully and fairly litigated by the parties and finally determined in the Nebraska courts, the federal court in Missouri was correct in ruling that further inquiry was precluded. Accordingly the judgment of the Court of Appeals is reversed, and that of the District Court is affirmed. It is so ordered.

Mr. Justice BLACK, concurring.

* * * I concur in today's reversal of the Court of Appeals' judgment, but with the understanding that we are not deciding the question whether the respondent would continue to be bound by the Nebraska judgment should it later be authoritatively decided, either in an original proceeding between the States in this Court or by a compact between the two States under Art. I, § 10, that the disputed tract is in Missouri.

Notes and Questions

1. In Chapters 3 and 4, you learned about both subject-matter and personal jurisdiction. Which type of jurisdiction is at issue in *Durfee*?

2. Is the Supreme Court saying that a state has the power to decide that a specific plot of land lies within the borders of that state? Would it make a difference if the parcel was not on the border, but instead in the center of Missouri?

3. Suppose that a person named Dumond also claims to own the land at issue in *Durfee v. Duke*. Dumond received notice of the Nebraska action, but failed to appear in that action. Instead, after the Nebraska judgment, Dumond brings her own quiet title action. Is Dumond's suit barred by the Nebraska judgment? The answer depends on whether she brings her case in Nebraska or in Missouri. Do you see why the location of her case makes a difference?

4. If our imaginary Dumond can avoid the Nebraska judgment by suing in Missouri, why can *Duke* not avoid it in the same way? What is the key difference between Duke and Dumond? Is Duke bound by claim preclusion (that is, is his "claim" to the property barred because it was presented in the Nebraska quiet title case) or by issue preclusion?

5. Although the Nebraska judgment in *Durfee* purported to be a quiet title action, does the judgment ultimately quiet title as against the world?

6. Suppose that after prevailing before the United States Supreme Court, Durfee returns to his land. Within a few weeks, he receives *two* property tax bills: one from Nebraska, the other from Missouri. Durfee challenges the bills, arguing that it is legally impossible for the land to be in both states. If he sues in Nebraska, can he argue that the land is not in that state? What about the earlier Nebraska judgment? If he sues in Missouri, is

Missouri bound by the earlier determination that the land was in Nebraska? Missouri did not appear in that case. If he cannot convince the Missouri court that the land is in Nebraska, is there any way for Durfee to avoid the double taxation?

7. *Equity and family law orders.* Equitable orders, as well as cases involving child custody and support orders, are by nature subject to modification. Therefore, although they are entitled to full faith and credit, F2 retains the ability to modify the order to reflect changed conditions. Congress has attempted to deal with some of the family law issues by statute. *See* 28 U.S.C. §§ 1738A (full faith and credit to child custody) and 1738B (full faith and credit to support orders). You will discuss these provisions in courses such as Family Law.

Problems

1. P sues D in F1 for breach of contract, and after a full trial recovers a judgment for $100,000. When D does not pay the judgment, P sues D in F2 based on the judgment. In this second action, D argues for the first time that the contract is invalid because D was a minor when it was signed. P argues that D cannot raise this issue in F2. Who is correct?

2. Same facts as Problem 1, except that in the F2 case D argues that the F1 court lacked personal jurisdiction over D. P argues that D cannot contest the F1 court's personal jurisdiction in the F2 courts. Who is correct?

3. Same facts as Problem 2, except assume that the F2 court holds (correctly or incorrectly) that the F1 court lacked personal jurisdiction. The case goes to trial, and the F2 court enters judgment for D. P now sues in F3, seeking to collect on the *F1* judgment. D argues that the F2 judgment bars this new action. Is D correct?

4. P sues D in F1 and recovers a judgment. P then sues D in F2 on the F1 judgment. The F2 court respects the F1 judgment, and enters a new judgment for P. However, when P discovers that D has no non-exempt assets of note in F2, P brings a new action in F3 , based on the F1 judgment. D argues that the F2 judgment bars this third case. Is D correct?

5. P1 sues D, a pilot, in F1 for injuries that P1 sustained in a rough airplane landing. P1 wins a judgment for $50,000. P2 then sues D in F2 for injuries that P2 sustained in the same landing. P2 correctly notes that under the preclusion law of F1, a plaintiff such as P2 could make non-mutual offensive use of the F1 judgment in the F1 courts to prevent D from relitigating the question of his negligence. Therefore, P2 argues, the F2 court should likewise allow P2 to use issue preclusion. However, D correctly notes that F2 preclusion law does *not* allow offensive non-mutual issue preclusion under any circumstances. Will the court allow P2 to use issue preclusion on the issue of D's negligence?

6. Same facts as Problem 5, except that the state's laws are reversed. That is, F1 law would not allow offensive non-mutual issue preclusion under any circumstances, while F2 would allow a party such as P2 to use issue preclusion offensively if the first judgment were also rendered by F2. Will the court allow P2 to use issue preclusion on the issue of D's negligence?

G.   DOCTRINES SIMILAR TO PRECLUSION

INTRODUCTORY PROBLEM

Last year, Paul won a $150,000 judgment against Donna for injuries that Paul sustained in an automobile collision. In that case, Donna had asserted that Paul was at least partly at fault because he had not repaired the brakes on his car. Paul denied there was any problem with the brakes. The court believed Paul, and rejected Donna's comparative fault argument.

Now, Paul has sued the state of Illiana under federal civil rights laws. As a condition to obtaining a license plate, Illiana requires an inspection by state officials. Paul had had his vehicle inspected two days before his collision with Donna. Paul claims that in this inspection the officials failed to detect that his brake pads were seriously worn, eventually leading to the collision two days later. Paul claims that because the official's negligence deprived Paul of his property—namely, his automobile—the state is liable to Paul for the value of the car. Paul did not seek property damage in his prior suit against Donna.

Illiana moves to dismiss the case, arguing that Paul should be precluded from arguing that the brakes were defective, given that he had argued that the brakes were *not* defective in the prior case.

Claim and issue preclusion are the main—but by no means the only—ways in which what happens in one case can bind one or more of the parties in later litigation. Two other doctrines, *law of the case* and *judicial estoppel*, operate in a roughly similar way. Although these doctrines are sometimes confused with preclusion (even by the courts), there are significant differences in when they apply and who can invoke them. In addition, law of the case and judicial estoppel are more flexible doctrines than claim and issue preclusion, and you will find that courts sometimes refuse to invoke them out of a sense of fairness.

1. Law of the Case

Claim and issue preclusion begin to operate after the court in Case One renders a final judgment. The doctrine of law of the case, by contrast, gives preclusive effect to rulings that occur before Case One is complete. At its core, the doctrine represents the quite sensible notion that a court should not generally revisit its rulings on disputed issues without good reason. Thus, although a ruling obviously cannot bind a higher court, it binds the court that rendered it, as well as the lower courts, for the course of a particular case. In other words, the ruling has become the "law of the case."

To illustrate, suppose P sues D for a novel claim. The trial court grants D's 12(b)(6) motion, concluding that the claim is not recognized in that jurisdiction. P appeals, and the court of appeals reverses and remands, holding that the claim is valid. The appellate court's ruling binds the trial court on remand, of course. In addition, however, if P should prevail on the remand, the law of the case doctrine prevents D from asking the appellate court to change its mind as to whether the claim is recognized by law.

As its name implies, the law of the case applies only to the actual case in question. The court of appeals in the above example would be ˙ee to reverse its position in a later case, and reject the claim.

The law of the case doctrine is not always strictly applied. There are ˙me common exceptions. Most importantly, if, after the court of ˙rules, a higher court issues a contrary ruling on the same ˙ law in a different case, most courts will allow the parties to ˙e of the newer decision.

˙oppel

˙W HAMPSHIRE v. MAINE

˙2, 121 S.Ct. 1808, 149 L.Ed.2d 968 (2001)

˙ered the opinion of the Court.

˙ at the southeastern end of New Hamp-
˙ The river begins at the headwaters of
˙to Portsmouth Harbor (also known as
˙2000, New Hampshire brought this
˙ that the Piscataqua River bound-
˙hat the entire river and all of
˙hire. Maine has filed a motion
˙ceedings—a 1740 boundary
˙consent judgment entered
˙ River boundary at the

* * *

the two States
˙dgment fixing
˙he boundary
˙aine, from
Gosport
˙63, 48
U.S.
˙cation
˙tch of the
westward to

˙oundary, we summa-
˙n the Piscataqua River

region. See *New Hampshire v. Maine*, 426 U.S. at 366–367. The boundary, we said, "was in fact fixed in 1740 by decree of King George II of England" as follows:

" 'That the Dividing Line shall pass up thro the Mouth of Piscataqua Harbour and up the Middle of the River. . . . And that the Dividing Line shall part the Isles of Shoals and run thro the Middle of the Harbour between the Islands to the Sea on the Southerly Side. . . .' "

Id. at 366 (quoting the 1740 decree). [The Court then stated that meaning of the phrase "Middle of the River" was crucial to determining the off-shore boundary between the states.] * * *

In the course of litigation, New Hampshire and Maine proposed a consent decree in which they agreed, *inter alia*, that the words "Middle of the River" in the 1740 decree refer to the middle of the Piscataqua River's main channel of navigation. The Special Master, upon reviewing pertinent history, rejected the States' interpretation * * * . This Court determined, however, that the States' interpretation "reasonably invested imprecise terms" with a definition not "wholly contrary to relevant evidence." *New Hampshire v. Maine*, 426 U.S. at 369. On that basis, the Court declined to adopt the Special Master's construction of "Middle of the River" and directed entry of the consent decree. The final decree entered in 1977, defined "Middle of the River" as "the middle of the main channel of navigation of the Piscataqua River." *New Hampshire [v.] Maine*, 434 U.S. at 2.

The 1977 consent judgment fixed only the lateral marine boun[dary] and not the inland Piscataqua River boundary. In the instant a[ction] New Hampshire contends that the inland river boundary "runs [along] the low water mark on the Maine shore," and asserts sovereign[ty over] the entire river and all of Portsmouth Harbor, including the Por[tsmouth] Naval Shipyard on Seavey Island located within the harbor just [off] Kittery, Maine. Relying on various historical records, New H[ampshire] urges that "Middle of the River," as those words were use[d in 1740,] denotes the main branch of the river, not a mid-channel bo[undary, and] that New Hampshire, not Maine, exercised sole jurisdicti[on over ship]ping and military activities in Portsmouth Harbor durin[g the years] before and after the 1740 decree.

While disagreeing with New Hampshire's understan[ding of history,] Maine primarily contends that the 1740 decree and t[he 1977 consent] judgment divided the Piscataqua River at the middle of [the main channel] of navigation—a division that places Seavey Island wi[thin Maine's juris]diction. Those earlier proceedings, according to Main[e, bar New Hamp]shire's complaint under principles of claim and issu[e preclusion, as well] as judicial estoppel.

We pretermit the States' competing historic[al records and] their arguments on the application *vel non* of th[e doctrines] commonly called claim and issue preclusion. [Under the] circumstances this case presents, we conclude [that a third doctrine,] judicial estoppel, best fits the controversy. Und[er . . .]

New Hampshire is equitably barred from asserting—contrary to its position in the 1970's litigation—that the inland Piscataqua River boundary runs along the Maine shore.

II

"Where a party assumes a certain position in a legal proceeding, and succeeds in maintaining that position, he may not thereafter, simply because his interests have changed, assume a contrary position, especially if it be to the prejudice of the party who has acquiesced in the position formerly taken by him." *Davis v. Wakelee*, 156 U.S. 680, 689, 39 L. Ed. 578, 15 S. Ct. 555 (1895). This rule, known as judicial estoppel, "generally prevents a party from prevailing in one phase of a case on an argument and then relying on a contradictory argument to prevail in another phase." *Pegram v. Herdrich*, 530 U.S. 211, 227, n. 8, 147 L. Ed. 2d 164, 120 S. Ct. 2143 (2000); see * * * 18 C. Wright, A. Miller, & E. Cooper, Federal Practice and Procedure § 4477, p. 782 (1981) ("absent any good explanation, a party should not be allowed to gain an advantage by litigation on one theory, and then seek an inconsistent advantage by pursuing an incompatible theory") (hereinafter Wright).

Although we have not had occasion to discuss the doctrine elaborately, other courts have uniformly recognized that its purpose is "to protect the integrity of the judicial process," *Edwards v. Aetna Life Ins. Co.*, 690 F.2d 595, 598 (CA6 1982), by "prohibiting parties from deliberately changing positions according to the exigencies of the moment," *United States v. McCaskey*, 9 F.3d 368, 378 (CA5 1993). See * * * *Allen v. Zurich Ins. Co.*, 667 F.2d 1162, 1166 (CA4 1982) (judicial estoppel "protects the essential integrity of the judicial process"); *Scarano v. Central R. Co.*, 203 F.2d 510, 513 (CA3 1953) (judicial estoppel prevents parties from "playing 'fast and loose with the courts' " (quoting *Stretch v. Watson*, 6 N.J. Super. 456, 469, 69 A.2d 596, 603 (1949))). Because the rule is intended to prevent "improper use of judicial machinery," *Konstantinidis v. Chen*, 200 U.S. App. D.C. 69, 626 F.2d 933, 938 (CADC 1980), judicial estoppel "is an equitable doctrine invoked by a court at its discretion," *Russell v. Rolfs*, 893 F.2d 1033, 1037 (CA9 1990).

Courts have observed that "the circumstances under which judicial estoppel may appropriately be invoked are probably not reducible to any general formulation of principle," *Allen*, 667 F.2d at 1166. Nevertheless, several factors typically inform the decision whether to apply the doctrine in a particular case: First, a party's later position must be "clearly inconsistent" with its earlier position. Second, courts regularly inquire whether the party has succeeded in persuading a court to accept that party's earlier position, so that judicial acceptance of an inconsistent position in a later proceeding would create "the perception that either the first or the second court was misled," *Edwards*, 690 F.2d at 599. Absent success in a prior proceeding, a party's later inconsistent position introduces no "risk of inconsistent court determinations," *United States v. C. I. T. Constr. Inc.*, 944 F.2d 253, 259 (CA5 1991), and thus poses little threat to judicial integrity. A third consideration is whether the party seeking to assert an inconsistent position would derive an unfair advantage or impose an unfair detriment on the opposing party if not estopped.

In enumerating these factors, we do not establish inflexible prerequisites or an exhaustive formula for determining the applicability of judicial estoppel. Additional considerations may inform the doctrine's application in specific factual contexts. In this case, we simply observe that the factors above firmly tip the balance of equities in favor of barring New Hampshire's present complaint.

New Hampshire's claim that the Piscataqua River boundary runs along the Maine shore is clearly inconsistent with its interpretation of the words "Middle of the River" during the 1970's litigation. As mentioned above, interpretation of those words was "necessary" to fixing the northern endpoint of the lateral marine boundary. New Hampshire offered two interpretations in the earlier proceeding—first agreeing with Maine in the proposed consent decree that "Middle of the River" means the middle of the main channel of navigation, and later agreeing with the Special Master that the words mean the geographic middle of the river. Both constructions located the "Middle of the River" somewhere other than the Maine shore of the Piscataqua River.

Moreover, the record of the 1970's dispute makes clear that this Court accepted New Hampshire's agreement with Maine that "Middle of the River" means middle of the main navigable channel, and that New Hampshire benefited from that interpretation. New Hampshire, it is true, preferred the interpretation of "Middle of the River" in the Special Master's report. But the consent decree was sufficiently favorable to New Hampshire to garner its approval. Although New Hampshire now suggests that it "compromised in Maine's favor" on the definition of "Middle of the River" in the 1970's litigation, that "compromise" enabled New Hampshire to settle the case on terms beneficial to both States. * * *

New Hampshire also contends that the 1977 consent decree was entered without "a searching historical inquiry into what that language ['Middle of the River'] meant." According to New Hampshire, had it known then what it knows now about the relevant history, it would not have entered into the decree. We do not question that it may be appropriate to resist application of judicial estoppel "when a party's prior position was based on inadvertence or mistake." *John S. Clark Co. v. Faggert & Frieden, P. C.*, 65 F.3d 26, 29 (CA4 1995). We are unpersuaded, however, that New Hamsphire's position in 1977 fairly may be regarded as a product of inadvertence or mistake.

The pleadings in the lateral marine boundary case show that New Hampshire did engage in "a searching historical inquiry" into the meaning of "Middle of the River." * * *

Nor can it be said that New Hampshire lacked the opportunity or incentive to locate the river boundary at Maine's shore. In its present complaint, New Hampshire relies on historical materials—primarily offi-

cial documents and events from the colonial and postcolonial periods—
that were no less available 25 years ago than they are today. And New
Hampshire had every reason to consult those materials: A river boundary running along Maine's shore would have placed the northern termi-
nus of the lateral marine boundary much closer to Maine, "resulting in
hundreds if not thousands of additional acres of territory being in New
Hampshire rather than Maine," Tr. of Oral Arg. 48 (rebuttal argument
of Maine). * * *

In short, considerations of equity persuade us that application of
judicial estoppel is appropriate in this case. Having convinced this Court
to accept one interpretation of "Middle of the River," and having
benefited from that interpretation, New Hampshire now urges an inconsistent interpretation to gain an additional advantage at Maine's expense. Were we to accept New Hampshire's latest view, the "risk of
inconsistent court determinations," *C.I.T. Construction,* 944 F.2d at 259,
would become a reality. We cannot interpret "Middle of the River" in
the 1740 decree to mean two different things along the same boundary
line without undermining the integrity of the judicial process.

Finally, notwithstanding the balance of equities, New Hampshire
points to this Court's recognition that "ordinarily the doctrine of estoppel or that part of it which precludes inconsistent positions in judicial
proceedings is not applied to states," *Illinois ex rel. Gordon v. Campbell,*
329 U.S. 362, 369, 91 L. Ed. 348, 67 S. Ct. 340 (1946). Of course, "broad
interests of public policy may make it important to allow a change of
positions that might seem inappropriate as a matter of merely private
interests." 18 Wright § 4477, p. 784. But this is not a case where
estoppel would compromise a governmental interest in enforcing the law.
Nor is this a case where the shift in the government's position is "the
result of a change in public policy," *United States v. Owens,* 54 F.3d 271,
275 (CA6 1995); cf. *Commissioner v. Sunnen,* 333 U.S. 591, 601, 92 L.
Ed. 898, 68 S. Ct. 715 (1948) (collateral estoppel does not apply to
Commissioner where pertinent statutory provisions or Treasury regulations have changed between the first and second proceeding), or the
result of a change in facts essential to the prior judgment. Instead, it is a
case between two States, in which each owes the other a full measure of
respect.

What has changed between 1976 and today is New Hampshire's
interpretation of the historical evidence concerning the King's 1740
decree. New Hampshire advances its new interpretation not to enforce
its own laws within its borders, but to adjust the border itself. Given
Maine's countervailing interest in the location of the boundary, we are
unable to discern any "broad interest of public policy," 18 Wright
§ 4477, p. 784, that gives New Hampshire the prerogative to construe
"Middle of the River" differently today than it did 25 years ago.

For the reasons stated, we conclude that judicial estoppel bars New
Hampshire from asserting that the Piscataqua River boundary runs

along the Maine shore. Accordingly, we grant Maine's motion to dismiss the complaint.

JUSTICE SOUTER took no part in the consideration or decision of this case.

Notes and Questions

1. Note that the United States Supreme Court was the trial court in this case. In cases involving a dispute between two states, both Article III, § 2 of the Constitution and 28 U.S.C. § 1251(a) give the Supreme Court original jurisdiction. However, the Justices rarely conduct the trial themselves. Instead, they assign the case to a special master, who hears the evidence and makes suggested findings to the Court. It was a special master who heard the actual trial between Maine and New Hampshire.

2. Claim and issue preclusion usually bind a party who *lost* an argument in the first case, and is trying to make that same (or a similar) argument again in the second case. By contrast, you should think in terms of judicial estoppel when a party *prevailed* on an argument in the first case, and is now taking a contrary stance. As *New Hampshire v. Maine* demonstrates, the doctrine is more concerned with issues of fairness and appearances than with any strictly formal logic.

3. Like law of the case, courts are not completely consistent in applying judicial estoppel. However, during the last decade courts have begun to invoke the doctrine more frequently, perhaps out of a sense of frustration with attorneys and parties who change their position whenever there is something to be gained from doing so.

4. Because of the need to allow government to establish policy, most courts do not apply judicial estoppel to a government entity that changes its view on a legal issue.

5. Judicial estoppel binds a party who takes inconsistent positions. Does it also bind people in privity with that party? *See Whitacre Partnership v. Biosignia, Inc.*, 358 N.C. 1, 591 S.E.2d 870 (2004).

Chapter 12

APPEALS

Much of the reading in law school involves appellate court opinions. And yet, at this point in your law school career you probably have only a vague idea of how the appellate process works. A basic understanding of appeals will help you understand why appellate opinions make such good teaching tools. First, appellate courts usually concentrate their attention on one or a few crucial issues, instead of rehashing all the evidence presented at trial. Second, appeals tend to focus on issues of law. Although an appellate court can overturn a trial court's findings of fact, it will afford considerable deference to the trial court on most factual issues.

This Chapter provides a short, but systematic, study of the appellate process. However, time considerations prevent an in-depth study of all the myriad issues that arise in appeals. This Chapter accordingly only hits the "highlights": issues that arise with some regularity, and for which the law is either non-obvious or subject to stark differences of opinion.

A. WHO MAY APPEAL

INTRODUCTORY PROBLEM

While crossing the street on a sunny day, Pedro Pedestrian was struck and injured by an automobile operated by Diane Driver. Pedro sues Diane in state court for his injuries, asking for $100,000 in damages. Pedro's complaint sets forth two counts of negligence. First, Pedro claims that Diane was negligent because she failed to have her brakes maintained. Second, Pedro claims that Diane was negligent because she was drunk while operating the automobile. The case goes to trial, and both sides submit extensive evidence. The judge directs the jury to deliver a special verdict. The jury returns with a $100,000 verdict for Pedro. In the special verdict, the jury specifically states that Diane was not drunk, but that she did fail to maintain the brakes on her vehicle. The court enters judgment in accordance with the verdict.

Although Pedro was awarded the full $100,000, he nevertheless wants to appeal the jury's finding that Diane was not drunk. Pedro has heard a rumor that Diane is about ready to file for bankruptcy. If she does, she can discharge most of her debts, including any liability for ordinary negligence. However, a debtor in bankruptcy cannot discharge a debt arising from driving while intoxicated. Pedro therefore wants his judgment to state that Diane was drunk, so that the $100,000 debt would not be dischargeable in the event that Diane files for bankruptcy.

Ignoring the issue of whether he would *win* an appeal, may Pedro even file an appeal in this case?

Only a party who loses at trial has the right to appeal. That rule makes perfect sense. Parties who win everything they wanted at trial have no incentive to appeal, other than possibly to harass the judgment loser. But what does it mean to "lose" a case? Suppose that a court in a trespass case enters a $20,000 judgment for plaintiff. Defendant may, of course, appeal. Yet plaintiff can also appeal if, for example, her complaint asked for anything more than $20,000 in damages. In essence, in the context of appeal it is entirely possible—and indeed fairly common—for *all* parties to lose a case.

The next case presents a more subtle variation on this theme. In the case, defendant technically won at trial. However, defendant claims that its victory is Pyrrhic, as it has potentially negative consequences for the defendant. See if you can identify the possible consequences, and why the court ends up deciding that defendant cannot appeal.

IN RE DES LITIGATION

7 F.3d 20 (2d Cir. 1993)

JON O. NEWMAN, Chief Judge:

* * *

BACKGROUND

Some background information concerning DES and the varying approaches to DES liability adopted by different states will assist in understanding Boehringer's motivation in attempting to appeal from the interlocutory rulings. Between 1941 and 1971, approximately 300 pharmaceutical companies marketed DES, a synthetic form of estrogen, for the prevention of miscarriages. In 1971, the FDA banned DES after determining that the drug caused vaginal adenocarcinoma, a form of cancer, and adenosis, a precancerous vaginal or cervical growth, in the daughters of women who took the drug. Although it was made in pills of different shapes and colors, all DES was chemically identical, and druggists generally filled prescriptions from whatever stock they had on hand. Most women ingesting DES did not know the identity of the manufacturer, and by the time their daughters realized they had been injured by DES, it was often impossible to determine the manufacturer.

Faced with this situation, the California Supreme Court adopted a "market share" theory of liability. See *Sindell v. Abbott Laboratories*, 26 Cal.3d 588, 163 Cal.Rptr. 132, 607 P.2d 924, *cert. denied*, 449 U.S. 912 (1980). The Court held that a plaintiff could recover by showing that her injuries had been caused by DES and by joining as defendants "the manufacturers of a substantial share of the DES which her mother might have taken." *Id.* at 612, 163 Cal.Rptr. at 145, 607 P.2d at 937. Each manufacturer would "be held liable for the proportion of the judgment represented by its share of [the] market unless it demonstrates that it could not have made the product which caused plaintiff's injuries." *Id.* In a later case, the California Court clarified that liability was several only, with the consequence that if less than all manufacturers are joined, a plaintiff will recover less than 100 percent of her damages.

The New York Court of Appeals substantially adopted the *Sindell* approach. * * *

On September 30, 1991, a group of plaintiffs, comprising women allegedly injured by DES, along with their husbands, filed the instant suit in the Eastern District of New York against 33 manufacturers, or successors to manufacturers, of DES. The plaintiffs, who are New York or foreign residents, asserted jurisdiction on the basis of diversity of citizenship. The sole appellant, Boehringer, is a Delaware corporation authorized to do business in New York. Boehringer never sold or manufactured DES, but it is the successor to Stayner Corporation, which manufactured limited amounts of DES in Berkeley, California, between 1949 and 1971. Stayner sold products in California, Washington, Oregon, and Montana. It never marketed any products in New York, was not licensed to do business in New York, and had no significant contacts with New York. * * *

On October 25, 1991, Boehringer moved to dismiss for failure to state a claim and for lack of personal jurisdiction. Judge Weinstein denied the motion in his April 13, 1992, opinion. He concluded (1) that the New York long arm statute reached Boehringer; (2) that this exercise of jurisdiction was constitutional; (3) that New York would apply its law to Boehringer; (4) that application of this choice of law rule was constitutional; (5) that the complaint stated a claim against Boehringer under New York substantive law; and (6) that New York substantive DES law was constitutional. * * *

On September 14, 1992, apparently at Boehringer's request, the District Court entered a judgment that provides:

> [T]he case having been fully resolved as to all parties and claims by settlement or adjudication on the merits, It is ORDERED AND ADJUDGED that all of the claims in this action, including specifically cross-claims, are DISMISSED, without costs, subject to the right of any party to re-open the final judgment if any settlement is not consummated.

At oral argument, Boehringer attempted to give a fuller explication of the procedural history behind this judgment. Boehringer stated that all the other defendant DES manufacturers settled with plaintiffs, but that Boehringer refused to do so. Trial then commenced against Boehringer, but the plaintiffs declined to present any evidence. The District Court then orally dismissed the complaint as to Boehringer for want of prosecution.

DISCUSSION

* * * The only appellant is Boehringer, the defendant in the District Court. The plaintiffs have declined to contest Boehringer's appeal, neither filing a brief nor appearing for argument. Apparently their settlements with other defendants diminished their interest in attempting to establish Boehringer's liability. * * *

It is the defendant's lack of standing that impels us to dismiss this appeal. Boehringer prevailed on the merits by successfully moving to have the plaintiffs' complaint dismissed with prejudice for lack of prosecution. Ordinarily, a prevailing party cannot appeal from a district court judgment in its favor. There are, however, two exceptions to this rule. One exception arises when the prevailing party is aggrieved by the collateral estoppel effect of a district court's rulings. Boehringer observes that at least 42 DES cases are pending against it in New York, and states that it fears that the trial courts in these cases will accord preclusive effect to Judge Weinstein's jurisdictional and choice of law rulings. We disagree, however, that the matters resolved in the April 13 order have collateral estoppel effect. Relitigation of an issue in a second action is precluded only if "the judgment in the prior action was dependent upon the determination made of the issue." 1B James W. Moore, et al., *Moore's Federal Practice* ¶ 0.443[1], at 760 (2d ed. 1993). The judgment in this case is not dependent upon the interlocutory rulings in favor of the plaintiff. Upon the failure of the plaintiffs to prosecute their suit, the District Court was free to enter a judgment dismissing the complaint whether or not there was personal jurisdiction over Boehringer and whether or not New York law applied to Boehringer. * * *

[O]ur decision to decline appellate review of the District Court's order confirms the lack of any possible collateral estoppel effect arising from the District Court's interlocutory rulings. See *Restatement (Second) of Judgments* § 28(1) (1982) (relitigation of an issue not precluded if "party against whom preclusion is sought could not, as a matter of law, have obtained review of the judgment in the initial action"). Thus, whether or not other trial judges find Judge Weinstein's opinion a persuasive precedent, they are not bound to apply it in any subsequent litigation against Boehringer.

The second exception to the rule prohibiting appeal by a prevailing party arises, in some circumstances, where a prevailing party can show that it is aggrieved by some aspect of the trial court's judgment or decree. In *Electrical Fittings Corp. v. Thomas & Betts Co.*, 307 U.S. 241 (1939), the District Court had entered a judgment for the defendant, finding that the defendant had not infringed the plaintiff's patent but also finding that the patent was valid. We dismissed the defendant's appeal, since the finding of validity did not support the decree and would not have estoppel effect. The Supreme Court reversed and held that we should have "entertain[ed] the appeal, not for the purpose of passing on the merits, but to direct the reformation of the decree." Id. at 242. Judge Learned Hand later explained the Supreme Court's terse decision as follows:

> The Supreme Court did not differ with us in thinking that the finding [of validity] was immaterial, but nevertheless it directed us to strike it from the decree. The rationale of that decision was that the defendant was entitled to have it out because, although it was not an estoppel, it might create some presumptive prejudice against him.

Harries v. Air King Products Co., 183 F.2d 158, 161 (2d Cir.1950) (footnote omitted).

Electrical Fittings is distinguishable in at least two ways. First, Boehringer's appellate brief does not ask us to vacate any portion of the judgment; what Boehringer seeks is a reversal of the interlocutory rulings. * * *

Second, and more importantly, the District Court's rulings on personal jurisdiction and choice of law do not appear on the face of the judgment, as was the case with the finding of validity in *Electrical Fittings*. The judgment in this case says only that the complaint is dismissed. We therefore are confronted with an "appellant" that seeks no modification of the judgment as entered. In these circumstances, appellate jurisdiction is improperly invoked.

Accordingly, the appeal is dismissed. Boehringer's motion for a ruling on the merits is denied.

Notes and Questions

1. Defendant in *DES* claimed that although it was held not liable in the case, the decision might negatively affect it in other cases. Be prepared to explain how defendant claimed the judgment could harm it in the future.

2. If you have studied issue preclusion (Chapter 11, Part D), try to restate the *DES* court's argument as to why issue preclusion (which the court calls collateral estoppel) would not apply. Is the court's analysis correct?

3. Do you agree that the distinctions the court draws between the case at bar and *Electrical Fittings*, a case in which appeal was allowed, are meaningful? Why should it matter whether the findings appear on the face of the judgment?

4. Why does the law deny a prevailing party the opportunity to appeal? Isn't the simple fact that a party is going to the time and expense of filing an

appeal sufficient evidence in itself that there is something about the ruling that is unsatisfactory to that party?

B.   THE TIMING OF AN APPEAL—THE "FINAL DECISION" RULE

INTRODUCTORY PROBLEM

Like law school, United States presidents often look better in hindsight. The past few years have witnessed the birth of a popular movement to place the image of a recent president on Mount Rushmore, a national monument. However, the site's physical limitations make it impossible simply to add a face to the monument. The only option is to reshape one of the existing faces into a new image. The obvious candidate for such an "extreme makeover" is Teddy Roosevelt, the least influential of the presidents currently enshrined on Mount Rushmore.

When the federal government refuses to accede to its demands, a group of interested citizens sues the United States for an order requiring the government to replace Roosevelt's face with that of their idol. The government responds by moving to dismiss for failure to join a necessary party. The government argues that Roosevelt's descendents are necessary because they would be directly affected by the removal of Roosevelt's face. The government also fears that the descendents will sue the United States for damages based on harm to their reputation.

The court rejects these argument and denies the motion to dismiss. May the government appeal immediately after the motion is denied?

Governing law: 28 U.S.C. §§ 1291, 1292; Federal Rule 54(b).

1.   The Basic Rule

The primary rule governing when a party may appeal a decision from the federal district courts to the courts of appeal is 28 U.S.C. § 1291, which provides:

> The courts of appeals (other than the United States Court of Appeals for the Federal Circuit) shall have jurisdiction of appeals from all final decisions of the district courts of the United States * * *.

Many states have a similar provision, although it is not necessarily interpreted the same way. Courts and commentators use the term *interlocutory appeal* to refer to an appeal of a decision that does not qualify as "final" under § 1291 or the related state provisions.

Note that the statute speaks in terms of jurisdiction. If a party tries to appeal a decision that is not final, and that decision does not fall into one of the exceptions discussed below, the court of appeals lacks subject-matter jurisdiction over the appeal. As with all issues of subject matter jurisdiction, any party may raise the question of whether § 1291 has been satisfied at any time, or the court may raise the issue of its own accord.

Although § 1291 uses the term "final decision", the standard it establishes is better thought of as a final *judgment* rule. The classic statement interpreting § 1291 is set out in *Catlin v. United States*, 324 U.S. 229, 233, 65 S.Ct. 631, 89 L.Ed. 911 (1945):

> A "final decision" generally is one which ends the litigation on the merits and leaves nothing for the court to do but execute the judgment.

For a judgment to be final under this standard, it must completely dispose of *all* claims in the case. Therefore, a partial summary judgment is not final for purposes of § 1291. Similarly, a summary judgment for defendant on all of plaintiff's claims is not final under § 1291 if a counterclaim or cross-claim remains pending (although this and the prior example may be immediately appealable under one of the exceptions; see Part 2.A). However, notwithstanding the language in *Catlin* about executing on a judgment, a complete victory for defendant on all claims is final and can be appealed.

The purpose of § 1291 is to prevent what are often called "piecemeal appeals." An appeal requires the parties to educate a new set of judges about the case. Therefore, for the sake of efficiency it makes sense to limit the total number of appeals. Moreover, allowing an appeal before a case is complete complicates the proceedings in the trial court. The basic approach of § 1291 is accordingly to require the appellant to present the case to the court of appeals as a complete package, allowing the court to focus its attention on all grounds—and *only* those grounds—that might require reversal.

To test your understanding of the *Catlin* rule, make sure you can explain why the following are, or are not, final judgments under § 1291:

- The grant of a motion for a new trial based on the weight of the evidence is not a final judgment.

- The denial of a motion for a new trial based on a procedural error is a final judgment.

- The grant or denial of a motion to certify a case as a class action is not a final judgment.

- The denial of a motion to intervene in a case as of right is not a final judgment.

- Dismissal of all claims in a case for lack of subject matter jurisdiction is a final judgment.

- Dismissal of fewer than all claims in a case is not a final judgment, regardless of the reason for dismissal.

- If two cases are consolidated under Federal Rule 42(a), and the court disposes of all claims in one of the original cases, that ruling is not a final judgment. *See Brandon, Jones, Sandall, Zeide, Kohn, Chalal & Musso, P.A. v. MedPartners, Inc.*, 312 F.3d 1349 (11th Cir. 2002).

• If after summary judgment is entered against a party on one claim, that party dismisses all remaining claims, courts are split as to whether the entry of summary judgment is final. *Compare Chrysler Motors Corp. v. Thomas Auto Co., Inc.*, 939 F.2d 538 (8th Cir. 1991) (final judgment) *with Swope v. Columbian Chemicals Co.*, 281 F.3d 185 (5th Cir. 2002) (not appealable where dismissal was without prejudice).

2. Limitations on and Exceptions to the Rule

Although piecemeal appeals are generally undesirable, there are certain situations in which allowing immediate appeal of a crucial ruling could be highly beneficial. The following exceptions each deal with a different concern. Taken together, do the exceptions cover all the cases in which an interlocutory appeal would be desirable?

A.   Federal Rule 54(b)

N.A.A.C.P. v. AMERICAN FAMILY MUTUAL INSURANCE CO.

978 F.2d 287 (7th Cir. 1992), *cert. denied* 508 U.S. 907, 113 S.Ct. 2335, 124 L.Ed.2d 247

EASTERBROOK, Circuit Judge.

Is redlining in the insurance business a form of racial discrimination violating the Fair Housing Act? "Redlining" is charging higher rates or declining to write insurance for people who live in particular areas (figuratively, sometimes literally, enclosed with red lines on a map). The NAACP, its Milwaukee Branch, and eight of its members contend in this class action that redlining violates the Fair Housing Act, 42 U.S.C. §§ 3601–19, and four other rules of state and federal law when insurers draw their lines around areas that have large or growing minority populations. * * *

The complaint asserts that American Family Mutual Insurance Company engages in redlining in and near Milwaukee. The district judge concluded that two of plaintiffs' five theories are legally insufficient. See Fed.R.Civ.P. 12(b)(6). Following *Mackey v. Nationwide Insurance Cos.*, 724 F.2d 419, 423–24 (4th Cir.1984), he held that the Fair Housing Act (Title VIII of the Civil Rights Act of 1968) does not apply to the property and casualty insurance business. And he held that Wisconsin would not recognize a private right of action to enforce the antidiscrimination portions of its insurance code. At the conclusion of his oral ruling, the judge entered a partial final judgment on these two theories under Fed.R.Civ.P. 54(b). * * *

Appellate jurisdiction is the first question. Rule 54(b) allows a court to "direct the entry of a final judgment as to one or more but fewer than all of the claims or parties" but does not employ a special meaning of "final". So it does not authorize appeal of decisions that, if made in stand-alone litigation, would not be final. Unless the court enters judgment on an entire "claim," or wraps up the case with respect to all claims involving a particular party, Rule 54(b) does not permit an immediate appeal.

The district judge did not discuss the legal and factual overlap between the two counts being dismissed and the three being retained and did not explain why he viewed them as separate claims. A "claim for relief" seeks redress of a distinct wrong; a distinct legal underpinning differs from a new claim and is not independently appealable. Yet the district judge appears to have equated theories with claims. He observed that because a trial lay more than a year in the future there was ample time to resolve these two legal disputes on appeal so that all theories could be handled during one trial. This suggests that the judge confused Rule 54(b) with 28 U.S.C. § 1292(b), which permits a court to certify the case for discretionary appeal when interlocutory resolution of important issues could advance the final disposition of the litigation. Because of the mismatch between the district court's stated rationale and the scope of Rule 54(b)—and the apparent overlap of the two dismissed counts with the three retained—our jurisdiction is in doubt.

Plaintiffs' complaint begins with 66 paragraphs and then states five "claims," each of which incorporates these paragraphs and asserts one reason why the conduct is wrongful. The Fair Housing Act and the state insurance code are two. The other three: Wisconsin's Fair Housing Act, 42 U.S.C. § 1981 (the right to be free of racial discrimination in making contracts), and 42 U.S.C. § 1982 (the right to be free of racial discrimination in buying real property). Perhaps the judge was led astray by the structure of the complaint. Identifying legal theories may assist defendants and the court in seeing how the plaintiff hopes to prevail, but this organization does not track the idea of "claim for relief" in the federal rules. * * *

One set of facts producing one injury creates one claim for relief, no matter how many laws the deeds violate. Plaintiffs could not litigate and lose a suit asserting that American Family's redlining violates Title VIII, pursue another asserting that redlining violates § 1981, and then crank up a third asserting that redlining violates § 1982. If these principles— well understood when dealing with the preclusive effects of judgments— define a "claim" for purposes of Rule 54(b), then this appeal must be dismissed.

Language in some of our cases equates "claim" in Rule 54(b) with "claim" for purposes of res judicata, but as we observed in *Olympia Hotels Corp. v. Johnson Wax Development Corp.*, 908 F.2d 1363, 1367 (7th Cir.1990), this equivalence cannot accommodate the many cases that permit separate appeals of claims and compulsory counterclaims. It follows that two "claims" may arise out of the same transaction for purposes of Rule 54(b), provided that the facts and theories are sufficiently distinct. Two legal theories sufficiently distinct that they call for proof of substantially different facts may be separate "claims." *Stearns v. Consolidated Management, Inc.,* 747 F.2d 1105, 1108–09 (7th Cir. 1984).

"Sufficiently" and "substantially" are hedges. Ideally the facts and theories separated for immediate appeal should not overlap with those retained; to the extent they do, the court of appeals is "deciding" claims still pending in the district court, and may have to cover the same ground when the district court acts on the residue. A combination of anticipation with overlap leads to wasteful duplication and increases the likelihood of conflict (or error). In disdaining bright lines and asking how much duplication is too much, we enter the zone of shadings traditionally committed to a district judge's discretion. * * *

Although the district judge in our case confused Rule 54(b) with § 1292(b), we do not believe that he abused his discretion in permitting an immediate appeal. American Family stated, in its memorandum concerning appellate jurisdiction, that "the dismissed Fair Housing Act claim, would, if it were viable, be subject to proof under a disparate impact formula, rather than under the 'intentional racial discrimination' test applicable to all the counts remaining in the district court." * * * We therefore assume that plaintiffs' burden under Title VIII is lighter than their burden under the other legal theories. Different burdens may imply different "claims" even for purposes of preclusion. Resolving the Title VIII issue in plaintiffs' favor implies that the other legal theories will fall away. If they prevail under Title VIII, they obtain all the relief they seek; if they lose at trial under Title VIII, they necessarily lose on all other theories; either way, there will not be duplicative appellate review. *Stearns* holds that this is enough, if barely, to justify treating a legal theory as a "claim" for purposes of Rule 54(b). * * *

[The court then upheld the lower court's ruling on the Wisconsin state-law claim, but reversed on the Fair Housing Act claim, finding that the federal law did cover redlining.]

Notes and Questions

1. Do you understand why the court concluded that the Title VIII claim was separate? Didn't the court find that that claim arose out of the exact same facts as the others? If so, how can it be separate?

2. *NAACP* sets out one approach to determining whether a particular ruling involves a separate claim for relief. The court in *Eldredge v. Martin Marietta Corp.,* 207 F.3d 737, 741 (5th Cir. 2000) discusses different tests that courts have employed:

> [V]arious methods to determine what constitutes a "claim for relief" for purposes of Rule 54(b) have percolated amongst the circuits. One approach "focuses upon the possibility of separate recoveries under arguably separate claims." *Samaad v. City of Dallas,* 940 F.2d 925, 931 (5th Cir. 1991). If the alleged claims for relief do not permit more than one possible recovery, then they are not separately enforceable nor appropriate for Rule 54(b) certification. See *Brandt v. Bassett (In re*

Southeast Banking Corp.), 69 F.3d 1539, 1547 (11th Cir. 1995) (concluding that allegations seeking damages against holding company's directors for failing to consider merger possibilities over several years stated one claim because relief could only be recovered once); *Local P–171, Amalgamated Meat Cutters v. Thompson Farms Co.*, 642 F.2d 1065, 1070 (7th Cir. 1981) (Wisdom, J.) ("At a minimum, claims cannot be separate unless separate recovery is possible.").

Another approach "concentrates on the facts underlying the putatively separate claims." *Samaad*, 940 F.2d at 931. If the facts underlying those claims are different, then those claims may be deemed separate for Rule 54(b) purposes. "By the same token, if there is a great deal of factual overlap between the decided and the retained claims they are not separate, and appeal must be deferred till the latter are resolved." *Jack Walters & Sons v. Morton Bldg.*, 737 F.2d 698, 702 (7th Cir. 1984)). A prime basis for the factual approach is "to spare the court of appeals from having to keep relearning the facts of a case on successive appeals." *Id.*

Finally, at least one circuit has expressed that claims are not distinct when they are " 'so closely related that they would fall afoul of the rule against splitting claims if brought separately.' " *Tolson v. United States*, 235 U.S. App. D.C. 396, 732 F.2d 998, 1001 (D.C. Cir. 1984) (quoting *Local P–171*, 642 F.2d at 1071).

3. Federal Rule 54(b) is usually listed as an "exception" to § 1291. However, it is also possible to treat the rule as a procedural ploy to alter the case in a way that makes it satisfy § 1291. To illustrate, suppose that the judge in *N.A.A.C.P.*, immediately before granting the summary judgment, had severed the case under Federal Rule 20(b) or 42(b) into two separate cases—one comprising the two legally insufficient claims, the other comprising the remaining three claims. Is there any doubt that the court's grant of summary judgment on the two legally insufficient claims would be a final decision within the meaning of § 1291? In this regard, Federal Rule 54(b) can be thought of as a response to the liberal joinder provisions of the Federal Rules.

4. Determining which claims constitute a distinct claim for relief is only half the battle under Federal Rule 54(b). It is also important for the trial judge to include the specific language called for in that rule when she makes the ruling. Without an express determination that there is no just reason to delay entry of the judgment, a ruling cannot be appealed even if it clearly involves a claim for relief that is separate from the remaining claims.

5. Are there any limits on a judge's authority to make, or to refuse to make, the express determination called for by Federal Rule 54(b)? *Curtiss–Wright Corp. v. General Electric Co.*, 446 U.S. 1, 100 S.Ct. 1460, 64 L.Ed.2d 1 (1980), discusses this issue at length. It indicates that the trial judge must consider not only the equities of the individual case, but also the "administrative interests" of the court system. Most significantly, if a technically separate claim for relief nevertheless shares certain factual issues with other claims yet to be adjudicated, the trial judge should usually decline to make the express determination, in order to save the appellate court the possible trouble of reviewing those same issues twice. 446 U.S. at 8.

6. In *Chiles v. Thornburgh* on page 388, the court allowed a party whose motion to intervene as of right was denied to appeal immediately. Other circuits (although not all) agree that interlocutory appeals are available in this situation. Courts sometimes invoke Federal Rule 54(b) as the basis for this rule. Can you reconstruct the argument concerning how denial of a motion to intervene as of right involves a "separate claim" for purpose of Rule 54(b)?

7. At first glance, it might seem that the main risk posed by Federal Rule 54(b) is that a party will appeal too early, either because the issue that was resolved is not a distinct claim for relief, or because the trial judge did not make the express determination. The most likely consequence of an early appeal is merely added expense: the appellate court will dismiss, and make the party wait until later to appeal.

However, a far more serious risk posed by Federal Rule 54(b) is that appeal may occur too *late*. Federal Rule of Appellate Procedure 4(a)(1)(A) provides that a party must generally file notice of an appeal within 30 days of entry of judgment. If a timely notice is not filed, the party cannot appeal. The problem that arises in some Rule 54(b) cases is that the party does not realize that a final decision triggering the 30–day period has been issued. Compounding the problem is the nature of the express determination that the trial judge makes under the Rule. The judge need only say that there is no just reason to delay *entry of the judgment*. She need say nothing about appeals.

B.   § 1292(a)

Section 1292 represents Congress's attempt to soften the sting of § 1291's final decision rule. Section 1292(a) provides for immediate appeals of certain interlocutory orders. Unless you practice debtor-creditor or maritime law, you are unlikely to encounter the exceptions set out in § 1292(a)(2) and (3). However, many attorneys will be affected by § 1291(a)(1). This provision allows immediate appeals of orders involving injunctions. The rationale for the exception is that an injunction by its very nature changes the *status quo ante*, and can in some cases cause significant hardship. Note that the exception also applies when injunctive relief is *denied*. Do you see why?

What does the section mean by an "injunction?" The statute applies both to permanent injunctions granted at the end of a case, and to preliminary injunctions issued at an early stage in the proceedings. However, a grant or denial of a temporary restraining order is not appealable under § 1292(a)(1). A temporary restraining order, or "TRO", is a ruling that one party obtains in an emergency that is so pressing that there is no time to serve notice on the other parties.* To obtain a TRO, the moving party must show that the situation is so urgent that irreparable harm could occur during the time it would take to notify the other side and schedule a hearing. If granted, the order remains in force only until notice and a hearing can occur, at which time the court may convert the TRO into a preliminary injunction. Therefore, a TRO has a built-in review process—the trial judge

---

* Note that the terminology in this area differs. Some states refer to all preliminary injunctions as "temporary restraining or-ders." As used in this discussion, the key difference is whether notice is given to the opposing party.

herself will revisit the merits at the hearing to convert the TRO into a preliminary injunction. Given that built-in review, there is no need to allow an appeal of the TRO itself. Of course, the judge's later ruling on the preliminary injunction can be appealed under § 1292(a)(1).

C.   § 1292(b)

UNITED STATES v. BEAR MARINE SERVICES

696 F.2d 1117 (5th Cir. 1983)

RUBIN, Circuit Judge:

* * * The United States filed suit against Bear Marine Services (Bear Marine), International Matex Tank Terminals, Inc. (IMTT), and others for the cost of cleaning up an oil spill in the Mississippi River. The complaint alleged that a tug towing an oil-carrying barge laid the tow alongside IMTT's dolphin. When the barge struck the dolphin, a metal beam or object attached to the dolphin punctured one of the barge's oil tanks.

The basis of the government's claim against IMTT is that the spill was caused by its "negligence . . . in maintaining an unauthorized obstruction to navigation, namely a metal beam or object attached to a dolphin in violation of 33 U.S.C. 403." IMTT moved to dismiss the complaint against it for failure to state a claim upon which relief could be granted. One basis for this motion was IMTT's assertion that the Federal Water Pollution Control Act, 33 U.S.C. §§ 1251–1376 (1976) (FWPCA), provided the exclusive means for the government to recover the cost of cleaning up oil spills.

The district court denied IMTT's motion. The court held that the FWPCA had not affected the government's right to proceed under fault-based maritime tort doctrines against non-sole cause, non-discharging third parties. The court certified for appeal under 28 U.S.C. § 1292(b), however, its holding that the FWPCA "is not the exclusive means by which the United States may recover oil clean-up costs from 'third parties'." A motions panel of this court granted leave to pursue the interlocutory appeal.

After this appeal had been preliminarily approved, this court decided *United States v. M/V Big Sam*, 681 F.2d 432 (5th Cir.1982). *Big Sam* held that the FWPCA does not preclude a fault-based maritime tort action against a sole-cause, non-discharging third party. * * * Therefore, if the government establishes that IMTT was negligent, even if it is shown that this was concurrent with the negligence of some other party and that IMTT was not alone at fault, the government may recover from IMTT. * * *

Thus, our decision in *Big Sam* resolves the primary issue upon which the interlocutory appeal was granted. The parties, nevertheless, contend that there are still issues we could decide. The United States asks us to decide whether maintenance of an unauthorized obstruction to navigation constitutes a per se violation of the federal common law, noting "expressions at the highest level" that such an action may not exist. IMTT, on the other hand, suggests that we should decide whether the United States may ever assert a cause of action against IMTT under the FWPCA.

The final judgment rule is the hallmark of federal appellate jurisdiction. * * * The foundation of the principle codified by 28 U.S.C. 1291, which permits appeals of only "final decisions," is the avoidance of piecemeal litigation. The policy that cases are ordinarily to be reviewed only once, and then comprehensively, conserves judicial energy and eliminates the delays, harassment, and costs that would be occasioned by a succession of separate interlocutory appeals.

The Judicial Code, however, authorizes appeals from interlocutory orders in exceptional cases such as those in which the potential shortening of litigation warrants such an extraordinary procedure. One such unusual appeal is permitted when a district judge certifies that the order to be appealed "involves a controlling question of law as to which there is a substantial ground for difference of opinion" and that immediate appeal will materially advance the end of the litigation. 28 U.S.C. § 1292(b). Upon receiving this certification, the court of appeals may, in its discretion, permit the appeal.

In this circuit, as in many others, a motion for leave to appeal an interlocutory order is first presented to a motions panel. That panel, prior to the filing of briefs on the merits, makes a preliminary decision to allow or refuse the appeal. Thereafter, the case is briefed and assigned to a panel for disposition on the merits.

The merits panel has the benefit of full briefs and frequently, as in this case, oral argument. It also has the opportunity to consider events that took place after the motions panel preliminarily allowed the appeal. With this perspective, the merits panel may conclude that the initial decision to hear the appeal was, or was later rendered, improvident. If the merits panel reaches that conclusion, it must vacate the earlier order granting leave to appeal and must remand the case to the district court. * * *

Prior to our decision in *Big Sam*, it was unclear whether the FWPCA provided the exclusive remedy for the claim against IMTT in the present case. Now, it is clear that the FWPCA does not. Therefore, nothing that we can do will prevent a trial of the negligence claim in this case. At the very least, both parties agree that the complaint states a cause of action against IMTT sounding in fault-based maritime tort.

We decline to address the additional theories of liability. We do not sit to decide moot questions, or to issue advisory opinions. The appropriate time to consider these theories is at trial, in the context of the actual proof of the case.

The United States suggests that considerable time of the court and counsel have been invested in considering this appeal. That is no reason for the court to dissipate further energies on the appeal or to decide questions that may prove to be hypothetical. Moreover, it is evident the trial will be short, and nothing we might do is likely to abbreviate it significantly. Action by this court will not, therefore, materially advance the ultimate termination of this litigation. For these reasons, we VACATE the order granting leave to appeal and REMAND to the district court for further proceedings.

Notes and Questions

1.   Although both Federal Rule 54(b) and § 1292(b) both turn on the willingness of the trial judge to allow immediate appeal, the two exceptions are in no way redundant. List all of the differences between the grounds for, and procedures governing, the two provisions.

2.   *Controlling.* An issue is "controlling" within the meaning of § 1292 if resolution of that issue is very likely to affect the outcome of one or more claims in the case. *Sokaogan Gaming Enterprise Corp. v. Tushie–Montgomery Associates, Inc.*, 86 F.3d 656 (7th Cir. 1996); *In re City of Memphis*, 293 F.3d 345 (6th Cir. 2002). Would an order denying a motion to submit the dispute to arbitration be a "controlling" issue? *See Faber v. Menard, Inc.*, 267 F.Supp.2d 961 (N.D. Iowa 2003), *rev'd on other grounds* 367 F.3d 1048 (8th Cir. 2004).

3.   *Question of Law.* The issue of whether a ruling involves a question of law has proven surprisingly problematic. Of course, a ruling that is based in whole or in part on an evaluation of the evidence does not involve a question of law. *Christy v. Pennsylvania Turnpike Comm.*, 912 F.Supp. 148 (E.D. Penn. 1996) (ruling on summary judgment motion); *Genentech, Inc. v. Novo Nordisk A/S*, 907 F.Supp. 97 (S.D.N.Y. 1995). Similarly, a challenge to the trial judge's exercise of discretion cannot be appealed under § 1292(b). *White v. Nix*, 43 F.3d 374 (8th Cir. 1994). But in other cases, determining whether something is a question of law is more difficult. In *Faber*, discussed in the prior note, the court held that whether a contract clause that required arbitration was "unconscionable" was a question of law. Do you agree?

4.   *Substantial Ground for Difference of Opinion.* If the law on a given issue is well settled, appeal under § 1292(b) is unavailable. Ironically, this means that § 1292(b) cannot be used when the trial judge makes a blatant and easily-corrected mistake on the governing law.

5.   *Materially Advance Termination.* The final factor is one of the most difficult to satisfy. Many rulings of law may meet the other parts of the test, but flounder on this last requirement. The main case is one example of a case where allowing an appeal would not advance termination of the litigation. Another is *Piazza v. Major League Baseball*, 836 F.Supp. 269 (1993), where a baseball player brought antitrust and other claims against Major League Baseball. The trial court denied defendant's motion to dismiss the antitrust claim. At first glance, it might seem that immediate appeal of this ruling would advance termination, for if the trial court was wrong, there would be no need to litigate the factually complicated antitrust claim. However, the court found that because the antitrust issue was factually intertwined with other issues that would have to be tried anyway, immediate appeal would not really speed up the case.

6. Unlike Federal Rule 54(b), the entry of an order qualifying for immediate appeal does not commence the running of the thirty-day period to appeal. The losing party may, at its choice, either seek certification under § 1292(b) or wait to appeal until after a final judgment.

D. Federal Rule 23(f)

Federal Rule 23(f) allows for an immediate appeal of any district court order granting or refusing class action certification. Such orders are crucial, and often prove to be as important as the merits of the case itself. However, it is difficult to appeal these non-final orders under the other exceptions discussed in this section. Rule 23(f) was added in 1998 to allow for immediate appeals of certification rulings. Note that appeal is not a matter of right, but is up to the discretion of the court of appeals.

Unlike most of the other Federal Rules, Rule 23(f) was not enacted pursuant to the Rules Enabling Act, 28 U.S.C. § 2072. Instead, the Supreme Court promulgated the Rule under the special grant of authority contained in 28 U.S.C. § 1292(e). This different source of Court authority means that an *Erie* analysis of Rule 23(f) would proceed along different lines than the analysis employed for the other Federal Rules.

E. Mandamus and Prohibition

The writs of mandamus and prohibition allow a party to challenge the acts of a government official in court. Technically, mandamus orders the official to do something, while prohibition orders the official *not* to do something. However, the distinction between the two is often a matter of semantics. For example, if a judge refuses to grant a party's motion to amend her complaint, the party might seek a mandamus ordering the judge to allow amendment, or a prohibition preventing the judge from proceeding any further with the case without the amendment.

Although the writs of mandamus and prohibition are by no means limited to challenges to trial judge decisions, they can in certain cases provide a safety valve from the final judgment rule. Mandamus and prohibition actually involve a new, separate action brought against the official. Because it is a new action rather than an appeal, a mandamus or prohibition case falls outside the restrictions of the final judgment rule of 28 U.S.C. § 1291. Potentially, then, the writs could prove to be a useful way to challenge a wide array of interlocutory rulings.

However, at least in federal court, mandamus and prohibition are of little use as a substitute to appeal. Mandamus and prohibition are "extraordinary writs." To obtain relief, the party must usually demonstrate that the judge has abdicated her jurisdictional duties. Merely showing error is not enough, even if the error is fairly clear. Nor can mandamus or prohibition be used to challenge decisions falling within the discretion of the trial judge.

Nevertheless, there is one issue where mandamus is frequently used in the federal system as an avenue of appeal. As discussed in Chapter 9, in certain cases the parties have a constitutional right to a jury trial. In part because of these constitutional concerns, a decision by the trial judge to deny a jury trial can often be challenged by mandamus. A decision to *grant* a jury trial, by contrast, violates no one's constitutional rights, and cannot be appealed by mandamus.

F.   The Collateral Order Doctrine

The statutes and Federal Rules discussed to this point allow a variety of important interlocutory decisions to be appealed immediately, rather than after a final judgment. Taken together, these exceptions help to avoid many of the situations in which the final judgment rule imposes serious hardship on the losing party. However, they do not provide a solution for all the problem cases. The subject of this section—the "collateral order" doctrine—represents the courts' attempt to fill in the gaps.

IN RE DIET DRUGS (PHENTERMINE/FENFLURAMINE/ DEXFENFLURAMINE) PRODUCTS LIABILITY LITIGATION

401 F.3d 143 (3d Cir. 2005)

GARTH, Circuit Judge.

* * *

I

In November 1999, American Home Products Corporation ("AHP"), which had sold two prescription drugs for the treatment of obesity, fenfluramine and dexfenfluramine, marketed as "Pondimin" and "Redux," entered into a Nationwide Class Action Settlement Agreement (the "Settlement Agreement") with a coalition of plaintiffs' attorneys. These attorneys represented those individuals * * * who had sought monetary damages and other relief from their purchase and ingestion of the diet drugs.

Comprehensive in its description of the various classes or categories of claimants which it comprised, the Settlement Agreement also made provision for the payment of legal fees. In particular, the Settlement Agreement established two accounts (to be funded by Wyeth)—the Fund A Legal Fee Escrow Account and the Fund B Legal Fee Escrow Account—to provide for an appropriate award of attorneys' fees. Additionally, the District Court ordered a percentage of fees from settlements or other recoveries achieved by opt-out plaintiffs in individual actions to be paid into a separate account * * * to compensate the Plaintiffs' Management Committee (the "PMC") for its common benefit work in MDL 1203. The District Court's interim award of attorneys' fees ($153,722,-911.25) was comprised of funds from all three accounts.

The overarching question presented by four of the seven current appeals is whether the District Court properly sequestered a percentage of funds from individual settlements or recoveries to compensate the PMC in cases where individual plaintiffs and their attorneys did not utilize the PMC's discovery or trial preparation materials and thus received no ostensible benefit from the PMC. * * *

A threshold issue here, however, is that of our appellate jurisdiction, for absent jurisdiction we cannot decide the many issues raised before us. We are confronted with appeals from an award of attorneys' fees, which, by their interim nature, may lack the necessary elements of finality to properly invoke this Court's appellate jurisdiction. At the outset, therefore, but not before we describe the nature of the interim fee award within the broader context of this litigation, we turn to the resolution of our jurisdiction. * * *

II

Between 1995 and 1997, four million people took Pondimin and two million people took Redux. In September 1997, the U.S. Food and Drug Administration ("FDA") issued a press release reporting abnormal echocardiograms in a "higher than expected percentage of" patients taking the drugs. Subsequent studies suggested that the drugs may have been linked to serious cardiopulmonary side effects, including heart-valve regurgitation (the reverse flow of blood through a closed valve of the heart) and primary pulmonary hypertension (a progressive and fatal disease affecting pulmonary circulation).

After the withdrawal of the diet drugs, 18,000 individual suits and 130 class actions were filed in state and federal courts. In December 1997, the federal cases were transferred to the Eastern District of Pennsylvania for consolidated or coordinated pretrial purposes by the Judicial Panel on Multidistrict Litigation pursuant to 28 U.S.C. § 1407. In November 1999, Wyeth entered into the Settlement Agreement with users of the diet drugs in the United States. After conducting fairness proceedings, the District Court in the Eastern District of Pennsylvania certified a settlement class and approved the Settlement Agreement. * * *

IV.

Courts of Appeals acquire jurisdiction over appeals through final orders under 28 U.S.C. § 1291; collateral orders under the doctrine of *Cohen v. Beneficial Indus. Loan Corp.*, 337 U.S. 541, 546 (1949); interlocutory orders concerning injunctions under 28 U.S.C. § 1292(a); questions certified for appeal by the district court and then certified by the appellate court under 28 U.S.C. § 1292(b); or certification by the district court pursuant to Fed.R.Civ.P. 54(b) of a "final" judgment when disposition has been had of less than all parts or issues in a given case.

We are not here concerned with the jurisdictional routes provided by § 1292 or Fed.R.Civ.P. 54(b), inasmuch as certification was neither sought nor granted by the District Court and the appeals filed here do not involve the denial, modification or grant of injunctive relief. The Appellants essentially rely on "finality" pursuant to § 1291 and the collateral order doctrine as sources of appellate jurisdiction. We hold that their reliance is misplaced. * * *

A decision of the district court is "final" if it "ends litigation upon the merits and leaves nothing for [the] court to do but execute the judgment." *Catlin v. United States*, 324 U.S. 229, 233 (1945). Accordingly, then, an interim award of attorneys' fees is not, in almost all cases, an appealable final order because it foresees further and additional action by the district court, thus continuing, but not concluding, the fee litigation.

Appellants urge, however, that the fee award determined by the District Court possesses the necessary elements of finality to constitute a final, appealable order for purposes of 28 U.S.C. § 1291. In Appellants' view, there was nothing tentative about the fee award, which they claim differentiates this case from those cases holding that interim fee awards are non-appealable. The signal characteristic of a non-appealable interim award, they argue, is the partial compensation paid to counsel "amidst ongoing litigation" such that the determination of the ultimate amount of the award becomes entwined with a consideration of the merits. Here, by contrast, they claim the merits of the underlying litigation is now complete because the District Court has approved the class action settlement, leaving only ministerial or administrative tasks associated with the implementation of the settlement to be completed. Properly understood, then, they argue that this case involves an advance or partial payment of a finite fee award, not an "interim" award of unquantifiable total fees.

In so arguing, however, Appellants mistakenly assume that the total fee award has been firmly established by the District Court. * * *

Only after the remaining issues, affecting the overall value and efficacy of the settlement, have been resolved will the District Court be in a position to consider making a final fee award to Class Counsel. In other words, the total fee award relates to the overall settlement value, which is undetermined at this time. * * *

The collateral order doctrine, as first annunciated in *Cohen v. Beneficial Indus. Loan Corp.*, "relaxes the strict standard of finality by permitting [the court] to entertain appeals from certain orders that would not otherwise be appealable final decisions." *Martin v. Brown*, 63 F.3d 1252, 1258 (3d Cir.1995) (citations omitted). The order sought to be appealed must (1) conclusively determine the disputed question, (2) resolve an important issue completely separate from the merits of the action, and (3) be effectively unreviewable on appeal from a final judgment. *Coopers & Lybrand v. Livesay*, 437 U.S. 463, 468 (1978). We have described these three requirements as (1) the "conclusiveness" prong, (2) the "importance/separateness" prong, and (3) the "unreviewability" prong. *Martin*, 63 F.3d at 1259. Failure to satisfy any one prong defeats collateral order jurisdiction.

Applying the *Cohen* factors here, it is evident that Pretrial Order Nos. 2622 and 2859 do not qualify as collateral orders, for each fails to satisfy both the "conclusiveness" and "unreviewability" prongs.

1. The "Conclusiveness" Prong

An order is conclusive when no further consideration is contemplated by the district court, which excludes from review any decision which is tentative, informal or incomplete. Analyzing the first *Cohen* criteria [*sic*], we cannot conclude that the pretrial orders conclusively determined the question of attorneys' fees. To the contrary, the District Court has expressed unequivocally that it intends to revisit the issue and make a final award after applying the Gunter factors. The fee award leaves unresolved the *total* or *final* amount of fees due to Class Counsel. * * *

2. The "Unreviewability" Prong

On the unreviewability prong of the *Cohen* requirements, we consider whether the District Court's orders will be "effectively unreviewable" absent immediate review. *Martin*, 63 F.3d at 1261. To meet this requirement, an order must be such that review postponed will, in effect, be review denied. For purposes of the collateral order doctrine, unreviewability means that failure to review immediately may well cause significant harm.

It is well established that an award of interim fees may be effectively reviewed after final judgment is entered. The one possible exception to this conclusion, as suggested in *Palmer v. City of Chicago*, 806 F.2d 1316, 1319–20 (7th Cir.1986), is when the mere payment of fees would make them unrecoverable. That is, to satisfy the "unreviewability" prong, there must be a showing that disbursement of the fees might very well make them unrecoverable at the end of the litigation should they turn out to have been awarded in error. Appellants have made no such showing here.

Appellants cite to *Palmer* to support their argument that the interim fee award is collaterally appealable under *Cohen* because of the irreparable harm that may be inflicted by an order to pay interim fees. In *Palmer*, a district court ordered a city to pay immediately interim fees that might not have been recoverable if the award was later held invalid. The Seventh Circuit held that the order threatened sufficient harm to justify appellate review. *Palmer*, however, does not support Appellants' position here.

As explained by the Ninth Circuit in *Rosenfeld*, "the 'irrevocable harm' in Palmer would arise because interim fees were to be paid directly to a 'revolving fund' of prisoners and defendants whose class members might, by the close of the litigation, be insolvent, have disappeared, or no longer even be parties, making recovery upon appeal impossible." 859 F.2d at 721. In contrast, the *Palmer* court stated,

> If (but for this appeal) the fees would have been disbursed to the lawyers rather than retained by the prisoners and defendants, the problem would be less serious ... [w]e assume that the district court has an inherent power to order attorneys to whom fees were paid over by their clients pursuant to court order to repay the fees should the order be reversed.

Palmer, 806 F.2d at 1319.

Rosenfeld distinguished *Palmer* on the basis that the interim fees were paid directly to counsel, thus satisfying *Palmer*'s concern. 859 F.2d at 721. In this case, too, the interim fees will go directly to counsel and the threat of insolvency is entirely conjectural. * * *

At least two of the three Cohen criteria have not been met in this case. Accordingly, we hold that the appeals taken from Pretrial Order Nos. 2622 and 2859 cannot be entertained under the collateral order doctrine of Cohen.

V

We have examined the grounds of jurisdiction advanced by the Appellants, and we have explored with them our own jurisdictional analysis. We have concluded that there is no theory of jurisdiction that permits us to entertain any of the merits arguments or issues presented by the seven Appellants. We have been instructed that absent jurisdiction, we are to dismiss the appeals filed and take no further action. See *Firestone Tire & Rubber Co. v. Risjord*, 449 U.S. 368, 379 (1981) ("If the appellate court finds that the order from which a party seeks to appeal does not fall within [its appellate jurisdiction], its inquiry is over.").

We do so here.

[The concurring opinion of Judge AMBRO is omitted.]

Notes and Questions

1. The collateral order doctrine applies only to "important" issues. What issue are important? According to one court of appeals, determining whether something is important involves balancing the harm to the appellant that would be caused by delaying appeal and the efficiency costs of allowing appeal. *United States v. Philip Morris, Inc.*, 314 F.3d 612 (D.C. Cir. 2003). Isn't that akin to comparing apples and oranges?

2. Why does the exception apply only to "collateral" orders; *i.e.*, orders that do not involve the merits? What would be the consequences of allowing immediate appeal of orders that touched on the merits of the case?

3. The most difficult part of the test to satisfy is the "effectively unreviewable" requirement. Do you understand why the ruling in *Diet Drugs* failed this prong? Won't *every* ruling fail this requirement? Is there ever a situation where a court of appeals, waiting until after final judgment, cannot "undo" the harm done by an erroneous ruling at trial? At the very least, can't the court of appeals grant a new trial?

Consider the situation in *Cohen*, the Supreme Court case mentioned in *Diet Drugs* that established the collateral order doctrine. In that case, the issue was whether a plaintiff in a shareholders derivative action had to file a bond. The bond would be used to compensate defendant if the case proved frivolous. The trial court held that no bond was required, and defendant tried to appeal. The Supreme Court held that the ruling was immediately appealable. Note that if defendant had to wait until after final judgment to appeal, it would suffer the very harm—frivolous litigation—that the bond was intended to deter. Once the defendant had litigated the frivolous suit, nothing the court of appeals could do would fix the problem. A new trial would only make matters worse.

In general, then, one class of cases where the "effectively unreviewable" prong will be met is where the harm caused is the *trial itself*. Relying on this logic, courts often allow collateral order appeals when the defendant claims that he is immune from suit under the Eleventh Amendment or some other doctrine. *See, e.g., Nanda v. Board of Trustees of University of Illinois*, 303 F.3d 817 (7th Cir. 2002). To the extent that immunity is a freedom from being sued at all (as opposed to freedom from having to pay damages), forcing a defendant whose claim of immunity has been rejected to delay its appeal until after a final judgment would deprive that defendant of the main benefit of the immunity. Recent decisions have expanded the exception to "qualified" immunity, where protection turns on a finding that the defendant acted in good faith. *See, e.g., International Action Center v. United States*, 365 F.3d 20 (D.C. Cir. 2004); *Coleman v. Parkman*, 349 F.3d 534 (8th Cir. 2003). However, denial of a motion to dismiss based on *forum non conveniens* is not effectively unreviewable. *In re Ford Motor Co.*, 344 F.3d 648 (7th Cir. 2003).

4. Is the collateral order exception constitutional? The final judgment rule of 28 U.S.C. § 1291 is a rule of subject matter jurisdiction. Under Article III of the Constitution, only Congress has the power to define the jurisdiction of the federal appellate courts. To the extent that the appellate courts have expanded their jurisdiction beyond that allowed by §§ 1291 and 1292, the collateral order doctrine raises serious constitutional concerns.

But is the collateral order doctrine really an exception? Can you make an argument that the rule is simply an interpretation of the word "final" in § 1291?

Problems

1. P sues D for breach of contract. The court enters judgment for P for $50,000. However, because D refuses to pay, P will need to obtain a garnishment order from the trial court to seize D's bank account. May D appeal now, or must it wait until after the garnishment order?

2. P sues D1 and D2 for negligence. The trial judge grants D1's motion to dismiss the case against it for lack of personal jurisdiction. Is dismissal of the case against D1 a final judgment under 28 U.S.C. § 1291?

3. P sues D, his neighbor, in federal court. P's complaint contains two counts. In Count One, P seeks recovery for a window that D broke while playing baseball in her yard. Count Two seeks recovery for nuisance, based on D's annoying habit of playing her stereo at loud levels during the middle of the night. P seeks damages under Count One, and both damages and an injunction under Count Two. The trial court grants partial summary judgment to P on the broken window claim. May D appeal immediately?

4. Same as Problem 3, except that the court grants partial summary judgment for P on the question of nuisance instead of the broken window, and awards damages to P. However, the court does not decide whether to issue the injunction.

5. Same as Problem 3, except that the court grants partial summary judgment for P on the question of nuisance instead of the broken window,

and grants an injunction. However, the court does not decide what P's damages are for the nuisance.

6.   P sues D for unfair competition. During discovery, P asks D to disclose its customer list. D argues that the list is a trade secret, and asks the court for a protective order against disclosure of the list. The court agrees with D and grants the protective order. May P appeal this ruling immediately?

7.   Same as Problem 6, except that the court agrees with P, and orders D to disclose the list.

8.   P sues D, an internet service provider, for negligence and breach of contract based on D's transmission of a computer virus to P. The court enters judgment as a matter of law for D on the negligence claim, finding that D's acts were not unreasonable as a matter of law. Other courts, dealing with similar facts, have reached the opposite conclusion. Recognizing this difference in views, the trial judge certifies the ruling as ripe for interlocutory appeal, and the court of appeals agrees to hear the case. Did the courts act properly?

C.   SCOPE OF APPELLATE REVIEW

Sections A and B of this Chapter deal with who can appeal a case, and when an appeal may occur. But what does the appellate court do with the case once it gets there? Many of you are aware from your course in legal research or legal writing that the court of appeals will often have a hearing at which each side may present its arguments. Beyond that, however, you may never have focused specifically on an appellate court's power to review what the trial court has done.

At the risk of oversimplification, there are two main issues that arise in appellate review. First, the appellate court cannot necessarily review all issues that were adjudicated by the trial court. For many issues, appellate review is possible only if the appealing party raised the issue at trial. Second, even when an issue was properly raised below, the court of appeals may not try the issue anew. Instead, the appellate court will give a certain degree of deference to the trial court's decision. Each of these issues is addressed in turn.

1.   Need to Raise the Issue Below

At the risk of sounding trite, the role of an appellate court is to *review* what the trial judge did. Therefore, as a general matter a court of appeals will not hear arguments that did not form part of the trial court's decision. As with every general rule, however, there are exceptions. The first is *subject matter jurisdiction*. As you learned in Chapter 2, in federal court a party can raise subject matter jurisdiction at any time, even for the first time on appeal. The limits on federal subject matter jurisdiction are so fundamental, and so important, that the ordinary rules about waiver of rights by failure to assert them is set aside.

The second main exception to the general rule applies to the party who won at trial. A prevailing party may ask the appellate court to affirm on *any* ground, even if the trial court did not rely on that ground as a basis for its judgment. Although a few courts have suggested that an appellee may raise entirely new theories on appeal in order to sustain a judgment, the weight of the precedent makes it clear that the argument must have been presented at trial in some form:

> (I)t is likewise settled that the appellee may, without taking a cross-appeal, urge in support of a decree any matter appearing in the record, although his argument may involve an attack upon the reasoning of the lower court or an insistence upon matter overlooked or ignored by it. By the claims now in question, the [appellant] does not attack, in any respect, the decree entered below. It merely asserts additional grounds why the decree should be affirmed.

United States v. American Rwy Express Co., 265 U.S. 425, 435–36, 44 S.Ct. 560, 68 L.Ed. 1087 (1924). *See also Dandridge v. Williams*, 397 U.S. 471, 475–76 n. 6, 90 S.Ct. 1153, 25 L.Ed.2d 491 (1970); *Skipper v. French*, 130 F.3d 603, 610 (4th Cir. 1997); *Boggs v. West*, 188 F.3d 1335 (Fed. Cir. 1999).

As noted in section A of this chapter, in some circumstances a prevailing party may also appeal. However, a party need not appeal if all it wants to do is offer alternate arguments to affirm the holding. Filing a cross-appeal is necessary only of the party seeks either to increase his own rights or to diminish the rights of his adversary. *Montgomery v. City of Ardmore*, 365 F.3d 926, 944 (10th Cir. 2004).

Contemporaneous Objection Rule. The contemporaneous objection rule is a corollary to the general principle that a party may only argue issues that were tried below. To preserve the right to appeal based on a supposed error that occurred at trial, the aggrieved party must object to the error in timely fashion. A timely objection is one raised in time to prevent significant harm from occurring. For example, objections to the proposed jury instructions must be raised before those instructions are submitted to the jury, or those objections are lost. Moreover, if the mistake continues to manifest itself later in the trial, the party may be required to restate its objection on one or more additional occasions. For example, if the judge wrongfully allows hearsay evidence, and the plaintiff's attorney refers to that evidence in his closing argument, the defendant should object again to preserve the right to appeal.

The contemporaneous objection rule is tempered by certain exceptions. First, there are limits on the requirement that a recurring objection must be repeated. For example, if a judge rules that a particular witness is an expert, the opposing side should enter an objection into the record at that point. However, most courts would not require the party to restate its objection every time that witness offers an opinion.

Second, if the trial judge makes a "clear error," the party need not object at all. The clear error exception is exceedingly limited, however.

An error will be deemed clear only if it is so manifestly incorrect that it leads one to believe that the judge has a basic bias against the party.

The rationale for the contemporaneous objection rule is fairly obvious. No trial is free from errors. However, to deal with those errors by way of the appellate process is very inefficient, as each appeal involves considerable "start up" time for the appellate panel. To encourage efficiency, then, the rule requires the parties to give the trial judge at least one chance to correct her own mistake.

Note that the contemporaneous objection rule applies only to mistakes that occur during trial. If a party wants to appeal based on the judgment itself, no formal objection is necessary. More importantly, although a party who loses a verdict is free to seek a new trial or judgment as a matter of law from the trial judge, neither of those motions is a prerequisite to an appeal. If a party feels that the trial judge is not inclined to provide post-judgment relief, she can appeal directly to the appellate court.

2. The Standard of Review

The role of the appellate court is not to retry the case. Thus, the appellate court will give a certain amount of deference to the rulings of the trial court. However, the appellate court does not give equal deference to all findings. The amount of deference varies depending on the nature of the particular issue being reviewed.

Basically, the standard of review turns on whether the issue is one of fact, law, or something committed to the trial court's discretion. With respect to findings of *fact*, the appellate court gives a great deal of deference, assuming that the trial court's findings are correct unless it is clearly demonstrated otherwise. Federal Rule 52(a) calls this standard of review "clearly erroneous"; some states use different terminology to express the same basic idea. For questions of *law*, by contrast, the appellate court gives no deference at all. This standard of review is commonly referred to as *"de novo"*, and allows the appellate court to reverse merely if it disagrees with the trial court. Because determining the governing rule of law does not depend on an evaluation of the evidence presented at trial, there is no need for the court of appeals to give any deference on pure issues of law. Finally, there are certain issues—for example, the decision whether to grant a new trial—that are left to the *discretion* of the trial judge. For these issues, the appellate court will overturn only if the trial judge's decision was an "abuse of discretion." The abuse of discretion standard is even more deferential than the clearly erroneous standard.

This division between questions of fact, law, and discretionary matters is not nearly as clear as it may seem at first glance. What exactly do we mean by a question of "fact" or "law?" The following materials provide a brief glimpse into this complex issue.

LAVOIE v. PACIFIC PRESS & SHEAR CO., 975 F.2d 48 (2d Cir. 1992). Lavoie, an industrial worker, was hurt by a machine. Lavoie sued the manufacturer of the machine for negligence. The jury found defendant negligent, and defendant appealed. Defendant argued that the jury erred in finding both that defendant was negligent and that its negligence was the proximate cause of plaintiff's injuries. Defendant argued that the acts of his employer (GE) were an intervening cause. The court refused to overturn the jury findings:

> Defendant's burden in this regard is a substantial one. In Vermont, only verdicts that are not "justified by 'any reasonable view of the evidence'" will be overturned. See *Claude G. Dern Electric, Inc. v. Bernstein*, 144 Vt. 423, 479 A.2d 136, 138 (1984) (quoting *Crawford v. State Highway Board*, 130 Vt. 18, 285 A.2d 760, 764 (1971)). A jury finding of negligence will be preserved unless reasonable persons reviewing the record, construed in favor of the prevailing party could not draw different conclusions and would reach a different result. Federal law applies a similar standard. The record reveals an ample basis for the finding of negligence by Pacific, and we therefore need not select between federal and state standards.

> Defendant contends further that a finding of negligence against it may not stand because it was not a proximate cause of plaintiff's injuries. Pacific points to testimony that Lavoie would not have been injured if her co-workers had not turned off the non-integrated light curtain which GE had installed to protect operators of the machine. The alleged negligence of plaintiff's co-workers constituted, defendant continues, an efficient intervening cause of the injuries, making any negligence by defendant merely a contribution to but not a cause of the accident. We disagree.

> Like the predicate question of negligence, the issue of proximate cause is one for the jury, and nonprevailing parties who seek to challenge such findings face similar substantial burdens. The law in Vermont makes clear that more than one act of negligence, each contributing to produce a harm, may be a concurring proximate cause. * * * If negligent conduct by a third person was a foreseeable consequence that, "in the eye of the law, the person charged was bound to anticipate, the causal connection is not broken." *Beatty v. Dunn*, 103 Vt. 340, 154 A. 770, 772 (1931). * * *

> Once again defendant fails to sustain its heavy burden for overturning findings of the jury, this time that defendant's negligence was a proximate cause of plaintiff's injuries. Sufficient evidence is present in the record that supports the finding that Pacific should have anticipated, first, that GE would install a light curtain that was not integrated with the power supply to the press brake and, second, that a GE employee might turn on the press brake without using the light curtain. Reasonable persons could conclude that GE, a company not in the business of equipping press brakes with safety devices, might have become aware of the danger posed by the brake press but nevertheless failed adequately to retrofit the machine due to its own inexperience. Such a failure on GE's part would not work

to absolve defendant of liability if Pacific should have anticipated that GE's efforts would not be adequate.

OREGON TRAIL ELEC. CONSUMERS COOP., INC. V. CO–GEN CO., 168 Or.App. 466, 7 P.3d 594 (2000). Oregon Trail, an electric cooperative, bought electricity from Co–Gen under a written contract. Oregon Trail later filed suit for a declaratory judgment that the price should be modified to reflect the public interest. The trial court determined that the contract did not allow Oregon Trail to seek to modify the purchase price, and accordingly entered judgment for Co–Gen. The court of appeals affirmed. However, it reviewed the trial judge's rulings on the meaning of the contract partly under a "clearly erroneous" standard, and partly under a *de novo* standard:

> The pertinent principles we follow in construing a contract are well-settled. In the absence of an ambiguity, the trial court in the first instance, and this court on appeal, determines the meaning of a contract as a matter of law. A contract provision is legally ambiguous if it has no definite significance or if it is capable of more than one reasonable and sensible construction in the context of the agreement as a whole. In deciding whether an ambiguity exists, the court is not limited to mere text and context but may consider parol and other evidence. Likewise, if the contract is ambiguous, the trier of fact may consider other evidence of the parties' intentions and construe the language of the agreement accordingly. Where the trial court's construction of the contract depends on factual inquiries, we review the court's factual findings for "any evidence." Our review otherwise is for legal correctness, which means that we determine, as though in the first instance, how the contract should be construed.

AETNA CASUALTY AND SURETY CO. V. LEAHEY CONSTRUCTION CO., INC., 219 F.3d 519 (6th Cir. 2000). Aetna provided a surety bond to Leahey in connection with a construction project. When Aetna was called upon to pay under the bond, it sued Leahey, a bank, and an accounting firm, alleging that Leahey's financial condition had been misrepresented in the negotiations for the surety agreement. The jury entered judgment for Aetna, and the judge denied defendants' motion for judgment as a matter of law. On appeal, one of defendants' claims was that the judge should have entered judgment as a matter of law on two of plaintiff's claims; namely, aiding and abetting fraud and conspiracy to commit fraud. The appellate court upheld the trial judge's ruling on aiding and abetting, but overturned the ruling on conspiracy. In so ruling, the court also had to determine whether the state or federal standard of review applied in a diversity case:

> The standard of review applicable to a district court's determinations pursuant to Rule 50 of the Federal Rules of Civil Procedure in a diversity action has been summarized by this court as follows:

>> [A] federal court sitting in diversity reviews *de novo* legal determinations raised by a Rule 50 motion, and must apply the

forum state's standard of review "only when a Rule 50 challenge is mounted to the sufficiency of the evidence supporting a jury's findings. No deference is appropriate in diversity cases to the trial court's resolutions of legal questions."

Palmer v. Fox Software, Inc., 107 F.3d 415, 418 (6th Cir.1997) (quoting *K & T Enters., Inc. v. Zurich Ins. Co.*, 97 F.3d 171, 176 (6th Cir.1996)); see also *J.C. Wyckoff & Assocs., Inc. v. Standard Fire Ins. Co.*, 936 F.2d 1474, 1482 (6th Cir.1991) ("In federal court diversity cases, this circuit adheres to the minority rule that state law governs the standard for granting motions for directed verdicts and judgments notwithstanding the verdict.").

An appellate court reviewing a diversity action, however, "need show no deference to the trial court's assessment of the sufficiency of the evidence before a jury, even if state law so requires." *K & T Enters.*, 97 F.3d at 176 (emphasis in original). As will become apparent, the defendants' challenge to the district court's denial of their Rule 50 motions is "mounted to the sufficiency of the evidence" and, therefore, this court must apply Ohio's standard of review. * * *

In reviewing the evidence presented at trial, the court held that the jury could reasonably have found that defendants aided and abetted fraud. However, on the conspiracy claim, the court held that it was unreasonable on the evidence presented for the jury to infer a conspiracy.

Notes and Questions

1. Can *Lavoie* and *Oregon Trail* be reconciled? How can a finding of negligence involve a question of fact, while a finding of the meaning of a contract—which like negligence deals with the state of mind of the parties—involve a question of law?

2. In *Oregon Trail*, how important is it that the contract was in writing? Would an appellate court apply the *de novo* standard of review to a finding of negligence *per se* based on a violation of a statute?

3. In *Aetna*, do you understand why the court applied the *de novo* standard to a trial judge's ruling on judgment as a matter of law, given that the grant of judgment as a matter of law requires evaluation of the evidence?

4. When an appellate court reviews a finding of fact, does it matter whether that finding was made by a judge or a jury? Most courts hold that when reviewing a jury verdict, the standard applied by the court of appeals is the same as a trial judge would apply when asked to set aside a jury verdict. Is that standard more or less deferential than the clearly erroneous standard?

5. Are there limits to how much deference a court can give to a jury verdict? In *Honda Motor Co., Ltd. v. Oberg*, 512 U.S. 415, 114 S.Ct. 2331, 129 L.Ed.2d 336 (1994), the Court was faced with a provision in the Oregon Constitution which forbade judicial review of the amount of punitive damages awarded by a jury "unless the court can affirmatively say there is no

evidence to support the verdict." The Court held that the provision violated the due process clause of the fourteenth amendment to the United States Constitution. Due process, the Court reasoned, requires some meaningful judicial review of a jury's award of punitive damages.

6. *Abuse of discretion.* The abuse of discretion standard is reserved for certain rulings that are subject to the discretion of the trial judge, such as rulings on a new trial, rulings on preliminary injunctions and temporary restraining orders, and the scope of sanctions for discovery and Federal Rule 11 violations. How does the abuse of discretion standard differ from the clearly erroneous standard?

Unfortunately, there is no single accepted definition of "abuse of discretion." As one appellate court noted, "Abuse of discretion is famously slippery—its meaning can vary between contexts, and there has been little consensus over the years as to precisely what the phrase means." *Zervos v. Verizon New York, Inc.*, 252 F.3d 163, 169 note 4 (2d Cir. 2001). Another court surveyed various definitions of the term:

> One view is represented by the statement in *Delno v. Market St. Ry.*, 124 F.2d 965, 967 (9 Cir. 1942):
>
>> Discretion, in this sense, is abused when the judicial action is arbitrary, fanciful or unreasonable, which is another way of saying that discretion is abused only where no reasonable man would take the view adopted by the trial court. If reasonable men could differ as to the propriety of the action taken by the trial court, then it cannot be said that the trial court abused its discretion.
>
> A sharply contrasting view was voiced by Chief Judge Magruder in *In re Josephson*, 218 F.2d 174, 182 (1 Cir. 1954):
>
>> "Abuse of discretion" is a phrase which sounds worse than it really is. All it need mean is that, when judicial action is taken in a discretionary matter, such action cannot be set aside by a reviewing court unless it has a definite and firm conviction that the court below committed a clear error of judgment in the conclusion it reached upon a weighing of the relevant factors.
>
> The Ninth Circuit, without citation of *Delno*, has since followed or even gone beyond the Josephson formulation, see *Pearson v. Dennison*, 353 F.2d 24, 28 n. 6 (9 Cir. 1965) (Duniway, J.):
>
>> We do not much like the term "abuse" in this context. It has pejorative connotations not here appropriate. But it has become the customary word. Perhaps "misuse" is milder. What we mean, when we say that a court abused its discretion, is merely that we think that it made a mistake. There are, however, cases in which the term abuse is appropriate.

Buffalo Courier–Express, Inc. v. Buffalo Evening News, Inc., 601 F.2d 48, 59 note 18 (2d Cir. 1979).

D. UNITED STATES SUPREME COURT REVIEW

So far, this chapter has focused almost exclusively on appeals from the federal district courts to the courts of appeal. The next step in the federal appeals process, of course, is the United States Supreme Court. Because of its special role in the United States federal system, Supreme Court review is governed by its own special statutes, and in some respects its own principles.

A case can reach the Supreme Court by three different routes, depending on the parties and issues. As the highest federal court, the Supreme Court reviews lower federal court decisions. However, unlike the other federal courts, the Supreme Court also has the authority to review cases heard in the *state* court systems.* Review of state cases raises issues of federalism, some of which are addressed in Part 2 of this section. Finally, in certain rare cases the Supreme Court actually serves as a *trial* court. *See, e.g., New Hampshire v. Maine*, set out on page 791, which involves a suit between two states.

As a technical matter, the United States Supreme Court hears very few true appeals. Instead, review of both federal court of appeals decisions and state court decisions is initiated by a writ of *certiorari*. See 28 U.S.C. §§ 1254 and 1257. The main distinction between appeals and *certiorari* is that the latter is entirely discretionary, giving the Supreme Court the ability to pick and choose the cases it will decide. Congress has over the years narrowed the cases in which a party may actually appeal to the Supreme Court. Today, the only direct appeals occur under 28 U.S.C. § 1253, which provides for direct appeal of a case that must be heard by a three-judge panel. Note that in these rare cases involving a three-judge panel, the party appeals directly from the district court to the Supreme Court.

1. Supreme Court Review of the Federal Courts of Appeal

Review of cases in the federal courts of appeal is governed by 28 U.S.C. § 1254. The most important distinction between that section and § 1291 is that § 1254 has no final judgment requirement. Therefore, a party can seek *certiorari* for any decision by the court of appeals as soon as it occurs. However, because appellate proceedings are resolved in a fairly short time window, and because the Supreme Court has the discretion whether to grant *certiorari*, review of interlocutory rulings of an federal court of appeals are rare.

Section 1254(2) allows the appellate court to certify questions of law to the Supreme Court. Such certification could be useful in a case where

---

* The writ of *habeas corpus* admittedly gives lower federal courts the power to review state judicial proceedings that result in imprisonment or other confinement. Like the writs of mandamus and prohibition, however, the federal court in these cases is not technically involved in an "appeal." Because the writ applies mainly in criminal cases, and involves a number of significant restrictions, study of *habeas corpus* is best deferred to an upper level course in Criminal Procedure or Federal Courts.

the law is unclear. The Supreme Court may, if it chooses, issue a ruling clarifying the issue for the appellate court, or it may take the entire case itself, bypassing the court of appeals.

2.   Supreme Court Review of the States' High Courts

Section 1257 governs appeals from the state courts. Unlike § 1254, § 1257 *does* have a final judgment rule. Thus, a party cannot seek *certiorari* from the Supreme Court for a state case until the state courts have completely wrapped up the case. The definition of a "final" judgment under § 1257 and 1291 is essentially the same. However, most of the exceptions discussed in section B.2 of this chapter do not apply under § 1257. The only exception that does apply is the "collateral order" doctrine. In fact, the collateral order doctrine was developed primarily under § 1257. As with the definition of "final", precedent involving the collateral order doctrine is equally valid for appeals under § 1291 and review of state court opinions under § 1257.

The Supreme Court can only hear rulings of "the highest court of a State in which a decision could be had." Typically, this will be the state's supreme court. However, if a particular case cannot be appealed to the state supreme court because of a procedural issue, the United States Supreme Court can review decisions of the lower state courts.

Perhaps the most important limitation imposed by § 1257, however, is that Supreme Court review is confined to issues of *federal* or *constitutional* law. The Supreme Court cannot review a state's rulings on *state* law, even if the litigants are of diverse citizenship.* This limitation reflects a somewhat unusual—and often forgotten—feature of the United States Supreme Court. The United States Supreme Court is misnamed, for it is not a true supreme court. Instead, it is a supreme *federal* court, bound by the jurisdictional limitations of Article III of the United States Constitution. The Supreme Court of Canada, by contrast, is a real supreme court, capable of reviewing all legal issues regardless of their source.

This feature of § 1257 raises a number of intriguing problems. Most of these are beyond the scope of a basic Civil Procedure course. However, one important issue—the "adequate and independent state ground" doctrine—arises with sufficient frequency that it warrants mention here. The doctrine has played a major role in defining the Supreme Court's perception of its proper function.

HERB v. PITCAIRN, 324 U.S. 117, 65 S.Ct. 459, 89 L.Ed. 789 (1945). After suffering serious injuries in a railroad accident, plaintiff sued defendant, his employer, under the Federal Employers' Liability Act. Plaintiff sued in an Illinois City Court. One of the core issues in the case was whether the federal law allowed recovery. While the case was pending, the Illinois Supreme Court ruled that City Courts could not hear cases brought by

---

* Note that this restriction is contained only in § 1257, not in 1254. Thus, when the Supreme Court reviews a decision of a lower federal court, it can hear all questions properly before that lower court, including questions of state law.

railroad employees under federal law. Plaintiff then sought and obtained an order of the City Court transferring venue to Circuit Court, which clearly had jurisdiction to hear these claims. Defendant, however, argued that the City Court was completely powerless to hear the case, and so the order transferring venue was invalid. The Illinois Supreme Court agreed with defendant, holding that under state law, plaintiff's case was not currently pending in any state court. Because the statute of limitations had run on his claim, plaintiff sought *certiorari* from the United States Supreme Court. The Supreme Court refused to hear the case:

> This Court from the time of its foundation has adhered to the principle that it will not review judgments of state courts that rest on adequate and independent state grounds. *Murdock v. Memphis,* 20 Wall. 590, 636; *Berea College v. Kentucky,* 211 U.S. 45, 53; *Enterprise Irrigation District v. Farmers' Mutual Canal Co.,* 243 U.S. 157, 164; *Fox Film Corp. v. Muller,* 296 U.S. 207. The reason is so obvious that it has rarely been thought to warrant statement. It is found in the partitioning of power between the state and federal judicial systems and in the limitations of our own jurisdiction. Our only power over state judgments is to correct them to the extent that they incorrectly adjudge federal rights. And our power is to correct wrong judgments, not to revise opinions. We are not permitted to render an advisory opinion, and if the same judgment would be rendered by the state court after we corrected its views of federal laws, our review could amount to nothing more than an advisory opinion. If the Illinois court means to hold that the city courts could not adjudge, transfer, or begin these cases and that no case is pending in its courts at the present time, it is manifest that no view we might express of the federal Act would require its courts to proceed to the trial of these actions.

MICHIGAN v. LONG

463 U.S. 1032, 103 S.Ct. 3469, 77 L.Ed.2d 1201 (1983)

Justice O'CONNOR delivered the opinion of the Court.

* * * David Long was convicted for possession of marijuana found by police in the passenger compartment and trunk of the automobile that he was driving. The police searched the passenger compartment because they had reason to believe that the vehicle contained weapons potentially dangerous to the officers. We hold that the protective search of the passenger compartment was reasonable under the principles articulated in * * * decisions of this Court. We also examine Long's argument that the decision below rests upon an adequate and independent state ground, and we decide in favor of our jurisdiction. * * *

Before reaching the merits, we must consider Long's argument that we are without jurisdiction to decide this case because the decision below rests on an adequate and independent state ground. The court below referred twice to the state constitution in its opinion, but otherwise relied exclusively on federal law.[3] Long argues that the Michigan courts have provided greater protection from searches and seizures under the state constitution than is afforded under the Fourth Amendment, and the references to the state constitution therefore establish an adequate and independent ground for the decision below. * * *

Although we have announced a number of principles in order to help us determine whether various forms of references to state law constitute adequate and independent state grounds,[4] we openly admit that we have thus far not developed a satisfying and consistent approach for resolving this vexing issue. In some instances, we have taken the strict view that if the ground of decision was at all unclear, we would dismiss the case. In other instances, we have vacated or continued a case in order to obtain clarification about the nature of a state court decision. In more recent cases, we have ourselves examined state law to determine whether state courts have used federal law to guide their application of state law or to provide the actual basis for the decision that was reached. * * *

This ad hoc method of dealing with cases that involve possible adequate and independent state grounds is antithetical to the doctrinal consistency that is required when sensitive issues of federal-state relations are involved. Moreover, none of the various methods of disposition that we have employed thus far recommends itself as the preferred method that we should apply to the exclusion of others, and we therefore determine that it is appropriate to reexamine our treatment of this jurisdictional issue in order to achieve the consistency that is necessary. * * *

Respect for the independence of state courts, as well as avoidance of rendering advisory opinions, have been the cornerstones of this Court's refusal to decide cases where there is an adequate and independent state ground. It is precisely because of this respect for state courts, and this desire to avoid advisory opinions, that we do not wish to continue to decide issues of state law that go beyond the opinion that we review, or to require state courts to reconsider cases to clarify the grounds of their

---

3. On the first occasion, the court merely cited in a footnote both the state and federal constitutions. On the second occasion, at the conclusion of the opinion, the court stated: "We hold, therefore, that the deputies' search of the vehicle was proscribed by the Fourth Amendment to the United States Constitution and art. 1, § 11 of the Michigan Constitution."

4. For example, we have long recognized that "where the judgment of a state court rests upon two grounds, one of which is federal and the other non-federal in character, our jurisdiction fails if the non-federal ground is independent of the federal ground and adequate to support the judgment." *Fox Film Corp. v. Muller*, 296 U.S. 207, 210 (1935). We may review a state case decided on a federal ground even if it is clear that there was an available state ground for decision on which the state court could properly have relied. Also, if, in our view, the state court " 'felt compelled by what it understood to be federal constitutional considerations to construe ... its own law in the manner that it did,' " then we will not treat a normally adequate state ground as independent, and there will be no question about our jurisdiction. *Delaware v. Prouse*, 440 U.S. 648, 653 (1979) Finally, "where the non-federal ground is so interwoven with the [federal ground] as not to be an independent matter, or is not of sufficient breadth to sustain the judgment without any decision of the other, our jurisdiction is plain." *Enterprise Irrigation District v. Farmers Mutual Canal Company*, 243 U.S. 157, 164 (1917).

decisions. Accordingly, when, as in this case, a state court decision fairly appears to rest primarily on federal law, or to be interwoven with the federal law, and when the adequacy and independence of any possible state law ground is not clear from the face of the opinion, we will accept as the most reasonable explanation that the state court decided the case the way it did because it believed that federal law required it to do so. If a state court chooses merely to rely on federal precedents as it would on the precedents of all other jurisdictions, then it need only make clear by a plain statement in its judgment or opinion that the federal cases are being used only for the purpose of guidance, and do not themselves compel the result that the court has reached. In this way, both justice and judicial administration will be greatly improved. If the state court decision indicates clearly and expressly that it is alternatively based on bona fide separate, adequate, and independent grounds, we, of course, will not undertake to review the decision.

This approach obviates in most instances the need to examine state law in order to decide the nature of the state court decision, and will at the same time avoid the danger of our rendering advisory opinions. It also avoids the unsatisfactory and intrusive practice of requiring state courts to clarify their decisions to the satisfaction of this Court. We believe that such an approach will provide state judges with a clearer opportunity to develop state jurisprudence unimpeded by federal interference, and yet will preserve the integrity of federal law. "It is fundamental that state courts be left free and unfettered by us in interpreting their state constitutions. But it is equally important that ambiguous or obscure adjudications by state courts do not stand as barriers to a determination by this Court of the validity under the federal constitution of state action." *National Tea Co.*, supra, 309 U.S., at 557.

The principle that we will not review judgments of state courts that rest on adequate and independent state grounds is based, in part, on "the limitations of our own jurisdiction." *Herb v. Pitcairn*, 324 U.S. 117, 125 (1945). The jurisdictional concern is that we not "render an advisory opinion, and if the same judgment would be rendered by the state court after we corrected its views of federal laws, our review could amount to nothing more than an advisory opinion." *Id.*, at 126. Our requirement of a "plain statement" that a decision rests upon adequate and independent state grounds does not in any way authorize the rendering of advisory opinions. Rather, in determining, as we must, whether we have jurisdiction to review a case that is alleged to rest on adequate and independent state grounds, we merely assume that there are no such grounds when it is not clear from the opinion itself that the state court relied upon an adequate and independent state ground and when it fairly appears that the state court rested its decision primarily on federal law.

Our review of the decision below under this framework leaves us unconvinced that it rests upon an independent state ground. Apart from its two citations to the state constitution, the court below relied exclusively on its understanding of * * * federal cases. Not a single state case was cited to support the state court's holding that the search of the passenger compartment was unconstitutional. Indeed, the court declared that the search in this case was unconstitutional because "[t]he Court of Appeals erroneously applied the principles of *Terry v. Ohio* ... to the search of the interior of the vehicle in this case." The references to the state constitution in no way indicate that the decision below rested on grounds in any way independent from the state court's interpretation of federal law. Even if we accept that the Michigan constitution has been interpreted to provide independent protection for certain rights also secured under the Fourth Amendment, it fairly appears in this case that the Michigan Supreme Court rested its decision primarily on federal law.

Rather than dismissing the case, or requiring that the state court reconsider its decision on our behalf solely because of a mere possibility that an adequate and independent ground supports the judgment, we find that we have jurisdiction in the absence of a plain statement that the decision below rested on an adequate and independent state ground.

[The Court then held that the search was illegal under the Fourth Amendment.]

[The concurring opinion of Justice BLACKMUN, and the dissenting opinions of Justice BRENNAN (joined by MARSHALL) and Justice STEVENS are omitted.]

Notes and Questions

1.   Conceptually, there are two types of adequate and independent state grounds, *substantive* and *procedural*. A case involves a substantive ground when the ruling is based on two claims or defenses, one state, the other federal or constitutional. A procedural state ground, by contrast, exists when some question of state procedural law prevents the state court from reaching a federal issue. What type of state ground was involved in *Herb*? In *Long*?

2.   The test set out by the court in *Long* explores whether the state ground is truly "independent" of the federal ground. If you were a state supreme court judge writing an opinion after *Long*, is there anything you could do to "insulate" your decision from being reviewed by the Supreme Court?

3.   There are also a few decisions involving whether a state ground is "adequate." *See, e.g., Henry v. Mississippi*, 379 U.S. 443, 85 S.Ct. 564, 13 L.Ed.2d 408 (1965) (failure to satisfy state contemporaneous objection rule did not prevent Supreme Court from reviewing illegality of search). These cases typically involve "procedural" state grounds. Reviewing state grounds for adequacy may have fallen into disfavor, as in recent years it has become increasingly difficult for a party to obtain review by arguing that a state ground is inadequate.

4.   Is there something problematic about the Court's test in *Long*? Even if the state court relied heavily on federal precedent, isn't the state constitutional ground still purely a question of state law?

5.   Suppose a state supreme court is dealing with a case involving an illegal search. The court finds that the search is constitutional under the

fourth amendment to the United States Constitution, but violates the analogous state constitutional provision. However, the court's reasoning with respect to the state ground is nothing more than a bare-bones conclusion. Moreover, the opinion does not contain any language stating that the state grounds are independent from the United States constitutional grounds. Why will the Supreme Court not review the case, even though it lacks the "clear statement" called for by *Long*?

Problems

1. P sues D in federal court, alleging three claims. The trial judge dismisses the complaint for failure to state a claim, and P appeals. The appellate court summarily affirms the dismissal with respect to claim one, but schedules a hearing to hear arguments concerning the other two claims. May P appeal now, or must she wait until the appellate court has ruled on all three claims?

2. P sues D in a state court in State Alpha. In his answer, D argues that because he has no minimum contacts with Alpha, it would violate the United States Constitution for an Alpha court to exercise personal jurisdiction over him. Unlike the Federal Rules, however, the Alpha Rules of Procedure require a party to raise personal jurisdiction in a pre-answer motion, or the defense is lost. The trial judge therefore refuses to consider D's personal jurisdiction argument. The case goes to trial, and judgment is entered for P. D appeals on the personal jurisdiction grounds, but the state's high court affirms the trial judge's ruling, based on the Alpha procedure rule. Will the United States Supreme hear the case?

3. Same as Problem 2, except that D properly raises the personal jurisdiction defense. The trial judge, however, denies D's motion to dismiss. The case goes to trial, and judgment is entered for P. D appeals. The Alpha Supreme Court affirms the trial judge's rulings on jurisdiction, but reverses the judgment for P, finding that P's complaint failed to state a claim because it omitted a vital element. The Alpha Supreme Court remands the case to the trial judge with orders to dismiss for failure to state a claim. However, because the statute of limitations has not yet run on P's claim, P could amend the complaint and refile the action. D seeks review of the state Supreme Court judgment. May the United States Supreme Court hear the case?

Chapter 13

SPECIAL ISSUES IN FEDERAL COURT

Almost all of the cases in this book are from federal court. However, most of the issues in Civil Procedure arise in both the state and federal systems. Although the governing rules may differ, all courts must deal with matters such as pleading, personal jurisdiction, joinder, discovery, controlling the jury, and appeals. This book, like all Civil Procedure books, concentrates on the Federal Rules and federal cases mainly because it is the one system that exists throughout the nation.

On the other hand, there are three significant topics in Civil Procedure that are virtually unique to the federal courts: federal subject-matter jurisdiction, the Seventh Amendment right to a jury trial, and the *Erie* doctrine. Each of these topics has been dealt with to some extent earlier. However, because the discussion of federal question jurisdiction and *Erie* was fairly basic, this Chapter explores these two topics in greater depth. Whether your professor chooses to cover this material turns on several factors, especially whether these issues are addressed in upper-level courses at your school.

A. ADVANCED ISSUES IN FEDERAL QUESTION JURISDICTION

INTRODUCTORY PROBLEM

A little over a year ago, Ivan Inventor invented a better mousetrap. However, contrary to the popular adage, the world has not beaten a path to his door. Sales of Ivan's mousetrap have been very slow despite his intensive marketing efforts.

While watching an infomercial on television one day, Ivan discovers the reason for his slow sales. Mimi Cry, an aspiring entrepreneur, is peddling her own mousetrap. Mimi's trap is almost identical to Ivan's, using the same irresistible yet deadly bait, and a similar foolproof mechanism that prevents escape. After further investigation, Ivan is convinced that Mimi copied his trap.

Ivan therefore sues Mimi in a state court in the State of The Union. Because he never filed for a patent, Ivan cannot bring a federal patent infringement claim against Mimi. Ivan's complaint instead contains two state-law claims. First, he sues Mimi for common-law misappropriation, based on her intentional copying of his invention. Second, he brings a claim under the state's false advertising statute. Under this statute, false advertising occurs either when a person makes a false statement about his product, or when he "fails to disclose a fact that he is required by law to disclose." Ivan's complaint correctly asserts that the Federal Insecticide, Fungicide, and Rodenticide Act (FIFRA) requires Mimi to disclose to consumers the rodenticides that she uses in her bait. As Mimi does not disclose the information required by federal law, Ivan contends that she has violated the state false advertising statute.

Mimi files a timely notice of removal. Ivan moves to remand, contending that removal was improper. It is clear that diversity jurisdiction is not available. However, Mimi argues that both of Ivan's claims, although ostensibly based on state law, actually constitute federal questions. With respect to the misappropriation claim, Mimi correctly points out that the federal patent laws preempt all state laws that allow recovery for copying of inventions. Indeed, the scope of preemption under the federal patent laws is quite broad, as state laws are preempted even if they are entirely consistent with federal patent laws. Mimi argues that the issue of preemption introduces a federal issue into the misappropriation claim, making it a federal question.

With respect to the false advertising claim, Mimi takes a different tack. FIFRA does not preempt state false advertising laws. However, because Ivan has invoked FIFRA as proof that Mimi did not make a disclosure required "by law," Mimi argues that the court must interpret FIFRA in order to resolve the false advertising claim. This federal "element," Mimi contends, is enough to make the false advertising claim a federal question.

How should the federal district judge rule on Ivan's motion to remand?

Governing law: 28 U.S.C. §§ 1331 and 1441 (mainly to refresh your memory).

In *Louisville & Nashville Railroad v. Mottley* on page 56, you learned that courts use the "face of the complaint" rule to determine whether a case involves a federal question under § 1331 and similar statutes. Under that rule, federal law must be the foundation of plaintiff's claim. A court does not consider defenses and counterclaims asserted by the defendant when applying that rule.

The examples discussed in Chapter 3 are in one sense the "easy cases," where plaintiff's right to recover clearly does (or does not) arise under federal law. And in truth, the vast majority of cases involve that relatively straightforward analysis. But on occasion, a federal court must deal with a claim that, although purporting to arise under state law, also involves one or more issues governed by federal law. The following two cases discuss two ways in which this federal "ingredient" can lead a court to treat the state claim as a federal question.

NICODEMUS v. UNION PACIFIC CORPORATION

318 F.3d 1231 (10th Cir. 2003)

TACHA, Chief Circuit Judge

BACKGROUND

Plaintiffs-appellees are Wyoming landowners (1) Warren Nicodemus, trustee, and (2) John Morris, Norma Morris, and John H. Bell Iron Mountain Ranch Company. Defendants-appellants, Union Pacific Corporation and Union Pacific Railroad Company ("Union Pacific"), own railroad rights-of-way over plaintiffs' respective properties. Union Pacific acquired the rights-of-way at issue in this case under numerous federal land-grant statutes, dating from 1852 to 1875.

The dispute between the parties arose from agreements entered into by Union Pacific and numerous telecommunications providers, in which Union Pacific "licensed" to the telecommunications providers the right to install and maintain fiber-optic cables in the rights-of-way over plaintiffs' land. Union Pacific has received and continues to receive revenue from these license agreements.

Plaintiffs brought suit in federal court, arguing that Union Pacific's actions exceeded the scope of Union Pacific's rights under the federally granted rights-of-way. Plaintiffs claim that Union Pacific's rights-of-way over their land are easements and that plaintiffs retain the servient tenement in the underlying land, subject only to Union Pacific's undisputed right to conduct railroad operations along the rights-of-way. In the district court, Nicodemus sought various forms of relief, including: (1) damages for trespass; (2) damages for unjust enrichment; (3) an accounting and disgorgement of rents and profits; (4) a permanent injunction "ordering Union Pacific to cease offering, negotiating, or undertaking leases, licenses, sales, or other conveyances of any claimed interest in the [plaintiffs'] lands;" and (5) a declaratory judgment establishing, *inter alia,* that "Union Pacific's interest in the right-of-way land across which it still operates railroad cars is limited to that necessary for the operation of the railroad and does not entitle Union Pacific to use the land beyond that use which is necessary for railroad operations . . . and Union Pacific's purported or asserted interest(s) in the lands owned by [plaintiffs] was terminated upon abandonment of the railroad rights of way and/or discontinuation of railroad operations on these rights of way." The Morris plaintiffs advanced similar claims, and in addition, requested the following: (1) damages for slander of title; (2) damages for inverse condemnation; and (3) "an injunction that requires Union Pacific to remove the trespassing fiber optical telecommunications cables."

Union Pacific raised numerous affirmative defenses in response to plaintiffs' respective complaints, including the existence of a "license" and the fact that "Defendants have acted within their rights and have engaged in uses of their property interests that are permitted." * * *

On December 6, 2001, the district court ... dismissed plaintiffs' causes of action for lack of subject-matter jurisdiction, concluding that it lacked jurisdiction under both 28 U.S.C. § 1331 and 1332. * * *

Union Pacific brought this appeal, contending that the district court erred in concluding that it lacked subject-matter jurisdiction under 28 U.S.C. § 1331.

Discussion

[The court first determined that Union Pacific could appeal even though it had won below. As discussed in Chapter 11, even a prevailing party may appeal if it can show that the judgment is not exactly what it wanted.] * * *

1. Overview

"Federal courts are courts of limited jurisdiction; they must have a statutory basis for their jurisdiction." *Morris v. City of Hobart,* 39 F.3d 1105, 1111 (10th Cir.1994). There are two statutory bases for federal subject-matter jurisdiction: diversity jurisdiction under 28 U.S.C. § 1332 and federal-question jurisdiction under 28 U.S.C. § 1331. Federal-question jurisdiction exists for all claims "arising under the Constitution, laws, or treaties of the United States." 28 U.S.C. § 1331. "A case arises under federal law if its 'well-pleaded complaint establishes either that federal law creates the cause of action or that the plaintiff's right to relief necessarily depends on resolution of a substantial question of federal law.'" *Morris,* 39 F.3d at 1111 (quoting *Franchise Tax Bd. of Cal. v. Construction Laborers Vacation Trust for S. Cal.,* 463 U.S. 1, 27–28 (1983)).

Thus, to find jurisdiction under 28 U.S.C. § 1331, two conditions must be satisfied. First, a question of federal law must appear on the face of plaintiff's well-pleaded complaint. *Rice v. Office of Servicemembers' Group Life Ins.,* 260 F.3d 1240, 1245 (10th Cir.2001). Second, plaintiff's cause of action must either be (1) created by federal law, or (2) if it is a state-created cause of action, "its resolution must necessarily turn on a substantial question of federal law." *Id.* (citing *Merrell Dow Pharms. Inc. v. Thompson,* 478 U.S. 804, 808 (1986)). "A court examining whether a case turns on a [substantial] question of federal law [must] focus on whether Congress evidenced an intent to provide a federal forum." *Morris,* 39 F.3d at 1111 (citation omitted).

2. The well-pleaded complaint rule

"[W]hether a claim 'arises under' federal law must be determined by reference to the 'well-pleaded complaint.'" *Merrell Dow,* 478 U.S. at 808 (citing *Franchise Tax Bd.,* 463 U.S. at 9–10). It is well settled that "[a] defense that raises a federal question is inadequate to confer federal jurisdiction." Federal-question jurisdiction is not present "even if the [federal] defense is anticipated in the plaintiff's complaint, and even if both parties admit that the defense is the only question truly at issue in the case." *Franchise Tax Bd.,* 463 U.S. at 14.

In this case, we assume without deciding that plaintiffs' various causes of action satisfy the well-pleaded complaint rule. Accordingly, we proceed to consider plaintiffs' claims under the second prong of the federal-question jurisdictional analysis.

3. *Plaintiffs' state-created causes of action do not give rise to federal-question jurisdiction*

The "vast majority" of federal-question jurisdiction cases fall within Justice Holmes' statement that a " 'suit arises under the law that creates the cause of action.' " *Merrell Dow,* 478 U.S. at 808 (quoting *American Well Works Co. v. Layne & Bowler Co.,* 241 U.S. 257, 260 (1916)). Federal-question jurisdiction also exists, however, where "it appears that some substantial, disputed question of federal law is a necessary element of one of the well-pleaded state claims." *Franchise Tax Bd.,* 463 U.S. at 13. But the "mere presence of a federal issue in a state cause of action does not automatically confer federal-question jurisdiction." *Merrell Dow,* 478 U.S. at 813. In considering whether a substantial federal question exists, we must exercise "prudence and restraint." *Id.* at 810. After *Merrell Dow,* "[a] court examining whether a case turns on a [substantial] question of federal law should focus on whether Congress evidenced an intent to provide a federal forum." *Morris,* 39 F.3d at 1111.

In this case, plaintiffs sought damages under numerous theories, including: (1) trespass; (2) unjust enrichment; (3) slander of title; and (4) inverse condemnation. Plaintiffs also requested injunctive and declaratory relief. Union Pacific raised numerous defenses in response to plaintiffs' allegations, including (1) license and (2) legal authorization.[7]

Union Pacific argues that federal-question jurisdiction exists in this case because of the substantial federal interest in the railroad rights-of-way held by Union Pacific. In support of this contention, Union Pacific notes the following: (1) the federal government's subsidization of the construction of a transcontinental railroad through right-of-way grants; (2) the federal government's limited right of reverter in the railroad rights-of-way, and (3) the applicability of federal common law in construing the federal land-grant statutes, *see N. Pac. Ry. Co. v. Townsend,* 190 U.S. 267, 270–71 (1903) (" 'The courts of the United States will construe the grants of the general government without reference to the rules of construction adopted by the states for their grants . . . .' ").

---

7. Specifically, Union Pacific pled the following affirmative defense: "In all respects pertinent to this action, Defendants have acted within their rights and have engaged in uses of their property interests that are permitted."

a. *There is no evidence that Congress intended to provide a federal forum.*

Union Pacific amply demonstrates, and we acknowledge, the existence of a considerable federal interest in the present case. However, separation-of-power principles mandate that Congress, not the courts, decide whether the federal interest is sufficiently substantial to justify the creation of federal-question jurisdiction. "[D]eterminations about federal jurisdiction require sensitive judgments about congressional intent, judicial power, and the federal system." *Merrell Dow,* 478 U.S. at 810. Thus, in considering the substantiality of the federal interest, "[we] focus on whether Congress evidenced an intent to provide a federal forum." *Morris,* 39 F.3d at 1111 (citing *Merrell Dow,* 478 U.S. at 812).

To determine whether Congress intended to provide a federal forum, the surest indicator is whether the federal statute under consideration created a private right of action. In the absence of a federal private right of action, "it would flout congressional intent to provide a private federal remedy for the violation of the federal statute ... [and] it would similarly flout, or at least undermine, congressional intent to conclude that federal courts might nevertheless exercise federal-question jurisdiction." *Merrell Dow,* 478 U.S. at 812.

In the present case, Union Pacific does not contend that the federal land-grant statutes at issue in this case create a private right of action. Nor could it. Further, Union Pacific points to no alternative evidence of congressional intent to provide a federal forum. As the district court noted, "[there] is no suggestion that Congress intended to confer federal question jurisdiction over the construction of [federal] land grants." Under *Merrell Dow,* this absence is fatal. *Cf.* 478 U.S. at 814 ("[T]he congressional determination that there should be no federal remedy for the violation of this federal statute is tantamount to a congressional conclusion that the presence of a claimed violation of the statute as an element of a state cause of action is insufficiently 'substantial' to confer federal-question jurisdiction.").

b. *Plaintiffs' causes of action involve subjects traditionally relegated to state law.*

Focusing on the nature of plaintiffs' claims bolsters our conclusion. In conducting our jurisdictional inquiry, we must consider principles of federalism. *Morris,* 39 F.3d at 1112. "We hesitate to exercise jurisdiction where the 'cause of action is a subject traditionally relegated to state law.'" *Id.* (citing *Merrell Dow,* 478 U.S. at 811). In this case, plaintiffs' causes of action all arise under Wyoming property and tort law. "Because [trespass and unjust enrichment] actions are traditionally reserved for state courts to resolve, federalism concerns also militate against our exercise of jurisdiction here." *See id.*

c. *The Kansas Pacific case*

Union Pacific attempts to avoid this result, relying on the Supreme Court's decision in *Kan. Pac. Ry. Co. v. Atchison, Topeka & Sante Fe.*

R.R. Co., 112 U.S. 414 (1884). In *Kansas Pacific,* two railroad corporations each "claim[ed] title to the same land in Kansas under different acts of congress." *Id.* at 416. Plaintiff claimed a right to the property under 1862 and 1864 acts of Congress. Defendant claimed a right to the same property based on an 1863 act of Congress, in essence arguing that the 1863 act withdrew a certain section of property from the 1864 act under which plaintiff derived part of its rights. The Supreme Court concluded that the suit fell within the district court's statutory federal-question jurisdiction, noting that its "decision [would necessarily] depend[ ] upon the construction given to those acts." *Id.*

Union Pacific's reliance on *Kansas Pacific* is misplaced. First, Kansas Pacific did not hold that federal land-grant statutes create a private right of action in the grantee. In *Kansas Pacific,* the *sole* question before the Court was the reconciliation of two ostensibly conflicting federal land-grant statutes. So construed, the existence of federal-question jurisdiction is obvious. In the present case, however, we deal with federal land-grant statutes in the context of numerous state-created causes of action. Thus, federal law is but one element in plaintiffs' causes of action under Wyoming property and tort law. This is insufficient to confer federal-question jurisdiction, even assuming that the federal question is likely dispositive.

Second, since *Kansas Pacific,* the Supreme Court has construed the "arising under" jurisdictional grant in 28 U.S.C. § 1331 as conferring a more limited power than the Article III jurisdictional grant. Although *Kansas Pacific* dealt with the statutory grant of federal-question jurisdiction under the March 3, 1875, act of Congress, rather than the constitutional jurisdictional grant under Article III, the district court was likely correct in concluding that "the *Kansas Pacific* Court applied the broad constitutional 'ingredient' test in finding jurisdiction, not the more narrow 'federal remedy' test." *Nicodemus,* 204 F.R.D. at 485.

Thus, while *Kansas Pacific* has some bearing in our analysis, we must consider the peculiar posture of the case and the historical context in which the case was decided. Here, we have already concluded that Congress did not intend to provide a federal forum under the federal land-grant statutes. *Kansas Pacific* does not fill this void. Thus, we may not exercise federal-question jurisdiction over plaintiffs' state-created causes of action.

d. *Plaintiffs' requests for a declaratory judgment*

* * * In this case, both plaintiffs requested a declaratory judgment in the district court, establishing the scope of Union Pacific's rights under the numerous federal land-grant statutes. As discussed in sections II(B)(3)(a)-(c), plaintiffs' "coercive" actions do not give rise to federal-question jurisdiction. * * *

Similarly, a coercive action brought by Union Pacific to enforce its rights under the federal land-grant statutes would fall outside of 28 U.S.C. § 1331. As the Supreme Court noted in *Townsend,* " 'whatever incidents or rights attach to the ownership of property conveyed by the government will be determined by the states, subject to the condition that their rules do not impair the efficacy of the grants or the use and enjoyment of the property by the grantee.'" 190 U.S. at 270–71. Thus, because Union Pacific's rights incident to its ownership of federally-granted rights-of-way must be determined under state law, any "coercive action" brought by Union Pacific to enforce its rights would fall outside of 28 U.S.C. § 1331's jurisdictional grant, since the federal land-grant statutes contain no evidence of congressional intent to provide a federal forum.

e. *Plaintiffs' requests for injunctive relief*

Here, plaintiffs sought injunctive relief in order to protect rights granted under Wyoming property and tort law. Because the requested injunctions would protect *state-created rights,* and since the federal land-grant statutes at issue lack any evidence of congressional intent to provide a federal forum, we have no jurisdiction under 28 U.S.C. § 1331 to consider these claims.

Conclusion

The district court properly held that it lacked subject-matter jurisdiction under 28 U.S.C. § 1331. Accordingly, we AFFIRM.

Notes and Questions

1. The railroad received its right-of-way through a grant from the federal government. That federal grant defined the scope of the rights held by the railroad. Why, then, does the case not involve a federal question? Isn't it necessary to construe exactly what the federal government granted to the railroad in order to determine whether the railroad may license some of its rights to others?

In twenty-five words or less, restate the court's reasoning concerning why the case does not arise under federal law for purposes of § 1331.

2. In the Introductory Problem, would it affect your analysis to learn that FIFRA does not provide a private cause of action to enforce its labeling requirements? Instead, those requirements are enforced by the federal Environmental Protection Agency through fines.

3. Whether a federal statute creates a private cause of action can be a difficult question. If the federal statute explicitly addresses the issue, of course, the answer is clear. But courts will sometimes *imply* a private cause of action from the language of a statute that does not discuss who may enforce it. *Merrill Lynch, Pierce, Fenner & Smith, Inc. v. Curran,* 456 U.S. 353, 102 S.Ct. 1825, 72 L.Ed.2d 182 (1982) (private right of action under Commodities Futures Trading Commission Act). The implied cause of action analysis turns on several factors, the most important of which is a "clear indication" of Congress's intent. *Karahalios v. National Federation of Federal Employees,* 489 U.S. 527, 109 S.Ct. 1282, 103 L.Ed.2d 539 (1989). Because

evidence of intent is difficult to find, most of the recent cases refuse to imply causes of action.

4. What if plaintiff's complaint relies on federal law for one element, but that element could also be decided in plaintiff's favor without interpreting federal law? For example, suppose that plaintiff sues defendant for negligence in the operation of a commercial airplane. Plaintiff alleges that defendant is negligent because she violated a federal law dictating the altitude at which a plane may fly. That federal law would afford plaintiff a private right of action. However, plaintiff could also prevail by showing that defendant was negligent in some other way. In this case, federal law is an element, but not a necessary element, of the claim. Is the case a federal question? See *Columbia Gas Transmission Corp. v. Drain*, 191 F.3d 552 (4th Cir. 1999) (no jurisdiction).

5. The court also indicates that the Supreme Court's earlier decision in *Kansas Pacific* could be readily distinguished. First, that case applied a now-discarded interpretation of § 1331. As we have seen, the modern cases take a much narrower view of the statutory language.

On the other hand, the court also indicated that the different facts of *Kansas Pacific* presented an "obvious" federal question. Do you agree? Even if both parties were granted rights to the same land by the federal government, isn't the ultimate right being litigated—the right to exclusive possession—a right created by state law? In that respect, is *Kansas Pacific* really any different than *Nicodemus*?

6. Does the test applied in *Nicodemus* (commonly called the "*Merrell–Dow* test") make sense? Why does the fact that Congress chose not to allow private parties to sue under the federal statute affect whether a *state* claim that incorporates that federal statute qualifies as a federal question? How would it "flout Congress's intent" to allow a federal court to hear the state-law claim? Isn't the real issue whether a private party, who otherwise could not enforce the federal statute, should be able to "back door" his way into court (*any* court, state or federal) by incorporating the federal standard into a state claim?

7. *Nicodemus* is in one respect an unusual case. *Merrell–Dow* questions most often arise in the context of removal. Plaintiff would rather sue in state court. When it attempts to remove, defendant asserts that plaintiff, through "artful pleading," has disguised a federal claim in state-law clothing. Several cases make it clear that a party cannot prevent removal by phrasing what is in essence a federal claim as a state-law tort or other state action. *Franchise Tax Board v. Construction Laborers Vacation Trust*, 463 U.S. 1, 103 S.Ct. 2841, 77 L.Ed.2d 420 (1983); *Paige v. Henry J. Kaiser Co.*, 826 F.2d 857 (9th Cir. 1987).

8. In the Introductory Problem, suppose that FIFRA *did* provide a private cause of action. Under the *Merrell–Dow* test, Ivan's false advertising claim would qualify as a federal question. Could Ivan nevertheless prevent removal by explicitly waiving any reliance on his FIFRA claim? Under *Merrell–Dow*, is the court saying that when a federal private right exists, the complaint, measured by the "notice pleading" standards of Federal Rule 8, also automatically states a "hidden" federal claim—in which case a plaintiff could waive the federal claim by explicit language? Or is the Court saying

that the state claim itself becomes a federal question (in which case waiver would not work)? Several cases, including *ARCO Environmental Remediation, L.L.C. v. Department of Health and Environmental Quality, State of Montana*, 213 F.3d 1108 (9th Cir. 2000) and *Dunlap v. G & L Holding Group, Inc.*, 381 F.3d 1285 (11th Cir. 2004), appear to adopt the latter view.

BENEFICIAL NATIONAL BANK v. ANDERSON

539 U.S. 1, 123 S.Ct. 2058, 156 L.Ed.2d 1 (2003)

Justice STEVENS delivered the opinion of the Court.

The question in this case is whether an action filed in a state court to recover damages from a national bank for allegedly charging excessive interest in violation of both "the common law usury doctrine" and an Alabama usury statute may be removed to a federal court because it actually arises under federal law. We hold that it may.

I

Respondents are 26 individual taxpayers who made pledges of their anticipated tax refunds to secure short-term loans obtained from petitioner Beneficial National Bank, a national bank chartered under the National Bank Act. Respondents brought suit in an Alabama court against the bank and the two other petitioners that arranged the loans, seeking compensatory and punitive damages on the theory, among others, that the bank's interest rates were usurious. Their complaint did not refer to any federal law.

Petitioners removed the case to the United States District Court for the Middle District of Alabama. In their notice of removal they asserted that the National Bank Act, 12 U.S.C. § 85, is the exclusive provision governing the rate of interest that a national bank may lawfully charge, that the rates charged to respondents complied with that provision, that § 86 provides the exclusive remedies available against a national bank charging excessive interest, and that the removal statute, 28 U.S.C. § 1441, therefore applied. The District Court denied respondents' motion to remand the case to state court but certified the question whether it had jurisdiction to proceed with the case to the Court of Appeals pursuant to 28 U.S.C. § 1292(b).

A divided panel of the Eleventh Circuit reversed. The majority held that under our "well-pleaded complaint" rule, removal is generally not permitted unless the complaint expressly alleges a federal claim and that the narrow exception from that rule known as the "complete preemption doctrine" did not apply because it could "find no clear congressional intent to permit removal under §§ 85 and 86." Because this holding conflicted with an Eighth Circuit decision, *Krispin v. May Dept. Stores Co.*, 218 F.3d 919 (2000), we granted certiorari.

II

A civil action filed in a state court may be removed to federal court if the claim is one "arising under" federal law. § 1441(b). To determine whether the claim arises under federal law, we examine the "well pleaded" allegations of the complaint and ignore potential defenses: "a suit arises under the Constitution and laws of the United States only when the plaintiff's statement of his own cause of action shows that it is based upon those laws or that Constitution. It is not enough that the plaintiff alleges some anticipated defense to his cause of action and asserts that the defense is invalidated by some provision of the Constitution of the United States." *Louisville & Nashville R. Co. v. Mottley*, 211 U.S. 149, 152 (1908). * * * As a general rule, absent diversity jurisdiction, a case will not be removable if the complaint does not affirmatively allege a federal claim.

Congress has, however, created certain exceptions to that rule. [Discussion of other case omitted.]

We have also construed § 301 of the Labor Management Relations Act, 1947 (LMRA), 29 U.S.C. § 185, as not only preempting state law but also authorizing removal of actions that sought relief only under state law. *Avco Corp. v. Machinists*, 390 U.S. 557 (1968). We later explained that holding as resting on the unusually "powerful" pre-emptive force of § 301:

> The Court of Appeals held, and we affirmed, that the petitioner's action "arose under" § 301, and thus could be removed to federal court, although the petitioner had undoubtedly pleaded an adequate claim for relief under the state law of contracts and had sought a remedy available only under state law. The necessary ground of decision was that the pre-emptive force of § 301 is so powerful as to displace entirely any state cause of action "for violation of contracts between an employer and a labor organization." Any such suit is purely a creature of federal law, notwithstanding the fact that state law would provide a cause of action in the absence of § 301. *Avco* stands for the proposition that if a federal cause of action completely pre-empts a state cause of action any complaint that comes within the scope of the federal cause of action necessarily "arises under" federal law.

Franchise Tax Bd., 463 U.S., at 23–24 (footnote omitted).

Similarly, in *Metropolitan Life Ins. Co. v. Taylor*, 481 U.S. 58 (1987), we considered whether the "complete pre-emption" approach adopted in *Avco* also supported the removal of state common-law causes of action asserting improper processing of benefit claims under a plan regulated by the Employee Retirement Income Security Act of 1974 (ERISA), 29 U.S.C. § 1001 et seq. For two reasons, we held that removal was proper even though the complaint purported to raise only state-law claims. First, the statutory text in § 502(a), 29 U.S.C. § 1132, not only provided an express federal remedy for the plaintiffs' claims, but also in its jurisdiction subsection, § 502(f), used language similar to the statutory language construed in *Avco*, thereby indicating that the two statutes should be construed in the same way. 481 U.S., at 65. Second, the legislative history of ERISA unambiguously described an intent to treat such actions "as arising under the laws of the United States in similar fashion to those brought under section 301 of the Labor–Management Relations Act of 1947." *Id.*, at 65–66 (internal quotation marks and emphasis omitted).

Thus, a state claim may be removed to federal court in only two circumstances—when Congress expressly so provides, such as in the Price–Anderson Act, or when a federal statute wholly displaces the state-law cause of action through complete pre-emption.[3] When the federal statute completely pre-empts the state-law cause of action, a claim which comes within the scope of that cause of action, even if pleaded in terms of state law, is in reality based on federal law. This claim is then removable under 28 U.S.C. § 1441(b), which authorizes any claim that "arises under" federal law to be removed to federal court. In the two categories of cases where this Court has found complete pre-emption— certain causes of action under the LMRA and ERISA—the federal statutes at issue provided the exclusive cause of action for the claim asserted and also set forth procedures and remedies governing that cause of action.

III

Count IV of respondents' complaint sought relief for "usury violations" and claimed that petitioners "charged ... excessive interest in violation of the common law usury doctrine" and violated "Alabama Code. § 8–8–1, et seq. by charging excessive interest." Respondents' complaint thus expressly charged petitioners with usury. *Metropolitan Life*, *Avco*, and *Franchise Tax Board* provide the framework for answering the dispositive question in this case: Does the National Bank Act provide the exclusive cause of action for usury claims against national banks? If so, then the cause of action necessarily arises under federal law and the case is removable. If not, then the complaint does not arise under federal law and is not removable.

Sections 85 and 86 serve distinct purposes. The former sets forth the substantive limits on the rates of interest that national banks may charge. The latter sets forth the elements of a usury claim against a national bank, provides for a 2–year statute of limitations for such a claim, and prescribes the remedies available to borrowers who are charged higher rates and the procedures governing such a claim. If, as petitioners asserted in their notice of removal, the interest that the bank charged to respondents did not violate § 85 limits, the statute unquestionably pre-empts any common-law or Alabama statutory rule that would treat those rates as usurious. The section would therefore provide the petitioners with a complete federal defense. Such a federal defense, however, would not justify removal. Only if Congress intended § 86 to provide the exclusive cause of action for usury claims against national

---

3. Of course, a state claim can also be removed through the use of the supplemental jurisdiction statute, 28 U.S.C. § 1367(a), provided that another claim in the complaint is removable.

banks would the statute be comparable to the provisions that we construed in the *Avco* and *Metropolitan Life* cases.[5]

In a series of cases decided shortly after the Act was passed, we endorsed that approach. * * * In *Evans v. National Bank of Savannah*, 251 U.S. 108 (1919), we stated that "federal law * * * completely defines what constitutes the taking of usury by a national bank, referring to the state law only to determine the maximum permitted rate." See also *Barnet v. National Bank*, 98 U.S. 555, 558 (1879) (the "statutes of Ohio and Indiana upon the subject of usury ... cannot affect the case" because the Act "creates a new right" that is "exclusive"); *Haseltine v. Central Bank of Springfield*, 183 U.S. 132, 134 (1901) ("[T]he definition of usury and the penalties affixed thereto must be determined by the National Banking Act and not by the law of the State").

In addition to this Court's longstanding and consistent construction of the National Bank Act as providing an exclusive federal cause of action for usury against national banks, this Court has also recognized the special nature of federally chartered banks. Uniform rules limiting the liability of national banks and prescribing exclusive remedies for their overcharges are an integral part of a banking system that needed protection from "possible unfriendly State legislation." *Tiffany v. National Bank of Mo.*, 18 Wall. 409, 412 (1874). The same federal interest that protected national banks from the state taxation that Chief Justice Marshall characterized as the "power to destroy," *McCulloch v. Maryland*, 4 Wheat. 316, 431 (1819), supports the established interpretation of §§ 85 and 86 that gives those provisions the requisite pre-emptive force to provide removal jurisdiction. In actions against national banks for usury, these provisions supersede both the substantive and the remedial provisions of state usury laws and create a federal remedy for overcharges that is exclusive, even when a state complainant, as here, relies entirely on state law. Because §§ 85 and 86 provide the exclusive cause of action for such claims, there is, in short, no such thing as a state-law claim of usury against a national bank. Even though the complaint makes no mention of federal law, it unquestionably and unambiguously claims that petitioners violated usury laws. This cause of action against national banks only arises under federal law and could, therefore, be removed under § 1441.

The judgment of the Court of Appeals is reversed.

Justice SCALIA, with whom Justice THOMAS joins, dissenting.

* * * Under the well-pleaded-complaint rule, "a federal court does not have original jurisdiction over a case in which the complaint presents a state-law cause of action, but also asserts that federal law deprives the defendant of a defense he may raise, * * * or that a federal defense the

---

5. Because the proper inquiry focuses on whether Congress intended the federal cause of action to be exclusive rather than on whether Congress intended that the cause of action be removable, the fact that these sections of the National Bank Act were passed in 1864, 11 years prior to the passage of the statute authorizing removal, is irrelevant, contrary to respondents' assertions.

defendant may raise is not sufficient to defeat the claim." *Franchise Tax Bd. of Cal. v. Construction Laborers Vacation Trust for Southern Cal.*, 463 U.S. 1, 10 (1983). Of critical importance here, the rejection of a federal defense as the basis for original federal-question jurisdiction applies with equal force when the defense is one of federal pre-emption. "By unimpeachable authority, a suit brought upon a state statute does not arise under an act of Congress or the Constitution of the United States because prohibited thereby." *Gully v. First Nat. Bank in Meridian*, 299 U.S. 109, 116 (1936). "[A] case may not be removed to federal court on the basis of . . . the defense of pre-emption. . . ." *Caterpillar, supra*, at 393. To be sure, pre-emption requires a state court to dismiss a particular claim that is filed under state law, but it does not, as a general matter, provide grounds for removal.

This Court has twice recognized exceptions to the well-pleaded-complaint rule, upholding removal jurisdiction notwithstanding the absence of a federal question on the face of the plaintiff's complaint. [Justice Scalia discussed both *Avco*, which allowed removal based on complete preemption for claims that paralleled claims under § 301 of the LMRA, and *Taylor*, which applied the same logic to claims preempted by ERISA. In addition to criticizing the reasoning of those cases, Justice Scalia argued that they did not support the majority's conclusion in this case.] * * *

In an effort to justify this shift, the Court explains that "[b]ecause §§ 85 and 86 [of the National Bank Act] provide the exclusive cause of action for such claims, there is . . . no such thing as a state-law claim of usury against a national bank." But the mere fact that a state-law claim is invalid no more deprives it of its character as a state-law claim which does not raise a federal question, than does the fact that a federal claim is invalid deprive it of its character as a federal claim which does raise a federal question. The proper response to the presentation of a nonexistent claim to a state court is dismissal, not the "federalize-and-remove" dance authorized by today's opinion. For even if the Court is correct that the National Bank Act obliterates entirely any state-created right to relief for usury against a national bank, that does not explain how or why the claim of such a right is transmogrified into the claim of a federal right. Congress's mere act of creating a federal right and eliminating all state-created rights in no way suggests an expansion of federal jurisdiction so as to wrest from state courts the authority to decide questions of pre-emption under the National Bank Act. * * *

Notes and Questions

1. *Preemption.* Understanding *Beneficial* requires a basic understanding of the doctrine of preemption. Basically, for purposes of federal question jurisdiction there are two categories of preemption: "conflict" and "complete." The vast majority of preemption issues involve what the Court deems "conflict preemption." If you studied Chapter 3, you saw this type of preemption in *Caterpillar, Inc. v. Williams* on page 109. To the extent that a

state law directly clashes with federal law, that state law must give way. *Caterpillar* makes it clear that conflict preemption is a defense, and therefore cannot satisfy the well-pleaded complaint rule.

So-called "complete preemption" is much rarer, but is far more sweeping in its scope when it does apply. In some situations, Congress intends for federal law to fill up a particular subject area in its entirety. If Congress fills up an area, state law can play no role whatsoever. In cases of complete preemption, state law is preempted not only when it clashes with federal law, but even if it is perfectly consistent with federal law. Complete preemption usually applies in connection with broad federal statutory schemes. As *Beneficial* demonstrates, the Court has explicitly found complete preemption under only three statutes: §§ 85 and 86 of the National Bank Act (*Beneficial*), § 301 of the Labor Management Relations Act (*Avco*), and § 502 of the Employment Retirement Income Security Act of 1974 (ERISA) (*Metropolitan Life*). A case involving the property rights of Indian tribes is probably another category. In *Oneida Indian Nation v. County of Oneida*, 414 U.S. 661, 94 S.Ct. 772, 39 L.Ed.2d 73 (1974), the Court held that a claim by the tribe seeking possession of tribal land would always arise under federal law. Compare that result to the reasoning in *Nicodemus*.

2. The complete preemption rule discussed in *Beneficial* is fundamentally different than the *Merrell–Dow* rule discussed in *Nicodemus*. Complete preemption in essence transforms the state-law claim into a federal substantive claim. Once we recognize that federal law replaces state law as the source of the claim, it is easy to see how the claim qualifies as a federal question. Under *Merrell–Dow*, by contrast, the claim remains a state-law claim, but nevertheless is treated as a federal question claim for purposes of § 1331 because of the federal ingredient.

3. Isn't Justice Scalia's dissent correct? If federal law preempts state law—regardless of whether it is because of conflict or complete preemption—doesn't that simply mean that there is *no state law claim*? How can the fact of preemption somehow convert a state claim into a federal claim?

4. Consider a variation on the facts of *Beneficial* ... a variation that has *Merrell–Dow* implications. Suppose Plaintiff sues Defendant under a state claim that is completely preempted by federal law. However, unlike in *Beneficial*, the federal law provides no private right of action. Same result? What about in the Introductory Problem, where federal law does provide a cause of action, but Plaintiff cannot recover under that federal law?

5. *Federal party theory.* Federal question jurisdiction also exists in suits involving certain corporations and other entities created by Congress. If the statute creating the organization explicitly provides that the organization can sue and be sued *in federal court*, all claims by or against that organization are considered federal questions. *American National Red Cross v. S.G.*, 505 U.S. 247, 112 S.Ct. 2465, 120 L.Ed.2d 201 (1992).

6. *"Federal Interest" Jurisdiction.* Can a case that does not arise under federal law under any of the analyses discussed above nevertheless involve such a strong federal interest that it qualifies as a federal question? A recent Supreme Court case suggests that in certain rare cases the answer may be yes. In *Grable & Sons Metal Prods., Inc. v. Darue Engineering & Mfg.*, ___ U.S. ___, 125 S.Ct. 2363, 162 L.Ed.2d 257 (2005), Plaintiff's land was seized

by the IRS for failure to pay federal taxes. The IRS sold the land to Defendant at a tax sale. Plaintiff brought a quiet title action in state court, claiming that the IRS gave improper notice of the tax sale. Defendant tried to remove the case to federal court as a federal question. So far, the case looks somewhat like *Nicodemus*—a title dispute where one of the parties' property rights comes from the federal government. Nevertheless, the Court held that there was federal question jurisdiction. Because of the strong federal interest in having federal courts hear all claims relating to the federal tax laws, the federal issue inherent in the dispute was enough to satisfy 28 U.S.C. § 1331. Note that unlike *Nicodemus*, there was clear evidence of Congressional intent to provide a federal forum.

Problems

1. In the interest of uniformity, Congress enacts a national speed limit of 65 miles per hour on interstate highways. P is injured by D on an interstate highway. D was driving 70 miles per hour at the time of the accident. P sues D in federal court, alleging that D was negligent *per se* for violating the federal speed limit law. Does the court have federal question jurisdiction?

2. P sues D (a nearby factory) in federal court. P claims that D committed a nuisance by discharging hazardous fumes from its smokestacks. Under state law, nuisance is the unreasonable use of one's property. In his complaint, P alleges that D's use is unreasonable because it exceeds the limits established by the federal Clean Air Act. Although the Clean Air Act does contain a provision allowing aggrieved citizens such as P to sue, the only remedy that provision authorizes is an injunction. P has sued for nuisance in the hope that he can recover damages. Does the court have federal question jurisdiction?

3. City recently enacted a zoning ordinance for its historic district. This ordinance includes strict limits on the size and coloring of store signs. P operates a fast food franchise in the historic district. P wants to erect a sign with its logo, which is an especially hideous shade of puce. P's logo, including the puce color, is a registered trademark under federal trademark laws. Because that color is not allowed under the ordinance, City denies P's application to erect a sign. P sues City in federal court for an order requiring the City to approve the application. P's sole claim is that the provisions of the ordinance that regulate color cannot be applied to P. A section of the federal trademark law preempts state laws that prohibit a party from using a federally-registered mark on a sign or in advertising. Does the court have federal question jurisdiction?

4. Same as Problem 3, except that P erects the sign without seeking permission. City sues P in state court to force P to take down the sign. P removes the action to federal court. When City seeks a remand to state court because of lack of jurisdiction, P argues that the federal court has jurisdiction on two bases. First, P argues that federal trademark laws preempt the city ordinance. Second, P argues that the City's prohibition of puce represents a taking of property without compensation under the United States Constitution. Will the court remand the case?

B. AN IN–DEPTH LOOK AT
THE *ERIE* DOCTRINE

Chapter 5 of this book contains three modern cases dealing with the *Erie* doctrine; a doctrine that requires federal courts to apply certain state laws. If you studied those cases, you may have been left with the impression that the *Erie* analysis is relatively mechanical. The basic "test" in those cases turns on whether the federal law is a Federal Rule of Civil Procedure or other judge-made law.

That brief introduction to *Erie*, however, does not paint a complete picture. The *Erie* doctrine deals with more than the Federal Rules and judge-made law. Moreover, even though certain Supreme Court cases do suggest a specific test, more recent decisions have muddied the waters. Tracing the development of the *Erie* doctrine from its beginnings to the most recent decisions will provide you a much deeper understanding of the overall analysis. At the same time, you will better appreciate why some consider *Erie* to be one of the cornerstones of American federalism.

1. Genesis of the Doctrine

The roots of the *Erie* doctrine are almost as old as the United States itself. Congress laid the groundwork in the Judiciary Act of 1789, the first comprehensive statute dealing with the federal court system. Near the end of that Act was a short and little-noticed section, § 34, which provided simply:

> *And be it further enacted,* That the laws of the several states, except where the constitution, treaties or statutes of the United States shall otherwise require or provide, shall be regarded as rules of decision in trials at common law in the courts of the United States in cases where they apply.

Section 34, commonly called the "Rules of Decision Act," is still in force, although it has been expanded in certain ways we will consider later. The current version is codified at 28 U.S.C. § 1652. For the first three cases, however, it is important to keep the original language in mind.

The Rules of Decision Act contains an ambiguity, although one that is not obvious to the modern eye. The statute requires federal courts to apply "the laws of the several states." But what exactly is law? The Court answered that question in 1842 in *Swift v. Tyson*, establishing a basic view of law that would last for almost a century.

SWIFT v. TYSON, 41 U.S. (16 Pet.) 1, 10 L.Ed. 865 (1842). Defendant bought land from a person named Norton, giving a "bill of exchange" (a type of negotiable instrument) in return. However, Norton had made several fraudulent representations about the land. Norton later conveyed the bill of exchange to Plaintiff as payment for an existing debt. When Plaintiff presented the bill to Defendant for payment, Defendant refused to pay, arguing that Norton's fraud rendered the bill voidable. The law of negotiable instruments, however, includes a key rule called the "holder in due course" rule. Under this doctrine, a person who acquires a negotiable instrument for value and without knowledge of any problems is not subject to many of the defenses that might otherwise render the instrument unenforceable, including the defense of fraud. If Plaintiff was a holder in due course, he clearly could have recovered on the bill of exchange, even though Norton would have been barred from recovery because of his fraud.

The crucial issue was whether Plaintiff had given "value" for the bill of exchange. Under New York law, it was unclear whether accepting a negotiable instrument in payment of an antecedent debt constituted giving value sufficient to make one a holder in due course. Justice Story, writing for the Court, discussed the New York precedent. However, he then declared that the New York case law was not controlling:

But, admitting the doctrine to be fully settled in New York, it remains to be considered, whether it is obligatory upon this court, if it differs from the principles established in the general commercial law. It is observable, that the courts of New York do not found their decisions upon this point, upon any local statute, or positive, fixed or ancient local usage; but they deduce the doctrine from the general principles of commercial law. It is, however, contended, that the 34th section of the judiciary act of 1789 furnishes a rule obligatory upon this court to follow the decisions of the state tribunals in all cases to which they apply. * * * In order to maintain the argument, it is essential, therefore, to hold, that the word "laws," in this section, includes within the scope of its meaning, the decisions of the local tribunals. In the ordinary use of language, it will hardly be contended, that the decisions of courts constitute laws. They are, at most, only evidence of what the laws are, and are not, of themselves, laws. They are often re-examined, reversed and qualified by the courts themselves, whenever they are found to be either defective, or ill-founded, or otherwise incorrect. The laws of a state are more usually understood to mean the rules and enactments promulgated by the legislative authority thereof, or long-established local customs having the force of laws. In all the various cases, which have hitherto come before us for decision, this court have uniformly supposed, that the true interpretation of the 34th section limited its application to state laws, strictly local, that is to say, to the positive statutes of the state, and the construction thereof adopted by the local tribunals, and to rights and titles to things having a permanent locality, such as the rights and titles to real estate, and other matters immovable and intra-territorial in their nature and character. It never has been supposed by us, that the section did apply, or was designed to apply, to questions of a more general nature, not at all dependent upon local statutes or local usages of a fixed and permanent operation, as, for example, to the construction of ordinary contracts or other written instruments, and especially to questions of general commercial law, where the state tribunals are called upon to perform the like functions as ourselves, that is, to ascertain, upon general reasoning and legal analogies, what is the true exposition of the contract or instrument, or what is the just rule furnished by the principles of commercial law to govern the case. And we have not now the slightest difficulty in holding, that this section, upon its true intendment and construction, is strictly limited to local statutes and local usages of the character before stated, and does not extend to contracts and other instruments of a commercial nature, the true interpretation and effect whereof are to be sought, not in the decisions of the local tribunals, but in the general principles and doctrines of commercial jurisprudence. Undoubtedly, the decisions of the local tribunals upon such subjects are entitled to, and will receive, the most deliberate attention and respect of this court; but they cannot furnish positive rules, or conclusive authority, by which our own judgments are to be bound up and governed. The law respecting negotiable instruments may be truly declared in the languages of Cicero, adopted by Lord MANSFIELD in Luke v. Lyde, 2 Burr. 883, 887, to be in a great measure, not the law of a single country only, but of the commercial world. *Non erit alia lex Romae, alia Athenis; alia nunc, alia posthac; sed et apud omnes gentes, et omni tempore una eademque lex obtinebit.*

It becomes necessary for us, therefore, upon the present occasion, to express our own opinion of the true result of the commercial law upon the question now before us. * * *

The Court then concluded that under the general commercial law Plaintiff was a holder in due course even though he acquired the bill of exchange in satisfaction of an antecedent debt.

Notes and Questions

1. Joseph Story, the author of *Swift*, was one of the most brilliant legal minds in United States history. He was appointed to the Supreme Court in 1811 at the age of 32, the youngest person ever to serve on the Court. He wrote several Commentaries on certain topics in the law, which were frequently cited by the Court even while Story was a sitting Justice.

2. In 50 words or less, explain why, according to *Swift*, common-law rules such as tort and contract are not "state law."

3. Contrary to what seems to have become a modern popular myth, Justice Story's views of the nature of the common law were not universally accepted at the time of *Swift*. Indeed, the Supreme Court stated a very different view in a case decided only eight years prior to *Swift*. *Wheaton v. Peters*, 33 U.S. (8 Pet.) 591, 8 L.Ed. 1055 (1834), was a dispute indirectly involving the Court itself. Wheaton and Peters published reporters containing Supreme Court opinions, references to which (Wheat. and Pet.) still appear in official citations. Wheaton published from 1816 to 1827, and Peters published after that. However, Peters also decided to publish copies of Wheaton's older reporters. Wheaton sued Peters for violation of both common-law authors' rights and the federal copyright statute.

With respect to the common-law authors' rights, Wheaton argued that English law had recognized such a claim, and that the common-law right continued in the United States after independence. The Court disagreed:

> But, if the common law right of authors were shown to exist in England, does the same right exist, and to the same extent, in this country.
>
> It is clear, there can be no common law of the United States. The federal government is composed of twenty-four sovereign and independent states; each of which may have its local usages, customs and common law. There is no principle which pervades the union and has the authority of law, that is not embodied in the constitution or laws of the union. * * *
>
> When, therefore, a common law right is asserted, we must look to the state in which the controversy originated. * * *
>
> No one will contend, that the common law, as it existed in England, has ever been in force in all its provisions, in any state in this union. It was adopted, so far only as its principles were suited to the condition of the colonies; and from this circumstance we see, what is common law in one state, is not so considered in another. The judicial decisions, the usages and customs of the respective states, must determine, how far the common law has been introduced and sanctioned in each.

Because there was no proof that Pennsylvania (the state where the works were created) recognized authors' rights, the Court held that Wheaton could not recover on that claim. Justice Story did not write an opinion in the case.

4. During the century following *Swift*, the federal courts developed a body of "federal common law." The rules of this federal judge-made law often differed from the rules that would have been applied in the state courts had the same case been heard there. Federal common law grew to encompass not only the general commercial law at issue in *Swift*, but also most issues of contract, tort, and to some extent even property, law.

The next case, *Erie R. Co. v. Tompkins,* started out as a routine application of this federal common law. The plaintiff chose federal court in the hope that he would receive the benefit of the more favorable federal common law rule (when you read the case, make sure to identify the clash in governing law). Although the parties disagreed as to the content of the state and federal rules, no one on appeal questioned whether *Swift* ought to apply. And yet, as the first line of the Supreme Court's opinion makes clear, the Court had quite a different agenda in mind.

ERIE R. CO. v. TOMPKINS

304 U.S. 64, 58 S.Ct. 817, 82 L.Ed. 1188 (1938)

Mr. Justice BRANDEIS delivered the opinion of the Court.

The question for decision is whether the oft-challenged doctrine of Swift v. Tyson shall now be disapproved.

Tompkins, a citizen of Pennsylvania, was injured on a dark night by a passing freight train of the Erie Railroad Company while walking along its right of way at Hughestown in that state. He claimed that the accident occurred through negligence in the operation, or maintenance, of the train; that he was rightfully on the premises as licensee because on a commonly used beaten footpath which ran for a short distance alongside the tracks; and that he was struck by something which looked like a door projecting from one of the moving cars. To enforce that claim he brought an action in the federal court for Southern New York, which had jurisdiction because the company is a corporation of that state. It denied liability; and the case was tried by a jury.

The Erie insisted that its duty to Tompkins was no greater than that owed to a trespasser. It contended, among other things, that its duty to Tompkins, and hence its liability, should be determined in accordance with the Pennsylvania law; that under the law of Pennsylvania, as declared by its highest court, persons who use pathways along the railroad right of way—that is, a longitudinal pathway as distinguished from a crossing—are to be deemed trespassers; and that the railroad is not liable for injuries to undiscovered trespassers resulting from its negligence, unless it be wanton or willful. Tompkins denied that any such rule had been established by the decisions of the Pennsylvania courts; and contended that, since there was no statute of the state on the subject, the railroad's duty and liability is to be determined in federal courts as a matter of general law. * * *

The Erie had contended that application of the Pennsylvania rule was required, among other things, by section 34 of the Federal Judiciary Act of September 24, 1789, which provides: "The laws of the several States, except where the Constitution, treaties, or statutes of the United States otherwise require or provide, shall be regarded as rules of decision in trials at common law, in the courts of the United States, in cases where they apply."

Because of the importance of the question whether the federal court was free to disregard the alleged rule of the Pennsylvania common law, we granted certiorari.

First. Swift v. Tyson, 16 Pet. 1, 18, held that federal courts exercising jurisdiction on the ground of diversity of citizenship need not, in matters of general jurisprudence, apply the unwritten law of the state as declared by its highest court; that they are free to exercise an independent judgment as to what the common law of the state is—or should be; and that, as there stated by Mr. Justice Story, "the true interpretation of the 34th section limited its application to state laws, strictly local, that is to say, to the positive statutes of the state, and the construction thereof adopted by the local tribunals, and to rights and titles to things having a permanent locality, such as the rights and titles to real estate, and other matters immovable and intra-territorial in their nature and character. * * * "

The Court in applying the rule of section 34 to equity cases, in Mason v. United States, 260 U.S. 545, 559, said: "The statute, however, is merely declarative of the rule which would exist in the absence of the statute." The federal courts assumed, in the broad field of "general law," the power to declare rules of decision which Congress was confessedly without power to enact as statutes. Doubt was repeatedly expressed as to the correctness of the construction given section 34, and as to the soundness of the rule which it introduced. But it was the more recent research of a competent scholar, who examined the original document, which established that the construction given to it by the Court was erroneous; and that the purpose of the section was merely to make certain that, in all matters except those in which some federal law is controlling, the federal courts exercising jurisdiction in diversity of citizenship cases would apply as their rules of decision the law of the state, unwritten as well as written.[5] * * *

Second. Experience in applying the doctrine of Swift v. Tyson, had revealed its defects, political and social; and the benefits expected to flow from the rule did not accrue. Persistence of state courts in their own opinions on questions of common law prevented uniformity; and the impossibility of discovering a satisfactory line of demarcation between the province of general law and that of local law developed a new well of uncertainties.

On the other hand, the mischievous results of the doctrine had become apparent. Diversity of citizenship jurisdiction was conferred in order to prevent apprehended discrimination in state courts against those not citizens of the state. Swift v. Tyson introduced grave discrimination by noncitizens against citizens. It made rights enjoyed under the unwritten "general law" vary according to whether enforcement was sought in the state or in the federal court; and the privilege of selecting the court in which the right should be determined was conferred upon the noncitizen. Thus, the doctrine rendered impossible equal protection of the law. In attempting to promote uniformity of law throughout the United States, the doctrine had prevented uniformity in the administration of the law of the state.

The discrimination resulting became in practice far-reaching. This resulted in part from the broad province accorded to the so-called "general law" as to which federal courts exercised an independent judgment. * * *

In part the discrimination resulted from the wide range of persons held entitled to avail themselves of the federal rule by resort to the diversity of citizenship jurisdiction. Through this jurisdiction individual citizens willing to remove from their own state and become citizens of another might avail themselves of the federal rule. And, without even change of residence, a corporate citizen of the state could avail itself of the federal rule by reincorporating under the laws of another state * * *.

The injustice and confusion incident to the doctrine of Swift v. Tyson have been repeatedly urged as reasons for abolishing or limiting diversity of citizenship jurisdiction. Other legislative relief has been

5. Charles Warren, *New Light on the History of the Federal Judiciary Act of 1789* (1923) 37 Harv.L.Rev. 49, 51–52 , 81–88, 108.

proposed. If only a question of statutory construction were involved, we should not be prepared to abandon a doctrine so widely applied throughout nearly a century. But the unconstitutionality of the course pursued has now been made clear, and compels us to do so.

Third. Except in matters governed by the Federal Constitution or by acts of Congress, the law to be applied in any case is the law of the state. And whether the law of the state shall be declared by its Legislature in a statute or by its highest court in a decision is not a matter of federal concern. There is no federal general common law. Congress has no power to declare substantive rules of common law applicable in a state whether they be local in their nature or "general," be they commercial law or a part of the law of torts. And no clause in the Constitution purports to confer such a power upon the federal courts. As stated by Mr. Justice Field when protesting in Baltimore & Ohio R.R. Co. v. Baugh, 149 U.S. 368, 401, against ignoring the Ohio common law of fellow-servant liability: I am aware that what has been termed the general law of the country—which is often little less than what the judge advancing the doctrine thinks at the time should be the general law on a particular subject—has been often advanced in judicial opinions of this court to control a conflicting law of a state. I admit that learned judges have fallen into the habit of repeating this doctrine as a convenient mode of brushing aside the law of a state in conflict with their views. And I confess that, moved and governed by the authority of the great names of those judges, I have, myself, in many instances, unhesitatingly and confidently, but I think now erroneously, repeated the same doctrine. But, notwithstanding the great names which may be cited in favor of the doctrine, and notwithstanding the frequency with which the doctrine has been reiterated, there stands, as a perpetual protest against its repetition, the constitution of the United States, which recognizes and preserves the autonomy and independence of the states,—independence in their legislative and independence in their judicial departments. Supervision over either the legislative or the judicial action of the states is in no case permissible except as to matters by the constitution specifically authorized or delegated to the United States. Any interference with either, except as thus permitted, is an invasion of the authority of the state, and, to that extent, a denial of its independence.

The fallacy underlying the rule declared in Swift v. Tyson is made clear by Mr. Justice Holmes. The doctrine rests upon the assumption that there is "a transcendental body of law outside of any particular State but obligatory within it unless and until changed by statute," that federal courts have the power to use their judgment as to what the rules of common law are; and that in the federal courts "the parties are entitled to an independent judgment on matters of general law":

> But law in the sense in which courts speak of it today does not exist without some definite authority behind it. The common law so far as it is enforced in a State, whether called common law or not, is not the common law generally but the law of that State existing by the

authority of that State without regard to what it may have been in England or anywhere else. * * *

The authority and only authority is the State, and if that be so, the voice adopted by the State as its own (whether it be of its Legislature or of its Supreme Court) should utter the last word.

[*Kuhn v. Fairmont Coal Co.*, 215 U.S. 349 (1910).] Thus the doctrine of Swift v. Tyson is, as Mr. Justice Holmes said, "an unconstitutional assumption of powers by the Courts of the United States which no lapse of time or respectable array of opinion should make us hesitate to correct." In disapproving that doctrine we do not hold unconstitutional section 34 of the Federal Judiciary Act of 1789 or any other act of Congress. We merely declare that in applying the doctrine this Court and the lower courts have invaded rights which in our opinion are reserved by the Constitution to the several states.

Fourth. The defendant contended that by the common law of Pennsylvania as declared by its highest court in Falchetti v. Pennsylvania R. Co., 307 Pa. 203, 160 A. 859, the only duty owed to the plaintiff was to refrain from willful or wanton injury. The plaintiff denied that such is the Pennsylvania law. In support of their respective contentions the parties discussed and cited many decisions of the Supreme Court of the state. The Circuit Court of Appeals ruled that the question of liability is one of general law; and on that ground declined to decide the issue of state law. As we hold this was error, the judgment is reversed and the case remanded to it for further proceedings in conformity with our opinion.

Mr. Justice CARDOZO took no part in the consideration or decision of this case.

Mr. Justice BUTLER (dissenting).

* * * [*Swift v. Tyson*] has been followed by this Court in an unbroken line of decisions. So far as appears, it was not questioned until more than 50 years later, and then by a single judge. * * *

It is hard to foresee the consequences of the radical change * * * [this Court has] made. * * * It extends to all matters of contracts and torts not positively governed by state enactments. Counsel searching for precedent and reasoning to disclose common-law principles on which to guide clients and conduct litigation are by this decision told that as to all of these questions the decisions of this Court and other federal courts are no longer anywhere authoritative. * * *

The Court's opinion in its first sentence defines the question to be whether the doctrine of Swift v. Tyson shall now be disapproved; it recites that Congress is without power to prescribe rules of decision that have been followed by federal courts as a result of the construction of section 34 in Swift v. Tyson and since; after discussion, it declares that "the unconstitutionality of the course pursued (meaning the rule of decision resulting from that construction) * * * compels" abandonment of the doctrine so long applied; and then near the end of the last page, the Court states that it does not hold section 34 unconstitutional, but merely that, in applying the doctrine of Swift v. Tyson construing it, this Court and the lower courts have invaded rights which are reserved by the Constitution to the several states. But, plainly through the form of words employed, the substance of the decision appears; it strikes down as unconstitutional section 34 as construed by our decisions; it divests the Congress of power to prescribe rules to be followed by federal courts when deciding questions of general law. In that broad field it compels this and the lower federal courts to follow decisions of the courts of a particular state. * * *

Mr. Justice McREYNOLDS, concurs in this opinion.

Mr. Justice REED (concurring in part).

I concur in the conclusion reached in this case, in the disapproval of the doctrine of Swift v. Tyson, and in the reasoning of the majority opinion, except in so far as it relies upon the unconstitutionality of the "course pursued" by the federal courts. * * *

Notes and Questions

1. *Swift* adopted a particular interpretation of the Rules of Decision Act. Does *Erie* change that interpretation? After *Erie*, what does the reference to "laws" in the Rules of Decision Act mean?

2. The Court in *Erie* supports its decision by declaring that *Swift*'s view of the common law was based on a "fallacy." *Erie* substituted a modern view of the common law, a view grounded in the emerging legal philosophy of legal realism. Yet was the view in *Swift* really that outdated? Consider your own studies as a law student. In your courses in Torts, Contracts, and Property, do you study only the law of one state? Moreover, don't courts in one state often cite decisions from *other* states when dealing with new questions? Isn't there in fact a sense of universality to the common law, notwithstanding Justice Brandeis's views?

3. Canada, another federal state with a common-law heritage, has not adopted anything resembling the *Erie* doctrine. There remains in Canada a sense that the common law is a shared body of law (except in Québec), even if the particular rules may on occasion differ between provinces. Could this difference be systemic? To what extent could it be relevant that the Supreme Court of Canada, unlike its American counterpart, is a general court of appeals that can review all decisions rendered by the provinces, even those involving common-law issues? Would it affect your answer to learn that in practice the Supreme Court of Canada rarely reviews cases turning solely on the interpretation of the common law?

4. Even if *Erie*'s view of the common law is correct, is there an internal inconsistency to the decision? If the general common law is purely state law, then isn't the philosophical *nature* of that law also entirely up to the states? Suppose, for example, that a state continues to adhere to *Swift*'s view of the common law. In that state, at least, shouldn't a federal court be free to ignore state-court precedent and determine for itself what the "proper" rule should be? Can the United States Supreme Court change that? Doesn't *Erie*

stand for the proposition that federal courts—including the United States Supreme Court—are powerless to change the nature of the common law?

5. Like *Swift* before it, *Erie* deals with the Rules of Decision Act. Suppose Congress were to repeal that statute. Would the federal courts immediately revert to an approach like that in *Swift*? What does the Court mean when it says, "If only a question of statutory construction were involved, we should not be prepared to abandon a doctrine so widely applied throughout nearly a century. But the unconstitutionality of the course pursued has now been made clear, and compels us to do so."?

6. Note that only a bare majority of the Court explicitly signed on to the notion that the rule in *Erie* is constitutionally required. Even Justice Reed, who agreed that *Swift* should be overturned, disavowed the idea that *Swift* was unconstitutional.

7. *Equal protection?* If *Erie* is a constitutional decision, upon which provision of the Constitution is it based? The only specific provision mentioned by the Court is the equal protection clause (which is in the fourteenth amendment). However, the practice under *Swift* could not violate that clause. Under *Swift*, federal courts would apply a different rule than their state counterparts. There is no equal protection violation merely because the state and federal governments have two different rules governing the same behavior. (If it were, which government would be violating the clause?) As just one example, both the federal government and some states have laws that regulate unfair trade practices; laws that often differ in several important respects.

8. *Federalism?* The Court's other constitutional references are more subtle. In part *"First"* of the opinion, the Court states that federal courts under *Swift* would "declare rules of decision which Congress was confessedly without power to enact as statutes." In part *"Third"*, the Court indicates that "Congress has no power to declare substantive rules of common law * * *. And no clause in the Constitution purports to confer such a power upon the federal courts." Finally, later in the same paragraph, the Court mentions how the Constitution "recognizes and preserves the autonomy and independence of the states,—independence in their legislative and independence in their judicial departments." Can you cobble from these quotes—all of which relate to federalism—a constitutional theory supporting *Erie*?

Consider the references to Congressional power in the first two quotes. If you have taken Constitutional Law, you should know that Congress could, under its Article I power to regulate interstate commerce, pass a law regulating the substantive issue in *Erie* (the liability of a railroad), even given the restrictive interpretation of the commerce power that prevailed in 1938. But does it matter that Congress could have passed such a law? In *Erie* itself, would *Congress* be deciding what the standard of care would be? On the other hand, as long as the federal government has the authority to pass a law, does it really matter which branch does so? Who selects Congress? The courts?

9. In certain situations, Congress may delegate some of its lawmaking powers. In fact, the notion of delegation is central to the Court's reasoning in *Hanna v. Plumer* on page 869. Of course, in *Erie* itself there was no evidence of a delegation from Congress to the federal courts; indeed, the

Rules of Decision Act is clear evidence that Congress had not given the federal courts a general power to make law. But could Congress delegate to the federal courts the power to create governing law for all cases heard in federal court? Although Congress could have passed the rule in *Erie*, could it enact statutes governing every case heard in federal court—especially *diversity* cases? Consider again the quotes set out in note 8 above. Do they make more sense when viewed in this light?

10.   Is there something a bit facile about analogizing pre-*Erie* federal common law to a federal statute? If Congress enacts a statute, is there anything a state can do to overcome it? By contrast, did pre-*Erie* federal common law apply in the state courts? And couldn't a state control the result even in federal court merely by enacting a statute?

11.   Many courts and commentators have suggested that *Erie* is an issue only in diversity cases. These statements are simply incorrect. The doctrine also applies when a federal court hears the "non-federal" portion of a case heard under its supplemental jurisdiction. Moreover, you will see later in this chapter that the doctrine can apply even in pure federal question cases.

12.   The *Erie* case was litigated in a New York federal court. So why does the Supreme Court hold that the federal court should apply *Pennsylvania* law? Given that most *Erie* cases are diversity cases, and accordingly have connections with two or more states, how does a federal court choose *which* state's law to apply?

The Supreme Court answered this question in *Klaxon Co. v. Stentor Electric Mfg. Co.*, 313 U.S. 487, 61 S.Ct. 1020, 85 L.Ed. 1477 (1941). The Court noted that every state had its own "choice of law rules" that dictated what law would be used to decide a case that had connections with more than one jurisdiction. (For an overview of these rules, see the *Paul* case in Chapter 5). These choice of law rules, the Court reasoned, were included among the state laws that federal courts must apply under *Erie*.

The *Erie* court may not even have considered the choice of law issue. Under the dominant choice of law methodology in use in 1938, it was clear that the law of the place of the accident—Pennsylvania—would govern the case. This rule was in force in all states, and would probably also would have represented the federal approach.

————————

The *Erie* opinion paints with a very broad brush. Read literally, it suggests that federal courts are completely powerless to enact rules of law. But a court, by its very nature, makes a number of binding proclamations that are not directly supported by a statute. Suppose, for example, that a judge wants to close a potentially sensitive trial to the media. State law, however, allows media into all trials. Would the federal court have to follow the state practice and allow the media into the courtroom? Wouldn't a rule barring the media be a form of "federal common law?"

Certainly *Erie* does not go that far. Yet, because the opinion is written in such broad terms, the Court had to revisit the basic issue only seven years after its decision in *Erie*. Before diving into *Guaranty Trust Co. of New York v. York*, however, it is useful to discuss the issue facing the Court. *Guaranty Trust* was a suit in equity. The case involved an action for breach of trust, a historically equitable claim (see Chapter 5). Courts sitting in equity typically did not consider themselves bound by statutes of limitation. Instead, they would apply the judge-made doctrine of *laches*. Laches is not a fixed period of time. Instead, a suit is barred by laches only if the defendant was somehow harmed by the plaintiff's delay in bringing the case. The issue in *Guaranty Trust* is whether the federal court should apply laches (under which the action could proceed because defendant had not been harmed by the delay) or, like the state courts, apply the state statute of limitations (under which the action would be barred).

GUARANTY TRUST CO. OF NEW YORK v. YORK

326 U.S. 99, 65 S.Ct. 1464, 89 L.Ed. 2079 (1945)

Mr. Justice FRANKFURTER delivered the opinion of the Court.

* * * In May, 1930, Van Sweringen Corporation issued notes to the amount of $30,000,000. Under an indenture of the same date, petitioner, Guaranty Trust Co., was named trustee with power and obligations to enforce the rights of the noteholders in the assets of the Corporation and of the Van Sweringen brothers. In October, 1930, petitioner, with other banks, made large advances to companies affiliated with the Corporation and wholly controlled by the Van Sweringens. In October, 1931, when it was apparent that the Corporation could not meet its obligations, Guaranty co-operated in a plan for the purchase of the outstanding notes on the basis of cash for 50% of the face value of the notes and twenty shares of Van Sweringen Corporation's stock for each $1,000 note. * * *

Respondent York received $6,000 of the notes as a gift in 1934, her donor not having accepted the offer of exchange. * * *

The suit, instituted [by York] as a class action on behalf of non-accepting noteholders and brought in a federal court solely because of diversity of citizenship, is based on an alleged breach of trust by Guaranty in that it failed to protect the interests of the noteholders in assenting to the exchange offer and failed to disclose its self-interest when sponsoring the offer. * * * [The lower federal courts held that the action was barred by the New York statute of limitations, even though the suit was in equity.]

We put to one side the considerations relevant in disposing of questions that arise when a federal court is adjudicating a claim based on a federal law. Our problem only touches transactions for which rights and obligations are created by one of the States, and for the assertion of which, in case of diversity of the citizenship of the parties, Congress has made a federal court another available forum.

Our starting point must be the policy of federal jurisdiction which Erie R. Co. v. Tompkins embodies. In overruling Swift v. Tyson, Erie R. Co. v. Tompkins did not merely overrule a venerable case. It overruled a particular way of looking at law which dominated the judicial process long after its inadequacies had been laid bare. Law was conceived as a "brooding omnipresence" of Reason, of which decisions were merely evidence and not themselves the controlling formulations. Accordingly, federal courts deemed themselves free to ascertain what Reason, and therefore Law, required wholly independent of authoritatively declared State law, even in cases where a legal right as the basis for relief was created by State authority and could not be created by federal authority and the case got into a federal court merely because it was "between Citizens of different States" under Art. III, § 2 of the Constitution of the United States. * * *

In relation to the problem now here, the real significance of Swift v. Tyson lies in the fact that it did not enunciate novel doctrine. Nor was it restricted to its particular situation. It summed up prior attitudes and expressions in cases that had come before this Court and lower federal courts for at least thirty years, at law as well as in equity. The short of it is that the doctrine was congenial to the jurisprudential climate of the time. Once established, judicial momentum kept it going. Since it was conceived that there was "a transcendental body of law outside of any particular State but obligatory within it unless and until changed by statute", 276 U.S. 518, 532, 533, State court decisions were not "the law" but merely someone's opinion—to be sure an opinion to be respected—concerning the content of this all-pervading law. Not unnaturally, the federal courts assumed power to find for themselves the content of such a body of law. The notion was stimulated by the attractive vision of a uniform body of federal law. To such sentiments for uniformity of decision and freedom from diversity in State law the federal courts gave currency, particularly in cases where equitable remedies were sought, because equitable doctrines are so often cast in terms of universal applicability when close analysis of the source of legal enforceability is not demanded.

In exercising their jurisdiction on the ground of diversity of citizenship, the federal courts, in the long course of their history, have not differentiated in their regard for State law between actions at law and suits in equity. Although § 34 of the Judiciary Act of 1789 directed that the "laws of the several States * * * shall be regarded as rules of decision in trials of common law * * * ", this was deemed, consistently for over a hundred years, to be merely declaratory of what would in any event have governed the federal courts and therefore was equally applicable to equity suits. * * *

Partly because the States in the early days varied greatly in the manner in which equitable relief was afforded and in the extent to which it was available, Congress provided that "the forms and modes of proceeding in suits * * * of equity" would conform to the settled uses of courts of equity. Section 2, 1 Stat. 275, 276. But this enactment gave the federal courts no power that they would not have had in any event when courts were given "cognizance", by the first Judiciary Act, of equity. From the beginning there has been a good deal of talk in the cases that federal equity is a separate legal system. And so it is, properly understood. The suits in equity of which the federal courts have had "cognizance" ever since 1789 constituted the body of law which had been transplanted to this country from the English Court of Chancery. But this system of equity "derived its doctrines, as well as its powers, from its mode of giving relief". Langdell, Summary of Equity Pleading (1877) xxvii. In giving federal courts "cognizance" of equity suits in cases of diversity jurisdiction, Congress never gave, nor did the federal courts ever claim, the power to deny substantive rights created by State law or to create substantive rights denied by State law.

This does not mean that whatever equitable remedy is available in a State court must be available in a diversity suit in a federal court, or conversely, that a federal court may not afford an equitable remedy not available in a State court. Equitable relief in a federal court is of course subject to restrictions: the suit must be within the traditional scope of equity as historically evolved in the English Court of Chancery; a plain, adequate and complete remedy at law must be wanting; explicit Congressional curtailment of equity powers must be respected; the constitutional right to trial by jury cannot be evaded. That a State may authorize its courts to give equitable relief unhampered by any or all such restrictions cannot remove these fetters from the federal courts. State law cannot define the remedies which a federal court must give simply because a federal court in diversity jurisdiction is available as an alternative tribunal to the State's courts. Contrariwise, a federal court may afford an equitable remedy for a substantive right recognized by a State even though a State court cannot give it. Whatever contradiction or confusion may be produced by a medley of judicial phrases severed from their environment, the body of adjudications concerning equitable relief in diversity cases leaves no doubt that the federal courts enforced State-created substantive rights if the mode of proceeding and remedy were consonant with the traditional body of equitable remedies, practice and procedure, and in so doing they were enforcing rights created by the States and not arising under any inherent or statutory federal law. * * *

And so this case reduces itself to the narrow question whether, when no recovery could be had in a State court because the action is barred by the statute of limitations, a federal court in equity can take cognizance of the suit because there is diversity of citizenship between the parties. Is the outlawry, according to State law, of a claim created by the States a matter of "substantive rights" to be respected by a federal court of equity when that court's jurisdiction is dependent on the fact that there is a State-created right, or is such statute of "a mere remedial character", which a federal court may disregard?

Matters of "substance" and matters of "procedure" are much talked about in the books as though they defined a great divide cutting across the whole domain of law. But, of course, "substance" and "procedure" are the same key-words to very different problems. Neither "substance" nor "procedure" represents the same invariants. Each implies different variables depending upon the particular problem for which it is used.

And the different problems are only distantly related at best, for the terms are in common use in connection with situations turning on such different considerations as those that are relevant to questions pertaining to ex post facto legislation, the impairment of the obligations of contract, the enforcement of federal rights in the State courts and the multitudinous phases of the conflict of laws.

Here we are dealing with a right to recover derived not from the United States but from one of the States. When, because the plaintiff happens to be a nonresident, such a right is enforceable in a federal as well as in a State court, the forms and mode of enforcing the right may at times, naturally enough, vary because the two judicial systems are not identic. But since a federal court adjudicating a state-created right solely because of the diversity of citizenship of the parties is for that purpose, in effect, only another court of the State, it cannot afford recovery if the right to recover is made unavailable by the State nor can it substantially affect the enforcement of the right as given by the State.

And so the question is not whether a statute of limitations is deemed a matter of "procedure" in some sense. The question is whether such a statute concerns merely the manner and the means by which a right to recover, as recognized by the State, is enforced, or whether such statutory limitation is a matter of substance in the aspect that alone is relevant to our problem, namely, does it significantly affect the result of a litigation for a federal court or disregard a law of a State that would be controlling in an action upon the same claim by the same parties in a State court?

It is therefore immaterial whether statutes of limitation are characterized either as "substantive" or "procedural" in State court opinions in any use of those terms unrelated to the specific issue before us. Erie R. Co. v. Tompkins was not an endeavor to formulate scientific legal terminology. It expressed a policy that touches vitally the proper distribution of judicial power between State and federal courts. In essence, the intent of that decision was to insure that, in all cases where a federal court is exercising jurisdiction solely because of the diversity of citizenship of the parties, the outcome of the litigation in the federal court should be substantially the same, so far as legal rules determine the outcome of a litigation, as it would be if tried in a State court. The nub of the policy that underlies Erie R. Co. v. Tompkins is that for the same transaction the accident of a suit by a non-resident litigant in a federal court instead of in a State court a block away, should not lead to a substantially different result. * * * A policy so important to our federalism must be kept free from entanglements with analytical or terminological niceties.

Plainly enough, a statute that would completely bar recovery in a suit if brought in a State court bears on a State-created right vitally and not merely formally or negligibly. As to consequences that so intimately affect recovery or non-recovery a federal court in a diversity case should follow State law. * * * [I]f a plea of the statute of limitations would bar

recovery in a State court, a federal court ought not to afford recovery.
* * *

To make an exception to Erie R. Co. v. Tompkins on the equity side of a federal court is to reject the considerations of policy which, after long travail, led to that decision. Judge Augustus N. Hand thus summarized below the fatal objection to such inroad upon Erie R. Co. v. Tompkins: "In my opinion it would be a mischievous practice to disregard state statutes of limitation whenever federal courts think that the result of adopting them may be inequitable. Such procedure would promote the choice of United States rather than of state courts in order to gain the advantage of different laws. The main foundation for the criticism of Swift v. Tyson was that a litigant in cases where federal jurisdiction is based only on diverse citizenship may obtain a more favorable decision by suing in the United States courts." 2 Cir., 143 F.2d 503, 529, 531.

Diversity jurisdiction is founded on assurance to non-resident litigants of courts free from susceptibility to potential local bias. * * * And so Congress afforded out-of-State litigants another tribunal, not another body of law. The operation of a double system of conflicting laws in the same State is plainly hostile to the reign of law. Certainly, the fortuitous circumstance of residence out of a State of one of the parties to a litigation ought not to give rise to a discrimination against others equally concerned but locally resident. The source of substantive rights enforced by a federal court under diversity jurisdiction, it cannot be said too often, is the law of the States. Whenever that law is authoritatively declared by a State, whether its voice be the legislature or its highest court, such law ought to govern in litigation founded on that law, whether the forum of application is a State or a federal court and whether the remedies be sought at law or may be had in equity. * * *

The judgment is reversed and the case is remanded for proceedings not inconsistent with this opinion.

Mr. Justice ROBERTS and Mr. Justice DOUGLAS took no part in the consideration or decision of this case.

Mr. Justice RUTLEDGE.

I dissent. * * *

If any characteristic of equity jurisprudence has descended unbrokenly from and within "the traditional scope of equity as historically evolved in the English Court of Chancery," it is that statutes of limitations, often in terms applying only to actions at law, have never been deemed to be rigidly applicable as absolute barriers to suits in equity as they are to actions at law. That tradition, it would seem, should be regarded as having been incorporated in the various Acts of Congress which have conferred equity jurisdiction upon the federal courts. So incorporated, it has been reaffirmed repeatedly by the decisions of this and other courts. It is now excised from those Acts. If there is to be excision, Congress, not this Court, should make it. * * *

The words "substantive" and "procedural" or "remedial" are not talismanic. Merely calling a legal question by one or the other does not resolve it otherwise than as a purely authoritarian performance. But they have come to designate in a broad way large and distinctive legal domains within the greater one of the law and to mark, though often indistinctly or with overlapping limits, many divides between such regions. * * *

It may be true that if the matter were wholly fresh the barring of rights in equity by statutes of limitation would seem to partake more of the substantive than of the remedial phase of law. But the matter is not fresh and it is not without room for debate. A long tradition, in the states and here, as well as in the common law which antedated both state and federal law, has emphasized the remedial character of statutes of limitations, more especially in application to equity causes, on many kinds of issues requiring differentiation of such matters from more clearly and exclusively substantive ones. * * * The tradition now in question is equally long and unvaried. I cannot say the tradition is clearly wrong in this case more than in that. Nor can I say, as was said in the Erie case, that the matter is beyond the power of Congress to control. If that be conceded, I think Congress should make the change if it is to be made. The Erie decision was rendered in 1938. Seven years have passed without action by Congress to extend the rule to these matters. That is long enough to justify the conclusion that Congress also regards them as not governed by Erie and as wishing to make no change. This should be reason enough for leaving the matter at rest until it decides to act. * * *

Mr. Justice MURPHY joins in this opinion.

Notes and Questions

1. The state law in question in *Guaranty Trust* was a statute. Even under *Swift*, federal courts would apply state statutes as "state law" under the Rules of Decision Act. Why is *Guaranty Trust* even an *Erie* case?

2. The version of the Rules of Decision Act in effect at the time of *Guaranty Trust* is set out on page 849. Re-read that statute. Do you see why the statute, as written, technically did not apply to the litigation in *Guaranty Trust*? Because the Court nevertheless ordered the federal court to apply state law, *Guranty Trust* reinforces the notion that the *Erie* doctrine is grounded in the Constitution.

Now read the current version of the Rules of Decision Act, codified at 28 U.S.C. § 1652. Do you see why the current version would apply to a case like *Guaranty Trust* brought today?

3. Consider again the hypothetical set out in the text prior to the case. After *Guaranty Trust*, would a federal court be free to close a case to the media? Why or why not?

4. How does the Court arrive at the conclusion that a federal court need not apply state "procedural" law? Under *Erie*, a federal court is

required to follow state law by default; *i.e.*, because it is powerless to fashion a contrary rule. If federal courts can ignore state procedural rules, it means that the federal courts have the power to make federal procedural law. Where do the courts get this power?

5.   The problem with applying a straightforward substance/procedure analysis in *Guaranty Trust* is that for many purposes statutes of limitation are considered *procedural*. For example, courts generally consider statutes of limitation procedural for purposes of choice of law, which means that a court applies its own state's limitations period even when applying some other state's law to the other issues in the case. *C.f. Restatement of the Law (Second), Conflicts* § 142. The Court in *Guaranty Trust*, however, does not consider itself bound by this precedent. Because the Court says that the considerations underlying *Erie* are different than those underlying issues such as choice of law, the definition of "substance" and "procedure" might also be different. The Court devotes much of the opinion to defining substance and procedure in the *Erie* context. It ends up adopting what is commonly referred to as the "outcome determinative" test. Under this test, when is a rule procedural?

6.   Do you agree with the Court that the considerations underlying *Erie* and choice of law are different? Isn't *Erie* merely a type of choice of law rule that applies in federal court? On the other hand, is a court faced with an *Erie* issue really choosing one of two valid but competing laws?

7.   Apply the outcome determinative test to the following situation: State X has a maniacal obsession with its state university's athletic program. The school colors are an obnoxious shade of blue. To show its school spirit, the state legislature passes a statute that requires all state judges to wear blue robes. In addition, the law provides that no pleadings will be accepted unless printed in blue ink. Does a federal judge in State X have to replace her black robe with an obnoxious blue one when she hears a diversity case? May the federal court clerk accept a complaint printed in black ink for such a case?

8.   The Court in *Guaranty Trust* explicitly reserves judgment on whether a federal court must apply a state limitations period when adjudicating a case arising under federal law. Today, the rule is that the limitations period on a federal claim is a question of *federal* law, although in many cases the court will borrow the most analogous state limitations period. *Reed v. United Transp. Union*, 488 U.S. 319, 109 S.Ct. 621, 102 L.Ed.2d 665 (1989).

9.   *Remedies*. The Court also indicates that a federal court is not bound by state law when it is called upon to fashion an appropriate equitable remedy. Is that consistent with the rest of the opinion? Isn't the remedy the heart and soul of the "outcome" in a case, insofar as different remedies change the outcome?

For a discussion of how *Erie* applies to equitable remedies and other issues in equity, see John T. Cross, *The* Erie *Doctrine in Equity*, 60 La. L. Rev. 173 (1999). The author concludes that federal courts do in fact have a significant, albeit limited, power to ignore state laws dealing with equitable remedies.

As the discussion above suggests, *Guaranty Trust*'s "outcome determinative" test is problematic. Many matters that on their face seem clearly procedural can nevertheless change the outcome of a particular case. For the next twenty years, the Court continued to struggle with how to define the federal courts' power to regulate their procedure, as the following case demonstrates.

BYRD V. BLUE RIDGE RURAL ELECTRIC CO-OPERATIVE, INC., 356 U.S. 525, 78 S.Ct. 893, 2 L.Ed.2d 953 (1958). Plaintiff worked for a construction contractor. Plaintiff's employer was retained by Defendant, an electric utility, to install new power lines. While working on this job, Plaintiff was injured. Plaintiff sued Defendant for negligence in federal court, based on diversity. Defendant argued that because Plaintiff was injured on the job, his sole remedy lay under the South Carolina Workmen's Compensation Act.

One of the key issues in the case was who would decide whether Plaintiff was a "statutory employee" of Defendant, in which case his sole right to monetary relief would be workmen's compensation. In the South Carolina courts, the judge would decide that threshold issue. Plaintiff, however, wanted the federal court to try that issue to a jury. The Court held that the state practice of having the judge decide did not apply in the federal courts. Its analysis turned on three factors. First, the Court found that the state practice of using a judge was not an integral part of the right to recover against the employer:

> We find nothing to suggest that this rule was announced as an integral part of the special relationship created by the statute. Thus the requirement appears to be merely a form and mode of enforcing the immunity, *Guaranty Trust Co. of New York v. York*, 326 U.S. 99, and not a rule intended to be bound up with the definition of the rights and obligations of the parties. The situation is therefore not analogous to that in *Dice v. Akron, C. & Y.R. Co.*, 342 U.S. 359, where this Court held that the right to trial by jury is so substantial a part of the cause of action created by the Federal Employers' Liability Act that the Ohio courts could not apply, in an action under that statute, the Ohio rule that the question of fraudulent release was for determination by a judge rather than by a jury.

Second, the Court indicated that there was a countervailing federal interest; namely, the federal custom of using juries to decide contested factual issues. Although the Court in footnote 10 declined to hold that the Seventh Amendment required a jury in this case, that federal "tradition" nevertheless entered the calculus:

> It may well be that in the instant personal-injury case the outcome would be substantially affected by whether the issue of immunity is decided by a judge or a jury. Therefore, were "outcome" the only consideration, a strong case might appear for saying that the federal court should follow the state practice.

> But there are affirmative countervailing considerations at work here. The federal system is an independent system for administering justice to litigants who properly invoke its jurisdiction. An essential characteristic of that system is the manner in which, in civil common-law actions, it distributes trial functions between judge and jury and, under the influ-

ence—if not the command—of the Seventh Amendment, assigns the decisions of disputed questions of fact to the jury. The policy of uniform enforcement of state-created rights and obligations, cannot in every case exact compliance with a state rule—not bound up with rights and obligations—which disrupts the federal system of allocating functions between judge and jury.

Third, the Court also noted that the state law was not "outcome determinative" to the same degree as the rules in *Erie* and *Guaranty Trust*:

> We have discussed the problem upon the assumption that the outcome of the litigation may be substantially affected by whether the issue of immunity is decided by a judge or a jury. But clearly there is not present here the certainty that a different result would follow, cf. *Guaranty Trust Co. of New York v. York, supra,* or even the strong possibility that this would be the case. There are factors present here which might reduce that possibility. The trial judge in the federal system has powers denied the judges of many States to comment on the weight of evidence and credibility of witnesses, and discretion to grant a new trial if the verdict appears to him to be against the weight of the evidence. We do not think the likelihood of a different result is so strong as to require the federal practice of jury determination of disputed factual issues to yield to the state rule in the interest of uniformity of outcome.

Notes and Questions

1.   The Court's analysis invokes the Seventh Amendment. However, the Court dodges the issue of whether the Amendment actually requires a jury. But isn't that the crucial issue? If the Seventh Amendment requires a jury to decide the particular issue, of course, that specific requirement overrides the general federalism concerns of *Erie*. If the Seventh Amendment does not require a jury, how is it even relevant to the analysis?

2.   Can you think of any other areas where there is a federal interest strong enough to affect the *Erie* analysis?

3.   Does *Byrd* modify the *Guaranty Trust* test, or does it simply create an exception? Try to restate the rule of *Byrd* as a three-step exception, based on the three excerpts set out above.

4.   How would your three-part test apply to the blue robe/blue ink example set out in note 7 following *Guaranty Trust*?

5.   *Byrd* holds that a federal court may sometimes ignore state law governing use of a jury. However, as the Court indicates, the Supreme Court's decision in *Dice v. Akron, Canton, and Youngstown R. Co.*, 342 U.S. 359, 72 S.Ct. 312, 96 L.Ed. 398 (1952), held that a *state* court was required to use a jury when hearing a claim under a *federal* statute, even though the state practice was not to use a jury on those issues. Can *Byrd* and *Dice* be reconciled? Is it relevant that in both cases the Court held that a jury would be used to decide the crucial question?

HANNA v. PLUMER

380 U.S. 460, 85 S.Ct. 1136, 14 L.Ed.2d 8 (1965)

Mr. Chief Justice WARREN delivered the opinion of the Court.

The question to be decided is whether, in a civil action where the jurisdiction of the United States district court is based upon diversity of citizenship between the parties, service of process shall be made in the manner prescribed by state law or that set forth in Rule 4(d)(1) of the Federal Rules of Civil Procedure.

On February 6, 1963, petitioner, a citizen of Ohio, filed her complaint in the District Court for the District of Massachusetts, claiming damages in excess of $10,000 for personal injuries resulting from an automobile accident in South Carolina, allegedly caused by the negligence of one Louise Plumer Osgood, a Massachusetts citizen deceased at the time of the filing of the complaint. Respondent, Mrs. Osgood's executor and also a Massachusetts citizen, was named as defendant. On February 8, service was made by leaving copies of the summons and the complaint with respondent's wife at his residence, concededly in compliance with Rule 4(d)(1) * * *.

Respondent filed his answer on February 26, alleging, *inter alia*, that the action could not be maintained because it had been brought "contrary to and in violation of the provisions of Massachusetts General Laws Chapter 197, Section 9." That section provides:

> Except as provided in this chapter, an executor or administrator shall not be held to answer to an action by a creditor of the deceased which is not commenced within one year from the time of his giving bond for the performance of his trust, or to such an action which is commenced within said year unless before the expiration thereof the writ in such action has been served by delivery in hand upon such executor or administrator or service thereof accepted by him or a notice stating the name of the estate, the name and address of the creditor, the amount of the claim and the court in which the action has been brought has been filed in the proper registry of probate.
> * * *

On October 17, 1963, the District Court granted respondent's motion for summary judgment, * * * [concluding] that the adequacy of the service was to be measured by § 9, with which, the court held, petitioner had not complied. On appeal, petitioner admitted noncompliance with § 9, but argued that Rule 4(d)(1) defines the method by which service of process is to be effected in diversity actions. The Court of Appeals for the First Circuit, finding that "(r)elatively recent amendments (to § 9) evince a clear legislative purpose to require personal notification within the year," concluded that the conflict of state and federal rules was over "a substantive rather than a procedural matter," and unanimously affirmed. Because of the threat to the goal of uniformity of federal procedure posed by the decision below, we granted certiorari.

We conclude that the adoption of Rule 4(d)(1), designed to control service of process in diversity actions, neither exceeded the congressional mandate embodied in the Rules Enabling Act nor transgressed constitutional bounds, and that the Rule is therefore the standard against which the District Court should have measured the adequacy of the service. Accordingly, we reverse the decision of the Court of Appeals.

The Rules Enabling Act, 28 U.S.C. § 2072, provides, in pertinent part:

The Supreme Court shall have the power to prescribe, by general rules, the forms of process, writs, pleadings, and motions, and the practice and procedure of the district courts of the United States in civil actions.

Such rules shall not abridge, enlarge or modify any substantive right and shall preserve the right of trial by jury * * *.

Under the cases construing the scope of the Enabling Act, Rule 4(d)(1) clearly passes muster. Prescribing the manner in which a defendant is to be notified that a suit has been instituted against him, it relates to the "practice and procedure of the district courts."

The test must be whether a rule really regulates procedure,—the judicial process for enforcing rights and duties recognized by substantive law and for justly administering remedy and redress for disregard or infraction of them. *Sibbach v. Wilson & Co.*, 312 U.S. 1, 14. * * *

Thus were there no conflicting state procedure, Rule 4(d)(1) would clearly control. However, respondent, focusing on the contrary Massachusetts rule, calls to the Court's attention another line of cases, a line which—like the Federal Rules—had its birth in 1938. *Erie R. Co. v. Tompkins*, 304 U.S. 64, overruling *Swift v. Tyson*, 16 Pet. 1, held that federal courts sitting in diversity cases, when deciding questions of "substantive" law, are bound by state court decisions as well as state statutes. The broad command of *Erie* was therefore identical to that of the Enabling Act: federal courts are to apply state substantive law and federal procedural law. However, as subsequent cases sharpened the distinction between substance and procedure, the line of cases following *Erie* diverged markedly from the line construing the Enabling Act. *Guaranty Trust Co. of New York v. York*, 326 U.S. 99, made it clear that *Erie*-type problems were not to be solved by reference to any traditional or common-sense substance-procedure distinction * * *.

Respondent * * * suggests that the *Erie* doctrine acts as a check on the Federal Rules of Civil Procedure, that despite the clear command of Rule 4(d)(1), *Erie* and its progeny demand the application of the Massachusetts rule. Reduced to essentials, the argument is: (1) *Erie*, as refined in *York*, demands that federal courts apply state law whenever application of federal law in its stead will alter the outcome of the case. (2) In this case, a determination that the Massachusetts service requirements obtain will result in immediate victory for respondent. If, on the other hand, it should be held that Rule 4(d)(1) is applicable, the litigation will continue, with possible victory for petitioner. (3) Therefore, *Erie* demands application of the Massachusetts rule. The syllogism possesses an appealing simplicity, but is for several reasons invalid.

In the first place, it is doubtful that, even if there were no Federal Rule making it clear that in-hand service is not required in diversity actions, the *Erie* rule would have obligated the District Court to follow the Massachusetts procedure. "Outcome-determination" analysis was never intended to serve as a talisman. Indeed, the message of *York* itself is that choices between state and federal law are to be made not by application of any automatic, "litmus paper" criterion, but rather by reference to the policies underlying the *Erie* rule.

The *Erie* rule is rooted in part in a realization that it would be unfair for the character of result of a litigation materially to differ because the suit had been brought in a federal court. * * *

The decision was also in part a reaction to the practice of "forum-shopping" which had grown up in response to the rule of *Swift v. Tyson*. That the *York* test was an attempt to effectuate these policies is demonstrated by the fact that the opinion framed the inquiry in terms of "substantial" variations between state and federal litigation. Not only are nonsubstantial, or trivial, variations not likely to raise the sort of equal protection problems which troubled the Court in *Erie*; they are also unlikely to influence the choice of a forum. The "outcome-determination" test therefore cannot be read without reference to the twin aims of the *Erie* rule: discouragement of forum-shopping and avoidance of inequitable administration of the laws.

The difference between the conclusion that the Massachusetts rule is applicable, and the conclusion that it is not, is of course at this point "outcome-determinative" in the sense that if we hold the state rule to apply, respondent prevails, whereas if we hold that Rule 4(d)(1) governs, the litigation will continue. But in this sense every procedural variation is "outcome-determinative." For example, having brought suit in a federal court, a plaintiff cannot then insist on the right to file subsequent pleadings in accord with the time limits applicable in state courts, even though enforcement of the federal timetable will, if he continues to insist that he must meet only the state time limit, result in determination of the controversy against him. So it is here. Though choice of the federal or state rule will at this point have a marked effect upon the outcome of the litigation, the difference between the two rules would be of scant, if any, relevance to the choice of a forum. Petitioner, in choosing her forum, was not presented with a situation where application of the state rule would wholly bar recovery; rather, adherence to the state rule would have resulted only in altering the way in which process was served. Moreover, it is difficult to argue that permitting service of defendant's wife to take the place of inhand service of defendant himself alters the mode of enforcement of state-created rights in a fashion sufficiently "substantial" to raise the sort of equal protection problems to which the *Erie* opinion alluded.

There is, however, a more fundamental flaw in respondent's syllogism: the incorrect assumption that the rule of *Erie R. Co. v. Tompkins* constitutes the appropriate test of the validity and therefore the applicability of a Federal Rule of Civil Procedure. The *Erie* rule has never been invoked to void a Federal Rule. It is true that there have been cases where this Court has held applicable a state rule in the face of an argument that the situation was governed by one of the Federal Rules. But the holding of each such case was not that *Erie* commanded displacement of a Federal Rule by an inconsistent state rule, but rather that the scope of the Federal Rule was not as broad as the losing party urged, and therefore, there being no Federal Rule which covered the point in dispute, *Erie* commanded the enforcement of state law. * * * (Here, of course, the clash is unavoidable; Rule 4(d)(1) says—implicitly, but with unmistakable clarity—that inhand service is not required in federal courts.) At the same time, in cases adjudicating the validity of Federal Rules, we have not applied the *York* rule or other refinements of *Erie*, but have to this day continued to decide questions concerning the scope of the Enabling Act and the constitutionality of specific Federal Rules in light of the distinction set forth in *Sibbach*.

Nor has the development of two separate lines of cases been inadvertent. The line between "substance" and "procedure" shifts as the legal context changes. "Each implies different variables depending upon the particular problem for which it is used." *Guaranty Trust Co. of New York v. York, supra*, 326 U.S. at 108. It is true that both the Enabling Act and the *Erie* rule say, roughly, that federal courts are to apply state "substantive" law and federal "procedural" law, but from that it need not follow that the tests are identical. For they were designed to control very different sorts of decisions. When a situation is covered by one of the Federal Rules, the question facing the court is a far cry from the typical, relatively unguided *Erie* Choice: the court has been instructed to apply the Federal Rule, and can refuse to do so only if the Advisory Committee, this Court, and Congress erred in their prima facie judgment that the Rule in question transgresses neither the terms of the Enabling Act nor constitutional restrictions.

We are reminded by the *Erie* opinion that neither Congress nor the federal courts can, under the guise of formulating rules of decision for federal courts, fashion rules which are not supported by a grant of federal authority contained in Article I or some other section of the Constitution; in such areas state law must govern because there can be no other law. But the opinion in *Erie*, which involved no Federal Rule and dealt with a question which was "substantive" in every traditional sense (whether the railroad owed a duty of care to Tompkins as a trespasser or a licensee), surely neither said nor implied that measures like Rule 4(d)(1) are unconstitutional. For the constitutional provision for a federal court system (augmented by the Necessary and Proper

Clause*) carries with it congressional power to make rules governing the practice and pleading in those courts, which in turn includes a power to regulate matters which, though falling within the uncertain area between substance and procedure, are rationally capable of classification as either. Neither *York* nor the cases following it ever suggested that the rule there laid down for coping with situations where no Federal Rule applies is coextensive with the limitation on Congress to which *Erie* had adverted. * * *

Erie and its offspring cast no doubt on the long-recognized power of Congress to prescribe housekeeping rules for federal courts even though some of those rules will inevitably differ from comparable state rules. * * * To hold that a Federal Rule of Civil Procedure must cease to function whenever it alters the mode of enforcing state-created rights would be to disembowel either the Constitution's grant of power over federal procedure or Congress' attempt to exercise that power in the Enabling Act. Rule 4(d)(1) is valid and controls the instant case.

Reversed.

Mr. Justice BLACK concurs in the result.

Mr. Justice HARLAN, concurring. * * *

Erie was something more than an opinion which worried about "forum-shopping and avoidance of inequitable administration of the laws," although to be sure these were important elements of the decision. I have always regarded that decision as one of the modern cornerstones of our federalism, expressing policies that profoundly touch the allocation of judicial power between the state and federal systems. *Erie* recognized that there should not be two conflicting systems of law controlling the primary activity of citizens, for such alternative governing authority must necessarily give rise to a debilitating uncertainty in the planning of everyday affairs. And it recognized that the scheme of our Constitution envisions an allocation of law-making functions between state and federal legislative processes which is undercut if the federal judiciary can make substantive law affecting state affairs beyond the bounds of congressional legislative powers in this regard. Thus, in diversity cases *Erie* commands that it be the state law governing primary private activity which prevails. * * *

To my mind the proper line of approach in determining whether to apply a state or a federal rule, whether "substantive" or "procedural," is to stay close to basic principles by inquiring if the choice of rule would substantially affect those primary decisions respecting human conduct which our constitutional system leaves to state regulation. If so, *Erie* and the Constitution require that the state rule prevail, even in the face of a conflicting federal rule.

---

* U.S. Const. Art. 1, § 8, gives Congress the power to enact laws that are "necessary and proper" for implementing any of its enumerated powers. This clause, commonly referred to as the "Necessary and Proper Clause," augments Congress's powers not only under Article I, but also under any other provision of the Constitution. *Eds.*

The Court weakens, if indeed it does not submerge, this basic principle by finding, in effect, a grant of substantive legislative power in the constitutional provision for a federal court system, and through it, setting up the Federal Rules as a body of law inviolate. * * * So long as a reasonable man could characterize any duly adopted federal rule as "procedural," the Court, unless I misapprehend what is said, would have it apply no matter how seriously it frustrated a State's substantive regulation of the primary conduct and affairs of its citizens. Since the members of the Advisory Committee, the Judicial Conference, and this Court who formulated the Federal Rules are presumably reasonable men, it follows that the integrity of the Federal Rules is absolute. Whereas the unadulterated outcome and forum-shopping tests may err too far toward honoring state rules, I submit that the Court's "arguably procedural, *ergo* constitutional" test moves too fast and far in the other direction. * * *

It remains to apply what has been said to the present case. The Massachusetts rule provides that an executor need not answer suits unless in-hand service was made upon him or notice of the action was filed in the proper registry of probate within one year of his giving bond. The evident intent of this statute is to permit an executor to distribute the estate which he is administering without fear that further liabilities may be outstanding for which he could be held personally liable. If the Federal District Court in Massachusetts applies Rule 4(d) (1) of the Federal Rules of Civil Procedure instead of the Massachusetts service rule, what effect would that have on the speed and assurance with which estates are distributed? As I see it, the effect would not be substantial. It would mean simply that an executor would have to check at his own house or the federal courthouse as well as the registry of probate before he could distribute the estate with impunity. As this does not seem enough to give rise to any real impingement on the vitality of the state policy which the Massachusetts rule is intended to serve, I concur in the judgment of the Court.

Notes and Questions

1. Like all *Erie* cases, *Hanna* involves a clash between state and federal law. What is the federal law involved in the case? Did any of the earlier cases involve this type of federal law?

2. Although the Federal Rules are codified, they are nevertheless a type of judge-made law. The Supreme Court, with the help of an Advisory Committee, promulgates the Rules pursuant to the authority granted in the Rules Enabling Act, 28 U.S.C. § 2072. Unless Congress rejects or modifies a proposed Rule, it automatically takes effect on December 1 of the year it was promulgated. 28 U.S.C. § 2074(a).

3. Review the Rules Enabling Act. Does it give the Supreme Court the power to enact a wide variety of rules? What explicit limits does the Act place on the Court's authority to enact laws?

4. Conceptually, both *Guaranty Trust* and *Byrd* dealt with the federal courts' inherent ability to regulate their own procedure. The issue in *Hanna*

is fundamentally different. Because the Rules Enabling Act represents a delegation to the Supreme Court of some of Congress's lawmaking powers, the issue in a case like *Hanna* is not the courts' inherent power, but rather whether the Supreme Court has acted within the scope of the Congressional delegation.

5.   With this background, consider the portion of *Hanna* that discusses whether a federal court should apply a Federal Rule in lieu of state law (which oddly enough comes at the end of the opinion). What test does the Court adopt? Is that test anything more than a restatement of the restrictions imposed by the Rules Enabling Act?

6.   Note that when considering whether to apply a Federal Rule, a court does not ask whether the difference in state and federal law would be outcome determinative. If the Rule is valid under the Rules Enabling Act, it automatically applies. Why is outcome determination not relevant to the Rules? Recall that the Rules Enabling Act delegates Congressional power. Does Congress have the ability to change the outcome of cases?

7.   Justice Harlan's concurrence criticizes the majority's test for evaluating the Federal Rules. How does he propose a court should deal with a Federal Rule? Do you find his argument persuasive? Does Justice Harlan's approach gauge the federal court's inherent or delegated power to make law?

8.   *Other Rules*. The Federal Rules of Civil Procedure are not the only body of law promulgated by the federal courts pursuant to a delegation by Congress. The Rules Enabling Act also allows the Supreme Court to create rules of evidence. How would you modify the *Hanna* test to determine whether a rule of evidence would apply in federal court in lieu of state law?

Other statutes delegate additional powers. 28 U.S.C. § 2075 allows the Supreme Court to promulgate procedural rules for the Bankruptcy Courts. Section 2071 allows all federal courts to enact local rules governing practice in those courts. The analysis of rules promulgated under these statutes is similar to the Rules Enabling Act analysis in *Hanna*.

9.   Suppose that the federal law at issue in *Hanna*—the rule allowing service at the defendant's abode—was not codified in the Federal Rules, but was instead a common practice followed by the federal courts. Now, the "arguably procedural" test would not apply. Under *Guaranty Trust* and *Byrd*, the court would have to apply the state law requiring in-hand service, because to apply the federal "law" would change the outcome. Does *Hanna* offer any insight into this situation? According to the Court, would a federal court in our hypothetical apply the federal custom or state law? Why?

10.   Although the Court's "likely to cause forum shopping" test is technically *dictum*, it has become the accepted way to deal with *Erie* issues involving federal rules established by precedent, as opposed to rules promulgated pursuant to the Rules Enabling Act or similar laws. Apply that test to the federal laws in *Erie*, *Guaranty Trust*, and *Byrd*. Would the outcome of any of these cases have changed?

11.   Consider the following two hypothetical situations:

Situation One. A state legislature enacts a statute imposing a special $10,000 filing fee for complaints in malpractice cases. The filing fee for federal courts in that state is $150. The federal fee is set by the district clerk, not by the Federal Rules or any local rule. Must the federal court charge a $10,000 filing fee for federal diversity malpractice cases?

Situation Two. The judges in State X have proven to be extremely biased against out-of-state litigants, at least when those litigants are suing or being sued by citizens of State X. Plaintiff, from State Y, sues Defendant, from State X, in a federal court in State X. Must the federal judge adopt a bias against Plaintiff?

In both of these situations, won't the difference in federal and state practice lead to forum shopping? Does that mean that the federal court should ape the state court? If so, does that make sense?

Re-read the portion of *Hanna* dealing with judge-made law. What is the Court trying to say when it talks about the "twin aims" of *Erie*? What is the "inequitable administration of the laws?" Does that second aim affect how one applies the likely to cause forum shopping test? Is all forum shopping equally objectionable?

12. Both *Hanna* and *Guaranty Trust* make it clear that *Erie* applies to state statutes of limitations, at least when the case itself is based on state law. Does it follow that the federal court must calculate the limitations period in exactly the same way? In many states, the statute of limitations is tolled not when the case is filed, but only once the defendant is served. By contrast, Federal Rule 3 provides, "A civil action is commenced by filing a complaint with the court." Does Federal Rule 3 allow a plaintiff to beat out a state statute of limitations in federal court merely by filing the complaint? If so, is the Rule valid?

The Supreme Court dodged the issue in *Walker v. Armco Steel Corp.*, 446 U.S. 740, 100 S.Ct. 1978, 64 L.Ed.2d 659 (1980). It held that Federal Rule 3 did not govern the application of state statutes of limitations. Instead, the Rule simply was an internal timing device for purposes of applying other Federal Rules. Because Rule 3 did not apply, the Court in *Walker* applied the "likely to cause forum shopping" analysis of *Hanna*, finding that state law controlled the issue of what a plaintiff must do to satisfy the state statute of limitations.

Does the Court's argument in *Walker* make sense? Why—other than for purposes of the statute of limitations—do we care about when a case commences? Are any of the time periods in the Federal Rules measured by the date the action is commenced?

Note that when a case is governed by a federal limitations period, courts look to the date of filing rather than service to determine whether the complaint is timely. Does this undermine the Court's argument that Rule 3 is nothing more than an internal timing mechanism?

13. *Walker* is evidence that a court will sometimes construe a Federal Rule narrowly so as to avoid a clash with state law. Another case in which the Court may have chosen a narrow interpretation is *Semtek*, set out below at page 883.

In other situations, however, the Court will take the Federal Rule at face value. Consider *Burlington Northern Railroad v. Woods*, 480 U.S. 1, 107 S.Ct. 967, 94 L.Ed.2d 1 (1987). In that case, state law required a party who appealed a trial court's money judgment to pay an additional penalty of ten percent of that judgment if she also lost the appeal. Federal Rule of Appellate Procedure 38, by contrast, gives a federal appellate court the ability to impose sanctions in cases involving "frivolous" appeals. Plaintiff argued that the rules did not conflict, as the federal court could impose both the ten percent penalty called for by state law, and, if it found the appeal frivolous, an additional amount under the Federal Rule. The Supreme Court disagreed, holding that the rules clashed. Because the Federal Rule was valid under the Rules Enabling Act analysis, the Court held that it applied.

14. Does the *Klaxon* rule (discussed in note 12 following *Erie*) survive *Hanna*? Are State X's choice of law rules—rules which almost invariably apply only in the courts of State X—rules of substance or procedure? Which of the two *Hanna* tests would apply? *See Day & Zimmerman, Inc. v. Challoner*, 423 U.S. 3, 96 S.Ct. 167, 46 L.Ed.2d 3 (1975).

15. If the choice of law question is governed by the likely to cause forum shopping test, what happens in a situation where state court is not a viable option? Recall that in a statutory interpleader case, federal courts may exercise personal jurisdiction over claimants located anywhere in the United States. State courts, by contrast, would have to have minimum contacts with all claimants. As a result, in many situations a party could bring an interpleader action only in federal court.

In *Griffin v. McCoach*, 313 U.S. 498, 61 S.Ct. 1023, 85 L.Ed. 1481 (1941), a companion case to *Klaxon*, the Court held that the *Klaxon* rule applied even to a statutory interpleader case that could not have been heard in any state court. Even if *Klaxon* is still good law, does *Griffin* survive *Hanna*? Is there any chance of forum shopping when the state courts could not have heard the case? *See* John T. Cross, *State Choice of Law Rules in Bankruptcy*, 42 Okla. L. Rev. 531 (1989), which argues that both *Klaxon* and *Griffin* are still good law.

2. Applying the Modern Doctrine

STEWART ORGANIZATION v. RICOH CORPORATION

487 U.S. 22, 108 S.Ct. 2239, 101 L.Ed.2d 22 (1988)

Justice MARSHALL delivered the opinion of the Court.

This case presents the issue whether a federal court sitting in diversity should apply state or federal law in adjudicating a motion to transfer a case to a venue provided in a contractual forum-selection clause.

The dispute underlying this case grew out of a dealership agreement that obligated petitioner company, an Alabama corporation, to market copier products of respondent, a nationwide manufacturer with its principal place of business in New Jersey. The agreement contained a forum-selection clause providing that any dispute arising out of the contract could be brought only in a court located in Manhattan.[1] Busi-

---

1. Specifically, the forum-selection clause read: "Dealer and Ricoh agree that   any appropriate state or federal district court located in the Borough of Manhattan,

ness relations between the parties soured under circumstances that are not relevant here. In September 1984, petitioner brought a complaint in the United States District Court for the Northern District of Alabama. The core of the complaint was an allegation that respondent had breached the dealership agreement, but petitioner also included claims for breach of warranty, fraud, and antitrust violations.

Relying on the contractual forum-selection clause, respondent moved the District Court either to transfer the case to the Southern District of New York under 28 U.S.C. § 1404(a) or to dismiss the case for improper venue under 28 U.S.C. § 1406. The District Court denied the motion. It reasoned that the transfer motion was controlled by Alabama law and that Alabama looks unfavorably upon contractual forum-selection clauses. * * *

On appeal, a divided panel of the Eleventh Circuit reversed the District Court. The panel concluded that questions of venue in diversity actions are governed by federal law, and that the parties' forum-selection clause was enforceable as a matter of federal law. * * *

A district court's decision whether to apply a federal statute such as § 1404(a) in a diversity action * * * involves a considerably less intricate analysis than that which governs the "relatively unguided *Erie* choice." *Hanna v. Plumer*, 380 U.S. 460 (1965). Our cases indicate that when the federal law sought to be applied is a congressional statute, the first and chief question for the district court's determination is whether the statute is "sufficiently broad to control the issue before the Court." *Walker v. Armco Steel Corp.*, 446 U.S. 740, 749–750 (1980). This question involves a straightforward exercise in statutory interpretation to determine if the statute covers the point in dispute.

If the district court determines that a federal statute covers the point in dispute, it proceeds to inquire whether the statute represents a valid exercise of Congress' authority under the Constitution. If Congress intended to reach the issue before the District Court, and if it enacted its intention into law in a manner that abides with the Constitution, that is the end of the matter * * *. Thus, a district court sitting in diversity must apply a federal statute that controls the issue before the court and that represents a valid exercise of Congress' constitutional powers.

Applying the above analysis to this case persuades us that federal law, specifically 28 U.S.C. § 1404(a), governs the parties' venue dispute. * * *

Section 1404(a) is intended to place discretion in the district court to adjudicate motions for transfer according to an "individualized, case-by-case consideration of convenience and fairness." *Van Dusen v. Barrack*, 376 U.S. 612, 622 (1964). A motion to transfer under § 1404(a) thus calls on the district court to weigh in the balance a number of case-specific

New York City, New York, shall have exclusive jurisdiction over any case or controversy arising under or in connection with this   Agreement and shall be a proper forum in which to adjudicate such case or controversy."

factors. The presence of a forum-selection clause such as the parties entered into in this case will be a significant factor that figures centrally in the district court's calculus. In its resolution of the § 1404(a) motion in this case, for example, the District Court will be called on to address such issues as the convenience of a Manhattan forum given the parties' expressed preference for that venue, and the fairness of transfer in light of the forum-selection clause and the parties' relative bargaining power. The flexible and individualized analysis Congress prescribed in § 1404(a) thus encompasses consideration of the parties' private expression of their venue preferences. * * *

It is true that § 1404(a) and Alabama's putative policy regarding forum-selection clauses are not perfectly coextensive. Section 1404(a) directs a district court to take account of factors other than those that bear solely on the parties' private ordering of their affairs. The district court also must weigh in the balance the convenience of the witnesses and those public-interest factors of systemic integrity and fairness that, in addition to private concerns, come under the heading of "the interest of justice." It is conceivable in a particular case, for example, that because of these factors a district court acting under § 1404(a) would refuse to transfer a case notwithstanding the counterweight of a forum-selection clause, whereas the coordinate state rule might dictate the opposite result. But this potential conflict in fact frames an additional argument for the supremacy of federal law. Congress has directed that multiple considerations govern transfer within the federal court system, and a state policy focusing on a single concern or a subset of the factors identified in § 1404(a) would defeat that command. * * * The forum-selection clause, which represents the parties' agreement as to the most proper forum, should receive neither dispositive consideration (as respondent might have it) nor no consideration (as Alabama law might have it), but rather the consideration for which Congress provided in § 1404(a). * * *

Because § 1404(a) controls the issue before the District Court, it must be applied if it represents a valid exercise of Congress' authority under the Constitution. The constitutional authority of Congress to enact § 1404(a) is not subject to serious question. As the Court made plain in *Hanna*, "the constitutional provision for a federal court system . . . carries with it congressional power to make rules governing the practice and pleading in those courts, which in turn includes a power to regulate matters which, though falling within the uncertain area between substance and procedure, are rationally capable of classification as either." 380 U.S., at 472. See also *id.*, at 473 ("*Erie* and its offspring cast no doubt on the long-recognized power of Congress to prescribe housekeeping rules for federal courts"). Section 1404(a) is doubtless capable of classification as a procedural rule * * *. It therefore falls comfortably within Congress' powers under Article III as augmented by the Necessary and Proper Clause.

We hold that federal law, specifically 28 U.S.C. § 1404(a), governs the District Court's decision whether to give effect to the parties' forum-selection clause and transfer this case to a court in Manhattan.[11] We therefore affirm the Eleventh Circuit order reversing the District Court's application of Alabama law. The case is remanded so that the District Court may determine in the first instance the appropriate effect under federal law of the parties' forum-selection clause on respondent's § 1404(a) motion.

[The concurring opinion of Justice KENNEDY, joined by Justice O'CONNOR, is omitted.]

Justice SCALIA, dissenting.

* * * The Court largely attempts to avoid acknowledging the novel scope it gives to § 1404(a) by casting the issue as how much *weight* a district court should give a forum-selection clause as against other factors when it makes its determination under § 1404(a). I agree that if the weight-among-factors issue were before us, it would be governed by § 1404(a). That is because, while the parties may decide who between them should bear any inconvenience, only a court can decide how much weight should be given under § 1404(a) to the factor of the parties' convenience as against other relevant factors such as the convenience of witnesses. But the Court's description of the issue begs the question: what law governs whether the forum-selection clause is a *valid* or *invalid* allocation of any inconvenience between the parties. If it is invalid, i.e., should be voided, between the parties, it cannot be entitled to any weight in the § 1404(a) determination. Since under Alabama law the forum-selection clause should be voided, in this case the question of what weight should be given the forum-selection clause can be reached only if as a preliminary matter federal law controls the issue of the validity of the clause between the parties.

Second, § 1404(a) was enacted against the background that issues of contract, including a contract's validity, are nearly always governed by state law. It is simply contrary to the practice of our system that such an issue should be wrenched from state control in absence of a clear conflict with federal law or explicit statutory provision.

[After concluding that § 1404 did not apply to the issue, Justice Scalia argued that the federal courts could not, under *Erie*, fashion a judge-made rule to govern the question of forum selection clauses.]

Notes and Questions

1. The Court in *Stewart* finds that 28 U.S.C. § 1404 clashes with state law. Review that statute. Does it say anything about forum selection clauses? If not, how can the Court conclude that it applies? What motion was presented to the trial court?

2. Is Justice Scalia correct when he argues it is logically necessary to determine if the forum selection clause is valid and enforceable? Does the

---

11. Because a validly enacted Act of Congress controls the issue in dispute, we have no occasion to evaluate the impact of application of federal judge-made law on the "twin aims" that animate the *Erie* doctrine.

Court need to find the clause valid in order to give it any weight in a § 1404 analysis? Even if the clause is invalid, how might it be relevant to a court's decision whether to transfer the case?

3. According to *Stewart*, how does a court deal with an *Erie* dispute involving a federal statute? Does it ask whether the statute would cause forum shopping? Whether the statute is "arguably procedural?" Why is the analysis different?

4. Suppose the Court had concluded that § 1404 did not apply. How would it have analyzed the case? Would Alabama's rule refusing to enforce forum selection clauses apply in federal court?

5. Note that defendant had also moved to dismiss under 28 U.S.C. § 1406 based on the forum selection clause. The Court did not deal with that issue. If it had, how should it have ruled? Does § 1406 itself govern whether the forum selection clause is valid? Does any other federal statute or rule deal with the issue? What about 28 U.S.C. § 1391?

GASPERINI V. CENTER FOR HUMANITIES, INC., 518 U.S. 415, 116 S.Ct. 2211, 135 L.Ed.2d 659 (1996). Gasperini, a photographer, loaned 300 photos to Defendant. After Defendant lost the photos, Plaintiff sued in federal court to recover their value. The trial court awarded Plaintiff damages of $1500 per photograph, for a total of $450,000. Defendant appealed. The usual practice in federal court is that a court of appeals will overturn a jury verdict only if the result "shocks the conscience"—a very difficult standard to satisfy. However, Defendant argued that the federal appellate court was bound to apply a New York statute, CPLR § 5501(c), that required a court of appeals to overturn a judgment based on a jury verdict "if it deviates materially from what would be reasonable compensation." This standard would be considerably easier for the judgment loser to satisfy.

The Supreme Court first held that the New York law was "substantive" for purposes of *Erie*:

> We start from a point the parties do not debate. Gasperini acknowledges that a statutory cap on damages would supply substantive law for *Erie* purposes. Although CPLR § 5501(c) is less readily classified, it was designed to provide an analogous control. * * *

> We think it a fair conclusion that CPLR § 5501(c) differs from a statutory cap principally "in that the maximum amount recoverable is not set forth by statute, but rather is determined by case law." *Brief for City of New York as Amicus Curiae* 11. In sum, § 5501(c) contains a procedural instruction, but the State's objective is manifestly substantive.

> It thus appears that if federal courts ignore the change in the New York standard and persist in applying the "shock the conscience" test to damage awards on claims governed by New York law, " 'substantial' variations between state and federal [money judgments]" may be expected. See *Hanna*, 380 U.S., at 467–468. We therefore agree with the Second Circuit that New York's check on excessive damages implicates

what we have called *Erie*'s "twin aims." * * * *Erie* precludes a recovery in federal court significantly larger than the recovery that would have been tolerated in state court.

However, the Court also concluded that the state-law standard should be applied by the *trial* court, rather than the court of appeals as would have been the case in the New York state courts. Its reasoning turned on the Seventh Amendment and *Byrd*:

The Seventh Amendment, which governs proceedings in federal court, but not in state court, bears not only on the allocation of trial functions between judge and jury, the issue in *Byrd*; it also controls the allocation of authority to review verdicts, the issue of concern here. * * *

Byrd involved the first Clause of the Amendment, the "trial by jury" Clause. This case involves the second, the "Reexamination" Clause. In keeping with the historic understanding, the Reexamination Clause does not inhibit the authority of trial judges to grant new trials "for any of the reasons for which new trials have heretofore been granted in actions at law in the courts of the United States." Fed. Rule Civ. Proc. 59(a). That authority is large. "The trial judge in the federal system," we have reaffirmed, "has ... discretion to grant a new trial if the verdict appears to [the judge] to be against the weight of the evidence." *Byrd*, 356 U.S., at 540. This discretion includes overturning verdicts for excessiveness and ordering a new trial without qualification, or conditioned on the verdict winner's refusal to agree to a reduction (remittitur).

In contrast, appellate review of a federal trial court's denial of a motion to set aside a jury's verdict as excessive is a relatively late, and less secure, development. Such review was once deemed inconsonant with the Seventh Amendment's Reexamination Clause. * * *

Before today, we have not "expressly [held] that the Seventh Amendment allows appellate review of a district court's denial of a motion to set aside an award as excessive." *Browning–Ferris Industries of Vt., Inc. v. Kelco Disposal, Inc.*, 492 U.S. 257, 279, n. 25 (1989). But in successive reminders that the question was worthy of this Court's attention, we noted, without disapproval, that courts of appeals engage in review of district court excessiveness determinations, applying "abuse of discretion" as their standard. * * * [I]n *Browning–Ferris*, we again referred to appellate court abuse-of-discretion review:

"[T]he role of the district court is to determine whether the jury's verdict is within the confines set by state law, and to determine, by reference to federal standards developed under Rule 59, whether a new trial or remittitur should be ordered. The court of appeals should then review the district court's determination under an abuse-of-discretion standard." 492 U.S., at 279.

* * * [A]ppellate review for abuse of discretion is reconcilable with the Seventh Amendment as a control necessary and proper to the fair administration of justice * * *.

New York's dominant interest can be respected, without disrupting the federal system, once it is recognized that the federal district court is capable of performing the checking function, i.e., that court can apply the State's "deviates materially" standard in line with New York case law evolving under CPLR § 5501(c). * * *

Within the federal system, practical reasons combine with Seventh Amendment constraints to lodge in the district court, not the court of appeals, primary responsibility for application of § 5501(c)'s "deviates materially" check. * * *

District court applications of the "deviates materially" standard would be subject to appellate review under the standard the Circuits now employ when inadequacy or excessiveness is asserted on appeal: abuse of discretion. * * *

Notes and Questions

1. The Court bifurcates the New York law into two discrete components. What are these, and does state or federal law apply to each?

2. Do you agree with the court that refusing to follow the New York "damages cap" would be likely to cause forum shopping? Do parties really base their choice of forum on what the appellate courts might do?

3. With respect to the second part of the case—whether the federal appellate court should apply the state standard—do you understand the Court's reasoning? If the Reexamination Clause of the Seventh Amendment prevents a court from setting aside a jury verdict, why does it matter whether the appellate court or trial court sets it aside? In this context, you may find it helpful to review the materials on the Reexamination Clause in the chapter on jury trials (Chapter 9, section A.3.).

SEMTEK INTERNATIONAL INC. v. LOCKHEED MARTIN CORP.

531 U.S. 497, 121 S.Ct. 1021, 149 L.Ed.2d 32 (2001)

Justice SCALIA delivered the opinion of the Court.

This case presents the question whether the claim-preclusive effect of a federal judgment dismissing a diversity action on statute-of-limitations grounds is determined by the law of the State in which the federal court sits.

I

Petitioner filed a complaint against respondent in California state court, alleging inducement of breach of contract and various business torts. Respondent removed the case to the United States District Court for the Central District of California on the basis of diversity of citizenship, and successfully moved to dismiss petitioner's claims as barred by California's 2–year statute of limitations. In its order of dismissal, the District Court, adopting language suggested by respondent, dismissed petitioner's claims "in [their] entirety on the merits and with prejudice." Without contesting the District Court's designation of its dismissal as "on the merits," petitioner appealed to the Court of Appeals for the Ninth Circuit, which affirmed the District Court's order. Petitioner also brought suit against respondent in the State Circuit Court for Baltimore City, Maryland, alleging the same causes of action, which were not time barred under Maryland's 3–year statute of limitations. * * * Following a hearing, the Maryland state court granted respondent's motion to dismiss on the ground of res judicata. * * * After the Maryland Court of Appeals declined to review the case, we granted certiorari.

II

Petitioner contends that the outcome of this case is controlled by *Dupasseur v. Rochereau*, 21 Wall. 130 (1875), which held that the res judicata effect of a federal diversity judgment "is such as would belong to judgments of the State courts rendered under similar circumstances," and may not be accorded any "higher sanctity or effect." Since, petitioner argues, the dismissal of an action on statute-of-limitations grounds by a California state court would not be claim preclusive, it follows that the similar dismissal of this diversity action by the California federal court cannot be claim preclusive. While we agree that this would be the result demanded by *Dupasseur*, the case is not dispositive because it was decided under the Conformity Act of 1872, which required federal courts to apply the procedural law of the forum State in nonequity cases. That arguably affected the outcome of the case.

Respondent, for its part, contends that the outcome of this case is controlled by Federal Rule of Civil Procedure 41(b), which provides as follows:

> Involuntary Dismissal: Effect Thereof. For failure of the plaintiff to prosecute or to comply with these rules or any order of court, a defendant may move for dismissal of an action or of any claim against the defendant. Unless the court in its order for dismissal otherwise specifies, a dismissal under this subdivision and any dismissal not provided for in this rule, other than a dismissal for lack of jurisdiction, for improper venue, or for failure to join a party under Rule 19, operates as an adjudication upon the merits.

Since the dismissal here did not "otherwise specif[y]" (indeed, it specifically stated that it *was* "on the merits"), and did not pertain to the excepted subjects of jurisdiction, venue, or joinder, it follows, respondent contends, that the dismissal "is entitled to claim preclusive effect."

Implicit in this reasoning is the unstated minor premise that all judgments denominated "on the merits" are entitled to claim-preclusive effect. That premise is not necessarily valid. The original connotation of an "on the merits" adjudication is one that actually "pass[es] directly on the substance of [a particular] claim" before the court. *Restatement [(Second) of Judgments]* § 19, Comment a, at 161. That connotation remains common to every jurisdiction of which we are aware. And it is, we think, the meaning intended in those many statements to the effect that a judgment "on the merits" triggers the doctrine of res judicata or claim preclusion.

But over the years the meaning of the term "judgment on the merits" "has gradually undergone change," R. Marcus, M. Redish, & E. Sherman, *Civil Procedure: A Modern Approach* 1140–1141 (3d ed.2000), and it has come to be applied to some judgments (such as the one involved here) that do not pass upon the substantive merits of a claim and hence do not (in many jurisdictions) entail claim-preclusive effect. That is why the *Restatement of Judgments* has abandoned the use of the term—"because of its possibly misleading connotations," *Restatement* § 19, Comment a, at 161.

In short, it is no longer true that a judgment "on the merits" is necessarily a judgment entitled to claim-preclusive effect; and there are a number of reasons for believing that the phrase "adjudication upon the merits" does not bear that meaning in Rule 41(b). To begin with, Rule 41(b) sets forth nothing more than a default rule for determining the import of a dismissal (a dismissal is "upon the merits," with the three stated exceptions, unless the court "otherwise specifies"). This would be a highly peculiar context in which to announce a federally prescribed rule on the complex question of claim preclusion, saying in effect, "All federal dismissals (with three specified exceptions) preclude suit elsewhere, unless the court otherwise specifies."

And even apart from the purely default character of Rule 41(b), it would be peculiar to find a rule governing the effect that must be accorded federal judgments by other courts ensconced in rules governing the internal procedures of the rendering court itself. Indeed, such a rule would arguably violate the jurisdictional limitation of the Rules Enabling Act: that the Rules "shall not abridge, enlarge or modify any substantive right," 28 U.S.C. § 2072(b). In the present case, for example, if California law left petitioner free to sue on this claim in Maryland even after the California statute of limitations had expired, the federal court's extinguishment of that right (through Rule 41(b)'s mandated claim-preclusive effect of its judgment) would seem to violate this limitation.

Moreover, as so interpreted, the Rule would in many cases violate the federalism principle of *Erie R. Co. v. Tompkins*, 304 U.S. 64, 78–80 (1938), by engendering " 'substantial' variations [in outcomes] between state and federal litigation" which would "[l]ikely ... influence the choice of a forum," *Hanna v. Plumer*, 380 U.S. 460, 467–468 (1965). With regard to the claim-preclusion issue involved in the present case, for example, the traditional rule is that expiration of the applicable statute of limitations merely bars the remedy and does not extinguish the substantive right, so that dismissal on that ground does not have claim-preclusive effect in other jurisdictions with longer, unexpired limitations periods. Out-of-state defendants sued on stale claims in California and in other States adhering to this traditional rule would systematically remove state-law suits brought against them to federal court— where, unless otherwise specified, a statute-of-limitations dismissal would bar suit everywhere. * * *

We think the key to a more reasonable interpretation of the meaning of "operates as an adjudication upon the merits" in Rule 41(b) is to be found in Rule 41(a), which, in discussing the effect of voluntary dismissal by the plaintiff, makes clear that an "adjudication upon the merits" is the opposite of a "dismissal without prejudice" * * *. The primary meaning of "dismissal without prejudice," we think, is dismissal without barring the plaintiff from returning later, to the same court, with the same underlying claim. That will also ordinarily (though not always) have the consequence of not barring the claim from *other* courts, but its primary meaning relates to the dismissing court itself. * * *

We think, then, that the effect of the "adjudication upon the merits" default provision of Rule 41(b)—and, presumably, of the explicit order in the present case that used the language of that default provision—is simply that, unlike a dismissal "without prejudice," the dismissal in the present case barred refiling of the same claim in the United States District Court for the Central District of California. That is undoubtedly a necessary condition, but it is not a sufficient one, for claim-preclusive effect in other courts.

III

Having concluded that the claim-preclusive effect, in Maryland, of this California federal diversity judgment is dictated neither by *Dupasseur v. Rochereau*, as petitioner contends, nor by Rule 41(b), as respondent contends, we turn to consideration of what determines the issue. Neither the Full Faith and Credit Clause, U.S. Const., Art. IV, § 1, nor the full faith and credit statute, 28 U.S.C. § 1738, addresses the question. By their terms they govern the effects to be given only to state-court judgments (and, in the case of the statute, to judgments by courts of territories and possessions). * * *

It is also true, however, that no federal textual provision addresses the claim-preclusive effect of a federal-court judgment in a federal-question case, yet we have long held that States cannot give those judgments merely whatever effect they would give their own judgments, but must accord them the effect that this Court prescribes. * * * [E]ven when States are allowed to give federal judgments (notably, judgments in diversity cases) no more than the effect accorded to state judgments, that disposition is by direction of this Court, which has the last word on the claim-preclusive effect of all federal judgments * * *.

In other words, in *Dupasseur* the State was allowed (indeed, required) to give a federal diversity judgment no more effect than it would accord one of its own judgments only because reference to state law was the federal rule that this Court deemed appropriate. In short, federal common law governs the claim-preclusive effect of a dismissal by a federal court sitting in diversity.

It is left to us, then, to determine the appropriate federal rule. And despite the sea change that has occurred in the background law since *Dupasseur* was decided—not only repeal of the Conformity Act but also the watershed decision of this Court in Erie—we think the result decreed by *Dupasseur* continues to be correct for diversity cases. Since state, rather than federal, substantive law is at issue there is no need for a uniform federal rule. And indeed, nationwide uniformity in the substance of the matter is better served by having the same claim-preclusive rule (the state rule) apply whether the dismissal has been ordered by a state or a federal court. This is, it seems to us, a classic case for adopting, as the federally prescribed rule of decision, the law that would be applied by state courts in the State in which the federal diversity court sits. As we have alluded to above, any other rule would produce the sort of "forum-shopping ... and ... inequitable administration of the laws" that *Erie* seeks to avoid, *Hanna*, 380 U.S., at 468, since filing in, or removing to, federal court would be encouraged by the divergent effects that the litigants would anticipate from likely grounds of dismissal.

This federal reference to state law will not obtain, of course, in situations in which the state law is incompatible with federal interests. If, for example, state law did not accord claim-preclusive effect to dismissals for willful violation of discovery orders, federal courts' interest in the integrity of their own processes might justify a contrary federal rule. No such conflict with potential federal interests exists in the present case. Dismissal of this state cause of action was decreed by the California federal court only because the California statute of limitations so required; and there is no conceivable federal interest in giving that time bar more effect in other courts than the California courts themselves would impose.

* * *

Because the claim-preclusive effect of the California federal court's dismissal "upon the merits" of petitioner's action on statute-of-limitations grounds is governed by a federal rule that in turn incorporates California's law of claim preclusion (the content of which we do not pass upon today), the Maryland Court of Special Appeals erred in holding that the dismissal necessarily precluded the bringing of this action in the Maryland courts. The judgment is reversed, and the case remanded for further proceedings not inconsistent with this opinion.

Notes and Questions

1.   The Supreme Court holds that dismissal of the earlier case "on the merits" does not prevent the plaintiff from refiling the action in state court. If dismissal on the merits does not mean that a later suit is precluded, what does it mean? After *Semtek*, what difference is there between a dismissal on the merits and a dismissal that is not on the merits?

2.   The Court's narrow construction of Federal Rule 41(b) certainly helps it find that the Rule is valid under the Rules Enabling Act, 28 U.S.C. § 2072. How does the Court's reading (which limits the preclusive effect to actions filed in the same district) make the Rule look more procedural?

3. The opinion also suggests that a broader reading of Federal Rule 41(b) might also result in forum shopping. This discussion is technically *dictum*. However, based on what you read prior to this case, is that reasoning proper? Under *Hanna*, does it matter whether a Federal Rule might lead to forum shopping?

4. Once the Court determines that Federal Rule 41(b) does not apply, it still must determine whether the state law controls in federal court. How does the Court analyze this question? Given that the clash is now one between federal judge-made law and state law, is it surprising that the Court makes no mention of forum shopping in this portion of the opinion?

5. Is the way the Court deals with the element of forum shopping—employing it in the Rules Enabling Act analysis, but omitting it from the federal judge-made law analysis—simply carelessness? Or is the Court suggesting that the *Erie* analysis is not as rigidly compartmentalized as the *Hanna* opinion might lead one to believe?

6. The Court ultimately holds that the preclusive effect of a Rule 41(b) dismissal is governed by federal judge-made law, but that the *content* of that law will typically be borrowed from the state in which the dismissing court sits. Although it may seem unusual for federal law to incorporate local state law, there are actually several situations in which such incorporation takes place. For example, on many federal enclaves (such as military bases), the basic law of tort and contract is borrowed state law. In any situation involving borrowing, the federal law will vary from state to state, at least to some degree. Is this inconsistency a problem?

3. Federal Common Law

The *Semtek* case in the prior section holds that "federal common law" governs the preclusive effect of a federal involuntary dismissal. This reference to a federal common law may have surprised you. There are a number of sources (including some student aids) that declare that *Erie* abolished federal common law. But if you reread that opinion, you will see that the Court did not paint with so broad a brush. Instead, *Erie* declares, "There is no federal *general* common law." (emphasis added) Use of the qualifier "general" suggests that there could be *specific* pockets of federal judge-made law.

In fact, there is a considerable amount of federal common law. Moreover, you already know about one category of this law. Many of the Supreme Court cases set out above explore the federal courts' ability to fashion a body of *procedural* law to govern proceedings in the federal courts. This procedural common law remains the largest body of federal common law. However, it is not the only category. The following case indicates that there are also areas in which the federal courts can create rules that would clearly be substantive under any definition of that word.

TEXAS INDUSTRIES, INC. v. RADCLIFF MATERIALS, INC.

451 U.S. 630, 101 S.Ct. 2061, 68 L.Ed.2d 500 (1981)

Chief Justice BURGER delivered the opinion of the Court.

This case presents the question whether the federal antitrust laws allow a defendant, against whom civil damages, costs, and attorney's fees have been assessed, a right to contribution from other participants in the unlawful conspiracy on which recovery was based. * * *

I

Petitioner and the three respondents manufacture and sell ready-mix concrete in the New Orleans, La., area. In 1975, the Wilson P. Abraham Construction Corp., which had purchased concrete from petitioner, filed a civil action in the United States District Court for the Eastern District of Louisiana naming petitioner as defendant; the complaint alleged that petitioner and certain unnamed concrete firms had conspired to raise prices in violation of § 1 of the Sherman Act, 15 U.S.C. § 1 * * *.

Through discovery, petitioner learned that Abraham believed respondents were the other concrete producers that had participated in the alleged price-fixing scheme. Petitioner then filed a third-party complaint against respondents seeking contribution from them should it be held liable in the action filed by Abraham. The District Court dismissed the third-party complaint for failure to state a claim upon which relief could be granted, holding that federal law does not allow an antitrust defendant to recover in contribution from co-conspirators. * * *

On appeal, the Court of Appeals for the Fifth Circuit affirmed, holding that, although the Sherman and the Clayton Acts do not expressly afford a right to contribution, the issue should be resolved as a matter of federal common law. The court then examined what it perceived to be the benefits and the difficulties of contribution and concluded that no common-law rule of contribution should be fashioned by the courts.

II

The common law provided no right to contribution among joint tortfeasors. * * * Since the turn of the century, however, 39 states and the District of Columbia have fashioned rules of contribution in one form or another, 10 initially through judicial action and the remainder through legislation. Because courts generally have acknowledged that treble-damages actions under the antitrust laws are analogous to common-law actions sounding in tort, we are urged to follow this trend and adopt contribution for antitrust violators.

The parties and *amici* representing a variety of business interests—as well as a legion of commentators—have thoroughly addressed the policy concerns implicated in the creation of a right to contribution in antitrust cases. With potentially large sums at stake, it is not surprising that the numerous and articulate *amici* disagree strongly over the basic issue raised: whether sharing of damages liability will advance or impair the objectives of the antitrust laws. * * *

III

The contentions advanced indicate how views diverge as to the "unfairness" of not providing contribution, the risks and trade-offs perceived by decisionmakers in business, and the various patterns for contribution that could be devised. In this vigorous debate over the advantages and disadvantages of contribution and various contribution schemes, the parties, *amici*, and commentators have paid less attention to a very significant and perhaps dispositive threshold question: whether courts have the power to create such a cause of action absent legislation and, if so, whether that authority should be exercised in this context.

Earlier this Term, in *Northwest Airlines, Inc. v. Transport Workers*, 451 U.S. 77, we addressed the similar question of a right to contribution under the Equal Pay Act of 1963 and Title VII of the Civil Rights Act of 1964. We concluded that a right to contribution may arise in either of two ways: first, through the affirmative creation of a right of action by Congress, either expressly or by clear implication; or, second, through the power of federal courts to fashion a federal common law of contribution.

A

[The Court held that the antitrust laws did not create a right to contribution, either expressly or by implication.] * * *

B

There is, of course, "no federal general common law." *Erie R. Co. v. Tompkins*, 304 U.S. 64, 78 (1938). Nevertheless, the Court has recognized the need and authority in some limited areas to formulate what has come to be known as "federal common law." These instances are "few and restricted," *Wheeldin v. Wheeler*, 373 U.S. 647, 651 (1963), and fall into essentially two categories: those in which a federal rule of decision is "necessary to protect uniquely federal interests," *Banco Nacional de Cuba v. Sabbatino*, 376 U.S. 398, 426 (1964), and those in which Congress has given the courts the power to develop substantive law.

(1)

The vesting of jurisdiction in the federal courts does not in and of itself give rise to authority to formulate federal common law, nor does the existence of congressional authority under Art. I mean that federal courts are free to develop a common law to govern those areas until Congress acts. Rather, absent some congressional authorization to formulate substantive rules of decision, federal common law exists only in such narrow areas as those concerned with the rights and obligations of the United States, interstate and international disputes implicating the conflicting rights of States or our relations with foreign nations, and admiralty cases. In these instances, our federal system does not permit the controversy to be resolved under state law, either because the authority and duties of the United States as sovereign are intimately involved or because the interstate or international nature of the controversy makes it inappropriate for state law to control.

In areas where federal common law applies, the creation of a right to contribution may fall within the power of the federal courts. For example, in *Cooper Stevedoring Co. v. Fritz Kopke, Inc.*, 417 U.S. 106 (1974), we held that contribution is available among joint tortfeasors for injury to a longshoreman. But that claim arose within admiralty jurisdiction, one of the areas long recognized as subject to federal common law * * *. *Copper Stevedoring* thus does not stand for a general federal common-law right to contribution.

The antitrust laws were enacted pursuant to the power of Congress under the Commerce Clause, Art. I, § 8, cl. 3, to regulate interstate and foreign trade, and the case law construing the Sherman Act now spans nearly a century. Nevertheless, a treble-damages action remains a private suit involving the rights and obligations of private parties. Admittedly, there is a federal interest in the sense that vindication of rights arising out of these congressional enactments supplements federal enforcement and fulfills the objects of the statutory scheme. Notwithstanding that nexus, contribution among antitrust wrongdoers does not involve the duties of the Federal Government, the distribution of powers in our federal system, or matters necessarily subject to federal control even in the absence of statutory authority. In short, contribution does not implicate "uniquely federal interests" of the kind that oblige courts to formulate federal common law.

(2)

Federal common law also may come into play when Congress has vested jurisdiction in the federal courts and empowered them to create governing rules of law. In this vein, this Court has read § 301(a) of the Labor Management Relations Act, not only as granting jurisdiction over defined areas of labor law but also as vesting in the courts the power to develop a common law of labor-management relations within that jurisdiction. *Textile Workers v. Lincoln Mills*, 353 U.S. 448 (1957). A similar situation arises with regard to the first two sections of the Sherman Act, which in sweeping language forbid "[e]very contract, combination ... , or conspiracy, in restraint of trade" and "monopoliz [ing], or attempt[ing] to monopolize, ... any part of the trade or commerce...." 15 U.S.C. §§ 1, 2. We noted in *National Society of Professional Engineers v. United States*, 435 U.S. 679, 688 (1978):

> Congress, however, did not intend the text of the Sherman Act to delineate the full meaning of the statute or its application in

concrete situations. The legislative history makes it perfectly clear that it expected the courts to give shape to the statute's broad mandate by drawing on common-law tradition.

It does not necessarily follow, however, that Congress intended to give courts as wide discretion in formulating remedies to enforce the provisions of the Sherman Act or the kind of relief sought through contribution. The intent to allow courts to develop governing principles of law, so unmistakably clear with regard to substantive violations, does not appear in debates on the treble-damages action created in § 7 of the original Act. * * *

In contrast to the sweeping language of §§ 1 and 2 of the Sherman Act, the remedial provisions defined in the antitrust laws are detailed and specific" * * *.

> The presumption that a remedy was deliberately omitted from a statute is strongest when Congress has enacted a comprehensive legislative scheme including an integrated system of procedures for enforcement.

Northwest Airlines, Inc. v. Transport Workers Union, supra, 451 U.S., at 97. That presumption is strong indeed in the context of antitrust violations; the continuing existence of this statutory scheme for 90 years without amendments authorizing contribution is not without significance. There is nothing in the statute itself, in its legislative history, or in the overall regulatory scheme to suggest that Congress intended courts to have the power to alter or supplement the remedies enacted. * * *

We are satisfied that neither the Sherman Act nor the Clayton Act confers on federal courts the broad power to formulate the right to contribution sought here.

IV

The policy questions presented by petitioner's claimed right to contribution are far-reaching. In declining to provide a right to contribution, we neither reject the validity of those arguments nor adopt the views of those opposing contribution. Rather, we recognize that, regardless of the merits of the conflicting arguments, this is a matter for Congress, not the courts, to resolve. * * *

Because we are unable to discern any basis in federal statutory or common law that allows federal courts to fashion the relief urged by petitioner, the judgment of the Court of Appeals is *Affirmed*.

Notes and Questions

1. Federal common law is actually as old as the *Erie* doctrine itself. On a case decided on the same day as *Erie*, the Supreme Court applied a rule that it called "federal common law" to resolve a dispute involving the allocation of water in an interstate stream. *Hinderlider v. La Plata River & Cherry Creek Ditch Co.*, 304 U.S. 92, 58 S.Ct. 803, 82 L.Ed. 1202 (1938).

2. Part III.B of the *Texas Industries* opinion suggests that there are two broad categories of substantive federal common law. In fact, these two categories correspond nicely to the two categories of procedural common law discussed after *Hanna*. In the first category (where federal common law is "necessary to protect uniquely federal interests"), the federal courts have the *inherent* power to make law. In the second, Congress has *delegated* part of its lawmaking power to the federal courts.

3. The second category is the easier of the two to understand. If Congress has delegated authority to the courts, the only real issues are whether Congress had the power to begin with, and whether the court is acting within the scope of the delegation (a third issue—constitutional limits on Congress's power to delegate its legislative power—is best left to a course in Constitutional or Administrative Law). When you dealt with the Rules Enabling Act, you were basically analyzing the scope of the delegation. That Act places explicit limits on the Supreme Court's rulemaking power, limiting the Rules to those that do not abridge, enlarge, or modify substantive rights.

Determining the scope of delegation in areas of substantive federal common law, by contrast, is a far trickier proposition. Unlike the Rules Enabling Act, there is almost never a statute that explicitly delegates substantive lawmaking authority to the courts. Instead, the courts typically find such a delegation by implication. In *Textile Workers v. Lincoln Mills*, 353 U.S. 448, 77 S.Ct. 912, 1 L.Ed.2d 972 (1957), a case discussed in *Texas Industries*, the Court found a delegation of lawmaking authority in a statute that simply gave the federal courts exclusive jurisdiction over certain labor contracts. Similarly, the power to fashion equitable remedies described in *Guaranty Trust* may stem from the grant of equity jurisdiction to the federal courts.

4. Although *Texas Industries* lists it as an area of inherent power, could maritime law actually be an area where lawmaking power has been delegated? To what extent is it relevant that federal courts have always had exclusive jurisdiction in admiralty? *See* Judiciary Act of 1789, § 9. If *Erie* applied in admiralty, would there be any state judge-made maritime law for the federal courts to apply?

5. Turn now to the first category of substantive federal common law: situations where there is a strong federal interest. The cases finding federal common law in this area are summarized in Part III.B(1) of the opinion. Is there a thread that ties them together?

6. Is there any doubt that a uniform national law would usually be desirable in the first category of federal common law? But does it necessarily follow that federal courts should have the ability to make law in such areas? If there is truly a strong federal interest in areas such as foreign affairs, isn't the usual solution for *Congress* to enact a statute setting out a nationwide rule? Why shouldn't the same be required in the areas listed by the Court?

7. Like a federal statute, federal common law is a federal question. Therefore, a claim arising under federal common law can be heard in the federal courts regardless of the citizenship of the litigants or amount in controversy. *Illinois v. City of Milwaukee*, 406 U.S. 91, 92 S.Ct. 1385, 31 L.Ed.2d 712 (1972).

Problems

1.   Defendant, a Michigan citizen, has a 20-year-old son who attends the University of Northern Florida. Every spring break, students from the University travel to Daytona Beach, Florida. While driving to Florida last spring, Defendant's son negligently collided with car driven by Plaintiff, a Florida citizen, in a small town in northern Florida.

Since Defendant's son has no assets, Plaintiff decides to sue Defendant. To avoid a battle over personal jurisdiction, Plaintiff brings the action in the federal district court for the Western District of Michigan. Defendant immediately files a motion to dismiss under Federal Rule of Civil Procedure 12(b)(6), citing a recent case of the Michigan Supreme Court holding that a parent may not be held vicariously liable for the actions of a non-minor child. A person reaches majority in Michigan at age 18.

How will the district court rule on Defendant's motion to dismiss?

2.   Because of the substantial variation in filing fees among the federal district courts, the Supreme Court recently amended Federal Rule of Civil Procedure 3 to read as follows:

A civil action is commenced by (a) filing a complaint with the court, and (b) paying a $100.00 filing fee to the clerk of court.

Plaintiff is contemplating bringing a class action against Defendant in the state of Dakota. Upon reviewing state law, however, she discovers that Dakota Rule of Civil Procedure 6.02 imposes a special filing fee of $20,000 for all lawsuits brought in the form of a class action. Dakota adopted this special fee because of the tremendous burden that class actions place on the courts. In order to avoid this expense, Plaintiff brings her suit in the federal district court for the District of Dakota by filing her complaint and paying the $100.00 fee. Defendant moves to dismiss, claiming that Plaintiff's lawsuit was not properly commenced because she failed to comply with the filing fee requirements of Dakota law.

How should the court rule on Defendant's motion?

3.   You are the attorney for Defendant in a breach of contract action currently pending in the district court for the District of Superior. Plaintiff filed the lawsuit back in 1999, and has done nothing since serving the summons and complaint upon your client. Therefore, you file a motion to dismiss the case "for failure to prosecute."

Under Federal Rule of Civil Procedure 41(b), all involuntary dismissals are deemed to be "with prejudice," unless the court specifically says otherwise. This means that, following dismissal, Plaintiff would be barred from ever bringing the breach of contract claim against your client.

The hearing on your motion is scheduled for 8:00 a.m. tomorrow. At 10:30 in the evening, your client calls and says, "Isn't this motion just a waste of my money? I just talked to my cousin, a Superior state court judge. She said that under Superior law all dismissals are deemed to be *without prejudice* unless the court indicates otherwise [you may assume that this is a correct statement of Superior law]. Even if we win tomorrow, can't Plaintiff simply sue me again for the breach of contract claim?''

What do you tell your client?

4. The legislature of the state of Carolina has become extremely concerned about the profusion of personal injury litigation in that state. To combat this problem, the legislature passes a statute that requires a plaintiff who *loses* a personal injury lawsuit to pay the attorney's fees of the prevailing defendant. This new statute is clearly at variance with the traditional American common-law rule in effect in the other 49 states, which requires each party to pay his own attorney's fees.

Plaintiff sues Defendant in a federal district court in Carolina for injuries sustained when Plaintiff slipped and fell on the sidewalk in front of Defendant's house. The jury finds for Defendant. Defendant moves for an order requiring Plaintiff to pay Defendant's attorney's fees in the action. How will the judge rule?

5. Bugs lives in Iowa, on the Iowa/Missouri state line. Just across the state line lives Elmer Fudd, a small-time farmer who ekes out a living growing carrots. To increase his profits, Elmer quits growing carrots and takes up raising horseradish. Infuriated, Bugs immediately sues Elmer in a federal district court in Missouri, asking for an injunction ordering Elmer to sell his horseradish and resume growing carrots.

Under the law of most states, a jury will not be empaneled in a suit involving solely equitable relief [recall that an injunction is equitable relief]. The federal courts follow this practice. Under the Missouri constitution, however, all parties in a civil lawsuit have the right to a jury trial, even when the case involves equitable relief.

Bugs requests a jury trial in his case with Elmer. Elmer resists Bugs' request. How should the district judge rule?

6. Same facts as Problem 5. Elmer has asked the district court to dismiss Bugs's suit under the equitable doctrine of "unclean hands." Historically, courts of equity would only hear cases in which the plaintiff had not acted improperly. If the plaintiff came to court with unclean hands, the court would refuse to lend any assistance to the plaintiff.

Elmer claims that Bugs has unclean hands because he has been pilfering Elmer's carrots. Bugs, however, cites a recent decision of the Missouri Supreme Court which holds that that the doctrine of unclean hands does not apply in Missouri actions in equity.

How should the judge rule on Elmer's motion to dismiss?

7. The St. Croix river defines part of the boundary between the states of Minnesota and Wisconsin. In areas where the river forms the boundary, all land east of the river is in the state of Wisconsin; while all land to the west is in Minnesota.

After a particular snowy winter, the April thaw causes the St. Croix to "jump its banks;" thereby carving out a new channel. As a result, 3,000 acres of land (the "3,000 acres") which were formerly located east of the St. Croix are now on the west side of the river.

Although Wisconsin and Minnesota are neighbors, they differ in the celebration of one very important religious holiday. In Wisconsin, the walleye season begins on the first of May. In Minnesota, it begins on the second Saturday in May.

On May 1st, Wally Fisher, a Wisconsin citizen, is fined by the Minnesota Department of Natural Resources (the "DNR") for reeling in a walleye from a small lake situated on the 3,000 acres. Infuriated, the state of Wisconsin immediately sues the DNR in a federal district court in Minnesota, asking for a declaratory judgment that the 3,000 acres is still a part of the state of Wisconsin. The DNR, citing Minnesota law, moves to dismiss Wisconsin's complaint.

Under the law of Minnesota and 24 other states, the new river channel would be used to establish the boundary. Under the law of Wisconsin and 24 other states, however, the doctrine of "avulsion" would apply, and the sudden change in the river's course would not serve to redefine the boundary.

How should the court rule on the DNR's motion? *Variation*: What if Wisconsin had sued the DNR in a Minnesota *state* court? Is there any reason for Minnesota not to follow its own law?

Index

References are to Pages

ALTERNATIVE DISPUTE RESOLUTION
Arbitration, 526
Mediation, 536

APPEALS, 797

COLLATERAL ESTOPPEL, 744

DEFAULT JUDGMENTS, 663

DISCOVERY, 456
Depositions, 487
Discovery of relevant and non–privileged
    information, 459
Discovery sanctions, 517
Experts, 480
Interrogatories, 495
Mandatory disclosure, 457
Physical and mental examinations, 513
Request for admissions, 508
Request for production of documents, 502
Scope of discovery, 457
Work product, 469

DISMISSALS, 647
Involuntary dismissals, 655
Voluntary dismissals, 648

DISPOSITIVE MOTIONS, 647
Failure to state a claim, 305, 673
Judgment as a matter of law, 694
Judgment on the pleadings, 673
Summary judgment, 674

JOINDER OF CLAIMS AND PARTIES, 9,
    387
Class actions, 430
Counterclaims, 18
Cross–claims, 26
Impleader, 29
Interpleader, 412
Intervention, 387
Merger and bar, 43, 730
Multiple claims, 37
Multiple parties, 10
Necessary parties, 400

JURY TRIALS, 576
Constitutional right, 577
Demanding a jury trial, 610
Jury instructions, 635
Jury verdicts, 640
Selecting group of prospective jurors, 612

JURY TRIALS—Cont'd
Voir dire of prospective jurors, 617

PERSONAL JURISDICTION, 120
Change of venue, 244
Forum non conveniens, 251
Personal jurisdiction, 120
Rule 12(b) challenges, 259
Service of process, 216
Venue, 238

PLEADING, 262
Affirmative defenses, 340
Amending pleadings, 368
    Amendments filed after the limitations
        period has expired, 377
    Amendments to add issues at trial, 374
Choice of law, 313
Determining the applicable law, 310
Erie doctrine, 319, 849
Federal rules, 273
Form of the complaint, 300
Heightened pleading standards, 291
Objecting to the statement of a claim, 305
Philosophy and history of pleading, 263
Prayer for relief, 299
Responding to the answer, 346
Responding to the complaint, 333
Supplemental pleadings, 383
Veracity standards for filed documents, 351

POST-TRIAL MOTIONS, 694
Judgment as a matter of law, 694
New trial, 705
Relief from judgment, 716

PRECLUSION, 730
Applying preclusion across state lines, 776
Claim, 732
Doctrines similar to preclusion
    Judicial estoppel, 791
    Law of the case, 790
Issue, 744
Parties affected by preclusion, 762

RES JUDICATA, 732

SERVICE OF PROCESS, 216

SETTLEMENT, 542

SUBJECT MATTER JURISDICTION, 51
Amount in controversy, 76
Challenging subject matter jurisdiction, 117

897

SUBJECT MATTER JURISDICTION
—Cont'd
Diversity of citizenship, 64
Federal question, 54
Removal, 109
Supplemental, jurisdiction, 87

VENUE, 238
Change of venue, 244
Federal statutory standards, 239
Forum non conveniens, 251

†